Poetry
Criticism

Guide to Gale Literary Criticism Series

For criticism on	You need these Gale series
Authors now living or who died after December 31, 1959	*CONTEMPORARY LITERARY CRITICISM (CLC)*
Authors who died between 1900 and 1959	*TWENTIETH-CENTURY LITERARY CRITICISM (TCLC)*
Authors who died between 1800 and 1899	*NINETEENTH-CENTURY LITERATURE CRITICISM (NCLC)*
Authors who died between 1400 and 1799	*LITERATURE CRITICISM FROM 1400 TO 1800 (LC)* *SHAKESPEAREAN CRITICISM (SC)*
Authors who died before 1400	*CLASSICAL AND MEDIEVAL LITERATURE CRITICISM (CMLC)*
Authors of books for children and young adults	*CHILDREN'S LITERATURE REVIEW (CLR)*
Black writers of the past two hundred years	*BLACK LITERATURE CRITICISM (BLC)*
Short story writers	*SHORT STORY CRITICISM (SSC)*
Poets	*POETRY CRITICISM (PC)*
Dramatists	*DRAMA CRITICISM (DC)*
Major authors from the Renaissance to the present	*WORLD LITERATURE CRITICISM, 1500 TO THE PRESENT (WLC)*

For criticism on visual artists since 1850, see

MODERN ARTS CRITICISM (MAC)

ISSN 1052-4851

Poetry Criticism

Excerpts from Criticism of the Works of the Most Significant and Widely Studied Poets of World Literature

VOLUME 6

Drew Kalasky
Editor

Gale Research Inc. • DETROIT • WASHINGTON, D.C. • LONDON

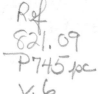

STAFF

Drew Kalasky, *Editor*

Laurie Di Mauro, James P. Draper, Christopher Giroux, Jelena O. Krstović, Marie Lazzari, Kyung-Sun Lim, David Segal, Joseph C. Tardiff, Bridget Travers, Thomas Votteler, *Associate Editors*

Jennifer Brostrom, Jeffery Chapman, Ian A. Goodhall, Michael Magoulias, Brigham Narins, Debra Wells, Lynn M. Zott, *Assistant Editors*

Jeanne A. Gough, *Permissions & Production Manager*
Linda M. Pugliese, *Production Supervisor*
Donna Craft, Paul Lewon, Maureen Puhl, Camille Robinson, Jennifer VanSickle, Sheila Walencewicz, *Editorial Associates*

Sandra C. Davis, *Permissions Supervisor (Text)*
Maria L. Franklin, Josephine M. Keene, Michele Lonoconus, Denise Singleton, Kimberly F. Smilay, *Permissions Associates*
Jennifer A. Arnold, Brandy C. Merritt, Shalice Shah, *Permissions Assistants*

Margaret A. Chamberlain, *Permissions Supervisor (Pictures)*
Pamela A. Hayes, Keith Reed, *Permissions Associates*
Arlene Johnson, Barbara Wallace, *Permissions Assistants*

Victoria B. Cariappa, *Research Manager*
Maureen Richards, *Research Supervisor*
Robert S. Lazich, Mary Beth McElmeel, Tamara C. Nott, *Editorial Associates*
Kelly Hill, Donna Melnychenko, *Editorial Assistants*

Mary Beth Trimper, *Production Manager*
Catherine Kemp, *Production Assistant*

Cynthia Baldwin, *Art Director*
Nicholas Jakubiak, C. J. Jonik, Yolanda Y. Latham, *Keyliners*

Library of Congress Catalog Card Number 91-118494
ISBN 0-8103-8334-9
ISSN 1052-4851

Printed in the United States of America
Published simultaneously in the United Kingdom
by Gale Research International Limited
(An affiliated company of Gale Research Inc.)
10 9 8 7 6 5 4 3 2 1

The trademark **ITP** is used under license.

Contents

Preface   vii

Acknowledgments   xi

Preface

A Comprehensive Information Source on World Poetry

*P*oetry Criticism (PC) provides substantial critical excerpts and biographical information on poets throughout the world who are most frequently studied in high school and undergraduate college courses. Each *PC* entry is supplemented by biographical and bibliographical material to help guide the user to a fuller understanding of the genre and its creators. Although major poets and literary movements are covered in such Gale Literary Criticism Series as *Contemporary Literary Criticism (CLC), Twentieth-Century Literary Criticism (TCLC), Nineteenth-Century Literature Criticism (NCLC), Literature Criticism from 1400 to 1800 (LC),* and *Classical and Medieval Literature Criticism (CMLC), PC* offers more focused attention on poetry than is possible in the broader, survey-oriented entries on writers in these Gale series. Students, teachers, librarians, and researchers will find that the generous excerpts and supplementary material provided by *PC* supply them with vital information needed to write a term paper on poetic technique, examine a poet's most prominent themes, or lead a poetry discussion group.

Coverage

In order to reflect the influence of tradition as well as innovation, poets of various nationalities, eras, and movements are represented in every volume of *PC*. Each author entry presents a historical survey of the critical response to that author's work; the length of an entry reflects the amount of critical attention that the author has received from critics writing in English and from foreign critics in translation. Since many poets have inspired a prodigious amount of critical explication, *PC* is necessarily selective, and the editors have chosen the most significant published criticism to aid readers and students in their research. In order to provide these important critical pieces, the editors will sometimes reprint essays that have appeared in previous volumes of Gale's Literary Criticism Series. Such duplication, however, never exceeds fifteen percent of a *PC* volume.

Organization

Each *PC* author entry consists of the following components:

- **Author Heading:** the name under which the author wrote appears at the beginning of the entry, followed by birth and death dates. If the author wrote consistently under a pseudonym, the pseudonym will be listed in the author heading and his or her legal name given in parentheses in the lines immediately preceding the Introduction. Uncertainty as to birth or death dates is indicated by question marks.

- **Introduction:** a biographical and critical essay introduces readers to the author and the critical discussions surrounding his or her work.

- **Author Portrait:** a photograph or illustration of the author is included when available. Most entries also feature illustrations of people and places pertinent to an author's career, as well as holographs of manuscript pages and dust jackets.

- **Principal Works:** the author's most important works are identified in a list ordered chronologically by first publication dates. The first section comprises poetry collections and book-length poems. The second section gives information on other major works by the author. For foreign authors, original foreign-language publication information is provided, as well as the best and most complete English-language editions of their works.

- **Criticism:** critical excerpts chronologically arranged in each author entry provide perspective on changes in critical evaluation over the years. All individual titles of poems and poetry collections by the author featured in the entry are printed in boldface type to enable a reader to ascertain without difficulty the works under discussion. For purposes of easy identification, the critic's name and the publication date of the essay are given at the beginning of each piece of criticism. Unsigned criticism is preceded by the title of the journal in which it originally appeared. Publication information (such as publisher names and book prices) and parenthetical numerical references (such as footnotes or page and line references to specific editions of a work) have been deleted at the editor's discretion to enable smoother reading of the text.

- **Explanatory Notes:** introductory comments preface each critical excerpt, providing several types of useful information, including: the reputation of a critic, the importance of a work of criticism, and the specific type of criticism (biographical, psychoanalytic, historical, etc.).

- **Author Commentary:** insightful comments from the authors themselves and excerpts from author interviews are included when available.

- **Bibliographical Citations:** information following each piece of criticism guides the interested reader to the original essay or book.

- **Further Reading:** bibliographic references accompanied by descriptive notes at the end of each entry suggest additional materials for study of the author. Boxed material following the Further Reading provides references to other biographical and critical series published by Gale.

Other Features

Cumulative Author Index: comprises all authors who have appeared in Gale's Literary Criticism Series, along with cross-references to such Gale biographical series as *Contemporary Authors* and *Dictionary of Literary Biography*. This cumulated index enables the user to locate an author within the various series.

Cumulative Nationality Index: includes all authors featured in *PC,* arranged alphabetically under their respective nationalities.

Cumulative Title Index: lists in alphabetical order all individual poems, book-length poems, and collection titles contained in the *PC* series. Titles of poetry collections and separately published poems are printed in italics, while titles of individual poems are printed in roman type with quotation marks. Each title is followed by the author's name and the volume and page number corresponding to the location of commentary on specific works. English-language translations of original foreign-language titles are cross-referenced to the foreign titles so that all references to discussion of a work are combined in one listing.

Citing *Poetry Criticism*

When writing papers, students who quote directly from any volume in the Literary Criticism Series may use the following general formats to footnote reprinted criticism. The first example pertains to material drawn from periodicals, the second to material reprinted from books:

[1]David Daiches, "W. H. Auden: The Search for a Public," *Poetry* LIV (June 1939), 148-56; excerpted and reprinted in *Poetry Criticism*, Vol. 1, ed. Robyn V. Young (Detroit: Gale Research, 1990), pp. 7-9.

[2]Pamela J. Annas, *A Disturbance in Mirrors: The Poetry of Sylvia Plath* (Greenwood Press, 1988); excerpted and reprinted in *Poetry Criticism*, Vol. 1, ed. Robyn V. Young (Detroit: Gale Research, 1990), pp. 410-14.

Comments Are Welcome

Readers who wish to suggest authors to appear in future volumes, or who have other suggestions, are cordially invited to contact the editors.

Acknowledgments

The editors wish to thank the copyright holders of the excerpted criticism included in this volume, the permissions managers of many book and magazine publishing companies for assisting us in securing reprint rights, and Anthony Bogucki for assistance with copyright research. We are also grateful to the staffs of the Detroit Public Library, Wayne State University Purdy/Kresge Library Complex, and the University of Michigan Libraries for making their resources available to us. Following is a list of the copyright holders who have granted us permission to reprint material in this volume of *PC*. Every effort has been made to trace copyright, but if omissions have been made, please let us know.

COPYRIGHTED EXCERPTS IN *PC*, VOLUME 6, WERE REPRINTED FROM THE FOLLOWING PERIODICALS:

AWP Newsletter, May, 1979 for "Apollo's Harsher Songs: 'Desire without an Object of Desire'" by Helen Vendler. Copyright © 1980 by Helen Vendler. Reprinted by permission of the author.—*Black American Literature Forum,* v. 19, Fall, 1985 for a review of "From the Auroral Darkness: The Life and Poetry of Robert Hayden" by Marcellus Blount; v. 21, Fall, 1987 for a review of "Thomas and Beulah" by John Shoptaw. Copyright © 1985, 1987 Indiana State University. Both reprinted by permission of Indiana State University and the respective authors.—*Callaloo,* v. 9, Winter, 1986. Copyright © 1986 by Charles H. Rowell. All rights reserved. Reprinted by permission of the publisher.—*The Century,* v. 106, June, 1923. Copyright, 1923, renewed 1950 by Current History, Inc. Reprinted by permission of Current History.—*CLA Journal,* v. XX, December, 1976. Copyright, 1976 by The College Language Association. Used by permission of The College Language Association.—*The Georgia Review,* v. LXIV, Spring-Summer, 1990. Copyright, 1990, by the University of Georgia. Reprinted by permission of the publisher.—*Grand Street,* v. 2, Winter, 1983 for "All That Again" by Peter Green. Copyright © 1983 by Grand Street Publications, Inc. All rights reserved. Reprinted by permission of the publisher and the author's agents, Harold Ober Associates Incorporated.—*The Hudson Review,* v. 9, Summer, 1956 for "Graves, Gods, and Scholars" by Northrop Frye. Copyright © 1956, renewed 1984 by The Hudson Review, Inc. Reprinted with the permission of the Literary Estate of Northrop Frye.—*The Iowa Review,* v. 19, Fall, 1989 for an interview with Rita Dove by Steven Schneider. Copyright © 1989 by The University of Iowa. Reprinted by permission of the publisher and Rita Dove.—*Journal of Women's Studies in Literature,* v. 1, Spring, 1979 for "Edna St. Vincent Millay and the Tradition of Domestic Poetry" by Jeannine Dobbs. Copyright © 1979 Eden Press Women's Publications, Inc. Reprinted by permission of the author.—*MELUS,* v. 8, Spring, 1981. Copyright MELUS, The Society for the Study of Multi-Ethnic Literature of the United States, 1981. Reprinted by permission of the publisher.—*Michigan Quarterly Review,* v. XXII, Fall, 1983 for "Struck by Lightning: Four Distinct Modern Voices" by G. E. Murray. Copyright © The University of Michigan, 1983. Reprinted by permission of the author.—*The Nation,* New York, v. 179, October 16, 1954. Copyright 1954, renewed 1982 *The Nation* magazine/ The Nation Company, Inc. Reprinted by permission of the publisher.—*The New Criterion,* v. VII, October, 1988 for "The Poetry of Robert Graves" by Robert Richman; v. 8, November, 1989 for "The Example of Robert Hayden" by William Rice. Copyright © 1988, 1989 by The Foundation for Cultural Review. Both reprinted by permission of the respective authors.—*The New England Quarterly,* v. XLVIII, June, 1975 for "Millay's 'Ungrafted Tree': The Problem of the Artist as Woman" by Walter S. Minot. Copyright 1975 by *The New England Quarterly.* Reprinted by permission of the publisher and the author.—*The New York Herald Tribune Books,* December 15, 1935; December 6, 1936. Copyright 1935, renewed 1963; copyright 1936, renewed 1964, New York Herald Tribune Inc. All rights reserved. Both reprinted by permission.—*The New York Times Book Review,* October 16, 1921; August 9, 1931; October 24, 1937; November 29, 1942. Copyright 1921, 1931, 1937, 1942 by The New York Times Company. All reprinted by permission of the publisher.—*Obsidian,* v. VIII, Spring, 1981 for "In the Darkness A Wellspring of Plangency: The Poetry of Robert Hayden" by Gary Zebrun. Copyright © 1981 by Alvin Aubert. All rights reserved. Reprinted by permission of the author.—*Parnassus: Poetry in Review,* v. 16, 1991 for "A Dissonant Triad" by Helen Vendler. Copyright © 1991 Poetry in Review Foundation, NY. Reprinted by permission of the author.—*Philological Quarterly,* v. 63, Winter, 1984 for "Tennyson, Nature, and Romantic Nature Poetry" by Timothy Peltason. Copyright 1984 by The University of Iowa. Reprinted by permission of the publisher and the author.—*Poetry,* v. 85, February, 1955 for "Without the Inventions of Sorrow" by Hayden Carruth. © 1955, renewed 1983 by the Modern Poetry Association. Reprinted by permission of the Editor of *Poetry* and the author.—*The Saturday Review of Literature,* v. XXIX, March 23, 1946. Copyright 1946, renewed 1973 *Saturday Review* magazine.—*The Southern Review,* Louisiana State University, v. 26, Spring, 1990 for a review

COPYRIGHTED EXCERPTS IN *PC,* VOLUME 6, WERE REPRINTED FROM THE FOLLOWING BOOKS:

Elizabeth Barrett Browning

1806-1861

English poet, translator, and essayist.

INTRODUCTION

Considered one of the preeminent love poets of Victorian English literature, Browning is most remembered for her emotionally charged *Sonnets from the Portuguese* and her ambitious verse novel, *Aurora Leigh,* which treats women's search for identity and their role within the English class system. Although she was lavishly praised in her own lifetime, Browning's posthumous reputation has declined as a result of what critics perceive to be her reliance on overly extravagant language and sentiment. Nevertheless, her works continue to command interest for their treatment of social issues, and she endures in the popular imagination as a writer of intense love poetry.

The eldest of eleven children born to a wealthy and overbearing father, Browning demonstrated at an early age a prodigious aptitude for classical languages. When she was fourteen her father privately published her epic *The Battle of Marathon: A Poem.* Around this time she injured her spine in a riding accident and seemed destined to a life of infirmity and confinement. She continued to study and write, publishing *An Essay on Mind, with Other Poems* in 1826 and a translation of Aeschylus's *Prometheus Bound* in 1833—both of which appeared anonymously. These works, together with *The Seraphim, and Other Poems,* her first signed volume, earned for Browning the status of an accomplished poet. In the 1840s she entered into correspondence with Robert Browning, then a little-known poet, whose volume *Bells and Pomegranates* she had praised. In 1846 the two poets eloped to Italy and established themselves in Florence, where Browning's physical condition profoundly improved. Her literary reputation continued to grow, and when William Wordsworth died in 1850, she was among those seriously considered to replace him as Poet Laureate. Browning died in Florence in 1861.

Browning's early poems typically focus on religious and social themes. Writing from the standpoint of Evangelical Christianity, a faith she later abandoned, Browning initially viewed composing poetry as a religious pursuit. In "A Sea-Side Meditation," for example, she argued that the poet's mission is to free humanity from the bonds of sensory experience and guide it to the realm of the spirit. "A Drama of Exile" employs an ancient Greek dramatic form both to elucidate the expulsion of Adam and Eve from Eden and to attempt to harmonize Evangelical Christianity with the tradition of Classical Humanism. Demonstrating Browning's concomitant emphasis on humanity's worldly condition, "The Cry of the Children" laments the victimization of child factory workers. "The Rhyme of the

Duchess of May," a ballad dealing with the betrothal of a medieval orphan girl, attacks the conception of women as commercial objects to be bought and sold in marriage. In *Casa Guidi Windows: A Poem* Browning deals with the political theme of Italian nationalism. This work charts the struggle for Italian independence in the mid-nineteenth century. Celebrated by contemporary Italian nationalists, *Casa Guidi Windows* has also been praised by modern critics for its depiction of political complexities.

Sonnets from the Portuguese, the work most closely associated with Browning's name, documents the romance that developed between Elizabeth Barrett and Robert Browning: first Browning's surprise that she, an ailing, middle-aged woman, could be the object of romantic love; then her initial refusal to consider her lover's proposal of marriage; and finally—having overcome her doubts concerning the ephemeral nature of love—Browning's confidence in Robert Browning's love and the profundity of her emotional attachment. Due to the intensely personal quality of the verse, the title *Sonnets from the Portuguese* was selected with a view to presenting the poems as translations rather than as original compositions. Upon publication the *Sonnets* were overlooked by most critics; it was only when the autobiographical nature of the verse became generally known that the collection received widespread attention. Early commentators praised the sincerity and intensity of the sonnets, arguing that Browning's emotionalism was effectively balanced by her technical mastery of the restraints of the sonnet form. Later critics, however, have tended to reverse this judgment, pointing to the excessive quality of Browning's self-revelation and her calculated display of sentiment.

Browning's verse novel, *Aurora Leigh,* was lauded by the influential Victorian critic John Ruskin as "the greatest *poem* in the English language." Written in the form of an epic, it focuses on the evolution of a female writer's consciousness, deftly portraying her intellectual and emotional enlightenment as she vacillates between marriage and a life dedicated to art. Browning shifted the focus of the poem from the privileged background of Aurora's childhood to the world of poverty and sexual exploitation represented by the character Marion Erle, thereby returning to the political and social issues found in her earlier work. Initially well-received, *Aurora Leigh* was soon perceived as an artistic failure on the basis of its poorly developed characterization and occasionally prosaic passages. In the early twentieth century, Virginia Woolf argued for the poem's rehabilitation, calling it "a masterpiece in embryo" that "still commands our interest and inspires our respect." Modern critics concur with Woolf's assessment arguing that *Aurora Leigh* possesses literary and historical value as a vigorous assertion of female independence. Although the extravagant praise which Browning received in her lifetime is no longer regarded as justifiable, critics recognize her importance in English literary history as one of the first female poets to seek independence from the male tradition and to address social concerns in her works.

PRINCIPAL WORKS

POETRY

The Battle of Marathon: A Poem   1820
An Essay on Mind, with Other Poems   1826
Prometheus Bound, Translated from the Greek of Aeschylus; and Miscellaneous Poems   1833
The Seraphim, and Other Poems   1838
Poems   1844
*Poems: New Edition   1850
Casa Guidi Windows: A Poem   1851
Poems: Third Edition   1853
Poems: Fourth Edition   1856
Aurora Leigh   1857; also published in revised form as *Aurora Leigh,*   1859
Poems before Congress   1860
Last Poems   1862

OTHER MAJOR WORKS
The Greek Christian Poets and the English Poets   (essays) 1863
The Letters of Elizabeth Barrett Browning.   2 vols.   (letters)   1897

*This collection includes *Sonnets from the Portuguese.*

CRITICISM

Littell's Living Age   (essay date 1857)

[*In the following review, the critic argues that* Aurora Leigh, *despite passages of powerful writing, is weakened by Browning's melodramatic, discursive style and the static nature of her characters.*]

There was always something of the Titaness about Mrs. Browning: her instincts were towards the vague, the vast, the indefinite, the unutterable; and the ideal world in which her imagination lived was a world of formless grandeur, of radiant mist, in which shapes of superhuman majesty moved and loomed dimly glorious. In her art she was a Pythoness struggling for utterance, too full of the god to do more than writhe her lips in convulsed agony; her speech was inarticulate, often because she meant so much; the note she sounded became a hollow noise, because it was so deep. In this state of mind she wrote lyrical dramas on the Fall of Man and the Crucifixion of Christ, which were little more than hysterical spasms; poured herself forth in improvisations which in one stanza stirred every heart and thrilled every soul, and in the next moved inextinguishable laughter, so strangely were strength and weakness mingled, grand thought and deep feeling with nonsense, affectation, and wilful puerility. *Casa Guidi Windows* was a great advance, though still there was much to do before she became mistress of her own powers—before she could guide the metal coursers of her chariot with a light finger on the silken reins of art. *Aurora Leigh* is in point of execution another great step forward; if the steeds still toss their heads somewhat wildly for wellbred carriage-horses, still snuff the air as if the trackless desert were their native home, it is that their mistress prefers to drive with a loose reign, and would rather ride with Mazeppa than take a ticket by the Great Western or a canter round Rotten Row.

But the old anarchic nature of the Titaness is still discernible; still there is something of the old contempt for limitation and the littleness of completeness; still the conception vast and vague and only half-realized; rich elements of force and beauty in chaos and confusion, the waters heaving and boiling with life ere yet the demiurgic spirit has brooded over them and given to each thing its definite form and its separate place. The poem professes to be the autobiography of a woman of genius, who early in life refuses to marry a man she likes, because he, being a philanthropist, seems to her to seek her for his wife not so much as a woman whom he loves, and whose love he wants, as to be his helper in his social work. She is further offended by his slight estimate of art and literature, and by his disbelief in a woman's ability to attain high excellence in either. So far as concerns herself, the record is one more of feelings than of facts, a history of mental growth and the development of character rather than of fortune and outward incidents. But there is no lack of incidents, and those of so startling a character that they might serve for the plot of a Victorian melodrama. Indeed, nothing can be more evident than that Mrs. Browning has not cared to throw an air of every-day probability over her story, or to propitiate in the least that sort of refinement which avoids almost with equal horror violent emotions and eccentric actions. The two principal characters in the book, besides the autobiographer Aurora Leigh, are her cousin Romney Leigh, whom she refuses to marry for the motives before assigned, and a girl of the lowest station, named Marian Erle, who is pure and good, though abjectly poor and the child of brutal tramps. There are other characters incidentally introduced, one of whom, a fashionable young widow, Lady Waldemar, plays a leading part in the development of the story; but the three we have mentioned are the principal dramatis personæ, and it is in their mutual relations that the interest of the poem consists. Thus we have already two very distinct elements of poetic excitement in the growth of Aurora's character, in her experience as woman and artist, and in the strange fortunes of Romney Leigh and Marian Erle. But along with these, we have on the one hand, as appropriate enough to Aurora's autobiography, frequent discursive reflections on art and life in general, sketches of people in society, the brilliant talk of London evening-parties, and all that might naturally enter into the journalizing of a literary woman mixing in the literary and fashionable society of London; and on the other, as Romney Leigh is a philanthropist to begin with, and loses his wife through an overstraining on the practical side of life and marriage, he too passes through the various phases of Socialistic opinion; and the book not only abounds in discussion and allusions to the various and conflicting theories and schemes for the regeneration of society, but its deepest object consists, we should say, in the contrast and final reconcilement of Aurora's artistic cultivation of the individual, with Romney's mechanical and materialistic plans for the improvement of the masses. It would require not perhaps more genius and intellect than Mrs. Browning has shown, to organize all this material, all these elements, into a poem of which each part should grow from the expanding life of the central idea, and be necessary to the completeness of the whole; but it would require a more patient endurance of intellectual toil, a more resolute hand upon the reins, more thought, more pains, less self-indulgence in composition, less wilfulness. She has succeeded in writing brilliantly and powerfully almost throughout this long poem of more than ten thousand lines of blank verse; she has touched social problems with the light of her penetrating intellect and the warmth of her passionate heart; has painted scenery with a free outline and a glowing color; has sketched characters as a sensitive and observant woman can sketch them; above all, she has dramatized passion with a force and energy that recall the greatest masters of tragedy: but these various excellences, though they make a book interesting, and prove genius of a high order, do not make a great poem, and will never be held to do so by any persons who know and feel that a work of art is something different in kind from the finest discursive talk, or even from a collection of studies however masterly, and though they may be ingeniously patchworked into a cleverly-devised frame.

It may be that Mrs. Browning cares little for this distinction; and that she would tell us, that, provided the wine be good, the shape of the glass matters not—that she never aimed at writing a great poem in our sense of the word, but only at writing fine sense and deep feeling. Be it so, if she really is satisfied with that explanation. We do not understand an artist who ignores art, especially when the consciousness of high moral and artistic aims is evidently present, and only the patient effort, the resolute will to conquer difficulties, is wanting. For the rest, she has succeeded in saying a number of beautiful things in a free and natural manner, that loses little of its ease and lightness in the more prosaic parts of the poem, and gains in much larger proportion in the impassioned parts by being in verse. (pp. 427-28)

The essential fault of this book is that the plan is too large and complex for the mental power brought to bear upon it; that the characters do not sufficiently act upon each other, and are too stationary in their own development. They neither grow from mutual influence nor from the expansion of their own individuality. Aurora is much the same person at thirty as at twenty; the accident which finally brings about the denouement would have brought it at any period in her mental growth. Marian Erle is a statue of heroic goodness, out of whom circumstances bring the varying expressions of that goodness, but who can scarcely be said to change, to learn any thing, to develop powers or virtues though she manifests them. And Romney Leigh is a somewhat vaguely-conceived type of a particular kind of self-sacrifice and intellectual narrowness, invested with the outward form and circumstances of an English gentleman. All this comes of not conceiving the work as a whole, but looking mainly to the separate effect of particular passages and scenes. The characters have no true continuity and development of life in the book, because the writer never conceived them from beginning to end of their careers in one coherent effort of imagination.

We do not know whether Mrs. Browning has ever read *Clarissa Harlowe,* Mrs. Gaskell's *Ruth,* and Miss Bronte's *Jane Eyre;* but in the story of Marian Erle she has joined together the central incident of Clarissa Harlowe with the leading sentiment of Ruth—that healing and reconciling influence of the maternal passion for a child whose birth is, according to common worldly feeling, the mother's disgrace. The combination is striking and original, not to say courageous in a lady. We mention it to disavow any feeling of repugnance to the moral, though we certainly do question the propriety and good taste of introducing the Clarissa Harlowe calamity under any amount of reserve, or for any emotional effect, in poem or novel. The bar of the Old Bailey is the only place where we wish to hear of such things. The same objection does not of course apply to the incident borrowed from *Jane Eyre.* But it is disagreeable to be so forcibly reminded of a recent and popular work, when a small expenditure of ingenuity would have avoided the resemblance; which is enhanced by the fact that the incident proves in each case the solution of the story's knot. (pp. 429-30)

"Mrs. Browning's 'Aurora Leigh'," in Littell's Living Age, *Vol. LII, No. 663, February 7, 1857, pp. 427-30.*

The Christian Examiner (essay date 1862)

[*In the following excerpt, the critic offers extravagant praise for* Sonnets from the Portuguese *and Browning's own character.*]

In tenderness and pathos Mrs. Browning is unsurpassed. As love-poems there is nothing finer in the language than **Sonnets from the Portuguese.** They are not only of deep interest, as disclosing passages in the life of two great poets, but have rare merit in themselves. Such purity, sweet humility, lofty self-abnegation, and impassioned tenderness have never before found utterance in verse. Shakespeare's sonnets, beautiful as they are, cannot be compared with them, and Petrarch's seem commonplace beside them. (p. 74)

"Fortitude, constancy, and devotion" have been termed the crowning excellence of the feminine character. To these must be added a gentle nature and a pure heart, and Mrs. Browning possessed them all in no stinted measure. . . . The woman who took far more pride and pleasure in being identified as "the mother of that beautiful boy," than as [an author], . . . had certainly no craving ambition for either power or fame to gratify. Her actions were prompted by a self-forgetting love, and she sought the welfare of her age far more than its applause. Such a union of whatever is great and lofty in genius with all that is pure and lovely in woman, is very rare; so rare that it will be interesting to trace some of the causes that contributed to the exquisitely blended development. Grief, the first agent, did its work thoroughly. Insight is one of the attributes of genius, but a great grief quickens marvellously the perceptive faculties. "Eyes that have wept much see clear," and Mrs. Browning owed not a little of her intimate knowledge of the human heart and her entire and earnest sympathy with all phases of suffering to those sad years unavoidably so introspective. Patience and submission are the compensating blessings the invalid may gain, and these were hers to the fullest extent. The silent heroism of this period of her life is inexpressibly touching. There is no pining wretchedness in the bearing of her cross. Sorrow and illness wrought their best discipline, bringing to her that peace which is akin to blessedness. The poems written during the season of seclusion and grief breathe a subdued thankfulness, and tell of a serene resignation. The **Sonnets from the Portuguese** reveal what life had been to Elizabeth Barrett, and also what life became to her when, by the recuperative power of a great passion, she triumphed over sorrow and the grave. For love was the next teacher, perfecting what grief began. Moved by this, she looked out upon the world with still deeper and clearer vision, her sphere of duty growing wider as her heart expanded. New light and brilliancy are reflected in her verses. As a great happiness steals into her life, her song rings out with a richer and more triumphant tone. Peace has risen to joy; but still to joy partaking largely of the nature of peace.

Underlying these mighty influences was yet another and a mightier, her deep and steadfast religious faith. This was as strong and active as her reasoning powers were acute and subtle, and the pride of the latter never overcame the convictions of the former. With nothing morbid or narrow in her piety, she held to the doctrines of the church in which she was born and nurtured. (pp. 85-6)

Mrs. Browning's moral strength equalled her intellectual. Virtue with her was no passive sentimentality, no vain aspiration. She who worked by precept worked also by example. A thorough understanding of the mission of the poet did not make her unmindful of the weighty import of the duty of the woman. . . . [Her spirit] will endure and act far into the future; and generations to come will reverence and honor the great woman-poet of our time. (p. 88)

"Mrs. Browning," in The Christian Examiner, *Vol. LXXII, No. CXXIX, January, 1862, pp. 65-88.*

Edmund Gosse (essay date 1896)

[*A distinguished English literary historian, critic, and biographer, Gosse wrote extensively on seventeenth- and eighteenth-century English literature. In the following excerpt, he assesses the emotional intent of* Sonnets from the Portuguese, *outlines its merits, and ranks it within the body of Browning's writings.*]

[The] **Sonnets from the Portuguese,** although they are by no means of equal merit, reach at their best the highest art of which their author was capable, and if we did not possess them, we should be forced to form a considerably lower estimate of her possibilities as an artist than we now do. She seems in the very best of her work, outside the volumes of 1844, to be utterly indifferent to technical excellence. Even in those volumes we see that her laxity was absolutely inherent, and that she is always liable to imperfection and licence. But the **Sonnets from the Portuguese** prove that she could, at her purest, throw off these stains and blemishes, and cast her work in bronze, like a master. They show her to us at her very best, and they form the pinnacle of her edifice as an artistic constructor. Perhaps, and to some readers, they may be neither the most attractive nor the most amusing of her writings, but to the critic they are certainly the least imperfect.

The natural bent of Elizabeth Barrett was certainly not to the sonnet. She was too dithyrambic, too tumultuous, to be willingly restrained within a rigid form of verse. She employed none other of the regular English metres, except blank verse, which she treated with a sort of defiant desperation, and *terza rima,* in which she successfully strangled her genius. Her lyrics are all of her own invention or adaptation, and they are commonly of a loose, wild form, fit to receive her chains of adverbial caprices and her tempestuous assonances. But her love of Shakespeare and Wordsworth drove her to emulation, and once and again she strove to bind her ebullient melodies down to the strict mould of fourteen rhymed iambics. It is evident that the difficulties she encountered piqued her to return to the attack, for her occasional sonnets became more and more frequent. It is interesting to note that, as befitted so learned a student of the Italians, her sonnets, from the first, were accurately built on the Petrarchan model. We might have expected from her usual laxity of form an adherence to the Elizabethan quatorzain, or, at least, to some of those adaptations in which Wordsworth, Coleridge, and even Keats indulged. But Miss Barrett, throughout her career, was one of the most rigid of Petrarchans, and no fault can be found with the structure of her octetts and sestetts. (pp. 5-7)

Great technical beauty, therefore, is the mark of these wonderful poems. Not merely are the rhymes arranged with a rare science and with a precision which few other English poets have had the patience to preserve, but the tiresome faults of Miss Barrett's prosody, those little foxes which habitually spoil her grapes, are here marvellously absent. Her very ear, which sometimes seemed so dull, with its "morning" and "inurning," its "Bacchantes" and "grant us," here seems to be quickened and strung into acuteness. There is a marked absence, in the *Sonnets from the Portuguese,* of all slovenly false rhymes, of all careless half-meaningless locutions, of all practical jokes played upon the parts of speech. The cycle opens with a noble dignity, and it is, on the whole, preserved at that high ethical level of distinguished poetic utterance. (pp. 8-9)

[Miss Barrett] is left, on this occasion, with but two competitors. Rossetti excels her by the volume and impetus of his imagery, and by his voluptuous intrepidity, but she holds her own by the intense vivacity of her instinct and the sincerity of her picture of emotion. Beside the immortal melodies of Shakespeare, hers may be counted voluble, harsh, and slight; but even here, her sympathy with a universal passion, the freshness and poignancy with which she treats a mood that is not rare and almost sickly, not foreign to the common experience of mankind, but eminently normal, direct, and obvious, give her a curious advantage. It is probable that the sonnets written by Shakespeare to his friend contain lovelier poetry and a style more perennially admirable, but those addressed by Elizabeth Barrett to her lover are hardly less exquisite to any of us, and to many of us are more wholesome and more intelligible. (p. 10)

[The] keynote of Elizabeth Barrett as an artist was sincerity. It is this quality, with all that it implies, which holds together the edifice of her style, built of such incongruous materials that no less-tempered mortar could bind it into a compact whole. At no period of her literary life, even when she was too slavishly following obsolete or tasteless models, was she otherwise than sincere. She was not striving to produce an effect; she was trying with all the effort of which her spirit was capable, to say exactly what was in her heart. When sorrow possessed her, her verse sobbed and wailed with impatient human stress, and when at last, while she waited for Death to take her by the hair, it was Love instead who came, she poured forth the heart of a happy woman without stint or concealment. The typical instance of the former class is the poem called **"De Profundis,"** written as soon after the drowning of her brother Edward as the shattered nerves and beaten brain permitted her to taste the solace of composition. It should be read, in spite of its comparative inferiority, in connection with the *Sonnets from the Portuguese,* for the power it reveals is the same; it is the capacity, while feeling acutely and deeply, to find appropriate, sufficient, and yet unexaggerated expression for the emotion. This great neuropath-

ic artist was a physician as well as a sufferer, and could count her pulses accurately through all the spasms of her anguish and her ecstasy.

When, in 1866, Robert Browning published the first selection from his wife's poems, he arranged the pieces in such a way as to give unobtrusive emphasis to the connection between the *Sonnets from the Portuguese* and two short lyrics. Even if he had not placed **"Question and Answer,"** and **"Inclusions"** immediately in front of the sonnet-cycle, we might have been justified in conjecturing that they belonged to the same period and the same mood. The arrangement of the *Sonnets* is historical. They are not heaped together in accidental sequence, as Spenser's and Shakespeare's seem to be, but they move on from the first surprise of unexpected passion to the final complete resignation of soul and body in a rapture which is to be sanctified and heightened by death itself. It is therefore possible, I think, by careful examination of the text, to insert in the sequence of sonnets, at their obvious point of composition, the two lyrics I have just mentioned; and for that purpose I will quote them here.

Taking the *Sonnets* in our hands, we meet first with the record of the violent shock produced on the whole being of the solitary and fading recluse by the discovery that Love—laughing Love masquerading under the cowl of Death—has invaded her sequestered chamber. Then to amazement succeeds instinctive repulsion; she shrinks back in a sort of horror, in her chilly twilight, from the boisterous entrance of so much heat and glow. But this quickly passes, also, submerged in the sense of her own unworthiness; her hands are numb, her eyes blinded and dazed—what has this guest of kings to do with her, a mourner in the dust? Then follows, in a crescent movement of emotion, the noble image of Electra, pouring her sepulchral urn and all its ashes at the feet of Love, ashes that blight and burn, an affection so morbid and vain that it may rather destroy than bless the heart which provokes the gift. It is at this moment, I think, between sonnets 5 and 6, that **"Question and Answer"** should be read, repeating the same idea, but repeating it in a lower key, with less violence and perhaps a shade less conviction:

> Love you seek for, presupposes
>   Summer heat and sunny glow.
> Tell me, do you find moss-roses
>   Budding, blooming in the snow?
> Snow might kill the rose-tree's root—
> Shake it quickly from your foot,
>   Lest it harm you as you go.
>
> From the ivy where it dapples
>   A grey ruin, stone by stone,
> Do you look for grapes or apples,
>   Or for sad green leaves alone?
> Pluck the leaves off, two or three—
> Keep them for mortality
>   When you shall be safe and gone.

But above these flutterings of the captured heart the captor hangs enamoured and persistent, smiling at the fiat which bids him begone: and the heart begins to thaw with the unrelieved radiation. The poetess acknowledges that she feels that she will stand henceforward in his shadow, that he has changed for her the face of all the world. Still, she dares not yield. The tide of her unworthiness flows up, and floods all the creeks of her being; she can but hide her eyes, from which the tears are flowing, and bid him, if he will not go and leave her, if he will persist in standing there with eloquent eyes fixed upon her, to trample on the pale stuff of her life, too dead to be taken to his arms. She is scarcely reasonable; we feel her pulses reeling, her limbs failing, and in the next sonnet the wave recedes for the final forward rush. She will not pour her poison on to his Venice-glass, she will not love him, will not see him—and in the next line she is folded to his arms, murmuring, "I love thee . . . I love thee!"

From this point forward the sonnets play, in their exquisite masque, as if to celestial dance-music, with the wild thoughts and tremulous frolics of accepted love, with a pulse that ever sinks into more and more normal beat, with an ever steadier and deeper flush of the new-born life. And here, if the reader will lay down the book at the close of sonnet 18, he may interpolate the lovely lyric called **"Inclusions"**:

> Oh, wilt thou have my hand, Dear, to lie along
> in
>   thine?
> As a little stone in a running stream, it seems to
> lie and
>   pine.
> Now drop the poor pale hand, Dear, unfit to
> pledge
>   with thine.
>
> Oh, wilt thou have my cheek, Dear, drawn
>   closer to
>   thine own?
> My cheek is white, my cheek is worn, by many
>   a tear
>   run down.
> Now leave a little space, Dear, lest it should wet
>   thine
>   own.
>
> Oh, must thou have my soul, Dear, commingled
>   with
>   thy soul?
> Red grows the cheek, and warm the hand; the
>   part is in
>   the whole:
> Nor hands nor cheeks keep separate, when soul
>   is
>   joined to soul,

We may pursue no further, save in the divine words of the sonnets themselves, the record of this noble and exquisite "marriage of true minds." But we may be thankful that the accredited chronicle of this episode in life and literature, lifted far out of any vagueness of conjecture or possibility of misconstruction, exists for us, distinguishing, illuminating, perfuming a great page of our national poetry. Many of the thoughts that enrich mankind and many of the purest flowers of the imagination had their roots, if the secrets of experience were made known, in actions, in desires, which could not bear the light of day, in hot-beds smelling quite otherwise than of violet or sweetbriar. But this cycle of admirable sonnets, one of the acknowledged glories of our literature, is built patently and unquestionably on the union in stainless harmony of two of the most

distinguished spirits which our century has produced. (pp. 12-17)

Edmund Gosse, "The Sonnets from the Portuguese," in his Critical Kit-Kats, *1896. Reprint by Scholarly Press, Inc., 1971, pp. 1-17.*

The Saturday Review   (essay date 1898)

[*In the following review of her collected poems, the anonymous critic praises Browning as the preeminent British woman poet.*]

No faults of style—and they are more serious and offensive than exist in any other poet known to fame—no deficiencies as an artist, no errors of undisciplined energy, no lack of breadth, of sanity, of repose, can shake Mrs. Browning's claim to a first place among British poetesses. In intensity and passion she was excelled by Emily Brontë. An enthusiasm as pure and noble, a nature as finely touched, inspired and informed the lyrics of Christina Rossetti, to whose pathos, at once so subtle and so simple, to whose visionary insight, to whose music, to whose perfection of felicitous expression, she had no pretension. Other women, notably Lady Nairn, Jane Elliott and Lady Barnard, have left single poems which many perhaps would not exchange for any one poem of Mrs. Browning's. But taking the whole mass of her writings and surveying her manifold genius on all its sides, who could fail to see that so far from having any rival among her sisters she has no second? She stands alone, alone in her extraordinary gifts, alone in her unparalleled fertility and many-sidedness. A scholar whose attainments astonished all who knew her, she resembled Macaulay in her devotion to books, being not only versed in the Hebrew, Greek, Latin, Italian, French, Spanish and Portuguese languages; but, as her poems, prefaces, letters, and dissertation on the Greek Christian poets prove, in their literatures as well. Her knowledge of our own literature, particularly our poetry from Chaucer to Scott and Wordsworth, was as minute and extensive as Southey's. And if she touched Macaulay on one side, she touched Jacob Boehmen and Swedenborg on the other. She was a Mystic, and never since Norris of Bemerton had rapt mysticism found such a voice as it finds in **"The Seraphim"** and in **"The Rhapsody of Life's Progress."** But she was neither a pedant nor a dreamer. She entered heart and soul into all the social and political questions of her time, both in England and in Italy. A religious devotee, it would not be going too far to describe her as the poet-missionary of the creed which for her summed up all spiritual and ethical truth. In the "Inni Sacri" of Manzoni alone have we any modern parallel to the fervour and rapture of her sacred poetry. But, above all things, she was a woman—"very woman of very woman," and here lies the secret of her real power and charm as a poetess. In such works as **"A Drama of Exile"** she astonishes and perplexes us; by such works as *Aurora Leigh* we are alternately attracted and repelled: few could now take pleasure in the poems in which her mysticism finds expression, and still fewer in her political poems, her *Casa Guidi Windows,* for example, or her *Poems before Congress.* But the *Sonnets from the Portuguese,* **"The Cry of the Children," "Cowper's Grave," "A Child's Grave at Florence," "To**

Flush my Dog," "The Ragged Schools of London," "The Cry of the Human," and the like go straight to every heart. Nor will the world easily forget such poems as **"A Vision of Poets," "The Lost Bower"** and **"The Dead Pan."** The great characteristic of Mrs. Browning was her very serious conception of the ends and functions of her art. It was due partly to this exquisite sensibility, partly to the intensity of her religious conviction, and partly to the stern discipline of pain and suffering to which during the whole of her early life she had been submitted. It was a return to the ideal of Milton. "Poetry has been as serious a thing to me," she wrote, "as life itself, and life has been a very serious thing. I never mistook pleasure for the final cause of poetry; nor leisure for the hour of the poet." She may have been right; she may have been wrong; but at any rate she was desperately sincere.

In one of her early poems she had attempted, she said, to express her view of the mission of the poet, "of the self-abnegation implied in it, of the great work involved in it, of the duty and glory of what Balzac has beautifully and truly called *la patience angélique du génie,* and of the obvious truth, above all, that if knowledge is power, suffering should be acceptable as a part of knowledge." Mr. Ruskin stands alone, and will probably always stand alone in his judgment that *Aurora Leigh* is the greatest poem which this century has produced in any language"; but of one thing there can be no doubt, that its authoress is in the true sense of the term one of the greatest, as well as one of the most interesting, of women. (pp. 497-98)

> *"Elizabeth Barrett Browning," in* The Saturday Review, *London, Vol. 86, No. 2215, April 9, 1898, pp. 497-98.*

Francis Thompson   (essay date 1901)

[*Thompson was one of the most important poets of the Catholic Revival in nineteenth-century English literature. Like other writers of the* fin de siècle *period, Thompson wrote poetry and prose noted for rich verbal effects and a devotion to the values of aestheticism. In the following essay, originally published in the* Academy *in 1901, he criticizes the stylistic shortcomings and facile optimism in Browning's* Casa Guidi Windows.]

This handy little reissue of one of Mrs. Browning's later poems, *Casa Guidi Windows,* has a short preface by a fellow-poet, Mme. Duclaux, better known as Miss Mary Robinson. Mme. Duclaux briefly relates the circumstances under which the poem came to be written, and interprets its spirit with sympathetic enthusiasm. But neither here nor anywhere in the book do we find what is essentially needed in a good reissue of *Casa Guidi Windows*—explanation of its crowded references to the Italian and Florentine politics of the day; references intelligible enough at the time, but now grown dim as the political references of Dryden and Pope. An unannotated edition of [John Dryden's] "Absalom and Achitophel" were but a degree more unsatisfactory. A very little trouble would have removed this defect, and caused the book to supply a real want, which in its present form we can scarcely think it does. For the rest, it is well printed on good paper and satisfactory in all other respects.

Casa Guidi Windows shows the turn of the tide towards Mrs. Browning's final manner, fully developed in *Aurora Leigh*; which, with all respect to Mme. Duclaux's judgment, we cannot think an improvement on her previous manner. On the whole, it seems to us a decided change for the worse. In this poem it is still tentative, and even Mme. Duclaux frankly admits its deficiency. The poem is entirely political, and not unnaturally it is in Mrs. Browning's rhetorical rather than her poetical style. Few poets can treat a political theme without falling into this style, which it were perhaps more accurate to call oratorical than rhetorical. It takes the lyric power of Shelley to write a "Hellas," and even Shelley fell from poetry in "The Masque of Anarchy," while he did not uniformly maintain it in "The Revolt of Islam." Still, this would be a mere question of species, were the eloquence good, as Mrs. Browning's sometimes is. But in this poem it is strained, tense, excited, often downright shrill. This defect of execution is not mended by the absence of construction. The poem is desultory, a string of reflections conditioned by passing events. It is a woman's meditations on the Italian politics of four years, taking for starting-point that Florentine portion of them which she witnessed from her windows. But her reflections are sufficiently divagatory to embrace the international exhibition at the Crystal Palace, which, as we know, was to inaugurate an era of peace and universal brotherhood. Of course, the poem is intentionally desultory. But to compensate the absence of definite scheme, the wilful invertebrateness of it, there needs a felicity of execution, an inspired caprice, an opulent luxuriance of impulse, which are unfortunately lacking. A voluntary [lack of definite scheme] must be very rich in detail to excuse the deliberate lack of unity.

Mme. Duclaux would palliate the shortcomings of style by having us admire Mrs. Browning in the part of prophetess. Now, it is true she prophesies the ultimate triumph of Italian unity, at a time when the cause had come to grief. But it needs no large power of prophecy to foresee that a great national movement, the chief barrier against which is a steadily decadent power like Austria, will ultimately win its way. Moreover, when one's whole hopes are bound up with the success of a cause, it is human nature, and woman's nature above all, to believe that the cause must ultimately triumph, no matter how dark its destinies may temporarily be. What forlorn hope but has had some woman to believe in it? When we come to things less vague and general than the triumph of *Italia Irredenta*, Mrs. Browning's fallacy as a prophetess seems blazoned large over *Casa Guidi Windows.* She believed that the day of universal brotherhood was nigh at hand, the era when wars should cease, and thinkers replace fighters as the peaceful warriors of the future. It is there in black and white. Are we any nearer it than when she shared these generous illusions with a crowd of others, who mistook the cravenness of the stay-at-home *bourgeois,* anxious to fill his moneybags in peace, for a change of heart in mankind?

> The poet shall look grander in the face
> Than ever he looked of old, when he began
> To sing that "Achillean wrath which slew
> So many heroes."

Yet the Poet Laureate is not noticeably a better model for a bust than Homer. Her Britannic prophecies are peculiarly belied by time:

> Send abroad thy high hopes and thy higher
> Resolves, from that most virtuous altitude,
> Till nations shall unconsciously aspire
> By looking up to thee, and learn that good
> And glory are not different.

Is that precisely the way in which the admiring nations now look up to England?

> No war!
> Disband thy captains, change thy victories,
> Be henceforth prosperous as the angels are—
> Helping, not humbling!

Which would be excellent, were earth Heaven. But even the angels (if we are rightly informed) humble demons. In other words, Mrs. Browning's prophecies represent the current enthusiasms of her age, and are no more nor less right than those enthusiasms. Had she lived, she would seemingly have been a Little Englander—unless, being the child of the enthusiasms of her age, she had been an ardent Imperialist.

But, being withal Elizabeth Barrett Browning, she could not escape frequent lapses into lofty eloquence, or even rank poetry. Ever and again they blow on us with triumphant refreshment. So in the finely summarised description of the nations meeting at the Crystal Palace Exhibition, each with her characteristic product in her hand:

> Imperial England draws
> The flowing ends of the earth, from Fez, Canton,
> Delhi and Stockholm, Athens and Madrid,
> The Russias and the vast Americas,
> As a queen gathers in her robes amid
> Her golden cincture. . . .
> "I wove these stuffs so subtly, that the gold
> Swims to the surface of the silk, like cream,
> And curdles to fair patterns. Ye behold?" . . .
>
> "These carpets—you walk slow on them like kings,
> Inaudible like spirits, while your foot
> Dips deep in velvet roses and such things."— . . .
>
> "This model of a steamship moves your wonder?
> You should behold it crushing down the brine
> Like a blind Jove who feels his way with thunder."— . . .
>
> "Methinks you will not match this steel of ours."—
> "Nor you this porcelain! One might think the clay
> Retained in it the larvae of the flowers,
> They bud so, round the cup, the old spring way."

That is Mrs. Browning at her best—the large, masculine way which no other woman has compassed, and which she, ever passionately and daringly trying, only seized aright by fits and starts.

> You should behold it crushing down the brine

> Like a blind Jove who feels his way with thunder.

Of what majestic grasp is that—insolently easy, not to be disdained of Shakespeare's self! No other woman has reached her hand to such things; and Elizabeth Browning could not keep her grasp on them, but clutched desperately for them, capturing them only at moments. She was best when she was content with a lesser scope. But that she could seize such images at times, all honour to her fervid, ultra-feminine soul in a frame too weak! In this poem one sees the influence of her husband beginning, not (on the whole) to her advantage; making her careless of form (of which she was never too careful), and self-indulgent in jerkinesses of style, wherein she tries to copy his native brusqueness and abruptness. The beginning of a decline (as we think) largely induced by her husband; but with splendid flakes of the old Elizabeth Barrett still clinging about her. As, indeed, even in *Aurora Leigh*, they did not abandon her. (pp. 159-63)

Francis Thompson, "Mrs. Browning as Prophetess," in his Literary Criticisms, edited by Rev. Terence L. Connolly, S. J., E. P. Dutton and Company, Inc., 1948, pp. 159-63.

G. K. Chesterton (essay date 1903)

[*Regarded as one of England's premier men of letters during the first half of the twentieth century, Chesterton is best known today as a witty essayist and the creator of the Father Brown mysteries and the fantasy* The Man Who Was Thursday *(1908). Chesterton's essays are characterized by their humor, frequent use of paradox, and chatty, rambling style. The following review of* Casa Guidi Windows *was originally published in 1903. Chesterton comments on Browning's extravagant and ambitious poetic conceits and places her in the context of nineteenth-century liberalism.*]

The delightful new edition of Mrs. Browning's *Casa Guidi Windows* . . . ought certainly to serve as an opportunity for the serious criticism and inevitable admiration to which a great poet is entitled. For Mrs. Browning was a great poet, and not, as is idly and vulgarly supposed, only a great poetess. The word poetess is bad English, and it conveys a particularly bad compliment. Nothing is more remarkable about Mrs. Browning's work than the absence of that trite and namby-pamby elegance which the last two centuries demanded from lady writers. Wherever her verse is bad it is bad from some extravagance of imagery, some violence of comparison, some kind of debauch of cleverness. Her nonsense never arises from weakness, but from a confusion of powers. If the phrase explain itself, she is far more a great poet than she is a good one.

Mrs. Browning often appears more luscious and sentimental than many other literary women, but this was because she was stronger. It requires a certain amount of internal force to break down. A complete self-humiliation requires enormous strength, more strength than most of us possess. When she was writing the poetry of self-abandonment she really abandoned herself with the valour and decision of an anchorite abandoning the world. Such a couplet as:

> Our Euripides, the human,
> With his dropping of warm tears,

gives to most of us a sickly and nauseous sensation. Nothing can be well conceived more ridiculous than Euripides going about dropping tears with a loud splash, and Mrs. Browning coming after him with a thermometer. But the one emphatic point about this idiotic couplet is that Mrs. Hemans would never have written it. She would have written something perfectly dignified, perfectly harmless, perfectly inconsiderable. Mrs. Browning was in a great and serious difficulty. She really meant something. She aimed at a vivid and curious image, and she missed it. She had that catastrophic and public failure which is, as much as a medal or a testimonial, the badge of the brave.

In spite of the tiresome half-truth that art is unmoral, the arts require a certain considerable number of moral qualities, and more especially all the arts require courage. The art of drawing, for example, requires even a kind of physical courage. Anyone who has tried to draw a straight line and failed knows that he fails chiefly in nerve, as he might fail to jump off a cliff. And similarly all great literary art involves the element of risk, and the greatest literary artists have commonly been those who have run the greatest risk of talking nonsense. Almost all great poets rant, from Shakespeare downwards. Mrs. Browning was Elizabethan in her luxuriance and her audacity, and the gigantic scale of her wit. We often feel with her as we feel with Shakespeare, that she would have done better with half as much talent. The great curse of the Elizabethans is upon her, that she cannot leave anything alone, she cannot write a single line without a conceit:

> And the eyes of the peacock fans
> Winked at the alien glory,

she said of the Papal fans in the presence of the Italian tricolour:

> And a royal blood sends glances up her princely
> eye to trouble.
> And the shadow of a monarch's crown is soft-
> ened in her hair,

is her description of a beautiful and aristocratic lady. The notion of peacock feathers winking like so many London urchins is perhaps one of her rather aggressive and outrageous figures of speech. The image of a woman's hair as the softened shadow of a crown is a singularly vivid and perfect one. But both have the same quality of intellectual fancy and intellectual concentration. They are both instances of a sort of ethereal epigram. This is the great and dominant characteristic of Mrs. Browning, that she was significant alike in failure and success. Just as every marriage in the world, good or bad, is a marriage, dramatic, irrevocable, and big with coming events, so every one of her wild weddings between alien ideas is an accomplished fact which produces a certain effect on the imagination, which has for good or evil become part and parcel of our mental vision forever. She gives the reader the impression that she never declined a fancy, just as some gentlemen of the eighteenth century never declined a duel. When she fell it was always because she missed the foothold, never because she funked the leap.

Casa Guidi Windows is, in one aspect, a poem very typical of its author. Mrs. Browning may fairly be called the peculiar poet of Liberalism, of that great movement of the first half of the nineteenth century towards the emancipation of men from ancient institutions which had gradually changed their nature, from the houses of refuge which had turned into dungeons, and the mystic jewels which remained only as fetters. It was not what we ordinarily understand by revolt. It had no hatred in its heart for ancient and essentially human institutions. It had that deeply conservative belief in the most ancient of institutions, the average man, which goes by the name of democracy. It had none of the spirit of modern Imperialism which is kicking a man because he is down. But, on the other hand, it had none of the spirit of modern Anarchism and scepticism which is kicking a man merely because he is up. It was based fundamentally on a belief in the destiny of humanity, whether that belief took an irreligious form, as in Swinburne, or a religious form, as in Mrs. Browning. It had that rooted and natural conviction that the Millennium was coming to-morrow which has been the conviction of all iconoclasts and reformers, and for which some rationalists have been absurd enough to blame the early Christians. But they had none of that disposition to pin their whole faith to some black-and-white scientific system which afterwards became the curse of philosophical Radicalism. They were not like the sociologists who lay down a final rectification of things, amounting to nothing except an end of the world, a great deal more depressing than would be the case if it were knocked to pieces by a comet. Their ideal, like the ideal of all sensible people, was a chaotic and confused notion of goodness made up of English primroses and Greek statues, birds singing in April, and regiments being cut to pieces for a flag. They were neither Radicals nor Socialists, but Liberals, and a Liberal is a noble and indispensable lunatic who tries to make a cosmos of his own head.

Mrs. Browning and her husband were more liberal than most Liberals. Theirs was the hospitality of the intellect and the hospitality of the heart, which is the best definition of the term. They never fell into the habit of the idle revolutionists of supposing that the past was bad because the future was good, which amounted to asserting that because humanity had never made anything but mistakes it was now quite certain to be right. Browning possessed in a greater degree than any other man the power of realising that all conventions were only victorious revolutions. He could follow the mediæval logicians in all their sowing of the wind and reaping of the whirlwind with all that generous ardour which is due to abstract ideas. He could study the ancients with the young eyes of the Renaissance and read a Greek grammar like a book of love lyrics. This immense and almost confounding Liberalism of Browning doubtless had some effect upon his wife. In her vision of New Italy she went back to the image of Ancient Italy like an honest and true revolutionist; for does not the very word "revolution" mean a rolling backward. All true revolutions are reversions to the natural and the normal. A revolutionist who breaks with the past is a notion fit for an idiot. For how could a man even wish for something which he had never heard of? Mrs. Browning's inexhaustible sympathy with all the ancient and essential passions of humanity was nowhere more in evidence than in her conception of patriotism. For some dark reason, which it is difficult indeed to fathom, belief in patriotism in our day is held to mean principally a belief in every other nation abandoning its patriotic feelings. In the case of no other passion does this weird contradiction exist. Men whose lives are mainly based upon friendship sympathise with the friendships of others. The interest of engaged couples in each other is a proverb, and like many other proverbs sometimes a nuisance. In patriotism alone it is considered correct just now to assume that the sentiment does not exist in other people. It was not so with the great Liberals of Mrs. Browning's time. The Brownings had, so to speak, a disembodied talent for patriotism. They loved England and they loved Italy; yet they were the very reverse of cosmopolitans. They loved the two countries as countries, not as arbitrary divisions of the globe. They had hold of the root and essence of patriotism. They knew how certain flowers and birds and rivers pass into the mills of the brain and come out as wars and discoveries, and how some triumphant adventure or some staggering crime wrought in a remote continent may bear about it the colour of an Italian city or the soul of a silent village of Surrey. (pp. 261-69)

> G. K. Chesterton, "Elizabeth Barrett Browning," in his Varied Types, Dodd, Mead and Company, 1909, pp. 261-69.

Browning on the immortality of the soul (in a letter to Madame Braun dated 1858):

'More and more life is what we want' Tennyson wrote long ago, and that is the right want. Indifference to life is disease, and therefore not strength. But the life here is only half the apple—a cut out of the apple, I should say, merely meant to suggest the perfect round of fruit—and there is in the world now, I can testify to you, *scientific proof* that what we call death is a mere change of circumstances, a change of dress, a mere breaking of the outside shell and husk. This subject is so much the most interesting to me of all, that I can't help writing of it to you. Among all the ways of progress along which the minds of men are moving, this draws me most. There is much folly and fanaticism, unfortunately, because foolish men and women do not cease to be foolish when they hit upon a truth. There was a man who hung bracelets upon plane trees. But it was a tree—it is a truth—notwithstanding; yes, and so much a truth that in twenty years the probability is you will have no more doubters of the immortality of souls, and no more need of Platos to prove it.

Elizabeth Barrett Browning in her The Letters of Elizabeth Barrett Browning, *1897.*

Virginia Woolf (essay date 1931)

[*Woolf is considered one of the most prominent literary figures of twentieth-century English literature. Her works, noted for their subjective explorations of characters' inner lives and their delicate poetic quality, have* *had a lasting effect on the art of the novel. A discerning and influential critic and essayist as well as a novelist, Woolf began writing reviews for the* Times Literary Supplement *at an early age. Her critical essays, which cover almost the entire range of English literature, contain some of her finest prose and are praised for their insight. In the following essay, originally published in 1931, Woolf analyzes* Aurora Leigh *as "a masterpiece in embryo."*]

By one of those ironies of fashion that might have amused the Brownings themselves, it seems likely that they are now far better known in the flesh than they have ever been in the spirit. Passionate lovers, in curls and side whiskers, oppressed, defiant, eloping—in this guise thousands of people must know and love the Brownings who have never read a line of their poetry. They have become two of the most conspicuous figures in that bright and animated company of authors who, thanks to our modern habit of writing memoirs and printing letters and sitting to be photographed, live in the flesh, not merely as of old in the word; are known by their hats, not merely by their poems. What damage the art of photography has inflicted upon the art of literature has yet to be reckoned. How far we are going to read a poet when we can read about a poet is a problem to lay before biographers. Meanwhile, nobody can deny the power of the Brownings to excite our sympathy and rouse our interest. **"Lady Geraldine's Courtship"** is glanced at perhaps by two professors in American universities once a year; but we all know how Miss Barrett lay on her sofa; how she escaped from the dark house in Wimpole Street one September morning; how she met health and happiness, freedom, and Robert Browning in the church round the corner.

But fate has not been kind to Mrs Browning as a writer. Nobody reads her, nobody discusses her, nobody troubles to put her in her place. One has only to compare her reputation with Christina Rossetti's to trace her decline. Christina Rossetti mounts irresistibly to the first place among English women poets. Elizabeth, so much more loudly applauded during her lifetime, falls farther and farther behind. The primers dismiss her with contumely. Her importance, they say, 'has now become merely historical. Neither education nor association with her husband ever succeeded in teaching her the value of words and a sense of form.' In short, the only place in the mansion of literature that is assigned her is downstairs in the servants' quarters, where, in company with Mrs Hemans, Eliza Cook, Jean Ingelow, Alexander Smith, Edwin Arnold, and Robert Montgomery, she bangs the crockery about and eats vast handfuls of peas on the point of her knife.

If, therefore, we take **Aurora Leigh** from the shelf it is not so much in order to read it as to muse with kindly condescension over this token of bygone fashion, as we toy with the fringes of our grandmothers' mantles and muse over the alabaster models of the Taj Mahal which once adorned their drawing-room tables. But to the Victorians, undoubtedly, the book was very dear. Thirteen editions of **Aurora Leigh** had been demanded by the year 1873. And, to judge from the dedication, Mrs Browning herself was not afraid to say that she set great store by it—'the most mature of my works,' she calls it, 'and the one into which my highest convictions upon Life and Art have entered'. Her letters show that she had had the book in mind for many years. She was brooding over it when she first met Browning, and her intention with regard to it forms almost the first of those confidences about their work which the lovers delighted to share.

> . . . my chief *intention* [she wrote] just now is the writing of a sort of novel-poem . . . running into the midst of our conventions, and rushing into drawing-rooms and the like, 'where angels fear to tread'; and so, meeting face to face and without mask the Humanity of the age, and speaking the truth of it out plainly. That is my intention.

But for reasons which later become clear, she hoarded her intention throughout the ten astonishing years of escape and happiness; and when at last the book appeared in 1856 she might well feel that she had poured into it the best that she had to give. Perhaps the hoarding and the saturation which resulted have something to do with the surprise that awaits us. At any rate we cannot read the first twenty pages of *Aurora Leigh* without becoming aware that the Ancient Mariner who lingers, for unknown reasons, at the porch of one book and not of another has us by the hand, and makes us listen like a three years' child while Mrs Browning pours out in nine volumes of blank verse the story of Aurora Leigh. Speed and energy, forthrightness and complete self-confidence—these are the qualities that hold us enthralled. Floated off our feet by them, we learn how Aurora was the child of an Italian mother 'whose rare blue eyes were shut from seeing her when she was scarcely four years old'. Her father was 'an austere Englishman, Who, after a dry life-time spent at home In college-learning, law and parish talk, Was flooded with a passion unaware', but died too, and the child was sent back to England to be brought up by an aunt. The aunt, of the well-known family of the Leighs, stood upon the hall step of her country house dressed in black to welcome her. Her somewhat narrow forehead was braided tight with brown hair pricked with grey; she had a close, mild mouth; eyes of no colour; and cheeks like roses pressed in books, 'Kept more for ruth than pleasure,—if past bloom, Past fading also'. The lady had lived a quiet life, exercising her Christian gifts upon knitting stockings and stitching petticoats 'because we are of one flesh, after all, and need one flannel'. At her hand Aurora suffered the education that was thought proper for women. She learnt a little French, a little algebra; the internal laws of the Burmese empire; what navigable river joins itself to Lara; what census of the year five was taken at Klagenfurt; also how to draw nereids neatly draped, to spin glass, to stuff birds, and model flowers in wax. For the Aunt liked a woman to be womanly. Of an evening she did cross-stitch and, owing to some mistake in her choice of silk, once embroidered a shepherdess with pink eyes. Under this torture of women's education, the passionate Aurora exclaimed, certain women have died; others pine; a few who have, as Aurora had, 'relations with the unseen', survive, and walk demurely, and are civil to their cousins and listen to the vicar and pour out tea. Aurora herself was blessed with a little room. It was green papered, had a green carpet and there were green curtains to the bed, as if to match the insipid green-

ery of the English countryside. There she retired; there she read. 'I had found the secret of a garret room Piled high with cases in my father's name, Piled high, packed large, where, creeping in and out . . . like some small nimble mouse between the ribs of a mastodon' she read and read. The mouse indeed (it is the way with Mrs Browning's mice) took wings and soared, for 'It is rather when We gloriously forget ourselves and plunge Soul-forward, headlong, into a book's profound, Impassioned for its beauty and salt of truth—'Tis then we get the right good from a book'. And so she read and read, until her cousin Romney called to walk with her, or the painter Vincent Carrington, 'whom men judge hardly as bee-bonneted Because he holds that paint a body well you paint a soul by implication', tapped on the window.

This hasty abstract of the first volume of *Aurora Leigh* does it of course no sort of justice; but having gulped down the original much as Aurora herself advises, soul-forward, headlong, we find ourselves in a state where some attempt at the ordering of our multitudinous impressions becomes imperative. The first of these impressions and the most pervasive is the sense of the writer's presence. Through the voice of Aurora the character, the circumstances, the idiosyncrasies of Elizabeth Barrett Browning ring in our ears. Mrs Browning could no more conceal herself than she could control herself, a sign no doubt of imperfection in an artist, but a sign also that life has impinged upon art more than life should. Again and again in the pages we have read, Aurora the fictitious seems to be throwing light upon Elizabeth the actual. The idea of the poem, we must remember, came to her in the early forties when the connection between a woman's art and a woman's life was unnaturally close, so that it is impossible for the most austere of critics not sometimes to touch the flesh when his eyes should be fixed upon the page. And as everybody knows, the life of Elizabeth Barrett was of a nature to affect the most authentic and individual of gifts. Her mother had died when she was a child; she had read profusely and privately; her favourite brother was drowned; her health broke down; she had been immured by the tyranny of her father in almost conventual seclusion in a bedroom in Wimpole Street. But instead of rehearsing the well-known facts, it is better to read in her own words her own account of the effect they had upon her.

> I have lived only inwardly [she wrote] or with *sorrow,* for a strong emotion. Before this seclusion of my illness, I was secluded still, and there are few of the youngest women in the world who have not seen more, heard more, known more, of society, than I, who am scarcely to be called young now. I grew up in the country—I had no social opportunities, had my heart in books and poetry, and my experience in reveries . . . And so time passed and passed—and afterwards, when my illness came . . . and no prospect (as appeared at one time) of ever passing the threshold of one room again; why then, I turned to thinking with some bitterness . . . that I had stood blind in this temple I was about to leave— that I had seen no Human nature, that my brothers and sisters of the earth were *names* to me, that I had beheld no great mountain or river, nothing in fact . . . And do you also know what

a disadvantage this ignorance is to my art? Why, if I live on and yet do not escape from this seclusion, do you not perceive that I labour under signal disadvantages—that I am, in a manner as a *blind poet?* Certainly, there is compensation to a degree. I have had much of the inner life, and from the habit of self-consciousness and self-analysis, I make great guesses at Human nature in the main. But how willingly I would as a poet exchange some of this lumbering, ponderous, helpless knowledge of books, for some experience of life and man, for some . . .

She breaks off, with three little dots, and we may take advantage of her pause to turn once more to *Aurora Leigh.*

What damage had her life done her as a poet? A great one, we cannot deny. For it is clear, as we turn the pages of *Aurora Leigh* or of the *Letters*—one often echoes the other—that the mind which found its natural expression in this swift and chaotic poem about real men and women was not the mind to profit by solitude. A lyrical, a scholarly, a fastidious mind might have used seclusion and solitude to perfect its powers. Tennyson asked no better than to live with books in the heart of the country. But the mind of Elizabeth Barrett was lively and secular and satirical. She was no scholar. Books were to her not an end in themselves but a substitute for living. She raced through folios because she was forbidden to scamper on the grass. She wrestled with Aeschylus and Plato because it was out of the question that she should argue about politics with live men and women. Her favourite reading as an invalid was Balzac and George Sand and other 'immortal improprieties' because 'they kept the colour in my life to some degree'. Nothing is more striking when at last she broke the prison bars than the fervour with which she flung herself into the life of the moment. She loved to sit in a café and watch people passing; she loved the arguments, the politics, and the strife of the modern world. The past and its ruins, even the past of Italy and Italian ruins, interested her much less than the theories of Mr Hume the medium, or the politics of Napoleon, Emperor of the French. Italian pictures, Greek poetry, roused in her a clumsy and conventional enthusiasm in strange contrast with the original independence of her mind when it applied itself to actual facts.

Such being her natural bent, it is not surprising that even in the depths of her sick-room her mind turned to modern life as a subject for poetry. She waited, wisely, until her escape had given her some measure of knowledge and proportion. But it cannot be doubted that the long years of seclusion had done her irreparable damage as an artist. She had lived shut off, guessing at what was outside, and inevitably magnifying what was within. The loss of Flush, the spaniel, affected her as the loss of a child might have affected another woman. The tap of ivy on the pane became the thrash of trees in a gale. Every sound was enlarged, every incident exaggerated, for the silence of the sick-room was profound and the monotony of Wimpole Street was intense. When at last she was able to 'rush into drawing-rooms and the like and meet face to face without mask the Humanity of the age and speak the truth of it out plainly', she was too weak to stand the shock. Ordinary daylight, current gossip, the usual traffic of human

beings left her exhausted, ecstatic, and dazzled into a state where she saw so much and felt so much that she did not altogether know what she felt or what she saw.

Aurora Leigh, the novel-poem, is not, therefore, the masterpiece that it might have been. Rather it is a masterpiece in embryo; a work whose genius floats diffused and fluctuating in some pre-natal stage waiting the final stroke of creative power to bring it into being. Stimulating and boring, ungainly and eloquent, monstrous and exquisite, all by turns, it overwhelms and bewilders; but, nevertheless, it still commands our interest and inspires our respect. For it becomes clear as we read that, whatever Mrs Browning's faults, she was one of those rare writers who risk themselves adventurously and disinterestedly in an imaginative life which is independent of their private lives and demands to be considered apart from personalities. Her 'intention' survives; the interest of her theory redeems much that is faulty in her practice. Abridged and simplified from Aurora's argument in the fifth book, that theory runs something like this. The true work of poets, she said, is to present their own age, not Charlemagne's. More passion takes place in drawing-rooms than at Roncesvalles with Roland and his knights. 'To flinch from modern varnish, coat or flounce, Cry out for togas and the picturesque, Is fatal—foolish too'. For living art presents and records real life, and the only life we can truly know is our own. But what form, she asks, can a poem on modern life take? The drama is impossible, for only servile and docile plays have any chance of success. Moreover, what we (in 1846) have to say about life is not fit for 'boards, actors, prompters, gaslight, and costume; our stage is now the soul itself '. What then can she do? The problem is difficult, performance is bound to fall short of endeavour; but she has at least wrung her life-blood on to every page of her book, and, for the rest 'Let me think of forms less, and the external. Trust the spirit . . . Keep up the fire and leave the generous flames to shape themselves'. And so the fire blazed and the flames leapt high.

The desire to deal with modern life in poetry was not confined to Miss Barrett. Robert Browning said that he had had the same ambition all his life. Coventry Patmore's 'Angel in the House' and Clough's 'Bothie' were both attempts at the same kind and preceded *Aurora Leigh* by some years. It was natural enough. The novelists were dealing triumphantly with modern life in prose. *Jane Eyre, Vanity Fair, David Copperfield, Richard Feverel* all trod fast on each other's heels between the years 1847 and 1860. The poets may well have felt, with Aurora Leigh, that modern life had an intensity and a meaning of its own. Why should these spoils fall solely into the laps of the prose writers? Why should the poet be forced back to the remoteness of Charlemagne and Roland, to the toga and the picturesque, when the humours and tragedies of village life, drawing-room life, club life, and street life all cried aloud for celebration? It was true that the old form in which poetry had dealt with life—the drama—was obsolete; but was there none other that could take its place? Mrs Browning, convinced of the divinity of poetry, pondered, seized as much as she could of actual experience, and then at last threw down her challenge to the Brontës and the Thackerays in nine books of blank verse. It was in blank verse that she sang of Shoreditch and Kensington; of my aunt and the vicar; of Romney Leigh and Vincent Carrington; of Marian Erle and Lord Howe; of fashionable weddings and drab suburban streets, and bonnets and whiskers and four-wheeled cabs, and railway trains. The poets can treat of these things, she exclaimed, as well as of knights and dames, moats and drawbridges and castle courts. But can they? Let us see what happens to a poet when he poaches upon a novelist's preserves and gives us not an epic or a lyric but the story of many lives that move and change and are inspired by the interests and passions that are ours in the middle of the reign of Queen Victoria.

In the first place there is the story; a tale has to be told; the poet must somehow convey to us the necessary information that his hero has been asked out to dinner. This is a statement that a novelist would convey as quietly and prosaically as possible; for example, 'While I was kissing her glove, sadly enough, a note was brought saying that her father sent his regards and asked me to dine with them next day'. That is harmless. But the poet has to write:

> While thus I grieved, and kissed her glove,
>   My man brought in her note to say,
> Papa had bid her send his love,
>   And would I dine with them next day!

Which is absurd. The simple words have been made to strut and posture and take on an emphasis which makes them ridiculous. Then again, what will the poet do with dialogue? In modern life, as Mrs Browning indicated when she said that our stage is now the soul, the tongue has superseded the sword. It is in talk that the high moments of life, the shock of character upon character, are defined. But poetry when it tries to follow the words on people's lips is terribly impeded. Listen to Romney in a moment of high emotion talking to his old love Marian about the baby she has borne to another man:

> May God so father me, as I do him,
> And so forsake me, as I let him feel
> He's orphaned haply. Here I take the child
> To share my cup, to slumber on my knee,
> To play his loudest gambol at my foot,
> To hold my finger in the public ways . . .

and so on. Romney, in short, rants and reels like any of those Elizabethan heroes whom Mrs Browning had warned so imperiously out of her modern living-room. Blank verse has proved itself the most remorseless enemy of living speech. Talk tossed up on the surge and swing of the verse becomes high, rhetorical, impassioned; and as talk, since action is ruled out, must go on and on, the reader's mind stiffens and glazes under the monotony of the rhythm. Following the lilt of her rhythm rather than the emotions of her characters, Mrs Browning is swept on into generalisation and declamation. Forced by the nature of her medium, she ignores the slighter, the subtler, the more hidden shades of emotion by which a novelist builds up touch by touch a character in prose. Change and development, the effect of one character upon another—all this is abandoned. The poem becomes one long soliloquy, and the only character that is known to us and the only story that is told us are the character and story of Aurora Leigh herself.

Thus, if Mrs Browning meant by a novel-poem a book in which character is closely and subtly revealed, the relations of many hearts laid bare, and a story unfalteringly unfolded, she failed completely. But if she meant rather to give us a sense of life in general, of people who are unmistakably Victorian, wrestling with the problems of their own time, all brightened, intensified and compacted by the fire of poetry, she succeeded. Aurora Leigh, with her passionate interest in social questions, her conflict as artist and woman, her longing for knowledge and freedom, is the true daughter of her age. Romney, too, is no less certainly a mid-Victorian gentleman of high ideals who has thought deeply about the social question, and has founded, unfortunately, a phalanstery in Shropshire. The aunt, the antimacassars, and the country house from which Aurora escapes are real enough to fetch high prices in the Tottenham Court Road at this moment. The broader aspects of what it felt like to be a Victorian are seized as surely and stamped as vividly upon us as in any novel by Trollope or Mrs Gaskell.

And indeed if we compare the prose novel and the novel-poem the triumphs are by no means all to the credit of prose. As we rush through page after page of narrative in which a dozen scenes that the novelist would smooth out separately are pressed into one, in which pages of deliberate description are fused into a single line, we cannot help feeling that the poet has outpaced the prose writer. Her page is packed twice as full as his. Characters, too, if they are not shown in conflict but snipped off and summed up with something of the exaggeration of a caricaturist, have a heightened and symbolical significance which prose with its gradual approach cannot rival. The general aspect of things—market, sunset, church—have a brilliance and a continuity, owing to the compressions and elisions of poetry, which mock the prose writer and his slow accumulations of careful detail. For these reasons *Aurora Leigh* remains, with all its imperfections, a book that still lives and breathes and has its being. And when we think how still and cold the plays of Beddoes or of Sir Henry Taylor lie, in spite of all their beauty, and how seldom in our own day we disturb the repose of the classical dramas of Robert Bridges, we may suspect that Elizabeth Barrett was inspired by a flash of true genius when she rushed into the drawing-room and said that here, where we live and work, is the true place for the poet. At any rate, her courage was justified in her own case. Her bad taste, her tortured ingenuity, her floundering, scrambling, and confused impetuosity have space to spend themselves here without inflicting a deadly wound, while her ardour and abundance, her brilliant descriptive powers, her shrewd and caustic humour, infect us with her own enthusiasm. We laugh, we protest, we complain—it is absurd, it is impossible, we cannot tolerate this exaggeration a moment longer—but, nevertheless, we read to the end enthralled. What more can an author ask? But the best compliment that we can pay *Aurora Leigh* is that it makes us wonder why it has left no successors. Surely the street, the drawing-room, are promising subjects; modern life is worthy of the muse. But the rapid sketch that Elizabeth Barrett Browning threw off when she leapt from her couch and dashed into the drawing-room remains unfinished. The conservatism or the timidity of poets still leaves the chief spoils of modern life to the novelist. We have no novel-poem of the age of George the Fifth. (pp. 202-13)

Virginia Woolf, "Aurora Leigh," in her The Second Common Reader, *edited by Andrew McNeillie, Harcourt Brace Jovanovich, 1986, pp. 202-13.*

Gardner B. Taplin   (essay date 1956)

[*In the following excerpt, Taplin focuses on the revisions Browning made to her* Poems (1850) *prior to publication and provides a general overview of early critical reaction to the collection.*]

Robert Browning and his wife were busy with their poetry in the winter of 1849-50. Robert was writing his *Christmas-Eve and Easter-Day,* and Elizabeth was revising her volumes of 1838 and 1844 in preparation for a new edition. Elizabeth thought that Browning's poem, brought out by Chapman and Hall, was "full of power," but the work received few acceptable reviews and the sales were poor.

Indeed, during Elizabeth's lifetime all of Browning's poetry failed to win general recognition, and his reputation was very much overshadowed by that of his wife. For example, when the post of poet laureate became vacant after Wordsworth's death in April, 1850, it was Elizabeth, not Robert, whom the *Athenaeum* recommended to the position. The first paragraph of a column, probably written by H. F. Chorley, entitled "Our Weekly Gossip" in the *Athenaeum,* June 1, said that to grant the laureateship "to a female would be at once an honourable testimonial to the individual, a fitting recognition of the remarkable place which the women of England have taken in the literature of the day, and a graceful compliment to the Sovereign herself." The writer added that, "There is no living poet of either sex who can prefer a higher claim than Mrs. Elizabeth Barrett Browning." Three weeks later the *Athenaeum* reported that Leigh Hunt was being considered for the post. Although the author of the article believed that Hunt had a claim, he thought that is was "not of the kind which can be properly recognized by the laureateship," and again suggested Elizabeth's name. After the position was granted to Tennyson, Chorley regretted the decision because the award had not gone to a woman and because Tennyson already had a pension. Elizabeth had at first favored Leigh Hunt, who was "a great man and a good man in spite of all," but she later said that Tennyson was "in a sense" worthier of the laureateship than Hunt; "only Tennyson can wait, that is the single difference."

Although Elizabeth had not published much poetry since her volume of 1844, she had not been altogether forgotten either in America or England before the discussion about the laureateship. An American critic and traveler, Henry Theodore Tuckerman, who had been for a while editor of the *Boston Miscellany of Literature and Fashion,* in which Elizabeth had published in 1842, wrote an appreciative review of her work in his *Thoughts on the Poets,* which appeared in New York in 1846. He emphasized her classical scholarship and declared that her poems were "imbued with the spirit of antique models." An American clergy-

man, musician, and minor poet, George W. Bethune, wrote in 1848 in his volume *The British Female Poets* of Elizabeth's "high religious faith, her love of children, her delight in the graceful and beautiful, her revelations of feminine feeling, her sorrow over the suffering, and her indignation against the oppressor." In 1849 an English editor and author, Frederick Rowton, paid tribute to her genius in his *Female Poets of Great Britain.* He found in her precisely the qualities she lacked: "She is chief amongst the learned poetesses of our land: at least, I know of no British female writer who exhibits so intimate an acquaintance with the *spirit* of both antique and modern philosophy, or so refined a perception of intellectual purity and beauty. Her poetry is the poetry of pure reason."

Elizabeth probably did not know of all these flattering articles, but she was much pleased to have been suggested for the laureateship. While she was awaiting the critical reception of her new volumes, she suffered in the summer of 1850 from her fourth and last miscarriage, her most serious setback since she had left England. For six weeks afterwards she was gravely ill. Her physician, Dr. Harding, realized that she would have to move to the country as soon as she was well enough to travel.

In the morning of August 31, the Brownings left Florence by railroad for Siena. They spent September in a small villa, which cost only eleven shillings a week, about two miles from the city. It was in the midst of a vineyard, olive orchard, and flower garden, and was on a hill called *poggio dei venti.* The villa was cool and had splendid views in all directions. Elizabeth wrote that, "From one window you have a view of Siena, with its Duomo and its campanile, and its Italian colouring over all! . . . From another, the whole country leaps under the sun, alive with verdure and vineyards." Her health soon improved, so that during the first week of October, which they spent in Siena, she was able to walk through the cathedral and through the Academy, where she admired "the divine Eve of Sodoma." Although she was to live in Siena parts of the summers of 1859 and 1860 and to pass through the city many times on her journeys between Florence and Rome, she was never again strong enough to climb the steps into the cathedral.

About the first of November Elizabeth's "new edition" was brought out by Chapman and Hall, who had published Browning's *Christmas-Eve and Easter-Day.* The *Poems* were issued in two octavo volumes bound in dark gray-blue cloth boards. Elizabeth included all of the poems in the volume of 1844, and all but nine of the poems in the volume of *The Seraphim* (omitting the weakest, such as **"The Little Friend," "Victoria's Tears,"** and **"The Weeping Saviour"**)—and all the verses which had appeared in periodicals since 1844, most of them in *Blackwood's,* two in the *Christian Mother's Magazine,* and one each in the *Liberty Bell* of Boston and the *Athenaeum;* also **"A Sabbath Morning at Sea"** from an annual in 1839 and **"The Claim,"** which had been published in the *Athenaeum* in 1842. She had not been writing so frequently for magazines as before her marriage. Browning strongly disapproved of the publication of poetry in a periodical before it should appear in a book, because he felt the practice was

Casa Guidi, the palace in Florence where the Brownings had an apartment.

a deception to the public. The most important of her works being published for the first time were the new translation of the *Prometheus Bound,* a translation of Bion's *Lament for Adonis,* and the **Sonnets from the Portuguese,** as well as three short poems which also were inspired by her love for Browning: **"Life and Love," "Inclusions,"** and **"Insufficiency."**

In the preparation of her new edition she made many revisions among the poems of 1844 and had to rewrite many pages of the volume of 1838. "Oh, such feeble rhymes, and turns of thought—such a dingy mistiness!" she wrote of *The Seraphim, and Other Poems.* "Even Robert couldn't say a word for much of it. I took great pains with the whole, and made considerable portions new." First of all, she improved many of the rhymes: "shaped"—"heaped" became "deep"—"heap"; "spade"—"led" was changed to "spade"—"laid." Obsolete words such as "een," "eyne," "pleasaunce," "eke," "aye," "erst," "anear," "enow" were eliminated. Dyssyllabic past participles like "kneeled," "laughed," "looked" were revised to "knelt," "her laugh," "did look," and outmoded words such as "waxed" and "tranced" were removed. She took out adverbs which had been overused and were sometimes meaningless; for instance, "striking on thy ringlets sheenly."

Many adjectives were placed in their normal position: "water colourless" became "the gray water" and "her small feet bare" was changed to "her small bare feet." The indicative form of the verb was substituted for the old-fashioned subjunctive: "There be (later "are") none of England's daughters." Several of her emendations were of words which had done violence to parts of speech; for example, "verduring the hills" became "to beautify thy hills. Occasionally when a passage was filled with archaic diction, she entirely rewrote the lines. To illustrate, the following verses seemed so unpromising that she eliminated them altogether from the revised version of the **"Stanzas to Bettine"** :

> I ween, thy smile is graver—
> Paler thy cheek, I ween:
> For thou the mystic sight hast seen,
> Which maketh quail the braver—

She also removed many of the mottoes for individual poems: verses by Beaumont and Fletcher, Burton, Spenser, Habington, Hawes, Gascoigne, Wither, and others; also Latin verses by Milton and passages in Greek by Plato, St. Chrysostom, and Orpheus; and she discarded a long footnote on the derivation of the name of Homer and two shorter footnotes referring to Biblical passages. Her reason for the deletions may have been that she was weary of her reputation as an uncomfortably learned poet. Since her marriage she had no longer been reading Hebrew, Greek, Latin, nor English literature of earlier periods. The only long poem she had written was the first part of *Casa Guidi Windows,* which was still in manuscript, on current affairs in Italy. After the bleak years at Wimpole Street she had achieved fulfillment as a wife and mother. It may have been therefore that she wished to come before the public in 1850 as a writer who had moved away from the world of books toward "life."

Prometheus Bound had been finished in 1845 and was later sent to William Blackwood in Edinburgh. In 1848 he also had the manuscript of **"A Meditation in Tuscany"** but returned both works because of their unsuitability for publication in his magazine; and so Elizabeth included them in the *Poems* of 1850. Her translation of the *Prometheus Bound,* which received Browning's careful attention, is a great improvement upon her earlier attempt. It is a spirited and readable, rather than a pedantically literal version; and, although in many passages she does not pretend to convey every idiosyncrasy of the Greek, she nowhere misleads the reader. She did not make the mistake that Browning made years later in his translation of the *Agamemnon,* which remained so close to the original that it was generally considered incomprehensible. Indeed throughout her version she happily reproduces many of the original figures of speech.

Among the poems with personal associations are three sonnets to H. S. Boyd: **"His Blindness," "His Death,"** and **"Legacies,"** the last filled with lachrymose recollections. The copies of Aeschylus and of Gregory Nazianzen which came to her after his death were

> those I used to read, thus

> Assisting my dear teacher's soul to unlock
> The darkness of his eyes: now, mine they mock,
> Blinded in turn, by tears: now, murmurous
> Sad echoes of my young voice, years agone,
> Entoning, from these leaves, the Graecian
>   phrase,
> Return and choke my utterance.

Another poem with the background of Herefordshire was **"Hector in the Garden,"** which had been written before she left Italy and published in *Blackwood's* in October, 1846. Elizabeth recalls the pleasure she experienced at the age of nine from tending in the Hope End garden a "huge giant" of many different kinds of flowers—daffodils, violets, lilies, daisies, and others. In spite of its descriptive charm, the poem is spoiled by the "moral" of the concluding stanzas. The poet will not allow herself "this dreaming" about the past, but she thirsts for action, "Life's heroic ends pursuing."

It was in the new edition of her *Poems* that Elizabeth first published the sonnet sequence she had composed before her marriage. On July 22 of her last summer in London she had said to Browning, "You shall see some day at Pisa what I will not show you now. Does not Solomon say that 'there is a time to read what is written.' " Except for that cryptic remark she told him nothing of the sonnets she had

been writing on the miracle of her life: her former isolation, ill-health, and sense of deep grief followed by the triumph of love over doubts and fears. Just below the last, the forty-fourth of the sonnets which Elizabeth copied into her small white notebook, she wrote, "50 Wimpole Street 1846, Sept." In this poem she spoke of the many flowers Browning had brought her from his garden, and in return she presented him with her sheaf of sonnets:

> So, in the like name of that love of ours,
> Take back these thoughts, which here unfolded
>   too,
> And which on warm and cold days I withdrew
> From my heart's ground.

But neither at Pisa nor for the next two years at Florence did she show her husband these sonnets. It was not until they were at Bagni di Lucca in the summer of 1849 that Elizabeth first placed "that wreath of Sonnets" on Robert "one morning unawares, three years after it had been twined." Her reluctance to let him see them all this time may have been due to her shyness or to a chance remark Browning had once made "against putting one's loves into verse." At Lucca he had suddenly spoken "something else on the other side," and the following morning Elizabeth "said hesitatingly 'Do you know I once wrote some poems about you?'—and then—'There they are, if you care to see them,'—and there was the little Book"—the same one which Browning had beside him when he later wrote these words to Julia Wedgwood three years after Elizabeth's death. When Robert saw the manuscript, he was "much touched and pleased" and thought so highly of the poetry that he "could not consent," Elizabeth wrote Arabel, "that they should be lost" to her volumes.

Browning and she decided "to slip them in under some sort of veil" and chose the title *"Sonnets from the Portuguese,"* which might seem to mean *"from the Portuguese language,"* but which really referred to **"Catarina to Camoëns,"** the poem immediately preceding the *Sonnets.* Browning had read this poem before he made Elizabeth's acquaintance, and it "had affected him to tears . . . again and again." Ever since then he had "in a loving fancy" associated her with the Portuguese Catarina. According to legend, she was the girl with whom the Portuguese poet Camoëns fell in love, and she is supposed to have died during his absence abroad and to have left him "the ribband from her hair," as Browning said. And so Elizabeth and Robert gave the *Sonnets* their ambiguous name and allowed the public, "who are very little versed in Portuguese literature," as Elizabeth wrote, to interpret the title as they pleased.

Forty-three of the *Sonnets from the Portuguese* came at the end of the second volume of the new edition. **"Future and Past,"** which was the last poem of the first volume, later became the forty-second of the sonnet sequence in the fourth edition of 1856. Elizabeth did not place the sonnet with the others in 1850 because of its association with **"Past and Future"** published in the *Poems* of 1844, and she thus hoped to preserve the anonymity of the new sequence. In the earliest of the three manuscripts of the *Sonnets* which had been preserved, she gave titles to eight of the poems: **"Death and Love"** (I), **"Love's Obstacles"**

(II), **"Love's New Creation"** (VII), **"Love's Expression"** (XIII), **"Love's Causes"** (XIV), **"Love's Repetitions"** (XXI), **"Love's Refuge"** (XXII), and **"Love's Sacrifice"** (XXIII). But she wisely decided that forty-three titles all somewhat similar to one another would have a monotonous effect and crossed out the eight she had tentatively chosen so that in the published form the individual poems were designated only by Roman numerals. Elizabeth took more pains in the composition of the *Sonnets* than in any of her former poems. For once the expression was concise and coherent, the rhymes almost all conventional, the imagery in better taste, the syntax clear, and the diction simple and unaffected.

A study of the significant revisions of one of the sonnets will illustrate the great care with which she wrote and later emended them. The *Sonnets* may be seen in five different stages of development: the manuscript in the Pierpont Morgan Library, the George Murray Smith Memorial Manuscript in the British Museum, the new edition of the *Poems,* the third edition of 1853 (in which she made only three or four slight revisions of the *Sonnets*), and the fourth edition of the *Poems* in 1856. The earliest manuscript reading of **"Sonnet XVI,"** for example, is as follows:

> 1 And yet because thou art above me so,
> 2 Because thou art more strong, and like a king,
> 3 Thou canst prevail against my fears and fling
> 4 Thy purple round me till my heart shall grow
> 5 Too close against thy heart to henceforth know
> 6 Its separate trembling pulse. Oh, conquering
> 7 May prove as noble and complete a thing
> 8 In lifting upward as in beating low!
> 9 And as a soldier, struck down by a sword,
> 10 Cries "Here my strife ends", and sinks dead
>   to earth,—
> 11 Even so, beloved, I, at last, record . . .
> 12 "My doubt ends here—" If *thou* invite me
>   forth,
> 13 I rise above abasement at the word!—
> 14 Make thy love larger to enlarge my worth.

The words "art above me" were given a stronger meaning with "overcomest." "Strong" in line 2 was changed to "princely" and later to "noble." The awkward and needless splitting of the infinitive in line 5 was corrected so that the phrase became "henceforth to know." Since the movement of the first four words in line 6 was hindered by the excessive number of *s* and *t* sounds, she eliminated the expression and substituted "How it shook when alone." The word "noble" had been used in the revision of line 2 and was therefore removed from line 7 in favor of "lordly." In line 8 "beating" was replaced by the more vivid "crushing." In the change of the next two lines, the figure became much happier: the wounded soldier raised by his gallant enemy is compared to the poet herself, whose hesitations were conquered by a generous lover.

> 9 And as a vanquished soldier yields his sword
> 10 To one who lifts him from the bloody
>   earth,—

The first four words of line 12 became in 1850 the more emphatic sentence, "Here ends my doubt!" and in 1856 the meaning was enlarged by the change: "Here ends my strife."

Yet despite Elizabeth's conscientious craftsmanship the freshness of the *Sonnets* has faded, and they no longer evoke the eager response of earlier generations. With all their singing angels, floods of tears, chrisms, lutes, and golden thrones, they are in the idiom of the period, but no poems were ever called into being by a love more true and sincere.

She received fewer reviews of her new edition than she had in either 1838 or in 1844. The *Poems* of 1850 were almost unnoticed in the United States, because no separate American edition was issued. A Boston publisher had agreed to reprint her two volumes and to pay for the rights, but he was anticipated by C. S. Francis of New York, who pirated the two volumes of her *Poems* without the alterations or new material. "I don't know when I have been so provoked," Elizabeth wrote to Arabel of the failure of the Boston publisher to honor his agreement because the volumes had already appeared in New York. "So I lose everything—both money and reputation." A brief, perfunctory notice of one paragraph in the *Christian Examiner* of Boston referred to Elizabeth's "possession of the richest poetical gifts," and an equally short paragraph in *Harper's Magazine* spoke of her "peculiar boldness, originality, and beauty" and said that the new edition would be "thankfully accepted by the wide circle which has learned to venerate Mrs. Browning's genius."

In England the most favorable review was in the *Athenaeum* and was probably written by Elizabeth's friend H. F. Chorley. He quoted from many of her best-known poems, such as **"The Cry of the Children"** and **"Catarina to Camoëns"** and concluded with the handsome praise "Mrs. Browning is probably, of her sex, the first imaginative writer England has produced in any age:—she is, beyond comparison, the first poetess of her own." *The Electric Review,* which was also extravagant in its commendation of the *Poems,* spoke of her "splendid poetry," her "profound thought," and her "pervading spirit so pure and so womanly." The writer thought that the romantic ballad **"Bertha in the Lane"** was "unrivalled in its pathetic beauty" and that the carelessly written **"Lady Geraldine's Courtship"** was "one of the most charming and finely-elaborated poems in the language" and had an effect which was "indescribably beautiful." No other woman writer, in the reviewer's opinion, had such a combination of "solemn purpose with large intellect and the same intensity of imagination."

However, the *Guardian,* the *Examiner, Fraser's Magazine,* and the *English Review* were more temperate in their praise and believed that even her most recent poetry had the same faults of style mentioned in the reviews of earlier volumes: diffuseness, obscure and affected diction, ungrammatical syntax, inappropriate and absurd images, confusion of the parts of speech, slovenly versification, and incorrect rhymes. Each of the four reviews, however, found something to commend. The *Guardian,* for example, said that "in melody of verse, in tenderness, in true pathos, in abundant language, command of rhyme, and affluence of imagery, she is quite in the first ranks of living writers." The *English Review* asserted that Elizabeth took "high rank among the bards of England" and that there was perhaps none who surpassed her "in her especial beauties—in the combination of romantic wildness with deep, true tenderness and most singular power." Yet, unlike many critics at that time, the reviewer considered Browning a greater poet than his wife: "Upon the whole, we think Browning's the higher and the master spirit; hers the more tender, and the more musical also." A remark in the *Examiner* on **"Lady Geraldine's Courtship"** and **"The Romaunt of the Page"** was expressed with the characteristic glibness of reviewers: that both poems "show how delicate, pure, and intense a spirit of womanly love is connected with this masculine and far-reaching intellect."

On the whole the reviews had curiously little to say about either the new translation of the *Prometheus Bound* or the **Sonnets from the Portuguese.** It is doubtful whether the writer of the notice in the *English Review* understood Elizabeth's responsibility as a translator, for he wrote of her **Prometheus Bound** that the hero's "complaints are rather too rhetorically rendered, without sufficient dramatic earnestness." The *Eclectic Review* called her version of the drama "a noble achievement" and one of the many evidences of the poet's "solid classical scholarship." None of the reviews made a close examination of the **Prometheus Bound** by comparing it with the original, nor did any of them appear to know that the new translation was her second of the same drama.

The reviews were equally imperceptive in their comments on the **Sonnets from the Portuguese.** They mostly ignored these new poems, and the two or three which mentioned them failed to grasp their significance. The writer in *Frazer's Magazine* did not understand that the sonnets were a revelation of the poet's own love, but he suggested that they were more than translations: "From the Portuguese they may be: but their life and earnestness must prove Mrs. Browning either to be the most perfect of all known translators, or to have quickened with her own spirit the framework of another's thoughts, and then modestly declined the honour which was really her own." The *Examiner* described the themes of the **Sonnets,** which it thought a "remarkable series," but it gave no hint that they might have been based upon Elizabeth's personal experiences.

The *Spectator* was the only important journal which found almost nothing of merit in the new edition. The reviewer believed that, although Elizabeth had shown great promise in her earlier volumes, she had made almost no progress in her art: "Mrs. Browning has given no single instance of her ability to compose finished works. Diffuseness, obscurity, and exaggeration, mar even the happiest efforts of her genius." It seemed to the writer that most of her poems were only "rough sketches, thrown off, it is to be supposed, in one or two sittings."

Elizabeth was not affected by the notices of her volumes of 1850, as she had been in 1844, probably because copies of the journals did not arrive in Italy until months after they had been published. Since many of the reviews had been kind to her, she could not have been disappointed. The article in the *Guardian,* which she had read early in May, 1851, just as she was beginning her journey to England, gave her in fact great pleasure. But the reviewers

had mostly read her poems with the same carelessness and haste they had imputed to her writing, and they had expressed themselves superficially and in clichés.

In November and December Charles Eliot Norton, who had been graduated four years earlier from Harvard and was on a leisurely tour of the East and of Europe, paid a number of calls upon the Brownings at Casa Guidi. He found them "sitting in a pleasant home-like room, surrounded with pictures and books, with an open fire shedding a genial light through it." Browning, as Norton described him, had "a pleasant open expression and manner" and seemed in his looks and conversation quite unlike the idea of him he had received from his poems. Elizabeth's appearance was also altogether different from what he had expected after reading her works. He noticed her slight and delicate figure, her "reserved and timid" manner, her quiet plaintive voice. At first she had little to say, and Norton felt "as if she were so distrustful of herself that she kept back the expression of her sentiments and thoughts from all but those with whom she was familiar." Her face, like her voice, was "melancholy and full of sensibility" so that she looked like "the most delicate and sensitive of poets," rather than the author of poems of "very great intellectual strength and power of expression."

The more Norton saw of the Brownings, the more he liked them. Browning's conversation he thought extraordinary, with its quick flow of ideas and its inexhaustible fund of anecdotes told "with such entire straightforward earnestness that one cannot but like him." He continued, "He is quite unconscious and never even in the slightest way claims any regard for himself as a poet, or shows that he expects you to remember that he is one. Indeed one of the most charming characteristics of both him and his wife is their self-forgetfulness." (pp. 181-93)

Gardner B. Taplin, "Mrs. Browning's Poems of 1850," in The Boston Public Library Quarterly, *Vol. 8, No. 4, October, 1956, pp. 181-94.*

Hoxie Neale Fairchild   (essay date 1957)

[*An American educator, Fairchild was the author of numerous essays and books on literary and religious subjects. His major works include* The Noble Savage: A Study in Romantic Naturalism *(1928), a lengthy discussion of the depiction of the unspoiled primitive life in literature and its relationship to romantic naturalism, and a six-volume study,* Religious Trends in English Poetry *(1939-1968), which traces religious thought and feeling in English poetry from the eighteenth to the twentieth century. In the following excerpt, Fairchild examines the religious nature of Browning's poetry, tracing the development of her themes from the period of her youth to that after her marriage to Robert Browning.*]

Edward Barrett Moulton Barrett did not long remain satisfied with the colorless and perfunctory Anglicanism of his childhood. At Trinity he responded to the influence of the Cambridge Evangelicals. By 1806, the year of Elizabeth's birth, he had gone further: he and his dutifully negligible wife now worshipped with the Wesleyan Methodists. His sectarianism, however, was not extremely rigid.

He had only two grudges against the Church of England: not enough of its clergy had a firm grasp of saving truth, and in any case the idea of an officially established Church was repugnant. Later, in the Wimpole Street days, he apparently regarded himself as an Independent; otherwise Elizabeth would not have said that he would never permit a daughter of his to marry "Even if a prince of Eldorado should come, with a pedigree of lineal descent from some signory in the moon in one hand, and a ticket of good behaviour from the nearest Independent chapel in the other." But he never frequented such a chapel as the one described in Browning's *Christmas-Eve.* The type of Nonconformity which Mr. Barrett cultivated was barely distinguishable from the Anglicanism of the Clapham Sect— prosperous, cultivated, not very grim Evangelicals like William Wilberforce and Zachary Macaulay, pious men of affairs who knew how to make the best of both possible worlds.

Elizabeth and the other children at Hope End did not live in constant terror of the wrath to come. They seem to have enjoyed their religion as part of the general stir of imaginative vividness which characterized the household. In those early years, before business worries and family sorrows had aggravated the morbid side of his nature, Mr. Barrett's despotism was usually jolly and stimulating. He must never be crossed, but he was seldom so unpleasantly oppressive that a loving child would wish to cross him. Far from being opposed to secular culture, he was rather demoralizingly proud of the little bluestocking who had begun to study Greek at the age of eight. His indulgence conditioned the headstrong, willful girl to think of scholarship and poetry as the best means of getting her own way and satisfying her intense craving for distinction. Once beyond the tomboy stage she too complacently accepted her father's stereotype of the dreamy, delicate, nervous female genius. Of course certain books were strictly prohibited, but with incredible carelessness Papa had shelved on the unforbidden side of his library Voltaire, Hume, Gibbon, Rousseau, Paine, Mary Wollstonecraft, and *Werther.* The adolescent Elizabeth read them as avidly as the adolescent Robert Browning read *Queen Mab.*

But we are looking too far ahead. Little Elizabeth's nursery poems are mostly humorous family occasional pieces but sometimes dutifully echo the pious precepts of her rearing. Once at least she combined the spirit of the two *genres* in a song which contrives to be both jolly and edifying:

> Peter Quarry he called all his vices together
> To meet on the green field, or bright yellow
>   meadow.
> Says he our acquaintance I fear will be short,
> For of going to virtue I've a great thought.
>   Singing fal lal, etc.
>
> So you must be gone
> With your weeds and your bushes,
> And sweet virtue must come
> With her larks and her thrushes.
>   Singing fal lal, etc.

An astonishing performance for a child of eight. Three years later she was aiming much higher with less agreeable

results. She was only eleven when she began *The Battle of Marathon,* a frigid imitation of Pope's imitation of Homer which her proud father privately printed in 1820.

For *An Essay on Mind* (1826) her model is Pope as moralist, not as translator. But although the poem is ploddingly ethical rather than religious, there are a few indications that she has been reading more pious eighteenth-century poets—chiefly, we may conjecture, Mrs. Elizabeth Rowe. She lauds "Divinest Newton" for having been

> Rich in all nature, but her erring side:
> Endow'd with all of Science—but its pride;

and she dreams of a heaven where pure minds, stripped of words no less than of flesh, will communicate ideas only through "voiceless intercourse." Two of the fourteen short pieces published with the *Essay* may owe their more explicit piety to her first serious illness in 1821. **"The Prayer"** explains that the purpose of unhappiness is to prevent us from falling too deeply in love with this delightful world. In **"The Dream"** she has a vision of the whole sinful sweep of pre-Christian history, until at last

> . . . a God came to die, bringing down
>   peace—
> *"Pan was not;"* and the darkness that did
>   wreathe
> The earth, past from the soul—Life came by
>   death!

Here is the first of several attempts to be as pleased about the death of Pan as she knows she should be. Nobody, however, would think of the 1826 volume as primarily a book of sacred poetry. Learned young Miss Barrett has not yet firmly combined her literary ambitions with her creed.

The pietistic element is much stronger in *Poems* (1833) and *The Seraphim and Other Poems* (1838). Despite hints of coming change to be noted later, the *Poems* of 1844 are also a body of religious verse. A close study of Elizabeth's writings in relation to the circumstances of her life would show that the poems become more urgently Evangelical as she becomes more saddened by family sorrows, more aware of the deterioration of her father's character, more oppressed by illness both physical and psychosomatic. In 1834 or thereabouts there is also some indication that she is sentimentally interested in a Nonconformist minister named George Barrett Hunter. In that case her piety might to some extent be an expression of her need for love.

During this most emphatically religious stage of her career she gives an Evangelical twist to the Puritan theory of Christian poetry as it had been carried from the seventeenth century into the eighteenth by Dennis, Watts, and Blackmore. In **"The Dead Pan"** she calls upon Christian poets to hymn the Crucified in refutation of Schiller's idea in *Die Götter Griechenlands* that the death of Pan means the death of poetry—"a doctrine still more dishonoring to poetry than to Christianity." It also blasphemes the Victorian faith in progress. Of course, she grants in *The Greek Christian Poets,* the modern world has had its pious versifiers. Also there are true poets who sing as if man had never fallen, and others who sing "as if in the first hour of exile, when the echo of the curse was louder than the whisper of the promise. But the right 'genius of Christianism' has done little up to this moment [1842], even for Chateaubriand. We want the touch of Christ's hand upon our literature, as it touched other dead things—we want the sense of the saturation of Christ's blood upon the souls of our poets, that it may cry *through* them in answer to the ceaseless wail of the Sphinx of our humanity."

Although Elizabeth writes much better than other simon-pure Victorian Evangelicals, she is far from achieving a richly satisfying expression of "the genius of Christianism." In religious no less than in secular verse her considerable gift for making warmly emotionalized rhetoric move to incantatory rhythms is largely vitiated by her diffuseness, messiness, sentimentality, and lack of organic relation between thought and image. But as a sacred poet she is beset by additional handicaps. Her vocation as a leader in a campaign to Christianize English poetry burdens her with a stultifying self-consciousness, tempts her to force her powers beyond their modest bounds. Even in asserting that poetry is essentially religious she is haunted by pious scruples about her craving to win fame through aesthetic creativity. She is quite enough of an artist to know that poetry is sensuous, but she does not see how she can be sensuous without succumbing to a soulless naturalism. Remembering her frigid *Essay on Mind,* she dreads being entrapped by the sensationalism and associationism of Locke, Hartley, and the Utilitarians. **"A Sea-Side Meditation"** asserts that the mission of the poet is to show men how to break the manacles of sense and soar into the world of the spirit. And yet, she continues, is there not too much of sinful pride in the poet's assertion of visionary power? Victory over the flesh is the gift of God, not the exploit of man. We must await that Final Day when "God's arm shall meet God's foe, and hurl him back!"

She cannot bear, however, to relinquish the belief that if angels may sing in heaven, poets may sing on earth:

> Sing, seraph with the glory! heaven is high;
> Sing, poet with the sorrow! earth is low:
> The universe's inward voices cry
> "Amen" to either song of joy and woe:
> Sing, seraph,—poet,—sing on equally!

"Equally" claims too much. On the other hand she feels that complete attainment of **"The Soul's Expression"** in poetry would be tantamount to death, for

> . . . if I did it,—as the thunder-roll
> Breaks its own cloud, my flesh would perish
>   there
> Before that dread apocalypse of soul.

She thinks too much *about* writing religious poetry.

Although she would like to feel religious about nature she resists the temptation. Once a beautiful scene drew her toward pagan animism, but she gathered up all her strength, expelled "the heathen dream" from her mind, and prophetically heard "Nature's death-shrieking" in that great day when the world will be nothing to us and Christ will be all in all. Vainly do we seek **"The Image of God"** in nature: He only is "like to God" who died that we might live. Sometimes, however, she concedes to the Christian, and

to him alone, the right to praise Mother Earth because he knows that she has been granted a little of God's mercy:

>   . . . Oh, beautiful
> Art thou, Earth, albeit worse
> Than in heaven is called good!
> Good to us, that we may know
> Meekly from thy good to go;
> While the holy, crying Blood
> Puts its music kind and low
> 'Twixt such ears as are not dull,
>   And thine ancient curse!

"We want the sense of the saturation of Christ's blood upon the souls of our poets" because it is only the Blood that heals and saves. In **"Sounds"** she runs through a catalogue of the noises of Vanity Fair, including the chatter of a ritualistic priest who "disserts / Upon linen shirts." The hubbub muffles the voice of God murmuring in our souls:

> *I* am the end of love! give love to *Me*!
> O thou that sinnest, grace doth more abound
> Than all thy sin! sit still beneath My rood,
> And count the droppings of My victim-blood,
>   And seek none other sound!

In **"The Seraphim"** (1838), two angels behold the Crucifixion from heaven and exclaim their way to the conclusion that henceforward man's love for God will outstrip their own. Seraphs indeed love, but

> . . . not with this blood on us—and this face,—
> Still, haply, pale with sorrow that it bore
> In our behalf, and tender evermore
> With nature all our own, upon us gazing—
> Nor yet with these forgiving hands upraising
> Their unreproachful wounds, alone to bless!

This is truly Christian and Evangelical; but when one angel tells the other that "Heaven is dull, mine Ador, to man's earth," the anticipation of the glory-of-the-imperfect doctrine of *Rephan* reminds us that Miss Barrett is destined to marry Robert Browning.

Much more ambitious is **"A Drama of Exile"** (1844), a full-dress Aeschylean lyrical drama in which the plan of redemption is revealed to Adam and Eve after their expulsion from Eden. Despite her almost too anxious insistence that Pan is dead, she had never wholly abandoned her beloved Greeks. Not only Hugh Stuart Boyd but Shelley had taught her to think of Prometheus as the forerunner of Christ. There was no incongruity in imposing the form of Aeschylus upon the matter of Milton, who himself had written not only a Christian classical epic but a Christian classical tragedy. We cannot blame her for failing to divulge a more immediate and a stronger influence—that of Byron's *Cain* and *Heaven and Earth.* In the dedication to her father she describes **"A Drama of Exile"** as "the longest and most important work (*to me!*) which I ever trusted into the current of publication." That is just the trouble. She is not equipped to compete with Aeschylus and Milton, or even with Byron, in a poetic drama whose characters are Jesus Christ, Adam, Eve, and Satan, with the Spirits of Organic and Inorganic Nature thrown in for good measure. That the result is neither absurd nor offensive is after all a high tribute. Here as elsewhere, also, she deserves praise for her intelligent and by no means wholly unsuccessful attempt to reconcile Evangelical Christianity with the traditions of humanistic culture. But she is a more appealing religious poet when she is less ambitious. Surely it is not only the Christian believer who still finds himself moved by some of her short lyrics of personal spiritual experience—**"The Sleep"**, **"My Doves,"** **"Comfort,"** and **"Cowper's Grave."**

In the 1844 volume the sonnets placed just after **"A Drama of Exile"** are heavy with bitterness and self-accusation. At Torquay, four years earlier, had occurred the tragedy which haunted Elizabeth throughout the remainder of her life—her brother Edward's death by drowning. Quite irrationally, Mr. Barrett blamed her for the disaster: Edward would not have been sailing on that fatal day had Elizabeth not teased him to stay on with her at the seashore against her father's wishes. She accepted the burden of guilt and the pain of estrangement from the beloved parent who now became the man we loathe as Mr. Barrett of Wimpole Street. Elizabeth was thinking of herself when she said in a letter that the subject of **"A Drama of Exile"** was "especially the grief of Eve, under that reproach of soul which must have afflicted her with so peculiar an agony." The first effect of this situation was to make her cling to the Cross with the convulsive strength born of her misery and remorse; the ultimate effect was a weakening of her grasp as estrangement from her father brought estrangement from his religion.

The process was far advanced before she was willing to acknowledge the outcome. **"A Drama of Exile"** and some of its companion pieces represent the painful climax of her Evangelical fervor, not its decay. Nevertheless the 1844 *Poems* as a whole are somewhat less redolent of the chapel than the volume of 1838. Her Christian objectivity seems to be as solid as ever, but there is a less insistently technical emphasis on the atoning Blood. For the first time, such poems as **"The Cry of the Children"** and **"The Cry of the Human"** suggest the beginning of a trend away from Evangelical theology toward a slightly broadened Evangelical humanitarianism:

> The curse of gold upon the land
>   The lack of bread enforces;
> The rail-cars snort from strand to strand,
>   Like more of Death's White Horses.
> The rich preach "rights" and "future days,"
>   And hear no angel scoffing,
> The poor die mute, with starving gaze
>   On corn-ships in the offing.
>   Be pitiful, O God.

In the darkened room at Wimpole Street her mind was much less secluded than her body. The letters of Miss Martineau and R. H. Horne, the visits of Kenyon and the rest, and the parliamentary Blue Books made her more up-to-date that she had been in less inactive years. Her father's no longer amiable tyranny prompted rebellious thoughts about the position of woman in society. In the year when this volume was published she had begun to plan a resolutely unconventional treatment of modern life: *Aurora Leigh* was stirring in her mind.

Thus even before the advent of her "rosy, rough rescuer"

there are symptoms of approaching change. Those hints, however, are too obscure to prevent us from being startled as we move onward from the 1844 volume into the poems of her married life. Miss Elizabeth Barrett Moulton Barrett is an Evangelical poet; Mrs. Robert Browning is nothing of the sort. Even those who think her unworthy of close study for her own sake will grant that the fact is of some importance for interpretation of her husband's changing thought. It casts doubt upon the familiar notion that his movement away from chapel Christianity to subjectivist theism was retarded by her uncompromising Evangelicalism.

Mr. De Vane tells us [in *Nineteenth-Century Studies*] that Browning was becoming distinctly heterodox when he began to court Elizabeth, but that "Miss Barrett stopped all that in no time, and the first poetic product of their union was *Christmas-Eve and Easter-Day*." But we know that she was puzzled by the asceticism of the latter poem; and when we look back to the letters of 1845 and 1846 we find no evidence of desire to bind her lover to the foot of the Cross. She is quick to grant that "There is a narrowness among the dissenters which is wonderful; an arid, grey Puritanism in the clefts of their souls: but it seems to me clear that they know what the 'liberty of Christ' means better than those who call themselves Churchmen." What she now values in the chapel is not its doctrinal purity but its freedom. A year later, discussing the question of where they are to be married, she declares herself "unwilling . . . to put on any of the liveries of the sects. The truth, as God sees it, must be something so different from these opinions about truth." She feels able to worship "anywhere and with all sorts of worshippers, from the Sistine Chapel to Mr. Fox's." In every denomination "there is a little to revolt, and a good deal to bear with." But she greatly prefers a chapel—of the sort "where the minister is simple-minded and not controversial." She is quite ready, however, to marry Robert anywhere—even at an Anglican church if the service is free from Puseyite embellishments. "After all, perhaps the best will be what is easiest." Browning warmly agrees with all this in a letter which adumbrates the theme of *Christmas-Eve*.

As we have seen, the adolescent Elizabeth had read Voltaire, Gibbon, and Paine in her father's library. In maturity she confined neither her reading nor her friendships to the sphere of the Saints. During the years when she was writing her most fervently Evangelical poems she was corresponding with Harriet Martineau, an ex-Unitarian who now believed in nothing except Positivism and mesmerism, and with the highly unorthodox R. H. Horne. She had even planned to collaborate with the future author of *Orion* in a lyrical drama about the birth and growth of the soul. The scheme was abortive, but in 1844 they joined forces in a volume of critical essays, *A New Spirit of the Age*.

In 1842 she writes to Hugh Boyd, who has charged her with Calvinism: "I believe simply that the saved are saved by grace, and that they shall hereafter know it fully; that the lost are lost by their choice and free will—by choosing to sin and die." At this time and during the courtship she was deep in Carlyle and Emerson. she was reading novels, many of them French. Balzac she warmly admired and she preferred Hugo to Dickens. George Sand was then her ideal of emancipated creative womanhood—an illusion later damaged in Paris but never completely repudiated. She always liked the relaxed uncensorious atmosphere of Europe more genuinely than Robert did. "On the continent," she assures Henrietta, "you escape a quantity of Mrs. Grundyism, and can live as you like, nobody making you afraid." In Italy she consorted happily with pagans like Landor, left-wing Unitarians like Miss Cobbe, and transcendentalists like Margaret Fuller. Probably she always remained a more definitely believing Christian than her husband eventually became, but we can hardly suppose that she did much to curb his growing heterodoxy during their life together.

In 1857 she writes Leigh Hunt: "I receive more dogmas perhaps . . . than you do. I believe in the divinity of Christ in the intensest sense—that he was God absolutely. But for the rest, I am very unorthodox . . . In fact the churches do all of them, as at present constituted, seem too narrow and low to hold true Christianity in its proximate developments." The proximate developments are spirit-rappings and the like. Although she is somewhat distressed by the vulgarity of Yankee mediums, she has been assured by a friend "that the mediumship in England will be of a higher character than in America by much." Quite! Her spiritualism—which might well have disgusted Browning into clinging to his Christianity a little longer than he otherwise might have done—was the most absorbing of a cluster of neurotic fads which included homeopathic medicine, mesmerism, and Swedenborg—"I'm a Swedenborgian, you know, and believe in 'spheres,' 'atmospheres,' and 'influences.'" Although she held that the spirits were at last conclusively demonstrating the truth of Christianity, she received no messages from the shades of departed Evangelicals. More appropriately it was "Dr. Channing's spirit (or one giving himself for such)" who told her that her sins were forgiven, that the veil between this life and the next is very thin, and that the spirit world is a place of "transcendent beauty." It seems strange that the poems of her married years contain hardly a hint of this obsession. Perhaps she was unwilling to distress Robert, or perhaps Miss [Jeannette Marks in her *The Family of the Barrett*] is correct in supposing that spiritualism was not so much a part of her actual religious experience as it was a hysterical attempt to shake off the clutch of morphine.

Although her Evangelicalism melted away with surprising rapidity after her marriage, there is no need to doubt that it had been sincere while it lasted. What had always been fundamental in her nature was a loving heart, an abundance of warm, slack, diffused feeling, a desire to expand her personality by voicing that feeling in poetry, and a tendency to ascribe a kind of holiness to anything that pleasantly excited her. Between about 1828 and the receipt of Robert's first letter, Evangelical Christianity was the most exciting thing she knew and therefore the most propitious stimulus to self-expression. Its dominant mood was in keeping with the sorrow and illness and confinement which shadowed those years. Why should she question its truth so long as she could feel it as the supremely poetic

subject? In her mundane extrapoetic life she had no great enthusiasm for the fine points of Puritan theology, still less for the mentality of the average chapel-goer. But when she donned her singing robes she was converted and reconverted by her own facile emotions, her own fluent rhythms; and then she sensed the saturation of Christ's blood upon her soul.

Robert Browning stopped all that in no time. He gave her something else to be excited about:

> . . . My own, my own,
> Who camest to me when the world was gone,
> And I who looked for only God, found *thee*!
> I find thee; I am safe, and strong, and glad.

Although the lines do not imply the complete substitution of Robert for the Deity, "only God" is not a phrase which William Wilberforce would have approved. This Pompilia is quite explicit saying that she has found in her Caponsacchi a safety and strength and gladness which she has not derived from the Blood of the Lamb. The angel's words in **"The Seraphim,"** "Heaven is dull, / Mine Ador, to man's earth," have taken on new meaning.

Of course Mrs. Browning is not the woman to proclaim to the Victorian public that divinity is most potently revealed and mediated by whatever human being one loves most deeply. She will not say this unequivocally even to her husband. *Sonnets from the Portuguese,* never intended by her for publication, barely nibbles at a theme which Robert was to treat more boldly. Clearer in this respect than any of her sonnets is the passage in *Aurora Leigh* which tells how the heroine's future father, attending Mass as a sightseer in Florence, first saw the girl who was to become his wife:

> A face flashed like a cymbal on his face
> And shook with silent clangour brain and heart,
> Transfiguring him to music. Thus, even thus,
> He too received his sacramental gift
> With eucharistic meanings; for he loved.

We are to infer that he thus discovers the truly human, and hence most deeply religious, meaning of "This is my Body, which is given for you."

If Miss Betty Miller's interpretation of Robert Browning's psychology is correct—and with some reservations it probably is—Elizabeth's enjoyment of this type of sacramental experience may after all have proved somewhat limited. Fortunately, at all events, her new life provided her with other sources of excitement. She responded to them with one eye turned toward heaven and the other cocked in the direction of George Sand, Victor Hugo, George Eliot, and Charlotte Brontë. She now attaches her religiosity chiefly to politico-social liberalism, humanitarianism, the gospel of service, feminism, and the mission of the poet to complement the work of the practical reformer by being eloquently idealistic on such topics. Her indignation sometimes strikes a prophetic note; she can cite Scripture for her purpose; she frequently invokes God and occasionally Jesus Christ. But the divine names are now primarily emotive symbols which gather up the man-made spiritual values of the social causes and ideals which her benevolism has espoused. In escaping from Wimpole

Street she seems to have crossed the line which separates "God is love" from "Love is God."

Aurora Leigh shocked most of her old admirers but delighted Ruskin, Rossetti, and Swinburne. It is a courageous, high-minded, sentimental problem novel in verse. There are moments—not very many—when it is also a fine poem. The book is saturated in a spirituality which achieves its clearest expression in the closing lines:

> . . . The world's old,
> But the old world waits the time to be renewed:
> Toward which, new hearts in individual growth
> Must quicken, and increase to multitude
> In new dynasties of the race of men,—
> Developed whence, shall grow spontaneously
> New churches, new œconomies, new laws
> Admitting freedom, new societies
> Excluding falsehood: HE shall make all new.
> My Romney!—Lifting up my hand in his,
> As wheeled by Seeing spirits towards the east,
> He turned instinctively, where, faint and far,
> Along the tingling desert of the sky,
> Beyond the circle of the conscious hills,
> Were laid in jasper-stone as clear as glass
> The first foundations of that new, near Day
> Which should be builded out of heaven, to God.

Men and women are to strive upward through higher and higher stages of individual development, the highest level being the identification of complete self-expression with complete social love. Before long there will be a whole race of creative and altruistic beings like Aurora and Romney, and then the brand-new world will automatically emerge. But the model and inspiration for the making of this world will be the Heavenly Jerusalem; and somehow all this human work, including the "new churches," will also be God's work. The question is whether the supernaturalistic element is organically essential to Mrs. Browning's social ideal or whether it is merely hitched onto that ideal to add a tinge of numinousness to her humanitarianism. To me the latter interpretation seems more probable. It is as if George Eliot, in some unguarded moment, had enlivened her gospel of the Choir Invisible with a bit of Swedenborg.

I shall not attempt to refute the anticipated rejoinder that Mrs. Browning is more *truly* Christian than Miss Barrett because she transcends the death-dealing letter and applies to contemporary problems the life-giving spirit of Love. It may be so. Let us be content to agree that she strikingly illustrates the failure of Evangelicalism to retain the loyalty of many of its most intelligent and gifted adherents. Whether she found something better or something worse is a matter of opinion. (pp. 49-60)

> *Hoxie Neale Fairchild, "Miss Barrett and Mrs. Browning," in her* Religious Trends in English Poetry, Vol. IV, 1830-1880: Christianity and Romanticism in the Victorian Era, *Columbia University Press, 1957, pp. 49-60.*

Alethea Hayter   (essay date 1962)

[*Hayter is an English critic who has written extensively on the English Romantics and Elizabeth Barrett Browning. In the following excerpt, she examines the themes and imagery in Browning's* Last Poems.]

Jeannette Marks on Browning's morphine addiction:

When Elizabeth Barrett was forty years old, she had lived in a nest of fears,—fears that friends would wish to come to see her, fears when she did see them, fears of what might happen, fears about going out. Now in husband, child, outward moving life, and many friends, she knew that she had gained—although it was not complete freedom from the family domination and the domination of opium—more than she had lost. Nevertheless, her father's death brought "sudden desolation" from which she was never to recover. In proportion to the love for Robert Browning which she had won in conflict with her love for her father, was she destined to collapse at the time of her father's death. It was this collapse which in 1857 had set in, and which made any final escape from dependence on morphine impossible.

> *Jeanette Marks, in her* The Family of the Barrett, *1938.*

The *Last Poems* are a puzzle. Only four of them (**'De Profundis'**, **'A Song for the Ragged Schools of London'**, **'My Kate'** and **'Amy's Cruelty'**) are known to have been written more than a year before [Browning's] death, but the whole collection is so various and uneven that it might have been written twenty years apart, or by three or four different poets. Among them are four of the strongest most direct lyrics Mrs. Browning ever wrote, **'A Musical Instrument'**, **'My Heart and I'**, **'Bianca Among the Nightingales'**, **'A View across the Roman Campagna'**, but nothing except their adult feeling and technical mastery unites even these four—they represent quite different moods and themes. *Last Poems* includes a group of songs on different types of women—**'My Kate'**, **'Amy's Cruelty'**, **'A False Step'**—which are faint far-off echoes of Cowper and Campbell and would have done for the gilt-edged Christmas annuals for which she used to write twenty-five years before. But it also includes the splendid **'De Profundis'** which *was* written nearly twenty years before, and which she herself described as in her 'early manner', but which much more closely resembles another poem in this volume, **'My Heart and I'**, which can fairly confidently be dated, by parallels in one of her letters, as late as August 1860. The volume contains a group of political poems in which the vehement energy of the *Poems before Congress* has died down; it is still to be heard a little in the opening of **'First News from Villafranca'**, but it has mostly trickled away into the sorrows, not made real to the imagination, of parting lovers and bereaved mothers and dead conscripts at Solferino. The fiercest poems in the volume are three which depict treacherous, falsely sweet women. In them there is a new note of powerful dramatic characterization which may owe something to Browning's influence, but is probably more directly due to a personal experience of Mrs. Browning's last years—the only time in her life in which she ever broke off a friendship from her side. In 1858 the Brownings made friends with an American couple, the Eckleys, and there was soon an enthusiastic affection, cemented by a common interest in spiritualism, between Sophia Eckley and Elizabeth Barrett Browning, though Browning early recognized Mrs. Eckley as an inveterate liar. But it was two years before Mrs. Browning was disillusioned—by what means will never be known exactly; it is generally said that she discovered that Mrs. Eckley had been deceiving her by fraudulent claims to mediumistic powers, but some of Browning's references to Mrs. Eckley suggest that she had spread lies about her husband's fidelity, even to his own family, because she fancied herself in the role of the injured wife, on the model of Lady Byron. Browning wrote furiously to William Whetmore Story about the 'daily-sprouting toadstools of that dunghill of a soul—lies about this, lies about that'. Mrs. Browning's comment was 'She sticks - - - like treacle,—or dissolved lollipop. Once I praised the sweetness—now I feel very sick at the adhesiveness. Oh if I could believe in the honesty of an inch of her or if she said she hated me; how much easier I should feel. These last words are directly echoed in the savage little poem **'May's Love'**, about a woman who professed to love everyone, who dealt out her sweet looks indiscriminately, and whom the writer implores to turn off her sickening love and hate him instead.

It is curious that Browning never identified the nauseating May of this poem with Mrs. Eckley, but did tell his friends that another poem in this volume, **'Where's Agnes?'**, was about her. He said that his wife had disguised Mrs. Eckley's identity by changing the circumstances in the poem, and that this was done at his request, partly for the sake of Mr. Eckley and partly because Mrs. Browning herself deserved some blame for having been so easily deceived. **'Where's Agnes?'** is a ruthless violent poem about a sickly sweet woman, a Dora Spenlow gone rotten, whose 'sweetness strained the sense Of common life and duty'. So far, a recognizable portrait of Mrs. Eckley; the disguise of changed circumstances consisted in making Agnes a false woman in the conventional sense of the term—an adulteress—for all her pose of white-rose purity. It was the pose, not the adultery, that sickened the broadminded but truthloving Mrs. Browning. Her sympathy with straightforward passion shows in the most remarkable poem in this volume, the astonishing **'Bianca Among the Nightingales'**, the outcry of an Italian woman whose lover has been stolen by a cold-hearted English girl. The first three stanzas, with their intense outspoken love-imagery of flames and arrows and leaping blood, brilliantly patterned with moonlight and black cypress-shade and firefly spirals, are the most explicitly sensual lines Mrs. Browning ever wrote. How was it that, now for the first time when she was a dying woman in her fifties, she was able to convey the passionate intensity and excitement of young lovers? Giulio and Bianca, afloat on the Arno on the feast day of Saint John, watching the soaring rockets, see the luminous city reflected in the river, and the boats, laden with singers, skimming over the glittering towers. Their own boat almost collides with another, and in the sudden flare of a torch Giulio sees the golden hair, the 'leaping eyeballs' wide with fright, of the Englishwoman in the other boat, and catches her as she falls—and Bianca wishes that she and Giulio had drowned together the moment before, the moment when they still loved each other perfectly. Like Madame de Staël's Corinne, Bianca follows her lover and

his new love to England, and there pines miserably at the contrast between

> our Tuscan trees that spring
> As vital flames into the blue,
> And dull round blots of foliage meant
> Like saturated sponges here
> To suck the fogs up.

The images of flame and of nightingale song throb together all through this fierce poem, a heat of passion which is contrasted with the clay coldness, the creeping corruption of the Englishwoman's unfeeling vanities which

> hunt
> Like spiders, in the altar's wood.

The revelation of Mrs. Eckley's real nature undoubtedly gave a violent shock to Mrs. Browning's trusting nature, but it was not enough to account for all the impetus of these vigorous poems. Some change of direction was beginning in Mrs. Browning's poetry which makes one long to know what she would have written if she had lived another ten years. In *Last Poems* there are two poems about the deaths of children (a subject which always haunted Mrs. Browning), **'Only a Curl'** and **'Little Mattie'**. The angel consolations of the former seem strangely perfunctory, in the latter there is a real chill of separation.

> Just so young but yesternight,
> Now she is as old as death
> You can teach her nothing else.
> She has seen the mystery hid
> Under Egypt's pyramid:
> By those eyelids pale and close
> Now she knows what Rhamses knows.

This pyramidal cold is completely at variance with what Mrs. Browning was writing at that time in her letters about continuity and close communion with the dead. Perhaps as her own death drew nearer, the trust which she had put in spiritualist revelations of the life to come failed in her poetic imagination, though not in her conscious mental processes. In her poetry she now writes about death, not as the gentle transition 'perhaps scarcely a greater one than the occurrence of puberty', which her letters call it, but in that drastic image of the lyric called **'Died . . .'**, of the two men following a third along a gallery, criticizing his walk and manner;

> Sudden in the sun
> An oubliette winks. Where is he? Gone.

Death need not be either welcomed or feared, she still believed, but perhaps it was more momentous poetically than she had made it before; and casting round for an image of false security, she found that shattering one at the end of **'First News from Villafranca'**, of

> such a peace as the ear can achieve
> 'Twixt the rifle's click and the rush of the ball,
> 'Twixt the tiger's spring and the crunch of the
> tooth,
> 'Twixt the dying atheist's negative
> And God's Face—waiting, after all!

She was no dying atheist. She knew and had always known that God's Face was waiting for us all when we die. But perhaps she was content now not to be so confident that she knew all about the life after death. She had been hot for certainties, but now perhaps she had achieved Keats' negative capability 'when a man is capable of being in uncertainties, mysteries, doubts, without any irritable reaching after fact and reason'. She was content to think that her heart and she were tired out, and that perhaps she needed to feel and know no more. (pp. 222-26)

> *Alethea Hayter, in her* Mrs Browning: A Poet's Work and Its Setting, *Faber & Faber, 1962, 261 p.*

Helen Cooper   (essay date 1979)

[*In the following excerpt, Cooper considers the extent to which Browning's poetry departs from the literary tradition established by male English poets.*]

A year after the publication of Elizabeth Barrett Browning's [*Poems* (1844)] which established her as Britain's foremost woman poet, she was painfully aware of the absence of foremothers:

> . . . England has had many learned women, not merely readers but writers of the learned languages, in Elizabeth's time and afterwards—women of deeper acquirements than are common now in the greater diffusion of letters; and yet where were the poetesses? The divine breath . . . why did it never pass, even in the lyrical form, over the lips of a woman? How strange! And can we deny that it was so? I look everywhere for grandmothers and see none. It is not in the filial spirit I am deficient, I do assure you—witness my reverent love of the grandfathers!

Chaucer, Spenser, Shakespeare, Milton, Pope, Wordsworth: British poetry embodied four hundred years of male practice of the art. Unlike Arthur Quiller-Couch, who describes how Britain nurtured the men who became its major poets—claiming a university education as a virtual prerequisite for "poetical genius"—Barrett Browning never formulated a penetrating political or social analysis of the factors contributing to the absence of great women poets. However, in letters of 1845 she demonstrates some ambivalence over this issue. To Robert Browning she confesses:

> . . . let us say & do what we please & can . . there *is* a natural inferiority of mind in women—of the intellect . . not by any means, of the moral nature—& that the history of Art . . & of genius testifies to this fact openly. . . .

Seeming "to justify for a moment an opposite opinion," her admiration for George Sand undercuts this:

> Such a colossal nature in every way—with all that breadth & scope of faculty which women want—magnanimous, & loving the truth & loving the people—and with that "hate of hate" too. . . .

In the same year she admits to a Miss Thompson, who had solicited some classical translations for an anthology:

> Perhaps I do not . . . partake quite your 'divine fury' for converting our sex into Greek scholarship. . . . You . . . know that the Greek language . . . swallows up year after year of studious life. Now I have a 'doxy' . . . that there is no exercise of the mind so little profitable to the mind as the study of languages. It is the nearest thing to a passive recipiency—is it not?—as a mental action, though it leaves one as weary as ennui itself. Women want to be made to *think actively:* their apprehension is quicker than that of men, but their defect lies for the most part in the logical faculty and in the higher mental activities.

It is not women's "natural inferiority of mind" that hinders them, but their training into a "passive recipiency." Such a mental state is incompatible with the active thinking necessary for a poet.

Deprived of "grandmothers," Barrett Browning energetically explored what it meant to be a woman poet writing out of a male tradition, in which she was thoroughly self-educated. In 1857 she formulated a clear statement of the material appropriate to the woman poet when she challenged the critical reception to her discussion of prostitutes in *Aurora Leigh:*

> What has given most offence in the book . . . has been the reference to the condition of women in our cities, which a woman oughtn't to refer to . . . says the conventional tradition. Now I have thought deeply otherwise. If a woman ignores these wrongs, then may women as a sex continue to suffer them; there is no help for any of us—let us be dumb and die.
>
>   (pp. 65-6)

To realize her aesthetic Barrett Browning took the idea of excellence from, yet resisted the domination of, the male poetic tradition. Increasingly she absorbed a woman's culture: her letters are peppered with references to [Felicia] Hemans, [Letitia] Landon, and other women poets, to Jane Austen, Charlotte Brontë, George Eliot, George Sand, Mrs. Gaskell, and Harriet Beecher Stowe, to Harriet Martineau and Margaret Fuller, and to the young American sculptor Harriet Hosmer. She probes their work, their assessment of themselves, their strengths and weaknesses, creating for herself a network of support while systematically breaking through the limiting proprieties ascribed to women poets.

Informing this sense of community was the memory of the love between herself and her mother, who died suddenly away from home in 1828 when Barrett Browning was twenty-two. Three years later she records in her diary:

> How I thought of those words *"You will never find another person who will love you as I love you"*—And how I felt that to hear again the sound of those beloved, those ever ever beloved lips, I wd barter all other sounds & sights—that I wd in joy & gratitude lay down before her my tastes & feelings each & all, in sacrifice for the love, the exceeding love which I never, in truth, can find again.

The relationship between Barrett Browning and Edward Moulton Barrett, her father, has become legend, but the love between the poet and Mary Graham-Clarke, her mother, has been ignored by critics. Certainly her father educated her from the full bookcases in his study and was intensely a part of her adult life. However, the education the young poet received from her mother about the nurturing power of love between women also needs exploration and documentation, for it is this that resonates through such poems as her sonnets to George Sand and *Aurora Leigh.*

By the age of twelve Barrett Browning had read Mary Wollstonecraft's *A Vindication of the Rights of Woman.* Taplin, her biographer, records her reading in 1828 in *The Literary Souvenir:*

> . . . a sentimental poem by Miss Landon called "The Forsaken," which represented the lament of a country girl whose lover had left her to look for city pleasures. Elizabeth thought the verses were "beautiful and pathetic." She was also much affected by a poem by Mrs Hemans—it "goes to the heart," she wrote—describing the death of a mother and her baby in a shipwreck.

Yet her second book, *An Essay on Mind,* privately published in the same year, bears the unmistakable imprint of Pope's style:

> Since Spirit first inspir'd, pervaded all,
> And Mind met Matter, at th' Eternal call—
> Since dust weigh'd Genius down, or Genius gave
> Th' immortal halo to the mortal's grave;

and so on for more than a thousand lines.

The Seraphim and Other Poems (1838) and [*Poems* (1844)] were Barrett Browning's first widely published volumes and the first in which a new sense of herself as a woman poet emerged. The latter especially brought good reviews:

> Mr. Chorley, in the *Athenaeum,* described the volume as "extraordinary," adding that "between her poems and the slighter lyrics of the sisterhood, there is all the difference which exists between the putting-on of 'singing robes' for altar service, and the taking up lute or harp to enchant an indulgent circle of friends and kindred."

"The Seraphim" (1838) and "The Drama of Exile" (1844) are both long dramatic poems, influenced by Milton's work. "A Vision of Poets" (1844) and "Lady Geraldine's Courtship" (1844), both about poets, seem traditional because the writers are male. In each case, however, the writer's vision is clarified through interaction with a strong and intelligent woman. In the former the woman specifically instructs the poet as to his true function. Although the poet is not yet identified as a woman, as she will be ten years later in *Aurora Leigh* (1856), this is a radical departure from male tradition, where the woman's function is not to know about poetry but to "inspire" the poet from afar through her beauty or to seduce him away from his work.

Barrett Browning was certain of her dedication to poetry:

> I cannot remember the time when I did not love it—with a lying-awake sort of passion at nine years old, and with a more powerful feeling since. . . . At this moment I love it more than ever—and am more bent than ever, if possible, to work into light . . not into popularity but into expression . . whatever faculty I have. This is the object of the intellectual part of me—and if I live it shall be done. . . . for poetry's own sake . . . for the sake of my love of it. Love is the safest and most unwearied moving principle in all things—it is an heroic worker.

To this poet love is not self-denial and resignation, but a powerful energy source for the transformation of vision into poetry. Sloughing off the male mask in "The Soul's Expression" (1844), she describes forcefully her own creative process:

> With stammering lips and insufficient sound
> I strive and struggle to deliver right
> That music of my nature, day and night
> With dream and thought and feeling interwound,
> And inly answering all the senses round
> With octaves of a mystic depth and height
> Which step out grandly to the infinite
> From the dark edges of the sensual ground.
> This song of soul I struggle to outbear
> Through portals of the sense, sublime and whole,
> And utter all myself into the air:
> But if I did it,—as the thunder-roll
> Breaks its own cloud, my flesh would perish there,
> Before that dread apocalypse of soul.

Her determination to "work into light" necessitates the "stammering lips and insufficient sound" with which she struggles to "deliver right / That music of my nature." Her vision comes through her senses, as she seeks transcendence to "step out grandly to the infinite / From the dark edges of the sensual ground." As a woman trained to a "passive recipiency," she experiences the active energy of creativity as potentially destructive. Compelled to deliver the "music of my nature," she fears to give herself totally to her imagination "and utter all myself into the air," fears "my flesh would perish there, / Before that dread apocalypse of soul." And yet it was through the power of her imagination that she created her identity and her ability to deal with her eight-year "captivity" as a Victorian female invalid, as "The Prisoner" (1844) reveals:

> . . . Nature's lute
>
> Sounds on, behind this door so closely shut,
> A strange wild music to the prisoner's ears,
> Dilated by the distance, till the brain
> Grows dim with fancies which it feels too fine:

"Behind this door" she responded passionately to George Sand's novels, and her sonnet "To George Sand: A Recognition" (1844) contains a clear statement about the special nature of a woman's voice writing of women's concerns:

> True genius, but true woman! dost deny
> The woman's nature with a manly scorn,
> And break away the gauds and armlets worn
> By weaker women in captivity?

Ah, vain denial! that revolted cry
Is sobbed in by a woman's voice forlorn,—
Thy woman's hair, my sister, all unshorn
Floats back dishevelled strength in agony,
Disproving thy man's name: and while before
The world thou burnest in a poet-fire,
We see thy woman-heart beat evermore
Through the large flame. Beat purer, heart, and
　　higher,
Till God unsex thee on the heavenly shore
Where unincarnate spirits purely aspire!

The male mask can never hide the "revolted cry . . . sobbed in by a woman's voice forlorn." She implies no woman can "break away the gauds and armlets worn / By weaker women in captivity." Barrett Browning recognized that if women generally are exploited and oppressed, then all women as a class suffer, no matter any individual woman's apparent privilege. She identifies herself here as part of a community of women, "we," as opposed to "the world" of men.

In [*Poems* (1844)] there is a strongly evolving consciousness of herself as a woman poet and of her belief that the "sole work" of the poet "is to represent the age," as **"The Cry of the Children"**—about child factory-workers—shows. But this new voice and subject matter were not supported by nor obvious to all of her old friends. In September 1843 she articulates to an early mentor, Hugh Boyd, her belief in this new poetry:

Will you see the **'Cry of the (Children)'** or not?

It will not please you, probably. It wants melody. The versification is eccentric to the ear, and the subject (the factory miseries) is scarcely an agreeable one to the fancy. Perhaps altogether you had better not see it, because I know you think me to be deteriorating, and I don't want you to have farther hypothetical evidence of so false an opinion. Frankly, if not humbly, I believe myself to have gained power since . . . the **'Seraphim'**. . . . I differ with you, the longer I live, on the ground of what you call the 'jumping lines' . . . and the tenacity of my judgement (arises) . . . from the deeper study of the old master-poets—English poets—those of the Elizabeth and James ages, before the corruption of French rhythms stole in with Waller and Denham, and was acclimated into a national inodorousness by Dryden and Pope.

Barrett Browning asserts her "power," the "tenacity of her judgement," and her defiance of both her critics and the established poetic tradition. In the following year, August 1844, she explains to John Kenyon:

I wish I could persuade you of the rightness of my view about **'Essays on Mind'** and such things, and how the difference between them and my present poems is not merely the difference between two schools, . . . nor even the difference between immaturity and maturity; but that it is the difference between the dead and the living, between a copy and an individuality, between what is myself and what is not myself.

She grew increasingly convinced that women writers should actively concern themselves with social conditions. In 1853 she exhorts the art critic and her life-long correspondent, Mrs. Jameson:

Not read Mrs. Stowe's book! But you *must*. Her book is quite a sign of the times, and has otherwise and intrinsically considerable power. For myself, I rejoice in the success, both as a woman and a human being. Oh, and is it possible that you think a woman has no business with questions like the question of slavery? Then she had better use a pen no more. She had better subside into slavery and concubinage herself, I think, as in the times of old, shut herself up with the Penelopes in the 'women's apartment,' and take no rank among thinkers and speakers.

"A Curse for a Nation" confirms Barrett Browning's refusal to "subside into slavery and concubinage." Written for the abolitionist movement in America and published in *Poems Before Congress* (1860), the poem incurred the wrath of critics disturbed by her interference in politics. Tough poetry results from her conviction that this is precisely her role:

'Therefore,' the voice said, 'shalt thou write
　　My curse to-night.
Because thou hast strength to see and hate
A foul thing done *within* thy gate.'

'Not so,' I answered once again.
　　'To curse, choose men.
For I, a woman, have only known
How the heart melts and tears run down.'

Manuscript page of a poem published in The Seraphim and Other Poems.

'Therefore,' the voice said, 'shalt thou write
   My curse to-night.
Some women weep and curse, I say
(And no one marvels), night and day,

And thou shalt take their part to-night,
   Weep and write.
A curse from the depths of womanhood
Is very salt, and bitter, and good.'

Barrett Browning specifically repudiates her assigned role as "lady" who knows only "How the heart melts and tears run down." She designates herself as spokesperson for those less-privileged women who "weep and curse, I say / (And no one marvels), night and day," thereby defying patriarchy's division of "ladies" from working-class women.

Her anger against critics who disavowed her right to step beyond the limits laid down for "lady poets" had been revealed some years earlier in a fascinating discussion of Florence Nightingale, whom she came to see as performing an age-old role, that of angel on the battlefield:

I know Florence Nightingale slightly. . . . I honour her from my heart. . . .

At the same time, I confess to be at a loss to see any new position for the sex, or the most imperfect solution of the 'woman's question,' in this step of hers. . . . Since the seige of Troy and earlier, we have had princesses binding wounds with their hands; it's strictly the woman's part, and men understand it so. . . . Every man is on his knees before ladies carrying lint, calling them 'angelic she's,' whereas, if they stir an inch as thinkers or artists from the beaten line (involving more good to general humanity than is involved in lint), the very same men would curse the impudence of the very same women and stop there. . . . For my own part (and apart from the exceptional miseries of the war), I acknowledge to you that I do not consider the best use to which we can put a gifted and accomplished woman is to *make her a hospital nurse.* If it is, why then woe to us all who are artists!

Barrett Browning wants to start healing the wounds of women by naming them. She writes of the Crimean War:

War, war! It is terrible certainly. But there are worse plagues, deeper griefs, dreader wounds than the physical. What of the forty thousand wretched women in this city? The silent writhing of them is to me more appalling than the roar of the cannons.

The "homely domestic ballad" which Chorley sees as being purified on "passing into female hands" is subverted by Barrett Browning to condemn men's seduction and exploitation of women. **"The Rhyme of the Duchess of May"** (1844), a long ballad-poem set in the Middle Ages, tells of an orphaned girl betrothed by her guardian at twelve to his son. Grown into womanhood, she refuses this marriage, having chosen her own lover. The viewing of women as a commercial commodity is pointed up by her guardian's response to her decision:

'Good my niece, that hand withal looketh

somewhat soft and small
For so large a will, in sooth.'

To which the niece astutely replies:

'Little hand clasps muckle gold, or it were
   not worth the hold
Of thy son, good uncle mine!'

The duchess secretly marries her lover. When her uncle's soldiers try to reclaim his "property," even her husband intends to kill himself on the assumption that his wife will be forgiven. She refuses to see herself as property and dies with her chosen husband to avoid life with a man she detests.

The finely honed ballad **"Amy's Cruelty"** (1862) hinges on the ironic observation that what seems to be a woman's cruelty to her lover is in fact her only defense against exploitation:

Fair Amy of the terraced house,
   Assist me to discover
Why you who would not hurt a mouse
   Can torture so your lover. . . .

But when *he* haunts your door . . . the town
   Marks coming and marks going . . .
You seem to have stitched your eyelids down
   To that long piece of sewing!

Amy's life is circumscribed. She sits daily in the "terraced house" fulfilling her sewing duties. Yet she has the power to protect herself and the insight to know the dangers of love:

He wants my world, my sun, my heaven,
   Soul, body, whole existence. . . .

I only know my mother's love
   Which gives all and asks nothing;
And this new loving sets the groove
   Too much the way of loathing.
Unless he gives me all in change,
   I forfeit all things by him:
The risk is terrible and strange—
   I tremble, doubt, . . . deny him.

The "risk is terrible": in **"Void in Law"** (1862) a court finds a marriage void because only one witness was competent. The husband can now marry another woman, approved by society, one whose:

. . . throat has the antelope curve,
And her cheek just the color and line
   Which fade not before him nor swerve.

The first wife and child are legally abandoned.

"Bianca Among the Nightingales" (1862), one of Barrett Browning's most technically exciting ballad-poems, opens with a frank celebration of sexuality. Bianca remembers embracing her lover in the Italian moonlight:

And *we,* too! from such soul-height went
   Such leaps of blood, so blindly driven, . . .

The nightingales, the nightingales!

We paled with love, we shook with love,
   We kissed so close we could not vow. . . .

The nightingales, whose singing "throbbed" in Italy with the passion of their love, haunt Bianca in "gloomy England," where she follows her lover who has abandoned her to pursue a woman of great beauty: "These nightingales will sing me mad." Bianca delineates the difference between his love for her and for the other woman:

> He says to her what moves her most.
>   He would not name his soul within
> Her hearing,—rather pays the cost
>   With praises to her lips and chin.

She is physically to be praised as ritualistically as any sonneteer's mistress. She has a "fine tongue" and "loose gold ringlets," but to Bianca she is "mere cold clay / As all false things are." The only person who will know this woman's soul is Bianca: "She lied and stole, / And spat into my love's pure pyx / The rank saliva of her soul." Barrett Browning explores the reality that a woman who truly wishes to be herself, to experience her sexuality and some kind of fruitful relationship with the male world will be challenged by the more acceptable norm of the woman who has learned to remain all beautiful surface, hidden both from herself and from the men she must please. The refrain "The nightingales, the nightingales" moves relentlessly from an affirmation of love to a taunting that drives Bianca to madness. In the last stanza the extended refrain and repetition enact her frenzy:

> —Oh, owl-like birds! They sing for spite,
>   They sing for hate, they sing for doom,
> They'll sing through death who sing through night,
>   They'll sing and stun me in the tomb—
> The nightingales, the nightingales!

Bianca knows she can never be like the other woman, but neither can she bear the ostracism attendant on being different.

The woman who is not abandoned is just as easily prey to exploitation. **"Lord Walter's Wife"** (1862) sets her husband's friend straight when he is horror-stricken at her suggestion of an affair—the logical conclusion to his flirtatious innuendoes:

> 'A moment,—I pray your attention!—I
>   have a poor word in my head
> I must utter, though womanly custom
>   would set it down better unsaid. . . .
>
> You did me the honour, perhaps to be
>   moved at my side now and then
> In the senses—a vice, I have heard, which
>   is common to beasts and some men. . . .
>
> And since, when all's said, you're too
>   noble to stoop to the frivolous cant
> About crimes irresistible, virtues that swindle, betray, and supplant,
>
> I determined to prove to yourself that,
>   whate'er you might dream or avow
> By illusion, you wanted precisely no more
>   of me than you have now.'

This poem caused Thackeray much embarrassment when it was submitted to him for publication in the *Cornhill Magazine* in 1861:

> . . . one of the best wives, mothers, women in the world writes some verses which I feel certain would be objected to by many of our readers. . . . In your poem, you know, there is an account of unlawful passion, felt by a man for a woman, and though you write pure doctrine, and real modesty, and pure ethics, I am sure our readers would make an outcry, and so I have not published this poem.

Barrett Browning replies in no uncertain terms:

> I am not a 'fast woman.' I don't like coarse subjects, or the coarse treatment of any subject. But I am deeply convinced that the corruption of our society requires not shut doors and windows, but light and air: and that it is exactly because pure and prosperous women choose to *ignore* vice, that miserable women suffer wrong by it everywhere. Has paterfamilias, with his Oriental traditions and veiled female faces, very successfully dealt with a certain class of evil? What if materfamilias, with her quick sure instincts and honest innocent eyes, do more towards their expulsion by simply looking at them and calling them by their names?

This strong conviction in the last year of her life that the responsibility of the woman poet was to confront and name the condition of women had manifested itself in her poetry from the **Seraphim** on, as she sought to delineate the complexity of female experience. She wrote powerfully about the institution of motherhood in patriarchy, and the experience of biological motherhood. **"The Virgin Mary to the Child Jesus"** (1838) is a meditation in Mary's voice. She begins poignantly, unsure what name she can call this child who is both of her flesh and also her Lord. She watches Jesus sleeping, imagines he dreams of God his father, whereas the best she can give him is a mother's kiss. Patriarchal Christian tradition exalts Mary as most honored; a woman writes of the pain Mary would experience mothering a child simultaneously hers and not hers:

> Then, I think aloud
> The words 'despised,'—'rejected,'—every word
> Recoiling into darkness as I view
>   The DARLING on my knee.
> Bright angels,—move not—lest ye stir the cloud
> Betwixt my soul and his futurity!
> I must not die, with mother's work to do,
>   And could not live—and see.

The implications of the poem point beyond the immediate meditation to a consideration of how patriarchy always destines its sons for a life beyond their mothers. Another early poem, **"Victoria's Tears"** (1838), explores how the young woman is jolted from her childhood into mothering her country as its queen (when women were not even enfranchised). Barrett Browning contrasts the grandiose coronation with her sense of what the young woman has lost:

> She saw no purples shine,
>   For tears had dimmed her eyes;
> She only knew her childhood's flowers
>   Were happier pageantries!
> And while her heralds played the part,
>   For million shouts to drown—

'God save the Queen' from hill to mart,—
She heard through all her beating heart,
    And turned and wept—
She wept, to wear a crown!

Both poems pinpoint the isolation of the "token woman," whose position of supposed privilege is actually one of loneliness and confusion.

In **"The Cry of the Children"** (1844), she exposes how hopeless it is for the child factory workers to cry to mothers powerless to alleviate their suffering:

Do ye hear the children weeping, O my brothers,
    Ere the sorrow comes with years?
They are leaning their young heads against their
    mothers,
And *that* cannot stop their tears. . . .

But the young, young children, O my brothers,
    Do you ask them why they stand
Weeping sore before the bosom of their mothers,
    In our happy Fatherland?

The capitalization of "Fatherland" but not of "mothers" underlines the power structure: the natural flesh bond between the child and mother is helpless before the demands of patriarchy. The children mourn Alice, who died from the brutal working conditions: "Could we see her face, be sure we should not know her, / For the smile has time for growing in her eyes. . . ." That it is a girl who dies from such work in a society that draped its middle-class women with prudery, passivity and sentimentality should not go unnoticed. Repetition creates the delirium of these children's exhaustion, pulling us into their experience:

'For all day the wheels are droning, turning;
    Their wind comes in our faces,
Till our hearts turn, our heads with pulses burn-
    ing,
    And the walls turn in their places:
Turns the sky in the high window, blank and
    reeling,
    Turns the long light that drops adown the
    wall,
Turn the black flies that crawl along the ceiling:
    All are turning, all the day, and we with all.
And all day the iron wheels are droning,
    And sometimes we could pray,
"O ye wheels" (breaking out in a mad moaning),
    "Stop! be silent for to-day!" '

Victimization is again exposed in **"The Runaway Slave at Pilgrim's Point"** (1850), spoken in the voice of a young black woman slave being flogged to death where the pilgrims landed. On the plantation she had loved a black male slave. The white overseers, learning of this love, beat the man to death and, seeing her grief, her owner rapes her. Her initial response to the child born of this rape is love:

Thus we went moaning, child and mother,
One to another, one to another,

but

. . . the babe who lay on my bosom so,
    Was far too white, too white for me;
As white as the ladies who scorned to pray
Beside me at church but yesterday.

Soon she cannot look at her son and strains a handkerchief over his face. He struggles against this, wanting his freedom: "For the white child wanted his liberty— / Ha, Ha! he wanted the master-right." The dichotomies her son represents overwhelm her. She loves him but hates that, being male and white, he will grow up with the right to violate a woman as her rapist, his father, did. She loves him but:

Why, in that single glance I had
    Of my child's face, . . . I tell you all,
I saw a look that made me mad!
    The *master's* look, that used to fall
On my soul like his lash . . . or worse!
And so, to save it from my curse,
    I twisted it round in my shawl.

She strangles her son so she will neither have to repudiate him later, nor experience her rape reenacted every time she looks into his face. She runs from the plantation holding the child to her for many days before burying him. Her owner catches her and flogs her to death. Taplin's dismissal [Gardner B. Taplin in his *The Life of Elizabeth Barrett Browning,* 1957] of the poem as "too blunt and shocking" only underscores the poem's explosive exposure of racism and sexism.

Barrett Browning had four pregnancies in the four years after her marriage. Only the third ended with a birth, that of her son, Robert Wiedeman ("Penini") in 1849. The experience of childbirth and biological motherhood informs **"Only a Curl"** (1862), written on receiving a lock of hair from the parents of a dead child unknown to the poet. In language movingly reminiscent of **"The Soul's Expression,"** written twenty years earlier about the creative process, Barrett Browning comforts by saying how once a mother has known her power in childbirth her child is always in some way part of the mother's experience:

. . . I appeal
    To all who bear babes—in the hour
When the veil of the body we feel
    Rent round us,—while torments reveal
    The motherhood's advent in power,

And the babe cries!—has each of us known
    By apocalypse (God being there
Full in nature) the child is our own,
Life of life, love of love, moan of moan,
    Through all changes, all times, everywhere.

She records in her letters what a powerful and health-giving experience childbirth was. Even today, forty-three is considered "late" for giving birth to a first child. For Barrett Browning, almost given up as dead three years earlier, to have that much physical power was exhilarating.

One of her last poems, **"Mother and Poet"** (1862), confronts, like **"The Virgin Mary to the Child Jesus,"** the conflict between a mother's relationship with her sons and their destiny within patriarchy. It is spoken in the voice of Laura Savio, an Italian poet and patriot dedicated, as was Barrett Browning, to the unification of Italy. Savio's two sons were killed fighting for "freedom." The poet reconsiders the meaning of both motherhood and patriotism after their deaths:

To teach them . . . It stings there! I made them
   indeed
   Speak plain the word *country*. I taught them,
   no doubt,
That a country's a thing men should die for at
   need.
    I prated of liberty, rights, and about
      The tyrant cast out.

She imagines the victory celebrations:

Forgive me. Some women bear children in
   strength,
   And bite back the cry of their pain in self-
   scorn;
But the birth-pangs of nations will wring us at
   length
   Into wail such as this—and we sit on forlorn
    When the man-child is born.

Dead! One of them shot by the sea in the east,
   And one of them shot in the west by the sea.
Both! both my boys! If in keeping the feast
   You want a great song for your Italy free,
    Let none look at *me*!

To Barrett Browning, whose son had grown up listening to her passionate political talk and at twelve spoke eagerly of his own desire to fight for freedom, this is an assessment of great integrity about her own complicity in patriarchy. She understands that the energetic womanhood manifest in the bearing of children is undermined by mothers, like herself, who incorporate patriarchal values into their own consciousness and become breeders of cannon fodder. Taplin brushes the poem off as "devoid of inspiration," quite missing the poet's sophisticated insight into women's contribution to their own oppression.

"Mother and Poet" fuses three of Barrett Browning's preoccupations in her writing—art, politics, and motherhood—as a manifestation of powerful womanhood. "What art's for a woman?" she has Laura Savio ask. In her own career she was increasingly convinced that women as "artists and thinkers" must be concerned with social interaction, social conditions, and political events. Realizing that the "personal is the political," she used her physical and emotional experiences as a woman to illuminate the public sphere. In doing so she created a voice and vision for herself as a woman poet and became truly our "grandmother." Like many grandmothers, she has been unjustly ignored; like many grandmothers, she has healing wisdom to share. As early as 1845 she believed:

. . . we should all be ready to say that if the secrets of our daily lives & inner souls may instruct other surviving souls, let them be open to men hereafter, even as they are to God now. Dust to dust, & soul-secrets to humanity— there are natural heirs to all things.

(pp. 68-81)

Helen M. Cooper, "Working into Light: Elizabeth Barrett Browning," in Shakespeare's Sisters: Feminist Essays on Women Poets, *edited by Sandra M. Gilbert and Susan Gubar, Indiana University Press, 1979, 65-81.*

David Loth on Browning's thoughts about her marriage:

The wedding had been definitely fixed for the autumn. Ba and Robert sent each other books and travelers' letters dealing with the weather in Italian towns, the state of the roads, the food, the quality of the inns, the exposure to tourists. But Ba was still oppressed with occasional qualms that it was too good to last. She worried about Robert's future happiness when he should find what life with an invalid really meant. Robert was defying the world to call him a fortune-hunter, and Ba assured him that "people are more likely to say that I have taken you in." But at last, in her perplexity, she hit upon a solution that marked the only real breach with the conventions that either of them ever contemplated in all their lives. She proposed a trial marriage. They would go off together, legally tied of course, in the fall. But if at winter's end he were tired of the arrangement, she would leave him, taking only so much of her own money as would support her alone in Greece.

David Loth, in his The Brownings: A Victorian Idyll, *1934.*

Kathleen Blake   (essay date 1983)

[*In the following excerpt, Blake discusses the ambivalent handling of the theme of love in Browning's poetry, focusing on* Aurora Leigh *as "a comprehensive treatment of E.B.B.'s complicated feelings about love."*]

[Elizabeth Barrett Browning] is certainly a poet of love. Yet her poetry, letters and diaries also reveal a profound ambivalence. Her early verse explores predominantly religious themes and develops a Christian theology of love, as in **"A Supplication for Love"** in the 1838 volume ***The Seraphim,*** which asks "that we may love like THEE". This theology is interestingly linked to an aesthetic and a theory of womanhood in the 1844 **"A Drama of Exile"**, a Sophoclean version of the exile from Eden, with unmiltonic emphasis on Eve. Damnation means to suffer as Lucifer does "the great woe of striving against Love". A Romantic aesthetic theory emerges from the theological framework. The earth has been betrayed by human sin and blames Adam and Eve for causing its suffering. But Christ admonishes the earth spirits to pardon, serve and love humanity. Mankind's grateful love for the wronged earth that yet willingly ministers to human needs will spiritualise natural phenomena above their own capacity. They will become "Suggesters to his soul of higher things / Than any of your highest", material for his "golden fantasies". To this is added a theory of womanly love. As Eve's sin takes precedence in the drama, so does her expiation, which works itself out through the pains of love: childbirth, the weariness and cold returns of motherhood, mistrust from those she serves, treason from those she cares for, cruelty and tyranny from man, the stronger. Love forms Eve's difficult "crown". One pain is left out of this catalogue, the conflict to be developed in ***Aurora Leigh*** between the crown of love and the laurel crown of art and fame. But **"A Drama of Exile"** supplies a good introduction to E.B.B.'s glorification of love in terms of the price paid for it, especially by women. In a number of her poems the price is so high that the glory is hard to keep sight of.

In October of 1846, a month after her marriage to Browning, E.B.B. published five poems in *Blackwood's*. One treats the woman's capacity for fatally absolute love. The companion poem treats the fickleness of the man, who demands more than he returns. **"A Year's Spinning"** and **"Change Upon Change"** describe a woman's abandonment by a false lover. These poems seem odd when considered in relation to the author's recent marriage, but they really present a standard theme for her. She doesn't drop it because Browning made her happy. **"Void in Law"** and **"Bianca Among the Nightingales"** offer two relatively straightforward examples from her last *Poems* (1862). These treat the woman's abandonment and sorrow, and they explain the dread of love expressed in another poem in the volume, **"Amy's Cruelty"**: "He wants my world, my sun, my heaven, / Soul, body, whole existence / . . . . Unless he gives me all in change, / I forfeit all things by him: / The risk is terrible and strange— / I tremble, doubt, . . . deny him."

Risk reverberates through E.B.B.'s poems of love. *The Seraphim* contains **"The Romaunt of Margret"**, a dialogue between a woman and her shadow-double who challenges her for the stakes of life or death to demonstrate whether she is loved as much as she loves. Brother, little sister, father and lover all fall short (though it is this lover's death that causes his fickleness), and the woman confronts "failing human love" (XXVII) and dies. **"The Romaunt of the Page"** of the *Poems* of 1844 tells the story of a devoted wife who disguises herself as a page and follows her knight-husband into battle. But when she covertly enquires what he would think of such a woman, he says he would find her actions admirable but unwomanly, and he would not care for her. After this rebuke the page-wife puts herself into the way of death at the hands of the paynim. She doesn't blame her husband, but neither does the poem validate his idea of women and love, for the page-wife wishes him "A lady to thy mind, / More woman-proud and *half as true* / As one thou leav'st behind!" (italics mine).

Risk is here associated with non-requital, but in **"The Romance of the Swan's Nest"** and **"Confessions"** risk stems from the woman's own desire and its usurpation of other values. Little Ellie of **"The Romance of the Swan's Nest"** presents a familiar figure. Awaiting a romantic saviour, she daydreams of a perfect hero of knightly chivalry, a righter of wrongs, a rider of a silver-shod steed. But at the end of her afternoon of dreaming she goes to look at her swan's nest by the river and finds it deserted and rat-gnawed. The poem concludes with uncertainty about the lover—whether he will ever arrive—but certainty that Ellie will never have the swan's nest to show him. By implication, what she actually has, has been lost to something she may never get. This poem does not celebrate love, but makes its dreams into self-betrayal.

"Confessions" also raises doubts about desire for salvation through love. The poem represents a confrontation within the soul as a dialogue between "I" and "She", heard only

by God. "She" confesses her sin. It consists of the failure to shine out, to burn with the spark of God's creation, developed in imagery of light versus dark. Yet "She" justifies herself in the one claim that "I have *loved*". The "I" of the poem does not fully accept this justification, but regards the love of the human as a substitute for the love of the divine, which should express itself through the shining forth of the self created by God. Not only has "She" forfeited her own light, but she has not been recompensed by the warmth of returned affection, and the poem ends with more guilt and terror than consolation for the one who has made love her only claim. The last lines are obscure and suggestive:

> God, over my head
> Must sweep in the wrath of his judgment-seas
> If *He* shall deal with me sinning, but only indeed
>   the
>   same
> And no gentler than these.

"These" are the ones she loved without return. As I read the lines, "She" accepts God's judging wrath as a just desert for her sin of self-darkening love, but implies by her "if" his possible choice not to punish her sin. If he does not choose mercy, he will seem the same and no gentler than those who failed to requite her love. Manifold ambivalence informs this peculiar and powerful poem. Love becomes implicated in the sin against God in oneself, and it does not provide an adequate plea of innocence or for mercy. Still, God himself risks the poem's judgement should he prove as harsh as his creatures, who give so sparing a return on love.

The *Sonnets from the Portuguese* (1850) are the flower of E.B.B.'s actual love for Robert Browning, of which their magnificent correspondence is the full growth. I will use both, as well as other personal writings, as I press toward E.B.B.'s archetype of the woman artist in *Aurora Leigh,* whose trouble is love. Heroines of literature have awaited lovers as if they had been angels, and like little Ellie and the "She" of **"Confessions"**, have sometimes found such awaited salvation problematical. But Browning came to E.B.B. with hardly less than angelic grace. He quite literally saved her from invalidism, isolation, hopelessness, guilt and virtual incarceration in her father's house. The sonnets worshipfully acknowledge his "dovelike help", his "strong divineness", his "saving kiss": "I who looked for only God, found *thee*!" (XXXI, XXXVII, XXVII). One letter calls him "my angel at the gate of the prison". E.B.B. believed that "love is so much more to me naturally—it is, to all women", but she also knew that vulnerability attends need, and in the sonnets and letters she remains troubled by the miraculous visitation of love. Reluctance and dismay play a role that the grateful rejoicing should not make us overlook.

For instance, Browning may have come to her like an angel, but in doing so he had to overmaster her to some degree and make her accept an earthly salvation after she had fixed her eyes on death and heaven. The speaker of the sonnets hears love's voice "in mastery". She must be drawn back to him by the hair (I). The letters, too, indicate a sense of being overmastered: "I felt as if you had a power over me & meant to use it, & that I could not breathe or speak very differently from what you chose to make me". According to the sonnets, "I yield the grave for thy sake", letting go the "near sweet view of Heaven" for "life's lower range" (XXIII). According to the letters, "mournful and bitter would be to me this return into life, apart from you".

E.B.B. suffered from the idea that one bond must break another; so here too romance demanded concession. She knew that her father's bizarre exaggeration of patriarchal rights would make him disavow her for marrying. She also knew that marriage and happiness would break the constancy of her grief for her beloved brother Edward, for whose death she blamed herself since he had drowned while remaining with her at the seaside upon her special request, and against the will of their father. She felt that she had not only challenged family unity but caused a tragic break in it, from which feelings came her qualms about leaving with a lover:

> Shall I never miss
> Home-talk and blessing and the common kiss
> That comes to each in turn, nor count it strange,
> When I look up, to drop on a new range
> Of walls and floors, another home than this?
> Nay, wilt thou fill that place by me which is
> Filled by dead eyes too tender to know change?
> That's hardest
>
> (XXXV)

"You stand in between me & not merely the living who stood closest, but between me and the closer graves, . . . & I reproach myself for this sometimes". "I, who had my warmest affections on the other side of the grave, feel that it is otherwise with me now—quite otherwise. I did not like it at first to be so much otherwise".

Much of E.B.B.'s hesitation came from knowing that love can bring injury as well as boon. She had suffered such injury. With great pain did she finally recognise that her father's strangely heartless affection would have buried her in her sickroom, for how else could she interpret his squelching of her plan to travel south for her health in 1846, when the doctors practically ordered the journey to Italy as a last hope? She had to face the fact that she cared for him more warmly than he for her. E.B.B. had had previous experience of one-sided affection, as we see in her diary of 1831-2, which concerns her relationship with the Greek scholar H.S. Boyd. For a year her entries calculate the bitter difference between his regard and her own, and she wonders if she can ever hope for reciprocation. In fact, she finds her womanly capacity for feeling a liability and wishes she could feel less—"I am not of a cold nature, & cannot bear to be treated coldly. When cold water is thrown upon hot iron, the iron *hisses.* I wish that water *wd.* make my iron as cold as itself ".

Besides being hurt in love, E.B.B. felt she had done hurt, and this too made her cautious. She felt that she had actually caused her brother's death by wanting him with her, and done violence to a tight-knit family. She fearfully questioned what sort of gift her heart would make to Browning since she was not young (thirty-eight), six years an invalid, broken-spirited in guilt and sorrow. She writes

to Browning, "May God turn back the evil of me!" "Can it be right to give what I can give? / To let thee sit beneath the fall of tears?" (IX). Also she feared to involve him in an unequal relationship. She felt that she could only care for someone higher than herself, and in so doing would condemn him to attachment to an inferior. One can only drag down a man loved for standing at the level of the angels: "We are not peers, / So to be lovers" (IX).

Browning had constantly to challenge "your strange disbelief in yourself ". He thought she crippled herself to maintain the holding power of the bond with her father— "chop off your legs, you will never go astray". This might suggest self-stultification in the name of love like that of Dorothea Brooke, who puts her best soul in prison in order to please her husband. However, "the process of my selfscorning", as E.B.B. calls it, also apparently served a different purpose. It seems to be abject, but it could also operate self-protectively, as a defence against the encroachments of love. E.B.B. remarks that her life had been as restricted as any nun's, but this had provided a certain safety, too.

Thus she achieved a curious integrity through the process of her selfscorning. She constantly repudiated Browning's extravagant praises because she thought that in conjuring an amorous ideal he might overlook her actual self. She sounds a bit like Jane Eyre resisting Rochester: "I shall end by being jealous of some ideal Czarina who must stand between you & me. I shall think that it is not I whom you look at". From the outset E.B.B. had wanted to bar a sexual element from their relationship to render it more genuine and valuable. Chivalrous addresses disgusted her. On one occasion she complains hotly to Browning of the insolence under the name of worship she had endured in the past. A letter to Mary Russell Mitford complains of the masculine ideal of female perfection that justifies contempt of the living woman. One might almost say that E.B.B. vaunts her inadequacies and sometimes, as in the letter to Mitford, those of her sex, for at least they represent the real thing, like the poetic faults that she vigorously claims as her own and refuses to lay at Tennyson's door.

If selfscorning contained an element of defence, E.B.B. could also take the offensive and directly express her distrust of men, love and marriage. Sonnet XXXVII confesses a "doubt, a dread" about the sincerity of Browning's suit. After a year of letters and meetings she admits that she still falls prey to black remissions of confidence in him. The precipitousness of his love seems suspect: "Quickloving hearts, I thought, may quickly loathe" (XXXII). A number of accounts appear in her diary and letters of jiltings, breach-of-promise cases, courtship *débâcles.* She jokes on love as the word that rhymes with glove and comes as easily on and off. One of her correspondents, Anna Jameson, was the victim of an unhappy marriage. She recounts the story to another favourite correspondent, Miss Mitford, who was sure to appreciate it, being a foe of matrimony. To Miss Mitford she excoriates the double standard, "the crushing into dust for the woman and the 'oh you naughty man'ism for the betrayer". She assures Browning that she knows something about men, and it is not good: "As for *men,* you are not to take me to be quite ignorant of what they are worth in the gross. The most blindfolded of women may see a little under the folds . . . & I have seen quite enough to be glad to shut my eyes". "Men are nearly all the same in the point of *wanting generosity to women*. It is a sin of the sex, be sure". Browning proves to be the exception in his freedom from "the common rampant man-vices which tread down a woman's peace".

According to E.B.B.'s analysis of marriage, it typically and contemptibly revolves around worldly convenience; often even when it begins in affection, it turns to hate; it invites the tyranny of the stronger and the hypocrisy of the weaker; it degrades women because men do not seek companionship but ministration. More than once in her early diary she resolves not to marry. She records a dream of being married that was a nightmare. She tells Browning that she never forgot a conversation overheard in childhood on the disillusionment of the first year after the wedding when the suitor turns into the husband.

Not surprisingly, she recalls to Browning another childhood memory, her uncle's warning: "Do you beware of ever loving!—If you do, you will not do it half: it will be for life & death". She sounds a warning note in advising a Miss Haworth to review the real worth of her single state before deciding whether to accept a proposal, to consider her freedom "to live out, in short, your individual life, which is so hard to do in marriage, even where you marry worthily". A woman has need of her "instinct of preservation", according to E.B.B., who can say even to Browning well into their courtship, "you are a man, & free to care less". E.B.B. writes to Miss Mitford, "the truth is, that I who always did certainly believe in love, yet was as great a sceptic as you about the evidences thereof". "As to marriage . . . it never was high up in my ideal". "A happy marriage was the happiest condition, I believed vaguely—but *where were the happy marriages?*" E.B.B. did not particularly ally herself with the women's movement. She does not sound like a feminist when in one letter, for instance, she calls her sex intellectually inferior. On the other hand, the obituary in *The Englishwoman's Journal* applauds *Aurora Leigh* and the fact that the author had signed a petition for married women's property rights. My point is that E.B.B. shared the distaste of many feminists for Byron's precept that "man's love is of man's life a thing apart", while it is woman's whole existence. She wryly comments that this notion spawns the typical husband, a fellow uninterested in conjugal companionship who expects to have his prunes stewed for him while he reads classics by himself.

Aurora Leigh is a "verse novel" in blank verse and nine books, longer than *Paradise Lost,* and it offers a comprehensive treatment of E.B.B.'s complicated feelings about love. Love forms the highest religious imperative, as we have seen in her **"A Drama of Exile"**. Aurora's father dies with the words, "Love, my child, love, love!", and the pauper girl Marion Erle has only to look up at the sun to be taught a "grand blind Love. . . . She learnt God that way". But in this life and on this earth the ways of love prove difficult to follow. To the probings of its injuries, inequities and conflicts found in her other poems and her personal writings, E.B.B. adds the question of its role for the woman artist. *Aurora Leigh* tells the story of the development of a woman poet largely as the story of her struggle to understand how her life and art can accommodate love. Aurora Leigh envies male poets because they find it possible to write poetry *for* their wives and mothers. In a woman's case art and love are connected by a "but": "Art is much, but Love is more". To be an artist means living as a lone woman. This wrongs the artist's feminine nature and, in turn, undermines her art because "No perfect artist is developed here / From any imperfect woman". *Aurora Leigh* assumes a feminine instinct of love, from which it develops the woman artist's dilemma: she cannot become a full artist unless she is a full woman, but she can hardly become an artist at all without resisting love as it consumes women, subsuming them to men.

Men literally consume women in the poem. *Aurora Leigh* gained notoriety and went into multiple editions for its treatment of prostitution. Marion Erle's mother tries to sell her to a man, and later she is conveyed unknowingly into the hands of a bawd, raped in a continental brothel, and made mad with the indignity. No complete recovery can follow such a thing. Some power of feeling perishes. Only her child can rouse response, and Marion refuses to marry the noble-hearted Romney Leigh, even though marriage would redress dishonour. From her drugged violation she "waked up in the grave", and she remains enshrouded, never to be decked out in nuptial imagery.

Yet Marion Erle ends with a curious dignity, her life lopped of everything except her feeling for her child, but also having gained a certain bleak freedom from dependence on a man or his wedding ring. Before the disaster she had been betrothed to Romney. He had taken her up as one of "the people", to whom he ministers with selfless philanthropy. His feeling for her derived from principle, not equal affection. She doted on him like a dog, like a handmaid more than a wife, because he lifted her up. According to Aurora, more than a little arrogance coloured his condescension. He intended to take a wife as he would sign a subscription cheque. The poem exposes in their engagement the misguidedness of the highest intentions. Because of its imbalance Marion runs away into danger. She comes to grief partly because Romney put her in such an untenable position. Moreover, her suffering is ultimately more tenable for a self-responsible human being than marriage to him would have been. When she turns down his second proposal, she explains that she used to feel unworthy of him or only worthy by his miraculous bestowal of worth. But now through her grief she has learned "a woman . . . is a human soul". For all of her external degradation, she values herself without needing restoration by an offer of marriage. For Marion, developing consciousness comes from utter casting down. She emerges from her period of madness to confront herself, "I, Marion Erle, myself, alone, undone". She is cast upon her own resources and thereby finds them. Presumably she would not have found them in a marriage of grateful, worshipful subservience to grace-conferring Romney Leigh. She would have forgone more than she lost by being raped.

Aurora Leigh runs the same risk from Romney in a very

different form. His ideas about the relation of the sexes invite her also to forgo herself out of feeling for him. Romney Leigh has little use for poets and less for women poets. He believes that art finds its only excuse in being the best, and that female art usually fails to quality. He thinks that women possess a too personal and circumstantial vision for the disinterested ideality of art. This follows from his own bias for the general and systematic. He is a philanthropist on a scale too grand to allow for individual sentiment. A debate on art versus practical benevolence and the role of women in each ensues when Romney discovers the young Aurora crowning herself with laurels in playful symbolism, a would-be Corinne crowned at the Capitol. He wants her to marry him instead, initiating a contest between love and art, for though Aurora's heart belongs to Romney, as later becomes clear, she must resist him. He wants to turn the artist into the philanthropist's handmaid. Aurora reacts bitterly to his lordly charity in offering to put her to use. She accuses him of wanting "a wife to help your ends,—in her no end". Romney typifies the man, "Who sees the woman as the complement / Of his sex merely. You forget too much / That every creature, female as male, / Stands single in responsible act and thought". Aurora views such a relationship to a husband as dangerous and common because of the difference between the sexes, she amorously self-dissolving and he self-aggrandising:

> . . . where we learn to lose ourselves
> And melt like white pearls in another's wine,
> He seeks to double himself by what he loves,
> And make his drink more costly by our pearls.

Knowing her own susceptibility—"I love love"—Aurora is also dismayed by what love does to women—"for love, / They pick much oakum". She chooses vocation by turning Romney down. The two acts are one.

A good portion of the rest of the poem is devoted to showing Aurora's heart-starvation as the price of her accomplishment. She neither finds happiness in working nor full belief in the value of the work. Once in London, writing, successful, she is told by an admirer, "You stand outside, / You artist women, of the common sex / . . . your hearts / Being starved to make your heads: so run the old / Traditions of you". Aurora says, "Books succeed, / And lives fail". Her looks and health decline much faster than Romney's. She becomes "a printing woman who has lost her place / (The sweet safe corner of the household fire / Behind the heads of children)". She believes that her poetry gains power from what she gives up in her life, fire from her own unkissed lips, but she takes no satisfaction in sublimation:

> How dreary 't is for women to sit still,
> On winter nights by solitary fires,
> And hear the nations praising them far off,
> Too far! Ay, praising our quick sense of love,
> Our very heart of passionate womanhood,
> Which could not beat so in the verse without
> Being present also in the unkissed lips.

She becomes so demoralised that she even experiences her fame in ironical terms, first, because she suspects that popular success signals inferiority, and, second, because she thinks women are so constituted as to find the adulation of the crowd no substitute for a personal affection. In fact, she wonders whether this hankering for the love of the one instead of the many weakens her art, and she suspects that Romney's critique may stand confirmed: "There it is, / We women are too apt to look to one, / Which proves a certain impotence in art".

Besides forfeiting love, and believing that her art depends on the forfeiture, but doubting whether her work is good enough to be worth it, Aurora Leigh also suffers from guilt over the effect of her denial upon Romney. Just as Jane Eyre has to resist feeling responsible for Rochester's reprobation when she leaves him, and Sue Bridehead feels guilty for rejecting men and making them desperate, Aurora suspects that Romney would have escaped dangerous entanglement with Marion Erle and Lady Waldemar if she had married him:

> . . . 'Now, if I had been a woman, such
> As God made women, to save men by love,—
> By just my love I might have saved this man,
> And made a nobler poem for the world
> Than all I have failed in.' But I failed besides
> In this; and now he's lost! through me alone!

The worst of her choice of the artist over the woman is that neither obliterates and each rebukes the other. After her outburst in favour of femininity she suffers the rebound, and "It seems as if I had a man in me, / Despising such a woman". Her ambivalence produces a certain misogyny, reminiscent of Rhoda Nunn's. Romney observes, "you sweep your sex / With somewhat bitter gusts from where you live / Above them". Some of *Aurora Leigh*'s most powerful sequences evoke her disgust with herself: "I live self-despised for being myself". Some of E.B.B.'s oddest and most compelling imagery results:

> . . . is all a dismal flat,
> And God alone above each, as the sun
> O'er level lagunes, to make them shine and
>   stink—
> Laying stress upon us with immediate flame,
> While we respond with our miasmal fog,
> And call it mounting higher because we grow
> More highly fatal?

A section follows on Aurora's gloomy satisfaction in wandering as a mere observer in Italy unrecognised as if without past or future. The satisfaction comes from the "most surprising riddance of one's life". In an effectively nauseous image, she finds herself dissolving slowly until lost, like a lump of salt that spoils the drink into which it disappears.

According to *Aurora Leigh,* women dissolve in love like pearls in men's wine, but without love like salt in a ruined drink. Feminine or feminist self-postponement (the artist's version of these)—there is little to choose between them. The first precludes poetry; the second enables but ultimately demoralises it. And yet by holding out until the latter dissolution, after which Aurora lacks spirits to write, she produces a great poem. It is so great that it even converts Romney to appreciation of art and the woman artist. He himself is brought low, as his humanitarian schemes fail and he loses his eyesight in a melodramatic débâcle, symbolising his former lack of true perception. Stripped of his masculine arrogance, he declares his love again, and Aurora accepts him. Like Jane Eyre, she is vindicated and compensated, and also assured of power enough to balance the relationship by her husband's new-found debility. The rift between art and love is pronounced healed near the end of the poem as Aurora and Romney vow to "Distort our nature never for our work". "Beloved, let us love so well, / Our work shall still be better for our love, / And still our love be sweeter for our work".

But the conflict remains more compelling than its resolution in *Aurora Leigh,* as E.B.B. had also found to be so in *Consuelo.* Denial of love was necessary to the production of Aurora's great poem while steadily eroding the capacity to go on writing great poems, that is, when the writer is a woman. Aurora's continued vocation as a poet doesn't seem very likely at the end because she so completely identifies her former achievements with abdication of love, and because she so completely repudiates the abdication:

> Art symbolizes heaven, but Love is God
> And makes heaven. I, Aurora, fell from mine.
> I would not be a woman like the rest,
> A simple woman who believes in love
> . . . I must analyse,
> Confront, and question.

If she had not analysed, confronted and questioned, and been complicated enough to distrust love, Romney would never have come around to see that women can produce great poems, because she would not have produced one.

Both Aurora and Romney sound abject in the final speeches, filling Book IX with lengthy confessions of having been wrong and proud. But there is a difference between their reasons for abjection, which makes all the difference: he is brought low by having failed; she is brought low by having succeeded. His philanthropic schemes go to pieces, and so he rethinks his position and yields more credence to hers. Her poetry gains success—with the public, with Romney—and yet at such internal expense in doubt and conflict that her self-blame only increases as his admiration for her work seems to validate her means of achieving it.

I think the *Athenaeum*'s reviewer speaks for the poem's overall impact when he characterises *Aurora Leigh* as a "confession of failure", for ultimately it reveals the insufficiency of artistic ambition and success to make up for the lack of love on which they depend. "As in all the works of its kind, which women have so freely poured out from their full hearts during late years, we see the agony more fully than the remedy".

It is deeply curious that E.B.B.'s most extended work should devote itself to this agony because she had certainly experienced the remedy herself in her romance and marriage with Browning. A one-man refutation of virtually all of her anxieties, he brought her almost literally back to life, health and happiness, and he encouraged her work. Browning was emphatically unlike the doctors humorously described by E.B.B., who carried the inkstand out of her room as part of the cure because if poetry involves malady

even for men, "for women it was . . . incompatible with any common show of health under any circumstances".

Their relationship began in his admiring her poetry. His audacious first letter moves from loving her books to loving her. E.B.B. was alarmed by his "extravagance", and worried that he might substitute lioness-worship for real feeling, with something of Aurora Leigh's distaste for merely literary adulation. So for a long time he had to accede to her formula, urged in the *Sonnets,* that he loved her for nothing at all, just because he loved her. But once he had overcome her mistrust, he began to campaign for his right to include her poetic gift among his reasons for being smitten: "How can I put your poetry away from you?" She must keep up her writing for "Ba herself to be quite Ba". He worried that she might scant her own work in order to help him and write him letters, for he knew how self-sacrificing affection could make her. She answered that she felt better and stronger for his interest and did not grow so idle as he thought. She was composing the *Sonnets* during their letter-writing courtship, and she also outlined her rough idea for *Aurora Leigh.* Browning comments that he would like to undertake something as ambitious himself, and "you can do it, I know and am sure".

Though E.B.B. did not do a great deal of work for a year or so after her marriage—as she says, before she could go forward she had to learn how to stand up steadily after so great a revolution—the intermission was brief and the follow through impressive. Before her death in 1861: *Poems* of 1850, *Casa Guidi Windows* (1851), *Aurora Leigh, Poems Before Congress* (1860), and her last *Poems.* Bearing a son put no stop to her enterprise. She writes in 1850, "As for poetry, I hope to do better things in it yet, though I *have* a child to 'stand in my sunshine,' as you suppose he must; but he only makes the sunbeams brighter with his glistening curls, little darling". A charming picture emerges of the Brownings' mutual aid, to the pouring out of the coffee. She benefited from their unconstraint, their regimen of hard work, their interchange of encouragement.

Browning was a helpful critic from the beginning, for instance, from his earliest letter commenting on her translation of *Prometheus Bound.* But E.B.B. was not easily influenced and often stood up for her originality even when people thought it amounted to eccentricity, as they more than once did. On her controversial *Poems Before Congress* she says, "I never wrote to please any of you, not even to please my own husband". She did not emulate Browning directly because she thought she shouldn't, and because she thought she couldn't anyway. As Susan Zimmerman has shown [in her essay " 'Sonnets from the Portuguese': A Negative and Positive Context," *Mary Wollstonecraft Newsletter* (1973)], the *Sonnets* differ from the traditional sonnet sequence in praising the beloved—Browning—as a singer far beyond the speaker in power—he is a "gracious singer of high poems", while she is a worn-out viol (IV; XXXII). In breaking the traditional identity between lover and poet, E.B.B. forecasts the split between woman-in-love and artist developed in *Aurora Leigh.* At the same time, her awe of Browning as a specifically masculine poet discouraged her in a way that also guaranteed integrity because it put imitation out of the question: "You are 'masculine' to the height—and I, as a woman, have studied some of your gestures of language & intonation wistfully, as a thing beyond me far! and admirable for being beyond".

Browning's benefit to her work went beyond encouragement, criticism and provision of a model to study but not to copy. E.B.B. had felt the limits of her own experience as limits to her poetry. She had known a filial and invalid exaggeration of feminine enclosure. Browning gave her Italy, gave her travel, gave her experience. Her letters after her marriage run over with the high spirits of the wanderer and observer, which she was at heart, in spite of the years of willing Wimpole Street incarceration.

Besides expanding her material, Browning also restored her to her own aesthetic. E.B.B.'s *ars poetica* stressed self-expression, made it a first principle to "looke in thine heart, and write", according to her *Essays on the English and the Greek Christian Poets.* Yet in the reduced state in which Browning found her, she experienced separation between her inmost feelings and her poetry:

> I . . . sate here alone but yesterday, so weary of my own being that to take interest in my very poems I had to lift them up by an effort & separate them from myself & cast them out from me into the sunshine where I was not—feeling nothing of the light that fell on them even—making indeed a sort of pleasure & interest about the factitious personality associated with them . . . but knowing it to be all far on the outside of *me . . . myself.*

E.B.B. scouts the idea that "selfrenunciation" constitutes poetic genius. Yet her own being had become so nearly defunct that she could not produce poetry except from a factitious personality. This is not looking into one's heart to write. A revitalised self meant revitalised self-expression.

A final demonstration of Browning's healthy impact comes from his commentary on a letter that E.B.B. received from Harriet Martineau. . . . [This] letter shows Martineau's attraction to a certain sort of domesticity. It describes her life in the Lake District and meetings with Wordsworth. Two elements drew Browning's criticism. One is Martineau's picture of Wordsworth as the genuis dependent on his wife's domestic ministrations. The other is her account of her own pleasure in housekeeping, to the extent of preferring it to authorship. She declares her horror of "mere booklife", and, importantly, "I like a need to have some express & daily share in somebody's comfort" (not that of a husband, but of maids, friends and relatives). Browning is not charmed by Wordsworth's dependence on a helpmate, and he is suspicious of Martineau's eagerness to lay down the pen to keep house. Most significantly, he refuses to value even ministration to others over authorship. E.B.B. felt no inclination toward housework, but he knew that she did crave to be needed, that she had practically "chopped off her legs" to serve and please her father and secure his love. He didn't want her to care for others more than for herself and her writing. He did not promote the conflict that forms the theme of *Aurora Leigh.* (pp. 175-92)

Kathleen Blake, "Elizabeth Barrett Browning (and George Eliot): Art versus Love," in her Love and the Woman Question in Victorian Literature: The Art of Self-Postponement, *The Harvester Press, Sussex, 1983, pp. 171-201.*

Helen Cooper   (essay date 1988)

[*In the following excerpt, Cooper traces the development of Browning's poetic identity from "A Drama of Exile," through* Sonnets from the Portuguese, *to "The Runaway Slave."*]

In selecting which 1838 and 1844 poems to publish in *Poems* (1850), Barrett Browning explained to Mitford, "I gave much time to the revision, and did not omit reforming some of the rhymes, although you must consider that the irregularity of these in a certain degree rather falls in with my system than falls out through my carelessness." To her Florentine friend, Mrs. Ogilvy, she lamented, "[the volume] contains *all* my poems worth a straw, though many which I should like to burn as stubble & cant. It is difficult to recover one's misdeeds from the press." Barrett Browning's experiments with rhyme, claiming them as her "system" rather than her "carelessness," indicate her desire to question formal conventions. She designated her earlier work as including "stubble & cant" and "misdeeds." Although the *Poems* (1850) included previously published work, a new voice emerges in the *Sonnets from the Portuguese* and **"The Runaway Slave at Pilgrim's Point,"** poems that drew little interest from nineteenth-century reviewers.

Although biographical explanations for literary texts open up a Pandora's box, the parallel between Barrett's description of her relationship as a daughter with her father and her relationship as a poet with her male precursors is illuminating. *Sonnets from the Portuguese* and **"The Runaway Slave at Pilgrim's Point"** demonstrate how Barrett's refusal of her father's authority enabled Barrett Browning to appropriate male literary authority to her purposes. Recording sexual desire in the *Sonnets,* Barrett defied her father's refusal to "tolerate in his family . . . the development of one class of feelings." This was not merely a projection of repressed sexuality on Barrett's part, as exemplified by her description of her father's treatment of her younger sister, Henrietta, when she wanted to marry:

> Yet how she was made to suffer—Oh, the dreadful scenes!—and only because she had seemed to feel a little. I told you, I think, that there was an obliquity . . . an eccentricity—or something beyond . . . on one class of subjects. I hear how her knees were made to ring upon the floor, now!—she was carried out of the room in strong hysterics, & I, who rose up to follow her, though I was quite well at that time & suffered only by sympathy, fell flat down upon my face in a fainting-fit. Arabel thought I was dead.

Barrett suffers "by sympathy" with her sister, but in falling down as though "dead" she seems to obey her father's edict denying passion. However, her disobedience in choosing " 'Not Death, but Love' " (*Sonnets,* I) with Robert Browning defies her father and echoes Eve's transgression: eating of the tree of knowledge is identified as Eve's sexually assertive act. Barrett's ballads focused on woman's desire for authority; not, however, until she disobeyed the paternal edict against passion and self-determination was she able to realize an authoritative protagonist and a confident female poetic "I."

The *Sonnets* first bring into harmony "I" a woman and "I" the poet, separated in **"The Poet's Vow," "A Vision of Poets"** [*Poems* (1844)], and **"Lady Geraldine's Courtship."** The *Sonnets* record the transformation of woman from muse/helpmeet/object into poet/creator/subject. That act allowed Barrett Browning to transform earlier ballad narratives into dramatic monologues—**"The Runaway Slave at Pilgrim's Point"** and **"Bianca Among the Nightingales"** (*Last Poems,* 1862)—and the epics and dramas modeled on the Greek poets and Milton into the first-person female narratives of the long political poem, *Casa Guidi Windows,* and of her fictional autobiography, *Aurora Leigh.*

Barrett wrote the *Sonnets from the Portuguese* during her courtship of 1845-46. She only hinted of their existence to Browning, informing him on July 22, 1846, "You shall see some day at Pisa what I will not show you now." Browning insisted on their publication in 1850, and to disguise their personal nature he, master of masks, suggested their title, an allusion to Barrett's **"Catarina to Camoens"** (1844), which he admired. This history of the *Sonnets* is crucial: the privacy surrounding their composition, and the fact that Barrett did not write them for publication, empowered her voice.

Contemporary critics have too often judged Barrett's achievement not by the standards of poetry, but of maleness. Hayter writes [in her *Mrs. Browning: A Poet's Work and its Setting,* 1962], "Mrs. Browning's sonnets express the love of one particular individual for another; they are personal, even idiosyncratic. Most love poems are written by, or in the character of, a young man. The *Sonnets from the Portuguese* are written by a mature invalid woman. . . . They are not enough removed from personal relationship to universal communication." Lorraine Gray criticizes the *Sonnets* for failing to "express the universal wisdom expressed in the love sequences of Dante, Petrarch, Sidney, Spenser, Shakespeare and Meredith, poets who narrated man's failure to translate his ideals into the actual world." Only Dorothy Mermin acknowledges [in "The Female Poet," *ELH* 48, No. 2 (1981)] the sequence as an attempt to create a female poetic voice in a male tradition; she sees the lack of irony in the *Sonnets* as resulting from Barrett's desire to locate her place within the literary tradition rather than to replicate her male contemporaries' concern to reveal "the disjunction between the passionate certainties of literature, and the flawed complexities of life."

"Hope End," the Barrett estate in Herefordshire, where Browning spent her early childhood.

Barrett's *Sonnets* do not have the traditional "young man" as speaker, nor do they address "man's failure to translate his ideals into the actual world"; yet they should not be dismissed as "personal, even idiosyncratic." Instead of the young man's conventional lament, the mature woman starts from a known world and uses the sonnets as a process of discovery in transforming that world into one hitherto unimagined, a world created in art that she can then inhabit. The *Sonnets* enact the process whereby the speaker resolves the tensions inherent in being both poet and also the object of another's narrative into at last being the subject of her own story, able to speak in the first person of her passion.

The basic plot of the amatory tradition, as with all courtly lyrics, was "a poet reiterating his plaint eight hundred, nine hundred, a thousand times; and a fair lady who ever says 'No.' " [Wendell Stacy Johnson, in his *Sex and Marriage in Victorian Poetry* (1975)] Shakespeare had already added sonnets addressed to a young man and refused the elaborate tributes to the mistress: "My mistress when she walks treads on the ground"; and the speaker in Spenser's *Amoretti* found a fair lady who finally said, "Yes." Barrett, however, by adopting the Petrarchan form, rather than the English developments enacted in the Shakespearean form, implies a return to the conventions of the sonnet's Italian origins, although, like Spenser's, her sequence ends happily.

The *Sonnets* fall into three groups: in 1 and 2 the speaker portrays woman as the object of man's love, 3-40 record the speaker's wavering between objectifying herself and claiming her own creative and sexual subjectivity, and 41-44 demonstrate the poet's arrival at her own subjectivity, which displaces her allegiance to the conventions of the male tradition and reveals her confidence in the voice which that subjectivity elicits.

The first two sonnets, in which the speaker is initiated into love as the traditional object, are located in the past tense. The speaker remembers,

> a mystic Shape did move
> Behind me, and drew me backward by the hair;
> And a voice said in mastery, while I strove,—
> "Guess now who holds thee?'—"Death," I said.
>   But, there,
> The silver answer rang,—"Not Death, but
> Love."

The conversational tones of Sidney and Donne echo in these lines; by splitting the last one to create a seven-line sestet, Barrett delays the startling revelation at the end. The reference is to the *Iliad*, 1.204: as Athene prevented Achilles from fighting Agamemnon, so the "mystic Shape," imagined here as male "in mastery," pulls the speaker from Death and into Love. The subject-object arrangement is announced in the second sonnet, "Thee speaking, and me listening!" (made problematic by an unspoken "and me writing"). Yet Barrett transforms the convention such that the lovers are separated, not by the woman's capricious "No," but by divine prohibition: " 'Nay' is worse / From God than from all others." The power attributed to the cruel ladies who scorned their poet

lovers had little reality under a patriarchal authority that determined women's lives.

The third sonnet, rejecting the conventions that made woman the object, moves the sequence out of the past tense of the first two sonnets into the present. Here the speaking statue of **"Lady Geraldine's Courtship"** finds human form:

> Thou, bethink thee, art
> A guest for queens to social pageantries,
> With gages from a hundred brighter eyes
> Than tears even can make mine, to play thy part
> Of chief musician. What hast *thou* to do
> With looking from the lattice-lights at me,
> A poor, tired, wandering singer, singing through
> The dark, and leaning up a cypress tree?
> The chrism is on thine head,—on mine, the
>   dew,—
> And Death must dig the level where these agree.

The female speaker's role is complex. She is the humble lover, "A poor, tired, wandering singer," who admires the beloved, perceived as exalted, "A guest for queens to social pageantries." She is also the woman whose eyes are bright with "tears," receiving the poet lover's attentions,—"What has *thou* to do / With looking from the lattice-lights at me?"—only to reject them: "The chrism is on thine head,—on mine, the dew,— / And Death must dig the level where these agree." Her rejection is not capricious, however, but from her own closeness to death. Her description of herself as "A poor, tired, wandering singer" is conventional as a description of a courtly poet. It is also realistic; her rejection of the lover stems from the distance she recognizes between them, not because of social status, but because his involvement in the "social pageantries" of life contrasts with her own preoccupation with death. The speaker's spatial allegiances here identify her with the poet as subject, rather than with the woman as object. She is the object of his "looking"; nevertheless she places the man, beloved, poet lover, and "chief musician" in the domestic interior the woman usually inhabits, while she, the speaker, is outside in the dark "leaning up a cypress tree." Both the "dark" and "a cypress tree" function here primarily as reminders of death; this reversal of the spheres conventionally inhabited by men and women contributes, however, to the dilemma over gender roles that informs this sonnet.

The speaker's acceptance of the distance to be maintained between the beloved/lover and herself is emphasized by the perfect Petrarchan form of the fourth sonnet: the first quatrain focuses on the beloved, the "most gracious singer of high poems"; the second elaborates on the "golden fulness" of his "music," which he brings to the speaker's house, too poor for the beloved; and the sestet shifts the speaker's focus to the desolation of the house (reminiscent of the poet's house in **"The Poet's Vow"**) where she lives with "the casement broken in, / The bats and owlets builders in the roof." The sestet answers the importuning of the "most gracious singer" by stressing the necessity that each one stay "alone, aloof" from the other. The speaker maintains her stance of inadequacy as a poet beside the beloved: "My cricket chirps against thy mandolin"; she "weeps" while he "sing[s]."

Such stasis cannot be maintained, however: the very images of decay that convince the speaker of the impossibility of love are also indicative of action and energy. The subsequent poems record both the woman's struggle to risk the unknown terrain of love rather than embrace the familiar territory of death, and also the poet's struggle to become confident in her own subjectivity. The brisk commands and argumentative linguistic structures of juxtaposed sonnets—"Stand farther off then! go" (5) followed by "Go from me. Yet I feel" (6)—express her struggle, as do her contradictory feelings. She acknowledges that "the face of all the world is changed" by the beloved who has "taught the whole / Of life in a new rhythm" (7), and she admits, *I love thee* (10). Yet convinced she must renounce her beloved to his face (11), she imagines herself as object, who in "the silence of [her] womanhood" is "unwon, however wooed," as a strategy for refusing to "fashion into speech" the love to which she does not feel entitled because of her "grief" (13). The speaker argues her way into being overpowered by the beloved: "noble and like a king, / Thou canst prevail against my fears and fling / Thy purple round me" (16). Yet her acceptance of love is on male terms and on strangely violent ones: "And as a vanquished soldier yields his sword / To one who lifts him from the bloody earth, / Even so, Beloved, I at last record, / Here ends my strife" (16). She cannot authorize herself to be the subject of her own passion, but yields as object of the beloved's will, imagining herself only as his muse. She offers herself to him:

> How, Dearest, wilt thou have me for most use?
> A hope, to sing by gladly? or a fine
> Sad memory, with thy songs to interfuse?
> A shade, in which to sing—of palm or pine?
> A grove, on which to rest from singing? Choose.
>
> [17]

The speaker extends her objectification as one conquered by love into the offering of herself as muse or object for the beloved. Although Barrett's authorship modifies the speaker's passive vision of herself, "this extreme self-abnegation," as Mermin says, "is also an incisive commentary on male love poems . . . since the alternatives require not only the woman's passivity and silence but her absence and finally her death." Previous sonnets record the speaker's rescue from death; this final line in which she offers to lie in her grave for the poet's inspiration highlights the absurdity of the sacrifice traditional sonneteers require.

Subsequent sonnets ponder not the speaker's unworthiness but the difference between "life's great cup of wonder" and the previous year when

>   I sat alone here in the snow
> And saw no footprint, heard the silence sink
> No moment at thy voice, but, link by link,
> Went counting all my chains.
>
> [20]

However, not only does she declare, "I yield the grave for thy sake, and exchange / My near sweet view of Heaven, for earth with thee!" (23), but she anxiously questions,

> If I leave all for thee, wilt thou exchange
> And be all to me? Shall I never miss
> Home-talk and blessing and the common kiss

> That comes to each in turn, nor count it strange,
> When I look up, to drop on a new range
> Of walls and floors, another home than this?
>
> [35]

The speaker realizes that choosing love means losing all she has previously held dear. When the "common kiss" given her as daughter of the family is transformed, however, into a lover's kiss, she rejects innocence for experience and confidently claims her passions:

> First time he kissed me, he but only kissed
> The fingers of this hand wherewith I write;
> And ever since, it grew more clean and white,
> Slow to world-greetings, quick with its "Oh, list,"
> When the angels speak. A ring of amethyst
> I could not wear here, plainer to my sight,
> Than that first kiss. The second past in height
> The first, and sought the forehead, and half missed,
> Half falling on the hair. O beyond meed!
> That was the chrism of love, which love's own crown,
> With sanctifying sweetness, did precede.
> The third upon my lips was folded down
> In perfect, purple state; since when, indeed,
> I have been proud and said, "My love, my own."
>
> [38]

The kiss on the fingers makes the speaker "clean and white," more a companion of the angels than of "world-greetings." The kiss on the forehead, suggestive of an increasing sexuality in the carelessness of its being "half missed / Half falling on the hair," "pass[es] in height" the first and is accompanied with "sanctifying sweetness." Eschewing metaphoric definitions of the kiss—the "ring of amethyst," the chrism or crown of love—the speaker concisely records, "The third upon my lips was folded down." The attempt to spiritualize physical love collapses with this kiss "upon my lips." In contrast to "height" this kiss is "folded down," suggesting physicality rather than spirituality. The speaker's response to this kiss is no longer to deny it by purifying it, but to enjoy it—"I have been proud"—and to claim it—" 'My love, my own.' "

This portrait of a Victorian "angel" enjoying passionate encounters in her stern father's house is refreshing. First, it commits Barrett to a belief in physical pleasure as an essential manifestation of love, reaffirmed both at the end of **Aurora Leigh** and in **"Bianca Among the Nightingales"** (**Last Poems,** 1862). Second, it positions her in relation to an aspect of Victorian thinking in which "mere" sexual passion is "half-akin to brute."

The speaker's proud claim, "My love, my own," ushers in the crucial turning point in the sequence (41). The early sonnets had dramatized Barrett's attempt to find a voice as both poet and woman, fusing in the process the traditional self-abnegation of the courtly lover with the conventional humility attributed to nineteenth-century woman. The later sonnets record a speaker who assesses a changed world in which she is "caught up in love, and taught the whole / Of life in a new rhythm" (7). The last four sonnets reflect on the transformation of the speaker's voice from her early attempt to accommodate to male convention into a later security in her own subjectivity. The speaker is grateful to all "Who paused a little near the prison-wall / To hear [her] music in its louder parts" (41), yet the true timbre of her voice only the beloved appreciates who "own'st the grace / To look through and behind this mask of [her]" (39). The speaker gains confidence in her voice, transforming the beloved from the one who perceives her to the one who listens to her:

> But thou, who, in my voice's sink and fall
> When the sob took it, thy divinest Art's
> Own instrument didst drop down at thy foot
> To hearken what I said between my tears.
>   [41]

The female "I" is authoritative once she no longer allows the male poet's "divinest Art" to compete with, appropriate, or trivialize her voice. She silences the male voice of the opening sonnets, so the beloved is object to her realized subjectivity. She can now imagine, confidently, a future as a poet in which she will "shoot / [Her] soul's full meaning into future years, / That *they* should lend it utterance." This theme is elaborated in the next sonnet, in which, quoting from **"Past and Future"** [*Poems* (1844)], " '*My future will not copy fair my past,*' " the speaker reflects on how once she imagined her future to be in heaven, whereas now it is to be in the world. The beloved becomes her Muse:

> I seek no copy now of life's first half:
> Leave here the pages with long musing curled,
> And write me new my future's epigraph,
> New angel mine, unhoped for in the world!
>   [42]

The "angel," culturally associated in the nineteenth century with woman, is here used in an ambiguous way—as the earlier Seraphim had been. Barrett draws on a Biblical and Miltonic tradition that considered the angel as male, and yet the asexual quality of the angel associates the "new angel mine" as her muse with the young boy at the end of **"A Vision of Poets"** and the little boy whose singing would be the inspiration for *Casa Guidi Windows.*

The famous penultimate sonnet, "How do I love thee? Let me count the ways," is, in fact, less sentimental than authoritative about its speaker's desire. The "I" is confidently female, while the object of her attention is assuredly male. There is none of the hysterics of Bertram's love for Geraldine, none of the tortuous love conventions with which the ballad heroines tried to articulate their passions, none of the unfortunate and cloying images found earlier in the sonnets, such as when the crying speaker asks the beloved to "Open thine heart wide, / And fold within the wet wings of thy dove" (35). Instead the voice is as confident in its passion as it had earlier been in its sonnet of despair, **"Grief"** [*Poems* (1844)].

Barrett's disobedience of her father's edict against "the development of a certain class of feelings" meant eating of the tree of knowledge and entering the world of experience. She did not perceive this as a fall, which necessitated woman's suffering, but as a liberating act that allowed her imaginative freedom. In her rejection of what she wrote in "life's first half" and in her commitment to write a

"new . . . future's epigraph" she also rejected her literary fathers' edict. This is exemplified in her last sonnet:

> Belovèd, thou hast brought me many flowers
> Plucked in the garden, all the summer through
> And winter, and it seemed as if they grew
> In this close room, nor missed the sun and show-
>   ers.
> So, in the like name of that love of ours,
> Take back these thoughts which here unfolded
>   too,
> And which on warm and cold days I withdrew
> From my heart's ground. Indeed, those beds and
>   bowers
> Be overgrown with bitter weeds and rue,
> And wait thy weeding; yet here's eglantine,
> Here's ivy!—take them, as I used to do
> Thy flowers, and keep them where they shall not
>   pine.
> Instruct thine eyes to keep their colours true,
> And tell thy soul their roots are left in mine.
>   [44]

Both the room and the texts which so long imprisoned her and in which she "lived with visions for my company / Instead of men and women" (26), have been simultaneously transformed to a place of imaginative freedom. The very invalid isolation that had freed Barrett from conformity to literary expectations about women poets also protected her from the normal chaperoned routine of upper-middle-class courtship. The freedom to experience her passion unhampered by parental physical presence, and the fact that a male poet set his own work aside to listen to hers, translated into a female "I," confident in "these thoughts which here unfolded too." Whereas the "Beloved" brings flowers, she gives back poems, which she expects him to "keep . . . where they shall not pine." The last two lines record the assurance she feels in a poetic voice identified as female, and an admonition to the male poet reader that he read her desire, not his own: "Instruct thine eyes to keep their [her poems] colours true."

These were Barrett's last sonnets. Their formal discipline substitutes for the speaker's imprisonment, a substitution that allows the speaker freedom to engage in the process of transformation I have described. It is appropriate that the sonnet sequence, which by definition had hitherto hinged on the objectification of woman, should be the arena for the self-conscious transformation of the poetic "I" of English poetry to include the female voice. But the form ultimately proved as confining as the "close room" for Barrett; like her creator, Aurora Leigh felt the poet "can stand / Like Atlas, in the sonnet,—and support / His [sic] own heavens pregnant with dynastic stars; / But then he must stand still, nor take a step." Barrett fully intended to "take a step" beyond.

The decision to leave the "close room" of the *Sonnets* was paralleled by Barrett's decision to leave her room in Wimpole Street. She justified this to her friend Mrs. Martin:

> I had made up my mind to act upon my full right
> of taking my own way. I had long believed such
> an act (the most strictly personal act of one's
> life) to be within the rights of every person of
> mature age, man or woman, and I had resolved
> to exercise that right in my own case by a resolu-

tion which had slowly ripened. All the other doors of life were shut to me, and shut me in as in a prison. . . . Therefore, wrong or right, . . . I did and do consider . . . I sinned against no duty.

Barrett, in marrying Browning and moving to Italy, received the approval of her sisters but was repudiated by her brothers, who had grown "used to the thought of a tomb; [where she] was buried." She refused, however, to concur with their desire that she "drop like a dead weight into the abyss, a sacrifice without an object and expiation." Onora's death, for choosing love, passion, and life in defiance of her father and of God, is eerily prophetic of Barrett's own situation. But Barrett refused the fate for herself that she had earlier imposed on her heroine.

The transformation that the *Sonnets* wrought on Barrett's work is exemplified by the fact that **"Lady Geraldine's Courtship,"** with its male protagonist, was one of the last poems written before the *Sonnets* in 1844, and that **"The Runaway Slave at Pilgrim's Point,"** with its first-person narration by a black slave woman, was one of the first written after them in 1846, after her secret marriage and departure for Italy, after her father's (and brothers') refusal to talk, write, or see her again. The last sonnet, whose pastoral echoes demonstrate the female speaker's ability to manipulate male poetic conventions to her own uses, is the culmination of Barrett's work; **"The Runaway Slave,"** in which the poet engaged the protagonist in a natural landscape far from the domestic interior so familiar to the speaker of the *Sonnets,* is the beginning of Barrett Browning's.

Barrett Browning's first mention of **"The Runaway Slave at Pilgrim's Point"** is in a letter to Mitford, dated January 12, 1842. Her uncle, Richard Barrett (first cousin to her father and an influential Jamaican land and slave owner), had years previously given her "a subject for a poem about a run away negro . . . in his handwriting." She finally took his "subject" and wrote a "rather long ballad . . . at request of anti-slavery friends in America." She confided to her friend, Mr. Boyd, that it was "too ferocious, perhaps, for the Americans to publish: but they asked for a poem and shall have it." **"The Runaway Slave"** was first published in 1848 in *The Liberty Bell,* which was sold at the Boston National Anti-Slavery Bazaar of 1848. It has been described as a "horrifying story" of a "slave forced into concubinage," dismissed as "too blunt and shocking to have any enduring artistic worth," and toned down to a description of a "negro slave-woman with her voodoo ideas of angels sucking souls." Only recently has its subject been acknowledged; a black slave woman is "raped by her white master."

"The Runaway Slave at Pilgrim's Point" is not the first of Barrett's poems of social criticism. [*Poems* (1844)] had included **"The Cry of the Children,"** written after R. H. Horne had sent her the government's blue book on child labor in the factories and mines. It is a powerful poem, technically and politically:

> "For all day the wheels are droning, turning;
>   Their wind comes in our faces,

> Till our hearts turn, our heads with pulses burning,
>   And the walls turn in their places:
> Turns the sky in the high window, blank and reeling,
>   Turns the long light that drops adown the wall,
> Turn the black flies that crawl along the ceiling:
>   All are turning, all the day, and we with all.
> And all day the iron wheels are droning,
>   And sometimes we could pray,
> 'O ye wheels' (breaking out in a mad moaning),
>   'Stop! be silent for to-day!' "

The droning tedium of these exploited children's lives is suggested by the repetition of "turn," as though to recreate the factory wheels that surrounded them. Politically, the poem exposes the powerlessness of "mothers" in the industrial "Fatherland" and also addresses the religious hypocrisy accompanying zeal for progress. The children imagine that God "Our Father" should spare them their miserable conditions saying, "Come and rest with me, my child."

> "But, no!" say the children, weeping faster,
>   "He is speechless as a stone:
> And they tell us, of His image is the master
>   Who commands us to work on.
> Go to!" say the children,—"up in Heaven,
>   Dark, wheel-like, turning clouds are all we find.
> Do not mock us; grief has made us unbelieving:
>   We look up for God, but tears have made us blind."
> Do you hear the children weeping and disproving,
>   O my brothers, what ye preach?
> For God's possible is taught by His world's loving,
>   And the children doubt of each.

The idea that God is only manifest through people's actions, and is cold and "speechless as a stone" to society's victims, reappears in **"The Runaway Slave."** But, whereas the children's protest is controlled by the quotation marks that separate their words from the narrator's, there is no such mediation in **"The Runaway Slave,"** where for the first time one of Barrett's angry female speakers narrates her story. Not without years of struggle could Barrett Browning begin this poem with an unmediated "I."

Hemans's *Records of Woman* (1828) and Browning's *Dramatic Lyrics* (1842) and *Dramatic Romances* (1845) suggest possible female and male influences for this poem. Hemans's poems are tales of women, all of whom suffer with varying degrees of resignation or resentment the pangs of love, leading usually to death. They are mainly third-person narratives, although some women narrate their stories. None has the forceful rhetoric of Barrett Browning's style, but they do center experience in female consciousness, and such titles as the "Indian Woman's Death-Song" or "The American Forest Girl" suggest, as much as Wordsworth, a genre that encompasses the lives of hitherto insignificant people as poetic material. However, none of Hemans's titles bears the irony that Barrett Browning's does in yoking the runaway slave with the oppressive descendants of the pilgrims, themselves once oppressed. Nor do the accounts of woman's suffering in love touch on the social and political complexities that Barrett Browning brings to her slave's story. The "Indian Woman's Death-Song" does, however, offer a model for a story of infanticide: the speaker, deserted by her husband for another woman, rows a canoe down the Mississippi toward a cataract, intending that she and her child should drown. The woman's dying song echoes the conventional lament of the poetesses until she addresses her daughter:

> "And thou, my babe! though born, like me, for
>   woman's weary lot,
> Smile!—to that wasting of the heart, my own! I
>   leave thee not;
> Too bright a thing art *thou* to pine in aching love
>   away—
> Thy mother bears thee far, young fawn! from
>   sorrow and decay."

There is here no serious engagement with the issue of infanticide; and the mother's suicide, while killing her daughter to protect her from "woman's weary lot," is much less audacious than Barrett Browning's speaker's action. Without committing suicide, she suffocates her infant son to deny him "the master right."

Although Barrett Browning might have imagined her poem as belonging to literary "records of woman," Browning may well have influenced the authority expressed in this "record." By the time Barrett Browning wrote **"The Runaway Slave,"** Browning had published both his *Dramatic Lyrics* (1842) and *Dramatic Romances* (1845) which included his early dramatic monologues, "My Last Duchess," and "The Bishop Orders His Tomb at St. Praxed's Church." When the two poets started corresponding early in 1845, they were already admirers of each other's work. In one of her earliest letters to Browning, Barrett had written, "You are 'masculine' to the height—and I, as a woman, have studied some of your gestures of language & intonation wistfully, as a thing beyond me far!" Her admiration for Browning's unconventional "gestures of language and intonation" must have assured her of his sympathy with her commitment to "new *forms . . .* as well as thoughts. The old gods are dethroned. Why should we go back to the antique moulds . . . classical moulds, as they are so improperly called? . . . Let us all aspire rather to *Life*—& let the dead bury their dead." Most of Tennyson's early dramatic monologues, spoken through such classical figures as Ulysses or Tithonus, would not have been as liberating as Browning's conversational tone, his focus on obscure (even if titled) characters, and the essential contemporaneity of his settings (even when his subjects were in fact taken from the Renaissance). Peculiarly appropriate to Barrett Browning's concerns in **"The Runaway Slave"** were Browning's murderers' monologues, "My Last Duchess," and "Porphyria's Lover," and his hypocritical—if persuasive—representative of religious institutions, the dying Bishop. By 1846 Barrett Browning had empowered herself to appropriate the confidence of Browning's speakers in expressing the slave's worldview.

However, if Browning's triumph enables us to sympathize with speakers such as the Duke, Porphyria's lover, or the Bishop, even as we judge them for their actions, Barrett Browning's task was quite different: she identifies our sympathy with the despised outsider and our judgement with the privileged law-abiding citizen. She thereby makes the "unnatural" act of infanticide (made monstrous by such mythic women as Medea) seem natural in a culture that violently distorts the bond between mother and child.

The slave, appropriated as a potent symbol for nineteenth-century women's oppression (as in Harriet Beecher Stowe's *Uncle Tom's Cabin*), had peculiar importance for Barrett Browning because her family had owned slaves in Jamaica for several generations. Mr. Barrett returned, as a young man, to England, leaving his plantations under the management of overseers. However, as Barrett grew in the luxury of Hope End, her family's home, her father and brothers made trips to Jamaica; slavery informed the first thirty years of her life. The loss of Hope End was precipitated by the financial decline attendant on the Proclamation of Freedom for the Slaves in 1833. Barrett wrote to a friend, "The late Bill has ruined the [white] West Indians. That is settled. The consternation here is very great. Nevertheless I am glad, and always shall be, that the negroes are—virtually—free!" Sixteen years later the slave speaker's repudiation of the unjust power of white slave owners resonates with Barrett Browning's rejection of her once slave-owning father's irrational authority in refusing to allow his children, both sons and daughters, to marry and leave his home. The request by the abolitionists that she write such a poem empowered the rage she had suppressed by years of opium as she lay on her invalid couch.

"The Runaway Slave at Pilgrim's Point" is a dramatic monologue in ballad form. The speaker, a young black slave woman, has escaped from the plantation the day before her narrative begins and has run to Pilgrim's Point, where "exile turned to ancestor." Her story is in three parts. The first two she addresses to "the pilgrim-souls" at Pilgrim's Point, those who first came to America as a land of freedom, and whose descendants now own the slaves whom she represents: initially, the slave meditates on being black in a world privileging God's "white creatures"; in a flashback she tells her story to these "pilgrim-souls." Finally, she addresses the "hunter sons" of the original pilgrims who have pursued her to stone her to death.

The assertive opening, "I stand," sets the tone. The speaker never falters in presenting the complexity of her situation, as a woman, a black, and a slave—a thoroughly marginal protagonist—in the white man's violent system. She recognizes that it divides women, black from white, "As white as the ladies who scorned to pray / Beside me at church but yesterday." Although she dies, she finds freedom outside of that system, by shaping her own discourse.

As she describes the "pilgrim-souls" clustering around her—"round me and round me ye go"—we feel the dizziness and exhaustion of one who has "gasped and run / All night long from the whips." Her purpose is to "speak" to the pilgrim-souls: "lift my black face, my black hand, / Here, in your names, to curse this land / Ye blessed in freedom's." She claims her racial identity, "I am black, I am black," and describes how such an identity imprisons her: "About our souls . . . / Our blackness shuts like prison-bars." The slave employs metaphors, which Barrett

Browning used in her letters to Browning describing her invalidism in a room cut off from sun, to dramatize imprisonment behind a dark skin in a world where God's work of creating black people has been cast away "under the feet of His white creatures." She celebrates that the "little dark bird sits and sings", the "dark stream ripples out of sight", the "dark frogs chant in the safe morass", and the "darkest night" is host to the "sweetest stars." In the natural world, unlike the human one, there is no equation of dark with bad and light with good, and no discrimination between black and white people: the sun and frost "they make us hot, they make us cold," while the "beasts and birds, in wood and fold, / Do fear and take us for very men."

The slave argues for the equality of black and white before detailing her particular oppression. Like her meditation on blackness, her story begins with her assertion, "I am black, I am black." Love for her fellow slave engaged her in a human emotion that united her with rather than distinguished her from white people, making her feel "unsold, unbought." Her white owner, denying such common humanity, insisted that the lovers had "no claim to love and bliss," to basic human emotions, and brutally separated them. His actions mirrored those of God, who silently and "coldly . . . sat'st behind the sun," offering no comfort to the slaves. The owner and his men "wrung [her] cold hands out of his / They dragged him—where?" She knows only that they left her lover's "blood's mark in the dust."

The white men deny the slave not only the communal human emotion of love, but also that of grief. Denial of and control over the slave's emotions were essential to the owner's supremacy: "Mere grief's too good for such as I." To dramatize his ownership of the slaves' bodies, the owner beats the man and rapes the woman: "Wrong, followed by a deeper wrong! / . . . the white men brought the shame ere long / To strangle the sob of my agony." Barrett Browning's description of rape is tactful but explicit when the "wrong" is immediately followed by "I am black, I am black! / I wore a child upon my breast," a child who was "far too white, too white" for her. The violation and control inherent in rape is "worse" than the "lash."

Susan Brownmiller in *Against Our Will: Men, Women and Rape* discusses the notorious system of rape, euphemistically termed "concubinage"—literally, "cohabiting of man and woman not legally married"—in which white male slave owners assumed sexual rights over their black slave women: the mulatto children of such "breeder women" were sold for the owner's financial gain. Barrett Browning expressed no surprise at her uncle's story of the runaway slave; she was probably quite familiar with the iniquitous system. As Jeanette Marks records in *The Family of the Barrett*: "That the problem of black and white connections had since the second generation in Jamaica been embedding itself in the family ramifications of the Barrett family is based on direct evidence. . . . Concubinage as 'custom of the country' was an inescapable part of slavery." Whereas such novels as *Adam Bede* and *Ruth* center on the seduction of women, Barrett Browning

dramatizes both here and in Marian Erle's story in *Aurora Leigh* the violence that threatens and controls women. (Pompilia's description of her enforced sexual relations with Guido in Browning's later *The Ring and the Book* would now be described as marital rape.) She examines the way sexual and racial politics warp the emotions.

The slave's maternal feelings are in conflict: in a representation of a mother-child relationship, she carries the child on her breast; however, he appears as an "amulet that [hangs] too slack"; neither mother nor child can rest—they go "moaning, child and mother, / One to another"; and there is an ominous note in "all ended for the best." The speaker's complex maternal feelings dramatize a conflict between her love for her child and her hatred of the way he was conceived and of what he represents. From birth he was different, so that she "dared not sing to the white-faced child / The only song [she] knew," the song of her black lover's name, feeling that "A child and mother / Do wrong to look at one another / When one is black and one is fair." Once she has seen her child, she can never forget his conception:

> Why in that single glance I had
>   Of my child's face, . . . I tell you all,
> I saw a look that made me mad!
>   The *master's* look, that used to fall
> On my soul like his lash . . . or worse!

Her "far too white" son resembles his father: the sight of him is like a reenactment of her rape. It also reminds her of what his moaning and struggling represent: "the white child wanted his liberty— / Ha, ha! he wanted the master-right." She fears he will claim it, scorning his dark mother as much as the "white ladies" in church do. The white male child, even as an infant, proclaims his mother's dispossession. (I should point out here that Barrett Browning was operating not in accordance with the American system, whereby any child born of one black parent was classified and disenfranchised as a black, but according to the Jamaican system. In the latter, the children of white owners and black slaves could be sent to England along with the father's "legal" white children for schooling. Hence the lighter the skin the more a male child could claim the "master-right.")

The speaker gradually unfolds her child's story, anticipating the final tragedy in her references to his "little feet that never grew"; and to how he lies now between the mango roots. To hide his white face she covers it with a handkerchief "close and tight"; he struggles against this imposed darkness. She kills the child to protect herself from the rapist she sees in him: "I twisted it round in my shawl" because of the "*master's* look, that used to fall / On my soul like his lash . . . or worse," till the child lay "too suddenly still and mute." Clutching his dead body, she escapes from the plantation. As she runs, she reiterates God's abandonment of black people, imagining that the trees, and by implication God, ignore her: "They stood too high for astonishment, / They could see God sit on his throne." However, God's "angels far, / With a white sharp finger from every star, / Did point and mock." This separation of God and his angels from herself results not from her being a murderer cast out of Heaven, but from being black and marginalized by the white God, angels, and people.

Though horrible, this infanticide becomes, within the terms of the poem, tragically grand and inevitable, the logical conclusion to the slave's situation. She blames, not herself, but the "fine white angels (who have seen / Nearest the secret of God's power)" who "sucked the soul" of her child. The cultural signifiers, black and white, are now reversed: the "white angels" are murderers claiming "the white child's spirit." So liberating is the dramatic monologue for Barrett Browning (even if, as with Browning's Pompilia in *The Ring and the Book,* the language is that of an educated middle-class poet rather than of a raped teenage girl) that we accept the slave's reasoning: she is made so marginal by the white man's system that she cannot be judged by its laws. What from their white perspective seems a crazed black woman strangling her child and clutching him "on [her] heart like a stone" is a brutalized woman's totally coherent act. Her behavior, although resembling madness, is, in fact, governed by her victimization in an alien system. If God's silence convinces Porphyria's lover that he is morally right, it convinces the slave that God's system, epitomized by his "white angels," is morally wrong.

Although she kills him, the speaker's love for her child is manifest in the confusion she exhibits between her own self and her son: "My little body," refers to her son; running till "I felt it was tired" indicates her own exhaustion. This merging anticipates the union that becomes possible once the white child is buried in the dark earth:

> Yet when it was all done aright,—
> Earth, 'twixt me and my baby, strewed,—
> All, changed to black earth,—nothing white,—
> A dark child in the dark!—ensued
> Some comfort, and my heart grew young;
> I sate down smiling there and sung
> The song I learnt in my maidenhood.
>
> And thus we two were reconciled,
> The white child and black mother, thus;
> For as I sang it soft and wild,
> The same song, more melodious,
> Rose from the grave whereon I sate:
> It was the dead child singing that,
> To join the souls of both of us.

"Song" here is an important issue. First, it evokes the slave practice of singing in the fields to survive the grueling work. Second, it draws attention to the ballad form that ties this poem to Barrett Browning's earlier works. Although **"The Runaway Slave"** rejects the medievalism of the 1838 and 1844 ballads, its speaker is connected to their protagonists' questioning of the white man's courtly ideology. Third, the emphatic repetition of "I sang" asserts the slave's right to narrate her story.

Initially, the slave addresses the "pilgrim-souls"—"I speak to you." Her intention is to tell her tragic story and to "curse this land / Ye blessed in freedom's" name. She recalls the man she loved and how:

> I sang his name instead of a song,
> Over and over I sang his name, . . .

> I sang it low, that the slave-girls near
> Might never guess, from aught they could hear,
> It was only a name—a name.

The slave's initial song exemplifies the work of the poetesses; her "song" is confined to love and to her lover's name. However, in an ironic reversal, this does not prove to be safe subject matter for a woman: like love and grief, use of language threatens the white men's power.

After the birth of her "too white" son, who struggled against the blackness imposed by the slave's kerchief because, she imagines, he wanted his white male "master-right," the slave is fearful: "I might have sung and made him mild, / But I dared not sing to the white-faced child / The only song I knew." Even a white male infant dispossesses her of her right to sing. Her only song is of her slavery; that cannot be told to the masters. So angry is she at being silenced that she suffocates the child, rendering him as "still and mute" as he has made her. Only when she has transformed him into a "dark child in the dark" by burying him in the earth, which knows no discrimination, can she sing to him. "The song I learnt in my maidenhood" may literally refer to her lover's name, but it also functions on a more complex level. Now the subject of her story rather than the object of his, she sings to her son "soft and wild." He no longer signifies the white male world, but inhabits her dark earth. She centers herself and transforms the young white boy into her muse, making her song "more melodious."

The sun rises as she tells her story. While the "free sun rideth gloriously," the pilgrim-souls become more menacing, and yet as insubstantial "pilgrim-ghosts" they fade away at the arrival of this new dawn in which the slave "glares with a scorn." The speaker, once frightened to imagine herself as subject in the presence of her white child, now renders the white pilgrim-souls into objects frightened by her power. By singing to her son, the slave wins her freedom and confronts in strength "the hunter sons" eager to whip her to death.

Although the speaker knows her death is at hand, she directs this last scene. As the white men armed with whips approach her "in a ring," she shouts, "Keep off." Her words do not represent hope for escape, but rather an order to listen before stoning her. As one picks up a stone, she commands him to drop it, charging the men with following the double standard in that their wives "May keep live babies on [their] knee, / And sing the song [they] like the best," while also indicating their actions of moving in and threatening her. She taunts "the Washington-race," who, "staring, shrinking back," are now afraid of her, with the mockery they have made of language. "This land is the free America" is an empty phrase beside "this mark on my wrist . . . / Ropes tied me up here to the flogging-place."

Facing her death, the slave imagines being rendered into a Christ-like martyr. She remembers the silence surrounding her frequent floggings: "Not a sound! / I hung, as a gourd hangs in the sun," identifying both with the nondiscriminatory natural world again and with the image of Christ on the cross. But she refuses this sop:

Our wounds are different. Your white men
  Are, after all, not gods indeed,
Nor able to make Christs again
  Do good with bleeding. *We* who bleed
(Stand off!) we help not in our loss!
We are too heavy for our cross,
  And fall and crush you and your seed.

In this bitter denunciation, white men are no longer the "gods" they claim to be, and black people, exemplified by this black woman, refuse to be cast as Christ figures whose suffering can be justified as doing "good by bleeding." Their suffering is so great it will destroy the structures designed to contain and exploit it, and will kill the white man's "seed." When the slave "look[s] at the sky," she feels the "clouds are breaking on [her] brain"; the white man's Heaven crushes the dying slave, whereas she eagerly joins her white child and lover in the nondiscriminating "death-dark" earth. In her fall she will crush the white "seed."

Unlike her foremothers in Barrett's poetry, this woman is not submissive. She dies at the height of her power, but in death, though "broken-hearted," she rejects the system that marginalizes and violates her. Her initial desire "to curse this land," strengthens into leaving the white men "all curse-free / In [her] broken heart's disdain." The formulaic gibberish of a curse, which enjoins supernatural aid and which the slave imagined was her only strength, yields to the power she gains by centering herself in her own discourse. She dies holding her hypocritical persecutors in "disdain" at Pilgrim's Point.

The dramatic monologue proved a powerful medium for Barrett Browning. Yoking her need to produce a public poem about slavery to her own developing poetics, Barrett Browning incorporated rape and infanticide into the slave's denunciation of patriarchy. Barrett Browning did not shrink from the unsayable, in contrast to American women like Angeline Grimké who toiled for the abolitionist movement yet felt bound by women's silence concerning their bodies and the belief that "a man's private life was beyond the pale of political scrutiny." The violence visited on slave women did not inform the speech even of those most horrified by it. Barrett Browning exploits the slave's triumphant cry, "Your white men / Are, after all, not gods indeed," to speak to her own liberation from both her own once slave-owning father and also from the literary fathers who for so long held her in thrall.

Eve's songs of experience celebrate woman's refusal both to be bound by patriarchal authority and also to accept her "alloted grief" for such a refusal. Unlike Eve in **"A Drama of Exile,"** when the slave disavows identification with Christ in suffering, she excoriates her pain rather than accepting it. This disavowal also symbolizes Barrett Browning's outgrowing the necessity to justify her poetic ambition by identifying both the woman's and the poet's task with Christ's suffering on behalf of "mankind." ***Sonnets from the Portuguese*** were the testing-ground for the female "I": the black slave woman exemplifies Barrett Browning's conviction that on her own authority woman can locate her consciousness at the center of poetry. Her two long poems, ***Casa Guidi Windows*** and ***Aurora Leigh,*** demonstrate what such a vision reveals. (pp. 99-123)

Helen Cooper, in her Elizabeth Barrett Browning: Woman & Artist, *The University of North Carolina Press, 1988, 219 p.*

FURTHER READING

Bibliography

Ehrsam, Theodore G.; Deily, Robert H.; and Smith, Robert M. "Elizabeth Barrett Browning." In their *Bibliographies of Twelve Victorian Authors,* pp. 47-66. New York: H. W. Wilson Co., 1936.
  A bibliography of writings on Browning.

Biography

Ingram, John H. *Elizabeth Barrett Browning.* London: W. H. Allen & Co., 1888, 194 p.
  The first biography of Browning.

Taplin, Gardner B. *The Life of Elizabeth Barrett Browning.* New Haven: Yale University Press, 1957, 482 p.
  The definitive biography, which includes a detailed account of the creation, publication, and critical reception of Browning's poetry.

Criticism

Churchill, Kenneth. *Italy and English Literature 1764-1930.* Totowa, N.J.: Barnes & Noble Books, 1980, 230 p.
  Discusses the influence of Italy on Victorian poets and includes a brief section on Browning.

Cunliffe, John W. "Elizabeth Barrett (1806-1861); Robert Browning (1812-1889)." In his *Leaders of the Victorian Revolution,* pp. 118-30. New York: D. Appleton-Century, 1934.
  Assessment of the "literary and spiritual achievements of Victorian England" that contains a general overview of Browning's life and work.

Falk, Alice. "Elizabeth Barrett Browning and Her Prometheuses: Self-Will and a Woman Poet." *Tulsa Studies in Women's Literature* 7, No. 1 (Spring 1988): 69-85.
  Examines classical influences in Browning's poetry, focusing in particular on her two translations of Aeschylus's *Prometheus Bound.*

Gilbert, Sandra M., and Gubar, Susan. "The Aesthetics of Renunciation." In their *The Madwoman in the Attic: The Woman Writer and the Nineteenth-Century Imagination,* pp. 539-80. New Haven: Yale University Press, 1979.
  Feminist study that discusses *Aurora Leigh* as Browning's masterpiece of "feminist self-affirmation."

Leighton, Angela. *Elizabeth Barrett Browning.* Bloomington: Indiana University Press, 1986, 184 p.
  Overview of Browning's life and career.

Lupton, Mary Jane. *Elizabeth Barrett Browning.* New York: The Feminist Press, 1972, 103 p.
  Study of Browning's work from a feminist perspective.

Mermin, Dorothy. *Elizabeth Barrett Browning: The Origins*

of a New Poetry. Chicago: The University of Chicago Press, 1989, 297 p.

Critical study of Browning from the point of view of women's studies.

Miller, Betty. "Elizabeth and Emily Elizabeth." *The Twentieth Century* 159, No. 952 (June 1956): 574-83.

Compares the poetry and personalities of Browning and Emily Dickinson.

Radley, Virginia L. *Elizabeth Barrett Browning.* New York: Twayne Publishers Inc., 1972, 156 p.

Study of Browning's poetic themes and techniques.

Smith, Fred Manning. "Mrs. Browning's Rhymes." *PMLA* LIX, No. 3 (September 1939): 829-34.

Argues that Browning's rhyme schemes were experiments going against Victorian poetic conventions.

Turner, Paul. "Aurora versus the Angel." *The Review of English Studies* XXIV, No. 95 (July 1948): 227-35.

Compares *Aurora Leigh* with Coventry Patmore's verse novel *The Angel in the House.*

Additional coverage of Browning's life and career is contained in the following sources published by Gale Research: *Dictionary of Literary Biography,* Vol. 32; *Nineteenth-Century Literary Criticism,* Vols. 1 and 16; and *World Literature Criticism, 1500 to the Present,* Vol. 1.

Robert Burns

1759-1796

(Born Robert Burnes) Scottish poet and lyricist.

INTRODUCTION

Considered the national poet of Scotland for his efforts to preserve Scottish language and traditions, Burns is revered as the poet of the "common man" because he extolled love, fellowship, and equality in expressing the thoughts and emotions of ordinary people. Burns, whose poetry is regarded as the culmination of the Scottish literary tradition, is admired for his ironic wit, his adept use of Scots and English, his mastery of traditional literary forms, and his fervent concern for the human condition.

Burns was born in Alloway, Scotland. His father, an impoverished tenant farmer, sought to provide his sons with as much formal education as his resources allowed. He employed a private tutor for Burns and also managed to pay for several years of formal though intermittent schooling. An avid reader, Burns had acquired a grounding in English before studying the poetry of his Scottish heritage. During his youth Burns endured the hard work and progressively worsening financial difficulties which beset his family as they moved from one rented farm to another. As was the case with his father, Burns lacked the capital to purchase modern farming implements and fared little better in his own attempts at farming. Burns's biographers have argued that, as a poor and disenfranchised farmer, Burns was well qualified to speak for the common Scot and condemn social injustice. As a young man Burns developed a reputation for charm and wit, indulging in several love affairs that brought him into conflict with the Presbyterian Church. Burns also angered the church by criticizing such accepted beliefs as the Calvinist tenets of innate sinfulness and predestination, which he considered incompatible with human nature and satirized in "Holy Willie's Prayer."

In 1786 Burns proposed marriage to Jean Armour, then pregnant with twins by Burns. Yet her parents rejected his offer and demanded financial restitution. As a result, Burns determined to sail to Jamaica and begin a new life. However, with the successful publication that year of the Kilmarnock edition of *Poems, Chiefly in the Scottish Dialect,* Burns abandoned his plans and traveled to Edinburgh, where he became the chief object of the literati's admiration and published an enlarged edition of the earlier volume. Composed of poems written between 1784 and 1786, *Poems, Chiefly in the Scottish Dialect* brought Burns a year of sudden fame followed by relative obscurity. After his marriage in 1788 to Jean Armour, Burns balanced his time between writing poetry and tenant farming until moving to Dumfries to accept a position in the excise service. Except for "Tam o' Shanter," Burns did not produce

any major poems after 1786. Some critics have attributed this decline to his move away from his native heath, which, they have argued, distanced Burns from the people, places, and politics of his earlier work. Others attribute the decline to Burns's association with a loose-knit movement to preserve the relics of Scottish culture which the ongoing assimilation of English culture threatened. As a result of his involvement, Burns devoted the latter part of his creative career to collecting, revising, and in some cases composing new lyrics for the vast number of extant Scottish folk songs, an undertaking for which he refused payment. Among the most famous songs revitalized by Burns are "Green Grow the Rashes O" and "Auld Lange Syne." In 1796 Burns died from rheumatic heart disease.

Most commentators consider the universality of Burns's poems to be the most important distinguishing characteristic of his work. Although Burns's poems are set in the context of rural Scotland, his themes, with their attention to the problems of ordinary people and solutions derived from common wisdom, transcend national boundaries. In "To a Mouse," for instance, a farmer realizes that he and a mouse share a common connection to the earth and nature. "The Cotter's Saturday Night," an idealized vision of a farm worker's life, extols the love and fellowship to be found among family members, while "The Holy Fair" satirizes religious hypocrisy and celebrates the survival of life-creating sexuality in the wake of puritan repression. In other poems, such as "Epistle to Davie" and "Second Epistle to J. Lapraik," Burns commented on class conflict and individualism by contrasting capitalism with humanistic values. Happiness, according to Burns, emanates from love and the fellowship evident in an alehouse rather than the pursuit of profit, and the genuine individual is emancipated from the norms of society but still possesses, unlike the rich, the ability to cooperate with others.

Burns's universal appeal also centers on his ability to convincingly present opposing viewpoints. For instance, "The Jolly Beggars" appeals to both radicals and conservatives because advocates of each political persuasion can find support for their views in either the socially orthodox opinions of the narrator or the iconoclastic precepts of the beggars. Burns's presentation of these conflicting attitudes, critics contend, reveals his sympathy for the beggars' position as well as his respect for the values of an organized though imperfect society. Critics, such as John Weston, Jr., have observed another aspect of Burns's divided nature in "Tam o' Shanter," a narrative poem in which the narrator, through his commentary on the hero, reveals himself as an individual torn between body and soul as well as Scots and English culture. Thomas Crawford has described Burns's work as the expression of "a mind in motion" that gives in to conflicting emotions and principles while struggling to understand a complex world.

Some critics have dismissed Burns's poetry as overly accessible and transparent, arguing that these qualities render his themes trite and reveal that he wrote poetry absentmindedly with little concern for artistic expression. The majority of critics, however, identify the language and structure of his poetry as indicators of his self-conscious concern with art and tradition. For example, Raymond Bentman has noted Burns's conscious efforts to achieve rhyme, alliteration, and proper meter by intermixing Scots and English words. Burns's pastoral imagery and metaphors have also elicited favorable commentary. In "The Holy Fair" Burns employed ambiguous imagery as he mixed the carnal and spiritual meanings of words to accent the contrast between appearance and reality. Also typical of Burns is the extended metaphor used in "The Holy Tulzie" wherein a minister and his congregation are portrayed as a shepherd and his flock. Numerous critics have also commented favorably upon Burns's adaptation of traditional Scottish literary forms. John Weston, for instance, has noted that by employing a sheep as the subject of "Poor Mailie's Elegy," Burns created inherent irony in the whole concept of the poem, making it the first true mock elegy in the Scottish tradition of humorous elegies. Although the Scottish vernacular of Burns's poems is no longer spoken, John Spiers has written that "Burns's Scots verse is still contemporary with the modern reader who in reading relives it and shares its viewpoint and criticism of human life."

PRINCIPAL WORKS

POETRY

Poems, Chiefly in the Scottish Dialect   1786; also pub-
lished as *Poems, Chiefly in the Scottish Dialect* [enlarged edition], 1787
"Tam o' Shanter"   1791; published in *The Antiquities of Scotland*
Poems Ascribed to Robert Burns, the Ayrshire Bard   1801
Reliques of Robert Burns, Consisting Chiefly of Original Letters, Poems, and Critical Observations on Scottish Songs   (poetry, letters, and criticism)   1808
The Poetry of Robert Burns. 4 vols.   (poetry and songs) 1896-97
The Poems and Songs of Robert Burns. 3 vols.   (poetry and songs)   1968

OTHER MAJOR WORKS

The Letters of Robert Burns. 2 vols.   (letters)   1931

CRITICISM

John Logan   (review date 1787)

[*Logan was a Scottish clergyman and poet. In the following excerpt from a review of* Poems, Chiefly in the Scottish Dialect *(1786), he praises Burns's humorous and satirical poems but claims that Burns's use of Scottish words will limit his readership to fellow Scots.*]

In an age that is satiated with literary pleasures, nothing is so grateful to the public taste as novelty. This ingredient will give a gust to very indifferent fare, and lend a flavour to the produce of the home-brewed vintage. Whatever excites the jaded appetite of an epicure will be prized; and a red herring from Greenock or Dunbar will be reckoned a *delice*. From this propensity in human nature, a musical child, a rhyming milkwoman, a learned pig, or a Russian poet, will "strut their hour upon the stage," and gain the applause of the moment. From this cause, and this alone, Stephen Duck the thresher, and many other *nameless* names, have glittered and disappeared like those bubbles of the atmosphere which are called *falling* stars.

Robert Burns, the Ayrshire ploughman [and the author of ***Poems, Chiefly in the Scottish Dialect***], does not belong to this class of *obscurorum virorum*. Although he is by no means such a poetical prodigy as some of his *malicious* friends have represented, he has a genuine title to the attention and approbation of the public, as a *natural,* though not a *legitimate,* son of the muses.

The first poems in this collection are of the humorous and satirical kind; and in these our author appears to be most at home. In his serious poems we can trace imitations of almost every English author of celebrity; but his humour is entirely his own. His **"Address to the Deil"** (Devil), **"The Holy Fair"** (a country sacrament), and his **"Epistle,"** in which he disguises an amour under the veil of partridge-shooting, are his masterpieces in this line; and happily in these instances his humour is neither local nor transient; for the devil, the world, and the flesh, will always keep their ground. **"The Vision"** is perhaps the most poetical of all his performances. Revolving his obscure situation, in which there was nothing to animate pursuit or gratify ambition; comparing his humble lot with the more flourishing condition of mercantile adventures; and vowing to renounce the unprofitable trade of verse for ever; there appeared to him a celestial figure; not one of the nine muses, celebrated in fiction; but the real muse of every inspired poet, the GENIUS of his native district and frequented scenes. This is an elegant and happy imagination. The form of Nature, that first met his enamoured eyes, is the muse of the rural poet. The mountains, the forests, and the streams, are the living volumes that impregnate his fancy, and kindle the fire of genius. The address of this rural deity to him marks the character, and describes the feelings of a poet.

> With future hope I oft would gaze,
> Fond, on thy little, early ways,
> Thy rudely-caroll'd, chiming phrase,
>   In uncouth rhymes,
> Fir'd at the simple, artless lays
>   Of other times.
>
> I saw thee seek the sounding shore,
> Delighted with the dashing roar;
> Or when the North his fleecy store
>   Drove through the sky,
> I saw grim Nature's visage hoar,
>   Struck thy young eye.
>
> Or when the deep-green-mantl'd earth
> Warm-cherish'd ev'ry flowret's birth,
> And joy and music pouring forth
>   In ev'ry grove,
> I saw thee eye the gen'ral mirth
>   With boundless love.
>
> When ripen'd fields and azure skies
> Call'd forth the reaper's rustling noise,
> I saw thee leave their ev'ning joys,
>   And lonely stalk,
> To vent thy bosom's swelling rise,
>   In pensive walk.
>
> When youthful Love, warm blushing, strong,
> Keen-shivering shot thy nerves along,
> Those accents, grateful to thy tongue,
>   Th' adored Name,
> I taught thee how to pour in song,
>   To sooth thy flame.
>
> I saw thy pulse's maddening play
> Wild send thee Pleasure's devious way,
> Misled by Fancy's meteor-ray,
>   By Passion driven:
> But yet the light that led astray
>   Was light from Heav'n.

"Halloween," or **"Even,"** gives a just and literal account of the principal spells and charms that are practised, on that anniversary, among the peasants of Scotland, from the desire of prying into futurity, but it is not happily executed. A mixture of the solemn and burlesque can never be agreeable.

"The Cotter's (cottager's) Saturday Night," is, without exception, the best poem in the collection. It is written in the stanza of Spenser, which probably our bard acquired

from Thomson's "Castle of Indolence," and Beattie's "Minstrel." It describes one of the happiest and most affecting scenes to be found in a country life; and draws a domestic picture of rustic simplicity, natural tenderness, and innocent passion, that must please every reader whose feelings are not perverted.

The Odes **"To a Mouse on turning up her Nest,"** and **"To a Mountain Daisy,"** are of a similar nature, and will strike every reader for the elegant fancy and the vein of sentimental reflection that runs through them. (pp. 89-91)

The stanza of Mr. Burns is generally ill-chosen, and his provincial dialect confines his beauties to one half of the island. But he possesses the genuine characteristics of a poet; a vigorous mind, a lively fancy, a surprizing knowledge of human nature, and an expression rich, various, and abundant. In the plaintive or pathetic he does not excel; his love-poems (though he confesses, or rather *professes,* a *penchant* to the *belle passion*) are execrable; but in the midst of vulgarity and common-place, which occupy one half of the volume, we meet with many striking beauties that make ample compensation. One happy touch on the Eolian harp from fairy fingers awakes emotions in the soul that makes us forget the antecedent mediocrity or harshness of that natural music.

The liberal patronage which Scotland has extended to this self-taught bard reflects honour on the country. If Mr. Burns has flourished in the shade of obscurity, his country will form higher expectations from him when basking in the sunshine of applause. His situation, however, is critical. He seems to possess too great a facility of composition and is too easily satisfied with his own productions. Fame may be procured by novelty, but it must be supported by merit. We have thrown out these hints to our young and ingenious author, because we discern faults in him, which, if not corrected, like the *fly in the apothecary's ointment,* may give an unfortunate tincture and colour to his future compositions. (p. 93)

> *John Logan, in a review of "Poems, Chiefly in the Scottish Dialect" (1786), in* The English Review, *Vol. IX, February, 1787, pp. 89-93.*

Robert Burns   (letter date 1787)

[*In the following excerpt from an autobiographical letter to his patron Dr. John Moore, Burns recounts some of the events and circumstances of his youth that influenced his poetry.*]

For the first six or seven years of my life, my father was gardener to a worthy gentleman of small estate in the neighbourhood of Ayr. Had he continued in that station, I must have marched off to be one of the little underlings about a farmhouse; but it was his dearest wish and prayer to have it in his power to keep his children under his own eye, till they could discern between good and evil; so with the assistance of his generous master, my father ventured on a small farm on his estate. . . . I owe much to an old woman who resided in the family, remarkable for her ignorance, credulity, and superstition. She had, I suppose, the largest collection in the country of tales and songs concerning devils, ghosts, fairies, brownies, witches, war-locks, spunkies, kelpies, elf-candles, dead-lights, wraiths, apparitions, cantraips, giants, enchanted towers, dragons and other trumpery. This cultivated the latent seeds of po-etry; but had so strong an effect on my imagination, that to this hour, in my nocturnal rambles, I sometimes keep a sharp look-out in suspicious places; and though nobody can be more sceptical than I am in such matters, yet it often takes an effort of philosophy to shake off these idle terrors. The earliest composition that I recollect taking pleasure in, was "The Vision of Mirza," and a hymn of Addison's beginning, "How are thy servants blest, O Lord!" I particularly remember one half-stanza which was music to my boyish ear—

> For though in dreadful whirls we hung
> High on the broken wave—

I met with these pieces in *Mason's English Collection,* one of my schoolbooks. The first two books I ever read in pri-vate, and which gave me more pleasure than any two books I ever read since, were *The Life of Hannibal,* and *The History of Sir William Wallace.* Hannibal gave my young ideas such a turn, that I used to strut in raptures up and down after the recruiting drum and bagpipe, and wish myself tall enough to be a soldier; while the story of Wallace poured a Scottish prejudice into my veins, which will boil along there till the flood-gates of life shut in eter-nal rest.

Polemical divinity about this time was putting the country half mad, and I, ambitious of shining in conversation par-ties on Sundays, between sermons, at funerals, etc., used a few years afterwards to puzzle Calvinism with so much heat and indiscretion, that I raised a hue and cry of heresy against me, which has not ceased to this hour.

My vicinity to Ayr was of some advantage to me. My so-cial disposition, when not checked by some modifications of spited pride, was like our catechism definition of infini-tude, without bounds or limits. I formed several connex-ions with other younkers, who possessed superior advan-tages; the youngling actors who were busy in the rehearsal of parts, in which they were shortly to appear on the stage of life, where, alas! I was destined to drudge behind the scenes. It is not commonly at this green age, that our young gentry have a just sense of the immense distance be-tween them and their ragged play-fellows. . . . They would give me stray volumes of books; among them, even then, I could pick up some observations, and one, whose heart, I am sure, not even the "Munny Begum" scenes have tainted, helped me to a little French. Parting with these my young friends and benefactors, as they occasion-ally went off for the East or West Indies, was often to me a sore affliction; but I was soon called to more serious evils. My father's generous master died; the farm proved a ruinous bargain; and to clench the misfortune, we fell into the hands of a factor, who sat for the picture I have drawn of one in my tale of **"Twa Dogs."** My father was advanced in life when he married; I was the eldest of seven children, and he, worn out by early hardships, was unfit for labour. My father's spirit was soon irritated, but not easily broken. There was a freedom in his lease in two years more, and to weather these two years, we retrenched

our expenses. We lived very poorly: I was a dexterous ploughman for my age; and the next eldest to me was a brother (Gilbert), who could drive the plough very well, and help me to thrash the corn. A novel-writer might, per-haps, have viewed these scenes with some satisfaction, but so did not I; my indignation yet boils at the recollection of the scoundrel factor's insolent threatening letters, which used to set us all in tears.

This kind of life—the cheerless gloom of a hermit, with the unceasing moil of a galley slave, brought me to my six-teenth year; a little before which period I first committed the sin of rhyme. You know our country custom of cou-pling a man and woman together as partners in the labours of harvest. In my fifteenth autumn, my partner was a be-witching creature, a year younger than myself. My scarci-ty of English denies me the power of doing her justice in that language, but you know the Scottish idiom: she was a "bonnie, sweet, sonsie lass." In short, she, altogether un-wittingly to herself, initiated me in that delicious passion, which, in spite of acid disappointment, gin-horse pru-dence, and bookworm philosophy, I hold to be the first of human joys, our dearest blessing here below! How she caught the contagion I cannot tell; you medical people talk much of infection from breathing the same air, the touch, etc.; but I never expressly said I loved her. Indeed I did not know myself why I liked so much to loiter behind with her, when returning in the evening from our labours; why the tones of her voice made my heart-strings thrill like an Æolian harp; and particularly why my pulse beat such a furious ratan, when I looked and fingered over her little hand to pick out the cruel nettle-stings and thistles. Among her other love-inspiring qualities, she sung sweet-ly; and it was her favourite reel to which I attempted giv-ing an embodied vehicle in rhyme. I was not so presump-tuous as to imagine that I could make verses like printed ones, composed by men who had Greek and Latin; but my girl sung a song which was said to be composed by a small country laird's son, on one of his father's maids, with whom he was in love; and I saw no reason why I might not rhyme as well as he; for, excepting that he could smear sheep, and cast peats, his father living in the moorlands, he had no more scholar-craft than myself.

Thus with me began love and poetry; which at times have been my only, and till within the last twelve months, have been my highest enjoyment. My father struggled on till he reached the freedom in his lease, when he entered on a larger farm, about ten miles farther in the country. (pp. 264-67)

It is during the time that we lived on this farm, that my little story is most eventful. I was, at the beginning of this period, perhaps the most ungainly, awkward boy in the parish—no *solitaire* was less acquainted with the ways of the world. What I knew of ancient story was gathered from Salmon's and Guthrie's *Geographical Grammars;* and the ideas I had formed of modern manners, of litera-ture, and criticism, I got from the *Spectator.* These, with Pope's *Works,* some Plays of Shakspeare, *Tull and Dick-son on Agriculture, The Pantheon,* Locke's *Essay on the Human Understanding,* Stackhouse's *History of the Bible,* Justice's *British Gardener's Directory,* Boyle's *Lectures,*

Allan Ramsay's *Works,* Taylor's *Scripture Doctrine of Original Sin, A Select Collection of English Songs,* and Hervey's *Meditations,* had formed the whole of my reading. The collection of songs was my *vade mecum.* I pored over them, driving my cart, or walking to labour, song by song, verse by verse; carefully noting the true, tender, or sublime, from affectation and fustian. I am convinced I owe to this practice much of my critic-craft, such as it is. (p. 268)

Another circumstance in my life which made some alteration in my mind and manners, was, that I spent my seventeenth summer on a smuggling coast, a good distance from home, at a noted school, to learn mensuration, surveying, dialling, etc., in which I made a pretty good progress. But I made a greater progress in the knowledge of mankind. The contraband trade was at that time very successful, and it sometimes happened to me to fall in with those who carried it on. Scenes of swaggering riot and roaring dissipation were, till this time, new to me; but I was no enemy to social life. Here, though I learnt to fill my glass, and to mix without fear in a drunken squabble, yet I went on with a high hand with my geometry, till the sun entered Virgo, a month which is always a carnival in my bosom, when a charming *fillette,* who lived next door to the school, overset my trigonometry, and set me off at a tangent from the spheres of my studies. I, however, struggled on with my sines and co-sines for a few days more; but stepping into the garden one charming noon to take the sun's altitude, there I met my angel—

> Like Proserpine gathering flowers,
> Herself a fairer flower—.

It was in vain to think of doing any more good at school. The remaining week I staid I did nothing but craze the faculties of my soul about her, or steal out to meet her; and the two last nights of my stay in the country, had sleep been a mortal sin, the image of this modest and innocent girl had kept me guiltless.

I returned home very considerably improved. My reading was enlarged with the very important addition of Thomson's and Shenstone's Works: I had seen human nature in a new phasis; and I engaged several of my schoolfellows to keep up a literary correspondence with me. This improved me in composition. I had met with a collection of letters by the wits of Queen Anne's reign, and I pored over them most devoutly. I kept copies of any of my own letters that pleased me, and a comparison between them and the composition of most of my correspondents flattered my vanity. I carried this whim so far, that though I had not three-farthings' worth of business in the world, yet almost every post brought me as many letters as if I had been a broad plodding son of the daybook and ledger.

My life flowed on much in the same course till my twenty-third year. *Vive l'amour, et vive la bagatelle,* were my sole principles of action. The addition of two more authors to my library gave me great pleasure; Sterne and Mackenzie—*Tristram Shandy* and the *Man of Feeling*—were my bosom favourites. Poesy was still a darling walk for my mind, but it was only indulged in according to the humour of the hour. I had usually half-a-dozen or more pieces on hand; I took up one or other, as it suited the momentary

tone of the mind, and dismissed the work as it bordered on fatigue. My passions, when once lighted up, raged like so many devils, till they got vent in rhyme; and then the conning over my verses, like a spell, soothed all into quiet! None of the rhymes of those days are in print, except, **"Winter: a Dirge,"** the eldest of my printed pieces; **"The Death of Poor Mailie," "John Barleycorn,"** and Songs first, second, and third. Song second was the ebullition of that passion which ended the forementioned school-business.

My twenty-third year was to me an important æra. Partly through whim, and partly that I wished to set about doing something in life, I joined a flax-dresser in a neighbouring town (Irvine), to learn his trade. This was an unlucky affair. My * * * and to finish the whole, as we were giving a welcome carousal to the new year, the shop took fire and burned to ashes, and I was left, like a true poet, not worth a sixpence.

I was obliged to give up this scheme; the clouds of misfortune were gathering thick round my father's head; and, what was worst of all, he was visibly far gone in a consumption; and to crown my distresses, a *belle fille,* whom I adored, and who had pledged her soul to meet me in the field of matrimony, jilted me, with peculiar circumstances of mortification. The finishing evil that brought up the rear of this infernal file, was my constitutional melancholy being increased to such a degree, that for three months I was in a state of mind scarcely to be envied by the hopeless wretches who have got their mittimus—depart from me, ye cursed!

From this adventure I learned something of a town life; but the principal thing which gave my mind a turn, was a friendship I formed with a young fellow, a very noble character, but a hapless son of misfortune. (pp. 270-72)

His mind was fraught with independence, magnanimity, and every manly virtue. I loved and admired him to a degree of enthusiasm, and of course strove to imitate him. In some measure I succeeded; I had pride before, but he taught it to flow in proper channels. His knowledge of the world was vastly superior to mine, and I was all attention to learn. He was the only man I ever saw who was a greater fool than myself where woman was the presiding star; but he spoke of illicit love with the levity of a sailor, which hitherto I had regarded with horror. Here his friendship did me a mischief, and the consequence was, that soon after I resumed the plough, I wrote the *Poet's Welcome.* My reading only increased while in this town by two stray volumes of *Pamela,* and one of *Ferdinand Count Fathom,* which gave me some idea of novels. Rhyme, except some religious pieces that are in print, I had given up; but meeting with Fergusson's *Scottish Poems,* I strung anew my wildly-sounding lyre with emulating vigour. When my father died, his all went among the hell-hounds that growl in the kennel of justice; but we made a shift to collect a little money in the family amongst us, with which, to keep us together, my brother and I took a neighbouring farm. My brother wanted my hair-brained imagination, as well as my social and amorous madness; but in good sense, and every sober qualification, he was far my superior.

I entered on this farm with a full resolution, "come, go to, I will be wise!" I read farming books, I calculated crops; I attended markets; and in short, in spite of the devil, and the world, and the flesh, I believe I should have been a wise man; but the first year, from unfortunately buying bad seed, the second from a late harvest, we lost half our crops. This overset all my wisdom, and I returned, "like the dog to his vomit, and the sow that was washed, to her wallowing in the mire."

I now began to be known in the neighbourhood as a maker of rhymes. The first of my poetic offspring that saw the light, was a burlesque lamentation on a quarrel between two reverend Calvinists, both of them *dramatis personæ* in my **"Holy Fair."** I had a notion myself that the piece had some merit; but, to prevent the worst, I gave a copy of it to a friend, who was very fond of such things, and told him that I could not guess who was the author of it, but that I thought it pretty clever. With a certain description of the clergy, as well as laity, it met with a roar of applause. **"Holy Willie's Prayer"** next made its appearance, and alarmed the kirk-session so much, that they held several meetings to look over their spiritual artillery, if haply any of it might be pointed against profane rhymers. Unluckily for me, my wanderings led me on another side, within point-blank shot of their heaviest metal. This is the unfortunate story that gave rise to my printed poem, **"The Lament."** This was a most melancholy affair, which I cannot yet bear to reflect on, and had very nearly given me one or two of the principal qualifications for a place among those who have lost the chart, and mistaken the reckoning of rationality. I gave up my part of the farm to my brother; in truth it was only nominally mine; and made what little preparation was in my power for Jamaica. But before leaving my native country for ever, I resolved to publish my poems. I weighed my productions as impartially as was in my power; I thought they had merit; and it was a delicious idea that I should be called a clever fellow, even though it should never reach my ears—a poor negro-driver—or perhaps a victim to that inhospitable clime, and gone to the world of spirits! I can truly say, that *pauvre inconnu* as I then was, I had pretty nearly as high an idea of myself and of my works as I have at this moment, when the public has decided in their favour. It ever was my opinion that the mistakes and blunders, both in a rational and religious point of view, of which we see thousands daily guilty, are owing to their ignorance of themselves. To know myself had been all along my constant study. I weighed myself alone; I balanced myself with others; I watched every means of information, to see how much ground I occupied as a man and as a poet; I studied assiduously Nature's design in my formation—where the lights and shades in my character were intended. I was pretty confident my poems would meet with some applause; but at the worst, the roar of the Atlantic would deafen the voice of censure, and the novelty of West Indian scenes make me forget neglect. I threw off six hundred copies, of which I had got subscriptions for about three hundred and fifty. My vanity was highly gratified by the reception I met with from the public; and besides I pocketed, all expenses deducted, nearly twenty pounds. This sum came very seasonably, as I was thinking of indenting myself, for want of money to procure my passage. As soon as I was master of nine guineas, the price of wafting me to the torrid zone, I took a steerage passage in the first ship that was to sail from the Clyde, for

> Hungry ruin had me in the wind.

I had been for some days skulking from covert to covert, under all the terrors of a jail; as some ill-advised people had uncoupled the merciless pack of the law at my heels. I had taken the last farewell of my few friends; my chest was on the road to Greenock; I had composed the last song I should ever measure in Caledonia—*The Gloomy Night is Gathering Fast,* when a letter from Dr Blacklock to a friend of mine, overthrew all my schemes, by opening new prospects to my poetic ambition. The doctor belonged to a set of critics for whose applause I had not dared to hope. His opinion, that I would meet with encouragement in Edinburgh for a second edition, fired me so much, that away I posted for that city, without a single acquaintance, or a single letter of introduction. The baneful star that had so long shed its blasting influence in my zenith, for once made a revolution to the nadir; and a kind Providence placed me under the patronage of one of the noblest of men, the Earl of Glencairn. *Oublie moi, grand Dieu, si jamais je l'oublie!*

I need relate no farther. At Edinburgh I was in a new world; I mingled among many classes of men, but all of them new to me, and I was all attention to "catch" the characters and "the manners living as they rise." Whether I have profited, time will show. (pp. 272-75)

Robert Burns, in a letter to Dr. Moore on August 2, 1787, in Life of Robert Burns, *by John Gibson Lockhart, J. M. Dent & Co., 1907, pp. 264-75.*

John Gibson Lockhart   (essay date 1828)

[*Although Lockhart wrote several novels, his fame rests on his biography of Sir Walter Scott and his critical contributions to* Blackwood's Edinburgh Magazine *and the* Quarterly Review. *He is regarded as a versatile, if somewhat severe critic whose opinions of his contemporaries, though lacking depth, are generally considered accurate when not distorted by political animosities. In the following excerpt from his* Life of Robert Burns, *which was originally published in 1828, he praises Burns and his poetry for revitalizing Scottish culture.*]

It is possible, perhaps for some it may be easy, to imagine a character of a much higher cast than that of Burns, developed, too, under circumstances in many respects not unlike those of his history—the character of a man of lowly birth, and powerful genius, elevated by that philosophy which is alone pure and divine, far above all those annoyances of terrestrial spleen and passion, which mixed from the beginning with the workings of his inspiration, and in the end were able to eat deep into the great heart which they had long tormented. Such a being would have received, no question, a species of devout reverence, I mean when the grave had closed on him, to which the warmest admirers of our poet can advance no pretensions for their unfortunate favourite; but could such a being have delighted his species—could he even have instructed them like Burns? Ought we not to be thankful for every new variety of form and circumstance, in and under which the ennobling energies of true and lofty genius are found addressing themselves to the common brethren of the race? Would we have none but Miltons and Cowpers in poetry—but Brownes and Southeys in prose? Alas! if it were so, to how large a portion of the species would all the gifts of all the muses remain for ever a fountain shut up and a book sealed! Were the doctrine of intellectual excommunication to be thus expounded and enforced, how small the library that would remain to kindle the fancy, to draw out and refine the feelings, to enlighten the head by expanding the heart of man! From Aristophanes to Byron, how broad the sweep, how woeful the desolation!

In the absence of that vehement sympathy with humanity as it is, its sorrows and its joys as they are, we might have had a great man, perhaps a great poet, but we could have had no Burns. It is very noble to despise the accidents of fortune; but what moral homily concerning these, could have equalled that which Burns's poetry, considered alongside of Burns's history, and the history of his fame, presents! It is very noble to be above the allurements of pleasure; but who preaches so effectually against them, as he who sets forth in immortal verse his own intense sympathy with those that yield, and in verse and in prose, in action and in passion, in life and in death, the dangers and the miseries of yielding? (pp. 222-23)

That some men in every age will comfort themselves in the practice of certain vices, by reference to particular passages both in the history and in the poetry of Burns, there is all reason to fear; but surely the general influence of both is calculated, and has been found, to produce far different effects. The universal popularity which his writings have all along enjoyed among one of the most virtuous of nations, is of itself, as it would seem, a decisive circumstance. Search Scotland over, from the Pentland to the Solway, and there is not a cottage-hut so poor and wretched as to be without its Bible; and hardly one that, on the same shelf, and next to it, does not possess a Burns. Have the people degenerated since their adoption of this new manual? Has their attachment to the Book of Books declined? Are their hearts less firmly bound, than were their fathers', to the old faith and the old virtues? I believe, he that knows the most of the country will be the readiest to answer all these questions, as every lover of genius and virtue would desire to hear them answered.

On one point there can be no controversy; the poetry of Burns has had most powerful influence in reviving and strengthening the national feelings of his countrymen. Amidst penury and labour, his youth fed on the old minstrelsy and traditional glories of his nation, and his genius divined, that what he felt so deeply must belong to a spirit that might lie smothered around him, but could not be extinguished. The political circumstances of Scotland were, and had been, such as to starve the flame of patriotism; the popular literature had striven, and not in vain, to make itself English; and, above all, a new and a cold system of speculative philosophy had begun to spread widely among us. A peasant appeared, and set himself to check the creeping pestilence of this indifference. Whatever genius has

since then been devoted to the illustration of the national manners, and sustaining thereby of the national feelings of the people, there can be no doubt that Burns will ever be remembered as the founder, and, alas! in his own person as the martyr, of this reformation.

That what is nowadays called, by solitary eminence, the *wealth* of the nation, had been on the increase ever since our incorporation with a greater and wealthier state—nay, that the laws had been improving, and, above all, the administration of the laws, it would be mere bigotry to dispute. It may also be conceded easily, that the national mind had been rapidly clearing itself of many injurious prejudices—that the people, as a people, had been gradually and surely advancing in knowledge and wisdom, as well as in wealth and security. But all this good had not been accomplished without rude work. If the improvement were valuable, it had been purchased dearly. "The spring fire," Allan Cunningham says beautifully somewhere, "which destroys the furze, makes an end also of the nests of a thousand song-birds; and he who goes a-trouting with lime leaves little of life in the stream." We were getting fast ashamed of many precious and beautiful things, only for that they were old and our own.

It has already been remarked, how even Smollett, who began with a national tragedy, and one of the noblest of national lyrics, never dared to make use of the dialect of his own country; and how Moore, another most enthusiastic Scotsman, followed in this respect, as in others, the example of Smollett, and over and over again counselled Burns to do the like. But a still more striking sign of the times is to be found in the style adopted by both of these novelists, especially the great master of the art, in their representations of the manners and characters of their own countrymen. In *Humphry Clinker,* the last and best of Smollett's tales, there are some traits of a better kind—but, taking his works as a whole, the impression it conveys is certainly a painful, a disgusting one. The Scotsmen of these authors are the Jockeys and Archies of farce—

Time out of mind the Southrons' mirthmakers—

the best of them grotesque combinations of simplicity and hypocrisy, pride and meanness. When such men, high-spirited Scottish gentlemen, possessed of learning and talents, and, one of them at least, of splendid genius, felt, or fancied, the necessity of making such submissions to the prejudices of the dominant nation, and did so without exciting a murmur among their own countrymen, we may form some notion of the boldness of Burns's experiment; and on contrasting the state of things then with what is before us now, it will cost no effort to appreciate the nature and consequences of the victory in which our poet led the way, by achievements never in their kind to be surpassed. "Burns," says Mr Campbell, "has given the elixir vitæ to his dialect:" [Thomas Campbell, *Specimens of the British Poets,* 1819]—he gave it to more than his dialect.

The moral influence of his genius has not been confined to his own countrymen. "The range of the *pastoral,*" said Johnson,

> is narrow. Poetry cannot dwell upon the minuter
> distinctions by which one species differs from

another, without departing from that simplicity of grandeur which *fills the imagination;* nor dissect the latent qualities of things, without losing its *general power of gratifying every mind by recalling its own conceptions.* Not only the images of rural life, but the occasions on which they can be properly applied, are few and general. The state of a man confined to the employments and pleasures of the country, is so little diversified, and exposed to so few of those accidents which produce perplexities, terrors, and surprises, in more complicated transactions, that he can be shown but seldom in such circumstances as attract curiosity. His ambition is without policy, and his love without intrigue. He has no complaints to make of his rival, but that he is richer than himself; nor any disasters to lament, but a cruel mistress or a bad harvest.

Such were the notions of the great arbiter of taste, whose dicta formed the creed of the British world, at the time when Burns made his appearance to overturn all such dogmata at a single blow; to convince the loftiest of the noble, and the daintiest of the learned, that wherever human nature is at work, the eye of a poet may discover rich elements of his art—that over Christian Europe, at all events, the purity of sentiment and the fervour of passion may be found combined with sagacity of intellect, wit, shrewdness, humour, whatever elevates and whatever delights the mind, not more easily amidst the most "complicated transactions" of the most polished societies, than

> In huts where poor men lie.

Burns did not place himself only within the estimation and admiration of those whom the world called his superiors—a solitary tree emerging into light and air, and leaving the parent underwood as low and as dark as before. He, as well as any man,

> Knew his own worth, and reverenced the lyre;

but he ever announced himself as a peasant, the representative of his class, the painter of their manners, inspired by the same influences which ruled their bosoms; and whosoever sympathised with the verse of Burns, had his soul opened for the moment to the whole family of man. If, in too many instances, the matter has stopped there—the blame is not with the poet, but with the mad and unconquerable pride and coldness of the worldly heart—"man's inhumanity to man." If, in spite of Burns, and all his successors, the boundary lines of society are observed with increasing strictness among us—if the various orders of men still, day by day, feel the cord of sympathy relaxing, let us lament over symptoms of a disease in the body politic, which, if it goes on, must find sooner or later a fatal ending: but let us not undervalue the antidote which has all along been checking this strong poison. Who can doubt that at this moment thousands of "the first-born of Egypt" look upon the smoke of a cottager's chimney with feelings which would never have been developed within their being, had there been no Burns?

Such, it can hardly be disputed, has been and is the general influence of this poet's genius; and the effect has been accomplished, not in spite of, but by means of the most exact contradiction of, every one of the principles laid down by

Dr Johnson in a passage already cited; and, indeed, assumed throughout the whole body of that great author's critical disquisitions. Whatever Burns has done, he has done by his exquisite power of entering into the characters and feelings of individuals, as Heron has well expressed it, "by the effusion of particular, not general sentiments, and in the picturing out of particular imagery."

Dr Currie says, that "if *fiction* be the soul of poetry, as some assert, Burns can have small pretensions to the name of poet." The success of Burns, the influence of his verse, would alone be enough to overturn all the systems of a thousand definers; but the Doctor has obviously taken *fiction* in far too limited a sense. There are indeed but few of Burns's pieces in which he is found creating beings and circumstances, both alike alien from his own person and experience, and then by the power of imagination, divining and expressing what forms life and passion would assume with, and under these—But there are some; there is quite enough to satisfy every reader of **"Hallowe'en,"** the **"Jolly Beggars,"** and **"Tam o' Shanter"** (to say nothing of various particular songs, such as **"Bruce's Address," "Macpherson's Lament,"** etc.), that Burns, if he pleased, might have been as largely and as successfully an inventor in this way, as he is in another walk, perhaps not so inferior to this as many people may have accustomed themselves to believe; in the art, namely, of recombining and new-combining, varying, embellishing, and fixing and transmitting the elements of a most picturesque experience, and most vivid feelings.

Lord Byron, in his letter on Pope, treats with high and just contempt the laborious trifling which has been expended on distinguishing by air-drawn lines and technical slang-words, the elements and materials of poetical exertion; and, among other things, expresses his scorn of the attempts that have been made to class Burns among minor poets, merely because he has put forth few large pieces, and still fewer of what is called the purely imaginative character. Fight who will about words and forms, "Burns's rank," says he, "is in the first class of his art;" and, I believe, the world at large are nowadays well prepared to prefer a line from such a pen as Byron's on any such subject as this, to the most luculent dissertation that ever perplexed the brains of writer and of reader. *Sentio, ergo sum,* says the metaphysician; the critic may safely parody the saying, and assert that that is poetry of the highest order, which exerts influence of the most powerful order on the hearts and minds of mankind.

Burns has been appreciated duly, and he has had the fortune to be praised eloquently, by almost every poet who has come after him. To accumulate all that has been said of him, even by men like himself, of the first order, would fill a volume—and a noble monument, no question, that volume would be—the noblest, except what he has left us in his own immortal verses, which—were some dross removed, and the rest arranged in a chronological order—would I believe form, to the intelligent, a more perfect and vivid history of his life than will ever be composed out of all the materials in the world besides. "The impression of his genius," says Campbell,

> is deep and universal; and viewing him merely

as a poet, there is scarcely another regret connected with his name, than that his productions, with all their merit, fall short of the talents which he possessed. That he never attempted any great work of fiction, may be partly traced to the cast of his genius, and partly to his circumstances, and defective education. His poetical temperament was that of fitful transports, rather than steady inspiration. Whatever he might have written, was likely to have been fraught with passion. There is always enough of *interest* in life to cherish the feelings of genius; but it requires knowledge to enlarge and enrich the imagination. Of that knowledge, which unrolls the diversities of human manners, adventures, and characters, to a poet's study, he could have no great share; although he stamped the little treasure which he possessed in the mintage of sovereign genius.

"Notwithstanding," says Sir Walter Scott,

the spirit of many of his lyrics, and the exquisite sweetness and simplicity of others, we cannot but deeply regret that so much of his time and talents were frittered away in compiling and composing for musical collections. There is sufficient evidence, that even the genius of Burns could not support him in the monotonous task of writing love verses, on heaving bosoms and sparkling eyes, and twisting them into such rhythmical forms as might suit the capricious evolutions of Scotch reels and strathspeys. Besides, this constant waste of his power and fancy in small and insignificant compositions, must necessarily have had no little effect in deterring him from undertaking any grave or important task. Let no one suppose that we undervalue the songs of Burns. When his soul was intent on suiting a favourite air to words humorous or tender, as the subject demanded, no poet of our tongue ever displayed higher skill in marrying melody to immortal verse. But the writing of a series of songs for large musical collections, degenerated into a slavish labour which no talents could support, led to negligence, and, above all, diverted the poet from his grand plan of dramatic composition. To produce a work of this kind, neither, perhaps, a regular tragedy nor comedy, but something partaking of the nature of both, seems to have been long the cherished wish of Burns. He had even fixed on the subject, which was an adventure in low life, said to have happened to Robert Bruce, while wandering in danger and disguise, after being defeated by the English. The Scottish dialect would have rendered such a piece totally unfit for the stage; but those who recollect the masculine and lofty tone of martial spirit which glows in the poem of Bannockburn, will sigh to think what the character of the gallant Bruce might have proved under the hand of Burns. It would undoubtedly have wanted that tinge of chivalrous feeling which the manners of the age, no less than the disposition of the monarch, demanded; but this deficiency would have been more than supplied by a bard who could have drawn from his own perceptions the unbending energy of a hero sustaining the desertion of friends, the persecution of enemies, and

the utmost malice of disastrous fortune. The scene, too, being partly laid in humble life, admitted that display of broad humour and exquisite pathos, with which he could, interchangeably and at pleasure, adorn his cottage views. Nor was the assemblage of familiar sentiments incompatible in Burns, with those of the most exalted dignity. In the inimitable tale of **"Tam o' Shanter,"** he has left us sufficient evidence of his abilities to combine the ludicrous with the awful, and even the horrible. No poet, with the exception of Shakspeare, ever possessed the power of exciting the most varied and discordant emotions with such rapid transitions. His humorous description of death in the poem on **"Dr Hornbook"** borders on the terrific, and the witches' dance in the kirk of Alloway is at once ludicrous and horrible. Deeply must we then regret those avocations which diverted a fancy so varied and so vigorous, joined with language and expression suited to all its changes, from leaving a more substantial monument to his own fame, and to the honour of his country.

The cantata of the **"Jolly Beggars,"** which was not printed at all until some time after the poet's death, and has not been included in the editions of his works until within these few years, cannot be considered as it deserves, without strongly heightening our regret that Burns never lived to execute his meditated drama. That extraordinary sketch, coupled with his later lyrics in a higher vein, is enough to show that in him we had a master capable of placing the musical drama on a level with the loftiest of our classical forms. *Beggar's Bush,* and *Beggar's Opera,* sink into tameness in the comparison; and indeed, without profanity to the name of Shakspeare, it may be said, that out of such materials, even his genius could hardly have constructed a piece in which imagination could have more splendidly predominated over the outward shows of things—in which the sympathy-awakening power of poetry could have been displayed more triumphantly under circumstances of the greatest difficulty.—That remarkable performance, by the way, was an early production of the Mauchline period; I know nothing but the **"Tam o' Shanter"** that is calculated to convey so high an impression of what Burns might have done.

As to Burns's want of education and knowledge, Mr Campbell may not have considered, but he must admit, that whatever Burns's opportunities had been at the time when he produced his first poems, such a man as he was not likely to be a hard reader (which he certainly was), and a constant observer of men and manners, in a much wider circle of society than almost any other great poet has ever moved in, from three-and-twenty to eight-and-thirty, without having thoroughly removed any pretext for auguring unfavourably on that score, of what he might have been expected to produce in the more elaborate departments of his art, had his life been spared to the usual limits of humanity. In another way, however, I cannot help suspecting that Burns's enlarged knowledge, both of men and books, produced an unfavourable effect, rather than otherwise, on the exertions, such as they were, of his later years. His generous spirit was open to the impression of every kind of excellence; his lively imagination, bending its own vigour to whatever it touched, made him admire even what other people try to read in vain; and after travelling, as he did, over the general surface of our literature, he appears to have been somewhat startled at the consideration of what he himself had, in comparative ignorance, adventured, and to have been more intimidated than encouraged by the retrospect. In most of the new departments in which he made some trial of his strength (such, for example, as the moral epistle in Pope's vein, the *heroic* satire, etc.), he appears to have soon lost heart, and paused. There is indeed one magnificent exception in **"Tam o' Shanter"**—a piece which no one can understand without believing, that had Burns pursued that walk, and poured out his stores of traditional lore, embellished with his extraordinary powers of description of all kinds, we might have had from his hand a series of national tales, uniting the quaint simplicity, sly humour, and irresistible pathos of another Chaucer, with the strong and graceful versification, and masculine wit and sense of another Dryden.

This was a sort of feeling that must have in time subsided.—But let us not waste words in regretting what might have been, where so much is. Burns, short and painful as were his years, has left behind him a volume in which there is inspiration for every fancy, and music for every mood; which lives, and will live in strength and vigour— "to soothe," as a generous lover of genius has said—"the sorrows of how many a lover, to inflame the patriotism of how many a soldier, to fan the fires of how many a genius, to disperse the gloom of solitude, appease the agonies of pain, encourage virtue, and show vice its ugliness;" [Sir Egerton Brydges, *Censura Literaria,* 1815]—a volume, in which, centuries hence, as now, wherever a Scotsman may wander, he will find the dearest consolation of his exile. (pp. 225-34)

John Gibson Lockhart, in his Life of Robert Burns, *J. M. Dent & Sons, 1907, 322 p.*

Matthew Arnold   (essay date 1880)

[Arnold was one of the most important English critics of the nineteenth century. Although a poet and a commentator on the social and moral life in England, Arnold was essentially an apologist for literary criticism. He argued that the major purpose of the critic is to inform and liberate the public at large and to prepare the way–through the fostering of ideas and information–for his or her country's next creative epoch. Arnold was a forceful advocate of the doctrine of "disinterestedness," which he defined as a flexible and non-utilitarian approach to culture and art. He also advocated–though often failed to achieve in his own writing–the "real estimate" of created object, which demands that the critic judge a work of art according to its own qualities apart from the influence of history and the limitations of subjective experience. In the following excerpt from an essay originally published as the introduction to an 1880 critical anthology of English poetry, Arnold assesses Burns's verse.]

[As] we draw towards the end of the eighteenth century, we are met by the great name of [Robert] Burns. We enter now on times where the personal estimate of poets begins to be rife, and where the real estimate of them is not reached without difficulty. But in spite of the disturbing pressures of personal partiality, of national partiality, let us try to reach a real estimate of the poetry of Burns.

By his English poetry Burns in general belongs to the eighteenth century, and has little importance for us.

> Mark ruffian Violence, distain'd with crimes,
> Rousing elate in these degenerate times;
> View unsuspecting Innocence a prey,
> As guileful Fraud points out the erring way;
> While subtle Litigation's pliant tongue
> The life-blood equal sucks of Right and Wrong!

Evidently this is not the real Burns, or his name and fame would have disappeared long ago. Nor is Clarinda's love-poet, Sylvander, the real Burns either. But he tells us himself: 'These English songs gravel me to death. I have not the command of the language that I have of my native tongue. In fact, I think that my ideas are more barren in English than in Scotch. I have been at **"Duncan Gray"** to dress it in English, but all I can do is desperately stupid.' We English turn naturally, in Burns, to the poems in our own language, because we can read them easily; but in those poems we have not the real Burns.

The real Burns is of course in his Scotch poems. Let us boldly say that of much of this poetry, a poetry dealing perpetually with Scotch drink, Scotch religion, and Scotch manners, a Scotchman's estimate is apt to be personal. A Scotchman is used to this world of Scotch drink, Scotch religion, and Scotch manners; he has a tenderness for it; he meets its poet half way. In this tender mood he reads pieces like the **"Holy Fair"** or **"Halloween."** But this world of Scotch drink, Scotch religion, and Scotch manners is against a poet, not for him, when it is not a partial countryman who reads him; for in itself it is not a beautiful world, and no one can deny that it is of advantage to a poet to deal with a beautiful world. Burns's world of Scotch drink, Scotch religion, and Scotch manners, is often a harsh, a sordid, a repulsive world; even the world of his **"Cotter's Saturday Night"** is not a beautiful world. No doubt a poet's criticism of life may have such truth and power that it triumphs over its world and delights us. Burns may triumph over his world, often he does triumph over his world, but let us observe how and where. Burns is the first case we have had where the bias of the personal estimate tends to mislead; let us look at him closely, he can bear it.

Many of his admirers will tell us that we have Burns, convivial, genuine, delightful, here—

> Leeze me on drink! it gies us mair
>   Than either school or college;
> It kindles wit, it waukens lair,
>   It pangs us fou o' knowledge.
> Be 't whisky gill or penny wheep
>   Or ony stronger potion,
> It never fails, on drinking deep,
>   To kittle up our notion
>
>   By night or day.

There is a great deal of that sort of thing in Burns, and it is unsatisfactory, not because it is bacchanalian poetry, but because it has not that accent of sincerity which bacchanalian poetry, to do it justice, very often has. There is something in it of bravado, something which makes us feel that we have not the man speaking to us with his real voice; something, therefore, poetically unsound.

With still more confidence will his admirers tell us that we have the genuine Burns, the great poet, when his strain asserts the independence, equality, dignity, of men, as in the famous song **"For a' that and a' that"**—

> A prince can mak' a belted knight,
>   A marquis, duke, and a' that;
> But an honest man's aboon his might,
>   Guid faith he mauna fa' that!
>   For a' that, and a' that,
>   Their dignities, and a' that,
>   The pith o' sense, and pride o' worth,
>   Are higher rank than a' that.

Here they find his grand, genuine touches; and still more, when this puissant genius, who so often set morality at defiance, falls moralising—

> The sacred lowe o' weel-placed love
>   Luxuriantly indulge it;
> But never tempt th' illicit rove,
>   Tho' naething should divulge it.
> I waive the quantum o' the sin,
>   The hazard o' concealing,
> But och! it hardens a' within,
>   And petrifies the feeling.

Or in a higher strain—

> Who made the heart, 'tis He alone
>   Decidedly can try us;
> He knows each chord, its various tone;
>   Each spring, its various bias.
> Then at the balance let's be mute,
>   We never can adjust it;
> What's *done* we partly may compute,
>   But know not what's resisted.

Or in a better strain yet, a strain, his admirers will say, unsurpassable—

> To make a happy fire-side clime
>   To weans and wife,
> That's the true pathos and sublime
>   Of human life.

There is criticism of life for you, the admirers of Burns will say to us; there is the application of ideas to life! There is, undoubtedly. The doctrine of the last-quoted lines coincides almost exactly with what was the aim and end, Xenophon tells us, of all the teaching of Socrates. And the application is a powerful one; made by a man of vigorous understanding, and (need I say?) a master of language.

But for supreme poetical success more is required than the powerful application of ideas to life; it must be an application under the conditions fixed by the laws of poetic truth and poetic beauty. Those laws fix as an essential condition, in the poet's treatment of such matters as are here in question, high seriousness;—the high seriousness which comes from absolute sincerity. The accent of high seriousness, born of absolute sincerity, is what gives to such verse as

> In la sua volontade è nostra pace . . .

to such criticism of life as Dante's, its power. Is this accent felt in the passages which I have been quoting from Burns? Surely not; surely, if our sense is quick, we must perceive that we have not in those passages a voice from the very inmost soul of the genuine Burns; he is not speaking to us from these depths, he is more or less preaching. And the compensation for admiring such passages less, from missing the perfect poetic accent in them, will be that we shall admire more the poetry where that accent is found.

No; Burns, like Chaucer, comes short of the high seriousness of the great classics, and the virtue of matter and manner which goes with that high seriousness is wanting to his work. At moments he touches it in a profound and passionate melancholy, as in those four immortal lines taken by Byron as a motto for "The Bride of Abydos," but which have in them a depth of poetic quality such as resides in no verse of Byron's own—

> Had we never loved sae kindly,
> Had we never loved sae blindly,
> Never met, or never parted,
> We had ne'er been broken-hearted.

But a whole poem of that quality Burns cannot make; the rest, in the **"Farewell to Nancy,"** is verbiage.

We arrive best at the real estimate of Burns, I think, by conceiving his work as having truth of matter and truth of manner, but not the accent or the poetic virtue of the highest masters. His genuine criticism of life, when the sheer poet in him speaks, is ironic; it is not—

> Thou Power Supreme, whose mighty scheme
>   These woes of mine fulfil,
> Here firm I rest, they must be best
>   Because they are Thy will!

It is far rather: "Whistle owre the lave o't!" Yet we may say of him as of Chaucer, that of life and the world, as they come before him, his view is large, free, shrewd, benignant,—truly poetic, therefore; and his manner of rendering what he sees is to match. But we must note, at the same time, his great difference from Chaucer. The freedom of Chaucer is heightened, in Burns, by a fiery, reckless energy; the benignity of Chaucer deepens, in Burns, into an overwhelming sense of the pathos of things;—of the pathos of human nature, the pathos, also, of non-human nature. Instead of the fluidity of Chaucer's manner, the manner of Burns has spring, bounding swiftness. Burns is by far the greater force, though he has perhaps less charm. The world of Chaucer is fairer, richer, more significant than that of Burns; but when the largeness and freedom of Burns get full sweep, as in **"Tam o' Shanter,"** or still more in that puissant and splendid production, **"The Jolly Beggars,"** his world may be what it will, his poetic genius triumphs over it. In the world of **"The Jolly Beggars"** there is more than hideousness and squalor, there is bestiality; yet the piece is a superb poetic success. It has a breadth, truth, and power which make the famous scene in Auerbach's Cellar, of Goethe's *Faust,* seem artificial and tame beside it, and which are only matched by Shakspeare and Aristophanes.

Here, where his largeness and freedom serve him so admirably, and also in those poems and songs where to shrewdness he adds infinite archness and wit, and to benignity infinite pathos, where his manner is flawless, and a perfect poetic whole is the result,—in things like the address to the mouse whose home he had ruined, in things like **"Duncan Gray," "Tam Glen," "Whistle and I'll come to you, my lad," "Auld Lang Syne"** (this list might be made much longer),—here we have the genuine Burns, of whom the real estimate must be high indeed. Not a classic, nor with the excellent σπουδαιοτηδ of the great classics, nor with a verse rising to a criticism of life and a virtue like theirs; but a poet with thorough truth of substance and an answering truth of style, giving us a poetry sound to the core. We all of us have a leaning towards the pathetic, and may be inclined perhaps to prize Burns most for his touches of piercing, sometimes almost intolerable, pathos; for verse like—

> We twa hae paidl't i' the burn
>   Frae mornin' sun till dine;
> But seas between us braid hae roar'd
>   Sin auld lang syne . . .

where he is as lovely as he is sound. But perhaps it is by the perfection of soundness of his lighter and archer masterpieces that he is poetically most wholesome for us. For the votary misled by a personal estimate of Shelley, as so many of us have been, are, and will be,—of that beautiful spirit building his many-coloured haze of words and images

> Pinnacled dim in the intense inane—

no contact can be wholesomer than the contact with Burns at his archest and soundest. Side by side with the

> On the brink of the night and the morning
>   My coursers are wont to respire,
> But the Earth has just whispered a warning
>   That their flight must be swifter than fire . . .

of "Prometheus Unbound," how salutary, how very salutary, to place this from **"Tam Glen"**—

> My minnie does constantly deave me
>   And bids me beware o' young men;
> They flatter, she says, to deceive me;
>   But wha can think sae o' Tam Glen?

But we enter on burning ground as we approach the poetry of times so near to us—poetry like that of Byron, Shelley, and Wordsworth—of which the estimates are so often not only personal, but personal with passion. For my purpose, it is enough to have taken the single case of Burns, the first poet we come to of whose work the estimate formed is evidently apt to be personal, and to have suggested how we may proceed, using the poetry of the great classics as a sort of touchstone, to correct this estimate. (pp. 32-40)

> *Matthew Arnold, "The Study of Poetry," in his* Essays in Criticism, Second Series, *AMS, 1970, pp. 1-41.*

Edwin Muir   (essay date 1947)

[*Muir was a distinguished Scottish novelist, poet, critic, and translator. In his critical writings, Muir emphasized the philosophical issues raised by works of art—such as the nature of time or society—rather than the particulars of the work itself, such as style or characterization. In the following essay, which was originally published in 1947, he comments on Burns's popularity and significance to the Scottish people.*]

For a Scotsman to see Burns simply as a poet is almost impossible. Burns is so deeply imbedded in Scottish life that he cannot be detached from it, from what is best and what is worst in it, and regarded as we regard Dunbar or James Hogg or Walter Scott. He is more a personage to us than a poet, more a figurehead than a personage, and more a myth than a figurehead. To those who have heard of Dunbar he is a figure, of course, comparable to Dunbar; but he is also a figure comparable to Prince Charlie, about whom everyone has heard. He is a myth evolved by the popular imagination, a communal poetic creation, a Protean figure; we can all shape him to our own likeness, for a myth is endlessly adaptable; so that to the respectable this secondary Burns is a decent man; to the Rabelaisian, bawdy; to the sentimentalist, sentimental; to the Socialist, a revolutionary; to the Nationalist, a patriot; to the religious, pious; to the self-made man, self-made; to the drinker, a drinker. He has the power of making any Scotsman, whether generous or canny, sentimental or prosaic, religious or profane, more wholeheartedly himself than he could have been without assistance; and in that way perhaps more human. He greases our wheels; we could not roll on our way so comfortably but for him; and it is impossible to judge impartially a convenient appliance to which we have grown accustomed.

The myth is unlike the man; but the man was its basis, and no other could have served. We cannot imagine Wordsworth or Shelley or Tennyson or Shakespeare turning into a popular myth; and Burns did so because his qualities made it possible, and because he deserved it. No other writer has said so fully and expressly what every man of his race wanted him to say; no other writer, consequently, has been taken so completely into the life of a people. The myth may in some ways be absurd, but it is as solid as the agreement which rises in Scotsmen's minds whenever Burns utters one of his great platitudes:

> O wad some Pow'r the giftie gie us
> To see oursels as ithers see us!

> The hert aye's the part aye
>   That makes us right or wrang.

> The best laid schemes o' mice and men
>   Gang aft a-gley.

When the Burnsites are assembled on the Night, they feel Burns invisibly present among them as one of themselves, a great man who by some felicitous stroke has been transformed into an ordinary man, and is the greater because of it—a man indeed more really, more universally ordinary than any mere ordinary man could ever hope to be. This feeling is a tribute to Burns' humanity; it is a claim to kinship; it is also a grateful recognition that here is a poet for everybody, a poet who has such an insight into ordinary thoughts and feelings that he can catch them and give them poetic shape, as those who merely think or feel them cannot. This was Burns' supreme art. It appears to be simple. People are inclined to believe that it is easier to express ordinary thoughts and feelings in verse than complex and unusual ones. The problem is an artificial one, for in the end a poet does what he has a supreme gift for doing. Burns' gift lay there; it made him a myth; it predestined him to become the Rabbie of Burns Nights. When we consider Burns we must therefore include the Burns Nights with him, and the Burns cult in all its forms; if we sneer at them, we sneer at Burns. They are his reward, or his punishment (whichever the fastidious reader may prefer to call it) for having had the temerity to express the ordinary feelings of his people, and for having become a part of their life. What the Burns Nights ignore is the perfection of Burns' art, which makes him one of the great poets. But there is so much more involved that this, his real greatness, is scarcely taken into account.

Ordinary thoughts and feelings are not necessarily shallow, any more than subtle and unusual ones are necessarily profound. It may be said that Burns was never shallow and never profound. He did not have

> Those thoughts that wander through eternity

which consoled Milton's Belial in Hell; and he could not be shallow as Tennyson sometimes was. He was sentimental, but sentimental with a certain solidity and grossness; there is genuine feeling behind his mawkishness, not merely a sick refinement of sensibility striving to generate the illusion of feeling. He could rise to the full height of the ordinary, where simplicity and greatness meet:

> Thou'll break my heart, thou bonie bird,
> That sings beside thy mate;
> For sae I sat, and sae I sang,
> And wist na o' my fate.

His rhetoric, his humour, his satire, his platitude have all the same solidity, the same devastating common sense. There is a great difference between **"A Man's a Man for a' that"** and

> Kind hearts are more than coronets,
> And simple faith than Norman blood.

The one speaks positively to us; the other says nothing. Burns became as amorphous as a myth because he was as solid as a ploughman. He became legendary because he was so startlingly ordinary. He was the ordinary man for whom Scotland had been looking as it might have looked for a king; and it discovered him with greater surprise and delight than if it had found a king, for kings are more common. His poetry embodied the obvious in its universal form, the obvious in its essence and its truth, the discovery of which is one of the perennial surprises of mankind. If Burns' poetry had not been obvious, he could never have become the national poet of Scotland.

But the national poet of Scotland is too conventional a term for him; the poet of the Scottish people is better, for all claim him. And by the people I do not mean merely the ploughman and the factory worker and the grocer's assistant, but the lawyer, the business man, the minister, the bailie—all that large class of Scotsmen who are not very interested in literature, not very cultivated, and know little

poetry outside the poetry of Burns. It is these who have fashioned the popular image of Burns; and this is what really happens when a poet is taken into the life of a people. He moulds their thoughts and feelings; but they mould his too, sometimes long after he is dead. They make current a vulgarised image of him, and a vulgarised reading of his poetry; they take him into their life, but they also enter into his; and what emerges as the popular picture is a cross between the two. What is good in this bargain is self-evident—that the words and thoughts and feelings of a great poet become the common property of his people. The disadvantages I have tried to describe; they are natural and inevitable; compared to the single great advantage they do not matter very much, unless to those who cannot endure a normal dose of vulgarity. But they exist, and those who are advocating a more popular note in poetry at present should take them into account. For Burns is an object-lesson in what poetic popularity really means—the prime object-lesson in the poetry of the world, perhaps the unique instance.

It is good, then, that there should be 'poetry for the people', as its advocates call it. But there is another side of the question, and I found it illustrated while turning over an old number of the *Criterion* the other day, and coming on an editorial note by Mr. T. S. Eliot. A letter by the Poet Laureate and his friends had appeared in *The Times* under the heading, 'Art in the Inn'. Mr. Masefield proposed making use of the country public-house for 'verse-speaking, drama and readings of prose, and thus encouraging a wider appreciation of our language and literature in its highest forms'. Mr. Eliot was disconcerted by this proposal, as a number of us would be; for he 'had always thought of the public-house as one of the few places to which one could escape from verse-speaking, drama and readings of prose. If the public-house is to fall into the hands of the English Association and the British Drama League, where, one must ask bluntly, is a man to go for a drink?'

With this most people would agree; propaganda of this kind rests on a false basis; but Burns, at any rate, does not need it; when he is quoted or recited in pubs, the act is quite natural and spontaneous. But the more serious part of Mr. Eliot's comment comes later.

> I suspect that two distinct intentions, both laudable, have been confused. One is, that there should be a public for poetry. But what is important is not that this public should be large, but that it should be sensitive, critical and educated—conditions only possible for a small public. The other intention is, that people should be made happier, and be given the best life of which they are capable. I doubt whether poetry can be made to serve this purpose for the populace; if it ever does, it will never come as a result of centralised planning.

Now, when Mr. Eliot doubts 'whether poetry can be made to serve this purpose' (of giving people the best life of which they are capable), he is evidently thinking of poetry as everyone who takes it seriously thinks of it; the poetry, to guess at his own tastes, of Dante, Shakespeare, Webster, Donne, Dryden, Baudelaire, the French Symbolists; but the list can be indefinitely extended, and for the genuine lover of poetry it will include Burns, shorn of his popularity, a name of the same kind as those other great names. If there is to be a public for these poets, and for what is good in the poetry of our own time, obviously Mr. Eliot is right in saying that it must be 'sensitive, critical and educated'; for without such a public, poetry could not be preserved, and its traditions would be lost. Mr. Eliot asserts that this public is bound to be small, and no doubt that is so; but there is a fringe surrounding it which is not small, a working liaison between the discriminating few and the undiscriminating mass. Nothing can be done by propaganda or organisation to extend that fringe; but by merely existing it produces an effect among the mass which is different from the effect produced by popular poetry; for it is qualitative. What the advocates of poetry for the people should aim at is the dissemination of a feeling for quality, not the production of poetry which will be read in greater and greater quantity. This cannot be done by propaganda for popular poetry; but a beginning might be made by reform of our schools, where poetry is so often 'taught' in a way to make the pupil dislike it and misunderstand it.

Burns exists in both worlds—the world of quality and the world of quantity. The world of quantity has grown so powerful and established such a firm hold on him that it is difficult to extricate him from its grip. He has certainly fulfilled one of the functions which Mr. Eliot doubted whether poetry could fulfil—'that people should be happier'; he has done much more than that; and what he has done is good beyond doubt, with this limitation which does not apply to other poets—that he has not brought poetry to people, but simply Burns. It may be that Burns is enough for many people who read him; but Shakespeare, or Milton, or Keats is not; to read one of them is to wish to read the others, and to discover poetry. Yet though Burns invisibly appears on Burns Nights, obedient to the summons, one feels that he too would have agreed with Mr. Eliot's opinion that the public for poetry should be 'sensitive, critical and educated'; for he knew something by experience which his admirers do not know—the desire for perfection and the endless pains of the artist. (pp. 58-64)

> *Edwin Muir, "Burns and Popular Poetry," in his* Essays on Literature and Society, *revised edition, Harvard University Press, 1965, pp. 58-64.*

John C. Weston, Jr.   (essay date 1960)

[*Weston is an American educator and author who has written extensively on Burns. In the following excerpt, he praises Burns for his innovations in the Scottish tradition of humorous elegies.*]

Burns worked self-consciously within the Scots tradition. He says, in his "Preface" to the Kilmarnock edition, that he belongs to a definite school, the chief representatives of which are Allan Ramsay and Robert Fergusson. He undoubtedly was acquainted with the poems in James Watson's famous three-part *Choice Collection of Comic and*

Serious Scots Poems (1706, 1709, 1711), which was the first in a series of eighteenth-century anthologies of Scots poetry to revive the Lowland Scots tradition, and to make possible the work of Ramsay and Fergusson.

From this tradition emerged Burns' **"Poor Mailie's Elegy,"** a mock lament for the death of a favorite sheep, first printed in the Kilmarnock edition and probably written not long before. Those poems of the tradition from which **"Mailie"** emerges and which we would expect Burns to know are three in Watson's *Choice Collection,* four by Ramsay, and two by Robert Fergusson.

The most distinguished poem in and the prototype of the tradition is Robert Sempill's of Beltrees "The Life and Death of the Piper of Kilbarchan, or, The Epitaph of Habbie Simson," originally printed in a number of broadsides but first made generally popular by its inclusion in part one of Watson's *Collection* (1706). The poem is most famous for popularizing an earlier and rare but afterwards typical Scots six-line stanza ($AAA_4B_2A_4B_2$) called in recognition of its source the Habbie Simson stanza (and later the Standard Scots, Standard Habbie, or the Burns Stanza). Because the poem is the direct source of the eighteenth-century Scots humorous elegies which culminate in Burns' poem here under consideration, we should inspect it closely.

"The Piper," a poem of fourteen stanzas, treats in a lightly tender and nostalgic way the former activities of a recently deceased bagpipe musician. Sempill first calls upon the village of Kilbarchan to lament the passing of their famous entertainer, then asks who will now play the favorite old songs for the kirktown and perform at various village functions, and then presents a picture of the life and times of Habbie Simson—his playing at military parades, stage plays and horse races, his skill in sports, his entertainment and amusing conduct at weddings, his attempt to kill a man who thrust a knife into his pipe-bag, and finally his appearance and character. In the final stanza a shift is made from the bagpiper to the poet, who owes a debt to the piper for former pleasures. There is, then, a loose organization in the poem. It is framed with lament stanzas. There is a suggestion of chronology in the treatment of Habbie's life: his skill at sports in times of his youth is treated in stanza 8, and his toothless old age is mentioned in stanza 12—but this progression might be accidental. A unity is maintained by reminding the reader in the final two lines of each stanza, a turn characteristic of the Standard Habbie, that all these happy times will be no more "Sin Habbie's dead." And this final refrain is ingeniously integrated by always referring to the aspect of Habbie's character or conduct with which the stanza is concerned.

There is no humor of language in the poem. Certain of Habbie's activities described are quietly amusing:

> At Bridals he wan many Placks, *an old Scotch*
> *coin*
> He bobbed ay behind Fo'ks backs,
>   and shook his Head.

The picture of the piper furtively bowing, and jesting and mimicking at a wedding is wistfully pleasant. But the humour goes no further. The language comes from that which Sempill spoke or which he read in Scots poetry. The main object of the poem, to present a light, nostalgic portrait of a character, is accomplished with some skill. The poem expresses more nostalgia for the past than grief for the subject. The tone of the poem is one of whimsical melancholy tending in a few lines to true pathos:

> In the Kirk-yard, his Mare stood tedder'd,
> where he lies dead!

And,

> We need not look for Piping mair,
> sen *Habbie's* dead.

"The Piper" begins a tradition of poems written in its stanza the main purpose of which is to paint a humorous and vigorous portrait of a departed person while at the same time to lament his passing with various shades of irony and emphasis. The other two representatives of the type in Watson's *Collection* are anonymous and closely derivative. The source of the first imitation is made quite clear in its full title: "Epitaph on Sanny Briggs, Nephew to Habbie Simson, and Butler to the Laird of Kilbarcan (1706)." "Sanny Briggs" has not as much lively local imagery, the emphasis being shifted somewhat from the life of the dead man toward the emotions of the "mourner": the writer shows an ironic grief over the death of one who provided food, drink, companionship, and tender care after too much drinking. There are some amusing scenes (Briggs beats the drunken kitchen help), but the poem is not very funny, the ironic exaggerated grief coming through often with boyish lack of subtlety:

> When first I heard the waeful Knell,
> And Dool ring o's Passing Bell,   *sorrowful*
> It made me yelp, and yeul and yell,
> and skirl and skreed.   *shriek, screech*

And there is an unsophisticated, robust braggadocio in the display of the writer's love of drink, which now is frustrated. Like "The Piper" the stanzas end in "dead," many of them in "since Sanny's dead," with the resulting contrasting turn from life to death in the last two lines. And like "The Piper" the language is all Scots. (pp. 634-37)

In the final representative of the type in Watson's *Collection,* "William Lithgow, Writer in Edinburgh, His Epitaph (1709)," we see exaggerated a characteristic that Ramsay will seize upon, that is, the celebration of the exploits of a local memorable eccentric who lived outside the ordinary proprieties, in this instance a drunkard, whoremaster, brawler, and boon companion to lusty riffraff. It shares many features with "The Piper," but it, like "Sanny Briggs," is a rather silly and juvenile poem. There is some ironic lament, but the emphasis is on the description of the life of the dead man. . . . The language is again Scots, except perhaps for that in the lame and anti-climactic last stanza, which introduces an innovation that does not effect the tradition (except very slightly in a poem by Fergusson) until Burns, a moral application almost Chaucerian in flavor:

> Ye Gentlemen that given be
> To *Bacchus* and sweet Lecherie,
> Now take Example when you see
> Your Neighbour bleed:

> As Willie is so must you be,
> Alace, he's dead.

(p. 637)

Allan Ramsay next contributes to the developing tradition with his "The Life and Acts of, or an Elegy on Patie Birnie, The Famous Fidler of Klinghorn (1721)." That Ramsay used "The Piper" as a model is made clear by an epigraph, a two-line quotation from that poem. The title shows the ambivalence of the tradition at this point, the purpose hovering between the biography of a portrait and the lament of an elegy. The poem treats the life and character of a village fiddler, again an off-beat social type. The first stanza announces the poet's intention to sing the departed one; the second admonishes his village to lament his passing, but the rest of the twenty-two-stanza poem except the last stanza, which returns to lamentation, is a portrait.

There is less of an attempt to justify this portrait as an elegy, with a consequent failure in unity, than there was in "The Piper," for, since there is no variable refrain, the last two lines in each stanza do not remind us of the death. The emphasis is almost altogether on biography, but there is a greater use of the elegiac conventions at the beginning and the end of the poem:

> In Sonnet slee the Man I sing,
> His rare Engine in Rhyme shall ring.

The first line solemnly announces the intention; the second substitutes the elevated phrase "rare engine" for fiddle. In the second stanza,

> *Klinghorn* may rue the ruefou Day
> That lighted *Patie* to his clay,

shows at once the use of the elegiac conventions and the sly humor of language which "The Piper" lacked. . . . Ramsay's main innovations come from a knowledge of classical, not Scots, literature: some classical diction and the final consolation, traditional in elegiac poetry since the Renaissance, that the subject really is not dead. The poem lacks even a touch of the pathos and tenderness about its object which "The Piper" possessed. It shows no depth of feeling, although the situations are amusing and the minuteness of observation admirable. It uses certain elegiac features—the opening, the close, the classical analogies, the occasional heightened language—in a portrait of a man to produce a lusty, humorous effect.

This main branch of the developing tradition before Burns ends with Robert Fergusson's "Elegy on John Hogg," a portrait of a porter at the University of St. Andrews. The first stanza admonishes Death for taking Hogg; the second calls on the scholars to mourn, the bells to ring, and the steeples to fall down; and the third informs the students that they previously have never had good reason to wear their accustomed black attire. But the remaining thirteen stanzas of the poem paint the portrait of Hogg with only one additional passing reference to grief over the death when the poet asks, in a stanza reminiscent of the second and third stanzas of "The Piper" and a number in "Sanny Briggs," who will provide a student *esprit de corps* since Hogg's death. After the first three stanzas there is no attempt to recall the elegiac occasion: like "Patie Birnie" there is no repeated refrain to keep the focus on death; nor is there an elegiac ending in the classical tradition as there is in "Patie Birnie." The poem concludes by instructing students to use Hogg's practice as an example of wise frugality, a conclusion which recalls the final moral application of "William Lithgow." This poem then, is further from the elegiac occasion than even Ramsay's poem. The language is all Scots and there is, as to a greater degree there is in Ramsay, fine humor of language, for example in the first stanza:

> Death, what's ado? the de'il be licket
> Or wi' your stang ye ne'er had pricket,
> Or our auld Alma Mater tricket
>   O' poor John Hogg,
> And trailed him been thro' your mirk wicket
>   As dead's a dog.

There are two minor cul-de-sac offshoots from the tradition which deserve some attention. First there is the elegy on a place of amusement. Ramsay wrote two poems like his "Patie Birnie" which are ostensibly humorous elegies on the deaths of lady proprietors of places of amusement ("Elegy on Maggy Johnstoun" and "Elegy on Lucky Wood" [both 1721]) but which are really laments for the passing of and reminiscences of the days associated with those establishments. . . . Second, there is the elegy used for satire. Ramsay's "Elegy on John Cowper (1721)," perhaps Ramsay's best effort in the humorous elegy, pretends to lament the passing of a kirk-treasurer's man, whose duty it is to expose fornicators, but in reality simultaneously exposes his dishonest practices: the emphasis is again on biography and anecdote, this time for the purpose of humorous attack not humorous praise. . . . Fergusson also wrote a satirical elegy, "Elegy on the Death of Mr David Gregory, Late Professor of Mathematics in the University of St. Andrews," a slight but excellent piece of only seven stanzas which makes fun of the academic accomplishments of his subject. The emphasis is on biography as usual. Unlike his "John Hogg," the stanzas end (except for the last one) in refrain lines of "dead," a practice unique after the three pieces in the *Collection* and before Burns. And a further unity is achieved by framing the poem with elegiac elements.

At this point a definition of the tradition as Burns inherited it can be attempted. A pre-Burns eighteenth-century Scots humorous elegy is a topical poem written in Lowland Scots which uses the Standard Habbie stanza and takes the occasion of the death of some eccentric, usually from the lower classes, most commonly to give a portrait of the character and activities of that person during his life, but sometimes to describe the place associated with him or to satirize him. The emphasis is not on the grief for the departed. Although the activities of the subject are often humorous, there is not much humor of language; but there is an almost consistent lightness of tone, which is at the same time rollicking and vigorous. There is very little pathos. A mechanical unity is sometimes achieved by framing the main part of the poem with Scots and occasionally classical elegiac formulas and by presenting an ironic turn in the last two lines of each stanza and a repeated end-line terminating with the word "dead."

It is clear from this necessarily qualified descriptive definition that the tradition had not hardened into any firm convention. Its looseness makes the question of Burns' use of it all the more interesting because he had considerable freedom to pick and choose.

"Poor Mailie's Elegy"

Lament in rhyme, lament in prose,	
Wi' saut tears tricklin' down your nose;	
Our bardie's fate is at a close,	
Past a' remead;	
The last sad cape-stane of his woes—	
Poor Mailie's dead!	
It's no the loss o' warl's gear	
That could sae bitter draw the tear,	
Or mak our bardie, dowie, wear	*sad*
The mourning weed:	
He's lost a friend and neibor dear	
In Mailie dead.	
Thro' a' the toun she trotted by him;	
A lang half-mile she could descry him;	
Wi' kindly bleat, when she did spy him,	
She ran wi' speed:	
A friend mair faithfu' ne'er cam nigh him	
Than Mailie dead.	
I wat she was a sheep o' sense,	*know*
An' could behave hersel wi' mense;	*good manners*
I'll say't, she never brak a fence	
Thro' thievish greed.	
Our bardie, lanely, keeps the spense	*parlor*
Sin' Mailie's dead.	
Or, if he wanders up the howe,	*hollow*
Her living image in her yowe	*ewe*
Comes bleating to him, owre the knowe,	*knoll*
For bits o' bread,	
An' down the briny pearls rowe	
For Mailie dead.	
She was nae get o' moorland tups,	*rams*
Wi' tawted ket, an' hairy hips;	*matted fleece*
For her forbears were brought in ships	
Frae yont the Tweed:	
A bonnier fleesh ne'er cross'd the clips	
Than Mailie's, dead.	
Wae worth the man wha first did shape	
That vile wanchancie thing—a rape!	*unlucky, rope*
It maks guid fellows girn and gape!	*grin*
Wi' chokin' dread;	
An' Robin's bonnet wave wi' crape	
For Mailie dead.	
O a' ye bards on bonnie Doon!	
An' wha on Ayr your chanters tune!	
Come, join the melancholious croon	
O' Robin's reed;	
His heart will never get aboon	*above*
His Mailie dead!	

Burns' poem, although shorter than all its predecessors except "David Gregory," is clearly in the tradition. Here is the Standard Habbie with its characteristic turn and refrain, the elegiac conventions, the humor, the pathos, the biography, the conventional tear passage, the inevitable rime of "remead" and "dead." But there are significant innovations and changes of emphasis. The most obvious departure from the tradition is the bold one that the manifest subject is a sheep. But unlike almost all his predecessors (the author of "Sanny Briggs" is a possible exception here), who lacked an organic unity because the emphasis was on the portrait or the description while the ostensible elegiac occasion received only token attention, Burns achieves such a unity by focusing the poem on himself, that is, on his state of mind at the loss of his sheep.

Consequent to this emphasis on the one who is doing the mourning rather than on the person or thing mourned, there is a much greater amount of pathos than in the poems of any of his predecessors. In fact, we saw that only Sempill imparted any pathos whatsoever and that only in a very small measure. Admitting that the pathos is mixed with a tongue-in-cheek humor, it is nevertheless sentimentally affecting, in the same sense as the scene with Uncle Toby and the fly is in *Tristram Shandy:* we rationally *understand* the ridiculous disproportion between the sentiment and its object, but we cannot help but *feel* a kind of ambiguous pathos.

From having an animal as a subject and the focus on himself, Burns achieves a humor of exaggeration and outrageous inappropriateness, or what Wittig calls—commenting on this form and claiming its intimate connection with Scottish life and literary tradition—"a clash of appearance and reality, of pretentious solemnity and shrewd realism" [Kurt Wittig, *The Scottish Tradition in Literature*, 1958]. Mailie's death is lamented as that of a most-loved kinsman and in language appropriate to a human death. Mailie is treated as having a human's character: she showed a love for the poet, she would call to him, she had good manners and was honest, she left offspring, she had a good lineage. But, with cunning timing, we are made aware that she is a sheep. After informing us proudly of her lineage, the poet reminds us (like the practice of Chaucer with Chaunt(icleer) that she is a sheep by saying,

> A bonnier fleesh ne'er cross'd the clips
> Than Mailie's, . . .

None of the earlier poets in this tradition had a humor which was inherent in the idea of the whole poem.

It is a question whether we can call the poems of this tradition before Burns true mock elegies at all because their "mockness" consists merely in lightness, in *occasional* irony, in utterance which we take to impart something other than what is imparted in traditional elegy from the time of Theocritus on: *real* praise, grief, and consolation. None of them has any basic irony in the very idea of the poem as a whole, that is, a sustained and organic irony. There is in the previous poems the irony which emerges from the occasional expression of grief in terms which are felt to be extravagant for the low object. In the two satirical Scots elegies prior to **"Mailie's,"** there is the complete reversal of meaning: sorrow is expressed for the death although joy is really felt. But real mock elegy, like mock any-other genre, involves something else: a polarity between the subject matter and the expression. Low pursuits are expressed in high terms—mock epic: "The Rape of the

Lock" expresses the trivial flirtations and tea-time maneuverings at Hampton in traditional epic terms and conventions; mock pastoral: Gay's *The Shepherds' Week* expresses the barnyard activities of country clowns in terms appropriate to the shepherds and shepherdesses of the Spenserian tradition; mock-opera: Gay's *Beggar's Opera* expresses the affairs of thieves in terms appropriate to lords and ladies and with the conventions of the Italian opera; mock elegy: Gray's "Ode on the Death of a Favorite Cat" relates the occasion of the death of a household pet in the conventional terms of classical elegy. Burns is certainly not closer to the English than to the Scots tradition of humorous elegy, but in this one important respect he brought a loose Scots tradition into a form which has the basic feature of all mock writing: a totally-informing ironic polarity between *res* and *verba*. Burns received hints for this form from the Scots tradition: the occasional but not informing ironic treatment of Habbie Simson, Sanny Briggs, Patie Birnie, John Hogg. But Burns was the first to write a true Scots *mock* elegy.

It was either Burns' natural genius ("heaven-born" in Mackenzie's sentimental phrase) which discovered the true nature of mock-writing independent of example or, more probably, his knowledge of English literature that can account for this addition to the Scots tradition in this poem. Consequently it is with some caution that we should accept such sweeping statements about Burns' Scottish verse as, "It has no connection with English verse at any point" [John Spiers, *The Scots Literary Tradition*, 1940]. To admit that Burns' poems written with Augustan English diction and in his genteel persona are invariably poor is one thing; to claim that Burns did not put into his fine Scots poems anything he had learned from Pope, Gay, Gray, or Shenstone is entirely another.

Only Ramsay and to a lesser degree Fergusson had any humor of language. Burns greatly excels these two in this. If we compare the traditional tear-passages in poems by Ramsay and Fergusson to the one in this, we discover that the thought and order is remarkably similar and that the striking superiority of Burns' lines are accounted for only by a richer comic sense:

> Auld Reeky, mourn in sable hue   *Old
> Smokey* (Edinburgh)
> Let fouth of tears dreep like May dew.   *plenty*
>   (Ramsay, "Maggie Johnstoun")
>
> Now mourn, ye college masters a';
> And frae your een a tear let fa':
>   (Fergusson, "David Gregory")
>
> Lament in rhyme, lament in prose,
> Wi' saut tears tricklin' down your nose:
>   (Burns)

Burns' lines show a sly and cunning humor which is very distinctive to him and which here derives principally from riming the noble "prose" with the ignoble "nose," an ironic coupling of diction organic to the mock contrast of opposites which informs the entire poem. The flavor of the lines is evidence of what Arnold called Burns' "infinite archness and wit."

Burns' diction is Scots like all his predecessors, but we

should not miss the one word which suggests an influence other than native: in the last stanza all the local poets are bid to add their songs to Burns' "reed." Here is diction of the classical pastoral elegy, perhaps deriving second-hand through Ramsay, whose poems in the Scots humorous elegiac tradition alone show a similar influence (although in those poems "reed" is not found), but more probably deriving from Burns' knowledge of English poets, particularly his favorite Shenstone.

To buttress the unity of theme discussed above, Burns added both the devices of framing the main portion of the poem with elegiac elements and of ending every stanza with a final refrain. Thus he went back to the early tradition to follow the lead of the poems in Watson's *Collection*. Ramsay did not use the refrain throughout any of his elegies and Fergusson did so only in "David Gregory" (and in that poem there is one stanza without the end-word "dead"). But Burns went further in this particular than even the early poems. Burns always precedes "dead" with a form of the name, Mailie, and often, unlike any of his predecessors, enjambs the two last lines to achieve a unity in the ironic final twist. To be sure, this means that the adjective "dead" must follow the noun, but in two stanzas he varies this in the traditional way by making "dead" a predicate adjective, thus:

> Sin' Mailie's dead.

In the sixth stanza he must just tack the word on at the end where it has no grammatical connection with the sentence, and this is unfortunate. But that Burns imposed these added restrictions on himself shows a certain boldness in versification reminiscent of the old makaris and a willingness to work within tight forms.

In the seventh stanza Burns curses the man who first made a rope because that was the instrument of Mailie's death. Here Burns is indulging in a favorite poetic occupation. He takes off from a lowly object and develops a moral feeling applicable to all mankind or applies the feeling of all men to the object. Burns could have received the suggestion from the overt moralizing in "William Lithgow," but Burns' moralizing is indirect. He goes from a rope to a fear of the gallows among guilty men, and implies a grave moral feeling without drawing a moral. The same sort of extension outward from the homely and lowly to the general world of men is found in many of Burns' poems, such as **"To a Mouse"** and **"To a Louse."** And this moral extension, in this poem at least, is closer to English neo-classic poetry than to his Scots models; closer, for instance, to Gray's moral extensions from the boys rolling hoops at Eton and the insects in spring than to the last stanza of "William Lithgow."

One last feature of the poem must be mentioned. The half-humorous, half-pathetic lament of a poet for a dead sheep has a much greater universal appeal than a description of a village musician or of a bawdy-house and its mistress or of a college porter. Certainly a poet can work through the topical to the universal, as Burns often does and as I feel Sempill in "The Piper" does to some extent, but Ramsay and Fergusson failed to give us a universal quality in their elegies and part of the reason for the failure is that the sub-

ject matter was too local. Burns chose a subject that we can all understand.

We can perceive now the extent of Burns' achievement. Inheriting a loose tradition, he selectively used most of its particular elements but by avoiding its main fault of a divided purpose and by a bold change of the traditional subject, he achieved the true mock elegy. We see exemplified, thus, Burns' claim in the "Preface" to the Kilmarnock edition that he belongs to the tradition of Ramsay and Fergusson but that he kept their poems in mind "rather with a view to kindle at their flame, than for servile imitation." Burns is, if we can generalize somewhat from this single poem, what marks all great poets, both traditional and original. The innovations in this poem, some probably deriving from English literature—unity, the informing mock discrepancy of *res* and *verba,* the humor of language, the rigorous mechanical restrictions, the implied moral extensions—all improve the tradition without destroying it. We cannot but be made melancholy to think that there came after him no great Scots poets to carry it on. This poem shows, indeed, what David Daiches in speaking of all Burns' poetry has aptly called, "the Indian Summer of a Scottish literary tradition" [*Robert Burns,* 1950]. (pp. 637-47)

John C. Weston, Jr., "An Example of Robert Burns' Contribution to the Scottish Vernacular Tradition," in Studies in Philology, *Vol. LVII, No. 4, October, 1960, pp. 634-47.*

Thomas Crawford   (essay date 1960)

[*Crawford is an English educator who has stated that his work reflects "a passionate involvement with the literature of Scotland and a wish to make it more widely known." In the following excerpt from his critical work* Burns: A Study of the Poems and Songs, *he analyzes the contradictory themes of Burns's epistles.*]

[The **"Epistle to John Rankine, enclosing some Poems,"** the earliest of Burns's verse epistles,] is a light, confident, even impudent poem exhibiting many traits characteristic of the mature Burns. Rankine's personality is indicated by a few bold strokes only, so that the reader feels he has known this crude hard-drinking old sinner all the years of his life; and in the third and fourth stanzas essentially the same method is employed as in **"Holy Willie's Prayer."** The trick consists in the apparent acceptance of the real or imputed ideas of those attacked, which here takes the form of a despairing, almost whining appeal to Rankine to spare Hypocrisy:

> Hypocrisy, in mercy spare it!
> That holy robe, O, dinna tear it!
> Spare't for their sakes, wha aften wear it—
>   The lads in black;
> But your curst wit, when it comes near it,
>   Rives 't aff their back.
>
> Think, wicked sinner, wha ye're skaithing:
> It's just the Blue-gown badge an' claithing
> O' saunts; tak that, ye lea'e them naething
>   To ken them by
> Frae onie unregenerate heathen,

Like you or I.

It is only in the seventh stanza that the main subject appears—an account of Burns's dealings with Elizabeth Paton [a servant in the Burns household who in May, 1785, gave birth to Burns's first illegitimate child] in a comic allegory of guns and partridges and poaching. In the tenth, he swears that in revenge for having to make public confession before the Holy Willies, he'll make havoc next year on all the girls in sight:

> But, by my gun, o' guns the wale,
> An' by my pouther an' my hail,
> An' by my hen, an' by her tail,
>   I vow an' swear!
> The game shall pay, owre moor an' dale,
> For this, niest year!

This is the humour of the lads of the village: rough, full of energy and pride in physical prowess, but not to be taken too seriously. It is an example of Burns making real poetry out of the commonest bawdy material.

The ideas and emotions out of which the best pieces in the Kilmarnock Edition were made can be traced in a series of poems less disciplined and more informal than his set pieces—the epistles to "Davie," J. Lapraik, William Simpson, John Goldie, and James Smith.

The first **"Epistle to Davie [David Sillar], a Brother Poet,"** written in January 1785, is concerned with the contrast between riches and poverty which underlies "Man was made to Mourn," as well as with another subject—the Rousseauistic glorification of "the heart." Beginning with a firm and brisk impression of winter, the poem soon moves to those "greatfolk" who are well-housed and comfortable in winter. Burns feels, however, that it is very wrong of him to envy the rich—a sentiment that rather takes the edge off his criticism of their "cursed pride." In the second stanza he introduces one of his major preoccupations, the possibility of beggary, and decides—like many a member of the class of agricultural labourers into which the Burnses were always afraid of falling—that the prospect is less fearsome when treated philosophically:

> But Davie, lad, ne'er fash your head,
>   Tho' we hae little gear;
> We're fit to win our daily bread,
>   As lang's we're hale and fier:
> 'Mair spier na, nor fear na,'
>   Auld age ne'er mind a feg;
> The last o't, the warst o't,
>   Is only but to beg.

When utterly destitute, Burns and Sillar have nowhere to sleep except in kilns or deserted barns—

> Nae mair then, we'll care then,
>   Nae farther can we fa'.

He imagines Davie and himself enjoying an equality of perfect comradeship as "commoners of air," taking pleasure in landscapes of "sweeping vales" and "foaming floods," complete with daisies and blackbirds. In springtime on the hillsides they will set words to traditional tunes, proud and free in their mendicancy like the beggars of W. B. Yeats:

> It's no in titles nor in rank:
> It's no in wealth like Lon'on Bank,
>   To purchase peace and rest.
> It's no in makin muckle, mair;
> It's no in books, it's no in lear,
>   To make us truly blest:
> If happiness hae not her seat
>   An' centre in the breast,
> We may be wise, or rich, or great,
>   But never can be blest!
>   Nae treasures nor pleasures
>   Could make us happy lang;
>   The heart ay's the part ay
>   That makes us right or wrang.

The Puritan "inner light" has after many vicissitudes become with Burns the "heart" of an eighteenth-century rustic Man of Feeling.

In the sixth stanza Burns comes back to the contrast with which he began, between the labouring poor and the idle rich. It is confidently asserted that men who "drudge and drive thro' wet and dry" are just as happy as those who live in palaces and mansions:

> Think ye, are we less blest than they,
> Wha scarcely tent us in their way,
>   As hardly worth their while?
> Alas! how oft, in haughty mood,
>   God's creatures they oppress!
> Or else, neglecting a' that's guid,
>   They riot in excess!

Burns's solution of this class conflict, which fills him with such detestation of the aristocracy, is not a social one, but something personal and private—the cultivation of a contented state of mind, "making the best of a bad job." The epistle begins to deteriorate from this point. Surely these lines from the eighth stanza are as nauseating as any adjuration of "the lads in black," and come perilously close to "All is for the best in the best of all possible worlds":

> And, even should misfortunes come,
> I here wha sit hae met wi' some,
>   An's thankfu' for them yet,
> They gie the wit of age to youth;
>   They let us ken oursel;
> They make us see the naked truth,
>   The real guid and ill. . . .

In this eighth stanza Burns asserts that inner happiness (the positive Good of the poem) can be realised only in love and friendship—or as we would say today, in personal relationships—and in the ninth stanza he even depicts his feelings for [his future wife] Jean Armour as an escape from the woes of daily life:

> When heart-corroding care and grief
>   Deprive my soul of rest,
> Her dear idea brings relief
>   And solace to my breast.

If poetically the tenth stanza is not much superior to the ninth, yet intellectually it is one of the key passages in the epistle. One might paraphrase it, cockney-fashion, as "It's bein' so tender as keeps me goin' ":

> All hail! ye tender feelings dear!
> The smile of love, the friendly tear,

The sympathetic glow!

Burns is in this poem taking himself seriously as a Man of Feeling, having apparently forgotten the self-criticism of such moods as the following:

> Beware a tongue that's smoothly hung,
>   A heart that warmly seems to feel!
> That feeling heart but acts a part—
>   'Tis rakish art in Rob Mossgiel.

Yet the thought is one he returned to again and again, in various guises—that love is the only thing that makes life worth living for the poor. In slightly more robust form it is the ground and foundation of that well-known lyric **"Green grow the Rashes, O,"** while the same idea (this time quite unashamedly equated with four-lettered words) is a recurrent theme of all the "cloaciniad" verse in *The Merry Muses of Caledonia:*

> And why shouldna poor folk mowe, mowe,
>   mowe,
>   And why shouldna poor folk mowe:
> The great folk hae siller, & houses & lands,
>   Poor bodies hae naething but mowe.

Thus if the eighth, ninth and tenth stanzas of the **"Epistle to Davie"** appear a trifle mawkish to modern readers, it is important to realise that they express but one variant—a refined and somewhat tenuous one, it is true—of a concept which would surely have met with the approval of D. H. Lawrence. In part, it is a gospel of "Joy through Sex" that Burns is preaching here—not simply the sexual act itself (which receives its tributes in the **The Merry Muses**), but all the emotions and sentiments which grow out of its soil. The other "positive" in the poem is friendship; and these two values of the heart are held to be sufficient to compensate for the exploitation of man by man. Was it because Burns knew in his heart of hearts that these "positives" are not in themselves enough to offset the real ills of life that the poem remained an interesting but imperfect experiment clogged by abstract monstrosities of diction like "sympathetic glow" and "tenebrific scene"? Perhaps Burns flew to the pompous-sounding English words because he did not really believe what he was saying.

The first **"Epistle to J. Lapraik, An Old Scottish Bard, April 1, 1785,"** has none of these verbal infelicities. Written in the traditional "Standard Habbie" measure, so eminently suited to poetic gossip and conversational topics, it is the very perfection of occasional verse. On Fastene'en, the evening before Lent, Burns had attended a traditional "rockin" or small social gathering where women spun on the distaff or wove stockings while each member of the company sang a song in turn. One piece in particular pleased Burns—

> Thought I, 'Can this be Pope, or Steele,
>   Or Beattie's wark?'
> They told me 'twas an odd kind chiel
>   About Muirkirk.

It was Lapraik's "When I upon thy Bosom Lean," which happens to bear an extraordinary resemblance to a song published in Ruddiman's *Weekly Magazine* for 11 Oct. 1773, under the *nom-de-plume* of "Happy Husband": a circumstance which has led many editors to brand La-

praik as a plagiarist. But there is no evidence for this whatsoever; Lapraik himself may have been "Happy Husband." Burns longed to make the acquaintance of the man who could compose such a song and was, he felt, a kindred spirit. He sent him a verse epistle suggesting a meeting at Mauchline Races or Mauchline Fair—or, at the very least, that Lapraik should write him a few lines in reply.

The **"Epistle to J. Lapraik"** is an important document because it is in some respects Burns's poetic manifesto, proclaiming the superiority of inspiration over the learned "Jargon o' your Schools," and the relevance (to Burns at least) of the vernacular tradition:

> Gie me ae spark o' Nature's fire,
> That's a' the learning I desire;
> Then, tho' I drudge thro' dub an' mire
>   At pleugh or cart,
> My Muse, tho' hamely in attire,
>   May touch the heart.
>
> O for a spunk o' Allan's glee,
> Or Fergusson's, the bauld an' slee,
> Or bright Lapraik's, my friend to be,
>   If I can hit it!
> That would be lear eneugh for me,
>   If I could get it.

Nevertheless, it should never be forgotten that this often-quoted statement expresses Burns in only one mood. In the very same poem in which the credo occurs, in a stanza already cited (Stanza IV), he mentions the greatest English poet of the century, and finds it not in the least incongruous to praise Lapraik by saying he thought that Pope, or else Beattie—a Scotsman who usually wrote in English—had composed "When I upon thy Bosom lean." What he implies in this epistle is simply that creative imitation of vernacular verse is the way for him (indeed, it is perhaps only one of several possible ways), and that Scots poetry is a worthy kind in its own right, though not to the exclusion of others which might, for all we know, be superior to anything in the northern tongue. The famous condemnation of the classically-educated pedants who go into college as "stirks" and come out "asses," and the claim that he himself has "to learning nae pretence," but relies entirely on inspiration—

> Whene'er my Muse does on me glance,
>   I jingle at her . . .

—all this is suspiciously like the disguise adopted in the prefaces to the Kilmarnock and Edinburgh Editions. But as a corrective to the self-portrait in these verses, one should remember the **"Elegy on the Death of Robert Ruisseaux,"** where he appears as a voracious reader, pleased above all else when praised for his learning:

> Tho' he was bred to kintra-wark,
> And counted was baith wight and stark,
> Yet that was never Robin's mark
>   To mak a man;
> But tell him, he was learned and clark,
>   Ye roos'd him then!

This Robert, too, is something of a *persona,* ironically ridiculing his own pretensions to learning; but both pictures—

the Child of Nature and the Eager Student—have their share of truth, for each reflects a characteristic mood.

The **"Epistle to J. Lapraik"** contains one of the most thorough-going condemnations of money-grubbing and selfish calculation in the whole of Burns:

> Awa ye selfish, warly race,
> Wha think that havins, sense, an' grace,
> Ev'n love an' friendship, should give place
>   To Catch-the-Plack!
> I dinna like to see your face,
>   Nor hear your crack.
>
> But ye whom social pleasure charms,
> Whose hearts the tide of kindness warms,
> Who hold your being on the terms,
>   'Each aid the others,'
> Come to my bowl, come to my arms,
>   My friends, my brothers!

Exactly as in the first **"Epistle to Davie,"** money-economy and the values of humanity are irreconcilable opposites; but in this poem the antithesis is much more completely realised, without abstraction and without sentimentality. Those who chase after the yellow dirt subordinate everything—brains, reason and the generous feelings—to a frenzied pursuit of wealth. They live separate and alone; they abstain from consumption (and therefore from pleasure) in order to save. Real men are the direct contrary of such caricatures of humanity; they co-operate with one another. Individualism is the supreme evil, and mutual aid the greatest good—surely a tremendous advance on the "tender feelings" of the **"Epistle to Davie."**

Even in this epistle, with its frank and unqualified homage to Ramsay and Fergusson, Burns modulates into something which on the printed page is indistinguishable from Standard English. The change of diction takes place right at the climax of the poem, in the twenty-first stanza; but the reader does not feel that the transition to "social pleasure" and the "tide of kindness" is in the least discordant. When one considers the whole context of the poem, it is evident that Burns can scarcely have regarded the passage as essentially un-Scottish: rather, as spoken by a Scot it is related to the early vernacular of the stanzas beginning

> What's a' your jargon o' your Schools . . .

as, in music, one key is to another.

The **"Second Epistle to J. Lapraik"** contains, in the sixth and seventh stanzas, one of the most astonishingly spontaneous outbursts in the whole of Burns:

> Sae I gat paper in a blink,
> An' down gaed stumpie in the ink:
> Quoth I: 'Before I sleep a wink,
>   I vow I'll close it:
> An' if ye winna mak it clink,
>   By Jove, I'll prose it!'
>
> Sae I've begun to scrawl, but whether
> In rhyme, or prose, or baith thegither,
> Or some hotch-potch that's rightly neither,
>   Let time mak proof;
> But I shall scribble down some blether
>   Just clean aff-loof.

Here Burns transcends both Scots and English tradition in order to make a statement that is above all personal—one man speaking to another in his own individual voice, with little thought of models.

Written only three weeks after the first, in content the **"Second Epistle"** strikes a completely new note. Fortune is still there in the background, but she is no longer all-powerful, as in **"Man was made to Mourn"**:

> Ne'er mind how Fortune waft an' warp;
>   She's but a bitch.

Though ultimate beggary is still a possibility, the dancing lines are radiant with a light-hearted comedy that takes away all terror from the prospect. The rich are no longer an undifferentiated mass, but particularised as two separate groups, the town merchants, and the country landlords, whom Burns specifically terms "feudal":

> Do ye envý the city gent,
> Behint a kist to lie an' sklent;
> Or purse-proud, big wi' cent. per cent.
>   An' muckle wame,
> In some bit brugh to represent
>   A bailie's name?
>
> Or is't the paughty feudal thane,
> Wi' ruffl'd sark an' glancing cane,
> Wha thinks himsel nae sheep-shank bane,
>   But lordly stalks;
> While caps an' bonnets aff are taen,
>   As by he walks?

Three weeks before, positive value had resided in sociability and co-operation; now (and this constitutes the innovation) it resides in a kind of individualism, which is however rather different from the individualism of calculating utilitarians soullessly planning their own advantage. The **"Second Epistle to Lapraik"** presses the claims of the free man, glorying in "wit an' sense," and, emancipated from the bonds of custom, turned adrift to fend for himself in a hostile Scotland. There is nothing to prevent this new and genuine individual from cooperating with others; he too is "social"—but he is a person first, a friend and reveller second. Whatever is of worth in this kind of man would be destroyed if either the "city gent" or the "feudal thane" were according to nature; but, mercifully, it is the rich who are twisted and distorted, while men like Burns and Lapraik are after nature's stamp:

> Were this the charter of our state,
> 'On pain o' hell be rich an' great,'
> Damnation then would be our fate,
>   Beyond remead;
> But, thanks to heaven, that's no the gate
>   We learn our creed.
>
> For thus the royal mandate ran,
> When first the human race began:
> 'The social, friendly, honest man,
>   Whate'er he be,
> 'Tis he fulfils great Nature's plan,
>   And none but he.'

In the sixteenth and seventeenth stanzas the isolated Individual, uncircumscribed, free as air, who can yet join together with others in "social glee," is identified with the archetypal figure of the Artist in a passage which makes amusing play with the doctrines of reincarnation. The poem ends with a hilarious vision of pie-in-the-sky for Lapraik and Burns, while all the moneyed classes are reduced to bestial shapes. Everything is bathed in a warm humorous glow—and yet the irreconcilable opposition between Art and Money, which was to take on almost tragic form in the nineteenth century, is already prefigured in the ending.

From the fourteenth stanza onwards, as he nears the end of the epistle, Burns once more modulates into Scots-English, without, however, leaving the vernacular completely behind; he retains the liberty to use words like "remead," or Scots "gate," or "neivefu'." I cannot agree that the final stanzas are greatly inferior to most of the earlier ones—that is, if the magnificent sixth and seventh stanzas are left entirely out of consideration. One has only to look at the texture of the verse to realise that Burns's mastery of sound-patterns has not deserted him in Anglo-Scots:

> Tho' here they scrape, an' squeeze, an' growl,
> Their worthless neivefu' of a soul
> May in some future carcase howl,
>   The forest's fright;
> Or in some day-detesting owl
>   May shun the light.

We are entitled to condemn the poem's ending only if we are prepared to reject all the English poetry of the mid-eighteenth century. If Burns thought that the translation of himself and Lapraik

> To reach their native, kindred skies,
> And sing their pleasures, hopes an' joys,
>   In some mild sphere

was the only possible artistic conclusion for the work, then he had no alternative but to employ Anglo-Scots; by itself, the vernacular did not have the resources to deal with such an abstract idea.

Like the first **"Epistle to Lapraik,"** the epistle **"To William Simpson of Ochiltree, May 1785,"** contains some lines which suggest that Burns was dreaming of publication nearly a year before he circulated his proposals for the Kilmarnock Edition. Simpson had written in praise of Burns's verse, to which he replied:

> My senses wad be in a creel,
> Should I but dare a hope to speel,
> Wi' Allan, or wi' Gilbertfield,
>   The braes o' fame;
> Or Fergusson, the writer-chiel,
>   A deathless name.

These lines exhibit, perhaps, the assumed modesty of a conventional disclaimer; one cannot reject the idea of becoming famous without at least having considered it as a possibility, and this in Burns's case surely implied a printed volume. As in the first **"Epistle to Lapraik"** he is anxious to place himself in the vernacular tradition, which (he now claims) the upper classes have tried to strangle; for that is surely the implication of his statement that a tenth of what the Edinburgh gentry were accustomed to waste at cards would have been sufficient to keep Fergusson from destitution. Verse-writing in Scots has, for Burns, an

essentially cathartic function—"It gies me ease," and is therefore a supremely natural activity. In the sixth, seventh, eighth and ninth stanzas, he relates his local patriotism to this general Lowland Scots tradition by stating his intention of making the rivers of Ayrshire as well-known as Forth and Tay, Yarrow and Tweed, so often mentioned in vernacular poetry; but he enumerates the streams of Ayrshire in the wider context of the whole of Western culture, indeed of the whole known world, as revealed by geographical exploration. Irwin, Lugar, Ayr and Doon are part of a complex which includes "Illissus, Tiber, Thames an' Seine," New Holland and the remotest seas:

> Or whare wild-meeting oceans boil
>   Besouth Magellan.

In the tenth stanza the poem moves from a level which is both local and international to one which is national and patriotic, by way of allusion to William Wallace, who often triumphed over the English on "Coila's plains an' fells." At this point, in the eleventh stanza, there occurs one of the most vivid and startling images in the whole of Burns, presented by means of a compound adjective:

> Oft have our fearless fathers strode
>   By Wallace' side,
> Still pressing onward, *red-wat-shod,*
>   Or glorious dy'd!

The next development is a return to the locality in order to describe its natural scenery, as a prelude to the introduction of something wider than either country or nation—Nature herself. The twelfth and thirteenth stanzas are as fine as any descriptive poetry written during the century:

> O, sweet are Coila's haughs an' woods,
> When lintwhites chant amang the buds,
> And jinkin hares, in amorous whids,
>   Their loves enjoy;
> While thro' the braes the cushat croods
>   With wailfu' cry!
>
> Ev'n winter bleak has charms to me,
> When winds rave thro' the naked tree;
> Or frosts on hills of Ochiltree
>   Are hoary gray;
> Or blinding drifts wild-furious flee,
>   Dark'ning the day!

The transition to Nature in general is made through the intermediary of the Man of Feeling. Nature has charms for "feeling, pensive hearts," and a poet ought to wander by himself, letting his emotions well up within him till they issue forth in "a heart-felt sang." The isolated individual of the **"Second Epistle to Lapraik"** is now viewed from another angle, in a mood which is far removed from even the joys of convivial drinking or friendly argument. Burns praises pensive pondering and the abjuration of rational thought, the sort of self-indulgent daydreaming condemned by Dr Johnson in the famous chapter on the dangerous prevalence of imagination in *Rasselas.* In complete contrast to Johnson, Burns here considers such sensuous mind-wandering to be an essential part of the poetical character. Nature contemplated in this way, has now become the antidote to Mammon, as Art fulfilled the same function in the **"Second Epistle to Lapraik"**:

BURNS

POETRY CRITICISM, Vol. 6

The warly race may drudge an' drive,
Hog-shouther, jundie, stretch, an' strive;
Let me fair Nature's face descrive,
    And I, wi' pleasure,
Shall let the busy, grumbling hive
    Bum owre their treasure.

It is a fine stanza, with its images of jostling animals and buzzing hoarding bees—the real conclusion of the poem. The next two stanzas are simply an easy fade-out, while the Postscript, with its fable of the Auld and New Lichts, serves to heighten still further the informality of the piece.

Each of the epistles so far examined counterpoises some positive value to the mechanical utilitarianism of philistine hucksters and canting hypocrites. The epistle **"To John Goldie, August 1785,"** which belongs rather with the ecclesiastical satires, sets the fellowship of the alehouse above that of the Church; a similar praise of alcohol is at the centre of the third epistle **"To J. Lapraik":**

But let the kirk-folk ring their bells!
Let's sing about our noble sel's:
We'll cry nae jads frae heathen hills
    To help or roose us,
But browster wives an' whisky stills—
    They are the Muses!

Though the second epistle **"To Davie"** is in some ways a disappointing performance—the second stanza in particular is almost as sickly-sentimental and falsely rustic as the productions of the nineteenth-century Kailyard school—it provides contemporary evidence of the tremendous energy expended by Burns (both in living and in writing) during his great creative period:

For me, I'm on Parnassus' brink,
Rivin the words to gar them clink;
Whyles daez't wi' love, whyles daez't wi' drink
    Wi' jads or Masons,
An' whyles, but ay owre late I think,
    Braw sober lessons.

In the following stanzas he holds fast once more to the convenient myth of the thoughtless, improvident "Bardie clan" who are constitutionally incapable of behaving like ordinary mortals, and again (as at the end of that far more successful work, the **"Second Epistle to Lapraik"**) he sees in poetry the one sure buckler in a hostile world. Even in a bad poem the same preoccupations recur, as they do in the rather bathetic conclusion, with its hint of the beggar theme at the very end:

Haud to the Muse, my dainty Davie:
The warl' may play you monie a shavie;
But for the Muse, she'll never leave ye,
    Tho' e'er sae puir;
Na, even tho' limpin wi' the spavie
    Frae door to door!

The **"Epistle to James Smith"** is generally preferred to the other verse epistles. It is certainly a remarkable work, overflowing with effortless spontaneity and bubbling humour. Written a little earlier than April 1786, just before Burns had definitely decided to bring out an edition, it shows him once again in the role of the completely uneducated poet:

Something cries, "Hoolie!
I red you, honest man, tak tent!
Ye'll shaw your folly. . . . "

How can such a man as he possibly hope for immortality when so many literate poets have faded from remembrance after their brief day of glory? Surely it would be safer to eschew print altogether, and remain simply an unknown bard who rhymes for fun. In the twelfth stanza, the ills of life, inevitable suffering and death, even the cosy retirement enjoyed by profiteers in their old age—all are viewed through a golden haze of humour and well-being:

This life, sae far 's I understand,
Is a' enchanted fairy-land,
Where Pleasure is the magic-wand,
    That, wielded right,
Maks hours like minutes, hand in hand,
    Dance by fu' light.

Not that he is utterly oblivious of Time's chariot. As with Marvell, "To his Coy Mistress," the injunction is to

. . . tear our Pleasures with rough strife,
Thorough the Iron gates of life.

In an equally vigorous image, Burns puts it in his own way:

Then top and maintop crowd the sail,
    Heave Care o'er-side!
And large, before Enjoyment's gale,
    Let's tak the tide.

He wants nothing from life except the opportunity to make poetry: the varied positives of the earlier epistles now give way to a single positive, an idea which unites poetry and "real, sterling wit." The worshippers of Mammon are now *identified* with the "unco guid," the main target of the ecclesiastical satires. Holy Willie and Cent.-per-Cent. are fundamentally one and the same:

O ye douce folk that live by rule,
Grave, tideless-blooded, calm an' cool,
Compar'd wi' you—O fool! fool! fool!
    How much unlike!
Your hearts are just a standing pool,
    Your lives a dyke!

Nae hair-brained, sentimental traces
In your unletter'd, nameless faces!
In *arioso* trills and graces
    Ye never stray,
But *gravissímo,* solemn basses
    Ye hum away.

Ye are sae grave, nae doubt ye're wise;
Nae ferly tho' ye do despise
The hairum-scairum, ram-stam boys,
    The rattling squad:
I see ye upward cast your eyes—
    Ye ken the road!

I suppose the modern equivalents of the "rattling squad" are the juvenile delinquents, teddy-boys, rock-and-roll fiends, and all rebels with or without a cause. Translated into these terms, the **"Epistle to James Smith"** states that the iconoclastic young (not the angry young men of the middle classes, but those who make the street and the milk-bar their *rendez-vous*) represent Life and Libido and the Horn of Plenty, while the ordinary suburbanite wor-shipper of the god in the garage stands for death, debility, and the crucifixion of essential humanity. It is an opposi-tion of this sort which lies at the heart of the **"Epistle to James Smith,"** and indeed at the centre of Burns's own soul. On the one hand, the peasantry's old, half-pagan lust for life, survivals of which take on somewhat distorted shapes in twentieth-century dormitory towns; on the other, puritanism, rationality, calculation, and control. During these two momentous years especially, Burns him-self was one of the "hairum-scairum, ram-stam boys." But he was also the man who preached Common-sense, whose favourite quotation was:

> on reason build resolve,
> (That column of true majesty in man) . . .

This other side of Burns—Burns the Champion of Society, paying his tribute to all the established virtues like any company-director, executive or racing reporter after a spree—is exhibited in the last of the early epistles, the **"Epistle to a Young Friend"** of May 1786, composed at the very height of the Armour crisis, when he was also (so it would seem) deeply involved with Mary Campbell. He advises his young friend to keep to the path of convention-al virtue:

> The sacred lowe o' weel-plac'd love,
>   Luxuriantly indulge it;
> But never tempt th' illicit rove,
>   Tho' naething should divulge it:
> I waive the quantum o' the sin,
>   The hazard of concealing;
> But, och! it hardens a' within,
>   And petrifies the feeling!

Amusingly enough, the young man is given a homily on the value of thrift—provided that he does not use his sav-ings to lord it ostentatiously over others:

> To catch Dame Fortune's golden smile,
>   Assiduous wait upon her;
> And gather gear by ev'ry wile
>   That's justify'd by honor:
> Not for to hide it in a hedge,
>   Nor for a train-attendant;
> But for the glorious privilege
>   Of being independent.

This is indeed the morality of small farmers and petty traders! Established ethics, the maxims which his own fa-ther taught him, are of inestimable value in life; the only trouble with them is that they are so difficult to put into practice:

> And may ye better reck the rede,
>   Than ever did th' adviser!

Into this *pot-pourri* of all the bourgeois virtues—complete with

> An atheist-laugh's a poor exchange
>   For Deity offended!

—Burns intrudes the concept of personal honour, perhaps in the last resort derived from clan morality. Most signifi-cantly, he sets it side by side with the Calvinists' fear of

Hell, so that the one doctrine appears as the negation of the other:

> The fear o' Hell's a hangman's whip
>   To haud the wretch in order;
> But where ye feel your honour grip,
>   Let that ay be your border. . . .

A good way of appreciating the variety of Burns's moods is to place the **"Epistle to James Smith"** side-by-side with the **"Epistle to a Young Friend."** The latter is as much a fruit of experience as the former; it has taken some of its colouring from the remorseful mood of the fifth stanza of **"Despondency, an Ode":**

> O enviable early days,
> When dancing thoughtless pleasure's maze,
>   To care, to guilt unknown!
> How ill exchang'd for riper times,
> To feel the follies or the crimes
>   Of others, or my own!

The man who takes the tide before "enjoyment's gale" is liable to find that his fairyland turns into a desert because his actions have caused suffering to others; as Burns re-marks at the end of the second stanza of the ode the life of ordinary mortals striving for worldly success may have its compensations after all:

> You, bustling and justling,
>   Forget each grief and pain;
> I, listless yet restless,
>   Find ev'ry prospect vain.

Burns on religion:

As the grand end of human life is to cultivate an intercourse with that BEING to whom we owe life, with every enjoyment that renders life delightful; and to maintain an integritive conduct towards our fellow-creatures; that so, by forming piety and virtue into habit, we may be fit members for that society of the pious and the good which reason and revela-tion teach us to expect beyond the grave, I do not see that the turn of mind and pursuits of such an one . . . who spends the hours and thoughts which the vocations of the day can spare with Ossian, Shakspeare, Thomson, Shen-stone, Sterne, etc.; or, as the maggot takes him, a gun, a fid-dle, or a song to make or mend; and at all times some heart's-dear bonnie lass in view—I say I do not see that the turn of mind and pursuits of such an one are in the least more inimical to the sacred interests of piety and virtue, than the even lawful bustling and straining after the world's riches and honours: and I do not see but he may gain heaven as well—which, by the by, is no mean consideration—who steals through the vale of life, amusing himself with every little flower that fortune throws in his way, as he who, straining straight forward, and perhaps bespattering all about him, gains some of life's little eminences, where, after all, he can only see and be seen a little more conspicuously than what, in the pride of his heart, he is apt to term the poor, indolent devil he has left behind him.

Robert Burns in his Commonplace Book, *reprinted by J. G. Lockhart in his* Life of Robert Burns, *1828.*

However, it would be wrong to represent this last position as final; like the others, it is the reflexion of a mood. The self-dramatisations of the epistles express a mind in motion, giving itself over at different times to *conflicting* principles and feelings; they mirror that mind as it grappled with a complex world. In order to body it forth, Burns had to be, in himself, and not simply in play, both Calvinist and anti-Calvinist, both fornicator and champion of chastity, both Jacobite and Jacobin, both local and national, both British and European, both anarchist and sober calculator, both philistine and anti-philistine. He had to write in both Braid Scots and Scots-English and in a blend of the two, being at one and the same time a man of the old homely Scotland of village communities, a forerunner of the Scotland of capitalist farmers employing wage-labour and the new agricultural implements, and a poet who shared—even before he went to Edinburgh—something of the Anglo-Scottish culture of the capital. The occasional and informal nature of the epistle was ideal for the expression of a plethora of moods together with the transitions between them; consequently, Burns's experiments with the *genre* contain much of his finest work. (pp. 82-104)

> *Thomas Crawford, in his* Burns: A Study of the Poems and Songs, *Oliver and Boyd, 1960, 400 p.*

David Daiches (essay date 1963)

[*Daiches is a prominent English scholar and critic who has written extensively on English and American literature. He is especially renowned for his in-depth studies of such writers as Robert Burns, Robert Louis Stevenson, and Virginia Woolf. His criticism in general is best characterized as receptive and attached to no single methodology. In the following excerpt, he provides an overview of Burns's poetry and songs.*]

Robert Burns is not merely the national poet of Scotland; he is a world-wide symbol, a universal excuse for celebration and sentimentality. Further, the Burns cult developed soon after the poet's death and has been maintained at a steady level of irrational enthusiasm ever since. It is a cult participated in by people who do not normally have any interest in poetry and indeed by not a few who do not even read Burns's poetry but who cherish his memory, adore his furniture, his snuffbox, his masonic apron, and his wife's pinkie-ring, memorize the names of the girls he made love to, and fiercely challenge anybody who denies that Burns was the greatest poet who ever lived anywhere in the world. Who was Burns and what was his relation to the Scotland of his day? What kinds of poems did he write and how good are they and why? What is there about his character and achievement that can throw light on the way in which he is remembered and celebrated? (p. 323)

[Robert Burns] was the proud and ambitious son of a struggling Scottish tenant farmer, born into a Scotland whose culture was deeply divided between a superficial genteel tradition and a half submerged and attenuated national tradition, who captured an audience for his Scots poetry among the educated classes of his day by cashing

in on contemporary interest in the primitive sources of poetry and the virtues of the "natural man," and who in considerable degree, but not wholly or consistently, resisted the demands of that audience that he should play up to their sentimental expectations of the ideal peasant poet. The sources on which he drew were the oral folk tradition of his own people, such older Scottish poetry (and it was a fairly small segment) as was available to him in contemporary collections, the Scottish poems of Ramsay and Fergusson, and a variety of anthologies of songs and ballads, all this stiffened by a sense of craftsmanship he learned partly from his study of older English poetry and intermittently threatened by his immersion in the late eighteenth-century sentimental movement.

Though Burns began his poetic career as a song writer (under the joint influence of love, music, and the desire to emulate the son of a local laird who had written a song for *his* girl), it was in the latter part of his life that he wrote most of his songs: his earliest real successes were satirical poems dealing with local church politics, poems projecting with vivid particularization aspects of experience in a farming community, and verse epistles, a traditional Scottish form in which Burns rapidly acquired remarkable skill. His satirical poems—**"The Holy Fair," "Holy Willie's Prayer," "The Ordination,"** among others—show a high technical virtuosity and indicate that Burns had learned his trade from a variety of sources both Scottish and English. Most of them derive from his taking sides with those who believed that the essence of religion was a good heart, against the extreme Calvinists who stressed original sin, the inability of good works to save man, the predestined damnation of the vast majority of all men as a result of Adam's fall and the similarly predestined salvation of a tiny minority not through any virtuous acts of their own but through the arbitrary bestowal of God's grace. **"Holy Willie's Prayer"** is a dramatic monologue in which the speaker all unconsciously damns the creed he professes by revealing the sanctimoniousness and hypocrisy that it inevitably breeds: it is one of the great verse satires of all time. **"The Holy Fair"** gives an account, in an old Scottish stanza-form, of an outdoor communion celebration, then a feature of Scottish religious life, mischievously using accepted biblical and religious phraseology to stress the contrast between what really goes on and what is supposed to go on. The whole thing is done in a mood not of bitterness but of joyful exposure of the indomitable claims of the flesh. The brilliance of the ambiguous imagery, the adroit intermingling of the carnal and the spiritual meanings of the same word, the variations of tempo and the manipulation of levels of suggestiveness show a high art: here is no spontaneous bubbling-up of simple peasant emotion but a conscious use of the multiple resources of a complex verse form. On a simpler level, but in its own way equally impressive, is such a poem as **"To a Louse,"** where with affectionately ironic humor Burns reduces to her proper size the proud country lass, masquerading as a fine lady in church because of her new bonnet, by the way he contemplates the louse crawling on the bonnet, visible to the poet as he sits behind her though unknown to the girl herself. It is a perfect little poem, dealing with loving particularization with an aspect of a subject that is the theme of many of Burns's poems, especially of his satires—the relation between appearance and reality, between what is pretended and what really is.

Burns's greatest poetic achievement is his satires. These show a command of a greater variety of poetic skills, a subtler and more complex use of the medium of poetry, than any other kind of poetry he wrote. They are not, however, the poems quoted by orators at Burns suppers. Indeed, such orators generally quote the worst of Burns, the platitudinous or sentimental or jingling or crudely rhetorical Burns. Another important group are his verse letters. This is not a kind of poetry that has ever been popular in England. But in Scotland it had been a tradition since the beginning of the eighteenth century, and Burns learned of the tradition from Ramsay. It represented a handling of language peculiarly suited to his genius, counterpointing the formal and colloquial, moving out from the carefully localized picture of the poet in a specific time and place to his reflections as they arise naturally from the given situation to a progressively widening circle of comment that culminates in a series of clinching epigrams before the poet returns to himself and his correspondent to sign off in an adroitly turned conclusion. These verse letters show remarkable skill in combining a colloquial ease with a formal pattern in such a way that each brings out new significance in the other.

To Burns the satirist and Burns the writer of masterly verse letters I would add Burns the narrative poet. Even though he wrote only one narrative poem, **"Tam o' Shanter,"** it is enough to enable us to list narrative poetry among his claims to high poetic distinction. This rendering in octosyllabic couplets of a local folk story is a triumph of *pace;* the variations in tempo are handled with the utmost adroitness to achieve not only a narrative style that follows the curve of the action most cunningly but also a wealth of humorously ironic comment on human frailty and human imagination. The opening sets the scene in the local pub where the hero sits happily boozing in a cosy interior while outside the storm rises. This contrast between the cosy interior and the harsh weather outside is an old tradition in Scottish poetry: it can be found as far back as the opening of Henryson's *Testament of Crisseid,* perhaps the first medieval narrative poem to tell the truth about the weather in these islands. . . . Tam's climax of conviviality is soon reached, and splendidly described. There follows a mock-serious passage in pulpit-English describing the evanescence of pleasure, culminating in a sudden switch back to Scots, this time in a tone of homely proverbial wisdom. Then comes the description of the storm, growing ever more rapid in movement until it has reached the point at which the name of the Devil can be appropriately introduced. The superstitious and drunken imagination of Tam is built up by a remarkable progression of comically horrible images until at last he reaches Alloway Kirk, sees the Devil and the dance of the witches, and, his fancy caught by a "winsome wench and wawlie" dancing in a particularly short shift, he calls out to her in approval and thus betrays his presence. In a flash the witches are after him, and he gallops madly along on his faithful mare Maggie. It looks as though the end has come. But Maggie escapes by crossing a running stream (which witches cannot cross) just as the leader is on her. Her tail,

however, has been seized and plucked off. Tam arrives home with a tailless mare. The poem ends with a mock-solemn warning against drink and girls, in language that is a parody of Scottish pulpit moralizing. The whole story can of course be explained by the fact that Tam was drunk and only imagined the witches. But how do we explain Maggie's loss of her tail? Every incident *except one* can be rationally explained. This is a formula for supernatural tales told to a modern skeptical audience that has been followed ever since, notably in Scott's "Wandering Willie's Tale."

So I think we can grant Burns's skill as a narrative poet even though we have only one example to judge by. **"Tam o' Shanter"** was written in 1790 when Burns was combining farming at Ellisland with his duties as a recently appointed excise officer. He had returned reluctantly to

Manuscript page of Burns's "The Jolly Beggars; or, Love and Liberty: A Cantata."

farming after his prolonged visit to Edinburgh—reluctantly, because he knew from experience that the back-breaking work and economic risks of farming at that time would seriously cut down his opportunities of writing poetry. He wanted some sort of government job to enable him to have the leisure for writing and the opportunity for meeting and talking with interesting people that were so important for him. Even after he gave up his farm and settled in Dumfries as a full-time exciseman, he never had the leisure a poet really requires. **"Tam o' Shanter"** makes us realize what Burns might have done had he had time and opportunity to cultivate all his poetic faculties properly. One single poem in a vein of which he was clearly a past master—it is a tantalizing glimpse of what we might have had if Burns had had health, leisure, and a more congenial environment for poetic creation.

By a more congenial environment, I do not simply mean more educated friends, though it is true that Burns was hampered by the fact that the people he could talk to as intellectual equals (and he found few if any) tended to patronize him socially. I mean a society that did not condemn him to be a performing peasant poet as an illustration of primitivist theories of poetry. . . . Burns's admirers did him harm, or did their unconscious best to do so. Though Burns resisted the advice that many of them gave him to abandon the Scottish tradition in language and form, he was often content to give them the kind of attitudinizing they wanted. His duty poem in praise of Edinburgh, **"Edina, Scotia's Darling Seat!"** is a shocking bad performance in a neo-classic English idiom that he was never really able to handle, though some aspects of eighteenth-century English poetic idiom he could use with real skill. If we want to see the real Burns side by side with the bogus Burns, we have only to set **"To a Mouse"** beside **"To a Mountain Daisy."** The former recognizes with wry humor the fellow feeling that joins the poet and the little creature and skillfully turns the theme round at the end to project his own unhappy situation. The unsentimental use of diminutives to strengthen the note of friendly concern ("Thy wee-bit housie, too, in ruin!"), the effective introduction of a rustic proverbial idiom that both bridges the worlds of mice and men and sounds an appealing note of rueful wisdom ("The best-laid schemes o' Mice an' Men, / Gang aft a-gley"), the mastery of tone and movement throughout—these show Burns working with a fine assurance in a medium of which he was complete master. But **"To a Mountain Daisy"** is an exercise in sentimental attitudinizing for the benefit of the tender feelings of his genteel readers. The poetic device known as the pathetic fallacy—the attribution of human thought and feeling to an inanimate object—is a dangerous one at best, and Burns's use of it here, in addressing the daisy, is clumsy and histrionic. In particular, the comparison of the daisy to a country maid betrayed by a rustic seducer—the betrayed maiden is a standard property in sentimental fiction of the period—is grotesquely inappropriate. We know that Burns was attitudinizing when he wrote this poem. He enclosed a copy in a letter to a friend with the remark: "I am a good deal pleased with some sentiments myself, as they are just the native querulous feelings of a heart which, as the elegantly melting Gray says, 'Melancholy has marked for her own.' "

We can see similar defects in parts of **"The Cotter's Saturday Night,"** an attempt to improve on Robert Fergusson's poem on the same theme, "The Farmer's Ingle." But Fergusson's poem remains the more successful, a shrewdly affectionate account of an evening in a farm kitchen set against a sense of the underlying rhythm of the seasons and of agricultural labor. Burns opens the **"Cotter"** with a monstrous stanza addressed to the prosperous Ayr lawyer Bob Aiken: "My lov'd, my honor'd much respected friend!" And the stanza ends with the suggestion that this bustling and prosperous townsman would be happier in a humble rustic cottage than in his comfortable house in Ayr:

> What Aiken in a Cottage would have been;
> Ah! tho' his worth unknown, far happier there,
> I ween!

This is sentimental nonsense, and Burns knew it; even the verse echoes dully and mechanically to such forced sentiments. The real opening of the poem is the fine second stanza, setting the time and place with an intimate sense of the quality of living that is involved here, and adding just a suggestion of controlled melancholy in the observation of rustic rest after rustic toil that he got from Gray's *Elegy*. There are other stanzas equally fine; but at intervals Burns the professional sentimentalist showing off his ideal rustics to a genteel Edinburgh audience steps in and wrecks the poem.

I am not maintaining that Burns wrote good poems only when he wrote in Scots and not in English. Many of his finest poems are in an English tipped with Scots, and many of his best songs contain only an occasional Scots word. The linguistic situation in Burns's Scotland was so confused that only by creating a synthetic language of his own, out of his native spoken dialect, standard southern English, and Scots of other times and regions, could Burns have achieved any flexibility in operation at all: this language was in the nature of things neither consistent nor arbitrary, but varied according to the demands of particular kinds of poetic situations. I *am* maintaining, however, that when Burns kept his eye on the literary fashions of educated Scotsmen of his day and wrote for the taste of the literati instead of in one of the ways that he knew suited his own genius, his poetry is generally bad. And there is no doubt that in English literature of his own time his taste was very uncertain. But he was not alone in that. He learned much, however, from English poetry, whose influence we can trace in his work in all sorts of ways. He used what he learned, of course, for his purposes in his own way, sometimes, for example, transforming an elegant piece of Augustan wit into the idiom of Scottish folk song. In the Second Epistle of Pope's "Moral Essays" occur the lines

> Heaven, when it strives to polish all it can
> Its last best work, but forms a softer Man.

Burns gave this thought a completely different kind of expression in the last stanza of **"Green grow the rashes O":**

> Auld Nature swears, the lively Dears
> Her noblest work she classes, O:
> Her prentice han' she try'd on man,

An' then she made the lasses, O.

I have claimed Burns as a great poet in virtue of his satires, his verse letters, and his one narrative poem. There remain, of course, his songs. In April 1787, Burns met in Edinburgh James Johnson, a self-educated lover of Scottish songs, who had invented a cheap process for printing by using stamped pewter plates, a combination that led him to project a series of volumes of songs. He enlisted Burns's assistance, and gradually, as Burns became more and more the dominant partner in the project, the original character of the enterprise changed: it became a vast six-volume anthology of Scottish songs, old and new. Later, Burns was approached by George Thomson, a more educated and genteel publisher of Scottish songs, for help in *his* collection. Burns responded to both requests avidly, with the result that the great majority of his own songs were written for and first appeared in either Johnson's *Scots Musical Museum* or Thomson's *Select Scottish Airs.* It is important to understand exactly what Burns did for Scottish song. He found Scottish folk song in a confused and fragmentary state. The decay of the courtly musical tradition after 1603, Presbyterian disapproval of popular secular song, and indeed the whole confused condition of Scottish culture all contributed to this. Scottish airs had been popular since the latter part of the seventeenth century, and many collections of Scottish songs and song tunes appeared both in Edinburgh and London in the eighteenth century. But the great majority of older songs survived only in fragments, as an odd chorus or a few garbled lines. One of the favorite sports of Scottish ladies and gentlemen of the period was writing new words to old airs, and these words were generally frigid and derivative. Burns's aim was to recover as many airs and sets of words as he could and, where the existing words were fragmentary or impossibly coarse or equally impossibly genteel, to re-create the song in the true spirit of the folk tradition. It was a staggering program, nothing less than the single-handed recreation of the whole body of Scottish folk song. Further, Burns undertook to provide words to tunes which, though they may originally have had words, now existed only as dance tunes. He was anxious that all Scotland should be represented, and in his journeys in Scotland scrupulously collected such songs and fragments as he could find, to rework them into complete songs. . . . If Burns had not been uncannily in tune with the folk spirit in Scottish song, he would be execrated today for having spoiled the original fragments by bogus improvements. But in fact he did not spoil them; he saved them from total corruption and disappearance and gave them new life and meaning and popularity.

The greater part of Burns's poetic activity in the last years of his life was taken up with these songs. He collected, revised, completed, rewrote, and re-created hundreds of songs, devoting an immense amount of energy to the task and refusing all payment from Johnson or Thomson, declaring that he did it for Scotland's sake. And this was no theatrical gesture: it was true. He regarded this vast work as a contribution to the preservation and renewal of his country's culture. The amount of work he did on a particular song would vary in accordance with the state of the original and the amount of time at his disposal. If only a chorus or a few fragments of verse survived, he might substantially rewrite the whole song. Often the first verse and the chorus survived, and Burns provided more verses. Sometimes he rewrote an old bawdy song as a tender and passionate love song or, as in the case of "John Anderson My Jo," as a poem of married affection. On many occasions, he took a popular dance tune, slowed down the tempo to bring out musical qualities obscured by the fast dancing pace, and wrote a song for it. Burns, though no singer, had an acute ear for melody and a genius for fitting words to music such as few poets have possessed. His correspondence with Thomson about the words and the music of the songs he sent him is full of technical discussions of prosody and of musical rhythm and time.

Burns wrote all his songs to known tunes, sometimes writing several sets of words to the same air in an endeavor to find the most apt poem for a given melody. Roughly speaking, we can divide Burns's songs into three categories: those he rewrote from old fragments, completely new songs he wrote to old tunes, and new songs he wrote for dance tunes which, though they may originally have been song tunes, did not exist as such in Burns's day. But the categories are not always separate and sometimes fade into one another. Many songs that we know from a variety of evidence must have been substantially written by Burns he never claimed as his. He never claimed **"Auld Lang Syne,"** for example, which he described simply as an old fragment he had discovered, but the song as we have it is almost certainly his, though the chorus and probably the first stanza are old. . . . Many of the songs are extremely slight and trivial. But many others are splendid examples of the embodiment of passionate experience in art.

It is the uncanny ability to speak with the great anonymous voice of the Scottish people that must be part of the explanation for the special feeling Burns arouses. But his songs are not all in a simple folk idiom, though most of them have that air of simplicity (whatever the subtleties below the surface) so necessary to a sung poem. There is the symbolic color and imagery of **"Open the Door to Me Oh!"** which so impressed W. B. Yeats:

> The wan moon is setting ayont the white wave,
>   And time is setting with me, oh!

There is that wonderful mixture of tenderness and swagger—so characteristic of the male in love—in **"A Red, Red Rose,"** Burns's rewriting of an old fragment. There is the magnificent abandonment to the moment of experience in **"Yestreen I Had a Pint o' Wine":**

> The kirk and state may gae to hell,
>   And I'll gae to my Anna.

There is the controlled historical melancholy of the Jacobite songs, where Burns gives this romantic lost cause a new meaning in terms of human emotion:

> Now a' is done that men can do,
>   And a' is done in vain:
> My Love and Native Land farweel,
>   For I maun cross the main, my dear,
>   For I maun cross the main.

There is that splendid drinking song, **"Willie Brew'd a Peck o' Maut,"** with its rollicking chorus:

> We are na fou, We're nae that fou,
> But just a drappie in our e'e, . . .

There is a wonderful counterpointing of folk feeling and high ceremony, of simple emotion and pageantry, in **"Go, Fetch to Me a Pint o' Wine,"** where the whole atmosphere of medieval romance and ballad is concentrated in two stanzas. There is the magical tenderness of **"O Lay Thy Loof in Mine, Lass"**—though here I would particularly emphasize the importance of taking the words with the tune: it is the tune that lights up the words. There is the lilting love song he composed to one of his wife's favorite airs, **"The Posie"**:

> O Luve will venture in, where it daurna weel be
>   seen,
> O luve will venture in, where wisdom ance has
>   been. . . .

(Again, it is lost without the music.) There is that sprightly piece of ironic self-compliment, **"There Was a Lad Was Born in Kyle."** There is the moving benedictory cadence, so perfectly wrought together with the music, in **"Ca' the Yowes to the Knowes"**:

> Ghaist nor bogle shalt thou fear;
> Thou'rt to love and Heaven sae dear,
> Nocht of ill may come thee near,
>   My bonnie dearie.

A final word on Burns as a man. He was a man of great intellectual energy and force of character who in a class-ridden society never found an environment in which he could fully exercise his personality. After his death, the lively literary lady Maria Riddell wrote a character sketch of him in the *Dumfries Journal* in which she said that his powers of conversation, his impromptu wit, his ability to grasp new ideas, his intolerance of stupidity and arrogance, his capacity for devastating ironic comment, were in her opinion even more impressive than his poetry. "I believe no man was ever gifted with a larger portion of the *vivida vis animi,*" she wrote. But it was not only the class structure of his society, which led to his being alternately patronized and sentimentalized over, that constricted him. Coming to Edinburgh between the age of Hume and the age of Scott, Burns found no one really worthy of his mettle. The problem was, however, more than one of personalities. The only substitute for the rejected Calvinism available to Burns in the Scotland of his day was a sentimental Deism, a facile belief in the good heart as all, which though also part of late eighteenth-century English culture, was in England likely to be involved with other and more profound currents of thought. Let us be clear on one point. In spite of the annual Burns orators, the truth is that Burns in his adult life was not a Christian. He was in a vague sort of way a Deist, who believed in a benevolent designer of the universe and who believed in good-heartedness, generosity, and openness as the supreme virtues. He was also an egalitarian in politics, a sympathizer with the French Revolution, and an unremitting opponent of the class system of his time. He was at the same time a shrewd and penetrating observer of contemporary politics and of human psychology as he found it in the ladies and gentlemen who entertained and patronized him. As for his famous amours, the fact here is that Burns was unable to be on terms of sexual equality with his intellectual equals (or near-equals): the result was that he could only flirt with the well-born ladies, while he sought physical satisfaction with country lasses. His sex life is part of the schizophrenia of the Scottish culture of his time and of the split personality that this forced on him.

I have tried to answer the questions I began with. Who was Burns and what was his relation to the Scotland of his day? What kind of poems did he write and how good are they and why? It remains for me to try and relate what I have said to the Burns cult, which I began by referring to. How can this be explained? I think, very roughly, there are three reasons for the Burns cult. One is the fact that Burns was a humble peasant who stood up for human worth regardless of rank or possessions: he is the most spectacular example in our literature of a humble rustic who really made good in the literary world. Another is that in his songs he identified himself with the folk tradition and spoke with moving authenticity for the daily experiences of men and women as they are encountered in ordinary life. The third reason, which is bound up with the second, is his ability to speak for man's "unofficial self," his total lack—in his best and most characteristic poems—of any idealizing haze or of anything that the reader not professionally interested in literature might regard as pretentious expansion of significance. His love songs are worlds apart from say, Shelley's *Epipsychidion,* and Shelley is not a poet normally celebrated in country pubs or city clubs. I am not now talking of degrees of poetic merit, but differences in poetic *kind.* The odd thing is that in spite of the fact that the popular feeling about Burns—on which, after all, the Burns cult is based—derives from a true insight into the nature of one side at least of his poetry, the kind of thing spouted annually at Burns suppers does not: it derives from and seeks inspiration in the sentimental-rhetorical Burns, who is not the real Burns at all. (pp. 329-39)

Soon after Burns's death, the Industrial Revolution changed the face of much of the part of Scotland he knew best, and later generations looked back from black cities and slag heaps to Burns and saw him through the mists of nostalgia for a lost rustic way of life as the singer of a sentimentalized countryside, the "wee hoose amang the heather" sort of thing. This vulgarization of Burns in the nineteenth century led to his having a bad influence on subsequent Scottish poetry. But that was not Burns's fault. And if we go back, not to what is said about his poetry, but to the poems themselves, especially the great satires, the verse letters, **"Tam o' Shanter,"** and the songs, we shall hear that disturbingly human voice, in mockery, in gaiety, or in passion, laying bare the essence of *la condition humaine* as it is known to daily living. It is a voice that compels assent; and we respond, as Joyce's Molly Bloom responded to life at the end of *Ulysses,* with acquiescence and affirmation: "Yes," we say, "Yes . . . yes." (p. 340)

David Daiches, "The Identity of Burns," in Restoration and Eighteenth-Century Literature: Essays in Honor of Alan Dugald McKillop, *edited by Carroll Camden, The University of Chicago Press, 1963, pp. 323-40.*

Raymond Bentman   (essay date 1965)

[*Bentman has written several essays on Burns. In the following excerpt, he investigates Burns's use of Scottish and English words in his poetry and lyrics in order to refute the commonly held view that Burns wrote in the same manner that he spoke.*]

Scottish and English are so closely related that they are little more than different dialects of the same language. It is often difficult to distinguish between them. But in Burns's poetry the distinction between "Scottish" and "English" is inaccurate and misleading. Burns wrote some poems in pure English, most of them in neoclassic style, but he wrote no poems in pure vernacular Scottish. The "Scottish" poems are written in a literary language, which was mostly, although not entirely English, in grammar and syntax, and, in varying proportions, both Scottish and English in vocabulary. "Scots wha hae," as Sir James A. H. Murray points out, "is fancy Scotch." Spoken vernacular Scottish would be "Scots at haes." [*The Dialect of the Southern Counties of Scotland,* 1873]

These mixed poems, which I call the "vernacular" poems, vary from poems like **"Halloween,"** parts of which are difficult to understand without a glossary, to songs like **"Sweet Afton"** or **"A Red, Red Rose,"** which differ from English in only a few words. Throughout the vernacular poems Burns interchanges, arbitrarily, the grammatical suffixes "an," "in," "in'," and "ing." Franklyn Bliss Snyder points out [in "Notes on Burns's First Volume," *Modern Philology* (1919)] that even in the 1786 Kilmarnock Edition, where the Scottish endings are most frequent, they are concentrated in a few poems and are neither uniform nor predominant in those. Burns denotes the past indicative and past participle at times by the Scottish suffix "it" and at times by the English "ed." He interchanges the Scottish forms "keepit" and "foughten" with the English "kept" and "fought." He employs the relative pronouns "wha," "whase," and "wham" and the interrogative "wham," none of which exist in spoken Scottish. He even changes some of the sources to make them closer to English grammar. He changes "Green grows the rashes" to "Green grow the rashes" which is grammatical English but ungrammatical Scottish—in the present tense of the verb the Scottish uses an "s" suffix for the plural unless the proper personal pronoun immediately precedes: "they grow" but "the rashes grows" and "green grows the rashes."

In spite of the evidence of Sir James Murray and of all other philologists who have written on the subject, the belief persists that Burns wrote as he spoke. I have heard this belief expressed by many literary scholars; and it has been written, since Murray's monograph, by Robert Louis Stevenson ["Some Aspects of Poetry," *The Cornhill Magazine* (1879)], Matthew Arnold ["General Introduction," *The English Poets,* 1880], William Ernest Henley ["Life: Genius: Achievement," *The Poetry of Robert Burns,* Vol. IV, 1896-97], and recently by John Speirs—to mention

only a few. Speirs's beliefs are typical: "Poetry made, as are these poems, out of a spoken language . . . is almost necessarily counter to pretension and affectation both literary and moral" ["Burns and English Literature," *From Blake to Byron: The Pelican Guide to English Literature,* Vol. V, 1957]. While the advocates of this belief seem to rely mostly on their feelings to establish linguistic details, they do present some evidence from Burns's prose statements, usually one comment: "I have not that command of the language [English] that I have of my native tongue.—In fact, I think my ideas are more barren in English than in Scotish."

Other prose comments of Burns's, if looked at with sufficient haste, may also be made to say that he claimed to be writing in Scottish. In the Preface to the Kilmarnock Edition he says of himself: "Unacquainted with the necessary requisites for commencing Poet by rule, he sings the sentiments and manners he felt and saw in himself and his rustic compeers around him, in his and their native language." But other prose comments are in direct contradiction. In his correspondence with the song editors James Johnson and George Thomson he constantly makes such remarks as:

> The sprinkling of Scotch in it, while it is but a sprinkling, gives it an air of rustic naïveté, which time will rather increase than diminish.

> I will vamp up the old Song, & make it English enough to be understood.

> I could easily throw this into an English mould; but to my taste, in the simple & tender of the Pastoral song, a sprinkling of the old Scotish, has an inimitable effect.

> I have sprinkled it with the Scots dialect.

> If you are for *English* verses, there is, on my part, an end of the matter.—Whether in the simplicity of the *Ballad,* or the pathos of *the Song,* I can only hope to please myself in being allowed at least a sprinkling of our native tongue.

A "sprinkling" accurately describes his changes. In **"Wha Is That at My Bower Door,"** based on an older Scottish song in English, "Who But I, Quoth Finlay," he changes "come no further" to "gae your gate," "who" to "wha," and "quoth" to "quo'." Often he simply drops the final "g" of an "ing" ending, or makes minor spelling changes like "summer" to "simmer," "good" to "guid," or "oft" to "aft." At other times he interchanges a few words which do not alter the meaning in context, as "then" to "syne" and "one" to "ae."

Why Burns referred to his "native language" when he meant a "sprinkling" can be speculated upon: an attempt, also in the epistles, to create an elaborate *persona* for the Kilmarnock volume, much as Housman did later in *A Shropshire Lad;* a cynical attempt to attract attention from the sentimental admirer of the heaven-taught plowman; a self-delusion; too great a reliance on Ramsay's confused theories, which were in turn part of certain confusions in other British Augustan theories; or an ambiguity in terms, similar to the ambiguity which often causes a misreading of Wordsworth's theories of poetic diction.

Many modern biographers and critics agree that Burns did not write in vernacular Scottish but offer little concrete explanation of his contradictory statements or his artificial language. Burns was most probably following, for personal and nationalistic reasons, the tradition established partly by Ramsay and Fergusson and partly by older Scottish writers. But great poets use traditions; they are not enslaved by them. Any evaluation of Burns's ability as a poet and of his place in the trends of British poetry must take into large account his use or misuse of the tradition he follows.

Burns shows little compunction about interchanging Scottish and English words to fit his needs. He uses "sword" in both neoclassic and vernacular poems, but "glaive" once when it rhymes with "save" (**"When Guilford Good"**). He uses "Gizz" once (**"Address to the Deil"** and "wig" twice (**"To John Goldie"** and **"The Kirk's Alarm"**) always in vernacular poems and always to facilitate the rhyme. "Hawk" is the usual word in both neoclassic and vernacular poems, except where "gled" rhymes (**"Killiecrankie"** and **"Ballad Fourth: The Trogger"**).

The distinction between Scottish and English words is not always so easy to make as in the examples above. Since Scottish of the eighteenth century had no standard spelling, Scottish dialect poets often used the English spelling when a Scottish word had a near-English equivalent. Intermixing such words as "fae" and "foe" or "gi'e" and "give" may only indicate that Burns is, like most writers who have attempted dialect, an inconsistent speller. But Burns takes care to spell "have" when the rhyme demands the English pronunciation, even in such vernacular poems as **"Kellyburn Braes,"** where "have" rhymes with "crave," or as **"When First I Saw,"** where "have her" is supposed to rhyme with "favour." "Foe" is frequently substituted for "fae" to help the rhyme, as in **"Scots Wha Hae,"** where it rhymes with "low" and "blow," words which could never be brought to rhyme with "fae." "Fight" replaces the more common "fecht" to rhyme with "wight," "sight," and "tight" in **"The Author's Earnest Cry and Prayer."**

Burns is equally free in interchanging words to facilitate alliteration. "Chapman" is the standard word used in vernacular poems except for **"Kellyburn Braes"**: "And like a poor pedlar he's carried his pack." He uses "Callet" in all vernacular poems except in **"Tam O'Shanter"**: "There was ae winsome wench and wawlie" and in the **"Soldier's Song"** of **"The Jolly Beggars"** for rhyme, even though in the same song there is the line: "I'm as happy with my wallet, my bottle and my callet." Again, he uses an English word consistently except when the Scottish helps alliterate: "Corbies and Clergy are a shot right kittle" (**"The Brigs of Ayr"**) but "Your locks were like the raven" (**"John Anderson, My Jo"**); in **"Willie Wastle"**: "The cat has twa [eyes] the very colour" but "Auld Baudrons by the ingle sits." One function of using both Scottish and English, then, is expediency; to facilitate rhyme and alliteration.

But sometimes Burns, for no apparent reason, interchanges Scottish and English words of almost identical meaning where neither rhyme nor alliteration nor meter

is aided: "ragged"—"duddie" (**"Second Epistle to John Lapraik"** and **"The Twa Dogs"**); "coft"—"bought" (**"Tam O'Shanter"** and **"The Weary Pund o' Tow"**). Interestingly, he more often uses an English word mistakenly for a Scottish word than the other way around. For example, "daisy" is used in **"Lament of Mary Queen of Scots"**: "And spreads her sheets o' daisies white," but never is "gowan" used in a passage which is clearly neoclassic. The only error of this type that I have found is "lug" used for "ear" in a neoclassic passage in **"The Brigs of Ayr."**

Apparently Burns did not even attempt to write a pure Scottish. Words like "gowan," "gled," "chapman," "baudron," and "corbies" had no magical power for him. He discarded them when it fit his convenience to do so and did not, at other times, watch them closely.

Many Scottish words which Burns uses have specific, unambiguous meanings and point to concrete objects. The great majority of these words refer to farming, peasant home life, or Scottish institutions. For example, farming: "braik," "cairn," "calf-ward," "calker," "crap," "fell," "graip," "thraive," "icker," "ripp," "ripple"; peasant home life: "but and ben," "cake," "cootie," "cotter," "cran," "creel," "fecket," "girdle," "tacket"; Scottish institutions: "bowkail," "philibeg," "creepie-chair," "ell," "ferintosh," "groat." These words offer an advantage which other Scottish words offer less obviously. They help define the speaker and place of the poem. The words may not always be those which an eighteenth-century Scottish peasant would have used, but they suggest that the speaker is a person who has an easy familiarity with the minute details of farm implements or kitchenware.

Such a concretely defined speaker helps avoid the sentimentality which always hovers near in poetry about rustic life. The farmer in **"The Auld Farmer's New-Year Morning Salutation to His Auld Mare, Maggie"** remains probable and realistic when he draws his doggedly optimistic conclusion, "Here to crazy age we're brought, / Wi' something yet" because he so clearly speaks out of concrete experience; because he shows the frank materialism of a farmer when he recalls the exact details of his dowry and lists, as one of his fondest recollections of Maggie, that her colts "drew me thretteen pund and twa, / The vera warst"; and because he knows and talks about the hardships they both went through in an obviously "weary warl'."

The syntax of the poems written before 1790 often sounds like conversation but proves rather formal on close examination. The sentences are long and well-constructed, the rhetoric is often balanced ("Come to my bowl, come to my arms, / My friends, my brothers!"), the adjective often follows the noun ("prospects drear"), lines almost invariably end with a comma or period. Burns achieves the sound of conversational syntax through the use of the short line in the Standard Habbie stanza for emphatic afterthoughts ("They gang in stirks, and come out asses, / Plain truth to speak") or asides ("So dinna ye affront your trade, / But rhyme it right"), through the use of words of familiarity or endearment, and through simple, direct diction. Burns can re-create the rhythms of conversation ("Ha! whare ye gaun") even when he retains, often ironically, Augustan parallelism ("He's stampin, an' he's jumpin!").

Burns often uses provincial words, picturesque spelling, and conversational-sounding diction in his satiric poems to create an ironically oafish speaker, one who looks at the world with wide-eyed astonishment and little apparent understanding. In **"To a Louse,"** the speaker finds an ostensibly trivial object worthy of discussion. But he misses the point, in fact he turns the argument upside down by blaming the louse for the disorder in the scheme of things ("in some beggar's hauffet squattle"), rather than by blaming Jenny and those other humans who pretend to an order that does not exist. In the last stanza the irony disappears, as do the provincial words and Scottish idioms. The picturesque spelling and Scottish diminutive, however, enforce the theme stated here satirically, and in other poems lyrically, that there is a wisdom to be found in homely experience ("What airs in dress an' gait wad lea'e us, / An' ev'n devotion!"). The oafish diction allows Burns to have it both ways, for the speaker's mock-awe denies the sentimental inference that wisdom is necessarily and only found in the simplest men; but the truth behind his wonder, his realization that something is wrong, confirms in essence what the poem pretends to deny in tone. There is, Burns says, a native, uneducated wisdom which derives from one's feelings and which is neither better nor worse than other kinds of wisdom.

About half the Scottish words of specifics which Burns uses were used by either Ramsay or Fergusson. But Ramsay never mentions a detail of Scottish peasant life without making a sermon, most of it in rather Augustan English:

> Be that time Bannocks, and a Shave of Cheese,
> Will make a Breakfast that a Laird might please;
> Might please the daintiest Gabs, were they sae
>   wise,
> To season Meat with Health instead of Spice
>   ("The Gentle Shepherd")

Burns uses the same bannocks with both greater humor and greater affection and suggests, without overt statement, that bannocks, however they may compare to other foods, are still deserving of attention:

> Tell yon guid bluid of auld Boconnock's,
> I'll be his debt twa mashlum bonnocks,
> An' drink his health in auld Nanse Tinnock's,
>   Nine times a-week.
>   **("The Author's Earnest Cry and Prayer")**

Fergusson has a lighter touch than Ramsay and appears to have a more genuine affection for the homely details. But he does little with them. For example:

> The readied *kail* stand by the chimley cheeks,
> And had the riggin het wi' welcome steams,
> Whilk than the daintiest kitchen nicer seems.
>   ("The Farmer's Ingle")

Such comparisons inevitably entail a note of self-righteousness and insincerity even when the diction gives the sense that a peasant is speaking. Fergusson and Burns knew that the only advantage of peasant cooking is its economy. When Burns follows Fergusson too closely, as he does in **"The Cotter's Saturday Night,"** which is modeled after and distinctly inferior to Fergusson's "Farmer's

Ingle," he is as patronizing as Fergusson and as sanctimonious as Ramsay. In his best poetry, like **"Epistle to James Smith,"** he cares much less about lowering and raising kitchen items according to their social class:

> "While ye are pleased to keep me hale,
> I'll sit down o'er my scanty meal,
> Be't water-brose or muslin-kail,
>   Wi' cheerfu' face,
> As lang's the Muses dinna fail
>   To say the grace"

Burns only says that when we accompany kail with health, with cheer, with poetry, and with grace (in both senses), the meal may not become less scanty but it does gain something. Even the most humble parts of life can become symbols of a joyous scheme which includes art, emotions, and perhaps God.

Among the hundred and sixty-odd words which Burns uses more than fifty times, a considerable majority are English and most of the others differ from English in spelling but not in meaning, as "amang," "gae," "guid," "hae," "lang," "mair," "mony," "sae," "sair," "twa," and "wha." I have found only six words whose meanings differ from English which are used frequently, "ay," "bonie," "brae," "braw," "fou," and "ken." The indication, however, is not that Burns found few Scottish words useful but that he found so many useful that he did not have to depend on them repeatedly, as he seems to have with such English words as "sweet," "fair," "heart," "soul," "nature," and "love." Burns apparently found Scottish words to have a suggestiveness, a poetic ambiguity, a fluidity, which he seems to have found in late eighteenth-century English in only self-consciously "poetic" and rather tired words.

The **"Epistle to J. Lapraik"** offers many examples of his facility with diction. Stanzas XIII and XIV are among the best known of the poem:

> Gie me ae spark o' Nature's fire,
> That's a' the learning I desire;
> Then, tho' I drudge thro' dub an' mire
>   At pleugh or cart,
> My Muse, tho' hamely in attire,
>   May touch the heart.
>
> O for a spunk o' Allen's glee,
> Or Fergusson's, the bauld an' slee,
> Or bright Lapraik's, my friend to be,
>   If I can hit it!
> That would be lear eneugh for me,
>   If I could get it.

The metaphor of fire runs through the two stanzas. "Spunk" can mean "spark" or "small fire" but it extends to mean "life," "spirit," and "mettle," in the sense it still has in colloquial English. The metaphor is sustained by "glee," which in both English and Scottish implies "brightness" as well as "mirth" and "joy"; by "bauld," which in Scottish retains some of the implications of "fiery" and some of the older meaning of "to kindle"; and by "bright." The bright and fiery suggestion of Stanza XIV contrasts, on one hand, to the "spark" of the previous stanza to suggest, with characteristic modesty, that Burns hopes only for the beginnings of what the older poets have all excelled in, and contrasts further with the drudgery and "dub an' mire" in which Burns, both in livelihood and in poetry-writing, finds himself. The English "bold" and "sly" had settled in the eighteenth century into discretely separable words. "Bold" meant "vigorous" or "courageous"; but in Scottish it retained some pejorative sense of "fierce." "Sly" meant "cunning"; in Scottish it retained some of the more favorable sense of "skillful" and "dextrous." In English the two separable words would have indicated only two kinds of behavior. In Scottish the two flow into one another to create a scope which allows no clear distinction between "courageous" and "cunning" but suggests that the whole of man, good and bad, contributes to poetry.

The setting, described in the early stanzas, is rich in connotations of simple life warmly expressed: "rockin," "ca' the crack," "weave our stockin," and "hearty yokin." "Rockin" means "social gathering" but retains implications of its origin, the "rock" which is the distaff of a spinning wheel. "Hearty yokin" employs both the English advantages of "hearty" and the dialect "yokin," which means "bout" or "contest." Together, they sustain the ideas of "weaving," "being together," and "simplicity" and carry them further to the instinctive, passionate qualities of a peasant contest. The following three stanzas express the concept of the unity of the whole being by using words that describe both emotional and physical reactions to poetry and marital love. The line "thirl'd the heart-strings thro' the breast" uses the Scottish "thirl'd," which goes beyond the English "thrilled" (the word Burns had originally used) to mean "cause to vibrate," and exploits the English "heart-strings" and "breast." "Fidgin-fain" combines the meaning of a physical restlessness (the English "fidgit") with emotional excitement. Stanza VI indicates that poetry is by no means limited to the simplicity of a peasant "rockin"; it can be "douce," "merry," or "witty." The three adjectives, standing out in the relatively unconnotative stanza in which they appear, flow into one another: "merry" to mean "pleasant" and "friendly" as well as "joyous" (hence picking up the setting); "douce" to mean "pleasant" and "kind" as well as "sedate" and "sober"; and "witty" to mean "amusing" and "clever" as well as "intelligent."

The effect of the poem, a brilliant one, is to suggest the universal range of poetry, which can grow out of the simple life and be written by humble men, but which extends to works of great masters. That the whole of man reacts to poetry serves both to exalt man and exalt poetry. Burns concludes the poem amusingly, gaily, humbly, profoundly, by rhyming "epistle" to recall poetry; "grissle" which emphasizes that the pen originated in something alive; "fissle" which combines physical and emotional "tingling"; and "sing or whistle" which recalls his own humility.

In **"To a Mouse"** much of the diction conveys physical details which are in close approximation to the actuality of a farmer's life rather than to an idealized portrait. The speaker uses many homely words, "daimen icker," "thrave," "foggage," and "coulter," all of which suggest that a farmer is speaking, someone well acquainted with the details of peasant work. But highly suggestive words are intermixed. "Cowrin" conveys, in both Scottish and English, the state of fear and the physical position assumed in fear, but in Scottish it can refer to the normal squatting position of an animal. Hence the word both conveys the continuity of physical state and emotional sensation, and allows the farmer to attribute a human reaction to the animal without becoming unconvincingly imaginative. "Bickering" in Scottish means "hastening" but also carries the English "fighting," "squabbling," "brawling," and thus conveys antagonism as well as fear in the mouse. "Breastie," by its diminutive form, conveys some of the affection of the farmer but also gives the mouse human implications, both physical and emotional, by virtue of the breadth of meaning of the word, while its rhyme with "beastie" recalls that the mouse's human qualities do not make it human. "Ill" goes further in Scottish than in English, suggesting "annoyed," "vexed," "hostile," (still in the English "ill-tempered") thus picking up the sense of antagonism in the first stanza and, with "dominion," contrasting "social union" and "companion." "Nature's social union" is a rare example of Burns's ironic use of English; perhaps it is inappropriate diction for a farmer, but it expresses, through its irony, Burns's contempt for abstract theodicies, for well-laid schemes. "Silly," in Stanza IV, carries the Scottish meaning of "deserving of pity," "frail," "meager," while retaining the English and Scottish "plain," "simple," "homely." Hence the word conveys both the physical state of the shelter and the farmer's compassion for it, while demonstrating the continuity of the two.

The farmer states explicitly what the two have in common; they are both "earth born" and "mortal." Burns enriches the relationship of the two by the farmer's tender language, through words which suggest that there is something human about the mouse, and through words which convey the emotional contact between the two living and dying beings. But in the undertone of hostility and fear he says that something is "agley," that is, "off the straight," "irregular," "wrong." The two "poor" companions, "impoverished," "pathetic," "ill-fortuned," are united in a scheme which makes prospects "drear" or frightening, in which living and dying is the only certain pattern, in which life justifies "ill opinion," not "social union." Yet life can offer some consolation, although few accept it, through sympathetic contact between living beings and through recognition that "dreary winter" and the "cruel coulter" are far more serious problems than "a daimen icker in a thrave."

Burns is not saying the farmer is a philosopher any more than he is saying the mouse is a human. His point is that such distinctions are unimportant. The philosophic understanding of the farmer may be limited, but it is the best understanding we are likely to have.

A diction of discrete, unambiguous words would express a degree of clarity or organization which Burns considers outside actuality. The fluid, suggestive diction conveys poetically that rigid distinctions have little to do with the world as it is, that we must be satisfied with the consolation which comes from the sympathy of all living beings, that schemes to organize nature, either philosophically or practically, will only delude us with "promis'd joy."

In these, as in other vernacular poems, Burns does not rely entirely on Scottish words. He readily employs any English words which help convey his poetic intent. But Scottish words provide a higher proportion of the poetically effective words. Further, the Scottish words lend something else, not so easily defined, but which calls for more investigation.

I have found no evidence that Burns learned his use of Scottish from Ramsay and Fergusson. They probably gave him the idea of using the mixed language, but taught him few of its specific advantages. The use of highly concrete diction to convey a poetry which comes out of everyday experience occurs rarely in their poetry and then in such a stylized and unconvincing way, especially in Ramsay's poetry, as to make it more like Ambrose Philips than Burns. Nor do either of them use the poetic suggestiveness of Scottish in the way Burns does. The Scottish words and meanings which Burns uses with great facility, as "bauld," "thirl'd," "douce," "fissle," "bicker," "silly," "cowrin," and "ill," Ramsay uses either not at all or rarely and uninterestingly. Fergusson uses less than half of the words and never the techniques of Burns. For example, "spunk," which Burns uses to help create a rich suggestive metaphor in **"Epistle to J. Lapraik,"** Fergusson uses once:

> Then what is Man? why a' this Phraze?
> Life's Spunk decay'd, nae mair can blaze.
> Let sober Grief alone declare
> Our fond Anxiety and Care:
> Nor let the Undertakers be
> The only waefu' Friends we see.
>
> ("Auld Reikie")

Fergusson picks up figures and uses them as befits his point, so that the fire metaphor is only a passing convenience for the sake of articulation, to be discarded when another point must be made. There is nothing to suggest that fire and life are joined in a poetic or philosophic scheme. "Slee," which Burns uses in **"Epistle to J. Lapraik,"** Fergusson uses in "Elegy on the Death of Scots Music" combined with "pawky":

> Macgibbon's gane: Ah! waes my heart!
> The man in music maist expert,
> Wha cou'd sweet melody impart,
>   And tune the reed,
> Wi' sic a slee and pawky art;
>   But now he's dead.

Burns also combines the two words in **"Epistle to James Smith"**:

> Dear Smith, the slee'st, pawkie thief,
> That e'er attempted stealth or rief!
> Ye surely hae some warlock-breef
>   Owre human hearts;
> For ne'er a bosom yet was prief
>   Against your arts.

Burns follows Fergusson in using the words to describe a reaction of affection mingled with a sense of magic, but Burns also uses their favorable and unfavorable connotations to describe the happy reluctance with which one gives up his heart. Fergusson . . . did not express, in either themes or diction, the idea, which Burns developed so successfully, that distinction must be subordinated to connection. Whatever he gained through the use of Scottish, he did not use the dialect in the same way as Burns.

The most obvious change in Burns's diction from his earlier to his later career is, as everyone notes, toward more English and less exclusively Scottish words. The most apparent reason, as everyone also notes, is that after 1790 he wrote mostly songs. The one important poem written after 1790, **"Tam O'Shanter,"** uses a great many Scottish words. The few songs written before 1790 use fewer Scottish words than the poems written during those years.

One unfortunately inescapable reason for more English words in the songs is that songs are made to be sung. The listener cannot consult a glossary such as Ramsay, Fergusson, and Burns put at the back of their collected poems. Notably, Burns continues in the songs to use Scottish words which are easily understandable to an English-speaking listener, as "auld," "fa," "fit," "aft," "fause," "rin," "saft." When he alters the source from English to Scottish the change is usually to an easily understood word. In **"O, Let Me in This Ae Night,"** based on a song in [David Herd's *Ancient and Modern Scottish Songs*, 1776], he changes "would" to "wad," "waking" to "waukin" and "foot" to "fit."

But another reason emerges from the subject matter. Most of the songs express a simple feeling—love, friendship, loneliness, regret, contentment, yearning. They less often need a provincial speaker, whether for purposes of self-ridicule, or to express the wisdom found in concrete experience, or to create any of the shadings of irony Burns often employs. The few songs which have this irony, like **"The Deuk's Dang O'er My Daddy," "Willie Wastle,"** or **"Landlady, Count the Lawin,"** have more Scottish. Likewise, the songs whose subject matter calls for a provincial setting, such as patriotic songs, use more Scottish words. But generally, Burns uses the simplicity of the song to express what the provincialism of the poems expresses. He need not, in an expression of love, remind us that this feeling is available to all classes.

Franklyn Bliss Snyder hypothesizes that the larger proportion of English words in the songs was in part the result of Burns's greater assurance with the language as a result of his Edinburgh visit and the favorable reception of his poetry. Yet an examination of the diction of the songs fails to uphold this speculation.

Burns bases the first stanza of **"I Do Confess Thou Art Sae Fair"** on a seventeenth-century English metaphysical poem, "To His Forsaken Mistress." He changes English words to Scottish but leaves the grammar and syntax intact, a practice which is typical of his method. The source is:

> I do confess thou'rt smooth and fair,
>   And I might have gone near to love thee,
> Had I not found the slightest prayer
>   That lip could move, had power to move thee;
> But I can let thee now alone
>   As worthy to be loved by none.

I do confess thou'rt sweet, but find
    Thee such an unthrift of thy sweets:
Thy favours are but like the wind
    Which kisseth ev'rything it meets;
And since thou canst with more than one
    Thou'rt worthy to be kiss'd by none.

Burns's first stanza is:

I do confess thou art sae fair,
    I wad been o'er the lugs in luve,
Had I na found the slightest prayer
    That lips could speak thy heart could muve.
I do confess thee sweet, but find
    Thou art so thriftless o' thy sweets,
Thy favours are the silly wind
    That kisses ilka thing it meets.

Some of the changes are simply the improvements of a better poet but some are improvements that the latitude of using both Scottish and English allows. The change of "every-" to "ilka" smooths out the sound of the line with the repeating "i" sound, emphasizes the word with the hard stop on "k," and connects the word, amusingly, contemptuously, with the sound of "kisseth." The advantage depends entirely on the sound, since the two words have no difference in meaning and Burns uses them interchangeably, often using "every" in vernacular poems and songs. "Lugs" allows Burns to alliterate with "love," creating an amusing comparison which helps the speaker satirize both himself and passionate, misplaced love. Some changes achieve greater simplicity and avoid self-conscious poeticisms. "Kisseth" to "kisses" is one example. "But like" to "silly" smooths out the syntax and further clarifies the speaker's feeling for the woman, since "silly" means both "frail" or "weak," "dear" or "innocent," as well as "foolish" (cf. "Its silly wa's the winds are strewin") and thus refers to both the woman and the wind. The removal of the appurtenance of the simile is a typical simplification, in spite of "O, my luve is like a red, red rose." Burns has added a few easy Scotticisms, like "na," "o," "muve," which give some informality, but he has retained the poetic second-person singular pronoun. The rhetoric is obviously controlled. Burns removes the source's pun on "move," substituting an Augustan parallelism, satiric and sardonic in emphasis rather than metaphysical in implication.

The tendency, then, is toward a simplified, easy-flowing, and unself-conscious diction, but one of restrained gentle familiarity rather than one that is vernacular. Yet again, as in the poems, Burns seems able to use an almost Augustan rhetoric and still attain the rhythms of common speech which give the sense that the poet is writing as the thoughts and phrases first occur to him ("As fair art thou, my bonnie lass, / So deep in luve am I").

The changes Burns makes over his songs tend to be largely, although not invariably, away from concreteness. I had expected to find a general pattern of changes toward racy, sensuous detail. This kind of change does occur, as in **"The White Cockade,"** based on "Ranting Roving Lad" in Herd. But more often he lessens the specificity and adds more suggestive diction.

In **"How Lang and Dreary Is the Night,"** based on "The Day Begins to Peep" in the Herd manuscript, he changes:

I ne'er can sleep a wink,
Tho' ne'er so wet and weary,
But ly and cry and think

to:

I restless lie frae e'en to morn
Tho' I were ne'er sae weary.

Burns shortens the poem from nine stanzas to three stanzas and a chorus, mostly by eliminating the concrete and sensuous details of the source. This decrease allows the highly suggestive rhyme-words, "dearie," "weary," "dreary," and especially "eerie" to attain much greater importance; for in the source all are obscured by the quantity of details. "Eerie" in eighteenth-century English was limited to the current sense of "weird," but in Scottish retained its older senses of "superstitiously fearful," "lonely from fear," "fearful of something unknown," "uneasy," "melancholy." This word is reflected by "lanely nights," "dreams," "absent," "restless," "heavy hours," and "joyless" as well as the rhyme words, so that the girl's many fears and sorrows spread out over the poem, indicating the terror of both loneliness and the unknown.

In **"The Lea-Rig"** he removes the specific indecent "rowe" from the source (Herd MS. pages 100-101), substituting "meet," and changes the poem from a proposition to a statement of love. He changes "dark" to "mirkest," which combines the English "dark" and the English "murky." He adds "eerie" and "wild," which combine with the original "weary," to contrast with "scented birks," "dew . . . hangin clear," "morning sun," and "heart sae cheery"; and he changes the social comment of:

While others herd their ewes and lambs
And toil for warldly gear, my jo

to:

When . . .
    . . . owsen frae the furrow'd field
    Return sae dowf and weary, O.

"Dowf" includes "weary" but puts the emphasis on "dullness" and "listlessness" rather than on the physical part of tiredness, and adds "melancholy," "numbness," and "dreariness." The result is that the two moods run through the poem; the mood of darkness, weariness, melancholy, fear, superstition, the unknown, the wild; and the mood of light, clearness, joy, and love. Within a life where fear, weariness, and gloom are the commonplace, the lovers find brightness and joy, even, or especially, at "gloamin grey." The emphasis is entirely on the mood and feelings of the lovers; the obvious comment on life is left unspoken and only slightly implied.

There is not much evidence, then, that Burns turns toward more English words in the songs because of his greater facility or assurance. He uses both English and Scottish words with facility in both poems and songs. It is more likely that he turned away from Scottish because of the change in form which needed less concreteness in subject and in definition of the speaker, and, perhaps, required more clarity for an English-speaking person.

Since Burns's use of Scottish does not come from Ramsay, Fergusson, or the Scottish folk song and since he shows facility with English as well as Scottish, he may have learned the techniques from his favorite English poets, Pope, Thomson, Goldsmith, or Cowper. A separate study is needed of Burns's English diction and its relation to that of other eighteenth-century writers. Yet, even if a similarity does appear, it will raise as many questions as it answers. If Burns learned techniques of diction from English writers and then applied them to Scottish, the pattern of his diction would probably be reversed. We would expect Burns to employ more English words in the earlier poems, then turn to more Scottish words as he acquired facility with the techniques. While we cannot exclude, without further exploration, the possibility of English influence on his diction, we must at least allow for considerable originality in his way of handling diction. His prose comments suggest that he was indeed trying something new. In his *First Commonplace Book* Burns says:

> It may be some entertainment to a curious observer of human-nature to see how a ploughman thinks, and feels, under the pressure of Love, Ambition, Anxiety, Grief with the like cares and passions, which, however diversified by the Modes, and Manners of life, operate pretty much alike I believe, in all the Species.

Burns is a poet of common ideas and common emotions, "which, however diversified by the Modes and Manners of life, operate pretty much alike . . . in all the Species." We need accept in his poetry no philosophic or religious schemes; no tradition of love, courtly or otherwise; outside of **"Is There for Honest Poverty,"** no political or economic system; not even, the diction reminds us, a tradition of literature ("But I shall scribble down some blether / Just clean aff-loof "). Burns's argument is that man can find ethical and aesthetic direction in life without elaborate schemes. What better symbol of the freedom from political, aesthetic, or religious systems than a poor independent farmer, an uneducated poet, or a love-sick peasant girl? But it is vastly minimizing his accomplishment to say that he simply creates, through Scottish words and picturesque spellings, the sense of a provincial speaker.

Since Burns admits that he does not write as he speaks, surely we can give his statement that he writes in his "native language" some metaphoric interpretation. A statement which Burns made in a letter to Margaret Chalmers and considered worth recording in his *Second Commonplace Book* helps explain his theory of poetry: "The whining cant of love, except in real passion, and by a masterly hand, is to me as insufferable as the preaching cant of old Father Smeaton. . . . Darts, flames, Cupids, loves, graces, and all that farrago, are just a Mauchline [sacrament], a senseless rabble." He speaks elsewhere against both poetry written without passion and emblematic poetry. Neither denunciation is surprising in Burns. But the sequence in the quotation, which equates overly-stylized poetry with love poetry written without passion, has particular significance. His denunciation is directed not only against stylized imagery but against highly stylized poetry

generally. A large part of contemporary British poetry had become over-intellectualized, abstract, lifeless. Poets frequently described love, misery, poverty, and the simple life as if their only experiences with them were literary, and wrote in a language which had gone sterile with inbreeding. Burns advocates poetry which describes "incidents and situations from common life" and which expresses "the spontaneous overflow of powerful feelings" in a "language really used by men."

His attempt to write poetry which has suggestive, fluid diction and which expresses feelings at once passionate and commonplace leads him to theorize about and to attempt the same renewal of the language of poetry which Wordsworth and Coleridge demand. The many poets and critics, Stevenson, Arnold, Henley, Speirs, who insist, in spite of contrary evidence, that Burns writes as he speaks, are eloquent attestations to Burns's success in creating "a plainer and more emphatic language" which keeps "the reader in the company of flesh and blood" and which has the power "to give the charm of novelty to things of every day, and to excite a feeling analogous to the supernatural, by awakening the mind's attention from the lethargy of custom, and directing it to the loveliness and the wonders of the world before us." (pp. 239-57)

Raymond Bentman, "Robert Burns's Use of Scottish Diction," in From Sensibility to Romanticism: Essays Presented to Frederick A. Pottle, *edited by Frederick W. Hilles and Harold Bloom, Oxford University Press, Inc., 1965, pp. 239-58.*

Alexander Scott   (essay date 1975)

[*Scott is an English educator, poet, and dramatist. In the following essay, he remarks on the style and themes of Burns's satires, paying particular attention to the time and place established in their narratives.*]

The unanimity of praise for the satires among modern Scottish critics of Burns is remarkable in a literary scene where controversy is more usual than consent. To David Daiches, **'The Holy Tulzie'** is 'brilliant' and 'extraordinarily effective'; **'Holy Willie's Prayer'** possesses 'cosmic irony' and 'perfect dramatic appropriateness'; **'The Holy Fair'** is at once 'the finest of those [poems] in the Kilmarnock volume which show the full stature of Burns as a poet working in the Scots literary tradition' and a creation with 'revolutionary implications'; **'The Twa Dogs'** is 'brisk, sharp-toned . . . with wit and point'; **'Address to the Deil'** is 'effective' in that it 'blows up' the doctrine of original sin; **'The Ordination'** is (again) 'effective', this time in 'the contrast between the form and the ostensible theme'; and **'Address of Beelzebub'** is 'bitter and biting' [*Robert Burns,* 1950]. To Thomas Crawford, **'The Holy Tulzie'** shows 'developing still further the technique used in . . . the **"Epistle to John Rankine"**—the apparent assumption of the standards, beliefs and language of the opposite party'; **'Holy Willie's Prayer'** is 'one of the finest satires of all time'; **'The Holy Fair'** shows 'complete mastery of traditional poetic skills'; **'The Twa Dogs'** has 'a pleasing manner'; **'The Ordination'** is 'one of the finest and

freshest things Burns ever did'; and **'Address of Beelzebub'** is 'the most savage of all Burns' satires' [*Burns,* 1960].
To David Craig, despite his distrust of 'reductive criticism' and 'the reductive idiom and the poor man's defensive pose' in much eighteenth-century Scots satirical writing, 'Burns was in a wonderfully original and rich vein in
the poems that may be called his satires' [*Scottish Literature and the Scottish People 1680-1830,* 1961].

All these works had been written before the publication
in July 1786 of the Kilmarnock edition which created for
Burns the national—and international—reputation he has
enjoyed ever since. Yet references to the satires in the contemporary reviews are few and far between. The *Edinburgh Magazine* of October 1786, noting that 'some of his
subjects are serious, but those of the humorous kind are
the best', illustrates the point by quoting **'Address to the
Deil'** and excerpts from **'The Holy Fair'**, but none of the
other satirical pieces is so much as mentioned by name;
the *Monthly Review* (London) of December 1786 expresses the opinion that 'our author seems to be most in his element when in the sportive humorous strain', but neither
discusses nor illustrates the work which would exemplify
that remark—perhaps because of a view that 'the poems
of this cast . . . so much abound with provincial phrases
and allusions to local circumstances, that no extracts from
them would be sufficiently intelligible to our English readers'; the *Lounger* (Edinburgh) of December 1786, where

the reviewer was the novelist Henry Mackenzie, mentions
the **'Dialogue of the Dogs'** [*sic*] among other 'lighter and
more humorous poems' which demonstrate 'with what
uncommon penetration and sagacity this heaven-taught
ploughman, from his humble unlettered station, has
looked upon men and manners', but in defending Burns
against the charge of 'irreligion' by remarking that 'we
shall not look upon his lighter muse as the enemy of religion (of which in several places he expresses the justest
sentiments) though she has been somewhat unguarded in
her ridicule of hypocrisy', Mackenzie leaves the religious
satires unrecorded by either title or quotation; and the *English Review* (London) of February 1787, while adducing
'Address to the Deil' and **'The Holy Fair'** to exemplify its
view that 'the finest poems . . . are of the humorous and
satirical kind, and in these our author appears to be most
at home', devotes most of its space to the discussion of
poems from which humour and satire are entirely absent.

The temptation to berate those early critics of Burns for
obtuseness, however strong it may be, and however apparently justified in the eyes of readers of his collected poems,
does not survive reference to the Kilmarnock edition. For
of all the satires mentioned in the first paragraph above,
only three, **'The Holy Fair'**, **'The Twa Dogs'** and **'Address
to the Deil'**, find a place in its pages. The others have been
suppressed, either by the poet himself, or by the poet following the views of his adviser, the lawyer Robert Aiken,
'Dear Patron of my Virgin Muse'. When Burns made his
first bow to the public, he chose to do so with his strong
right arm tied behind his back.

If at first sight this seems to be extraordinary behaviour
for a novice, who might be expected to wish to make the
maximum impact upon his readers, the appearance is deceptive. Burns and his adviser had sufficient reasons for
deciding against the inclusion in the Kilmarnock edition
of those satires which are now among the most highly
praised of all his works. Most of them were certainly libel-
lous—and, in the eyes of some of those local readers in the
west of Scotland for whom the Kilmarnock edition was
printed by subscription, they might have appeared blasphemous at worst, and at best in extremely poor taste.

The clue to the situation lies in Burns's famous autobiographical letter to Dr Moore where, discussing the earliest
of his satires, **'The Holy Tulzie'**, he writes:

> The first of my poetic offspring that saw the light
> was a burlesque lamentation on a quarrel be-
> tween two reverend Calvinists, both of them dra-
> matis person in my Holy Fair.—I had an idea
> myself that the piece had some merit; but to pre-
> vent the worst, I gave a copy of it to a friend who
> was very fond of these things, and told him I
> could not guess who was the Author of it, but
> that I thought it pretty clever.—With a certain
> side of both clergy and laity it met with a roar
> of applause. [*Letters,* edited by J. De Lancey
> Ferguson, 1931]

But there are always two sides (at least) to any Scottish
reaction to works of art of a controversial kind, and how
others among 'both clergy and laity' must have reacted to
'The Holy Fair' is indicated by their reception of its imme-

diate successor, **'Holy Willie's Prayer'**—'It alarmed the kirk-session so much that they held three successive meetings to look over their holy artillery, if any of it was pointed against profane Rhymers'.

Both **'The Holy Tulzie'** and **'Holy Willie's Prayer'** were attacks on *local* personalities in the church—hence the caution, 'to prevent the worst', which led Burns to pretend ignorance of the authorship of the former when passing it out in manuscript. Rural Ayrshire in the late eighteenth century was still under a clerical discipline—or Calvinist dictatorship—whose restrictive power was all the greater for its basis in a public opinion which Henry Mackenzie, reflecting 'moderate' Edinburgh views, described as 'the ignorance and fanaticism of the lower class of the people in the country where these poems were written, a fanaticism of that pernicious sort which sets faith in opposition to good works'. Moreover, at the time **'The Holy Tulzie'** and **'Holy Willie's Prayer'** were composed, early in 1785, Burns had placed himself in a highly vulnerable position *vis-à-vis* the kirk: 'Unluckily for me, my idle wanderings led me, on another side, point-blank within the reach of their heaviest metal.' Less metaphorically, he was responsible for the pregnancy of Elizabeth Paton, the Burns family's domestic servant, who bore him a daughter on 22 May 1785, and consequently he would be required to appear on the church's stool of repentance, 'arrayed . . . in the black sackcloth gown of fornication', for three successive Sundays. After that penance he would be regarded as having made his peace with the kirk, provided there were no other scandals appertaining to his person. But if his authorship of **'The Holy Tulzie'** and **'Holy Willie's Prayer'** had been avowed, or even acknowledged, the clerical authorities would have had every reason (in their own view) to continue to hold him under the ban of their baleful displeasure.

A year later, in the spring of 1786, when Burns was selecting poems for the Kilmarnock edition, he would have been in even worse trouble had all the facts of his sexual irregularities come to light, for at that time he had made himself a bigamist by contracting two irregular marriages, firstly with Jean Armour—who bore him twins on 3 September—and secondly (and secretly) with Mary Campbell. From the consequences of those follies he was rescued, through no merit of his own, by the sudden death of 'Highland Mary' in the autumn of that year. By then, however, the Kilmarnock edition had already been published, with most of the anti-clerical satires omitted.

Yet, ironically enough, the same system of clerical dictatorship which compelled Burns to deny the dignity of print to some of his liveliest poems would appear to have been responsible for their original composition. While the poet's Commonplace Book makes it plain that he had reached a 'moderate' view in religion, opposed to the narrow fundamentalist ('Auld Licht') principles of his local kirk-session, at least as early as 1784, it was not until 'the thorns were in his own flesh' and he found himself in peril of the kirk's censure as a result of his affair with Elizabeth Paton that he was stimulated into writing about the Calvinists of his own district in terms of the kind of attack

which has traditionally been regarded as the best means of defence.

A notorious dispute about parish boundaries between two 'Auld Licht' ministers, 'hitherto sworn friends and associates', who 'lost all command of temper' when the matter was discussed at the Presbytery of Ayr, and 'abused each other . . . with a fiery violence of invective' [J. G. Lockhart, *Burns,* 1828], presented the poet with a golden opportunity for satire. The whole of **'The Holy Tulzie'** is an extended metaphor, the nature of which is succinctly indicated by the poem's alternative title **'The Twa Herds'**, but the very orthodoxy of the time-hallowed images of the minister as shepherd and the congregation as his flock gives a keener edge to the mockery of the treatment, and the poet's adoption of the persona of an Auld Licht sympathizer, professing horror and dismay at the 'bitter, black outcast' between the two guardians of sanctity, sharpens the irony to a more penetrating point. Again, the presentation of the two pastors as actual—as well as metaphorical—Scottish shepherds, their business to protect the sheep 'frae the fox / Or worrying tykes', their practice to trap 'the Fulmart, Wil-cat, Brock and Tod' and 'sell their skin', deprives them of dignity and makes their blowing of 'gospel horns' and swinging of 'the Gospel-club' all the more ludicrous by the brilliantly daring association of the scriptural with the mundane—while the presentation of their flocks as real sheep ('the Brutes') puts beyond argument the propriety of patronage in the presentation of parish ministers, since it would appear that the only alternative is to 'get the Brutes the pouer themsels / To chuse their Herds'. Technically, too, the poet's command of the Habbie Simson stanza is already consummate, although this is only the third occasion he has employed it.

Despite those various virtues, however, the poem falls short of being a masterpiece. As Hilton Brown remarks, '[Burns] was always lazy . . . even in his best days many of his most promising openings peter out for lack of just that finish and pulling together which an extra ounce of effort would have supplied' [*There Was a Lad,* 1949], and he gives **'The Holy Tulzie'** as an example of this fault. The poem ends too abruptly, as if the writer had suddenly run out of steam. But even before that point is reached, readers from other airts than eighteenth-century Ayrshire find themselves in difficulty and compelled to start grubbing in editorial notes. During the first fifty-four lines, no such grubbing is necessary, for even although we know nothing about the two protagonists, 'Moodie man and wordy Russell' as Burns punningly names them, their natures and their functions emerge so clearly from the verse that they quickly establish themselves in our minds as recognizable clerical types, as true to life now as then. But in the next thirty lines the poet lets loose an avalanche of ministers' names, all of them familiar enough to his original local audience, but now unknown to fame except for their appearance here and elsewhere in Burns's work, and none of them sufficiently delineated to achieve a living reality in the verse. From being a local poem which yet contains implications of wider significance, **'The Holy Tulzie'** here becomes parochial, concerned with personalities of interest only to a limited circle of readers. Those very elements which gave the poem much of its notoriety among Burns's

Ayrshire contemporaries decrease its appeal to the present day.

Some stanzas of **'Holy Willie's Prayer'** suffer from the same disability. To say as much is not to deny a jot of the brilliance of Burns's parody of the style of 'the Scottish Presbyterian eloquence' with its incongruous combination of the Biblical and the broad, or the satirical skill of the presentation of his protagonist, the arch-hypocrite of Calvinist fanaticism, disguising yet revealing his lust and greed under 'a veil that is rent', a tattered screen of sanctified self-interest, and betraying himself out of his own all too awfully eloquent mouth. For the first sixty-six of the poem's one hundred and two lines, Holy Willie is a prototype as well as a local personality, and given the slightest acquaintanceship on the reader's part with the doctrines of original sin and predestination, the theme of Christianity unchristianized is of universal—and ageless—relevance. Even the introduction, by name, of Willie's most hated 'enemy', Gavin Hamilton, requires no external explanation, for he too is not only individual but representative, a personality who enjoys the pleasures frowned upon by the kirk ('He drinks, and swears, and plays at cartes') while possessing such charm that he commits the even greater 'crime' of winning more regard than the community's religious leader ('Frae G—d's ain priest the people's hearts / He steals awa').

But then occur two stanzas in which Willie demands that the Lord should 'hear my earnest cry and prayer / Against that Presbytery of Ayr!' and describes 'that glib-tongu'd Aiken' who created such terror among the godly that even 'Auld wi' hingin lip gaed sneaking'. These lines are a good deal less than self-explanatory to readers unaware of what occurred when Gavin Hamilton appealed to the 'moderate' Presbytery of Ayr, against the adverse judgment on his alleged absence from public worship passed by the 'Auld Licht' kirk in the parish of Mauchline, and won his case thanks to the successful pleading of his lawyer and friend Robert Aiken. To 'the rustic inmates of the hamlet' who constituted Burns's first audience, the affair was so recent, and the gossip concerning it so rife, that detailed description would have been otiose, but what was daylight to them is darkness to us unless we are given editorial assistance, for the parochial nature of the subject-matter defeats unaided comprehension.

Both **'The Holy Tulzie'** and **'Holy Willie's Prayer'** are concerned with specific local religious scandals, so notorious in the west country that, had the poems been printed, the characters who feature in them could not have failed to be recognized, even if their names had been omitted and replaced by asterisks. The risk of a libel action, or of clerical condemnation, or of both, was too great for that unconfessed bigamist among 'rakish rooks', Robert Burns, to include them in the Kilmarnock edition—even although there can be little doubt, human nature being what it is, that those subjects of scandal and concern had created much of that local interest in the author which led to his first publication being so heavily subscribed by his neighbours. **'The Holy Tulzie'** remained unpublished during the poet's lifetime, the first to appear in print being **'Holy Willie's Prayer'**, in an anonymous pamphlet of

1789, when it was accompanied—appropriately—by 'quotations from the Presbyterian eloquence'.

This linking of Burns's late-eighteenth-century poem with a work published in 1694 as a result of the religious strife in seventeenth-century Scotland is significant, for although Professor James Kinsley indicates a more recent model for **'Holy Willie's Prayer'** ('Burns may have taken a hint from Ramsay's "Last Speech of a Wretched Miser to his hoard" ' [*Poems and Songs,* edited by J. Kinsley, 1968]), it has much in common with Drummond of Hawthornden's late near-vernacular poem, 'A Character of the Anti-Covenanter, or Malignant', first published among the posthumous poems in the 1711 edition of Drummond's works. Here Drummond, himself an 'anti-Covenanter, or Malignant' (or Cavalier), adopts the persona of a Covenanter in order to 'attack' the Cavalier view, in exact anticipation of the way in which Burns, himself a moderate (with the same dislike of Presbyterian extremism as the Cavaliers had possessed before him), adopts the persona of an Auld Licht in order to 'attack' the moderate standpoint, and in each poem the Calvinist fanatic who is the protagonist brings down the reader's condemnation upon himself while seeking to destroy the opposition.

'A Character of the Anti-Covenanter', 106 lines long—only four lines longer than **'Holy Willie's Prayer'**—is written in octosyllabic couplets instead of the 'standard Habbie' of Burns, but its jaunty, irregular rhythms, its at least equally irregular rhymes, its brutal jocularity, its plain blunt energy—at the opposite pole of style from the stately and mellifluous decorum of Drummond's earlier verse, published during his lifetime—give it a force no less devastating, and no less remarkable for its counterpointing of the profound and the profane, than the later work. There is, however, one major difference between the two poems, for the speaker in Drummond is not identified by any nickname; he represents all extreme Calvinists rather than, like Holy Willie, a particular spokesman speaking for all. In the same way, the targets at which the earlier extremist fires his musket are not specific opponents like Gavin Hamilton and Robert Aiken, but each and every member of the 'malignant' party. It may be argued that Burns's particularity of characterization gives **'Holy Willie's Prayer'** more point (although in fact Hamilton is as much a type as an individual, and Aiken is scarcely particularized at all, except as 'glib-tongu'd), or it may be held that this very particularization narrows the range of Burns's attack, compared with Drummond's; but it is beyond dispute that the present-day reader of Drummond does not require to acquaint himself with seventeenth-century Scottish biography in order to gain full appreciation of his poem, as must be done with regard to the following century in respect of **'Holy Willie's Prayer'**.

Unlike that dramatic lyric, Burns's next religious satire, **'The Holy Fair'**, which followed in the autumn of the same year, was considered 'safe' enough for inclusion in the Kilmarnock edition—although that safety was ensured only by a liberal substitution of asterisks for proper names whose owners would have regarded their appearance in print in such a context as being highly improper. A further measure of safety arises from the fact that **'The**

Holy Fair' is less personal than public, less concerned with the follies committed by particular individuals than with the festivities enjoyed by a whole community, for the poem belongs to a Scots tradition of 'come-to-the-fair' verse-comedy traceable to the medieval celebration of village life in 'Christ's Kirk on the Green' (which had been brought up to date earlier in the eighteenth century by Allan Ramsay, with the addition of extra cantos of his own).

Again, **'The Holy Fair'** is not concerned with one specific, easily recognizable occurrence—an undignified row between two Calvinist ministers, or a legal battle between fundamentalist priest and liberal parishioner—but might derive from observation of any and every public communion held in the open air in the west of Scotland. The scene is in fact set in Burns's local parish of Mauchline, as we now know (from the manuscript), but the asterisks in the Kilmarnock edition give no clue to this, and there are no merely parochial descriptive details (except perhaps the mention of 'Racer Jess', the half-witted daughter of 'Poosie Nansie' Gibson, who kept a local tavern) which might give the game—and the name—away to readers not already in the know. Moreover, the references to the various preachers who waste the sweetness (or sourness) of their eloquence on the desert air—while 'the godly . . . gie the jars an' barrels / A lift that day' and 'the lads an' lasses . . . are cozie i' the neuk'—are of such a generalized kind that their actual identities, indicated in the printed text only by asterisks, matter little or nothing.

> Now a' the congregation o'er,
>   Is silent expectation;
> For ****** speels the holy door,
>   Wi' tidings o' s-lv-t–n:
> Should *Hornie,* as in ancient days,
>   'Mang sons o' G– present him,
> The vera sight o' ******'s face,
>   To's ain *het hame* had sent him
>   Wi' fright that day.

Who cares, or needs to care, that scholarly research has revealed the minister there as 'Sawnie', otherwise Alexander Moodie (of **'The Holy Tulzie'**), 'educated at Glasgow, ordained to Culross in 1759, and minister of Riccarton from 1762'? What difference does it make to the reader's enjoyment to know that the asterisks in '***** opens out his cauld harangues' represent that grand old Caledonian cognomen, Smith? Yet Burns himself, publishing his volume while he poised precariously on the razor's edge dividing acknowledged fornication from unadmitted bigamy, was compelled to care, and the difference between asterisks and actuality was vital. He might risk revealing the truth in **'The Holy Fair'**, but not the whole truth. The real identities of his preaching protagonists remained 'underground'.

Of all the many poems in the 'Christ's Kirk' tradition, **'The Holy Fair'** is the most masterly, in its command of verse technique, the idiomatic cut and thrust of its style, the combination of comedy and criticism in its action and characterization, and the cunning of its transitions between panoramic views of general activities and close-ups of individuals and particularities. Yet Hilton Brown, while finding the poem 'excellent as a descriptive piece', dismiss-

es it as 'surely too crude for successful satire', a view which seems eccentric—unless the critic is using 'crude' in the sexual sense, expressing disapproval of such scenes as the lover taking advantage of everyone else's eyes being fixed on the preacher, and engaging meantime in intimate caresses of his 'ain dear lass'. But this is surely to have overlooked the central theme of the poem, the triumphant survival of life-creating sexuality even under the dreary domination of the most repressive puritanism.

The satire on Calvinism in **'Address to the Deil'** (written in the winter of 1785-6) is so indirect, and so devoid of specific local references, that it was included in the Kilmarnock edition almost as written. Almost, but not quite. In lines 61-6 the demands of decorum have led to the toning down of the tragic tale of how devilish witchcraft deprives the new bridegroom of his virility at the most vital of all moments; and in lines 85-90 'my bonie Jean, / My dearest part' is removed from the poem. The first of these departures from the manuscript is significant in showing how Burns, despite his contempt for convention, was the kind of rebel poet who is not above deciding, on occasion, that discretion is the better part of valour where the interests of publication are concerned—and even then he was not discreet enough for some, since the Rev. Hugh Blair advised [in his *Burns Chronicle,* 1932] that even the revised stanza 'had better be left out, as indecent' from the Edinburgh edition of 1787.

Of the revision of lines 85-90 Kinsley takes the view that it was 'probably made just before going to press, to remove the allusion to Jean Armour, from whom he was estranged', but this does much less than justice to the difficulty and danger of Burns's situation in June 1786, when he was secretly married not only to a pregnant Jean Armour but also to Mary Campbell (whose reputation was far from being impregnable). 'Estranged' from Jean Armour, Burns undoubtedly was, when her parents compelled her to acquiesce in the defacement of the 'marriage certificate' which the poet had given her and then packed her off to Paisley in the hope that she might contrive a more suitable match; but he did not languish after her for long. On the contrary, the speed with which he was off with the old love and on with the new, and his recklessness in giving the second girl the same kind of documentary evidence of his 'honourable intentions' as he had already presented to the first, put him in a position of vulnerability to the law—if his secrets were discovered—that would have weakened even the steeliest nerves. For Burns to have published a declaration of his regard for Jean ('A dancin, sweet, young, handsome queen / Wi' guileless heart') at a time when he was risking a charge of bigamy—against which he could have defended himself only by swearing that she had no claim upon him whatsoever—would have been an act of self-destruction too apparent for even the most impractical poet to ignore. As far as his published work was concerned, it was imperative that Jean be kept 'underground', consigned to oblivion, become a nonperson. And so it happened, Burns replacing her person with 'the Soul of Love', an unconscious irony which was lost upon those of his original readers who had not already encountered the poem in manuscript. Even in its altered state, the **'Address'** remains one of his most attractive works, a humorous mock-attack on the Great Enemy which reduces more orthodox assaults upon him to the status of superstitious nonsense, but the excised stanzas have a bite and a particularity lacking from their published counterparts.

The last of the religious satires composed before the Kilmarnock edition made Burns famous, **'The Ordination'** (written early in 1786) was as parochial in origin as **'The Holy Tulzie'** and **'Holy Willie's Prayer'**, and it suffered the same fate, exclusion. For all the asterisks with which the text is bespattered fail to conceal from even the most cursory reader that the scene is Kilmarnock and the occasion the presentation to the ministry of the Laigh Kirk there of a fundamentalist minister, the Rev. James Mackinlay, who owed his preferment to the favour of the patron, the Earl of Glencairn. Written to console the moderate party in their defeat, the poem uses the pastoral imagery of **'The Holy Tulzie'** to present a ludicrously grotesque picture of Kilmarnock's Auld Licht congregation in the shape of a ram which has had only 'scanty' feeding while the Moderates held the field but which can now revel in rich repasts of *'gospel kail'* and *'runts o' grace'* provided by the fundamentalist Mackinlay. The work's daring juxtapositions of the sacred and the profane must have seemed blasphemous to contemporary readers of the evangelical persuasion, and the concluding episode, when Orthodoxy flogs Learning, Common Sense and Morality through the town as if they were rogues and vagabonds, possesses a brutal jocularity, equating 'righteousness' with sadistic revenge, which lays it open to the same charge. This is the only one of Burns's pre-Kilmarnock satires occasioned by a Moderate defeat rather than by an Evangelical upset, and the sharper bitterness of its tone may well reflect the rage felt by the poet's party, and by the author himself, at their discomfiture on a battleground where they had begun to believe that they were on the winning side.

But Burns did not leave **'The Ordination'** unacknowledged and underground for very long. Although he omitted it from the Kilmarnock, he found it a place in the Edinburgh edition of 1787, and one can only speculate on the reasons which led him on that occasion to accept a risk which he had refused to take a year earlier, and which he still refused on behalf of **'The Holy Tulzie'** and **'Holy Willie's Prayer'**. Perhaps he had realized that irony remains unnoticed by persons without a sense of humour, and that a poem written in the style of a victory-song for the fundamentalists might well be interpreted as such by them and hence escape their strictures? Whatever the explanation, there is no doubt that Burns experienced some difficulty in finding sufficient previously unpublished poems for the Edinburgh edition to justify it in the eyes of readers who had already bought the earlier book—this accounts for his inclusion in the Edinburgh collection of **'Death and Dr Hornbook'**, a *jeu d'esprit* which has been greatly admired for its witty command of dialogue but which the poet himself had considered 'too trifling and prolix' to publish in the Kilmarnock volume. He may have felt that, having 'got away' with **'The Holy Fair'** in the Kilmarnock, where it had even been praised and quoted in the reviews, he might now take a chance on the publication of another re-

ligious satire, and chose **'The Ordination'** as being less of a pointed personal attack on individuals than **'The Holy Tulzie'** and **'Holy Willie's Prayer'**. The question must remain in doubt, but—given the necessity of finding some 'new poems' for the Edinburgh volume—the hypothesis seems not unreasonable.

In his religious satires, Burns is the artist-intellectual in rebellion against the obscurantism of local public opinion, and his allies are the men of education who favoured patronage (exercised by land-owning heritors) in the establishment of parish ministers, rather than election by the elders of individual kirks, as the uneducated majority preferred. In his social satires, however, Burns becomes the lower-class radical hostile to the gentry, and his allies are the same peasant masses—the crofters and small farmers—for whose fundamentalist religious opinions he had the highest contempt. **'The Twa Dogs'** (early 1786), an eclogue consisting of canine comparisons between the virtues and vices of the rich and the poor, much to the latter's advantage, eschews all discussion of religion, and its implicit Biblical moral, that 'Satan still finds work for idle hands to do', in contrasting the idle aristocracy with the hard-working peasantry, avoids any scriptural association. This is perhaps 'natural' enough, in the sense that the dialogue is conducted between a pair of brute beasts to whom the spiritual aspects of existence might be expected to remain unknown, but in view of Burns's own religious alignment, the omission is also highly significant.

Radical as **'The Twa Dogs'** is in its attack on the privileged, its inclusion in the Kilmarnock volume placed its unprivileged author in no danger of any kind of prosecution or persecution by authority. When social criticism emerges from the mouths—or muzzles—or dogs, it is bound to create the effect that their bark is worse than their bite. Moreover, Burns takes care to make exceptions to his general strictures on the gentry—'there's some exceptions, man an' woman'—and thereby provides the opportunity for any reader belonging to the upper classes to include himself among the exceptional few to whom the satire does not apply. Again, the introductory descriptions of the two canine characters have such charm as to make it well-nigh impossible to take offence at anything they say. Their dialogue is both racy and pointed, and Burns's success in giving his octosyllabic couplets the cadence of Scots vernacular speech is so remarkable as to be quite unremarked in the reading. Yet, at the same time, one can appreciate the doubt in Hilton Brown's mind when he commented that 'to talk of . . . **"The Twa Dogs"** . . . as "poetry" seems to strain a little the accepted meaning of words' and preferred to consider the work's medium as being verse; for in capturing the tone of conversation Burns frequently strays so far from the poetical that passage after passage is no more than rhythmical rhyming prose, entirely devoid of imagery.

Different in every way, except its octosyllabic couplets, is **'Address of Beelzebub'**, also written in 1786, but never published in Burns's lifetime. Dated from 'Hell 1st June Anno Mundi 5790', and signed by Beelzebub, the poem is only too particular in the point of its attack, being directed to the Rt Honble JOHN, EARL OF BREADALBANE, President of the Rt Honble the HIGHLAND SOCIETY, which met, on the 23d of May last, at the Shakespeare, Covent garden, to concert ways and means to frustrate the designs of FIVE HUNDRED HIGHLANDERS who, as the Society were informed by Mr McKenzie of Applecross, were so audacious as to attempt to escape from theire lawful lords and masters whose property they are by emigrating from the lands of Mr McDonald of Glengary to the wilds of CANADA, in search of that fantastic thing—LIBERTY.

The savage sarcasm of the poem's sixty-two lines makes it one of the most fiercely effective of Burns's works, a furious condemnation of aristocratic arrogance, which lashes authority with as stinging a whip as his lordship is pictured as using on 'the tatter'd gipseys' who are wives to those 'Poor, dunghill sons of dirt an' mire', his Highland tenants. For attempting to interfere with their freedom of choice, Breadalbane is not only doomed but also pre-eminently damned, fated to a special place in hell, 'The benmost newk, aside the ingle / At my right hand', and the brutality of the punishment to be inflicted by him upon the lower orders ('smash them! crush them a' to spails!') is evoked by Burns in a passage of such ferocious energy as to make eternal hell-fire seem no outrageous sentence when compared with the crime.

Yet the power in the land which permitted Breadalbane and his associates among the Scottish gentry to curtail the liberties of their tenants was also too great for a mere tenant-farmer such as Burns to risk defying it by publication, however violently he might denounce that power in manuscript. In a Scotland where political—and judicial—authority was concentrated in the 'happy few' who constituted the landed interest, and where that authority was well-nigh absolute (as Burns and other radicals were to discover to their cost when they dared to favour the French Revolution a few years later), the public defiance of a belted earl by an untitled nobody from the hilts of a plough might well have exposed the latter to a legal system for which the social hierarchy was still sacrosanct, and would certainly have placed him beyond the pale so far as any prospect of public employment was concerned. It is even a matter of doubt whether he could have continued as a tenant-farmer, for as a 'marked man', a radical who had published an attack on one of the greatest landlords in the country, he would have found most other landlords refusing to rent him a farm. Such were the perils daunting enough to force the freest spirit in eighteenth-century Scotland to confine **'Address of Beelzebub'** to an underground existence.

Ironically, it seems to have been safer to satirize the monarch in far-off London than a mere magnate with a Scottish estate. When King George III's birthday was celebrated on 4 June 1786 with a Pindaric ode by the poet-laureate, Burns immediately retorted with **'A Dream'**, and inserted it into the copy for the Kilmarnock edition just before it went to press. Although his aristocratic acquaintance Mrs Dunlop informed him that the work was disliked by 'numbers at London' and suggested that he amend it for the Edinburgh edition, Burns rejected her advice on the grounds that 'I set as little by kings, lords, cler-

gy, critics etc. as all these respectable Gentry do by my bardship'. This appears to be very bold, but in fact it is little more than bravado. For while some readers of **'A Dream'** might take offence at its tone of impudent familiarity, addressing the king and his family as if they were near neighbours, the poem is innocent of any attack on the institution of monarchy. On the contrary, it protests the author's 'loyal, true affection' alongside its waggish depreciation of the flattery of courtiers and the pecadilloes of the royal princes. Its publication might be regarded as being in doubtful taste, but it could scarcely be denounced for advocating revolutionary principles of equality, since its democratic attitude remains implicit, as a matter of manner, and is never explicitly stated, and even stressed, as in the overt onslaught upon aristocracy in **'Address of Beelzebub'.**

After the publication of the Kilmarnock edition in July 1786 and Burns's consequent departure from his native heath to become consecutively a literary lion in Edinburgh, a farmer in Dumfries-shire, and an exciseman in Dumfries, there was a marked decline in his satirical production, both in quantity and in quality. For this there would appear to have been two reasons—rootlessness and respectability. Burns the famous poet, elevated out of the ranks of the tenantry and commissioned as an officer in the Excise, and domiciled in a district different from that in which he had shared the trials and tribulations of the labouring life, was inevitably distanced from the people and the places, the pulpits and the politics, which had provided his radical attacks on religious orthodoxy and aristocratic privilege. Occasionally he attempted to hark back to his parochial past in Ayrshire, but **'A New Psalm for the Chapel of Kilmarnock'** (25 April 1789), written in the mock-scriptural style of **'Holy Willie's Prayer'**, was innocuous enough—in its avoidance of personalities—for immediate publication in the London *Morning Star,* while **'The Kirk of Scotland's Garland'** (autumn 1789), published as an anonymous broadsheet, is a repetitive catalogue of individual insults rather than a rounded poem. Well might the author ask himself, 'Poet Burns, Poet Burns, wi' your priest-skelping turns, / Why desert ye your auld native shire?' The short answer, financial necessity (' 'tis luxury in comparison of all my preceding life'), had been expressed more poignantly by the poet a twelvemonth earlier, in his **'Extemporaneous Effusion on being appointed to the Excise'**—

> Searching auld wives' barrels,
>   Ochon, the day!
> That clarty barm should stain my laurels;
>   But—what'll ye say?
> These muvin' things ca'd wives and weans
> Wad muve the very hearts o' stanes!

With the solitary exception of **'Tam o' Shanter'**—his only excursion into narrative—the rest of the best of Burns is not satire but song. (pp. 90-104)

Alexander Scott, "The Satires: Underground Poetry," in Critical Essays on Robert Burns, *edited by Donald A. Low, Routledge & Kegan Paul, 1975, pp. 90-105.*

Allan H. MacLaine   (essay date 1978)

[*A Canadian educator, MacLaine has written extensively on Burns and Scottish poetry. In the following excerpt, he proposes that "The Jolly Beggars" is a complex mix of Burns's radical and conservative sympathies.*]

> A fig for those by law protected!
> *LIBERTY'S* a glorious feast!
> Courts for Cowards were erected,
>   Churches built to please the *PRIEST.*

These lines from the final song of the Bard are the most often quoted in **"The Jolly Beggars,"** and that fact in itself points up the problem with which I intend to deal.

It often happens in the history of literature that an early stereotype becomes affixed to a poem or play or novel, and persists without critical challenge for generations. In many cases the stereotype begins with superficial or facile judgments by influential people which color all subsequent reactions to the work. Succeeding critics never really look at the work directly for what it is, but always tend to see it through the distorting glass of the time-honored view. Such has certainly been the fate of Burns's **"The Jolly Beggars."** From the beginning this magnificent cantata was labeled with adjectives like "revolutionary," "radical," "anarchic," and so forth, recalling Lady Bracknell's dictum (in a very different context) in Oscar Wilde's *The Importance of Being Earnest*—"It reminds one of the worst excesses of the French Revolution."

In our own time, recent Burns critics have followed the same line in a somewhat more sophisticated fashion. David Daiches, [in *Robert Burns,* 1952], clearly views **"The Jolly Beggars"** as a revolutionary work and says that it makes its appeal to "humanity's unofficial self" (George Orwell's phrase). Similarly, Thomas Crawford in [*Burns: A Study of the Poems and Songs,* 1960] calls it "a root-and-branch criticism of organized community life and morality from a point of view as extreme in its own way as those sometimes found in Byron and Shelley." He says, further, that "the cantata effectively demolishes the presuppositions of eighteenth-century society." I propose to dispute this traditional view of **"The Jolly Beggars,"** to show that it is at least a badly lopsided conception of what the poem actually has to say to us.

Burns's own attitude toward **"The Jolly Beggars"** is somewhat enigmatic. He withheld the poem from the press during his lifetime, and his only recorded comment on it occurs in a letter to the publisher George Thomson written in 1793, eight years after the time of composition: "I have forgot the Cantata you allude to, as I kept no copy, and indeed did not know that it was in existence; however, I remember that none of the songs pleased myself except the last—something about

> Courts for cowards were erected,
> Churches built to please the priest."

None of these statements is believable. The brilliant finish of the cantata, the evidence of hard work and extensive revision by Burns [that John C. Weston has documented in "The Text of Burns' 'The Jolly Beggars'," *Studies in Bibliography* (1960)], show that he certainly intended it for

publication in 1786. But he withheld it, and in 1793, the time of the letter, he was under fire and his Excise position threatened as a result of his open sympathies with the French Revolution. At this juncture, writing to Thomson who was an influential man of very conservative views, Burns had strong reasons to dissociate himself as much as possible from **"The Jolly Beggars."** Hence the conscious attempt to play down the importance of **"The Jolly Beggars"** and to pass it off to Thomson as a sort of bagatelle, a trivial and unsuccessful work of his earlier years, not to be taken seriously since the author himself has "forgot" it. Yet it is curious that Burns chose to quote the two most radical lines in the cantata; as a consequence his own comment tended to support the idea that **"The Jolly Beggars"** was a dangerous work.

Rightly or wrongly, and no doubt on the advice of prudent literary friends in Ayrshire and later in Edinburgh, Burns concluded that **"The Jolly Beggars"** was too risky a production to put into "guid black prent." It was not published until 1799, three years after the poet's death.

Yet it is an extraordinary fact that **"The Jolly Beggars"**, this reputedly radical and dangerous work, has been consistently praised by critics of all political persuasions. John Gibson Lockhart, the biographer of Carlyle and hardly a sympathizer with social revolutions, had this to say about **"The Jolly Beggars"** in 1828:

> *Beggar's Bush,* and *Beggar's Opera,* sink into tameness in the comparison; and indeed, without profanity to the name of Shakespeare, it may be said, that out of such materials, even his genius could hardly have constructed a piece in which imagination could have more splendidly predominated over the outward shows of things—in which the sympathy-awakening power of poetry could have been displayed more triumphantly under the circumstances of the greatest difficulty.

And later in the same year (1828) Thomas Carlyle himself, that thunderer against "big, black Democracy," echoed Lockhart's enthusiastic assessment of **"The Jolly Beggars"** [in his "Essay on Burns," *Edinburgh Review* (1828)], calling it "the most strictly poetical" of all Burns's poems, and the most perfect thing of its kind in literature.

Similarly, Matthew Arnold, a critic who was often unsympathetic and generally completely wrong-headed on the subject of Burns, was overwhelmed by **"The Jolly Beggars."**

> "That puissant and splendid production," he called it; "the piece is a superb poetic success. It has a breadth, truth, and power which make the famous scene in Auerbach's Cellar, of Goethe's 'Faust,' seem artificial and tame beside it, and which are only matched by Shakespeare and Aristophanes."
>
> ["The Study of Poetry"]

At the end of the nineteenth century (1896), W. E. Henley and T. F. Henderson, in their fine edition of [Burns's poetry], summed up **"The Jolly Beggars"** in a now famous phrase as "this irresistible presentation of humanity caught in the act and summarized forever in the terms of art." And twentieth-century critics have been equally effusive. This chorus of praise, extending all the way from reactionary Carlyle to socialistic Crawford, suggests not only a purely aesthetic appreciation of the artistry of **"The Jolly Beggars,"** but also some degree of approval of the thought content in the work. There must be something politically appealing for every kind of reader in **"The Jolly Beggars."** Besides the nihilistic philosophy of the songs on which so much emphasis has been laid ("Courts for cowards," etc.), there must be a guiding intelligence in the cantata that is basically conservative and eminently sane. I submit that there is such a counterbalance and that it is to be found in the attitude of the narrator.

I have already quoted Daiches' comment on the universal appeal to "humanity's unofficial self." This is undoubtedly true, but it does not get us very far in explaining the secret of **"The Jolly Beggars,"** because it is also true of *all* beggar literature. The shoddiest, third-rate eighteenth-century song in celebration of beggars' "freedom" also appeals to this universal instinct. The difficult question is: Why does **"The Jolly Beggars"** have a unique kind of potency? My thesis is that the special power of **"The Jolly Beggars"** arises out of a tension between two opposed points of view: (a) that of the beggars themselves, and (b) that of the narrator. The beggars in their songs speak in voices that are indeed radical, anarchic, amoral, contemptuous of all the institutions of Western society. They express the traditional beggar philosophy as found in the literature of roguery through the centuries. The narrator's attitude, on the other hand, is basically conservative, realistic, and socially orthodox. And it is the thrust of the one idea against the other that gives **"The Jolly Beggars"** its extraordinary power.

A brief review of the immensely rich literary background to **"The Jolly Beggars"** will support my contention that the high originality and uniqueness of the cantata lie in its presentation of two opposed attitudes in the songs and narrative framework. All commentators agree that in composing **"The Jolly Beggars,"** Burns had a voluminous international literary tradition to draw upon—the literature of roguery, of beggars, thieves, and vagabonds, extending back to medieval times and including some of the poems of François Villon in France, the narrative song of "The Gaberlunzieman" in Scotland, and dozens of English ballads, songs, and prose tracts. . . . Songs glorifying the carefree, irresponsible, "free" life of beggars and vagabonds were much in vogue in the early eighteenth century. Of the scores of such songs in common circulation, many were accessible to Burns in two large collections—Thomas D'Urfey's *Wit and Mirth: or Pills to Purge Melancholy* (1719-20) and Allan Ramsay's *Tea-Table Miscellany* (1723). In the latter, which grew from one to four volumes in successive editions and which Burns certainly knew in detail, there are several beggar songs, including "The Happy Beggars" and "The Merry Beggars." "The Merry Beggars," wherein six characters tell their stories in turn, unquestionably suggested to Burns the basic structure for **"The Jolly Beggars."** In the same collection there is a brief, undistinguished effort, attributed to Ramsay himself, called "A Scots Cantata," with two

recitative sections and two songs, which surely provided the specific model for Burns's cantata form.

In all of the suggestive wealth of beggar songs, there is a consistent theme of celebration of the beggar philosophy, of beggars' "freedom"; there is no hint of any contrasting point of view. This is true also of the immensely popular *Beggar's Opera* (1728) of John Gay which Burns almost certainly knew. Nevertheless, Gay's brilliant ballad opera, with its many new songs written to old and popular tunes and set in a dramatic framework exposing the lives of Macheath and his gang of thieves and vagabonds, is an important part of the background to **"The Jolly Beggars."** Furthermore, Gay draws parallels between the mores and morality of the London underworld (where Peachum, the master "fence," functions as chief manipulator or prime minister) with those of the British Court circle, a device of social satire that reappears in **"The Jolly Beggars."** Of course, *The Beggar's Opera* has implications that go far beyond the simplicities of the beggar songs and the beggar philosophy. It is, in fact, a penetrating comment—at once hilarious and devastating—on the depravity of human nature in general and on the amorality of the ruling class in particular. But in his *method* Gay stays strictly within the limits of the beggar tradition in literature. *The Beggar's Opera* is, in short, a self-contained world in which we get a seemingly straight-forward exposition of the values of the beggar philosophy. In Gay's work no other set of values is directly expressed; on the contrary, Gay suggests that "polite" society has basically the same amoral values as the underworld of the beggars. Consequently, *The Beggar's Opera* provided no precedent for the kind of dual vision we find in Burns's **"The Jolly Beggars."**

Such a precedent, however, was readily at hand for Burns. He found it in native Scots poetry, outside of the beggar tradition, in the genre of *Christis Kirk.* . . .Burns, of course, was steeped in this Scots poetic form, from its fifteenth-century prototypes, *Christis Kirk on the Green* and *Peblis to the Play,* through the later work of Alexander Scott, Ramsay, Fergusson, and others. He had already tried his own hand in this genre in a **"A Mauchline Wedding," "The Holy Fair,"** and **"Halloween,"** and he turned the wealth of knowledge and skill thus acquired to good account in the composition of **"The Jolly Beggars."**

The crucial thing about the *Christis Kirk* tradition with respect to **"The Jolly Beggars"** is that in the *Christis Kirk* poems we have a satirical narrator who describes, comments on, and laughs at the antics of the characters. In other words, in these poems there are two very different points of view presented: (a) that of the lower class characters as revealed in their speeches, and (b) that of the superior narrator as expressed in his satiric description of and comment on the behavior of the characters. In essence, this is exactly the method of **"The Jolly Beggars,"** with its opposed and contrasting attitudes of beggars and narrator. In terms of literary precedent, therefore, the special quality of **"The Jolly Beggars"** results from Burns's unique fusion of the beggar tradition with its themes of "freedom" and defiance of convention and the *Christis Kirk* tradition with its methods of genial satirical narration.

Before examining the text in detail, let us first consider the overall structure of the work to see how Burns's dual vision is embodied in its poetic architecture.

If we exclude the "Merry-andrew" section which Burns wisely chose to delete, the cantata as we have it consists of seven "recitativo" passages and seven songs, the whole forming a tightly integrated dramatic structure. In all, seven distinct characters are presented: a Soldier and his "doxy," a Pickpocket ("raucle Carlin"), a Fiddler, a Caird (tinker), a "Dame," and a Bard (ballad-singer). Each of these, with the exception of the Dame, sings a song; the Bard sings two. In organizing this material, Burns cleverly interrelates all seven characters.

Burns opens with a brilliant narrative section, depicting first with bemused tolerance the wild scene of merriment in Poosie-Nansie's, and then focussing in on his first vignette of the Soldier and his Doxy with sharper comic emphasis on their squalor and lust. At this point the Soldier staggers to his feet with a swaggering song of praise for his two careers, first as a soldier, now as a beggar. In the second recitative, the Fiddler is momentarily brought in, foreshadowing the large part he plays later, and then the Soldier's Doxy rises to match the Soldier's song with a rousing and uninhibited one of her own, recounting her sexual "life story" as a camp follower. (Apparently, Soldier and Doxy are a couple who mated in youth, separated, and are now reunited in middle age.) The third recitative introduces a husky female Pickpocket, whose song of mourning for her dead "John Highlandman" is an envious reaction to the Doxy's joy in rediscovering her "old boy." The "pigmy" Fiddler, depicted in two brilliant, farcical stanzas (fourth recitative), is stricken by the charms of the massive Pickpocket and, moved by her grief, he consoles her with his song and offer of love. The song, of course, is lively, sexual, amoral. At this point (fifth recitative), the "sturdy *CAIRD,* " also smitten by the Pickpocket, intervenes; the narrator in a passage of hilarious satire shows the Caird thrusting the trembling Fiddler aside, then embracing and serenading the "raucle Carlin." After the Caird's song we get the superlative sixth recitative in which the Caird "prevails" with the Pickpocket, while the poor Fiddler finds consolation "behint the Chicken cavie" with a Dame who turns out to be one of the three "wives" of the Bard. The latter, catching them *in flagrante delicto,* is not offended; since he still has two wives left he wishes Fiddler and Dame luck in a rousing song. This sixth narrative section, full of sharp but genial satire, is the richest in the whole work. The Bard's second song, ("A fig for those by law protected!") demanded by the whole company, brings the scene of drunkenness and profligacy to its crashing climax.

This brief summary of the cantata reveals not only its tight dramatic organization, but also suggests Burns's ambivalence in the contrasting ideas and attitudes of beggars and narrator. (The style of the poetry itself is also highly significant, as we shall see later.) As for ideas or views of life, these are expressed directly only in the songs, and they are the traditional ones of beggar literature: "freedom" (all characters), sexual amorality (Doxy, Fiddler, Bard), contempt for property values (Pickpocket, Caird, Bard), contempt for the requirements of social respectability (all characters; but especially the Bard), and so forth. The narrator, on the other hand, has no ideas; he pretends simply to report what he sees, without comment or evaluation. But the narrator's *attitude* emerges indirectly through his selection of detail (as well as language), and in this way his point of view is differentiated sharply from that of the beggars. The narrator is under no illusions; he is relentlessly realistic, choosing details which tend cumulatively to bring out both the absurdity of the beggars' pretensions and the squalor of their lives. Burns, after all, had seen much of actual beggary in Ayrshire, and had feared being reduced to it himself. His sympathy for these vagabonds comes out in the heroics of the songs, but his clear grasp of the realities of their way of life is shown in the satiric attitude of the narrator.

The language of **"The Jolly Beggars"** supports the central thesis of this essay in broad terms. The situation, however, is complex; the differentiation between narrator and beggars is not marked by a clear-cut stylistic dichotomy. Indeed the beggars themselves sing in a variety of voices. Nevertheless, certain general tendencies may be discerned and set forth as follows:

(1) The language of the songs tends to be more idealized than that of the narrative framework, with frequent use of heroic or romantic touches and echoes of serious sentimental-aristocratic literature. The idealization is made to seem natural in songs presented (as these are) as spontaneous outbursts of lyric emotion. At the same time, we are allowed in some of the songs (especially those of Doxy, Fiddler, Caird, and Bard) to catch glimpses of the sordid realities, and this technique heightens the comic incongruity of the highflown diction.

(2) The language of the narrator is, on the whole, much more sober, realistic, and down-to-earth, often with deliberate emphasis on squalid images. However, the narrator also introduces mock-heroic devices for hilarious satiric effects. These effects are used sparingly at first, but become very prominent toward the end in recitatives 4, 5, and 6, as though Burns, pleased with the comic power of incongruous language in the early songs, decided to exploit it further in narrative sections. The difference is that whereas in the songs the fancy diction is made to seem unconscious and ludicrously naive, in the recitatives it is clearly deliberate and satiric.

(3) Burns's juxtaposition of styles enhances the total satiric effect; that is, each song is "set up" in the preceding narrative passage. The recitative is always realistic, giving a clear picture of the gamey goings-on in Poosie Nansie's; then this is immediately followed by a song—heroic or sentimental—in high style. The contrast is devastatingly funny. In this way, moving from narrative to song and back to narrative, Burns achieves a kind of contrapuntal comedy.

Let us turn now to the text to see how some of these stylistic effects are worked in practice.

The opening stanza, with superb economy of expression brings us inside from bitter November weather into the warm, hectic conviviality of Poosie Nansie's, as Burns immediately begins to establish the narrator's attitude toward the beggars by means of the style of his first description of them:

Ae night at e'en a merry core	One; evening
O' randie, gangrel bodies,	carefree; vagrant
In Poosie-Nansie's held the splore,	riotous frolic
To drink their orra dudies.	spare rags

Here we have clearly the point of view of an amused, tolerant outsider. The witty line "To drink their orra dudies," that is, to pawn their spare rags to buy drink, is particularly effective in showing the narrator's clear-eyed perception of the essence of the beggars' way of life—their combination of abject poverty with utterly irresponsible profligacy or "randiness." Similarly, in the second stanza we see the narrator stressing in his choice of language the degradation of the beggars, especially in the phrase "the tozie drab" (drunken slut) for the Doxy, and the earthy image of her holding up "her greedy gab" for more kisses.

The first song, that of the Soldier, is a lively piece of swaggering bravado, followed by a recitative which merits full quotation:

He ended; and the kebars sheuk,	rafters shook
Aboon the chorus roar;	Above
While frighted rattons backward leuk,	rats; look
An' seek the benmost bore:	inmost hole
A fairy *FIDDLER* frae the neuk,	corner
He skirl'd out, *ENCORE,*	cried out shrilly
But up arose the martial *CHUCK,*	
An' laid the loud uproar— . . .	

In this stanza the narrator brings in his first slight touches of mock-heroic. The picture of the frightened rats scurrying for shelter is, of course, a wonderfully comic way of suggesting both the volume of noise and the squalor of the place; but the whole opening quatrain is also an ironic reminiscence of Milton's *Paradise Lost,* I, 541-3: "At which the universal Host upsent / A shout that tore Hell's Concave, and beyond Frighted the Reign of *Chaos* and old Night." This Miltonic echo enhances the narrator's genial mockery of the beggars. More obviously, his use of the grandiose "martial *CHUCK* " when he means simply "soldier's whore" has the same kind of ludicrous effect.

The Doxy's song which follows, regarded by Cedric Thorpe Davie as one of Burns's supreme achievements as a songwriter in its perfect matching of words to music, is a small masterpiece of ironic language. Here the grubby, abandoned life story of the camp follower, always vulnerable to sudden dire poverty and venereal disease, is recounted in the exalted idiom of sentimental literature. The underlying realities, however, are never lost sight of, as we can see in the opening lines.

I *ONCE* was a Maid, tho' I cannot tell when,
And still my delight is in proper young men . . .

The Doxy's total promiscuity, made clear in the first line, clashes ironically with "proper young men" in the second. In the next stanza, there is similar comic ambiguity in the line "Transported I was with my *SODGER LADDIE.* " The surface meaning of "transported" is, of course, the genteel one—"carried away by powerful emotion," or

something like that. In this context, however, the term might also mean "shipped to a prison colony"—and Burns surely intended the line to be read as a delightfully unconscious *double entendre.* In stanza 3 we get even more brilliant examples of the comic contrast between high language and low life:

But the godly old Chaplain left him in the lurch,
The sword I forsook for the sake of the church;
He ventur'd the *SOUL,* and I risked the *BODY,*
'Twas then I prov'd false to my *SODGER LADDIE.*

Yet another kind of comic irony comes out in the latter part of the song in single adjective-noun phrases in which one element is connotatively polite, the other debased, as in "sanctified *Sot*" (stanza 4) or "His *RAGS REGIMENTAL*" (stanza 5).

Altogether, the Doxy's song is of special significance for my thesis, since it expresses perhaps more clearly than any other section of **"The Jolly Beggars"** the real ambivalence of Burns's attitude. On the one hand, the comic incongruities of language in the song tend to make fun of the beggars, to explode the pretensions of the beggar philosophy, and to suggest that the Doxy (like the others) lives in a world of illusions. Yet, at the same time, these same incongruities give a kind of innocence, even a kind of heroism, to the Doxy's undaunted view of herself and her world. In the end her song becomes a triumphant celebration of total sexual freedom and *joie de vivre.*

The third recitative brings us back to the narrator and his brief sketch of the Pickpocket, the "raucle Carlin." Here the language is generally earthy ("raucle Carlin," sturdy old woman, has a fine Scots pithiness) and realistic:

For mony a pursie she had hooked,
An' had in mony a well been douked.

After giving us, in a few broad strokes, these details of the Pickpocket's disreputable career and the fact that her lover had been a Highlander who was hanged, the narrator brings in just a touch of the mock-sentimental:

Wi' sighs an' sobs she thus began
To wail her braw *JOHN HIGHLANDMAN.*

This touch prepares us for further ironic language in the Pickpocket's very lively song (of grief) which follows— lines like "The ladies' hearts he did trepan," or "adown my cheeks the pearls ran." The employment by this thieving trull of stilted formulas (tears like "pearls") from sentimental literature has the effect of turning her grief into comedy.

With the re-entrance of the Fiddler in the fourth recitative, the cantata moves into a phase of uproarious farce. The narrator describes this "pigmy Scraper" and his sudden amour with the strapping Pickpocket in a single *Habbie* stanza:

A pigmy Scraper wi' his Fiddle,	
Wha us'd to trystes an' fairs to driddle,	cattle markets; totter
Her strappan limb an' gausy middle,	buxom
(He reach'd nae higher)	
Had hol'd his *HEARTIE* like a riddle,	pierced; sieve

An' blawn't on fire.

The narrator here begins with four lines of straightforward, earthy description of this absurdly ill-matched pair. In the last two lines, however, he gives us a brilliant travesty of a romantic stereotype from aristocratic literature—the hero's heart is pierced, and blown "on fire." This is made doubly amusing here, first by the absurdity of using this exalted formula to describe a crude and ridiculous situation, and second by the couching of the formula in colloquial Scots—"hol'd," "*HEARTIE,*" "riddle," "blawn't." His use of the Scots diminutive "*HEARTIE*" (little heart), with very non-heroic connotations, is especially funny and, of course, appropriate to the tiny Fiddler. The second stanza follows roughly the same pattern, with braid Scots description in the first two lines, followed by a passage of macaronic wit wherein the fiddling talents of the "wee Apollo" are portrayed with formal Italian musical terms ingeniously embedded in the Scots texture. The Fiddler is thus made to seem as absurd and pretentious as possible.

The Fiddler's song itself, set to the old tune of *Whistle owre the lave o't* (the refrain has sexual connotations), carries on this method of burlesque of serious literary conventions. The tiny Fiddler, reaching upwards toward the Pickpocket's face, begins:

> Let me ryke up to dight that tear,   reach; wipe
> An' go wi' me an' be my *DEAR* . . .

The first line is again a travesty (concealed in vernacular Scots) of the common formula in sentimental novels or poems where the hero consoles the weeping heroine and wipes tears from her eyes. Similarly, the second line is a faint but definite parody of Marlowe's *The Passionate Shepherd to his Love;* and, indeed, the remainder of the song follows the general rhetorical structure of Marlowe's poem. Within this elevated poetic pattern, however, the pleasanter realities of vagabond life are earthily depicted—drinking, fornicating, and so forth. Then, in the final stanza a special burlesque effect is achieved:

> But bless me wi' your heav'n o' charms,
> An' while I kittle hair on thairms   tickle; guts
> *HUNGER, CAULD,* an' a' sic harms   such
> May whistle owre the lave o't.   over the rest

In the first line the phrase "heav'n o' charms" is a euphemism for the female genitals drawn from sophisticated courtly literature. But in the second line we have a sudden drop in style from the courtly to the "hamely" with "kittle hair on thairms" (tickle hair on guts; that is, play the fiddle), clearly a bawdy pun. The overall result of these devices is, of course, to make the Fiddler's "fine" language seem ludicrous in the light of the very vulgar things he is actually saying.

In the fifth recitative, the narrator comes back with further verbal ironies, as we learn that the Pickpocket's "charms" had smitten the robust Caird as well as the Fiddler. The Caird brutally forces the Fiddler, under threat of violent death, to "relinquish her for ever," another example of the narrator's deft burlesque of serious styles. He then introduces internal rimes to enhance the farcical effect of the whole vignette:

> Wi' ghastly e'e poor *TWEEDLEDEE*   eye
> Upon his hunkers bended,   haunches
> An' pray'd for grace wi' ruefu' face,
> An' so the quarrel ended.

The Caird's own song which shortly follows—another serenade to the Pickpocket ("My bonie lass I work in brass")—carries on the internal rime device. The Caird heaps scorn, in earthy and sexual language, upon the hapless Fiddler ("Despise that *SHRIMP,* that wither'd *IMP*") and embraces the portly Pickpocket.

Next comes the sixth recitative, the richest and most imaginatively conceived part of **"The Jolly Beggars"**. In three *Christis Kirk* stanzas, the narrator manages the final resolution of the Fiddler-Pickpocket-Caird conflict and presents a wholly new dramatic situation—the seduction by the frustrated Fiddler of one of the three "wives" of the Bard and the latter's goodnatured acquiescence. In these stanzas the narrator's (and Burns's) play with contrasting levels of style reaches its peak of brilliance:

> The Caird prevail'd—th'unblushing fair
> In his embraces sunk;
> Partly wi' *LOVE* o'ercome sae sair,
> An' partly she was drunk.

Here again the narrator makes use of courtly stereotypes to portray the squalid promiscuity of the beggars. The prettified stock image of "the blushing fair," the heroine of sentimental literature, becomes "th' unblushing fair" in the amoral world of Poosie-Nansie's. Similarly, the reference to capitalized "*LOVE*" in this context is deliciously funny and foreshadows the appearance of Cupid himself in the next stanza:

> But hurchin Cupid shot a shaft,   urchin
> That play'd a *DAME* a shavie—   trick
> The Fiddler *RAK'D* her *FORE AND AFT,*
> Behint the Chicken cavie.   coop

With devastating irony the copulation of Fiddler and Dame is thus explained in terms of Greek mythology; and, as in the previous passage, there is a sudden dropping from the realms of romance or classical myth to the sordid, startling reality ("An' partly she was drunk"). The mind of the reader exults in the sheer brilliance of satiric effects such as these. We are reminded of comparable passages in **"The Holy Fair"** (e.g., "There's some are fou o' *love divine*; / There's some are fou o' *brandy*"), and elsewhere in Burns. As for **"The Jolly Beggars,"** can any reader viewing these passages doubt that the narrator is consciously *making fun* of his beggars?

The Bard's first song which follows this trenchant recitative carries on some of the same stylistic techniques: the juxtaposition of genteel and "hamely" levels of language, the sprinkling of bawdry, and the device of sinking from the ideal to the earthy. The thrust of the Bard's use of high style, however, is rather different from that of the earlier singers. Whereas in the preceding songs the beggars have tended to exalt their way of life by naively comparing it with the romantic or heroic, the Bard instead, through his ironic use of the refrain "an' a' that," implies a rejection of the dream world of classical poetry and chivalric love as so much mumbo-jumbo. Like Robert Fergusson in *The*

King's Birth-Day in Edinburgh, the Bard finds his poetic inspiration, his "Muse," in strong drink:

I never drank the Muse's *STANK,*	pool
Castalia's burn an' a' that,	brook
But there it streams an' richly reams,	froths
My *HELICON* I ca' that.	call

Similarly, he finds his "love" not in the clichés of the sentimental novel but in earthy, promiscuous sex:

In raptures sweet this hour we meet	
Wi' mutual love an' a' that;	
But for how lang the *FLIE MAY*	
STANG,	fly; sting
Let *INCLINATION* law that!	determine

In this context the refrain "an' a' that" clearly means "and all that *nonsense.*" The last stanza and final chorus, full of sexual metaphors—"They've ta'en me in" or "My *DEAREST BLUID*" (semen)—are wholly earthy and wholly Scots in language, so that the real world of the beggars appears to prevail at the end.

In the seventh and final recitative the narrator reverts to *The Cherrie and the Slae* stanza of the opening and to a panoramic overview of the whole scene in Poosie-Nansie's as the orgy of the beggars reaches its wild climax. Again we have an ironic stylistic dropping from the elevated, faintly Miltonic tone of the first three lines to the coarse and graphic quality of the second three:

So sung the *BARD*—and	
Nansie's waws	walls
Shook with a thunder of applause	
Re-echo'd from each mouth!	
They toom'd their pocks, they	emptied;
pawn'd their duds,	bags
They scarcely left to coor	
their fuds	cover their
	buttocks
To quench their lowan drouth.	burning
	thirst

On this note of frenzied drunkenness and excitement the Bard rises, by popular demand, to sing his second song, the finale of **"The Jolly Beggars."**

This song, with its famous radical chorus ("A fig for those by law protected!"), sums up the total beggar view of life that has gradually been unfolded in the six preceding lyrics. It gives us, in standard English, Burns's most conventional expression in the cantata of the grand delusion of the vagabond in literary tradition—the notion that he is truly "free," that he enjoys life more than respectable folk:

Does the sober bed of *MARRIAGE*
Witness brighter scenes of love?

Life is all a *VARIORUM,*
We regard not how it goes;
Let them cant about *DECORUM,*
Who have character to lose.

With great skill Burns weaves these commonplaces from the literature of roguery into a kind of final ritualistic statement of the beggar philosophy, ending significantly with the word "*AMEN!*" The result is impressively powerful.

Indeed, Burns's very success with this climactic finale, with its rousing, nihilistic chorus, has tended to obscure the satiric role of the narrator and his countervailing, conservative point of view—his mockery of the beggars. Critics have generally equated the Bard and his statement with the poet Burns, and have lost track of the fact that Burns's voice is at least equally-present in that of the narrator, that Burns is also the author of the socially orthodox recitatives. A recent commentator, for example, has characterized the final song as "one of the most superb things that ever came from his pen, a proclamation of his faith and of his philosophy which may have shocked the conservative of his day, but which stands firm after nearly two centuries in company with his finest creations" [Cedric Thorpe Davie, "Robert Burns, Writer of Songs," in *Critical Essays on Robert Burns,* 1975]. Such a comment, however valid as an aesthetic judgment, fails to take account of that *other* Burns who wrote the narrative sections in this same work in which he makes fun of the beggars and their "philosophy." To suppose that the drunken Bard's "faith" is identical with that of Burns, his creator, is to oversimplify, to ignore the genuine ambivalence in Burns's attitude toward the beggars. To say that the Bard's final song is a proclamation of Burns's faith is to say that Burns really believed that courts for cowards were erected and that might should make right (as it does in Poosie-Nansie's). Surely not. No doubt the dazzling impressiveness of the finale is at least partly responsible for this lopsided view.

The foregoing stylistic analysis of **"The Jolly Beggars,"** stressing verbal incongruities and Burns's deft play with contrasting levels of style, demonstrates the conservative side of Burns's attitude toward the beggars. He is satirizing their view of life in two basic ways (with some variations). In the songs the satire is indirect and arises out of the absurdity of the beggars' pretending, in their use of elevated language, to the ideals of heroic myth and sentimental romance in the light of the coarseness and squalor of what they are actually doing. In the recitatives the satire is direct and even more devastating as the narrator—detached, amused, and tolerant—depicts the crude goings-on at Poosie-Nansie's with hilarious touches of the mock-heroic and mock-sentimental in his language and imagery.

Of course there is another side to the coin. This essay deals with the matter of radicalism and conservatism in Burns's view of the beggars, but obviously my main effort has been to bring out the conservative aspect. That is by no means to deny the radicalism. Clearly Burns had a great deal of sympathy for these outcasts. He saw them as victims of the same kinds of social and economic injustice and hypocrisy from which he himself suffered. He admired their spirit in the face of adversity; on one side of his mind he applauded their fierce pride and bravado, absurd as these often seemed, recognizing that the beggars had no other resources in facing a hostile world; above all, he relished their humanity, and, like John Gay, saw that in essence they were not unlike their "betters." Certainly, burdened as he was by social pressures, he half envied the beggars' independence and utter irresponsibility. He celebrates their irrepressible *joie de vivre.* In all of these ways, Burns is on the side of the beggars, so to speak, and his cantata is a radical statement concerning the injustice and hypocrisy of society as he knew it. The radicalism is there, and has been more than adequately commented on by others.

The trouble is that nearly all Burns critics have seen *only* the radicalism, and have been blind to the counterbalancing orthodoxy of the narrator, to the contrasting conservative attitude that is also there and is implied in the poetic technique of the entire cantata, both in recitatives and in songs.

The fact is that **"The Jolly Beggars"** is one of the very few masterpieces by Burns which give expression to the full range of his rich and complex personality. In it we hear different voices, as we do in **"Tam O' Shanter"** and one or two other poems. Yet, paradoxically, all the voices are those of Burns in various moods and attitudes, expressing different facets of his mind but somehow unified by the vibrant force of the one personality. The mixture of styles and perspectives in **"The Jolly Beggars"** is rare in Burns's work; we are more accustomed to the kind of poem, whether satiric or romantic (**"Holy Willie's Prayer"** or **"To a Mouse,"** for examples), where a single overwhelming effect is aimed at and achieved. Perhaps the habit of expecting single effects partly accounts for the exclusive stress by critics on the radical point of view in **"The Jolly Beggars"**. Yet there is copious evidence in Burns's other poetry, even more in his letters, of the extraordinary range of his sympathies. We know that the composer of the bawdiest obscenities in **"The Merry Muses"** was also the author of such orthodox moralities as **"Epistle to a Young Friend."** We know that "rantin, rovin' Robin" was also the solid family man who wrote "To make a happy fireside clime / To weans and wife, / That's the true *Pathos* and *Sublime* / Of Human life." The paradoxes and strange contradictions of Burns's personality can be documented ad infinitum from individual poems, songs, and letters. Why, then, should we be surprised to find them together in a single work? **"The Jolly Beggars"** gives us just that: a radical-conservative paradox, the separate contrasting perspectives of beggars and narrator, the dual vision of the creator Burns. And both points of view have their own kinds of validity.

What I am arguing for, then, is a balanced view of **"The Jolly Beggars"** as a profound and moving commentary on the human predicament, on the tension between "freedom" and social responsibility. Burns's point is that the beggars' way is not the answer; their vaunted "freedom" is *not* free to have his way with the Pickpocket, but is swept aside by the brutal Caird. In the realm of Poosie-Nansie, might makes right; there is no justice ("Courts for Cowards were erected") and therefore no genuine freedom; the people live and love like animals. Burns saw clearly enough that for himself and for the mass of mankind such a life was impossible. He realized that if most people chose the beggars' way civilized society, which he valued in spite of its own kinds of injustice, would collapse. Consequently, **"The Jolly Beggars"** is at the same time both a celebration of and a satire on the beggar philosophy; the poet admires and laughs at his characters simultaneously. It is this double vision, this thrust of one point of view against the other, which gives the cantata its tension and much of its unique appeal to all classes of readers. In this masterly work Burns has it both ways. (pp. 125-41)

Allan H. MacLaine, "Radicalism and Conservatism in Burns's 'The Jolly Beggars'," in Studies in Scottish Literature, *Vol. XIII, 1978, pp. 125-43.*

Iain Crichton Smith (essay date 1982)

[*One of Scotland's most prolific contemporary writers, Smith is best known for his poetry in both English and Gaelic. Often compared to his countryman Hugh MacDiarmid, Smith writes analytic verse, avoiding the sentimentality found in much Scottish poetry. In the following excerpt, he argues that the emotion and power of Burns's poetry arise from its universality.*]

I must say that I have never considered Burns a great poet in the same sense as I think of Dante as a great poet. I believe that Burns wrote one indisputably great poem, that is, **'Holy Willie's Prayer',** and I consider this a great poem because it is artistically articulated, and because it expresses perfectly the hypocrite immersed in his own accepted way of life. As for the rest of Burns's work I do not think that it reached the pitch of artistic perfection that this particular poem reaches. **'The Cotter's Saturday Night'** seems to me to be responsible for much of the very bad sentimental poetry that we had in Scotland up until the time that MacDiarmid opened his little country out to the universe, and set it by implication in its true perspective. His parody of a Burns Supper as delivered by a Chinaman says much of what I myself think of that extraordinary ceremony. There is also in Burns an unhealthy Scottish chauvinism which I find disquieting.

Thus it seems to me that Burns has been responsible for much of the inferior poetry that depends on the idea of the 'heart'. The kailyard for example is implicit in **'The Cotter's Saturday Night',** and I often think it odd that Burns himself could see no discrepancy between his own mode of life and that which he praised in **'The Cotter's Saturday Night'.** His attack on the villain who might remove the daughter's virginity might very well have been an attack on himself if he could have seen more clearly than he did. **'The Cotter's Saturday Night'** is a perfect example of much that is wrong with a certain kind of Scottish poetry.

Nevertheless the cult of Burns has to be explained, and I do not simply mean by that the admiration which the Russians and the Chinese have for him, an admiration which is probably political. There is in Burns a quality which makes an appeal to ordinary people and which obviously has little to do with 'artistic articulation'. They read him, for example, when they do not read Ezra Pound or Eliot or, for that matter, MacDiarmid. MacDiarmid is a poet's poet in a way that Burns is not. We go to MacDiarmid for interesting ideas, for a larger vision than we can find in Burns. Where we find in MacDiarmid a continual interest in life itself and man as merely one manifestation of that life, we obviously do not find this in Burns, for Burns is not interested in ideas, and in comparison with MacDiarmid—and for that matter Wordsworth and Coleridge—he is almost naïve. He is not in fact a self-conscious poet in the way that we expect of our moderns and even in the way that Pope was self-conscious.

There is not in Burns's work any artistic obsession, and it seems to me that the corpus of his work looks disturbingly occasional. In a sense Burns was more like Clare than he was like a Wordsworth or Coleridge, except that he is more universal than Clare. For his philosophy is not a complicated one, and amounts to little more than an adage, 'A man's a man for a' that'.

And yet and yet . . . Burns cannot be as easily dismissed as this. In spite of saying that he is not philosophical, that he does not use language in a specifically artistic way, that he is often sentimental and that he is naïve, there is a quality in Burns that cannot easily be turned aside. It is a quality that one finds in his lyrics and that haunts and lingers. It is not the case that any weight of modern learning can be brought to bear on these lyrics, for they are not, for instance, ironical, and irony is perhaps the most common weapon in modern consciousness. Irony implies that a writer is not only concerned with his writing but is also concerned with himself being concerned. What I find in Burns is an unusual simplicity and transparency. It seems to me that Burns was a poet as a 'rose is a rose'; that is to say, we hardly ever find any sense of strain in his work, and especially in the lyrics. We never feel that he is looking for a variant to what he is writing down, and in this sense the lyrics look as if they have been made almost without intervention. There is a speed and rightness in these lyrics which make them almost become part of our poetic corpus, without our wishing to attribute them to anyone. It is useless to say, 'This is a Burns lyric' in the same way as one can say, 'This is a Stevens poem' precisely because the poetry is so naïve. It is as if we were looking through the poet to the universal things that he is writing about.

When I say that we can talk of a 'Stevens poem', what we are concerned with is not only the poem that we are reading but all the other poems that are leading up to this poem and of which this poem forms a part. It is also a question of language and of a specific tone which can be seen as belonging to Stevens alone. But all the time we are aware of a particular mind and consciousness behind these poems in a way that we are not when we read a Burns lyric. In a sense nothing much can be said of a Burns lyric except that it is there. No resources of modern scholarship can be brought to bear on it. And yet it speaks of intense emotion, it is powerful, and it resonates.

For instance, suppose we have a look at the lyric 'The Silver Tassie', which runs as follows:

> Go fetch to me a pint o' wine,
> And fill it in a silver tassie;
> That I may drink before I go,
> A service to my bonie lassie:
> The boat rocks at the Pier o' Lieth
> Fu' loud the wind blaws frae the Ferry,
> The ship rides by the Berwick-law,
> And I maun leave my bony Mary.
>
> The trumpets sound, the banners fly,
> The glittering spears are ranked ready,
> The shouts o' war are heard afar,
> The battle closes deep and bloody.
> It's not the roar o' sea or shore,
> Wad make me langer wish to tarry;
> Nor shouts o' war that's heard afar—

> It's leaving thee, my bony Mary!

I can imagine a scholar trying to find something to say about this poem. For instance he might point to the internal rhymes, or he might remark that the colours in the poem are silver and red, that for instance the silver tassie is linked up with the silver spears and trumpets, or that the wine in the cup links up with the blood mentioned in the second stanza. He might say all these things but they would be irrelevant. In a Stevens poem they might not be irrelevant for he might have used silver and red in other poems for a specific reason. But in Burns they would be irrelevant for Burns does not use these colours significantly as part of an artistic consciousness. All we can say about this poem is found in the cadence, 'It's leaving thee, my bony Mary' or 'And I maun leave my bony Mary'. The poem is there on the page. It is easy to forget about Burns and simply look at what he has created as if it were a stone. There is no sense of strain, no sense of alternative possibilities.

If we look at Blake's lyrics we can imagine other possibilities, other ironies. But Burns's lyrics are presented to us, whole and fresh, and they are open to any reader in a way that Blake's lyrics are not. Of course behind those words are the cadences of the songs based on them, and it is very difficult for one to see and read them without being haunted by these cadences. Nevertheless, what astonishes is their extreme self-confidence and simplicity.

One of his very great lyrics is **'Ae Fond Kiss'**, and again there is this naïve self-confidence as in

> I'll ne'er blame my partial fancy,
> Naething could resist my Nancy:

where the girl is so specifically and easily named.

The fact that the greatest verse perhaps in Burns's lyrics could flow so effortlessly shows not merely the self-confidence of the poet but also the strength of a tradition:

> Had we never lov'd sae kindly,
> Had we never lov'd say blindly!
> Never met—or never parted,
> We had ne'er been broken-hearted.

There is no sense in which this verse makes the rest of the poem seem inferior, because the poet does not in any way strain after the greatness of the verse. As on a piece of land a flower might grow beside an old tin can, so this verse lies with the others and does not appear out of place. For the following lines are not so fine, especially the ones:

> Thine be ilka joy and treasure,
> Peace, Enjoyment, Love and Pleasure!

However, if we compare this with a love lyric by MacDiarmid we are immediately in a different country. The lyric is called 'In the Hedge-Back':

> It was a wild black nicht,
> But i' the hert o't we
> Drave back the darkness wi' a bleeze o' licht,
> Ferrer than men could see.
>
> It was a wild black nicht,
> But o' the snell air we
> Kept juist eneuch to hinder the heat
> Meltin' us utterly.

It was a wild black nicht,
But o' the win's roar we
Kept juist eneuch to hear oor herts beat
Owre it triumphantly.

It was a wild black nicht,
But o' the Earth we
Kept juist eneuch underneath us to ken
That a warl' used to be.

Now it seems to me that this is a great lyric, but it is different from Burns's lyrics in many ways. For one thing the last two lines are beyond Burns. He didn't have that kind of imagination, and perhaps it was not possible to have written like that in the eighteenth century in any case. But there is a drive towards these last two lines which is not typical of Burns, though it is typical of MacDiarmid. But the real difference is this, that this poem does not have the lucid universality that Burns's lyrics have.

A poet who I think derives more from Burns than Mac-Diarmid does is Sidney Goodsir Smith, as for instance in 'Loch Leven':

Tell me was a glorie ever seen
As the morn I left my lass
Fore licht in the toun o snaw,
And saw the dawn
O' burnan cramasie
Turn the grey ice
O' Mary's Loch Leven
Til sheenan brass—
And kent the glorie and the gleen
Was but the waukenin o her een . . .

It seems to me that there is a Burnsian quality haunting that poem, and yet it is not as great a lyric for us as Mac-Diarmid's lyric is. There is a thinness here precisely because the poet relies so much on the cadences. The simplicity that is to be found in this poem looks too simple for the twentieth century. Yet, in their own context, though Burns's poems are simple, they are not irritatingly so.

It is possible that the reason why Wordsworth admired Burns so much was not just because of his creed of independence and humanity, but rather because he envied the tradition that could allow a poet to speak so clearly and so confidently and so unself-consciously. It is rather as if Eliot were envying MacDiarmid for the way in which he can move up and down the ladder of a Scottish democratic language, while, for instance, Eliot's pub scene in *The Waste Land* sounds artificial and strained. There are, for instance, in **'Auld Lang Syne'** two verses which are powerful because Burns could almost take for granted that his readers would have done exactly what is being described in these verses, and indeed we have.

We twa hae run about the braes,
And pou'd the gowans fine;
But we've wander'd mony a weary fitt,
Sin auld lang syne.

We twa hae paidl'd in the burn,
Frae morning sun till dine;
But seas between us braid hae roar'd

Sin auld lang syne.

I think that these lines are very close to great poetry because they are so universal. Again they are written with supernatural ease and self-confidence and are things which neither Wordsworth nor for that matter Coleridge could have written. And I think that this has a great deal to do with a Scottish tradition. It is true that Wordsworth wrote about childhood, but I am sure he did not write as simply and with such naturalness and resonance as this. This union of the familiar and the large was one of Burns's outstanding gifts. There is a directness about these lines which Wordsworth never attained (though he did great things in another mode) and perhaps by the nature of things never could have attained, unless, perhaps, he had written in the Cumberland dialect.

Burns can even do it in **'John Anderson my Jo'** which seems to me to be sentimental and gooey in the verse:

But now your brow is beld, John,
Your locks are like the snaw;
But blessings on your frosty pow,
John Anderson my Jo.

Nevertheless, in spite of these lines, which seem to me to be analogous with **'My Granny's Hieland Hame'** for sentiment, he can be pure and clear as in:

John Anderson my jo, John,
We clamb the hill the gither;
And mony a canty day, John,
We've had wi' ane anither.

Better and very fine indeed is the verse:

The soger frae the war returns,
The sailor frae the main,
But I hae parted frae my Love,
Never to meet again, my dear,
Never to meet again . . .

Where the pause at 'my dear' is like a catch at the heart.

It is possible that much of the simplicity and emotional strength of these lyrics comes from the language and from a tradition, and yet this may not wholly be true, for a poem on childhood which I myself have much admired is 'A Boy's Song' by James Hogg:

Where the pools are bright and deep,
Where the gray trout lies asleep,
Up the river and o'er the lea,
That's the way for Billy and me.

Where the blackbird sings the latest,
Where the hawthorn blooms the sweetest,
Where the nestlings chirp and flee,
That's the way for Billy and me.

Where the mowers mow the cleanest,
Where the hay lies thick and greenest;
There to trace the homeward bee,
That's the way for Billy and me.

Where the hazel bank is steepest,
Where the shadow falls the deepest,
Where the clustering nuts fall free,
That's the way for Billy and me.

Why the boys should drive away

Little sweet maidens from the play,
Or love to banter and fight so well,
That's the thing I never could tell.

But this I know, I love to play,
Through the meadow, among the hay;
Up the water and o'er the lea,
That's the way for Billy and me.

This poem seems to me to have the purity of the verses I have quoted from **'Auld Lang Syne',** and it occurs to me that the reason for this purity is perhaps not so much to do with language as with the nature of Scotland. It may be that these poems have their power because of the fact that the poet could assume that most of the people of Scotland could have done something like this in their childhood: in other words, that the power has to do with the relative democratic nature of a country, for in a sense these poems seem to me to get closer to the pathos of childhood than Wordsworth's poems do, precisely because they are unweighted by a philosophy. As I have said already, Clare would have got closer to this than either Wordsworth or Coleridge, and as far as Blake is concerned it is possible that the cadences he created are more personal and idiosyncratic than those which Burns employed.

Now it is quite impossible for a poet to write like this in the twentieth century, and indeed, if he were directly influenced by these lyrics, he would, I think, appear out-of-date, for we cannot look on women and children as Burns did. A poem like **'A Red Red Rose'** begs too many questions, is too set in one inflated mood for us to write like it, because we would be far more concerned with the shadows. How could we possibly, in our world, speak of such permanency?

> Till a' the seas gang dry, my Dear,
> And the rocks melt wi' the sun:
> I will love thee still, my Dear,
> While the sands o' life shall run.

That is why I think Goodsir Smith's lyrics, some of them I think deriving from Burns, seem so thin in this century simply because of what they have left out. A largeness such as this is beyond us. We could not speak with such eloquence.

In fact, though nothing can diminish my admiration for Burns's lyrics, I feel that they are less individual poems than emanations from a people. And however much we may regret the fact that poetry can no longer be the voice of the people, it is nevertheless the case. When Burns wrote these lyrics he was not speaking out of his own dark life, he was articulating moods. (pp. 22-30)

An early poem of Goodsir Smith's like 'Kinnoul Hill' reads rather like a Burns lyric:

> Kinnoul Hill lies white wi snaw,
> The lyft is pale as stane,
> My burd's dark een 're far awa—
> It's dreich tae bide alane.
>
> It's cauld an gurl on Kinnoul Hill
> As Janiveer gaes oot,
> But neer a blast sae shairp an fell
> As whorls my saul aboot.

> O black's the ice on Kinnoul Brae,
> Dark scaurs like wa's o doom—
> But nane sae mirk 's this dumb wae
> That maks aa Perth a tomb.
>
> My loo, I lang yir airms the nicht,
> My lane's sae fremt an drear—
> An Kinnoul Hill stans bleak an white
> I' the goulin wunds o Janiveer.

The Burnsian cadence can be heard in this lyric, but at the same time it is to be noticed that Smith feels it necessary to break it in the last line as if he felt that the lyric was moving too smoothly.

MacDiarmid once remarked that the most beautiful line in Scottish poetry was that one, **'Ye are na Mary Morison'.** But I do not think that **'Mary Morison'** is a typical Burns lyric. It seems to me to be too vitiated by a foreign poetic diction, such as in the second verse:

> Yestreen when to the trembling string
> The dance gaed through the lighted ha',
> To thee my fancy took its wing,
> I sat, but neither heard nor saw . . .

The directness and speed which are the true characteristics of the Burns lyric seem to me to be missing.

I come back again to a lyric like **'It Was a' for our Rightfu' King',** which has these qualities:

> It was a' for our rightfu' king
> We left fair Scotland's strand;
> It was a' for our rightfu' king,
> We e'er saw Irish land, my dear,
> We e'er saw Irish land.—
>
> Now a' is done that men can do,
> And a' is done in vain:
> My Love and Native Land fareweel,
> For I maun cross the main, my dear,
> For I maun cross the main.
>
> He turned him right and round about,
> Upon the Irish shore,
> And gae his bridle-reins a shake,
> With, Adieu for evermore, my dear,
> And adieu for evermore.
>
> The soger frae the wars returns,
> The sailor frae the main,
> But I hae parted frae my Love,
> Never to meet again, my dear,
> Never to meet again.
>
> When day is gane, and night is come,
> And a' folk bound to sleep;
> I think on him that's far awa',
> The lee-lang night and weep, my dear,
> The lee-lang night and weep.

This lyric seems to me perfect of its kind. There is an energy which is never dissipated by hesitation on the part of the poet. Burns shows complete confidence in the way he moves from description to generalization, as in the fourth verse. It is as if he wrote his best verses as absentmindedly as he wrote the other verses, so that we never feel with him that he is building up to something special. In other words, we are in the presence of an unself-conscious poetry which is, because of its purity and simplicity, universal. What is even more interesting is that this directness and simplicity can be found in his comic poems as well as in his 'romantic ones', and this is the sign of an unusual talent. We find these qualities for instance in **'Duncan Gray'**:

>   Duncan Gray cam here to woo,
>   Ha, ha, the wooing o't,
>   On blythe Yule night when we were fu',
>   Ha, ha, the wooing o't.
>
>   Maggie coost her head fu' high,
>   Look'd asklent and unco skiegh,
>   Gart poor Duncan stand abiegh;
>   Ha, ha, the wooing o't.

It seems to me that Burns in these lyrics has an unusual speed of thought which allows the poem to move very fast and with great energy. It is not, however, the kind of thought that will issue in ideas. It is rather the speed of thought of a poetically gifted mind, sure of itself at all times.

I know no other writer in Scottish literature able to write this sort of universal lyric, dealing so intimately and with such great power with the concerns of ordinary humanity. MacDiarmid's lyrics are something else again: they are new and almost idiosyncratic in a way that Burns's lyrics are not. They are the product of a highly conscious artistic mind. They show genius of a different kind from Burns's. It was possible for Burns to write at a particular moment in history with a freedom and assurance and ease that allowed him to articulate the passions of ordinary people as if they were his own.

There is of course much that these lyrics do not touch on, but they do touch on many important aspects of our emotional lives. They tell us about forsaken love, happy love, about love in old age, about domestic comedy. Time and time again their cadences have a piercing quality as in for instance:

>   There's wild-woods grow, and rivers row,
>   And mony a hill between;
>   But day and night my fancy's flight
>   Is ever wi' my Jean.

There seems to me nothing that he cannot handle in the territory that he has chosen for himself. What we do not have, in all this perfection, is the idiosyncrasy of Burns himself, of the darknesses that he must at times have felt. What we do not have is the slant oddness of a Blake, or the strangeness of some of Wordsworth's lyrics. What we do have is the pure universality of the moods and thoughts of the ordinary person. (pp. 30-3)

The lyrics of Burns are perfect of their kind, and their perfection, poised precariously between sentiment and universal truth, tells us that nothing more can be added. We do not have the confidence to write like this now. We do not have the extraordinary control over the cadence that Burns had. And in any case, after Freud and the rest, we do not have the lack of self-consciousness to write like this. We are no longer able as poets to speak so universally and with such authority and rightness. All we can do is write from within ourselves alone. (p. 35)

Iain Crichton Smith, "The Lyrics of Robert

Burns," in The Art of Robert Burns, *edited by R. D. S. Jack and Andrew Noble, London: Vision Press, 1982, pp. 22-35.*

FURTHER READING

Biography

Fitzhugh, Robert T. *Robert Burns, the Man and the Poet: A Round, Unvarnished Account.* Boston: Houghton Mifflin Co., 1970, 508 p.

>   Portrays Burns as a sophisticated, original poet and a man of remarkable paradoxes. The author quotes extensively from Burns's poetry and correspondence, maintaining that the poet himself is the most worthy biographical source.

Hecht, Hans. *Robert Burns: The Man and His Work.* Translated by Jane Lymburn. Rev. ed. London: William Hodge and Co., 1950, 301 p.

>   Account of Burns's life which strives "to show the universal aspect of Burns by presenting him against the broad backgrounds of British civilization, of the eighteenth century, and of European culture in general."

Criticism

Beaty, Frederick L. "Burns's Comedy of Romantic Love." *PMLA* 83, No. 2 (May 1968): 429-38.

>   Analysis of the comic elements in Burns's poems on love.

Bentman, Raymond. "Robert Burns's Declining Fame." *Studies in Romanticism* 11, No. 3 (Summer 1972): 207-24.

>   Contends that "Burns figures in the major tradition of British poetry and is indeed significant in the transition from the style of poetry written in the early eighteenth century to the style of poetry written in the early nineteenth century."

Brooke, Stopford A. "Robert Burns." In his *Naturalism in English Poetry,* pp. 113-34. New York: E. P. Dutton, 1920.

>   Praises Burns's poetry for its wit, sincerity, and attention to nature.

Brown, Mary Ellen. *Burns and Tradition.* London: Macmillan Press, 1984, 176 p.

>   Investigates the effect of the Scottish oral tradition on Burns's poetry and songs as well as Burns's effect on Scottish culture and tradition.

Daiches, David. *Robert Burns.* Rev. ed. London: Andre Deutsch, 1966, 334 p.

>   Critical examination of Burns's poetry and his development as a poet.

Damico, Helen. "Sources of Stanza Forms Used by Burns." *Studies in Scottish Literature* XII, No. 3 (January 1975): 207-19.

>   Traces Burns's stanza forms to medieval sources.

Davison, Edward. "Robert Burns: Some Reconsiderations."

In his *Some Modern Poets and Other Critical Essays,* pp. 43-74. New York: Harper and Brothers Publishers, 1928.
   Discusses Burns and his poetry in relation to other eighteenth-century poets.

Granger, Byrd Howell. "Folklore in Robert Burns' 'Tam o' Shanter'." In *Folklore International: Essays in Traditional Literature, Belief, and Custom in Honor of Wayland Debs Hand,* edited by D. K. Wilgus, pp. 83-8. Hatboro, Pa.: Folklore Associates, 1967.
   Discusses the elements of folklore in "Tam o' Shanter."

Jack, R. D. S., and Noble, Andrew, eds. *The Art of Robert Burns.* London: Vision Press, 1982, 240 p.
   Collection of essays on Burns and his work.

Keith, Christina. *The Russet Coat: A Critical Study of Burns' Poetry and of Its Background.* London: Robert Hale, 1956, 235 p.
   Analysis of Burns's background, poetry, thought, and significance to Scottish culture.

Kroeber, Karl. "Narrative Poetry and the Romantic Style." In his *Romantic Narrative Art,* pp. 3-11. Madison: University of Wisconsin Press, 1960.
   Discusses "Tam o' Shanter" in relation to the Romantic tradition of narrative poetry.

Low, Donald A., ed. *Robert Burns: The Critical Heritage.* London: Routledge and Kegan Paul, 1974, 447 p.
   Excerpts of critical reaction to Burns's poetry from 1786 through 1859.

———, ed. *Critical Essays on Robert Burns.* London: Routledge and Kegan Paul, 1975, 191 p.
   Collection of essays addressing Burns's language, poems, songs, and his relation to other poets.

MacLaine, Allan H. "Burns's Use of Parody in 'Tam o' Shanter'." *Criticism* 1, No. 4 (Fall 1959): 308-16.
   Identifies "parody as an important stylistic method in 'Tam o' Shanter'."

McGuirk, Carol. *Robert Burns and the Sentimental Era.* Athens: University of Georgia Press, 1985, 193 p.
   Argues that Burns's use of Scots dialect does not limit his significance to English poetry and that sentimental influences on Burns's poetry were far from disastrous.

Montgomerie, William, ed. *New Judgements: Robert Burns.* Glasgow: William McLellan and Co., 1947, 84 p.
   Collection of essays on Burns and his poetry.

Morton, Richard. "Narrative Irony in Robert Burns's 'Tam o' Shanter'." *Modern Language Quarterly* XXII, No. 1 (March 1961): 12-20.
   Contends that the poem's ironic effect is a result of the tension between the story and the storyteller's narrative style.

Sampson, David. "Robert Burns: The Revival of Scottish Literature?" *The Modern Language Review* 80, No. 1 (January 1985): 16-38.
   Discusses the themes of Burns's work and assigns him a unique position in the Scottish and English literary traditions.

Schneider, Mary W. "The Real Burns and 'The Study of Poetry'." *Victorian Poetry* 26, No. 1-2 (Spring-Summer 1988): 135-40.

Comments on the debate between John Campbell Shairp and Matthew Arnold over the nature of Burns's poetry.

Short, Douglas D. "Robert Burns, 'Tam o' Shanter,' and the Authorship of 'Duncan Macleerie'." *Studies in Scottish Literature* XIII (1978): 32-42.
   Suggests that Burns wrote the lyrics for the Scottish folk song "Duncan Macleerie" based on its parallels with "Tam o' Shanter."

Snyder, Franklin B. "Notes on Burns's First Volume." *Modern Philology* XVI, No. 9 (January 1919): 475-83.
   Comments on the omissions and language of the Kilmarnock edition of Burns's poetry.

———. "A Note on Burns's Language." *Modern Language Notes* XLIII, No. 8 (December 1928): 511-18.
   Argues that Burns's use of Scottish dialect in poetry was revolutionary. Snyder also refutes claims that Burns spoke in the dialect of his poems.

———. *Robert Burns: His Personality, His Reputation, and His Art.* 1936. Reprint. Port Washington, N. Y.: Kennikat Press, 119 p.
   Biographical and critical consideration of Burns and his poetry.

Speirs, John. "Burns and English Literature." In *From Blake to Byron.* The New Pelican Guide to English Literature, rev. ed., edited by Boris Ford, vol. 5, pp. 100-09. Harmondsworth, England: Penguin Books, 1982.
   Overview of Burns's poetry.

Weston, John C., Jr. "The Text of Burns' 'The Jolly Beggars'." In *Studies in Bibliography.* Papers of the Bibliographical Society of the University of Virginia, edited by Fredson Bowers, vol. 13, pp. 239-47. Charlottesville, Bibliographical Society of the University of Virginia, 1960.
   Observes that the most commonly reprinted version of Burns's posthumously published poem contains a passage which, he argues, Burns omitted from the poem's finished version.

———. "The Narrator of 'Tam o' Shanter'." *Studies in English Literature, 1500-1900* VIII, No. 3 (Summer 1968): 537-50.
   Considers "Tam o' Shanter" a burlesque of the spiritual and cultural conflicts of Burns's divided self.

———. "Robert Burns' Use of the Scots Verse-Epistle Form." *Philological Quarterly* XLIX, No. 2 (April 1970): 188-210.
   Comments on how Burns modified the Scots verse-epistle form and used it to express his vision of self.

Whitman, Walt. "Robert Burns as Poet and Person." In *Rivulets of Prose: Critical Essays by Walt Whitman,* edited by Carolyn Wells and Alfred F. Goldsmith, pp. 73-91. New York: Greenberg, 1928.
   Enumerates the weaknesses of Burns's poetry but praises his concern for nature and humanity.

Wilbur, Richard. "Explaining the Obvious." In his *Responses: Prose Pieces, 1953-1976,* pp. 139-45. New York: Harcourt Brace Jovanovich, 1976.
   Explication of "A Red, Red Rose."

Wittig, Kurt. "Robert Burns." In his *The Scottish Tradition in Literature,* pp. 199-220. Edinburgh: Oliver and Boyd, 1958.

Assesses Burns's position in the Scottish literary tradition and argues that Burns's best work reveals his intimate contact with his social and natural environment.

Additional coverage of Burns's life and career is contained in the following sources published by Gale Research: *Concise Dictionary of British Literary Biography, 1789-1832;* *Dictionary of Literary Biography,* Vol. 109; *Literature Criticism from 1400 to 1800,* Vol. 3; and *World Literature Criticism.*

Rita Dove

1952-

(Full name Rita Frances Dove) American poet and short story writer.

INTRODUCTION

Best known for *Thomas and Beulah,* which received the 1987 Pulitzer Prize in poetry, Dove is considered one of the leading poets of her generation. In her work she draws on her own perceptions and emotions while also integrating an awareness of history and social issues. These qualities are best evidenced in *Thomas and Beulah,* which commemorates the lives of her grandparents and offers a chronicle of the collective experience of African-Americans during the twentieth century.

Critics have noted a steady development in Dove's poetic career. From the publication of *The Yellow House on the Corner* in 1980, her first book to attract significant criticism, to the release of *Grace Notes* in 1989, Dove has refined her style and technique. Her poetry is characterized by tight control of words and structure, use of color imagery, and a tone that combines objectivity and personal concern. Although many of Dove's poems incorporate black history and directly address racial themes, they present issues, such as prejudice and oppression, that transcend racial boundaries. Dove explained in an interview: "Obviously, as a black woman, I am concerned with race. . . . But certainly not every poem of mine mentions the fact of being black. They are poems about humanity, and sometimes humanity happens to be black." In *The Yellow House on the Corner,* for example, a section is devoted to poems about slavery and freedom. "Parsley," a poem published in *Museum,* recounts the massacre of thousands of Haitian blacks because they allegedly could not pronounce the letter "r" in *perejil,* the Spanish word for "parsley." *Thomas and Beulah* combines racial concerns with historical and personal elements. Loosely based on the lives of Dove's maternal grandparents, *Thomas and Beulah* is divided into two sections. "Mandolin," the opening sequence of poems, is written from the viewpoint of Thomas, a former musician haunted since his youth by the death of a friend. "Canary in Bloom," the other sequence, portrays the placid domestic existence of Thomas's wife, Beulah, from childhood to marriage and widowhood. Through allusions to events outside the lives of Thomas and Beulah—including the Great Depression, the black migration from the rural South to the industrial North, the civil rights marches of the 1960s, and the assassination of President John F. Kennedy—Dove emphasizes the couple's interconnectedness with history. Dove remarked: "I'm always fascinated with seeing a story from different angles, but also, in the two sequences, I'm not interested in the big moments. . . . I was interested in the

thoughts, the things which were concerning these small people, these nobodies in the course of history." Critics have noted that *Thomas and Beulah* successfully recounts Dove's story through vivid imagery and character development.

Grace Notes contains autobiographical poems that delineate Dove's various roles as mother, wife, daughter, sister, and poet. "Pastoral," for example, describes Dove's observations and feelings while nursing her daughter, and "Poem in Which I Refuse Contemplation" relates a letter from her mother that Dove received while in Germany. Like her previous works, *Grace Notes* has been favorably reviewed by critics. Sidney Burris observed that *Grace Notes* "might well be [Dove's] watershed because it shows her blithely equal to the ordeal of Life-After-A-Major-Prize: she has survived her fame."

PRINCIPAL WORKS

POETRY

Ten Poems 1977

The Only Dark Spot in the Sky 1980
The Yellow House on the Corner 1980
Mandolin 1982
Museum 1983
Thomas and Beulah 1986
The Other Side of the House 1988
Grace Notes 1989

OTHER MAJOR WORKS

Fifth Sunday (short stories) 1985

CRITICISM

Arnold Rampersad (essay date 1986)

[*Rampersad is an African-American educator, critic, and the author of the highly respected two-volume biography* The Life of Langston Hughes *(1986-88). In the excerpt below, he praises Dove as one of the most important black writers of the late twentieth century and admires her poetic voice, wide range of subjects, and technique.*]

For the past few years Afro-American poetry has been in a state of inactivity not unlike a deep slumber. Ten or fifteen years ago, black poets stood so very close to the center of the movement for civil rights and black power that they seemed almost to defy W. H. Auden's celebrated lament that poetry makes nothing happen. Then, slowly but steadily, much of the air went out of their practice of the genre. Although the times are hard for all black artists, the losses in this particular area have far exceeded the rate of attrition, so to speak, in fiction or even in drama—for all of the many onerous demands of the stage. Not only is one hard pressed to come up with the name of a black poet of any consequence today who did not first make his or her reputation during the late sixties and very early seventies, it is also very difficult to assert that any of the poets of that period have grown *as poets* in any remarkable way since then. Although writers such as Audre Lorde, June Jordan, and Mari Evans have continued to be effective and influential, no poet, as far as I can tell, has built on his or her beginnings in the late sixties in anything like the way that Toni Morrison, Alice Walker, John Wideman, Gloria Naylor, and David Bradley, for example, have built on their own starts in fiction during the same period.

If one looks at *male* poets, as a separate category, the contrast is perhaps even more severe and puzzling. Unlike the leading role and the plentiful number of male poets, such as Amiri Baraka, Don L. Lee, and Etheridge Knight, at the height of the movement, impressive young black male poets seem to have all but disappeared from the scene. There are exceptions, of course—but my sense is of a particular dearth of black men as poets today; it seems to be almost unfashionable now to be both a black male and a poet. However, the weak performance by young male

writers is probably only a token of the general decline in the art of verse in recent years within black culture, especially as compared to what has happened in fiction.

Now, on the other hand, with the consistently accomplished work of thirty-three year old Rita Dove, there is at least one clear sign if not of a coming renaissance of poetry, then at least of the emergence of an unusually strong new figure who might provide leadership by brilliant example. Thus far, Rita Dove has produced a remarkable record of publications in a wide range of respected poetry and other literary journals. Two books of verse, *The Yellow House on the Corner* (1980) and *Museum* (1983), have appeared from Carnegie-Mellon University Press. A third book-length manuscript of poetry, *Thomas and Beulah,* is scheduled to be published early in 1986 by the same house. Clearly Rita Dove has both the energy and the sense of professionalism required to lead other writers. Most importantly—even a first reading of her two books makes it clear that she also possesses the talent to do so. Dove is surely one of the three or four most gifted young black American poets to appear since LeRoi Jones ambled with deceptive nonchalance onto the scene in the late nineteen fifties, and perhaps the most disciplined and technically accomplished black poet to arrive since Gwendolyn Brooks began her remarkable career in the nineteen forties.

These references to the sixties and early seventies are pointed. Rita Dove's work shows a keen awareness of this period—but mainly as a point of radical departure for her in the development of her own aesthetic. In many ways, her poems are exactly the opposite of those that have come to be considered quintessentially black verse in recent years. Instead of looseness of structure, one finds in her poems remarkably tight control; instead of a reliance on reckless inspiration, one recognizes discipline and practice, and long, taxing hours in competitive university poetry workshops and in her study; instead of a range of reference limited to personal confession, one finds personal reference disciplined by a measuring of distance and a prizing of objectivity; instead of an obsession with the theme of race, one finds an eagerness, perhaps even an anxiety, to transcend—if not actually to repudiate—black cultural nationalism in the name of a more inclusive sensibility. Hers is a brilliant mind, reinforced by what appears to be very wide reading, that seeks for itself the widest possible play, an ever expanding range of reference, the most acute distinctions, and the most subtle shadings of meaning.

In what I take to be Dove's determination to break new ground and set fresh standards in relation to the black writers of the half-generation before her, there are some dangers. The most subtle of these she may not have completely avoided: some of her work seems to have been conceived and written, however unconsciously at times, in a spirit of reaction. This is almost to be expected, since Dove must be acutely aware of herself as a poetic reformer, one with great potential as a leader, even if she hardly ever condescends to expose her indignations. One must assume, however, that her hostility to the "black arts" tradition is at least in part behind her astonishing poem **"Upon**

Meeting Don L. Lee, in a Dream," from *The Yellow House on the Corner:*

> . . . Moments slip by like worms.
> "Seven years ago . . ." he begins; but
> I cut him off: "Those years are gone—
> What is there now?" He starts to cry; his eye-
>   balls
>
> Burst into flame. I can see caviar
> Imbedded like buckshot between his teeth.
> His hair falls out in clumps of burned-out wire.
> The music grows like branches in the wind.
>
> I lie down, chuckling as the grass curls around
>   me.
> He can only stand, fists clenched, and weep
> Tears of iodine, while the singers float away,
> Rustling on brown paper wings.

Dreaming or awake, Dove in her art certainly confronts Lee in his own once dominating, or domineering, version of the poet's role. Her opposition may be couched in this poem in highly personal terms (neutralized by the idea that the perception of Lee here is in a dream), but it is in fact mainly philosophic. Dove sees poetry, its dignity, nature, and functions, in a way quite different from most of the writers who came just before her. These writers sometimes used poems the way a Jacobin mob used cobblestones—because there was nothing more destructive at hand. Not so Dove, who clearly comes to verse with a profound respect and love, and an appropriate solicitude for its tradition and future. For some people, such an approach is hopelessly retrograde; for Dove, I suspect, it is as necessary as life itself.

As a poet, Dove is well aware of black history. One of the five sections of *The Yellow House* is devoted entirely to poems on the theme of slavery and freedom. These pieces are inspired by nameless but strongly representative victims of the "peculiar institution," as well as by more famous heroic figures (who may be seen as fellow black writers, most of them) such as Solomon Northrup, abducted out of Northern freedom on a visit to Washington ("I remember how the windows rattled with each report. / Then the wine, like a pink lake, tipped. / I was lifted—the sky swivelled, clicked into place"), and the revolutionary David Walker ('Compass needles, / eloquent as tuning forks, shivered, pointing north. / Evenings, the ceiling fan sputtered like a second pulse. / *Oh Heaven! I am full!! I can hardly move my pen!!!*"). In these works and others such as **"Banneker"** in the later volume, *Museum,* Dove shows both a willingness and a fine ability to evoke, through deft vignettes, the psychological terror of slavery. She is certainly adept at recreating graphically the starched idioms of the eighteenth and early nineteenth centuries, at breathing life into the monumental or sometimes only arthritic rhythms of that vanished and yet still echoing age. Her poems in this style and area are hardly less moving than those of Robert Hayden, who made the period poem (the period being slavery) virtually his own invention among black poets. Dove's special empathy as a historical poet seems to be with the most sensitive, most eloquent blacks, individuals of ductile intelligence made neurotic by pain, especially the pain of not being understood and of not being able to express themselves. The scientist Benjamin Banneker:

> What did he do except lie
> under a pear tree, wrapped in
> a great cloak, and meditate
> on the heavenly bodies?
> *Venerable,* the good people of Baltimore
> whispered, shocked and more than
> a little afraid. After all it was said
> he took to strong drink.
> Why else would he stay out
> under the stars all night
> and why hadn't he married?
>
> But who would want him! Neither
> Ethiopian nor English, neither
> lucky nor crazy, a capacious bird
> humming as he penned in his mind
> another inflamed letter
> to President Jefferson—he imagined
> the reply—polite, rhetorical . . .

Dove writes few poems about racism today. One might say that she apparently declines to dwell on the links between past history and present history. Sensitive to the demands of her art, she perhaps is wary of what she perceives as the trap set by race for the black writer. She writes of black experience, but mainly in the course of "ordinary" things—where a given human situation is recognizably black but not defined even in part by the tension that many of us see as ever-present between the races. The situations she describes that involve blacks are almost always very close to the poet's private experience, part of her personal and family history; both inside and outside of this tight little circle there is little sense of racial identification even in the objective sense of the term. Such meagerness of racial feeling may have curious, even dubious roots—a question that surfaces disturbingly when one searches for the final meaning of a poem such as **"Nigger Song: An Odyssey":**

> We six pile in, the engine churning ink:
> We ride into the night.
> Past factories, past graveyards
> And the broken eyes of windows, we ride
> Into the gray-green nigger night.
>
> We sweep past excavation sites; the pits
> Of gravel gleam like mounds of ice.
> Weeds clutch at the wheels;
> We laugh and swerve away, veering
> Into the black entrails of the earth,
> The green smoke sizzling on our tongues . . .
> In the nigger night, thick with the smell of cab-
>   bages,
> Nothing can catch us.
> Laughter spills like gin from glasses,
> And "yeah" we whisper, "yeah"
> We croon, "yeah."

Further complicating the matter are poems that indicate that Dove, who sometimes poetically masks herself as a shy, withdrawing spirit, knows something about rage inspired by political and social injustice. **"Parsley,"** the last poem in *Museum,* is a chilling evocation of the madness that led General Trujillo allegedly to order the massacre of thousands of Haitian blacks in the Dominican Republic apparently because they could not pronounce the letter "r" in *perejil,* the Spanish word for "parsley." The Haitians speak, to open the poem:

> There is a parrot imitating spring
> in the palace, its feathers parsley green.
> Out of the swamp the cane appears
>
> To haunt us, and we cut it down. El General
> searches for a word; he is all the world
> there is. Like a parrot imitating spring,
>
> we lie down screaming as rain punches through
> and we come up green. We cannot speak an
>   R— . . .

As a theme in verse, Dove seems to say, indignation at social injustice has a place but one that should not be too prominent; *racial* indignation must be even more discreet. Indignation tends to destroy art itself, she apparently believes, especially black art; a confrontation with racism appears to open the world but often only opens a void that gapes deceitfully between the poet and her possession of the wide world. Dove wishes nothing less than possession of that wide world; she longs for the complete freedom of her imagination:

> I prove a theorem and the house expands:
> the windows jerk free to hover near the ceiling
> the ceiling floats away with a sigh.
>
> As the walls clear themselves of everything
> but transparency, the scent of carnations
> leaves with them. I am out in the open
>
> and above the windows have hinged into butter-
>   flies,
> sunlight glinting where they've intersected.
> They are going to some point true and unproven.

"The house expands"—but Dove's expansions begin, as they should, with the familiar. The reader can easily be distracted by the many sophisticated or even arcane references in *The Yellow House on the Corner* and *Museum* from seeing the extent to which the poet, for all her ambition, breathes an affection for the homely and the familiar that is signalled in the title of her first book before being countered (as if on purpose, in fear of too much familiarity?) in the title of her second. I referred earlier to the mask of a shy, withdrawing spirit she sometimes wears; nevertheless, that spirit ("My heart, shy mulatto," as she puts it in one place when she writes of her adolescence), as a transcended part of her psychological history, remains authentic in its way. Many of her most affecting poems take us back to those years when romantic doubt, intimidation by the complex newness of life, and a survivor's gift for fantasy stepped in spontaneously between emotion and calm intelligence. So uncompromising is Dove's later, adult intelligence that we cling to some of these "softer" poems in relief.

In *The Yellow House,* one finds **"A Suite for Augustus"** and the three-part **"Adolescence"** grounding the larger work and then sanctioning Dove's more ambitious flights; the same is true for the beautiful section "My Father's Telescope" in *Museum.* **"A Suite for Augustus"** sketches the passage of years between a knob-kneed virginity and the arrival of womanhood, between nervous black adolescences, male and female, and the final "making" of the cool world. With deft wordplay, an excellent dramatic sense, and a sure ability to choose just the right fragment of experience and expose it to precisely the correct amount of light, Dove takes us—within the space of relatively few lines—on a historical tour of a sensibility. The suite opens with **"1963"**:

> That winter I stopped loving the President
> And loved his dying. He smiled
> From his frame on the chifforobe
> And watched as I reined in each day
> Using buttons for rosary beads.
>
> Then tapwater rinsed orange through my under-
>   wear.
> You moved away . . .

Adolescent waywardness, its haunted, quixotic eye and self-absorbed, self-caressing languor of temperament, merge gradually with the will towards monumentality of a gifted, ambitious persona who eventually will look back mainly to help her chart the way ahead. Unafraid of temporary obscurity, of the surreal half-note, but always seeking finally the representation of clear vision, Dove moves stylishly from effect to effect. **"Planning the Perfect Evening"**:

> . . . Stardust. The band folds up
> resolutely, with plum-dark faces.
> The night still chirps. Sixteen cars
>
> caravan to Georgia for a terrace,
> beer and tacos. Even this far south
> a thin blue ice shackles the moon,
>
> and I'm happy my glass sizzles with stars.
> How far away the world! And how hulking
> you are, my dear, my sweet black bear!

As a poet, Dove loathes sentimentality; she is so hypersensitive to false sweetness that her work will sometimes seem far too demanding to the reader who takes honey with his poetry. Perhaps this general principle, as much as anything else, also explains her tough-minded attitude to race. Certainly she is only modestly sentimental about her own past; she insists on looking back with dancing irony and a disciplined will to understand, and not simply evoke or indulge. Dove's aim in her evocations of her past, her "roots," is a glistening but really scrubbed and unvarnished remembrance of lost time. **"Grape Sherbet,"** from "My Father's Telescope":

> The day? Memorial.
> After the grill
> Dad appears with his masterpiece—
> swirled snow, gelled light.
> We cheer. The recipe's
> a secret and he fights
> a smile, his cap turned up
> so the bib resembles a duck.
>
>   . . .
> Everyone agrees—it's wonderful!
> It's just how we imagined lavender
> would taste. The diabetic grandmother
> stares from the porch,
> a torch of pure refusal . . .

Dove insists on a more austere governance of intimacy than many poets, and most people, are willing to concede.

Even when she looks back with affection on the memory of growing up with her father, her manner is one of mock chastisement. The stars are *not* far apart, as he had taught her. No; with passing time

> . . . houses
> shrivel, un-lost,
>
> and porches sag;
> neighbors phone
>
> to report cracks
> in the cellar floor,
>
> roots of the willow
> coming up. Stars
>
> speak to a child.
> The past
>
> is silent. . . .

Between father and daughter, now man and grown woman, "Outer space is / inconceivably / intimate."

As much as she values home, Dove ranges widely as writer; it is an essential part of her commission to herself as a poet. Europe, as the prime example, is a neighboring field to be mastered like the field of home. The composer Robert Schumann, a German woman who has lost her man in war and lives thereafter crazed by grief ("She went inside, / fed the parakeet, / broke its neck"), the age-old science and mystery and ritual of making champagne—Rita Dove sees everywhere a continuity of human experience. Africa and Asia come more lightly within her frame of reference, but nowhere is she a perfect stranger. The past, too, for her is everything in human history of which she can be made aware, not least of all in the antiquity of Europe and Asia, or the Middle Ages. Dove's approach is neither panoramic nor political; still less is it for cultural genuflection. Cerebral, skeptical, and yet at the same time intensely human, she looks on the wide world and the fallen centuries, with the same essentially ironic consciousness, the same shrewd intelligence that does not absolutely forbid love, but conditions it, that marks the recreation of her own private past. **"Catherine of Alexandria"** memorializes a celebrated would-be martyr of the early Christian church:

> Deprived of learning and
>   the chance to travel,
> No wonder sainthood
>   came as a voice
>
> in your bed—
>   and what went on
> each night was fit
>   for nobody's ears
>
> but Jesus'. His
>   breath of a lily.
> His spiraling
>   pain. Each morning
>
> the nightshirt bunched
>   above your waist—
> a kept promise,
>   a ring of milk.

Dove's imaginative flights are tacked down again and gain

by homey details: "the woolens stacked on cedar / shelves back home in your / father's shop," in **"Catherine of Siena"**; the "two bronze jugs, worth more / than a family pays in taxes / for the privilege to stay / alive, a year, together," in **"Tou Wan Speaks To Her Husband, Liu Sheng."** On the patina of dust obscuring the humanity of the past from our eyes Rita Dove quietly traces a finger. She writes in a colloquial, familiar idiom that subdues the glittering exotic and makes the ultimate effect of most of these "foreign" poems to be nothing less than a documentation of her claim to the whole world as her home.

The absence of strain in her voice, and the almost uncanny sense of peace and grace that infuses this wide-ranging poetry, suggest that Dove has already reached her mature, natural stride as a poet. I suspect that this judgment might be premature in itself. Both volumes are so tightly controlled, so guarded against excess, that some readers may find them in certain places—perhaps even as a totality—too closely crafted, too reserved, for unqualified appreciation. I think that what we may have in these two books—although they already outclass the complete works of many other poets, and virtually all black poets of Dove's generation—is in fact only the beginning of a major career. In which direction will Dove's great talent take her? I believe that, paradoxically for someone so determined to be a world citizen, she may yet gain her greatest strength by returning to some place closer to her old neighborhood.

Very carefully, I do not say her "home"—much less her "real home" or her "true home." Such terms, made shabby by the hucksters, are millstones to a poet like Dove; for her, a house is not necessarily a home. In the end, she may yet as a poet redefine for all of us what "home" means. Dove herself would probably benefit in her own way as an artist from this active redefinition. Then one should perhaps see in her work a loosening of rhythms and a greater willingness to surrender to improvisational and other gifts that she has kept in check but certainly earned the right to indulge. I would expect a vision growing more and more—again paradoxically—into narrower focus and consistency, with the emphasis shifting from irony and learning and calm intelligence towards the celebrations of the more wayward energy that springs naturally out of human circumstance. (pp. 52-60)

Arnold Rampersad, "The Poems of Rita Dove," in Callaloo, *Vol. 9, No. 1, Winter, 1986, pp. 52-60.*

Robert McDowell   (essay date 1986)

[*McDowell is an American critic, educator, and poet whose work, like Dove's, is praised for its lyrical quality. In the following excerpt, he presents an overview of Dove's poetry up to the publication of* Thomas and Beulah *and discusses her development as a poet.*]

Rita Dove has always possessed a storyteller's instinct. In **The Yellow House on the Corner** (1980), **Museum** (1983), and . . . **Thomas and Beulah** [1986], this instinct has found expression in a synthesis of striking imagery, myth, magic, fable, wit, humor, political comment, and a sure knowledge of history. Many contemporaries share Dove's mastery of some of these, but few succeed in bringing them together to create a point of view that, by its breadth and force, stands apart. She has not worked her way into this enviable position among poets without fierce commitment.

Passing through a graduate writing program (Iowa) in the mid-seventies, Dove and her peers were schooled in the importance of sensation and its representation through manipulation of The Image. The standard lesson plan, devised to reflect the ascendancy of Wallace Stevens and a corrupt revision of T. S. Eliot's objective correlative, instructed young writers to renounce realistic depiction and offer it up to the province of prose; it promoted subjectivity and imagination-as-image; it has strangled a generation of poems.

How and why this came to pass is less important, really, than admitting that it is so. Literary magazines are gorged with poems devoid of shapeliness and scope. Imagistic, cramped and confessional, they exist for the predictably surprising, climactic phrase. An historically conscious reader, aware of literary tradition, might understandably perceive an enormous cultural amnesia as the dubiously distinguishing feature of such poems. Such a reader will rue the fact that the writing and interpretation of poetry has diminished to a trivial pursuit, a pronouncement of personal instinct. If this is the dominant direction of a discouraging Moment, then Rita Dove distinguishes herself by resolutely heading the other way.

Unlike the dissembling spirit indicted above, Dove is an assembler who gathers the various facts of this life and presents them in ways that jar our lazy assumptions. She gives voice to many positions and many characters. Like the speaker / writer of classic argumentation, she shows again and again that she understands the opposing sides of conflicts she deals with. She tells all sides of the story. Consider the titles of her books, their symbolic weight. The personal turning point *House on the Corner* evolves, becoming the public Museum (symbol of preserved chronology); that, in turn, gives way to the names of two characters whose lives combine and illustrate the implicit meanings of the personal House and the public Museum.

The Yellow House on the Corner, first of all, is a showcase for Dove's control of the language. This is our first encounter with the powerful images we have come to associate with her work:

> The texture of twilight made me think of
> Lengths of dotted Swiss.
>
> As the sun broke the water into a thousand nee-
> dles
> tipped with the blood from someone's finger . . .
>
> This nutmeg stick of a boy in loose trousers!

These are the observations of original sight.

There is also the rich and heavily symbolic use of color—red, orange, blue, yellow, and black and white. They usually appear as adjectives, but her adjectival preoccupation comes across with a difference. For example, while repeatedly employing *black* as an adjective ("black place," "black table," "prune-black water," "horses black,"

"black tongues," "my black bear"), she never settles for quick agreement based on obvious connotations. Instead, she injects the adjectives with tantalizing ambiguity and new meanings based on their relationships to other words. She redefines our connotative relationship to them. She outdistances most poets simply because she understands that adjectives enhance nouns by better defining them; they are part of the equations we are born to cope with, not substitutes for weak noun counterparts.

The Yellow House also introduces the poet's devotion to myth, her determination to reveal what is magical in our contemporary lives. (pp. 61-2)

In ["This Life"], "The Bird Frau," "The Snow King," "Beauty and the Beast," and others, she echoes, distorts, and revises ancient myths; in "Upon Meeting Don L. Lee in a Dream" and "Robert Schumann, Or: Musical Genius Begins with Affliction," she focuses on characters whose actual lives have been the stuff of myths.

These and a number of short love poems comprise one side of Dove's Grand Equation. Travelogue poems (consistent throughout her work) erect a transitional bridge between her myth-making component and the historical, public side of the equation: poems examining race relations in America. At their best, poems from the myth-making category are lyrical and mysterious; poems from the latter category are heartbreakingly honest and inescapable. Though these last poems are placed throughout the volume, the third section is made up entirely of them, a fact which makes it the most relentless and coherent segment of the book.

In these poems, Dove makes the reader aware of the relationship between private and public events. "The Transport of Slaves from Maryland to Mississippi," for example, is based on an incident of 1839 in which a slave woman thwarts the escape of a wagonload of slaves by helping the driver regain his horse. The narrative point of view shifts three times, revealing the complexity of the incident and of the characters involved in it. No prescriptive strategy limits expression, as the woman's opening monologue makes clear. Describing the driver she says, " . . . his eyes were my eyes in a yellower face. . . . He might have been a son of mine." The justification of her act is poignant even though its consequences are disastrous for her fellows.

This section of *The Yellow House* is bold and beautifully elegiac, presenting the motives and gestures of all of the dramatic players. The poet's wise utterance peels back the rhetorically thick skin of injustice and exposes Man's inhumanity for what it is: unbearable, shameful, unforgettable.

> Well,
> that was too much for the doctor.
> Strip 'em! he ordered. And they
> were slicked down with bacon fat and
> superstition strapped from them
> to the beat of the tam-tam. Those strong enough
> rose up too, and wailed as they leapt.
> It was a dance of unusual ferocity.
>
> ("Cholera")

That final grim understatement intensifies the reader's outrage.

Dove's synthesis of an historical consciousness, devotion to myth, and virtuoso manipulation of parts of speech convey us into the world of her major thematic preoccupation. In one poem she writes "My heart, shy mulatto," which informs the closing lines of a later poem like **"Adolescence—III."**

> . . . I dreamed how it would happen:
> He would meet me by the blue spruce,
> A carnation over his heart, saying,
> "I have come for you, Madam;
> I have loved you in my dreams."
> At his touch, the scabs would fall away.
> Over his shoulder, I see my father coming to-
>   ward us:
> He carries his tears in a bowl,
> And blood hangs in the pine-soaked air.

This poem, and this volume's cumulative thrust, redefines the poet's need to reconcile the conventional, Romantic American wish (that life be a fairy tale) with the cruel facts of Black America's heritage.

Museum begins with travelogues, which prepare the reader for travel poems that eclipse the personal by introducing overlooked historical detail. **"Nestor's Bathtub,"** a pivotal poem in this respect, begins with the lines "As usual, legend got it all wrong." This announces a dissatisfaction with the conventional ordering of events and an intention to rejuvenate history by coming up with new ways of telling it. In successive poems (**"Tou Wan Speaks to Her Husband, Liu Sheng," "Catherine of Alexandria," "Catherine of Siena," "Boccaccio: The Plague Years,"** and its companion piece, **"Fiammetta Breaks Her Peace"**), Dove adopts a variety of personae that bear witness to the struggles of victimized women in societies in which men are dubiously perceived as gods.

This strategy continues into the book's second section, though the subjects and personae are primarily male (**"Shakespeare Say," "Banneker," "Ike"**). Here is the narrator in **"Reading Holderlin on the Patio with the Aid of a Dictionary"**:

> The meaning that surfaces
> comes to me aslant and
> I go to meet it, stepping
> out of my body
> word for word, until I am
> everything at once.

As in *The Yellow House,* in *Museum* Dove focuses on characters, and chooses characters to speak through, from the historical rosters of those whose lives have been the stuff of fable. Toward the end of this section, her identification with historical and mysterious male-female consciousness is most complete in **"Agosta the Winged Man and Rasha the Black Dove."** In this poem she tells the story of a pair of German circus performers, an inscrutable deformed man and an equally inscrutable black woman who dances with snakes. These characters are performers, who like the poet, look at the world in unique ways.

> Agosta in
> classical drapery, then,
> and Rasha at his feet.
> Without passion. Not
> the canvas
> >   but their gaze,
> >   so calm,
> was merciless.

The poem that follows, **"At the German Writers Conference in Munich,"** examines and exploits this preoccupation from another angle. In the poem another art—another way of performing—is described. The calm, stiff characters of a tapestry are not outwardly grotesque as are the characters in the preceding poem. Nevertheless, they appear to be out of step with their woven environment, existing as they do in a world of flowers. The two poems, together, illustrate a brilliant shifting of focus, a looking out of the eyes of characters, then a merciless looking into them.

The third section of *Museum* contains a focusing down of this strategy in a tight group of Family poems in which the father is the dominant character. He is perceived by the innocent narrator as the teacher, the bearer of all that is magical in the world.

> I've been trying
> to remember the taste,
> but it doesn't exist.
> Now I see why
> you bothered,
> father.
>
> > (**"Grape Sherbet"**)

Whether he is making palpable an impalpable taste or miraculously rescuing roses from beetles (**"Roses"**), or deftly retrieving what is magical from a mistake (**"My Father's Telescope"**), he is clearly the narrator's mentor, inspiring a different way of meeting the world:

> this
> magician's skew of scarves
> issuing from an opaque heart.
> > (**"A Father Out Walking On the Lawn"**)

Dove on the writing process:

I don't think poetry is going to make anyone a better person, and it is not going to save you. But writing is a constant for me. There's an edge that needs to be explored, the edge between being unconscious and then suddenly being so aware that the skin tingles. Let me be more precise. There is that moment in the writing of a poem when things start to come together, coalesce into a discovery. This is sheer bliss, and has something to do with discovering something about myself. It doesn't mean I understand myself; in fact, the more I write the less I know of myself. But I also learn more. Territory is being covered—excursions into the interior. I write for those moments of discovery really, but there are two steps in this process: one is the intimate revelation, and the second step is to take that revelation and to make it visible—palpable—for others.

Rita Dove, in "Coming Home: An Interview with Rita Dove," in The Iowa Review, *1989.*

But even in this tender, celebratory section, Dove includes one poem, **"Anti-Father,"** which satisfies her self-imposed demand that she tell all sides of the story.

> Just between
>
> me and you,
> woman to man,
>
> outer space is
> inconceivably
>
> intimate.

The innocent narrator, now a knowledgeable woman, reverses roles here, contradicting the father but offering magical insight in doing so.

The closing section of Rita Dove's second volume summarizes all that has preceded it, and in two remarkable poems, anticipates *Thomas and Beulah.*

The narrator of **"A Sailor in Africa"** spins off from a Viennese card game (circa 1910) and unravels the adventures of the characters in the game. A black slave, who is actually a sea captain, outwits his captors and takes over their ship. He is shipwrecked later, only to discover great wealth in his isolation. This effortless storytelling combines Dove's great strengths—memorable images, wit, travelogue, fable, complex representation of motive and gesture, historical awareness—and is a groundbreaking poem.

It is balanced and rivaled by **"Parsley,"** the book's concluding poem, which tells the story of a dictator who orders the annihilation of 20,000 blacks because they cannot pronounce the letter "r." The poem is constructed in two parts. The first, a villanelle, presents the entire drama; it is all the more terrifying because the facts smash against the stark and beautiful container of the form itself. In the second part of the poem, a third person narrator examines the dictator's relationship to his mother, who can "roll her 'r's' like a queen."

> As he paces he wonders
> who can I kill today . . .
>
>   Someone
> calls out his name in a voice
> so like his mother's, a startled tear
> splashes the tip of his right boot.
> *My mother, my love in death.*

As she often does, Dove unerringly combines private and public political history in this and in many other poems in *Museum.* It is a direction that flourishes on a book-length scale in *Thomas and Beulah.*

"These poems tell two sides of a story and are meant to be read in sequence." So begins *Thomas and Beulah.* Their story is told twice: from Thomas's point of view in the twenty-three poems of "Mandolin," and from Beulah's point of view in the twenty-one poems of "Canary in Bloom." The time, according to an extensive Chronology at book's end, covers the years 1919-1968. Most of the story takes place in Akron, Ohio, a city, which the Chronology also tells us, had a Negro population of 11,000 (out of a total population of 243,000) in 1940.

The chief narrative method employed, the story twice-told, does not rely so much on action; it relies on reactions of characters to events and circumstances that affect them even though they are wholly beyond them. The questions generated by this approach are chilling and clear: if two characters, deeply involved with one another, interpret events (inner and outer, private and public) so differently, what does this suggest about our manipulation of history; what does it say about our reliability as witnesses, as teachers of successive generations; what is true?

Truth in *Thomas and Beulah* is found in the characters themselves. In **"The Event,"** the first poem in the section entitled "Mandolin," Thomas leaves Tennessee for the riverboat life. He travels with a good friend, Lem, and a magical symbol, a talisman which gathers pain and wards it off—his mandolin. In a turn that explodes the deliberate echo of Mark Twain's *Huck Finn,* Lem dives overboard to collect chestnuts on a passing island and drowns. This tragedy, at the outset of his journey, will haunt Thomas for the rest of his life. We observe his arrival in Akron in 1921, deftly and desperately playing his mandolin for pay. He is a driven figure, confronting his guilt and his second-class citizenship in a racially divided country. His half-hearted attempts to sell himself in such a country will drive the more sheltered Beulah to find fault in him. It is a key element of his tragedy that he faults himself for it, too:

> He used to sleep like a glass of water
> held up in the hand of a very young girl.

and later,

> To him work is a narrow grief
> and the music afterwards
> like a woman
> reaching into his chest
> to spread it around.
>
>   ("Straw Hat")

After their marriage, the promise of equality and upward mobility is profoundly betrayed. The world is threatening, malicious after all. In **"Nothing Down,"** they buy a new car for a trip to Tennessee, but the symbol and the dream it represents are destroyed when they're passed by a carload of jeering whites; in **"The Zeppelin Factory,"** Thomas lands construction work, laboring on the largest building in the world without interior supports (another appropriate, unforgettable symbol for the world we make) and hates it; Thomas ponders the impending birth of a third daughter against the backdrop of union violence (**"Under the Viaduct"**); Thomas walks out of a movie house to witness a splendid natural phenomenon (**"Aurora Borealis"**), but even this double barreled symbolic magic is overpowered by the grim facts of the world around him. Finally, he finds even his oldest companion, his mandolin, estranged:

> How long has it been . . . ?
> Too long. Each note slips
> into querulous rebuke, fingerpads
> scarred with pain, shallow ditches
> to rut in like a runaway slave
> with a barking heart. Days afterwards
> blisters to hide from the children.

Hanging by a thread. *Some day,*
he threatens, *I'll just*
let go.
      ("Definition in the Face of Unnamed Fury")

Only in his own good heart is Thomas vindicated, and the physical manifestation of his goodness is his family. In **"Roast Opossum,"** he spins two tales for his grandchildren: hunting opossum for Malcolm, a tale of horses for the girls. This tender poem makes a case for salvation implicit in one generation's nurturing another by gathering and making palpable history and myth, fact and fiction. In such ritual we discover our one defense against the inhuman things we do to one another.

The section concludes with three elegiac poems covering the events of Thomas's declining health and eventual death. **"The Stroke"** contains a lovely memory of Beulah during pregnancy and his certainty that the pain he feels is Lem knocking on his chest. In the end, Thomas appropriately suffers his final heart attack behind the wheel of his car (**"Thomas at the Wheel"**).

Whereas Thomas's life is a perpetual scramble toward definition, Beulah's, as presented in "Canary in Bloom," is pre-ordained. She will marry; she will bear children. These restrictions force her to develop an inward, private life. For example, her fear and distrust of male figures is established early in **"Taking in Wash."** Her father comes home drunk:

> Tonight
>
> every light hums, the kitchen arctic
> with sheets, Papa is making the hankies
> sail. Her foot upon a silk
> stitched rose, she waits
> until he turns, his smile sliding all over.

This is the seed of her reaction to her suitor and future husband. She would prefer a pianola to his mandolin; she hates his yellow scarf. When they marry, "rice drumming / the both of them blind," she sees Thomas as "a hulk, awkward in blue serge." Her father places her fingertips in Thomas's hand, and men in collusion have delivered her up to her fate.

From this point on, Beulah's story seeks the form, the shape, of meditation. In **"Dusting"** she fondly remembers a boy at a fair, comparing that magical location and meeting with the hard news of her life. In **"Weathering Out"** she daydreams through her seventh month of pregnancy, glad to be rid of Thomas as he daily hunts for work. In the sad **"Daystar"** she reclines in the backyard while the children nap and dreams of a place where she is nothing. In **"The Great Palace of Versailles"** she works in a dress shop, frequents the library, and temporarily loses the facts of her own life in the magic of lords and ladies.

Beulah's development of a rich inner life is the result of meditation with an outward eye. Throughout her long battle with the prescribed role she was born to play, she continues to cope admirably and compassionately with the world outside. She manages her family; she feeds transients during the Depression; she shows kindness to the daughter of a prejudiced neighbor. As the poems progress her wisdom deepens. Her attitude toward Thomas softens,

too. While sweeping she recalls the drive to Tennessee, how

> Even then
> he was forever off in the woods somewhere in
>   search
> of a magic creek.
>   **("Pomade")**

And later, addressing him in **"Company"**:

> Listen: we were good,
> though we never believed it.

If she does not change her life, Beulah through wisdom comes to understand it. She also comprehends the lives of her daughters. At their husbands' company picnic—a segregated picnic—Beulah remembers the march on Washington and its effects on the lives of her children. Her meditative impulse blossoms. Her preferred inner life squares off against the world of iniquity, and the succeeding generation is better off for it.

When I consider the discouraging Moment I mentioned at the beginning of this article, when I despair of it, I turn to only a few poets of my generation and am revitalized. Rita Dove's development through three volumes reminds us of the necessity for scope in poetry. A wide range of talent in service to an assembling vision is the tonic we need for discouragement. (pp. 63-70)

> *Robert McDowell, "The Assembling Vision of Rita Dove," in* Callaloo, *Vol. 9, No. 1, Winter, 1986, pp. 61-70.*

John Shoptaw (essay date 1987)

[*In the following excerpt, Shoptaw commends* Thomas *and* Beulah *for its rich characterization, language, and structure.*]

At the beginning of Rita Dove's arresting new volume of poetry, we are given directions for reading which turn out to be true but impossible to follow: "These poems tell two sides of a story and are meant to be read in sequence." The impossibility is not physical, as in the instructions prefacing John Ashbery's long, double-columned poem *Litany,* which tell us that the columns "are meant to be read as simultaneous but independent monologues"; rather, the impossibility in reading the two sides of Rita Dove's book—Thomas's side (I. "Mandolin," 23 poems), followed by Beulah's side (II. "Canary in Bloom," 21 poems)—is biographical and historical. The lives of Thomas and Beulah, whether considered together or individually, lack what would integrate them into a single story. The events in ***Thomas and Beulah*** are narrated in a strict chronological order which is detailed in the appended chronology. The subjection of story time to historical time, unusual in modern narratives, gives Dove's sequence a tragic linearity, a growing sense that what is done cannot be undone and that what is not done but only regretted or deferred cannot be redeemed in the telling. The narrative runs from Thomas's riverboat life (1919) to his arrival in Akron (1921) and marriage to Beulah (1924), to their children's births, his jobs at Goodyear, and his stroke (1960) and death (1963); then the narrative begins again with Beulah—her father's flirtations, Thomas's flirtations and courtship (1923), their marriage (1924), a pregnancy (1931), her millinery work (1950), a family reunion (1964), and her death (1969). In the background, the Depression and the March on Washington mark, respectively, the trials of the couple's and their children's generations.

As a narrative, ***Thomas and Beulah*** resembles fiction more than a poetic sequence—Faulkner's family chronicles in particular. Dove's modernist narrator stands back, paring fingernails like an unobtrusive master or God. The cover shows a snapshot, of Thomas and Beulah presumably, and the volume may be considered as a photo album, or two albums, with only the date and place printed underneath each picture. Thomas and Beulah are probably Rita Dove's grandparents; the book is dedicated to her mother, Elvira Elizabeth, and the third child born to Thomas and Beulah is identified in the chronology as Liza. But whether the couple is actually Rita Dove's grandparents is less important than the fact that all evidence of their relation has been removed.

Any choice of genre involves an economy of gains and losses. Objective, dramatic narration—showing rather than telling—has the advantage of letting the events speak for themselves and the disadvantage of dispensing with the problematics of narrative distortion and a camera-eye or God's-eye view. ***Thomas and Beulah*** tells it like it is and assumes it is like it tells us.

The most surprising thing about ***Thomas and Beulah*** is the severance not between narrator and story but between story and story. In **"Wingfoot Lake"** Beulah's in-laws attend a segregated Goodyear picnic: "white families on one side and them / on the other, unpacking the same / squeeze bottles of Heinz, the same / waxy beef patties and Salem potato chip bags." The "two sides of a story" are similarly segregated in Dove's volume, cordoned off by the roman numerals I and II. ***Thomas and Beulah*** tells no joyous love story, as we might expect, nor a tragedy of love lost. The lives of Thomas and Beulah rarely intersect: There are few common events in their stories and no Faulknerian climax in which their worlds collide. They rarely think about each other (Beulah's name does not even appear in Thomas's side); and when they do, it is with an absent-minded fondness. Their lives' desires lie elsewhere. The love of Thomas's life is Lem, who dies in the volume's brilliant inaugural poem **"The Event."** The easygoing cadences of the opening stanzas obscure the irony that this is not the honeymooning couple we expected:

> Ever since they'd left the Tennessee ridge
> with nothing to boast of
> but good looks and a mandolin,
>
> the two Negroes leaning
> on the rail of a riverboat
> were inseparable: Lem plucked
>
> to Thomas' silver falsetto.

On Thomas's drunken dare, Lem dives into the water toward an island mirage, which sinks into the river like Atlantis along with Lem. All Lem leaves Thomas is "a stinking circle of rags, / the half-shell of a mandolin." The

commonest images, circles and lines, are the most capable of variation. One of the signs of Dove's poetic power is the changes she rings on that Orphic half-shell, the surviving Aristophanic hemisphere of their round of love. The other half rises to heaven, becoming the blue vault of the sky. A Zeppelin disaster in 1931 merely replays Thomas's own tragedy. In a wonderfully interlaced poem, **"Nothing Down,"** Thomas and Beulah pick out a "sky blue Chandler," while in the alternating italicized stanzas, Thomas combines the memories of a blue flower overhead and a young Lem in a tree into a prophetic, ghostly gesture of forgiveness. But the car, as we learn from the chronology (which adds its own silent ironies to the volume), is repossessed during the Depression. The sense of guilt and loss stemming from Lem's drowning in 1919 drives Thomas for the next half a century to his death. Thomas spends his wedding night playing Lem's mandolin; his disappointment over not having any sons stems from his not making another Lem; the parable of the possum playing dead recalls Lem; even his stroke is Lem's doing:

> he knows it was Lem all along:
> Lem's knuckles tapping his chest in passing,
> Lem's heart, for safekeeping,
> he shores up in his arms.

The closest relative of Thomas's elegiac side of the story turns out to be Tennyson's *In Memoriam,* in which the poet deals with the death of his friend Arthur Hallam.

The bifurcations and divisions in ***Thomas and Beulah*** extend to the very grammar of its sentences, which are marked by the frequent appearance of free modifiers and absolute phrases. These constructions, uncommon in modern poetry and fiction (Faulkner, again, uses them more than any other American writer, though less often than Dove), consist of a participial phrase (free modifier) or of a noun and a participial phrase (absolute) which are syntactically separated from the main clause or noun they modify. Both Thomas's sequence ("as the keys swung, ticking") and Beulah's ("the walls exploding with shabby tutus") end on these constructions. A stanza may employ several in a disjunctive series, as in **"Courtship,"** when Thomas asks Beulah's father for her hand:

> Then the parlor festooned
> like a ship and Thomas
> twirling his hat in his hands
> wondering how did I get here.
> China pugs guarding a fringed settee
> where a father, half-Cherokee,
> smokes and frowns.
> *I'll give her a good life—*
> what was he doing,
> selling all for a song?
> His heart fluttering shut
> then slowly opening.

This pronounced style can tell us much about ***Thomas and Beulah.*** Since their verbs are subordinated and nominalized, such constructions tend to fragment action into a series of still shots. Although there is persistent imagery of a bomb ticking and finally exploding ("the walls exploding in shabby tutus"), ***Thomas and Beulah*** is in fact a drama devoid of suspense in which nothing ever happens, or in which **"The Event,"** Lem's drowning, sets the narrative aftermath in motion. There is no Faulknerian passion or war or rape or murder or incest. Like most of us, Thomas and Beulah meet and marry and work and have kids and die without much intention or commotion. The book is realist not in the obvious sense of treating the sordid and grim elements of experience but in the essential sense of privileging ordinary experience over the strange. If the strange was the dark continent of the South, the ordinary is the undiscovered country of the Midwest.

Free modifiers and absolute phrases function in an additive syntax like a cinematic close-up. As we can see in the following passages from Dove's book, the focus is usually upon parts of the body or clothing: "his wingtips balanced / on a scuffed linoleum square," "the cigars crackling / in cellophane," "Lem's knuckles tapping his chest in passing," "storm door clipping her heel on the way in," "white arms jutting into the chevrons of high society." Since they are set off from their main clauses, these trailers can displace, in a synecdochal flourish, the sentences they supplement: "the cutout magazine cloud taped to the pane," "the white picket fence marching up the hill," "the pale eyes bright as salt," "cold drawing the yellow out," "a pod set to sea, / a kiss unpuckering," "white tongues of remorse / sinking into the earth," "the canary courting its effigy. / The girls fragrant in their beds." These unbound phrases contain the most striking poetry in Dove's book, set off like mirage islands from the syntactical mainland where the prosaic lives of Thomas and Beulah are lived. It is a region both inviolable and unreachable.

There is no loss in Beulah's side of the story equivalent to the loss of Lem; her side consequently lacks the haunting pathos of Thomas's. Because it is not a relic, Beulah's canary makes insignificant music when compared to Thomas's mandolin. The gap in Beulah's side is not an unrecovered loss but a promise unfulfilled. Beulah misses what she never knew; her never-never mirage island keeps its distance. An absence, however, is inevitably understood or felt as a loss. What we miss we must have had, and all empty names are markers. Dove dramatizes the positing of a loss in place of a fundamental absence in **"Dusting,"** the best poem in the second half of *Thomas and Beulah:*

>   Every day a wilderness—no
>   shade in sight. Beulah
>   patient among knicknacks,
>   the solarium a rage
>   of light, a grainstorm
>   as her gray cloth brings
>   dark wood to life.
>
>   Under her hand scrolls
>   and crests gleam
>   darker still. What
>   was his name, that
>   silly boy at the fair with
>   the rifle booth? And his kiss and
>   the clear bowl with one bright
>   fish, rippling
>   wound!
>
>   Not Michael—
>   something finer. Each dust
>   stroke a deep breath and
>   the canary in bloom.

>   Wavery memory: home
>   from a dance, the front door
>   blown open and the parlor
>   in snow, she rushed
>   the bowl to the stove, watched
>   as the locket of ice
>   dissolved and he
>   swam free.
>
>   That was years before
>   Father gave her up
>   with her name, years before
>   her name grew to mean
>   Promise, then
>   Desert-in-Peace.
>   Long before the shadow and
>   sun's accomplice, the tree.
>
>   Maurice.

Strong poems omit their linkages. That remembering is like unearthing (dusting), or diving for, or thawing out memories is just what **"Dusting"** must leave unsaid for its details to resonate. Beulah's memory of freeing her fish from its "locket of ice" ("locked in ice") is itself an allegory of remembering. Beulah's dusting stirs up a "grainstorm" of memories—a nonce word gathering "brainstorm," "rainstorm," and "dust storm." The "wavery" wood grain with its "crests" has its own depths to fathom. Diving into the past is in fact the characteristic activity of this volume, as the opening poem's buried signature attests (*"Them's chestnuts, / I believe.* Dove"). The forgotten name, Maurice, surfaces in its own final stanza but begins to sound earlier in "ice," "Promise," and "accomplice." The name Maurice itself echoes and marks all her unrecovered memories as the name beginning with M ("Not Michael") on the tip of Beulah's tongue ("Maurice," "memories").

But there is another name, appearing for the first time in **"Dusting,"** whose face or landscape cannot be remembered because it has not yet been discovered: Beulah. Coined first in *Isaiah* and most famously in *The Pilgrim's Progress,* Beulah names the Promised Land. In Hebrew *Beulah* means "married." As Thomas is separated from Lem, Beulah is divorced from Beulah. Beulah's heart is set on Beulah-Land, which goes by several names. In **"Magic,"** a giant Eiffel Tower appears in the sky as "a sign / she would make it to Paris one day." In **"Pomade,"** a friend's fragrance "always put her / in mind of Turkish minarets against / a sky wrenched blue." From **"The House on Bishop Street,"** it was nameless but nearly visible: "If she leaned out she could glimpse / the faintest of mauve—no more than an idea— / growing just behind the last houses." It appears last, and for what it is, in **"The Oriental Ballerina,"** as daylight comes to Beulah's deathbed. Beulah's last moments are accompanied by a mechanical ballerina, a paltry Angel of Death, pirouetting on her jewelbox to "the wheeze of the old / rugged cross" on her radio. Ironic juxtapositions of the exotic and the homely, the beautiful and the vulgar organize the poem. What finally dawns on Beulah is not a Beulah-Land but an unbridgeable nothing which the name has hidden:

>   The head on the pillow sees nothing
>   else, though it feels the sun warming

its cheeks. *There is no China;*
no cross, just the papery kiss
of a kleenex above the stink of camphor,

    the walls exploding with shabby tutus. . . .

This uncompromising, Shakespearean renunciation explodes Beulah's myths of Beulah. There is no China, no Promised Land, no Landlord. Beulah also explodes the fiction of her own story by denying the existence of the omniscient, absentee Narrator who relates it—the rest is ellipsis. In **"One Volume Missing"** Thomas buys a used encyclopedia "for five bucks / no zebras, no Virginia, / no wars." And no Zion, as in the "A.M.E. Zion Church" which sold it. *Thomas and Beulah*—with its gaps, divisions, and deletions—comes also as an incomplete set. But that is Dove's bargain. For us to read any of her fragmentary alphabet, the never-never volume which would integrate the Goodyear picnic, Thomas and Lem, Thomas and Beulah, the main clauses and their absolutes, Beulah and Beulah, and the narrator and her stories must remain missing. (pp. 335-41)

> *John Shoptaw, in a review of "Thomas and*
> *Beulah," in* Black American Literature
> Forum, *Vol. 21, No. 3, Fall, 1987, pp. 335-41.*

Dove on the genesis of *Thomas and Beulah*:

Thomas and Beulah is based very loosely on my grandparents' lives. My grandmother had told me a story that had happened to my grandfather when he was young, coming up on a riverboat to Akron, Ohio, my hometown. But that was all I had basically. And the story so fascinated me that I tried to write about it. I started off writing stories about my grandfather, and soon, because I ran out of real facts, in order to keep going, I made up facts for this character, Thomas.

> *Rita Dove, in "A Conversation with Rita Dove," in* Black
> American Literature Forum, *Fall 1986.*

Peter Harris   **(essay date 1988)**

[*In the excerpt below, Harris reviews* Thomas and Beulah, *focusing on the work's appeal and Dove's "reticent" lyrical style.*]

Rita Dove's ***Thomas and Beulah,*** winner of the 1987 Pulitzer Prize, has a distinctive, ambitiously unified design. It traces the history of two blacks who separately move North, to Ohio, meet and get married in the 1920's, and go on to raise four girls, enduring many vicissitudes before their deaths in the 1960's. Arranged serially and accompanied by an almost essential chronology, the poems, we are told in a note beforehand, are meant to be read in order. Much as Michael Ondaatje has done in his poem-like novel, *Coming through Slaughter,* Dove reconstructs the past through a series of discontinuous vignettes which enter freely into the psyches of the two main characters.

It is important that the poems are arranged chronological-

ly because we often need all the help we can get in clarifying many of the references. Even with chronology as a guide, the poems sometimes seem unnecessarily obscure and cryptic. More often, however, the difficulty of the work is justifiable because the insights are exactly as subtle as they are oblique. In exploiting the virtues of ellipsis, Dove evidently has faith we will have gumption enough to stare a hole in the page until our minds leap with hers across the gaps. For example, in the opening poem, **"The Event,"** Thomas dares his drunken friend, Lem, to jump off a riverboat and swim to a nearby island. Lem jumps and drowns. Later in the volume, we find out that Thomas is haunted by Lem's death for the rest of his life. But in the opening poem, the aftershock goes unmentioned:

> Thomas, dry
>
> on deck, saw the green crown shake
> as the island slipped
>
> under, dissolved
> in the thickening stream.
> At his feet
>
> a stinking circle of rags,
> the half-shell mandolin.
> Where the wheel turned the water
>
> gently shirred.

Given Dove's reticent lyricism, we can't be completely sure from this description that Lem has drowned; we can only guess. That leaves us uncertain and, therefore, vulnerable, which is quite appropriate because the world we are entering with Thomas is fraught with deceptive beauty and danger. Even the shirring of roiled water can indicate death.

One of the great strengths of this book is the depth of Dove's sympathetic understanding not only of Beulah but also of Thomas; she manages to convey the inner savor both of Thomas' early ebullience and of his later frustration and despair at not being allowed a part in the world equal to his considerable sensitivity. The mandolin provides him with a creative outlet, but it becomes the bittersweet outlet of the blues. As Dove's narrator puts it in **"Straw Hat:"**

> To him, work is a narrow grief
> and the music afterwards
> is like a woman reaching into his chest
> to spread it around.

The diction of this passage, which includes the elegant phrase "narrow grief," is a good indication of how Dove manages to use the more abstract resources of English to telling effect, without sacrificing the credibility of her account.

In her forays into the black vernacular, Dove chooses not to be phonetic; instead, she concentrates on diction and speech rhythm and does so with dialectical pizzazz, as in the conclusion to **"Jiving:"**

> The young ladies
>
> saying *He sure plays*
>
> *that tater bug*

like the devil!

sighing their sighs
and dimpling.

Here, the juxtaposition of two voices and styles highlights the virtues of both. It's difficult to make such switches in the level of diction while still maintaining a plausible narrative voice; yet Dove most often succeeds. Because she has thoroughly imagined her characters, Dove can handle her vernacular material convincingly from a decided stylistic remove.

Moreover, the poems appeal so directly to the five senses that we're convinced of their authenticity before, and after, we've had time to plumb their artfulness. Consider, for example, with what resourcefulness and immediacy Dove dramatizes Beulah's reluctant attraction to the wild mandolin player, Thomas, during their courtship:

Cigar-box music!
She'd much prefer a pianola
and scent in a sky-colored flask.

Not that scarf, bright as butter.
Not his hands, cool as dimes.

Beneath its sensuousness, the passage conceals a delicately comedic irony. Beulah may snobbishly prefer a pianola to the mandolin, but snobbery is no defense against the flamboyant appeal of Thomas' scarf and "cool" hands, whatever "cool" may mean, and it may mean many things, from graceful to calculatingly seductive. Thomas lives long enough to be worn down by time and by the lack of meaningful work, but in his prime, especially in his courtship of Beulah, he was a prodigy to behold, the "King of the Crawfish." And no less remarkable is Dove's portrayal of Beulah herself, whom we first see as an elegant woman, fending off Thomas in "pleated skirt [that] fans / softly, a circlet of arrows"; we follow her into a dignified, though sadly reduced widowhood, where the best she can say, in retrospect about her marriage is *we were good, / though we never believed it.*" The psychic cost of suffering makes itself keenly felt in **Thomas and Beulah,** a blues book that aims, through music and sympathy, to reach an affirmative answer to the question posed by Melvin B. Tolson, which Dove includes as the epigraph to the volume:

Black Boy, O Black Boy,
is the port worth the cruise?

(pp. 270-73)

Peter Harris, "Four Salvers Salvaging," in The Virginia Quarterly Review, *Vol. 64, No. 2, Spring, 1988, pp. 262-76.*

Rita Dove with Steven Schneider (interview date 1989)

[*In the following interview with Schneider, Dove discusses the writing of* Thomas and Beulah, *receiving the Pulitzer Prize, and the writing process.*]

[Steven Schneider]: *How does it feel to be the first black woman poet since Gwendolyn Brooks to win the Pulitzer Prize?*

[Rita Dove]: My first reaction was quite simply disbelief. Disbelief that first of all there hasn't been another black person since Gwendolyn Brooks in 1950 to win the Pulitzer Prize in poetry, though there certainly have been some outstanding black poets in that period. On a public level, it says something about the nature of cultural politics in this country. It's a shame actually. On a personal level, it's overwhelming.

Did you feel you had written something special when you completed Thomas and Beulah?

I felt I had written something larger than myself, larger than what I had hoped for it to be. I did not begin this sequence as a book; it began as a poem. The book grew poem by poem, and it wasn't until I was about a third of the way through that I realized it would have to be a book. So I grew with it and I had to rise to it. I started with the Thomas poems because I wanted to understand my grandfather more—what he was like as a young man, how he grew up and became the man I knew. To do that though, I realized pretty early on that I could rely neither on my memories of him nor on the memories of my mother or her sisters or brothers, but I had to get to know the town he lived in. What was Akron, Ohio like in the '20s and '30s? It was different from the Akron I knew. That meant I had to go to the library and read a whole bunch of stuff I never counted on researching to try to get a sense of that period of time in the industrial Midwest. On other levels, I had to enter male consciousness in a way which was—well, I knew I could do it for one or two poems but this was an extended effort. I was really, at a certain point, very very driven to be as honest as I could possibly be. Also, I didn't want to impose my language or my sensibility upon their lives. And things got—

Things got very complicated?

That's right.

Did you have a different kind of satisfaction about finishing this book than your other two books?

It was different. I am not going to say I was more satisfied; I don't think I have a favorite book of mine. But there was a feeling of relief because I had made it through.

How long did it take you to write Thomas and Beulah?

About five years. I was working on the *Museum* poems in the middle of that, too. So, altogether five years.

You've mentioned to me that your life has been quite hectic since you won the Pulitzer. How does this affect your life and your writing?

First of all, the act of writing is such a private, basic matter. It's you and the poem, you and the pencil and the paper in a room under a circle of lamplight. And that is the essence of writing. A public life, then, becomes schizophrenic; on the one hand, you have to extend yourself and talk to people about your writing, an experience which you cannot really articulate. To talk about private experience to total strangers is very schizophrenic. Once in a while it's good to get out and do readings because the shadows on the wall grow large when you are writing. But in this past year and a half, I sometimes feel I have been a little too public—or let's just say I feel the public encroaching on the private time.

Are things getting back to normal now? Do you find you are able to work on a regular schedule?

Things are getting back to normal for several reasons. One of them is that I think I've learned a little bit how to live with the public life and not let it affect the private sector. Also how not to feel guilty about saying "No."

For some writers, winning such a prize so young can block their creative output for years to come. How do you respond creatively to the pressures of fame?

I remember when I first got the Pulitzer, the question that came up in every interview was: "Does this put pressure on you now for your next book?" And in those first weeks afterward, the question always hit me out of left field. What did they mean?

You didn't feel pressured until they started asking you.

Exactly. I didn't feel it at all. So in a way, it is an artificial pressure. It's particularly artificial if one really sits down and thinks about the number of people who have gotten Pulitzers and how many of them stayed "famous." If you look at the list, it's very interesting. Nothing's guaranteed.

So some Pulitzer winners have declined in reputation?

Sure, some Nobel Laureates as well.

So that takes some pressure off?

Right. And taking that further, what does it mean? I mean it's wonderful, but in the end, what is important to me? When I go into the room and try to write a poem, the Pulitzer doesn't mean a thing. I am still just as challenged by the blank page.

Much has been said about the number of black writers who seem to have been ignored by the literary establishment. This surfaced again recently when James Baldwin died. Do you think the literary establishment has been unfair to black writers?

Of course it has been unfair—this is true not only for black writers, but for other minorities as well. It is outrageous that James Baldwin never got a Pulitzer Prize. It's outrageous that Ralph Ellison didn't get every literary award around for *Invisible Man.*

There have been recent attempts to revise the canon and to give more attention to women writers and to minority writers in America. Are you gratified by these attempts? Are they going far enough?

I think they are absolutely necessary. I can't say whether they are going far enough: it depends where, in what context. But it's important to try to round those things out. Let's face it: if Gwendolyn Brooks or Toni Morrison are not on the reading lists for Ph.D. dissertations, students aren't going to read them.

So what do you think your winning the Pulitzer Prize for poetry means to other young black American writers?

When I was growing up it would have meant a lot to me to know that a black person had been recognized for his or her writing. *Thomas and Beulah* is a book about black Americans, and two very ordinary ones at that. Nothing spectacular happens in their life. And yet this "non-sensational" double portrait is awarded a prize. That's what is important.

You mentioned you talked recently with some South African writers. Does winning the Pulitzer Prize give you more political leverage and visibility?

The Pulitzer does carry international credentials. In the past year and a half I have had increased opportunities to talk and to meet with writers of other countries and to see how they live. Because of the Pulitzer, I got the chance to do a conversation via satellite with some South African writers. I may have the chance of going there, which is certainly not going to be a pleasure trip. I feel the need to see the situation there for myself if it's possible.

Let's talk about **Thomas and Beulah.** *Your interest in these characters resulted from a story your grandmother told you as a child. Is that right?*

Yes. That story actually became the first poem in the book. I was about ten or twelve when she told me about my grandfather coming north on a river boat; it seems he had dared his best friend to swim the river, and the friend drowned. This was, for me, a phenomenal event. My grandfather had been a very gentle and quiet man. Frankly, I couldn't see how he could have carried that kind of guilt around all those years. I found it incredible that I had never heard the story before. In the writing, I had to confront several problems: How could he have borne it? How does anyone bear guilt that is irretrievable?

Did you set out consciously on a quest to reclaim your roots?

No. Not consciously. Though it was a conscious attempt to understand someone who had meant a lot to me, who was part of me. And in doing that I got drawn more and more into my family history which was perfectly fine and kind of wonderful. It gave me a doorway into my history. I had a hinge, something that I could work on and through. I ended up talking to a lot of people about my grandparents; I learned a lot about my roots that doesn't even appear in the book.

Certainly that knowledge becomes meaningful to you and who you are today.

Yes, exactly. I think I was always working toward that. Now, when I look back on the three books that I have done and see how they move, I understand that old adage about coming back to your own backyard. But it is almost as if I started out in *The Yellow House on the Corner* with a very domestic scene, a real neighborhood. The second book, *Museum,* was much more about art and artifact, and attempts to register personal human experience against the larger context of history.

There are some family poems in **Museum** *too.*

Yes—but the family poems in that book constitute one section only; the overwhelming majority are portraits of individuals in their particular historical context.

How did you go about recreating the era of Thomas and Beulah's migration?

I read everything I could get my hands on about the migration from the rural south to the industrial north. The WPA books that were done on each state were especially invaluable.

So there were lots of details you had to track down.

Exactly the stuff that will drop out of the next edition of the *Encyclopedia Britannica,* right? I was trying to get that feeling, that ambiance, so I talked to my mother an awful lot about what it was like growing up at that time. She was remarkable. At first she asked, "What do you want to hear?" But I didn't know what I wanted to hear. I just wanted her to talk, and that's what she did. I amassed so much material; then I had to kind of forget it all in order to write the poems.

You have said of **Thomas and Beulah** *that "less and less did it become based on my grandparents because after a while I was after a different kind of truth." What is the larger truth you were after?*

I was after the essence of my grandparents' existence and their survival, not necessarily the facts of their survival. That's the distinction I'm trying to make. So when I said it became less and less about them, I meant I was not so concerned about whether Thomas in the book was born the same year as my grandfather (he wasn't, incidentally) or whether in fact it was a yellow scarf he gave Beulah or not. What's important is the gesture of that scarf. One appropriates certain gestures from the factual life to reinforce a larger sense of truth that is not, strictly speaking, reality.

Is there something especially significant about a generation like Thomas and Beulah's which had to uproot itself—in this case, from the South, in order to work in northern cities?

Yes, of course. Only very recently have historians begun to explore that entire era in any depth and what impact the great migration, as they call it now, had on not only southern communities and northern communities but a host of other things. So much has been done or talked about the uprooting of the black family through slavery, but this was a second uprooting and displacement. It's the first time that blacks in this country had any chance, however stifled, of pursuing "the American dream." Obviously not with the same advantages as whites, not even as the otherwise ostracized European immigrants, and so it is a very poignant era. I never heard very much about it when I was a child. I wondered why my cousins from Cleveland spoke with a southern accent, but we didn't. It wasn't that unusual that entire communities were brought up and resettled around each other. It's a major population movement in our country that just went largely unrecorded.

Did you begin with the notion of writing such a closely knit sequence where many of the poems depend upon previous ones?

As I said earlier, when I started out I did not think in terms of a book. I did start out with a single poem. Then I thought, "This isn't enough," and I went on. I thought I was going to have a suite of poems, a group of six or seven. At that point I did want them narrative; I thought there must be a way to get back into poetry the grandness that narrative can give, plus the sweep of time. Lyric poetry does not have that sweep of time. Lyrics are discrete moments. On the other hand, a lot of narrative poems can tend to bog down in the prosier transitional moments. I didn't see very many long narrative poems that really weren't smaller poems linked together. So one of the things I was trying to do was string moments as beads on a necklace. In other words, I have lyric poems which, when placed one after the other, reconstruct the sweep of time. I wanted it all. I wanted a narrative and I wanted lyric poems, so I tried to do them both.

Some of the poems seem more capable of standing alone than others—"Jiving" and "Lightning Blues" for example. Many others depend on our reading of the previous ones.

At the beginning of the book I warn that these poems are meant to be read in sequence. I put that in there because the poems make most sense when read in order. But even though some of the poems are absolutely dependent on others, in the writing I was still trying very hard to make each poem wholly self-sufficient, of a piece. In other words, a particular poem may be dependent on an earlier poem for its maximum meaning, but in itself it is a complete poem. It just happens to need another beat to make the best connection.

A few of the poems have italicized song-like rhymes that sound like they might derive from southern minstrels or gospels. I am especially thinking of "Refrain." Let me just read you a few of these. This is the one I really love.

> Take a gourd and string it
> Take a banana and peel it
> Buy a baby blue Nash and wheel and deal it.
> Count your kisses sweet as honey
> Count your boss' dirty money.

What's the origin of those lyrics?

I made them up. They are in the spirit of country blues. They are also influenced by spirituals and gospels. The poem **"Gospel"** begins as a takeoff on "Swing Low Sweet Chariot." It starts off: "Swing low so I / can step inside." Both **"Refrain"** and **"Gospel"** are written in quatrains, and I think there's quite a kinship between them. The roots—no, let's say the connections—between gospel and blues are very close.

Were you listening to recent blues recordings?

No. Mostly older blues recordings though I have listened to recent ones too. While I was writing this book I was playing a lot of music, everything from Lightnin' Hopkins to older ones like Larry Jackson or some of the recordings that Al Lomax made of musicians, all the way up to Billie Holliday, stopping about in the '50s. It seemed to be the music for the book.

Let's talk about Akron, Ohio, the town where Thomas and Beulah lived. Your book serves as a commentary and history of that place with its zeppelin factory and Satisfaction

Coal Company, and its impoverishment during the Depression. This kind of social realism in your work seems striking and in some ways a departure from your earlier work.

At some point in the writing, I knew the poems needed background; I realized that I had to give a history of the town. I can't say I approached this task with joy. After all, Akron is not a tourist attraction. Let's face it: few of us were born in beautiful places. Yet I remember Akron, Ohio as a place of beauty. Rilke says in his *Letters to a Young Poet,* that if you cannot recount the riches of a place do not blame the place—blame yourself, because you are not rich enough to recall its riches. When I read that again, I realized that I'd be doing Akron an injustice if I would just dwell on its industrial ugliness, and if I could not explain or bring across some of its magic or make it come alive to others, then it was my problem, certainly not Akron's.

Does **Thomas and Beulah** *feel like a different book from your earlier ones?*

I think it is a departure from my other work—rather, I came home.

And, rather than a collection of poems, each working out a discrete universe, **Thomas and Beulah** is a string of moments that work together to define a universe much in the way a necklace defines the neck and shoulders. In my first book, **The Yellow House on the Corner,** there was an entire section dealing with aspects of slavery; **Museum** is somewhat of a hodgepodge of various social and political realities and how individuals work within them. **Thomas and Beulah** is the first sustained effort at sequence.

It seemed to me that especially in **Yellow House** *and in places in* **Museum** *there is more of a surrealistic feeling to some of the poems. In* **Thomas and Beulah** *we don't get as much of that. It seems much more grounded in the place and in the time and in the people.*

The word "surrealistic" has been used quite often in describing my work, and I must say I have always been amazed by it. I never thought of myself as being surrealistic.

Maybe "deep image."

No. Obviously, though, this is what people think of it. So now I kind of smile; I'm not going to escape this world. I mean, I accept it as a fair judgment. To me magic, or the existence of an unexplainable occurrence, is something I grew up with. One shouldn't try to explain everything. I learned to live with paradox, to accept strange happenings. I listened to older people talking about, for example, a person who refused to die easy and came back to haunt. In terms of memory and guilt, that makes a lot of sense to me. Now I'm not talking about ghost stories; I'm talking about how to live with strangeness. And for a minority, particularly black people growing up in America, a lot of surreal things are going on all the time.

One interesting thing about the Thomas section of the book is that Lem really haunts Thomas throughout. I find that very moving. Is this based on the story you referred to earlier from your grandmother?

Yes, yes. And you know the only facts that I had in the story were that my grandfather had come up the river with a good friend and that the friend had died. I knew nothing about the man. In fact, my grandfather never mentioned the story to us as children. The idea of Lem haunting him grew out of the poems—it actually grew out of the character of Thomas and what I felt he would have done.

Another question about Thomas. He comes across in some ways as a real lady's man. How did Beulah tie him down?

I don't know! I mean I think that . . . he might come across that way, but his being a lady's man was constrained by the death of his friend. In a way, he is trying to play his way out of hell.

Of course, the other side of it is he is very dedicated to his family.

He's a classic case in that he mourns the youth he had, but he can't get back to it anyway. I think it would be untrue for any of us to say we haven't felt that at some point. You feel you want to let go of all the stuff that starts attaching itself to you as you grow up, but you can't do it anymore.

The bills have to be paid. What is it that you admire about Beulah? And what is it you would like to honor in her?

I think of Beulah as being a very strong woman who still has no way of showing how strong she could be. She is the one who really wants to travel, to see the world. She is curious; she is intelligent; and her situation in life does not allow her to pursue her curiosity. If there is anything I want to honor in her, it is that spirit.

The sense of sacrifice?

Certainly that too, but lots of people make sacrifices. It's the way one handles sacrifice that's crucial.

She did it gracefully.

She did it gracefully, but not too gracefully—that is, not without spunk. It's important that people know there's a struggle involved, that the sacrifice is being made. You have to learn not to be crushed by what you can't do.

Both Thomas and Beulah seem relatively free of gnawing bitterness towards their environment, towards whites, despite some difficult circumstances, very difficult circumstances. Is there a lesson in this?

A lesson? Let me take a different tack. We tend to forget that there were generations upon generations of black Americans who did not have the luxury of bitterness. I don't mean to suggest that there was no bitterness, just that you had enough to do with surviving. You had to eat first. This drive for survival above all else could lead to a certain autism; one's personality freezes.

The civil rights movement and the rise of black consciousness in the 1960s made the release of emotion—anger, elation, fury, righteousness—possible. One could get emotions out without being poisonous and so still be able to go on with life. But Thomas and Beulah came from a different generation, from an era when there was no point in talking about what white people had and black people did not. That was a fact of life—it didn't mean they liked it, it didn't mean they thought it was right. But there were a few more pressing matters to talk about. Inequality was a given. I know how impatient we became with our grandparents in the '60s and our great aunts, when we would call ourselves Afro-Americans or black and they would continue to say "colored" and we'd go: "AHHHHH, come on." The impatience of youth. Why aren't Thomas and Beulah furious? Well, they were, but they had a different way of expressing it.

Both Beulah and Thomas grow old together, and sadness overtakes the readers as we read of their health problems and their demise. But they stick together and support each other. Is there a commentary on aging here for a society which is accused of neglecting its elderly?

Yes. Certainly one of the things I learned in writing **Thomas and Beulah** is that all of us are guilty at one time or another of not assigning other people their full human worth, for whatever reasons—men having preconceived ideas of women or vice versa, racial prejudice, misconceptions about the young and the old. In order to be able to understand my grandfather, or how my grandmother could be the woman she was, I had to go back and revision their youth. It was a humbling experience for me. And there are certain satisfactions with age that we tend not to think about.

Thomas and Beulah are there for each other to the very end. That kind of commitment through thick and thin, as sappy as it may sound, is a striking part of the book.

I received essays written in the form of letters from students at Brown University. One student thought Thomas and Beulah didn't like each other at all, that the marriage was very sad. I was absolutely amazed at that notion. It must have something to do with our concept of love—that if we are young it is going to be romantic all the way through. In the poem **"Company"** Beulah said: "Listen: we were good, / though we never believed it." I remember that absolutely calm feeling that my grandparents had, a sense of belonging together. Today I see young lovers struggling to find earth-shattering ecstasy in every second. That's a part of love, but it's a small part.

There is a kind of ripeness about their love that is unusual and that only comes with age.

Absolutely.

What does the future hold for Rita Dove? Do you plan on writing more poetry or trying a novel?

More poems, of course, and I definitely plan to write more fiction. I'm writing a novel right now. Why not?

Will you be doing a lot more teaching? Or traveling in the next couple of years?

I have this year off, but I will be going back to teaching in the fall. I enjoy teaching. Travel is always in my life. I'm always traveling, it seems.

We mentioned fiction and you do have that one book of short stories (Fifth Sunday). *Do you find the two activities—writing fiction, writing poetry—mutually supportive or do you think of them as separate, unrelated activities?*

Is there any kind of schizophrenia about it? Or is it just natural?

I think that they are part of the same process. It's all writing; there are just different ways of going about it. I don't find them compatible in the sense that when I am writing poetry I am not usually going to start a story. If I'm writing a story I am in a slightly different mode. I can't explain what it is—it's not as severe as speaking another language. Still, I think the notion of prose writing and poetry writing as separate entities has been artificially created, partly as a result of fitting writing into the academic curriculum where it is easiest to teach them separately. That's valid pedagogical methodology, but there is no reason for them to exist separately outside the workshop. One of the things I deplored when I was in graduate school was just how separate the two were kept; fiction writers and the poetry writers didn't even go to the same parties.

This is the final question. It's actually two. Does writing poetry enable you to be more fully aware of who you are? Is it the bliss of writing that attracts you?

(after some hesitation) No. It isn't the bliss of writing but the bliss of unfolding. I was hesitating with the question because I wanted to consider how to go about making my answer clear without making it sound corny. I don't think poetry is going to make anyone a better person, and it is not going to save you. But writing is a constant for me. There's an edge that needs to be explored, the edge between being unconscious and then suddenly being so aware that the skin tingles. Let me be more precise. There is that moment in the writing of a poem when things start to come together, coalesce into a discovery. This is sheer bliss, and has something to do with discovering something about myself. It doesn't mean I understand myself; in fact, the more I write the less I know of myself. But I also learn more. Territory is being covered—excursions into the interior. I write for those moments of discovery really, but there are two steps in this process: one is the intimate revelation, and the second step is to take that revelation and to make it visible—palpable—for others.

It's one thing to experience strong emotion; it's another thing to communicate it to others. I do believe that an experience inarticulated will be lost; part of my task as a writer, one of the things I take on and want to do, is to articulate those moments so they won't be lost. I think there is no greater joy than to have someone else say, "I know what you mean." That's real corny, but it's what literature does for all of us, the reader as well as the writer. An active reader longs to be pulled into another's world and to comprehend that world, to get into another's skin utterly and yet understand what's happening at the same time. That's an immensely exciting thing. And that's what I work for. (pp. 112-23)

Rita Dove and Steven Schneider, in an interview in The Iowa Review, *Vol. 19, No. 3, Fall, 1989, pp. 112-23.*

Sidney Burris   (essay date 1990)

[*In the following excerpt, Burris applauds* Grace Notes

as a watershed in Dove's career and discusses the autobiographical poems in the collection.]

Rita Dove's third volume of poetry, **Thomas and Beulah,** won the Pulitzer Prize in 1987, but **Grace Notes,** her fourth collection, might well be her watershed because it shows her blithely equal to the ordeal of Life-After-A-Major-Prize: she has survived her fame. In **Grace Notes,** Dove has switched her focus from the biographies of Thomas and Beulah, demanding the third-person narration, to the selected configurations of her own biography which have naturally called on her to deploy the first-person perspective. For Dove, this involves more than a syntactic distinction because the remarkable plasticity of her conception of the pronoun discloses a thoroughgoing critique of the gender distinctions that lie at the heart of our language. **"Pastoral,"** appearing in the third section of the book, provides a good example of this unusual talent; the poet describes the experience of nursing her daughter:

> Like an otter, but warm,
> she latched onto the shadowy tip
> and I watched, diminished
> by those amazing gulps. Finished
> she let her head loll, eyes
> unfocused and large: milk drunk.
>
> I liked afterwards best, lying
> outside on a quilt, her new skin
> spread out like meringue. I felt then
> what a young man must feel
> with his first love asleep on his breast:
> desire, and the freedom to imagine it.

The title alone makes Dove one of the wiliest nomenclators around: the privileged domain of pastoral writing, that exclusive and imperial union of English ascendancy and Classical grandeur, has been infiltrated by a black American woman, and the anarchic change ("I felt then / what a young man must feel") at the end of this distinctly maternal poem reveals the kind of iconoclastic intelligence that Dove has at her disposal. The formal resolution to the poem is gently androgynous, yet such a resolution is occasioned by the special perspective of motherhood; the governing perspective of the poem, then, is entirely maternal, entirely that of a woman.

Dove's architectural sensibility, readily apparent in **"Pastoral,"** represents perhaps the signal characteristic of **Thomas and Beulah,** a collection founded on a strongly sequential logic. **Grace Notes,** which comprises five sections, exhibits a similarly overarching sense of form, so much so that the individual sections seem, in one sense, more coherent than the poems that constitute them. Section I, for example, presents a whistle-stop tour of Dove's life, from the prosaically rendered **"Silos"** and the nostalgic piece, **"Fifth Grade Autobiography,"** to the twelfth and final poem of the section, **"Poem in Which I Refuse Contemplation,"** where Dove finds herself at the house of her German mother-in-law reading a letter from home. **"Fifth Grade Autobiography,"** the second poem of the section, had revolved around a photograph ("I was four in this photograph fishing / with my grandparents at a lake in Michigan"), and as Dove articulates the hidden tensions

that lie behind the pregnant silence of the photograph ("I am staring jealously at my brother; / the day before he rode his first horse, alone"), she is already setting the stage for the autobiographical revelations that will culminate in **"Poem in Which I Refuse Contemplation."** In the earlier poem, Dove had appeared as the grandchild of black American grandparents; in this last poem, her daughter appears as the grandchild of German grandparents, and it is the noisy efficacy of language—German, American, and "misspelled American"—that replaces the suffocating silence of the childhood photograph:

> A letter from my mother was waiting:
> read in standing, one a.m.,
> just arrived at my German mother-in-law
>
> six hours from Paris by car.
> Our daughter hops on Oma's bed,
> happy to be back in a language
>
> she knows. *Hello, all! Your postcard
> came on the nineth*—familiar misspelled
> words, exclamations. . . .

The poem continues with phrases excerpted from her mother's letter, and these phrases of simple piety and love are set in high contrast to the polished skepticism of Dove's verse. The entire first section chronicles Dove's growing engagement with her own ethics of articulation ("Haven't I always hated . . . English, too / Americanese's chewy twang?"), and the final poem of the section, distinguished by its adroit role reversals, by its variegated incorporation of culture, and by its several levels of locution, distinguishes Dove as one of our most gifted and thorough practitioners of the poetry of genealogy. (pp. 457-59)

Sidney Burris, in a review of "Grace Notes," in The Southern Review, *Louisiana State University, Vol. 26, No. 2, Spring, 1990, pp. 457-59.*

Judith Kitchen   (essay date 1990)

[*In the following excerpt, Kitchen praises Dove's feminine sensibility and its role in leading to fresh perceptions in* Grace Notes.]

Rita Dove is both a woman and black but her poems are not "about" being a woman, or being black; those facts are simply the context in which her poems occur. That does not mean she shrinks from issues related to being black or being female, and many of the poems in Dove's **Grace Notes,** her fourth collection, speak directly to the marginality of blacks and women in the larger culture. Clearly she cares about these issues, but she doesn't assume that dealing with them makes her a poet. She is a poet because of her fine ear, her keen perception, her love of the individual word. If there is a unity in this book, it is not the unity of theme or of character; it is the unity of an incisive mind applying itself to a particular life.

Grace Notes is a complex weave of personal experience, memory, dialectic, and visual imagination. Each poem adds a layer of experience or insight so that the whole is experienced much as a piece of music; one senses its shape long before one has words to describe it. It is nearly impossible to cite any single poem as exemplary of a specific thematic concern; instead, they overlap, giving the book a dense, luxurious structure. She has arranged the poems to resist categorization. For example, each of the five sections begins with an epigraph, but the epigraph does not necessarily apply to the section it heads. Dove did something similar in *Museum,* but here this displacement becomes part of the way in which the book must be read. The reader, in effect, must make the connections—and there are myriad connections to be made.

Dove resists ideology in all guises, preferring the inquisitive mind that discovers meaning rather than shapes it. And her strong sense of self allows room for such discovery. Because of the individual nature of the poems—ranging from childhood in Ohio to instances of black suppression, from Eugene's soliloquy under the sink to Dove's memory of her daughter's conception and her father-in-law's death, from landscapes in the Southwest to an old folk's home in Israel—it is nearly impossible to label them, even in terms of theme. Instead, they become parts of the larger picture, each offering up a small moment of observation or insight which, in turn, sheds light on another. The overall effect of the book is that of an interior voice dealing with the exterior world, often intruding on the act of observation with reflective comment. This happens from poem to poem, but the method of the book is reproduced in microcosm in **"Ozone,"** which is my personal favorite. In this twenty-nine-line poem, the poet alternates her own "take" on the hole in the ozone layer with an italicized, running response to a quote from Rilke. The effect is that of both seeing through the poet's eyes and simultaneously hearing her interior voice. The poems begins:

> *. . . Does the cosmic*
> *space we dissolve into taste of us, then?*
> —Rilke, *The Second*
> *Elegy*

> Everything civilized will whistle before
> it rages—kettle of the asthmatic,
> the aerosol can and its immaculate awl
> perforating the dome of heaven.

> We wire the sky for comfort:
> we thread it through our lungs for a perfect fit.
> We've arranged this calm, though it is con-
>   stantly
> unraveling.

> *Where does it go then,*
> *atmosphere suckered up*
> *an invisible flue?*
> *How can we know where it goes?*

The poem continues with a series of associative leaps until Rilke's cosmic question is contemplated on practical, present-day terms, and today's ecological issues merge with a spiritual quest: *"Rising, the pulse / sings: / memento mei."* What is the significance of the individual in the face of global destruction?

Rita Dove's female sensibility is the underpinning of the book. She is mother, wife, daughter, sister—but she lets

---

> **Rita Dove is both a woman and black but her poems are not "about" being a woman, or being black; those facts are simply the context in which her poems occur.**
>
> **—Judith Kitchen**

---

none of these roles substitute for individual consciousness and imaginative exploration. Her womanly roles are the means to new understanding of the world. In **"Pastoral,"** she describes the ultimate feminine act of nursing her infant in such a way that she, in fact, discovers a truth about male perception. Male and female experiences merge in the act of mutual understanding that constitutes a poem:

> I liked afterwards best, lying
> outside on a quilt, her new skin
> spread out like meringue. I felt then
> what a young man must feel
> with his first love asleep on his breast:
> desire, and the freedom to imagine it.

At the same time, Dove celebrates her womanhood. **"After Reading *Mickey in the Night Kitchen* for the Third Time Before Bed"** shows her daughter discovering "facts" about the vagina. It ends with an acknowledgment of their basic individuality, and their shared womanhood: "How to tell her that it's what makes us— / black mother, cream child. / That we're in the pink / and the pink's in us." Women are celebrated. They did not make the nuclear silos which rise above the plains. "They were masculine toys. They were tall wishes. They / were the ribs of the modern world." Significantly, the book begins with a poem that stands alone, **"Summit Beach, 1921,"** in which a young girl sits on the Negro beach, not dancing with the others, but fingering a scar and remembering her great moment of childish imagination:

> She could wait, she was gold.
> When the right man smiled it would be
> music skittering up her calf

> like a chuckle. She could feel
> the breeze in her ears like water,
> like the air as a child when
> she climbed Papa's shed and stepped off
> the tin roof into blue,

> with her parasol and invisible wings.

Rita Dove seems, in *Grace Notes,* to be offering today's adult women, and today's blacks, those same invisible wings—the faith to step into blue. Why should we reserve the territory of imagination for childhood? Poetry, then, is one of Dove's answers; it is, as in **"Ars Poetica,"** a "traveling x-marks-the-spot." She zeroes in on what is important by a faithful, close observance of the world. She gives us its particulars, and she makes it mysterious and fluid:

> *Mississippi*

> In the beginning was the dark
> moan and creak, a sidewheel

moving through. Thicker
then, scent of lilac,
scent of thyme; slight hairs
on a wrist lying down in sweat.
We were falling down
river, carnal
slippage and shadow melt.
We were standing on the deck
of the New World, before maps:
tepid seizure of a breeze
and the spirit hissing away . . .

The line breaks highlight words, demonstrate their own carnal slippage, layering the poem with black history, with individual experience, with a sense of the overall importance of this New World in which we all, male and female, black and white, share a future.

The jacket cover claims that grace notes are musical embellishments, but I like to think of them as the almost invisible thread that holds a piece together. Certainly the grace notes of this collection—the lyric poems that shimmer with a music all their own—are suggestive of the larger shape behind their singular subjects. "What are music or books if not ways / to trap us in rumors? The freedom of fine cages!" *Grace Notes* is such a fine cage—golden and filigreed, showing the boundaries of our vision at the same time that it offers us freedom of imagination, the possibility of soaring beyond the bars. (pp. 268-71)

*Judith Kitchen, in a review of "Grace Notes,"
in* The Georgia Review, *Vol. XLIV, Nos. 1 &
2, Spring-Summer, 1990, pp. 268-71.*

Helen Vendler   (essay date 1991)

[*Vendler is regarded as one of America's foremost critics
of poetry. Her* Part of Nature, Part of Us: Modern
American Poets *(1980) is considered a vital study of
contemporary poetry. In the following excerpt, she examines a selection of poems from* Grace Notes, *admiring its lyricism but faulting its occasional "flatness."*]

[Rita Dove] looks for a hard, angular surface to her poems. She is an expert in the disjunctive, often refusing the usual discursive signs of "the meditative." Crosscutting and elliptical jumps were her chief stylistic signature even in her first volume, *The Yellow House on the Corner. Grace Notes* is her fourth book, and represents both a return to the lyric from her successful objective sequence *Thomas and Beulah,* and an attempt to make her poems weigh less heavily on the page. Her poems are rarely without drama, however, and she has done a remarkable thing in making even the routines of motherhood become dramatic, in the best poems in this volume, a sequence occupying Part III of *Grace Notes.* Here is **"The Breathing, the Endless News"**:

Every god is lonely, an exile
composed of parts: elk horn,
cloven hoof. Receptacle

for wishes, each god is empty
without us, penitent,
raking our yards into windblown piles. . . .

Children know this: they are

the trailings of gods. Their eyes
hold nothing at birth then fill slowly

with the myth of ourselves. Not so the dolls,
out of the count, each toe pouting from
the slumped-over toddler clothes:

no blossoming there. So we
give our children dolls, and
they know just what to do—
line them up and shoot them.
With every execution
doll and god grow stronger.

This is at once mock-horrific (the angelic daughter lines up her dolls and shoots them) and culturally unnerving. The actors: the gods and ourselves; the godlike children and their not-godlike dolls; the picture of life as the successive killing of successive "dolls" by emergent "gods"; the declining parents; the fetishistic nature of consciousness and its gods (part noble elk horn, part indecent cloven hoof)—all these are immensely suggestive without ever becoming quite explicitly allegorical.

In **"Genetic Expedition,"** Dove (a black married to a white husband) contrasts her own looks to those of her blond daughter, with a frankness that sentimentality would blush at:

Each evening I see my breasts
slacker, black-tipped
like the heavy plugs on hot water bottles;

. . . . .

My child has
her father's hips, his hair
like the miller's daughter, combed gold.
Though her lips are mine, housewives
stare when we cross the parking lot
because of that ghostly profusion.

You can't be cute, she says. *You're big.*
She's lost her toddler's belly,
that seaworthy prow. She regards me
with serious eyes, power-lit,
atomic gaze
I'm sucked into, sheer through to

the gray brain of sky.

The disturbing ending—an atomic extinction of the parent back into the mind of the universe—draws the sensual immediacy of the opening into its component gray quanta, raw material for the next invention of the sky.

As these poems suggest, Dove's lines and stanzas are carefully aligned into dovetailed wholes. (The pun, unintended, seems legitimate.) Her **"Ars Poetica"** doesn't deal with the making of poems, only with the stance from which they are made. This is contrasted to the large ambitions, presented satirically, of two male straw men:

What I want is this poem to be small,
a ghost town
on the larger map of wills.
Then you can pencil me in as a hawk:
a traveling x-marks-the-spot.

This doesn't get to the heart of Dove's talent. Her true *ars poetica* in this volume is a harsh poem called **"Ozone,"** which is about arrangement and what it yields—which is precisely nothing (if you choose to see it that way). Life, says the poem, is "suckered up / an invisible flue"; it "disappear[s] into an empty bouquet." The maddening aspect of art is that life disappears into it once you've cleared out the space for life to fit into it. The weirdness with which, as [Wallace] Stevens said, "Things as they are / Are changed upon the blue guitar," is both the despair and the triumph of artists. Thinking to express feeling, they make a hole in reality:

> Everything civilized will whistle before
> it rages—kettle of the asthmatic,
> the aerosol can and its immaculate awl
> perforating the dome of heaven.
>
> We wire the sky for comfort;
> we thread it through out lungs for a perfect fit.
> We've arranged this calm, though it is con-
> stantly
> unraveling.
>
> . . . . .
>
> The sky is wired so it won't fall down.
> Each house notches into its neighbor
> and then the next, the whole row scaldingly
> white,
> unmistakable as a set of bared teeth.

Dove hasn't always this angry fatality, but there is an electricity (whistling, raging) about this wiring and notching and scalding and perforation that makes **"Ozone"** unforgettable. The poem speaks to the pain underlying Dove's work: the barely contained nervous tension which can only be appeased by notching one bared tooth into the next, carefully blowtorching a hole in the sky with awl-like precision, fixing the hole like "a gentleman [who] pokes blue through a buttonhole." Dove's combination of the domestic kettle, the artisanal awl, the aesthetic boutonniere, and the passional bared teeth convinces a reader that Dove's inner factions are in intense communication with each other.

Dove is interested by intransigency and its discontents. In one of the lesser poems here, a set of students respond to what they (and Dove, their teacher) take to be racism in a (white) lecturer (who may be William Arrowsmith; the poem is called **"Arrow"**):

> . . . We sat there.
> Dana's purple eyes deepened, Becky
> twitched to her hairtips
> and Janice in her red shoes
> scribbled [a note of rage]. . . .
>
>   My students
> sat there already devising
>
> their different ways of coping:
> Dana knowing it best to have
> the migraine at once, get the poison out quickly
> Becky holding it back for five hours and Janice
> making it to the evening reading and
> party afterwards
> in black pants and tunic with silver mirrors
> her shoes pointed and studded, wicked witch
> shoes:
> Janice who will wear red for three days or

> yellow brighter
> than her hair so she can't be
> seen at all

Janice's way, we suspect, is Dove's way; anger and tension are released in the scribbling of a note, the flaunting of color, the disappearance of self into raiment. The comparative slackness and "realism" here are a mode Dove carries off less well than she does her fierce and laconic "symbolic" mode. Here is her splendidly suggestive **"Medusa"**:

> I've got to go
> down where my eye
> can't reach
> hairy star
> who forgets to shiver
> forgets the cool suck
> inside
>
> Someday long
> off someone will
> see me
> fling me up
> until I look
> into sky
>
> drop his memory
>
> My hair
> dry water

Resistant though this is to analysis, it feels right, at least to me. That "hairy star," the eye, forgets (because of its visual and cerebral way of being) the shiver and the suck of the passional life. By descending into her subaqueous realm, Medusa gains the snaky locks that symbolize her knowledge. When another eye sees her, she is stellified and turned into the "dry water" of art. The beholder forgets his other life, stands rooted. This too is an *ars poetica*, though not only that.

I admire Dove's persistent probes into ordinary language, including the language of the black proletariat. Here, the most successful experiment in that genre is **"Genie's Prayer under the Kitchen Sink"**—a monologue by a grown son (Eugene, the "Genie" of the title) summoned by his mother to unclog the kitchen sink. The touch becomes uneasy here and there, though, as Dove wants a decorativeness in her poem that the voice can't sustain:

> . . . I came because I'm good at this, I'm good
>
> with my hands; last March I bought some 2 by
> 4s
> at Home Depot and honed them down
> to the sleekest, blondest, free-standing bar
> any mildewed basement in a cardboard housing
> tract
> under the glass gloom of a factory clock
> ever saw. . . .

One can believe in the first four lines of this, but not the last three.

Dove's youth, in this volume, is already shadowed, and one can see her trying to peer out of her present emotional riches into a savorless future. She visits an old poet in **"Old Folk's Home, Jerusalem"**:

> So you wrote a few poems. The horned

thumbnail hooked into an ear doesn't care.
The gray underwear wadded over a belt says So
what. . . .

Valley settlements put on their lights
like armor; there's finch chit and my sandal's
inconsequential crunch.

Everyone waiting here was once in love.

The flatness of "my sandal's inconsequential crunch" betokens a Dove to come, looking at intransigency become
inconsequential, though still held in the unyielding principle of her angular stanzas. (pp. 396-401)

> *Helen Vendler, "A Dissonant Triad," in* Par-
> nassus: Poetry in Review, *Vol. 16, No. 2, 1991,*
> *pp. 391-404.*

FURTHER READING

Brody, Jennifer. "Genre Fixing: An Interview with Rita

Dove." *Poetry Flash: A Poetry Review and Literary Calendar for the West,* No. 238 (January 1993): 1, 9-11, 22-3.

Interview with Dove in which she discusses her novel *Through the Ivory Gate,* the difference between writing prose and poetry, and the influence on her work.

Corn, Alfred. Review of *Grace Notes,* by Rita Dove. *Poetry* 157, No. 1 (October 1990): 37-9.

Admires Dove's poetic sensibility—"her Rilkean instinct for the textures and taste of the world, her ironic amusement at the world's absurdity—" and her "let-chips-fall-where-they-may fearlessness" in *Grace Notes.*

Steinman, Lisa M. "Dialogues between History and Dream." *Michigan Quarterly Review* XXVI, No. 2 (Spring 1987): 428-38.

Discusses Dove's incorporation of twentieth-century American history in *Thomas and Beulah* and notes that "the poems themselves are not about an individual's *relationship* to her history, nor about the weight of history. They are, more, history allowed to speak for itself."

Waller, Gary. "I and Ideology: Demystifying the Self of Contemporary Poetry." *Denver Quarterly* 18, No. 3 (Autumn 1983): 123-38.

Briefly reviews *Museum,* which focuses "on the intersection of the 'individual' and the history that has brought her into being."

Additional coverage of Dove's life and career is contained in the following sources published by Gale Research: *Black Writers; Contemporary Authors,* Vol. 109; *Contemporary Authors New Revision Series,* Vol. 27; *Contemporary Literary Criticism,* Vol. 50; and *Dictionary of Literary Biography,* Vol. 120.

Robert Graves

1895-1985

(Full name Robert von Ranke Graves; also wrote with Laura Riding under the joint pseudonym Barbara Rich) English poet, novelist, critic, nonfiction writer, short story writer, translator, playwright, librettist, editor, and author of children's books.

INTRODUCTION

Considered one of the most distinctive and lyrical voices in twentieth-century English poetry, Graves dismissed contemporary poetic fashions and precepts and developed his own poetic theory principally inspired by ancient mythology and folklore. In addition to mythical-archaic themes, Graves's verse typically encompasses love poems and grotesque depictions of war. Often employing short-lined verse structures and idiosyncratic meters derived from the Tudor poet John Skelton, Graves combined deft craftsmanship with dry humor and emotional intensity. In summing up his achievement, the critic Northrop Frye wrote that Graves's poetry exhibits a profound correspondence between thematic content and technique whereby "every poem is aimed directly at a definite human or mythical situation and usually hits it squarely in its central paradox."

Graves was born in Wimbledon, near London, in 1895. His father was an Irish poet and his mother was a relation of Leopold von Ranke, one of the founding fathers of modern historical studies. At the English public school Charterhouse, Graves studied classical literature and won a scholarship to continue his studies at St. John's College, Oxford, in 1913. Rather than pursuing an academic career, however, he volunteered for military service and at the outbreak of World War I was sent to France as a sub-altern with the Royal Welch Fusiliers. He fought in the Battle of Loos and was injured in the Somme offensive in 1916. Graves recorded his wartime experiences in *Good-Bye to All That,* an autobiography that many critics regard as one of the finest prose works to emerge from the First World War. In 1918 Graves married and moved to Oxford to begin his university studies. Although he failed to finish his degree, he wrote a postgraduate thesis entitled "The Illogical Element in English Poetry" which qualified him to teach English at Cairo University. In 1929 Graves separated from his wife as a result of his liaison with the American poet Laura Riding, whom he had met in 1926. Graves moved to Majorca with Riding, who lived with him until 1938.

In the 1930s and 1940s, Graves supported himself financially by writing historical novels which earned him both popular and critical acclaim. The celebrated novel *I, Claudius* imaginatively recreates the life and politics of the Roman Empire as represented in Suetonius's *Lives of the*

Caesars. In *The Story of Marie Powell, Wife to Mr. Milton* Graves disputes the traditional reputation of John Milton by depicting his wife as the greater creative force. This novel reflects Graves's dissatisfaction at that time with male values and intellectual abstractions, as well as his newly found regard for the feminine as the source of poetic inspiration—themes elaborated upon in his critical work *The White Goddess: A Historical Grammar of Poetic Myth.* Graves's poetry registers this shift in orientation by focusing on celebrations of love and woman. During the years 1961 to 1966 Graves lectured periodically at Oxford University in his capacity as Professor of Poetry, and in 1968 he received the Queen's Gold Medal for Poetry. Throughout his career he published and revised numerous editions of his *Collected Poems.* Graves died in Majorca in 1985.

Graves's early volumes of poetry, like the verse of the Georgians, his contemporaries, deal with natural beauty and bucolic pleasures in addition to the aftereffects of the First World War. Such works as *Over the Brazier* and *Fairies and Fusiliers* earned Graves a reputation as an accomplished war poet akin to Siegfried Sassoon. Recent critics have commented on the escapist and occasionally mawkish quality of many of these poems, however, and

Graves himself described them in 1923 as "bankrupt stock" originating from "the desire to escape from a painful war neurosis into an Arcadia of amatory fancy." Commentators have moreover tended to fault his war poems as unconvincing and lacking in control, often relying on gratuitously grotesque imagery and the piling up of adjectives for effect.

After meeting Laura Riding in 1926, Graves's poetry underwent a significant transformation. Douglas Day has written that the "influence of Laura Riding is quite possibly the most important single element in [Graves's] poetic career: she persuaded him to curb his digressiveness and his rambling philosophizing and to concentrate instead on terse, ironic poems written on personal themes." For instance, in Graves's second volume of collected poems, *Poems, 1926-1930,* his previous pastoral sentimentality is replaced by intensely personal poems that explore the themes of loss and salvation through love. Much of the poetry of this period is further concerned with the dichotomy between consciousness and the body. The poem "Certain Mercies," for example, expresses dissatisfaction with the vicissitudes of corporeal existence and employs the metaphor of the body as prison.

In the 1940s, after his break with Riding, Graves formulated his personal mythology of the White Goddess. Inspired by late nineteenth-century studies of matriarchal societies and goddess cults, Graves asserts in *The White Goddess* that "the true poet" receives inspiration from a female Muse, "the cruel, capricious, incontinent White Goddess," and seeks to be destroyed by her. Central to this mythology is the ancient Near Eastern story of Attis, the mortal male who becomes the consort of the goddess Cybele after she has driven him to madness and suicide. The yearly death and resurrection of Attis is a metaphor of the natural cycle to which Graves alludes in such poems as "To Juan at the Winter Solstice," "Theseus and Ariadne," and "The Sirens' Welcome to Cronos." Of these poems Randall Jarrell has written that they "are different from anything else in English; their whole meaning and texture and motion are different from anything we could have expected from Graves or from anybody else."

Graves's later poetry is based on further refinement of the White Goddess theme. In the early 1960s Graves had become interested in the Islamic mystical movement of Sufism. This led him to develop the theory that behind the cruel White Goddess there lies the Black Goddess of Wisdom who provides the poet with a "miraculous certitude in love." The poetry of these years sought to achieve a synthesis between realism and romanticism. In his *Collected Poems* (1965) Graves wrote: "My main theme was always the practical impossibility, transcended only by a belief in miracle, of absolute love continuing between man and woman." The critic Michael Kirkham has singled out the poem "Ambience" as representative of the tranquility of Graves's mature vision. Constructed of carefully modulated syntax, giving the effect of elegant prose, "Ambience" celebrates the Black Goddess as "the nymph of the forest," who infuses the natural order with rapture.

While critics acknowledge Graves's technical mastery and lyrical intensity, there is a divergence of opinion as to whether he is a major poet. Many critics have claimed that the work of poets such as W. B. Yeats and T. S. Eliot, whom Graves dismissed, is of a more enduring and memorable nature than that of Graves. Other critics, however, have argued that Graves's independence from twentieth-century trends has had a lasting impact on younger English poets. In 1962 W. H. Auden went as far as to assert that Graves was England's "greatest living poet." Having founded no school, and with few direct disciples, Graves, through his mythologically inspired love poetry, occupies a distinctive position among twentieth-century poets writing in English. As the scholar John Carey wrote in Graves's obituary, "He had a mind like an alchemist's laboratory: everything that got into it came out new, weird and gleaming."

PRINCIPAL WORKS

POETRY

Over the Brazier   1916
Fairies and Fusiliers   1917
Country Sentiment   1920
The Pier-Glass   1921
Whipperginny   1923
Mock Beggar Hall   1924
Poems (1914-1927)   1927
Poems, 1926-1930   1931
Collected Poems   1938
Collected Poems (1914-1947)   1948
Poems and Satires   1951
Collected Poems: 1955   1955
Collected Poems   1965
Collected Poems   1975

OTHER MAJOR WORKS

Goodbye to All That   (autobiography)   1929
I, Claudius   (novel)   1934
Count Belisarius   (novel)   1938
The Story of Marie Powell, Wife to Mr. Milton   (novel)   1943
King Jesus   (novel)   1946
The White Goddess: A Historical Grammar of Poetic Myth   (criticism)   1948
The Common Asphodel: Collected Essays on Poetry, 1922-1949   (criticism)   1949
The Greek Myths   (criticism)   1955
The Crowning Privilege: Collected Essays on Poetry   (criticism)   1956
Mammon and the Black Goddess   (criticism)   1963

CRITICISM

Edwin Muir (essay date 1926)

[*Muir was a distinguished Scottish novelist, poet, critic, and translator. In his critical writings, Muir was more concerned with the general philosophical issues raised by works of art—such as the nature of time or society—than with the particulars of the work itself, such as style or characterization. In the following review of several volumes of Graves's early poetry, Muir claims that Graves fails to achieve a synthesis between external reality and his own consciousness.*]

Mr. Graves is one of the most puzzling figures in contemporary literature. He is conspicuously honest, yet he is often evasive; he is bold—and suddenly cautious; he is more dogmatic than any other contemporary poet, and perhaps more really sceptical at the same time. And it is in his poems of conflict that he is most sceptical, in his poems of escape that he is most daring. The best poems in *Country Sentiment,* which he describes himself as poems of escape, are admirably sincere; they face the reality of things more concretely than most of the later poetry, concerned with more everyday problems. Their sincerity, moreover, is of a very rare kind. For it takes far less courage, as modern psychology tells us, to face external realities than it takes to recognize the realities within us, especially when these are unconscious realities becoming conscious, as they are in *Country Sentiment.* Like everybody else the poet must, of course, adapt himself to the world around him. To learn what one's environment is and to relate oneself to that is a utilitarian activity which cannot be avoided; but its attainment is not the work of poetry but of commonsense. Approaching reality directly in this way, we are working with the conscious mind on the raw fact; a harmony, therefore, cannot result, but only a compromise. Where Mr. Graves's poetry fails, as where a great deal of modern poetry fails, is where we have this bare confrontation of the conscious mind and the raw reality. The identity of the seer with the thing seen, the subjective-objective reality of vision, is not attained; this condition is only a stage towards its attainment; poetry in embryo, not poetry born. And though it is desirable that the modern world should find expression in poetry, that will never be done by one who sets out, in spite of his repugnance, to do so. It will only be done when a poet finds the modern world within himself, when not merely the outward, conscious adaptation to it has been made, but the inner, unconscious one as well. This is, indeed, a platitude; yet a number of modern theories of poetry ignore it and dogmatize as if it were not there. Mr. Graves does not do so; his observations on the function and aim of poetry are always enlightened and often true; but his practice is tending less and less to conform to his best theory. In the second section of *Whipperginny* and in *Mock Beggar Hall* he has no longer the integral approach to the theme which we find in his earlier poetry. He no longer attacks the problem with all his faculties, finding a resolution on the various planes of the mind, as he has said poetry should; he attacks it only with his intellect, enlisting the imagination, if at all, as a supernumerary. He does not reveal convictions and intuitions; he treats general ideas which, we feel, have not

been assimilated to his poetic nature and are perhaps alien to it. The will to adaptation is in his later work, rather than the living act of adaptation, and all that a will of this kind can give the poet is a compromise, not a reconciling vision of life, not a resolution.

And it is for a compromise that Mr. Graves seems to be out in his later poetry and in his criticism. His criticism is very illuminating, both for what it says and for what it tells us about himself. He is an out-and-out relativist. What is good poetry to one man, he claims, is bad poetry to another; what this age finds significant a later one will find meaningless. Bad poetry is poetry which does not ease or clarify our subconscious conflicts; but it may ease or clarify the complexes of another generation, and then it will become good poetry. The theory is consistent, but so are most theories of criticism; the important thing is to find out what by means of it the author wishes to prove. For problems of this kind are never resolved; their terms are only changed from time to time by the action of fresh intelligences. In what way has Mr. Graves's candid and unconventional intelligence changed them? In two ways chiefly: by casting doubt on the supreme utterances of poetry (for no poetry can be supreme which is good in one age and bad in another); and by making the criterion of poetry very largely a utilitarian one. Nothing could show more clearly Mr. Graves's compromising temper. For when a man becomes convinced that compromise is essential he will in time come to prefer the second-best to the best, or at any rate the good to the surpassing, recognizing that for his purposes the former is the more effective. Moreover compromise and a utilitarian preoccupation go together, the criterion of every compromise being essentially its usefulness. There would be no point in controverting Mr. Graves's theories. They are a stimulating addition to critical thought; they emphasize factors which literary criticism almost always ignores, factors at present of the first importance. The question is whether Mr. Graves has emphasized them in the right way.

To take an extreme example, even if in certain ages Shakespeare has been a bad poet (not touching their particular conflicts), there is still a vast difference between him, in any age, and a bad poet like Martin Tupper. It is for differences as important as this that Mr. Graves's critical theory does not provide. The psychological effect of poetry is so important to him that as a theorist he has an eye for very little else. "For the poet," he says, "the writing of poetry accomplishes a certain end, irrespective of whether the poem ever finds another reader but himself; it enables him to be rid of the conflicts between his subpersonalities. And for the reader, the reading of poetry performs a similar service; it acts for him as a physician of his mental disorders." As far as it goes this is no doubt true; but the poet may rid himself of his subconscious conflicts in an infinity of ways, and on various planes, and as important as his release is the manner in which he effects it. For to rid oneself of a conflict is to be in a different state, and the quality of that state is not a matter of indifference. Yet to Mr. Graves sometimes it seems to be indifferent what the state is so long as the conflict has been removed. "Francis Thompson's *Sister Songs* and Lear's *Nonsense Rhymes,*" he says, "are apparently the same sort of escape from the same sort of conflict; strange that Lear is treated less seriously. And who will say that the foolery in Edward Lear is less worthy of our tragic imagination than the terrible foolery at the crisis of *King Lear*?" The only thing that can be said in reply to this is that by the foolery in *King Lear* our conflicts are released into an infinitely greater world than they are by Edward Lear's nonsense verses. Although both help to rid us of our conflicts, they move us in completely different ways and with vastly different power. Nonsense verse does give our conflicts a certain relief. It presents us with a lively picture of the utter unintelligibility of our subconscious war, and the resignation to that unintelligibility loosens our tensions for a time. The mood of nonsense and the mood of mystery are alike in as far as they are evoked by things which seem unintelligible; the great difference between them is that while the one is a giving way to meaninglessness, the other is an attempt to impose meaning upon it. Not even to the curative psychologist concerned only to release the pressure of a conflict in the subconscious mind could these modes of relief appear of equal importance; to a poet interested in the positive temper of the soul it is quite impossible to see how they can.

It is when we come to Mr. Graves's later poetry that we see some of the bad effects of this curiously pragmatic evaluation of the act of poetic expression. The change is decisively marked in **Whipperginny,** and the preface to the volume tells us that the author was aware of it. The first part of the book, he says, continues the mood of **The Pier Glass,** "aggressive and disciplinary, rather than escapist." "But in most of the later pieces," he adds, "will be found evidences of greater detachment in the poet and the appearance of a new series of problems in religion, psychology and philosophy, no less exacting than their predecessors, but, it may be said, of less emotional intensity." In this later poetry and in some which Mr. Graves has written since, we are conscious that each poem is a theme chosen. We admire the manner in which the poet's mind deals with it; but subject and mind are not fused; and it is not an experience that is registered, but a hypothesis. Nor is that the worst, for we are often aware that the poetry is performing a set psychological function. The machinery is too apparent. Certain of the poems in **Whipperginny**— **"The Technique of Perfection,"** for instance, and **"The Bowl and the Rim"**—are simply hypothetical statements of the general conditions of psychological conflict, about which the poet is clarifying his mind. But in resolving our subconscious conflicts poetry does not inform us of them, as psycho-analysis does; its operation is different; it takes place on the various planes of the psyche, and not, as in psycho-analysis, on the one which gives the key to the others; its effect is thus a harmonizing of the mind, rather than a clarifying of it. When Mr. Graves informs us in his poetry of the subconscious conflicts, therefore, he is forcing the natural growth of poetry with his intellect, and forcing it for a utilitarian purpose, that the effects of poetry might be enjoyed. In a process such as this the impulses of the unconscious are given a ready-made shape before they appear; the poet is prepared for them, and therefore against them, in advance; and the result is that they never achieve an organic expression, but only a schematized one. They are categories by the time Mr. Graves handles them,

rather than energies. The only way one can mark the difference between

> Across two counties he can hear,
> And catch your words before you speak.
> The woodlouse or the maggot's weak
> Clamour rings in his sad ear,

from **The Pier Glass,** and

> Let us live upright, yet with care consider
> Whether, in living thus, we do not err,

from **Whipperginny,** is by saying that the first contains potentially all that is in the second, and contains as well something more. And when one compares the much earlier **"In the Wilderness"** with the recent **"The Clipped Stater,"** the discrepancy is still greater. **"In the Wilderness"** is not one of Mr. Graves's best poems, it is too inconclusive; but the difference between

> Basilisk, cockatrice,
> Flocked to his homilies,
> With mail of dread device,
> With monstrous barbed slings,
> With eager dragon eyes;
> Great rats on leather wings,
> And poor blind broken things,
> Foul in their miseries,

and

> Then Finity is true Godhead's final test,
> Nor does it shear the grandeur from Free Being;
> "I must fulfil myself by self-destruction."
> The curious phrase renews his conquering zest,

is definite and striking. It is the difference between a state imagined and a state hypothecated and only dipped in the imagination to be given an intellectual convincingness. The first passage has the immediacy of psychological reality, the second has not. It lacks the truth which we feel in poetry when there is an organic correspondence between the external image and the inner conflict or desire—that correspondence which clamps poetry to reality and gives it an absolute force. **"The Clipped Stater"** is a floating fancy thrown off by the inconstant mind; it has no necessity; it may or may not be true. The question is not whether **"The Clipped Stater"** is poetry. It is a question rather of the relative value of two kinds of work which Mr. Graves has produced and still continues to produce side by side. In literary criticism nothing can be proved; the only thing that one can say is that by poetry like **"In the Wilderness"** something is done that by **"The Clipped Stater"** is not done at all; that the first is real, the second—not certainly so; that they are consequently of different worth.

The interesting thing about Mr. Graves is that with such an effective equipment for compromise he sometimes deserts it and leads an attack on his own defences. Nothing could be more different from the temporizing relativity of the critical books and the stifling compromise of *Mock Beggar Hall* than an occasional poem like **"The Rock Below."** "Where speedwell grows and violets grow" the poet plucks up the flowers and finds stumps of thorn beneath. These come up and he sets a rose bush where they were.

> Love has pleasure in my roses
> For a summer space.

But the roots of the rose bush turn on stone, so he tears them up and far beneath strikes on the rock, "jarring hatefully." But "up the rock shall start."

> Now from the deep and frightful pit
> Shoots forth the spiring phoenix-tree
> Long despaired in this bleak land,
> Holds the air with boughs, with bland
> Fragrance welcome to the bee,
> With fruits of immortality.

The contradiction in Mr. Graves's poetry is fundamental. On the one hand we have the consistent relativism of his later poetry, on the other, a determination to dig down until his mind produces "fruits of immortality." There is the mass of his busy, temporizing, hypothetical verse, verse which seems to say, "This may be true, or it may not"; there are a few poems which leave no room for the relative or for questions of this kind. **"Lost Love"** and **"A Lover since Childhood"** have this incontestable seriousness; some of the poems at the beginning of *Country Sentiment* have it in a higher degree than any Mr. Graves has written since. In these, and still more clearly in poems like **"In the Wilderness"** and **"The Rock Below,"** Mr. Graves shows himself to be an original poet. In his later pseudo-philosophical poetry the thought, while lively and full of idiosyncrasy, is never very original; the supposititious form in which it is advanced makes it appear far more profound than it is in reality. It may be that Mr. Graves's excursion into philosophy will deepen his mind, and that later he will return with fuller powers to the kind of poetry which he seems so inevitably equipped to write. Meanwhile one can only note the passing phase. (pp. 163-76)

> *Edwin Muir, "Robert Graves," in his* Transition: Essays on Contemporary Literature, *The Viking Press, 1926, pp. 163-76.*

Stephen Spender   (essay date 1946)

[*Spender is an English man of letters who rose to prominence during the 1930s as a Marxist lyric poet and as an associate of W. H. Auden, Christopher Isherwood, C. Day Lewis, and Louis MacNeice. His poetic reputation declined in the postwar years, while his stature as a prolific and perceptive literary critic has grown. In the following excerpt, taken from a review of* Poems: 1938-1945, *Spender comments on the purity of Graves's poetry.*]

Mr. Robert Graves is opposed to all impurities, past and present. He writes of a purely poetic subject-matter, and here his Foreword to his *Poems 1938-1945* is most illuminating:

> Since poems should be self-explanatory I refrain from more foreword than this: that I write poems for poets, and satires or grotesques for wits. For people in general I write prose, and am content that they should be unaware that I do anything else. To write poems for other than poets is wasteful. The moral of the Scilly islanders who earned a precarious livelihood by taking

in one another's washing is that they never upset their carefully balanced island economy by trying to horn into the laundry of the mainland; and that nowhere in the Western Hemisphere was washing so well done.

This is not only a shrewd self-appraisal, it is also a shrewd criticism of Mr. Graves's fellow poets who 'horn into' religion, philosophy, psychology, politics, events and occasions. And Mr. Graves's own poems have the air often of being solid and wry little touchstones which, self-contained and unconcerned as they are with other poems than themselves, yet somehow imply a gritty comment on most of their contemporaries by other poets.

> The full moon easterly rising, furious,
> Against a winter sky ragged with red;
> The hedges high in snow, and owls raving—
> Solemnities not easy to withstand:
> A shiver wakes the spine.
>
> In boyhood, having encountered the scene,
> I suffered horror: I fetched the moon home,
> With owls and snow, to nurse in my head
> Throughout the trials of a new spring,
> Famine unassuaged.
>
> But fell in love, and made a lodgement
> Of love on those chill ramparts.
> Her image was my ensign: snows melted,
> Hedges sprouted, the moon tenderly shone,
> The owls trilled with tongues of the nightingale.
>
> These were all lies, though they matched the
>   time,
> And brought me less than luck: her image
> Warped in the weather, turned beldamish.
> Then back came winter on me at a bound,
> The pallid sky heaved with a moon-quake.
>
> Dangerous it had been with love-notes
> To serenade Queen Famine.
> In tears I recompensed the former scene,
> Let the snow lie, watched the moon rise, suffered
>   the owls,
> Paid homage to them of unevent.

I quote this exquisite poem, **"A Love Story,"** in full because it is not only an almost perfect example of Mr. Graves's manner but it also saves me trouble by supplying its own comment in the last line 'Paid homage to them of unevent'. For the point is that nothing happens, nothing is said, in Mr. Graves's poems except the poetry. One has the impression in this poem of a lifetime having been passed to no purpose, except to extract the poetic metal from the ore of experience. One is then given the pure ore, with no comment, no message, no consolation, and the poem exists by its complete negation of extra-poetic ambition. Mr. Graves writes a kind of pure poetry which is different from the search for the pure phrase, the pure line, the pure music of the French purists: it is the rather roughly hewn poetry of a purely poetic experience. (pp. 223-25)

> *Stephen Spender, "Poetry for Poetry's Sake and Poetry beyond Poetry," in* Horizon, *London, Vol. XIII, No. 76, April, 1946, pp. 221-38.*

George Fraser   (essay date 1947)

[*Fraser was a distinguished English critic who wrote extensively on twentieth-century poetry. In the following essay, originally published in 1947, he explores the dichotomy between mind and body in Graves's poetry.*]

If we wanted to introduce Robert Graves's poetry to some receptive and intelligent person who did not know much about it—and there are many such people, for Graves as a poet is merely a fine artist preoccupied with a rather strange personal theme, what he says has sometimes a good deal of philosophic interest, but he has neither a warning nor a consoling message for his age—where would we start? We would wish to illustrate the solid excellence of style in much of his poetry, its occasional intense lyricism, a certain defiant toughness of mood which it expresses; and we would also wish to hint at that strange personal theme. **'Ulysses'** might be as good a poem to start with as another. It opens in a workmanlike way:

> To this much-tossed Ulysses, never done
>   With woman whether gowned as wife or
>   whore,
> Penelope and Circe seemed as one:
> She like a whore made his lewd fancies run,
>   And wifely she a hero to him bore.

A cultivated reader would appreciate at once the rotundity and neatness of that, and the fashion in which the 'she' and 'she', standing for *illa* and *haec,* reproduce in a neat inverted antithesis (it is Penelope, though she is his wife, who makes his lewd fancies run, and Circe, though she is his whore, who bears a hero to him) the effect of an Ovidian elegiac couplet. It is of Ovid, in fact, that we think at once, rather than of later poets like Dante and Tennyson who have also seen what they could do with Ulysses. Once the reader, however, has settled down to expect a smooth

Ovidian treatment, he will be disturbed in the next stanza by two lines of bitingly vivid romantic imagery: these women.

> Now they were storms frosting the sea with
>   spray
> And now the lotus orchard's filthy ease.

The first of these images is too romantically beautiful for the Ovidian setting; the second, with the violent epithet, 'filthy', too full of sharp self-disgust. The next stanza is a piece of angry moralizing:

> One, two, and many: flesh had made him blind,
>   Flesh had one pleasure only in the act,
> Flesh set one purpose only in the mind—
> Triumph of flesh, and afterwards to find
>   Still those same terrors wherewith flesh was
>   racked.

And the last stanza clinches the thought: the brave hero, the great amorist, was really to himself a *worthless* person, in all his successes he was fleeing from something he was afraid of, yielding to a weakness that he despised.

> His wiles were witty and his fame far known,
> Every king's daughter sought him for her own,
>   Yet he was nothing to be won or lost.
> All lands to him were Ithaca: love tossed,
> He loathed the fraud yet would not bed alone.

Graves set out, like Ovid, to comment, from an unheroic point of view, on a well-known heroic story; but his comments are more searching than Ovid's, and though this poem can stand by itself, it also fits into the general body of his work as a variation on his favourite theme, which is the relationship particularly between love and sexuality, more generally between the spirit and the body, more generally still between the mind and nature. That relationship Graves sees as sometimes a comic, sometimes a tragic, but always essentially an *awkward* relationship; it is never happy and harmonious.

Graves is peculiar among poets in that (though unlike Leopardi, for instance, who had something of the same attitude, he is a man of robust physical energy) he has a sense of awkward and unwilling attachment to his own body; and that awkwardness and unwillingness are, again and again, the main *theme* of his poems. He can treat the topic in a thoroughly amusing fashion, as in the comic and rather indecent little poem which begins, 'Down, wanton, down!' Addressing an intractable part of himself, he says, with a sort of affectionate contempt:

> Poor bombard-captain, sworn to reach
> The ravelin and effect a breach—
> Indifferent what you storm or why
> So be that in the breach you die!

But his more common attitude to the body, to its lusts, to its energies, to its mortality, to the clogging foreign weight that it hangs about him, is a far more sombre one. In **'The Furious Voyage'** it is a ship, on a great uncharted sea, containing no land:

> And it has width enough for you,
> This vessel, dead from truck to keel,
> With its unmanageable wheel,

Its blank chart and its surly crew,

Its ballast only due to fetch
The turning point of wretchedness
On an uncoasted, featureless
And barren ocean of blue stretch.

In a perhaps less effective poem, **'The Castle',** it is a sort
of gothic bastille in which he is imprisoned:

Planning to use—but by definition
There's no way out, no way out—
Rope-ladders, baulks of timber, pulleys,
A rocket whizzing over the walls and moat—
Machines easy to improvise—

Baudelaire (but Baudelaire was a sick man, aware that his
body was breeding its own ruin) has similar images in
some rough notes of a dream: he explores a crumbling and
gothic interior, full of labyrinths and tottering statues, a
fabric which is at any moment going to fall and crush him,
but from which there is 'by definition no way out'. But
Graves is concerned not so much with the body's mortality as with what he regards as the bearable, just bearable,
nastiness of ordinary physical life. Should we after all, he
asks in one poem, be grateful

That the rusty water
In the unclean pitcher
Our thirst quenches?

That the rotten, detestable
Food is yet eatable
By us ravenous?

That the prison censor
Permits a weekly letter?
(We may write: 'We are well.')

That with patience and deference
We do not experience
The punishment cell?

That each new indignity
Defeats only the body,
Pampering the spirit
With obscure, proud merit?

Most of his emblems for the body, it should be noted, are
inorganic: a ship, a castle, a prison cell. (In the little comic
poem I have quoted, the male sexual organ, the 'poor bom-
bard-captain' is a sort of obstreperous puppet-character
like Mr Punch.) As a love poet, Graves is essentially a romantic, along the same lines as (though probably not consciously influenced by) the troubadours and the poets of
the *dolce stil nuovo*: a critic like Denis de Rougemont
would connect his hatred of the body with their alleged
Catharism, and it is true that Graves, in his latest novel,
shows a great interest in the Gnostics, for whom the real
fall was the creation of the world. But I think Graves's
philosophy, in so far as he has one, springs from a fact
about his personal nature: the fact does not spring from
a philosophy. This sense of awkward and unwilling attachment to his body is, as it were, a *given* factor for him.
A critic, too, must take it as a given factor.

Much of Graves's poetry, then, will be concerned with the
dissatisfaction of the lover with sex, of the spirit with the
body, of the mind with nature; and yet with facing the fact

that love is bound to sex, spirit to body, and mind to nature. It is revealing to read, in this connection, some of his
abundant and on the whole unsatisfactory early verses.
Graves's early work does not show much promise of his
present strikingly individual and distinguished style. He
became known first as a war poet. After the war he re-
lapsed for a little into very weak writing in the Georgian
bucolic style, and in the preface to **Whipperginny** (1923)
he describes some of these rustic pieces as 'bankrupt
stock', and this whole manner as the result of a mood of
1918, 'the desire to escape from a painful war neurosis into
an Arcadia of amatory fancy'. These escapist pieces have
most of the qualities that we dislike today in the Georgians, the bucolic-hearty strain,

Contentions weary,
    It giddies all to think;
Then kiss, girl, kiss,
    Or drink, fellow, drink.

the manly beer-drinking note,

'What do you think
    The bravest drink
Under the sky?'
    'Strong beer,' said I.

and what Belloc, in 'Caliban's Guide to Letters', calls the
prattling style,

No! No!
My rhymes must go
Turn 'ee, twist 'ee,
Will-o'-the-wisp like, misty;
Rhymes I will make
Like Keats and Blake
And Christina Rossetti,
With run and ripple and shake,
How pretty . . .

How pretty, indeed, we feel inclined to murmur. And
today when we come upon this self-conscious rusticity,
these awkward assumptions of innocence in verse, we remember the advice of Patrice de la Tour du Pin: 'Do not
play, like children, with the parts of yourself that are no
longer childish.' But if these escapist pieces are mostly
rather mawkish, the war neurosis did not itself produce
very memorable poetry. Consider this postscript to an otherwise rather sentimental **'Familiar Letter, to Siegfried
Sassoon'**:

. . . to-day I found in Mametz wood
A certain cure for lust of blood,
Where propped against a shattered trunk
    In a great mess of things unclean
Sat a dead Boche: he scowled and stunk
    With clothes and face a sodden green;
Big-bellied, spectacled, crop-haired,
Dribbling black blood from nose to beard.

In a passage like that there are the roots of the horror
which is a recurring theme in Graves's later poetry; just
as in the bucolic pieces he seeks in nature something
which, in later, better poems he will know he has not
found. But though the passage is obviously extremely sincere, it is poetically unconvincing. Compare the amount
of control in it with that shown in some verses on a similar
theme by the most mature battle poet of the war that re-

cently ended, Keith Douglas. Douglas is writing about another dead soldier, this time in the Western Desert:

> Three weeks gone and the combatants gone,
> returning over the nightmare ground
> we found the place again and found
> the soldier sprawling in the sun.
>
> The frowning barrel of his gun
> overshadows him. As we came on
> that day, he hit my tank with one
> like the entry of a demon . . .

Douglas's dead man has a picture of his girl in his pocket:

> But she would weep to see to-day
> how on his skin the swart flies move,
> the dust upon the paper eye
> and the burst stomach like a cave.
>
> For here the lover and killer are mingled
> who had one body and one heart;
> and Death, who had the soldier singled,
> had done the lover mortal hurt.

This is a very much better passage than Graves's, partly because Graves expresses more disgust (and mere disgust is itself disgusting); because the dead soldier in this passage is seen as a person, and the 'dead Boche' in the other a mere object. There are also technical reasons why it is a better passage. Some of them have to do with the changing technique, not of poetry, but of war; mobile warfare, more than trench warfare, permits a certain control and detachment; Keith Douglas, not quite perpetually having his nose rubbed in the smell of death, is able to look on his dead man as an example of the fortunes of war and the large paradoxes of human life. The horrid foreground does not block all background. But also Douglas is beginning to write in a handier period, with neater tricks of rhetoric available to him. His lines move on the verb (the repetitions of 'gone' and 'found' in the first stanza), his visual images are conveyed by the antiseptically exact epithet and the isolated noun ('the *swart* flies', 'the *paper* eye', 'the *burst* stomach', 'the *frowning* barrel', and even, deliberately trite but appropriate, 'the *nightmare* ground'; and the two similes, 'like a *cave*', 'like the entry of a *demon*', at once natural and surprising). Moreover the deliberate formality of the language ('*nightmare* ground', '*swart* flies', '*weep*' instead of 'cry', particularly) and of the balanced syntax,

> and Death, who had the soldier singled,
> had done the lover mortal hurt.

give an effect of aesthetic distance. With Graves that effect is not created, he merely presents unpleasant raw material, too close to him to be art. And neither verbs nor nouns are used in Graves's passage so as to activate the line. He has one terribly feeble inversion ('things unclean'), and he makes his main descriptive effect,

> Big-bellied, spectacled, crop-haired,
> Dribbling black blood . . .

in the weakest way, by piling up adjectives. Yet we may well suppose that the ardours and horrors of the 1914-18 war, and his retreat into 'an Arcadia of amatory fancy' afterwards, provided Graves with his main poetic material;

in his later work he has, we may say, been largely concerned with refining, controlling, and generalizing the practical attitudes that were forced upon him in these exacting years. He had a facile success as a war poet and a writer of bucolics; it is very much to his credit that he should have struggled through from that sort of success to one more lonely but very much more worth having.

Examples of his early style at its least satisfactory can be found in *Poems, 1914-1926.* Graves's second volume of collected poems, *Poems, 1926-1930,* has an epigraph from Laura Riding:

> It is a conversation between angels now
> Or between who remain when all are gone.

and his style in this volume has suffered the astonishing purgation that this epigraph suggests. The Arcadianism has gone. Nature and a self-conscious bucolic childishness are no longer considered as cures for a poetic, or a metaphysical unease that has become a far deeper and wider thing than any war-neurosis. In one of the rudest poems ever written about nature (a poem which, like much else in the volume, beautifully anticipates Auden's earliest manner), he says, with all the spite of a disillusioned lover (I quote the original version from that volume, not the revised version from '**No More Ghosts**'):

> Nature is also so, you find,
> That brutal-comic mind,
> As wind,
> Retching among the empty spaces,
> Ruffling the idiot grasses,
> The sheep's fleeces.
>
> Whose pleasures are excreting, poking,
> Havocking and sucking,
> Sleepy licking,
>
> Whose griefs are melancholy,
> Whose flowers are oafish,
> Whose waters, silly,
> Whose birds, raffish,
> Whose fish, fish.

The total effect of such a passage is probably indescribable in prose. The poem, in fact, like most of Graves's later pieces, is very much itself and not what a critic can say about it. But if you read these lines out to yourself aloud, you will find they have a slow, sad movement, a melancholy perched on the edge of a yawn, a humour on the edge of a sigh, that lulls and depresses, that seems at once to confirm and contradict what the poem says: for this oafish, idiotic, and melancholy nature has its own perverse charm, too, conveyed much more intensely in these lines than in Graves's earlier straight poems about rustic life, in such volumes as *Country Sentiment.* There will also be, in very much of his later work, that knack of flat and final statement,

> Whose birds, raffish,
> Whose fish, fish,

as well as that ability to make a jocular manner go with a sad tone of voice, that ability to seem, whatever is being said, not entirely committed to it. Graves's reader had better be suspicious and alert; or else choose another poet.

Graves, in his volume of 1930, anticipates Auden's early manner so often and so startlingly—as in the beautiful poem that begins:

> O Love, be fed with apples while you may,
> And feel the sun and go in royal array,
> A smiling innocent in the heavenly causeway—

that we may wonder why he did not enjoy a revival of prestige in the 1930s, on the tail, as it were, of Auden's sumptuous early renown. The chief reason was probably that, unlike Auden (who has had a succession of messages), Graves has no obvious message for the age. He is probably most moving and most beautiful as a poet in these love poems which are concerned entirely with themes from his personal life. As far as politics are concerned, he has expressed, in a poem called **'The Tower of Siloam'**, his objection to becoming a prophet, an announcer of calamities:

> It behoved us, indeed, as poets
> To be silent in Siloam, to foretell
> No visible calamity. Though kings
> Were crowned with gold coin minted still and
>   horses
> Still munched at nose-bags in the public streets,
> All such sad emblems were to be condoned:
> An old wives' tale, not ours.

About politics, as about war, as about life in general, his feeling seems to be that people are to do their duty and not to expect things to turn out well. His Belisarius hates the corrupt, cowardly Justinian, rather admires the straightforward virtues of the barbarians he is fighting against, but never thinks of ousting Justinian from his place, or going over to the other side; and Belisarius is a hero very much to Graves's taste. He has a poem about that period, **'The Cuirassiers of the Frontier'**: the soldiers who speak in it say

> We, not the city, are the Empire's soul:
> A rotten tree lives only in its rind.

Does Graves feel about the British Empire, or about western European civilization generally, more or less what he feels about Byzantium? He gives no hint about that. But whereas when he fought it was the horrors of war that came most closely home to him, in his later poetry he thinks more of the honour and nobility of a soldier's life, of the good fortune of an early death. As in the poem, **'Callow Captain'**, in which he may perhaps be thinking of the *persona* of himself, the young, gallant soldier, who stalks through *Goodbye to All That*.

> A wind ruffles the book, and he whose name
>   Was mine vanishes: all is at an end.
> Fortunate soldier: to be spared shame
>   Of chapter-years unprofitable to spend,
> To ride off into history, nor throw
>   Before the story-sun a long shadow.

Yet if he has managed, in retrospect, to purge war of its horror, horror of another kind has gathered in his later poetry around the love in which he sought an escape from war. His love poems are nearly all, though wonderfully touching, almost unbearably sad. That poem of which I

have quoted three lines closes (I quote again the earlier version) sadly and sinisterly enough:

> Be warm, enjoy the season, lift your head,
> Exquisite in the pulse of tainted blood,
> That shivering glory not to be despised.

> Take your delight in momentariness,
> Walk between dark and dark, a shining space,
> With the grave's narrowness, but not its peace.

'The tainted blood', 'the shivering glory' (the uncontrollable shivering of the body in a fit of lust), 'not to be despised'. Even in a love poem Graves cannot repress his faint grimace of disgust at the body; and in the saddest of all his love poems, **'A Love Story'**, he describes how love had dispersed the winter whose horror besieged him, transformed it, how his loved one, 'warped in the weather, turned beldamish', how the horror came back again, and how he realized that it had been a mistake 'to serenade Queen Famine'. His advice, in fact, about love, as about other things, seems to be to make the most of the good in the evil, of the good moment which heralds the bad change. But his final note is always sad:

> And now warm earth was Arctic sea,
>   Each breath came dagger-keen;
> Two bergs of glinting ice were we,
>   The broad moon sailed between;

> There swam the mermaids, tailed and finned,
> And love went by upon the wind
>   As though it had not been.

Only the lucid wintry fantasy there, and the compelling canorous voice, only the romantic trappings of which Graves had never entirely divested himself, console us for the cruel thing said.

It would be wrong to think of Graves as an entirely pessimistic poet. He is pessimistic about the world that exists. He has no message for the age, in that he does not think that things will turn out well (as, in their different ways, Auden and Eliot do). Some writers, like Orwell, who expect things to turn out badly, are at least very much concerned about this: and that also gives them, in a sense, a message; it is their part 'to foretell visible calamity—'. Graves seems, on the whole, to think that it is in the nature of things to turn out badly, and only a fool would make a fuss about it. But there is some realm or other of subsisting value (in a recent poem, he calls it 'excellence') which the change, which is the badness, cannot touch: the ravaging worms

> . . . were greedy-nosed
> To smell the taint and go scavenging,
> Yet over excellence held no domain.
> Excellence lives; they are already dead—
> The ages of a putrefying corpse.

And in his last volume there is also a religious poem (largely translated from ancient Greek texts), **'Instructions to the Orphic Adept'**, in which it is suggested that complete self-recollection is a way of escape from change. The regenerate soul is admonished:

> . . . Man, remember
> What you have suffered here in Samothrace,

Manuscript for "A Country Mood," first published in 1920.

What you have suffered.
Avoid this spring, which is Forgetfulness;
Though all the common rout rush down to
    drink,
Avoid this spring.

In his poetry, Graves has obeyed these instructions; he has remembered what he has suffered, and, in remembering, has transformed pain into the excellence of art. He is a very fine poet, and a poet whose vision of some things, of love, of suffering, of pain, of honour, is much deeper, stronger, and calmer than the vision that most of us can claim. His temperament may estrange intimacy; his chief preoccupations may be irrelevant to our most urgent contemporary problems. And when he deals with the theme of the body in a prison he may be dealing with a theme rather excessively private (in the sense that readers, like myself, who have not a parallel feeling about their own bodies, have to make a rather conscious effort of sympathy). Nevertheless, in his later work in verse—as, indeed, in his better work in prose—he is a model for young writers of a strong and pure style. His journeys may lie rather aside from what we think of as our main roads; but his is a very pure and individual talent, which, if we do care at all for good and honest writing, we ought not to ignore or decry. (pp. 125-35)

> *George Fraser, "The Poetry of Robert Graves,"*
> *in his* Essays on Twentieth-Century Poets,
> *Leicester University Press, 1977, pp. 125-35.*

Ronald Hayman   (essay date 1955)

[*In the following excerpt, Hayman argues that Graves's most important poems are those which deal directly with emotional experience.*]

The poet is defeated as often as the novelist by the difficulty of treating experience so as to communicate both his view of its significance and a sense of its reality. But while novels are less likely to lack reality than to lack significance, the poet is in greater danger of neglecting the reality of experience, whether by letting the process of analysis distract him or by keeping a subjective lens screwed into one eye and never opening the other. The most general failing of modern 'metaphysical' poets (Empson, Bottrall, Wain) is their lack of interest in the particular, the immediate and the personal, while the weakness of the 'Romantics' (Barker, Kathleen Raine, Watkins) is that they refuse to look at anything else and so see nothing in a perspective of values.

Of course this is all far too simple. I have said nothing about the vivid shots of individual scenes that can flash through a 'metaphysical' poem or about the effect of classical allusions in much romantic poetry or about a host of other relevant points. But I do not want to go on generalising about the opposition between 'Romantic' and 'Metaphysical'. I believe that the poets most worth discussing, Eliot, Thomas, Auden and Graves, cannot justly be classified under either head, and I want to argue that Graves's importance as a poet depends on a small corpus of poems which are neither metaphysical nor romantic, the strength of these poems lying in their complete freedom from either of the two weaknesses.

Of the large number of Graves's poems that are purely and incontrovertibly 'metaphysical', we can take **'In Broken Images'** as an example. Like most of Empson's verse it does not stem out of any experience nor even arise from an urge to make statements about experience in general. The argument is elaborated for the sake of the pattern of opposites that meet and mount like the vertical and horizontal surfaces of a staircase.

> He is quick thinking in clear images;
> I am slow thinking in broken images.
>
> He becomes dull trusting to his clear images;
> I become sharp mistrusting my broken images.
>
> Trusting his images he assumes their relevance,
> Mistrusting my images, I question their relevance. . . .

And it goes on to construct four more steps out of statements and counter-statements. The analysis might really have been as subtle as it looks if it had an object, but the 'I' and the 'he' exist only as opposites that can be balanced; and, since the poem is not about anything, its development is quite haphazard: its only incentive to go on seems to be the hope of finding chances to echo phrases or balance their opposites against them. He becomes dull only because 'dull' is an opposite of clear, whilst I do not become sharp because sharpness is a likely consequence of mistrusting broken images but because another opposite of 'dull' has to be found. With no virtues but its pattern, its poise and its virtuosity with words the poem, though pleasing, is very slight; and I would think such an analysis of it quite unsuitable and quite unnecessary if I had not heard a major claim for Graves based on it and poems like it.

If his range were limited to such work he would be a very minor poet. But even in poems similar in flavour to **'In Broken Images,'** we can often see, bubbling through, a much stronger feeling for the immediate situation than we ever see in Empson. In **'Cry Faugh'** it boils over. Graves deliberately takes a metaphysical saucepan that is too small, just for the pleasure of seeing the poem surge over the sides and pour down into Romanticism. The first five stanzas are conventionally metaphysical. They remind us of Empson by the way they arrange sober lines of learned facts in a pattern of witty summaries—

> Socrates and Plato burked the issue
> (Namely how man-and-woman love should be)
> With homosexual ideology.

> Apocalyptic Israelites, foretelling
> The immanent End, called only for a chaste
> Sodality: all dead below the waist

At first it seems that apart from the way they are unified by the verse, the only connection between the summaries is that they are all of attitudes to sexual love and that the poet disapproves of them all. But these abstract general statements are built up only to be knocked aside as we are jerked into the personal and particular—

> Cry Faugh! on science, ethics, metaphysics,
> On antonyms of sacred and profane—
> Come walk with me, love, in a golden rain

> Past toppling collonades of glory,
> The moon alive on each uplifted face:
> Proud remnants of a visionary race.

There is the same change from abstract to concrete in **'The Terraced Valley,'** though this does not begin with abstract statements but in an abstract world, perspectiveless, negative, unhealthy. It is described in more or less abstract terms and it is imagined as a projection not of the abstract, but, negatively, of a lack of the concrete. It represents a blind alley of consciousness into which the poet has strayed

> In a deep thought of you and concentration.

In the woman's absence, the concentration has led to a confused inversion of reality. When remote from palpable emotional experience, Graves's consciousness always is liable to be drawn into a vacuum where it may succumb to the nightmare visions of unreality in the real world which find expression in such outbursts of nihilism as **'The Castle.'** Or it may try to fill the gap with words, disguising the fact that they are mere words, fleshless, colourless and almost meaningless, by forming them into conceits. In this poem we find the nightmare vision expressed in patterned paradoxes, and it is impossible to say which produced which.

> Calm sea beyond the terraced valley
> Without horizon easily was spread
> As it were overhead

> Washing the mountain spurs behind me:
> The unnecessary sky was not there
> Therefore no heights, no deeps, no birds of the
> air.

> Neat outside-inside, neat below-above,
> Hermaphrodising love.
> Neat this-way-that-way and without mistake
> On the right hand could slide the left glove.

Speaking of such a perplexed world, the poem is itself perplexing. Unhealthy, isolated concentration produced this world—and played a part, evidently, in producing the poem—but the poem is healthier than its world because it shows awareness of how unhealthy the world, the isolation and the concentration are. Before it ends it restores reality as the reappearance of the woman shatters all three.

Graves is at his best when dealing directly with emotional experience. His early style was formed long before Eliot's influence inaugurated the cult of detachment, and throughout his development from the whimsy in which he tried to forget the 1914-18 war to the acuity of *Poems and Satires* (1951), he has consistently held aloof from the modes and movements of his contemporaries, scarcely even being influenced by them. It is partly owing to his complete independence that he has not received the recognition he deserves. There is some truth in what he wrote, with Laura Riding, in *Form in Modernist Poetry*:

> If a poet is to achieve even the smallest reputation today, his work must suggest a style capable of being exploited by a group; or he must either be a brilliant group member or quick-change parasite. Otherwise he is likely to be lost to the literary news sheet of every critical colour and not even to occur as subject of the plain reader's suspicion and the critic's caution; to exist, in fact, only unto himself.

As the bitterness of this passage suggests, isolation as a writer, and consciousness of it, did Graves a great deal of harm; but it also enabled him to go on writing from the centre of emotional experiences quite unaffected by the prevailing tendency to view them from outside and from a distance. Unlike the poets who may be called 'Romantics', he was not even influenced by the cult of detachment into reacting against it.

Dylan Thomas was; but he and Graves can both maintain a balance between living emotional experience and adequate awareness of it. They can both immerse themselves fully in the particular situation, yet see beyond it, and so judge it. Graves, however, projects the significance of the situations he treats beyond the particular contexts not, as Thomas does, by the enlarging suggestiveness of his images, but by the thoroughness of his investigation. (There is a parallel contrast between the fiction of the two poets.) His verse is formally more or less regular and straightforward in syntax, while, compared with Thomas's, it often seems almost as dry in tone and as economical in language as Eliot's. But it is emotional and dramatic. The situations are not first-personally dramatic as often as Thomas's are, but, in his best poems, he always penetrates deeply into them. He does not go outside his situations to draw ironical classical parallels as Eliot did in his earlier verse but he achieves ironical effects by means of a change of viewpoint or a time-shift. In both of the sequences in **'Theseus and Ariadne'** there is a time shift, and there is also a change of viewpoint between the two, so that the findings of one consciousness can be measured against the other's,—

> High on his figured couch beyond the waves
> He dreams, in dream recalling her set walk
> Down paths of oyster-shell bordered with flow-
> ers
> And down the shadowy path beneath the vine.
> He sighs: 'Deep sunk in my erroneous past
> She haunts the ruins and the ravaged lawns.'
>
> Yet still unharmed it stands, the regal house
> Crooked with age and overtopped by pines
> Where first he wearied of her constancy.
> And with a surer foot she goes than when
> Dread of his hate was thunder in the air,
>
> When the pines agonised by flaws of wind
> And flowers glared up at her with frantic eyes.
> Of him, now all is done, she never dreams
> But calls a living blessing down upon
> What he would have mere rubble and rank
> grass;
> Playing the queen to nobler company.

The precision of 'High on his figured couch' may at first seem to assort oddly with the vagueness of 'beyond the waves' but the vagueness is deliberate; the waves are to serve the double purpose of separating the two scenes and distancing them from us. Immediacy is not lost, though— the solid particularity and the penetration into the consciousnesses of the characters makes the experiences very vivid. The first half of the poem contrasts the purposeful gait he remembers with the form the memory now takes in his consciousness. But the phrases used for both, 'her set walk' and 'she haunts', are caught up, balanced and corrected by 'a surer foot'. The way she really moves now is beyond Theseus's awareness, which is incapable either of imagining her existence outside the past they shared or remembering that his is not the only possible valuation of that past. A quiet assertion of the present reality dismisses the dreams of Theseus and gives Ariadne best. She has no need to dream of their past, for she is better off now, living to enjoy the house and the landscape that for him no longer exist as they really are. The mistake Theseus makes about these symbolically parallels his mistake over Ariadne's present. Like her, the regal house, is no more of a ruin than it was before. His memory of the landscape background to the love affair is also countered in the second half of the poem by hers. The word 'flowers' is repeated with a quite different effect. (Graves often makes a new view of a landscape symbolise a change of attitude—in **'A Love Story'** and **'Full Moon,'** for example.) The whole structure of **'Theseus and Ariadne'** is—typically—based on opposition between the real thing and the false idea of it. The principle is simple, but the detail of the organisation is complex; modulated echoes and modifying backward glances make suggestions of meaning reverberate through the poem and carry beyond it.

No loss of immediacy is involved in the complexity of this

or of the love poetry, which often achieves a poise and an intensity reminiscent of the metaphysical love poetry of the seventeenth century. **'Sick Love,'** the poem that begins

> Oh Love be fed on apples while you may . . .

recalls Herrick by its movement and its cheerful willingness to face the transience of passion and pleasure. Complete awareness does not kill the emotion in this or in any of Graves's love poems because he is too deeply immersed in the particular experience to be over-conscious, as Auden often is, and because he can preserve a delicate poise between the elements. The jocular outrightness of **'Sick Love'** is played off gently against the passionate seriousness without reducing its urgency.

> Be warm, enjoy the season, lift your head,
> Exquisite in the pulse of tainted blood,
> That shivering glory not to be despised.
>
> Take your delight in momentariness,
> Walk between dark and dark—a shining space
> With the grave's narrowness, though not its
> peace.

Not even the explicitness of 'momentariness' can harm the spirit that phrase and movement have generated. And the dual consciousness of the whole poem is reflected in the balance of each single line, each with opposite suggestions caught and harmonised.

Mood and movement are graver in **'Counting the Beats,'** but there is the same clear-eyed awareness of all the facts, and the central image expresses perfectly the sense of loving in and against time.

> Counting the beats,
> Counting the slow heart beats,
> The bleeding to death of time in slow heart
> beats,
> Wakeful they lie.

She asks where they will be when death strikes home, and his answer is

> Not there but here,
> (He whispers) only here,
> As we are, here, together, now and here,
> Always you and I.

The faith in the moment is given a religious force by the incantatory movement, (which links the poem to some of Graves's magical poems,) and by the repetition, which also brings out the lover's urgency and his anxiety to believe in what he is saying.

'Il doutait de tout, même de l'amour', but in Graves, as in Donne, the balance of the poetry gives an edge of certainty to scepticism, so that its effect is to strengthen faith by implying a demarcation of its province.

The balance is accomplished by looking backwards in **'Theseus and Ariadne',** by looking forwards in **'Counting the Beats';** a third means is to look back at a major experience which may be repeated, asking whether it is worth having again, and using the answer to assess the future which will repeat it. In a number of his poems, Graves has seen himself as the only survivor in a world full of ghosts. This image, which originated from a wartime sensation, was at first used to indulge a sense of horror by projecting it into fancy. But in **'The Survivor'** (1951) the death is less fantastic. It is now partly symbolic of the death to an experience which comes simply from having had it once. A love affair is a dying-to-love for both lovers, and in the light of this, future love affairs can be assessed.

> And is this joy: after the double suicide
> (Heart against heart) to be restored entire,
> To smooth your hair and wash away your life-
>   blood,
> And presently seek a young and innocent bride,
> Whispering in the dark: 'for ever and ever'?

But this is scarcely written from the centre of the experience: the vantage point is at some distance away. The present weariness is well realised in the verse movement but the past is dim and perfunctorily recalled, while the future 'for ever and ever' is left till the end of a long question. Here the balance is just preserved, but in all too many of Graves's poems, the experience is so externalised in the process of judging it that the poetry is stiffened almost into satire. The energy is diverted into clever construction, equilibrium between the meanings of the parts becoming more apparent and more important than the meaning of the whole. **'Children of Darkness'** is one example. The parts are skilfully played off against one another, the viewpoint is skilfully varied between the children and the parents conceiving them, the scene varied between the world and the womb, and opposites are skilfully compounded into paradoxes. But actuality is no longer in focus.

It is impossible not to admire the architectonic accomplishment of such poems; it is impossible not to regret that, with metaphysical poems that virtually abandon the particular altogether, they account for such a large proportion of his verse. He might have come within reach of greatness if he had been able to concentrate on poetry as central to experience as his best poems are. They share the same balance, depth and intensity, and each explores a situation representing one part of a single area of emotional experience. But he allowed himself to be distracted from exploring it more thoroughly. His minor poems are often witty and nearly always accomplished and enjoyable, but (to echo what Eliot has said of W. B. Yeats's early poems) they are as satisfactory in isolation or in anthologies as they are in the context of his other poems. So perhaps the best service we can do Graves is to distinguish between these and the major poems which can be seen together as a single corpus. My list will provoke disagreement by leaving out a number of poems, such as **'To Juan at the Winter Solstice'** and **'The Challenge,'** which are very good in themselves and not unconnected with the corpus. But the corpus has no clear boundaries. The list is only meant to indicate the poems that belong to it most clearly, not to select 23 poems that are categorically better than any of his others: **'The Presence,' 'Pure Death,' 'The Pier-Glass,' 'The Clipped Stater,' 'The Felloe'd Year,' 'Ulysses,' 'Never Such Love,' 'Interruption,' 'Recalling War,' 'Return,' 'End of Play,' 'Sick Love,' 'The Fallen Tower of Siloam,' 'A Love Story,' 'The Worms of History,' 'To Sleep,' 'Through Nightmare,' 'To Lucia at Birth,' 'Theseus and Ariadne,' 'Counting the Beats,' 'Darien,' 'The Survivor,' 'Prometheus.'** Even if there were no border-line

poems, these 23 would be enough to demonstrate his importance as a poet. And, pointing to them, it is not hard to defend him from the usual limiting criticisms of him: that he is essentially a satirist, that his concern for craftsmanship is excessive, and that he writes 'pure poetry'.

The pains he takes over texture are enormous, as is obvious from his amendments to poems that have already appeared in print, amendments made not so much to modify the meaning, as for the sake of euphony. His note *Secondary Elaboration* reprinted in *The Common Asphodel* shows how four lines of his went through six drafts before he was satisfied with their sound. But that note also shows how changes made for euphony often tend to make the meaning more subtle. Graves once quoted with enthusiastic approval the old Chinese painter who said 'the art of portrait painting consists in putting the high-lights of the eyes at exactly the right spot'. This may well be true—if the assumption is justified that everything else is right. And in poetry, no degree of concern for the nuances can be excessive if the whole work is proportionately good. Dylan Thomas's poetry would not be what it is but for the painstaking calculations behind the appearance of haste. Like Thomas's, Graves's best poems deserve and need all the care they get. But the rest do not. It is infuriating to find him giving time to the revision of pieces as inconsequent as **'Traveller's Curse after Misdirection',** which might just as well have been revived unrevised if at all, when it would have been so much more worth while to revive **'The Clipped Stater'** or **'The Felloe'd Year,'** revised or unrevised. But the inordinate self-consciousness he shows and the choices he makes in his revisions, his suppressions and his uneasy forewords seem to indicate that he lacks a sense of proportion, a failing which may have something to do with the disparity between his poems. It is a considerable failing which may be due partly to his isolation from contemporary literary theory and practice. His own theories have, not surprisingly, been inconsistent and eccentric. He announced in the preface to his 1945 volume of poems that 'to write poems for other than poets is wasteful', contradicting everything he had said against the obscurity that violates 'the plain reader's rights'. And he has never been very certain of what poetry ought to communicate. In 1949 he declared that the only remaining function of poetry was to remind men that they have got out of harmony with the family of living creatures amongst which they were born. The vagaries of his critical opinions help to explain why he seems to have known what it is most worth while for the poet to do, only when he was actually doing it, in his best poems.

This accounts for the poems which are 'pure' in Stephen Spender's sense, the patterns of statement like **'In Broken Images'** and the whimsies like **'Lollocks.'** But Spender meant all Graves's poetry was 'pure'.—'Nothing happens, nothing is said, in Mr. Graves's poems except the poetry.' They represent 'the extraction of poetry from life' in contrast to *Little Gidding* which represents 'the judgement of life by poetry'. The comment is apparently meant as a compliment, certainly not as an attack, but none of his poems would be very considerable if it were true of all of them. The strength of the ones that are most worth while lies in the way they convey the sense that something is happening at the same time as saying something about it, combine actualisation with judgment.

Others have made the 'pure poetry' charge on the ground that there is no 'message' in Graves's poetry. Certainly there is no moral or social or political message. Graves has held as aloof from political movements as he has from groups of poets with a common cause, political or literary. This is what he has to say of them,—

> Goody-goody humanitarian causes draw them easily into membership by making them wince at the notion of all the injustices prevalent in the world of physical consciousness. Let it be declared as clearly as possible that the goodness of poetry is not moral goodness, the goodness of temporal action, but the goodness of thought, the loving exercise of the will in the pursuit of truth.

But the insistence on truth rather than beauty is what distinguishes this from a declaration of belief in 'art for art's sake'. His own 'pure' poems are trivial because there is no exercise of the will in the pursuit of truth. They assume the effort isn't worth making. The satirical poems are trivial because they assume that the pursuit is over. Omniscience has been won, untruth has been run down, and there is nothing to do but belabour the quarry with a show of bitterness or, if it is dead already, look abstractedly away from it. But the poems which chase truth out from the centre of an experience constitute an important achievement. (pp. 32-43)

> *Ronald Hayman, "Robert Graves," in* Essays in Criticism, *Vol. V, No. 1, January, 1955, pp. 32-43.*

Northrop Frye   (essay date 1956)

[*Frye was a Canadian critic who exerted a tremendous influence in the field of twentieth-century literary scholarship. In his seminal study,* Anatomy of Criticism *(1957), he contended that literary criticism should be an autonomous discipline similar to the sciences. Frye maintained that the structure and components of literature—such as genre, myth, and archetypal symbol—are constant and observable like the laws of nature, and thus subject to regulated, objective study. In the following review of* Collected Poems: 1955 *which first appeared in* The Hudson Review *in 1956, Frye discusses the mythological foundations of Graves's poetry.*]

The trouble with being a literary critic is that one gets filing cards in the memory, and one is continually having to fish them out and wonder if the clichés typed on them are really so very bright. I imagine a good many people roughly familiar with modern poetry have some sort of card in their memories reading in effect: "Graves, Robert. Does tight, epigrammatic lyrics in the Hardy-Houseman tradition; closer in technique to Blunden and de la Mare than to Eliot, Pound, or Yeats; a minor poet, but one of the best of the post-Georgians." There is some factual basis for such a note, but in terms of "covering" its subject, it would hardly make an honest woman of Lady Godiva. Whatever one thinks of Mr. Graves as a poet, novelist, critic, transla-

tor, mythographer, editor, anthologist, collaborator, surveyor of modernist poetry, or restorer of the Nazarene gospel, there can be no reasonable doubt that Mr. Graves is big, and bigness is certainly one important attribute of greatness. He is not a minor poet; he is not a minor anything.

Of all evidences of bigness, one of the most impressive is a sense of the expendable. The present volume [*Collected Poems: 1955*] is as much selected as collected poems: Mr. Graves has written many fine poems that are not here, which indicates, not only that he is highly self-critical, but that he believes that the poet always knows what his essential poems are. I have some reservations about this latter view, but, on the other hand, every poet has the right to his own canon, and it is as an author's canon that the present collection should be read.

Lyrical poetry normally begins in an associative process in which sound is as important as sense, a process much of which is submerged below consciousness. Such a process may go in either of two directions. It may become oracular, ambiguous in sense and echoic in sound, in which case it is addressed in part to an uncritical faculty, concerned with casting a spell and demanding emotional surrender. Or it may become witty, addressing itself to the critical intelligence and the detached consciousness. The ingredients of paronomasia and assonance are common to both, and it depends on the context whether, for instance, Poe's line "The viol, the violet and the vine" or Pope's "Great Cibber's brazen, brainless brothers stand" is oracular or witty.

Mr. Graves is an epigrammatic writer who remains in full intellectual control of his work. The meaning of his poem never gets away from him, never dissolves in a drowsy charm of sound. He is a poet to whom theme means a good deal: every poem is aimed directly at a definite human or mythical situation and usually hits it squarely in its central paradox. The technique corresponds. In the earlier pages, one watches him practicing forms with a sharp, rhythmical bite: Mother Goose rhythms, ballads, and eight-six quatrains, and, in the fine **"In Procession,"** Skeltonics reminding us how much Mr. Graves has done to rehabilitate Skelton. The deep incision produced by exact meter and clear thought makes some unforgettably sharp outlines:

> Courtesies of good-morning and good-evening
> From rustic lips fail as the town encroaches:
> Soon nothing passes but the cold quick stare
> Of eyes that see ghosts, yet too many for fear.

Later in the book we get more unrhymed poems, where the metrical and mental discipline have to stand alone, and finally, in the poems that come from or are contemporary with *The White Goddess*, incantation itself. But as the poet has approached incantation from the opposite end, his enchanters speak in a curiously reasonable and expository voice. Thus the Sirens urge Cronos:

> Compared with this, what are the plains
> Of Elis, where you ruled as king?
> A wilderness indeed.

The poetic personality revealed in the book is one of sturdy independence, pragmatic common sense, and a consistently quizzical attitude toward systematized forms of experience, especially the religious. From this point of view, Mr. Graves's collected poems could hardly have come at a better time. We have had a good deal of ecclesiasticized poetry, full of the dilemma of modern man, Kierkegaardian *Angst,* and the facile resonance of the penitential mood. Mr. Graves is strongly in revolt against all this, and he is old enough to have the authority of a contemporary classic, carrying on a tradition that goes back to the nineteenth century through Henley and Housman; a tradition that has more in common with Clough than with Arnold. He writes not humbly but defiantly of **"Self-Praise,"** and says:

> Confess, creatures, how sulkily ourselves
>   We hiss with doom, fuel of a sodden age—
> Not rapt up roaring to the chimney stack
>   On incandescent clouds of spirit or rage.

He is occasionally betrayed into cliché on this point, as in **"Ogres and Pygmies,"** but the sense of candor and freshness remains the primary one.

Mr. Graves is becoming an influence on contemporary British poetry in such a way as to suggest that we may be ready to repeat, on a very small scale of decades rather than millennia, Yeats's pattern of progress from Christian humility to the tragic pride of Oedipus the riddle-guesser. Certainly no one can doubt that Mr. Graves is by far the greatest riddle-guesser of our time: all the Gordian knots of antiquity, from the song of the sirens to the number of Antichrist, fall to pieces at the swing of his sword. Readers who are still bemused by the oracular, still accustomed to think of poetry as Lenten reading and of the poet as a psychopomp, may put their hands confidingly into Mr. Graves's with the hope of being led, like Prufrock, to some overwhelming question, perhaps even an answer. And as they proceed, whether through this book or through the formidable series of mythological works, a central myth begins to take shape. This, of course, is the myth of the White Goddess, the mother-harlot, virgin-slut, "Sister of the mirage and echo," whose elusive and treacherous beauty has inspired poets from prehistoric times to the last whimpers of courtly love in Baudelaire. "It's a poet's privilege and fate" to fall in hopeless love with her: condemned by his genius to go on trying to screw the inscrutable, he must stumble groaningly around the four seasons of her adoration, from the rapture of spring to the reviling of winter:

> But we are gifted, even in November
> Rawest of seasons, with so huge a sense
> Of her nakedly worn magnificence
> We forget cruelty and past betrayal,
> Heedless of where the next bright bolt may fall.

That's it, then: "There is one story and one story only." The key to all myths, the answer to all riddles, the source of all great poems, is the story of Attis and Cybele, where a feminine principle remains enthroned and a masculine one follows the cycle of nature, a Lord of the May who is soon "dethroned" and turned into a doomed victim, like Actaeon, while the poet urges:

> Run, though you hope for nothing: to stay your
>   foot

> Would be ingratitude, a sour denial
> That the life she bestowed was sweet.

The Attis-Cybele story is very important in mythology; it underlies a vast number of poems; its ramifications are nearly as widespread as those of poetry itself. All this no one would wish to deny. One feels, nevertheless, that there is something dismally corny about isolating a myth in this way and in this form; something of rotten-ripe late romanticism; something that suggests the masochism of Swinburne or some of the worst effects of Maud Gonne or Yeats, rather than anything typical of Mr. Graves. So we go back and run through his book again.

We notice that the central theme of a relatively early poem, **"Warning to Children,"** is that of the boxes of Silenus, the image with which Rabelais begins. In the next poem, a most important poem called **"Alice,"** we read:

> Nor did Victoria's golden rule extend
> Beyond the glass: it came to the dead end
> Where empty hearses turn about; thereafter
> Begins that lubberland of dream and laughter,
> The red-and-white-flower-spangled hedge, the
>   grass
> Where Apuleius pastured his Gold Ass,
> Where young Gargantua made whole
>   holiday . . .

We begin to wonder if perhaps Mr. Graves does not after all belong, not to the solemnly systematic mythographers, not to the tradition of Apollodorus and Natalis Comes and George Eliot's Casaubon, but to the tradition of the writers who have turned mythical erudition into satire, to Rabelais and Apuleius, or to the exuberantly hyperbolic Celtic mythical poets. The combination of erudite satire and lyrical gifts is not uncommon: we find it in Petronius, in Heine, in Joyce, and (counting his lethal scholarly essays as erudite satire) in Houseman. Perhaps Mr. Graves's oracle, too, is the oracle of the Holy Bottle: certainly the myths in his poetry, like the ghosts, seem to be not part of the objective system but a kaleidoscopic chaos of human fragments. As he says:

> Now I know the mermaid kin
>   I find them bound by natural laws:
> They have neither tail nor fin,
>   But are deadlier for that cause.

He does not lead us toward an objective or systematic mythology: he leads us toward the mythical use of poetic language, where we invent our own myths and apply them to an indefinite number of human themes. He has several doppelganger poems, in which he develops the theme of the looking-glass world as this world looked at mythically; as, in short, the world constructed by love and imagination. This is the theme of **"The Climate of Thought,"** of **"The Terraced Valley,"** and of several other poems.

Perhaps, then, his attraction to the white goddess myth is simply that it is an ironic myth, ambiguous in its moral values, and providing in its human incarnations what is essentially a heap of broken images. In contrast, the masculine protest myths of father-gods, introduced to our culture by the prophet Ezekiel, according to *The White Goddess,* stand for order, system, and the limiting of poetic themes by artificial standards of truth and morality. In such poems as the early **"Reproach,"** where Christ appears as an accusing father, in **"The Eremites,"** in **"The Bards,"** and elsewhere, we see the perversion of life that results from enthroning a male god in the sky in place of a mother. Perhaps we may understand from these poems how we are to read such a book as *Wife to Mr. Milton:* less as biography or literary criticism than as a blow struck in defense of the white goddess, and one in the eye for the prophet Ezekiel. The ambivalence of Mr. Graves's attitude to myth reminds one of Samuel Butler, whom he curiously resembles in many ways. Butler was so subtle and poker-faced an ironist that some of his parodies, such as the Book of the Machines in *Erewhon,* take in the casual reader, who is apt to assume that it's a straight Franken-stein fantasy. Others, such as *The Fair Haven,* took in nearly the whole reading public in their day. And there are still others so *very* subtle that they seem to have taken in Samuel Butler himself. His account of the Resurrection, for instance, reads like a deadly parody of Victorian pseudorationalism going to work on the gospel narratives, but Butler appears to have taken it seriously, as he did his notions about the *Odyssey* (some of them shared by Mr. Graves) and about Shakespeare's sonnets. Similarly, *King Jesus* and *The Nazarene Gospel Restored* impress one primarily as mythical satire: that is, as constructs so obviously hypothetical that they suggest an indefinite number of other possible constructs, each as ingenious and plausible as the author's—or as the orthodox version. But Mr. Graves appears to take them "seriously," as in some way definitive or exclusive. But fortunately we can dodge that

---

Graves on the role of reason in writing poetry:

Though I rely on intuition for the writing of poems and for the general management of my life, intuition must obviously be checked by reason whenever possible. Poets are (or ought to be) reasonable people; poems, though born of intuition, are (or ought to be) reasonable entities, and make perfect sense in their unique way. I should not, however, describe either poems or poets as 'rational'. 'Reasonable' has warm human connotations; 'rational' has coldly inhuman ones. Examine the abstract nouns that both adjectives yield. The stock epithet for 'reasonableness', first used by Matthew Arnold, is 'sweet'. The usual epithets for 'rationality' are not at all affectionate; and those for 'rationalization' are often positively crude.

Dear, useful Reason! The technique of isolating hard facts from a sea of guess, or hearsay, or legend; and of building them, when checked and counter-checked, into an orderly system of cause and effect! But too much power and glory can be claimed for this technique. Though helpful in a number of routine tasks, Reason has its limitations. It fails, for example, to prompt the writing of original poems, or the painting of original pictures, or the composing of original music; and shows no spark of humour or religious feeling.

Robert Graves, in his "The Case for Xanthippe," *in* The Oxford Book of Essays, *edited by John Gross, Oxford University Press, 1991.*

issue in reading the poetry, and find the central path to his mind through something like this:

> He is quick, thinking in clear images;
> I am slow, thinking in broken images.
>
> He becomes dull, trusting to his clear images;
> I become sharp, mistrusting my broken images . . .
>
> He in a new confusion of his understanding;
> I in a new understanding of my confusion.

(pp. 230-36)

> *Northrop Frye, "Graves, Gods, and Scholars," in his* Northrop Frye on Culture and Literature: A Collection of Review Essays, *edited by Robert D. Denham, The University of Chicago Press, 1978, pp. 230-36.*

Randall Jarrell   (essay date 1956)

[*A distinguished American poet and critic, Jarrell is considered one of the prominent figures among the "Middle Generation" of American poets. Including such noted writers as Robert Lowell and John Berryman, the Middle Generation poets borrowed from such Modernists as T. S. Eliot and W. H. Auden while adhering to no set artistic credo. Although Jarrell is considered a poet of great technical skill, many critics perceive his greatest contribution to twentieth-century literature to be in the field of criticism. In the following essay, which originally appeared in* The Yale Review *in 1956, he analyzes Graves's* Collected Poems: 1955, *paying particular attention to the mythical-archaic poems associated with* The White Goddess. *Jarrell also discusses certain autobiographical elements of Graves's* Goodbye to All That *and* The White Goddess, *examining how the experiences recorded in these works contributed to the poet's artistic and intellectual development.*]

At the beginning of Robert Graves's **Collected Poems** [1955] there is a list of thirty-three books and three translations. The list makes it seem foolish to talk only of the poems, and if you think of *Goodbye to All That* and *The White Goddess,* it seems foolish to talk only of the writing: there is a great deal of Graves's life in what he has written, and a great deal of his writing seems plausible—explicable, even—only in terms of his life. I want to write, in the first half of this essay, about what his poetry seems to me; and later, about how his life (all I know of it comes from him) has made his poetry and his understanding of the world into the inimitable, eccentric marvels that they are.

Looking along his list, I see that I have read two of the translations and twenty-nine and a half of the books—three haven't got to me yet, and I quit in the middle of *Homer's Daughter*—but I have read three or four of the books Graves doesn't list. And I have read *I, Claudius* (a good book singular enough to be immortal) and its slightly inferior continuation three or four times; *King Jesus,* a wonderfully imagined, adequately written novel, three times; *The White Goddess,* that erudite, magical (or, as Eliot calls it, "prodigious, monstrous, stupefying, indescribable") masterwork of fantastic exposition, twice; the poems scores or hundreds of times. In two months I have had time to read *The Greek Myths* only once, but it is, both in matter and in manner, an odd rare classic that people will be rereading for many years. And they will be reading, I think, the book with which, in 1929, I began: the thirty-three-year-old Robert Graves's autobiography, *Goodbye to All That*. If you are interested in Graves—and how can anyone help being interested in so good and so queer a writer?—there is no better place to begin. No better, except for the **Collected Poems:** that, with Graves, is where one begins and ends.

For Graves is, first and last, a poet: in between he is a Graves. "There is a coldness in the Graveses which is anti-sentimental to the point of insolence," he writes. The Graveses have good minds "for examinations . . . and solving puzzles"; are loquacious, eccentric individualists "inclined to petulance"; are subject to "most disconcerting spells of complete amnesia . . . and rely on their intuition and bluff to get them through"; and, no matter how disreputable their clothes and friends, are always taken for gentlemen. This is a fine partial summary of one side of Robert von Ranke Graves: of that professional, matter-of-fact-to-the-point-of-insolence, complacent, prosaic competence of style and imagination that weighs down most of his fiction, gives a terse, crusty, Defoe-esque plausibility to even his most imaginative nonfiction, and is present in most of his poetry only as a shell or skeleton, a hard lifeless something supporting or enclosing the poem's different life. Graves has spoken of the "conflict of rival sub-personalities," of warring halves or thirds or quarters, as what makes a man a poet. He differentiates the two sides of his own nature so sharply that he speaks of the first poem "I" wrote and the first poem "I wrote as a Graves"; he calls his prose "potboiling"—much of it is—and puts into his autobiography a number of his mother's sayings primarily to show how much more, as a poet, he owes to the von Rankes than to the Graveses. (One of these sayings was, "There was a man once, a Frenchman, who died of grief because he could never become a mother." I find it delightful to think of the mother bending to the child who was to become the excavator or resurrector of the White Goddess, and repeating to him this Delphic sentence.)

The sincere and generous von Rankes, with their castles, venison, blind trout, and black honey; their women who "were noble and patient, and always kept their eyes on the ground when out walking"; their great historian of whom Graves says, "To him I owe my historical method"—a tribute that must have made Leopold von Ranke's very bones grow pale—the von Rankes are certainly, as Graves considers them, the more attractive side of himself. He speaks of his "once aquiline, now crooked nose" as being "a vertical line of demarcation between the left and right sides of my face, which are naturally unassorted—my eyes, eyebrows, and ears all being notably crooked and my cheek-bones, which are rather high, being on different levels." I do not propose to tell you which is the Graves, and which the von Ranke, eye, eyebrow, ear, and cheekbone, but I am prepared to do as much for almost any sentence in Robert Graves—to tell you whether it was written by the cold, puzzle-solving, stamp-collecting, logic-chopping

Regimental Explainer; or by the Babe, Lover, and Victim howling, in dreadful longing, for the Mother who bears, possesses, and destroys; or, as happens sometimes, by both. But I am being drawn, not much against my will, into the second part of this essay; let me get back to the poetry.

Graves's poems seem to divide naturally into six or seven types. These are: mythical-archaic poems, poems of the White Goddess; poems about extreme situations; expressive or magical landscapes; grotesques; observations—matter-of-fact, tightly organized, tersely penetrating observations of types of behavior, attitude, situation, of the processes and categories of existence; love poems; ballads or nursery rhymes.

These last are early poems, and disappear as soon as Graves can afford to leave "what I may call the folksong period of my life," the time when "country sentiment," childlike romance, were a refuge from "my shellshocked condition." The best of these poems is his grotesquely and ambiguously moving, faintly Ransomesque ballad of the Blatant Beast, **"Saint."** Some others are **"Frosty Night," "Apples and Water," "Richard Roe and John Doe," "Allie," "Henry and Mary," "Vain and Careless," "The Bedpost,"** and the beautiful **"Love without Hope"**:

> Love without hope, as when the young bird-catcher
> Swept off his tall hat to the Squire's own daughter,
> So let the imprisoned larks escape and fly
> Singing about her head, as she rode by.

The young birdcatcher might have stepped from "Under the Greenwood Tree" or "Winter Night in Woodland (Old Time)"—and in all Italy where is there a halo like his, made from such live and longing gold?

Graves has never forgotten the child's incommensurable joys; nor has he forgotten the child's and the man's incommensurable, irreducible agonies. He writes naturally and well—cannot keep himself from writing—about bad, and worse, and worst, the last extremities of existence:

> Walls, mounds, enclosing corrugations
> Of darkness, moonlight on dry grass.
> Walking this courtyard, sleepless, in fever;
> Planning to use—but by definition
> There's no way out, no way out—
> Rope-ladders, baulks of timber, pulleys,
> A rocket whizzing over the walls and moat—
> Machines easy to improvise.
>
>   No escape,
> No such thing; to dream of new dimensions,
> Cheating checkmate by painting the king's robe
> So that he slides like a queen;
> Or to cry, "Nightmare, nightmare!"
> Like a corpse in the cholera-pit
> Under a load of corpses;
> Or to run the head against these blind walls,
> Enter the dungeon, torment the eyes
> With apparitions chained two and two,
> And go frantic with fear—
> To die and wake up sweating in moonlight
> In the same courtyard, sleepless as before.

This poem, "The Castle," and such poems as "Haunted House," "The Pier-Glass," "Down," "Sick Love," "Mermaid, Dragon, and Fiend," "The Suicide in the Copse," "The Survivor," "The Devil at Berry Pomeroy," "The Death Room," and "The Jealous Man" are enough to make any reader decide that Graves is a man to whom terrible things have happened.

At the end of the First World War, Graves says, "I could not use a telephone, I was sick every time I travelled in a train, and if I saw more than two new people in a single day it prevented me from sleeping. . . . Shells used to come bursting on my bed at midnight even when Nancy was sharing it with me; strangers in daytime would assume the faces of friends who had been killed." Graves has removed from his *Collected Poems* any poem directly about the war; only the generalized, decade-removed "Recalling War" remains. When he had said *Goodbye to All That* he had meant it—meant it more than he had known, perhaps. The worst became for him, from then on, a civilian worst, and his thoughts about war dried and hardened into the routine, grotesque professionalism that is the best way of taking for granted, canceling out, the unbearable actualities of war. Who would have believed that the author who wrote about these, in *Goodbye to All That,* with plain truth, would in a few years be writing such a G. A. Henty book as *Count Belisarius?*

To Graves, often, the most extreme situation is truth, the mere seeing of reality; we can explain away or destroy the fabulous, traditional mermaids or dragons or devils of existence, but the real "mermaids will not be denied / The last bubbles of our shame, / The dragon flaunts an unpierced hide, / The true fiend governs in God's name." In "A Jealous Man" Graves writes with this truth about another war in which he has fought—writes about it in nightmarishly immediate, traditional, universal terms. The objectively summarizing, held-in, held-back lines seem, in Hopkins's phrase, to "wince and sing" under the hammering of this grotesque, obscene, intolerable anguish—an anguish that ends in untouched, indifferent air:

To be homeless is a pride
To the jealous man prowling
Hungry down the night lanes,

Who has no steel at his side,
No drink hot in his mouth,
But a mind dream-enlarged,

Who witnesses warfare,
Man with woman, hugely
Raging from hedge to hedge:

The raw knotted oak-club
Clenched in the raw fist,
The ivy-noose well flung,

The thronged din of battle,
Gaspings of the throat-snared,
Snores of the battered dying,

Tall corpses, braced together,
Fallen in clammy furrows,
Male and female,

Or, among haulms of nettle
Humped, in noisome heaps,

Male and female.

He glowers in the choked roadway
Between twin churchyards,
Like a turnip ghost.

(Here, the rain-worn headstone,
There, the Celtic cross
In rank white marble.)

This jealous man is smitten,
His fear-jerked forehead
Sweats a fine musk;

A score of bats bewitched
By the ruttish odor
Swoop singing at his head;

Nuns bricked up alive
Within the neighbouring wall
Wail in cat-like longing.

Crow, cocks, crow loud!
Reprieve the doomed devil,
Has he not died enough?

Now, out of careless sleep,
She wakes and greets him coldly,
The woman at home,

She, with a private wonder
At shoes bemired and bloody—
His war was not hers.

Often these poems of extreme situation, like those of observation, are grotesques—this neither by chance nor by choice, but by necessity. Much of life comes to Graves already sharpened into caricature: "another caricature scene" and "plenty of caricature scenes" are ordinary remarks in his autobiography. ("Another caricature scene to look back on," he writes of his wedding.) The best of his grotesques have a peculiar mesmeric power, shock when touched, since they are the charged caricatures of children, of dreams, of the unconscious:

All horses on the racecourse of Tralee
Have four more legs in gallop than in trot—
Two pairs fully extended, two pairs not;
And yet no thoroughbred with either three
Or five legs but is mercilessly shot.
I watched a filly gnaw her fifth leg free,
Warned by a speaking mare since turned silentiary.

Somewhere in Kafka there is a man who is haunted by two bouncing balls; living with this poem is like being haunted by a Gestalt diagram changing from figure to ground, ground to figure, there in the silent darkness, until we get up and turn on the light and look at it, and go back to sleep with it ringing—high, hollow, sinister, yet somehow lyric and living—in our dream-enlarged ears. One can say about this poem of Graves's, as about others: "If I weren't looking at it I wouldn't believe it." According to Stalky and Company, the impassioned Diderot burst forth, "O Richardson, thou singular genius!" When one reads "It Was All Very Tidy," "The Worms of History," "Ogres and Pygmies," "Lollocks," "The Laureate," "The Death Room," one feels just like Diderot; nor is one willing to dismiss grotesques like "Song: Lift-Boy," "The Suicide in the Copse," "Grotesques" II, "The Villagers and Death,"

"Welsh Incident," "Wm. Brazier," "General Blood-stock's Lament for England," "Vision in the Repair Shop," and "Front Door Soliloquy" with a mere "Singular, singular!"

Sometimes these grotesques are inspired hostile observations, highly organized outbursts of dislike, revulsion, or rejection: where these observations (and much else) are concerned, Graves is the true heir of Ben Jonson, and can give to his monstrosities, occasionally, the peculiar lyric magnificence Jonson gives them in *The Alchemist*. It is easy for him to see God or Death as grotesque monsters; and the White Goddess, with all her calm, grave, archaic magnificence, is monstrous. But sometimes Graves writes grotesques of local color, traditional properties, comfortable-enough types, and these can be good-humored—are even, once, wistful:

> Even in hotel beds the hair tousles.
> But this is observation, not complaint—
> "Complaints should please be dropped in the
>   complaint-box"—
> "Which courteously we beg you to vacate
> In that clean state as you should wish to find it."
>
> And the day after Carnival, today,
> I found, in the square, a crimson cardboard
>   heart:
> "Anna Maria," it read. Otherwise, friends,
> No foreign news—unless that here they drink
> Red wine from china bowls; here anis-roots
> Are stewed like turnips; here funiculars
> Light up at dusk, two crooked constella-
>   tions. . . .
>
> "It is not yet the season," pleads the Porter,
> "That comes in April, when the rain most
>   rains."
> Trilingual Switzer fish in Switzer lakes
> Pining for rain and bread-crumbs of the season,
> In thin reed-beds you pine!
>
>   In bed drowsing,
> (While the hair slowly tousles) uncomplain-
>   ing. . . .
> Anna Maria's heart under my pillow
> Evokes no furious dream. Who is this Anna?
> A Switzer maiden among Switzer maidens,
> Child of the children of that fox who never
> Ate the sour grapes: her teeth not set on edge.

The reader can murmur: "Why—why, this is life." But Graves—as mercilessly good a critic of his own poetry as he is a mercilessly bad critic of everybody else's—has here had a most disconcerting spell of complete amnesia: "Hotel Bed" isn't included in his new *Collected Poems.* "My poetry-writing has always been a painful process of continual corrections and corrections on top of corrections and persistent dissatisfaction," he writes. He is the only one who can afford to be dissatisfied with the process or the poems it has produced: he is the best rewriter and corrector of his own poetry that I know. Lately I have gone over the new, and old, and very old versions of all the poems in *Collected Poems,* and I am still dazzled by the magical skill, the inspiration apparently just there for use when needed, with which Graves has saved a ruined poem or perfected a good one. Usually the changes are so

exactly right, so thoroughly called for, that you're puzzled at his ever having written the original; it grieves me that I have no space in which to quote them.

About sixty of Graves's collected poems are what one might call Observations—observations of types, functions, states; of characteristic strategies and attitudes, people's "life-styles"; of families, genetic development in general; of the self; of well-known stories or characters; of good reasons and real reasons; of dilemmas; of many of the processes and categories of existence. Ordinarily these observations are witty, detailed, penetrating, disabused, tightly organized, logical-sounding, matter-of-fact, terse: Graves sounds, often, as if he were Defoe attempting to get his Collected Works into the "Sayings of Spartans." Frequently an observation is put in terms of landscape or grotesque, organized as an approach to a limit or a *reductio ad absurdum;* sometimes a set of observations (for instance, **"To Bring the Dead to Life"** and **"To Evoke Posterity"**) reminds one of a set of non-Euclidean geometries, differing assumptions rigorously worked out. Such a poem seems an organized, individual little world, this and no other. Finishing one we may feel, as in Graves's dry masterpiece, that It Was All Very Tidy—tidier, certainly, than life and our necessities; we feel about it a gnawing lack, the lack of anything lacking, of a way out—between the inside of the poem and the great outside there is no communication, and we long for an explosion or an implosion, we are not sure which. But these local actions, limited engagements, punitive expeditions; these poems which do, with elegance and dispatch, all that they set out to do; these bagatelles—on occasion Beethoven bagatelles; these complete, small-scale successes, are poems in which Graves excels. Few poets have written more pretty-good poems: **"Midway," "The Devil's Advice to Story Tellers," "The Fallen Tower of Siloam," "The Reader over My Shoulder," "To Bring the Dead to Life," "To Walk on Hills," "The Persian Version," "The Furious Voyage," "The Climate of Thought,"** and **"The Shot"** are some examples of notably successful "observations," but there are many more; and the grotesques and landscapes and love poems are full of such small successes.

Landscapes have always been of particular importance to Graves; shell-shocked, he spent an entire leave walking through some favorite country, and went back to France half cured. When he writes about landscapes he puts into them or gets out of them meanings, attitudes, and emotions that Poets rarely get from Poetic landscapes; like Wordsworth, he is not interested in landscape as landscape. Some of the best of these poems describe magical landscapes—inside-out, box-inside-a-box, infinite regress—that seem to express, or correspond to, emotional or physiological states in Graves that I am not sure of, and that Graves may not be sure of: **"Warning to Children," "Interruption,"** and, especially, **"The Terraced Valley"** are better than I can explain, and I listen to

> . . . Neat outside-inside, neat below-above,
> Hermaphrodizing love.
> Neat this-way-that-way and without mistake:
> On the right hand could slide the left glove.
> Neat over-under: the young snake   .

Through an unyielding shell his path could
  break.
Singing of kettles, like a singing brook,
Made out-of-doors a fireside nook.

 . . . I knew you near me in that strange region,
So searched for you, in hope to see you stand
On some near olive-terrace, in the heat,
The left-hand glove drawn on your right hand,
The empty snake's egg perfect at your feet—

with, at the climax, a kind of rapt uneasy satisfaction.

But Graves's richest, most moving, and most consistently
beautiful poems—poems that almost deserve the literal
magical—are his mythical-archaic pieces, all those the
reader thinks of as "White Goddess poems": **"To Juan at
the Winter Solstice," "Theseus and Ariadne," "Lament
for Pasiphaë," "The Sirens' Welcome to Cronos," "A
Love Story," "The Return of the Goddess," "Darien,"**
and eight or ten others. The best of these are different from
anything else in English; their whole meaning and texture
and motion are different from anything we could have expected from Graves or from anybody else. **"The Sirens'
Welcome to Cronos,"** for instance, has a color or taste that
is new because it has been lost for thousands of years. In
the second part of this essay I mean to discuss exactly
what these poems are, and how they got to be that, along
with the more ordinary love poems which form so large
a part of Graves's work; but here I should like simply to
quote the poem that represents them best, **"To Juan at the
Winter Solstice"**:

There is one story and one story only
That will prove worth your telling,
Whether as learned bard or gifted child;
To it all lines or lesser gauds belong
That startle with their shining
Such common stories as they stray into.

Is it of trees you tell, their months and virtues,
Or strange beasts that beset you,
Of birds that croak at you the Triple will?
Or of the Zodiac and how slow it turns
Below the Boreal Crown,
Prison of all true kings that ever reigned?

Water to water, ark again to ark,
From woman back to woman:
So each new victim treads unfalteringly
The never altered circuit of his fate,
Bringing twelve peers as witness
Both to his starry rise and starry fall.

Or is it of the Virgin's silver beauty,
All fish below the thighs?
She in her left hand bears a leafy quince;
When, with her right she crooks a finger smiling,
How may the King hold back?
Royally then he barters life for love.

Or of the undying snake from chaos hatched,
Whose coils contain the ocean,
Into whose chops with naked sword he springs,
Then in black water, tangled by the reeds,
Battles three days and nights,
To be spewed up beside her scalloped shore?

Much snow is falling, winds roar hollowly,
The owl hoots from the elder,

Fear in your heart cries to the loving-cup:
Sorrow to sorrow as the sparks fly upward.
The log groans and confesses
There is one story and one story only.

Dwell on her graciousness, dwell on her smiling,
Do not forget what flowers
The great boar trampled down in ivy time.
Her brow was creamy as the crested wave,
Her sea-blue eyes were wild
But nothing promised that is not performed.

Graves's best poems, I think, are **"To Juan at the Winter
Solstice," "A Jealous Man," "Theseus and Ariadne,"
"Lament for Pasiphaë," "The Sirens' Welcome to
Cronos," "Ogres and Pygmies," "The Worms of Histo-
ry," "It Was All Very Tidy," "Saint," "The Terraced Valley," "The Devil at Berry Pomeroy," "Lollocks"**; poems
like **"The Laureate," "The Castle," "Hotel Bed," "A
Love Story,"** and **"The Death Room"** might end this list
and begin a list of what seem to me Graves's next-best
poems: **"Interruption," "Warning to Children," "The
Young Cordwainer," "Down," "Reproach," "Recalling
War," "Song: Lift-Boy"** (with the old coda), **"The
Bards,"** and **"The Survivor."** Quite as good as some of
these are the best of Graves's slighter poems, delicate or
witty or beautiful pieces without much weight or extent
of subject and movement: **"Love without Hope," "She
Tells Her Love While Half Asleep," "Advocates," "Dawn
Bombardment," "Sick Love," "Grotesques"** II and VI,
**"The Suicide in the Copse," "Like Snow," "An English
Wood," "The Shot," "On Dwelling," "The Portrait"**; and
I have already listed what seem to me some of his best gro-
tesques and observations.

Graves is a poet of varied and consistent excellence. He
has written scores, almost hundreds, of poems that are
completely realized, different either from one another or
from the poems of any other poet. His poems have to an
extraordinary degree the feeling of one man's world, one
man's life: what he loves and loathes; what he thinks and
feels and doesn't know that he feels; the rhythms of his
voice, his walk, his gestures. To meet Robert Graves is unnecessary: all his life has transformed itself into his poetry.
The limitations of his poetic world come more from limitations of temperament than from limitations of gift or
ability—anything Graves is really interested in he can do.
He writes, always, with economical strength, with efficient distinction. Both the wording and the rhythm of his
verse are full of personal force and impersonal skill: the
poems have been made by a craftsman, but a craftsman
whose heart was in his fingers. His wit; terseness; matter-
of-factness; overmastering organizational and logical skill;
penetrating observation; radical two-sidedness; gifts of
skewness, wryness, cater-corneredness, sweet-sourness, of
"English eccentricity," of grotesque humor, of brotherly
acceptance of the perverse random contingency of the
world; feeling for landscapes and for Things; gifts of ecstasy, misery, and confident command; idiosyncratic ency-
clopedic knowledge of our world and the worlds that came
before it; the fact that love—everyday, specific, good-and-
bad, miraculous-and-disastrous love, not the Love most
writers write about—is the element he is a native of; his—
to put it in almost childish terms—invariable *interesting-*

ness, are a few of the many qualities that make Graves extraordinary.

Later on I should like to discuss Graves's limitations, which are as interesting as any of his qualities—which are, so to speak, the grotesque shadow of his qualities. His poems seem to me in no sense the work of a great poet; when you compare Graves with Wordsworth or Rilke, you are comparing a rearrangement of the room with a subsidence of continents. But Graves's poems are a marvel and a delight, the work of a fine poet who has managed, by the strangest of processes, to make himself into an extraordinary one. In the **"Fiend, Dragon, Mermaid"** that is not included in this last ***Collected Poems,*** Graves tells how he escaped from the monstrous fiend, dragon, mermaid, each dying—and how, quit of them, "I turned my gaze to the encounter of / The later genius, who of my pride and fear / And love / No monster made but me." This is true: he is, now, somewhat of a monster, a marvelous and troubling one, and it is by means of this "later genius," the White Goddess, the monstrous Muse, that he has made himself into what he is. In the second half of this essay I shall try to show how it was done.

"There is one story and one story only," Graves writes; all poems have the same theme. "The theme," he says in *The White Goddess,*

> is the antique story . . . of the birth, life, death, and resurrection of the God of the Waxing Year; the central chapters concern the God's long battle with the God of the Waning Year for love of the capricious and all-powerful Threefold Goddess, their mother, bride, and layer-out. The poet identifies himself with the God of the Waxing Year and his muse with the Goddess; the rival is his blood-brother, his other self, his weird. All true poetry—true by Housman's practical test—celebrates some incident or scene in this very ancient story, and the main characters are so much a part of our racial inheritance that they not only assert themselves in poetry but recur on occasions of emotional stress in the form of dreams, paranoiac visions and delusions. . . . The Goddess is a lovely, slender woman with a hooked nose, deathly pale face, lips red as rowanberries, startlingly blue eyes and long fair hair; she will suddenly transform herself into sow, mare, bitch, vixen, she-ass, weasel, serpent, owl, she-wolf, tigress, mermaid or loathsome hag. . . . I cannot think of any true poet from Homer on who has not independently recorded his experience of her. . . . The reason why the hairs stand on end, the skin crawls and a shiver runs down the spine when one writes or reads a true poem is that a true poem is necessarily an Invocation of the White Goddess, or Muse, the Mother of All Living, the ancient power of fright and lust—the female spider or the queen-bee whose embrace is death.

> . . . The true poet must always be original, but in a simpler sense: he must address only the Muse—not the King or Chief Bard or the people in general—and tell her the truth about himself and her in his own passionate and peculiar words. . . . Not that the Muse is ever complete-

ly satisfied. Laura Riding has summed her up in three memorable lines:

> Forgive me, giver, if I destroy the gift:
> It is so nearly what would please me
> I cannot but perfect it.

The Muse or Triple Goddess

> was a personification of primitive woman— woman the creatress and destructress. As the New Moon or Spring she was girl; as the Full Moon or Summer she was woman; as the Old Moon or Winter she was hag. . . . The revolutionary institution of fatherhood, imported into Europe from the East, brought with it the institution of individual marriage. . . . Once this revolution had occurred, the social status of women altered: man took over many of the sacred practices from which his sex had debarred him, and finally declared himself head of the household.

Graves describes with disgust the progressive degradation of this patriarchal world, as it moved farther and farther from its matriarchal beginnings, and as the "female sense of orderliness" was replaced by "the restless and arbitrary male will." This "female sense of orderliness" seems a rationalization or secondary elaboration: usually Graves speaks, without any disguise, of "the cruel, capricious, incontinent White Goddess," and values above all things the prospect of being destroyed by her. *Though she slay me, yet will I trust in her* is his motto, almost; if one substitutes *if* and *then* for *though* and *yet,* the sentence exactly fits his attitude.

One sees both from *The White Goddess* and the lectures recently published in England that almost no poets seem "true poets" to Graves; most of the poets of the past belonged to the Apollonian or "Classical homosexual" tradition, and most modern poets have ceased "to make poetic, prosaic, or even pathological sense." Woman "is not a poet: she is either a Muse or she is nothing." (One of his poems to Laura Riding is dedicated "To the Sovereign Muse": of all the poets who erstwhile bore the name, he says, "none bore it clear, not one"; she is the first to do so.) A woman should "either be a silent Muse" or "she should be the Muse in a complete sense; she should be in turn Arianrhod, Blodenwedd and the Old Sow of Maenawr Penarrd who eats her farrow." For the poet

> there is no other woman but Cerridwen and he desires one thing above all else in the world: her love. As Blodenwedd, she will gladly give him her love, but at only one price: his life. . . . Poetry began in the matriarchal age. . . . No poet can hope to understand the nature of poetry unless he has had a vision of the Naked King crucified to the lopped oak, and watched the dancers, red-eyed from the acrid smoke of the sacrificial fires, stamping out the measure of the dance, their bodies bent uncouthly forward; with a monotonous chant of "Kill! kill! kill!" and "Blood! blood! blood!"

But the reader before now will have interrupted this summary of Graves's world picture with an impatient "Why repeat all this to me? It's an ordinary wish fantasy reinforced with extraordinary erudition—a kind of family romance projected upon the universe. Having the loved one the mother is the usual thing. Of course, some of the details of this Mother-Muse, female spider, are unusual: she always *has* to kill, so that she is called cruel, capricious, incontinent, and yet is worshipped for being so; she—but case histories always are unusual. Let's admit that it's an unusual, an extraordinary fantasy; still, why quote it to me?"

I quote it for two reasons:

(1) It is the fantastic theory that has accompanied a marvelous practice: some of the best poems of our time have been written as a result of this (I think it fair to say) objectively grotesque account of reality. If the Principle of Indeterminacy had been discovered as a result of Schrödinger or Heisenberg's theory that the universe is a capricious, intuitive Great Mother whose behavior must always rightfully disappoint the predictions of her prying son—*a fingering slave, / One that would peep and botanize / Upon his mother's grave*—the theory would have an extrinsic interest that it now lacks. Because of the poems it enabled Yeats to write, many of us read *A Vision.* That Graves's astonishing theories should be so necessary to him, so right and proper for him, that by means of them he could write **"To Juan at the Winter Solstice," "Theseus and Ariadne," "The Sirens' Welcome to Cronos,"** is a thing worthy of our admiration and observation.

(2) Graves's theories, so astonishing in themselves, are—when we compare them with Graves's life and with psychoanalytical observation of lives in general, of the Unconscious, of children, neurotics, savages, myths, fairy tales—not astonishing at all, but logical and predictable; are so *natural* that we say with a tender smile, "Of course!" We see, or fancy that we see, why Graves believes them and why he is helped by believing them. Few poets have made better "pathological sense." I wish to try to explain these theories in terms of Graves's life; I shall try as far as possible to use Graves's own words.

In *Goodbye to All That* Graves cannot speak with enough emphasis of the difference between the side of him that is Graves and the side that is von Ranke. He writes with rather patronizing exactness of the Graveses, who are made to seem dry English eccentrics, excellent at puzzle solving, but writes with real warmth of the "goodness of heart" of his mother and the von Rankes; he seems to associate her idealism and *Gemütlichkeit,* her *Children, as your mother I command you* . . . with all that is spontaneous and emotional in his own nature—he has a heartfelt sentence telling "how much more I owe, as a writer, to my mother than to my father." His father was a poet. Graves writes:

> I am glad in a way that my father was a poet. This at least saved me from any false reverence for poets. . . . Some of his songs I sing without prejudice; when washing up after meals or shelling peas or on similar occasions. He never once tried to teach me how to write, or showed any understanding of my serious work; he was always more ready to ask advice about his own work than to offer it for mine.

Graves also says that "we children saw practically nothing of him except during the holidays." It is not difficult to see why, in Graves's myth of the world, it is a shadowy left-handed "blood-brother" or "other self," and not the father in his own form, against whom the hero struggles for the possession of the mother.

Graves's mother was forty, his father forty-nine, when he was born; she "was so busy running the household and conscientiously carrying out her obligations as my father's wife that we did not see her continuously"; he writes about his nurse: "In a practical way she came to be more to us than our mother. I began to despise her at the age of twelve—she was then nurse to my younger brothers—when I found that my education was now in advance of hers, and that if I struggled with her I was able to trip her up and bruise her quite easily." Graves says that his religious training developed in him, as a child, "a great capacity for fear (I was perpetually tortured by the fear of hell), a superstitious conscience and a sexual embarrassment." Graves's reading was "carefully censored"; after two years of trench service he had still been to the theater only twice, to children's plays; his mother "allowed us no hint of its [humanity's] dirtiness and intrigue and lustfulness, believing that innocence was the surest protection against

Graves during his school days at Charterhouse.

them." Two of his earlier memories seem particularly important to him:

> And the headmaster had a little daughter with a little girl friend, and I was in a sweat of terror whenever I met them; because, having no brothers, they once tried to find out about male anatomy from me by exploring down my shirt-neck when we were digging up pig-nuts in the garden.

> Another frightening experience of this part of my life was when I once had to wait in the school cloakroom for my sisters. . . . I waited about a quarter of an hour in the corner of the cloakroom. I suppose I was about ten years old, and hundreds and hundreds of girls went to and fro, and they all looked at me and giggled and whispered things to each other. I knew they hated me, because I was a boy sitting in the cloakroom of a girls' school, and when my sisters arrived they looked ashamed of me and quite different from the sisters I knew at home. I realized that I had blundered into a secret world, and for months and even years afterwards my worst nightmares were of this girls' school, which was filled with coloured toy balloons. "Very Freudian," as one says now.

> My normal impulses were set back for years by these two experiences. When I was about seventeen we spent our Christmas holidays in Brussels. An Irish girl stopping at the same *pension* made love to me in a way that I see now was really very sweet. I was so frightened I could have killed her.

> In English preparatory and public schools romance is necessarily homosexual. The opposite sex is despised and hated, treated as something obscene. Many boys never recover from this perversion. I only recovered by a shock at the age of twenty-one. For every born homosexual there are at least ten permanent pseudo-homosexuals made by the public school system. And nine of these ten are as honorably chaste and sentimental as I was.

His strained affection for Dick, a boy at his school, ended disastrously only after two years of military service. Graves went directly from what seemed to him the organized masculine nightmare of the public schools into the organized masculine nightmare of the First World War. He was an excellent soldier. His sense of professional tradition, of regimental loyalty, was extreme ("we all agreed that regimental pride was the greatest force that kept a battalion going as an effective fighting unit, contrasting it particularly with patriotism and religion"), but it led him only into prolonged service at the front, murderous and routine violence, wounds so serious that he was reported dead, shell shock, neurosis, and an intense hatred for governments, civilians, the whole established order of the world. Jung says, in a sentence that might have been written to apply specifically to Graves: "It is no light matter to stand between a day-world of exploded ideals and discredited values, and a night-world of apparently senseless fantasy. The weirdness of this standpoint is in fact so great that there is nobody who does not reach out for security,

even though it be a reaching back to the mother who shielded his childhood from the terrors of night."

When, on sick leave, he met a young artist, Nancy Nicholson, Graves reached back.

> Of course I also accepted the whole patriarchal system of things," he writes. "It is difficult now to recall how completely I believed in the natural supremacy of male over female. I never heard it even questioned until I met Nancy, when I was about twenty-two, towards the end of the war. *The surprising sense of ease* that I got from her frank statement of equality between the sexes was among my chief reasons for liking her. . . . Nancy's crude summary: 'God is a man, so it must be all rot,' *took a load off my shoulders.* [My italics.]

Champagne was scarce at their wedding:

> Nancy said: "Well, I'm going to get something out of this wedding, at any rate," and grabbed a bottle. After three or four glasses she went off and changed into her land-girl's costume of breeches and smock. . . . The embarrassments of our wedding night were somewhat eased by an air-raid. . . . Nancy's mother was a far more important person to her than I was. . . . The most important thing to her was judicial equality of the sexes; she held that all the wrong in the world was caused by male domination and narrowness. She refused to see my experiences in the war as in any way comparable with the sufferings that millions of married women of the working-class went through. . . . Male stupidity and callousness became an obsession with her and she found it difficult not to include me in her universal condemnation of men.

In country cottages; living from hand to mouth; ashamed of himself "as a drag on Nancy"; a friend, rather than a father, to Nancy's children; helping with the housework, taking care of the babies; so hauntedly neurotic that he saw ghosts at noon, couldn't use a telephone, couldn't see more than two new faces without lying awake all that night; writing child-poems or "country sentiment" poems to escape from his everyday reality, or else haunted nightmarish poems to express that everyday reality—so Graves spent the next six or eight years. (The keenest sense of the pathetic strangeness of that household comes to me when I read Graves's "I realized too that I had a new loyalty, to Nancy and the baby, tending to overshadow regimental loyalty now that the war was over.") "I had bad nights," Graves writes.

> I thought that perhaps I owed it to Nancy to go to a psychiatrist to be cured; yet I was not sure. Somehow I thought that the power of writing poetry, which was more important than anything else I did, would disappear if I allowed myself to get cured; my ***Pier-Glass*** haunting would end and I would become a dull easy writer. It seemed to me less important to be well than to be a good poet. I also had a strong repugnance against allowing anyone to have the power over me that psychiatrists always seem to win over their patients.

Anyone, here, means *any man,* I think; in the end Graves decided that he "would read the modern psychological books and apply them to my case," and "cure myself."

Their marriage, regretted by both husband and wife, ended after the two read an American poem and invited its author to come and live with them. Its author was a violent feminist, an original poet, a more than original thinker, and a personality of seductive and overmastering force. Judging from what Graves has written about her (in many poems, in some novels, and in his ecstatic epilogue to *Goodbye to All That,* in which he tells how he and she "went together to the land where the dead parade the streets and there met with demons and returned with the demons still treading behind us," speaks of the "salvation" that, through her, he has neared, and calls her a being essentially different from all others, a mystic savior "living invisibly, against kind, as dead, beyond event"), I believe that it is simplest to think of her as, so to speak, the White Goddess incarnate, the Mother-Muse in contemporary flesh. She seems to have had a radical influence on Graves's life, poetry, and opinions until 1939; and it was only after Graves was no longer in a position to be dominated by her in specific practice that he worked out his general theory of the necessary dominance of the White Goddess, the Mother-Muse, over all men, all poets.

Graves's theoretical picture of what life necessarily must be is so clearly related to what his life actually has been that it is possible to make summaries or outlines of the two, to put these outlines side by side, and to see that they match in every detail: this is what I have tried to do. (If the reader feels that he understands no better than before how and why Graves's world picture came into existence, either I have made very bad summaries or else I have deluded myself with an imaginary resemblance.) One does not need much of a psychoanalytical or anthropological background to see that Graves's world picture is a projection upon the universe of his own unconscious, of the compulsively repeated situation in which, alone, it is able to find satisfaction; or to see that this world picture is one familiar, in structure and in much detail, in the fantasies of children and neurotics, in dreams, in fairy tales, and, of course, in the myths and symbols of savages and of earlier cultures. Many details of case histories, much of Freud's theoretical analysis, are so specifically illuminating about Graves's myth that I would have quoted or summarized them here, if it had been possible to do so without extending this essay into a third issue of the *Review.* That all affect, libido, mana should be concentrated in this one figure of the Mother-Muse; that love and sexuality should be inseparably intermingled with fear, violence, destruction in this "female spider"—that the loved one should be, necessarily, the Bad Mother who, necessarily, deserts and destroys the child; that the child should permit against her no conscious aggression of any kind, and intend his *cruel, capricious, incontinent,* his *bitch, vixen, hag,* to be neither condemnation nor invective, but only fascinated description of the loved and worshipped Mother and Goddess, She-Who-Must-Be-Obeyed—all this is very interesting and very unoriginal. One encounters a rigorous, profound, and quite unparalleled understanding of such cases as Graves's in the many volumes of Freud; but one can read

an excellent empirical, schematic description of them in Volume VII of Jung's *Collected Works,* in the second part of the essay entitled "The Relations between the Ego and the Unconscious." Anyone familiar with what Jung has written about the *persona* and *anima,* and what happens when a man projects this *anima* upon the world and identifies himself with it, will more than once give a laugh of astonished recognition as he goes through *The White Goddess.*

The double-natured Graves has continually written about this split in himself—thought of it, once, as the poet's necessary condition: "I regarded poetry as, first, a personal cathartic for the poet suffering from some inner conflict, and then as a cathartic for readers in a similar conflict." One side of Robert Graves was—and is—the Graves or Father-of-the-Regiment side: the dry, matter-of-fact, pot-boiling, puzzle-solving, stamp-collecting, "anti-sentimental to the point of insolence" side, which notes, counts, orders, explains, explains away, which removes all affect from the world and replaces it by professional technique, pigeonholing, logic chopping. When this side is haunted or possessed by the childish, womanly, disorderly, emotional nightside of things, by the irresistible or inconsequential Unconscious—when the *dusty-featured Lollocks, by sloth on sorrow fathered,* play hide and seek among the *unanswered letters, empty medicine bottles* of *disordered drawers; plague little children* who cannot sleep; *are nasty together in the bed's shadow,* when *the imbecile aged are overlong in dying;* are invisible to, denied by, the men they torment; are visible to women, *naughty wives* who *slyly allow them* to lick their *honey-sticky fingers*—when all this happens, the dry masculine Ego can protect itself from them only by *hard broom and soft broom, / To well comb the hair, / To well brush the shoe, / And to pay every debt / So soon as it's due.* These measures—so Graves says—are *sovereign against Lollocks.*

And so they are, much of the day, a little of the night; that they are ever sovereign against "the Mother of All Living, the ancient power of fright and lust—the female spider or the queen-bee whose embrace is death," I doubt. The whole Tory, saddle-soap, regimental-song-singing side of Graves can only drug, quiet temporarily, disregard as long as routine and common sense have power, the demands, manifestations, and existence of Graves's other side, the side that says: "Oh, *him!* He's just something I fool people with in the daytime."

Yet we should be foolish to believe its remark—to insist, with Graves's unconscious, that the male principle is without all affect, libido, mana. (We can see from Graves's early life, from his public-school experiences, why it is necessary for *him* to insist that this is so.) It would be equally foolish to believe that the White Goddess does not exist: she is as real as the Unconscious which she inhabits and from which she has been projected, first upon actual women and later upon the universe. (A car's headlights can rest upon a deer until the deer moves away, but then the beam of light goes out to the sky beyond.) The usefulness of this projection, the therapeutic value of Graves's myth, is obvious: it has been able to bring into efficient and fairly amiable symbiosis the antagonistic halves of his nature.

Graves understands men far better than he understands women; has taken as his own *persona* or mask or life style the terse, professional, matter-of-fact, learned Head of the Regiment—Colonel Ben Jonson of the Royal Welch Fusiliers, so to speak. Men are as dry and as known to him as his own Ego; women are as unknown, and therefore as all-powerful and as all-attractive, as his own Id. Salvation, Graves has to believe, comes through Woman alone; regimented masculinity can work only for, by means of, everyday routine, unless it is *put into the service of Woman.* Graves is willing to have the Ego do anything for the Id except notice that it *is* the Id, analyze it, explain it as subjective necessity; instead the Ego completely accepts the Id and then, most ingeniously and logically and disingenuously, works out an endless explanation of, justification for, every aspect of what it insists is objective necessity. (All of Graves's readers must have felt: "Here is a man who can explain anything.") Graves's Ego can dismiss any rebellion against the reign of Woman with a hearty matter-of-fact—next to the White Goddess, matter-of-factness is the most important thing in the world to Graves—"Nonsense! nonsense!"; can dryly, grotesquely, and cruelly satirize those who rebel; can pigeonhole them, explain them, explain them away—and all in the service of the Mother! No wonder that the once-torn-in-two Graves becomes sure, calm, unquestioning; lives in the satisfied certainty that he is right, and the world wrong, about anything, anything! He has become, so to speak, his own Laura Riding. *There is only one Goddess, and Graves is her prophet*—and isn't the prophet of the White Goddess the nearest thing to the White Goddess?

If you break your neck every time you climb over a stile, soon you will be saying that the necessary condition of all men is to break, not rib, not thigh, not arm, not shin, but always, without fail, THE NECK when climbing over stiles; by making the accidental circumstances of your life the necessary conditions of all lives, you have transformed yourself from an accident-prone analysand into an emblematic Oedipus. Instead of going on thinking of himself, with shaky hope, as an abnormal eccentric, a "spiritual Quixote" better than the world, perhaps, in his own queer way, Graves now can think of himself as representing the norm, as being the one surviving citizen of that original matriarchal, normal state from which the abnormal, eccentric world has departed. The Mother whom he once clung to in personal shame ("childishly / I dart to Mother-skirts of love and peace / To play with toys until those horrors leave me")—what will the Fathers of the Regiment say?—turns out to be, as he can show with impersonal historical objectivity, the "real" Father of the Regiment: the Father-Principle, if you trace it back far enough, is really the Mother-Principle, and has inherited from the Primal Mother what legitimacy it has. Graves wants all ends to be Woman, and Man no more than the means to them. Everything has an original matriarchal core; all Life (and all "good" Death) comes from Woman. Authority is extremely important to Graves: by means of his myth he is able to get rid of the dry, lifeless, external authority of the father, the public school, the regiment, and to replace it with the wet, live, internal authority of the mother. All that is finally important to Graves is condensed in the one figure of the Mother-Mistress-Muse, she who creates, nourishes, seduces, destroys; she who saves us—or, as good as saving, destroys us—as long as we love her, write poems to her, submit to her without question, use all our professional, Regimental, masculine qualities in her service. Death is swallowed up in victory, said St. Paul; for Graves Life, Death, everything that exists is swallowed up in the White Goddess.

Graves's poems will certainly seem to the reader, as they seem to me, a great deal more interesting than any explanation of their origin. This account is no more than a sketch: the psychoanalytically or anthropologically minded reader will find in the poems, in *Goodbye to All That,* in *The White Goddess,* many things that I should have liked to discuss, many that I should have liked to understand. Because of the White Goddess, some of the most beautiful poems of our time have come into existence. But our gratitude to her need not stop there: as we read Graves's account of her we can say to ourselves, "We *are* the ancients," for it furnishes an almost incomparably beautiful illustration of the truth of Freud's "The power of creating myths is not extinct, but still produces in the neuroses the same psychical products as in the most ancient times." (pp. 77-112)

> *Randall Jarrell, "Graves and the White Goddess," in his* The Third Book of Criticism, *Farrar, Straus and Giroux, 1969, pp. 77-112.*

Donald Davie   (essay date 1960)

[*Davie is an English poet and critic. In the following essay originally published in 1960, he comments on* Collected Poems *and asserts that Graves's use of the epigram constitutes his enduring achievement.*]

After reading through Robert Graves's **Collected Poems** (not the first Graves 'Collected,' nor perhaps the last), I am confirmed in my sense of where his surest achievement lies, though my sense of it is enriched by examples I hadn't noticed. His natural and characteristic form is the epigram. I think of such poems as **"Love Without Hope," "Flying Crooked," "On Portents," "Woman and Tree"** and (a new one to me) **"New Legends";** it seems that this sort of achievement has been possible for Graves at every stage of his career. And it would be easy to elaborate this into a view of Graves as the Landor of his age. Not only the addiction to epigram (in the fullest Greek-Anthology sense, with a special place for the sumptuous love-compliment in this form), but also the self-imposed long exile by the Mediterranean, and the face turned to the public at large (irascible, scornful, self-consciously independent) are things that Graves and Landor have in common. What's more, the difficulty we have in making Landor fit (into his age that is, with Wordsworth and Coleridge, Shelley and Keats) is just the difficulty we have seeing where Graves fits in with Eliot and Pound and Yeats, Auden and Thomas. As historians forget about Landor, so, I suspect, they will try to forget Graves. Each poet seems to be the exception that proves the rule about his time, the case which belies the generalisation but cannot disprove it because the case is so clearly a special one. Yet this last limitation (for that's what it is) is not at all so clear in Graves's case as in Landor's; and that's why the comparison shouldn't be pressed—not because it is 'academic' but because it prejudges the issue.

To begin with, the epigrams are only a small part of Landor's work as a whole, from which moreover they stand apart in a category of their own. And this isn't true of Graves: it is recognisably the virtues of the epigram which inform much work by Graves that is ampler and more relaxed than the epigram proper. And this means that to do him justice we have either to extend the term 'epigram' to a point where it's meaningless or else find a term more comprehensive. I believe the right term is 'emblem.' This can be applied to a poem like **"Vain and Careless,"** which develops in very leisurely fashion indeed (such as the strict epigram can never afford) through six quatrains which nevertheless stand to the moral discovery in the final quatrain—'Water will not mix with oil, / Nor vain with careless heart'—in precisely the same relation as the body of an epigram to its pay-off line. The story of the lady so careless she mislaid her child and the man so vain he walked on stilts is an emblematic fable, as **"The Glutton"** is an emblematic image:

> Beyond the Atlas roams a glutton
> Lusty and sleek, a shameless robber,
> Sacred to Aethiopian Aphrodite;
> The aborigines harry it with darts,
> And its flesh is esteemed, though of a fishy tang
> Tainting the eater's mouth and lips.
>
> Ourselves once, wandering in mid-wilderness
> And by despair drawn to this diet,
> Before the meal was over sat apart
> Loathing each other's carrion company.

This is the emblem in the form of riddle. (The answer to the riddle seems to be 'Lust.') Graves has been much interested in poetic riddles, and in those bodies of literature (e.g. Celtic poetry, and English and Irish folk-lore) which are especially rich in them. Not many of his own riddles are so easy to solve as **"The Glutton";** one of the finest and most extended is also one of the hardest, **"Warning to Children,"** which I now take to be just about the most ambitious poem Graves has ever written.

It is common, and reasonable, to define 'emblem' by distinguishing it from 'symbol.' And part of the difficulty we have with Graves has to do with his being an emblematic poet in an age when symbol has been most practiced and most highly esteemed. It seems important to insist that the one is not an inferior version of the other; every image in George Herbert, for instance, is an emblem. One can define the difference by saying that the symbol casts a shadow, where the emblem doesn't; the symbol aims to be suggestive, the emblem to be, even in its guise as riddle, ultimately explicit. Another difference might be that the emblem is made, fabricated, where the symbol is *found;* or rather, since it seems plain that both 'making' and 'finding' are involved in any act of imagination, let us say that the symbol aims to give the effect of having been discovered, where the emblem aims at the effect of having been

constructed. This is an important distinction, for it means that part of the impressiveness of the good symbol lies in the place and the circumstances of its finding, whereas with the emblem this isn't true. We think the better of Eliot and Baudelaire for finding their symbols in the unexpected because largely unexplored life of the industrial metropolis; but this is no warrant for thinking worse of Graves because he finds his emblems most often in a rural and agrarian England which has vanished. (It's not here that the label 'Georgian' can be made to stick, but rather on an occasional ponderous whimsey, like **"The General Elliott."**) Who can doubt that the rustic image of **"Love Without Hope"** was specifically constructed (perhaps out of memory, but perhaps not) to stand as full and explicit counterpart to the abstractions of its title—

> Love without hope, as when the young bird-
> catcher
> Swept off his tall hat to the Squire's own daugh-
> ter,
> So let the imprisoned larks escape and fly
> Singing about her head, as she rode by.

The fullness and explicitness, the dry sharp unshadowed silhouette, the lack of resonance and overtone—these are the virtues of this emblematic writing; and the air of fabrication, even of contrivance (but not laboured contrivance), the evidence of forethought, plan and design—these will displease only the reader who comes to this verse for what it never offered to supply.

Sometimes, it's true, Graves seems not to understand the nature of his own gift. We have implied that the emblem is fitted to deal with those experiences which can be made explicit, whereas the symbol exists to deal with just those experiences which cannot be grasped, which can only be hinted at, seen askance out of the corner of the eye, part of the penumbra which in our mental life hangs densely about the cleared area of experience which we can formulate. When Graves tries, as he does quite often, to render experiences of nightmare obsession and anxiety, of self-disgust or the fear of madness, his dry and definite technique fails him; and we get the disconcerting effect of a nicely adjusted and chiselled frame about a vaporous centre. The much admired **"Nature's Lineaments"** seems a case of this, and **"Welsh Incident"** virtually admits as much. Another example, and an instructive one, is *The Pier-Glass,* a piece which could certainly be spared, bearing as it does every evidence of being very early work. This is almost entirely parasitical on early Tennyson ("Mariana" and "The Lady of Shalott"), and it is interesting chiefly for being so much less 'modern' and 'symbolist,' so much more explicit (on a theme which defies explicitness) than Tennyson was in the last century.

One great advantage of emblematic writing is its impersonality. A poet who deals with symbols, a Mallarmé or an Eliot, has to struggle much harder to cut the umbilical cord between poet and poem, so that the poem will stand free and independent. Of course there are those, like Yeats and his admirers, to whom impersonality seems not worth striving for. They find nothing attractive or valuable in the illusion which other poets seek to create, by which the poem shall seem to be a product of the language, and the poet merely the medium through which the language becomes articulate. For them poetry-making is inevitably a histrionic faculty, and they are quite happy to see poetry as the vehicle of personality. It's worth making this point because of a curious passage in Graves's Foreword where, after pointing out that he has lived and written in many countries, he remarks, 'But somehow these poems have never adopted a foreign accent or colouring; they remain true to the Anglo-Irish poetic tradition into which I was born.' What is this Anglo-Irish tradition? It's true we may think of Father Prout and 'The Groves of Blarney,' the Irish tradition of comic and macaronic verse, when Graves turns the delicious joke of a poem written in the pidgin idiom of a Mallorcan pamphlet for English-speaking tourists. But there isn't enough of this sort of thing for Graves to have had it principally in mind. In view of what we know to be his opinion of Yeats, he can hardly mean that either. And yet, to the English reader (rightly or wrongly) the Anglo-Irish poetic tradition means Yeats first and the rest nowhere. Is there any point in comparing Graves with Yeats?

The comparison could be sustained about as far as the comparison with Landor (*The White Goddess,* for instance is a parallel case to Yeats's source-book, *A Vision*), but in the end it is no more fruitful. Yet the word 'histrionic,' as it comes to mind in relation to Yeats particularly and the Anglo-Irish in general, is worth pondering. Graves has shown himself thoroughly at home in the world of the TV screen and the news-reel cameraman; he is not at all reluctant or maladroit in projecting a public image of himself. And this goes along with a self-regarding element in his own poetry, as in poems about his own name or about his own face in a mirror. This is very Yeatsian. Yet in general it's true that Graves uses other media than poetry in which to project his public image. The poems are impersonal in effect, even when they are on very personal themes. And it is the emblematic style which brings this about, whether the poet intended it or not. The histrionic attitude shows through in some of the early poems, notably the much-anthologized **"Rocky Acres,"** which I was sorry to see had been chosen by George Hartley for his long-playing disc of Graves reading:

> Yet this is my country, beloved by me best,
> The first land that rose from Chaos and the
>   Flood,
> Nursing no valleys for comfort or rest,
> Trampled by no shod hooves, bought with no
>   blood.
> Sempiternal country whose barrows have stood
> Stronghold for demigods when on earth they go,
> Terror for fat burghers on far plains below.

What can the last lines mean except that the poet is himself one of the demigods, poised at the verge of his harsh and craggy kingdom, prepared to harry and pillage bourgeois society? And is this not indeed very like the talk and boastful rant of Yeats in many poems, and of the professional Irishman everywhere? And if Yeats is frequently superior to this, isn't it in so piling on the extravagance as to show that he's not taken in by his own performance, but can ironically recognize blarney even when he speaks it himself? It will be interesting to hear how Graves reads

this poem, for his very idiosyncratic reading manner, flat and casual seems designed specifically to avoid rant of any kind.

The precautions he takes against rant aren't characteristically ironical; one sees them almost at once when, a few pages after **"Rocky Acres,"** that poem is as it were rewritten in a much terser mode, as **"Angry Samson"** :

> Are they blind, the lords of Gaza
>   In their strong towers,
> Who declare Samson pillow-smothered
>   And stripped of his powers?
>
> O stolid Philistines,
>   Stare now in amaze
> At my foxes running in your cornfields
>   With their tails ablaze,
>
> At swung jaw-bone, at bees swarming
>   In the stark lion's hide,
> At these, the gates of well-walled Gaza
>   A-clank to my stride.

This isn't an important poem, but it has all the impersonality of the emblem, of a medallion; and it seems that not the poet but the English language wrote it, out of the range of meanings that, for instance, 'Philistine' has taken on between the Authorised Version and Matthew Arnold. A good way to see the de-personalizing virtue of the emblem is to compare **"The Reader over my Shoulder"** (direct and personal, with accordingly a disastrous thumping of the chest in the last lines) with **"The Legs,"** which stands beside it and treats the same subject—the poet's attitude to his readers, his public, i.e. his society at large—with completely assured and telling control, only possible after he had objectified it fully, in a contrived fable. Hereabouts in the collection—in Sections II and III—the fine poems come thick and fast: **"Full Moon," "Pure Death,"** the incomparable **"Sick Love," "Saint," "Gardener," "In Broken Images," "Flying Crooked"**—nearly all of these are emblems. **"Flying Crooked"** is one such, in which the poet distinguishes himself from other sorts of thinkers, such as logicians; **"In Broken Images,"** constructed in propositions in couplets, has the same theme, and thus mimics very effectively that very discourse, the logician's, from which it distinguishes itself—and this neatness attained by other means has just the distancing de-personalising effect of the emblems.

In Section IV there are abundant signs of an enormous bitterness, seldom defined and as seldom mastered: such emblems as **"Hell,"** or **"Nature's Lineaments"** or **"Ogres and Pygmies"** are off-centre, registering an experience they cannot comprehend. This shows up in minutiae like the word 'raffish' in the penultimate line of **"Nature's Lineaments,"** which would certainly have been another word if the poet hadn't wanted a rhyme for 'fish.' The effect of thin shallowness in these pieces seems the product not of writing that is superficial, insufficiently engaged, but of writing that is engaged in the wrong way, produced out of the jangle of raw nerves not from perturbation of imagination. In **"With her Lips Only,"** the shallowness shows up in another way, as knowledgeable glibness. In different ways two poems do establish imaginative control over the screaming nerves: there are **"Down, Wanton, Down!"** and the admirable **"Certain Mercies,"** and George Hartley takes them both for the disc. He's to be complimented also on choosing **"To Evoke Posterity,"** a less familiar poem which provides a text to hang in the study of every poet and still more of every poetry-reader.

> To evoke Posterity
> Is to weep on your own grave,
> Ventriloquizing for the unborn.

Another body of work that hangs together usefully is Section VII, where Graves seems to have herded together most of his poems that can be described as marginalia, witty but trivial pieces like **"The Persian Version," "Apollo of the Physiologists,"** and **"1805."** These are the graceful trivia with which he now appears every few weeks or so, in the weekly magazines; one wishes one could be sure that editors and readers are as aware as their author is, of how marginal such pieces are to his and poetry's central and exacting concerns. (pp. 38-44)

> *Donald Davie, "Impersonal and Emblematic," in* Shenandoah, *Vol. XIII, No. 2, Winter, 1962, pp. 38-44.*

Martin Seymour-Smith on a meeting between Graves and T. S. Eliot:

At the end of the discussion, as Graves was about to leave, Eliot somewhat awkwardly raised the matter of Ezra Pound's predicament. Pound was then in some danger of being tried for treason—and even executed—because he had made broadcasts, for money, from Rome in wartime. He was very well aware, he said, that Graves did not care for Pound or his work, but he thought he'd ask him if he would like to sign a petition that was being got up.

Graves declined: he was very sorry for Pound, but he could see no reason to sign the petition himself, as he had never valued Pound's poetry—and wasn't the poetry one of the grounds of the petition? He wished Eliot the best of luck. Eliot, who had not expected to succeed, was gracious. On the way home Graves told me that he thought it would have been dishonest to sign a petition for Pound, since he didn't think he had any more literary merit than other traitors. (It has been stated that he spitefully hoped that Pound would be executed; but this is not so: he hoped he would be let off as insane; he has never been a proponent of capital punishment.)

> *Martin Seymour-Smith, in his* Robert Graves: His Life and Work, *Holt, Rinehart and Winston, 1982.*

W. H. Auden   (essay date 1962)

[*Auden was an English-born poet and critic who is often considered the poetic successor of W. B. Yeats and T. S. Eliot. As a member of a generation of English writers strongly influenced by the ideas of Karl Marx and Sigmund Freud, he considered social and psychological commentary important functions of literary criticism. In* the following essay, Auden comments on the moral and artistic merits of Graves's poetry.]

I first came across Robert Graves's poems in the volumes of *Georgian Poetry* when I was a schoolboy, and ever since he has been one of the very few poets whose volumes I have always bought the moment they appeared. There were many others, no doubt, who did the same, but, until recently, Mr. Graves was not a Public Name in the way that Mr. Eliot, for example, was. Individuals who had discovered his poetry for themselves would talk about it to each other, but his name was not bandied about at cocktail parties to show that the speaker was *au courant,* nor was he made the subject of critical articles in little magazines or of Ph.D. theses.

But now the situation has changed.

> . . . though the Otherwhereish currency
> Cannot be quoted yet officially,
> I meet less hindrance now with the exchange
> Nor is my garb, even, considered strange;
> And shy enquiries for literature
> Come in by every post, and the side door.

wrote Mr. Graves a few years ago, and already the first two lines are out of date. I do not know whether to be glad or sorry about this. One is always glad when a writer one has long admired gains wide recognition—publicity at least means bigger sales—but public fame has its dangers, not so much for the poet himself, particularly if he has Mr. Graves's years and strength of character, as for his public. With his consent or without it, he becomes responsible for a fashion and, though some fashions may be better than others, in all there is an element of falsehood. No poet has been more concerned than Mr. Graves with poetic integrity, with being true, at all costs, to his real self. The difficulty is that it is precisely the man who is most obviously himself who can be the greatest threat to those who have not yet found themselves, for instead of taking him as an *example,* inspiring them to do in their way what he has done in his, they are all too apt to take him as a *model* whose style of writing and literary tastes they blindly follow.

As an example, nothing could be more admirable than the way in which at a time when most of his seniors and juniors were looking to the French poets of the post-Baudelaireian period or to the English metaphysicals for their poetic models, Mr. Graves had the courage to ignore them and remain faithful to his personal preferences—nursery rhymes, ballads, Skelton, Caroline poets like Lovelace and Rochester, even romantic poets like Blake, Coleridge, and Christina Rossetti—or that, in the age obsessed with experiment and innovation in meter and poetic organization, he should have gone on quietly writing genuine contemporary poetry within the traditional forms. It would not be equally admirable, however, if Pope and free verse, say, were to become taboo because Mr. Graves does not like the one or write in the other. But to turn to his poems themselves is enough to make one forget all such gloomy forebodings.

The kind of critic who regards authors as an opportunity for displaying his own brilliance and ingenuity will find

Mr. Graves a poor subject. A few of his poems, it is true, can benefit from a gloss, but this Mr. Graves has provided himself in *The White Goddess*. For the rest, though he happens to be a learned scholar, he demands no scholarship of his readers; his poems are short, their diction simple, their syntax unambiguous and their concerns, love, nature, the personal life, matters with which all are familiar and in which all are interested. About public life, politics, the world situation, etc., he has nothing to say.

This does not mean that he regards public events as of no significance—he could never have written his excellent historical novels if he did—only that it is not a realm with which he believes poetry should be concerned. He also believes, I suspect, that in our age the Public Realm is irredeemable and that the only thing a sensible man can do is ignore it and live as decently as he can in spite of it. I can picture Mr. Graves, under certain circumstances, as a guerilla fighter, but I cannot see him writing pamphlets for any cause.

Like nearly all writers worth reading, Mr. Graves is a moralist, and the artistic merits of his poems cannot be divorced from the conception of the good life which they express. Though Horace is one of his favorite poets—Horace is unpassionate and easygoing, Graves passionate and puritanical—they both attach great importance to measure and good sense, and have a common dislike for willful disorder and theatrical gestures. If Mr. Graves is the more convincing advocate, it is because one feels that measure and good sense are values he has had to fight to achieve. It is hard to believe that Horace ever suffered from nightmares or some passion so violent that it could have destroyed him, but he would have approved, I think, of Graves's description of the climate of thought.

> Wind, sometimes, in the evening chimneys; rain
> On the early morning roof, on sleepy sight;
> Snow streaked upon the hilltop, feeding
> The fond brook at the valley-head
> That greens the valley and that parts the lips;
> The sun, simple, like a country neighbor;
> The moon, grand, not fanciful with clouds.

Graves's good man, leaving aside the special case of the good poet, is somebody who leads an orderly, hardworking, independent life, a good husband and father who keeps his word and pays his debts, outwardly, in fact, a good bourgeois, but inwardly never losing his sense of his personal identity or his capacity for love and reverence.

On the subject of love, no poet in our time has written more or better. Most of Hardy's love poems are elegies, most of Yeats's are concerned with unrequited love, but Graves's deal with the joys and griefs of mutual passion. He shares with D. H. Lawrence a contempt for those who would deny the physical element in love and call

> . . . for a chaste
> Sodality: all dead below the waist.

but that is the only point on which they agree. He has none of Lawrence's hysterical aversion to conscious understanding between the sexes; on the contrary, any sexual relationship that does not lead to personal understanding and affection is, for him, base. Nothing could be further

from Lawrence than his priapic poem **"Down, Wanton Down!"** In this, as in many others, he shows his distaste for the vulgarity and crudeness of untamed male sexuality. Woman, to Graves, is the superior sex, and only a woman can teach a man the meaning of true love.

For the poet, as the messenger of the Mother Goddess, there is an additional obligation to speak no more and no less than the truth, and each poet, according to his nature and the time in which he lives, has his own kind of temptation to lie. Mr. Graves has told us of his. He was born—the term is inaccurate but convenient—with a natural faculty for writing verse. Ask him to improvise a poem on any subject, and in ten minutes he can turn out something competent and mellifluous. This is a very valuable gift, and a poet like Wordsworth who lacks it is deficient, but it is a dangerous one, for the poet who possesses it can all too easily forsake the truth for verbal display.

> But you know, I know, and you know I know
>   My principal curse:
> Shame at the mounting dues I have come to owe
>   A devil of verse,
> Who caught me young, ingenuous and uncouth,
>   Prompting me how
> To evade the patent clumsiness of truth—
>   Which I do now.

It is of this devil and not of another poet, I think that Graves is speaking in **"In Broken Images."**

> He is quick, thinking in clear images;
> I am slow, thinking in broken images.
> He becomes dull, trusting to his clear images;
> I become sharp, mistrusting my broken images. . . .
> He in a new confusion of his understanding;
> I in a new understanding of my confusion.

A comparison between his individual volumes and the *Collected Poems* which follow it, and then between the successive *Collected Poems* of 1926, 1938, 1947, 1955 and 1961 reveals how stern with himself Mr. Graves has been in discarding any poems that contained a trace of smartness. Among them, I remember a pastiche of *Speke Parrot* [a poem by John Skelton], which was an amazing tour de force. Personally, I regret its omission, but I can see why it has been excluded. The only virtuoso pieces he has retained are comic poems like **"Welcome to the Caves of Arta"** and **"Apollo of the Physiologists,"** for a comic poem must almost necessarily be a virtuoso performance. If I have a greater fondness for bravura in poetry than Mr. Graves, I suspect that we only differ in our notion of what is comic or what may be comically treated. To me, for example, *Lycidas* is a "comic" poem which I can learn "by heart not rote" as I can learn a poem of Edward Lear. It seems to me a verbal arcadia in which death, grief, religion, and politics are games which cannot possibly be taken seriously. On the other hand, because I am convinced of the reality of their emotions, there are religious sonnets by Donne and Hopkins in which I feel that the virtuosity of expression comes between them and the truth.

Mr. Graves's other temptation has been the tendency of the romantic imagination to regard the extraordinary and

remote as more "poetic," more luminous than everyday
events.

> The lost, the freakish, the unspelt
> Drew me: for simple sights I had no eye.
> And I did swear allegiance then
> To wildness, not (as I thought) to truth—
> Become a virtuoso, and this also,
> Later, of simple sights, when tiring
> Of unicorn and upas?

Again, a reading of his collected poems will show how successful he has been in disciplining his imagination and his
tongue. Occasionally, perhaps, he indulges his subjective
feelings at the expense of objective fact. Among his more
recent poems is one entitled **"Turn of the Moon"** which
concludes as follows:

> But if one night she brings us, as she turns
> Soft, steady, even, copious rain
> That harms no leaf or flower, but gently falls
> Hour after hour, sinking to the taproots,
> And the sodden earth exhales at dawn
> A long sigh scented with pure gratitude,
> Such rain—the first rain of our lives, it seems,
> Neither foretold, cajoled, nor counted on—
> Is woman giving as she loves.

The lines are beautiful and, at first reading, I was carried
away. But, then, a tiresome doubt obtruded itself: "Are
drought and rainfall *really* caused by the moon? What
would a meteorologist say?"

In addition to discarding many poems, Mr. Graves has revised some, and, to anyone who writes verses himself,
nothing is more instructive than a poet's revisions.

In Mr. Graves's case, they are particularly important because they prevent his doctrine of the subordination of art
to truth from being misunderstood. It is all right for him
to say

> And call the man a liar who says I wrote
> All that I wrote in love, for love of art.

But we all know the kind of poet who, when one points
out to him that a certain line is obscure or clumsy and
should be rewritten, replies: "But that is how it came to
me." Art without love is nothing, but love without art is
insufficient. Here for comparison are two verses of **"The
Sea Horse."**

> Tenderly confide your secret love,
> For one who never pledged you less than love,
> To this indomitable hippocamp,
> Child of your element, coiled a-ramp,
> Having ridden out worse tempests than you
>   know of:
> Make much of him in your despair, and shed
> Salt tears to bathe his taciturn dry head.
>
> (1953)
>
> Since now in every public place
> Lurk phantoms who assume your walk and face,
> You cannot yet have utterly abjured me
> Nor stifled the insistent roar of sea.
>
> Do as I do: confide your unquiet love
> (For one who never owed you less than love)
> To this indomitable hippocamp,

> Child of your elements, coiled a-ramp,
> Having ridden out worse tempests than you
>   know of;
> Under his horny ribs a blood-red stain
> Portends renewal of our pain.
> Sweetheart, make much of him and shed
> Tears on his taciturn dry head.
>
> (1961)

Only a craftsman as meticulous as Mr. Graves can afford
to speak lightly of his art.

To read his poems is both a joy and a privilege; they are
passionate, truthful, and well-bred. (pp. 5-11)

W. H. Auden, "A Poet of Honor," in Shenan-
doah, *Vol. XIII, No. 2, Winter, 1962, pp. 5-11.*

Michael Kirkham   (essay date 1969)

[*In the following excerpt, Kirkham examines the conception of love which Graves formulated in the early
1960s and associated with the Black Goddess.*]

In the first five years of the 'sixties Graves has already published four volumes of poetry—*More Poems 1961* (1961),
New Poems 1962 (1962), *Man Does, Woman Is* (1964),
and in a limited edition *Love Respelt* (1965)—and another
collection. His astonishing productivity in these years is
one sign that he has entered a new period in his writing.
It is not the only sign: from the vantage-point of his most
recent work it can be seen that these poems are a progression of moods and attitudes leading to a new experience
and a new conception of love; to this conception he has
given the name of the Black Goddess. While the most
complete embodiment of this experience is in *Love Respelt,* there are hints of it in the preceding volumes; the
poem actually entitled **'The Black Goddess'** appears in
Man Does, Woman Is, and several other poems in that
volume use imagery peculiarly descriptive of her; the beginning of these images are to be traced in *More Poems
1961* and *New Poems 1962.*

In all the poems of the 'sixties theme and manner express,
more than anything else, the poet's ability to survive and
then to transcend suffering. *Poems 1953* heralded this development; but angry robustness gives place in *More
Poems 1961* to a different kind of robustness. The poet-
lover neither resists his fate nor submits despairingly to it;
both would be more demonstrative postures than these
poems generally allow. Both, too, would indicate a flaw in
the quality of the poet's acceptance of his experience: underlying the attitude of this volume is the tight-lipped acknowledgment, more unquestioning than ever before, that
the lover's fate is irrevocable and that protest would be irrelevant—acknowledgment of, in the words of an earlier
poem, 'the thing's necessity' (**'Despite and Still'**). All the
poems start from the curt assumption that love necessarily
involves suffering; the only uncertainty is whether the
lover can bear it. The poet asks in **'Patience'**:

> Must it be my task
> To assume the mask
> Of not desiring what I may not ask?

The answer being implicitly affirmative, what is really in

question is the poet's ability to maintain such an attitude of stoical self-denial. His cry is not to be released from his 'task' but for the patience to carry it out: 'O, to be patient / As you would have me patient . . . ' The question is the same in **'Symptoms of Love'**: can the lover '*endure* such grief . . . ?' (my italics). This word is, as it were, the *leit-motif* in **More Poems 1961.** To his usual romantic list of epithets for love Graves can now, in **'Under the Olives'**, add one more: 'Innocent, gentle, bold, *enduring,* proud' (my italics).

The style of these poems is a more extreme development of the spare terse style of **Poems 1953.** In keeping with the stated theme of several of them, refraining from protest they express a tighter self-restraint than do the poems of the earlier volume. Emotion is not excluded but held in check, so that it is felt as a constant pressure behind the verse; the characteristic tone implies a severely curbed pain. The poems are frequently brief; either they run to no more than seven, eight or ten lines a piece, or if longer the lines themselves are short, composed sometimes of five and six syllables each. Their syntactical simplicity and the baldness of their statements, or the fact that occasionally a poem consists of but a single sentence, add to the effect of brevity. **'The Cure'**, a poem of seven lines, is typically short, swift in movement and direct. It opens brusquely, 'No lover ever found a cure for love'; except, it continues, by the inflicting of such a painful wound, killing hope, that it was worse than love itself. Here abruptly the poet breaks off, adding only the summary dismissive verdict, 'More tolerable the infection than its cure'. We are left with an impression of the poet's fierce taciturnity, of an incipient rebelliousness cut short.

In **'Symptoms of Love'** the economy of the means employed to make the poem's effect is as conspicuous as in **'Counting the Beats'**.

> Love is a universal migraine,
> A bright stain on the vision
> Blotting out reason.
> Symptoms of true love
> Are leanness, jealousy . . .

In lines so clipped much of the poem's intention is contained in the curt rhythms, expressing a self-punishing naked truthfulness—in, for example, the brutal stress on 'blotting'. Every word has the maximum impact: the telescoping of the two images in 'bright stain', for example, gives to the phrase a compressed, complex power: 'bright', implying instantaneous illumination and immediate pain (the brightness of a migraine flash), conflicts—the contrast is heightened by the contrasting vowel sounds—and combines with the suggestion of something slow, dark and indelible (as a migraine is not) in 'stain', to epitomize the paradox of love.

Most striking of all, Graves has in these poems carried to its limit the discipline of leaving unsaid what it is not absolutely necessary to say. **'Under the Olives'** is in this respect representative.

> We never should have loved had love not struck
> Swifter than reason, and despite reason:
> Under the olives, our hands interlocked,
> We both fell silent:

> Each listened for the other's answering
> Sigh of unreasonableness—
> Innocent, gentle, bold, enduring, proud.

What we have is the plainest of statements, but one which at every point connotes an ambience of unstated feeling. The last line gives us the most definite clue—though it is still only a hint—to its character. It is a mixture of pain and satisfaction; while love induces gentleness in its subjects, it also requires from them the tougher qualities of boldness and endurance. The epithet 'enduring', in particular, raises nearer to the surface of the poem a sense of the difficulty of the lovers' relationship: points to the element of pain in 'struck', for example, and of conflict in 'despite'. It explains the resoluteness enacted in the verse-movement, which is made thereby to carry the further implications of cruelties survived and obstructions overcome. There is an intimation of something unsimple and laborious in love in the mere doubling of negatives in the first line. Even the pause after 'We both fell silent' is eloquent—enacting the ensuing silence and the fullness of the moment that cannot be expressed; in the pause, as again in the line-division between 'answering' and 'sigh', we feel happiness, awe, uncertainty and an awareness of difficulty.

Stoicism is not the only attitude communicated in these

Graves in his Royal Welch Fusiliers uniform.

poems but it is the central one, out of which the attitudes of the next two volumes seem to have developed and which prepared the ground for the affirmation of *Love Respelt.* Graves's practice in the majority of these poems of keeping very close to an actual human relationship, using the mythology only sparingly and simply, is also indicative of the direction in which he is now moving. This new approach to his theme and the tone of resolute stoicism are evidently related phenomena, each expressions of the poet's now more naked exposure to his experience. In 'Intimations of the Black Goddess', a lecture given in 1963, Graves wrote: 'Only during the past three years have I ventured to dramatize, truthfully and factually, the vicissitudes of a poet's dealings with the White Goddess, the Muse, the perpetual Other Woman'. The stress is on 'dramatize' and 'factually': it is not in the subject-matter of his latest poems that he found evidence of a new daring—the 'vicissitudes' of love was his theme throughout the White Goddess period—but in the bare, unmetaphorical treatment of it. This preoccupation with the literal human experience of love goes with, and perhaps derives from, the poet's concentration on love as a joint venture: woman is man's partner, though still the dominant one, rather than his conscience or the impartial administrator of justice. In **'The Sharp Ridge',** for example, the poet at a crisis in their relationship pleads with her to

> Have pity on us both: choose well
> On this sharp ridge dividing death from hell.

The theme is now more often the 'difficult achievement' of love (**'The Starred Coverlet'**), an achievement towards which *both* struggle and which involves them *both* in suffering, than the cruelty and mystery of womanhood. In doing what she must do, periodically withdrawing her love, she is not exempt from the pain she inflicts. The lover who, in **'The Intrusion',** recoils with horror from the picture of 'her white motionless face and folded hands / Framed in such thunderclouds of sorrow', at the same time is made to realize that this is an image of her suffering. He is urged to 'give her no word of consolation' because her grief is 'Divine mourning for what cannot be', but nevertheless her evident need of 'consolation' accents her purely human plight; she is in the same position as the man—of having to suffer the fate of which she is only the involuntary instrument. It is a fate they share in common, and the separate roles they play are each as difficult as the other's. In **'The Falcon Woman'** Graves, for the first time, considers the woman's role from her point of view. To be a man who honourably keeps his promises and builds too much upon the loved woman's promises, made in 'carelessness of spirit', to which she cannot be held, is, he admits, hard; but is it less hard for *such* a woman 'in carelessness of spirit / To love such a man?'

In his third period Graves was concerned with, separately or as a whole, the phases of love and the pattern of events in the man-woman relationship; each position taken was in answer to this preoccupation. Implied or stated in many of the poems now is a more fundamental question: not 'what experiences must the lover undergo?' but 'what *is* love, what makes it as a *single* experience different from any other?' The exclusive concentration on the essence of

this reality accounts, in part, for the spareness and brevity of most of these poems.

The opening poem of *More Poems 1961,* **'Lyceia',** sets the tone, indicates the sort of interest that Graves now has in his theme. Lyceia is the wolf-goddess, and 'All the wolves of the forest / Howl for Lyceia'; they compete for her love but she keeps them at a distance. The poet therefore asks: 'What do the wolves *learn?*' (my italics). Love is regarded as offering a *schooling* in a radically different outlook than is available to the ordinary person. This view of love had to wait until *Love Respelt* for its complete expression. As yet, according to Lyceia, they learn nothing but 'Envy and hope, / Hope and chagrin'. But that there is more to be learned is the import of other poems in this volume: in **'The Starred Coverlet'** lovers are enjoined on different occasions to learn patience, to endure, and

> to lie mute, without embrace or kiss,
> Without a rustle or a smothered sigh,
> Basking each in the other's glory.

The 'glory' is that of a distinct reality, the nature of which is the theme of several poems. They agree precisely on their definition: it strikes 'Swifter than reason and despite reason' (**'Under the Olives'**). Graves presents this life of unreason as a positive and rare achievement: he explains in **'The Laugh'** that he had been at first baffled by it because 'the identity of opposites / Had so confused my all too sober wits'. The *marriage* of opposites—of two people 'unyielding in / Their honest, first reluctance to agree' (**'Joan and Darby'**)—has gained for them entry to this special world, which defies and is inaccessible to reason and logic: if they were 'birds of similar plumage caged / In the peace of every day', he asks in **'Seldom Yet Now',**

> Would we still conjure wildfire up
> From common earth, as now?

Not obeying known laws love is unpredictable, incalculable—to be 'Neither foretold, cajoled, nor counted on' (**'Turn of the Moon'**)—and is the more precious for being so. The most intensely romantic expression of this reality, **'Two Children',** comes the nearest to portraying the new kind of love celebrated in *Love Respelt.* In his youth, the poet records, it was 'a fugitive beacon' chased by him in his dreams; it 'set a nap on the plum, a haze on the rose'; it is 'Child of the wave, child of the morning dew': the stress here is on the elusiveness, the apparent insubstantiality, and the almost *miraculous* nature of love. (pp. 241-46)

> *Michael Kirkham, in his* The Poetry of Robert Graves, *The Athlone Press, 1969, 284 p.*

Helen Vendler   (essay date 1977)

[*In the following excerpt, Vendler argues that Graves is an accomplished, but predictable, poet.*]

Graves remains unchanged, a poet who found his styles long ago, still moving familiarly in his world of dragons, goddesses, planetary influences, and ogres. He is archaic when it pleases him, and his poems are always construable and rhymed. It is intellectual poetry (for all Graves's preoccupation with love), and structured by its point more than by any gusts of feeling. His more complacent love poems ("She knows, as he knows, / Of a faithful-always / And an always-dear") are less moving than the poems written in abandonment:

> The death of love comes from reiteration:
> A single line sung over and over again.

In both sorts, peaceful and dismayed, Graves finds satisfying, if old-fashioned, last lines:

> It was impossible you could love me less,
> It was impossible I could love you more
> > ["**Deliverance**"].

> It was not my fault, love, nor was it your fault
> > ["**The Sentence**"].

On the other hand, the love poems, hundreds of them, come to seem almost like finger-exercises in a void, and the interruption of Graves's ironic and satiric tones is felt as a relief. On Ulysses:

> All lands to him were Ithaca: love-tossed
> He loathed the fraud, yet would not bed alone.

And, in a later poem, a comment on the herd of the unimaginative:

> Innumerable zombies
> With glazed eyes shuffled around at their diurnal
> > tasks,
> Keep the machines whirring, drudge idly in
> > stores and bars,
> Bear still-born zombie children, pack them off to
> > school
> For education in science and the dead languages,
> Divert themselves with moribund travesties of
> > living.

Accomplished though he is, Graves is not a compelling poet, whether in voice or attentiveness. His style is generic rather than shaped by each poem, and he believes too strongly that there is one story and one story only. The preordained plot precludes entirely any possibility of the erratic vagary, the unforeseen counterinstance. His poems are finished before they are begun, and proceed imperturbably to their destined point, discursive and magisterial. Confusion, bafflement, and surprise play less of a part in Graves than they do in life. Or perhaps it is truer to say that he is more a man of letters, a man who writes things in any form handy to him, than a poet. (p. 80)

> *Helen Vendler, in a review of "New Collected Poems," in* The Yale Review, *Vol. LXVII, No. 1, October, 1977, pp. 80-1.*

Katherine Snipes (essay date 1979)

[*In the following excerpt, Snipes examines Graves's theory of the poetic process as expressed in* The White Goddess *and* Mammon and the Black Goddess.]

Although *The White Goddess* is probably the most famous (or notorious) of his critical works, Graves has a long history of literary criticism. Some of it he has later disavowed. Some seems unnecessarily vicious in dealing with

brilliant contemporaries, such as Yeats. (Is he so irritated with Yeats because he, too, created a private symbol system that rivals his own?) Yet Graves has a coherent theory of poetry, quite aside from his more arcane speculations about the relationship between ancient religious ritual and the poetic art. We will look first at some of the "pure" critical theory—pure, that is, in the sense of unencumbered by anthropological and mythological considerations.

In one of his Oxford lectures called "The Poet in a Valley of Dry Bone" (in *Mammon and the Black Goddess,* 1963), Graves has a particularly lucid explanation of the poetic process. The art of the poet is the result of long experience and attention to the meanings of words, a carefully developed craftsmanship, and an intuitive openness to what Graves calls the poetic trance. Though he started writing poems himself at age thirteen, he says there are no child prodigies in poetry, as there are in music. "A long, long experience with language is needed before words can fully collaborate with one another under the poetic trance. It seems necessary, too, to have read a great many poems by other writers, good and bad, before a poet can realize his powers and limitations."

The craftsmanship of poetry, Graves says, is self-taught. "A poet lives with his own language, continually instructing himself in the origin, histories, pronunciation, and peculiar usages of words, together with their latent powers, and the exact shades of distinction between what Roget's *Thesaurus* calls 'synonyms.'"

Some languages, such as French, have officially correct ways of expressing every thought, but English has only precedents. One needs to know the precedents and when it may be wise to create one's own precedent. Graves says that he consults the Oxford English Dictionary four or five times a day, checking the derivations of words, how their meanings have changed, who used them, in what contexts. "The exact rightness of words can be explained only in the context of a whole poem: each one being related rhythmically, emotionally, and semantically, to every other."

Graves rejects decorative elaborations that add nothing to meaning. In *5 Pens in Hand,* he proposes a game he calls "Cables" to test a poem for superfluous verbiage. Imagine you are short of cash and have to cable the *sense* of each verse. He then offers a twelve-word cable of the forty-three word first stanza of Wordsworth's "Solitary Reaper." But he defies anyone to save much money by converting to a cablegram Shakespeare's "Full fathom five thy father lies / Of his bones are coral made. . . ."

As previously mentioned, Graves scorns schools and movements in poetry. One does not write good poetry by imitating either a popular fashion or a real genius. The idea or experience one wishes to express should determine the form, the diction, the rhythm—and the style should always be the writer's own. "I never have much use for one whose poems I do not recognize at a glance as inimitably his own; even so, I reject them if they draw attention to a cultivated eccentricity, to pride in scholarship, or to the master of Classical or Modernist technique."

Technique, as used here, suggests a more mechanical process than the craftsmanship Graves favors. It is partly timing and emphasis that makes the difference. The master of technique may be more conveying a poetic message—like an orator who sounds impressive, but makes no sense. For Graves, a poem must make sense; deliberate obscurity is an affectation. (Graves condemns Ezra Pound on this score.) But the poem must begin "beyond reason" in inspiration, welling up from the poetic trance. After the initial rush of expression comes critical appraisal and meticulous rewriting, where all the poet's craft is put to the service of the unique requirements of this particular poem. Graves says he writes approximately ten drafts of a poem.

On the creative process in poetry, Graves writes, in *Mammon and the Black Goddess:*

> The Vienna school of psychology presumes a conscious and unconscious mind, as two separate and usually warring entities, but a poet cannot accept this. In the poetic trance, he has access not only to the primitive emotions and thoughts which lie stored in his childhood memory, but to all his subsequent experiences—emotional and intellectual; including a wide knowledge of English won by constant critical study. Words are filed away by their hundred thousand, not in alphabetical order but in related groups; and as soon as the trance seizes him, he can single out most of the ones he needs. Moreover, when the first heavily blotted draft has been copied out fairly before he goes to bed, and laid aside for reconsideration, he will read it the next morning as if it were written by another hand. Yet soon he is back in the trance, finds that his mind has been active while he was asleep on the problem of internal relations, and that he can substitute the exact right word for the stand-in with which he had to be content the night before.

This illuminating description probably does not disprove the theory of the subconscious mind. It does suggest, however, that the skillful poet has remarkable access to buried memories and emotions, and to so much verbal aptitude that experience leaps out fully clothed in words. Lines of poetry that emerge spontaneously from trance will choose their own rhythm and suggest their own best form.

Graves described this poetic trance in some of his first critical works in the 1920s. His collected essays entitled *The Common Asphodel,* containing observations on poetry dated from 1922-1949 (some of which were collaborations with Laura Riding) begins with that topic:

> The nucleus of every poem worthy of the name is rhythmically formed in the poet's mind, during a trance-like suspension of his normal habits of thought, by the supra-logical reconciliation of conflicting emotional ideas. The poet learns to induce the trance in self-protection whenever he feels unable to resolve an emotional conflict by simple logic. . . . As soon as he has . . . dissociated himself from the poem, the secondary phase of composition begins: that of testing and correcting on commonsense principles, so as to satisfy public scrutiny, what began as a private message to himself from himself—yet taking care that nothing of poetic value is lost or im

paired. For the reader of the poem must fall into a complementary trance if he is to appreciate its full meaning. The amount of revision needed depends largely on the strength and scope of the emotional disturbance and the degree of trance.

Graves goes on to say that the critical sense is not completely suspended in light trance. Some trances are so deep, however, that the poem evoked is close to dream, wherein thought connections are governed by free association and the atmosphere charged with emotions the writer himself may not understand. (This observation, one might note, suggests that there is, indeed, a subconscious mind.) The classic example of dream poetry is Samuel Taylor Coleridge's "Kubla Khan."

Graves did not, in his earlier career, speak disparagingly of Freud. When he was struggling with his war-neurosis, under the care of Dr. Rivers, Graves thought that the writing of poetry could be psychologically therapeutic. The insight gained during his protracted illness and treatment, as he says specifically in *Poetic Unreason* and *On English Poetry,* helped him to develop an aesthetic for the next ten years, until he came under the influence of Laura Riding.

Daniel Hoffman has analyzed the contribution of Dr. Rivers to Graves's aesthetic in *Barbarous Knowledge.* Hoffman quotes Rivers's *Conflict and Dream,* then explains that Graves derived support from Rivers for these convictions:

> First, the poem, like the dream, is a symbolic presentation and resolution of individual emotional conflicts. Graves holds this conception still, although he has modified an accompanying theorem he held in the 1920's that the chief value of poetry is therapeutic.
>
> Rivers's second point of use to Graves is that there is the *materia poetica* ('the unelaborated product of the poet's mind') which is subjected to 'a lengthy process of a critical kind, comparable with . . . the secondary elaboration of the dream.' Hence the completed poem requires the collaboration of both the intuitive and the critical faculties of the mind. . . .
>
> From Rivers's statement that 'the real underlying meaning or latent content of the poem' is in fact quite different from that suggested by its outward imagery, Graves takes warrant for a reading of the poetry of others that can only be called idiosyncratic. And finally, the assertion . . . that only the poet himself can reveal 'the real mechanism of artistic production' [as the individual is the best interpreter of his own dreams] leads Graves to deduce universal principles of poetry from the analysis of his own practice.

One of these universal laws of poetics that Graves derives from his own experience, as Hoffman points out, is that there is no such thing as a true long poem. Poems should be devoted to a single subject—a principle also advanced by Edgar Allan Poe. That is one, though by no means the only, reason Graves is harsh with Milton. Again, Graves is not much interested in verse drama, even Shakespeare's, except for the isolated poems that can be extracted from them. As Hoffman implies, Graves seems to have limited tolerance for kinds of poetry that seem foreign to his own practice.

In 1927, Graves collaborated with Laura Riding on *A Survey of Modernist Poetry.* It contains a perceptive discussion of modern methods of poetry, using such innovators as Cummings and Eliot, as well as some excellent comments on older poems, especially Shakespearean sonnets. It analyzes the reasons for and shortcomings of faddish movements in poetry, such as imagism and Georgianism. Dead movements, they explain, are focused on the problem of style. Yet every poem should be a "new and self-explanatory creature," dictating its own style.

Both Graves and Riding are known for their caustic judgments on poets whose methods they dislike. The work of the imagist poet H. D. (Hilda Doolittle), for instance, is "so thin, so poor, that its emptiness seemed 'perfection,' its insipidity to be concealing a 'secret,' its superficiality so 'glacial' that it created a false 'classical' atmosphere." Of Gertrude Stein, " . . . she was only divinely inspired in ordinariness: her creative originality, that is, was original only because it was so grossly, so humanly, all-inclusively ordinary. She used language automatically to record pure ultimate obviousness." (One can't help thinking of the "pop art" painting of a huge Campbell's soup can.)

Modern experimental poetry, Graves and Riding say, has been influenced by nonrepresentational art—especially in the abandonment of meter. But poetry is necessarily linked with metrical forms designed to create in the reader a hypersensitive awareness of meaning. Verse forms are not rigid; they accommodate considerable stress and variation. But to discard them entirely, as in free verse, is to abandon a major requirement of the poetic mood.

The change from meter to free verse occurred around 1911, when English poetry was at low ebb. It became fashionable for the poet, modeling himself after the nonrepresentational artist, to abandon coherent statement, but to create abstract arrangements of emotionally laden phrases and sounds. In "Legitimate Criticism of Poetry" in *5 Pens in Hand,* Graves praises John Crowe Ransom and Robert Frost as true masters of experimental form, adapting individual speech rhythm and diction to conventional verse forms, as Shakespeare did.

In a comment in 1949, when Graves republished some of his collaborations with Laura Riding in *The Common Asphodel,* he made some gloomy predictions on the fate of poets in the modern world. True poets literally have no place to go and little audience except each other. That, of course, is one reason Graves fled the modern world to the relatively primitive and remote Majorca.

> The Communist state demands verse which glorifies national achievement under the Marxist theory and shows a complete divorce from European literary models; the big-business state demands verse which soothes the vanity and condones the near-illiteracy of the Hollywood-educated populace. . . . The writing of poems

is therefore likely to become a more private affair than ever.

Most poets, he says in *Food for Centaurs,* gravitate to the teaching profession, where they may be able to write some poems, at least on vacations. Yet this is the "most damaging of all professions for a poet." There are just too many obligations and restrictions that fritter away his mental and emotional substance.

> He must not diverge from the curriculum; he must teach a great many things which he knows to be useless, boring, or even untrue; he must discipline his pupils; he must pretend to know the answer to every question; he must lead a life secure against moral objection even from the most narrow-minded critic.

Under the circumstances, a poet apparently ought to be independently wealthy or, like Graves, produce some more popular forms of literature on the side.

Graves's *magnum opus, The White Goddess,* which he calls "A Historical Grammar of Poetic Myth," is so complex a document that it almost defies analysis. Even a reader fairly knowledgeable in myth can become mired in the voluminous details and lose the thread of the argument. Although the book is obviously a synthesis of all his research and meditation on ancient religions, the purpose of poetry, and a traditional body of literature, Graves says his argument is based on a detailed examination of two Welsh minstrel poems of the thirteenth century, *Câd Goddeu* and *Hanes Taliesin,* which ingeniously conceal the clues to an ancient secret.

He summarizes his findings in the Foreword:

> My thesis is that the language of poetic myth anciently current in the Mediterranean and Northern Europe was a magical language bound up with popular religious ceremonies in honour of the Moon-goddess, or Muse, some of them dating from the Old Stone Age, and that this remains the language of true poetry—'true' in the nostalgic modern sense of 'the unimprovable original, not a synthetic substitute'. The language was tampered with in late Minoan times when invaders from Central Asia began to model or falsify the myths to justify the social changes. Then came the early Greek philosophers who were strongly opposed to magical poetry as threatening their new religion of logic, and under their influence a rational poetic language (now called the Classical) was elaborated in honour of their patron Apollo and imposed on the world as the last word in spiritual illumination: a view that has prevailed practically ever since in European schools and universities, where myths are now studied only as quaint relics of the nursery age of mankind.

The secret hidden in the Welsh minstrel poems involves an esoteric tree alphabet used by wandering bards, the master-poets of Wales. When the country became Christianized, the bards tried to express the traditional pagan theme of bardic poetry in terms so disguised that the Church could not accuse them of heresy. They did this, presumably, with puzzling riddles and the ancient symbolism of the tree alphabet, which the Christians did not know.

> The Theme, briefly, is the antique story, which falls into thirteen chapters and epilogue, of the birth, life, death and resurrection of the God of the Waxing Year; the central chapters concern the God's losing battle with the God of the Waning Year for love of the capricious and all-powerful Threefold Goddess, their mother, bride and layer-out. The poet identifies himself with the God of the Waxing Year and his Muse with the Goddess; the rival is his blood-brother, his other self, his weird.

The God of the Waxing Year is, of course, a variation of the primitive vegetation god. He revives in the spring but suffers death in the fall, like the Egyptian Osiris, murdered by his brother Set, god of desert and drouth, only to be restored by his wife Isis. The poet sees himself in both creative and sacrificial roles, alternately inspired by the love of the Goddess Muse and suffering ritual death when her love grows cold.

Graves first found what is called the Beth-Luis-Nion tree alphabet in seventeenth century Roderick O'Flaterty's *Ogygia.* O'Flaterty presented it as a genuine relic of the Druids, who used it for divination. Graves has the decency to warn us that he wrote to Dr. Macalister, "the best living authority on Oghams," who told him not to take O'Flaterty's alphabet seriously. Nevertheless, Graves does do so, insisting that the clue to understanding seemingly nonsensical riddles in the *Romance of Taliesin* lies in knowing the secret tree alphabet, which was correlated to a tree calendar.

The alphabet has five vowels and thirteen consonants. Each letter is named after a tree or shrub. Graves explains the mythological associations that surround each tree symbolized in a letter. *H,* for instance, is the ash, sacred to Poseidon, also to Woden, or Wotan, or Odin, or Gwidion (as it was variously written), who uses it as his steed in "The Battle of the Trees," a poem in *Câd Goddeu.* But *H* was originally associated with the Scandinavian Triple Goddess, who dispensed justice under the ash tree.

F is the alder, the tree of Bran. *S* is the willow, sacred to Hecate, Circe, Hera, and Persephone, all death aspects of the Triple Goddess. *D* is the oak, "the tree of Zeus, Jupiter, Hercules, The Dagda (the chief of the older Irish gods), Thor, and all other thunder gods, Jehovah in so far as he was 'El,' and Allah." This is the sacred oak that Sir James Frazer elucidated at such length in *The Golden Bough.*

Graves's remarks on the letter *T* illustrate his capacity for intuitive synthesis, which some may regret as untrustworthy. Whether or not it says something reliable about how people perceive Jesus, it does illuminate one of the great English classics, *Sir Gawain and the Green Knight.*

> The eighth tree is the holly, which flowers in July. The holly appears in the originally Irish *Romance of Gawain and the Green Knight.* The Green Knight is an immortal giant whose club is a holly-bush. He and Sir Gawain, who appears in the Irish version as Cuchulain, a typical Her-

cules, make a compact to behead one another at alternate New Years—meaning midsummer and midwinter—but when it comes to the point, the Holly Knight spares the Oak Knight. Since in medieval practice St. John, who lost his head on St. John's day, took over the oak-king's titles and customs, it was natural to let Jesus, as John's merciful successor, take over the holly-king's. The holly was thus glorified beyond the oak.

Thus, the medieval bard, versed in an ancient pagan tradition, would tell the Christ story as another version of the birth, death, and resurrection of the God of the Waxing Year. Later in the discussion, however, Graves regrets the association of Jesus with the holly as poetically inept. " . . . It was the oak-king, not the holly-king, who was crucified on a T-shaped cross."

"The Battle of the Trees" in *Câd Goddeu* is a perfect example of what Graves calls "mythographic shorthand," which "records what seems to have been the most important religious event in pre-Christian Britain." Though the action involves only anthropomorphized trees and shrubs, the subject of this legend, Graves tells us, is a battle for religious mastery between the armies of Dôn, "the folk of the God whose mother is Danu," and the armies of Arawn ("Eloquence"), the King of Annwfn, the British underworld or city of the dead. In other words, it celebrates the supplanting of one priesthood and cult by another.

> As soon as one has mastered the elementary grammar and the accidence of myth, and built up a small vocabulary, and learned to distinguish seasonal myths from historical and iconotropic myths, one is surprised how close to the surface lie the explanations, lost since pre-Homeric times, of legends that are still religiously conserved as part of our European cultural inheritance.

All this lore about archaic alphabets and solar and lunar calendars seems to be evidence of a mythographic frame of reference that permeated a more poetic age wherein the Great Goddess was supreme. The book explores a prodigious range of such evidence covering northern and southern Europe, north Africa, and the Middle East.

When J. M. Cohen sent the typescript of his critical appraisal to Robert Graves for approval, Graves made notes in the margin. Cohen had written in reference to *The White Goddess:* "But the work is never for a moment a work of scholarship." Graves wrote the following mild comment beside this remark: "The odd thing is that it is becoming more and more accepted by serious historians and anthropologists and the flaw in the argument, if there is one, has never been found."

As a matter of fact, much of what Graves says about the widespread worship of the Great Goddess can be verified in a volume of impeccable scholarship: *The Cult of the Mother Goddess* by E. O. James. James makes no reference whatever to Graves, though he does mention in a footnote the psychological approach of Erich Neumann in *The Great Mother.* Actually, the idea is not new, having been proposed in the nineteenth century by certain anthropologists, particularly J. J. Bachofen in *Myth, Religion &*

Mother Right, originally published in German, but translated in 1967 for Princeton University Press. The James book, however, is undoubtedly less speculative and less biased by value judgments than Bachofen's.

Bachofen believed, as Graves does, that matriarchal forms of social structure preceded patriarchal ones, a notion in far more doubt among scholars than the existence of goddess cults. In some circumstances, Graves uses the term matrilinear, which is more easily argued than that political power rested in women. Matrilinear refers only to line of descent through the mother, not the father. It does not necessarily mean that the clan would be ruled in practical and political matters by women. Graves says that Samson's leaving his own clan to join Delilah indicates a matriarchal arrangement. Also, in the Garden of Eden story, Adam says "Therefore shall a man leave his father and his mother, and shall cleave unto his wife." Yet, in a patriarchal clan system, it is the woman, not the man, who must leave father and mother to cleave to her husband. (pp. 13-24)

The most idiosyncratic part of Graves's message, however, is not that society was once matrilinear or that goddess-worship once existed and inspired poets, but that goddess-worship is even now the only source of inspiration for the "true" poet. That is why, as already noted, Graves considers the modern world, dominated by business, politics, science, and technology—in other words, "Apollonian reason"—to be a barren wasteland for poetry.

With this remarkable book, Graves gathered from multiple streams of thought, a reservoir of ideas, metaphors, and images that he has used ever since in poetry and even in fiction. He has remained primarily a love poet, since the poet identifies with the God of the Waxing Year, regarding the Queen with mingled love and dread. This orientation undoubtedly initiated a burst of creative achievement. It may be, however, that it has limited the scope of his work in the long run. Some of his earlier poems on psychological and philosophical subjects are at least the equal of his Goddess poems. Moreover, some of his latest poems seem repetitive, as though he had run out of original ways to tell the "one story only." But he did find an appropriate fair haven for his talent, which allowed his essentially romantic nature to stay young and vigorous into old age. He has certainly proved that romanticism need not be cloyed with sentimentalism and stock phrases.

Graves must be at least partially responsible for renewed contemporary interest in myth in a number of academic fields. His complaint at the beginning of *The White Goddess* that myths are now studied only as "quaint relics of the nursery age of mankind" no longer seems accurate. Curiously, one concentration of interest in the subject is in Jungian psychology, an orientation he openly despised. Perhaps he "doth protest too much," since Jungian psychology could probably offer a rather credible explanation of Graves's obsession with the White Goddess.

In the Jungian conception of the subconscious the *anima,* the feminine element in a man's nature, has a function somewhat analogous to the Muse. It presumably may communicate to the conscious mind some of the knowl-edge that normally lies buried in the subconscious (which Graves claims he doesn't have). This energy is personified in men's dreams, the Jungians tell us, sometimes as young girl, sometimes as alluring woman, sometimes as terrifying hag. *The White Goddess,* both in historical belief and in Graves himself, might thus be a projection of a psychological archetype. (Whether there are such things as animas and archetypes, I do not pretend to know. That there are *literary* archetypes is more demonstrable.)

Nevertheless, Graves has had a salubrious effect upon poetry, insisting upon both inspiration and craftsmanship, ridiculing cliché and insincerity, promoting a meticulous study of the meanings and emotional overtones of words. These values will surely always be valid. Moreover, for the "now" generation, he demonstrates that even the remote past may impart some unique wisdom to the perceptive mind. (pp. 24-5)

> *Katherine Snipes, in her* Robert Graves, *Frederick Ungar Publishing Co., 1979, 222 p.*

Stephen Spender on Graves's attitudes toward women and poetry:

He was a man who, in spite of his buoyancy and grand manner, was mysterious in a great many respects—certainly as regards poetry. In his relationships with women, for instance—some of them were just women, others were white goddesses or they were muses of the white goddess. He regarded poetry as something separate and sacred—he probably had quite a lot of affairs but they were really not scandalous. They were all according to his system of muses, and if he found a lady who was a muse he presumably had an affair with her, but not necessarily. I don't think from one or two things that he said to me that sex was very important to him: love was important to him and I think that he did realise that if you have love for a woman, sex comes into it.

> *Stephen Spender, in his* "Graves and the Muses" The Listener, *Vol. 114, No. 2940, December 19 and 26, 1985.*

Peter Green   (essay date 1983)

[*Green is a distinguished English-born scholar and critic who has translated the Latin poets Juvenal and Ovid and written studies of Hellenistic civilization, Alexander the Great, and the Tudor poet John Skelton. In the following excerpt, he examines Graves's approach to poetry and the nature of his literary achievement, arguing that while Graves is a fine craftsman, his concentration on the White Goddess theme kept him from attaining status as a major poet.*]

I last saw Robert Graves in 1954, outside a Cambridge lecture room. He had just delivered his notorious (and, in parts, very funny) broadside against Yeats, Pound, Eliot, Auden, and Dylan Thomas, under the title "These be your gods, O Israel!", with sideswipes at "sick, muddle-headed, sex-mad D. H. Lawrence who wrote sketches for poems, but nothing more," and "poor, tortured Gerard Manley

Hopkins." Now he stood his ground like the old boxer he resembled, surrounded by an angry pack of Leavisites, uncomfortable in a tight blue serge suit, and looking vulnerable. Academic rage had been sharpened by his wickedly parodying—for his own very different ends—the moralistic ex cathedra name-calling of *Scrutiny.* There are few flies on Graves when it comes to literary in-fighting. Inveighing against rhetoric, his Cambridge Clark Lectures (afterwards published as *The Crowning Privilege*) scored a scintillating rhetorical success: they were so outrageous, so irresponsible in their polemic, so scurrilously witty, that no one, at the time, could resist them. Yet in retrospect they left behind a decidedly bad taste. Why?

There were, I think, two fundamental reasons. The first was this: however much Graves might claim to be defining his critical judgments, *qua* poet, in terms of "religious invocation of the Muse," it became clear, on reflection, that this attitude was little more than old-fashioned nineteenth-century romanticism, sauced up with Greco-Roman myth (itself transmuted, fairly early on, into mere literary convention). Like most conservative middle or late Victorian poets up to and including Housman, Graves held to the classical precept of imitating given models, while finding poetic excellence in lyric originality, the emotions (love above all), and anti-rationalism: his touchstones were tranced inspiration, the phrase that made one's beard turn against the razor, and so on. His superimposition on these criteria of what Laura Riding recently (1977) dismissed as "all the *White Goddess* trumpery" did not alter its essential nature. In his *Oxford Addresses on Poetry* (1961) Graves wrote: "The hairs stand on end, the eyes water, the throat constricts, the skin crawls, and a shiver runs down the spine when one writes or reads a true poem." We do not need to subscribe to primitive matriarchy or triadic goddess-worship to recognize the timeless force of this statement: it was a staple of the Romantic Movement long before Graves ever let the bees of Frazer and Jane Harrison come buzzing round his creative bonnet. In earlier poems he was candid enough to acknowledge his major influences. . . . About the only noticeable change has been that with age the Romantic influence has been largely ousted by that of the Metaphysicals. Graves's constant efforts to deny or redefine his literary roots remind me of Satie's remark on hearing that Ravel had refused the Legion of Honor: "Yes, but all his music accepts it."

The second point, a logical consequence of the first, concerned his brutal dismissal of every major poet—including Milton, Pope, and the later Wordsworth—who did not fit into this romantic pattern. In 1933 Siegfried Sassoon exactly pinpointed Graves's lifelong attitude during an angry exchange of letters, characterizing him as (on his own terms) "omniscient and infallible . . . and dismissing 90% of the world's best literature because it doesn't fit in with your own recipes for writing." Since the Romantic Movement was precisely what modernist poets had been fighting against, out *they* went too: Eliot (despite his French-inherited preoccupation with verbal precision, one of Graves's fetishes), Pound, Auden, *et hoc genus omne.* Though Graves knows French well enough to write poems in that language, like Eliot, on sexually tricky subjects

(e.g., the witty *"Dans un seul lit"*), he seems to have known nothing about Mallarmé's efforts to "purify the language of the tribe"; and in general—despite his European base, chosen originally for its climate and cheap cost of living—his interest (with one or two fortuitous exceptions) has always been exclusively in Anglo-American literature. Indeed, his lifelong determination, in or out of self-imposed exile, to play the anti-Establishment *enfant terrible* tends to make one forget what a conventional, conservative old blimp he is at heart: even his distaste for *vers libre* represents a residual prejudice of the Squirearchy. (pp. 89-91)

Whom, then, did Graves set up as the worthier alternative to the Eliot-Pound-Auden tradition? Siegfried Sassoon, Robert Frost, E. E. Cummings, John Crowe Ransom, Norman Cameron, W. H. Davies, Laura Riding, and Alun Lewis (but not, significantly, Keith Douglas, an altogether better war poet in Graves's own Metaphysical style). The list is an odd mixture of personal friends and the old Georgian rural rear guard. Graves's argument has always been that the modernist movement represented a blind-alley divagation from the mainstream of English literature which he himself represented; but anyone who so sedulously pastiches his predecessors (however well), and whose instinct, far from wanting to break new linguistic or structural ground, is for conservation and proper definition in all areas (Fowler, as it were, rather than Chomsky), will always be open to the charge of reaction and dilettantism. On literature, too often, Graves sounds like a priest or theologian: not surprisingly, since that is precisely how he sees himself. And whatever our opinion of his preferred poets as individuals (Frost and Ransom, certainly, are candidates for anyone's twentieth-century canon), it is clear that his thesis, when followed through, produces an absurdly lopsided view of modern English poetry. Worse, it gives the unmistakable impression of logrolling. The poets approved by Graves all write, or wrote, very much in his own romantic mode (true even of Cummings, despite his typographical affectations: Riding is a special case). Worse still, some of the poets excluded did just the things Graves prescribed, and, unforgivably, did them rather better.

William Empson, for instance, not only took over the Graves-Riding critical method and showed, in *Seven Types of Ambiguity,* what a first-class mind could make of it; he also beat Graves at his own poetic game, both technically and in achieving that metaphysical *frisson* on which Graves so prided himself. . . . "Empson," Graves . . . declared, "is as clever as a monkey & I do not like monkeys"—presumably forgetting that in *The Marmosite's Miscellany* (1925) he had impersonated one. Both Yeats and Dylan Thomas caught, again and again, that genuine lyric singing perfection vouchsafed so seldom to Graves; both (not, perhaps, by coincidence) have come in for some of his most savage critical manhandling. The case of Yeats is particularly interesting, since he and Graves share so many characteristics: Anglo-Irish romanticism, an interest in Donne and Blake, and—above all—a crackpot lunar mythopoeia to keep the metaphorical stockpot bubbling. Both, also, changed their poetic style in mid-career. But Yeats won a Nobel Prize and universal fame: Graves, whose own later work here and there shows Yeatsian echoes, dissected Yeats's anthology pieces with malice, made bitchy remarks in his public lectures about the effects of Yeats's Voronoff operation (a case of pot calling kettle black), and carefully steered round the great poems of Yeats's burning old age. Graves may have come within spitting distance of "Sailing to Byzantium," but spit was all he could do. Eliot, who in *The Waste Land* (midwifed by Pound, another of Graves's bêtes noires) used Frazerian and other myths more effectively than Graves ever did in the poems that were spin-offs from his *White Goddess* phase, comes off only slightly better. Auden not only ran rings round Graves as a technical versifier—despite his knowing asides about the arcana of metre, the trip wires for critics who'd never heard, say, of Skeltonic rhymeroyal, Graves has always had a rhythmically clumsy ear—but in poems like "Lay your sleeping head, my love" showed himself a more moving erotic lyricist. In *The Common Asphodel* (1949) Graves argued that Milton's "virtuous scorn" for Skelton really concealed "retrospective jealousy." Since he has always had a trick of attributing his own poetic weaknesses to others—for example, his charge against Donne in *The Crowning Privilege* of finding one or two fine lyric lines for a poem and then padding the rest—it seems likely that his animus against Yeats and Auden may have a similar raison d'être.

Graves's view of the modernists typifies his approach to poets he dislikes. His criticisms are strictly ad hominem, and he has no truck with the contemporary fashion of separating person from persona. For him, as for all ideologues, art and life-style are one. This is a fundamental element in his approach to literature, and always has been: it deserves closer scrutiny than it has hitherto received. We should not dismiss it, with a quick embarrassed shrug, as mere eccentric affectation. Let us look at some of his charges. Auden he has, at various times, dismissed from the poetic elect as a fraud, a homosexual (the old Fusilier always tends to look askance at fairies), a parlor pink, and a plagiarizer (in particular from Laura Riding: a charge no more seriously sustainable than in Graves's own case from, say, Skelton or Coleridge). Similarly he has damned Roy Campbell as a fascist, D. G. Rossetti as a "wop," Henry Williamson as a pious crook, and Yeats as a spiritualist ("inconsistent with being a poet," presumably through plugging into the wrong hot line). MacNeice was out for keeping a borzoi and throwing plates back at Nancy Coldstream when she threw them at him ("You must never offer violence to a woman"). Lack of front-line military service in wartime are black marks against Yeats, Auden ("the rats return to the unsunk ship," he wrote in 1945), and, of all people, Virgil, who "never bore arms either for or against Caesar." In refusing a letter of support to Tambimuttu, the editor of *Poetry London,* he added, gratuitously, "And I heard a good deal about his private life: I hope it was all lies." Eliot, who knew his man, judged, correctly, that there was no hope of getting Graves to sign a petition for Pound's release from St. Elizabeth's Hospital. Graves fudged on this one, first telling Eliot that he refused because Pound lacked poetic merit, later claiming that he never interfered with the internal affairs of another country. It seems clear that his real objection was to Pound's treason. Of D. H. Lawrence he remarked: "He

was a bum poet, of course, *being a bum person*" (my italics): for him poetry has always been, in the fullest sense, a way of life. The criteria are moral rather than literary: Graves (like the ancient Greeks he studies) would not separate the two. Sexual puritanism, too, sometimes fuels his insults. Thus, he condemned Dylan Thomas as a Welsh demagogic masturbator who, in addition to not paying his bills, was syphilitic. When told that Thomas had no venereal disease, his argument was that while Thomas might not be suffering from the complaint ("at present," he added, darkly), "*philosophically* he was riddled with it."

In short, the bad taste left by Graves's Clark Lectures was generated by that familiar phenomenon, unacknowledged (and indeed possibly unconscious) literary jealousy, rationalized into an exclusive poetic credo, and applied with all the minimally scrupulous passion of the committed ideologue. Graves professed himself shocked by Yeats's comment to him (perhaps made mischievously, knowing Graves's proclivities, with the Hesiodic Muses as well as Nietzsche in mind) that "we poets should be good liars." Yet in 1944 Graves himself had written to Basil Liddell Hart: "To lie is a sacred duty to all people who wish to uphold sacred traditions." The stance implied is revealing. Graves, throughout his literary career, has always been committed—in exactly the same way as a Catholic or a Communist—to an exclusive program of belief that claimed the monopoly of truth. This explains, even if it does not always justify, a good many of his more outré assertions and inconsistencies. Poetry is his religion, his credo: he is at heart a proselytizer, who thinks in terms of disciples and heretics, and has, during a long literary life, maintained a fairly active Inquisition (as *The Crowning Privilege* demonstrates). Belief, for Graves, has never been a merely literary matter. Very early on it began—sometimes with disastrous results—to dictate its exponent's life-style. His life and work have been intertwined in such a way that it is almost impossible to treat them apart; and some of his more enigmatic poems—**"The Blow-Fly," "Beware, madam!", "The Succubus"** or **"A Love Story,"** for example—make real sense only when one possesses their private context.

The White Goddess may be, as one critic plausibly suggests, "a gigantic metaphor," "the testament of a practicing poet," but there are disquieting signs that for much of his life Graves was bent on acting out the metaphor he had created. This is nowhere more apparent than in his notorious succession of "incarnated" Muses: five of them, beginning with Laura Riding, the prototype, and proceeding by way of Judith ("unmistakable, wielding a Cretan axe"), Canadian Margot, and Mexican-American Laraçuen to teen-age Julie, presumably the last of the line ("Angels, goddesses, bitches, all have edged away," MacNeice wrote). Between them they have generated untold trouble—and (Riding apart) very few first-rate poems. It's hard, especially when looking back on the Graves-Riding partnership, which habitually enveloped common-orgarden human urges in a fog of cosmic high-mindedness, not to agree with the cynics who explained the older Graves as a senescent but puritanical Don Juan who wanted extramarital sex *and* a good poetic justification for it. Auden (who, despite Graves's repeated attacks, always maintained the liveliest respect for the older man's work, and backed him for the Oxford Chair of Poetry) claimed that Graves once (c. 1960) boasted to him that "he's the oldest poet still fucking." In itself a heartening assertion, this becomes one more item to add to the creative and emotional confusion, the shattering quarrels and shaky reconciliations, the revamped dogmas, fallen stars, and grandiose self-deceptions with which Graves's career has been littered. In 1961 he assured an Oxford audience that "the Muse is 'the perpetual other woman,' never the poet's wife." Who gets fucked, and who goes home?

The sacred duty of lying in a good, that is, an acceptable, poetic cause (the end justifies the means) has also been responsible for some of Graves's more suspect flirtations with the sirens of scholarship and pseudo-scholarship. Metaphor *The White Goddess* may be, but it also tries to have it both ways by using the expository mode of academic research to imply that the metaphor rests on some sort of solid factual base. *The Greek Myths* (1955) took this process one step further by buttressing—in what purported to be a reliable work of reference—a whole mass of tendentious interpretation and lunatic-fringe etymologizing with the impressive paraphernalia of seeming scholarship, including detailed footnotes and references (often transferred wholesale, errors and all, from some uncited secondary work). The Cambridge scholar M. J. C. Hodgart put his finger, precisely, on what was wrong with this approach when he wrote (*Twentieth Century*, February 1955): "A good poet tells the truth by the deliberate use of fictions, while Mr. Graves weaves a fantasy out of facts."

The Greek Myths, as it happens, marked my own first personal contact with Graves (I had been reading him since the 1930s). I was already conscious of having rather more in common with him than made for complete psychological comfort—not least a taste for intelligent and dominating women. We had both won scholarships to Charterhouse and had a classical education. We were both caught up in a world war, during which we both corresponded on literary matters with Sir Edward Marsh. We both took on an academic job which we dropped within a year, firmly determined never to accept a salaried post again, but to live by writing. We both had a special interest in Greek religion and magic. In 1953 I was also in the middle of writing my own first historical novel. Later (without ever indulging in conscious emulation: only now have I come to tot this account up) I was to spend some years as a man of letters on a Mediterranean island, to publish a monograph on Skelton, to translate Roman authors for Penguin Classics, even to live in a literary ménage of which the odder elements had singular parallels (as I now know) in Graves's own household. If reader-identification can give insights, I should, by anyone's standards, have Graves figured out. The crucial difference, of course (why of course?), was that I totally lacked, and lack, Graves's driving obsession to ferret out arcane truth by way of dotty theories. This indeed was what brought us into contact, since while reviewing Rachel Levy's *The Sword from the Rock* (*Spectator,* May 15, 1953) I referred to "a rank growth of symbolical exegesis, where fantasy borrowed a disreputable cloak of half-digested scholarship to prove

any and every theory: a road strewn with primitive matriarchies and incredible etymologies, that culminated in Robert Graves' *White Goddess.*"

This was inviting trouble; and sure enough, on June 5, from his Mallorcan retreat, the Sage of Deyá came back at me with a packed column of symbolical exegesis, half-digested scholarship, and incredible etymologies lifted wholesale (as I soon had good reason to know) from *The Greek Myths,* to the forthcoming publication of which Graves referred. In the issue of June 12 I had great fun demolishing this rickety edifice, and remarked that I looked forward to Graves's encyclopedia of Greek myths and pseudo-myths with the liveliest interest. Perhaps Graves caught the metaphorical rubbing of anticipatory critical hands; at all events, instead of the long and acrimonious *Spectator* correspondence I was expecting, I got a charming personal letter from Graves, inviting me to go through the proofs of the book in question, presumably on the sensible principle of "If you can't beat them, get *them* to join *you.*" Unwisely, I accepted. For the next few weeks not only I but also my first wife (a Cambridge-trained archaeologist and Egyptologist who had turned to novel-writing) wrestled with the Hydra we had taken on. Crazy theories proliferated. The moment we lopped off one lunatic head another popped up. Each galley generated more than its own length in annotation and remonstrance. Some of the citations were wrong; others bore little if any reference to what they were supposed to document. Most of the (allegedly misinterpreted) ancient pictures described by Graves were figments of his luxuriant imagination. When my wife objected to this kind of thing Graves wrote back: "I love baiting the scholars with moonshine and green cheese." After a few chapters we gave up the unequal struggle and left *The Greek Myths* to the Cretan or other axes of its professional reviewers. The experience, nevertheless, had been illuminating. Among other things, it impelled me to quarry into Graves's earlier work to seek the genesis of this strange (and, it then seemed to us, disquietingly dishonest) *furor poeticus.* The rearrangement or falsification of facts to prove a point turned out to be nothing new. **"Ovid in Exile,"** for instance, a poem long suppressed, contrived to get every single important fact about that much-maligned poet wrong except the fact of his banishment, simply in order to make a psychological point (*"post coitum triste omne animal"*) which Graves may well have believed, but to which Ovid was flatly opposed. Yet only now, with the biographical facts beginning to fall into place, can the true significance of Graves's various persistent obsessions begin to be appreciated.

The most remarkable fact to emerge is how *consistent* Graves has been, at the deepest level, from the very beginning. If his literary career shows a series of doctrinal upheavals and apostasies, the inner psychological forces driving him seem to have remained constant. Apart from an innocent, nonphysical homoerotic friendship at school (par for the adolescent course, I should have thought, even if the object of Graves's pure affection *did* shock him silly by getting arrested for propositioning a Canadian corporal), Graves has been fiercely heterosexual all his life, with a marked taste—modified only in his later years—for aggressive, demanding, cruel or capricious women, easily elevated into the role of goddess or Muse. At the same time there has always been a marked feminine streak in his own Protean literary psyche. Though he declared (*On Poetry, 1969*, p. 245) that "no man can decently speak in a woman's name," he has done so twice himself, in startlingly convincing impersonations of Nausicaä (*Homer's Daughter*) and Marie Powell (*Wife to Mr Milton*). As early as 1917 he was writing to Robert Nichols that "my idea of a poet is a woman suffering all the hardships of a man." The creative act of writing, of course, gave him a chance to "distance" this trait (as he also did with his Baudelairean nose for decay and filth): indeed, much of the poetic tension in his life and art has been generated by a violent conflict between his powerful sexual urges and his fiercely puritanical German-Irish conscience. ***Down, wanton, down*** indeed. The ideal, for Graves, must be lifted above mere rutting nature. . . . The sensual, guilty poet, ithyphallic yet high-minded, had a desperate need for some ideal—romantic, ritual, purificatory—in which his erotic impulses could be redeemed: not merely the Muse Incarnate, but a complete metaphorical (and metaphysical) system to combat the ghosts of terror and self-disgust that haunted his life.

Other characteristic traits were visible as early as his service in World War I with the Royal Welch Fusiliers. In Siegfried Sassoon's *Memoirs of an Infantry Officer,* where "David Cromlech" is an undisguised portrait of Graves, we find him already "a positive expert at putting people's backs up unintentionally," already making arrogant excluding assertions, for instance that "all sports except boxing, football and rock climbing were snobbish and silly," already spouting theories about "who really wrote the Bible," and claiming (presumably after reading Samuel Butler) that "Homer was a woman." The Shavian animus he was to display against St. Paul in *King Jesus* had long before been expressed more succinctly in verse: "If Mother Church was proud / Of her great cuckoo son / He bit off her simple head / Before he had done." All his life Graves was to retain the passion (a familiar staple, alas, of the lunatic fringe) for ferreting out new hermetic explanations—allegedly missed by all orthodox scholars over the centuries, or else the victim of Establishment censorship—for everything from Greek myth to the Gospels, from *David Copperfield* to Omar Khayyam. Yet in the last resort we should be grateful, since the same impulse has produced, not only his mythography, but also the great historical novels. In both cases, his aim is to recover lost truth. "To bring the dead to life," he wrote in one haunting poem, "is no great magic; blow on a dead man's embers, and a live flame will start." (The offhand attitude is characteristic; Graves has always, perversely, dismissed *I, Claudius* and its successors as potboilers.) What he rather pretentiously terms his analeptic method is no different from the intuitive flash (similarly based on exhaustive preparation) that heralds a scientific breakthrough. R. G. Collingwood, in *The Idea of History,* likewise propounded the notion that a writer in possession of the requisite knowledge and sympathetic intuition could *think himself into the truth* of any given historical scene or event. From Graves's first historical fiction, *My Head! My Head!* (1925), which set out to explain, first, the relation of Elisha and the Shunamite, and second, the secret of Moses'

magic, his prime aim has been not to boil pots but to solve mysteries, and the more arcane the mystery the better. The epigraph to *My Head! My Head!* is taken from Skelton's *Speke, Parot:* "Thus myche Parott hathe opynlye expreste; / Let se who daré maken up the reste"—a challenge Graves has never been able to resist.

He has sometimes referred to this obsession of his as a weakness for puzzle-solving, allegedly inherited from his Irish father. He is fond of contrasting this side of his ancestry with the genes he supposedly acquired, through his mother's line, from the great German historian Leopold von Ranke. Here he shows a certain sly irony. Ranke's ideal—indeed, the only thing for which many people remember him—was his determination to write history *wie es eigentlich gewesen,* "as it really happened." Graves, of course, makes an identical claim; but if Ranke (a methodical rationalist if ever there was one) could return from the dead and observe his descendant's cavalier treatment of evidence, he might feel something more than miffed to hear Graves boast of having taken over *his* historical methods.

Sassoon, with blunt directness, told "Cromlech" he was a "fad-ridden crank." Some of the fads, as we have seen, stuck for life. *Paradise Lost* (already in 1916!) was being pooh-poohed by Graves as "that moribund concoction," while Skelton was upheld, characteristically, as "one of the few really good poets" (the theological excluding principle again: "only five writers in England and America . . . were any good," he assured Sassoon). Music, except for the Border ballads, Graves wrote off *in toto.* At the same time Sassoon was alert to the mutability of Graves's literary dogmas. "Many of my friend's quiddities," he later wrote, "were as nicely rounded, and as evanescent, as the double smoke rings he was so adroit at blowing." (In ***Fairies and Fusiliers*** Graves had used smoke rings as an image of divine creation.) In 1933, during one of his bitter quarrels with Graves, Sassoon told him: "I had to adapt myself to *your* ground . . . which meant swallowing a series of theories about poetry, &c., which you have since discarded. . . . " On Graves's side, these dogmatic shifts of stance (as in most creeds or ideologies) tended to involve a thoroughgoing erasure of past "errors." It is in this light that we should view the constant radical revision of the ***Collected Poems.*** The technique was applied elsewhere: for instance, after 1939 Graves dropped any reference to Laura Riding from his *Who's Who* entry, and made similar excisions from the 1957 edition of his early autobiography, *Goodbye to All That.*

From a literary viewpoint, indeed, the changes have very often been for the worse (whatever embarrassing enthusiasms or discarded dogma may have been eliminated in the process). . . . As critics have not been slow to point out, there is something suspect, in literary terms, about the criteria governing Graves's dismissal or rewriting of poems in successive editions of his ***Collected Poems*** (in itself a downright misleading title). **"Recalling War,"** for instance, has been dumped simply because Graves had changed his own attitude to war. But by now this should not surprise us, and on Graves's own terms is logical enough. If his poetic *oeuvre* embodies his spiritual and moral testament, expressed in terms which poetry alone can encompass, then revisionism (human nature being what it is) will be built into it almost by definition. It has been objected that revisionism destroys the record of evolution in a creed; an obtuse complaint, I have always thought, since that is precisely what it is meant to do.

It follows that for most readers the available body of Graves's poetry—as currently represented by *New Collected Poems* (1977), already, ironically enough, out of print and unobtainable—is, to put it mildly, lopsided. The 1977 volume has added 160 pages of new poems to that of 1965, and few of these diffuse, emotionally self-indulgent Muse-offerings seem likely to enhance Graves's reputation. New readers, ploughing through a sea of mild erotic marginalia, may justifiably wonder what all the fuss was about. Once or twice they will get a glimpse of the old, *echt* Graves. . . . Yet even here the plangency is reduced for those who have no knowledge of Graves's personal life on Deyá since the last war, and who are unaware that Marpessa, in Greek mythology, was courted by Apollo (the god of, among other things, poetry), but preferred Idas, a mortal. In his foreword to the 1938 *Collected Poems*—the last to come under Riding's direct influence—Graves had written: "Poems either do or do not stand by their poetic meaning: learned explanation cannot give them more than they possess." Too many of the later ones demand just such glossing. . . . (pp. 92-104)

What tends, except by specialists, to be forgotten is that Graves, in the course of his long poetic career, has excised from the corpus very nearly as much as he has chosen to preserve. Only those with access to rare book collections in major libraries can, with careful research, follow his trail from 1916 onwards. We are dependent on his judgment, and it is often shaky, on occasion whimsically perverse. When a full variorum edition is finally published, it will undoubtedly spring surprises. True, a sizable proportion of the rejects are nobody's loss: watered-down *fin-de-siècle* pastiche, embarrassing rural trivia, exercises in the manner of Keats or Housman. (It would be hard to name another serious modern poet who has published so high a proportion of really bad work.) Too often, however, careless panning has tossed out small nuggets with the dross. **"Star-Talk,"** for example ("Are you awake, Gemelli, this frosty night?"), written just after Graves left school, may have been condemned as an anthology piece, but remains fresh, witty, and original. The war poems, in particular, are gone *en bloc,* and considering the indelible impact that exposure to battle made on Graves, this seems difficult to justify.

Again, it is true that many of them—flat, fey, or gory; pickled Kipling, Brooke-and-water—hardly deserve resurrection. Bad imitations of the last trend but one seldom inspire. But who could resist the offbeat quality in **"Limbo"**:

> And then one night relief comes, and we go
>   Miles back into the sunny cornland where
> Babies like tickling, and where tall white horses
> Draw the plough leisurely in quiet courses . . .

—or the marvelous, and moving, conceit of **"The Dead Fox Hunter":**

> . . . what's for him to do
> Up there, but hunt the fox?
> Angelic choirs? No, justice must provide
> For one who rode straight and in hunting died.
>
> So if Heaven had no Hunt before he came,
>   Why, it must find one now:
> If any shirk and doubt they know the game,
>   There's one to teach them how:
> And the whole host of Seraphim complete
> Must jog in scarlet to his opening Meet.

There were ghosts, too, glimpsed on postwar streets—perhaps not so different, after all, from those Eliot saw—a sense that (as his bête noire Yeats said) "Things fall apart, the centre cannot hold": yet who but Graves could have taken the Norse myth of Audhumla, the First Cow, and used it to tie off a vision of the Waste Land?

> Here now is chaos once again,
> Primaeval mud, cold stones and rain,
> Here flesh decays and blood drips red,
> And the Cow's dead, the old Cow's dead.

It is, precisely, that wry toughness, that ability to impose a pattern on chaos, which most impresses us in this early period—together with a curious vernal innocence, an Eden vision, which haunts even where it sentimentalizes, as in **"An English Wood":** "Here, poised in quietude / Calm elementals brood / On the set shape of things." **"A Dedication of Three Hats,"** on the other hand (the three being tin helmet, mortarboard, and foolscap for poetry) salutes the postwar era with all the wit of Auden's 1947 Phi Beta Kappa poem, "Under Which Lyre," and with no less technical brilliance.

From 1926, the year of the first encounter with Riding, Graves's poetry changed: became denser, bleaker, less romantic, more pessimistic, more consciously intellectual. Like Empson, Graves was now learning a style from a despair. The 1938 **Collected Poems,** assembled under Riding's critical scrutiny, jettisoned earlier work wholesale, including the powerful **"This is Noon,"** an erotic pseudo-sonnet with effective echoes of Shakespeare and Wyatt. Now, and in the White Goddess period that followed, Graves began writing many more *à clef* poems—often, but not always, camouflaged by mythopoeic trappings—and personal considerations seem, at times, to have determined their fate. There can be little doubt that the only reason for eliminating from postwar editions that superb poem **"The Nape of the Neck"** was its close, and known, association with Riding, who took the title of her own first published collection from its opening line. . . . But perhaps the most inexplicable omission—and one of the few White Goddess poems that really works, which makes its removal all the odder—is **"The Destroyer,"** Graves's stinging indictment of world conquerors in the mythic person of Perseus. . . . Since Graves's flat, expository style (*simplex munditiis,* as Horace said) seldom rises to the horripilating lyric pitch that is his ideal, it seems doubly perverse of him to sacrifice to vagrant revisionism one of the rare poems he has written that does unquestionably blunt razor blades. (pp. 105-07)

Crucial though the key events of Graves's life are in relation to his achievement, it seems clear that final clarification must wait until all the main characters in that long creative drama are dead, and that even then the chance of an objective, balanced judgment remains slim. Will it be any easier to assess his place in English letters? Of the mainstream, yet always standing aloof from its current thrust, he is (partly, of course, by intention) a teasing paradox. His traditionalism may get him dismissed, by some, as a Horatian *laudator temporis acti,* but (as he would be the first to point out) there's a good chance that Horace—and Graves—will still be around when the Beat poets and the epigoni of the Black Mountain school are long forgotten. The massive indifference Graves has always shown to changing poetic fashion has its advantages—not least since the change tends to be cyclic, giving a cynical onlooker, eventually, the chance to say: "This is where I came in." From his Spanish eyrie he has watched one ism after the other end up on the literary trash heap; he was the first to appreciate the mordant irony of his sudden rediscovery by the Movement poets of the '60s, the revived taste for metrical formalism and metaphysical wit which he—old scapegoat out in the cultural wilderness—had never abandoned. For Graves neo-realism held nothing new, being (as he saw it) no more than a long-overdue return to normality. He should, then, be enjoying a triumph; yet something is still lacking. As one critic puts it, "If pride, determination, length of dedicated service, and courage in the field were the only criteria"—he might also have tipped in craftsmanship and technical discipline—"Robert Graves would be second to no poet of this century, not even to Yeats" (Patrick J. Keane, *A Wild Civility,* 1980). Unfortunately, they aren't. Vision and universality remain central, and this is where Graves falls short. Roy Campbell's epigram on South African novelists comes to mind:

> You praise the firm restraint with which they
>   write:
> I'm with you there, of course;
> They use the snaffle and the bit all right,
> But where's the bloody horse?

Not, it seems safe to say, in the same paddock as loopy interpretations of Ogham tree-alphabets, or unofficially deified young ladies prowling round Deyá with invisible double axe in hand, and psychological decapitation in mind. For Graves, the horse has been handicapped throughout by a series of crippling taboos and even more restrictive totems, from the ghastly good taste of Georgian romanticism right through to the archaising straitjacket of the Muse-Goddess. Why, one asks oneself, has this professional literary bruiser always punished himself by insisting on fighting with one hand tied behind his back?

Until 1926 Graves was essentially a Georgian pasticheur, with a talent for derivative variations on given themes—one legacy, I suspect, of being forced to practice classical verse composition at school. While Pound was masterminding the Imagists, while Eliot was writing "Prufrock" and Joyce completing *Ulysses,* Graves, deaf to the voices of innovation (though of the same generation as the innovators) was turning out stuff like this:

> Come comrades, roam we round the mead
> Where couch the sleeping kine;
> The breath of night blows soft indeed,
> And the jolly yellow moon doth shine . . .

The watershed change came with his introduction to Laura Riding. Though Riding herself now—understandably—exaggerates both the exclusiveness and the lasting effect of the influence she had over him, there can be no doubt that at the time her energy and self-confidence, his psychological need to submit himself *in toto* to a dominant female mentor ("The female mind is the judge," Riding pronounced, "and the male mind the subject of judgment") between them produced, at an appalling price, remarkable results. Riding's obvious weakness was the recurrent temptation (fully shared by Graves) to define universal poetic principles in terms of her own practice; but she did have the queen bee's natural instinct for bringing out the best (i.e., her own beliefs) in others. Graves set her up—at the time nothing loath, whatever she may say now—as a Muse-Goddess, dutifully quarreled with all his friends on her behalf, and encouraged her to treat him like dirt; but she did, in the process, scour away the worst of his muzzy-headed Georgian flimflam, and instilled in him (perhaps from the Viennese tradition of Karl Kraus) a precise concern with words and meanings. "Laura," he wrote to Sassoon, "is gradually teaching me to ratiocinate clearly." Laureate, now, in a rather different sense from his idol Skelton, he also sharpened up his poetic style and extended its range. It is surprising, on examination, what a large percentage of his poetic output—including much of his best work—is not lyric in the strict sense at all, but rather wit, satire, metaphysical fancy, epigram or *vers d'occasion.*

Robert Graves, circa 1961.

Yet the sad, clear truth, so obvious in retrospect, is how incompatible Graves and Riding were from the start, in literary no less than personal terms. Joyce Wexler, in *Laura Riding's Pursuit of Truth* (1979), correctly points out that "Riding's need for stability impelled her to seek a constant value to believe in, and like many others looking for reliable values in the 1920s, she tried to make a religion of art." So, of course, did Graves—and yet how different their approach! Riding's cerebral abstractions (Auden called her the only philosophical poet alive), even when given wriggling embodiment in a tour de force like "The Quids," were bound to produce abrasive tensions when teamed up with Graves's own more visceral, sensuous imagery. She was an intellectual, while he, for all his wide learning, was not. ("What *is* this bloody *néant?*" he once inquired, apropos Sartre.) Though he dutifully did his best to follow the linguistic and conceptual rules she laid down for him, it went against the grain. She tried to inflate him into a major thinker (just as, he claimed, Milton tried to blow himself up from a minor into a major poet), but the intellectual oxygen she used was—in every sense—too heady, and ended by giving him a bad case of the literary bends. Both, as time went on, produced a crop of psychosomatic symptoms: boils, eyeaches, migraines, fainting fits. Graves convinced himself these were due to her enforced regime of sexual abstinence. By the end both of them were thoroughly unwell. One way and another, the events of April 1939 were probably inevitable. The intriguing question remains: how far was Graves's subsequent excursion into White Goddess mythopoeia a mere vulgarized surrogate—as Riding herself and, up to a point, Randall Jarrell seem to assume—for the loss of Riding's personal domination and tutelage?

All the evidence suggests that that streak of hysterical (and heavily repressed) masochism was there in Graves's make-up from the very beginning. It is also true that (as I suggested earlier) there is something fundamentally dishonest, as well as synthetic, about Graves's whole approach to ancient myth, which he seems to have seen, in effect, as the raw material for poetic exploitation and pseudo-religious self-therapy, and which he was quite ready to manipulate in his own favor. Riding's charge of "sham poetic religiosity" has a certain substance. (It is certainly true that his iconic obsession with an abstract Muse-figure tends to rob her living avatars, in his verse, of all individuality.) Seymour-Smith [Martin Seymour-Smith in his *Robert Graves: His Life and Works*, 1982] says that there is "little or nothing in the Graves canon that suggests itself for inclusion in [that famous anthology of risibly bad verse] *The Stuffed Owl*"; but to my mind Graves's wildly overpraised White Goddess poem **"Darien"** qualifies immediately, and it's tempting to apply to it the same irreverent techniques that Graves himself, with Riding, deployed to such lethal effect in *The Perfect Modern Lyric*. The narrator is addressing one Darien (place rather than person, one had thought, but no matter), who appears to be the narrator's son by a Muse whose ideas of sexual consummation involve the use of a Cretan double axe on her partner. We are further required to believe that pregnancy in this lady could be, indeed was, induced by eyeball contact, and was followed by the narrator's decapitation, leaving the Muse swinging his severed head by the hair, maenad-

fashion. Thus, unless the unfortunate consort is emulating the articulate severed head of Orpheus, it does not at once appear how he has survived to tell the story, or to discuss Mama with the fruit of this bizarre union. **"Darien,"** with its sub-Freudian displacement-fantasies of sadism and castration, is, in short, pretentious, if revealing, bosh. Fortunately, Graves normally keeps his eccentric psyche under better control, so that his queen bees or female spiders do their murderous work in a somewhat more plausible context.

What, then, is the sum of the whole matter? Perhaps two dozen poems (I doubt if Graves himself would claim more) will stand the test of time, though probably my list would not coincide with his. Whether this is a fair return on the Muse's part for a lifetime's surrender is arguable. Graves describes himself as a minor poet; and, bearing in mind the self-imposed limitations of this Muse's acolyte, the description is probably a fair assessment. (In **"To Juan at the Winter Solstice,"** another over-rated poem, cobbled together from the mythic property-box, he wrote: "There is one story and one story only"—the perennial hazard of all official religious, including Marxist, poetry.) Katherine Snipes's judgment, in her *Robert Graves* (1979), is perhaps the fairest: "While not truly a great poet, he has written some very good poems at almost every stage of his career." Obstinately timeless, he can afford to ignore trendy verdicts. He is a poet's poet, a fine craftsman justly honored by his peers. Above all, he has inspired generations, win or lose, with the *idea* of what a poetic vocation should be. Those "green fields of unrest" that lie at the heart of his last poem form an apt coda to his career. He would, I think, be proud to echo the claim of that other, equally tough, equally woman-oriented poet, the seventh-century B.C. Greek colonist Archilochus, who declared: "I am both the War-God's servant, and have understanding of the Muses' lovely gifts." In his rugged, smoldering, island-bound old age he stands as a symbol for something above and beyond plain tangible achievement. (pp. 114-19)

Peter Green, "All That Again," in Grand Street, *Vol. 2, No. 2, Winter, 1983, pp. 89-119.*

Robert Richman (essay date 1988)

[*Richman is an American critic, poet, and editor. In the following essay, he argues that Graves's poetry fails to achieve a broad range of emotional and thematic concerns as a result of its overly literal conception of poetic inspiration.*]

At the time of his death in December 1985, at the age of ninety, on the island of Majorca, Robert Graves had long been a legendary figure in the literary world. This was due in part to his immense production: nineteen novels and short-story collections, sixty-three books of nonfiction (including translations), and fifty-six volumes of poetry. Because of this extraordinary productivity, Graves is the only serious writer of our time whose career was on a scale we associate more with the previous century than with our own.

Yet there is another and more important reason why Robert Graves became a figure of legend in the literary world of his time. This was his reputation as a rebel. Graves's fame as a cranky individualist derives, first of all, from his well-known autobiography, *Goodbye to All That,* published to coincide with his departure from England in 1929. (He went to Majorca, where he remained until the Spanish Civil War caused him to leave in 1936; ten years later he returned to the island and lived out the rest of his life there.) No reader of *Goodbye to All That* will forget Graves's bitter account of his youth in Edwardian England—especially the grim years at Charterhouse, the public school he attended between 1910 and 1914—or his moving portrayal of the war that devastated his generation and almost cost him his life.

Graves was part of the literary generation that was profoundly altered by the war. For some, the response took a political form. In the case of Graves, the war only confirmed what he had learned to despise at school. To him, the nastiness of the generals was a larger and more lethal version of the nastiness of his masters at Charterhouse. As he writes in *Goodbye to All That:*

> . . . we [the soldiers] could no longer see the war as one between trade rivals: its continuance seemed merely a sacrifice of the idealistic younger generation to the stupidity and self-protective alarm of the elder.

Especially vile to Graves was the generals' cynical misuse of the army's regimental pride. His war experiences resulted in Graves's permanent alienation from his country.

When Graves left England in 1929, however, he was fleeing something more than painful memories. He was also running away from the modern world. Poetry, he said, was his "ruling passion," and he had come to believe that the modern world had little use for poetry, or for the myths that, in his view, it was derived from. The literary and historical works Graves began producing once he settled in Majorca—works which consistently confounded critics and scholars—were clearly conceived by Graves as a means of avenging himself on the modern world he found so loathsome.

These books were not the only strange things emanating from the island, however. Rumors of a liberated sexual atmosphere in the Graves's household also filtered to the world beyond Majorca. It was said—correctly—that Graves shared his bed with numerous "muses." It was also said—incorrectly—that Graves had fathered half the children born on Majorca between 1929 and 1975. So well known were Graves's emancipated views on such matters that in the Sixties Majorca became a mecca for hippies seeking escape from conventional moral taboos. Some no doubt also came for advice on the proper consumption of hallucinogens, the use of which Graves had advocated in his *Oxford Addresses on Poetry* (1962).

There are some ironies, to be sure, in Graves's posture as a rebel. For one thing, although the content of many of his books is unconventional, the writing itself isn't. The poems are in fact written in a traditional style. His prosody might even be described as conservative. In *Goodbye to All That,* he attempted to account for his dual literary nature by pointing to his family history. His father's side

of the family, he said, was cold, rational, and "anti-sentimental to the point of insolence," while his mother's side was gentle, "gemütlich," "noble and patient."

Another irony is that Graves in his own life craved guidance. This is nowhere better seen than in his thirteen-year association with the American poet Laura Riding. In the early Twenties, Riding was affiliated with John Crowe Ransom and Allen Tate, and with their Fugitive group, which espoused regionalism in literature. Ransom used the occasion of a review in *The Fugitive* of Graves's *On English Poetry* to praise the English poet for his ability to express his "charming personality . . . without embarrassment in prosodical verse," something certain unnamed "brilliant minds" (i.e., Pound and Eliot) were, in Ransom's view, unable to do. At Ransom's urging Graves initiated a correspondence with Riding in 1924. Two years later she arrived in England and moved into Graves's house. Graves's growing attachment to Riding resulted in his separation in 1929 from his first wife, Nancy Nicholson.

The Graves-Riding partnership was a curious one, to say the least. Judging from Martin Seymour-Smith's 1982 biography of Graves [*Robert Graves: His Life and Work,* 1982], it could easily be characterized by the title of one of Graves's poems: **"Sick Love."** For Graves, Riding was, variously, the incarnation of an ancient Mediterranean moon goddess, the embodiment of the perfection of poetry itself, and a feminist advocating the overthrow of male-dominated society. Whatever role she played, she demanded, and received, total fealty from her subject. The Graves-Riding bond involved far more than Graves's relinquishing the household to her, or submitting his poems to her for approval, or accepting a subordinate role in their "joint" literary endeavors—all of which he did. The fact is, she treated him, as Tom Matthews, an American writer who stayed with the couple in 1932, observed, "like a dog. There was no prettier way to put it." Matthews, whose testimony is recorded in Seymour-Smith's book, wrote that Graves

> seemed in a constant swivet of anxiety to please her, to forestall her every wish, like a small boy dancing attendance on a rich aunt of uncertain temper. . . . Since I admired him and looked up to him as a dedicated poet and a professional writer, his subservience to her and her contemptuous bearings towards him troubled and embarrassed me . . . she was not so much his mistress as his master. . . .

So enthralled was Graves with Riding that he even emulated her in a (pre-Majorca) 1929 suicide attempt, undertaken because she loved a third party (one Geoffrey Phibbs) and Phibbs loved Nancy Nicholson. Graves leapt from a third-story window after Riding had jumped from the floor above. (This had been preceded by Riding's drinking Lysol, to no effect.) Graves escaped unscathed; Riding suffered a compound fracture of the spine. According to Seymour-Smith, the police's grilling of Graves after this incident was "one of the experiences that made him want to leave England."

The sources of Graves's idealization of and submission to

Laura Riding are well documented in the recently published *Robert Graves: The Assault Heroic, 1895-1926* by Richard Perceval Graves, the first installment of a proposed three-volume biography of Graves by his nephew. This volume, which is based on heretofore unreleased family letters, diaries, and extracts from a memoir of Robert by Perceval Graves's father, is a biographical undertaking of a different kind from Seymour-Smith's. Seymour-Smith's narrative is a more or less objective rendering of events. Perceval Graves's book, on the other hand, is a chronology of Robert's shifting psychological states. As a means of understanding the poetry, this approach leaves much to be desired. But it is invaluable for comprehending the childhood sources of Graves's bizarre behavior toward Riding. One is certainly given a sense, by both Seymour-Smith and Graves himself in *Goodbye to All That,* of the moralistic tenor of the Graves family household. "We learned to be strong moralists, and spent much of our time on self-examination and good resolutions," writes Graves in *Goodbye to All That.*

But the revelations in those two volumes pale in comparison to what Perceval Graves divulges. It appears the demand for moral perfection in the Graves home was constant and shrill. The letters Robert's mother wrote to her children at school are the best evidence of this. These letters, none of which are quoted, "were so emotional and intense," writes Perceval Graves,

> that as I read them more than seventy years later I cannot help feeling terribly sad that my father's generation of the family were subjected to such intense moral pressure. So often, Amy [Graves's mother] seems to be equating personal worth with the almost impossibly saintly behavior and self-sacrifice which she was accustomed to demand of herself. Any falling short of the highest ideals is greeted with a terrible sorrow, all the more devastating for being couched in such loving language.

The mania for purity pervaded every aspect of the children's lives. According to Perceval Graves, Robert's father would become enraged when he saw "a corner of a page folded down to mark a place, or—still worse—a book left open and face down." The attempt to make the children morally spotless, Graves says in *Goodbye to All That,* gave him and his siblings "no hint of [the world's] dirtiness and intrigue and lustfulness." As Perceval Graves says about this remark: "the very words Robert chooses to describe this show the extent to which he had been affected by [his mother's] moralizing." The result is that it was "very hard," according to Perceval Graves, "for [Robert] to come to terms with the world as it really is."

This puts the matter too benignly, however. What Graves was left with was a truly disabling horror of reality, particularly sexual reality. The disgust Graves expresses in *Goodbye to All That* at the soldiers' custom of picking up local girls offers some indication of this, as does his reaction to a girl's advances in a Brussels pension in 1913: "I was so frightened," he said, "I could have killed her." Seymour-Smith observes that "physical desire and the sexual act, the 'thing,' is what terrifies [Graves]."

Graves's craving for purity was undoubtedly one source of his poetry, in which he creates a timeless realm beyond history. (In *Poetic Unreason,* his Oxford thesis that was published in 1925, Graves describes poetry as something as "remote and unrealizable an ideal as perfection.") It also helps one understand Graves's taste for Laura Riding's poetry, the principal feature of which is her self-chastisement for not having attained the requisite flawlessness.

Graves's craving for purity also sheds light on his attraction first to Nancy Nicholson—a feminist crusader—and then to Riding. In both cases, Graves tried to escape the world's "dirtiness and intrigue and lustfulness" by submitting himself to someone he invested with redemptive, cleansing powers. (So numinous a realm did Riding inhabit that after a point in their relationship she refused to sleep with him.) Riding's "unquiet nature and propensity to criticize," says Seymour-Smith, "was something that Graves was no doubt unconsciously seeking out." Perhaps it is not all that surprising that Graves, who went to such lengths to spurn what he deemed to be the suffocating moralism of England, became involved with strong-minded women like Nicholson and Riding. The fact is, in England or out, Graves could never escape the stern moralism of family, school, or military; he took it with him wherever he went.

Randall Jarrell believed that Graves's poetry, along with the theory of poetry he constructed around it, was a sublimation of his life with Laura Riding. There is little reason to disagree. At the heart of Graves's theory is the idea that all "true" poetry is an invocation of the Mother-Goddess who ruled the world up to the thirteenth century B.C. What Mother-Goddess? you might ask. Well, Graves claimed to have discovered evidence of an ancient matriarchal cult while reading for *Hercules, My Shipmate* (1945), a retelling of the travels of Jason and the Argonauts. With clues taken from Sir James Frazer's *The Golden Bough* and other anthropological works, Graves concluded that the Mother-Goddess had been ousted by thirteenth-century B.C. invaders of what is now Greece. These invaders installed in her place the Olympian gods. The legacy of this momentous shift in spiritual power is Western civilization as we know it, with its (in Graves's view) undue emphasis on rationality and order, and distrust of magic and myths—indeed, all forms of "poetic unreason."

The White Goddess: A Historical Grammar of Poetic Myth, Graves's 1948 study of Britain's own dethroned Goddess and her connection to the Mediterranean one, is without a doubt the author at his crankiest. In the words of the critic Douglas Day [in his *Swifter than Reason: The Poetry and Criticism of Robert Graves,* 1963], the book is "a curious blend of fact and fancy, an often impenetrable wilderness of cryptology, obscure learning, and apparently *non sequitur* reasoning brought to bear on a thesis that has its roots partly in historic fact, partly in generally accepted anthropological hypotheses, and partly in pure poetic intuition." Suffice to say that Graves's attempt to prove the existence of this matriarchal religion—which involved him in readings of medieval Welsh poems, analyses of secret Druidic alphabets, musings on ancient tree-worship, and correlations between Greek and Celtic myth—was fervently rejected by anthropologists and literary critics alike. But this never shook Graves's confidence, for *The White Goddess* was in his eyes a document of faith. And its debunking by "rational" critics—who (Graves would assert) are products of a patriarchal society and therefore on a covert search-and-destroy mission for every contemporary manifestation of the Goddess—only served to intensify his devotion. It was the same kind of devotion he had evinced for Riding, who appears to have been for Graves a rare embodiment of the long-lost Goddess.

Poetry, an invocation of this beleaguered antique Muse, was, according to Graves, the most meaningful writing a Goddess-worshipper could undertake. As a result, Graves was quite candid about the ancillary role his books of non-fiction and historical fiction played in his life. These volumes, Graves said, were the "show dogs I breed and sell to support the cat." This does not mean, however, that Graves ever passed up the chance to use these books as a means of correcting the false history propagated by various anti-Goddess forces. In *Wife to Mr. Milton* (1943), for example, the English poet is portrayed as a ranting Puritan and his wife Marie as the epitome of charm. (The reverse is closer to the truth.) *Hercules, My Shipmate,* the British title of which is *The Golden Fleece,* argues that the triumphs of Jason and the Argonauts in the Mediterranean, and their recapture of the fleece, occurred because Jason had been blessed by the White Goddess. *Homer's Daughter* (1955) takes off from Samuel Butler's conviction that the *Odyssey* was written not by Homer but by the woman who calls herself Nausicaa in the story. Not surprisingly, the books written before Graves's mythological "discovery"—*I, Claudius* (1934), *Claudius the God* (1935), *Count Belisarius* (1938), and *King Jesus* (1943)—show a deep need for some redeeming force. Throughout these popular historical novels is Graves's preoccupation with the unhappy fate of a pure soul in a corrupt and lustful world.

Graves's rewriting of the past was not his only means of demonstrating his obeisance to Riding and the White Goddess. It can also be seen in his refusal to develop original plots or psychologically persuasive characters. Judging from these novels, at least, it would appear that the Muse tolerated from her vassal no extra-poetic invention. "There is one story and one story only," goes the first line of Graves's well-known poem **"To Juan at the Winter Solstice,"** and Graves seems to have believed this with all his heart. As entertaining as many of these novels are—and *I, Claudius, King Jesus,* and *Count Belisarius* are certainly good reads—all have an extremely short imaginative reach.

Most of Graves's nonfiction is similarly scarred. The underlying assumption of both *The Greek Myths* (1955) and *The Hebrew Myths* (1964) is the suppression of the various manifestations of the Goddess in antiquity. Graves's literary criticism, the bulk of which is collected in *The Crowning Privilege* (1955), has the same narrow focus. Many of the essays seek to expose the rational impulse that has helped undermine "true" poetry throughout the centuries. As one would expect, Graves detests the poetry of Eliot,

Pound, and Stevens. In his view, the motives of these modernist poets are critical, not creative.

Perhaps the most important contribution Graves makes in his criticism is his advocacy of the plain style. In a letter from 1920, Graves declared that he wanted to be "able to write . . . with as much economy of words & simplicity of expression as possible." Whatever the other defects of his prose, his loyalty to this principle was unwavering.

The one book that does survive as a prose classic is *Goodbye to All That.* Graves's autobiography, which was revised thoroughly in 1957—the original edition was written hastily and poorly—is without a doubt his most important book. It captures the spirit of rebellion—of a young man's bursting free of the shackles of his elders—in a way that few other books of our time do. In the very first pages, Graves writes:

> About this business of being a gentleman: I paid
> so heavily for the fourteen years of my gentle-
> man's education that I feel entitled, now and
> then, to get some sort of return.

This refreshingly heady swagger continues to the end of the book.

Nevertheless, posterity will remember Graves best not as a novelist, mythographer, or biographical legend, but as a poet. Graves himself insisted on this, and his critics have obliged. But even if they are right to focus principally on the poetry—for it *is* the part of Graves's oeuvre that has the greatest claim on our attention—many have been inclined to make extravagant and faulty judgments of it. Jarrell declared **"To Juan at the Winter Solstice"** to be one of the century's greatest poems. Martin Seymour-Smith referred to Graves as "the foremost English-language love poet of this century—and probably of the two preceding ones, too." And Perceval Graves writes that his uncle "has come to be regarded as one of the finest poets of the twentieth century."

These claims are unwarranted. Reading through the newly re-issued 1975 edition of Graves's **Collected Poems,** one is struck by how fine some of them are. But one is also struck by how much the verse sinks from the weight of the "one story and one story only," especially the later poems. What impairs the majority of the poems, however, is not the presence of the Goddess theme so much as its treatment. For in a way, Graves is correct: good poetry is on some level an invocation of the Muse, if the Muse is indeed the embodiment of poetic intuition. The bulk of Graves's verse is marred because he persists in addressing the Muse directly instead of allowing the poem to invoke her implicitly. If Graves had not been so often compelled to be literal—that is, anti-symbolical and anti-metaphorical—he probably would have been freer to take on a wider range of emotional and thematic concerns in his verse. As it is, too large a percentage of his poems are like **"In Her Praise"**:

> This they know well: the Goddess yet abides.
> Though each new lovely woman whom she
>   rides,
> Straddling her neck a year or two or three,
> Should sink beneath such weight of majesty

And, groping back to humankind, gainsay
The headlong power that whitened all her way
With a broad track of trefoil—leaving you,
Her chosen lover, ever again thrust through
With daggers, your purse rifled, your rings
    gone—
Nevertheless they call you to live on
To parley with the pure, oracular dead,
To hear the wild pack whimpering overhead,
To watch the moon tugging at her cold tides.
Woman is mortal woman. She abides.

On the level of language and technique, this poem is unobjectionable. What undoes **"In Her Praise"** is its content. By discussing his conception of the Goddess, rather than presenting his emotional response to her, Graves diminishes the poem's effectiveness, and he shuts out those readers who do not share his almost religious devotion to her.

"To Juan at the Winter Solstice," the poem Randall Jarrell thought so much of, is a much better poem, if not a great one. It works as well as it does because its charged, resonant language redeems the "one story and one story only":

There is one story and one story only
That will prove worth your telling,
Whether as learned bard or gifted child;
To it all lines or lesser gauds belong
That startle with their shining
Such common stories as they stray into.

Is it of trees you tell, their months and virtues,
Or strange beasts that beset you,
Of birds that croak at you the Triple will?
Or of the Zodiac and how slow it turns
Below the Boreal Crown,
Prison of all true kings that ever reigned?

Water to water, ark again to ark,
From woman back to woman:
So each new victim treads unfalteringly
The never altered circuit of his fate,
Bringing twelve peers as witness
Both to his starry rise and starry fall.

Or is it of the Virgin's silver beauty,
All fish below the thighs?
She in her left hand bears a leafy quince;
When with her right she crooks a finger, smiling,
How may the King hold back?
Royally then he barters life for love. . . .

"On Portents," another fine poem, also survives the Goddess/Riding theme, not only because of its superb language and technique, but also because the female figure in the poem is more generalized than in **"To Juan at the Winter Solstice."** The fact that "she" could refer to anyone is crucial to the success of the poem:

If strange things happen where she is,
So that men say that graves open
And the dead walk, or that futurity
Becomes a womb and the unborn are shed,
Such portents are not to be wondered at,
Being tourbillions in Time made
By the strong pulling of her bladed mind
Through that ever-reluctant element.

"A Love Story" works well because in it Graves sketches

a symbolic landscape—rare for him—which gives the reader an equally rare chance to get an extra-literal sense of the poet's internal emotional state:

The full moon easterly rising, furious,
Against a winter sky ragged with red;
The hedges high in snow, and owls raving—
Solemnities not easy to withstand:
A shiver wakes the spine. . . .

Much more common is Graves's literalism, which spoils many of his love poems. **"Three Times in Love," "Crucibles of Love,"** and **"Depth of Love"** are almost entirely devoid of imagery. What one is left with are dry arguments that squeeze most of the inspiring passion out of the poem. Typical in this respect is **"The Falcon Woman,"** in which love's power is depleted by Graves's purely intellectual apprehension of it:

It is hard to be a man
Whose word is his bond
In love with such a woman,

When he builds on a promise
She lightly let fall
In carelessness of spirit.

The more sternly he asks her
To stand by that promise
The faster she flies.

"The Visitation," on the other hand, succeeds because it is invigorated by an image of a living presence: "Your slender body seems a shaft of moonlight / Against the door as it gently closes. . . . "

To my mind, Graves's best poems are the early ones, the majority of which predate his post-Thirties absorption in the Goddess. **"Like Snow," "The Pier Glass," "Love in Barrenness," "The Terraced Valley,"** and **"The Cool Web"** are some of the best among them. **"The Cool Web,"** in particular—in which the poet expresses his gratefulness for the protection from reality that language affords—is exquisitely written. It is also compelling for the way it seems to set the stage for the later poems—the poems in which Graves seeks similar protection from a fallen world in the cold arms of an abstract Goddess:

Children are dumb to say how hot the day is,
How hot the scent is of the summer rose,
How dreadful the black wastes of evening sky,
How dreadful the tall soldiers drumming by.

But we have speech, to chill the angry day,
And speech, to dull the rose's cruel scent.
We spell away the overhanging night,
We spell away the soldiers and the fright.

There's a cool web of language winds us in,
Retreat from too much joy or too much fear:
We grow sea-green at last and coldly die
In brininess and volubility.

But if we let our tongues lose self-possession,
Throwing off language and its watery clasp
Before our death, instead of when death comes,
Facing the wide glare of the children's day,
Facing the rose, the dark sky and the drums,
We shall go mad no doubt and die that way.

Robert Graves never let his tongue "lose self-possession," but his worship of the Goddess prevented him from securing major status as a poet, largely because it led him to adopt an anti-metaphorical, anti-symbolical stance toward poetry. (He once characterized this in a letter as his habit of discussing things "truthfully and factually.") The limited imaginative range of his work—the "one story and one story only"—obviously owes everything to her as well.

As reductive as it was, Graves's fixation seems to have been derived from the terror of reality instilled in him as a child. Laura Riding only exacerbated an existing condition. Reading through Graves's poems, one finds oneself aching for a dose of the hated world the poet seeks protection from—even that portion of reality which is no more than "dirtiness and intrigue and lustfulness."

It is the element of "real" emotion that gives the poem **"Through Nightmare"** its hint of greatness. Like **"On Portents,"** the poem is generalized enough to make the reader wonder if Graves is perhaps addressing himself, especially in the final stanza. If **"Through Nightmare"** is indeed Graves's confession of his timorousness in the face of the nightmare of the modern world, the poem could easily serve as his epitaph, and as a kind of lament for the unfulfilled promise of this enormously gifted, and tragically tormented, writer:

> Never be disenchanted of
> That place you sometimes dream yourself into,
> Lying at large remove beyond all dream,
> Or those you find there, though but seldom
> In their company seated—
>
> The untameable, the live, the gentle.
> Have you not known them? Whom? They carry
> Time looped so river-wise about their house
> There's no way in by history's road
> To name or number them.
>
> In your sleepy eyes I read the journey
> Of which disjointedly you tell; which stirs
> My loving admiration, that you should travel
> Through nightmare to a lost and moated land,
> Who are timorous by nature.

(pp. 66-73)

Robert Richman, "The Poetry of Robert Graves," in The New Criterion, *Vol. VII, No. 2, October, 1988, pp. 66-73.*

FURTHER READING

Bibliography

Bryant, Hallman Bell. *Robert Graves: An Annotated Bibliography.* New York: Garland Publishing, Inc., 1986, 206 p.
  Chronologically arranged bibliography of both primary and secondary sources.

Biography

Graves, Richard Perceval. *Robert Graves: The Assault Heroic, 1895-1926.* New York: Viking, 1986, 387 p.

The first volume in a trilogy on the life of the poet by his nephew.

——. *Robert Graves: The Years with Laura, 1926–40.* London: Weidenfeld & Nicolson, 1990, 379 p.
  The second installment of Graves's biographical trilogy, this volume focuses on Graves's relationship with Laura Riding.

Seymour-Smith, Martin. *Robert Graves: His Life and Work.* New York: Holt, Rinehart and Winston, 1982, 609 p.
  Critical biography written with Graves's cooperation.

Criticism

Bloom, Harold, ed. *Robert Graves.* New York: Chelsea House Publishers, 1987, 197 p.
  Compilation of critical essays on Graves's poetry and prose.

Day, Douglas. *Swifter than Reason: The Poetry and Criticism of Robert Graves.* Chapel Hill: The University of North Carolina Press, 1963, 228 p.
  Argues that Graves's career falls into four main phases: Georgian juvenilia; "anodynic" therapeutic writing; abstract and detached poetry; and writing influenced by Laura Riding.

Enright, D. J. "Robert Graves and the Decline of Modernism." *Essays in Criticism* XI, No. 3 (July 1961): 319-37.
  Finds Graves's poems to be prime examples of the spontaneity of art.

Hoffman, Daniel. *Barbarous Knowledge: Myth in the Poetry of Yeats, Graves, and Muir.* New York: Oxford University Press, 1967, 266 p.
  Views Graves as one of the "last romantics" and analyzes his poetry in the light of his conception of the White Goddess.

Keane, Patrick J. *A Wild Civility: Interactions in the Poetry and Thought of Robert Graves.* Columbia: University of Missouri Press, 1980, 110 p.
  Critical study that examines Graves's literary heritage as well as the mixture of emotion and artistry in his works.

Nemerov, Howard. "The Poetry of Robert Graves." In his *Poetry and Fiction: Essays,* pp. 112-17. New Brunswick, N.J.: Rutgers University Press, 1963.
  Comments on the origins and principles of Graves's poetry.

Seymour-Smith, Martin. *Robert Graves.* Writers and Their Work Series, no. 78. London: Longman Group Ltd, 1956, 44 p.
  Early survey of Graves's life, poetry, and prose.

Skelton, Robin. "Craft and Ceremony: Some Notes on the Versecraft of Robert Graves." *The Malahat Review,* No. 35 (July 1975): 37-48.
  Discussion of Graves's craftmanship and his fusion of Welsh and Anglo-Classical prosody.

Steiner, George. "The Genius of Robert Graves." *The Kenyon Review* XXII, No. 3 (Summer 1960): 340-65.
  Argues that Graves's lyrics, while being technically accomplished, lack the supreme intensities of language and

emotion; Steiner claims that Graves's most enduring achievement is in his prose.

Trilling, Lionel. "A Ramble on Graves." In his *A Gathering of Fugitives,* pp. 20-30. Boston: Beacon Press, 1956.
    Considers Graves as a "poet of the first rank."

Additional coverage of Graves's life and career is contained in the following sources published by Gale Research: *Contemporary Authors,* Vols. 5-8, rev. ed., 117 [obituary]; *Contemporary Authors New Revision Series,* Vol. 5; *Contemporary Literary Criticism,* Vols. 1, 2, 6, 11, 39, 44, 45; *Dictionary of Literary Biography,* Vols. 20, 100; *Dictionary of Literary Biography Yearbook: 1985*; and *Something about the Author,* Vol. 45.

Robert Hayden

1913-1980

(Born Asa Bundy Sheffey) American poet, essayist, editor, and playwright.

INTRODUCTION

Hayden is the author of highly admired works celebrating the history and achievements of African Americans. His poetry often employs traditional techniques, forms, and styles and has been praised for masterful use of rhythmic diction, mystical symbolism, and complex perspective. Hayden was criticized during his lifetime for his rejection of the racial aesthetic advanced by proponents of the Black Arts Movement during the 1960s, but more recent commentators appreciate both his polished craftsmanship and his insightful presentation of black life in the United States.

Hayden was born Asa Bundy Sheffey in Detroit, Michigan, in an impoverished neighborhood that he later recalled in his "Elegies for Paradise Valley." His mother moved to New York when he was eighteen months old, leaving him in the care of her neighbors William and Sue Ellen Hayden. The Haydens rechristened him Robert Hayden and provided him with a home and an education although he was never legally adopted by the couple. Hayden later acknowledged their efforts in two poetic tributes, "The Ballad of Sue Ellen Westerfield" and "Those Winter Sundays." He attended Detroit City College (now Wayne State University) and the University of Michigan, where he studied with the poet W. H. Auden. As a student Hayden admired the works of such Harlem Renaissance writers as Countee Cullen and Langston Hughes, and their influence is evident in much of his early poetry. In 1943 he adopted the Baha'i belief in the unity of all religions and worldwide brotherhood, convictions that are strongly evidenced in his poetry. After graduating from college in 1944, Hayden embarked on an academic career as an instructor of literature, first at Fisk University and then at the University of Michigan. However, he considered himself foremost a poet, who taught only to earn a living. During the 1960s Hayden came into conflict with writers associated with the Black Arts Movement, who produced a flurry of works—often militant in tone—for and about African Americans. Such writers as Haki R. Madhubuti accused Hayden of denying his black heritage and adopting writing standards prescribed and practiced by the white literary establishment. While Hayden addressed racial themes in his poetry, he refused to adapt his somewhat formal poetics to counteract these charges. Hayden maintained that black poets should be judged by the same criteria as other writers, thus rejecting the notion of an exclusively black aesthetic. Warning against "ghettoizing" writers, he argued that separating black writers from the rest of the literary community limited their audience. Such views damaged Hayden's reputation within African-American literary circles and distracted attention from his work. In 1976 Hayden was appointed poetry consultant to the Library of Congress. He died in 1980.

Much of Hayden's early poetry—particularly that collected in *Heart-Shape in the Dust, The Lion and the Archer,* and *Figure of Time*—addresses racial themes and depicts prominent figures and events in African-American history. "Runagate Runagate" (a deliberate corruption of the word *renegade*) pays tribute to Harriet Tubman and the underground railroad, and "Frederick Douglass" commemorates the accomplishments of the great abolitionist. "Middle Passage," a poem about the shipping of enslaved Africans to the Americas, depicts the famous mutiny on the slave ship *Amistad.* Hayden broadened his range of topics with *A Ballad of Remembrance* and the works that followed. While still focusing much of his attention on black history and culture, Hayden began writing poems about nature, travel, art, family, and the Baha'i religion. Like many of his earlier works, *American Journal* concerns social injustice while celebrating the lives and achievements of notable black Americans, including such figures as Phillis Wheatley, Paul Laurence Dunbar, Paul Robeson, and Matthew H. Henson, a servant who accompanied the expedition that first reached the North Pole with Commodore Robert E. Peary.

Hayden's poetry has been characterized as erudite and reserved in tone yet it also drew on the colloquial language of the people whose stories are presented in his works. While Hayden often utilized such traditional poetic forms as ballad, blank verse, and sonnet, he also wrote unconventional verses, according to Dudley Randall, "with patterns of lines of varying length, in flexible rhythms, unrimed or with imperfect rimes." Unlike the works of many contemporary black writers, Hayden's poetry is neither polemical nor didactic; he was more interested in accomplished craftsmanship than in protest writing and summarized his position in an interview in 1973: "There's a tendency today—more than a tendency, it's almost a conspiracy—to delimit poets, to restrict them to the political and the socially or racially conscious. To me, this indicates gross ignorance of the poet's true function as well as of the function and value of poetry as an art. . . . I resist whatever would force me into a role as politician, sociologist, or yeasayer to current ideologies. I know who I am, and pretty much what I want to say."

PRINCIPAL WORKS

POETRY

Heart-Shape in the Dust   1940
The Lion and the Archer [with Myron O'Higgins]   1948
Figure of Time   1955
A Ballad of Remembrance   1962
Selected Poems   1966
Words in the Mourning Time   1970
The Night-Blooming Cereus   1972
Angle of Ascent   1975
American Journal   1978; enlarged edition, 1982
Robert Hayden: Collected Poems   1985

OTHER MAJOR WORKS

In Memoriam Malcolm X   (drama)   1974
Collected Prose   (prose)   1984

CRITICISM

Charles T. Davis   (essay date 1973)

[*An American educator, Davis was respected for his studies on black literature and culture. In the following excerpt from an essay written in 1973 and later published in* Black Is the Color of the Cosmos *(1982), he discusses Hayden's depiction of historical figures and events.*]

History has haunted Robert Hayden from the beginning of his career as a poet. In 1941, when a graduate student

at the University of Michigan, he worked on a series of poems dealing with slavery and the Civil War called *The Black Spear,* the manuscript of which was to win for him a second Hopwood Award. This effort was no juvenile excursion, to be forgotten in the years of maturity. Though some of the poems have not been reprinted in *Selected Poems* (1966), *The Black Spear* survives in a severely altered form in Section Five of that volume. What remains is not simply **"O Daedalus, Fly Away Home"** and **"Frederick Douglass,"** but a preoccupation with a continuing historical ambition. This was the desire to record accurately the yearnings, the frustrations, and the achievement of an enslaved but undestroyed people. **"Middle Passage,"** **"The Ballad of Nat Turner,"** and **"Runagate, Runagate,"** all written later, share this concern. In these poems noble blacks, Cinquez, Nat Turner, and Harriet Tubman, rise from oppression and obscurity.

An extended period of study and research, as well as correspondence in theme, links these later poems with *The Black Spear.* Hayden had intended **"Middle Passage"** to be the opening work of *The Black Spear,* but the poems in 1941 would not assume a shape that would satisfy a meticulous craftsman. **"The Ballad of Nat Turner"** and **"Runagate, Runagate"** come from poring over journals, notebooks, narratives, and histories dealing with the slave trade, plantation life, slave revolts, and the Underground Railroad, reading begun about 1940 and continued for perhaps a decade, judging from his recollection of the activity of composition.

A generation later Hayden displays an attachment somewhat less strong to historical themes. In 1966 **"Frederick Douglass"** closed Section Five of *Selected Poems* and the book, a sign of a surviving commitment. **"El-Hajj-Malik El-Shabazz (Malcolm X)"** opens Section Three, "Words in the Mourning Time," of Hayden's most recent book of poems, bearing the title of the section and published in 1970. Though the commitment to interpreting history is still present, the emphasis has changed. The poems of *The Black Spear* emerge from the suffering of black people before Emancipation and record their assertion of manhood, more than the simple ability to survive, but those in "Words in the Mourning Time" describe the agony undergone by Malcolm and others to achieve spiritual liberation in our own day and the search for meaning in history upon which that liberation depends. What has endured through the years is the central importance of history in Hayden's poetry—not history as the poet would like it to be, but history as he has discovered it.

The birth of the historical impulse in Hayden is not easily described. He seems to have nourished always a sense of the past. Hayden said in conversation with Paul McCluskey, his editor at Harcourt Brace Jovanovich: "For some reason, I don't know why, I seemed to have a need to recall my past and to rid myself of the pain of so much of it." The poet, then, was discussing poems written in the 1950s, but the statement applies with equal force to his work at any stage in his career. The activity of truthtelling from memory, of reconstructing the past, is purgative—at least in part, and it is intimately connected with the necessity to write poems.

Hayden's predisposition acquired quite early a formal reinforcement. The record of this is bound up with the writing of the poems in *The Black Spear.* Though W. H. Auden, his mentor at Michigan, looked on when Hayden received a prize for *The Black Spear,* the British poet was not the dominant influence shaping the work. That, rather, was Stephen Vincent Benét, whose long historical narrative *John Brown's Body* (1927) moved Hayden to think of approaching slavery and the Civil War "from the black man's point of view." Indeed, Hayden has acknowledged that the title of his sequence of historical poems, *The Black Spear,* comes from Benét and has pointed to a passage appearing late in *John Brown's Body,* in which the reaction of the newly emancipated slaves to Sherman's march through Georgia is described. Benét, in this passage, commented upon his failure to register in verse the full range and depth of the black response to the trauma of freedom:

> Oh, black skinned epic, epic with the black
>   spear,
> I cannot sing you, having too white a heart,
> And yet, some day, a poet will rise to sing you
> And sing you with such truth and mellowness,
>
> That you will be a match for any song
> Sung by old, populous nations in the past, . . .

Hayden aspired to become the poet called for by Benét, one with a heart sufficiently black. Indeed, he told Benét, several years after reading *John Brown's Body* and a year or so before the commencement of serious work on *The Black Spear,* that he intended to write a poem on the materials pointed to by the white poet, though possibly not the "black skinned epic" so solemnly predicted.

Benét was a hindrance as well as a help, as every major influence must be for a poet struggling to find his own voice. The story of the writing of **"Middle Passage"** documents the point. This poem, in many ways the most impressive achievement of Hayden's early career, was completed in some form by the time that *The Black Spear* was submitted to the Hopwood judges. But Hayden refused to include it in his volume, even though he had planned it as the inaugural piece of the whole sequence. And his reasons for delay are good ones: "Actually I had tried writing the poem in blank verse—unrhymed iambic pentameter—but, then, it was too much like Benét, not only in form, but in diction and narrative organization also" [*How I Write/1,* 1972]. The statement prepares us for differences in the final form of the poem, published originally in *Phylon* in 1945, but it also requires us to look for correspondences with *John Brown's Body,* because Benét's influence has been so powerful and pervasive.

The section of *John Brown's Body* which is closest to Hayden's **"Middle Passage"** is the one that appears immediately after the "invocation," "Prelude—the Slaver." Benét presents here the captain of a slave ship who is moved to comment on a profession in which he is skilled, while actually transporting a cargo of black ivory from Africa to America. The impulse toward self-revelation is aroused by the questions, often not stated but implied, posed by a young mate, who is inexperienced and innocent. The bulk of the narrative consists of exchanges between the two.

The Captain is firm in his piety: he reads his Bible regularly and sees no contradiction between practicing Christianity and ferrying blacks for profit to a life of enforced and unending servitude. The Mate is less certain; he recoils from what he sees—the blacks in chains, the threat of the plague, the hatred of the enslaved—and he yearns for his and the Captain's native New England. Most of all, he is upset by what he calls the Blackness, the stench that is everywhere, the stain that will not wash out. His own emotions approach a mystical terror that seems to deny the Captain's pieties, a terror more appropriate for the sinning than for those who take comfort in the fact that they are adding heathen black souls to Christ's kingdom.

Hayden takes over the problem of reconciling Christianity and slavetrading in **"Middle Passage,"** though the machinery of his narrative is much more complicated. The first of three parts offers the log entries, the prayers, and the ruminations of a pious member of the crew of a slaver. The conflict, however, is internal rather than external. The spur toward self-revelation is not an innocent youth on a maiden voyage, but the consciousness of the speaker, as he feels the threat to body and soul in the hazards and the emotional excesses that come from participation in the slave trade. Once again we find black resistance, rebellion and implacable hatred, and the threat of the plague. To these familiar difficulties, Hayden adds a new trial—the temptation to lust with black wenches, the giving up wholly to sex and alcohol so that ship, slaves, and self are all lost.

Hayden's addition points to one of the differences separating Benét's poem from his own—the richness of his documentation. The accurate touches that come from Hayden's wide reading are impressive. His wealth of information is to be seen in Part One in the names of the slave ships, the form of the ship's log, the description of the creeping blindness (Ophthalmia), and the graphic account of the drunken orgy aboard *The Bella J.* Parts Two and Three, almost untouched by the example of Benét's poem, display evidences of extensive research in the slave trade in the library of the University of Michigan. The recollections of the bluff slave trader, undistorted by qualms of conscience, describe the slave factories, the collection methods, the corruption of black kings, and the good times on the West African coast. Following this straightforward statement, we hear in Part Three the testimony of a Spanish slaver, who supplies from his own point of view the details of the *Amistad* Mutiny in 1839. Now, the sources of Hayden's knowledge are many, but he recalls two as being especially rewarding, *Adventures of an African Slaver* and Muriel Rukeyser's biography *Willard Gibbs,* which presents an accurate description of the *Amistad* Mutiny and the trial that followed.

Though Benét's poem might have suggested to Hayden the technique of handling the poetic problems of **"Middle Passage"** through the use of voices, it could not provide a model for the subtle use of the technique which Hayden's poem displays. Benét's "Prelude" has three voices—the skipper's, the mate's, and the poet's. Actually the poet intrudes very little, only to utter prophecy in a brief section toward the end of the poem. According to the poet, the black seeds "robbed from a black king's storehouse" would fall on American earth, "lie silent, quicken" and then grow. A seed would become "A black shadow-sapling, a tree of shadow," and the tree, the poet promises, would ultimately blot out "all the seamen's stars." An ominous prediction, then, is offered, one that identifies the shaking of the leaves of the shadow tree with the trampling of the "horses of anger," the "Beat of the heavy hooves like metal on metal," the signs of war. The poet of the "Prelude" engages, then, in the necessary prefiguration of the Civil War that he will describe in later books.

The poet of **"Middle Passage"** has a good deal more to do. His is the central consciousness of the poem, providing a frame in Part One for the description of the painful voyage from Africa to America and, at the beginning of the poem, extracting meaning for the journey: "voyage through death to life upon these shores." A crew member of a slave ship provides the actual description of the middle passage itself. His narration is not simple because it is made complex by the fact of his piety. On the one hand, there is the sailor's prosaic voice, instructing us in entries in ship's logs and, finally, in a legal deposition, of the hazards of a rebellious cargo, disease, and lust. On the other hand, there is the voice praying for "safe passage" to bring "heathen souls" to God's "chastening." What the sailor tells has so much cruelty and depravity that it seems finally to overwhelm the teller of the tale. The secure sense of accomplishing God's design departs, and there is only the cry, despairing, now, rather than confident: "Pilot Oh Pilot Me."

The poet echoes, clearly, the cry of the sailor. He has been moved deeply by the prosaic account in rather different ways. For one thing, he is aware of the irony present in the crewman's piety, and he comments, in the language of Shakespeare's Ariel and with a precedent provided by *The Waste Land:*

> Deep in the festering hold thy father lies,
> of his bones New England pews are made,
> those are altar lights that were his eyes.

The allusion to Shakespeare's sea-change mocks a less spiritual transformation, though Hayden's too has a claim to religious motivation. The "altar lights" in a church in New England are vulgar consequences of an investment in black gold. Moreover, the poet speculates quite openly on the destiny of the Yankee slave ship, with the benefit of a greater perspective and more knowledge than the sailor:

> What port awaits us, Davy Jones'
> or home? I've heard of slavers drifting, drifting,
> playthings of wind and storm and chance, their
>   crews
> gone blind, the jungle hatred
> crawling up on deck.

The poet's historical perspective appears more clearly in subsequent parts. In Part Two the poet becomes the "lad," who listens to the recollections of a hardened and unrepentant slaver, reconstructing the beginnings of the wretched trade in Africa in greed, vanity, war, deception, devastation, and disease. In Part Three the historical perspective acquires an important spiritual dimension. Here

the slave ships become "shuttles in the rocking loom of history" and the pattern from the loom itself emerges. The ships, though they may bear "bright ironical names like 'Jesus,' 'Estrella,' 'Esperanza,' 'Mercy,'" contribute to "New World littorals that are / mirage and myth and actual shore." The poet promises the "actual shore," and the journey to it, the middle passage, becomes a descent into death resembling the dark night of the soul. The "shore" is life at the end of death, but first blacks must experience death, a "voyage whose chartings are unlove."

Cinquez, the leader of the *Amistad* Mutiny, assumes especial prominence in the poet-speaker's vision of **"Middle Passage."** The Spanish slaver considers Cinquez "that surly brute who calls himself a prince, / directing, urging on the ghastly work." But in the enlightened historical perspective of the poet, Cinquez is an expression of "The deep immortal human wish, / the timeless will." He is seen as an early sign of "life upon these shores," a "deathless primaveral image, / life that transfigures many lives." Hayden describes, then, a second sea-change, one more genuine than the transformation of the "festering hold" into pews and altar lights in New England because this change transfigures blacks. Cinquez, on the bloody deck of the *Amistad* and beyond the "butchered bodies" of the slave crew, points to the discovery of manhood and human dignity, even to recognition by law (thanks to "the august John Quincy Adams").

Nothing resembling this historical vision appears in *John Brown's Body.* Benét sees the Civil War as the "pastoral rebellion of the earth / Against machines, against the Age of Steam," and out of John Brown's body grows "the new, mechanic birth, / . . . the great, metallic Beast / Expanding West and East." Hayden is not concerned with these problems, but rather with the transformation of slave to man, a transfiguration frequently touched with mystical overtones in his poems.

All of the poems of Section Five of **Selected Poems** have this preoccupation of Hayden's. Nat Turner in the darkness of the Dismal Swamp has a vision of bright angels in fiery combat, and he rises from his dream "at last free / And purified, . . . " and committed to holy war. He knows, then, that the "conqueror faces" of his dream were like his. Harriet Tubman, in **"Runagate, Runagate,"** rises above the impulsive, headlong flight of slaves to the North to insert steel in the spines of the timid, to provide light and direction to the bewildered, and threaten death to the faltering and craven. She is "woman of earth, whip-scarred, / a summoning, a shining," asserting a single objective, "Mean to be free." Indeed, only she, "alias The General / alias Moses Stealer of Slaves," knows that one must be "mean" to be free. The spiritual justification of her purpose comes in lines echoing the language of a Negro spiritual toward the conclusion of the poem:

> Midnight Special on a sabre track movering
>   movering,
> first stop Mercy and the last Hallelujah

Though the mystical transformation of the desire to be free, to assert manhood, links all of Hayden's historical poems of this period, **"The Ballad of Nat Turner"** and **"Runagate, Runagate"** point to the importance for Hayden of another kind of source material. Behind these poems, indeed, lies the research of the 1940s that supported **"Middle Passage"** as well, an accumulation of materials so rich that Hayden was moved to write a play about Harriet Tubman, *Go Down, Moses.* He recalls, in reviewing formal sources, that *The Negro in Virginia,* a study completed in 1940 by the Writer's Program of the Works Projects Administration and supervised by Roscoe E. Lewis of Hampton Institute, had especial value for him as he prepared to write **"The Ballad of Nat Turner."** But this familiar pattern of research and rumination received support from a knowledge of a type of source material not found in **"Middle Passage."** This was the Negro folk tradition.

Nat Turner is struck by the cessation in the turning of the wheel within a wheel, an image that recalls the spiritual celebrating Ezekiel's illumination. The details of the celestial combat have the vividness and the primitive power of a folk sermon. Nat's account in a moment of intense excitement tends to employ the repetition found so frequently in the words of a folk preacher, suggesting with its incantatory rhythms the chant that accompanies traditionally God's direct influence upon his mortal instrument:

> But I saw I saw oh many of
>   those mighty beings waver.
> Waver and fall, go streaking down
>   into swamp water, and the water
> hissed and steamed and bubbled and locked
>   shuddering shuddering over.

There is a folk basis too for the references to Africa, for those intimations of the mother land that come to blacks frequently in darkness and in the forest:

> where Ibo warriors
> hung shadowless, turning in wind
>   that moaned like Africa.

"Runagate, Runagate" has linguistic touches that suggest a strong folk inspiration, with "jack-muh-lanterns," "patterollers," an "a-murbling" fear, a "movering" train, "jaybird-talk," and "oh Susyanna." The invitation to get aboard the coach to the North is extended to enslaved blacks in accents that show dialect roots:

> Come ride-a my train
> Mean mean mean to be free.

The language is just a sign of the rich reliance upon the materials that come ultimately from the folk imagination. We have the vision of the free North as the "star-shaped yonder Bible city," the association of the journey to freedom with the "North star and bonanza gold," the identification of the flight itself as "crossing over" or as the freedom train, and the assumed connection between the calling of the hoot-owl and the "hants in the air." Not the least of these evidences of the pressure of folk culture intimately known are the snatches from the spirituals. Though these are mostly echoes rather than direct quotations, there are two lines, indeed, that come without change from the great spiritual that begins with the phrase "Oh-h freedom":

> And before I'll be a slave
> I'll be buried in my grave.

Hayden relies upon folk materials almost exclusively in only one poem in Section V of *Selected Poems*—**"O Daedalus, Fly Away Home."** Like the others, this poem transforms mystically the desire for freedom. In the interview with Paul McCluskey, Hayden has identified the source of the poem as "a legend common among the Georgia Sea Island Negroes—the legend of the Flying African." He adds that it was their belief that certain slaves had the magical power to fly to freedom in Africa. The poetic machinery that supports this central idea uses other elements in a folk culture. The metrics of the poem suggest the rhythm of a folk dance called "juba," widely performed by slaves in the antebellum South. The instruments providing the musical background are a "coonskin drum" and a "jubilee banjo." The only touch in the poem that does not show the influence of Negro folk history is the reference to Daedalus in the title and the resonance that is achieved throughout from the comparison with an earlier and better-known historical flight.

History, formal and folk, serves Hayden's purpose, and that purpose in the early historical poems is to describe the mystical emergence of freedom from circumstances that appall and degrade, and the making of a man, a black man in America. No better description of the poet's objective exists than the first lines of the justly famous tribute to Frederick Douglass:

> When it is finally ours, this freedom, this liberty,
>   this beautiful
> and terrible thing, needful to man as air, usable
>   as earth; . . .

Contributing to Douglass's eminence is his own "middle passage," his painful exposure to death in various forms—physical violence, humiliation, and ostracism:

> this man, this Douglass, this former slave, this
>   Negro
> beaten to his knees, exiled, visioning a world
> where none is lonely, none hunted, alien, . . .

Following death comes life, not simply for Douglass, whose image survives in our memories, but for us all. In a voice touched with awe at the transformation, the poet concludes his tribute in this way:

> Oh, not with statues' rhetoric,
> not with legends and poems and wreaths of
>   bronze alone,
> but with the lives grown out of his life, the lives
> fleshing his dream of the beautiful, needful
>   thing.

The end of the Douglass sonnet echoes, then, the theme of **"Middle Passage"**:

> Voyage through death
>   to life upon these shores

and offers again the great theme of the historical poems of Hayden's early period.

Hayden's poems published in 1970, *Words in the Mourning Time,* reveal a persistence of an interest in historical materials, but they do not have the focus or the concentration which the ideal of *The Black Spear* provided. No doubt, the poet's own soul has yielded to "migratory habits," which the poet represents as being the theme of Socrates at his "hemlock hour." Like Socrates, Hayden faces a world not entirely reassuring to the firmness of his early vision. The startling carcasses, "death's black droppings," strewn about the Fisk University lawns are bad enough, but they suggest, with their troublesome presence, the existence of more serious challenges elsewhere.

The consequences of "middle passage" are not all good, nor all life. The poet travels to Lookout Mountain, the site of a great Civil War battle, where the agony of suffering, struggle, and death was most acute, and finds himself among "Sunday alpinists" who "pick views and souvenirs." The Union victory seems "dubious," to say the least, when from the perspective of "A world away" the poet is moved to say:

> . . . the scions of that fighting climb
> endless hills of war, amid war's peaks
> and valleys broken, scattered fall.

The Roman rhetoric heard at the *Amistad* trial in **"Middle Passage"** has become the song of the "stuffed gold eagle."

Confusion comes from something other than the failure of the time to live up to its brightest vision; it occurs in the minds of those who stand to benefit most from the realization of the dream—the oppressed blacks. Hayden's dramatic poem **"The Dream"** deals with this problem. Old Sinda remains behind in the slave quarters after "Marse Lincum's soldier boys" have brought freedom to the plantation. This "ragged jubilo" does not accord with Sinda's expectations, and she hides in the quarters rather than follow, rejoicing, in the wake of the army. Her dream of emancipation is infinitely more attractive, and Sinda sees the faces of her sons Cal and Joe, and that of Charlie, possibly their father, who was sold to the ricefields many years before, on "the great big soldiers marching out of gunburst," and she will not accept "those Buckcras with their ornery / funning cussed commands." These are not "the hosts the dream had promised her." Sinda fails to understand that war is prose, recorded in Cal's letters to her about the "Kernul" and the "contrybans," the rain, the hardtack and the bully beef, the "ficety gals," and the constant worry about the "Bullit" with his name "rote on it." And liberation is prose too. But Sinda will cling to her vision until she dies, until the very end of her waning, "brittle strength."

"On Lookout Mountain" and **"The Dream"** are comments on history that have especial value in light of *The Black Spear,* since they deal with the pain and the expectation attached to the Civil War, but they do not confront directly the problems of recent history. **"El-Hajj Malik El-Shabazz (Malcolm X)"** does this. Certain prefigurations come from **"On Lookout Mountain"** and **"The Dream"** that prepare us for Hayden's approach to the career of Malcolm X. One is the poet's objection to the vulgar and materialistic limitations in contemporary American culture; another is the poet's sense of the possibility of distortion, even corruption, in the mind of the holder of the dream. Both are related to the epigraph of **"El-Hajj Malik El-Shabazz"**: "O masks and metamorphoses of Ahab, Native Son."

Malcolm, like Douglass, is a folk hero. What is required to measure the man is an understanding of the folk milieu out of which he came as well as his position in history as a charismatic leader of black people. The two kinds of historical knowledge which Hayden displayed in **"The Ballad of Nat Turner"** and in **"Runagate, Runagate"** are present here as well. The folk mores that rest behind Malcolm's emergence are urban, however, not rural. No doubt, the poet's memory of his own childhood in black Detroit gives especial poignancy to the reconstruction of Malcolm's early years. There is no question about the authority of his description of "Dee-troit Red" on the street:

> He conked his hair and Lindy-hopped,
> zoot-suited jiver, swinging those chicks
> in the hot rose and reefer glow.

Hayden is equally prepared to face the thorny problem of Malcolm's place in history. His consideration must begin with Malcolm's sense of his role, with the facts of the *Autobiography* [*of Malcolm X*]. The reliance seems to be especially clear when the poet refers to the tragic end of Malcolm's father and mother, to his reputation in prison (" 'Satan' in The Hole"), and to his intimations of his own violent death. But Hayden moves beyond the *Autobiography* to comment on Malcolm's Black Muslim faith. What stirs the poet is something other than a casual interest in Islam; it is the concern of a man deeply touched by the power of an Eastern religion, a devoted Bahaist who can sympathize with a conversion to a faith that many think exotic. Personal factors as well as the passion for accuracy combine to describe the historical phenomenon that is Malcolm.

The documentation of Malcolm's commitment to Islam has impressive economy. Important to his faith is the narrative attributed to Elijah Muhammad, the leader of the Nation of Islam among black Americans, about the creation of the white man. "Yacub's white-faced treachery" refers to the original mistake in genetic experimentation that led to the ultimate suppression of blacks by upstart and diabolical whites. In this version of creation there is no doubt about the color, rather the lack of it, of Ahab, the unholy king. Arabic phrases in Hayden's poem are fortunate and functional additions. Something of the evangelical character of the faith and of the excitement that thrills the faithful is conveyed through these exclamations. The poet describes with precision Malcolm's role in the movement:

> He X'd his name, became his people's anger,
> exhorted them to vengeance for their past;
> rebuked, admonished them,
>
> their scourger who
> would shame them, drive them from
> the lush ice gardens of their servitude.

Malcolm becomes Christ in this passage, angrily driving the money changers from the temple. There is accuracy in this comparison, and there is irony, too, if we consider Christ something other than Calvin's creation, with the "hellward-thrusting hands" that so repelled Malcolm. The irony becomes explicit rather than potential when the poet adds: "Rejecting Ahab, he was of Ahab's tribe."

The presence of ironies ties **"El-Hajj Malik El-Shabazz"** to **"Middle Passage."** In the earlier poem the play upon "sea-change" adds dimension to Hayden's statement; in the poem about Malcolm the "dawn" functions in much the same way. A "false dawn of vision" precedes a true awakening. Malcolm is first converted, through the offices of Elijah Muhammad, to a faith in a "racist Allah," one whose "adulterate attars could not cleanse / him of the odors of the pit." His pilgrimage to Mecca sparks a "final metamorphosis," a truer revelation that eliminates hate as a necessary component of faith. Malcolm moves from neo-Islam to orthodox Islam, and Hayden celebrates the second conversion:

> He fell upon his face before
> Allah the raceless in whose blazing Oneness all
> were one. He rose renewed renamed, became
> much more than there was time for him to be.

Hayden's tribute to El-Hajj Malik El-Shabazz, formerly Malcolm X, renamed after the Hajj rituals or the rites of the pilgrimage to Mecca, expresses a view of what the movement in history should be. The early poems record Hayden's vision of a black man who has acquired freedom and humanity. The later poems, dealing with history after Emancipation, describe the confused wanderings and the tormenting frustrations of the liberated man, but they still maintain that modern man must become more human. The first part of the long poem **"Words in the Mourning Time,"** a lament for the deaths of Martin Luther King and Robert Kennedy, sketches this necessary development in our culture, upon which our survival depends. The destruction of King and Kennedy—and of El-Hajj Malik El-Shabazz—represents for us a "middle passage" to "life upon these shores":

> the agonies of our deathbed childbed age
> are process, major means whereby,
> oh dreadfully, our humanness must be achieved.

The heroes of history in this time of mourning are different from those in *The Black Spear.* They are more fallible, more vulnerable, more confused, and more easily destroyed, but El-Hajj Malik El-Shabazz matures to share a vision that Douglass has seen and which Hayden still enunciates with eloquence:

> a human world where godliness
> is possible and man
> is neither gook nigger honkey wop nor kike
>
> but man
>
> > > > permitted to be man.
> > > > > (pp. 253-67)

Charles T. Davis, "The Structure of the Afro-American Literary Tradition: Robert Hayden's Use of History," in his Black Is the Color of the Cosmos: Essays on Afro-American Literature and Culture, 1942-1981, *by Charles T. Davis, edited by Henry Louis Gates, Jr., Garland Publishing, Inc., 1982, pp. 253-68.*

Robert Hayden with John O'Brien   (interview date 1973)

[The following excerpt is from an interview that originally appeared in O'Brien's Interviews with Black Writers *in 1973. Here, Hayden discusses his development as a poet.]*

[O'Brien]: Are you sometimes struck by the mystery of your art?

[Hayden]: I've always felt that poetry and the poetic process are pretty mysterious. What is it that makes one a poet? What are you doing when you write a poem? What is poetry? The feeling of mystery is no doubt intensified because you can't deliberately set out to be a poet. You can't become one by taking courses in creative writing. You are born with the gift, with a feeling for language and a certain manner of responding to life. You respond in a particular way to yourself, to the basic questions that concern all human beings—the nature of the universe, love, death, God, and so forth. And that way of responding, of coming to grips with life, determines the kind of poetry you write. Once you discover you're a poet—and you have to find out for yourself—you can study the art, learn the craft, and try to become a worthy servitor. But you can't *will* to be a poet. This is an age of overanalysis as well as overkill, and we've analyzed poetry and the poetic process to a point where analysis has become tiresome, not to say dangerous for the poet. And for all our investigations, mysteries remain. And I hope they always will.

Do you see a progression in your work? Do you realize that you are writing poetry today that you could never have succeeded with ten years ago?

I've been very much aware of that. Yes. I think I'm now writing poems I couldn't have written ten or fifteen years ago. But I should add that some of my best-known poems were written back then. But there've been changes in outlook and technique since, and so I'm able to accomplish, when I'm lucky, what I once found too difficult to bring off successfully. I didn't know enough. Still, there are elements, characteristics in my work now, that seem always to have been present. Certain subjects, themes, persist, and—perhaps—will continue to give my work direction. My interest in history, especially Afro-American history, has been a major influence on my poetry. And I have a strong sense of the past in general, that recurs in much of my work. I don't have any nostalgia for the past, but a feeling for its relationship to the present as well as to the future. And I like to write about people. I'm more interested in people than in things or in abstractions, philosophical (so-called) ideas. In heroic and "baroque" people especially; in outsiders, pariahs, losers. And places, localities, landscapes have always been a favorite source for me. I once thought of using *People and Places* as the title for one of my books. Despite changes in outlook and technique over the years, the qualities I was striving for as a younger poet are the same ones I'm striving for today, basically. I've always wanted my poems to have something of a dramatic quality. I've always thought that a poem should have tension—dramatic and structural. And I've always been concerned with tone, with sound in relation to sense or meaning. I sometimes feel that I write by the word, not by the line. I'm perhaps oversensitive to the weight and color of words. I hear my words and lines as I write them, and if they don't sound right to me, then I know I'll have to go on revising until they do. I revise endlessly, I might add.

My interest in history, especially Afro-American history, has been a major influence on my poetry. And I have a strong sense of the past in general, that recurs in much of my work. I don't have any nostalgia for the past, but a feeling for its relationship to the present as well as to the future.

—Robert Hayden

Did you ever fear that you might stop developing as a poet, that perhaps in another year or two years you would have exhausted yourself?

Oh, yes. A year or so ago—before I'd completed **The Night Blooming Cereus**—I was afraid I'd never be able to write a new poem again. . . . I went stale, felt I was repeating myself, had nothing more to say. I've been through all this before, many times in fact. **Cereus** . . . was a breakthrough for me, and no doubt that's why it's my favorite book up to now. Writing it released me, also confirmed ideas and feelings I'd had before, but distrusted. I began to move in a new direction and to consolidate my gains, such as they were.

When you first started writing, were there poets that you tried to imitate and hoped you would be as good as, some day?

When I was in college I loved Countee Cullen, Jean Toomer, Elinor Wylie, Edna St. Vincent Millay, Sara Teasdale, Langston Hughes, Carl Sandburg, Hart Crane. I read all the poetry I could get hold of, and I read without discrimination. Cullen became a favorite. I felt an affinity and wanted to write in his style. . . . All through my undergraduate years I was pretty imitative. As I discovered poets new to me, I studied their work and tried to write as they did. . . . I reached the point, inevitably, where I didn't want to be influenced by anyone else. I tried to find my own voice, my own way of seeing. I studied with W. H. Auden in graduate school, a strategic experience in my life. I think he showed me my strength and weaknesses as poet in ways no one else before had done. (pp. 116-18)

*I know that your religion has greatly affected your poetry. Have your religious views changed since writing **"Electrical Storm,"** where you recorded a near encounter with death? There seems to be a skepticism in that poem, absent in your most recent volume of poetry,* **Words in the Mourning Time.**

No, not actually. I'm only suggesting the skepticism I might have felt earlier in my life. This wasn't a factor at the time I wrote the poem. I've always been a believer of sorts, despite periods of doubt and questioning. I've always had God-consciousness, as I call it, if not religion.

Do you think that there is a religious dimension to the work of the poet? Is there a special role that he must play in a century like ours?

Being a poet is role enough, and special enough. What else can I say? I object to strict definitions of what a poet is or should be, because they usually are thought up by people with an axe to grind—by those who care less about poetry than they do about some cause. We're living in a time when individuality is threatened by a kind of mechanizing anonymity. And by regimentation. In order to be free, you must submit to tyranny, to ideological slavery, in the name of freedom. And, obviously, this is the enemy of the artist; it stultifies anything creative. Which brings me to my own view of the role of the poet, the artist. I am convinced that if poets have any calling, function, *raison d'être* beyond the attempt to produce viable poems—and that in itself is more than enough—it is to affirm the humane, the universal, the potentially divine in the human creature. And I'm sure the artist does this best by being true to his or her own vision and to the demands of the art. This is my view; it's the conviction out of which I write. I do not set it up as an imperative for others. Poetry, all art, it seems to me is ultimately religious in the broadest sense of the term. It grows out of, reflects, illuminates our inmost selves, and so on. It doesn't have to be sectarian or denominational. There's a tendency today—more than a tendency, it's almost a conspiracy—to delimit poets, to restrict them to the political and the socially or racially conscious. To me, this indicates gross ignorance of the poet's true function as well as of the function and value of poetry as an art. With a few notable exceptions, poets have generally been on the side of justice and humanity. I can't imagine any poet worth his salt today not being aware of social evils, human needs. But I feel I have the right to deal with these matters in my own way, in terms of my own understanding of what a poet is. I resist whatever would force me into a role as politician, sociologist, or yea-sayer to current ideologies. I know who I am, and pretty much what I want to say.

There's an impersonal tone in almost all of your poetry. You're removed from what you write about, even when a poem is obviously about something that has happened to you.

Yes, I suppose it's true I have a certain detachment. I'm unwilling, even unable, to reveal myself as directly in my poems as some other poets do. Frequently, I'm writing about myself but speaking through a mask, a persona. There are troublesome things I would like to exteriorize by writing about them directly. One method for getting rid of your inner demons sometimes is to be able to call their names. I've managed to do so occasionally, but not very often. I could never write the confessional poems that Anne Sexton, Robert Lowell, John Berryman have become identified with. And perhaps I don't honestly wish to. Reticence has its aesthetic values too, you know. Still, I greatly admire the way Michael S. Harper, for example, makes poems out of personal experiences that must have been devastating for him. He's a marvelously gifted poet. I agree that poets like Harper and Lowell do us a service. They reveal aspects of their lives that tell us something about our own. One of the functions of poetry anyway. I think I tend to enter so completely into my own experiences most of the time that I have no creative energy left afterward. (pp. 119-21)

Do you think of yourself as belonging to any school of poetry? Do you place yourself in a romantic tradition as well as a symbolist?

I don't know what to say to that. I suppose I think of myself as a symbolist of a kind, and symbolism is a form of romanticism by definition. I've often considered myself a realist who distrusts so-called reality. Perhaps it all comes down to my being a "romantic realist." How would I know? Leave classification to the academicians. I do know that I'm always trying in my fumbling way to get at the truth, the reality, behind appearances, and from this has come one of my favorite themes. I want to know what things are, how they work, what a given process is, and so on. When I was writing **"Zeus over Redeye,"** for instance, I studied the booklets I picked up at the Redstone Arsenal so I'd learn the correct terminology, get the facts about rocket missiles. I scarcely used any of this information, but it gave me a background against which my poem could move. (p. 121)

Except when you are dealing with an obvious historical situation, you depend upon the present tense in your poems.

I've made a superficial—very superficial—analysis of the recurrence of the present tense in my poems, and I think I may be using it to achieve dramatic immediacy and because in a sense there is no past, only the present. The past is also the present. The experiences I've had in the past are now a part of my mind, my subconscious, and they are there forever. They have determined the present for me; they exist in it.

There appears to be a progression in your long poem "Words in the Mourning Time." The first few sections catalogue the madness of our age, particularly that of the 1960s. Yet love enters in the last section and restores what appeared to be a hopeless condition. I'm not sure how you move from the vision of the evils to one of love. Were you suggesting that love comes after the violence and killing, or perhaps because of them?

The final poem is the culmination, the climax of the sequence. For me, it contains the answers to the questions the preceding poems have stated or implied. If I seem to come to any conclusion about injustice, suffering, violence at all, it's in the lines about man being "permitted to be man." And it's in the last poem, written originally for a Bahá'í occasion. Bahá'u'lláh urged the absolute, inescapable necessity for human unity, the recognition of the fundamental oneness of mankind. He also prophesied that we'd go through sheer hell before we achieved anything like world unity—partly owing to our inability to love. And speaking of love, I try to make the point, in the elegy for Martin Luther King in the section we're discussing, that love is not easy. It's not a matter of sloppy sentimen-

tality. It demands everything of you. I think it's much, much easier to hate than to love. (pp. 123-24)

In "Monet's 'Waterlilies' " you refer to "the world each of us has lost." Is it a world of innocence, of childhood?

I'm absolutely cold to the voguish and overused theme of "lost innocence." Maybe I'm just too pseudo-Freudian. I might have been thinking about childhood, though surely not about innocence. But no, I can't honestly say I was even thinking about childhood. I grant you the poem could be so interpreted without doing too much violence to its meaning. Certainly, children, as we all know, live in a fantasy world, in a realm of the imagination that's forever lost to them when they grow up. But each of us has known a happier time, whether as children or as adults. Each of us has lost something that once gave the world a dimension it will never have again for us, except in memory. A botched answer, to be sure, but the best I can offer at the moment.

Is it through art that one is able to recapture it or at least become highly conscious of it?

Sometimes. That particular Monet helps me to recapture something—to remember something. I would say that one of the valuable functions of all the arts is to make us aware, to illuminate human experience, to make us more conscious, more alive. That's why they give us pleasure, even when their subjects or themes are "unpleasant." (pp. 127-28)

        Robert Hayden and John O'Brien, "A Romantic Realist'," in Collected Prose by Robert Hayden, edited by Frederick Glaysher, The University of Michigan Press, 1984, pp. 115-28.

Constance J. Post   (essay date 1976)

[*In the following excerpt, Post explores recurring images, the use of paradox, and the theme of struggle in Hayden's poetry.*]

In Robert Hayden's **"Kodachromes of the Island,"** the speaker of the poem roams about, thinking of Yeats' passionate search for a theme while seeking one of his own. For both men the search came long after their careers as poets had been established. Yeats, it will be recalled, wrote "The Circus Animals' Desertion," the poem in which he discusses his search for a new theme, fifty years after the publication of his first book of poetry. In Hayden's case, the search came in the middle of his career after he had already written some of his most celebrated poems, such as **"Middle Passage," "Runagate Runagate"** and **"Frederick Douglass."** These and other poems were included in his first book of poetry, *A Ballad of Remembrance,* published in 1962, ten years before the collection in which **"Kodachromes of the Island"** appears, entitled *Words in the Mourning Time* (1972).

Both men pursued the quest with dogged persistence. According to Yeats, the search preoccupied him daily for more than a month and culminated in his enumeration, resignedly, of old themes, among them the reconciling of what he called the three islands of incompatible things, "Vain gaiety, vain battle, vain repose." Hayden, eschewing any such enumeration, leaves it up to the reader to judge the degree of his success. Elsewhere, however, a clue is provided in an interview conducted with him by John O'Brien. Having acknowledged how stale and repetitious he thought his poetry had become, Hayden affirms that **The Night-Blooming Cereus** represented a real breakthrough for him. After that, he says, "I began to move in a new direction and to consolidate my gains, such as they were."

A careful study of Hayden's poetry will reveal, I believe, that any new direction he might have taken was primarily in the area of consolidation, if only to look at his old themes from a new angle. By his so doing, a thread of continuity is woven throughout his entire work, giving it a unity and a coherence it otherwise would lack. This is true in general of his themes and the means he uses to develop them, especially of his imagery. Considered together, his lyrics take on an almost epic quality. They therefore support Donald Stauffer's thesis that the imagery of some poets, whether consciously or unconsciously, is organized in such coherent patterns that an epic effect is achieved.

Struggle, for example, is a common theme running through Hayden's poetry, fortified not only by his choice of imagery but through his use of paradox. His chief symbol for it is the star. In the poem entitled **"Stars,"** he refers to the starlight which "crosses eons of meta-space to us" and asks, "How shall the mind keep warm save at spectral fires—how thrive but by the light of paradox?" The light of paradox *is* the light of the star since, by crossing eons of meta-space, it challenges our expectations about speed, distance and time just as paradox, literally meaning "beyond opinion," contradicts our expectations. (*Meta* and *para* share the same meaning of *beyond*.)

The star, moreover, is a paradox because of its physical properties. It exists only because of the careful balance of contradictory forces whereby "the energy generated by nuclear reactions in the interior is balanced by the outflow of energy to the surface"; similarly, "the inward gravitational forces are balanced by the outward-directed gas and radiation pressure" (*American Heritage Dictionary*). When such a balance of opposites is no longer present in the star, it collapses within itself. Starlight can thus be seen as a means of keeping the mind warm and thriving.

What additional meanings does Hayden attach to the stars? Of central importance in understanding the significance of the stars to him is the connection he makes between them and the Baha'i faith. In Section V of **"Stars,"** he mentions many different kinds of stars and then singles

Hayden in Detroit, 1979.

out the Nine-Pointed Star, "sun-star in the constellation of the nuclear Will." A symbol commonly used by the Navaho Indians, the nine-pointed star represents perfection according to Baha'ism, since after nine all numbers are repetitious. Furthermore, the number nine is seen as the numerical manifestation of the Greatest Name, Baha, says A. Q. Faizi, who gives the numerical value of the name Baha, based upon the Arabic alphabet, as follows: B = 2, A = 1, H = 5, A = 1 for a total of 9.

In Section III of **"Stars"** the number nine also assumes importance as Hayden, in groups of two, three and four, mentions the names of nine stars of various colors and constellations. All share one thing in common, however, and that is brightness. Five of the nine stars—Aldebaran, Arcturus, Altair, Vega and Polaris—are among the brightest stars in the sky, visible at latitude 40° N. Another two, Betelgeuse and Algol, are two of the brightest variable stars; even though their brightness fluctuates, it nevertheless exceeds that of most of the other 6,000 stars in the sky which are visible to the naked eye. Also visible without the use of a telescope are the last two, Almaak (also known as Almach) and Maia, the star for whom Hayden's daughter is named.

The significance of nine for Baha'ism, other than that already mentioned, varies somewhat. Because every Baha'i temple has nine openings and since the one in the United States, located in Wilmette, Illinois, has nine sides, a common interpretation among Western Baha'is is that each side represents one of the major religions of the world: Hinduism, Confucianism, Taoism, Buddhism, Judaism, Islam, Christianity, Zorastrianism and Baha'ism. The last religion, that of Baha'ism, is considered therefore by some as the latest in a series of manifestations of God, though not necessarily his final revelation to man. Baha'u'llah himself gave a different interpretation to the significance of the nine openings. According to his teachings, the temple of wood or stone is but a correspondence of the human body, itself the temple of God, which has nine openings. In either interpretation, the salient point is that God is not limited in the ways he manifests Himself. Our minds can thus be illuminated by any one of the nine stars or by the Nine-Pointed Star itself "whose radiance filtering down to us lights mind and spirit, signals future light."

That explains why in Section I of the poem, Orion, the giant hunter who pursued the Pleiades, is praised. As the lover of Eos, the Greek goddess of dawn, he represents, in a larger sense, those who love the dawning of this new manifestation of God. In **"Baha'u'llah in the Garden of Ridwan,"** he is equated with the auroral darkness. Aurora, the Roman equivalent of Eos, figures importantly in the Baha'i faith since the term "Dawnbreaker" has often been used to refer to thousands of early Persian Baha'is who were martyred. (A literal translation of the term from Arabic is "The Rising Place of the Lights of the Sun.") In the garden, all of nature joins in praising the Dawnbreaker Baha'u'llah. "Energies like angels dance glorias of recognition," their radiance as much an illumination as the pulsars and quasars of Section IV in **"Stars."**

Coming down to earth, we find that even the rocks praise Baha'u'llah as "Within the rock the undiscovered suns release their light." A mineral silicate, common in igneous and metamorphoic rock, is called mica. The word *mica* is influenced by the Latin *micare,* meaning *to shine.* Bearing a brightness similar to that of the stars, it participates in the general awakening of nature which accompanies the arrival of the Dawnbreaker.

Mica is used elsewhere by Hayden to refer to the sea and to the sky. In **"Gulls,"** for instance he speaks of the "mica'd fall of the sea," using mica to describe the dark sea as the waves, breaking upon it, appear as little suns. Thus mica, based upon a metaphor derived from the stars, is first transferred to rock and then to the sea and finally, to complete the circle, back to the sky again.

"The birds explode into mica sky" writes Hayden in **"A Plague of Starlings,"** a poem which describes the attempts of workmen at Fisk University to get rid of the troublesome birds by shooting into the leaves at evening time. Starlings themselves are reminders of the stars in their dark, often iridescent plumage. The irony which they present is not lost upon the speaker in the poem as he tries to avoid their carcasses while walking to class to lecture on what Socrates had told his friends about the migratory habits of the soul.

Not only do the rocks and the sea reflect the light of the stars. So do people. In **"Runagate Runagate"** Hayden praises Harriet Tubman, leader of the Underground Railroad, as a "woman of earth, whipscarred, a summoning, a shining." She, like Sojourner Truth, is a star, summoning others to her light as well as being the light. Similarly, Akhenaten in **"Two Egyptian Portrait Masks"** is spoken of as, "O Lord of every land shining forth for all." Finally, Baha'u'llah is the supreme reflection of that light. Of him Hayden says, "who by the light of suns beyond the suns beyond the sun and stars . . . alone can comprehend . . . and stars and stones and seas acclaimed."

Hayden's theme of struggle draws support not just from his imagery of the stars and other celestial bodies, as well as their correspondences in other aspects of Nature. Equally significant is his use of oxymorons whereby he achieves the maximum effect of combining opposites with a minimum number of words. For example, Sojourner Truth is called a 'childless mother' in Section III of **"Stars."** An apparent contradiction, it can be resolved by one's remembering that Hayden refers to this freed slave, originally called Isabella, as one who was following the star, her mind a star. Believing that she had received a special message from heaven, she left her job in New York, adopted the name Sojourner Truth and travelled throughout the North preaching emancipation and women's rights. By shedding light upon others, she consequently became the mother of countless children even though she physically did not give birth to any.

Likewise, the apparent contradiction contained in Hayden's reference to Akhenaten as "multi-single like the Sun" can be resolved by the examination of the image closely in the poem **"Two Egyptian Portrait Masks."** Akhenaten, King of Egypt from c. 1375–c. 1358 B.C.E., believed, as the name he adopted suggests (*Aten* meaning *sun*), that the sun was god and god alone. The universe was filled with his beneficent light and by it everything that lived had its being. So convinced was Akhenaten of the truth of his solar monotheism that in addition to taking a new name he also established a new capital. The spirit in his heart, says Hayden, was that of "Aten Jahveh Allah God." Akhenaten can therefore be multi-single because he contains within himself the spirit of God in several of its manifestations besides his own: that of Yahweh, worshipped by Jews; Allah, by Moslems; and God, by Christians, among others. Akhenaten is thus seen as one of the royal prophets in the progressive revelation of God.

Two of Hayden's oxymorons are somewhat similar in content although the position of the terms has been reversed. A striking contrast can thus be observed between "eudaemonic pain" in the poem **"Witch Doctor"** and "pained amusement" in the poem **"The Sphinx."** In the first of these two poems the witch doctor, a religious leader, is considering what new device he can use in order to "enmesh his flock in theopathic tension." The degree of his success is attested by the "cries of eudaemonic pain" from the audience, a pain that is happy since it comes from having a good spirit.

Just as pain may be accompanied by happiness, so happiness may be accompanied by pain, according to Hayden. The latter is illustrated in the second poem in which the Sphinx says that eventually "you will come to regard my questioning with a certain pained amusement." Causing pain, the Sphinx's riddle may concomitantly be a source of gaiety, enabling a person to tolerate a paradox. By the poet's own admission, this poem suggests that "something fundamentally negative, or apparently so, may be used in a positive, a creative way" (Interview with John O'Brien). Turning adversity into advantage is vintage Brer Rabbit, of course, and serves to remind us of the degree to which folk material from Hayden's Afro-American tradition permeates his poetry.

An apparently insolvable question also puzzles the participants in **"Electrical Storm."** In that poem the speaker muses over whether it was chance or choice that saved himself and others in the storm which killed several persons. While he is content to leave the question dangling as are the electrical wires strewn about the ground, he feels confident that he knows "what those cowering true believers would have said." True believers—the phrase is used by Eric Hoffer as the title of his book on religious fanaticism—supposedly do not find it necessary to cringe or shrink in fear. In this case, the speaker in the poem appears certain that the believers would have insisted that heavenly design determined who would be saved. The irony in this poem is that those who don't know the answer to the riddle can nevertheless live with it better than those who are so sure they have the answers.

The oxymorons in **"Theme and Variation"** will serve as the final examples of the compact paradox as used by Hayden. In this poem the speaker, identified as a stranger, ponders life's ephemerality. Referring in the first line to the four major categories of life—animal, plant, insect and man—and in the second to the four elements (earth, air, water and fire), the stranger avers that these "Are the revelling shadows of a changing permanence." This idea, at

least as old as Heraclitus, has been advanced more recently by the twentieth century philosopher Henri Bergson. According to his views, change takes on the pervasive character of reality. Such a constantly altering state of things makes man a voyeur, spying "upon the striptease of reality," says the stranger. Continuing to employ sexual imagery, he comments, upon seeing the transience occurring at the edge of things, that such an impending change turns to "curiosa all I know."

Such an imminence, moreover, "changes light to rainbow darkness wherein God waylays us and empowers." The oxymoron "rainbow darkness" is strikingly similar to the "golden darkness" found in the poem **"The Ballad of Nat Turner"** and the "auroral darkness" of the poem **"Baha'u'llah in the Garden of Ridwan."** The use of the word *rainbow,* however, adds a note of promise to this image, as Noah was given the rainbow as a sign of God's avowal not to destroy the earth again by water. In such a darkness God waylays and empowers. Reminiscent of the sexual imagery used by Donne and Crashaw, Hayden here depicts God as one who ambushes, *ambush* being synonymous with the word *waylay,* but also suggestive of a sexual overpowering.

Hayden also makes additional use of paradox in his frequent treatment of the theme of struggle, often associated with metamorphosis. Thus the energies of a paradox, resting in tension as they do in the stars, serve to inform much of Hayden's poetry. In **"Richard Hunt's 'Arachne',"** for example, Hayden focuses on the precise moment when Arachne is changed from a woman into a spider. Arachne, according to Greek myth, had challenged Athena to a weaving contest and was subsequently metamorphosed by her into a spider for her temerity.

Hayden stresses the tension of the moment structurally in at least two ways. First, by using present participles throughout the poem, as well as gerunds, he rivets the reader's attention on the metamorphosis itself:

> Human face *becoming* locked insect face
>   mouth of agony *shaping* a cry it cannot utter
>   eyes *bulging* brimming with the horrors
>   of her *becoming*
>
>   Dazed crazed
>   by godly vivisection *husking* her
>   *gutting* her
> *cutting* hubris its fat and bones away
>
> In *goggling* terror *fleeing* powerless to flee
>   Arachne not yet arachnid and no longer woman
>   in the moment's centrifuge of *dying*
>   *becoming*
>
> (Italics mine)

A second device used by Hayden to create structural tension in the poem is variation in the indentation pattern of the lines. The poem, composed of three stanzas of four lines each, is organized in the following manner: stanza one is indented so that each line following the first is indented a few more spaces to the right. The second stanza is indented in just the opposite manner: the first line is indented far to the right and each successive line indented a bit farther to the left side of the page. The third stanza repeats the pattern of the first. A zigzag effect is thereby achieved which graphically outlines the wrenching force of Arachne's metamorphosis.

In **"The Night-Blooming Cereus"** Hayden again focuses on the moment of metamorphosis. Waiting night after night to see the tropical cactus burst into flower, the on-lookers have been partially rewarded already by the grow-ing awareness of the "rigorous design" governing the pro-cess to which they bear witness. Even before the flower ap-pears, it prompts the desire "to celebrate the blossom, paint ourselves, dance in honor of archaic mysteries," just as in the poem **"Full Moon"** Hayden fondly remembers agrarian peoples who worshipped the moon and regulated their lives by it. When the onlookers "beheld at last the achieved flower," they were filled with reverence, recog-nizing the awful struggle by which so grand a moment had been attained. Thus the cereus, whose name comes from the Latin word for *candle* (because of the similarity in shape), sheds a light which, though ephemeral, stirs man's deepest religious impulses. In so doing it achieves a glory worthy of the struggle.

A glorious struggle is also recorded by Hayden in **"The Ballad of Nat Turner"** in which he achieves a dramatic tension of the first magnitude. At the beginning of the poem Nat Turner wanders into the Dismal Swamp, sees trees "where Ibo warriors hung shadowless" and wonders if it is the sign promised him by God. The sign he awaits is a go-ahead that the Day of Judgment is at hand which he is to lead. From his confession, we know that he had been identified as a prophet early in his life and that he be-lieved God had ordained him for some great purpose. Such a conviction impelled him, said Turner, to return to his master after a successful escape.

The tension of the poem is heightened considerably through the use of dialogue in the first nine stanzas. When Turner cries in the second stanza, "Speak to me now or let me die," an immediate reply is not forthcoming. In the fifth, the blackness whispers, in response to the same ques-tion, "Die." Later on, in the ninth stanza, he cries to the rock and the bramble, "Hide me," and they in turn antiph-onally utter the same cry, so dazzling is the vision that Turner beheld.

Of equal if not greater importance in establishing tension throughout the poem is Hayden's use of repetition, partic-ularly of the word *and*. Having already used it eight times by the ninth stanza, he then repeats it an additional twenty times in the last eight stanzas. Seven uses of *and* occur at the beginning of sentences; the other thirteen are used as connectives in phrases and dependent clauses. Hayden thereby heaps image upon image, accelerating the action in such a way that the reader reels from its cumulative force much as Turner reels from his vision of the dazzling combat of the angels.

For Hayden, the struggles of others may also help us in our own. In recalling the deaths of Martin Luther King and Robert Kennedy, he suggests that words in the mourning time may be transformed into a morning time. Through the Dawnbreaker's transilluminating word,

these deaths become the "major means whereby, oh dreadfully, our humanness must be achieved." Likewise, in Hayden's celebrated poem, **"Middle Passage,"** Cin-quez' "voyage through death to life upon these shores" is the life that now transfigures many lives, serving, as do the lives of King and Kennedy, as the means whereby others may effect their own metamorphoses.

Another example of such a transformation can be ob-served in the poem **"El-Hajj Malik El-Shabazz."** There Hayden traces the gradual metamorphosis of Malcolm X from his memory of the racist murder of his father when Malcolm X was quite young to his subsequent rise as a leader in the Black Muslim movement. His metamorpho-sis was not complete, says Hayden, until Malcolm recog-nized "Allah the raceless in whose blazing Oneness all were one."

Hayden's concern for the struggles of mankind is not lim-ited to publicly acclaimed figures. In **"The Diver,"** for in-stance, the speaker in the poem says that he strove against the conflicting desires to live and to die. He did so in "lan-guid frenzy," the phrase itself indicative of his contradic-tory feelings. Somehow, though, he began the "measured rise," finding in order the means whereby to contain his chaotic, opposing feelings. A similar struggle marks the attempts of the old man to fly again in the poem **"For a Young Artist."** After many painful attempts, he succeeds: "the angle of ascent achieved." Rising, whether from the bottom of the sea to its surface or from the earth to the sky, depends upon the struggle to establish the proper bal-ance. For the diver, it means gauging the speed of his as-cent; for the old man, finding the right angle.

Here Hayden is dealing not just with the struggle of a lone individual but with the struggle of the artist. Such a bal-ancing act is much like walking a tightrope. "Death is on either side, the way of life between," the man in the hospi-tal room in **"The Broken Dark"** recalls the Rabbi saying. The man is also reminded of Baha'u'llah's words, "I have come to tell thee of struggles in the pit."

Not just a figure of speech, the pit refers to an under-ground dungeon in Tihran where Baha'u'llah spent four months in heavy chains. Called **"The Black Pit,"** the room had only one opening and was crammed with more than a hundred murderers and thieves. Elsewhere, howev-er, Hayden does refer to the pit in a figurative sense. In the poem on Malcolm X he says that Malcolm's vision of a racist Allah "could not cleanse him of the odors of the pit." Representing the stench and foulness of hatred, the pit symbolizes for Hayden what we must struggle to extri-cate ourselves from, despite the pain it may cause us.

The consideration of the way Hayden uses struggle in his poetry must finally rest upon his tragicomic view of life. In **"'Lear is Gay'"** Hayden, recalling Yeats' "Lapis Lazuli," praises that gaiety found in an old man who "can laugh sometimes as at a scarecrow whose hobo shoulders are a-twitch with crows." Dedicated to his friend Betsy Graves Reyneau, the poem expresses admiration for someone whose attitude towards irrevocable defeat is tem-pered with gaiety. The defeat may be the physical deterio-ration of the body as one is metamorphosed into a "tat-

coat upon a stick," to draw a relevant image from Yeats. Or, generally speaking, it may be anything that is reduced to ineffectuality, which Hayden captures precisely in his image of the scarecrow that can no longer scare a crow.

For Hayden, to be able to laugh at the ravages of time is an achievement of the human spirit secure in the knowledge that everything alters even as we behold it. Thus as the jilted lover and the soul-weary people behold the singer in **"Homage to the Empress of the Blues,"** their sorrow is transformed by the power of her song. She not only "flashed her golden smile," lustrous and radiant, but "shone that smile on us and sang." The light of the stars, their tension in delicate balance, is thereby reflected as she sings the blues. Her song thus embodies Hayden's imagery of the stars, his theme of struggle and his use of paradox, bearing eloquent testimony to Hayden's artistry as well as to her own. (pp. 164-75)

> *Constance J. Post, "Image and Idea in the Poetry of Robert Hayden," in* CLA Journal, *Vol. XX, No. 2, December, 1976, pp. 164-75.*

Vilma Raskin Potter   (essay date 1981)

[*In the following obituary tribute, Potter admires Hayden's portrayal of the black experience in America.*]

He is dead and the honors are no longer important: not the Library of Congress, not Dakar, not the academic encomiums from Fisk to Michigan, the prizes, the fellowships. What is important is what has always been—the poems gathered into a single collection called ***Angle of Ascent.*** The gift of Robert Hayden's poetry is his coherent vision of the black experience in this country as a continuing journey both communal and private. This journey begins in the involuntary suffering of the middle passage and continues across land and into consciousness. His poems are full of travelers whose imagination transforms the journey. In the striking sonnet, **"Frederick Douglass,"** Hayden names the journey "this freedom, this liberty, this beautiful / and terrible thing, needful to man as air." He celebrates Douglass's dream that makes "lives grown out of his life." These lives become the various dreamers of Hayden's canon. From his earliest published volume, ***A Ballad of Remembrance,*** to the last, ***American Journal,*** a traveler's perspective of our American experience is his most striking theme.

The black epic journey, a "voyage through death" is the subject of his complex, brilliant early poem, **"Middle Passage."** An anonymous narrator controls the tone of the poem from horror to celebration. The narrator is concealed as a witness, yet his is the ironic intelligence that judges, condemns, celebrates. He hears and reports the testimonies of those oceanic voyagers who are the poem's European voices. The epic black journey is recounted in a collage of white voices: hypocrites hymning in New England of Jesus walking upon the waters, scoundrel shipowners, deck officers, maritime lawyers, sick seamen. Into this sequence is threaded Shakespeare's song of Ariel in a fine double irony. It parodies the European civilization's great poet while it extends Shakespeare's text to emphasize the profound rage of the enslaved.

Deep in the festering hold thy father lies,
of his bones New England pews are made,
those are altar lights that were his eyes.
Deep in the festering hold thy father lies,
the corpse of mercy rots with him,
rats eat love's rotten gelid eyes.

But oh, the living look at you
with human eyes whose suffering accuses you,
whose hatred reaches through the swill of dark
to strike you like a leper's claw.

You cannot stare that hatred down
or chain the fear that stalks the watches
and breathes on you its fetid scorching breath;
cannot kill the deep immortal wish,
the timeless will.

Here Ariel and, as an echoing voice, the narrator speak as the victims. In a vivid conclusion, all that suffering and hatred is transformed by "the timeless will." Now the white speaker is urbane, Spanish; the scene is the Connecticut courtroom, 1841; it is the trial of the *Amistad* resisters and particularly of Cinquez, the leader. At the end of the poem, Cinquez becomes the "deathless primaveral image" whose life "transfigures many lives." Thus the voyage through death of **"Middle Passage"** becomes a voyage into life, an affirmation of will, struggle, resistance.

Hayden created a group of poems which resonate with continuity of the theme of the Middle Passage and the unfulfilled but "deep immortal wish" of Ariel's song. One of these, **"Runagate Runagate,"** is designed like **"Middle Passage"**: a multitude of voices testify; some are famous, some anonymous. The oceanic voyage is now an overland journey of the underground railroad whose wheels and people hum together the poem's refrain, "Mean mean mean to be free." In **"The Dream (1863),"** Hayden combines a formal narrator's voice with the nineteenth-century folk voice of a young black soldier writing home to an old woman, Sinda:

> the judas trees is blossomed out
> so pretty same as if this hurt and truble wasn't
>   going on.
> Almos like somthing you mite dream about i
>   take it for
> a sign The Lord remembers Us . . .

For the letter writer, the change from slave into soldier completes the meaning of the journey into a free life. It is not so for Sinda, the dreamer with an African name: her imagination demands more than northern buckras in warrior postures. Hayden sets Sinda into a landscape of birdsong and blooming tree—but her dream is unfulfilled. These overland journey poems Hayden wrote acknowledge the incompleteness of the dream; they become, therefore, a poetry of dreamers, of scouts, of seekers.

Some of Robert Hayden's dreamers are historic figures. The star poems of ***Angle of Ascent*** celebrate Sojourner Truth; Nat Turner and Frederick Douglass are in ***A Ballad of Remembrance;*** in the newest group are Phillis Wheatley and Matthew Henson. But many dreamers are plain folks. Mattie Lee scurries joyfully aboard a U.F.O. wearing "the dress the lady she cooked / for gave her." Sometimes the anonymous dreamer seems to Hayden himself—alert, ironic, peering into the heart of things. In **"Tour 5"** and **"Locus,"** the Middle Passage continues in an ordinary trip south. It becomes the historial American journey, "the route / of highway men and phantoms, / of slaves and armies." The poet interlocks the dreamers (Indians, Blacks, Spanish, southern whites) in brutal historic ceremonies which produce our "adored and unforgiven past."

Hayden's poem for Malcolm X chronicles Malcolm's long journey from "a punished self / struggling to break free" through "false dawn of vision," through masks and metamorphoses to that last identity: Hayden called it a selfhood that acknowledges the Oneness of a raceless Godhead.

> He rose renewed, renamed, became
> much more than there was time for him to be.

In becoming El-Hajj Malik El-Shabazz, Malcolm X completes the meaning of the black journey:

> *mean, mean, mean to be free.*

The middle passage of the black experience can also be a personal travail no less imperative than the historic journey of a people. Twice Hayden speaks of the poet-as-journeyer in the image of Daedalus. In the early poem, **"O Daedalus, Fly Away Home,"** he refashions an old folk song:

> *O fly away home fly away*
> Do you remember Africa?
> *O cleave the air fly away home*
> My gran, he flew back to Africa,
> Just spread his arms and
>   flew away home.
>
> Night is mourning juju man
> weaving a wish and a weariness together
>   to make two wings
> *O fly away home fly away*

Later, he made a fly-away poem from a story by Marquez and called it **"For a Young Artist."** It is again a Daedalus tale without the gorgeous trappings of western fancy (the remarkable feathers, the sweet wax, the confident leap). This dreamer is stuck in a pigsty. The ugly, common dreamer with his lousy wooden wings, this object of vulgar gawking and idle curiosity is no brilliant artificer. There he lies, barely covered by castoffs, eating leftovers.

> Carloads of the curious paid
> his clever hosts to see the
> actual angel? carny freak?
> in the barbedwire pen

He is among them; perhaps, even, *of* them. But, compelled by an impulse "needful as air," he struggles

> He strains, an awk-
> ward patsy, sweating strains
>   leaping falling. Then—
>   silken rustling in the air,
> the angle of ascent
>   achieved.

The last Hayden work is called *American Journal.* At this writing only portions have been published, yet it is evident that the Black-American passage, the transfiguring immortal wish continued to be Hayden's theme. In **"A Letter from Phillis Wheatley"** the woman compares the middle passage with her own safe experience. Her imagination, like Hayden's, is free; her expressive voice is ironic and sedate. She recognizes the serpent in the English Eden. She marvels at God, not at the English.

Hayden chooses Matthew Henson, polar explorer, for **"The Snow Lamp,"** a poem in three voices: an Eskimo, an invisible poet-narrator, and Henson. The narrator speaks of the stuff of adventure: expansive wastes, pain, desolation, the dire dark. The Eskimos celebrate Henson-Miypaluk, skilled with sledges, dogs, the hunt, women—skilled with life. But only the voyager himself may say why he goes. Only Henson knows why for twenty years, he followed the meridians to their end. Hayden does not choose Henson's ultimate 1906 journey; his great journeyer illustrates the continuity of a dream, and, therefore, is taken at a point of incompleteness. Henson crosses "through darkness dire / as though God slept / in clutch of nightmare." And at the last, it is the voice of the traveler we hear in his note for a remote cairn: "We are verminous. We stink like the Innuits. We fight the wish to die."

The title poem of *American Journal* is a journal entry of a traveler from some Galactic Elsewhere who has reached out towards "life upon these shores." He reports ironically upon the strange Americans:

> . . . this baffling
> multi people   extremes and variegation their
> noise restlessness their almost frightening
> energy

He reports it all: the noisy buckras Sinda saw, the **"Tour 5"** paradoxes and vanities, the tensions between myth and experience. At last he points to a unifying, pervasive passion for life. This *élan vital* brought together in Hayden's imagination the middle passage and the whole unfinished American journey. Courage, say the poems of Robert Hayden, courage! We are all travelers to life upon these shores. (pp. 51-5)

Vilma Raskin Potter, "A Remembrance for Robert Hayden: 1913-1980," in MELUS, *Vol. 8, No. 1, Spring, 1981, pp. 51-5.*

If poetry nags at you, if it's something you feel incomplete without, then you'll go on because you'll have to. One cannot learn to be a poet. One is born a poet.

—*Robert Hayden, as quoted in* From the Auroral Darkness: The Life and Poetry of Robert Hayden, *1984.*

Gary Zebrun (essay date 1981)

[*In the following excerpt, Zebrun discusses the intellectual and emotional sources of Hayden's poetry.*]

The great poets of the 20th century *have* achieved angles of ascent, transcendences of beauty, even though modern pressures of cruelty and destructiveness have made these ascents seem more precarious and uncertain than ever before. Eliot's measured dance in his "Four Quarters," his great ascent, is forever shadowed by the first horror of "The Wasteland." William Carlos Williams, as his contemporary Wallace Stevens noted in the preface to the 1934 edition of Williams's *Collected Poems,* insisted that "life would be untolerable except for the fact that one has, from the top, such an exceptional view of the public dump . . . ". All the wonder and solace that Yeats's poems can provide have their genesis in what he called in his famous closure to "The Circus Animals' Desertion," *the foul rag and bone shop of the heart.* It is out of Robert Hayden's own version of these dark and dingy places, completely grounded in the history of America and his own lifetime, in **"Hiroshima Watts My Lai,"** that his wellspring of plangency—and transcendence—takes place.

The voice of the speaker in Hayden's best work twists and squirms its way out of anguish in order to tell, or sing, stories of American history—in particular the courageous and plaintive record of Afro-American history—and to chart the thoughts and feelings of the poet's own private space. Both histories—the personal and historical ones—are transfigured into Hayden's poems, which are striking examples of what Emerson said a poem must be: "spheres and cubes, to be seen and smelled and handled." What one sees, smells, and touches in his poetry is the human imagination *searching* for something else besides the muck of history or of one's own foul rag and bone shop:

> Sprawled in the pigsty,
>   snouts nudging snuffling him—
> a naked old man
>   with bloodstained wings.
>
>   Fallen from the August sky?
> Dead? Alive?
>   But he twists away
> from the cattle-prod, wings
>   jerking, lifts his grizzled head,
> regarding all
>   with searching eyes,
>   (from **"For a Young Artist"**)

The speaker in the 3rd section of the poem, **"Stars,"** describes another seeker, *Sojourner Truth,* who "comes walking barefoot/out of slavery/ancestress/childless mother/following the stars/her mind a star." One of the primary human truths, Hayden believes, is freedom, the first principle on which America was founded and from which it has repeatedly strayed. It is personified here as a childless mother, the ironic and complex figure of the first freed black American desiring to give birth to free sons and daughters. But this figure remains sheer desire, starlight; she is a paradoxically painful and encouraging reminder that freedom (especially in this crazy winding down of the 20th century) remains, for many Americans, an unfulfilled desire. There is a rift between what is and

what one desires, and these barren facts of life and brilliant dreams of the imagination become a compelling and *challenging* tension in much of Hayden's poetry.

Throughout his work this urge to find relief from the horror and constriction of ordinary life remains simply the wish for transcendence, a kind of prayer, expressed, for example, in the 5th section of the remarkable series, **"Beginnings,"** the first poem in the collection *Angle of Ascent:*

> Floyd Collins oh
> I guess he's agoner,
> Pa Hayden sighed,
> the Extra trembling
> in his hands.
> Poor game loner
> trapped in the rock
> of Crystal Cave, as
> once in Kentucky coal-
> mine dark (I taste the
> darkness yet)
> my greenhorn dream of
> life. Alive down there
> in his grave. Open
> for him, Blue Door.

In this poignant lyric about the trapped miner, Floyd Collins, Hayden portrays how inextricably tangled are our human dreams and the hard, like Kentucky coal, realities of our lives. Here is the greenhorn dream of life (reminiscent of both the speaker's childhood and our first innocence, our lost Eden), and the Blue Door (the hoped-for opening in the earth and way out for the trapped miner). These rich, appealing images of beauty and solace, however, are checked by the first appearance of the father, trembling with fear and grief from the bleak news of Collins's disaster and by the coal mine darkness itself, so powerful that the speaker can taste it, in which the splendor of crystal and innocence and relief is trapped. The lyric form itself becomes in Hayden's difficult style a troubled, almost imprisoned voice of the heart. Beginning here with the wholly plain lines "Floyd Collins oh / guess he's a goner, Pa Hayden sighed, the Extra trembling / suddenly in his hands," the poem suddenly shifts to the trapped, worried voice of sorrow, "trapped in the rock / of Crystal Cave, as / once in Kentucky coal-mine dark . . . ," until it makes its transcendence, or noble wish for it, which is perhaps the only solace left for late 20th century poets: "Open / for him, Blue Door." These changes in tone and language in this brief section illustrate the poetic process in our post-romantic time, beginning in the ordinary world—the so-called "outward things" of English romantics—, passing into the troubled place of human consciousness—the prison of the self—, and emerging into tentative song, the result of imaginative transformation: the Blue Door. It is in poems, like this one, so finely crafted, that Hayden earns a place in literary history as one of the few contemporary poets of major distinction—a knowledgeable, competent, and inspired craftsman—who illustrates what may be in store for our poetry descending from Dickinson, Whitman, Frost, and Williams.

Somehow a striking sense of beauty, precarious as it is amidst material ugliness and threatening social and political actions, does emerge in these poems. In **"The Night**

Blooming Cereus" the speaker describes a night vigil during which he waited, hoping to see the heavy bud break into flower. "We waited," he says, "aware / of rigorous design." And the design that Hayden witnesses is as bewildering and contradictory as the design that Robert Frost describes in his famous poem called "Design." As in Frost's poem where assorted characters of death and blight meet, the dimple fat spider devouring the dead moth, against the background of the beautiful white heal-all, Hayden's night blooming cereus, a promise of so much beauty, both repells and fascinates the speaker. So, although he imagined it "packed / tight with its miracle. . . ," it seems, as it struggles to bloom, like an "eyeless bird head,/beak that would gape / with grotesque life-squak." Notice how tight, how compressed the language of these lines themselves are, not only representing the closed bud of the flower, but the *enclosed* place of consciousness, both of which contain so much beautiful possibility struggling to break out. When the cereus flower blossoms, it appears as a symbol of the hard earned and short-lived beauty, older than man himself; as the cry of doom that is existential in its source:

> Lunar presence,
> foredoomed, already dying,
> it charged the room
>   with plangency
>
>   older than human
> cries, ancient as prayers
> invoking Osiris, Krishna,
>   Tezcatlipoca.

"Elegies for Paradise Valley," one of Hayden's recent poems included in the volume, *American Journal,* is a collection of ballad-like poems about Hayden's dead kin and acquaintances from his childhood: Madam Artelia, Auntie Belle, Miss Alice, Jim—the Watusi prince, and especially Uncle Crip. The Paradise Valley of the title is a city slum in which one of the many voices of the poem remembers a junkie who died in maggots there and recalls the hatred for his kind he saw glistening like tears in the policemen's eyes. The title is no mere display of cleverness, or bitterness, but a roadsign for the reader that is packed with irony and poignant half-truths. City slum that Paradise Valley is, it goes beyond its surface decay, for it contains the sacred or nearly sacred characters that the poet brings powerfully before us. In section IV of the poem, its core, the speaker, the adult recollecting his childhood, accompanies his mother and Auntie (Uncle Crip's wife) to Madam Artelia's parlor. Madame Artelia has a saintlike appearance, qualified by the irony of superstition that one associates with contemporary prophets, those readers of a crystal ball. This is the kind of check which acts to question transcendence, characteristic of all these poems. When Auntie and Ma return to the waiting room and to the child who was forbidden to participate in the seance, Auntie seems almost satisfied that Crip is happy in his afterlife. "And Crip came," she says. "Happy, yes, I am happy here, / he told us; dying's not death. Do not grieve." But the poem does not end on this naked assurance that "dying's not death." The poet knows that human truths, or at least our perception of them, are much more complicated than this kind of blind assurance sug-

gests. So he continues the recollection: "Remembering, Auntie began to cry / and poured herself a glass of gin." To make this uncertainty perfectly clear, the speaker concludes, "Didn't sound a bit like Crip, Ma snapped." **"Elegies for Paradise Valley"** is one of Hayden's finest poems. It provides a rich example of the numerous tonal variations present in his work, including humor, anger, uncertainty, and love. His characters seem at once real and mythic. His ability to shift into voices quickly and effortlessly might remind a reader of some of the dramatic scenes in *Moby Dick,* in which Melville has created a flurry of believable voices: Ishmael, Queequeg, Pip, Starbuck, and Ahab, all about to speak on the deck of the Pequod.

Robert Hayden, supremely concerned with crafts as he is insists on exploring the fictions and truths of the heart that only a poet fastened to experience can convey. In particular, he studies the noble and tragic history of Afro-Americans as he charts the contradictory feelings of a *thinking* man, black or white. There is throughout his poetry a recurring elegiac tone. It is this plaintive note, this wellspring of plangency, that gives Hayden's poetry a signature of its own and that places him as an important link in an American tradition of soul-searching. This tradition received its first brilliance with Hawthorne and Meville, with Whitman and Dickinson, was extended to Frost and Crane, and during our time has passed to Lowell and Hayden. They have sought the spiritual in the land and in the heart, they have insisted on keeping up the highest order of technical brilliance (the craft of writing), and they have not balked at the difficulty and darkness which threaten their searches.

In his poetry, Robert Hayden is ceaselessly trying to achieve his angle of ascent, his transcendence, which must not be an escape from the horror of history or from the loneliness of individual mortality, but an ascent that somehow transforms the horror and creates a blessed permanence. This task, as he indicates in the swirling contradictions of his verse, might well be a folly. Nonetheless, it is *his* necessary folly and the single glorious folly that the human race in its vast imagination holds dear:

> We look for ease upon these islands named
> to honor holiness; in their chromatic
> torpor catch our breath.
>
> Scorn greets us with promises of rum,
> hostility welcomes us to bargain sales.
> We make friends with Flamboyant trees.
>   (from **"The Islands"**)
>   (pp. 22-6)

Gary Zebrun, "In the Darkness a Wellspring of Plangency: The Poetry of Robert Hayden," in Obsidian, *Vol. VIII, No. 1, Spring, 1981, pp. 22-6.*

G. E. Murray   (essay date 1983)

[*Murray is an American educator and poet. In the following excerpt, he praises the "honesty and directness" of* American Journal.]

Ironically, as the last original work we shall have from

[Robert] Hayden, *American Journal* represents an array of new beginnings for this important yet long overlooked poet. It shows Hayden to be moving in a great many positive directions. The book's opening selection, for instance, **"A Letter from Phillis Wheatley,"** audaciously re-creates the voice of the black colonial poet, circa 1773:

> A supper—I dined apart
> like captive Royalty—
> the Countess and her Guests promised
> signatures affirming me
> True Poetess, albeit once a slave.
> Indeed, they were most kind, and spoke,
> moreover, of presenting me
> at Court (I thought of Pocahontas)—
> an Honor, to be sure, but one,
> I should, no doubt, as Patriot decline.

From these mellow and subservient tones, Hayden turns to a vastly more radical historical perspective, that of abolitionist John Brown:

> I slew no man but blessed
> the Chosen, who in the name
> of justice killed at my command.
>
> Bleeding Kansas:
>
> a son martyred
> there: I am tested I am trued
> made worthy of my servitude.
>
> Oh the crimes of this guilty
> guilty land:
>
> let Kansas bleed.

The entire five-part sequence **"John Brown"** is impressive for its tight metrical control, visual impact and the "haunting stark / torchlight images," as well as for its pursuit of "Fury of truth: fury / of righteousness." These are and have always been concerns for Hayden, in spite of his wide range of poetic forms, lyric measures and voices. But occasionally, "righteousness" overwhelms the art, as with **"Homage to Paul Robeson:"**

> Call him deluded, say that he
> was dupe and by half-truths betrayed.
> I speak him fair in death,
> remembering the power of his
> compassionate art. All else fades.

This seems as dull—and, one supposes, as necessary—as dishwater. While this "homage" to the black singer and social reformer might well be better suited to prose, Hayden remains true to his medium, which more often than not proves an acceptable vehicle for his thoughts and desires, even when a particular poem falls short of its artistic mark.

Hayden's poetry has an indelible honesty and directness. He stares at the world and his life intently. He is honestly sentimental. His carefully pitched voice operates as a well-conditioned boxer, throwing a burst of glancing jabs as set-up, then delivering other blows at considerable length and effect. The result is a fine coordination between eye and ear, and a sense of completeness to this final book, albeit one of fragments and new vistas. Indeed, as one re-reads and interrelates Hayden's work, something remark-

able begins to occur. The world Hayden observes comes into clearer focus by virtue of his ways of looking at it, what he manages to cope with and capture. The poems do not consist of extraordinary high points; instead each poem becomes part of a more intricate music. Each poem proceeds by small increments and builds into larger, more deliberate structures which peak unobtrusively. Only after the plain and forceful voice stops, the poem ends, and we are drifting back from it, do we have the opportunity to regard the echoes and reverberations for all they are worth.

The best example of this is **"Elegies for Paradise Valley,"** a series of eight diverse and far reaching poems set in Hayden's boyhood Detroit. The sequence opens abruptly and convincingly:

> My shared bedroom's window
> opened on alley stench.
> A junkie died in maggots there.
> I saw his body shoved into a van.
> I saw the hatred for our kind
> glistening like tears
> in the policemen's eyes.

Soon after, Hayden alters and expands his expression to summon all the personal troubles of the times he has recollected:

> Where's Jim, Watusi prince and Good Old Boy,
> who with a joke went off to fight in France?
> Where's Tump the defeated artist, for meals
> or booze
> daubing with quarrelsome reds, disconsolate
> blues?
> Where's Les the huntsman? Tough Kid Choco-
> late, where
> is he? Where's dapper Jess? Where's Stomp the
> shell–
> shocked, clowning for us in parodies of war?
> Where's taunted Christopher, sad queen of
> night?
> And Ray, who cursing crossed the color line?
> Where's gentle Brother Davis? Where's dope-
> fiend Mel?
> Let vanished rooms, let dead streets tell.

It is apparent what purpose is served by this litany of appellations as Hayden focuses on the secrets of growing up rough and, sometimes, ready. Hayden proves to be a poet willing to return or go out to whatever can tell him what he is. And this is no common trait among our many poets. Hayden's poems yield pleasure and wisdom. They are the learned, meditative, witty and melancholy leavings of a craftsman who won't constrain his art or his life for the sake of any accommodation, literary or otherwise.

Two of this book's most exceptional poems are memorable for their curious circumstances and renderings. First is the tantalizing **"The Snow Lamp,"** a poem described as "in progress" and now, with Hayden's passing, one that will remain fragmentary. The poem's subject is Peary's 1909 expedition to the North Pole. Its main character is Matthew Henson, a black man in Peary's group, who became a legend among the Greenland Eskimos. In the following passage, Henson, whom the Innuit have adopted and named "Miypaluk," begins to appreciate his new identity:

it is beginning oh
it begins now
breathes into me
becomes my breath

out of the dark
like seal to harpoon
at breathinghole
out of the dark

where I have wait-
ed in stillness that
prays for truth–
ful dancing words

ay-ee it breathes
into me becomes
my breath spiritsong
of Miypaluk

Composed with an ear for the sound and spirit of an Eskimo song-poem, this foreshortened work exhibits fascinating possibilities, especially as Hayden begins to explore the
nature of demon in both Eskimo and expeditionist souls.

Finally, the title poem purports to be the chronicle of an
alien from another galaxy here to observe our American
strangeness: The concept is well-executed, and appropriate, for Hayden, as a black man who lived in the United
States all his life, knew how it felt to be a socially risky outsider looking in. The poet's feelings are understandably
mixed:

america   as much a problem in metaphysics as
it is a nation earthly entity an iota in our
galaxy   an organism that changes even as i
examine it   fact and fantasy never twice the
same   so many variables

exert greater caution   twice have aroused
suspicion   returned to the ship until rumors
of humanoids from outer space   so their scoff
ing media voices termed us   had been laughed
away   my crew and i laughed too of course

confess i am curiously drawn   unmentionable
   to
the americans   doubt i could exist among them
   for
long however   psychic demands far too severe
much violence much that repels   i am attracted
none the less   their variousness their ingenuity
their élan vital   and that some thing   essence
quiddity   i cannot penetrate or name

Standing out in a lifetime of thunderstorms, free-spirited
and attentive, Hayden *did* penetrate and name his essences—his indefatigable quest for learning and analysis,
his ethnic virtues—in order to produce a testimony to
faith even in the face of social and cultural ignorance.
Dedication to the life of his art enabled Hayden to understand that "we are for an instant held shining / like memories in the mind of God." (pp. 651-54)

G. E. Murray, "Struck by Lightning: Four Dis-
tinct Modern Voices," in Michigan Quarterly
Review, *Vol. XXII, No. 4, Fall, 1983, pp. 643-*
54.

John Hatcher   (essay date 1984)

[*In the following excerpt from a stylistic analysis of Hay-*
den's poetry, Hatcher discusses subject, setting, and
point of view.]

The characters and experiences which are the raw materials, the essential building blocks from which Hayden's
poems are fashioned, are striking in their variety. Ca-
talogued and categorized, they reveal a man intrigued
with people, places, with history and art, but above all, a
man acutely sensitive to the anguish of others.

[In an interview with John O'Brien] Hayden said that he
was 'more interested in people than in things or in abstractions', especially in 'heroic and "baroque" people' and in
'outsiders, pariahs, losers'. Statistically his poems bear
him out since most of them focus on characters. He drew
these figures from history, from his own family, from Paradise Valley, from myth and art. As a poet with a flair for
drama Hayden had an uncanny ability to invade the psyches of these characters and study the human mechanism
at work. It mattered not if they were lynchers or window
washers, vagrants, prisoners or mystics, whether heroes,
sycophants, spiritual leaders or simply survivors.

From Afro-American history he took his portraits of Cinquez, the fictional Daedalus, Sojourner Truth (Isabella
Van Wagener), Nat Turner, Harriet Tubman, Crispus At-
tucks, Frederick Douglass, Matthew Henson, Malcolm X
and Martin Luther King, Jr. From his Afro-American
cultural heritage he took Phillis Wheatley, Paul Laurence
Dunbar, Bessie Smith, Billie Holiday, Tiger Flowers and
Paul Robeson. From his own family history he portrayed
Pa Hayden, Sue Hayden, Uncle Jed, Uncle Crip and
Sinda. From the rich resources of his own imagination he
constructed the Rag Man, Aunt Jemima, the 'mystery
boy', the 'Queen of Sunday', the tattooed man, 'the stranger', the alien visitor, the diver and the astronauts. From
myth and literature he borrowed Lear, Perseus, Márques'
'old man with enormous wings', Arachne, the Sphinx,
Daedalus, Akhenaten and Nefertiti. Of course, most engaging of all his characters is the persona himself. In such
lyrics as **'The Broken Dark'**, **'Words in the Mourning
Time'** and **'The Peacock Room'** we come to know him well
as we trace his struggle towards identity and transformation.

Another frequently used subject in Hayden's poems is setting. Here too the great variety of places betokens the variety of symbolic uses they serve. In classifying these places,
however, one finds that they form several distinct clusters
which indicate the sources for some of Hayden's inspiration. The natural settings predominate, sometimes a landscape, sometimes a powerfully evocative place. In **'Kodachromes of the Island'**, **'The Islands'**, **'The Point'**, **'Veracruz'** and **'Gulls'** Hayden focuses on detailed seascapes.
'Snow', **'October'** and **'Ice Storm'** contain seasonal landscapes. **'The Diver'** contains elaborate underwater imagery and **'The Mirages'** contains a succinct but effective desert image.

Possibly the most prominent source of settings was Hayden's association with the South and the ironic contrasts
he felt between the pastoral beauty of the countryside and

the violence and racial injustice that the places connoted, both in the past and in the present. **'Locus', 'Tour 5', 'Theory of Evil', 'Magnolias in Snow', 'A Ballad of Remembrance'** and **'Night, Death, Mississippi'** all focus on Southern settings as symbols of inherited evil. Likewise, Hayden's portrait of the Redstone Arsenal in **'Zeus over Redeye'** contrasts the floral beauty of Alabama with the lethal weaponry of modern ballistic missiles, just as the relic battlefield in **'On Lookout Mountain'** ironically recalls the principles for which that war was waged, as present wars are yet being fought for freedom and justice.

Rooms are another major subject for Hayden's poetry. Prison cells are important as subject and symbol in **'Soledad', 'The Prisoners', 'Belsen, Day of Liberation'** and **' "From the Corpse Woodpiles. . .".'** In **'The Return'** and **'Those Winter Sundays'** a homestead plays a major part in evoking philosophical reflection, as do the hospital room in **'The Broken Dark'** and the museum room in **'The Peacock Room'**.

A number of poems focus on depictions of Paradise Valley. **'Elegies for Paradise Valley'**, though a character study, relies importantly on setting, as does **'Double Feature', 'Free Fantasia . . . '** and **'Summertime and the Living . . .'**, possibly the most detailed of these poems. The literal subjects in most of the Mexican poems are also focused on setting—**'Mountains', 'Veracruz', 'Sub Specie Aeternitatis', 'Market'** and **'La Corrida'** all function as poetic snapshots from which the poet constructs **'An Inference of Mexico'**.

In keeping with the Hayden symbology of light versus darkness, a number of poems with strong negative connotation are set at night, among them **'Night, Death, Mississippi', 'Ice Storm'** and **'The Ballad of Nat Turner'**. Several others are set at night, but portray the light of renewal and hope piercing the dark, though not all of these are strictly focused on setting *per se*. In **'The Broken Dark', 'The Night-Blooming Cereus', 'Full Moon', 'Stars'** and **'Traveling through Fog'**, the nighttime setting is only the backdrop against which more important concerns are discussed, but setting is a necessary part of the symbolism in each poem. Setting is also vital in any number of other poems. In **'Middle Passage'** each narrative voice is importantly placed in a dramatic context—in the ship's hold, in the officer's cabin, in the courtroom. Likewise the depiction of the desolate wastes in **'From *The Snow Lamp*'** and **'Astronauts'** are essential in the interplay between character and environment, as is the sideshow context for the tattooed man and Aunt Jemima, and the barnyard for the winged man.

There are a few other discernible groups of subjects—the use of animals in **'The Moose Wallow'**, in **'The Lions'** and in the 'El toro' section of **'La Corrida'**. In each of these the animal is only vaguely characterized, since with each usage the poet is primarily interested in the quality the animals characterize. In this sense these poems function much as did the ancient lyric tradition of the *Physiologus*. Likewise in several poems Hayden uses flowers (zinnias, the night-blooming cereus, the sunflowers), and here too he has used the literal image to evoke immediately the symbolic implication, just as he has done in **'Gulls'** and

'Butterfly Piece'. Hayden also uses literal references to celestial bodies as the subject of several poems, again with immediate symbolic value: the moon in **'The Wheel'** and **'Full Moon'**, the stars in **'Stars'** and **'Runagate Runagate'**. But clearly the most important and frequently recurring literal subjects in Hayden's poetry are the array of characters and settings which he has chosen as his principal correlatives.

After subject, our attention in Hayden's poems naturally focuses on the perspective from which the images are presented to us, the narrative point of view. Of course, often the speaker and subject are the same in his first-person narratives, and sometimes, like a clear mirror, the speaker is transparent, an objective reporter of fact. But always these three ingredients of reader, subject and narrator are in some important relationship, and like a camera lens the narrative point of view determines how we view that interplay.

In much of Hayden's poetry we are aware of the evolving persona who guides us through his world of thought and experience. In his dramatic monologues we forget the persona and concentrate on the fictive voice of a dramatic character who always reveals much more than he is aware. But unlike many poets who when they find an amenable narrative technique, hold fast to it, Hayden employed numerous voices and narrative devices. To begin with he employed the first-person point of view with a number of variations. . . . [In] the 1982 *American Journal* he has a group of poems that seem clearly personal, almost confessional in tone. In **'Names'** he describes directly his anguish over discovering he was not legally Robert Hayden. In **'As my blood was drawn'** he seems to give vent to his fear and sadness at discovering the ominous progress of his disease. In one sense these poems are little different from his earlier personal poems like **'The Whipping'** and **'Those Winter Sundays', 'Electrical Storm'** or **'The Night-Blooming Cereus'**, all of which are mostly first-person narratives about the poet's life. But in the later poems, in **'Elegies for Paradise Valley'** for example, the subject seems to be biographical insight into Robert Hayden, whereas **'The Whipping'** concerns Sue Hayden, **'Those Winter Sundays'** concerns Pa Hayden as a symbol of parental love, **'Electrical Storm'** focuses on Divine intervention and **'The Night-Blooming Cereus'** on the flower.

It could be well argued that even in these later first-person poems our interest goes beyond Hayden the individual to Hayden the Bahá'í viewing his own death as evidence of the world's painful transition, and I think this is true. With virtually no poem I am aware of is the poet's primary goal to present himself as an individual. As Wilburn Williams, Jr., noted in his study of *Angle of Ascent* [*Chants of Saints*], Hayden had the capacity to 'objectivize his own subjectivity. His private anguish never locks him into the sterile deadend of solipsism; it impels him outward into the world'.

Hayden's most frequent use of the first-person viewpoint involves his consistent use of the persona. It is sometimes a thinly guised mask, a fact which has led many critics to view his work as amplifications of biographical fact rather than to consider them as tropes for larger concerns. The continuity of Hayden's poetry demonstrates that one can trace the progress of the persona as he struggles for identity and his own voice in poems like **'A Ballad of Remembrance'**, as he flees from his furies in **'The Broken Dark'** or from the world's turmoil in **' "From the Corpse Woodpiles . . . " '**, as he becomes dispirited in **'Words in the Mourning Time'** or reconciled in **'October'**. These poems also focus on the first-person poet/persona, his experiences and feelings, but more obviously as a character, as a representative of a particular historical perspective, a Bahá'í struggling in a period of wrenching transformation.

Another use of this same persona involves the speaker's recollection of himself in relation to something else— another character, an experience, a work of art, a powerfully evocative setting. All of the Mexico poems have this perspective—the speaker is involved, is affected by what he sees. But while we key on his reaction, our primary concern is with the symbolic materials he encounters—the ritualistic celebrations, the marketplace, the bull-fight. Likewise in **'The Night-Blooming Cereus'** or **'Monet's "Waterlilies" '** or **'The Peacock Room'** we are interested in the speaker's personal reaction to these external objects; we learn about him from the relationship, but our primary attention is on the objects themselves as he reflects them to us.

A substantial part of this effect is Hayden's use of tenses. **'The Peacock Room'** and **'Monet's "Waterlilies" '** are narrated in the present tense and have immediacy, a feeling of emotional action taking place, whereas **'The Night-Blooming Cereus'**, narrated in the past tense, displays before us the speaker and his wife in relation to the flower, but also the speaker remembering himself—we infer that he has learned something by remembering his reaction. **'The Moose Wallow'** and **'Electrical Storm'** are also in the past tense as the narrator recalls himself as a character in the remembered anecdotes, whereas **'A Plague of Starlings'** and **'Full Moon'**, which are in the present tense, have a more uncertain tone, since the persona is in the midst of experience, not reflection.

One of Hayden's most celebrated usages of the first-person persona point of view is in his childhood recollections. **'Those Winter Sundays'**, which Karl Shapiro called 'a fine example of the "pure lyric" ', is perhaps the best example, though most of the recollections of Paradise Valley are similar in mode and narrative construction. **'Elegies for Paradise Valley'**, **'Free Fantasia: Tiger Flowers'**, the middle portion of **'The Whipping'**, **'The Rabbi'** and **'Double Feature'** all have more or less the same intent. The persona is not overwhelmed with nostalgia—these scenes do not flow naturally or easily before him. The persona dredges up some with pain, guilt, anguish; others he recalls with a sense of loss, but all of these scenes imply a persona willfully attempting a panoramic review of his beginnings in order to understand the mechanisms of the present—his lost identity, his guilt, his need for love, his appreciation of colorful characters.

In yet another use of the first-person narrative technique Hayden wrote a number of poems where the speaker focuses on something not so pointedly related to his own life or emotional response. In **'The Prisoners'**, for example, the poet/speaker is certainly involved with the inmate, reads to him and ultimately is moved by the prisoner's reaction to the heartfelt attempt at communication, but the reader's attention is primarily on the prisoner himself as a symbol for our own condition, not on the speaker or the speaker's response. Likewise in **'The Performers'**, **'Homage to Paul Robeson'** and **'The Rag Man'** the 'I' is important, if only because we view the exterior world through his biased perspective. The resulting impressionistic portraits do indeed give us added information about this artist/companion who guides us through his life, but here too our primary focus is on the external world, the window washers, Paul Robeson's career, the philosophical implications of the street scene in **'The Rag Man'**.

Certainly the most dramatic distance between the poet and the poem with first-person narratives occurs when Hayden creates complete and complex characters who tell their stories. One of the most powerful of these is **'The Ballad of Nat Turner'**, in which Turner himself recounts his vision for his 'brethren'. This remarkable use of the dramatic monologue portrays Turner's mystic vision and, more importantly, Turner's interpretation of that experience:

> In scary night I wandered, praying,
>   Lord God my harshener,
> speak to me now or let me die;
>   speak, Lord, to this mourner.
>
> And came at length to livid trees
>   where Ibo warriors
> hung shadowless, turning in wind
>   that moaned like Africa . . .

Hayden similarly creates the character of Daedalus who recalls how his 'gran' 'flew back to Africa', and who chants his longing to escape his slavery. Likewise a good portion of **'John Brown'** is in the form of a dramatic monologue, though the narrator's voice takes us in and out of that first-person narrative, in the same way that he does with the figure of Aunt Jemima. But in both poems, the heart of the narrative is the first-person recounting of lives by the characters themselves.

There are other minor examples of the dramatic monologue in earlier poems—Perseus, the speaker in **'The Wheel'**, the bereft Medea figure in **' "Incense of the Lucky Virgin" '**. But in his last volume Hayden created some of his most powerful examples of this effective narrative device. **'A Letter from Phillis Wheatley'** is an epistolary dramatic monologue, and the last section of **'From *The Snow Lamp*'** is also presented as the written log entry of Henson's experience. Hayden's most powerful uses of this narrative technique in *American Journal,* and perhaps in his career, are the monologue of the speaker in **'The Tattooed Man'** and the journal of the alien visitor in **'[American Journal]'**. In fact, the emphatic use of the dramatic monologue in this last volume caused Fred Fetrow in his review of the work to observe that Hayden's 'narrative versatility' is one of his most distinguishing qualities as a poet:

> In retrospect, Hayden's final poems appropriately exhibit his deft talent for creating diversified voices. Indeed, as partially indicated in *Ameri-*

can Journal, a significant element of his unique voice derives from his narrative versatility, a range in modality perhaps unmatched among contemporary poets ["American Poet," *Poet Lore* 1982].

Hayden's uses of the third-person narrative point of view are no less varied or innovative. Most of the poems which focus on anecdotes and elliptically told stories in the ballad tradition are presented in the third-person point of view. Among these are **'The Ballad of Sue Ellen Westerfield', 'The Ballad of the True Beast', 'Unidentified Flying Object',** the more elaborate **'For a Young Artist'** and **'El-Hajj Malik El-Shabazz'.** Likewise most of the character pieces are presented in the third person, though in various forms. There is the formal sonnet **'Frederick Douglass',** the richly ornate portrait in **'Witch Doctor',** the tightly imagistic sketch of the drug addict in **'Soledad',** the surreal impression of the distraught boy in **' "Mystery Boy" Looks for Kin in Nashville'.** In some of these the third-person narrator is faceless, a dispassionate reporter, a clear mirror, as in **'Kid'** or **' "The Burly Fading One" ',** whereas in **'Frederick Douglass'** or **'Bahá'u'lláh in the Garden of Ridwan'** the narrator makes no pretense at objectivity.

This same distinction holds true for Hayden's use of the third-person point of view in presenting settings. Sometimes the narrative voice objectively presents a place, from which we infer symbolic implications. There may be some tonal qualities in presentation as clues to thematic intent, but the narration itself does not imply that the setting is being filtered through a personality. **'Mountains', 'Stars'** and **'Locus',** for example, are presented through a keen-eyed but essentially objective point of view, even though we have some sense of that narrator. In pieces like **'Magnolias in Snow', 'Figures'** or **'Market'** the narrator, though unidentified, charges the portrait with his personal emotions, whereas in the highly compressed imagistic pieces, Hayden uses a dispassionate third-person narration. In such poems as **' "Dance the Orange" ', 'Smelt Fishing'** or **'Snow'** we are not only unaware of the narrator; we are also left largely without tonal clues to guide us to the poet's meaning.

A variation on the third-person presentation occurs in several poems which are, strictly speaking, first-person narrations—there is a reference to an 'I' or 'we', but the focus is so importantly on the subject that we are really oblivious to the narrative point of view. In **'Kodachromes of the Island',** for example, we are until the end of the poem concentrating on the photographic images of the setting. Likewise, in **'Theory of Evil'** the only hint of the first-person speaker is in the lines 'We think of that/ as we follow the Trace'. The rest of the poem focuses on the legend of the trail and the story of 'Them Harpes'. The most weighty use of this narrative approach occurs in **'Homage to the Empress of the Blues'.** In this poem Hayden presents a third-person portrait of the singer Billie Holiday on stage before an assemblage of entranced onlookers. Our view of this, like the camera's perspective in cinematography, is objective; we watch this interplay between performer and audience until the final line when the poet inserts a simple personal pronoun to suddenly place him

there in the audience, and us there with him: 'She came out on the stage in ostrich feathers, beaded satin,/ and shone that smile on us and sang'.

The analogy of narrative point of view to cinematography is a useful one, for just as we see only what the camera can see so in poetry we view the literal imagery from a certain narrative perspective, and it is often crucial to discern the nature of that point of view, whether the lens is clear and whether the camera angle is distorting reality. Likewise, the camera sometimes presents the world as the character sees it, and sometimes it stands apart, above or beyond the character to show his relationship to the world. But always there is the artist controlling what that camera sees; therefore we must always be aware of what that camera eye represents.

Nowhere is this component of style more apparent than in variation of the third-person point of view in **'The Whipping'.** The poem begins in the third person with the narrator viewing objectively the 'old woman across the way' who is 'whipping the boy again'. Then, after three stanzas of describing the boy who is vainly trying to flee, the poem suddenly shifts in the fourth stanza to the first-person perspective as the narrator becomes the boy: 'My head gripped in bony vise'. Halfway through the fifth stanza, when the whipping is over, the poem shifts back to the third-person point of view. The effect, ostensibly a violation of narrative logic, is incredibly effective, implying among other things that the poet can be objective in recounting his past until the scene recalls 'woundlike memories' and he instantly loses that analytical perspective.

A similarly powerful use of this shift occurs in **'Night, Death, Mississippi'.** Interspersed with the last three of the poem's nine quatrains are italicized lines which apparently belong to the narrator. Until this point the poem is the gruesome narrative in the third person of the inhuman torture and mutilation of a lynching victim. But, similar to the use of an intervening narrative voice in **'Middle Passage',** the poet can no longer contain his reaction. Alluding to his childhood symbol of utter terror (rawhead and bloodybones), the speaker implies that this vision of reality fulfills the darkest possibilities of his childhood dread:

> *O Jesus burning on the lily cross*
>
> . . . . .
>
> *O night, rawhead and bloodybones night*
>
> . . . . .
>
> *O night betrayed by darkness not its own*

Another variation on the third-person narrative point of view is a reversal of the technique used in **'Homage to the Empress of the Blues',** where the poem is ostensibly in the first person, but through a phrasal attribution we are aware that the narration is being filtered through a character's perspective. In **' "Summertime and the Living . . . " '** the attribution occurs in the first line: 'Nobody planted roses, he recalls.' Later in the poem there is 'he remembers', but we are virtually oblivious to this 'he' and accept the account, like Hayden's own unfinished autobiographical sketch (also in the third person) as a first-person account. The same holds true for **'The Lions'.** The lion tamer explains throughout the poem how he makes his beasts perform, but in the first and last lines appears 'he said' to distance the poem from the poet himself. Clearly it is a narrative device used to create a more objective poetic image, to ensure that we treat the speaker not as Hayden or a thinly guised mask for the poet, but as an independent character with possibilities of perspective and meaning quite beyond the biographical fact of the poet's life. It is precisely the same technique that Hayden employs when he introduces the character of the Stranger as narrator in **'Theme and Variation', 'The Mirages'** and **'Ballad of the True Beast'.** Naturally we need to ponder this illusive 'he'. We need to consider whether it is an artist, the winged man, a wise Platonic guide or possibly the alien visitor who in Hayden's last poem takes leave of our company. Regardless, it is well worth noting the important effect of this simple shift in narrative point of view.

Hayden's most adept handling of narrative to achieve poetic effect is his synthesis of voices and points of view. He employs this technique infrequently, though most effectively in his epical account of the slave revolt in **'Middle Passage'.** In this magnificent poem he combines the voices of the crew, strains of Methodist hymnody, the voice of poet/persona and the speeches of litigants at court in a symphonic structure of theme and variation. As [Jackson Blyden and Louis Rubin, Jr. in] *Black Poetry in America* note:

> Myriad voices speak, indeed, in **'Middle Passage'.** Hayden, a careful, painstaking, deliberate workman, sensitive to the infinite possibilities for the management of form in poetry, close student of the poetic mode approved by the New Critics, and, like Tolson, an esteemed teacher as well as a dedicated poet, may be adjudged in his performance in **'Middle Passage'** virtually the artist whom he hopes to be in his conception of the ideal poet.

Often compared in technique to Eliot's synthesis of voices in 'The Wasteland', this poem has been widely praised in its use of narrative point of view as providing immediacy, dramatic credibility, and a quality of objectivity. Hayden himself enumerated the variety of poetic voices, citing the voice of the poet as moral commentator, 'the traders, the hymn-singers, and perhaps even of the dead' [in *How I Write/I,* 1972]. Hayden used a similar synthesis in **'Runagate Runagate'** when he blended the third-person narration with the nervous voices of the escaping slaves, quotes from wanted posters, from Negro Spirituals and the authoritative commands of the 'General' herself, Harriet Tubman. Likewise, in the original version of **'Words in the Mourning Time'** we hear several different voices, though most sections represent the changing emotional reactions of the speaker. But clearly **'Middle Passage'** is the best example of this innovative use of narrative point of view, and it demonstrates more than any other of Hayden's poems the shaping of subject into poem which this basic tool can effect. (pp. 253-62)

> *John Hatcher, in his* From the Auroral Darkness: The Life and Poetry of Robert Hayden, *George Ronald, 1984, 342 p.*

Marcellus Blount   (essay date 1985)

[*In the following excerpt from an overview of Hayden's poetry, Blount groups Hayden's works into three categories: "poems of reality," "prayers for transcendence," and "probings of Afro-American history."*]

Of the many scourges of this world, the problem of literary audience is the one that has most afflicted Afro-American poets. When Whitman wrote that without great audiences we cannot have great poets, he predicted the malaise of a good many innovators of poetic language, and well he described the disease that inflicts Afro-American poets regardless of their historical, cultural, or literary point of view, in spite of their ongoing struggle for health and prosperity, in condemnation of their search for authentic poetic voice. Although not always fatal, this disease has broken the spirit as well as the pens of many poets, and the pages of Afro-American literary history are stained with the anguish of its victims.

Robert Hayden's poems are among its survivors. An embolism of the lungs may have taken his life at the beginning of this decade, but his poetry has endured, pulsating still with his determination to overcome the ill effects of critical neglect and ignorance. Realizing early in his career that he had to protect his poems from the insensitivity of his readers, Hayden devoted much of his energy as a poet to revising existing poems—paring them down, making his images more precise, his symbolism more elusive—all to the service of fortifying his work against the intrusions of readers who felt compelled to oversimplify his art. Yet the irony of his endeavor, as Hayden realized all too well, was that he desperately needed the spiritual and financial support of literary success. Undoubtedly, had success come to him sooner than in the final years of his life, he would have been able to leave behind more proof that the Afro-American poet can survive and prosper.

As John Hatcher points out in his recent study of Hayden's life and work [*From the Auroral Darkness: The Life and Poetry of Robert Hayden,* 1984], much of Hayden's strength grew from his resistance to any rigid labeling of his work. Hayden felt uncomfortable with the terms his readers fashioned for his writing, and he especially resisted being categorized on the basis of his racial identity. While his stance may have earned him some degree of critical and academic respectability, it angered and confused many of his readers. The well-known exchanges among Hayden and other writers at the Black Writers' Symposium at Fisk University in 1966, and between Hayden and Amiri Baraka (then LeRoi Jones) in the pages of the 1968 issues of *Negro Digest* (later known as *Black World*), tainted Hayden's reputation in black literary circles, as he sacrificed his black readership for his sense of artistic honesty and clarity in arguing that he was a universal poet—not a black poet. In an interview with John O'Brien, he speaks about wanting to protect his options: "There's a tendency today—more than a tendency, it's almost a conspiracy—to delimit poets, to restrict them to the political and the socially or racially conscious." In an unpublished conversation with Joseph Gendron, he adds: "I am afraid today that 'black poet' carries the implication, has the connotation, that the poet is interested in one kind of thing and that he closes his mind upon the world and concentrates on the ethnocentric." These statements and others demonstrate Hayden's chief concern that such racial labeling was too constricting for his sense of his own poetic identity.

Hayden's fears of how his audiences might want to define his poetry are understandable, especially given the critical responses that black writers receive. Perhaps he had in mind the example of Paul Laurence Dunbar, whose work was censored when William Dean Howells' introduction to *Lyrics of a Lowly Life* (1896) brought Dunbar fame for his "dialect pieces," but in effect dictated the critical neglect of his verse experiments with the Alexandrine, rhyme royal, and the sonnet. In poems like "An Antebellum Sermon," Dunbar's literary versions of the Afro-American vernacular complicate the texture of American literature, yet many of Dunbar's "dialect pieces" are just that: figural representations of his audience's assumptions, carved with mockery and irony, served with his disdain for their undemanding and insatiable appetites for what he calls, in "The Poet," "a jingle in a broken tongue." Dunbar's career authenticates Hayden's fears that his identity as a black poet might restrict his poetic aspirations.

Hayden attempted to defend his work against the violations of critical ignorance, and he constructed a language of denial to protect himself. When he decided to edit an anthology of Afro-American poetry in the late 1960s, he aimed his introduction at those readers who might misread his intentions. In *Kaleidoscope: Poems by American Negro Poets,* he attacks what some of his contemporaries called " 'Negro poetry' "—especially the " 'poets of the Negro revolution' " and their "pseudo-poetry." He celebrates instead the work and pronouncements of Countee Cullen, who "insisted that he be considered a 'poet' not a 'Negro poet,' for he did not want to be restricted to racial themes nor have his poetry judged solely on the basis of its relevance to the Negro struggle." While it is understandable that Hayden wanted to move his work out of the "literary ghetto," he managed to associate the quality of Cullen's poetry—and his own—with the poet's disavowal of the racial dimensions of his poetic identity.

Yet, as a few of Hayden's most sensitive critics have demonstrated, much of his best poetry imbibes the languages of Afro-American history and culture. Even though Hayden sometimes attempted to transcend racial themes and subjects, in order to attain a universality of poetic identity, his poetic voice was the most distinctive when he explored his particular sense of history and identity. His poetic strength comes from his individuality, and not even Hayden would deny that he was an Afro-American.

Robert Hayden's poetry is rich in its variety of shapes and concerns. There are three major groupings: the poems of reality, the prayers for transcendence, and the probings of Afro-American history. In **"Butterfly Piece," "The Night-Blooming Cereus," "For A Young Artist," "The Peacock Room," "Kodachromes of the Island," "The Diver," "The Rabbi," " 'An Inference of Mexico,' "** and many other poems, Hayden writes as a modern poet of reality who commands a unique sense of the textures of the imagination and of experience. When, for example, the in-

sightful stranger in **"Theme and Variation"** reveals the shimmering illuminations and illusions that govern the act of perception, he initiates us as readers into some of the mystery and excitement of Hayden's poetry:

> I sense, he said, the lurking rush, the sly
> transience flickering at the edge of things.
> I've spied from the corner of my eye
> upon the striptease of reality.

Through this stranger, Hayden posits the basic epistemological concerns of his canon. His awareness of the changing nature of reality and its subtle attempts to deceive forms a persisting question: "How do we achieve understanding in a world that frustrates our attempts to master it?" Beneath the calm surface of all of these poems, his question reveals the ferment that is the undertow, against which he struggles to maintain his bearings. His poems of reality explore the complexities of perception, as Hayden braves the hidden dangers of existence.

Hayden was able to survive through his spiritual faith as a Bahá'í, and his religious poems constitute a major grouping of his work. Shaping **"Dawnbreaker," " 'From the Corpse Woodpiles, from the Ashes,' "** and **"Bahá'u'lláh in the Garden of Ridwan"** most directly, and pulsating through many of his other poems, is his faith in the moral and aesthetic force of the human movement toward the new world order prophesied in Bahá'u'lláh's teachings in the nineteenth century. The strength of that faith contains Hayden's agony in **"Words in the Mourning Time"**:

> I grieve. Yet know the vanity
> of grief—through power of
> The Blessed Exile's
> transilluminating word
>
> aware of how these deaths, how all
> the agonies of our deathbed childbed age
> are process, major means whereby,
> oh dreadfully, our humanness must be achieved.

Assuaged in his knowledge that religious order will eventually clarify the contradictions, he allowed his religious faith to guide his explorations of the tensions that activate reality. As he reveals in his **"Statement on Poetics,"** Hayden viewed the writing of poems as "one way of coming to grips with inner and outer realities—as a spiritual act, really, a sort of prayer for illumination and perfection." His poems on the Bahá'í faith are crafted to locate his spiritual bearings and to reaffirm his spiritual mission.

While many of Hayden's poems should and will be remembered, his major contribution to literature is the third grouping of his works, the poems that reach down in search of the obsidian of history, the smoky shards of the black experience. He joins T. S. Eliot, Wallace Stevens, and William Butler Yeats in their attempts to use poetry to reveal and to create the truths and forms of modern experience. Yet Hayden distinguishes himself as an artist when he accompanies Gwendolyn Brooks and Sterling Brown in their search for an Afro-American modernism in the rhythms and speech and performances of Afro-American culture. In his major poems of Afro-American history, **"Middle Passage," "The Ballad of Nat Turner,"** and **"Runagate Runagate,"** to name a few, Hayden accepts the challenge of revising the conventions of Euro-American literature so that they might more accurately portray Afro-American themes and sensibilities. His **"Frederick Douglass"** provides an example of this achievement. The poem explores aspects of the traditional European sonnet and the rhetorical strategies of the Afro-American folk sermon. Listen to his artful re-creation of the voice of the black preacher:

> this man, this Douglass, this former slave, this
>   Negro
> beaten to his knees, exiled, visioning a world
> where none is lonely, none hunted, alien,
> this man, superb in love and logic, this man
> shall be remembered. . . .

Here Hayden demonstrates that an Afro-American identity can be rediscovered *as an act of literary language,* not merely as a political or social imperative.

As a poet, Hayden sang in different keys, and his modulations and even the tremors make his performances exciting, but his voice was often the clearest and certainly the most distinctive when he submitted himself to the desires of a particular source of inspiration, which even Countee Cullen called upon as the "ebony muse." (pp. 169-71)

> *Marcellus Blount, in a review of "From the Auroral Darkness: The Life and Poetry of Robert Hayden," by John Hatcher, in* Black American Literature Forum, *Vol. 19, No. 4, Fall, 1985, pp. 169-71.*

William Rice (essay date 1989)

[*In the excerpt below, Rice recounts Hayden's ideological differences with the proponents of "black aesthetics," a concept that proposes a unique standard by which to judge black art.*]

It would be unfair to lay Hayden's ill luck with critics to his refusal to endorse the cultural program of his would-be allies in the literary world. Nevertheless, his name would probably be more familiar if he had not resisted the militant doctrines that were in the air in the 1960s, the pivotal years of his career. It was a time when artistic reputations were made on the cheap currency of politics. Hayden chose not to invest. He was no longer a young man then, of course, nor was he a stranger to deep and unpopular allegiances. He was a veteran of the black civil-rights movement from his youth in the 1930s; and in the 1940s he had joined the Bahá'í faith, a move unlikely to win him friends among radical intellectuals. As a writer he had early on stopped dabbling in fashionable protest poetry, and he gained a healthy, self-conscious distance from the Harlem Renaissance writers who gave him his first models. In his late twenties he could write sincere but ordinary lines like these:

> You should live naked,
> Naked and proud,
> Where black skin is neither
> God's curse, nor a shroud.

But as he matured—quickly—his thinking sought universals and his verse gained subtlety. Men and women of all ages and places were to be seen not for what separated

---

them but for what they had in common. In this Hayden may reflect the Bahá'í belief in world unity, although the idea of a transcultural, continuous, and ennobling human tradition was widely endorsed at the time. (Its status in our revisionist age is less certain, to say the least.)

All this is not to suggest that Hayden ever forgets the tragic history of his race. On the contrary, in the words of William Meredith, he penned "scarcely a line . . . which is not identifiable as an experience of black America." But there is also scarcely a line that is not a great deal more. Take, for example, the opening of the third part of **"Middle Passage,"** a long collage-like poem on the Atlantic slave trade:

> Shuttles in the rocking loom of history,
> the dark ships move, the dark ships move,
> their bright ironical names
> like jests of kindness on a murderer's mouth;
> plough through thrashing glister toward
> fata morgana's lucent melting shore,
> weave toward New World littorals that are
> mirage and myth and actual shore.

In these eight lines a particularly hideous aspect of slavery—that slave vessels were given names like "Amistad," "Esperanza," "Adventure," and "Mercy"—is universalized in the image of the sniggering killer. Likewise, the image of a shore shimmering in the distance fuses the mythic with the immediate. The passage of man from freedom into slavery is represented both as sensory trauma and real event. For Hayden, the crimes committed against his race by Europeans and Americans are to be understood not only as enduring historic wrongs but, more importantly, as evidence of the human race's enormous capacity for evil; and poets who wish to narrow the scope of this awesome subject risk becoming what he called "minotaurs of edict." Hayden held that in art the black experience of suffering and the white experience of moral culpability should serve to illuminate, for readers of all races, the complete *human* condition. Art, then, impels us toward unity and shared tradition. To preserve artistic integrity, Hayden held, the poet must remain "meditative, ironic / and richly human" and be content with "crafted confusion." Public poetry remains possible—Hayden wrote a number of occasional poems for large audiences—but it could never become a political tool. If it did, it would descend to partisan propaganda.

Needless to say, when the 1960s exploded and the Black Power movement advanced the idea of a Black Aesthetic, Robert Hayden was damned up and down for his alleged naïveté. He was called an Uncle Tom for cautioning, in **"A Ballad of Remembrance,"** against the rage that radicals were urging on black citizens:

> Hate, shrieked the gun-metal priestess
> from her spiked bellcollar curved like a fleur-de-lis:
>
> As well have a talon as a finger, a muzzle as a
> mouth,
> as well have a hollow as a heart. And she pin-wheeled
> away in coruscations of laughter, scattering
> those others before her like foil stars.

Hayden's dismissal of the program of separatist "Negro poetry" as "an ideological weapon" drew a bitter attack from Don L. Lee (later Haki Madhubuti): "Mr. Hayden," he wrote in *Negro Digest,* "what are television, radio, movies . . . and weekly news magazines if not ideological weapons—white ideology?" Lee denounced Countee Cullen and Hayden for "perpetrat[ing] a very dangerous myth . . . that poets other than black poets or black critics, are qualified to judge black or 'negro' poetry." On other occasions, the poet was denigrated by others for being an admirer of William Butler Yeats, for using difficult words, and for not using "black style and language."

An affable, noncombative man by nature, Hayden proved fearless in the face of these assaults on his art and character. He spoke of "literary nazis," of art being "displaced by argument," and "racist propaganda in a new guise." Once he echoed Oscar Wilde, stating that there is "no such thing as black literature. There's good literature, and there's bad. And that's all!" Hayden's courage brought him considerable stress and anxiety. Colleagues such as John W. Aldridge at Michigan remember him appearing in their offices, often very agitated. Would his adversaries never understand, he asked, that he was a poet first, that skin color was not to be exploited? Fortunately, he never let hostile attention slow his pursuit of craft.

The charge against Hayden alluded to above—that as a poet he owed something to Yeats—is at least accurate, even if there is no reason to regard this debt as a flaw. As already noted, Hayden was a student of Auden's and read deeply in the Harlem Renaissance poets. These three influences instilled in him a high regard for traditional poetic form: for the well-turned iambic line, for the subtle alternation of poetic feet to draw attention to the two- and three-sidedness of his rhetoric and imagery. But as Hayden matured he came to favor, even more than Auden and Yeats had, the metrically imperfect line that sounded right, rather than the strict line with cumbersome syllabic additions. He wrote the poem **"Middle Passage,"** for example, in blank verse, then revised it with only passing regard for scansion. I for one regret that at the peak of his powers Hayden no longer observed exacting poetic form, which alone can give the reader the pleasure of watching the exceedingly difficult done effortlessly. But Hayden knew the lessons of English prosody well, as almost all his work shows.

It is also to be regretted, I think, that Hayden stinted on the pleasures of rhyme. This may be a result of his unyoking of the Harlem Renaissance influence, but whatever its cause we find in its place a love of musical words. Even more interesting for their sound are his neologisms. His poems are sprinkled with "gangle," "upfling," and "oldrose." His usage is at times difficult, even quaint, as his unsophisticated critics complained, and his syntax can be fairly demanding, as in these lines, which describe Perseus's confrontation with Medusa:

> Her sleeping head with its great gelid mass
> of serpents torpidly astir
> burned into the mirroring shield—
> a scathing image dire
> as hated truth the mind accepts at last
> and festers on.

If passages like this are best re-read and studied, Hayden could also write speechlike and lyrical verse which easily moves from voice to voice and subject to subject. Of a housemaid in **"The Islands,"** he writes

> . . . She's full
>
> of raucous anger. Nevertheless brings gifts of
> scarlet hibiscus when she comes to clean,
> white fragrant spider-lilies too sometimes.
>
> The roofless walls, the tidy ruins
> of a sugar mill. More than cane
> was crushed. But I am tired today
>
> of history, its patina'd cliches
> of endless evil. Flame trees.
> The intricate sheen of waters flowing into sun.
>
> I wake and see
> the morning like a god
> in peacock-flower mantle dancing
>
> on opalescent waves—

These lines reveal how Robert Hayden commands subjects that are at once separate and complementary: daily life and human history, conversation and contemplation, the natural world and the imagery of myth, moral engagement and aesthetic sense. The representation of so wide a range of concerns in a single poem (and in an entire body of carefully crafted poetry) is no small feat in our age, and Robert Hayden's achievement is all the more admirable for the courage he showed when circumstances required.

To a surprising degree, those circumstances are still with us. The militants of the 1960s gain little notice now in the culture at large, but in the academy a self-interested critic or poet may find it hard to resist the fashion that relates art and vision insistently to race, class, and gender, the Trinity of new literary studies. For example, a highly placed figure on the academic scene, Henry Louis Gates, Jr., declared early this year in *The New York Times Book Review* that "the [traditional] teaching of literature is . . . the teaching of an esthetic and political order, in which no person of color, no woman, was ever able to discover the reflection or representation of his or her cultural image or voice." Unfortunately, this kind of thinking leads the academic literary establishment to draw crude political caricatures, as when Gates attributes to unnamed persons "on the cultural right" the appalling claim "that black literature can have . . . no masterpieces." Even more disastrously, literature itself becomes, according to this line of thought, merely a subfield of sociology.

If the new academic fashion widens Robert Hayden's readership, it will be mainly for the wrong reason—the isolated fact of his skin color. Even so, a new audience would also observe his dedication to the transcendent ideals of independence and integrity, craft and character. Looking ahead, we can hope with some confidence that Robert Hayden's example will not be lost and that, as he wrote of Frederick Douglass,

> . . . this Negro,
> . . . exiled, visioning a world
> where none is lonely, none hunted, alien,
> this man, superb in love and logic, this man
> shall be remembered

(43-5)

William Rice, "The Example of Robert Hayden," in The New Criterion, *Vol. 8, No. 3, November, 1989, pp. 42-5.*

FURTHER READING

Bibliography

Nicholas, Xavier. "Robert Hayden." *Bulletin of Bibliography* 42, No. 3 (September 1985): 140-53.
    Bibliography of works by and about Hayden.

Biography

Fetrow, Fred M. *Robert Hayden.* Boston: Twayne Publishers, 1984, 159 p.
    Critical biography of Hayden.

Criticism

Callahan, John F. " 'Mean to Be Free': The Illuminative Voice of Robert Hayden." *Obsidian* 8, No. 1 (Spring 1981): 156-74.
    Admires Hayden's ability to "illuminate," or depict, the past, especially historical black figures and his own experiences.

Campbell, Charles R. "A Split Image of the American Heritage: The Poetry of Robert Hayden and Theodore Roethke." *Midamerica* XII (1985): 70-82.
    Examines the poetry of Hayden and Theodore Roethke, determining: "Both Hayden and Roethke were searching for a heritage; Hayden seeking a reality to be found in brotherhood, in others, in the people he met, and in history; Roethke almost always seeking for himself within himself."

Cooke, Michael G. "Intimacy: The Interpenetration of the One and the All in Robert Hayden and Alice Walker." In his *Afro-American Literature in the Twentieth Century: The Achievement of Intimacy,* pp. 133-76. New Haven, Conn.: Yale University Press, 1984.
    Explores "intimacy"—a concept in which "the Afro-American protagonist (male or female, pugilist or philosopher, activist or ascetic) is depicted as realistically enjoying a sound and clear orientation toward the self and the world"—in Hayden's poetry and Alice Walker's fiction.

Fetrow, Fred M. "Portraits and Personae: Characterization in the Poetry of Robert Hayden." In *Black American Poets Between Worlds, 1940-1960,* edited by R. Baxter Miller, pp. 43-76. Knoxville: University of Tennessee Press, 1986.
    Analyzes Hayden's poetic representations of such figures as Frederick Douglass, John Brown, Malcolm X, Phillis Wheatley, and Paul Robeson, maintaining that the poet "disguised" himself in these portraits.

Gibbons, Reginald. "A Man That in His Writing Was Most Wise." *Obsidian* 8, No. 1 (Spring 1981): 182-87.
    Praises the "civilized" quality of Hayden's work.

Glaysher, Frederick. "Re-Centering: The Turning of the Tide and Robert Hayden." *World Order* 17, No. 4 (Summer 1983): 9-17.
    Examines the influence of the Bahá'í faith on Hayden's "matchless" poetry, which Glaysher believes has "justly won international acclaim."

Hatcher, John. *From the Auroral Darkness: The Life and Poetry of Robert Hayden.* Oxford, England: George Ronald, 1984, 342 p.
    Acclaimed work on Hayden. Provides a critical biography of the poet, an assessment of his conflicts with literary movements and trends, and an analysis of his major works of poetry.

Hirsch, Edward. "Mean to Be Free." *The Nation* 241, No. 21 (21 December 1985): 685-86.
    Lauds *Collected Poems,* declaring that it "should become one of our exemplary poetic texts."

Oehlschlaeger, Fritz. "Robert Hayden's Meditation on Art: The Final Sequence of *Words in the Mourning Time.*" *Black American Literature Forum* 19, No. 3 (Fall 1985): 115-19.
    Analysis of *Words in the Mourning Time,* a poetry collection that Oehlschlaeger believes "responded directly

to one of the most violent decades in American history"—the 1960s.

Review of *American Journal,* by Robert Hayden. *The Virginia Quarterly Review* 58, No. 4 (Autumn 1982): 134.

  Describes *American Journal* as a "wise and serene" collection of poems that reflects Hayden's "preoccupation with bigotry, hatred, and violence."

Williams, Pontheolla T. *Robert Hayden: A Critical Analysis of His Poetry.* Urbana: University of Illinois Press, 1987, 241 p.

  Examines Hayden's development as a poet of the American experience.

Williams, Wilburn, Jr. "Covenant of Timelessness and Time: Symbolism and History in Robert Hayden's *Angle of Ascent.*" *The Massachusetts Review* XVIII, No. 4 (Winter 1977): 731-49.

  Examines Hayden's use of history and symbolism in his poetry, noting that in *Angle of Ascent* "we can see clearly the remarkable fertility of the symbolist's union with the historian, the bipolar extremes of Hayden's singular poetic genius."

Additional coverage of Hayden's life and career is contained in the following sources published by Gale Research: *Black Literature Criticism; Black Writers; Concise Dictionary of American Literary Biography, 1941-1968; Contemporary Authors,* **Vols. 69-72, 97-100 [obituary];** *Contemporary Authors Bibliography Series,* **Vol. 2;** *Contemporary Authors New Revision Series,* **Vol. 24;** *Contemporary Literary Criticism,* **Vols. 5, 9, 14, 37;** *Dictionary of Literary Biography,* **Vols. 5, 76;** *Major 20th-Century Writers;* **and** *Something about the Author,* **Vols. 19, 26.**

Edna St. Vincent Millay

1892-1950

(Also wrote under the pseudonym Nancy Boyd) American poet, playwright, short story writer, essayist, librettist, and translator.

INTRODUCTION

Millay was a popular American poet whose best-known poems reflect the exuberant mood of social change that characterized the Jazz Age of the 1920s. She has been deemed one of the most accomplished sonneteers of the twentieth century and praised for her use of classic sonnet structure to present modern themes. Her verse is also notable for extending the scope of subject matter for twentieth-century women poets and portraying the feminine character with vastly expanded range and depth. Much of Millay's poetry is private and introspective in tone, exploring emotions associated with childhood, nature, love, and death.

Millay was born in Rockland, Maine. When she was eight years old, her parents divorced, and Millay lived with her two sisters and her mother. Encouraged by her mother, Millay began composing verse during her childhood. Several of her poems appeared in the children's magazine *St. Nicholas,* and she was first acclaimed as a poet at age twenty when her poem "Renascence" was published in the anthology *The Lyric Year.* With a scholarship obtained partly through the notoriety she gained from the publication of "Renascence," Millay attended Vassar College, where she studied literature and theater. In 1917, following her graduation from Vassar College, she published her first collection, *Renascence, and Other Poems,* which received positive reviews and established her in the literary world. During the early 1920s Millay lived in Greenwich Village where she continued writing and worked as an actress. During this time she was widely perceived as a free-spirited and rebellious social figure whose celebration of love and life is reflected in such works as *A Few Figs from Thistles* and *Second April.*

In 1923, following a nervous breakdown and a two-year sojourn in Europe, Millay published *The Ballad of the Harp-Weaver* for which she was awarded the Pulitzer Prize in poetry. Influenced by the escalation of global tensions in the years leading up to World War II, Millay began to address political and philosophical issues in such works as *The Buck in the Snow, and Other Poems* and the sonnet sequence "Epitaph for the Race of Man," included in *Wine from These Grapes.* Millay's works became increasingly political during the 1930s, but her efforts at propaganda in such volumes as *Make Bright the Arrows: 1940 Notebook* and *The Murder at Lidice* were generally criticized as overly sentimental and less successful than her writing on personal subjects. In 1944 Millay suffered

a nervous breakdown that prevented her from writing for several years. Her final volume, *Mine the Harvest,* was completed shortly before her death from a heart attack in 1950 and published posthumously.

Much of Millay's verse, particularly that written during the early 1920s, has been characterized as an effective representation of the atmosphere of the Jazz Age. Her public image of independence and rebellion during this time was strengthened by the flippant tone of her volumes *A Few Figs From Thistles* and *Second April.* This image was particularly evident in such poems as "Figs from Thistles": "My candle burns at both ends; / It will not last the night; / But ah, my foes, and oh, my friends— / It gives a lovely light!" In the poems "To the Not Impossible Him" and "Thursday" Millay playfully denigrated social conventions by depicting women who remain casual and unattached in love relationships.

Despite the common perception of Millay's verse as light-hearted and brash, many of her poems are deeply introspective. "Renascence," for example, expresses the poet's spiritual awakening and is noted for its vivid nature imagery and childlike tone. Critics have also praised the exuberance and insight of such poems as "Journey," which celebrates nature, and "The Bean-Stalk," which portrays feelings of fear and euphoria associated with artistic expression. Recent critics have suggested that aspects of Millay's poetry evince an affinity with the dark themes and subject matter and anguished feminine perspectives in the works of such modern American poets as Anne Sexton and Sylvia Plath, noting that many of Millay's poems present images of vulnerability, suffering, and victimization. In "Moriturus" Millay portrays a struggle between herself and the personification of death: "With his hand on my mouth / He shall drag me forth, / Shrieking to the south / And clutching at the north." Although early reviewers emphasized the poem's tone of defiance, later critics have asserted that Millay's language in this and other poems suggests an experience of violation and exploitation. "The Fitting," for example, depicts a woman's experience of rigid social conditioning and depersonalization through the metaphor of an uncomfortable dress alteration, and "Sonnets from an Ungrafted Tree" describes feelings of emptiness and disillusionment within an unsatisfying marriage.

In several works Millay addressed philosophical, political, and social themes. In her sonnet "Euclid Alone Has Looked on Beauty Bare," she associated the abstract concept of beauty in nature with the logical concepts of symmetry and perfection in mathematics. Her poem "Justice Denied in Massachusetts" bitterly decries the executions of Nicola Sacco and Bartolomeo Vanzetti, political radicals whose convictions on charges of murder and theft were widely protested. In the sonnet sequence "Epitaph for the Race of Man" Millay considers the dichotomy between humanity's penchant for self-destruction and its capacity for integrity and virtue. These and her other political works were considered an indication of her declining talents. Nevertheless, critics have assessed her best poems as significant reflections of an exciting and unconventional age in American culture and authentic expressions of what William Lyon Phelps called the "mysterious flashes of inspiration which reveal truth apart from any conscious process of reasoning."

PRINCIPAL WORKS

POETRY

"Renascence" 1912; published in *The Lyric Year*
Renascence, and Other Poems 1917
A Few Figs from Thistles 1920; also published as *A Few Figs from Thistles* [enlarged edition], 1922
Second April 1921
The Ballad of the Harp-Weaver 1922
The Harp-Weaver, and Other Poems 1923
The Buck in the Snow, and Other Poems 1928
Fatal Interview 1931
Wine from These Grapes 1934
Conversation at Midnight 1937
Huntsman, What Quarry? 1939
Make Bright the Arrows: 1940 Notebook 1940
Collected Sonnets 1941
Collected Lyrics 1943
Mine the Harvest 1954

Collected Poems 1956
Edna St. Vincent Millay: Selected Poems 1991

OTHER MAJOR WORKS

*Aria da Capo (drama) 1921
*The Lamp and the Bell (drama) 1921
*Two Slatterns and a King (drama) 1921
Distressing Dialogues [as Nancy Boyd] (essays) 1924
The King's Henchman (libretto) 1927
Letters of Edna St. Vincent Millay (letters) 1952

*These works were published as *Three Plays* in 1926.

CRITICISM

Harriet Monroe (review date 1918)

[*As the founder and editor of* Poetry *magazine, Monroe was a key figure in the American "poetry renaissance" of the early twentieth century.* Poetry *was the first periodical devoted primarily to the works of new poets and to poetry criticism, and from 1912 until her death Monroe maintained an editorial policy of printing "the best English verse which is being written today, regardless of where, by whom, or under what theory of art it is written." In the following review, she praises several poems included in* Renascence and Other Poems, *focusing on the title work.*]

[*Renascence and Other Poems*] is a very exceptional first book, a book which is achievement rather than promise. One would have to go back a long way in literary history to find a young lyric poet singing so freely and musically in such a big world. Almost we hear a thrush at dawn, discovering the ever-renewing splendor of the morning.

"Renascence" gave me the only thrill I received from Mr. Kennerley's 1912 anthology, *The Lyric Year*. It was so much the best poem in that collection that probably it's no wonder it didn't receive any one of the three prizes. Reading it once more, after six years' discipline in modern poetry, I am thrilled again. The surprise of youth over the universe, the emotion of youth at encountering inexplicable infinities—that is expressed in this poem, and it is a big thing to express. Moreover, it is expressed with a certain triumphant joy, the very mood of exultant youth; and the poet gets a certain freshness and variety into a measure often stilted. The poem is too compact for quotation—it should be read entire. Possibly its spiritual motive is summed up in the couplet:

> God, I can push the grass apart
> And lay my finger on Thy heart!

This poem is much the biggest thing in the book; indeed, one almost sighs with fear lest life, closing in on this poet as on so many others, may narrow her scope and vision. It requires a rare spiritual integrity to keep one's sense of infinity against the persistent daily intrusions of the world, the flesh and the devil; but only the poet who keeps it through the years can sing his grandest song.

But even without **"Renascence"** the book would be exceptional. Not so much for **"Interim,"** though its emotion is poignantly sincere and expressed without affectation, as for some of the briefer lyrics. Such songs as **"Kin to Sorrow," "Tavern," "The Shroud,"** are perfect of their very simple and delicate kind; and one or two of the sonnets are admirable—**"Time does not Bring Relief "** and **"Bluebeard."** (pp. 167-68)

> *Harriet Monroe, in a review of "Renascence and Other Poems," in* Poetry, *Vol. XIII, No. III, December, 1918, pp. 167-68.*

Louis Untermeyer   (review date 1919)

[*Although he was a poet during the early years of his literary career, Untermeyer is better known as an anthologist of poetry and short fiction, an editor, and a master parodist. Notable among his anthologies are* Modern American Poetry *(1919),* The Book of Living Verse *(1931),* A Treasury of Laughter *(1946), and* New Modern American and British Poetry *(1950). In the following review, he praises the poems in* Renascence and Other Poems *for their dramatic power and spiritual eloquence.*]

[In] the poems of Edna St. Vincent Millay one finds an . . . untutored simplicity accompanying an indefinable magic. Because of her very *naïveté,* her pages vibrate with a direct and often dramatic power that few of our most expert craftsmen can equal. Turn to the title-poem of *Renascence and Other Poems,* a poem written when Miss Millay was still in her 'teens, and observe how amazingly it combines a spiritual eloquence with a cool, colloquial lucidity. It begins, like a child's aimless verse or a counting-out rhyme:

> All I could see from where I stood
> Was three long mountains and a wood;
> I turned and looked another way,
> And saw three islands in a bay.
> So with my eyes I traced the line
> Of the horizon, thin and fine,
> Straight around till I was come
> Back to where I'd started from;
> And all I saw from where I stood
> Was three long mountains and a wood.

An almost inconsequential opening but, as the poem proceeds, one with a haunting and cumulative effect.

> Over these things I could not see
> These were the things that bounded me

it goes on. And then, without ever losing the straightforwardness of the couplets, it begins to mount. There is an exquisite idyllic passage beginning

> The grass, a-tiptoe at my ear,
> Whispering to me I could hear;
> I felt the rain's cool finger-tips
> Brush tenderly across my lips,
> Laid gently on my sealèd sight,
> And all at once the heavy night
> Fell from my eyes and I could see,—

> A drenched and dripping apple-tree,
> A last long line of silver rain. . . .

And suddenly, beneath the descriptive rapture, one is confronted by a greater revelation. Mystery becomes articulate. It is as if a child playing about the room had, in the midst of prattling, uttered some shining and terrific truth. This remarkable poem is in parts a trifle repetitious, but what it repeats is said so pointedly and, for all its obvious youth, so profoundly that one thinks of scarcely any lesser poet than Blake as one begins the ascending climax:

> O God, I cried, no dark disguise
> Can e'er hereafter hide from me
> Thy radiant identity!
> Thou canst not move across the grass
> But my quick eye will see Thee pass,
> Nor speak, however silently,
> But my hushed voice will answer Thee.
> I know the path that tells Thy way
> Through the cool eve of every day;
> God, I can push the grass apart
> And lay my finger on Thy heart!

The entire poem commands one not merely by its precocious power but by its sheer lyrical mastery.

A few pages later, Miss Millay sounds this same love of earth in an even brighter and more condensed ecstasy. None of our poets has ever communicated rapture more smitingly than she has in

God's World

> O world, I cannot hold thee close enough!
>   Thy winds, thy wide grey skies!
>   Thy mists that roll and rise!
>   Thy woods, this autumn day, that ache and sag
>   And all but cry with color! That gaunt crag
>   To crush! To lift the lean of that black bluff!
>   World, World, I cannot get thee close enough!
>
> Long have I known a glory in it all,
>   But never knew I this;
>   Here such a passion is
> As stretcheth me apart.—Lord, I do fear
> Thou'st made the world too beautiful this year;
> My soul is all but out of me,—let fall
> No burning leaf; prithee, let no bird call.

In her more austere and formal lines, Miss Millay is almost as authoritative. Genius, not a mere pretty talent, burns through them. Her sonnets, with the phrasing cut down to the glowing core, exhibit the same sensitive parsimony that one finds in the best of the Imagist poems plus a far richer sense of human values. Here is the first of the four exquisite unnamed sonnets; one that has, like **"Renascence,"** a mixture of world sadness and a painful hunger for beauty—a hunger so intense that no delight seems great enough to give her peace.

> Thou art not lovelier than lilacs,—no
>   Nor honeysuckle; thou art not more fair
>   Than small white single poppies. I can bear
> Thy beauty; though I bend before thee, though
> From left to right, not knowing where to go,

I turn my troubled eyes, nor here nor there
    Find any refuge from thee; yet I swear
So has it been with mist,—with moonlight so.

Like him who day by day unto his draught
    Of delicate poison adds him one drop more
Till he may drink unharmed the death of ten,
Even so, inured to beauty, who have quaffed
    Each hour more deeply than the hour before,
I drink—and live—what has destroyed some men.

Elsewhere (as in **"The Suicide"**) the tone is more derivative and disillusioned. The idiom is less personal; the results of reading begin to show. In **"Interim"** there is an intrusion of foreign accents; echoes of other dramatic monologs disturb one as the poem wanders off into periods of reflection and rhetoric. And there are several pages where all that was fresh and native to this young poet seems turned to a mere imitation of prettiness. **"Ashes of Life"** and **"The Little Ghost"** are sweet lispings that might have emanated from many a talented undergraduate. The inclusion of such merely pleasant pieces is all the more surprising when one notes the inexplicable omission of **"Journey,"** a youthful poem, but one sharpened and illuminated by a succession of brilliant and memorable touches. Here is a part of it:

                          Cat-birds call
Through the long afternoon, and creeks at dusk
Are guttural. Whip-poor-wills wake and cry,
Drawing the twilight close about their throats;
Only my heart makes answer. Eager vines
Go up the rocks and wait; flushed apple-trees
Pause in their dance and break the ring for
    me. . . .
Round-faced roses, pink and petulant,
Look back and beckon ere they disappear.

No doubt this, as well as other notable verse, will make her next volume distinctive. But whatever the second volume contains, **Renascence** alone assures her a high place among American lyrists. (pp. 271-75)

> *Louis Untermeyer, "Sara Teasdale and the Lyricists," in his* The New Era in American Poetry, *1919. Reprint by Scholarly Press, 1970, pp. 263-90.*

William Lyon Phelps (review date 1921)

[*An American critic and educator, Phelps was the author of two influential critical studies and a prominent literary journalist whose criticism was noted for its enthusiastic tone. In the following review of* Renascence, and Other Poems *and* Second April, *he praises the high quality and restraint of Millay's writing and asserts that her apparent interest in death is typical of a young poet.*]

No one can read **Renascence** without believing in the author's lyrical gifts. The only indubitable sign of youth in her work is the writer's pre-occupation with the theme of death. Nothing is more normal than for a young poet to write about death—the contrast is romantic and sharply dramatic; it is the idea of death that appeals to youth.

The eighth sonnet in the volume, **"Second April,"** is thoroughly typical of Youth standing in contemplation before Death:

> And you as well must die, belovèd dust,
> And all your beauty stand you in no stead:
> This flawless, vital hand, this perfect head,
> This body of flame and steel, before the gust
> Of Death, or under his autumnal frost,
> Shall be as any leaf, be no less dead
> Than the first leaf that fell—this wonder fled,
> Altered, estranged, disintegrated, lost.
> Nor shall my love avail you in your hour.
> In spite of all my love, you will arise
> Upon that day and wander down the air
> Obscurely as the unattended flower,
> It mattering not how beautiful you were,
> Or how belovèd above all else that dies.

In Tennyson's first volume, the details of dissolution appear again and again, and the thought of death shadows nearly every page. When a poet is old, he does not write about death so much or in his early manner. Death is too close; it has become a fact rather than an idea. To youth death is an astounding, amazing, romantic tragedy, and yet somehow remote from the writer; it may not cost as much worry as a dentist appointment or an ill-fitting gown; but when one is old, death seems more natural. In St. Paul's early letters, he talks about the second coming of his Lord; in the last ones, about his own imminent departure.

The manner of approaching the grim subject changes with advancing years. In Tennyson's first volume, we find:

> The jaw is falling,
> The red cheek paling,
> The strong limbs failing;
> Ice with the warm blood mixing;
> The eyeballs fixing.

When he was 80, he wrote

> Sunset and evening star,
>   And one clear call for me,
> And may there be no moaning of the bar
>   When I put out to sea.

Thus to find the constantly recurring idea of death in the first two volumes by Miss Millay is quite the opposite of anything abnormal; I imagine, apart from her poetic gift, that she must be a natural, healthy-minded young girl. It is only fair to add that, in addition to the romantic idea of death as material for poetry, there are in the second volume beautiful tributes to the memory of a college friend, sincere expression of profound grief.

No matter how long we live, or how rich and varied our experience, Beauty always comes to us as a surprise; thus the reader will be happily struck more than a few times in these pages. But it is not surprising that they should be the work of youth; for all poets of quality achieve some perfection in early years. If one has reached the age of 22 without writing some admirable poetry, one might as well resign ambition to become distinguished as a poet. Undergraduate verse is probably on a higher level at this moment in America than it has ever been before; but the wonder is that so little of permanent value is produced.

The mysterious flashes of inspiration which reveal truth apart from any conscious process of reasoning—and which are the glory of poetry and music—appear more than once in the poems of Miss Millay. In **"Interim,"** for example:

> Not Truth, but Faith, it is
> That keeps the world alive. If all at once
> Faith were to slacken—that unconscious Faith
> Which must, I know, yet be the cornerstone
> Of all believing—birds now flying fearless
> Across would drop in terror to the earth;
> Fishes would drown; and the all-governing reins
> Would tangle in the frantic hands of God
> And the worlds gallop headlong to destruction!

The rhetorical flourish in the last line quoted is not common in these volumes; there is usually a restraint in expression rather remarkable, by which, of course, feeling gains in intensity. Extravagance of language, the prevailing fault in this nervous and excitable age, where everybody either swears or talks in italics, is not characteristic of the work of Miss Millay. It is pleasant also to see that the greedy attitude toward life, so frequently seen just now in novels and poems, is here absent; she loves life as an artist loves beauty, without wanting to eat it. There can be no true love of beauty if it be mingled with desire. One often falls into the fallacy of thinking one loves beauty when all one really loves is one's self. Consider the appalling picture presented in May Sinclair's "Waddington."

Remembering that the following poem appears in the earliest volume, we can have no doubt of our author's originality:

> If I should learn, in some quite casual way,
> That you were gone, not to return again—
> Read from the back page of a paper, say,
>   Held by a neighbor in a subway train,
> How at the corner of this avenue
>   And such a street (so are the papers filled)
> A hurrying man—who happened to be you—
>   At noon today had happened to be killed,
> I should not cry aloud—I could not cry
>   Aloud, or wring my hands in such a place—
> I should but watch the station lights rush by
>   With a more careful interest on my face,
> Or raise my eyes and read with greater care
> Where to store furs and how to treat the hair.

She has the poet's sight and the poet's hearing, which are more to be envied by us outsiders than any renown. She sees visions in nature beyond our range, and hears sounds to us inaudible. These extra powers give to many of her verses a delicate charm.

City Trees

> The trees along the city street,
>   Save for the traffic and the rains,
> Would make a sound as thin and sweet
>   As trees in country lanes.
>
> And people standing in their shade
>   Out of a shower, undoubtedly
> Would hear such music as is made
>   Upon a country tree.
>
> Oh, little leaves that are so dumb
>   Against the shrieking city air,

I watch you when the wind has come—
    I know what sound is there.

Miss Millay would not be a child of the twentieth century if she did not occasionally attempt to write in the vein of light cynicism and disillusion, in a manner recalling the less valuable work of Rupert Brooke. The little volume published this year, ***A Few Figs from Thistles,*** is exceedingly well named, and the result is one more proof of the truth of what you find in the Bible. These whimsies are graceful and amusing enough, but of no importance—not even to their author. A fig for such poetry!

> *William Lyon Phelps, "Edna St. Vincent Millay, Poet and Dramatist," in* The New York Times Book Review, *October 16, 1921, p. 10.*

Carl Van Doren (essay date 1923)

[*Van Doren is considered one of the most perceptive critics of the first half of the twentieth century. He worked for many years as a professor of English at Columbia University and served as literary editor and critic of the* Nation *and the* Century *during the 1920s. A founder of the Literary Guild and author or editor of several American literary histories, Van Doren was also a critically acclaimed historian and biographer. In the excerpt below, he discusses Millay's poetry in relation to the renaissance of lyric poetry that took place in the United States during the early twentieth century, praising her verse for its lucid style, its representation of the mood of youthful rebellion against social conventions that characterized the 1920s, and its unique presentation of a woman's perspective on love and life.*]

The little renaissance of poetry which there has been a hundred historians to scent and chronicle in the United States during the last decade flushed to a dawn in 1912. In that year was founded [*Poetry*], a magazine for the sole purpose of helping poems into the world; in that year was published an anthology which meant to become an annual, though, as it happened, another annual by another editor took its place the year following. The real poetical event of 1912, however, was the appearance in *The Lyric Year,* tentative anthology, of the first outstanding poem by Edna St. Vincent Millay. Who that then had any taste of which he can now be proud but remembers the discovery, among the numerous failures and very innumerable successes which made up the volume, of **"Renascence,"** by a girl of twenty whose name none but her friends and a lucky critic or two had heard? After wading through tens and dozens of rhetorical strophes and moral stanzas, it was like suddenly finding wings to come upon these lines:

> All I could see from where I stood
> Was three long mountains and a wood;
> I turned and looked another way,
> And saw three islands in a bay.
> So with my eyes I traced the line
> Of the horizon, thin and fine,
> Straight around till I was come
> Back to where I'd started from;
> And all I saw from where I stood
> Was three long mountains and a wood.

The diction was so plain, the arrangement so obvious, that

the magic of the opening seemed a mystery; and yet the lift and turn of these verses were magical, as if a lark had taken to the air out of a dreary patch of stubble.

Nor did the poem falter as it went on. If it had the movement of a bird's flight, so had it the ease of a bird's song. The poet of this lucid voice had gone through a radiant experience. She had, she said with mystical directness, felt that she could touch the horizon, and found that she could touch the sky. Then infinity had settled down upon her till she could hear

> The ticking of Eternity.

The universe pressed close and crushed her, oppressing her with omniscience and omnisentience; all sin, all remorse, all suffering, all punishment, all pity poured into her, torturing her. The weight drove her into the cool earth, where she lay buried, but happy, under the falling rain.

> The rain, I said, is kind to come
> And speak to me in my new home.
> I would I were alive again
> To kiss the fingers of the rain,
> To drink into my eyes the shine
> Of every slanting silver line.

Suddenly came over her the terrible memory of the "multi-colored, multi-form, beloved" beauty she had lost by this comfortable death. She burst into a prayer so potent that the responding rain, gathering in a black wave, opened the earth above her and set her free.

> Ah! Up then from the ground sprang I
> And hailed the earth with such a cry
> As is not heard save from a man
> Who has been dead, and lives again.
> About the trees my arms I wound;
> Like one gone mad I hugged the ground;
> I raised my quivering arms on high;
> I laughed and laughed into the sky.

Whereupon, somewhat quaintly, she moralized her experience with the pride of youth finally arrived at full stature in the world.

> The heart can push the sea and land
> Farther away on either hand;
> The soul can split the sky in two,
> And let the face of God shine through.
> But East and West will pinch the heart
> That cannot keep them pushed apart;
> And he whose soul is flat—the sky
> Will cave in on him by and by.

"Renascence," one of the loveliest of American poems, was an adventure, not an allegory, but it sounds almost allegorical because of the way it interpreted and distilled the temper which, after a long drought, was coming into American verse. Youth was discovering a new world, or thought it was. It had taken upon itself burdens of speculation, of responsibility, and had sunk under the weight. Now, on fire with beauty, it returned to joy and song.

Other things than joy and song, however, cut across the track of this little renaissance. There was a war. Youth—at least that part of it which makes poems—went out to fight, first with passion for the cause and then with con-

tempt for the dotards who had botched and bungled. Gray Tyrtæuses might drone that here was a good war designed to end war, but youth meantime saw that it was dying in hordes and tried to snatch what ecstasy it could before the time should come when there would be no more ecstasy. Boys and girls who would otherwise have followed the smooth paths of their elders now questioned them and turned aside into different paths of life. Young men and maidens who would otherwise have expected little of love for years to come now demanded all that love offers, and demanded it immediately for fear it might come too late. The planet was reeling, or looked to be; all the settled orders were straining and breaking. Amid the hurly-burly of argument and challenge and recrimination a lyric had a good chance to be unheard; yet it was a lyrical hour, as it always is when the poet sees himself surrounded by swift moments hurrying to an end. Some sense of this in the air, even amid the hurly-burly, gave to the youth of the time that rash, impatient, wild ardor and insolence and cynicism which followed in such fleet succession, growing sharper as the war which was to have been good turned into the peace which was bound to be bad. (pp. 311-13)

The decade since the little renaissance began has created a kind of symbol for this irresponsible mood in the more or less mythical Greenwich Village, where, according to the popular legend, art and mirth flourish without a care, far from the stupid duties of human life. No one so well as Miss Millay has spoken with the accents credited to the village.

> My candle burns at both ends;
> It will not last the night;
> But ah, my foes, and oh, my friends—
> It gives a lovely light!

Thus she commences in **"A Few Figs from Thistles."** And she continues with impish songs and rakish ballads and sonnets which laugh at the love which throbs through them. Suckling was not more insouciant than she is in **"Thursday"**:

> And if I loved you Wednesday,
> Well, what is that to you?
> I do not love you Thursday—
> So much is true.
>
> And why you come complaining
> Is more than I can see.
> I loved you Wednesday—yes—but what
> Is that to me?

With what a friendliness for wild souls she tells the story of the singing woman "Whose mother was a leprechaun, whose father was a friar."

> In through the bushes, on any foggy day,
> My Da would come a-swishing of the drops away,
> With a prayer for my death and a groan for my birth,
> A-mumbling of his beads for all that he was worth.
>
> And there sit my Ma, her knees beneath her chin,
> A-looking in his face and a-drinking of it in,

And a-marking in the moss some funny little
  saying
That would mean just the opposite of all that he
  was praying!

He taught me the holy-talk of Vesper and of
  Matin,
He heard me my Greek and he heard me my
  Latin,
He blessed me and crossed me to keep my soul
  from evil,
And we watched him out of sight, and we con-
  jured up the devil!

Oh, the things I have n't seen and the things I
  have n't known,
What with hedges and ditches till after I was
  grown,
And yanked both ways by my mother and my
  father,
With a 'Which would you better?' and a 'Which
  would you rather?'

With him for a sire and her for a dam,
What should I be but just what I am?"

Speaking in this manner, Greenwich Village seems a long
way from the Village of Concord, heart of the old tradition, even though Hawthorne loved a faun when he met
one, and Thoreau was something of a faun himself. In the
classic village any such mixture as this of leprechaun and
friar would have been kept as close a secret as possible,
and conscience would have been set to the work of driving
the leprechaun taint out. In Greenwich Village the friar
is made to look a little comical, especially to the mother
and daughter who conspire to have their fling behind his
back.

This tincture of diablerie appears again and again in Miss
Millay's verse, perhaps most of all in the candor with
which she talks of love. She has put by the mask under
which other poets who were women, apparently afraid for
the reputation of their sex, have spoken as if they were
men. She has put by the posture of fidelity which women
in poetry have been expected to assume. She speaks with
the voice of women who, like men, are thrilled by the
beauty of their lovers and are stung by desire; who know,
however, that love does not always vibrate at its first high
pitch, and so, too faithful to love to insist upon clinging
to what has become half-love merely, let go without desperation. A woman may be fickle for fun, Miss Millay suggests in various poems wherein this or that girl teases her
lover with the threat to leave him or the claim that she has
forgotten him; but so may a woman show wisdom by admitting the variability and transience of love, as in this
crystal sonnet:

I know I am but summer to your heart,
And not the full four seasons of the year;
And you must welcome from another part
Such noble moods as are not mine, my dear.
No gracious weight of golden fruits to sell
Have I, nor any wise and wintry thing;
And I have loved you all too long and well
To carry still the high sweet breast of spring.
Wherefore I say: O love, as summer goes,
I must be gone, steal forth with silent drums,
That you may hail anew the bird and rose

When I come back to you, as summer comes.
Else will you seek, at some not distant time,
Even your summer in another clime.

What sets Miss Millay's love-poems apart from almost all
those written in English by women is the full pulse which,
in spite of their gay impudence, beats through them. She
does not speak in the name of forlorn maidens or of wives
bereft, but in the name of women who dare to take love
at the flood, if it offers, and who later, if it has passed, remember with exultation that they had what no coward
could have had. Conscience does not trouble them, nor
any serious division in their natures. No one of them
weeps because she has been a wanton, no one of them because she has been betrayed. Rarely since Sappho has a
woman voiced such delight in a lover's beauty as this:

What's this of death, from you who never will
  die?
Think you the wrist that fashioned you in clay,
The thumb that set the hollow just that way
In your full throat and lidded the long eye
So roundly from the forehead, will let lie
Broken, forgotten, under foot some day
Your unimpeachable body, and so slay
The work he had been most remembered by?

Rarely since Sappho has a woman written as bravely as
this.

What lips my lips have kissed, and where, and
  why,
I have forgotten, and what arms have lain
Under my head till morning; but the rain
Is full of ghosts to-night, that tap and sigh
Upon the glass and listen for reply;
And in my heart there stirs a quiet pain
For unremembered lads that not again
Will turn to me at midnight with a cry.

In passages like these Miss Millay has given body and ves-
ture to a sense of equality in love; to the demand by
women that they be allowed to enter the world of adventure and experiment in love which men have long inhabited. But Miss Millay does not, like any feminist, argue for
that equality. She takes it for granted, exhibits it in action,
and turns it into beauty.

Beauty, not argument, is, after all, Miss Millay's concern
and goal. She can be somewhat metaphysical about it, as
in her contention that

Euclid alone has looked on Beauty bare.
Let all who prate of Beauty hold their peace,
And lay them prone upon the earth and cease
To ponder on themselves, the while they stare
At nothing, intricately drawn nowhere
In shapes of shifting lineage.

For the most part, however, she stands with those who
love life and persons too wholly to spend much passion
upon anything abstract. She loves the special countenance
of every season, the hot light of the sun, gardens of flowers
with old, fragrant names, the salt smell of the sea along
her native Maine coast, the sound of sheep-bells and drip-
ping eves and the unheard sound of city trees, the homely
facts of houses in which men and women live, tales of
quick deeds and eager heroisms, the cool, kind love of

young girls for one another, the color of words, the beat of rhythm. The shining clarity of her style does not permit her to work the things she finds beautiful into tapestried verse; she will not ask a song to carry more than it can carry on the easiest wings; but in all her graver songs and sonnets she serves beauty in one way or another. Now she affirms her absolute loyalty to beauty; now she hunts it out in unexpected places; most frequently of all she buries it with some of the most exquisite dirges of her time.

These returning dirges and elegies and epitaphs are as much the natural speech of Miss Millay as is her insolence of joy in the visible and tangible world. Like all those who most love life and beauty, she understands that both are brief and mortal. They take her round and round in a passionate circle: because she loves them so ardently she knows they cannot last, and because she knows they cannot last she loves them the more ardently while they do. Dispositions such as hers give themselves to joy when their vitality is at its peaks; in their lower hours they weep over the graves of loveliness which are bound to crowd their courses. Having a high heart and a proud creed, Miss Millay leaves unwept some graves which other poets and most people water abundantly, but she is stabbed by the essential tragedy and pity of death. Thus she expresses the tragic powerlessness of those who live to hold those who die:

> Nor shall my love avail you in your hour.
> In spite of all my love, you will arise
> Upon that day and wander down the air
> Obscurely as the unattended flower,
> It mattering not how beautiful you were,
> Or how belovèd above all else that dies.

Thus she expresses the pitiful knowledge which the living have that they cannot help the dead:

> Be to her, Persephone,
> All the things I might not be;
> Take her head upon your knee.
> She that was so proud and wild,
> Flippant, arrogant and free,
> She that had no need of me,
> Is a little lonely child
> Lost in Hell,—Persephone,
> Take her head upon your knee;
> Say to her, "My dear, my dear,
> It is not so dreadful here."

Are these only the accents of a minor poet, crying over withered roses and melted snows? Very rarely do minor poets strike such moving chords upon such universal strings. Still more rarely do merely minor poets have so much power over tragedy and pity, and yet in other hours have equal power over fire and laughter. (pp. 313-16)

> *Carl Van Doren, "Youth and Wings," in* The Century, *Vol. 106, No. 2, June, 1923, pp. 311-16.*

Harriet Monroe   (essay date 1924)

[*In the following essay, Monroe praises Millay's early poetry and asserts that Millay* "*may perhaps be the greatest woman poet since Sappho.*"]

Long ago, when I was mooning and dreaming through the pig-tail period, I used to think how fine it would be to be the greatest woman poet since Sappho. The audacity of youth—of near-childhood—would have scorned any lower goal; and the young aspirant, gazing aloft and afar, seemed to detect a smile of encouragement on the inhumanly beautiful visage which glorified an imaginary shrine.

Well, failure is the lot of all—it were shame indeed for ardent youth to set up any attainable goal. The dream must outrun the fleetest foot, or else the trophy will wither in one's hand. "Success—there's no such thing!" I once made a "successful" man say in a play. It is more reasonable to take pride in the degree of one's failure than to measure with facile vanity one's achievement.

But I am reminded by that old dream to wonder whether we may not raise a point worthy of discussion in claiming that a certain living lady may perhaps be the greatest woman poet since Sappho. After all, the roll contains few names. Who are they, the woman-poets of the past twenty-five hundred years? Possessing few languages, I am incompetent in the search, but I can remember no names of importance in the Greek, Roman or mediaeval literature. Folk-lore may hide under its anonymity a few women—its motive and feeling are often feminine; but no one can search them out. *Poetry*'s wide shelf of more-or-less-modern anthologies—French, German, Italian, Russian, Jugo-Slavian, Armenian, Ukrainian, Swedish and others—all these contain few feminine names, and apparently none of importance. Two or three oriental ladies have been listed, but of their quality we cannot judge.

In short, the woman-poets seem to have written almost exclusively in the English language. Emily Bronte, Elizabeth Barrett Browning, Christina Rossetti, Emily Dickinson—these four names bring us to 1900. Differing profoundly each from the others, these women were alike in this—they were all recluses by instinct, leading shy lives more or less aloof from the world; three of them spinsters, and the fourth protected and enveloped by a singularly potent and sympathetic marriage.

Emily Bronte—austere, heroic, solitary—is of course the greatest woman in literature. Not even Sappho's *Hymn to Aphrodite* (ignorant of Greek, I speak timidly) can surpass *Wuthering Heights* for sheer depth and power of beauty, or match it for the compassing of human experience in a single masterpiece. But *Wuthering Heights,* though poetic in motive and essence, classes as a novel rather than a poem; and, if one omits that from the reckoning, Emily Bronte's rank as a poet, or more specifically as a lyrist, rests upon a single poem, the sublime *Last Lines* which made her faith in life immortal—for her other poems, some of them fine, are scarcely important. As a poet, she has not the scope, the variety, of Edna St. Vincent Millay, whose claim to pre-eminence we are considering.

Mrs. Browning?—well, some of the *Sonnets from the Portuguese,* another fine sonnet *Grief,* and lyric bits of longer (usually too long) poems, are beautiful and poignant, sincerely feminine in their emotional appeal. But they do not quite ascend to those higher levels which we are now trying to explore.

Nor Christina Rossetti. Religious poems like *Paradise* and *Marvel of Marvels* are finely fluted little altar-candles—burning rather pale, though, beside those of real ecstatics like Saint Teresa or Gerard Hopkins; and a few songs—*When I am dead, my dearest,* and others—are lovely in their sweet sincerity of renunciation. But these also breathe not that rarer air.

Emily Dickinson seems to climb higher than either Elizabeth or Christina. Her brief poems—many of them—have a swift and keen lyric intensity, a star-like beauty. They are sudden flashes into the deep well of a serene and impregnable human soul, sure of the truth in solitude.

Edna Millay is a very different person from any of these four. By no means a recluse, she has courted life and shunned none of its adventures. Her youth has been crowded with companions, friends, lovers; she has gone through college, earned her living at journalism, has travelled, acted, given readings, known poverty and comparative ease—in short, she has taken the rough-and-tumble of a modern American girl's life and has reached its usual climax, marriage. Beginning, before she was twenty and while still a little tomboy of the Maine coast, with **"Renascence,"** a poem of desperate faith, lithe as a faun in its naked search of the soul, the danger has been that life might lure her away from art. The complications of a hunted human soul in these stirring days—the struggle for breath, for food and lodging, the pot-boilers, the flirtations, the teasing petty trials and interruptions—how could the poet in her survive all these, and put out fresh flowers of beauty?

But the poet has survived and the flowers have sprung up richly along her path. If **"Renascence"** remains the poem of largest sweep which Miss Millay has achieved as yet—the most comprehensive expression of her philosophy, so to speak, her sense of miracle in life and death—yet she has been lavish with details of experience, of emotion, and her agile and penetrating mind has leapt through spaces of thought rarely traversed by women, or by men either for that matter.

For in the lightest of her briefest lyrics there is always more than appears. In the **"Figs,"** for example, in **"Thursday," "The Penitent," "The Not Impossible Him"** and other witty ironies, and in more serious poems like **"The Betrothal,"** how neatly she upsets the carefully built walls of convention which men have set up around their Ideal Woman, even while they fought, bled and died for all the Helens and Cleopatras they happened to encounter! And in *Aria da Capo,* a masterpiece of irony sharp as Toledo steel, she stabs the war-god to the heart with a stroke as clean, as deft, as ever the most skilfully murderous swordsman bestowed upon his enemy. Harangues have been made, volumes have been written, for the outlawry of war, but who else has put its preposterous unreasonableness into a nutshell like this girl who brings to bear upon the problem the luminous creative insight of genius?

Thus on the most serious subjects there is always the keen swift touch. Beauty blows upon them and is gone before one can catch one's breath; and lo and behold, we have a poem too lovely to perish, a song out of the blue which will ring in the ears of time. Such are the "little elegies" which will make the poet's Vassar friend, *D. C.* of the wonderful voice, a legend of imperishable beauty even though "her singing days are done." Thousands of stay-at-home women speak wistfully in **"Departure;"** and **"Lament"**—where can one find deep grief and its futility expressed with such agonizing grace? Indeed, though love and death and the swift passing of beauty have haunted this poet as much as others, she is rarely specific and descriptive. Her thought is transformed into imagery, into symbol, and it flashes back at us as from the facets of a jewel.

And the thing is so simply done. One weeps, not over *D. C.'s* death, but over her narrow shoes and blue gowns empty in the closet. In **"Renascence"** the sky, the earth, the infinite, no longer abstractions, come close, as tangible as a tree. **"The Harp-weaver,"** presenting the protective power of enveloping love—power which enwraps the beloved even after death has robbed him, is a kind of fairy-tale ballad, sweetly told as for a child. Even more in **"The Curse"** emotion becomes sheer magic of imagery and sound, as clear and keen as frost in sunlight. Always one feels the poet's complete and unabashed sincerity. She says neither the expected thing nor the "daring" thing, but she says the incisive true thing as she has discovered it and feels it.

Miss Millay's most confessional lyrics are in sonnet form, and among them are a number which can hardly be forgotten so long as English literature endures, and one or two which will rank among the best of a language extremely rich in beautiful sonnets. It is a pity that the poet ever broke up the series of *Twenty Sonnets* published in *Reedy's Mirror* during April and May, 1920, and afterwards scattered, all but two of them, through the volumes entitled *Second April, Figs from Thistles,* and *The Harp-weaver.* About three-fourths of the twenty belong together in a sequence which should be restored, a sequence which might be entitled *Winged Love* since it portrays the ecstasy and bitter brevity of passion. Among these are **"Into the golden vessel of great song," "Not with libations," "Oh think not I am faithful to a vow," "And you as well must die," "Cherish you then the hope I shall forget,"** and others in which verbal music, the winged phrase, the richly colored image, carry poignant emotion in triumph.

Beyond these, outside the love-sequence, the **"Euclid"** sonnet stands in a place apart, of a beauty hardly to be matched for sculpturesque austerity, for detachment from the body and the physical universe. Other minds, searching the higher mathematics, have divined the central structural beauty on which all other beauty is founded, but if any other poet has expressed it I have yet to see the proof. That a young woman should have put this fundamental law into a sonnet is one of the inexplicable divinations of genius. Those shallow critics who decry the modern scientific spirit as materialistic, who find no creative imagination in such minds as Willard Gibbs and Wilbur Wright, would do well to meditate upon this poem, one of the great sonnets of the language. If Miss Millay had done nothing else, she could hardly be forgotten.

But she has done much else. Wilful, moody, whimsical, loving and forgetting, a creature of quick and keen emotions, she has followed her own way and sung her own songs. Taken as a whole, her poems present an utterly feminine personality of singular charm and power; and the best of them, a group of lyrics ineffably lovely, will probably be cherished as the richest, most precious gift of song which any woman since the immortal Lesbian has offered to the world. (pp. 260-66)

Harriet Monroe, "Edna St. Vincent Millay," in Poetry, Vol. XXIV, No. V, August, 1924, pp. 260-66.

Allen Tate   (essay date 1931)

[*An American critic closely associated with the Agrarians and the New Critics, Tate attacked the tradition of Western philosophy which he felt had alienated persons from themselves, one another, and nature, while he considered literature the principal form of knowledge and revelation. In the following review of* Fatal Interview, *Tate praises Millay's skillful use of sharply defined imagery and classical symbols. He considers Millay "the spokesperson for a generation" but suggests that her poetic achievement is limited by her failure to present a "comprehensive philosophy."*]

More than any other living American poet, with the exception possibly of T. S. Eliot, Miss Millay has puzzled her critics. Contrary to the received opinion, her poetry is understood even less than Eliot's, in spite of its greater simplicity, its more conventional meters and its closer fulfilment of the popular notion of what the language of poetry should be. Of contemporary poets whose excellence is beyond much dispute, she is the most difficult to appraise. She is the most written about, but her critics are partisans: they like her too well or not enough. There is something like worship here, patronage or worse there; both views are unjust; and what is worse, they are misleading. Less interested readers of her verse are tired of violent opinion; the more skeptical, perhaps, are put off by her popularity in an age of famously indifferent taste.

This, too, is misleading. Apart from her merit as a poet, Miss Millay is, not at all to her discredit, the spokesman of a generation. It does not behoove us to enquire how she came to express the feelings of the literary generation that seized the popular imagination from about 1917 to 1925. It is a fact that she did, and in such a way as to remain as its most typical poet. Her talent, with its diverting mixture of solemnity and levity, won the enthusiasm of a time bewildered intellectually and moving unsteadily towards an emotional attitude of its own. It was the age of The Seven Arts, of the old Masses, of the Provincetown Theatre, of the figure and disciples of Randolph Bourne. It has been called the age of experiment and liberation; there is still experiment, but no one is liberated; and that age is now dead.

Miss Millay helped to form that generation, and was formed by it. But she has survived her own time. Her statement about those times, in *A Few Figs from Thistles* and *Second April,* was not, taken philosophically, very

profound; morally, it has been said, it did perceptible damage to our young American womanhood, whose virgin impatience competed noisily with the Armistice and the industrial boom. There were suicides after "Werther" and seductions after "Don Juan." Neither Byron nor Miss Millay is of the first order of poets. They are distinguished examples of the second order, without which literature could not bear the weight of Dante and Shakespeare, and without which poetry would dry up of insensibility.

Being this kind of poet, Miss Millay was not prepared to give to her generation a philosophy in comprehensive terms; her poetry does not define the break with the nineteenth century. This task was left to the school of Eliot, and it was predictable that this school should be—except by young men who had the experience to share Eliot's problem—ignored and misunderstood. Eliot penetrated to the fundamental structure of the nineteenth-century mind and showed its breakdown. Miss Millay assumed no such profound alteration of the intelligence because, I suppose, not being an intellect but a sensibility, she was not aware of it. She foreshadowed an age without bringing it to terms. Taking the vocabulary of nineteenth-century poetry as pure as you will find it in Christina Rossetti, and drawing upon the stock of conventional symbolism accumulated from Drayton to Patmore, she has created, out of shopworn materials, a distinguished personal idiom: she has been able to use the language of the preceding generation to convey an emotion peculiar to her own.

The generation of decadence—Moody, Woodberry and Louise Imogene Guiney—had more than Miss Millay has; but she has all that they had which was not dead. By making their language personal she has brought it back to life. This is her distinction. It is also her limitation. As a limitation it is not peculiar to her, her age or any age, but common to all; it is the quality that defines Collins and Gray, and, in the next century, poets like the Rossettis and Tennyson. Poets of this second order lack the power of creation in the proper sense in which something like a complete world is achieved, either in the vast, systematic vision of Milton, or in the allusive power of Webster and Shakespeare where, backed only by a piece of common action, an entire world is set up in a line or even in a single phrase. In these poets the imaginative focus is less on the personal emotion than on its substructure, an order of intellectual life, and thus their very symbolism acquires not only a heightened significance but an independent existence of its own. Not so with Miss Millay; we feel that she never penetrates to the depth of her symbols, but uses them chiefly as a frame of reference, an adornment to the tale. It has been frequently and quite justly remarked that Miss Millay uses her classical symbols perhaps better than any other living poet; we should add, I believe, that she uses them conventionally better. She takes them literally, subtracting from them always only what serves her metaphor; whereas even a modern like Yeats is capable, in his sonnet "Leda," of that violent addition to the content of the symbol as he finds it which is the mark of great poetry.

Miss Millay's success with stock symbolism is precariously won. I have said that she is not an intellect but a sensibility: if she were capable of a profound analysis of her imagery she might not use it: such an analysis might disaffect her with the style that she so easily assumed, without necessarily leading her, as Yeats was led in mid-career, to create a new style of her own. The beautiful final sonnet of the sequence [in *Fatal Interview*] is a perfect specimen of her talent, and it is probably the finest poem she has written:

> Oh, sleep forever in the Latmian cave,
> Mortal Endymion, darling of the moon!
> Her silver garments by the senseless wave
> Shouldered and dropped and on the shingle
>   strewn,
> Her fluttering hand against her forehead
>   pressed,
> Her scattered looks that trouble all the sky,
> Her rapid footsteps running down the west—
> Of all her altered state, oblivious lie!
> Whom earthen you, by deathless lips adored,
> Wild-eyed and stammering to the grasses thrust,
> And deep into her crystal body poured
> The hot and sorrowful sweetness of the dust:
> Whereof she wanders mad, being all unfit
> For mortal love, that might not die of it.

We have only to compare this, magnificent as it is, with Mr. Yeats's "Leda" to see the difference between the two kinds of symbol that I have described. The difference is first of all one of concentration and intensity; and finally a difference between an accurate picture of an emotion and an act of the imagination:

> A sudden blow: the great wings beating still
> Above the staggering girl, her thighs caressed
> By the dark webs, her nape caught in his bill,
> He holds her helpless breast upon his breast.
>
> How can those terrified vague fingers push
> The feathered glory from her loosening thighs?
> And how can body, laid in that white rush
> But feel the strange heart beating where it lies?
> A shudder in the loins engenders there
> The broken wall, the burning roof and tower
> And Agamemnon dead.
>   Being so caught up,
> So mastered by the brute blood of the air,
> Did she put on his knowledge with his power
> Before the indifferent beak could let her drop?

In an age which, in Mr. Pound's phrase, has "demanded an image"; an age which has searched for a new construction of the mind, and has, in effect, asked every poet for a chart of salvation, it has been forgotten that one of the most valuable kinds of poetry may be deficient in imagination, and yet be valuable for the manner in which it meets its own defect. Miss Millay not only has given the personality of her age, but has preserved it in the purest traditional style. There are those who will have no minor poets; these Miss Millay does not move. The others, her not too enthusiastic but perhaps misguided partisans, have seen too much of their own personalities in her verse to care whether it is great poetry or not; so they call it great.

It is doubtful if all of Miss Millay's previous work put together is worth the thin volume of these fifty-two sonnets. At no previous time has she given us so sustained a performance. Half of the sonnets, perhaps all but about fifteen, lack distinction of emotional quality. None is deficient in

an almost final technique. From first to last every sonnet has its special rhythm and sharply defined imagery; they move like a smooth machine, but not machine-like, under the hand of a masterly technician. The best sonnets would adorn any of the great English sequences. There is some interesting analysis to be made of Miss Millay's skillful use of the Shakespearean form, whose difficult final couplet she has mastered, and perhaps is alone in having mastered since Shakespeare.

The serious, austere tone of her later work must not deceive us: she is the poet of ten years ago. She has been from the beginning the one poet of our time who has successfully stood athwart two ages; she has put the personality of her age into the intellect and style of the preceding one, without altering either. Of her it may be said, as of the late Elinor Wylie, that properly speaking she has no style, but has subtly transformed to her use the indefinable average of poetic English. We have seen the limitations of this order of talent. When the personal impulse lags in a mind that cannot create a symbol and invent a style, we get the pastiche of *The Buck in the Snow:* the defects of such a talent are defects of taste, while the defects of Blake are blunders. Let us say no more of it. Miss Millay is one of our most distinguished poets, and one that we should do well to misunderstand as little as possible. (pp. 335-36)

> *Allen Tate, "Miss Millay's Sonnets," in* The New Republic, *Vol. LXVI, No. 857, May 6, 1931, pp. 335-36.*

Edmund Wilson on the influence of personal relationships on Millay's poetry:

Though [Millay] reacted to the traits of the men she knew—a face or a voice or a manner—or to their special qualifications—what they sang or had read or collected—with the same intensely perceptive interest that she brought to anything else—a bird or a shell or a weed—that had attracted her burning attention; though she was quick to feel weakness or strength—she did not, however, give the impression that personality much mattered for her or that, aside from her mother and sisters, her personal relations were important except as subjects for poems; and when she came to write about her lovers, she gave them so little individuality that it was usually, in any given case, impossible to tell which man she was writing about.

> *Edmund Wilson, in his* The Shores of Light: A Literary Chronicle of the Twenties *(1952).*

James McBride Dabbs   (essay date 1938)

[*Dabbs was an American critic who wrote primarily about the fiction and culture of the American South. In the following essay, he discusses the major conflicts Millay explores in her poetry, and asserts that her verse is weakened by its personal and rhetorical tone.*]

We make out of the quarrel with others, rhetoric, but of the quarrel with ourselves, poetry." Though Edna St. Vincent Millay has with the passing years achieved a weightier accent, she has written an increasingly large proportion of rhetoric. If Yeats is correct, she is more and more inclined to quarrel with others.

She was never inclined to quarrel with herself, though from the first she had sufficient reason. **"Renascence,"** which made her famous at twenty, was, and is, a remarkable poem, both in its lyricism and in its mysticism. But, for an understanding of her later development, her tendency toward rhetoric, its significance lies in the duality of its mystic vision. The two pictures do not fuse. Suddenly conscious of the misery of man, the poet is crushed beneath the weight, and dies. From this death she is revived by a vision of natural beauty, so convincing that at last she cries out:

> God, I can push the grass apart
> And lay my finger on Thy heart!

But how does this conclusion follow? Only, it seems to me, by an evasion of the problem the poet herself set. The sufferings of man are not resolved in the beauty of nature; they are forgotten. The poet's renewed life springs up without root, and is therefore destined to wither soon. "What we live by we die by," says Robert Frost. And what we die by we live by. But here the poet finds renewed life in something unrelated to her death. If anyone urges that the poem represents merely the development of a mood, a development to be judged only by itself, I reply that the development of one mood may be sentimental, the development of another honest, and that certainly, in the light of Miss Millay's career, the development here is, as we shall see, symptomatic. There is revealed here a fissure that cuts straight through the spiritual life: on one side tortured man, on the other a peaceful God. The poet flees from man to God. This is to flee from oneself. A greater poet would have remained to quarrel with himself until he should have made one picture out of the two. Avoiding for some reason this quarrel, Miss Millay has been forced inevitably into a quarrel with the world.

She kept this quarrel hidden for a while by her enthusiasm for even the shining fragments of life. She closes **"Renascence"** in an unjustifiably happy mood. In many of her later poems, she recounts with such force the struggle of her will with the world, and laments with such poignancy its frustration, that we are apt to overlook the incompleteness of her vision. By the time that she reaches *The Buck in the Snow,* however, her native enthusiasm is waning, and the inevitable somberness of her confused quarrel with the world is coming to the surface.

But the false optimism of **"Renascence"** is revealed here and there much earlier than this. The introductory poem to *Second April* contains these lines:

> To what purpose, April, do you return again?
> Beauty is not enough.
> . . .
> Life in itself
> Is nothing.

In so short a time she who had fled from the pain of human life to sing of the beauty of April has been disillusioned.

For that matter, the concluding vision of **"Renascence"** is denied in the same volume, in **"Interim."** Here, in the breathlessness of sudden insight, the poet sees even the natural universe unrolled before her in chaos and doom, and in the blackness of that vision cries out:

> Not Truth, but Faith, it is
> That keeps the world alive.

Truth has become black and faith is false. This is the inevitable reaction from the unjustified optimism of **"Renascence,"** and is itself as unjustifiable, as incomplete, as romantic as that. Allen Tate, though he does not mention Miss Millay, describes very well her development in a discussion of what he calls romantic poetry: "There is the assumption that Truth is indifferent or hostile to the desires of men . . . that, Truth being known at last in the form of experimental science, it is intellectually impossible to maintain illusion any longer, at the same time that it is morally impossible to assimilate Truth."

"The poet revolts from Truth; that is, he defies the cruel and naturalistic world to break him if it can; and he is broken." "The whole thing," says Ludwig Lewisohn, speaking of Miss Millay's career, "in its totality is like a medieval morality."

This spiritual fissure, which divides the supposedly single world of **"Renascence"** into two worlds, and which, if it could have been recognized by the poet and made the cause of a quarrel with herself, might have kept her more of a poet and less of a rhetorician, appears in Miss Millay's poetry in the form of several unresolved conflicts. First and basic is the one already suggested: man *versus* nature, with God on the side of nature. In such a conflict man is bound to fail. Wordsworth was conscious of no such dichotomy. He felt in nature

> A sense sublime
> Of something far more deeply interfused,
> Whose dwelling is the light of setting suns,
> . . . and in the mind of man.

And he heard oftentimes "The still, sad music of humanity." There is, indeed, in one of Miss Millay's poems, **"The Little Hill,"** an attempt to bridge this chasm between the calm of nature and the passion of man, but it is a rather sentimental attempt, in which the poet attributes to the "little hill" feelings that seem to be hers alone. There are two other poems that represent nature as a refuge, however poor, for the man who has failed: in Sonnet X, of the unnamed series in *The Harp-Weaver,* the poet is shown as returning from inconstant love to the sullen but changeless rocks and skies (they were not sullen in **"Renascence"**); and in the opening poem of *Wine from These Grapes* she represents man as returning, after the failure of wife and friend, to the warm but uncomprehending woods. For a moment in this volume she touches a quiet wisdom, when, in the lines **"From a Train Window,"** she sees even the rickety graveyard on the hill in a neighborly light: "As if after all, the earth might know what it is about." But on the next page, in **"The Fawn,"** she reveals herself as poignantly conscious of her rejection by nature: she does not belong. A poem to set beside this is Robert Frost's "Two Look at Two," in which the lovers, though separated from the buck and doe, are accepted by them, and are made happy in the certainty that earth returns their love. In general, in her last volume, Miss Millay represents the universe as indifferent to man. This is essentially what she said at first, in **"Renascence."**

A second conflict foreshadowed by **"Renascence"** and revealed throughout her work is that between human love and beauty. In the human love—the sense of humanity—that revealed to the young poet the pain of life there was hidden a tragic beauty. Unable, however, for some reason, to realize this, she turned from the pain to the "multicolored, multiform, Beloved beauty" of nature. In **"The Concert"** (*The Harp-Weaver*), she turns away from love, which, she says, is of the body, to live awhile in the abstract beauty of music. This conflict between love and beauty appears from time to time in *Fatal Interview.* The poet is ashamed she has brought beauty—her lover—to terms, and more ashamed that she cannot let him go. Again, she says beauty has never heard of love. But in Sonnet XLV, though she insists that beauty continues to exist despite the passing of love, she seems to admit that beauty came because of love. Unfortunately, however, this cause-and-effect relation between love and beauty is not generally perceived. Love is to her too much a function of the practical will, an endeavor in which the will either succeeds or fails; too much a quarrel with others, an occasion for rhetoric. She needs more of that imaginative insight that teaches the poet "to discover immortal moods in mortal desires, an undecaying hope in our trivial ambitions, a divine love in sexual passion."

In her last volume, she has turned clean away from untrustworthy man (whom, as we shall see, she has never trusted) to impersonal, uncomprehending Beauty. Though the poetry is good, the attitude is desperate, and leads nowhere; indeed, she revealed it for what it was years before in the introductory poem to *Second April:* "Beauty is not enough."

We may admit the excellence of her famous sonnet on Euclid and yet point out that it too suggests the division that cuts through her life. Beauty is mathematical; beauty is inhuman. This, as in **"The Concert,"** is a flight from human life instead of the discovery of immortal moods in mortal desires.

There is a third conflict apparent in **"Renascence,"** which, though not very important in that poem, assumes importance in Miss Millay's work as a whole. It is the implied conflict between the poet's fear of life in general and her intense delight in the sensory aspect of life, in sensation. It is probably this delight in sensation that has caused many to admire her for her love of life. If we consider what this phrase means as applied to Miss Millay, we shall understand better the conflict implied in **"Renascence"** between the fear and the love of life.

Miss Millay's love of life is largely practical. On the imaginative or spiritual level it is extremely weak. She has a desperate will for life (Harriet Monroe called **"Renascence"** a poem of desperate faith); it is this that has made her the spokesman of such a large audience, most of whom have, in greater or less degree, this same practical will. She is not noted, however, for that love which is understanding and that understanding which is love; for that detached love which is the mark of the artist, and of every man in so far as he is an artist. Nor, indeed, has she a quality that belongs to all love at its best—trust. She could never say with Job, "Though he slay me, yet will I trust in him." Even in her love of nature she is at times possessive. In the oft-quoted poem **"God's World,"** she expresses the desire, not to behold the world, but to establish herself among and in things.

> That gaunt crag
> To crush! To lift the lean of that black bluff!

"A poetry of the will," says Allen Tate, "is a poetry of sensation, for the poet surrenders to his sensations of the object in his effort to identify himself with it, and to own it."

As to that aspect of the love of life which is revealed in the love of persons, this, in Miss Millay, is shot through with distrust. There is rarely, if ever, relaxation and peace. "Even in the moment of our earliest kiss," she says, I knew our love was doomed. (Why? Because, being country-bred, she knew that the frost would blacken the leaves. This identification of spiritual and physical life is common in Miss Millay.) Neither Emerson nor Hawthorne were great lovers surely, but both were far nearer wisdom than this, when they discerned immortal moods in mortal desires; Dante found in his love for Beatrice the love that moves the sun and all the stars. Again, love has not come to her, like a gracious fate prepared from the beginning; she has sought for it, striven for it, been ready at any moment to desert one lover for another.

> Oh, think not I am faithful to a vow!
> Faithless am I save to love's self alone.

But what is love's self alone? One suspects that it is no more than the poet's will to be loved. She takes love, and holds it, by main force, in her hands. This is the dominant tone of *Fatal Interview;* and this desperate will to have her way is called the love of life. It would appear that Miss Millay has never learned to let go with the hands. She does not trust love: it will fly away. Of course it will—from anyone who does not trust it. Or it will die. Of course—unless we give it life.

There is too constantly in her love poems a fear of being trapped by love, of losing her freedom in love. She wishes to remain free of love, while having love as something to use, to make free with. Apparently she wishes to be loved without loving in return. If she were willing to accept absolute freedom—but she is not. A late poem, **"On the Wide Heath,"** tells of the traveler who returns to his loveless, unlovely home because it is "Too lonely, to be free." She does not understand freedom in love, being too concerned for the wreaking of her individual will upon the world.

Distrustful of human relationships, she is also distrustful of time as "a bringer of new things." "We'll to the woods no more," she cries, "The laurels all are cut." As for the cause of her distrust,

> It is that a wind too strong
> Bent my back when I was young,

> It is that I fear the rain
> Lest it blister me again.

She has a sulky mind, she says, slow to forget the tempest in the new morning light. In **"Pueblo Pot,"** she hears the voice of wisdom telling her that broken beauty cannot be consoled, it must be made whole. ("The ruins of time," said Blake, "build mansions in eternity.") But she fears wisdom, and turns, but now in vain, to consider the shards. "I was ever a ten-o'clock scholar at the school of experience," she says. And it is true. She has been so busy telling life what she wanted that she has only rarely heard life telling her what it can give.

Though it is partly her scorn of those conventional people who sacrifice the full-bodied present to an abstract future, it is more largely her distrust of the future that makes Miss Millay emphasize the moment. For if she trusted time, and life, and let herself go, she would find in the moment both future and past: the moment would take on something of the quality of timelessness. Instead of this, she grasps at the moment as she does at life; and of course the moment slips away—which is what she expected. In her attempt to seize life, she has merely succeeded in breaking it to pieces. But, for that matter, the very attempt to seize it indicates that it is already broken to pieces, or at least divided into spiritual and physical and so destroyed. The physical quality of a moment can be known sensuously, can be grasped, which means it will escape the grasp; the complete moment, physical and spiritual, can be known only imaginatively, and thus known it remains. Trying to grasp time, Miss Millay becomes time's slave. If I loved you Wednesday, then I do not love you Thursday, for now on Thursday Wednesday is gone. And, indeed, I could not be sure even on Wednesday that I loved you, for thousands of days, each with its possible love, still lay before me, and, about these,

> How shall I know, unless I go
> To Cairo or Cathay . . . ?

This is to break time up into an infinite series of moments and out of these to construct, if possible, life. It is not possible, for life is not a mathematical sum but a poetic experience, the moments of which are not fractions but symbols of the whole. Life is not quantitative, but qualitative. Occasionally Miss Millay realizes this, as in such a poem as **"Recuerdo."** Usually, however, she falls into the same error against which she revolted, and reduces life to an abstraction.

Distrusting life, grasping at time, feeling the moments slip like sand between her fingers, Miss Millay lives continually in the presence of death, fears it, and struggles, though she knows futilely, against it. Occasionally she is so weary that she longs for death. Generally, however, her attitude is one of rebellion. It is in this attitude that she becomes most rhetorical. Her practical will, continually thwarted by death, turns inward and laments its thwarting. "Rhetoric," says W. B. Yeats, "is the will trying to do the work of the imagination." Miss Millay seems to some very brave in her refusal to be resigned to death, but not very wise. For in the actual world death occurs regardless of our will. Rhetoric is useless against it. Only poetry, only the imagination, illumining the subject from within, understanding

it, can avail anything. Mankind generally has understood this and has written its dirges with music.

In spite of all her talk about death, Miss Millay understands, for a poet, far too little of what she is talking about. She attempts to make up for this lack of knowledge by intensity of will. She senses death too much, sees it too little.

This emphasis upon sensation, upon the material side of life, has fooled many of her admirers into the belief that she is intensely alive. But intensity of sensation is a quality of decadence as well as of health. Miss Millay has been called a belated Elizabethan: the phrase refers, at least in part, to the concrete, earthy quality of her writing. In one of her happier, early elegies she wrote:

> She is happy where she lies
> With the dust upon her eyes.

But the Elizabethan, from our point of view truly young, wrote this:

> Upon my buried body lie
> Lightly, gentle earth.

The earth itself is imagined as sentient and sympathetic. A child is not disturbed that its mother's body lies in the grave; its mother is in heaven. There is little childlikeness in either Miss Millay's experience or memory of life, or in her thought of death. Take the poem **"Spring in the Garden":** the lupine and monkshood pierce the earth, but the dead lies numb and stupid from his first winter underground. Anyone who has lived must admit that the body is important, but this is to make the person the body alone, and surely we do not think of persons like that. Miss Millay is not imagining death; not giving it spiritual form. She is breaking her will against death—and that is merely suicide.

Indeed, for Miss Millay, the physical world is more of a trap for the spirit than a means of spiritual life. (When the rhetorician writes, says Yeats, it is "The struggle of the fly in marmalade"—or on flypaper.) This appears most in her love poems, especially in the sonnet sequence ***Fatal Interview.*** Though there is evidence of passion here—"desire touched with imagination"—there is more evidence of simple desire. When we consider other subjects than sexual love, we find that, though earth—the physical, the felt—is important, it is well balanced by something more than earth. Now, in so far as we find life physical, we shall find death physical; in so far as we find life more than physical, we shall find death more than physical. It is the fact that Miss Millay finds life so much more than physical that makes unwarranted her black picture of death. Angered by the thwarting of her will—and death is surely a thwarting of the will—she attacks the disorder of death rhetorically instead of attempting to reduce it to order imaginatively. If only she would ponder her own experience, she would find that something is saved from the wreck. I shall mention a few of the poems that suggest this. She still has something of Pao-Chin, though Pao-Chin himself may be dead. "Immortal page after page" of the poet remains. Love is something more than the physical. Love will outwit time, its greatest foe. Or, if time does take love away, it will change it into "a jewel cold and pure." Death, though he conquers at last, is shaken by love. Finally, the two great lines:

> How far from home in a world of mortal bur-
> dens
> Is Love, that may not die, and is forever young!

But if this is so, where is the home of love? Miss Millay knows too much not to know more. Important answers lie in her own experience, but instead of asking herself questions she denounces and laments, instead of quarreling with herself she quarrels with the world. She demands of life why it thwarts her, instead of asking herself how it thwarts her.

Yet, though Miss Millay has worried life, and herself, with the wrong questions, she has come slowly, by means of her sensibility, to at least a deeper sympathy with men. Her self-pity is more and more a pity for mankind. In *Wine from These Grapes*, says Louis Untermeyer, "the poet turns from prettiness and the pangs of romantic love, concerning herself with the unhappy, bewildered, self-torturing human spirit." More and more she sees herself as symbolic, her troubles as "the troubles of our proud and angry dust." This is the road that opened to her at the very beginning, in **"Renascence"**; unfortunately she has followed it hesitatingly and unwillingly. In the human pity that at least in part motivated that poem, even in the self-pity of lesser poems, she had found an attitude which, if it could have been boldly adhered to, would have brought an inspiring sense of the oneness of men. "For sudden the worst turns the best to the brave." But she was not able boldly to adhere to it; indeed, as we have already seen, in **"Renascence"** she fled from it. In Sonnet IV, in the same volume, oppressed by earth's pain, she longs to gather up her little gods and go. In the poem **"To the Wife of a Sick Friend,"** she expresses pity, but a separate and ineffective pity. A modern sensibility, she feels the grief of life beating upon her, but her life is too separate, too uncertain of any place in the world (too modern), for her to move outward toward others on this tide of grief. The same attitude appears in **"The Anguish,"** and, slightly modified, in **"Hangman's Oak,"** both of which relate to the Sacco-Vanzetti case. The latter poem expresses the sense of the oneness of life, but it is a oneness, not in life, but in apathetic peace, in death. In another poem she is filled with pity for that "blithe spirit," the skylark, so lost in this hard world. Here are the tears that one must feel for life, but where is the strength that should follow the identification with life that the tears suggest?

Once or twice Miss Millay touches this strength. Winter brings into view, she says, the summer-hidden hill. Again, distress makes men neighborly. In Sonnet XI, of **"Epitaph for the Race of Man,"** she tells of how a man, ruined by disaster,

> . . . saw as in a not unhappy dream
> The kindly heads against the horrid sky,
> And scowled, and cleared his throat and spat,
>   and wept—

moved to tears both by his own disaster and by the suddenly recognized goodness of man. In the poem **"To a Young Girl"** Miss Millay speaks of the wisdom of weep-

ing, but it is all idyllic and picturesque, and she doesn't believe deeply what she says. As for herself, she wants to weep but cannot. Why not? She does not say. But I should guess it is because of our modern pride, our desire to be self-sufficient and free.

The strength of Miss Millay's poetry becomes plainly evident through her reading voice. It is, paradoxically, a powerful pathos. It is also a plangent pathos. She is evidently "making an endless battle without hope." But her voice also reveals the weakness of her poetry. It is a personal poetry. Unfortunately in such a poetry one can disagree personally with the poet. This is only another way of saying that Miss Millay's poetry leans toward rhetoric, and one is tempted to agree or disagree with the view she expresses as that view confirms or refutes one's own opinion. We agree with an argument; we do not agree with poetry. Now, we tend to take Miss Millay personally, not only, as I have been saying throughout this paper, because of her inclination to quarrel, like a rhetorician, with the world, but also because of her individual manner of speech. She has attained, I said, a weightier accent; but on which level, the rhetorical or the poetical?

Because of the general similarity of their views, it may be illuminating to compare for a moment Miss Millay and A. E. Housman. In spite of the apparently personal quality of his poems, Housman is far more dramatic: his own voice is veiled and transmuted by a complex screen, and comes to us, not as his own, but somewhat as the voice of life. J. B. Priestley points out several dramatic elements in Housman's poems: they are moods presented "in a more or less definite atmosphere, on a more or less consistent plan"; a Roman soldier, a sort of shadow against the sky of the Shropshire Lad, stands vaguely in the background; in their natural speech we seem to hear the voice of the people ("It is this that makes his mournful folk seem to cry from the heart, as few others do in the poetry of our time"); and their many references to death are in a definite tradition (the classic instead of the romantic).

Miss Millay's voice is not transmuted by any such complex screen, partly because this screen is not available to her (Housman was a thorough classical scholar), partly because she does not wish to use it. What screen has she had for modifying her personal voice? From the first she has had the very definite music of song, the formal quality of which served as a screen, but it is significant that with the passage of time she has begun to use also the more indefinite music of the speaking voice. She has, like Housman, a command of the language of the people ("What's out to-night is lost") but she relies more heavily upon her own personal language. Why does she not use more extensively these modes of speech that at least would modify her own personal voice? Because it is her own personal voice—her will—that she wishes to express: her poetry is largely the expression of her rebellious or frustrated will. There is in Housman's poetry an acceptance of life foreign to Miss Millay's. His poetry consequently describes, as Charles Williams says, "a single hard curve down to death." Since he does not quarrel with life, he does not arouse in his readers the desire to quarrel with him.

But even had Miss Millay been willing (or able) to transfer

her quarrel from the world to herself, and so hide her personal voice behind an imaginative screen, she would not have had available the screen that Housman had. It is probably safe to say that for both Housman and Miss Millay the Christian tradition had generally broken down. Housman had available, however, in the Stoic philosophy and the classical tradition, with which as a scholar he was acquainted, a scheme of reference in which he could lose, and find, himself. Miss Millay was a neo-pagan, set adrift from the modern wreck of Christianity, but unaware of any other tradition, and tossing rudderless on the open sea. There was little left for her but to be personal.

Her imagery of death is an illustration. After discussing Housman's classical imagery of death, Mr. Priestley adds: "But most of our poets, and indeed rhetoricians, have very naturally taken the medieval or romantic, as opposed to the classical, the Christian as opposed to the pagan, view of the matter." The medieval emphasis upon the material body of death was by way of contrast to man's immortal spirit. But Miss Millay has lost the central faith, the belief in the spirit's value, and retains merely a bit of the machinery by means of which the medieval mind intensified the value of the spirit. It is a striking fragment, but being a fragment it is senseless.

Perhaps, more than anything else, it is the poverty of her tradition that has so often forced Miss Millay, in spite of her splendid technical equipment, on to the rhetorical plane. "We make out of the quarrel with ourselves, poetry." But what is this quarrel with ourselves? May it not be, at least in part, the attempt to strike a balance between the personal and the traditional? between life as it is personally apprehended, and life as it is traditionally ordered? When the tradition is unquestioned, there is no inner struggle; after it has ceased to exist, there is none. Given a poetic talent, says Allen Tate, poetry results when "the intellectual and religious background of an age no longer contains the whole spirit, and the poet proceeds to examine that background in terms of immediate experience. . . . The poet in the true sense 'criticizes' his tradition . . . *discerns* its real elements and thus establishes its value. . . . The poet finds himself balanced upon the moment when such a world is about to fall. . . . This world order is assimilated . . . to the poetic vision; it is brought down from abstraction to personal feeling."

The scene upon which Miss Millay appeared no longer expressed a world order. Unable to quarrel, therefore, except spasmodically, with herself, she has quarreled splendidly with the world. (pp. 54-66)

James McBride Dabbs, "Edna St. Vincent Millay: Not Resigned," in South Atlantic Quarterly, *Vol. XXXVII, No. 1, January, 1938, pp. 54-66.*

Delmore Schwartz (essay date 1943)

[*Schwartz was a prominent American poet, short story writer, and literary critic. In the following essay, he discusses Millay's poetry as a reflection of the Jazz Age and suggests that her use of traditional images, subjects, and forms contributed to her popularity.*]

Miss Millay belongs to the ages. Posterity, which is an anachronism, may prove this strong impression an illusion. But we shall now know about that. Meanwhile Miss Millay has written a good many poems . . . which make her a great poet to most readers of poetry. These readers consider Edgar Allan Poe, Henry Wadsworth Longfellow, Blake, and Shakespeare great poets also; and if they read Poe, Longfellow, and Miss Millay, rather than Blake and Shakespeare, what else can be expected? How else can these readers sustain their view of what great poetry is? . . .

Miss Millay belongs to an age as well as to the ages. She is dated in a good sense. Like Scott Fitzgerald, H. L. Mencken, Sinclair Lewis, prohibition, and midget golf, she belongs to a particular period. No one interested in that period will fail to be interested in Miss Millay's poems. . . . Her lyrics were used by the period, and she was made famous by their usefulness; but now they are inseparable from the period, and they will always illuminate the liberated Vassar girl, the jazz age, bohemianism, and the halcyon days of Greenwich Village. Who can forget the famous quatrain in which a lady's candle burns at both ends, and will not last the night, but gives a lovely light? How could this point of view have been stated with greater economy of means or more memorably? Yet not all that is memorable is admirable. (p. 735)

Miss Millay has perhaps been defeated by her very success. *Fatal Interview* . . . is probably her best book, but there is nothing in it which represents an advance in perception or insight over her first book, which was published in 1917. To compare the two books is to see how all that is good in her work, all that is of permanent interest, is circumscribed by the period in which she became a famous poetess.

Consider, as an example, the view of love which recurs without exception in these lyrics and in many of Miss Millay's sonnets; in one of her best-known sonnets, "What lips my lips have touched and how and why / I have forgotten," Miss Millay compares the female protagonist of the poem to a tree and "the unremembered lads" who were her lovers to birds. Is this not the eternal feminine of the day when woman's suffrage was an issue and not yet an amendment? If one has a weakness for visualizing images, then the dominant image of the poem certainly presents the female and the lads in unfair proportions. Elsewhere some lovers are assured that a love affair is not any the less true love because it has been rapidly succeeded by several more love affairs, an assurance which might come gracefully from Catherine the Great, let us say, but which is not really the kind of attitude that makes great poetry. Is it not, indeed, just as shallow as its opposite, the squeezable mindless doll whom Hemingway celebrates? Yet just such attitudes explain Miss Millay's popular fame at the same time as they exhibit her essential failure. The late John Wheelwright remarked that Miss Millay had sold free love to the women's clubs. Yes, this has been at once her success and her failure; and one should add that another attribute of this kind of famous authoress is that of inspiring epigrams.

When we look closely at Miss Millay's poetic equipment—her images, diction, habits of style, and versification—we find the same twins of success and failure. Her diction especially is poetic in the wrong sense: the candles, arrows, towers, scullions, thou's, lads, girls, prithees, shepherds, and the often-capitalized Beauty and Death are words which come, not from a fresh perception of experience, but from the reading of many lyric poems. . . . If there is an alternative, it is perhaps to be seen flickering in the poems in which Miss Millay draws upon what she has actually looked at on the New England coast or in the Maine woods. . . . (pp. 735-36)

But if Miss Millay had cultivated and searched out the actuality of this experience instead of using it as a stage set, she would not be the first text of all the girls who are going to write poetry; she would not have depended upon attitudes which are as characteristic of literate youth as the sophomore year; after her second volume she would have abandoned the obvious and banal poses she has struck in the face of love and death. She would not be the most famous poetess of our time, and she might have composed a body of poetry characterized by the nonesuch originality—however often warped, thin, fragmentary, exotic, or ingrown—of Marianne Moore, Leonie Adams, Louise Bogan, and Janet Lewis. . . . (p. 736)

> *Delmore Schwartz, "The Poetry of Millay," in* The Nation, *New York, Vol. 157, No. 25, December 18, 1943, pp. 735-36.*

Mary M. Colum   (essay date 1951)

[*Colum, who contributed criticism regularly to such publications as the* New Republic *and the* Saturday Review of Literature, *was called "the best woman critic in America" by William Rose Benét in 1933, although others have argued that her critical judgment was sometimes colored by personal prejudice. In the following essay, she discusses Millay's status as a popular poet, her expression of unconventional ideas and personal emotion, and her use of traditional forms.*]

In the nineteen twenties Edna St. Vincent Millay was America's sweetheart. It was one of the rare periods when poetry, and especially lyrical poetry, was considered important. Now the fact is that this country has seldom been enthusiastic about lyrical poetry, and this largely explains the attitude to Edgar Allan Poe and to that troubadour, Vachel Lindsay. In a favored poet—Robert Frost—what gives him authority is not his lyrical but his narrative and meditative poetry. But Edna Millay struck a mood in American life when lyricism was being welcomed as something strange and moving. Then, what was called her philosophy roused to excitement not only the young men and women but their elders, too. Said philosophy was simply an attitude to life made familiar throughout the ages by the men poets—Herrick's "Gather ye rosebuds while ye may," Horace's "Carpe Diem," Catullus' "Vivamus mea Lesbia. . . . Give me a thousand kisses, then another thousand. . . . For when our brief life ends there is a never ending night and a never ending sleep." Edna Millay was probably the first woman in literature to back such ideas wholeheartedly, for women have been notoriously diffident in their support of hedonism. Her reputation for

unconventionality caused her to be discussed by people for whom her poetic expression was not of first interest. It also caused W. B. Yeats, who was not overly impressed by her poetry, and Thomas Hardy, who was, to be excitedly interested in her personality.

When Edna Millay first began to be noticed, American women still could not smoke in restaurants or swim in such garb as the European *maillot* or without stockings to cover their legs; it was a time when people confused the regulations of *The Book of Etiquette* with the highest principles of ethics. She seemed to be the standard-bearer for the breakdown of futile conventions and of taboos. She advertised her love affairs and her sex affairs, and in her work she really made a differentiation between the two with a nicety that male poets seldom matched. Of her sex affairs:

> I find this frenzy insufficient reason
> For conversation when we meet again

or:

> What lips my lips have kissed, and where and
>   why
> I have forgotten, and what arms have lain
> Under my head till morning.
>   . . . . . .
> I only know that summer sang in me
> A little while that in me sings no more.

Then of her love:

> Women have loved before as I love now;
> At least in lively chronicles of the past,
> Of Irish waters by a Cornish prow,
> Or Trojan waters by a Spartan mast.

These unconventional emotions and ideas she expressed in that most conventional form of verse, the sonnet, which has such an attraction for American women poets. The form enticed her to go on and on, expressing the same emotions and ideas in an unceasing flow of sonnetry. Even people expert in knowing poetry by heart after a couple of readings find it difficult to distinguish one sonnet from another, though this can readily be done in the case of Elinor Wylie's love sonnets, where each reveals a distinct emotion and thought. But Elinor Wylie was a trained and disciplined artist in a sense that Edna Millay never was. She had the faculty to become an artist and a scholar, too; she never let her mind and emotions ramble as did Edna Millay.

The sort of mental and professional training that teaches poets how to say effectively what they have to say was not to be found in the New York of Millay's time. No one was there to show her, not so much the technique of writing verse, which she could learn for herself, but that higher technique of getting beyond one's private world, which would have prevented her repetitiousness. A woman admirer of hers, confusing artistic with conventional education, sent her to college after the publication of her first poems. In no country do people learn the essentials of the art of literature in colleges, but they learn even less of them in America than elsewhere. Edna Millay probably had a good time in college, but she learned little if anything of what might be useful to her as an artist. She could have learned more by staying at home and reading poetry with a few fellow writers, for as Yeats says, "There is no singing school but studying Monuments of its own magnificence." And, to put it in prose, there is this sentence of T. S. Eliot's: "It is important that the artist should be highly educated in his own art, but his education is one that is hindered rather than helped by the ordinary processes of society which constitute education for the ordinary man."

Most of the delighted readers of [Millay's] poetry never noticed her concern in nearly every poem with death—her own personal death and her artistic death, the fear that her work might be forgotten.

—Mary M. Colum

In this sense, Edna Millay, in her art, had not sufficient education to allow her to use effectively her poetic endowment, though occasionally, and especially in her earlier poems, she did so use it. This inadequacy of artistic education also injured her self-criticism: in spite of her interest in ideas, she could not cope with them in writing, and this is seen explicitly in her symposium, *Conversation at Midnight,* and her later work, [*The Murder of Lidice*]. She plunged into translating Baudelaire, for which she was not only linguistically but temperamentally unfitted. She could talk French fluently, but she was no French scholar and got confused by genders and difficult constructions. Then she was too feminine a poet to be able to deal with such a masculine, revolutionary, powerful mentality as that of Baudelaire, who could make an ugliness of nature—decrepit old men and women, a corpse rotting in a ditch—into a high beauty of art. Edna Millay could only deal with the acceptedly beautiful. Death, however, did fascinate her, though in a romantic style. Most of the delighted readers of her poetry never noticed her concern in nearly every poem with death—her own personal death and her artistic death, the fear that her work might be forgotten. In **"The Poet and His Book,"** one of her best poems, she wrote:

> Down, you mongrel Death,
> Back into your kennel . . .
> You shall scratch and you shall whine,
> Many a night, and you shall worry
> Many a bone before you bury
> One sweet bone of mine.
> Boys and girls that lie
> Whispering in the hedges,
> Do not let me die. . . .

This was really the burthen of many of her poems, "Do not let me die." What aided her popularity in her heyday was her warmth of heart, her generosity, her compassion for the beaten, the downtrodden, and this not in the current way of an impersonal, generalized humanitarianism, but with a rich feeling that made her adherence a strong personal emotion. Few of her admirers realized her funda-

mental loneliness, her shyness, her sadness, which made her gladly leave the turmoil of New York for an isolated country house where she seldom saw anybody and where she died alone and lonely. As she has written:

> Lovers and thinkers, into the earth with you.
> Be one with the dull, the indiscriminate dust.
> A fragment of what you felt, of what you knew,
> A formula, a phrase remains—but the best is
>   lost.

> (pp. 17-18)

Mary M. Colum, "Edna Millay and Her Time," in The New Republic, *Vol. 124, No. 11, March 12, 1951, pp. 17-18.*

James Gray   (essay date 1967)

[*Gray was an American playwright and critic. In the following review, he praises Millay's poems for their artistic maturity and originality and asserts that her major theme was the search for spiritual integrity in the face of destructive forces.*]

Seen whole [Edna St. Vincent Millay] emerges out of myth not as a gay figure but as a tragic one; not as a precocious perennial schoolgirl but as an artist born mature and burdened with a scrupulous sense of responsibility toward her gift; not as a changeling child of mysticism but as a creature whose essential desire was to find identity with the balanced order of nature; not as a woman merely but as a creator who inevitably contained within her persona masculine as well as feminine attributes.

The theme of all her poetry is the search for the integrity of the individual spirit. The campaign to conquer and control this realm of experience is conducted always in terms of positive and rigorous conflict—the duel with death, the duel with love, the duel of mind pitted against heart, the duel with "The spiteful and the stingy and the rude" who would steal away possession of beauty.

It is not too fanciful to say that she was born old while she remained forever young. . . . (pp. 5-6)

[Quiet] reverence for vitality under discipline is the distinguishing quality of her poetry. At its best it is characterized by a kind of orderly surrender to ecstasy. (p. 8)

It is often said of the major figures of the arts that each seems to create a universe all his own and to measure its vast dimensions with untransferable techniques. (pp. 9-10)

No such gigantic stature can be claimed for a poet like Edna Millay. Her theme was too personal, too intimate to herself to fill out the dimensions of a supernatural realm of imagination. Indeed it might be said that her unique effort was to perform the miracle of creation in reverse. A universe already made pressed its weight on the sensibility, the aptitude for awareness, of one individual. . . . (p. 10)

The journey in search of wholeness for the individual, an adventure which has obsessed the minds of the philosophers of the past and the psychiatrists of the present cannot be left safely to further exploration by the computers of the future. It continues, therefore, to be of no trivial interest as it is presented in the poems of Edna St. Vincent Millay.

It should not be taken as an indication of a failure to grow that Edna Millay produced when she was only nineteen years old one of the most characteristic, most memorable, and most moving of her poems. The intuitions of artists do not reach them on any schedule of merely logical development. . . . In **"Renascence"** Edna Millay announced the theme to which four more decades of her life were to be spent in the most intense kind of concentration. "The soul can split the sky in two, / And let the face of God shine through." This confrontation with the divine can be dared and endured because man is one with the divine.

Edna Millay presented the inner life of the spirit always as a conflict of powerful forces. The will to live and the will to die are elementally at war in **"Renascence."** . . . The impulse toward surrender *itself* has roused the counter impulse toward a participation more passionate than ever before in the values of human existence. . . . The meaning of this battle of the wills is clear. The anguish of existence must be endured as the tribute owed to its beauty. (pp. 10-12)

An account of the running battle between life and death claimed first place among the poet's preoccupations through her writing career. The effectiveness of the report is heightened by an awareness, sometimes bitter and sometimes merely rueful, that now one side commands ascendancy over will and now the other. (p. 12)

[Variations] of tone in her report on the duel of life against death lend the best and most original of her personal qualities to the development of an old, familiar theme. The parallel may be suggested that, just as a mother must have faith in her child lacking any evidence to justify it, so the believer in life must show a similar courageous unreasonableness. Edna Millay is perhaps at her best when she casts her vote of No Confidence in death. (p. 14)

So many of Edna Millay's pages are devoted to critical moments of the love duel that it has been possible, even for reasonably well informed readers, to be aware only of her confidences about "what arms have lain / Under my head till morning." To their loss they have ignored her equal preoccupation with other themes. Still it is true that some of her most searching observations about the human condition are concerned with the approach to ecstasy through the identification of man with woman. It would, however, be to deceive oneself to approach these poems as if they were exercises in eroticism. Despite the many sidelong references to the physical relationship, the enclosing interest is that of human love as a total experience of the psyche involving, on the positive side, intellectual communication and sympathy of taste and, on the negative side, the endless warfare of two egos that cannot effect a complete surrender into oneness.

The limp endorsement of correct and appropriate sentiments which has made up so much of love poetry, particularly that written by women, is conspicuous for its total absence from these ardent but anxious confrontations of man and woman. It is significant of Edna Millay's approach to the psychological crisis of love versus hate—and

to the even more destructive tragicomedy of love slackening away into indifference by the influences of time, change, and disillusion—that she does not speak of these matters simply as a woman. Often in her highly dramatic representations of the love duel she assumes the man's role and she plays it with no nervous air of indulging in a masquerade. She is concerned with the mind as the retort in which all the chemical reactions of love take place and, because her own intelligence partook of both masculine and feminine characteristics, the poems convey the impression that the exactitude of science, in control of the impulses of intuition, has been brought to bear to reveal much that those changes involve in a man's temperament as well as in a woman's.

Again, as in her account of the conflict of the will to live and the will to die, the love duel is presented with high drama as one that is destined to go on and on indecisively because the adversaries are only too well matched in aggressiveness and submissiveness, in strength and weakness, in sympathy and treachery. (pp. 16-17)

[A reverential gaiety] which finds room for humor in the midst of the contemplation of bliss, characterizes much of Edna Millay's love poetry. Its popularity may be accounted for by the intoxicating quality that brings the immediacy of a highly personal emotion to the poetic statement. The merit that gives the work permanence is the fastidiousness of the style in which the spontaneity is captured.

The theme of all [Millay's] poetry is the search for the integrity of the individual spirit.

—James Gray

In her younger days Edna Millay sometimes allowed her exuberant vitality to escape into verses the levity of which made her famous, perhaps to the injury of her reputation as a serious poet. (p. 18)

These flourishes of audacity do not touch at all closely on the center of her understanding of the love duel. There she held a formidable awareness of the power of change which is not in the least like the vague consciousness of impermanence in which so many poetic spirits have fluttered with languid futility. . . . Edna Millay used the sharpest tools of her intelligence to hew out for herself a unique place among poets by undertaking to discover *why* no love endures. What she says is that the loophole in commitment offers the necessary escape route by which the self saves its integrity. There can be no such thing as total surrender except with degradation or with, what is worse, dishonesty. In love the giving must be generous and free, but there must be withholding, too, if the self is to remain whole. (pp. 18-19)

The immediacy of experience is communicated in images that are piercingly personal. Very often the suggestions of the figurative language are so unexpected that they seem to spring out of an immediate passion which catches deliberately and desperately at punishing words. . . .

It is because she was bold enough to examine the problem of the psychological distance between man and woman—one that cannot be breached and should not be violated—that Edna Millay may be said to have made an original contribution to the literature of the love duel. (p. 19)

[It] is the ability to capture in colloquial language and in one brief thunderclap of drama the essence of a tragic psychological struggle that lends to Edna Millay's long discussion of the love duel its effects of variety and flexibility.

The tone of melancholy misgiving in the face of the emotional crisis is pervasive in these studies, but the warming, the nourishing, the half-maternal aspects of the experience of love are not neglected. (pp. 20-1)

It is characteristic of Edna Millay's temper—not merely its prevailing but its almost uninterrupted mood—that she enters upon the search for beauty as if this, too, were a struggle. (p. 21)

This is to say that the mind has its right to evaluate beauty. It should not yield in limp acceptance as if faced by something of divine origin and therefore, like a god of Greek mythology, not to be denied its will. What Edna Millay persuades a reader that she does indeed know is that beauty must be endured as well as enjoyed. To surrender to beauty without resistance would be to lose an exhilarating aspect of the experience. It must be participated in, but the terms of one's compact with beauty must be understood to be one-sided. "Beauty makes no pledges." In return for the awe that the observer feels in its presence nothing is promised other than awareness itself. . . .

That she is not entirely consistent in developing her religion of beauty need not be found disturbing. She is no more given to shifts of interpretation than mystics must ever be. Beauty may be aloof and impersonal but it is also an element in the process of rebirth, the faith in which the poet takes her deepest comfort. It even becomes in certain poems the food on which she feeds. Her figures of speech suggest again and again that, as a woman, she felt an almost organic closeness to the working of gestation. (p. 22)

Part of the nourishment that she receives from awareness of beauty is provided by what is for her the immediate actuality of sensuous experience. (p. 23)

She was always an actor in the drama: a militant defender of herself against beauty, a militant defender of beauty against its defilers. And she was resolutely faithful to the integrity of her own perceptions. She never attempts to encompass more of a sense of the wonder of the natural world than her own eyes can see. What moves her is the recollection of a familiar scene, fixed in memory by some small detail of local color. . . . Armed with awareness, the one who is "waylaid" by beauty may find exultation in the simplest of experiences. Edna Millay did indeed seem to write all her poems to give permanence to a moment of ecstasy. (pp. 23-4)

From first to last, through every phase of her develop-

ment, Edna Millay continued to be intensely herself and no other. Whether her theme was death, love, beauty, or the refreshing impulse of the will to live she spoke always with an accent that was unique to her. Of language she made a homespun garment to clothe her passions and her faith.

That she was able to create effects of striking originality is discovered to be only the more remarkable when a characteristic poem is examined closely and its thought is found to wear "something old" and "something borrowed" from the left-over wardrobe of tradition. Edna Millay was a product as much of the nineteenth century as of the twentieth. The influence of tradition moved her a little backward in time. A too great reverence for her early instruction—not only at her mother's knee but also at Keats's—probably accounts for all the "O's" and "Ah's," the "would I were's," the "hast's," the "art's," the "wert's," the "Tis's." It must account also for the inversions of normal word order which sometimes impede the plunge of her hardihood in thought.

Even in more important matters of vocabulary, imagery, and symbolism her impulse toward expression was governed by convention. Despite her interest in science she felt its discipline to be alien to her always personal style of utterance. She did not find in its language a new source of imaginative power such as Auden has exploited. Despite her obsession in the late years with the crisis of war, such a reference as one to "Man and his engines" reveals an uninvolved attitude toward the special concerns of the machine age. . . . The familiar image, drawn from the treasury of metaphor upon which Shakespeare also depended for imaginative resource, seems never to have dismayed her. She was not inhibited by fear of intelligibility; she was not tempted to prod the imagination with tortured similes. For her, death still swung his scythe and the poems in which he does so with the old familiar ruthlessness betray no nervous apprehension that the instrument may have become rusty or blunted with the use of ages.

Because she absorbed tradition deeply into herself she seems able to revitalize its language with the warmth of her own temper. Her words become fertile from the nourishment which, as woman, she communicated to them as if by an umbilical link.

Simplicity, spontaneity, the seeming absence of calculation combine to produce her best effects. (pp. 27-8)

More often than with either definitely declared voice she speaks as a detached observer of natural sights and sounds. These souvenirs of experience are shared with a reader in language that seems entirely casual; it has been borrowed for the moment from more studied performers in the realm of poetry simply to convey a passing impression. . . . More typical of the poet's method is the device of catching a symbolic significance, some warning of the threat against survival, in an image that seems to be, all at once, spontaneous, startling, and inescapably true. (p. 29)

Edna Millay's wit was never petty. She was generous toward all her adversaries except mediocrity, war, and death. And in fashioning an epigram she revealed her most fastidious respect both for truth and for elegance. In the later poems her wit is so unobtrusive, so modest, that it might be missed entirely by a reader hoping to find a showy attribute identified by a capital letter. But it is always subtly present, embedded in a theme, as is the wit of Henry James. The tight-packed phrase, the unexpected revelation of how opposites of impulse may be found to blend, the sudden illumination of an ambiguity—these are the veins of wisdom through which wit runs in the sonnets. (p. 32)

A close examination of the work of any artist is certain to reveal flaws. The very urgency of the desire to communicate must tempt any poet sometimes to override obstacles recklessly. With Edna Millay the individual line seldom limps though it may now and again betray an obvious determination to be vigorous. There is little sense of strain in the use of rhyme and, even in the early poems when her effects threaten to become self-conscious, she avoids the temptation to indulge in the verbal acrobatics of clever versifiers as even Byron does. What troubles her appraisers most of all is the willingness to snatch up old trophies of metaphor and set them up among her own inspirations as if she were unaware of the difference of freshness between them.

But in the end vigor and spontaneity prevail in technique as they do in passion. The singing quality of the lyrics, of the free forms of verse and of the formal sonnets, too, is consistently clear and true. (pp. 33-4)

She wrote prose, as she wrote poetry, with an at once witty and intensely sober regard for her own values. The personal letters glow—sometimes they seem feverishly to glitter—with the élan that sustained her, however precariously, through the crucial moments of her experience. Her preface to the volume of Baudelaire translations reveals a critical intelligence of distinction. Only the adroit satiric sketches written under the pseudonym Nancy Boyd depart from her preoccupation with poetry. These exercises, too, display a kind of coloratura virtuosity. They draw freely on her gift of wit and have importance as lucid indirect reflections of her attitudes: her unwavering honesty, her distaste for pretense, sentimentality, and concessiveness. (p. 34)

Conversation at Midnight remains pseudo-drama, lacking a concentrated drive toward effective vicarious experience. . . .

The faults of the work are inherent in the original concept. This requires a group of men, met for a session of late-night drinking and ratiocination, to use the occasion for a kind of war game in which they fire rounds of ammunition over each other's heads, hitting only distant, theoretical targets. Each guest represents a point of view, aesthetic, social, or moral; each in turn has his say, in a piece of stylized elocution, about capitalism, Communism, commercialism, Nazism, and, of course, love in a world that is out of sorts with spontaneity. All is spoken in earnest; much of the talk is witty and stimulating; some of it inevitably seems trivial in its cloudy references to situations in the lives of the characters which there has been neither time nor occasion really to evoke. Nothing resembling

dramatic tension can rise out of these arguments which never intermingle, never affect each other, never in the end manage to clarify idea. (p. 36)

There were crises of social life which gave gross affront to the most fundamental of her convictions and she could not withhold her protests. These took poetic form but—as she later knew to her chagrin—she was able at such times only to rear up the framework of a poem, gaunt and horrifying. To the lines with which she clothed the structure she could communicate her impotent rage but not the essence of compassion which she wished to memorialize.

There was, for example, her involvement in the Sacco and Vanzetti case. (p. 38)

When Sacco and Vanzetti were finally ordered to be executed, Edna Millay wrote the poem **"Justice Denied in Massachusetts,"** a desperate and bitter threnody. . . . The unwilling, half-stifled protest that a reader makes in his turn against these utterances springs from the impression that a just and honest sentiment is being overdramatized. Is the abject surrender to despair really congenial to the poet's spirit or does this lamentation have to be brought under the charge of being tainted by hysteria? The conviction is clearly genuine but the excess of passion with which it is expressed still seems dubious. The literary crisis is not ameliorated when the poet yields her mind to the most cliché of imaginings: "We shall die in darkness, and be buried in the rain."

It is right for a poet to be a participant in the affairs of everyday living. With her special talent for doing precisely this, Edna Millay could not withhold her word. Nor is it relevant that the guilt or innocence of the two men whose part she took is still a moot question. The respect must be paid her of considering anything she wrote as a work of art. Viewed in that light it becomes evident that poems written for occasions come forth misshapen at their birth by the influence of propaganda. In work that was truly her own even her bitterest protests against the will to destroy were informed by a still abiding faith; such poems reveal her militant spirit at its most staunch. The weakness of **"Justice Denied in Massachusetts"** must be attributed to the fact that it was not nourished by an inner will but fed on the inadequate substitute of propaganda. (pp. 39-40)

Edna St. Vincent Millay has been praised extravagantly as the greatest woman poet since Sappho. She has also been dismissed with lofty forbearance as a renegade from the contemporary movement in poetry and sometimes been treated almost as a traitor because she never broke defiantly with the past. But both eulogy and denigration seem to hang upon her figure like whimsical investitures. Neither costume suits the occasion when her enduring presence rises up before us to bespeak a mind that has not lost its vigor. (p. 43)

She belongs to an impressive company of artists who came to maturity and found their voices during the second quarter of this century. Many of these have undertaken to explore the darkest caves of the secret mind of man and they have developed new poetic forms in which to record their experiences. Among them the figure of Edna St. Vincent Millay is conspicuous because she stands alone and in a blaze of light. It is impossible not to understand what she has to say, impossible not to be moved by the simple, direct, eloquent statements of her convictions. The world, which she had held no closer at the beginning of her life than she did at the end, gave her as much of pain as it did pleasure. Love, beauty, and life itself had all to be endured as well as enjoyed. But the human experience had meaning for her. The round of the seasons still kept to its pledge of rebirth and renewal. From that faith she drew the strength to impart dignity and beauty . . . to even the most cruel phases of the adventure of our time. (pp. 45-6)

> *James Gray, in his* Edna St. Vincent Millay, *University of Minnesota Press, Minneapolis, 1967, 48 p.*

Walter S. Minot   (essay date 1975)

[*In the following essay, Minot presents a biographical interpretation of Millay's "Sonnets from an Ungrafted Tree" and suggests that Millay's artistic achievement was impeded by unresolved psychological conflicts reflective of the problematic nature of the woman as artist in America.*]

The reputation of Edna St. Vincent Millay as an American poet is small, and despite recent attempts to show that critical reaction against her work has been too harsh, her position in our letters is unlikely to change much, even with a sympathetic reassessment. She is, and probably will be considered, a minor poet. Nevertheless, her work and life are worth examining; perhaps they may help explain why a talented artist, who wrote as promising a poem as **"Renascence"** in her late adolescence, never achieved poetic greatness. Millay's career may be especially useful in explaining why so many talented American women have failed to attain the stature of major poets.

This essay will consider the biographical implications of Millay's neglected sequence, **"Sonnets from an Ungrafted Tree,"** especially in relation to the *Harp-Weaver* volume in which it appears. Its thesis is that the sonnets are a symbolic attempt, perhaps subconscious, at murdering her father. From there, I shall suggest how her unresolved psychological conflicts led to her later severe neurosis and perhaps disabled her as a poet and as a person. Then I hope to suggest how Millay's situation reflects the problem of the woman as artist in America.

The **"Sonnets from an Ungrafted Tree"** are unlike most of Millay's other sonnets in several respects. Their subject is not passionate love, but love turned cold and bitter. The *persona* is not her usual first-person lover, but a third-person narrator who describes her protagonist coldly and objectively. Indeed, critics have commented on Millay's use of objective details, and Jean Morris Petitt compares Millay's realism to that of Frost and Masters. Moreover, this sequence is notable for its consistently grim tone. There are very few tonal shifts or emotional peaks and valleys such as one finds in most of Millay's sonnets, and especially in *Fatal Interview* (1931). Finally, the sonnets do not follow the Shakespearean rhyme scheme strictly, and each closing couplet contains seven feet per line. In technique and form, **"Sonnets from an Ungrafted Tree"** is dif-

ferent from most of Millay's other work, especially her work up to this time.

"Sonnets from an Ungrafted Tree," as a whole, traces the actions and thoughts of a woman who returns to care for her estranged, dying husband. As the first sonnet indicates, she returns out of a sense of duty rather than love; she is described as "Loving him not at all."

The basis for this sonnet sequence is the visit which Millay made to Kingman, Maine in 1912, when her father, Henry Tolman Millay, was seriously ill. Thus, the dying husband would be Henry Millay, and the wife a combination of Cora Millay, who had divorced her husband, and Edna, who went to visit him in March, 1912. I hope to establish the basis for this interpretation with details from the poems that can be confirmed biographically, and then to discuss the significance of these details.

The very title, **"Sonnets from an Ungrafted Tree,"** suggests the metaphor of a family tree in which the fruits, or children, are left untended and uncared for. The children, like fruit from an ungrafted tree, grow up bitterly resentful of their father who abandoned them. This may describe Millay's feelings, perhaps unconscious, toward her father.

That the woman in the sequence is partially Cora Millay is borne out in several ways. First of all, she was divorced from her husband. Second, she made her living as a private nurse, often living-in with others to tend the sick, just as the woman in the poems is doing for her estranged husband. Third, as sonnet ix of this sequence indicates—"[he] had come into her life when anybody / Would have been welcome . . . "—their marriage was not based on any great mutual sympathy, but was basically one of incompatible spirits. Fourth, like the woman in the sonnets, Mrs. Millay loved to plant flowers, especially nasturtiums, which are mentioned in the second sonnet. While some of this evidence may seem slight, the basic situation and details seem to refer to Cora Millay, the estranged wife and professional nurse.

That the woman in the sonnets is also partially Edna Millay is shown in several ways. First, she actually did visit her father when he was seriously ill. Second, the time of year was late winter or early spring, as indicated in sonnet ix, though that poem mentions April rather than March. Third, the character of the woman bears some strong resemblances to the poet. Sonnet v, describes how "whirred / Her heart like a frightened partridge" and how the woman hid from the grocer's man. The motive seems to be an irrational fear, much like that of the aberration Vincent Sheean attributes to her: "At times she was so afflicted by self-consciousness and dislike for the external world that she could hardly utter a word; I have seen her cringe . . . actually physically cringe, when she felt herself being observed." Perhaps, too, the fear has a more reasonable basis in the inability of the Millays to pay their bills. Several sources suggest that they may have spent money on books and music when they hadn't paid the bills for the necessities. In the next sonnet, the grocer's man is described as "he forced the trade-slip on the nail"— certainly a reminder of unpaid bills. Moreover, the woman's refusal to go to the door and meet women who brought jellies for her husband is another reminder of Millay's fear of strangers. Grace Shaw Tolman remembers that on her visit to Kingman, Edna Millay seemed distant and hard to get to know.

There are other details in the poems that may also have biographical significance. For instance, in the final sonnet of the sequence, there is one outstanding simile in which the woman goes into the bedroom to view her husband's body and compares herself to "one who enters, sly, and proud, / To where her husband speaks before a crowd, / And sees a man she never saw before—". Henry Millay, the Superintendent of Schools and First Selectman of Kingman, was considered a fine speaker. Edna marvels in her letter from Kingman that her father is so important a personage in Kingman, and her tone is similar to that of the simile in the last sonnet.

Now whether this biographical analysis of **"Sonnets from an Ungrafted Tree"** seems justifiable and worth pursuing might be open to question if this sonnet sequence were not considered in relation to both the volume in which it appears and the larger pattern of Millay's life. Such consideration should justify a close analysis.

The Harp-Weaver and Other Poems was dedicated by Millay "To My Mother," and the title poem, **"The Ballad of the Harp-Weaver"** tells how a destitute widow magically weaves a beautiful suit of clothes for her son on her harp. The action takes place on Christmas Eve, an extremely cold night, and next morning the widow is frozen to death, but her son has "the clothes of a king's son" and is saved by his mother's heroic love and sacrifice. Despite the substitution of a son for a daughter and a widow for a divorced woman, critics and biographers agree that the poem is Millay's idealization of her relationship with her mother. Moreover, as Floyd Dell points out, Cora Millay told him that she "brought her [Edna] up . . . like a son—to be self-reliant, fearless and ambitious. She was called 'Vincent' rather oftener than [sic] 'Edna.' "

In a volume dedicated to her mother and with a title poem that idealized her mother, whom Millay deeply loved, the placing of **"Sonnets from an Ungrafted Tree"** is quite significant, especially since these sonnets appear as the last section of the book. These sonnets are Millay's symbolic repudiation of her father, while she glorifies and embraces her mother. The sonnet sequence is Millay's punishment of her father for abandoning her, and it may be a symbolic murder, probably unconscious, by the Edna-Cora woman, who is Edna's psychic projection of herself and her mother, who have suffered greatly and now triumph over this male figure. Perhaps, too, this symbolic murder was necessary in that it somehow set Millay free to marry Eugen Boissevain in 1923, the same year in which these sonnets were published.

The significance of Millay's relationship with her father has probably been greatly underestimated, though Jean Gould's recent biography and Joan Dash's recent study have gone a long way toward correcting the picture of Millay's relationship with her parents. Dash sums up effectively the formative forces on Millay's character: "Edna . . . adored her mother and saw life . . . through her mother's eyes; accordingly she called herself by the boy's name and became . . . the boy of the family. It was a tendency only strengthened by there being, in Henry Millay's absence, no other male in it. There was . . . no one to act out for her the differences between male and female, neither was there a model of womanliness . . . who took pride and pleasure in being female. . . . " The lack of fatherly affection and the general dominance and aggressiveness of her mother produced in Millay an uncertainty about sexual roles and a distrust of men that may have crippled her as a person, and could be the cause of her failure to achieve the poetic greatness that many predicted for her.

If we accept Dash's interpretation of Millay's personality, at least as a working hypothesis, some significant patterns emerge. Vincent Millay grew up in a fatherless home with an aggressive and ambitious mother whom she adored. She went to Vassar, a woman's college, and was graduated in 1917, the year that *Renascence,* her first volume of poetry, was published. She was already in love with Arthur Davison Ficke, a fellow poet who was married. She moved to Greenwich Village, and there had love affairs, either actual or hoped for by her suitors, with various literary men, including Floyd Dell, Witter Bynner, Edmund Wilson, and John Peale Bishop. But whenever it appeared that one of these affairs was moving toward the permanency of marriage, it was Millay who seemed to want to avoid marriage. For example, when Witter Bynner proposed to her by mail, she hedged so much that marriage would have been demeaning for Bynner. Indeed Millay, half-jokingly but perhaps half-seriously, talked of having her mother join her in Europe for a honeymoon and of publishing the *Love Letters of Edna St. Vincent Millay and Her Mother.* Another indication that she saw men as rivals to her mother is evident in this comment from a letter to her mother: "I have a curious feeling that someday I shall marry, and have a son; and that my husband will die; and that you and I and my little boy will all live together on a farm." This attempt to create a husband for herself out of her mother seems a serious distortion of rôles, but it reveals Millay's intense distrust of men.

Millay's poetry was concerned with such themes as the inconstancy and brevity of love, the frailty of love and beauty, and the need of women to be as sexually free as men. Although Millay's work was first published, it now seems almost compulsive. Such lyrics as **"The Spring and the Fall"** and **"Keen"** and such famous sonnets as **"What Lips My Lips Have Kissed," "I Know I Am but Summer,"** and **"Pity Me Not"** (all taken, for emphasis, from *The Harp-Weaver*) reveal Millay's fears of committing herself to love or of trusting men.

When Edna St. Vincent Millay finally did marry, it was to Eugen Jan Boissevain, who was an unusual husband for an unusual marriage. Eugen, a Dutchman by birth, had previously been married to Inez Milholland, a suffragette leader and graduate of Vassar. In this marriage, Eugen and Inez had, according to Max Eastman, taken vows of unpossessive love, which meant complete freedom for both partners, and had maintained their love without possessiveness until Inez's untimely death. This same freedom apparently also characterized the marriage of Eugen and Edna.

The marriage was indeed an unusual one. According to Max Eastman, who shared an apartment with him for several years, Eugen was a rare and lovable character: "He is handsome and muscular and bold, boisterous in conversation, noisy in laughter, yet redeemed by a strain of something feminine that most men except the creative geniuses lack." Eugen Boissevain's feminine instincts were revealed in his management of the housework and his wife's business affairs, along with the duties of managing the farm they bought in Austerlitz, New York. Eugen did everything he could to free Millay from the tasks of normal living in order that she could devote herself to writing poetry. He was not only a husband to her, but a kind of father, mother and nursemaid—an arrangement that both of them seemed to accept. They accepted, too, childless marriage at Steepletop, their farm in Austerlitz, perhaps because, as Janet Gassman suggests, she considered poetry more important and enduring than any human relationships.

Despite their mutual acceptance of this unconventional marriage and despite their mutual devotion to Millay's poetic achievements, the couple's retreat to pastoral bliss did not remain happy. After the early 1930's, Millay's poetry declined sharply in quality as she began to write about social and political issues unsuited to her lyric gifts. Her health, both physical and emotional, led her to a kind of perpetual nervous exhaustion, probably intensified by excessive drinking. The degeneration of her personality is evident in Edmund Wilson's description of her in 1948: "She was terribly nervous; her hands shook . . . Eugen brought us martinis. Very quietly he watched her and managed her. At moments he would baby her in a way . . . that had evidently become habitual, when she showed signs of bursting into tears over not being able to find a poem. . . . My wife said afterwards that Gene gave the impression of shaking me at her as if I had been a new toy. . . . " Although she did manage to write some good poetry again, which is to be found in the posthumous *Mine the Harvest,* she lived only a bit more than a year after Eugen's death in 1949.

Joan Dash has questioned Eugen's excessive protectiveness of Edna Millay, suggesting that this protectiveness was partly selfish and possessive and that Millay's decline as poet and her disintegration as a person may have been a result of her failure to have to face the realities of daily life. Whether Eugen is to be praised or blamed is a matter of conjecture, though Nancy Milford's projected biography, with the help of Norma Millay Ellis, may do much to confirm or deny some of these speculations.

Nevertheless, Millay's life and poetic career do tell us a good deal about the situation of the woman writer in America. That her great promise was never fulfilled may have many causes, but it seems clear that her inner conflicts, unresolved and so basic to life, were formidable obstacles to personal and poetic maturity. Millay's struggle to be independent and sexually free was probably too great a strain on a girl who grew up in a small town in Maine.

The psychic price that she, as a woman, had to pay to achieve the independence and artistry that her mother desired for her was too high a penalty for her spirit to pay. And, unfortunately, that very high price seems to be one that women have had to pay if they wanted to be poets in our society. The suicide of Sylvia Plath and the breakdowns of Millay and Anne Sexton bear witness to the pressures that being a poet places on a woman in American society. The eschewing of a more conventional style of living brings conflicts that may be too great, especially for women who also desire marriage and children.

In an even larger social perspective, we can see that any woman who goes against accepted customs and mores creates conflicts and problems for those around her. When Cora Millay divorced Henry Millay, she followed a brave and independent course, especially when one considers the prim morality of small towns at the turn of the century. Not only did she have to pay a heavy price to be independent, but part of the debt devolved upon her children, especially Vincent. The results can be seen in Millay's life and work.

Whether, in the long run, the heavy price is worth paying is impossible to determine. But Edna St. Vincent Millay's life and work illustrate both the glory and the misery of a woman who is determined to be an artist and independent person in our society. (pp. 260-69)

> *Walter S. Minot, "Millay's 'Ungrafted Tree':*
> *The Problem of the Artist as Woman," in* The
> New England Quarterly, *Vol. XLVIII, No. 2,*
> *June, 1975, pp. 260-69.*

Frederick Eckman (essay date 1976)

[*Eckman is an American poet and critic. In the following essay, he disputes the validity of Millay's "Roaring Twenties" public image in light of her frequent focus on death and desolation in her poetry, and concludes that Millay has more in common with such contemporary poets as Sylvia Plath and Anne Sexton than with poets of the Jazz Age.*]

The year 1912 is well enough remembered in modern literary history as that *annus mirabilis* which marked the founding of the Imagist Movement and the first appearance of *Poetry: A Magazine of Verse.* At the time, however, neither of these events seemed so auspicious to the American literary world as the publication of Edna St. Vincent Millay's precocious visionary poem, **"Renascence"** in a widely-publicized anthology, *The Lyric Year.* Though the poem had received only fourth place, and no prize, in the anthology's national competition, the book's readers, its editors (after agonizing post-publication reappraisal), and even its prize winners, all agreed that **"Renascence"** deserved much better than a runner-up position.

For the next twenty-five years or more, Edna Millay, the tiny auburn-haired woman from Maine, enjoyed a combination of popularity, public notice, and high esteem unmatched by any other American poet in this century. Even though Millay's critical reputation has languished since her death in 1950, at least a few of her poems hold a sacred place in the hearts of the American reading public hitherto occupied only by the most familiar verses of Poe, Longfellow, Whittier, and Dickinson. In Hayden Carruth's *The Voice That Is Great Within Us,* a 1970 anthology of American poetry since Frost, only two of the twenty-four women poets represented (H. D. and Denise Levertov) have more poems than Millay. Even in the trend-conscious 1973 *Norton Anthology of Modern Poetry,* she is represented by ten poems, one more than Stevens, H. D., and Wilfred Owen; only one less than Marianne Moore, and a mere two less than either Whitman or Auden. Her poems continue to appear in high school and college textbooks, as well as specialized anthologies: poetry by women, poetry for children, social-protest verse, and love poetry. Cloth-bound editions of her **Collected Sonnets** (1941), **Collected Lyrics** (1943), and **Collected Poems** (1956) have remained constantly in print since their publication.

It should not, however, surprise anyone familiar with patterns of American popular taste to find that the public, the beloved, the prestigious poet is not the *essential* poet. In literature, as in music and art, Americans exercise their democratic rights: rather predictably they choose the sunny, the funny, the sentimental and nostalgic, the pleasantly instructive, and the mildly scandalous. Even grim works, when not truly terrifying but merely scary, can delight American readers. Partisan considerations of "high culture" and "developed taste" aside, the general reading public is quite as selective, according to its lights, as the most discriminating connoisseur. Interestingly enough, the legends it forms about its favorite writers are almost identical to those formed by the high-brow reading public.

What appealed to readers in **"Renascence,"** I suspect, was the image of none other than Howells' ideal reader of a generation before, the saintly "girl of sixteen," given a voice and a habitation. Even the young woman who emerged immediately thereafter in the most widely quoted and reprinted of her "Jazz Age" poems was a logical 20th-century transformation: the clever, vivacious, slightly wicked (but still sensitive and intelligent) Greenwich Village soul-sister of Daisy Buchanan, Lady Brett Ashley, and Lorelei Lee. Probably no other poet in recorded history has acquired a more enduring public image from six lines than Millay did from these two epigrams in her second volume, *A Few Figs From Thistles* (1920):

First Fig

My candle burns at both ends;
  It will not last the night;
But ah, my foes, and oh, my friends—
  It gives a lovely light.

Second Fig

Safe upon the solid rock the ugly houses stand;
Come and see my shining palace built upon the
    sand!

These two "figs," along with certain other poems in the volume, not only revived a moribund tradition of light verse in America, through the work of such disciples and contemporaries as Dorothy Parker, Samuel Hoffenstein, Richard Armour, Phyllis McGinley, and Ogden Nash; they fixed in the American mind a simulacrum of the modern woman poet that has only recently begun to change into the troubled likeness of a Sylvia Plath. Yet, as later portions of this essay will imply, the poetic imaginations of these two poets—questions of relative excellence aside—are a good deal more alike than their public images.

The first impression that comes from reading Millay's **Collected Poems** from beginning to end (as I have done three times in as many months) is that she is so totally a *literary* poet. One expects the early work of any writer to reflect various admirations and influences. Most poets at any age are bookish, if not always imitative or allusive. But Millay's poems simply never stop drawing from the imagery, language, rhythms, forms, and allusions of other poets. If there is truth in Eliot's mock-solemn dictum that major poets commit grand larceny while minor poets are guilty only of shoplifting, then Millay is indisputably major. In another, more serious context, Eliot discusses this matter:

> Immature poets imitate; mature poets steal; bad poets deface what they take, and good poets make it into something better, or at least something different. The good poet welds his theft into a whole of feeling which is unique, utterly different from that from which it was torn; the bad poet throws it into something which has no cohesion.

At best, certainly, Millay makes her thefts from Shakespeare, Shelley, Keats, Tennyson, E. B. Browning, the Pre-Raphaelites, Housman, the Georgian Poets (especially de la Mare), Yeats, Frost, Sandburg, MacLeish, Jeffers, and such women contemporaries as Anna Hempstead Branch, Elinor Wylie, and Sara Teasdale into "something different." She is a true and good mockingbird. Allen Tate's conclusions on this aspect of Millay's poetry are more perceptive than anything I could hope to write:

> Taking the vocabulary of nineteenth-century poetry as pure as you will find it in Christina Rossetti, and drawing upon the stock of conventional imagery accumulated from Drayton to Housman, she has created out of shopworn materials an interesting personal attitude: she has been able to use the language of the preceding generation to convey an emotion peculiar to her own. . . . She has been from the beginning the one poet of our time who has successfully stood athwart two ages: she has put the personality of her age into the style of the preceding age, without altering either.

There can be little doubt that Millay's constant echoing of the familiar has done much to increase her popularity. By Pound's much harsher standards of excellence, she is the sort of "diluter" who is often preferred by a casual reader of poetry to the genuine article. But both Eliot and Tate make a distinction about derivative work that Pound—himself a compulsive borrower—failed to make: the difference between imitation and transformation. And though Millay's poems cannot always stand up to this test, she is quite often able to employ another's style in the best interests of her own poem.

The next, and deepest, impression that comes to me from reading Millay's poetry *in toto,* and the central topic of this essay, has already been hinted at in my epigraphs: its overwhelming, obsessive concern with death and desolation. Frequently it is human death, in the most literal, naturalistic sense: graves, tombstones, decaying corpses, drowned bodies, shrouds, skulls, and skeletal bones. Even her ubiquitous nature imagery—which arises from the precise, loving observation of a person totally at home in the natural world—is strongly impelled toward falling leaves, bare fields and hills, stagnant pools, withered flowers, slain or hunted wild creatures, snow, frost, cold winds, floods, blighted grain, weeds, maggots, voracious dogs and wolves, venomous snakes and gnawing rodents. Likewise, her domestic imagery always seems to be moving away from the warm, comfortable, and secure, toward burnt-out fires, empty cupboards, blank and hostile windows, gaping doors, shabby furnishings, rancid and sour household odors, decayed food scraps, irritating daytime and ominous night noises, funerals, sickrooms, dim or extinguished lamps, cobwebs, broken or unwashed crockery, leaking roofs, and mortgages. Since Millay is seldom a poet of verbal paradox or irony, we can usually accept this accumulation of images at face value. And more important than their conventional sign-values is their totality of impact from poem to poem, over the entire canon.

At this point I would like to brush away all temptation to indulge in amateur psychoanalytic criticism, especially that of the Freudian persuasion, which seems always to end with patronizing moral-esthetic judgments that reduce both poet and poem to mere curious objects of pathology. Death is, after all, one of the givens of the natural world; in the human realm, coming to terms with it is such an agonizing central struggle that, existentially speaking, we are better served by suspecting as abnormal the person who boasts of not being disturbed about it. As a critic I am not at all interested in determining whether the woman Edna St. Vincent Millay had a death wish, an immature horror of death, or even a creepy fascination with decay. I *am* interested in trying to demonstrate that themes of death and desolation in her poetry are evidence that her work needs reassessment, deliverance from the stock opinion (largely unchanged from her earliest reviews) that she is primarily a poet of praise, affirmation, and celebration. It is possible, of course, to select from such a large body of work enough images, or even complete poems, to prove almost anything. And I am well aware that death, dying, desolation, loss, and grief can, routinely employed, be no more than empty literary postures.

More convincing to my argument than any of the numerous poems *about* death are those in which such imagery works to another purpose. A simple instance is the lyric, **"Passer Mortuus Est"** from Millay's first volume:

> Death devours all lovely things;
>   Lesbia with her sparrow
> Shares the darkness,—presently
>   Every bed is narrow.
>
> Unremembered as old rain
>   Dries the sheer libation;
> And the little petulant hand
>   Is an annotation.
>
> After all, my erstwhile dear,

> My no longer cherished,
> Need we say it was not love,
>   Just because it perished?

In this elegantly clever little poem, the "turn" of the third stanza serves to remind us that *carpe diem* is, after all, grounded in a darker view of existence than its surface frivolity would indicate. We note also that the oft-borrowed Catullan tag in the title and first stanza is put to an altogether original use.

Another poem from the early 1920's employs a personified Death, to purposes beyiond mere mortality:

> **Siege**
> This I do, being mad;
> Gather baubles about me,
> Sit in a circle of toys, and all the time
> Death beating the door in.
>
> *White jade and an orange pitcher,*
>   *Hindu idol, Chinese god,—*
> *Maybe next year, when I'm richer*
>   *Carved beads and a lotus pod . . .*
>
> And all this time
> Death beating the door in.

From the traditional form of the "mad song," a splendidly compact and original poem emerges. On a first level, it is a personal parable of the poet, collecting at great cost a small hoard of rare and beautiful artifacts against, or in defiance of, the ravages of mortality. At another level, the poem can be read as a statement about the human necessity to create order—any order—against the chaos of existence. Read as a woman's poem, it would seem to refute Thoreau's sneer at "the ladies of the land, weaving toilet cushions against the Last Judgment." Whatever the reading, Death cannot be dismissed as a stock poetic device: he is hammering down the door like a stormtrooper or a National Guardsman; whether the speaker's lack of response to him comes from indifference, preoccupation, or defiance might be arguable, but one is not obliged to make a choice.

[Millay's] domestic imagery always seems to be moving away from the warm, comfortable, and secure, toward burnt-out fires, empty cupboards, blank and hostile windows, gaping doors, shabby furnishings, rancid and sour household odors, decayed food scraps, irritating daytime and ominous night noises, funerals, sickrooms. . . .

—*Frederick Eckman*

In Millay's fourth volume, *The Harp-Weaver and Other Poems* (1923), there appears a remarkable seventeen-poem sequence entitled **"Sonnets From an Ungrafted Tree."** Only one critic, [Walter S. Minot], to my knowledge, has paid it more than cursory attention; and I am in total agreement with Sister Mary Madeleva's 1925 opinion that it is a really outstanding work. In its language, rhythms, and imagery, the sequence is heavily indebted to Frost; yet somehow Millay managed to repay her debt by making Frost's familiar idiom sound as if it were her own. The plot of the narrative is about dying and death, but the central concern is with the altering consciousness of a survivor. A woman has come back to her estranged and dying husband, after an indefinite absence, to care for him in his last weeks. For most of the sequence, the dying man is only an object in another room; the real focus is on the woman and the house, with glimpses of the New England village where the story takes place.

> So she came back into his house again
> And watched beside his bed until he died,
> Loving him not at all. The winter rain
> Splashed in the painted butter-tub outside,
> Where once her red geraniums had stood,
> Where still their rotted stalks were to be seen;

The details are lovingly rendered, perhaps from memory: early in 1912 Millay had gone to care for her seriously-ill father, who had been divorced from her mother for a dozen years. Although the father recovered, her memories of the event—especially her own ambivalent emotions— must have remained fresh and poignant over the ensuing decade. The woman in the sequence hears the grocer's delivery man outside; in panic she flees to the cellar until he has left:

> Sour and damp from that dark vault
> Arose to her the well-remembered chill;
> She saw the narrow wooden stairway still
> Plunging into the earth, and the thin salt
> Crusting the crocks; until she knew him far,
> So stood, with listening eyes upon the empty
>   doughnut jar.

The theme of a marriage gone sour, along with Millay's uncharacteristic bending of the sonnet form, suggests another debt: George Meredith's *Modern Love;* but again, the borrowing becomes a transformation. An entire tract on the randomness of choice in marriage could not cover more ground than this quatrain:

> Not over-kind nor over-quick in study
> Nor skilled in sports nor beautiful was he,
> Who had come into her life when anybody
> Would have been welcome, so in need was she.

The boy has attracted her attention by flashing a mirror in her eyes at school. Soon there is an episode of swimming and seduction at the lake:

> So loud, so loud the million crickets' choir . . .
> So sweet the night, so long-drawn-out and
>   late . . .
> And if the man were not her spirit's mate,
> Why was her body sluggish with desire?

Thus they marry, and the sequence moves back into the grim present:

> Tenderly, in those times, as though she fed
> An ailing child—with sturdy propping up
>
> Of its small feverish body in the bed,

And steadying of its hands about the cup—
> She gave her husband of her body's strength,
> Thinking of men, what helpless things they
>   were,
> Until he turned and fell asleep at length,
> And stealthily stirred the night and spoke to her.

Her days become dream-like and hallucinatory. Fact and fantasy, in her deathbed attendant's routine, become confused:

> Upstairs, down other stairs, fearful to rouse,
> Regarding him, the wide and empty scream
> Of a strange sleeper on a malignant bed,
> And all the time not certain if it were
> Herself so doing or some one like to her,
> From this wan dream that was her daily bread.

I hesitate to summon again the august shade of Mr. Eliot, but passages like these inevitably suggest his concept of the "objective correlative": "a set of objects, a situation, a chain of events which shall be the formula of that *particular* emotion. . . . "

The heroine of this sequence is not unusually perceptive or even, beyond her household and nursing chores, able; what makes her heroic is her honesty. When the doctor asks her about preparations for the inevitable funeral,

> She said at length, feeling the doctor's eyes,
> "I don't know what you do exactly when a per-
>   son dies."

Finally, viewing her husband's dead body from the bedroom door,

> She was as one who enters, sly, and proud,
> To where her husband speaks before a crowd,
> And sees a man she never saw before—
> The man who eats his victuals at her side,
> Small, and absurd, and hers: for once, not hers,
>   unclassified.

So the sequence ends. I have not been able to give more than fragmentary glimpses of a suite of poems where emotion is skillfully controlled—dammed up, as it were, by precisely-rendered and composed details; and where dramatic power is released smoothly in the flat, lucid flow of the narration, like Williams' "river below the falls." Throughout the poems, images of death and loss are in the employ of answering that ultimate question posed by Frost's oven bird: "what to make of a diminished thing." That is to say, of existence itself. If the answer here seems to be no more than the stoic formula, "See things through," then we must be reminded that extracting messages and "paraphrasable content" from poems is only another intellectual game: the poem *is* the message, and ever so much more than the message.

Any reassessment of Edna Millay's poetry, then, should come from the poetry itself—the body of work. All but a few of her critics are useless, except perhaps as bad examples. John Crowe Ransom, the most eminent critic of that moment, chose in ["The Poet As Woman" in *The Southern Review,* Spring 1937] to set her record straight through a review of Elizabeth Atkins' critical study, [*Edna St. Vincent Millay and Her Times*], published a year earlier. The essay, surely the silliest, most pretentious and patronizing thing Ransom ever wrote, attacks the poet—through her perhaps equally silly champion—for (a) being a woman in the first place, (b) her "lack of intellectual interest," and (c) not being John Donne or a modern facsimile thereof. His method is the usual New-Critical strategy of attack: to pick apart, word by word, a few chosen poems, then set bleeding and mutilated passages beside those of poets he admires. About Ransom's first objection, a writer in our time can only shake his head sadly; about the second and third, he may reflect nostalgically on fashions in critical taste, wondering if perhaps the New Critics are by now at least as shopworn as Millay's Jazz Age flippancies. But from Ransom's method one can surely draw a lesson: that no poet (with the necessary exception of Chidiock Tichbourne) ought to, or need to, have a lifetime of accomplishment balancing on the point of one poem—or two, or even three.

My discussion of **"Sonnets From an Ungrafted Tree,"** then, is intended only to point a direction. If a poet can be read first of all in terms of the large patterns in the work, then a critic may well proceed, depth by depth, to what is at once the most important and the most elusive of critical goals: a true understanding of the individual poetic imagination in all its range and complexity. Such a study as I have outlined might well show us that Millay's imagery of death and desolation gives her more in common with the contemporary poets we now most prize— Roethke and Berryman, Plath and Sexton—than with the Roaring Twenties bohemians, the Depression radicals, and the quivering sensibilities of small-town poetry societies, where she is usually found nowadays. (pp. 193-203)

> Frederick Eckman, "Edna St. Vincent Millay: Notes toward a Reappraisal," in A Question of Quality: Popularity and Value in Modern Creative Writing, edited by Louis Filler, Bowling Green University Popular Press, 1976, pp. 193-203.

Jeannine Dobbs (essay date 1979)

[*In the following excerpt, Dobbs asserts that although Millay's domestic poems have suffered critical neglect, they are among her best works.*]

Despite the quality and quantity of Millay's domestic poetry, her reputation was built on poems expressing disillusionment with people and on those celebrating sexual freedoms for women. Two of her sonnet sequences, **"Epitaph for the Race of Man"** and *Fatal Interview* typify these concerns. The former is abstract philosophizing on the folly of humankind; the latter a proficient but somewhat academic exercise in the tradition of the courtly love sonnet sequence.

Many of Millay's New Women type poems are successful and interesting; but the speakers usually are not portrayed as real, individualized women. They are witty and clever and sexually emancipated, but as women they are a stereotyped abstraction. The speaker of the following sonnet, for example, is a disembodied voice:

    I, being born a woman and distressed

By all the needs and notions of my kind,
Am urged by your propinquity to find
Your person fair, and feel a certain zest
To bear your body's weight upon my breast:
So subtly is the fume of life designed,
To clarify the pulse and cloud the mind,
And leave me once again undone, possessed.
Think not for this, however, the poor treason
Of my stout blood against my staggering brain,
I shall remember you with love, or season
My scorn with pity,—let me make it plain:
I find this frenzy insufficient reason
For conversation when we meet again.
                                   The Harp-Weaver, 1923

The impersonal speaker works here because she represents all women: "I, being born women . . . " There is no personality here. There is no environment, no dramatic interplay. There is no real man involved, only a "person fair," a "body." There is not even any particularized emotion, just generalities: a "certain zest," a "frenzy." When the speaker is stereotyped and the situation generalized in this way, identification with the speaker must be made totally on an intellectual level. Many of Millay's burning-the-candle-at-both-ends type poems portray only a voice, and all portray the same voice.

In more successful poems, Millay places the speakers in a setting or in a situation with which women can identify. **"The Fitting"** (*Huntsman, What Quarry?* 1939) is such a poem. Here the speaker's body is portrayed as being impersonally, even roughly handled by dressmakers, "doing what they were paid to do." As this activity proceeds, the woman thinks of her lover. The brief mention of the lover invites comparisons between the present touch of the dressmakers and the anticipated evening with the lover, when his touch, as [Norman A. Brittin in his *Edna St. Vincent Millay*] notes, will not have to be paid for.

It was these kinds of love poems—love poems declaring or illustrating women's independence in the face of social conventions—which most interested Millay's public. Many of these poems appear to be autobiographical, confessional. Therefore, as much attention was paid to guessing the identity of the lover(s) as to the poems themselves. With the appearance of this type of heroine and this kind of love poem (especially in *A Few Figs from Thistles*), Millay began to be encouraged to write for all the wrong reasons: shock, titillation, idle speculation. "Gossip and scandal . . . enhanced her sales," Dorothy Thompson reports [in "The Woman Poet" in *Ladies Home Journal*, January 1951]. The fact that *Fatal Interview* describes an illicit affair may help to explain the popularity of that sonnet sequence. Also, it was undomestic, academic, and abstract. It was, therefore, pronounced "intellectual" and "masculine," a superior work according to Millay's critics. Thus, Millay's public, her editors and critics have emphasized and praised some of her less successful and actually less important work and have neglected or ignored work that best reveals her talent, her domestic poetry.

Millay was one of the number of bright, young women who converged on New York and the capitals of Europe in the early 1920s to pursue the new liberated life women felt they had won along with suffrage. By this time, Millay was a published and recognized poet; and, for a while, she undertook a simultaneous career as an actress. During this time, she half-heartedly agreed to marry two or three of her numerous suitors; meanwhile she practiced her belief in free love. She feared marriage because she thought it might kill her creative voice. Floyd Dell, one of the rejected lovers, recalls "that she was probably afraid that by becoming a wife and mother, she might be less the poet. She wanted to devote herself exclusively to her poetry and did not want to 'belong' to any one except herself. She did not want to spend her energies on domestic affairs." In spite of her fears, Millay married Eugene Boissevain in 1923. She was thirty-one; he was forty-three. He gave up his career in order to take up the household duties and free Millay for her writing. When Allan Ross MacDougall interviewed Boissevain for an article in the *Delineator* some years after the marriage, Boissevain recalled: "When we got married I gave up my business. It seemed advisable to arrange our lives to suit Vincent. It is so obvious to anyone that Vincent is more important than I am. Anyone can buy and sell coffee—which is what I did . . . But anyone cannot write poetry."

In the same year as her marriage, Millay published a sonnet that warns a husband what may happen if he scorns his wife's intellect and insists instead on subjugating her to stereotyped wifely roles—to being submissive, non-intellectual and vain:

> Oh, oh, you will be sorry for that word!
> Give back my book and take my kiss instead.
> Was it my emeny or my friend I heard,
>
> "What a big book for such a little head!"
> Come, I will show you now my newest hat,
> And you may watch me purse my mouth and
>   prink!
> Oh, I shall love you still, and all of that.
> I never again shall tell you what I think.
> I shall be sweet and crafty, soft and sly;
> You will not catch me reading any more:
> I shall be called a wife to pattern by;
> And some day when you knock and push the
>   door,
> Some sane day, not too bright and not too
>   stormy
> I shall be gone, and you may whistle for me.
>   *The Harp-Weaver,* 1923

Perhaps because Millay was so aware of the potential threat to her career posed by her marriage and certainly because of Boissevain's willingness to accept an untraditional domestic situation, the marriage endured until his death twenty-six years later.

Although some of Millay's domestic poems seem clearly autobiographical, it is difficult to discern any over-all correlation between the events of her life and the periods when she wrote on domestic subjects. She alternates between writing some domestic poems and writing none at all, but for no apparent reasons. She wrote about marriage before she became a wife, culminating with **"Sonnets from an Ungrafted Tree."** After her marriage, domesticity virtually disappeared from her work until the 1939 volume *Huntsman, What Quarry?,* a rather strange mixture of war and domestic concerns. During the war years, propa-

ganda held her captive; but the poems collected posthumously in 1954 in *Mine the Harvest* reveal that she ultimately returned to her more basic subjects: nostalgia for childhood, nature, and domesticity. Hence, it is more useful and enlightening to see her domestic poetry not in terms of chronological progression, but in terms of certain recurrent themes.

The same domestic themes run through all three of the periods of Millay's career in which she wrote about her own or other women's experiences. The **"Sonnets from an Ungrafted Tree"** sequence deals with one of the most common: the relationship between husband and wife. This sequence appeared in the May 1923 issue of *Harpers* before it was collected in *The Harp-Weaver* volume. Millay did not marry until August 30th of that year. Thus, the poems were written before she herself could have had any actual experience as a wife. This fact makes the sequence all the more remarkable since it is one of the most striking portraits of a wife's situation in twentieth-century American poetry.

These sonnets tell the story of a wife who returns to the deathbed of her estranged husband. The wife Millay creates or describes here is a woman whose body has trapped her into marriage with a man she knows to be her intellectual and spiritual inferior. The woman was aware that her husband was "not over-kind nor over-quick in study / Nor skilled in sports nor beautiful" when she met him in school, but she married him anyway. Apparently even his physical passion did not prove to be a match for hers. In Sonnet IV, the woman's "desolate wish for comfort" and her intense efforts at starting a fire among "the sleeping ashes" seem a metaphorical experience suggesting the woman's frustrated efforts to kindle a physical passion in her past marital relationship. The woman is "mindful of like passion hurled in vain / Upon a similar task in other days." She brings her whole body to bear upon the "hilt" of the coals.

The woman's story is told primarily through such small domestic actions, rather than through explicit statements. We are told that the man does not measure up to the woman's dreams, that she married him because she was "so in need." But we are not told explicitly how their previous life together progressed or why they separated. What we are given are subtle insights into the woman's character and flashes of what her life in the house once was. Thus, we see her in Sonnet I in the past, presumably a new wife, "big-aproned, blithe, with stiff blue sleeves . . . plant[ing] seeds, musing ahead to their far blossoming." There is something promising and maternal in this picture of the woman planning ahead to a distant crop. In contast are the geraniums, the "rotted stalks" of the present. She has not provided the necessary care to ensure that her plants survive the winter season. She abandoned them when she left her husband.

Sonnet I provides a further contrast with the woman's actions later in the sequence. Her figure, "big-aproned" and "blithe" in a past spring is contrasted to her discovery in Sonnet XI of an apron which she had lost in a long ago snowstorm. Finding the apron, she is struck "that here was spring, and the whole year to be lived through once more." It is as if the resurrection of the apron represents not a new year at all, but only the same year to be lived again. In fact, none of the promise of the image of the woman from her past is fulfilled. She comes back only to mother her dying husband and to muse, in the end, upon his corpse.

These poems do not reveal what has motivated the woman to return to care for her dying husband. Perhaps is is a sense of guilt or perhaps a sense of duty—certainly it is not love that has brought her. Her behavior, her desire to remain invisible to the eyes of the neighbors, suggests guilt. Her instinct is always to flee. She leaves only the fanning of a rocker to the eyes of the grocer, just as the small bird she thinks she may have seen has left only its flash among the dwarf nasturiums (shades of Emily Dickinson!). And the train's whistle at night brings her magic visions of cities that call to her as the whistle must have done when she first lived with the man as his wife.

The woman immerses herself in housekeeping as a distraction from her dying husband's "ever-clamorous care." She discovers that there is a "rapture of a decent kind, / In making mean and ugly objects fair." (It is to this kind of rapture that her desires have come.) She polishes the kitchen utensils, changes shelf paper, and replaces the table's oilcloth; but she is now only a visitor to the kitchen that once was hers. She has not been the one to position the soda and sugar; thus, they seem strange to her.

It is unclear whether or not the woman views domestic chores as a part of the trap of marriage. Perhaps it is only her disillusionment with the man and not her functions in the house which have caused the estrangement. The clean kitchen seems to give her pleasure; on the other hand, she finds saving the string and paper from the groceries a routine that is "treacherously dear" and "dull." And this is a woman who needs magic in her life, a woman for whom the common and everyday must be transformed.

As a girl she was blinded by a reflected light in a mirror held by the boyfriend, not by the vision of the boy himself. When it occurs to her that his dazzling her with a mirror is unmiraculous, she persists in viewing him by moonlight rather than by the clear and truthful light of day. The unsuccessful outcome of her marriage has not disillusioned the woman in general; she is still affected by the magic of the train's whistle. Only in matters concerning her husband has she given up hope of magic or surprise. She anticipates that in death he will be "only dead." But there is irony here. In Sonnet XVII, the last and perhaps the finest of the sequence, the woman is surprised by her dead husband. Considering him as "familiar as the bedroom door," she is surprised to discover in him a new dimension. In death he has a mystery about him that, in life, he had long since lost, or that she had only pretended was his.

These sonnets are serious, quiet, delicate pieces of work. Except for the epiphany in the final poem, the grand emotions of these characters are over. But the work is not slight or trivial. Much of Millay's work is uneven; however, except for the somewhat weak concluding couplet to Sonnet IX, this sequence is extremely well-written. Also, the sequence reveals a remarkable degree of imagination and insight into the female condition. Even though the essence of the story is said to be true [according to Jean Gould in her *The Poet and Her Book*], and even though Millay had done some housekeeping as the eldest daughter of a divorced and working mother, her understanding of the woman's emotional responses toward her husband—especially the epiphany in the concluding sonnet—is unaccounted for by what we know of her actual experience.

Whenever Millay writes about marriage, it is usually in the sad tone of **"Sonnets from an Ungrafted Tree,"** or in a disillusioned or cynical voice. A person is trapped, biologically, into marriage, or, like the husband in **"On the Wide Heath"** (*Wine from These Grapes,* 1934), trapped out of loneliness. This husband goes home "to a kitchen of a loud shrew" and

> Home to a worn reproach, the disagreeing,
>   The shelter, the stale air, content to be
> Pecked at, confined, encroached upon,—it being
> too lonely, to be free.

Also, the married person is one who resists being totally possessed. The speaker of **"Truck-Garden-Market Day"** (*Mine the Harvest*) for example, is happy to remain at home while her husband takes the produce to town because solitude gives her relief from his "noises." The time she is left alone represents to her the small part of herself she keeps from giving to him. She has already given him so much: "More than my heart to him I gave," she says, "who now am the timid, laughed-at slave." But she must not allow him to see how she feels, because:

> He would be troubled; he could not learn
> How small a part of myself I keep
> To smell the meadows, or sun the churn,
> When he's at market, or while he's asleep.

The woman is portrayed as preferring even a small housekeeping chore to the man's company. The woman's experience is different from her husband's, but by choice; and it is not necessarily inferior.

Perhaps Millay's most successful poem about marriage is one titled, **"An Ancient Gesture"** [from *Mine the Harvest*]:

> I thought, as I wiped my eyes on the corner of
>   my apron:
> Penelope did this too.
> And more than once; you can't keep weaving all
>   day
> And undoing it all through the night;
> Your arms get tired, and the back of your neck
>   gets tight;
> And along towards morning, when you think it
>   will never be light,
> And your husband has been gone, and you don't
>   know where, for years,
> Suddenly you burst into tears;
> There is simply nothing else to do
>
> And I thought, as I wiped my eyes on the corner
>   of my apron:
> This is an ancient gesture, authentic, antique,
> In the very best tradition, classic, Greek;
> Ulyssess did this too.
> But only as a gesture,—a gesture which implied

> To the assembled throng that he was much too
>   moved to speak.
> He learned it from Penelope . . .
> Penelope, who really cried.

This combining of the classic and the homely is surprising but perfectly appropriate. The poem expresses the universality of domestic experience for women as well as the differences in the nature of experience between women and men: Penelope, the stay-at-home, the weaver, contrasted with Ulysses, the venturer, adventurer, orator. Penelope's weaving, which according to myth never gets done, is a perfect symbol for woman's condition. Ulysses learns something from his wife but then uses it superficially—to further his own ends. The sincerity and suffering of the woman are contrasted effectively with the political expediency of the man.

"Menses" (*Huntsman, What Quarry?*) is another poem that deals with marriage and with the differences between the sexes. The speaker is a man who humors the woman in a patronizing way. When the woman attacks him brutally, however, he forgives her, thinking to himself merely that she is "unwell." (She says at one point: "Lord, the shame, / The crying shame of seeing a man no wiser that the beasts he feeds— / His skull as empty as a shell!") The poem ends with the woman's denunciation of her own weakness: "Just heaven consign and damn / To tedious Hell this body with its muddy feet in my mind!" Thus, it seems that the woman is as much or more concerned with the effect psychologically of her menstrual period on her intellect as with the effect on her relationship with the man.

The relationships between women and men and the differences between the sexes are thematically important to Millay's work. Maternity as subject or theme concerns her much less, although **"The Ballad of the Harp-Weaver,"** the poem for which she won the Pulitzer, tells the story of a mother's sacrifice for her child. In other poems, Millay oddly enough envisions herself (or her speakers) in strangely intense, maternal relationships with nature. Sometimes these visions are bizarre. In the apocalyptic poem **"The Blue-Flag in the Bog"** (*Second April,* 1921) she adopts a maternal posture toward the last flower left on earth. In **"The Little Hill"** (also *Second April*), she pictures herself as the mother of the hill where Christ died. But these conceits are mere oddities. Millay, although she had no children, could and did write successful poems about them. One example is an untitled poem [included in *Mine the Harvest*] in which she identifies with a child rather than with its mother. This poem deals with an adult's perception of birth as a betrayal. The second half reads:

> If you wish to witness a human countenance
>   contorted
> And convulsed and crumpled by helpless grief
>   and despair,
> Then stand beside the slatted crib and say There,
>   there, and take the toy away.
>
> Pink and pale-blue look well
> In a nursery. And for the most part Baby is
>   really good:

> He gurgles, he whimpers, he tries to get his toe
>   in his mouth; he slobbers his food
> Dreamily—cereals and vegetable juices—onto
>   his bib:
> He behaves as he should.
>
> But do not for a moment believe he has forgottn
>   Blackness; not the deep
> Easy swell; nor his thwarted
> Design to remain for ever there;
> Nor the crimson betrayal of his birth into a yel-
>   low glare.
> The pictures painted on the inner eyelids of in-
>   fants just before they sleep
> Are not pastel.

The sentiment almost inherent in this subject—baby in its pretty crib—is played off effectively against the strong ending of the poem. Removing the child's toy, which to the child is imcomprehensible loss, signifies the incomprehensible losses and terrors life holds. The child still recalls the "betrayal" of its birth; and thus its dreams are not, as we might sentimentally like to believe, "pastel."

Another major theme, although not a familial one, is the preference for nature to housekeeping. One early (1920) and possibly autobiographical poem entitled **"Portrait by a Neighbor"** describes this preference. The poem begins:

> Before she has her floor swept
>   Or her dishes done
> Any day you'll find her
>   A-sunning in the sun!
>   *A Few Figs from Thistles*

And the same subject is more effectively treated in a late (1954), untitled poem in which the speaker recalls the discovery of nature's beauty and wonders how as mere child she could have withstood "the shock / Of beauty seen, noticed, for the first time." The speaker, now adult, still is staggered by the experience of encountering natural beauty—to the extent that she finds it impossible to turn from it to mundane, domestic chores:

> How did I bear it?—Now—grown up and en-
>   cased
> In the armour of custom, after years
> Of looking at loveliness, forewarned
>   And face to face, and no time
>   And too prudent,
> At six in the morning to accept the unendurable
>   embrace,
>
> I come back from the garden into the kitchen,
>   And take off my rubbers—the dew
> Is heavy and high, wetting the sock above
>   The shoe—but I cannot do
> The housework yet.
>   *Mine the Harvest*

"Cave Canem" (*Mine the Harvest*), another seemingly autobiographical poem (probably written after Boissevain's death), also reveals her preference for nature as well as continued concern over the encroachment of domesticity on her writing. In this lyric, the speaker complains that she must "throw bright time to chickens in an untidy yard"; and that she is "forced to sit while the potted roses wilt in the case or the / sonnet cools."

In **"The Plaid Dress"** (*Huntsman, What Quarry?*), Millay uses something feminine in much the same way that Edward Taylor used the homely and commonplace as an emblem through which to treat larger concerns:

> Strong sun, that bleach [sic]
> The curtains of my room, can you not render
> Colourless this dress I wear?—
> This violent plaid
> Of purple angers and red shames; the yellow
>   stripe
> Of thin but valid treacheries; the flashy green of
>   kind deeds done
> Through indolence, high judgments given in
>   haste;
> The recurring checker of the serious breach of
>   taste?
>
> No more uncoloured than unmade,
> I fear, can be this garment that I may not doff;
> Confession does not strip it off,
> To send me homeward eased and bare;
>
> All through the formal, unoffending evening,
>   under the clean
> Bright hair,
> Lining the subtle gown . . . it is not seen,
> But it is there.

The speaker's violently-coloured dress is used as a metaphor to represent her emotions—her "purple angers and red shames." She can suppress these, but she cannot purge them from her personality.

Millay's letters to her editors reveal her own opinions about some of her work. They indicate that she preferred poems such as **"The Plaid Dress"** to what she called her more "modern" poems, poems of "the revolutionary element" concerning "the world outside myself today." It is revealing that she felt it necessary to defend her more personal, feminine poems, almost to apologize for them. The reason for her attitude undoubtedly lies in the critical reception to her work: when she wrote in the male tradition—that is, "abstract" and "intellectual" poetry—or when she wrote "shocking" verse, she was praised; when she wrote outside that tradition—the domestic poems—she was usually ignored or downgraded.

Of course Millay's "feminist" verse is important. It was flippant, fresh, and fun. It was popular with the public and helped gain her fame, and it was widely imitated by Dorothy Parker and other women poets of the period. But a reassessment of Millay suggests that her greater contribution and achievement have been in the poems she wrote of a more personal, more immediate nature, poems out of her own experience as a woman and out of her understanding of that experience on the part of other women. (pp. 94-105)

Jeannine Dobbs, "Edna St. Vincent Millay and the Tradition of Domestic Poetry," in Journal of Women's Studies in Literature, *Vol. 1, No. 2, Spring, 1979, pp. 89-106.*

Jane Stanbrough (essay date 1979)

[*In the essay below, Stanbrough argues that despite Millay's public image of liberation and self-assurance, the language and structural patterns of her poetry suggest an inner world of vulnerability, submission, confinement, and frustration.*]

In 1917, when Edna St. Vincent Millay moved to Greenwich Village, her image as a woman of spirit and independence was already legendary. Previously, at Vassar, Millay had become a notorious public figure. She was a publishing poet, an impressive actress, and a dramatist of growing reputation. She had all along flaunted her independence impudently, smoking against the rules, cutting classes that were boring, earning a severe faculty reprimand which nearly deprived her of participation in her graduation ceremonies. This image of defiance was enhanced by her move to Greenwich Village, known as a hotbed of free-thinking radicals, and by her publication of five poems under the heading **"Figs from Thistles"** in *Poetry* in 1918, poems which vivified her inclination toward bohemianism and promiscuity. The famous first fig—"My candle burns at both ends; / It will not last the night; / But ah, my foes, and oh, my friends— / It gives a lovely light!"—immortalized her public image of daring and unconventional behavior. It came as no real shock, then, when in 1920 she published an entire volume of poetry (including the first five figs) entitled *A Few Figs from Thistles,* dominated by a narrative voice that irreverently mocked public opinion and public morality, that scorned imposed values and prescribed behavior.

This image of liberation and self-assurance is the public image Millay deliberately cultivated, the self-projection that stole the show, demanded applause and attention, suited a loud and raucous jazz-age temper. For half a century it has captivated readers and critics and minimized or veiled entirely a private anxiety-ridden image of profound self-doubt and personal anguish with which Millay contended all her life. The braggadocio of the public image is, in fact, contradictory to experience as Millay inwardly felt it and is belied by both the language and the form through which she reflected her deepest sense of that experience. Although the poetry in *Figs* solidified that public image of defiance and independence, it did so in language and structural patterns that divulge a private image of submission and constriction. The dominant tone of the body of her work—the tone of heart-rending anguish—is apparent when she works at flippancy. Millay is unquestionably a woman who suffers, and the greatest source of her suffering seems to lie in an overwhelming sense of personal vulnerability—and ultimately of woman's vulnerability—to victimization by uncontrollable conditions in her environment.

This sense of vulnerability provides one of the richest linguistic patterns in her poetry, for in spite of her efforts to repress and protect a part of her emotional life, Millay is exposed and betrayed through a language pattern which calls attention to the emotional conflicts and tensions, the psychic realities of her existence. This pattern of self-revelation appears consistently throughout her work, though sometimes disguised by attitudes associated with the public image. **"Grown-up,"** for example (from *Figs*), seems to be merely a cute, little versified cliché about the disillusioning process of growing up.

Was it for this I uttered prayers,
And sobbed and cursed and kicked the stairs,
That now, domestic as a plate,
I should retire at half-past eight?

Notice the violence in the verbs; aptly, they do evoke an image of an unruly child, but they also suggest the strength of the frustration of the narrator for something absent from her life. The contrasting image, domestic as a plate, is perfectly appropriate to imply the flatness and brittleness and coldness that condition her existence. Growing into adult domesticity for this woman has been a process of subduing the will and shrinking the soul. The last line carries the shrinking image to its ultimate conclusion: oblivion, implied by the verb "retire." The woman is painfully aware of the disparity between her childhood hopes and the realities of her adult experience, a theme Millay treats at length in **"Sonnets from an Ungrafted Tree."** Here, the emptiness of the woman's life is made explicit by the fact that she retires at half-past eight, when for many the evening's activities have barely begun. This poem is a strong statement of protest against the processes that mitigate fulfilling and satisfying experience. Certainly, the poem might be read simply as a statement of the inadequacy of experience to measure up to the imaginative conception of it. But it is more. It is a specific statement about woman's experience. "Domestic as a plate" is an image that fits woman into her conventional place at rest on a shelf and out of the way. The poem reflects Millay's fears of her own fate and aids our understanding of the poet's excessive urge to proclaim herself a free and unconfined spirit.

Other poems in the *Figs* volume seem just as adolescently superficial as **"Grown-up"** but under closer analysis corroborate this deep sense of confinement and frustration. Both **"The Unexplorer"** and **"To the Not Impossible Him"** employ a central metaphor of limited travel to suggest the nature of the oppression and restriction felt by the narrators. In **"The Unexplorer,"** the child-narrator is inspired to "explore" the road beyond the house, but on the basis of information provided by her mother—"It brought you to the milk-man's door"—she has resigned herself to confinement. She rather wistfully explains, "That's why I have not travelled more." The implications of familial repression in the socialization process of the female are rather grim. In **"To the Not Impossible Him,"** while the tone is light and the pose coyly provocative, the issue again is serious. The last stanza concludes:

The fabric of my faithful love
No power shall dim or ravel
Whilst I stay here,—but oh, my dear,
If I should ever travel!

Confining the female, denying her experience, the narrator suggests, is the only sure way of forcing her into the social mold. Millay says a great deal more about this process in *Fatal Interview,* a collection of fifty-one sonnets published in 1931.

The structural simplicity and childlike narrative voice are techniques Millay used frequently in her early work. **"Afternoon on a Hill,"** published in 1917, appears to be too simple a poem to give a serious reading. In imitation of childhood speech and thus childhood experience, its regular meter and rhymed quatrains, its childlike diction and sentence structure effectively convey the notion of woman as child. The stanzas, significantly without metrical variation, measure out their syllables as repetitiously as the child's days:

I will be the gladdest thing
Under the sun!
I will touch a hundred flowers
And not pick one.

I will look at cliffs and clouds
With quiet eyes,
Watch the wind bow down the grass,
And the grass rise.

And when lights begin to show
Up from the town,
I will mark which must be mine,
And then start down!

Though appearing to lack subtlety and complexity, the poem does create a tension through an ironic disparity between the directness in tone and structure and the implications of the experience. The speaker seems to symbolize childhood's innocence and freedom. But the freedom, in fact, is artificial, for the child is regulated and restrained. She reaches out; she withdraws. "I will touch a hundred flowers," she decides, but then promises obediently: "And not pick one." The passivity outlined in this poem—looking, watching, obeying—again ends with the narrator's total retreat. It is, on the surface, an innocent-looking action. But it is a form of surrender. Throughout the poem one hears the promises of the "good little girl." She will do what is expected of her; she will watch quietly and disturb nothing.

Psychological experiences merely hinted at in this poem are verified directly and harshly in later poems. In **"Above These Cares"** Millay's narrator nearly screams out her recognition of her state:

Painfully, under the pressure that obtains
At the sea's bottom, crushing my lungs and my
    brains
(For the body makes shift to breathe and after
    a fashion flourish
Ten fathoms deep in care,
Ten fathoms down in an element denser than air
Wherein the soul must perish)
I trap and harvest, stilling my stomach's needs;
I crawl forever, hoping never to see
Above my head the limbs of my spirit no longer
    free
Kicking in frenzy, a swimmer enmeshed in
    weeds.

The woman's vulnerability is absolute because she is so helplessly ensnared. Her feelings of oppression and spiritual suffocation are excruciatingly described, and she craves a numbing of her consciousness to dull the pain of her awareness. The psychological disintegration resulting from thwarted experience shown in this poem is further displayed in **"Scrub,"** where the disillusioned narrator reflects bitterly on the meaning of her oppression and recognizes its origins in childhood:

If I grow bitterly,
Like a gnarled and stunted tree,
Bearing harshly of my youth
Puckered fruit that sears the mouth;
If I make of my drawn boughs
An inhospitable house,
Out of which I never pry
Towards the water and the sky,
Under which I stand and hide
And hear the day go by outside;
It is that a wind too strong
Bent my back when I was young,
It is that I fear the rain
Lest it blister me again.

Made vulnerable by its natural inclination to stretch and grow, the tree is thus subjected to attack and mutilation by forces in its environment; it is bent and blistered into submission. Terrorized and intimidated in the process, the woman—like the child who reaches to touch the flowers—makes a complete withdrawal inside "An inhospitable house, / Out of which I never pry / Towards the water and the sky, / Under which I stand and hide. . . . " Imagining herself like the tree to be deformed and grotesque, the mutilated narrator bemoans the psychological crippling of denied opportunities and punitive restrictions.

Millay found the child-narrator device very suggestive of woman's susceptibility to intimidation. In her vulnerability to victimization, the child in **"Afternoon on a Hill"** is psychologically parallel to the terrorized woman of **"Assault,"** a poem first published in 1920 in *The New Republic.*

I had forgotten how the frogs must sound
After a year of silence, else I think
I should not so have ventured forth alone
At dusk upon this unfrequented road.

I am waylaid by Beauty. Who will walk
Between me and the crying of the frogs?
Oh, savage Beauty, suffer me to pass,
That am a timid woman, on her way
From one house to another!

Here, ostensibly, is the narrator's expression of her sensitivity to and appreciation for the beauties of nature. But the word choice and the ideas evoked call into question so superficial a reading. The speaker describes the experience as an ambush where she is assaulted, "waylaid," forced by a savage attacker into terrified submission, an image obviously suggestive of rape. The woman is confused as well as terrified, and her bewilderment is apparent in the ambiguity of her perceptions. She calls her assailant Beauty, suggesting a benign, even attractive attacker. Yet, she describes the attack as savage and further qualifies its nature by defining Beauty in the shape of frogs. She thinks she hears them crying, and in a spontaneous outburst of identification with their pain, she too cries. "Oh, savage Beauty, suffer me to pass." The choice of "suffer" is brilliantly placed to capsulize the poem's theme, which is a vivid description of the author's sense of vulnerability and the suffering that accompanies it. The speaker feels isolated, unprotected, intimidated. In this poem Millay has cleverly succeeded in defining woman's sense of her true condition by capitalizing on a common assumption about the exces-

sive emotional nature of women. At the same time, she has implied that woman's oppressor is a deceptively disguished external force.

> Millay's victims are all alike: innocent, helpless, unsuspecting, unarmed, in every way vulnerable. And they are all embodiments of Millay, the anguished, writhing, defenseless, and finally defeated victim.
>
> —*Jane Stanbrough*

Millay's insistent use of verbs of assault and bombardment is an index to her concept of reality. She may title a poem **"Spring,"** but she really sees the brains of men eaten by maggots; she may claim that she sorrows over the **"Death of Autumn,"** but she portrays a malign force controlling the world, for the autumn rushes are "flattened"; the creek is "stripped"; beauty, "stiffened"; the narrator, crushed. All around her in the systematic operation of the elements Millay perceives the processes of barbaric intrusion and fatal attack. Millay's use of nature, which seems to depict typical romantic disillusionment with the transcience of beauty, is in fact loaded with psychological and social implications. In **"Low-Tide,"** the tide's movements, like the conditions of her existence, are inexorable. There are beautiful surfaces, but treacherous realities: "No place to dream, but a place to die." Here, again, the figure of a child qualifies the state of vulnerability. The narrator lacks knowledge and experience. Trusting and unsuspicious, she is susceptible to betrayal. This childlike susceptibility is consciously rendered in **"Being Young and Green"**:

Being young and green, I said in love's despite:
Never in the world will I to living wight
Give over, air my mind
To anyone,
Hang out its ancient secrets in the strong wind
To be shredded and faded. . . .
Oh, me, invaded
And sacked by the wind and the sun!

Millay's use of "ancient secrets" is highly suggestive of the private self she wishes to protect, but neither consciousness nor will is a strong enough defense against attack and exposure. The words "invaded and sacked," like "waylaid" in **"Assault,"** indicate both the treacherousness of the assailant and the devastation of the attack. Fearing ridicule as well as exposure, the narrator tries to forearm herself, but she is helpless against the assaulting invisible powers, which she names here as wind and sun. The intrusion is forced and, in a social context, implies the act of rape. The intensity of Millay's sense of personal violation is felt in the imagery of **"Moriturus"**:

I shall bolt my door
    With a bolt and cable;
I shall block my door
    With a bureau and a table;

> With all my might
> 　My door shall be barred.
> I shall put up a fight,
> 　I shall take it hard.
>
> With his hand on my mouth
> 　He shall drag me forth,
> Shrieking to the south
> 　And clutching at the north.

The attacker in this poem is identified as death, but for Millay the horror of the experience is not in the idea of dying, but in the vision of the brutalizing attack by which she is forced to a complete surrender. Millay's narrator is vulnerable to attack and to exploitation because of some basic inferiority, and, as the rape image implies, it lies in her sexuality.

When Millay left Vassar in 1917 to do whatever she liked with the world, as President McCracken had assured her she could, she must soon have been stunned and distressed at the world's reception of her. She tells her family:

> Mrs. Thompson, a lovely woman who helped put me through college wants me to come & be her secretary for a while— . . . but I just don' wanna! . . . Of course, I feel like the underneath of a toad not to do what she wants me to do—but I can't make up my mind to address envelopes and make out card catalogues all fall . . . be called on to answer the telephone and make appointments & reject invites. I might have been governess to the Aults, except for a similar feeling about my independence.

Professionally, at graduation, she wanted more than anything to be an actress. She hoped also to continue to write plays and poetry. She believed in her own genius, and **"The Bean-Stalk,"** published in 1920 in *Poetry*, seems to reflect the *Figs'* public image of self-confidence:

> Ho, Giant! This is I!
> I have built me a bean-stalk into your sky!
> La,—but it's 'lovely, up so high!
>
> This is how I came,—I put
> Here my knee, there my foot,
> Up and up, from shoot to shoot—

The possibilities are exhilarating:

> What a wind! What a morning!—

But imagery in a middle section of the poem counteracts that sense of exhilaration and faith with a description of the real effects of the climb and the wind upon the climber. Even the first line's intention to emphasize the speaker's identity is undercut by the notion of "giant." The climber becomes suddenly insecure and uncertain in her position; she realizes that she is open to the wind, vulnerable to attack. She may even doubt her talent:

> . . . bean-stalks is my trade,
> I couldn't make a shelf,
> Don't know how they're made.

The wind, first viewed as an exhilarating force, is soon felt as an assailant which nearly dislodges her, an assailant which she can neither see nor combat:

> And the wind was like a whip
> Cracking past my icy ears,
> And my hair stood out behind,
> And my eyes were full of tears,
> Wide-open and cold,
> More tears than they could hold,
> The wind was blowing so,
> And my teeth were in a row,
> Dry and grinning,
> And I felt my foot slip
> And I scratched the wind and whined,
> And I clutched the stalk and jabbered,
> With my eyes shut blind,—
> What a wind! What a wind!

The blowing, whipping, cracking force of the wind strips her to a skeleton. Though the experience is terrifying and the climber confounded by the violence of the attack and the wind's capriciousness, the climber holds her position, struggling to resist the devastating power of her adversary. It is a tentative position, however, for the wind is a treacherous force, invisible, deceptive—an excellent symbol for the undefined powers which seem to impede Millay's efforts and cause her such suffering, powers she ultimately associates with social oppression and political tyranny.

Millay did not become an actress. She wrote few plays. She spent her life struggling for survival as a poet. This may be difficult for readers to understand who know that Millay was a Pulitzer Prize winner, a popular lecturer, a well-known and sought-after personality whose poems were published, reviewed, and read. But we are not dealing with external data merely; we are examining the poetry for insights into the truth of Millay's inner sense of herself and her achievements. The language pattern of vulnerability suggests strongly that Millay saw herself as a misfit and a failure and that she believed that some external forces in her life impeded her development and inflicted permanent injury. An untitled poem in her posthumous collection, *Mine the Harvest,* conveys an understanding of the power and insidiousness of the enemy and a resignation to her fate. Again the verb pattern defines the sense of vulnerability and impending disaster felt by the narrator; the image of the overpowering force of the wave summarizes a lifetime of futile effort to transcend and resist a society which she feels has conspired to destroy her.

> Establishment is shocked. Stir no adventure
> Upon this splitted granite.
>
> I will no longer connive
> At my own destruction:—I will not again climb,
> Breaking my finger nails, out of reach of the
> 　reaching wave,
> To save
> What I hope will still be me
> When I have slid on slime and clutched at slippery rock-weed, and had my face towed under
> In scrubbing pebbles, under the weight of the
> 　wave and its thunder.
> I decline to scratch at this cliff. *If* is not a word.
> I will connive no more
> With that which hopes and plans that I shall not
> 　survive:
> Let the tide keep its distance;
> Or advance, and be split for a moment by a thing
> 　very small but all resistance;

Then do its own chore.

Here Millay identifies the malignant force assailing her as the establishment, and the causes for her deep sense of victimization are less opaque. She feels outside the establishment, in opposition to social tradition and authority. She had sensed as a young woman that the world was "no fit place for a child to play." She had discovered that for women, as for children, the beautiful things were out of reach. For Millay, the realities of her life were found in the rigidly structured patterns of social behavior: you must not smoke at Vassar; you must not be an actress if you want Lady Caroline's financial assistance; you must consider being a social secretary if you really seek employment; you must marry; you must have children; you must not offend conventional morality if you want recognition; you must be male if you want serious criticism of your poetry.

Millay concedes in this untitled poem that society does not tolerate its individualists; especially does it not tolerate its independent women. To be a nonconformist is to be exposed and intimidated, like the woman in **"Assault"**; it is to feel like the lone traveler in **"How Naked, How Without a Wall,"** chilled by the night air, struck by sharp sleet, buffeted by wind, vulnerable to the wolf's attack. The social ramifications are explicit in this poem. For this traveler, since he chooses to venture "forth alone / When other men are snug within," the world is a terrifying place of loneliness, alienation, inevitable catastrophe. Most people, Millay feels, are vulnerable to social pressures; some will compromise. Some will suffer self-betrayal rather than isolation, as another of Millay's travelers does in **"On the Wide Heath,"** surrendering himself to a loud shrew, a poaching son, a daughter with a disdainful smile:

> Home to the worn reproach, the disagreeing,
> 　The shelter, the stale air; content to be
> Pecked at, confined, encroached upon,—it being
> 　Too lonely, to be free.

The imagery of confinement and attack offer an unbearable alternative to the individual who is forced to acknowledge, as this narrator does in that haunting statement of vulnerability: "it being / Too lonely, to be free."

For Millay, reality is oppression and victimization, and she feels attacked by forces that tyrannize, whether she names them sun and wind, as she does in her early poetry, or hangmen and huntsmen, as she does later. The shift in focus is significant, for it marks a deliberate attempt by Millay to explain her sense of victimization in a larger context of social injustices. She sees that justice is denied in Massachusetts and that the huntsman gains on the quarry.

Victimization by totalitarian powers is subtly suggested in **"The Buck in the Snow,"** where we see death, as in slow motion, "bringing to his knees, bringing to his antlers / The buck in the snow." Horrified, with the narrator, we witness the capitulation, the ultimate defeat of beauty and freedom and life. The buck, vulnerable, defenseless, goes down before an invisible, armed, socially sanctioned slaughterer. In **"The Rabbit,"** the speaker, suffering excruciatingly for her greater awareness of reality than the rabbit has, screams a warning to the rabbit.

> 'O indiscreet!
> And the hawk and all my friends are out to kill!
> Get under cover!' But the rabbit never stirred;
> 　she never will.
> And I shall see again and again the large eye
> 　blaze
> With death, and gently glaze;
> The leap into the air I shall see again and again,
> 　and the kicking feet;
> And the sudden quiet everlasting, and the blade
> 　of grass green in the strange mouth of the in-
> 　terrupted grazer.

The real significance of the whole range of verbs of assault is crystalized here in the verb "kill." Millay's victims are all alike: innocent, helpless, unsuspecting, unarmed, in every way vulnerable. And they are all embodiments of Millay, the anguished, writhing, defenseless, and finally defeated victim. Millay's profound suffering and her constant rendering of personal vulnerability become increasingly comprehensible in the context of her imagery of woman as victim.

Virginia Woolf understood the agonies and stresses of gifted women struggling against conditions of oppression. "For it needs little skill in psychology," she wrote in *A Room of One's Own,* "to be sure that a highly gifted girl who had tried to use her gift for poetry would have been so thwarted and hindered by other people, so tortured and pulled asunder by her own contrary instincts, that she must have lost her health to a certainty." Millay's personal feelings of oppression and the realities of social restrictions imposed on her own professional ambitions and desires are poignantly stated in Section V of **"Not So Far as the Forest,"** where the figure of the wounded and confined bird suggests an authentic self-projection:

> Poor passionate thing,
> Even with this clipped wing how well you
> 　flew!—though not so far as the forest.

The bird initially presents an appearance of freedom and capability, striking for the top branches in the distant forest. But the bird's weakness, his vulnerability to defeat, invisible at first in his attempted flight, is ultimately disclosed. It is his ambition, described in the poem as "the eye's bright trouble," that has made him vulnerable. He has been victimized by "the unequal wind," that seductive environmental force with its seeming beneficence but real destructive power; and he has been chained by a human hand:

> Rebellious bird, . . .
> Has no one told you?—Hopeless is your flight
> Toward the high branches. . . .
>
> Though Time refeather the wing,
> Ankle slip the ring,
> The once-confined thing
> Is never again free.

Millay responded passionately and deeply to visions of suffering victims, from the starving man in Capri to the war victims of Lidice. These visions correspond closely to her view of herself as victim, and her use of language patterns of vulnerability take on greater significance as she develops her understanding of herself as a woman in a world where women's values and feelings are either prede-termined or discarded. Millay's frequent use of the child-like narrator is increasingly understandable in the context of her vulnerability to the world's view and treatment of her as a woman. The nature of her existence, like the na-ture of her vulnerability, is thus qualified by the fact that she experiences the world as a woman.

"The Fitting" is well titled to suggest Millay's sense of woman's social conditioning to fit the narrow role pre-scribed for her. Through verbs that attempt to mask the degree of harm inflicted in the process, the narrator bitter-ly expresses her sense of personal violation. She submits to the fitting in a state of mannikin-like paralysis.

> The fitter said, *'Madame, vous avez maigri,'*
> And pinched together a handful of skirt at my
>   hip.
> *'Tant mieux,'* I said, and looked away slowly,
>   and took my under-lip
> Softly between my teeth.
>
>   Rip—rip!
> Out came the seam, and was pinned together in
>   another place.
> She knelt before me, a hardworking woman with
>   a familiar and unknown face,
> Dressed in linty black, very tight in the arm's-
>   eye and smelling of sweat.
> She rose, lifting my arm, and set her cold shears
>   against me,—snip-snip;
> Her knuckles gouged my breast. My drooped
>   eyes lifted to my guarded eyes in the glass, and
>   glanced away as from someone they had never
>   met.
>
> *'Ah, que madame a maigri!'* cried the *vendeuse,*
>   coming in with dresses over her arm.
> *'C'est la chaleur,'* I said, looking out into the
>   sunny tops of the horse-chestnuts—and in-
>   deed it was very warm.
>
> I stood for a long time so, looking out into the
>   afternoon, thinking of the evening and
>   you. . . .
> While they murmured busily in the distance,
>   turning me, touching my secret body, doing
>   what they were paid to do.

The narrator suffers both indignity and depersonalization in the fitting process. For one moment only—in a single line in the poem—does Millay allow the imaginative es-cape to seem a possibility. This emphasis is quite different from that of **"The Bean-Stalk,"** where fantasized possibili-ty is the poem's overriding effect.

Two of Millay's best and longest sonnet sequences, *Fatal Interview* and **"Sonnets from an Ungrafted Tree,"** drama-tize further through metaphors of love and marriage the fatality of woman's vulnerability to social conditioning. *Fatal Interview* is an extended metaphorical illustration of the consequences to women of their limited range of ex-perience and their susceptibility to emotional exploitation. "Women's ways are witless ways," Millay states in a *Figs* poem, and *Fatal Interview* dramatically narrates how woman is trained to react emotionally to her environment and how devastating the results of such training are. The title suggests the nature of the results. Sonnet xvii of the

sequence portrays woman's naiveté and lack of prepara-tion for such an "interview" as she encounters:

> Sweet love, sweet thorn, when lightly to my
>   heart
> I took your thrust, whereby I since am slain,
> And lie disheveled in the grass apart,
> A sodden thing bedrenched by tears and rain,
>   . . . . .
> Had I bethought me then, sweet love, sweet
>   thorn,
> How sharp an anguish even at the best,
> When all's requited and the future sworn,
> The happy hour can leave within the breast,
> I had not so come running at the call
> Of one who loves me little, if at all.

An innocent believer in the value of her feelings, the woman opens herself to her lover's thrust. The sexual im-plications of "thrust" give emphasis to the irony of the woman's willing surrender to rape and murder. Through the image of happy submission to her slayer, Millay sharp-ly renders the utter pathos of woman's susceptibility. Too late she discovers the insignificance of her self, her life. The sequence dramatizes the spiritual disintegration that must occur through the social conditioning that explains woman's nature as essentially emotional and her greatest need as love. The entire sequence is relentless in its presen-tation of love's ravaging and immobilizing effects upon women whose lives are so isolated and confined. Sonnet lxxi epitomizes the victim's scarred state:

> This beast that rends me in the sight of all,
>   . . . . .
> Will glut, will sicken, will be gone by spring.
>   . . . . .
> I shall forget before the flickers mate
> Your look that is today my east and west.
> Unscathed, however, from a claw so deep
> Though I should love again I shall not go. . . .

Throughout the sonnets, the narrator exposes her emo-tional vulnerability to assault, humiliation, abuse, aban-donment, annihilation.

> How drowned in love and weedily washed
>   ashore,
> There to be fretted by the drag and shove
> At the tide's edge, I lie— . . .
>   . . . . .
> Small chance, however, in a storm so black,
> A man will leave his friendly fire and snug
> For a drowned woman's sake, and bring her
>   back
> To drip and scatter shells upon the rug. . . .

Brutalization and victimization characterize woman's ex-istence.

In "Sonnets from an Ungrafted Tree" the New England woman narrator poignantly and unforgettably reveals how she has been trapped by her illusions of romance and by her dreams of beauty into a relationship which stran-gles her emotionally and spiritually. One of Millay's most brilliant images of woman's spiritual suffocation is found in Sonnet xi of this sequence:

> It came into her mind, seeing how the snow
> Was gone, and the brown grass exposed again,

And clothes-pins, and an apron—long ago,
In some white storm that sifted through the pane
And sent her forth reluctantly at last
To gather in, before the line gave way,
Garments, board-stiff, that galloped on the blast
Clashing like angel armies in a fray,
An apron long ago in such a night
Blown down and buried in the deepening drift,
To lie till April thawed it back to sight,
Forgotten, quaint and novel as a gift—
It struck her, as she pulled and pried and tore,
That here was spring, and the whole year to be
    lived through once more.

Representing woman's condition, the apron, confined to the clothesline, is contrasted to the figure of clashing armies, suggestive of her imagined dreams of adventure and romance—dreams fulfilled only in a masculine world. The apron, obviously an article of domestic servitude, is a symbol for the woman's relinquished self, "Board-stiff," "blown down and buried" years before. Even then, this woman had half perceived the futility of her dreams and had gone out reluctantly to pull and pry and tear at the apron to try to resurrect it. Ultimately, the woman surrenders

                    . . . her mind's vision plain

    The magic World, where cities stood on end . . .
    Remote from where she lay—and yet—between,
    Save for something asleep beside her, only the
        window screen.

The restrictive realities of her life—something asleep beside her and the window screen—are stark contrasts to the waning dreams of her imagined self.

It is understandable why Millay's two extended narratives of woman's psychological disintegration are presented in sonnet sequences. Millay persistently resorts to the constraints of traditional verse forms. Given her time and place in the history of American poetry and given the external evidence of her unconventional childhood and youthful radicalism, one would expect to find her in the company of the avant-garde of American poetry. But Millay is no true Imagist. She eschews the freedoms of form which Ezra Pound had defined as essential to the new poetry. The sonnet, her best form, is a fit vehicle to convey her deepest feelings of woman's victimization. Through it, Millay imaginatively reenacts her constant struggle against boundaries. The wish for freedom is always qualified by the sense of restriction; couplets and quatrains suit her sensibility.

In Millay's poetry, women, in their quiet lives of fatal desires and futile gestures, are tragic and heroic. She identifies herself with suffering women, women whose dreams are denied, whose bodies are assaulted, whose minds and spirits are extinguished. She states her consciousness of the universality of women's vulnerability and anguish in **"An Ancient Gesture,"** contrasting Penelope's tears with those of Ulysses:

    I thought, as I wiped my eyes on the corner of
        my apron:
    Penelope did this too.

And more than once: you can't keep weaving all
    day
And undoing it all through the night;
Your arms get tired, and the back of your neck
    gets tight;
And along towards morning, when you think it
    will never be light,
And your husband has been gone, and you don't
    know where, for years,
Suddenly you burst into tears;
There is simply nothing else to do.

And I thought, as I wiped my eyes on the corner
    of my apron:
This is an ancient gesture, authentic, antique,
In the very best tradition, classic, Greek;
Ulysses did this too.
But only as a gesture,—a gesture which implied
To the assembled throng that he was much too
    moved to speak.
He learned it from Penelope . . .
Penelope, who really cried.

From the earliest volume, **Renascence,** where even her youthful awakening is accompanied by its grief-laden songs of shattering, through her posthumous harvest of mature experience, Millay records, unrelentingly, her life of pain and frustration. If she too loudly insisted on the public self's claims for freedom to love and think and feel and work as she pleased, she nevertheless quietly throughout her work continued to send out her linguistic distress signals. It is her profound insight into her self's inevitable capitulation that makes Millay ultimately so vulnerable and her poetry so meaningful. (pp. 183-99)

Jane Stanbrough, "Edna St. Vincent Millay and the Language of Vulnerability," in Shakespeare's Sisters: Feminist Essays on Women Poets, *edited by Sandra M. Gilbert and Susan Gubar, Indiana University Press, 1979, pp. 183-99.*

Debra Fried   (essay date 1988)

[*In the following essay, Fried discusses Millay's use of traditional sonnet form in relation to the influence of modernism on her poetry, her repudiation of social conventions, and her status as a woman poet.*]

In a critical climate in which we are rediscovering the powerful experiments of American women poets in the modernist era, the tidy verses of Edna St. Vincent Millay have remained something of an embarrassment. Tough-minded as they can be about sex, betrayal, and the price of being a woman who can write candidly about such matters, Millay's poems, particularly her sonnets, can often seem like retrograde schoolgirl exercises amidst the vanguard verbal dazzle of H. D., Mina Loy, Gertrude Stein, and Marianne Moore. In revising the history of modernism to make more central the achievements of these innovative poets, it has been convenient to dismiss Millay's work as copybook bohemianism. Millay may rightly be judged as a minor star in this constellation, but this is not, I think, why there have been so few serious investigations of Millay of late. Our silence attests rather to a failure to ask the right questions about how traditional poetic forms such as the sonnet may serve the needs of women poets. Why does a woman poet in this century elect to write sonnets? What sort of gender associations can a poetic form such as the sonnet accumulate, and how may such associations, and consequent exclusions, make that genre an especially lively arena for the revisionary acts of women's poetry? What model of the relation between generic restraints and expressive freedom is suggested by the sonnet? How does genre shape the meanings of allusion within a sonnet, particularly allusions to other sonnets? And, most centrally for thinking about Millay, how has the sonnet historically implied connections between formal (generic, metrical, rhetorical) constraints and sexual ones?

Instead of asking such questions, we have tended to assume that we know just how and why a poet like Millay must use circumscribed, traditional poetic forms: to rein in her strong, unruly feelings. This idea is a commonplace in earlier writing on the poet, as in Jean Gould's observation in her popular biography [*The Poet and Her Book*] that Millay "found security in classical form: the sonnet was the golden scepter with which she ruled her poetic passions." We can find similar claims in two recent essays on Millay's poetry. Jane Stanbrough caps a persuasive analysis of the deep sense of submission and constriction that lies behind Millay's seemingly defiant, unharnessed poetry [in her "Edna St. Vincent Millay and the Language of Vulnerability" in *Shakespeare's Sisters: Feminist Essays on Women Poets,* edited by Sandra Gilbert and Susan Gubar] with the observation that Millay's sonnets and sonnet sequences illustrate her tendency to "resort to the constraints of traditional verse form":

> The sonnet, her best form, is a fit vehicle to convey her deepest feelings of woman's victimization. Through it, Millay imaginatively reenacts her constant struggle against boundaries. The wish for freedom is always qualified by the sense of restriction; couplets and quatrains suit her sensibility.

This claim, sensible as it sounds, calls for considerable scrutiny. What poetic "sensibility," we may ask, is not in some degree suited to the strictures of poetic form? (Isn't that what it would mean to have a poetic sensibility?) The identification of sonnets with a creative temperament that both needs boundaries and needs to strain against them is by no means applicable exclusively to Millay or to women poets. Too many assumptions go untested in Stanbrough's implication that in Millay's dependence on poetic constraints to embody the drama of vulnerability and resistance we witness a particularly female response to lyric form. A full declaration of those assumptions would require an inquiry into the ways a potentially stifling poetic form may amplify—give pitch, density, and strength to—a poet's voice. If we are to isolate the particular resources, if any, with which a woman poet may rebel against formal constraints, we must begin with an examination of the tropes for the sonnet that are part of the history of that genre. Only then can we determine the particular uses a woman poet can make of the liberating fetters of the sonnet form. The power of Millay's sonnets, and their usefulness for the study of the relations between gender and genre in twentieth-century poetry, derives from

the readiness with which, while working within formal boundaries, they challenge the figurations for which the sonnet has been traditionally a receptive home. Through her revisions of those tropes and related devices—particularly as found in sonnets of Wordsworth and Keats—Millay's allusive sonnets, I will contend, reclaim that genre as her plot of ground, not chiefly by planting it with "woman's" themes or using it as mouthpiece for the woman's voice (though she does both these things), but by rethinking the form's historical capacity for silencing her voice.

It is this kind of reflectiveness about what it means to work within traditional forms that another recent essay would seem to deny to Millay. In a study of the Elizabethan sonnets of Millay and Elinor Wylie,[in *Poetic Traditions of the English Renaissance* edited by Maynard Mack and George de Forest Lord], Judith Farr argues that Millay's particular temperaments, attitudes, and skills sometimes led her to

> marshall against the lively but serene mathematics of contained forms like the sonnet, quatrain, or couplet a battery of disheveled impulses expressed in terms calculated to shock. . . . Millay's best work exhibits a tutored sensibility that enabled her to compose effectively within literary traditions she respected. The Petrarchan conventions to which she submitted in *Fatal Interview* served her well, moreover, disciplining her imagination yet encouraging the emotional scope her poetry instinctively sought.

One may readily take Farr's point that all of Millay's efforts in the Elizabethan mode are not equally successful. More questionable is the assumption here that the poet Millay is a creature of raw emotion or instinct who, when she is good, submits to a form that will tame that rawness, and when she is bad, invades the decorous parlors of poetic form like a spoiled child with her mad manners. The language of power in this passage from Farr's essay is also tellingly confused: the process whereby conventions to which the poet "submits" may then in turn submit to or "serve" her is a complicated one that needs to be explained and argued in specific instances. To assume, as Farr would appear to do, that in choosing "contained forms" Millay either bombards them with mischievous, whimsical "impulses" (are these the same as the "emotional scope her poetry instinctively sought"?) or submissively "composes" within them lest impulse get the better of her, is to imply that Millay worked unwittingly at the mercy of these opposed moods. But the question of whether writing in an established lyric genre is an act of taking command or of being commanded is one upon which Millay's sonnets reflect.

It is, moreover, a reflection to which Millay found the sonnet is supremely suited, in part because it is a subject explored in the English Romantic sonnets Millay knew well. One of the dubious things about Stanbrough's and Farr's accounts of why Millay found the sonnet suited to her poetic needs is that they so strikingly resemble Wordsworth's claim that he turned to the sonnet to find relief from "too much liberty." The sonnet is such a difficult form that from its inception in English it took as one of its topics the paradoxical release and scope to be derived from its intricate formal requirements. (pp. 1-4)

Edna St. Vincent Millay found herself in what was perhaps a unique position in the history of women writing poetry; she was called upon to uphold the tradition of binding lyric forms against the onslaught of what her supporters saw as a dangerously shapeless modernism. In 1917 the prodigious schoolgirl who wrote **"Renascence"** represented "an alternative to the 'new' poetry . . . whose work could serve as a rallying point for the rejection of free verse, imagism, and Prufrockian ennui" [according to Elizabeth P. Perlmutter in "A Doll's Heart: The Girl in the Poetry of Edna St. Vincent Millay and Louise Brogan," *Twentieth Century Literature,* Vol. 23, 1977]. At the same time Millay was identified with the bohemian literary life of Greenwich Village, seen as a kind of poetic flapper who, as Elizabeth Atkins put it in 1936, "represents our time to itself." It was, in short, an interesting time for a woman to be writing sonnets. The issues of poetic and sexual freedom were being explicitly linked; why should free-spirited Millay stick to the sonnet when other women poets were experimenting with free verse? It would be easy to suspect the poet of merely posturing at promiscuity, aping a man's freedom in order to earn the respite of poetic formalism on a man's ground. But for her the sonnet's formal patterns and its brevity both come to figure the price of freedom rather than a welcome retreat from it.

The power of Millay's sonnets, and their usefulness for the study of the relations between gender and genre in twentieth-century poetry, derives from the readiness with which, while working within formal boundaries, they challenge the figurations for which the sonnet has been traditionally a receptive home.

—*Debra Fried*

To the degree that Millay identifies the working of the sonnet with the poetics of the bohemian life, she rejects the Wordsworthian figuration of the sonnet as controlled respite from freedom. The self-fulfilling prophecies of the sonnet's tight formalities—the set of interlocking rules and obligations any sonnet sets itself early on and its "metrical contract," in Hollander's terms, not to waver from it—Millay found useful as a trope for a poetics of burning one's candle at both ends, of using one's life up completely. The sonnet can embody metrically, sonorously, and syntactically a kind of perfectly efficient hedonism, culminating in a closure with no residue. The sestet of **"Thou famished grave, I will not fill thee yet"** from *Huntsman, What Quarry?* defiantly tells Death how lives and poems are to be ended:

> I cannot starve thee out: I am thy prey
> And thou shalt have me; but I dare defend
> That I can stave thee off; and I dare say,

What with the life I lead, the force I spend,
I'll be but bones and jewels on that day,
And leave thee hungry even in the end.

The poet "staves off" death by the achieved design of her stanzas. Here the sonnet's closure—completing its metrical and rhyming requirements, leaving nothing formally unsatisfied, filling its staves—mimes the way the poet vows to use up her force completely and leave nothing behind. Millay allows her life to end with no residue of unlived days, as the completed sonnet, ending "in the end," permits no residue of unpaired rhymes, unbalanced argument, or dangling syntax. Not a matter of wanton wastefulness but of almost methodical, tasking exhaustiveness, the bohemian project is thus aptly figured in the seemingly opposite, straitlacing, vow-keeping, binding contract any sonnet must be. Recalling Farr's charge that Millay "marshall[s] against the lively but serene mathematics of contained forms like the sonnet, quatrain, or couplet a battery of dissheveled impulses," we might rather say that the self-fulfilling equations of poetic forms provide the formula whereby Millay makes sure that those impulses play themselves out to the full.

All this insistence on the scrupulous hard work of being liberated suggests the occupational hazards this job has for women. For them, the weight of too much liberty too often can be translated into a demanding lover's "weight upon my breast" ("I, being born a woman and distressed" from *The Harp-Weaver*). Free love itself can be a prison. Dazzled by the sight of her lover, the speaker of "When I too long have looked upon your face" (*Second April*) compares her condition, when she "turn[s] away reluctant" from his "light," to a very scanty plot of ground indeed:

> Then is my daily life a narrow room
> In which a little while, uncertainly,
> Surrounded by impenetrable gloom,
> Among familiar things grown strange to me
> Making my way, I pause, and feel, and hark,
> Till I become accustomed to the dark.

The new woman may fret a great deal in her freedom's "narrow room," it seems; and we may take Millay's soft but audible allusion to the opening line of **"Nuns Fret Not"** as a reflection on the different kinds of narrowness to which their own freedom may condemn men and women. The enclosing solace of the Wordsworthian sonnet becomes here an almost tomblike, if chosen, claustrophobia, a prison into which the woman dooms herself when she turns away, a "silly, dazzled thing deprived of sight," from the overpowering brilliance of her lover's face.

In Millay's posthumous sonnet on the sonnet [included in *Mine the Harvest*], the form appears not as a small plot of ground or a chosen cloister, but as an erotic prison:

> I will put Chaos into fourteen lines
> And keep him there; and let him thence escape
> If he be lucky; let him twist, and ape
> Flood, fire, and demon—his adroit designs
> Will strain to nothing in the strict confines
> Of this sweet Order, where, in pious rape,
> I hold his essence and amorphous shape,

Till he with Order mingles and combines.
Past are the hours, the years, of our duress,
His arrogance, our awful servitude:
I have him. He is nothing more or less
Than something simple not yet understood;
I shall not even force him to confess;
Or answer. I will only make him good.

When Millay claims that her sonnets "put Chaos into fourteen lines," she does more than simply repeat the inherited fiction of the sonnet as brief solace or momentary stay against profusion. The stakes seem higher than in Wordsworth's poem, the tasks put upon poetic form more demanding; this sonnet figures poetic form as a cage for a wild creature. Millay may have in mind Donne's dictum that "Grief brought to numbers cannot be so fierce, / For he tames it, that fetters it in verse" (**"The Triple Fool"**). But the fourteen lines of this sonnet's cage are not rigid iron bars or fetters but tethers whose strength derives from their flexibility. In refusing to make Chaos "confess," Millay refuses to use the machinery of rhyme and meter to force her stubborn, resistant subject into saying something against his will, perhaps with a glance at Ben Jonson's "A Fit of Rhyme against Rhyme," where rhyme is figured as a torture device to extort false words from the poem: "Rime the rack of finest wits / That expresseth but by fits / True conceit." She will not use the sonnet form to urge a confession or reply, to reveal the "something simple" that his complicated "designs" conceal. The simple goodness—virtuosity, well-craftedness—of the poem is sufficient, will "answer" or be adequate to the job of capturing Chaos. That alone will yield the solution, that is the way to make the prisoner speak up—to reform him, not punish him or make him squeal. This is a mildly coercive inquisition, a "pious rape." The curt, determined vows that close the sonnet leave us with a sense that this poetic mastery over an old rival takes its sweetest revenge from its substitution of an inescapable gentleness for the rival's former cruelty and "arrogance."

This late poem gathers up a recurring image in Millay's sonnets of eros as prison. In the fifth poem of the sequence *Fatal Interview,* the speaker counts herself the most abject of prisoners of love since "my chains throughout their iron length / Make such a golden clank upon my ear," and she would not escape even if she had the strength to do so. By sonnet XVIII in the sequence, the speaker questions her voluntary incarceration more closely: "Shall I be prisoner till my pulses stop / To hateful Love and drag his noisy chain?" Chaos is like a fugitive, faithless lover captured at last, his amorphousness like that of the unapproachable man of whom the woman says "I chase your colored phantom on the air. . . . Once more I clasp,—and there is nothing there" ("Once more into my arid days like dew" from *Second April*). **"I Will Put Chaos into Fourteen Lines"** explicitly equates sexual and poetic dominance in its insistence on the control and compression required of the woman poet who seizes upon traditional forms in order to free herself from the forces that would deny her the power to order poetic forms—forces that include traditional male accounts of the need for poetic order.

Like [Wordsworth's] "Nuns Fret Not," Millay's **"I Will Put Chaos"** ends in such a way as to suggest that the con-

trolling process it describes has been enacted in the sonnet as we read it. Wordsworth's closing hope that in the sonnet the liberty-weary "Should find brief solace there, as I have found" fulfills the promise it expresses, as it refers to the solace afforded by this very sonnet as well as by the poet's habitual writing of them. In the same way, Millay's final promise—"I will only make him good"—points to her goal in all her sonnets as well as to the technical excellence of this one she has just finished. A pun gives this closure a double force. Millay makes the sonnet aesthetically good by tempering the behavior of the unruly subject in its artful cage, making him "good" in the sense of training him to be well-mannered, obedient, and orderly. In Millay's figure, the woman poet binds "Chaos"—a kind of male anti-muse, perhaps the divisive forces of sexuality, or whatever the force may be that tears poems apart rather than inspires them—with the "strict confines" of her ordering art [according to Norman A. Britten in his *Edna St. Vincent Millay*]. The entire sonnet is almost an allegory of Judith Farr's somewhat paradoxical formula that the "conventions to which [Millay] submitted . . . served her well."

"I Will Put Chaos into Fourteen Lines" presents the struggle of the syntactic unit to find its completion, and to fit into the metrical and rhyming requirements of the sonnet (here, particularly of the octet), as an erotic tussling. The octet of **"I Will Put Chaos"** entertains the fiction that the single long sentence that comprises it is allowed free rein to flow from line to line, but is gently curbed (by the poet or by Order itself) at each line ending by the bars of rhyme and meter. The sestet, written in short sentences, largely end-stopped, looks back with precarious assurance on the struggles of the octet. The sonnet's trope for its own procedures is a peculiar one: the poet who dooms her subject into the prison of form acts almost like a pander supervising the mating of Chaos and Order. The twisting of the sentence from line to line illustrates Chaos' snaky attempts to wriggle out of the poem's snare, but the "adroit designs" the poem attributes to Chaos are, of course, the poet's designs by whose grace the caged creature may be as lively and various and protean as he wants. Only the sonnet's strict order of meter, rhyme, and syntax allows us to register the twists taken by the long sentence (lines 3-8) describing Chaos' ineffectual attempts to escape. Millay here makes enjambment positively sexy.

Perhaps this is merely to say that Millay makes good use of the resources of the sonnet, combining Miltonic or Romantic use of heavy enjambment with a strict Petrarchan division between octet and sestet. But, as we shall see, in the context of Millay's allusive polemic against the tradition of sexual myths for the sonnet, it is to say rather more. Again the figurative status of poetic closure is at issue. For Wordsworth, when in a sonnet "the sense does not close with the rhyme," the result desired is a "pervading sense of Unity." The way in which that unity is achieved is made invisible in favor of the satisfying fullness of the closure. In Milton's sonnets Wordsworth admires not the unfolding spell of the "sense variously drawn out" in run-on lines, but the achieved plenitude of the completed experience. Once the "brief solace" is found, the poem is over, and the poet can go on to other things, to wander and soar at liberty. For Millay, such run-over lines in the orderly sonnet figure rather the difficult wrestling of the poet to achieve unity, a wrestling that is inseparable from a rallying of opposed sexual forces. Wordsworth's sonnet ends with a sigh of satisfaction, the remedy having done the trick ("as I have found"), Millay's with the challenge still ahead, a vow the poet makes to herself ("I will only make him good"). She focuses on the syntactic drama itself, rather than the feeling of satisfaction after the curtain is rung down. The tug of line against syntax figures the poet's constant struggle with "Chaos," not the assurance of Miltonic authority, or the comforting sense of respite and accomplishment Wordsworth claims to derive from the sweet order of sonnet constraints. Intricate play with enjambment is a way Millay demonstrates and monitors that she is in charge of the words, not in some "awful servitude" to them. It is a game she knows she is playing, and knows which rules she has invented and which she has inherited. The critical view of Millay that judges her as in need of poetic form to control her emotional impulses merely repeats Millay's own strategic presentation of herself as such, a self-presentation that itself is in need of interpretation and cannot be taken as a straightforward outline of her poetics.

A sonnet from *Second April,* Millay's third volume (1921) brings together the two main figurations for the sonnet which we have been examining. Here a small plot of ground becomes an imprisoning site of too much liberty:

> Not with libations, but with shouts and laughter
> We drenched the altars of love's sacred grove,
> Shaking to earth green fruits, impatient after
> The launching of the colored moths of Love.
> Love's proper myrtle and his mother's zone
> We bound about our irreligious brows,
> And fettered him with garlands of our own,
> And spread a banquet in love's frugal house.
> Not yet the god has spoken; but I fear
> Though we should break our bodies in his flame,
> And pour our blood upon his altar, here
> Henceforward is a grove without a name,
> A pasture to the shaggy goats of Pan,
> Whence flee forever a woman and a man.

Again we see the high price exacted by the bohemian life: the sonnet, and presumably the affair it commemorates, ends with the sickening sense of loss and satiety that follows from banqueting on unripe fruits. No sacrifice to love can make the grove suitable for proper worship again; such overeager illicit lovers can never thereafter become spouses, dutifully bound in marriage. This may be an illicit and transient affair, but as we expect from Shakespearean sonnets, the transient is transformed into something permanent, and the agent of this permanence is the poem itself; Millay's final vision of the goatish couple fleeing "forever" borrows from this expectation while giving it a bohemian twist. But instead of two lovers frozen in the instant before a kiss, as on Keats's urn, this overheated pair is caught in a gesture of self-exile from a hot pastoral they have sullied with their excesses.

As a character in Millay's all-male verse drama *Conversa-*

tion at Midnight (1937) argues, with a glance sidelong at Shakespeare's Sonnet 94,

> it seems
> Even to my nostrils that the lilies are beginning
> to smell;
> And that the time has come to deck our amorous
> themes
> With the honester stenches.

With its bracing candor about modern love, **"Not with Libations"** lets fresh air into the sonnet, but that air is already tainted with the stench of overindulgence. We might find it a sufficiently revisionary move on Millay's part simply to give the female half of the couple room to admit that she too knows desire and has a sexual will (Millay gives us simply "a woman and a man," no longer poet and disdainful mistress, burning lover and dark lady), and Millay's sonnets often testify that women, too, know the lust that the Renaissance sonnet traditionally allowed only men to feel. But it would be too simple to say that through its act of bestowing on the woman desires as impatient as the man's the poem bestows on the woman poet the capacity to write sonnets as weighted as a man's. The woman's desire cannot resonate in the room of the sonnet with the same force as his desire; it is a room that has been designed to amplify his tones and to silence hers. To bring these issues to the fore, Millay treats the sonnet as an echo chamber, where we can listen to the voices this improperly proper sonnet has appropriated and revised.

"Not with Libations, but with Shouts and Laughter" is burdened with the weight of too much literature. The poem addresses "Nuns Fret Not at Their Convent's Narrow Room" in its marking for erotic indulgence the scanty plot of ground Wordsworth identifies with serene retreat. The narrow room of conventional passion is too restrictive for these lovers, who turn their erotic bonds into a prison in which they doom themselves. Despite the Wordsworthian figures and the Shakespearean design, however, this poem's grove is drenched with Keats, from incidental glances at the hymn to Pan in *Endymion,* the "Ode to Psyche," and the sonnet "On Solitude," to more importantly polemical allusions to Keats's sonnet on the sonnet.

Typically, the Keatsian echoes resound in a coarser tone in Millay's **"Not with Libations."** The lovers crowning themselves with "love's proper myrtle" have plucked some foliage from the "many that are come to pay their vows / With leaves about their brows" (*Endymion*) in the hymn to Pan, but Millay's lovers consign their grove to "the shaggy goats of Pan," not to an uplifted, Keatsian deity who is "the leaven / That spreading in this dull and clotted earth, / Gives it a touch ethereal." The music that drifts over from the "Ode to Psyche" becomes likewise sensualized. The closing prophecy in **"Not with Libations"** that "Henceforward is a grove without a name" alludes audibly enough to the vow in the ode to dress Psyche's sanctuary "With buds, and bells, and stars without a name" ("Ode to Psyche"). Like the speaker of the ode, Millay's lovers consecrate themselves as their own priests to a form of love which does not have its proper cult in poetry, and like him they adapt the available religious emblems to serve their new god and build him an altar that is erected more in the mind than in any special spot. Keats's ode closes with an invitation to "let the warm Love in," while Millay's sonnet ends with the exile of the warm lovers who, once they have celebrated their inventive rites, must abandon the spot. **"Not with Libations"** closes on a note from Keats's early sonnet beginning "O Solitude! if I must with thee dwell." Locating solitude on a natural prospect or "'mongst boughs pavilioned," the sonnet ends with the anticipation, addressing Solitude, that "it sure must be / Almost the highest bliss of humankind, / When to thy haunts two kindred spirits flee." Whereas Keats's kindred spirits are left fleeing into the grove of solitude, to engage in "sweet converse of an innocent mind," Millay's lovers "flee forever" from the carnal pasture they have desanctified. Keats's gentle sensualism of anticipation becomes in Millay the disheartening aftermath of consummation.

The most resounding echo in Millay's **"Not with Libations"** is to Keats's sonnet on the sonnet, "If by Dull Rhymes Our English Must Be Chained." As in "Nuns Fret Not," in Keats's self-reflexive sonnet the poet effects the cure his poem complains of:

> If by dull rhymes our English must be chained,
> And, like Andromeda, the Sonnet sweet
> Fettered, in spite of pained loveliness,
> Let us find out, if we must be constrained,
> Sandals more interwoven and complete
> To fit the naked foot of Poesy:
> Let us inspect the lyre, and weigh the stress
> Of every chord, and see what may be gained
> By ear industrious and attention meet;
> Misers of sound and syllable, no less
> Than Midas of his coinage, let us be
> Jealous of dead leaves in the bay wreath crown;
> So, if we may not let the Muse be free,
> She will be bound with garlands of her own.

Like the "Ode to Psyche" and **"Not with Libations,"** this sonnet adapts and loosens the instruments of tribute to a deity who is ultimately the muse. In contrast to the trope of the sonnet as a binding place—a scanty plot, writer's colony for one—the sonnet here is explicitly figured as a bound woman, the muse as Andromeda, with the poet as Perseus to the rescue. But rather than free the damsel in distress, this hero simply makes her chains less chafing. It is the fettering, the rules and rhymes and restrictions, that make the sonnet "sweet," for she is sweetest not when she is free but when she is "sweet / Fettered." The intricacies of the sonnet form guarantee that in some measure the poet "must be constrained" in writing it; the poet's task is to make that multiple manacling—of poet to set pattern, of each line handcuffed to its rhyming partner—less constricting, less strictly ornamental and thereby more graceful. The "dull rhymes" of the English sonnet as Keats inherited it are "more interwoven" in this poem's muted, complex rhyme scheme, a double liberation in that it led Keats to develop the pattern of his ode stanzas.

Poetic form itself is the sea-monster that has chained Andromeda to the rock of dull rhyme and stony, unyielding traditions. The poet does not release her, but reweaves her chains, turning them into honoring garlands. The poetic tradition he works in itself has tightened the strands from

which Keats is to release her by binding her with new ones, with the assurance that then "She will be bound with garlands of her own." The trick is to make Andromeda her own sea-monster, to craft a chain for her so cleverly natural that she can believe she has woven it herself as an adornment. In this sonnet Keats has woven a very powerful myth of poetic convention as a prison into which poetry willingly dooms itself, and part of its power derives from the identification of a constricting form with a willingly bound woman.

What are we to make of the echoes from Keats's sonnet of gentle shackling that resound in Millay's sonnet of unbridled eros? What in particular are echoes from a man's sonnet about the sonnet as bound woman doing in a woman's sonnet about the (perhaps enslaving) price of throwing off the conventional shackles of love between men and women? Keats promises Andromeda that she will be "bound with garlands of her own," while Millay's improper modern lovers, celebrating Love in their own reckless way, "fettered him with garlands of our own." They impose their own shackles on Love, whereas Keats works to impose no shackles on the sonnet from outside poetry herself. Millay's lovers reject the miserly care marking Keats's project for the sonnet. In their profligacy they "spread a banquet in [Love's] frugal house"; they reinterpret the traditional cestus and myrtle of restrained love as celebratory garlands, binding their brows as a mark of erotic victory with the cinctures designed to bind the waist as a mark of purity in love.

In both sonnets, then, the iconography of celebratory, erotic, and poetic garlanding is playfully unraveled and rewoven into a new pattern. Millay's "grove without a name" should perhaps be named the grove of the Romantic poetics of the sonnet, a lightly constraining enclosure which Millay turns into a bower of irreverent excess. Just as traditionally the woman poet is denied the kind of freedom that may drive the male poet into the retreat of the sonnet's boundaries, so neither can she be given the responsibility of a poetic Perseus to free the muse from her formal strictures, since she is supposed herself to be the muse. Even if a poet wishes to bind her with "garlands of her own" they will be the garlands he has experimentally determined are proper to her, garlands of his own after all. Millay does not take up Keats's call to reshuffle the sonnet's pattern of rhyming, knowing that no rearrangement can make the form more "natural." Poetic forms and genres are not natural but ideological. Andromeda's unfelt, self-willed fetters can figure a perfect marriage (of man and woman, form and subject) or a perfectly crippling ideology. Looking at Keats through the lens of Millay, we can begin to see Andromeda as torn between having to stand for a poetic form herself or for a free spirit that the form holds chained. For a woman writing poetry in the years between the wars, the brittleness of oaths and the shaky fiction of new sexual freedom for women made the sonnet an apt form in which to scrutinize the inherited stances of men toward women and poets toward their muses. By identifying the sonnet's scanty plot of ground with an erotic grove of excess, turning the chastity belt of poetic form into a token of sexual indulgence, Millay invades the sanctuary of male poetic control with her unsettling formalism in the service of freedom, a freedom that can, as the lovers learn in **"Not with Libations,"** turn into another kind of entrapment.

In **"Not with Libations,"** as in **"I Will Put Chaos into Fourteen Lines,"** Millay addresses the Romantic myths of the sonnet as liberating prison and pleasing fetters, the figurations governing Wordsworth's "Nuns Fret Not" and Keats's "If by Dull Rhymes." Her sonnets reshape those myths with the revisionary force of a woman poet who, however rearguard in the phalanx of modernism, recognizes that she has inherited a genre laden with figurations exclusive to a male poetic authority, and who knows that her adaptations of that genre must engage those very myths and figurations that would bar her from the ranks of legitimate practitioners of the sonnet. While more work on Millay along these lines is not likely to result in the elevation of her to the status of a major twentieth-century poet, it should lead to a more searching understanding of why we judge her to be minor, and to our estimate in general of poets in the modernist period who continued to write in traditional forms. Current feminist work on Millay suggests that in her use of poetic forms "the wish for freedom is always qualified by the sense of restriction": such an estimate, I believe, even when intended as evidence of Millay's virtuosity, echoes older dismissals of Millay on the grounds that she moodily concedes to poetic forms or, crippled by emotional turmoil, desperately leans on them, because it tends to see the poet as an unwitting victim of these two desires rather than as working consciously in light of the fact that the tradition itself is constantly troping on just this very debate. I have only suggested how a few of Millay's most effective sonnets engage in and reflect upon the struggle between poet and form as to which shall be master. Such engagement is a sign not only that Millay has mastered these inherited forms, but also that she has taken into account the full implications for the woman poet of the figure of poetic "mastery." (pp. 8-18)

> *Debra Fried, "Andromeda Unbound: Gender and Genre in Millay's Sonnets," in* Twentieth Century Literature, *Vol. 32, No. 1, Spring, 1986, pp. 1-22.*

FURTHER READING

Bibliography

Nierman, Judith. *Edna St. Vincent Millay: A Reference Guide.* Boston: G. K. Hall & Co., 1977, 191 p.
   Annotated primary and secondary bibliography.

Yost, Karl. *A Bibliography of the Works of Edna St. Vincent Millay.* New York: Harper & Brothers Publishers, 1937, 248 p.
   Provides publishing history of Millay's works through 1937. Contains an introductory essay by Harold Lewis

Cook in which he traces the progression of Millay's poetry as an expression of her personal development.

Biography

Brenner, Rica. "Edna St. Vincent Millay." In her *Ten Modern Poets,* pp. 61-82. New York: Harcourt, Brace & Co., 1930.
   Critical biography.

Brittin, Norman A. *Edna St. Vincent Millay.* Boston: Twayne, 1982, 167 p.
   Critical biography focusing on Millay's role as a feminist and considering her works in the context of the poetic movement "High Modernism."

Cheney, Anne. *Millay in Greenwich Village.* University: University of Alabama Press, 1975, 160 p.
   Biography of Millay's years in Greenwich Village that is only incidentally concerned with her poetry.

Dash, Joan. "Edna St. Vincent Millay." In her *A Life of One's Own: Three Gifted Women and the Men They Married,* pp. 115-227. New York: Harper & Row, 1973.
   Biographical sketch with a psychological slant that suggests that Millay was ambivalent about her femininity and that this uncertainty was a critical influence on her life and writings.

Gould, Jean. *The Poet and Her Book: A Biography of Edna St. Vincent Millay.* New York: Dodd, Mead & Co., 1969, 308 p.
   Standard critical biography.

Gurko, Miriam. *Restless Spirit: The Life of Edna St. Vincent Millay.* New York: Thomas Y. Crowell Co., 1962, 271 p.
   Treats Millay's poetry in an autobiographical context.

Hahn, Emily. "Mostly about Vincent." In her *Romantic Rebels: An Informal History of Bohemianism in America,* pp. 231-41. Boston: Houghton Mifflin Co., Riverside Press, 1966.
   Discussion of Millay's life in Greenwich Village during the 1920s.

Sprague, Rosemary. "Edna St. Vincent Millay." In her *Imaginary Gardens: A Study of Five American Poets,* pp. 135-82. Philadelphia: Chilton Book Co., 1969.
   Biographical survey of Millay's career.

Criticism

Atkins, Elizabeth. *Edna St. Vincent Millay and Her Times.* Chicago: University of Chicago Press, 1936, 266p.
   Critical discussion of Millay's major works through *Wine from These Grapes,* characterizing Millay as the "most popular and representative" poet of her time.

Benét, William Rose. Introduction to *Second April and The Buck in the Snow,* by Edna St. Vincent Millay, pp. v-xii. New York: Harper & Brothers Publishers, 1950.
   Discusses Millay's writing style and her themes of nature and childhood.

———. "Round about Parnassus." *The Saturday Review of Literature* XI, No. 17 (10 November 1934): 279.
   Positive assessment of *Wine from These Grapes,* highlighting several poems.

Burch, Francis F. "Millay's 'Not in a Silver Casket Cool with Pearls'." *The Explicator* 48, No. 4 (Summer 1990): 277-79.
   Discusses Sonnet XI of *Fatal Interview,* concluding that

"Millay introduces a feminine viewpoint to the English sonnet sequence, but her views are not new."

Clark, Suzanne. "Jouissance and the Sentimental Daughter: Edna St. Vincent Millay." *North Dakota Quarterly* 54, No. 2 (April 1986): 85-108.

 Examines issues relating to femininity and motherhood in Millay's poetry, particularly her poem "Renascence."

Colum, Padraic. "Miss Millay's Poems." *The Freeman* IV, No. 86 (2 November 1921): 189-90.

 Asserts that the poems in *A Few Figs from Thistles* and *Second April* are characterized by a child-like tone and often fail to reveal mature experience.

Davison, Edward. "Edna St. Vincent Millay." *The English Journal* XVI, No. 9 (November 1927): 671-82.

 Focuses on Millay's metrical skill, epigrammatic style, and exaggeration of language and emotion, and classifies her as a minor poet.

DuBois, Arthur E. "Edna St. Vincent Millay." *The Sewanee Review* 43, No. 1 (January-March 1935): 80-104.

 Considers Millay's poetry as a manifestation of her various personas: "precocious child, authentic poet, woman, and mystic."

Gould, Jean. "Edna St. Vincent Millay—Saint of the Modern Sonnet." In *Faith of a (Woman) Writer,* edited by Alice Kessler-Harris and William McBrien, pp. 129-42. New York: Greenwood Press, 1988.

 Originally presented at a conference on twentieth-century women writers held at Hofstra University in 1982. Examines the origins of the sonnet sequences "Fatal Interview" and "Epitaph for the Race of Man" through the events in Millay's life that made her "a twentieth-century sonneteer of the first rank."

Gregory, Horace, and Zaturenska, Marya. "Edna St. Vincent Millay and the Poetry of Feminine Revolt and Self-Expression." In their *A History of American Poetry, 1900-1940,* pp. 265-81. New York: Harcourt, Brace & Company, 1946.

 Discusses the development of Millay's literary personality and the structure and lyricism of her sonnets.

Jones, Phyllis M. "Amatory Sonnet Sequences and the Female Perspective of Elinor Wylie and Edna St. Vincent Millay." *Women's Studies: An Interdisciplinary Journal* 10, No. 1 (1983): 41-61.

 Compares Elinor Wylie's sonnet sequence "One Person"

with Millay's *Fatal Interview,* asserting that both works represent a Modernist reworking of earlier styles and forms from a female perspective.

Parks, Edd Winfield. "Edna St. Vincent Millay." *The Sewanee Review* XXXVIII, No. 1 (January-March 1930): 42-9.

 Asserts that *The Buck in the Snow* is superior to Millay's earlier works, focusing on its skillful craftmanship and presentation of Millay's philosophy of life.

Ransom, John Crowe. "The Poet As Woman." *The Southern Review* 2, No. 4 (Spring 1937): 783-806.

 Criticizes Millay's poetry for its "lack of intellectual interest."

Scott, Winfield Townley. "Millay Collected." *Poetry* LXIII, No. VI (March 1944): 334-42.

 Discusses the emotional and dramatic tone of Millay's poems in relation to critical reception of her work and her presentation of personal and universal themes.

Sheean, Vincent. *The Indigo Bunting: A Memoir of Edna St. Vincent Millay.* New York: Harper & Brothers, 1951, 131 p.

 Memoir of the critic's acquaintance with Millay during the 1940s that recounts significant events and relationships in Millay's life in those years and considers her verse in relation to her philosophical and spiritual perspectives.

Tate, Allen. "Edna St. Vincent Millay." In his *Reactionary Essays on Poetry and Ideas,* pp. 221-27. New York: Charles Scribner's Sons, 1936.

 Describes Millay as a poet of the second order who is limited by her failure to transcend personal emotions.

Untermeyer, Louis. "Edna St. Vincent Millay." In his *American Poetry Since 1900,* pp. 214-21. New York: Henry Holt & Co., 1923.

 Laudatory assessment of *Renascence and Other Poems, A Few Figs from Thistles,* and *Second April,* focusing on Millay's use of language.

Wood, Clement. "Edna St. Vincent Millay: A Clever Sappho." In his *Poets of America,* pp. 199-213. New York: E. P. Dutton & Co., 1925.

 Review of Millay's first three volumes of poetry that praises her work but denigrates her use of antiquated poetic techniques as self-conscious.

Additional coverage of Millay's life and career is contained in the following sources published by Gale Research: *Contemporary Authors,* **Vols. 104, 130;** *Concise Dictionary of American Literary Biography,* **1917-1929;** *Dictionary of Literary Biography,* **Vol. 45;** *Major 20th-Century Writers;* **and** *Twentieth-Century Literary Criticism,* **Vol. 4.**

Boris Pasternak

1890-1960

(Full name Boris Leonidovich Pasternak) Russian poet, novelist, short story writer, essayist, memoirist, playwright, and nonfiction writer.

INTRODUCTION

Awarded the 1958 Nobel Prize in literature, which he declined under pressure from the Soviet government, Pasternak is regarded as among the foremost Russian poets of the twentieth century. While his complex, ethereal poetry often defies translation, Western critics laud his synthesis of unconventional imagery and formalistic style as well as his vision of the individual's relationship to nature and history.

The son of an acclaimed artist and a concert pianist, Pasternak benefitted from a highly creative household that counted novelist Leo Tolstoy, composer Aleksandr Scriabin, and poet Rainer Maria Rilke among its visitors. Encouraged by Scriabin, Pasternak began studying music as a fourteen-year-old but abandoned this pursuit six years later due to what he perceived as a lack of technical skill. He then turned to philosophy, eventually enrolling in Germany's prestigious Marburg University where he studied Neo-Kantianism. In 1912, however, Pasternak abruptly left Marburg when his childhood friend, Ida Vysotskaia, rejected his marriage proposal, compelling Pasternak to reevaluate his professional and personal choices. Deciding to commit himself exclusively to poetry, he eventually joined Centrifuge, a moderate group of literary innovators associated with the Futurist movement. Rejecting the poetic conventions of such nineteenth-century authors as Alexander Pushkin and Leo Tolstoy, the Futurists advocated greater poetic freedom and attention to the actualities of modern life. Pasternak's first two poetry collections, *Blitzhets tuchakh* and *Poverkh barerov,* largely reflect these precepts as well as the influence of Vladimir Mayakovsky, Pasternak's close friend and among the most revered of the Futurist poets.

Injured by a childhood riding accident, Pasternak was declared unfit for military service and spent the first years of World War I in the Ural Mountains as a clerical worker. When news of the Bolshevik Revolution reached Pasternak in 1917 he returned to Moscow, but the capital's chaotic atmosphere forced him to leave for his family's summer home in the outlying countryside. There he composed *Sestra moia zhizn: leto 1917 goda (My Sister, Life: Summer 1917)*. Considered Pasternak's greatest poetic achievement, this volume celebrates nature as a creative force that permeates human experience and impels historical and personal change. Often uniting expansive, startling imagery with formal rhyme schemes, *My Sister, Life: Summer 1917* is lauded as an accomplished and innova-

tive synthesis of the principal poetic movements of early twentieth-century Russia, including Futurism and Imagism. Pasternak's next poetry collection, *Temi i variatsi* (which may be translated as *Themes and Variations*), solidified his standing as a major modern poet in the Soviet Union.

In 1923, enthusiastic about the possible artistic benefits of the Revolution, Pasternak joined Mayakovsky's Left Front of Art (LEF), an alliance between Futurist writers and the Communist party that used the avant-garde movement's literary innovations to glorify the new social order. His work from this period, *Vysockaya bolezn, Deviatsot piatyi god (The Year Nineteen-Five), Leitenant Shmidt,* and *Spektorsky,* are epic poems that favorably portray events leading up to and surrounding the uprisings of 1917. However, socialist critics faulted the distinctly meditative, personal tone of the poems as bourgeois. During the late 1920s Pasternak grew disillusioned with the government's increasing social and artistic restrictions which, in his opinion, directly opposed the individualistic nature of humanity. He then broke with the LEF, a decision finalized by Mayakovsky's suicide in 1930.

The following year, Pasternak divorced his first wife, Evgeniya Lurie, as a result of his affair with Zinaida Neigauz, whom he later married. Critics often cite this new relationship and the couple's friendships with several Georgian writers as the source of the revitalized poetics found in *Vtoroye rozhdenie.* A collection of love lyrics and impressions of the Georgian countryside, *Vtoroye rozhdenie* presented Pasternak's newly simplified style and chronicled his attempt to reconcile his artistic and social responsibilities in a time of political upheaval. Pasternak's newfound optimism, however, was subdued following the inception of the Soviet Writer's Union, a government institution that abolished independent literary groups and promoted conformity to the precepts of socialist realism. Recognized as a major poet by the Communist regime, Pasternak was invited to participate in several official literary functions, including the First Congress of Writers in 1934. Increasingly disturbed by and wary of Josef Stalin's intensified repressive policies, Pasternak gradually withdrew from public life and began translating the works of others. His many translations include Johann Wolfgang von Goethe's *Faust* as well as the major tragedies of Shakespeare, which remain the standard texts for staging the plays in Russian.

During World War II Pasternak published *Na rannikh poezdakh* and *Zemnoy proster.* These volumes eschewed conventional political rhetoric while reflecting the renewed patriotic and creative spirit that flourished in the Soviet Union during this time. Suppression of the arts resumed following the war, and many of Pasternak's friends and colleagues were imprisoned or executed. Historians and critics disagree as to why Pasternak, who had publicly condemned the actions of the government, escaped Stalin's purges of the intelligentsia. While some credit Pasternak's translation and promotion of writers from Stalin's native Georgia, others maintain that the poet's focus on nature rather than politics prompted the dictator, while glancing over Pasternak's dossier, to write "Do not touch this cloud-dweller."

In 1958, the Swedish Academy selected Pasternak for the Nobel Prize in literature, citing his achievements as both a poet and novelist. However, it was implied that the award had been given solely for his recently published novel *Doctor Zhivago,* an epic portrayal of the socialist revolution and its consequences, which government authorities deemed condemnatory of communism. Although the novel was published only in the West, the award prompted the Soviet government to launch a bitter campaign against Pasternak that ultimately forced him to decline the prize. Despite his decision, the Soviet Writer's Union expelled Pasternak from its ranks, and one Communist party member characterized the author as a "literary whore" in the employ of Western authorities. Disheartened but undaunted, Pasternak published two more works outside the Soviet Union before his death in 1960: a volume of reflective verse entitled *Kogda razgulyayetsya* (which may be translated as *When the Weather Clears*), and *Autobiogratichesey ocherk* (*I Remember: Sketch for an Autobiography*). At his funeral, Pasternak was not accorded the official ceremonies normally accompanying the death of a member of the Soviet Writer's Union. However, thousands of admirers accompanied his family to the grave site, which remains a place of pilgrimage in Russia.

In 1987, under Communist leader Mikhail Gorbachev's policy of social reform, or *glasnost,* the Writer's Union formally reinstated Pasternak, and in 1988, *Doctor Zhivago* was published in the Soviet Union for the first time.

Although much literary study of Pasternak is focused on *Doctor Zhivago,* many critics consider his poetry among the finest of the twentieth century, due to his skillful blending of traditional and unorthodox poetic elements to represent common human experience. C. M. Bowra asserted: "In a revolutionary age Pasternak [saw] beyond the disturbed surface of things to the powers behind it and found there an explanation of what really matters in the world. Through his unerring sense of poetry he has reached to wide issues and shown that the creative calling, with its efforts and its frustrations and its unanticipated triumphs, is, after all, something profoundly natural and closely related to the sources of life."

PRINCIPAL WORKS

POETRY

Blitzhets tuchakh   1914
Poverkh barerov   1917
Sestra moia zhizn: leto 1917 goda   1923
   [*My Sister, Life: Summer 1917,* 1967; also published in
      My Sister, Life; and Other Poems, 1976]
Temi i variatsi   1923
Vysockaya bolezn   1924
Deviatsot piatyi god   1926
   [*The Year Nineteen-Five,* 1989]
Spektorsky   1926
Leitenant Shmidt   1927
Vtoroye rozhdenie   1932
Poemy   1933
Stikhotvoreniia v odnom tome   1933
Stikhotvoreniia   1936
Na rannikh poezdakh   1943
Zemnoy proster   1945
Kogda razgulyayetsya   1959
   [*Poems, 1955-1959,* 1960]

OTHER MAJOR WORKS

†*Detstvo Luvors*   (short story) 1919
   [*Childhood,* 1941; also published as *The Adolescence of
      Zhenya Luvers,*   1961]
†*Rasskazy*   (short stories) 1925
†*Okhrannaya gramota*   (autobiographical nonfiction)
   1931
Povest   (novella)   1934
   [*The Last Summer,* 1959]
Il dottor Zivago [translated in Italian]   (novel) 1957
   [1957; Published as *Doctor Zhivago* in English, 1958;
      published as *Doktor Zivago* in Russian, 1988]
I Remember: Sketch for an Autobiography   (memoirs;

from the Russian manuscript "Autobiogratichesey ocherk") 1959

Sochineniya (collected works) 1961

Lettere agli amici georgiani (letters; from the Russian manuscript "Pis'ma k gurinskim druz'iam") 1967

[*Letters to Georgian Friends,* 1968]

Slepaia Krasavista (drama) 1969

[*The Blind Beauty,* 1969]

Boris Pasternak: Perepiska s Ol'goi Friedenberg (letters) 1981

[*The Correspondence of Boris Pasternak and Olga Friedenberg, 1910-1954,* 1982]

Letters, Summer 1926 (letters) 1985

*Published together as *Deviatsot piatyi god* in 1927.

†Translated and published in *The Collected Prose Works of Boris Pasternak,* 1977.

CRITICISM

J. M. Cohen (essay date 1944)

[*Cohen was an English critic, translator, and editor whose works include a translation of Pasternak's verse,* Selected Poems *(1958). In the following essay, he outlines Pasternak's distinctive lyrical style.*]

Boris Pasternak's early leanings were toward painting. The son of a painter of repute who had painted Tolstoy's portrait, a painter he remained even though his education at Moscow and later at Marburg was academic; but the medium that he chose was poetry.

Born in 1890, he first saw the shape of things to come as a schoolboy when he witnessed the 1905 outbreak at St. Petersburg. He studied; he travelled; he worked at an art school and studied music under Scriabin. But the war and the revolution were to interrupt his development into a cultivated man of letters. His early verse is slight, in contrast to the solemn poetry of the time, but a very early lyric, written in 1912, reveals already several characteristics of his mature style.

> The sleepy garden scatters beetles
> like bronze cinders from chafing pans.
> Level with me and with my candle
> the multicoloured worlds hang down.
>
> And as to some unheard of secret
> I step across into that night
> where damp in its decay the poplar
> covers the edges of the moon.
>
> A pond there's like a revealed secret,
> there whispers surf of apple trees,
> the garden hangs, a house on piles, there
> and holds in front of it the sky.

A pleasant enough little lyric written in regular rhymed verses, though slight liberties are taken with the rhymes,

sad (garden) rhyming with *visiat* (hang) and the feminine *táina* (secret) with *sváynoy* (on piles), a licence already taken by Blok and his contemporaries. But this differs from the conventional impressionist lyric written in most countries after Verlaine; it has two marks of individuality. The detail is visualized with a painter's eye, with an eye trained in the impressionist school to see not objects, but the space before the eye in which objects and their surroundings mingle in light, shape and colour, before separating into their individual forms. With a painter's eye Pasternak sees the garden suspended like a building on piles, foliage supported by the stems of the trees; the beetles are seen as if for the first time and an unexpected comparison made, a comparison based on visual similarity, the germ of the provocative image that is the hallmark of his later style and the second characteristic that that looks forward to his maturity. This poem is one of many written before 1916; among them are pieces as individual and delicately visualized as **"Wintry Sky,"** a skating scene in which Pasternak renders a landscape with less conventional touches than in the garden poem.

In other poems he develops this characteristic simile, the Pasternakian conceit, based sometimes like the seventeenth-century conceit on a mental comparison rather than a visual. In the last of a series of poems on St. Petersburg occur two images that show the strength and weakness of this device.

> 'The streets strive like thought towards the port
> like a dark stream of manifestos.'

Here the bird's eye view of the streets hung with banners and posters is well conveyed. The second simile is more violent. Addressing the city he says:

> 'You do not hold back with your piles the waves'
> inundations
> There talk is like the hands of blind midwives.'

One is reminded of the talk of the laundresses in *Finnegans Wake,* but the strain on the reader of tracing two comparisons and placing them side by side is severe. The sound of the waves is compared to the chatter of the midwives, their blind probing of the land to the groping of the midwives' hands.

Cutting across Pasternak's development in these years came the Futurist movement with its violence, its manifestos and its deliberate formlessness. There was not much that he could learn from Khlebnikov's naïve rejoicing in horror nor from Mayakovsky's brazen shout, but the movement releases two more components of the poet's character, his rejoicing in violence and his provocativeness. His first important book ***My Sister, Life,*** containing poems written in and before 1917, fully reveals both these features, though perhaps the provocative image is at its most vivid rather earlier, in the sequence *Spring.* A prose translation shows the style at its most outrageous.

> 'The wood is throttled with a knot of feathered throats, like a buffalo with a lasso and moans in the nets, as in sonatas the steel gladiator of the organ groans.'

> 'Poetry, be a Grecian sponge with suckers and

among the sticky green I will put you down on
the wet board of a green garden seat.'

'Grow a fine frill and farthingale, soak up cloud
and ravines and at night I will wring you out for
the good of greedy paper.'

My Sister, Life contains little as perverse as this, but there
is a deliberate attempt to make the reader sit up, to shock
him into seeing with the poet's eyes.

At the same time the impressionism gives way to expressionism. The landscape is in movement:

'And then the summer said goodbye
to the station. Taking off its cap,
at night for souvenirs the thunder
took a hundred blinding snaps,'

he says in **"Thunder, momentarily instantaneous."**

The book is uneven and its standards of taste most uncertain. It contains lyrics of appalling saccharinity, though of
perfect craftsmanship, and others in which romantic violence stops short and as violently laughs at itself.

The Kerensky revolution is celebrated in a poem of crude
imagery, **"Spring Rain,"** which concludes:

'It's not the night nor rain nor the peoples' rend-
ing choruses
Kerensky! hurrah!
It's the blinding march from catacombs, that
had no issue
yesterday
to the great forum.
It's not roses, it's not mouths, nor the murmur
of the crowd;
It's before this theatre, here,
that the surge of night is rising over Europe and
her pride
is breaking on our streets.'

But this acceptance of revolution is not the prelude to political adherence. Characteristically the poem occurs in a
section of the book with the sub-title *Distractions for the
beloved.*

His own attitude to political change is shown in the romantic pose of the poem **"About these verses,"** in which
he sets out the subject matter of his poems.

'Muffled, my hand before my eyes
down from the window I shall call:
"Children, what century is it
that's down in our courtyard, my dears?" '

'Who's cleared a pathway to the door
to that hole that's filled up with sleet,
whilst I was smoking with Lord Byron,
drinking with Edgar Allan Poe?'

The book is full of a theatrical swagger at its most pronounced when Pasternak is attacking the bourgeois, as in
the first poem of the series *Postscript:* **"Darling, it's frightening"**. He sees himself as another Lermontov, to whose
memory he dedicates the book, but there is a good deal of
excuse for those who dismissed him as deliberately obscure and provocative and accused him of flouting all traditional standards, Lermontov's among them. But there
are in the book several poems of real beauty. The two

pieces in the section, *Songs in letters, to save her from boredom,* have a pleasantly personal note of love in a country
cottage, a week-end simplicity that contrasts pleasantly
with the week-day exuberance of much of the book. Both
show Pasternak's most constant and most individual quality, a revelling in life and in the small things of life, in nature and the small, entrancing glimpses of her that are
vouchsafed to the innocent eye, the eye free of pre-
conception and clichés. Lines like these from **"Vorobyev
Hills"** are of the poet's best.

Here the town tram stops; the rails are laid no
further.
Beyond, the pines will serve. Beyond, they cannot run.
Beyond there's only Sunday. Plucking down the
branches
the glade goes running onward, slipping through
the grate.

Another genuine note is struck in the petulant gloom of
"Cape Mootch", in which the landscape is coloured by a
love affair gone wrong, and the lightness of **"English Lessons"** with its cryptic ending shows that the poet can bring
off lyrics that are charming in an individual vein yet with
a reminiscence of Laforgue.

The technical innovations that were marked in the first
poem quoted were continued and more variations of half
rhymes, both consonantal and vowel, invented. The only
test of validity seems to be the spoken word. Russian is a
strongly accented language and the vowels lose their full
value progressively as they lie further from the accentuated syllable; consequently his feminine and three syllable
rhymes look strange on the page, but are effective when
the poem is read. His metres are various and occasionally
the length of line is varied in the course of a poem; but a
sound instinct and real technical mastery save the poet
from the sprawling *vers libre* of his contemporaries and his
innovations, like Browning's rhymes, rather help than
hinder the vigour of his expression.

The next book, containing poems written from 1917 onwards, bears the title of its most ambitious poem, **"Theme
and Variations"**, an attempt rather deliberately to compose after a musical pattern. The motives are stated in the
theme, and repeated in the variations, one of which, the
third, is Pasternak's most common anthology piece—'The
stars rushed headlong by', a romantic statement, high
sounding, highly coloured and obscure, ending characteristically in self-irony.

A small wind from Morocco stirred the sea
The simoon blew. In snows Archangel snored.
The candles guttered. Rough draft of 'the
Prophet'
dried and the morning dawned above the Gan-
ges.

It was the romantic poet of 'The Prophet', Pasternak's
other self, that conceived the idea of this ambitious poem,
but the poet's approach to music was academic, to painting natural and it is to the landscapes of the section entitled *The Tireless Garden* that one turns for his best work.

The revolution had come, but the revolutionary poet of
My Sister, Life was less provocative; and it is a real proof

of his integrity that he could write in 1917 two pieces of pure and exact vision, **"The Hazel Grove"** and **"In the Wood"**, and in 1918 a piece of vision regret for the coming of winter to the pleasant country house, **'Spasskoye'**—was it in a sense for the coming of revolution to break up the carefree week-end life of **"Vorobyev Hills"**? But if these poems are remarkable for feelings more subtle and genuine, they are even more remarkable for the clarity of the painter's eye. He was not escaping from the revolution into a country refuge: there was none. Yet was not the drawing of the country more careful for the threat to the existence of that kind of life?

But in those years Pasternak greeted the new age with optimism. Two poems, one for the new year, **"January 1919"**, the other **"Will be"**, a jaunty piece of affirmation with the refrain 'Thus, even thus will life be new' look forward and the last has an oblique reference to the revolution:

> 'Boss us then, while the handkerchief's
> still fluttering, you're the lady yet,
> while we remain in darkness still
> and while the fire is not blown out.'

But it is a very personal symbolism that identifies the old régime with a lady imperiously fluttering her handkerchief, nor can Pasternak sufficiently pervert his own cultured background to identify himself with those who in a more real sense were in the darkness. The fire is the spark of a bullet wad and for the second of its flight the old régime might keep its power. It is only the date 1919 that makes us seek this explanation; in another year the poem's source might have seemed a purely personal anecdote.

Two other themes come into Pasternak's poetry in this volume. Regret for childhood lost, for childish innocence perverted in the section *I can forget them* gives rise to a spiritual autobiography rather more objective than the theatrical posturing of the earlier poetry.

> 'What does the siren on the bench
> mean by the menace of her beauty,
> if stealing children's not allowed?
> So there arise the first suspicions.
>
> So terrors ripen. Can he let
> a star surpass him in achievement,
> when he's a Faust, he's an enchanter?
> And so the gipsy ways begin.'

In this poem too Pasternak broaches the second fresh theme; begins to analyse the nature and the functions of a poet, both obvious enough in the days of the pontifical symbolists, but now like much else to be questioned. His solution of the problem varies from poem to poem; in the piece just quoted the poetry arises from the terror, but by 1922 in two poems he stresses the automatic nature of his inspiration:

> 'Images fly askew in showers,
> gather themselves from hinge, from wall
> and high road that's blown out the candle—
> and fall in rhythm. I don't stop them.'

In another piece, **"Poetry"**, written in the same year, the answer is more aggressive and more cynical:

> Poetry, when once an empty truism,
> like a zinc bucket's at the tap,
> then, only then it's sure to flow.
> The copy book's spread open—spout!

Pasternak's strength lies in his absolute independence; an individualist in the midst of a totalitarian revolution he makes no compromises. . . . He has been true to his own experience wherever it has led him.

—J. M. Cohen

The poet's place in society had been dwelt on before Pasternak's first dramatic piece **"Shakespeare"**, in which the poet, a Villon figure, is taken to task by his own sonnet, which confronts him on the morning after a 'thick' night in an inn and attacks him for demeaning himself to win 'billiard-room popularity'. The poet, with a sound instinct, sends his sonnet packing. This piece deals summarily with the theory of art for art's sake. In its deliberate anachronism it compares with Mayakovsky's *Christopher Columbus*. Pasternak did not believe in the 'ivory tower', though he wavers between the attitude suggested by the last three quotations and the claim that he makes for Balzac in a later poem, when he describes him as 'weaving a requiem service for Paris'. On the whole he is content like Kästner to own *eine gleine Versfabrik* in which he converts experience or nature into poetry 'for the benefit of greedy paper'. A training in philosophy at Marburg may have made him distrust dogmatism.

In contrast to the first book, ***Theme and Variations*** is smoother texture; the violent images are on the whole less arbitrary and, particularly in the beautiful poem **"In the Wood"**, much more fully worked out. These two books were published in the early days of the revolution, when, under the guidance of Lunacharsky, communists were proud to support and read advanced literature, but by 1921 this era was over, and the writer was required to show an adherence to the working class by writing works of a propagandist kind. For most of the poets of the day, for Anna Akhmatova and for Mandelstam, this was the end. They had written for a cultured audience that was no more, and the newly won proletarian couldn't understand their work. But Pasternak was in a different position for he strongly believed that he belonged to Russia and accepted the revolution, as is clear from the poem **"We're few"**. It was consequently not difficult for him to produce a set of poems, '1905', based on his schoolboy reminiscences of that outbreak. Technically he could do anything that Mayakovsky could and this staccato sequence, printed some years ago in *New Writing* in an English version by Alec Brown, is no less turgid, but considerably more obscure in its images and considerably more personal than other work of this kind. Another sequence, *Lieutenant Schmidt,* deals with a hero of that revolution in a series of lyrics perhaps more individual but hardly more interesting. These two works were written between 1925 and 1927, and they were followed by a fragmentary novel in verse, **"Spektorsky"**, smoother and much closer to the traditional style than anything he had so far written and, in part at least, autobiographical. But during these years Pasternak's output of lyrical poetry was small, though the few pieces included under the title of *Miscellaneous poems* dating from that year are of his best. Two, **"The Cocks"** and **"Lyubka"**, are among the most beautiful of his landscapes; and, true to the ambivalence of the poet, the first is a poem that greets the new world and its promise of change, while the second regrets the passing of the old. In the first he writes of the cocks:

> 'Examining each several year by name,
> each in his turn, they call upon the dark
> and so begin their prophecy of change
> in rain, in earth, in love, in all, in all.'

In the second, after describing a shower, the shower that occurs so often, each time with surprising freshness, in his poems he presents in four lines a vignette that contains regret for a whole age, the age of Turgenev.

> They're drinking evening tea in country houses,
> the mist swells the mosquito's sail and night,
> jungling with sudden music of guitars,
> stands in a milky darkness mid the cow-wheat.

These years were, however, hardly justified by a few lyrics even though these were richer and smoother than any except the best: **"Vorobyev Hills,"** **"In the Wood,"** and **"Spasskoye."** The poet's vigour, the images which had come to him in showers, the subjects for poetry, were growing less, and if we can blame the bleak background of socialist construction and its tight censorship on ideas in part, we must attribute the situation in part also to the poet's failure to look inwards. The poems were all the work of a young man, exuberant, bold, self dramatizing, a young man of amazing virtuosity, whose mastery of his own medium grew steadily and whose work had improved with the greater restraint he had displayed in his second book. He was capable of turning out the poetic journalism that the Soviet expected of him because he was in sympathy with the Soviet achievement. But he was not capable of any great advance as a poet. Unless he could recapture his own youthful feelings, Pasternak at the age of forty was not likely to write more than a little more genuine poetry, and it is to such a reconquest of his old powers that we owe his next book of poems, *Second Birth* (1932). From this book we learn the occasion of the miracle; it seems that he fell in love with a girl much younger than himself. His love lyrics for her are far tenderer than those in the early books, and the poet has now a charm that he rarely had as a young man.

The Pasternakian image had lost none of its element of surprise; on the first page we find the print of the waves on the beach compared with waffles, and the two ballads also contain a good deal of obscurity despite their simple form. But the poet's style is now less angular, though none the less individual. The painter's eye is as keen as ever, particularly in the two poems that give a meticulous de-

Cover of Vtoroye rozhdenie *(1932).*

scription of a journey in the Caucasus and in the impressionist **"Darkness of Death"**.

Never has he given such pictures as those of the Caucasus in the true romantic tradition.

> Afar where clouds in rings were coiling
> like serpents on their eggs, more dread
> than forays of the long dead Tartars,
> a range of Chinese shadows spread.
>
> A row of gravestones on a backcloth
> of paths, they were, blocked up by snow,
> beyond the scenery of those skies, where
> Prometheus languished, ceased to glow.

The love poems have a naïve and tempestuous flow that is pure delight and even a rather touching humility. For the first time the poet reveals his heart, and it is the heart of a young man.

> O, how bold she was, when hardly
> gone from her beloved mother's
> wing, in jest she gave her childish
> laugh to me and, never offering
> opposition or impediment,
> her childish peace and childish laugh,
> her concerns and cares, a child
> innocent of injury.

And rather wistfully he hopes to recapture in himself a childish directness that has been long overlaid with self-consciousness. The responsibility of love weighs upon him and he sighs:

> Lightly to waken, see again,
> shake from the heart its wordy letter
> and live in future days unsoiled.
> Surely all that needs no great cunning.

But though the keynote of *Second Birth* is the return of youth, other notes creep in, and the old optimism about the good times that the revolution will bring is tempered by irony and by the feeling that he may not survive to see them:

> In time to come, I tell them, we'll be equal
> to any living now. If cripples, then
> no matter we shall just have been run over
> by 'New Man' in the waggon of his Plan.
> And when from death the tablet doesn't save us,
> then time will hurry on more freely still
> to that far point where Five Year Plan the sec-
>   ond
> prolongs the dissertations of the soul.

But most revealing of all that the shades of the prison house are closing is the little poem: 'O had I known, that's how it happens'. Here old age, first stressed in **"Vorobyev Hills"** as a spur to enjoyment of the week-end life, now for the first time applies to himself, the old actor who had been prepared to stake so little when he made his stage debut:

> But old age is like Rome, demands
> instead of wisecracks and of tricks,
> actors must give not easy readings
> but death outright in sober earnest.
> And when the heart dictates the line
> it sends a slave upon the stage
> and there's an end of art and there's
> a breath of earth and destiny.

Though not the last in published sequence, this poem must be thought of as the last in the collected volume, which contains no poems written after *Second Birth.*

In the last years Pasternak has translated poetry from the Georgian, and is now engaged in translating Shakespeare. It has been suggested that the Soviet government, disapproving of his personal lyrics has directed him to this work, but after reading *Second Birth* one must doubt whether he had much more lyrical poetry to write.

By turning to translation it may be that he is saving himself from the fate of many poets who have spent the second half of their lives repeating their early work in vain attempts to relive the experience that made it real. It is given to few contemporary poets, to few indeed in any age, to deepen and widen their early inspiration in middle age, and nothing in *Second Birth* suggests that Pasternak is among those few.

In his later work his æstheticism has grown more clear-sighted, his dramatizations less violent and less perverse; technically his poetry has shed some of its most flamboyant features and its quick transitions from one image to another, each more surprising than the last, that destroyed

the unity of many poems in *My Sister, Life.* With age some of the pungency that must have won him young admirers is toned down, but there remains a prodigious talent that has added twenty or thirty fine poems to Russian literature, that has been able to write the poems that were required of him during the Soviet government's first 'Gleichschaltung', that must be capable of translating some of Shakespeare as well as it has ever been translated; for Pasternak's tremendous inventiveness, his enormous vocabulary and his vigour are admirably suited to the work of translation.

There remains the task of placing Pasternak in the contemporary scene, of suggesting the relationship of his poetry to that of others. To Blok, the master of his young days and one of Russia's greatest poets, he owes little. Only to read Blok's few poems about the war of 1914, those addressed to his native land and his poem about the Revolution, 'The Twelve', is to see the contrast between the poet of spiritual values, aloof yet sensitive to the cataclysm of his days, and the æsthete who sees the world in all its manifold aspects, makes an artist's choice among them, but fails to establish a stable sense of values, though he never surrenders to the ready-made values of the revolution.

There is little to connect Pasternak with the symbolists; his affinities are with the brood of Laforgue rather than with them. His natural settings of the steppe and snow, his distances and his wide horizons he shares with the Russian poets, but he takes over from the west, from Verlaine and from George and the German romantics, the haunted landscape that is foreign to all Russian poets except Tyutchev. Like Laforgue he is essentially a would-be romantic, brought up short by the unlikeness of the actual world to the highly-coloured world with its simple values that the romantics, Lermontov or Lenau, drew. But the actual world, far from revolting him, attracts him: to him because of his painter's eye it has an even greater beauty. The third variation, quoted earlier in this article, shows only one aspect of the poet's ambivalence, one closely related to T. S. Eliot's in the Sweeney poems. The real dualism in Pasternak's mind is not Laforgue's and not Eliot's; the world attracts him too much and robs his experience of vital core; instead there is a vague melancholy and unease of the man of action forced to reflect, the occasional thought of how it will all look afterwards that comes increasingly into such later poems as that beginning 'Some day in years to come they'll play me Brahms' and into the last lines of **"Lyubka":**

> Then everything is scented with night violet:
> the years and faces. Thoughts. And each event
> that may perhaps be rescued from the past
> and taken in the future from fate's hands.

Occasionally, even in *My Sister, Life,* he is overwhelmed with the sadness of things, and we see what lies below the surface of buoyant optimism, below his truculent challenge of the bourgeois values in everything including art. In **"The Definition of the creative power"**, as in the poems that lament the loss of childish innocence, we see that the art really emerges from the terror:

> Gardens, ponds, palings, the creation,

foamed with purity of tears,
are only categories of passion
hoarded by the human heart.

He remains in the 'Waste land', but the desert smiles on
him; only occasionally does its vegetation fail to attract.
Hence a poetic growth into the second half of life fails to
take place. Pasternak's development did not lead him into
a clear realization of the Waste Land position nor through
it and out the other side. The world was too prone to spill
beauty, yet the underlying melancholy serves to show that
the poet was not convinced by it; he was only too readily
attracted by the thunder, the rain and the revolution, all
of which may strip off nature's covering and reveal its essence: but none of them does.

Perhaps a truer comparison is with Auden, with whom he
shares his early success. Both as young men had marked
out one manner as their own. It is as easy to recognize a
poem by Pasternak as by Auden; both were victims of
their own fatal facility, yet it is possible to foresee from
Auden's continuous search for truth, even in so disappointing a poem as 'New Year's Letter', a possibility of future development. Pasternak looked for a second birth
outside himself, and he found it for an instant that he records for us in his poems of 1932.

The weakness in the poetry is its subjectivity; apparently
inspired more than most poets by external events, Pasternak is in fact never held by the world outside him. It is
clear from his quick movement from one image to the next
that his joy is feverish. His moods do not hold long. For
that reason it is difficult to compare him to his great contemporaries, Eliot, Lorca, Alberti or Aragon, all of whom
have moved on from one set of experiences to another and
attained maturity. Pasternak's vital experiences were adolescent and adolescence pervades the poetry, giving it both
its freshness and its violence, its changing moods and the
underlying melancholy and fear, which emerge strongly
from some of his very best poems; giving it also the gaiety
and promise that emerge just as strongly from others.

Pasternak's strength lies in his absolute independence; an
individualist in the midst of a totalitarian revolution he
makes no compromises. His acceptance of the revolution
is best understood from the line:

> Once We were people. Now we're epochs.

He is 'above the barriers' of politics; refusing to be interfered with, he stands honestly for the revolution, neither
sacrificing himself to it like Mayakovsky nor going into
exile and silence. He has been true to his own experience
wherever it has led him. (pp. 23-36)

*J. M. Cohen, "The Poetry of Boris Pasternak,"
in* Horizon, *London, Vol. X, No. 55, July,
1944, pp. 23-36.*

C. M. Bowra (essay date 1949)

[*Bowra, an English critic and literary historian, was considered among the foremost classical scholars of the first
half of the twentieth century. He also wrote extensively
on modern literature, particularly European poetry, in
studies noted for their erudition, lucidity, and straight-*

*forward style. In the following essay, Bowra examines
the influence of Imagism on* My Sister, Life *and*
Themes and Variations.]

Pasternak's resemblance to the Imagists was more personal than intellectual. He was not of their number and was
too good a craftsman to accept their extreme claims. But,
like other modern poets, he saw that the images has a special part to play and that it is almost impossible to express
complex states of mind without an adventurous and extensive use of it. It is customary to say that his use of images
reflects the world of painting in which he grew up, but
though Pasternak's visual sensibility is extremely keen, it
does much more than mark and record. It carries with it
something which is more than visual. Indeed we might say
that his musical training has been quite as important as his
knowledge of painting, since it has taught him to give a
precise sensuous form to otherwise undefined feelings and
to realise what strength can be added to words through
combinations of sound. What he sees awakes in him so
many remarkable trains of thought and sound that his poetry is packed and complex. It deals with many obscure
states which might be material for a musician but are beyond the scope of a painter. Everything that he notices is
fraught with mystery and meaning for him. He lives in the
real world and observes it intently, but his rapt observation uncovers much more than meets the seeing eye. In the
inextricable combination of his senses and emotions he
both sees and interprets nature, both marks its manifestations and understands what they mean and what relations
they suggest beyond the immediate "given". No doubt the
Imagists hoped to do something of this kind through their
cult of the image, but they defined its purpose too narrowly. Pasternak, consciously or unconsciously, has picked up
their doctrine and shown how it should really be applied.

Pasternak did not burst into poetry in extreme youth. His
early verses are not numerous and still show an experimental quality. At moments there are forecasts of his most
mature manner, at others mere attempts to write like
other men. Then in 1917 he flowered astonishingly and
marvellously. His volume *My Sister, Life,* which was not
published until 1922, was written in the summer of 1917
and shows how perfectly Pasternak had found himself.
The flood of inspiration in which he wrote this book continued for the next few years and produced the no less remarkable *Themes and Variations* in 1923. These two volumes are the essential core of his work, the climax of his
first endeavours and the inspired product of his young
manhood. In them his temperament and his circumstances combined to produce the new kind of poetry
which was his to give and which his time needed. His later
work contains many beauties, is always truthful and original, but it is sometimes too experimental, too much at war
with his circumstances, to have the final harmony of these
two books. In them Pasternak has done something which
is unique in his time.

An outlook like Pasternak's demands its own technique,
and he has found a form which is firm and concentrated
and powerful. In an age of metrical experiments he normally uses stanzas of fixed length and regular rhythms. On
the printed page his verses look perfectly normal. He also
uses rhyme, though he goes far in his use of half-rhymes

and assonances. While the formal plan of his verses binds its different elements together and reduces them to order, the unusual character of his contents is marked by his unusual rhymes. By this means Pasternak avoids that looseness of form which suits the surging moods of the Futurists but is unsuitable to a poet who wishes to give to a poem some of the balance and pattern of a painting or of a musical composition. Pasternak makes us feel that even the most complex of his themes has its own harmony and order and that, however surprising what he says may be, it has a controlling design. The strictness of the form adds dignity to the rich and unusual vocabulary which is in turns allusive, conversational and majestic, and does not shrink from elliptical expressions or from neologisms: it even controls the imagery which is always original and sometimes startling. The formality of Pasternak's verse holds the rebellious material together. Without it the complex themes would not be fused into a unity, and the final result would be far less satisfying.

In his instinctive knowledge of what poetry is, Pasternak is determined that his work shall be essentially and purely poetry. No doubt his standards owe much to the great Russian writers like Blok who brought poetry back to itself in the first decade of this century, but he must also owe something to the discriminating devotion to the arts which he learned in his family circle, especially from his father. If his determination to maintain always a level of pure poetry sometimes makes him obscure or even awkward, it also means that he never writes below a certain standard and never wastes his time on irrelevant matters. The close texture of his verse, which at times makes it difficult to grasp all his implications at a first reading, is an essential feature of his art. It helps him to convey his intense, concentrated experience and is a true mirror of his moods. He looks at objects not in isolation but as parts of a wider unity, marks their relations in a complex whole, and stresses the dominant character of a scene as much as the individual elements in it. His work is therefore extremely personal, but not so personal as to be beyond the understanding of other men. He assumes that others will recognise the truth of his vision and come to share it with him. For, in his view, what he gives them is not a scientific, photographic transcript of an impersonal, external reality but something intensely human, since reality and value are given to things by our appreciation of them and by our absorption of them into our consciousness. Man is the centre of the universe, and human consciousness is its uniting principle. Therefore he can say with perfect sincerity:

> Gardens, ponds and palings, the creation
> Foam-flecked with the whiteness of our weeping,
> Are nothing but categories of passion
> That the human heart has had in keeping.

Pasternak is a poet of sensibility in the sense that for him sensibility is both physical and intellectual, the means by which he gets a full and firm grip on reality, and that nothing counts but those moments when he has a vivid apprehension of something that happens both inside and outside himself.

To convey the results of this sensibility and this outlook demands a special technique. Since what the senses give us must be presented in its fullness, it is not right to use conventional means of description which presuppose an artificial arrangement of experience. The poet must convey his sensations exactly as they strike him. So Pasternak often presents a visible scene in a way which at first seems paradoxical but later reveals its essential truth and exactness. For instance he writes of a road so polished in summer by cart-wheels that it reflects the stars by night:

> By the road age-old midnight stands,
> Sprawls on the trackway with its stars;
> You cannot pass the hedge without
> Trampling upon the universe.

At first sight this looks like an imaginative trope, but it is really a truthful transcript of the poet's sensations. On crossing the road in such conditions he notices the reflected stars and for the moment believes that he is treading on them. That is the experience which inspires him, and that is precisely what he says. So somewhat differently, when he tells of a journey in a train at night, he assumes that, in his seat, he is the fixed centre of reality and that what he sees is a passing phenomenon. Everyone will know what he means and recognise how precisely he records it:

> And, with its third splash, off the bell goes swimming,
> Still making apologies: "Sorry, not here,"
> And under the blind the night passes flaming,
> And the plain crumbles off from the steps to a star.

The train has just left the station to the usual Russian signal of a bell rung three times. When the journey begins, the train seems to be fixed, and the night behind the blind to move, so that the country slowly disappears between the steps of the railway-carriage and the distant star which is relatively stationary. The description is careful and accurate. This is just what he feels in a train, and to put it differently would be to falsify it. But just because Pasternak sees it so clearly and knows exactly what it is, he is able to awake a delighted and surprised admiration at his exactness and truth.

The same art is applied to sensations other than visual and to these mental states which begin with sensations of eye or ear but contain something else in their mental appreciation of a situation. Pasternak, for instance, writes of a thunderstorm at the end of summer:

> Summer then to the flag-station
> Said good-bye. That night the thunder
> Doffed its cap and as memento
> Took a hundred blinding snaps.

The sight and the sound of the thunderstorm are inextricably mingled with the thought that the summer is over, and this combination comes out in original and consistent imagery. In Pasternak's poetry visible and mental things are closely associated, and he hardly troubles to distinguish between them. . . . The ultimate setting is in the poet's mind: this holds the phenomena together and gives them their character, but the physical sensations are none the less acutely felt and recorded. The watching mind observes them as they really are and sees their significance. Indeed the actual facts take on a symbolical importance and convey the character and atmosphere of the poet's state as he observes them. Pasternak's images deepen his meaning not merely because they give a greater exactness, but because they show the relation between a given event and other events not immediately connected, which are none the less of the same kind. They show that no event can be treated in absolute isolation but that any proper appreciation of it must take into account its universal qualities and relations.

This poetry is difficult just because it reflects the poet's sensations so exactly, especially when he advances beyond visual effects to the associations which they awake and with which they are inextricably united. Pasternak has a remarkable gift for giving shape and colour to these inchoate states of the mind in its moments of excited sensibility and uses vivid concrete images for much that poets usually leave undefined. He seizes on some significant trait in what he sees and relates it to something wider by his choice of a significant image. When, for instance, he writes:

> But people in watch-chains are loftily grumbling
> And sting you politely like snakes in the oats,

the primary effect is visual, but the scene, so clearly portrayed, suggests the character and habits of a class of persons who are coldly polite and use good manners to inflict wounds. So, more strikingly, in **"Spring"** Pasternak moves from the seen to the unseen, from an actual place to its character and meaning for him:

> It's spring. I leave a street where the poplar is astonished,
> Where distance is alarmed, and the house fears it may fall,
> Where air is blue just like the linen bundle
> A discharged patient takes from hospital,
>
> Where dusk is empty like a broken tale,
> Abandoned by a star, without conclusion,
> So that expressionless, unfathomable
> A thousand clamouring eyes are in confusion.

This is a real place with its street, it houses, its poplar, its sky with the colour of a blue bundle. But the visual effect is made more significant by the imaginative and emotional tone which it gets from the imagery. The poet leaves the place because it is somehow frustrated and incomplete. It has the confused pathos of an interrupted story, and this spreads to all who are interested in it and have hopes for its future. We all know how a visual scene may excite emotions in this way and contain in itself a power to move us to grief or pity. Pasternak describes such a state with admirable truth and appropriateness. He does not exaggerate his feelings, but passes with easy skill from one aspect of the situation to another until the short poem gives a complete and faithful picture of what has struck him.

This pictorial method enables Pasternak to deal with undefined and impalpable feelings and to give them a remarkable brilliance of colour and outline. He finds his images in what his eyes and ears have noted. These become his instruments for showing the obscure movements of the human soul. In particular when he tells of some action and

wishes to show its full significance, he sometimes uses its actual features symbolically. The symbols exist both in themselves and for what they represent, and a poem written in this way seems to call for understanding at two levels, literal and symbolical. One of his most quoted poems will show how Pasternak faces this technique with all its difficulties:

> Stars raced headlong. Seaward headlands lathered.
> Salt spray blinded. Eyes dried up their tears.
> Darkness filled the bedrooms. Thoughts raced headlong.
> To Sahara Sphinx turned patient ears.
>
> Candles guttered. Blood, it seemed, was frozen
> In the huge Colossus. Lips at play
> Swelled into the blue smile of the desert.
> In that hour of ebb night sank away.
>
> Seas were stirred by breezes from Morocco.
> Simoon blew. Archangel snored in snows.
> Candles guttered. First draft of *The Prophet*
> Dried, and on the Ganges dawn arose.

The last verse explains the whole. "The Prophet" is Pushkin's famous poem and Pasternak's subject is its composition. To this all the themes are related. In the first place we hear of the circumstances in which the poem is written. It is begun at night, and finished at dawn. The dark bedrooms, the guttering candles, the racing stars, are the accompaniment of composition. The geographical setting, from Africa to Archangel, from the Ganges to Morocco, places the poem in its wider, cosmic relations and sets its birth on the stage of the world. But each of the details serves a second purpose. They are symbols for the act of composition as it takes place in the poet. The storm at sea is his tumultuous energy, the freezing Colossus his state when the work begins, the listening Sphinx his expectant consciousness on the verge of starting, the swelling lips his joy that expands into creation, the snoring city of Archangel his indifference to all around him, and the dawn his final triumphant achievement. But though we may treat the poem at two levels, literal and symbolical, they are fused into a single result. The actual circumstances illuminate the significance of such an event and become symbols of its character. The composition of "The Prophet" is a display of creative energy in which the workings of the poet's inspiration have the power of natural forces and closely resemble them.

Pasternak uses imagery to give to his poems a high degree of exactness and individuality. For instance, he often writes about rain, but he distinguishes between its different aspects. At one time, on a summer evening, it advances through a clearing as a surveyor walks with his clerk: at another time a solid sheet of rain is like charcoal in a drawing: in **"Sultry Rain"**

> Dust simply soaked the rain in pills
> Like iron in a gentle powder.

The different parallels show variously the gentle approach of rain, its black torrential downpour, its disappearance in a parched landscape. When this art is applied to mental and emotional states, it gives a new significance and clarity to them. The unmarked passage of time becomes "the hour is scuttling like a beetle". A mood of quiet satisfaction appears as

> In fur-coat and arm-chair purrs the soul
> In the same way, always, on and on.

So the methods of the Imagists are given a new and much more impressive purpose. The image, as Pasternak uses it, is as rare and striking as they could demand, but instead of being given pride of place as the only thing that matters, it concentrates the poem's essence in itself and at the same time serves to make clearer the complex unity with which the poem as a whole deals.

The desire to make his imagery exact sometimes leads Pasternak into curious results. We may even feel that, like Apollinaire, he enjoys startling us by unexpected effects as when he says that a frosty night is "like a blind puppy lapping its milk" or that the dew "runs shivering like a hedgehog". But if we look closely at these, we see how apt they are in that a frosty night has really something primitively greedy about it and that the shivering of the dew is like the shivering of a hedgehog. The danger of this method is that the desire to make the image extremely precise may give it too great an emphasis and upset the balance of tone. . . . This is a minor fault, and there are not many instances of it, but it shows the difficulty of using images which are both striking and exact.

Pasternak uses this technique to convey his own vision of reality. He is perfectly at home in a real, physical world, but he sees it in a special way and gives his own interpretation of it. He believes that it has its own powers and forces and that it is for him to understand these and bring them into closer touch with himself. Just as the Futurist Khlebnikov believed that the earth is full of unacknowledged or neglected powers which he identified with the old Slavonic gods, so Pasternak, more realistically and more reasonably, sees in nature real, living powers with whom he can enter into some kind of communion and whose influence he can to some extent fathom. For him trees and flowers, skies and winds, clouds and light, are in their own way alive with a special energy and character of their own. Naturally he speaks of them in the language of human actions and relations, but his conception of nature is not simply of something akin to mankind. He sees that it works differently, and he is content to observe it as it is and to show how it affects him and other men. He can mark natural details as attentively as Tennyson, but he does more than this. He passes from his delighted observation of them to interpreting what they mean, what dramatic parts they play, what effects they create, what powers lie behind these common and apparently innocent phenomena. For him the natural world is a busy active place, full of strange forces and energies, which are often almost unintelligible but none the less exciting or disturbing. He feels that he stands in some relation to them, and tries to show what this means. Few poets have approached nature quite with these beliefs. Pasternak delights in it and feels that it is alive and powerful, but does not make a god of it or expect it to reveal oracular messages.

Pasternak is so at home with nature and treats it with so easy and affectionate a familiarity that we do not always notice how special his vision is and may even assume that his treatment of a natural subject is fundamentally conventional. (pp. 131-40)

This familiarity with nature passes into a deeper and more significant poetry. How much it can mean to Pasternak may be seen from **"Sparrow Hills."** Reduced to its lowest terms this is a variation on the old theme of *carpe diem:* since no pleasure lasts for long, let us enjoy what we can, and especially let us enjoy our youth. This is perhaps the fundamental theme, but the variations are what matter and give a unique quality to the poem. Pasternak tells of a real situation—the poem is in a section called "songs to save her from boredom"—and a real landscape. But in this actual scene he shows how close he is to nature and what it means to him: he starts with a hint of active love and shows how into this doubts break with their disturbing presage that this happiness will not last for ever. Even the pleasures of love may become monotonous, and he looks for an escape which shall be more satisfying and more exciting:

> Kisses on the breast, like water from a pitcher!
> Not always, not ceaseless spurts the summer's well.
> Nor shall we raise up the hurdy-gurdy's clamour
> Each night from the dust with feet that stamp and trail.
>
> I have heard of age—those hideous forebodings!
> When no wave will lift its hands up to the stars.
> If they speak, you doubt it. No face in the meadows,
> No heart in the pools, no god among the firs.
>
> Rouse your soul to frenzy. Foaming all the day through.
> It's the world's midday. Have you no eyes for it?
> Look how in the heights thoughts seethe into white bubbles
> Of fir-cones, woodpeckers, clouds, pine-needles, heat.
>
> Here the rails are ended of the city tram-cars.
> Further, pines must do. Further, trams cannot pass.
> Further, it is Sunday. Plucking down the branches,
> Skipping through the clearings, slipping on the grass.
>
> Sifting midday light and Whitsunday and walking
> Woods would have us think the world is always so;
> They're so planned with thickets, so inspired with spaces,
> Spilling from the clouds on us, like chintz, below.

This is Pasternak's *L'Invitation au Voyage,* but he invites his beloved not to an imaginary paradise but to a real wood in a real summer, and the renewal of life which he seeks is to come not from intellectual or artistic pleasures but from the presence of nature. The almost pantheistic language of the second verse, with its fear that the years may turn the poet's beliefs into illusions, prepares the way to the enhancement of the senses which is to be found in the woods, to the frenzy and the foaming which he believes to be at his command. In such an expedition the driving force is the belief that nature provides an invigorating relaxation, not supernatural peace but an enlargement of faculties in young lovers.

In nature, as Pasternak sees it, human beings are a constituent part. It interpenetrates their being and controls them in such a way that they are in some sense its creatures, swayed by the moods and subject to the influences of their surroundings. This interrelation raises many questions, and Pasternak sometimes forces us to look in quite a new way at man in his natural setting. For instance in **"In the Wood"** the scene is again a summer day in a wood, where a couple are asleep while the dusk gradually advances. What holds the poem together is the idea that, as they sleep, nature constructs a kind of natural clock which tells the hours, though the couple are insensible to the passage of time. We might almost say that the fundamental theme of the poem is that time flies for lovers while they do not notice it; but this flight is vividly expressed through the actual place where the lovers sleep. They, their sleep, and their surroundings are a single unity. . . . The poem begins with a suggestion of love satisfied. The lovers rest in a state bordering on sleep, in which the man is vaguely conscious of the woman at his side. Then gradually nature gets to work and builds in the sky its own kind of clock, and this sign of passing time is not marked by the couple who are now asleep. To this extent the poem is concerned with the state that follows the consummation of love, but just as other poets set love against the menace of fleeting time, so Pasternak makes the passing of the hours an element in the whole situation. Nature herself marks the time, though the human beings do not notice what they are losing.

Nature, which displays so many different moods to human beings, needs a different symbol or myth for each of them, and Pasternak, who has no fixed mythology, creates a fresh myth for each new manifestation of natural powers. Nature is alive with presences whose character cannot be fully known but whose actions are observed with keen curiosity. Spirits are abroad, but spirits of no common sort and with few familiar traits. They can be mischievous and arouse annoyance and even dismay. They have some of the malice of Shakespeare's fairies, but they move in a familiar world and are quite recognisable once our attention is drawn to them. Everyone, for instance, knows the disturbed and disturbing air that comes after the end of winter, and nowhere is the change of season more gusty and more trying to the temper than in the Russian thaw. At such a time uneasy spirits seem to walk abroad, and Pasternak tells of one:

> The air is whipped by the frequent rain-drops;
> The ice is mangy and grey. Ahead
> You look for the skyline to awaken
> And start; you wait for the drone to spread.
>
> As always, with overcoat unbuttoned,
> With muffler about his chest undone,
> He pursues before him the unsleeping
> Silly birds and chases them on.
>
> Now he comes to see you, and, dishevelled,
> The dripping candles he tried to snuff,

> Yawns, and remembers that now's the moment
> To take the hyacinths' night-caps off.
>
> Out of his senses, ruffling his hair-mop,
> Dark in his thought's confusion, he
> Leaves you quite dumfounded with a wicked
> Stupid tale that he tells of me.

The chief character is not named; he is simply "he" and is known from what he does. He rises out of the uneasy atmosphere, and his character and actions embody its untidy, restless, teasing spirit. He starts trouble not only by frightening the birds and making the candles flicker but in human beings. The poet feels the uneasiness spread to his companion and have the effect of a story told against himself. The season has in it a disturbing and grating presence, a kind of Puck, but a Puck who rises out of the time of year and is known only from his disorderly and malicious pranks.

This sense of natural powers at work in the world may even take on an almost tragic intensity. The Russian autumn has been sung by many poets, and Tyutchev more than once told of its melancholy character. In **"Spasskoye"** Pasternak does something of the same kind, but with a more poignant and more personal note. He takes the moment when the summer is over and autumn comes with falling leaves, the felling of trees, rising mists and anticipations of winter. What strikes him is the sense of decay and death, of lessened vitality and of painful separation. His imagery contributes greatly to the emotional effect; for each image adds something to the interpretation of the situation and suggests sickness and death. But behind the imagery and the description there is something which only Pasternak can convey, a situation in which man is so entangled in his natural surroundings that they dictate his moods and make him seem part of themselves:

> Unforgettable September is strewn about Spasskoye.
> Is to-day not the time to leave the cottage here?
> Beyond the fence Echo has shouted with the herdsman
> And in the woods has made the axe's stroke ring clear.
>
> Last night outside the park the chilling marshes shivered.
> The moment the sun rose it disappeared again.
> The hare-bells will not drink of the rheumatic dew-drops,
> On birches dropsy swells a dirty lilac stain.
>
> The wood is melancholy. What it wants is quiet
> Under the snows in bear-dens' unawaking sleep;
> And there among the boles inside the blackened fences
> Jaws of the columned park, like a long death-list, gape.
>
> The birchwood has not ceased to blot and lose its colour,
> To thin its watery shadows and grow sparse and dim.
> He is still mumbling,—you're fifteen years old again now,
> And now again, my child, what shall we do with them?

So many of them now that you should give up
  playing,
They're like birds in bushes, mushrooms along
  hedges.
Now with them we've begun to curtain our horizon
And with their mist to hide another's distances.

On his death-night the typhus-stricken clown
  hears tumult,
The gods' Homeric laughter from the gallery.
Now from the road, in Spasskoye, on the tim-
  bered cottage
Looks in hallucination the same agony.

The poem is built on a clear pattern. The first three verses set out the scene in its melancholy and decay. The actors are the natural features of the landscape—the echo, the marshes, the harebells, the trees, all of which are ailing and suffering. This sense of doom reaches its climax in the comparison of the trees in the park to an obituary column in a newspaper. In the fourth verse the purpose of this detailed setting emerges mysteriously and allusively. The undescribed "he" is surely one of Pasternak's natural powers, the genius of the place at this season who haunts and dominates the wooded park. It makes the poet feel as if he were again fifteen years old and again suffering from some childish melancholy and uncertainty with the sense that comes at such an age that life has lost its range and contracted its horizon. This feeling dominates the present moment and gives to the cottage and its surroundings a tragic air, as if it were being mocked by inhuman powers, like the people in the gallery of a theatre, in the hour of its death. The tense poignancy of the close is enhanced by the suggestion that the poet has been thrown back into his childhood and feels some old misery, awakened by the chance air of the season. All this is forced on him by natural powers at work in Spasskoye. He is their victim, and in their dealings with him they show the callous indifference which the ancient gods showed to men. His keen ears and eyes miss nothing in the scene, and everything which Pasternak gets from them starts something else in his mind, some parallel or illustration or symbol, which drives home with compelling precision his full response to the situation. Nature is the first source of his poetry and calls out his finest powers.

Pasternak's view of nature is central to his work, and his poetry illustrates his belief that a creative force is at work in everything and that elements in the natural scene are as powerful as those in man and closely connected with them. His special interest is in his contact or conflict with such powers. He sees himself and other men as moved by strange energies and influences which are not fully intelligible but can be grasped only through a special insight and represented only through myth or symbol. Even when he writes specifically about himself and his own feelings, his outlook is the same. He still treats of strange, undefined forces which sweep into or rush over him and are outside his control and full comprehension. This outlook, which rises from his acute sensibility, gives a special character to his poems of love. For him love breaks the ordinary rules of life and creates its own world. In **"From Superstition"** Pasternak shows how love transforms his circumstances and gives a new meaning to everything. For him "a box

with a red orange in it" is all the lodging that he now needs: the dappled wall-paper becomes an oak-tree: the entry to this setting is gained by song: when he kisses his beloved, he tastes violets: her dress is like a snowdrop which chirrups a greeting to April. The casual encounter takes on all the charm of the country in spring, and it is not surprising that the poet feels as if his beloved has taken his life down from the shelf and blown the dust off it. Love imposes its laws on reality and makes the lover enjoy a state which is more real than the reality around him. A similar capacity to transform is more elaborately and more forcibly portrayed in **"Do not touch"** where what looks like a pretty trope takes command of the poem and gives to it an unusual power. . . . [In the poem], the transforming power of love is displayed in the image of the white light which comes from the beloved and changes the poet's world. And this power, which arises from what might seem to be an unhealthy or abnormal condition, exerts itself especially on the poet's melancholy until it makes even that luminous.

If love is like this, it is a little disturbing. Such an incalculable power is not to be welcomed lightly. It comes from unplumbed depths of nature and may well cause havoc. That is why Pasternak sometimes treats of the disintegrating effects of love and shows how afraid he is of them. In one poem he draws a strong contrast between the ordinary view of love and his own. While other people treat weddings as occasions to get drunk and to shut "life, that is like a pearly dream by Watteau, into a snuff-box", he finds that it releases primaeval energies in him:

> Chaos again crawls out upon the world
> As in the ages when the fossils lived.

Ordinary people are jealous of him and do not like it when he raises a girl from the earth "like a bacchante from an amphora". But against this critical opposition his own powers are all the more enhanced. The Andes melt in his kisses: it is like dawn on the steppe where stars fall in dust. The result is that in commonplace surroundings, amid the flat ritual of marriage, a strange, chaotic power is released. Pasternak sees love as brutal, irrational, and uncontrollable; it breaks into life and turns everything upside down. It is therefore appropriate that his most effective love-poetry should be the series called **"Rupture"** which treats love as a morbid condition in which the mind is infected with a kind of disease and the lovers are haunted by a sense of shame and guilt:

> O grief, infected with lies in its roots,
> O sorrow, leprous sorrow!

For a moment Pasternak may accept love's illusions and imagine that he and his beloved can escape, like Actaeon and Atalanta, into the woods, but the mood does not last, and reality soon asserts itself again. At the end the separation comes, quietly, but not without leaving a wound. . . . Pasternak accepts love and its results because it is a natural process, but he finds in it much that is disturbing and distressing.

Most of this highly personal and lyrical poetry was written by Pasternak at a time when his country was in great turmoil and confusion. *My Sister, Life* was composed for the most part in the summer of 1917 between the February Revolution of Kerensky and the October Revolution of Lenin. *Themes and Variations* was written during the no less crowded and eventful period between the triumph of Bolshevism and the end of the Civil War. In these years, when the poetry of Mayakovsky and Khlebnikov was inspired by popular emotions and largely directed to revolutionary ends, Pasternak might seem to have kept himself detached and independent outside the battle. We might think that this time of violent changes made little impression on him: so faithful is he to his personal vision and to such themes as his immediate circumstances suggest to him. But this is to misunderstand him. Pasternak was neither unpolitical nor reactionary. As a boy of fifteen he had shared the revolutionary fervour of 1905. The Futurists were his friends, whose political aims and ambitions he shared. For him, as for them, the Revolution was a prodigious manifestation of natural forces which had hitherto lain dormant in Russia, and he could hardly fail to see that it answered to his own dynamic conception of life. In his own way his poetry contributes to the revolutionary period and owes much of its inspiration to the spirit of the time. But it is very much in his own way. Pasternak's manner of writing, sensitive, personal and lyrical, is quite different from the broken epics of Khlebnikov or the enthusiastic rhetoric of Mayakovsky. His genius forces him to assimilate his political experiences until they are part of himself and to present them precisely as he feels them. He understood the Revolution through his insight into the powers which stir in nature and in man, and it was this side of it that challenged his creative energies. It belonged to the same order of things as his other subjects, whether nature or love, and he wrote of it in the same way, as of something that touched him deeply in the roots of his being and was yet another sign of strange forces at work in the world.

The result is that Pasternak assimilates his political experiences so closely to his central outlook that he seems for the moment to detract from their importance and to reduce them to mere natural events. Yet this is precisely the importance that he finds in them. They are indeed natural events and therefore full of majesty and mystery. They are a special manifestation of the strange powers that can be observed in physical nature. Pasternak believes that, like other human actions, they rise naturally from the landscape and stand in some close relation to it. Even the Revolution is a natural event in the sense that it rises from the Russian soil no less than from the Russian soul. (pp. 141-50)

Pasternak is fully aware of the human side of the Revolution and sees that, though it holds out great promises, it also brings many anxieties and troubles. A hint of what he himself suffered in the first months after the Revolution and what solution he found may be seen in **"January 1918"** where he greets with relief the coming of a new year with its promise of better times. . . . [In the poem], as so often with Pasternak, the actual situation provides the symbols for something more abstract. After the suicidal terrors and deathly chill of the old year, the new year promises light and comfort and, above all, peace. Peace comes alike from nature and from men, both of whom are in their separate ways philosophers and know what it means. None the less the new year is not quite what is expected. It is noisy and vulgar and embarrassing. After the agonies and the sacrifices, after the bold Utopian hopes, reality gives something of a shock. But Pasternak accepts it with philosophic wisdom and cheerfulness and humour. The last two lines proclaim his trust in the future. The snow stands for the purifying forces which are abroad and will in the end produce a cure for present discontents. This poem shows the quality of Pasternak's detachment. He sees the events from his own point of view and is not afraid to say what he feels, but at the same time he appreciates their importance and foretells the good things that lie ahead.

The optimistic note on which this poem ends shows Pasternak's feeling towards his time. True to his trust that such an eruption of natural forces must in the end be right and prevail, he finds in them a source of vitality and energy. What matters for him is this release of nature's powers which bring man closer to itself. Pasternak is not a partisan of particular causes but a poet of the whole movement for liberation and a new life. That is why he is not too hard on his opponents. He feels that they have lost the battle and that they do not deserve too much attention. So he dismisses them ironically or contemptuously. He knows that there is a vast difference between his own exultant confidence and the straitened outlook of his adversaries, and that he has something which they cannot hope to have. What this means can be seen from **"May it be,"** written in 1919:

> Dawn shakes the candle, shoots a flame
> To light the wren, and does not miss.
> I search my memories and proclaim
> "May life be always fresh as this!"
>
> Like a shot dawn rang through the night.
> Bang bang it went. In swooning flight
> The wads of bullets flame and hiss.
> May life be always fresh as this.
>
> The breeze is at the door again.
> At night he shivered, wanted us.
> He froze when daybreak brought up rain.
> May life be always fresh as this.
>
> He is astonishingly queer.
> Why rudely past the gate-man press?
> Of course he saw "No thoroughfare".
> May life be always as fresh as this.
>
> Still with a handkerchief to shake,
> While mistress still, chase all about,
> While yet our darkness does not break,
> While yet the flames have not gone out.

The dawn symbolises the coming of the new order, and it breaks like a rifle-shot. The breeze shows that new movements are active, though their meaning is not fully understood and they do not conform to old proprieties and prohibitions. The poet welcomes the situation and knows that all will be well. In the last verse, the woman whom he addresses stands for the old ruling class which may for the moment continue its sentimental or authoritarian tasks but will before long have to change its ways. The poem is written in gaiety and confidence. What others may find frightening, Pasternak finds inspiring and exciting.

Pasternak's political poetry in the first years of the Revolution is nearly all composed in this special way. He tells how events strike him personally and what part they take in his scheme of things. But the Revolution called for more than this, and it was almost impossible for Pasternak to be deaf to it. Just as in these years Khlebnikov wrote heroic poems about Russian characters who fought for liberty, from the old rebel Stepan Razin to a nameless seamstress of 1917, so others felt the need to display the events of their time with a full sense of their grandeur. (pp. 151-54)

In nature, in love, in stirring political events Pasternak found the subjects of his mature poetry. In all of them was something primaeval and forceful which appealed strongly to him and echoed something in himself. This something was the spirit in which he composed poetry. He felt himself at home with such subjects because in them he saw powers at work which were closely related to his own powers when the spell of composition was on him. And just as these subjects excite his curiosity and vivid interest, so his own creative spirit is a burning question for him. He more than once writes about it and seems to have more than one view of it. Its aspects strike him differently at different times. He is so modest and truthful that we cannot

expect him to produce a grandiose metaphysic of art or even to reveal his whole feelings about it. But his career shows how much it means to him and how he puts it first even when he feels a strong call to serve other ends. Sometimes when he speaks about poetry he seems to assume an ironical or paradoxical air as if he were on the defensive and unwilling to put forward his whole case. But this is the reflection of an extreme honesty which refuses to speak dogmatically about something which means a great deal to him but cannot really be grasped or explained. . . . Nor is he prepared to make vast claims for the mood in which the poet composes. There is nothing of Blok's "Artist" in what Pasternak says of his work, no timeless ecstasy or vision of Paradise. . . . He even denies that composition gives him any pleasure and says in **"Poetry"**:

> You're summer with a third-class ticket,
> A suburb and not a refrain.

It is as stifling as May or a crowded quarter of the town or a fort over which clouds pass. Even the final consummation is not claimed to be at all impressive or wonderful:

> Poetry, when an empty truism,
> Like a zinc bucket, stands below
> The tap, is certain to be spouting.
> The copy-book is open. Flow!

This is Pasternak's modest way of not claiming too much for his art. It is, it seems, a perfectly natural process and he must not pretend that it is more.

Yet it is a natural process and all that this means to Pasternak. Whatever difficulty he may find in explaining his art to others or in justifying its place in society, he is quite confident and explicit about what it means to himself. In one poem he admits that a poet is a peculiar kind of being, but insists that he follows a special destiny and wins special rewards. He looks back on childhood and tells how from the beginning he has known the magical power of words and found his own most vivid experiences through them:

> So they begin. With two years gone
> From nurse to countless tunes they scuttle.
> They chirp and whistle. Then comes on
> The third year, and they start to prattle.
>
> So they begin to see and know.
> In din of started turbines roaring,
> Mother seems not their mother now,
> And you not you, and home is foreign.
>
> What meaning has the menacing
> Beauty beneath the lilac seated,
> If to steal children's not the thing?
> So first they fear that they are cheated.
>
> So ripen fears. Can he endure
> A star to beat him in successes,
> When he's a **Faust**, a sorcerer?
> So first his gipsy life progresses.
>
> So from the fence where home should lie
> In flight above are found to hover
> Seas unexpected as a sigh.
> So first iambics they discover.
>
> So summer nights fall down and pray

Sketch of young Boris writing, by Leonid Pasternak, 20 July 1898.

"Thy will be done" where oats are sprouting,
And menace with your eyes the day.
So with the sun they start disputing.

So verses start them on their way.

This is Pasternak's apology. It tells how marvellous discoveries reward him for feeling that he is odd and unlike other men. His course follows an inevitable rhythm from the start, and though his early shocks are more violent than those of other men, his compensations are correspondingly great. He has his wonderful dreams, his moments of rapture and exaltation, his conviction that he is at one with nature and shares her strength. By such means Pasternak does more than defend himself against utilitarian or mechanistic notions of poetry: he shows that so far from being an artificial adjunct of society he is a magician who releases nature's powers through his art.

Pasternak responds to the special character of his calling by a special sense of the responsibilities which it puts upon him. He believes, above all, that everything that he writes must be a work of art, complete and independent with its own life, the final vehicle by which experience is selected and organised and transformed into a permanent shape. He also believes that no work of art has any value unless it is true in a rigorous and exacting sense, true not merely to fact but to experience, to all that the poet sees in it and feels about it. This double ideal is perhaps responsible for his complexities and roughnesses, but it is no less responsible for his final success and for his special importance. In a revolutionary age Pasternak has seen beyond the disturbed surface of things to the powers behind it and found there an explanation of what really matters in the world. Through his unerring sense of poetry he has reached to wide issues and shown that the creative calling, with its efforts and its frustrations and its unanticipated triumphs, is, after all, something profoundly natural and closely related to the sources of life. (pp. 155-58)

> *C. M. Bowra, "Boris Pasternak, 1917-1923,"*
> *in his* The Creative Experiment, *Macmillan &*
> *Co. Ltd., 1949, pp. 128-58.*

[Pasternak's] idiom is like a mosaic made of broken pieces. The fragments are shapeless, and if they finally fit within the pattern of a line, or within the design of a poem, it is only because of the poet's will.
The cement holding them together is either syntax or rhythm; more frequently, both. From his early beginnings, Pasternak tightened the syntax of Russian poetic speech as no modern poet had ever done.

—*Renato Pogglio*, "Poets of Today," *in his* The Poets of Russia: 1890-1930, *1960.*

Aleksis Rannit   (essay date 1959)

[Rannit was a Russian art historian and author. In the following excerpt, he delineates the symbolism, imagery, and rhythm in Pasternak's early poetry.]

Strongly influenced by the symbolist and impressionist tendencies of the times, Pasternak's first collection of poems, *Bliznetz v tuchakh* (*A Twin in the Clouds*), was completed in 1914 and published that same year in Moscow by the literary circle "Lirika." This volume has been strangely overlooked, bibliographically and critically, in even the best articles on Pasternak's poetry that have appeared in English, those by Sir C. M. Bowra, C. L. Wrenn, and Ernest J. Simmons. Pasternak's third book of poems, *Sestra moya Zhizn'* (*My Sister, Life*) (1922), has often been called, even by serious critics, his debutant work, and others have mistaken the second volume of his verses, *Poverkh barierov* (*Above the Barriers*) (1917), for the bibliographic beginning of his literary career.

In a solemn foreword to *A Twin in the Clouds,* the poet Nikolai Aseyev declared that Pasternak's verses would echo strongly in the dead silence of Russian symbolism, but the volume won only a limited recognition, for two reasons. In the first place his work was still imitative; the young poet had not yet achieved the intensity of rhythmic control nor the dramatic sharpness of imagery that were to become his conspicuous qualities. A deeper reason for his failure to win recognition, however, lay outside his own merits. These early poems, already somewhat like atonal chamber music, reveal the power of a fervent, if intellectually loose, imagination and the clear beginnings of individuality in rhythm and color. But they were quite overshadowed by the extraordinary renaissance of Russian poetry that occurred at this time, a re-birth comparable to the first great period led by Aleksander Pushkin and Mikhail Lermontov in the early nineteenth century. (pp. 557-58)

Boris Pasternak was organizationally involved with a Moscow group of Futurists and it is against this whole entangled background of the culmination of Symbolism, the violence of Futurism, and the austere discipline of Acmeism that his dramatic, well-trained voice must be judged. In his second volume of poems *Poverkh barierov* (*Above the Barriers*) Pasternak continued to search for a convincing synthesis between symbolism and futurism. This shows clearly that his futurist association was quite a loose one, because futurism stressed only the dynamism of the new era and opposed completely a culture which looks to the past. Pasternak was always aware of the great common laws of the past while at the same time penetrating with his visionary, prophetic eye, the regions of future imagery. (p. 559)

Impulsively accented rhythm is probably the most distinctive criterion of Russian futurist poetry. Whitman's work certainly gave impetus to this movement of unshackling verse from traditional metrical pattern. The rhythmical ideas of Whitman were, however, dynamized and brought to a new energy by the Russians, who prolonged the structural forms in space, opened them up, and revealed the violence in their rapidity. In this poetry, even though mostly rhymed, the patterns of time value are not allotted to consecutive elements, the implication being that a particular time scheme should recur un-systematically. Boris Pasternak has tried to write in this manner of the broken line, although with considerable circumspection. A provocative example of this kind of experiment is Pasternak's longer poem **"Gorod"** (**"The City"**) written in Tikhiye Gory in 1916. But notwithstanding such temporary programmatic agreement with his fellow futurists, he soon recognized that the particular quality of his own genius was not adapted to the loose framework of the futurist poetics. Even while applying the new formal elements of futurism, Pasternak could not accept the metric irregularity of Mayakovski and others. Even while writing "white verses" (free verse) he would maintain a regularity of rhythmic pattern within the line and in corresponding lines. He remained too much a man of tradition to break with the regularly repeated measure and the regular stanzaic configuration of classical verse. Though rejecting, early, the mystical ideas of Russian symbolism, he remained in his metrics a faithful disciple of the symbolistic and other previous poets.

Within the clearly emphasized strophic structure Pasternak creates, however, in accordance with his own psychophysical predestination, a new, elementary, and exciting rhythm. This is achieved, technically, by the use of a high proportion of strongly accented words and by a dramatic use of the caesura. In a typical Pasternakian stanza, the caesura comes at a different position in each line and is frequently employed for an exceptional emphasis. The natural pauses are sharply delineated, and even in short lines the reader experiences a swift, insistent musicality. . . . In the invention of new rhymes Pasternak has probably no rivals in modern Russian poetry. Specifically he explores a new method, attempted by Igor' Severyanin with certain classical or "perfect" rhymes but developed and successfully regulated by Pasternak, according to which only the consonants and vowels to the left of the accented syllable are of decisive importance. (Consonants and vowels in the reminder of the word may vary considerably without destroying the effective rhyme of the stressed sounds.) This kind of rhyming is done by Pasternak with far-reaching virtuosity in the creation of new masculine, feminine, and polysyllabic rhymes: zdés'—zvezdé, prostór—stó, svályan—razválin, ogné—gnév, zamerlá—Tamerlan, orátor—utrátoi, pomerántsem—marátsia, prodolzháya—luzháyek; etc.

Pasternak's next two volumes of poetry, *Sestra moya zhizn'* (*My Sister, Life*) and *Temy i variatzii* (*Themes and Variations*) appeared in 1922 and 1923 and are most striking for their profusion and magnificence of metaphor. For Pasternak, metaphor is the synthesis of several units of observation in one commanding image. Associated with and conditioned by the rhythms of thought and feeling, it becomes emotional, intellectual, spiritual at the same time. There are conflicting views concerning the tornado of Pasternak's images. One puts the accent on poetic *form* and its autonomy; the other on psychological *force* and its impetus—a debate which revives the traditional dichotomy of classicism and romanticism, of being and becoming, of the Latin and the Russian temperaments. Erenburg and many others have seen in Pasternak *the* incarnation of ro-

manticism. Yet the Pasternakian epistemology is not exclusively emotional and intuitive, although it stresses the necessity of fullness and depth of feeling.

Like most romanticists, Pasternak rejects a reason which is purely analytical and inadequate to the task of comprehending the Absolute. For him knowing is always living, and he approaches nature through inspiration, longing, and sympathy but also through rational comprehension. In Pasternak's case romanticism is a metaphysical form of expressionism, although in some of his debutant poems his metaphors are unable to convey both realistic meaning and expressionistic doctrine. His intense interest in nature and his attempt to seize natural phenomena in a direct and immediate manner link him strongly with German and English romantic poets. He is a classicist in poetic theory, however, constantly seeking the perfect balance between body and spirit and, as a formalist, always speaking for an inner perfective principle as the determinate essence of poetry. Again his form is a *forma non subsistens* and *materialis,* the existence of which depends on matter, without which it cannot endure or be active.

The metaphors of Pasternak create a reality through lyrical allusion rather than representative illusion. The problem of simultaneity and contraposition of sign and image has preoccupied the poet from the beginning of his career. In *My Sister, Life* and **Themes and Variations** he achieved, through successive juxtaposition and superimposition and fragmentation of images, effects similar to those of the cubist paintings of Braque, Picasso, and Juan Gris. Nevertheless even in this period of extremely analytic and systematic experimentation Pasternak escaped the danger of hermetism evident in cubist painting.

The idea of the fragmentation of empirical reality and of the language of poetry came from [Aleksander] Blok, of whom Pasternak says that he "had everything that goes to make a great poet: fire, tenderness, emotion, his own image of the world." "Of all these qualities and many more," Pasternak singles out the side of Blok's genius "that has, perhaps, left the deepest impression on me and for that reason seems to me to be the most important one, namely Blok's impetuosity, his roving intentness, the rapidity of his observation. . . . Adjectives without nouns, predicates without subjects, hide-and-seek, breathless agitation, nimbly darting little figures, abruptness—" and then he adds: "how that style seemed to agree with the spirit of the age, hiding, secretive, underground." How well, we may add, these observations match the quality of Pasternak's own work! With a much greater rapidity of thought than Blok's, and with a manly vigor seldom present with such intensity in Blok's poetry, Pasternak endeavors to destroy the materiality of objects and to depict kinetic and impelling effects by the principle of simultaneity, in ways only partially derived from Blok. In a great number of poems from the years 1914 to 1920 and poems in the two collections of 1922 and 1923, an impulsive imagination reigns supreme, as far as the free flow of images is concerned. Around 1914 the poet discovers in this free creative stream from the subconscious *the* expression of the super-reality, a concept that becomes known in 1924 as "surrealism." Yet at the same time a great measure of conscious and even rational control seems to be indicated by the high degree of formal organization in all this poetry of Pasternak's.

His metaphoric expressions and his unexpected adjectives owe much of their strength and violent effect to the fact that Pasternak retains enough of the natural direct style of everyday speech to make his deviations from its natural shapes and forms seem radical or brutal or even vulgar deformations. Slang occurs next to the most sophisticated reinterpretations of Plato or the most subtle suggestions of tenderness. The romantic melodiousness of the tonic-syllabic Russian verse, so prominent in Blok, does not satisfy the young Pasternak, who instead produces a flexible tonality and a new, swift, pointed and feverish rhythm, generally a rising rhythm based on iambic, and anapaestic forms. These poems of emotion and imagination, serious and exalted in mood and language, should really be called modern odes, for they have often also the choral qualities of the old Greek "songs." Pasternak's *tempi* tend to grow more and more pronounced, his contrasts more and more accentuated—and his meter more and more classical in regularity. A constantly pulsating flow of matching vowels and consonants, words, phrases, and symbols is transmitted as a sharp rhapsody of light. This light strikes the masses of metonymy to give the shadow of the simple wording its unifying principle and its full value. Hence even though many details are still treated in a realistic manner, Pasternak transmutes their reality into a vision, of stormy radiance. Marina Tsvetayeva, in a hymn-like essay on *My Sister, Life,* calls this work a downpour of light ("Svetovoi liven'") and "poetry of eternal masculinity," and we fully agree. The unique contribution of this volume lies in the successful creation of an "impossible" synthesis between a tempest of expressionistic imagery and a classical regularity of meter.

The thunderburst of similar literary monads, translogical ideas, depth paradoxes, and imagistic patterns is elegantly and at the same time vigorously transformed into crystalline metrical shapes arranged in poetic perspective with geometrical precision. Certainly this is possible only because of the poet's extraordinary command of the principles of rhythm—rhythm as a rational, sensorial, and psychological force. For both the vocal rhythm and the ideational rhythm are brought by Pasternak into a strongly felt and tersely articulated unity. In all his poetry what most strikes the student is its rhythmically creative zest and power. Readers unable to follow Pasternak's poetry in the original and forced to make shift with mostly mediocre translations, may approximate the aesthetic situation of *My Sister, Life* by imagining a generally irrelative but for once convincing union between the automatic expression of a Whitman and the Parnassian perfection of a José Maria de Hérédia.

The companion volumes *My Sister, Life* and *Themes and Variations* mark the end, aside from some independent poems written in 1923 and 1924, of the comparatively pure isolation of Pasternak as a free man and an individualistic artist. In 1924 he wrote a long poem called **"High Malady,"** with the vision of Lenin in the background. And other long poems with the social accent followed, *The*

Year 1905, Lieutenant Schmidt, and the novel in verse *Spektorski.* These new works brought out the violence of the historical scene of the Revolution and the drama of the poet's own idealism. An analysis of this new era in Pasternak's work would require another and different attempt at criticism, necessarily in part sociological.

The author of these first four books of poetry which we have surveyed is a neo-Kantian disciple and a free follower of symbolist aesthetics, who believes, with Newton, that time is independent of and prior to events, that it flows equally without regard to matter in its path. In a militant, ideological article published in the *Black Cup,* the second book of the literary circle "Tzentrifuga," Pasternak declares:

> There is no force on this earth which would compel us, even in our words, to start preparing the history of tomorrow. Neither will we, following our free volition, attempt such an action. In Art we see clearly the peculiar situation of the *extemporal,* the only task of which consists in the need of its brilliant artistic realization. . . . We will never touch the time as we have never done it in the past. . . . Among the objects which can be conquered by the unarmed eye, the phantom of history is now appearing to the armed eye. We do wish not to lull our cognition with pitiful and foggy generalities. And we must not cheat ourselves: the whole reality *is* in the process of self-decomposition. Decomposing itself, it moves towards two contrasted polarities: toward Poetry and History. Both of them are a priori independent and absolute.

In these lines the *morale esthétique,* the subjective philosophy of young Pasternak, rhythmicist and metaphorist, found its definitive expression. (pp. 560-65)

> *Aleksis Rannit, "The Rhythm of Pasternak,"*
> *in* Bulletin of The New York Public Library,
> *Vol. 63, No. 11, November, 1959, pp. 555-67.*

The Times Literary Supplement (review date 1962)

[*The following is a laudatory review of* In the Interlude: Poems 1945-1960, *an English translation of Pasternak's later poetry.*]

> Creation's way is—to give all.
> And not to bluster or eclipse:
> How mean, when you don't signify,
> To be on everybody's lips!

So runs . . . one of Pasternak's last poems, **"It's Unbecoming".** But Pasternak, who never blustered, will be "on everybody's lips" as far as one can see into the future. He has a wholeness, both as artist and as the man we see behind the art, that puts him effortlessly among the great.

Pasternak ended as he had begun, as a poet. Nevertheless it seems quite understandable, in retrospect, that he should have spent the most creative of his middle years writing *Dr. Zhivago.* The poems themselves, in their variety and in their humanity, reveal Pasternak as a man of a comprehensive naturalness who would wish to speak of "the prose" as well as "the passion" of his experience. In his early autobiography, *Safe Conduct,* a glittering and arcane piece of writing that, set against what followed, looks like the masterpiece of his anti-self, Pasternak tells how he became aware of the Bible as the "notebook of humanity . . . vital not when it is obligatory, but when it is amenable to all the comparisons with which the ages receding from it gaze back at it". These are phrases that have an aptness when applied to Pasternak's own later work. On the level of great art it has the ease and spontaneity of a personal notebook. But its language at its finest is the language of that symbolism which is "amenable to all the comparisons" that might be made, out of their own experience, by multitudes of readers in different times and places.

The poems written by Pasternak after the war, some of them brought out of Russia in manuscript by his friends, fall into three groups. First . . . come the supposed poems of Yury Zhivago, then some thirty poems that were to have formed a sequence called "When the Skies Clear", and finally ten poems written in the last year of the poet's life. All, in their very different ways, have a directness and simplicity quite unlike the ardent and ingenious struggle with language that goes on in Pasternak's early poetry. The change in Pasternak's style has been compared to Yeats's; but it catches the character of Pasternak's work better perhaps to say that we would have seen something similar in English poetry if Yeats had had Hardy's personality incorporated in him too, and lending its own influence to Yeats's last years.

The Zhivago poems have a special interest, since in them Pasternak did something original and dramatic. If part of the satisfaction and achievement of Yury Zhivago in the novel was to lie in his poetry, then it would give a particular resonance to the point if some of his poems were there to be read as well. Yet Pasternak could quite properly make these poems at the same time his own poems, alternative expressions of some of the themes and symbolic happenings in the novel: for if the poems were, so to speak, impossible to attribute confidently either to Zhivago or Pasternak, that would demonstrate perfectly the essential objectivity and impersonality of true poetry. Apart from their attribution to Zhivago, and the occasional transmuted reference to incidents described in Zhivago's life, then, these poems are no different from the others. In poems like **"Spring Floods"**, **"Explanation"**, or **"Autumn"**, the coincidence in the description of simple, vivid event and symbol is complete. No generalizing link is necessary between the experience described and the reader's experience—the description is done in such a way that it is the living counterpart of any reader's potential experience. The effect of these symbolic poems might be compared with a feeling described by Pasternak in a poem called **"Everything Came True"**:

> A jay flies screeching overhead
> Into a birch grove's emptiness
> That, like an uncompleted building.
> Uprears itself in nakedness:
>
> And through its archways I can see
> My whole life's future course lie bare
> For all its small particulars
> Are outlined and perfected there.

But, as has been said, there is extraordinary variety in these poems. Lucent pieces of sheer description of the Russian landscape; poems that concentrate in intense aphorism—**"In Hospital,"** the realization addressed to God " . . . my life and my fate Are gifts without price you have shed!"; blunt satire on literary critics; poems as frank in their personal complaints as some of Hardy's; eloquent pieces on love, laconic pieces on desire, serene returns to the past; all these are gathered around the richer symbolic presentations of events, or cross the borderline and join them. The poems of Pasternak's last year are outstandingly fine: the passionate evocation of the life of a city, partner to Yeats's "mackerel-crowded seas"—

> Porches and stairs and flats upcurled
> In which all passions are enwhirled
> In order to remake the world;

the rejection of Soviet charges that he was interested in political upheaval—

> It is not some upheaval or uprising
> Can lead us to the new life we desire—
> But open truth and magnanimity
> And the storm within a soul afire;

the desperation of **"Winter Festivities"**—

> We need Eternity to stand
> Among us like a Christmas tree.

> *"Pasternak the Poet," in* The Times Literary Supplement, *No. 3141, May 11, 1962, p. 340.*

Angela Livingstone (essay date 1963)

[*An English critic, editor, translator, and educator, Livingstone edited and translated* Pasternak on Art and Creativity *(1985). In the following essay, she discusses the implications stemming from Pasternak's concentration on ordinary life in* When the Weather Clears.]

These poems [in **When the Weather Clears**] are among the last that Boris Pasternak wrote; they were written during and after the writing of *Dr. Zhivago.* They can be divided into two main groups (although some will belong to both groups): poems of personal confession and—the larger group—poems that describe some natural or urban scene. I will speak of the latter first.

In 1923 Marina Tsvetaeva wrote, of Pasternak's relation to [*byt*]—the common environment of everyday life—that it was to him as the earth is to the foot of someone walking: a moment's contact and a flying off. This single image sums up much of his earlier poetry. The Pasternak of thirty years later has a different relation to reality. Now all the ordinary things of daily living (the trains and houses, cupboards and Christmas trees, stamp collections, drainpipes), as well as the woods and steppe and lakes, seem the firm, accepted ground to stand upon. So a less imaginative view of walking is appropriate: every step of the walker comes down on the ground.

But he believes now in that ground in a way he did not before. He no longer feels that, as poet, he will transform the given world into something new and intense and extraordinary. Instead, he will go along with it, letting its whole presence work on him, until it yields its own splendid moment, its promise, its own transformation. He no longer seizes, but patiently contemplates, until similes arise as of themselves. Thus, the sunlight's striking through the leaves recalls stained glass windows in a cathedral, with their pictures of saints 'looking into eternity'; warmly, thankfully, he accepts the image, and says:

> World's tabernacle, Nature,
> I stand through your long service,
> Seized by a sacred trembling,
> In tears of happiness.

This is the poem that gives its title to the volume. Many others have a similar pattern: a landscape is transformed by the weather or season so that the thought of some universal change or religious revelation is quickened in it. **'Avenue of limes'**, through imagery evoking the interior of a cathedral, describes a dark walk of trees, blossoming into something marvellous and light. **'Autumn forest'**, similarly constructed, has, not light dispersing darkness, but the wakeful communicative sound of cocks breaking through a sleepy silence: there is such a waking up that the forest itself, opening out, 'sees new sights/Fields, distance and blue skies.' In **'Ploughing'** he asks what has happened to the usual landscape; for, transformed by the season and its work, it seems new, as if the limits were erased from earth and sky and—again an unemphasized suggestion of biblical imagery—as if mountains had been made level and the valley had been swept, and the trees (like people?) had stretched out to their full height. Everything has become clean and clear.

In other poems, though there may be no such definite idea of transfiguration, yet there are often images like that of the sun lighting up small mushrooms in the dark woods, or of the elk that for one precarious moment enchants the grove as it stands there and drinks; or again, the impossibility of walking in the Autumn forest without making a great clatter of leaves 'so that everyone knows',—images which suggest that clarity, meaning, beauty are constantly being created and discovered. Frequent metaphors of book and speech and language add the idea that this is something readable, to be interpreted.

Pasternak does not exactly interpret anything. At his most explicit, he merely says that a better future is coming. In two or three poems he describes a sense of seeing the future. For instance, when the bare trees make the forest seem opened up and spacious, the poet feels he is looking right through time, sees what is to come and rejoices in its certainty and safety (**'Fulfilment'**, **'Round the Turning'**). And again, in **'After the Storm'**, 'everything is alive with the change of weather' and 'memories of half a century recede with the passing storm. . . . It is time to give way to the future.'

The epilogue of the long poem **'Bacchanalia'**, which is seemingly about Pasternak himself, reaffirms the theme of the clarity and purity that must follow the days of confusion and strain. But there sounds also a note of sadness or weakness, as though the poet is remembering that he himself is at an end. It is true that after the Bacchanalia flowers will shed their sweetness from a vase; after the heartless party the plates are washed and everything is forgot-

ten. But the lonely man who couldn't get intoxicated and could only find truth when he recognized the tradition of sacrifice still enacted in **'Maria Stuart'** and could only find happiness at moments with another isolated person, will also be forgotten and left in the past.

However, Pasternak is sure that he will come into his own for, like Maria Stuart and like the actress who represented her, he has played not to his own age but 'to the centuries'. The theme of the artist's fame—that he cannot have it in his life and should not seek it (he must hide away, work in secret, be unknown) but that if he works for eternity it will be his (and therefore, in a sense, already is)—this theme, which is thus also that of sacrifice and of faith, runs through much of the poetry in previous volumes, and also through the second group of poems in **When the Weather Clears.**

These poems contain certain conclusions about life and show a final attitude of simple-hearted love and acceptance, as well as a resolution to keep going to the end, 'to be alive, only alive, only alive to the end'. On the whole they partake of the tone of adopted commonsense and decision, of self-confidence mixed with careful understatement, which is heard in the opening stanza of the poem **'Bread'**:

> You've been heaping up unwritten
> Conclusions half a century,
> And now if you're not a halfwit
> You must have understood something.

It seems Pasternak is determined to be glad, grateful, responsive, and to work on with faith; but—and this is my main point—the poems are often unsatisfying because the determination seems to exceed the force of his feeling about these things. Addressing himself, with something like Chekhov's 'one must drill oneself' in mind, he repeats very simple injunctions and morals, such as:

> But one must live without imposture . . .

or:

> Don't sleep, don't sleep, keep working

or again:

> You understood that idleness is a curse,
> And there's no happiness without heroism.

Behind the bright faith lies a dull effort, which is sad, and all the more sad because it is not admitted as sadness. Pasternak does not have a tragic view of life, and he even seems to be carefully avoiding such a view. Part of his insistence on simplicity is the insistence on optimism. He resolutely praises and thanks wherever he can. Just as, in an earlier volume, he says 'blagodarstvuyte' (thank you) to nature for being so beautiful, here he says 'spasibo' (thank you) to women for having meant much in his life; he writes gratefully of Blok for having been what he was; and he thanks all the people who have written him letters in his time of trouble. If he finds himself risking a tone of despair or regret he immediately overcomes it and turns the poem's course back to the affirmative. Thus **'Soul'**, which is a poem of mourning for friends who have suffered and died, is laconic, almost noncommittal, and ends with a pointing back to life and construction: for, having compared his soul to a vault, a sobbing lyre, a funeral urn, and a morgue, he finally compares it to a mill, that can change dung, lost experience, ruined lives, into the elements of new growth. Life must come forth out of the very substance of death—this is also a main motif in *Dr. Zhivago.* It is a moving poem, and yet it is not strong with the sense of the survived struggle, the endured despair, that its writer must have known. Two other poems about his own unhappy position fail to be moving at all, except if the reader deliberately relates them to the biographical circumstances, but then he is moved by the memory of the man, not by his poem. These are **'God's World'** and—a poem not included in the London publication of *When the Weather Clears* but to be found in the Complete Works— **'The Nobel Prize'.** The sadness in the first poem tries to be humorous and succeeds in being trivial. In the second a bewildered grief is expressed, but slackly, and it is likewise subordinated to what is here a disturbingly vague faith in a good future:

> Yet, though almost at the grave,
> I believe a time will come
> When the force of malice and meanness
> Will be conquered by the good.

In spite of this example, Pasternak's faith in the possibility of change, his images of freshness and illumination—these are what is most impressive in the present volume; but this invites comparison with a similar faith and similar language in the work of his youth, and if we make this comparison we shall find that the later work (i.e. both groups of poems I have distinguished) is weaker. Though Pasternak himself might reject tragedy (to see himself tragically may well be for him part of the romantic exaltation of the 'life of the poet' which he renounced when he met Mayakovsky), yet something tragic seems to have happened to him as a poet.

His faith in the future does reasonably follow from ideas latent in his much earlier writings—it is in a way a development of the same thing—but now the immediacy and the tension—the fight—has gone out of it. It is more an expounded faith than an urgent experience.

The poems of *My Sister, Life* (1917) implied a world constantly in process, in movement; ceaselessly changing and developing. The images were full of a dynamism and force, as though everything were straining, rushing forward and colliding, leaning and impinging, one thing on another, more powerfully than our ordinary sight had supposed. Even leaves at a window did not merely grow there but—

> There's a pressing and crowding of leaves at the
>   window.

Dawn was not simply a change of light:

> Dawn, like a tick, bit into the bay.

The steppe itself changes, as a train passes through it:

> The steppe is crumbling between step and star

It was as if the poet, unable to pause in his vigilance and with no opportunity for reflection, had to capture the essence of one after another unique and amazing image

flung up by the continuous process of change. If February came he straightaway had to answer:

> February! Get ink and weep! . . .

One sensed some living creative power—its robustness and strength and pressure—working in nature and identically working in art.

In every moment there is new life: this was then a sensation, which came upon him as if from outside, and each poem seemed the result of an intellectual fight to control and form the jagged elements of intense perceptions, with always a risk of incomprehensibility. But now he is not overwhelmed, but more simply says: since something new is always coming, let us trust in the future. To support this trust, he notes all signs of hope and meaning in the world around him, to record them in a poetic form that is chiefly concerned to avoid extravagance. He even explains that he would like to write poetry now, not in the way he once recommended—as casually and generously as a garden scattering its colours of amber and lemon—but with a plan, laying out his verses like a planned garden in which lime-trees grow, one after the other, in rows. All is to be modest and regular.

Now this does describe the poems in the present volume. Instead of the old casual splendour, they do contain rows of rather general and simple abstractions. Abstract words, in the early verse, always dissolved immediately into particular images, but here they are ranged together without concrete detail. There are many lines of this sort that one would like to set against lines from his earlier poetry, to the advantage of the latter. In **'After the Storm',** for instance, which says that the artist washes all things clean and dyes them so that there come forth, in a transformed state,

> life, reality and past,

these words in their deliberately imprecise attempt to indicate everything at once, recall such an earlier use of the word 'life' as:

> My sister is life and today in a flood
> She is shattered in spring rain over all . . .

The two abstractions in the line:

> In the forest is quietness, silence . . .

could be contrasted with a line from **'The Weeping Garden'** (1917), with its greater delicacy of alliteration then characteristic of Pasternak:

> But quiet. Not a leaf rustles.

Or again, when reading the now typically summarizing lines:

> Amid the earthly rotation
> Of births, sorrows and deaths.

one may well recall the description of an actual birth in **'The Urals'** (from *Above the Barriers,* 1917), of a definite grief—in **'The End'** (from *My Sister, Life*), and of a particular death—**'Death of the Poet'** (from *Second Birth,* 1932).

Pasternak stands at a greater distance from the world than before; and the chief stylistic effect (or means) of this distance is, besides the use of abstractions, the device of listing, or enumeration. Nouns are put side by side, their connotations cut short by the comma, and offered to the reader in a kind of silence. The first poem of the volume consists very largely of lists, such as 'meadows, sedge and harvest, / peals of the storm', or 'the miracle / of farms, parks, groves and graves'. The unrhetorical, harmonious addition of word to word seems to indicate—without evoking—a bigger harmony that the poems will not deal with; and often it is an attempt to give discreet, unexaggerated praise to all the things of the earth, to get everything in that is worthy, to leave nothing out.

> We shuffle away
> To look for mushrooms.
> Road. Forests. Ditches.
> Milestones to left and right.

But there are also instances where the lists produce no other effect than that of a rather cautious flinging wide of arms and a calling out: look at all the things there are, for all are included and all are good! This thankful all-comprehension is often monotonous and unimaginative as in the poem **'In Hospital',** where an injured man, in emphatically commonplace and stupid circumstances, suddenly realizes he is to die. The poem's climax is:

> O Lord, how perfect
> Are your works, the sick man thought,
> Beds and people and walls,
> Night of death and the town in the night.

And at its worst it is almost meaningless, as in **'God's World':**

> Mountains, lands, borders and lakes,
> Peninsulas and continents,
> Discussions, reviews, surveys,
> Children, youths and old men.

The use of enumeration is a weakness throughout the present volume. It appears as the result of a decision by a great poet of detail, a poet who once confessed:

> I don't know if the question
> Of the after-life is decided,
> But life, like silence
> In Autumn, is full of detail . . .

to go in for the generalities he then eschewed, the result of his attempt to see things more wholly—not only in the novel, which, as he recognised, was adapted to carrying such a vision, but also in his last poems.

There is one poem—that which opens the collection, and which, as I have noted, contains very many examples of nouns in lists—where Pasternak voices a certain sense of impotence. It begins:

> I want in everything
> The heart of the matter,
> In work, in the quest for a way,
> In the chaos of feelings.

This and the next two stanzas name over the things from which he wishes to obtain the essence: the past, its causes, its roots; fate. . . . They are recorded as if in a column,

with much repetition and wholly abstract vocabulary, which continues in:

> To live, think, feel, love . . .

Nothing could be further from an actual capturing and conveying of [the heart of the matter]. The poet goes on to express a particular wish for something he feels he cannot achieve:

> O if only I could,
> Though but in part,
> I would write eight lines
> On the properties of passion!
>
> On its lawlessness and sins,
> Pursuits and chases,
> Breathless impromptus,
> Elbows and palms.

Now, in fact, this very task has been accomplished, forty years before, almost to the last detail; for there is a poem in *Themes and Variations* (1923) which offers, in one line more than the eight here desired, the 'properties of passion', not abstractly but concretely, passionately; and not only does it include all the elements mentioned above but it even uses in prominent positions such words as pursuit, elbows, palms.

Pasternak has not forgotten his previous work, nor does he long for a lost capacity. He means, as is seen by the next line—'I would deduce its law'—that what he really thinks he should write about is not the essence of passion but its law, its principle. He wishes, not to present it any more, but to indicate and encompass it; not even to pronounce its 'names', but only their 'initials', in a poem that is to be delicate, distant, all-inclusive from a distance. This is his new ambition. Not that the new kind of poem is to be emptied of images in favour of philosophical comments: it is to be full, he says, of 'flowerscents, fields, harvest and thunder' (and these *are* the subjects of most of the poems in this book); but all these, I feel he is also saying, will point carefully and restrainedly to a reality of human fate and feeling which is beyond poetry, beyond Pasternak. The wish—indeed the sense of compulsion—to be simple and general is accompanied by a loss and a renunciation.

All critics who have praised Pasternak's early poetry have stressed above all an extraordinary power of perception, his seeing the world as if for the first time. In particular, two contemporary poetesses—Akhmatova and Tsvetaeva, whom I have already quoted—have spoken enthusiastically of this power and both have said that it is something childlike. Tsvetaeva even says:

> It is not Pasternak who is an infant, but the
> world is an infant in him. Pasternak himself I
> would regard as belonging to the very first days
> of creation; the first rivers, first dawns, first
> storms. He is created before Adam.

This seems to be written about an altogether different poet from the author of **When the Weather Clears.** For in this book, although there is certainly something uncorrupted and wholehearted which might be called childlike, yet the child's freshness, the wonder, the strong joy of acclamation of a world just created, is no longer there. Now the poet is seeing the world for the last time. He sees it at a distance—sees more of it than before, but much less of it in sharp detail; he loves it and finds truth and faith in it, but cannot really smell or taste it. He adds it up, recognizes its sum as right and good, and then leaves it: it is not any more his world. (pp. 388-95)

> *Angela Livingstone, "Pasternak's Last Poetry," in* Meanjin, *Vol. XXII, No. 4, December, 1963, pp. 388-96.*

Victor Erlich   (essay date 1964)

[*Erlich is a Russian critic and educator. In the following excerpt from his* The Double Image: Concepts of the Poet in Slavic Literatures, *he analyzes Pasternak's perspectives on the role of the self in his poetry and their effect upon his lyric style.*]

In his brilliant spiritual autobiography *Safe Conduct*, as well as in his more recent autobiographical sketch, Pasternak looks back reflectively on the forces which helped to shape the style of his early writings. He speaks of his profound affinity, and admiration as a budding poet, for Vladimir Maiakovskii and of his equally strong urge to evolve a distinctive poetic manner. "So as not to echo him [Maiakovskii] . . . and not to be taken for his imitator, I proceeded to get rid of the heroic tone, which in my case would have been false, and of any straining for effect." Elsewhere he put it thus: "I abandoned the Romantic manner. And that is how the non-Romantic style of *Above the Barriers* came about." He further suggests that this abandonment of the Romantic manner entailed a break with the "whole conception of life" which underlies it, more specifically, with the Romantic image of the poet. This image Pasternak described in a telling phrase as "the notion of biography as spectacle."

Few students of modern literature will fail to appreciate the import of this formula. As I have been trying to suggest above, the two interlocking attitudes which it highlights—the poet's tendency to dramatize himself in his work, and conversely to turn his life into lyrical drama—loom very large indeed in the early twentieth-century Russian poetry.

In Russian symbolism the boundary between life and art was perilously fluid. The poet's work served all too often to project the *fin-de-siècle* myth of the artist as a seer, a rebel, or both; the poet's biography—to bear witness to that myth. In this respect, as in some others, the Futurist iconoclast, Maiakovskii, was much closer to the Symbolist tradition than he knew or was ever prepared to admit. The "notion of biography as spectacle" is no less relevant to the life and work of Sergei Esenin. His confessional verses which time and again verge on lyrical exhibitionism were above all a vehicle for dramatizing the author's personal plight—that of a nostalgic and wayward peasant poet, "the last village bard," crushed by the inexorable demands of the iron age. Like Blok, both Maiakovskii and Esenin were regarded by their public primarily as literary figures, embodied poetic destinies, rather than as mere poets, i.e., creators of poetic values.

To at least one British critic the poetry of Boris Pasternak, seen against the background of "the agonies and perorations of Esenin and Maiakovskii," appears as nearly devoid of biographical traits: "a Parthenon of impersonality," writes George Reavey, in "A First Essay toward Pasternak." Reavey's assertion may seem to many of us highly questionable. The recent specious official charges of Pasternak's "narcissistic self-centeredness" or "individualistic subjectivism" can safely be disregarded. But how about Pasternak's own reference to the "fragmentary, personal" nature of his first writings? How about the lyrical excitement which pervades so many of Pasternak's poetic cycles, especially his incomparably vital *My Sister, Life* (1921), and the uniquely personal, idiosyncratic quality of the Pasternakian vision?

Clearly, the matter is highly complex, if not elusive. The poetry of Pasternak—introspective, but not self-oriented, deeply lyrical and yet more than personal, a poetry which combines the emotional intensity of a Dylan Thomas with an uncanny sharpness of sensory detail—plays havoc with hard-and-fast distinctions and discourages rigid dichotomies. But while it would be futile and presumptuous to try to resolve the apparent paradox of Pasternak's poetic craft, an attempt to redefine the problem might be useful and worth while. This calls for a somewhat closer look at the implicit as well as the explicit notions which Pasternak has of poetry and at the status of "the self" in the unique poetic world which bears his signature.

In a recent essay [in *Partisan Review* (Fall 1958)], Renato Poggioli makes an important observation: "The raw material of Pasternak's poetry is introspection. Yet Pasternak treats the self as object rather than as subject. Thus, in a nonmystical sense one could apply to him Rimbaud's formula: '*car je suis un autre.*'" This brings out an essential aspect of the Pasternakian manner—the virtual absence of the lyrical "hero." The "I" in Pasternak's poetry, or artistic prose for that matter, is not the pivot of a lyrical narrative, the principal point of reference. The self exists here, as it were, on a par with all other elements of this heterogeneous universe—natural phenomena, inanimate objects, indeed with its own objectified sensations and states of mind. An integral part of his physical environment, of nature, he is treated as "object" also in that he is no more likely to act than to be acted upon, looked at, appraised by, the things around him. This is how the remarkable poem **"Marburg"** (1916) describes its "hero" in a state of emotional shock: "I went out into the square. I could have been considered born anew. Each trifle lived and, setting little store by me, rose in its final significance." In a much later **"Ballad"** we find the following lines: "I wake up. I am encompassed by the discovered. / I am taken stock of." Indeed we might be tempted to say that the self is reduced here to the passive status of a mere thing if it were not for the apparent humanization of nature itself. The world of objects and natural phenomena to which the image of the author is assimilated throbs with lyrical dynamism, glows with an all-pervading emotion.

In an important theoretical passage in *Safe Conduct*, Pasternak says somewhat cryptically: "Focused on a reality which feeling has displaced, art is a record of this displacement." Clearly, the two key terms here are "displacement" and "feeling." The former seems to point towards that ultramodern quality of Pasternak's poetic art which could be described with Viktor Shklovskii as "semantic shift," and with Ezra Pound as a tendency towards the "unification of disparate ideas." Pasternak's bold, startling imagery reshuffles ordinary relationships and hierarchies by juxtaposing the most divergent notions and spheres of experience, by holding together within the compass of one stanza "seas stirred by breezes from Morocco, the simoon, . . . Archangel snoring in snows, . . . dawn on the Ganges," and the drying of a manuscript of Pushkin's "The Prophet."

It is feeling, Pasternak reminds us, which serves here as a reorganizing, displacing and yet integrating power. What kind of feeling is it? And how does the integration occur? Elsewhere, in a poem **"Definition of Creativity,"** this power is identified as "passion."

> Gardens, ponds and palings, the creation
> Foam-flecked with the whiteness of our weep-
> ing,
> Are nothing but categories of passion
> That the human heart has had in keeping.

As Sir Isaiah Berlin has already pointed out, it would be to misjudge the nature and the uses of this passion to consider these lines as merely another instance of the pathetic fallacy. For one thing, nature in Pasternak is not a screen on to which to project the author's personal feelings and moods. More broadly, it is not the Baudelairian *"forêt des symboles"* nor a set of T. S. Eliot's "objective correlatives" for specific human emotions. In Blok's poetry, the recurrent image of the snowstorm is typically a symbol of an emotional turmoil or a social cataclysm. Pasternak's favorite motif, that of a "shower," a "downpour," has a different status. The rain appears here as an elemental force. Its attractiveness to the poet may lie in its association with freshness, movement, transformation, renewal. But all these dynamic qualities or events are apprehended as part of nature. The image does not point beyond itself, does not serve as a proxy for any recognizable human situation. In **"After a Rain," "My Sister, Life"** and many other rain-soaked poems of Pasternak, the shower is a source of delight, the focus of lyrical excitement, but not its emblem.

More important, perhaps, the feeling which informs Pasternak's poems is not the stuff of which most lyrical narratives are made. This is not to minimize the importance of the erotic motif in Pasternak's work (some of his finest poems are love lyrics), or to ignore the personal genesis of lyrical cycles such as "Separation" in *Themes and Variations* (1923). Yet, when all is said and done, it is not the love of Boris Pasternak for another human being which provides the central theme and the integrating principle in this discordant welter of images, objects, and sensations. It is something much less tangible or personal— something akin to cosmic ecstasy, to an "oceanic feeling," as a Freudian would put it, or, in Sir Isaiah Berlin's words, to "a metaphysical emotion which melts the barrier between personal experience and brute creation." To put it rather differently, what is projected here is not a particular emotion but emotionality as a faculty of the human heart,

> Here for once was a master of the modern Russian poetic idiom who refused to serve as a banner or a symbol, who did not want to stylize his life into a Passion play spectacularly testifying to a larger truth or dramatically challenging the Philistines. Here for once was a poet who spurned the romantic temptations of prophecy and proposed to attend to his own business— the engrossing minutiae of the poetic craft.
>
> —*Victor Erlich*

as a generic form of the human psyche. What is celebrated is not a specific affective experience, but the very process of experiencing, the joy and the thrill of feeling, sensing, responding, of rubbing shoulders with "my sister, life." (What other poet would have thought of calling life his sister?)

This joy of existence is primordial, and is so fundamental an aspect of Pasternak's *Weltgefühl* as to be literally irrepressible, undaunted. Asserting itself time and again, as T. S. Eliot would phrase it, "in excess of facts as they appear," the Pasternakian ecstasy fills his more buoyant poems to the brim (in **"Our Storm"** the poet asks almost helplessly: "What shall I do with my joy?"), and proves nearly impervious to disappointment and defeat. "How can there be melancholy when there is so much joy?" he asks in *Safe Conduct.* The early poem **"Marburg,"** already quoted, is ostensibly about a major emotional setback: the poet proposes to his beloved and is turned down; from a characteristically vague passage in *Safe Conduct* it can be inferred that the poem echoes an actual occurrence. Yet not even the hero's anguish can silence the incongruous note of bliss. In Iurii Zhivago's solitary meditations about the nature of art this attitude to life is formulated and made an aesthetic canon: " . . . Every work of art, including tragedy, witnesses to the joy of existence." Pasternak seems to have espoused and actually voiced this notion even before he became a "practicing" poet. In his recent autobiographical sketch he restates the principal theses of a lecture entitled "Symbolism and Immortality" which he delivered in Moscow in 1910. He argued then that art is primarily concerned with the transcendent, suprapersonal aspect of "generic human subjectivity." He also said that "though an artist is naturally a mortal like everyone of us, the joy of existence which he experienced was immortal . . . Owing to his works, others will be able to experience it . . . , a hundred years later, in a kind of adherence to the personal and intimate form of his first sensations."

We may note, along with the linking of art with the joy of existence, which is the *idée maîtresse* of Pasternak's aesthetics, the further motif of self-transcendence. This is equally apparent in Pasternak's view of the creative process as reflected in *Doctor Zhivago:*

After two or three stanzas and several images by which he was himself astonished, his work took possession of him and he experienced the approach of what is called inspiration. At such moments . . . the ascendancy is no longer with the artist or the state of mind which he is trying to express, but with language, his instrument of expression. Language, the home and dwelling of beauty and meaning, itself begins to think and speak for man and turns wholly to music. . . .

At such moments Iurii felt that the main part of his work was not being done by him but by something which was above him and controlling him: the thought and poetry of the world as it was at that moment and as it would be in the future.

This passage does not necessarily imply a mystical notion of the creative act. It rather suggests a poetics which pays less heed to the poet and his personality than to the internal laws and exigencies of poetic language.

The connection between these tenets and the impersonal or nonsubjective tenor of much of Pasternak's poetry is apparent enough. His work does not so much project a coherent and dramatically effective image of the poet as dramatize what Edgar Allan Poe calls the poetic principle—the power which brings the poem into being. Is not that joy of heightened perception, of passionate seeing, which provides the emotional leitmotiv of Pasternak's poetry, the essential quality and the unique prerogative of creative imagination? No wonder that Pasternak's most characteristic collection of verse *My Sister, Life* contains so many, and highly unorthodox, attempts to define poetry and the creative process. In **"Definition of Poetry"** poetic creation is defined without any reference to the creator in a series of striking images, disparate but held together by some inner euphonic and emotional vibration:

> It's a whistle's precipitous rise,
> It is icicles broken and ringing,
> It is night when the frost on leaves lies,
> It's a duel of nightingales singing.

Perhaps even more revealing is **"Poetry"** where Pasternak says rather unexpectedly: "You are a summer with a third-class ticket / You are a suburb, not a refrain." One might be tempted to dismiss this as the most bizarre or whimsical "defence of poesie" yet offered. But the import of these lines is not as cryptic as it appears. Poetry, Pasternak seems to suggest, is not a soft musical background for, or a verbal accompaniment to, the life of action; it is the things themselves, the most prosaic, humdrum everyday objects or occurrences, rediscovered, displaced, transfigured. It is the world become language.

It was this immersion in the creative interplay between words and things, this intoxication with verbal magic, which made Pasternak, in a poem dated 1917, look out from his attic still dazed from an encounter with Byron and Edgar Allan Poe, and call to the children playing in the yard below: "What millennium is there outside, dears?" It was likewise a quiet dedication to the unheroic yet exacting task of rendering his vision with the utmost accuracy, a dedication coupled with his congenital reticence and shyness, which induced him to persist in shun-

ning the "notion of biography as spectacle." He expressed this more recently in somewhat more personal terms: "A life without secrets and without privacy, a life brilliantly reflected in the mirror of a show window is inconceivable for me."

Here for once was a master of the modern Russian poetic idiom who refused to serve as a banner or a symbol, who did not want to stylize his life into a Passion play spectacularly testifying to a larger truth or dramatically challenging the Philistines. Here for once was a poet who spurned the romantic temptations of prophecy and proposed to attend to his own business—the engrossing minutiae of the poetic craft.

But the events which followed the appearance of his *Doctor Zhivago* in translation abroad, when its publication in his own country was not allowed, abruptly propelled Pasternak into the very limelight which he had studiously sought to avoid and made his name an epitome and a symbol for many people all over the world who had never seen a single example of his work: the epitome of the inwardly free poet in an unfree society, the symbol of embattled creative integrity.

This does not necessarily mean that Pasternak had felt compelled to abandon his initial commitment to noncommitment, his unspectacular notion of biography. Paradoxically, it is precisely Pasternak's insistence on preserving his emotional and poetic privacy that has now made him a public figure. In choosing a life of contemplation and creativity, Pasternak followed his true nature or that of his poetic gift. But he reckoned without the nature of the age whose heavy shadow fell across his path.

Not that Pasternak has ever tried to insulate himself against the "body and pressure of time." His sense of history should not be judged solely or even primarily by the absent-minded question in his 1917 poem. Keeping his fine sensibility available to historical experience, he did not fail to respond to the elemental sweep of the Revolution, now with bewilderment, now with sympathetic fascination. As Marina Tsvetaeva put it: in the summer of 1917 "he walked alongside the revolution and listened to it raptly." He tried to absorb and accept the new realities, but on his own terms and at his own pace: that is, as an uncommitted poet rather than as a shrill propagandist. His interesting, though not altogether successful, epic fragments, **"Year 1905"** and **"Lieutenant Schmidt,"** represent an honest effort to grasp the meaning of the Revolution by recreating its antecedents. Yet he would not be used or rushed. "In an epoch of tempo," he once said, "one ought to think slowly." He would not be dragooned into "well-intentioned" (i.e., politically orthodox) platitudes: "Hell is paved with good intentions. A view has prevailed, that if one paves verses with them all is forgiven."

Characteristically it was not until the early thirties when Russian literature was whipped into conformity that the sense of grim foreboding entered the life-affirming poetry of Pasternak. At first, the note was sounded with Pasternak's characteristic cryptic reticence:

> It's vain in days when the great Soviet convenes,
> When highest passion runs in flooding tide,

To seek a place for poets on the scene,
It's dangerous, if not unoccupied.

But it became clearer in the following poem of 1932:

If only, when I made my debut,
There might have been a way to tell
That lines with blood in them can murder,
That they can flood the throat and kill.

I certainly would have rejected
A jest on such a sour note,
So bashful was that early interest,
The start was something so remote.

But age is pagan Rome, demanding
No balderdash, no measured breath,
No fine feigned parody of dying,
But really being done to death.

A line that feeling sternly dictates
Sends on the stage a slave and that
Means that the task of art is ended
And there's a breath of earth and fate.

"A breath of earth and fate." The obtrusive theme of modern Russian poetry—that of the poet's tragic destiny—had finally caught up with Boris Pasternak. Apparently, "life by verses" was proving increasingly incompatible with the kind of commitment and the style of life fostered by the Russian society of the 1930's.

When culture is treated as a weapon and literature as a source of moral edification, poetic detachment smacks of sabotage. When politics is viewed as the highest form of human activity, aesthetic contemplation seems an act of political defiance. When the dry-as-dust abstractions of an official ideology are increasingly used to displace reality and explain it away, even such politically innocuous qualities as delight in the sensory texture of things and worship of "the omnipotent god of details" are likely to appear as utter irrelevance and escapism.

This irreconcilable conflict between the outlook of the poet and the party activist lies at the core of *Doctor Zhivago* which is not merely Pasternak's first full-length work of fiction, but his first successful attempt to reach beyond the realm of lyrical emotion—of what he himself has called the "personal and fragmentary"—towards the fundamental moral dilemmas of our time. It is perhaps the crowning paradox of his paradox-ridden career that this one epic of his should be in a sense more personal and autobiographical than many of his lyrics. In spite of its panoramic scope and wide moral relevance, *Doctor Zhivago* is above all the poetic biography of a richly endowed individual and the story of his unremitting efforts to maintain his creative integrity amid the overwhelming pressures of an age of wars and revolutions. True, Iurii Andreevich Zhivago cannot wholly be identified with Boris Pasternak: to confuse a literary character with its creator is always a dubious procedure. But the kinship between the two is not easily overestimated; and it is nowhere more apparent than in Zhivago's religious reverence for life and love, in his striving for absolute freshness of perception and the utmost directness of statement, and in his stubborn refusal to subordinate the dictates of his poetic vision to the ever-shifting demands of totalitarian bureaucracy.

In what is one of the most sensitive essays on Pasternak in English, Helen Muchnic eloquently demonstrates the fundamental continuity of Pasternak's poetic vision from his earliest lyrics down to the *Doctor Zhivago* period. To be sure, the aging poet's much-touted repudiation of his early writings as "mere trifles" need not be taken literally. Yet such *dicta* cannot be altogether ignored either, especially where Pasternak's image of himself as a poet is concerned. Nor can it be denied that in the late phase of his career a partial shift of moral emphasis, a discernible change in the scope of the Pasternakian universe did indeed occur.

In the language of the early Pasternak, this change could have been described as a sudden coalescence of two poles of reality—lyricism and history. Viktor Frank, one of the most perceptive Russian *émigré* students of Pasternak, has put it a little differently: "A new dimension appeared in Pasternak's work, a social dimension."

Once again, let us beware of simplifications. As I have already indicated, none of Pasternak's previous works is properly or meaningfully described by such terms as "asocial," or for that matter, "self-centered," to quote Il'ia Erenburg's characteristically ambivalent memoir [*People and Life 1891-1921,* 1962]. The overflowing cosmic ecstasy of Pasternak's early verse, reaching as it does beyond the merely personal, militates against these labels. The fact remains, though, that in many a Pasternak lyric the poet, occasionally flanked by his beloved, is the only recognizable human protagonist. In the excited confrontation between the creator and his "sister, life" there is little room for others—for an explicit relatedness to, and active participation in, other human lives, for that sense of interconnectedness of human destinies, which is part and parcel of the late Pasternak's—and Iurii Zhivago's—Christian personalism.

My desire is to be among people,
And in crowds, in their bustle and ease

. . . . .

Just as though I were under their skin,
I can feel all their thoughts as my own,
And I melt as the melting of snow
Like the morning my brows wear a frown.

For with me are those without names,
The homebody, the child, the tree,
I am truly vanquished by them all . . .
Therein lies my sole victory.

This notion of self-transcendence as spiritual communion, as being "vanquished" by or merging with others, a notion born no doubt of the shared ordeal of "Russia's terrible years," is bound up with another theme which is essentially new here. The predicament of Iurii Zhivago clearly implies the inextricable connection between the fate of a man of sensibility and imagination, in short, of a poet, and the moral texture of his society. Though Pasternak's novel carefully avoids any narrowly political moral, the life and death of its main protagonist epitomizes the impossibility of poetry under the "reign of a lie," the inseparability of creative genius and freedom (Gerschenkron). Once again the death of a poet becomes an indictment of a society, an

273

ultimate proof of its spiritual enslavement. Once again the artist's right to creative integrity and emotional privacy appear as the embattled individual's last line of defense against the encroachments of the omnipotent state.

It is scarcely necessary to urge that the above represents not only the objective import of the novel, but the subjective intent of its author as well. Pasternak's increasing awareness of his role and responsibility as a spokesman for those who cannot speak was amply evidenced by his apparent determination to proclaim his message, to make his novel available to the world, whatever the cost to himself and those dearest to him.

"Mission," "testimony," "ordeal"—are we not back, after all, in Blok's and Maiakovskii's universe of discourse? Yes and no. The affinities between the author of _Doctor Zhivago_ and Aleksandr Blok are all too apparent. Pasternak's affection for, and sense of indebtedness to the Symbolist spellbinder may have derived additional poignancy from the fact that he had lived through the fulfillment of Blok's apocalyptic prophecies. In the epilogue to _Doctor Zhivago_ one of Iurii's surviving friends, Misha Gordon, muses thus: "When Blok was saying [in his much-quoted 1914 poem], 'We, children of Russia's terrible years,' the line was to be interpreted figuratively. The children were not children, terrors were not terrible, but providential, apocalyptic. Now the figurative has become literal, children are children, and terrors are terrible." In _I Remember_ Pasternak paid an eloquent tribute to Blok in words which could have been easily addressed to his own achievement: "Blok had everything that goes to make a great poet—fire, tenderness, emotion, his own image of the world, his own special gift for transforming everything he touched, and his own restrained, self-absorbed destiny." In a lyrical triptych **"The Wind,"** devoted to Blok's memory, he hailed the restless visionary as his generation's vital, indispensable companion.

There remains, however, a residual yet significant difference of moral thrust and self-image. While Blok was a seer, Pasternak was—or became increasingly—a witness.

In his thoughtful commentary appended to the recent English translation of Pasternak's post-1945 verse, G. Katkov offers a relevant distinction: "The mission of the poet in Blok's day had been prophecy; in Pasternak's it becomes one of apostolic service."

The analogy between Christ's Passion and the ordeal of Iurii Zhivago has been urged by a number of critics, on occasion, quite persuasively. Yet the point is easily overstated. Iurii Zhivago is all too human, all too fallible to be a Christ-figure. As Obolensky properly reminds us, "Pasternak's design lay not in making Zhivago Christ-like but in suggesting that his life and death acquire their true significance when they are illumined by the reality of Christ's sacrificial death and His Resurrection."

Pasternak's hero falters, suffers, endures, struggles and goes down in an unequal battle only to leave behind a batch of poems which, twenty years after his death, will sustain his countrymen in their overwhelming desire for freedom. Thus, his sacrifice has not been in vain. His fate, not unlike his creator's served to document the ultimate triumph of the spirit over the brute force of circumstance. Yet however strategic the embattled poet's mission, however trying his ordeal, it is not his job to point the way to salvation. Is it perhaps because the task of saving mankind is left here to Jesus Christ?

Clearly, the difference I am trying to highlight involves matters other than the poet's view of his own calling. Though Maiakovskii's radicalism was Bohemian rather than Marxist, though Blok's Dionysian romance with the November revolution proved in the end a tragic misunderstanding, both poets shared the political revolutionary's basic eschatology, his hankering for a climactic event, a liberating cataclysm, a total transformation of reality. Pasternak's temperament had never been that of a Utopian. By 1950 he had less use than ever for the notion of a millennium. He had lived to see the utopian _élan_ of the Russian radical intelligentsia debased into the doctrinaire madness of the 1930's. He had witnessed the hardening of the ideal of "reshaping life" into a tedious official cliché. Hence, perhaps the increasing distrust of ultimate goals and grand designs, shared by Zhivago and Lara, their profound conviction that life is more important than the meaning of life, hence the characteristic affinity of Iurii Andreevich for the unflamboyant, unprogrammatic stance of Pushkin and Chekhov. The late Pasternak's admiration for Tolstoy is amply documented. Nor is there any question as to his indebtedness to Dostoevsky. Yet there is good reason to assume that Zhivago speaks for his creator when he opts for Pushkin's and Chekhov's "shy unconcern" with "loud things," "the ultimate goals of humanity and their own salvation." "Such immodesties were not for them; their station was not high enough and they were too busy." [Gogol, Dostoevsky and Tolstoy] "prepared themselves for death, sought meanings, drew up accounts, whereas these others were to the end absorbed in the current particularities of the artist's calling and their life passed in recording its passage, like another private particularity which was no one's concern, and now this particularity turns out to be everybody's business, like an apple that is plucked when it is ripe and reaches usefulness of itself, and fills itself more and more with sweetness and meaning."

In this scheme of things the life of the artist is not a prefiguration of the _vita nuova,_ a sacrificial leap from the wilderness of an unbearable present into the promised land of an infinitely beautiful future. It is rather a poignant exemplification of basic human values, a telling restatement of eternal verities, the holiness of life, the enduring beauty of love, the indispensability of personal freedom, of "authenticity," of fidelity to one's self. In the end Pasternak makes no special claims for the poet as a human being. He doesn't expect him, ostensibly, to lead a special kind of life. He simply urges him to be himself, to be and remain fully, richly, and if need be, defiantly human—in a word, "alive."

> And never for a single instant
> Betray your true self or pretend—
> But be alive and only living,
> And only living to the end.

It is a grim commentary on the nature of the regime in

Pasternak in the 1920s.

whose shadow Pasternak was fated to live for thirty years, and on the tenor of the age which his fellow poet Mandelshtam, termed a murderous beast, that this ostensibly unspectacular program should have become a bone of contention and the source of an ordeal.

When all is said and done, in the late Pasternak's poetics as in his earlier statements, the last word belongs to poetry rather than the poet. If the claim made for the artist as man is modest—though in Soviet society this very modesty could have been a sign of quiet heroism—the poet's image-making power is exalted as a crucial, indeed central human faculty. The philosophy of history which informs *Doctor Zhivago* derives the meaning of each historical epoch not from the "sound and fury" of recorded political events, but from the era's major creative ferment. The "Poems of Iurii Zhivago" echo and reinforce the exuberant eulogy of the "wonder-working might" of the creative genius found in Pasternak's early lyrics. To Pasternak, the poetic image does not merely heighten or keep alive, as it renews, reshuffles and articulates, our perception of reality. It does not merely reveal the essence of each phenomenon. ("For things tear off their masks," says Pasternak in one of his early poems. "When they have a reason to sing," that is when they enter the realm of art.) It helps make ex-

istence what it is. Without the transforming and articulating impact of poetry, the universe would have been a "dumb place." As the world turns into words, as the matter becomes song, what would have otherwise remained inchoate, inert, and "deaf" acquires a form, a voice, a vibrancy. By the same token the poem does not merely verbalize our delight in existence; it makes nature itself aware of the joy which it is capable of generating:

> Surely it is my vocation,
> To prevent the loneliness
> Of distances, to keep the earth
> Outside the town from desolation.

Poetry thus is more than mimesis, an imitation or recreation of the given; it is a co-creator of existence, "a catalyst of reality." Is not this notion another echo of Romantic aesthetics? Undoubtedly. Yet here is a romanticism with a difference, a romanticism which sets more store by the artifact than by the *artifex,* which cares less for the myth of the poet than for the ineluctable reality of the poem. (pp. 133-54)

> *Victor Erlich, " 'Life by Verses': Boris Pasternak," in his* The Double Image: Concepts of the Poet in Slavic Literatures, *The Johns Hopkins Press, 1964, pp. 133-54.*

Dale L. Plank   (essay date 1966)

[*In the following excerpt from the introduction to his* Pasternak's Lyric: A Study of Sound and Imagery, *Plank discusses Pasternak's poetic sensibility and critical reaction to his works.*]

> [The pictures tilting, flying in torrents
> From the road that blew the candle out:
> I can't break them from tearing loose into rhyme
> From hooks and walls and falling in time.
> (from *Themes and Variations*)]

More than forty years afterward, Pasternak writes about how the poems of his first book came into being:

> To write these verses, rub out and restore what had been crossed out, was a profound necessity and brought me a pleasure—comparable to nothing else—that reduced me to tears.

He directs us to the mechanics of their composition: "to write" is first of all the graphic experience; the paper, with its marks and smudges, replaces the poem in remembrance.

He speaks of the book itself as immature and says that it should not have been published. Only about half of the poems of *Twin in Clouds* survived into later collections. He calls the title "pretentious to the point of stupidity", and "imitative of the cosmological profundities which were typical of the book titles of the Symbolists and the names of their publishing houses".

After forty years, in the pages of his autobiography, he is able, and finds it worthwhile, to describe the site of their composition: under the leaves of an old birch which, though toppled, continued to grow.

The birch may have wanted to be a lyrical hero, but what

is valuable to us right now is simply that the poet enjoyed writing these poems and that he needed to write them. Pasternak says that he did not "express, reflect, represent, or depict": "I needed nothing from myself, from the readers, or from the theory of art. I needed only that one poem should contain the city of Venice. . . ."

Pasternak's **"Venice"** seems to be "about" a single musical chord which wants so badly to persist that it becomes a spatial entity. It is, as he tells us, the water lights, fugitive like the chord from the anonymous guitar, that wanted longevity. An abstraction hangs on the end of an oar, and there are no streets or landmarks. The tourist will not find his Venice here.

Pasternak's remarks are meant not only to disarm, but to define. The word "contain" is too capacious to say much by itself, but he is clear about what he did not do in the poem. If we are not too intimidated, we may want to use words like "embody", but in the sense that we will be talking about the concrete properties of the verse itself; just as the sense of "contain" may be faithful to the analogy between the poem and a dipper of muddy water lights from the canal.

I have called attention to the author's own emphasis on the poetic act, its locale and mechanics, not because I want to bridge the dangerous gap between intention and realization, but because Pasternak's poems have the peculiar ability to engage the reader in the poetry as process, activity.

One result of this particular sort of realization is that ostensible, often conventional, themes are displaced by the act which originates them. As Jurij Tynjanov . . . put it: "The better half of Pasternak's verses are about poetry".

It is to be expected then that Pasternak would come to have the reputation of a poet's poet. The response from the critics to the "new thing" which Tynjanov said that Pasternak had brought was generally unfavorable. Vladimir Weidle, in an ambitious essay of 1928, wrote:

> One may read through two or three of Pasternak's poems and notice nothing in them, but it is impossible to read many of his poems and not see beyond them, in their depths, the opaque, elemental, chaotic gift that gave birth to them. And it is remarkable that as soon as we have caught that gift his verses begin to seem different from what they were before: no longer the cold experiment of an experimenter (one cannot however deny that this is present in them), but the cruel failure of a poet.

Meanwhile, a poet, Marina Cvetaeva, who reads him with the same sensibility that can distinguish the potentiality from the result, comes to the opposite conclusion:

> . . . concerning his poetic gift. I think that his gift is enormous, for its substance is enormous; it comes through in its entirety. His talent is obviously on a par with the substance, a most rare occurrence, a miracle . . .

Another poet, Eduard Bagrickij, honors him with a rhyme:

> Matches and tobacco
> In my pack,
> Tixonov,
> Sel'vinskij,
> Pasternak . . .

(In the Russian, Pasternak rhymes with another necessity of life, *tabak*.)

His name became eponymous for a generation of poetic sins. His influence is feared like a disease. Writing (under the spell of some inscrutable historical irony) of Nabokov's poetry, Georgij Adamovič said:

> He is undoubtedly the only genuine poet in the emigration who has studied Pasternak and learned something from him. Concerning the influence of Pasternak, we are constantly saying, while however for the most part citing him mechanically, uncritically: if a poem is not wholly intelligible it means that the author is following in the footsteps of Pasternak—and such opinions are not only to be overheard but seen in print as well.

Many of Pasternak's critics were admitting the success of his poetic accomplishment in the terms of their rejection of it, obscuring what was really a difference in philosophies. Maxim Gor'kij, for example, in a personal letter to Pasternak, dated November 30, 1927:

> To imagine means to bring form, a pattern into chaos. Sometimes I am painfully aware that the world's chaos overwhelms the force of your creativity and is reflected only as chaos in a disharmonic [sic] manner.

But, to Pasternak, poetry is not a drill-at-arms in a dishevelled landscape or a statement of withdrawals and deposits. To describe the poetics [of Pasternak], we will use the words, from a fairly remote context, of John Crowe Ransom:

> . . . the moral Universal of the poem does not use nature as a means but as an end; it goes out into nature not as a predatory conqueror and despoiler but as an inquirer, to look at nature as nature naturally is, and see what its own reception there may be.

It is an amiable poetry. Pasternak characteristically identifies it with its site, which gives us the smell of the sausages and sweat:

> Poetry, I will swear
> By you, and end croaking:
> You're not the sweetsinger's pose,
> You are a summer with a third-class seat,
> You are a suburb, not a refrain.

Irrepressibly familiar, it imputes its own emotions to its companion:

> Whose verses raised such a ruckus
> That even their thunder was dumbstruck with pain?
> One had better be delirious at least
> To give his consent to be a world.

Pasternak's statements of criticism, like those of most poets, make his own work the model of all art. The following dictum must be so understood, and it becomes the more valuable for that:

> Art is realistic as activity, and it is symbolic as fact. It is realistic in that it itself did not invent the metaphor, but found it in nature and reproduced it with reverence . . .

There is no mention of the poet or of the act of making poems. A number of writers, beginning with Jakobson, have emphasized the passive nature of Pasternak's lyrical hero. This is the thematic analogue to the effacement of the poet's will in the theory; but it is more than a demonstrative stylization. It is the necessary consequence of a poetics of discovery and surprise, of a poetry that is constantly attentive to the terms of its reception.

To be surprised, one might be looking for something other than what is finally found. When Jurij Živago sits down to write at Varykino near the end of his happiness, it is first the site that comes alive, humming with light and frost. An incidental, the gilded inner rim of the inkwell, puts us closer to his table than anything else could have done. Then we are told something about the activity of poetry:

> Primacy is given not to the man and the state of his soul, for which he seeks expression, but to the language with which he wants to express it. Language, the homeland and receptacle of beauty and meaning itself begins to think and speak for the man and it all becomes music, not in respect to the external acoustic properties of the verse, but in respect to the headlong drive and force of its internal current. Then like the rolling enormity of a river current, which by its very movement grinds the stones in its bed and turns millwheels, the flowing speech itself, by the power of its laws, creates along the way, in passing, meter and rhyme, and thousands of other forms and constructions that are still more important but are yet unknown, unstudied, and unnamed.
>
> (pp. 9-13)

The first question [related to Pasternak's poetics] is about one of the possible relations between poetry and music: the direct influence of the art of musical composition on the writing of poetry. When Adamovič says:

> The verses of Pasternak are densely worded and now and then come to the point of an actual uproar of words, images, sounds, and metaphors, which seem to crowd and drive each other along . . . Sounds? His sounds are absolutely barbaric, and the collision of five or six consonants doesn't bother Pasternak a bit . . .

we may be inclined to put to a test Northrop Frye's claim:

> . . . when we find sharp barking accents, long cumulative rhythms sweeping lines into paragraphs, crabbed and obscure language, mouthfuls of consonants, the spluttering rumble of long words, and the bite and grip of heavily stressed monosyllables, we are most likely to be reading a poet who is being influenced by music. Influenced, that is, by the music that we know, with its dance rhythm, discordant texture, and stress accent. The same principle suggests that

the other use of the term "musical" to mean a careful balancing of vowels and a dreamy sensuous flow of sound actually applies to poetry that is unmusical, that is, which shows no influence from the art of music.

In his autobiographical works, *Safe Conduct* (1931) and *An Autobiographical Sketch* (1957), Pasternak has told of his passionate devotion to music, under the spell of Scrjabin, between the ages of fourteen and twenty. The plausibility of a direct influence of Pasternak the composer on Pasternak the poet is reduced by the finality of his break with music: ". . . I decided to take stronger measures to enforce my abstinence. I stopped touching the piano, gave up going to concerts, and avoided meetings with musicians". He disavowed an interest in "musical" effects in his poetry:

> I was not trying to achieve the clear-cut rhythms of a song or a dance, under whose influence almost without the participation of words hands and feet begin to move by themselves . . .

> Later on, as a result of quite unnecessary attempts to find some sort of affinity between Mayakovsky and myself, people discovered oratorical and melodic tendencies in my poems. This is not correct. They are there no more than in the speech of any ordinary person.

Considering his renunciation of his poetry written before 1940, one may suspect that here Pasternak is telling us more about what that poetry should have been than what it was. Behind all this is an inner struggle between the uses of art, between music, elemental and non-cognitive, and a conception of art as a responsibility to history and descriptive truth, between poetry in some improbably ideal sense and prose. The conflict appears quite early: for example in these unexpected lines from a poem in ***Themes and Variations***:

> I'll say goodbye to poetry, my mania,
> I've set a date to meet you in a novel.
> As always, far from the parodies,
> We'll turn up side by side in nature.

Weidle, in a later essay, writes:

> The descriptive intention . . . is almost always before Pasternak from the very beginning. It has a direction that is rather less changeable, stronger than in many other poets; it is aimed at capturing not only the movements of the soul, but also the visible, audible, tangible images of the external world. It strives to describe, in the fullest sense of that word, even when the object of description is unnamed and escapes identification outside the poetry. The very lyrical emotion, or, what is the same thing, the rhythm itself, which engenders the verse, with him arises in a close connection with the external felt impressions; it is the impressions which suggest the words—but [word-sounds and images] alternate and vie with each other, so that the sound contends with the sense . . . [the poet] is not always able to overcome the very richness [of sounds] which he has not yet learned to sacrifice. . . . The whole course of his creative work, over a pe-

riod of decades, is determined by this unceasing struggle with himself.

(pp. 13-15)

Dale L. Plank, in his Pasternak's Lyric: A Study of Sound and Imagery, *Mouton & Co., 1966, 121 p.*

Pasternak's poetry is antispeculative, anti-intellectual. It is poetry of sensory perception. His worship of life meant a fascination with what can be called nature's moods: air, rain, clouds, snow in the streets, a detail changing, thanks to the time of the day or night, to the season.

—Czeslaw Milosz, "On Pasternak Soberly," in World Literature Today, *1989.*

Henry Gifford   (essay date 1977)

[*Gifford is an English critic, translator, and educator. In the following excerpt from his* Pasternak: A Critical Study, *he examines the poetry of* My Sister, Life, Themes and Variations, *and* When the Weather Clears.]

Pasternak's reputation as a poet became firmly established with the appearance of *My Sister Life* in 1922 and of its successor *Themes and Variations* [*Temy i variatsii*] in 1923. The former year is remarkable for other publications: Joyce's *Ulysses,* T. S. Eliot's *The Waste Land,* Rilke's *Duinese Elegies* and *Sonnets to Orpheus,* César Vallejo's *Trilce,* Mandelstam's *Tristia.* The list could be extended, and its effect is one of rebirth after the war—a resumption along the lines of discovery first plotted a decade before.

Themes and Variations was published by Helikon in Berlin, and there too in 1923 Grzhebin reissued the earlier volume which he had originally brought out in Moscow. At that time Berlin, with its vast influx of Russian refugees, and the coming and going of those who had taken Soviet citizenship, rivalled Moscow as a centre of Russian publishing. Pasternak had previously been known for his infrequent public readings in Moscow. Like most writers during the years of War Communism that followed the October Revolution he had lacked opportunity to publish. One result of newsprint being in scant supply was that poetry tended to flourish more than prose: a generally compact and more memorable form, verse at the beginning dominated Soviet literature.

Henceforth, these two volumes by Pasternak were to ensure that he could count on a public—fairly small perhaps but highly appreciative, and one that included among his admirers the best Russian poets of the time. Nadezhda Mandelstam's testimony can be supported: 'For many years Pasternak held undisputed sway over all other poets,

and none of them was immune to his influence. Akhmatova used to say that only Tsvetayeva came through this trial with honor.' Osip Mandelstam in 1922 had singled him out from all the Moscow futurists as combining 'invention and memory'. In an essay of 1923 he linked Pasternak's name with that of Khlebnikov for their achievement in freeing the Russian language so that it might realise in poetry its full native genius: 'After Khlebnikov and Pasternak Russian poetry again puts out to the open sea, and many of the customary passengers will have to say goodbye to its steamer.' He compared Pasternak's poetry with a series of breathing exercises to regulate the true voice of expression; and described it as 'a brilliant *Nike* [statue of victory] transposed from the Acropolis to the Sparrow Hills' outside Moscow. Marina Tsvetaeva, of whom Akhmatova further said that 'Pasternak enriched her and perhaps thanks to him she not only kept her true voice but even found it in the first place', wrote in lavish praise of his poetry in the same year 1923. Her addiction was shared by Mayakovsky, who used very often to repeat Pasternak's verses, and particularly, with such feeling that he might have written them himself, the first two stanzas of the 'Afterword' to *My Sister Life.*

Lilya Brik, who records this last detail, has described how Mayakovsky in those years was 'saturated with Pasternak', talking of him incessantly. Pasternak had been aware from their first meeting in 1914 of Mayakovsky as an exemplar whom it was hard not to accept totally. He explains in *Safe Conduct:* 'When they asked me to tell something of myself I would speak about Mayakovsky . . . I worshipped him. I embodied in him my own spiritual horizon.' But after the appearance of *My Sister Life* it became clear to Pasternak that their basic approaches to poetry were altogether different. Mayakovsky, engrossed in himself and in the revolution which he had unwisely made his own, tried for as long as possible to ignore the gulf between them. Every writer in those days had to ask himself where he stood in relation to the new order which was often as arbitrary and jealous in its dealings with the bourgeois artist as the God of the Puritans had been with the individual sinner. Mayakovsky knew the initial joys of the converted: his way had been marked out for him as a Soviet poet. Pasternak never became a Soviet poet in the true sense: he was more accurately a poet living under the Soviets, whose regime he could accept not as a mere *fait accompli* but as the fulfilment for that hour of Russia's destiny. But to recognise the Soviet order was not to abandon the sovereignty of art. Mayakovsky must have hoped that 'the social command' would positively enhance his powers as a poet. He needed the revolution to save him from the anarchy of his temperament, counting on Bolshevik discipline to regulate his artistic conscience. But evidently he looked with some envy on Pasternak's freedom. Once after hearing Pasternak read, Mayakovsky on his way home suddenly came out with the comment, made in an unusually wistful and subdued tone: 'Lucky Pasternak! See what lyric poetry he writes. While probably I never shall again.'

For a little while Pasternak contributed to Mayakovsky's journal *Lef*—three poems in all. In one of these he allows that public events will change him: . . .

Beyond the ocean of these storm spells
I foresee how, shattered as I am,
The year still to come
Will take in hand my education anew.

The year still to come was 1919. He refers, one would think, not to party directives but to the ordeals of common life as the source from which that teaching will flow. At times during the next decade, the 1920s, Pasternak wanted very definitely to write such poetry as would honour the revolution. He had no wish to stand aside from the Soviet people. But for him they were still the Russian people who found themselves in the Soviet epoch rather than a new species whose highest motivation must be political.

Themes and Variations has in many ways a resemblance to *My Sister Life.* Although it lacks a narrative frame, it adopts a similar division into cycles, of which there are six. These, however, serve principally to group poems which were written at different times. The volume does not bear the impression of a single continuing experience in the manner of *My Sister Life,* except in its fourth section 'The Break' ['*Razryv*']. This sequence, dated 1918, surpasses in passionate feeling anything the earlier book has to show. Pasternak wrote many of the poems collected in *Themes and Variations* during 1917 and 1918 when inspiration was running high and he 'wanted to bring his testimony as near as possible to the extemporised'. It carries forward the momentum of *My Sister Life.* As he explained in the letter to a Georgian poet from which I have just quoted, the principle behind both volumes of trusting to the immediate, natural and spontaneous phrase prevailed with him only during those two years. Yet there are some distinctions to draw. Certain emphases become more conspicuous in the second volume. Thus, its final section *Neskuchnyy sad* (the name of a Moscow park meaning 'the garden that isn't dull') consists for the greater part of impressionistic poems about the seasons in a country setting; and perception of this kind, original, momentary and intense, would continue throughout his work, being further refined and set down with an effect of unforced simplicity in his poems of the last decade. After *Themes and Variations* a new phase of imaginative effort begins when Pasternak attempts to write on an epic pattern. *Themes and Variations* twice appeared (in 1929 and in 1930) with *My Sister Life* as a single volume. What I said about the previous volume needs to be amplified a little in view of certain innovations, or more successful restatements of earlier discoveries, in this sequel to his first wholly authentic work.

Here perhaps even more than in *My Sister Life* there is apparent on every page a virtuosity not unlike that of the extemporising pianist elated by his audience. This virtuosity plays with syntax and form, with conceits caught in mid-air, with splendidly improvised rhymes, and with many changes of tone, from the colloquial or proverbial to an urgent complexity in which language, while not divorced from the speaking voice, enters into unprecedented relations. An example of this personal usage is the well known definition of poetry in the lyric by that name ['*Poeziya*']: . . .

You are not the posture of the euphonist,
You are summer with a seat travelling third,

The edge of town, not a refrain.

Pasternak may, as one contemporary critic [Chernyak] said, have passed through the Futurism with which he began; but he remained Futurist enough to prize novelty. In this Pasternak did not stand alone: the desire to shock and surprise by novelty was prominent in much poetry of that time, and T. S. Eliot and García Lorca escaped from it no more than he did. But they reveal an alert sophistication quite alien to him. Pasternak's elaborate mastery of technique went with a *naïveté* of feeling. Much of his subtlety rests at the level of very fine sensuous notation. He had the mind to discriminate between impressions, and to organise them beautifully. But sophisticated (in the tradition of Laforgue for Eliot, of Góngora for Lorca) he never became. And indeed that quality of mannered self-possession does not belong to any of the most considerable Russian writers.

Yet the poetry is self-conscious at least in technique, for all its freshness and innocence. The series entitled 'A Theme with Variations' ['*Tema s variatsiyami*'] might at a first reading suggest Picasso's game of parody and subversion with, for instance, a canvas by Velázquez. The whole sequence revolves round certain poems by Pushkin—the start of *The Bronze Horseman* [*Mednyy vsadnik*], 'The Prophet' ['*Prorok*'] and *The Gipsies* [*Tsygany*]—and it evokes the well known painting of him on a rocky coast by Ayvazovsky and Repin. One passage ('Imitation') ['*Podrazhatel' naya*'] not only adopts the movement of Pushkin's verse in *The Bronze Horseman,* but begins with the two opening lines of its Prologue. Instead of Peter by the Neva contemplating his future city, Pushkin stands by the sea contemplating the novel he will write. The conclusion of this passage, as Dale Plank has noted, acquires a density that is Pasternak's own, when the hero seems to merge with the landscape. There are ambiguities that Plank points out, and the texture of the verse thickens. Then, in the following section, where the metre has changed, the manner becomes wholly Pasternak's: . . .

The stars were rushing. In the sea washed the
    headlands.
Salt was blinded. And tears dried up.
Dark were the bedrooms. Thoughts were rush-
    ing,
And the sphinx listened to the Sahara.

All this series of 1918 is an engaging improvisation, but hardly more. Once the musical reference of its title has been taken, the object could no longer be supposed that of Picasso (wilful appropriation, mockery, almost a visual punning). This set of poems following the line of an improviser who makes up variations on a theme, does not, of course, remain merely an exercise. It explores, as so many of Pasternak's writings do, the process of creation. His poetry, like much modern poetry, watches itself in motion, whereas Pushkin, even when in 'Autumn' ['*Osen'* '] he describes the act of composition, cannot be said to show Pasternak's awareness of the description itself. Perhaps it is only in the modern age that a poet could say 'the best of the world's productions . . . are in effect recounting their own birth'.

Are the other series in this book virtually doing the same thing? The title might indicate that Pasternak was engrossed with technical problems and the delight of solving them. In the final section one poem is called **'In the Forest'** ['V lesu'], another group of poems 'Winter Morning' [*Zimnee utro'*], a third group 'Spring' [*'Vesna'*]—all of them subjects that are familiar enough from Tyutchev and Fet. The poems under these headings, or at least some of them, look very much like variations on Tyutchev or Fet by a poet who has formed his sensibility in the era of modernism. Those who value only the older poetry are going to complain that Pasternak has allowed his ingenuity to run away with him, so that the details get out of hand, and a restless ambition to innovate and to startle changes the mode of Tyutchev and Fet into a glittering mass of conceits. That is to put the case in its most hostile form, as Wladimir Weidlé did in an essay of 1928. He did not deny the talent of Pasternak, for him a genuine poet who had been spoiled by the age. When Weidlé came, thirty years later, to reconsider his views, in the light of all Pasternak had done since, he still regretted the one-sidedness that modernism had fostered in the poet's development, and which it took so many years to overcome. Here Weidlé, of course, gains support from the disenchanted comments made subsequently by Pasternak on his earlier work.

Themes and Variations is a more obvious target for such criticism than ***My Sister Life.*** It lacks the loose unity of the latter, and this causes the individual poems to stand out more on their own, sometimes rather showily. In the opening section 'Five Tales' ['*Pyat' povestey'*] each separate lyric is a virtuoso piece. The second of these, **'A Meeting'** ['*Vstrecha*'], may be taken as representative. Its action is very slight. The poet makes his way home from a gathering just before daylight in March, while the wind tears the puddles like sacking [*vretishche*]; we overhear the goodbye: . . .

> At six o'clock, like a bit of landscape
> From the staircase suddenly grown damp
> How it crashes into the water and how it
>   thumps,
> A weary 'Well then, till tomorrow!'

As the poet walks in the company of the March night, he is seen as belonging to the landscape: all this poem has been conceived in terms of a picture: . . .

> And the March night and the author
> Went side by side, and both of them quarrelling
> The cold hand of the landscape
> Led home, led from the gathering.

So they are met by the new day which is propelled towards them: . . .

> And the March night and the author
> Went fast, glancing now and then
> At a phantom that glimmered as if real
> And suddenly hid itself.
>
> That was the dawn. And like an amphitheatre
> That had appeared at the harbinger's call,
> There was borne towards both that tomorrow
> Uttered upon the staircase.

Dale Plank has commented on the ingenuity of the ending

to this poem, when trees and buildings are displaced as in a three-tiered hexameter (the line being echeloned, with its second and third clauses dropped in a descending sprawl): . . .

> It came with a baguette, like a picture-framer.
> Trees, buildings and fanes
> Seemed not to belong here, but there
> In the gap of the inaccessible frame.
>
> Like a three-tiered hexameter
> They were shifted to the right along a quadrat.
> Shifted they were carried out for dead,
> Nobody remarked the loss.

Plank takes the morning with its baguette or moulding-frame to be a stage-hand; and he translates the word *proval* in the last line of the penultimate stanza as 'pit'—the part of a theatre behind the stalls. For him the poet has now stepped on to the stage. However, despite the appearance of an amphitheatre, this poem is placed rather in a pictorial frame, as Plank also observes. The 'cold hand of the landscape' seems to conduct it all the way through.

'Meeting' is a difficult poem, with the features of a cubist painting, and its final dislocation [*smeshchenie*] relates to the cubist manner. Pasternak's highly-wrought idiom needs very close attention: . . .

> The automatic pulley's
> Torments further began,
> Where foretasting the gutters
> Dawn played the *shaman* mechanically.

We can see that *mashinal' no* grew out of *shamanil*, and *vostok* from *vodostokov*. But the adverb *mashinal' no* has to be explained by the presence of an automatic pulley in the previous couplet. This first image—of machinery to be put in motion with the day—cannot be disentangled from that of the dawn performing its rites.

In poetry like this, as in the variations on Pushkin, art is in danger of becoming over-obtrusive. English readers who know metaphysical verse of the seventeenth century will understand why [D. S.] Mirsky, writing in the 1920s when Donne was again widely read, found it 'very tempting' to compare him with Pasternak. Each, according to Mirsky, was a poet's poet; each combined passion with ingenuity, and broke up the smooth diction of an earlier school. For the Pasternak of **'A Meeting'** Crashaw might give the juster parallel. Here the conceits may seem forced in the manner of Crashaw's; and yet, as we have seen, they owe to a skilful organisation of syntax and sound their convincingness, their inevitability. Another poem, **'The Break'**, does indeed suggest Donne, and Donne at his finest, when he is struggling to clarify and to master a complex emotion. It is a sequence of nine lyrics in different metres that moves through the conflicting passions caused by a woman's deceit. There are tones in it not far from 'The Apparition', and again others that match the tenderness of 'A Valediction: forbidding mourning'. In the second lyric pain and indignation take on a depth and vibrancy that are new to Pasternak: . . .

> O shame, you are a burden to me. O conscience
>   in this early
> Break how many dreams are importunate still!

Had I been a man—I was a void collection
Of temples and lips and eyes, palms, shoulders,
   and cheeks!
Then by the hiss of my stanzas, their cry, their
   sign,
By the strong hold of my anguish, by its youth
I would yield to them all, lead them into attack,
And take you by storm, my humiliation.

Mayakovsky may have recalled this image in his last considerable poem *At the Top of My Voice* [*Vo ves' golos,* 1930] in which he calls on his verses to die like the nameless ordinary soldiers storming a position: . . .

Changes of inflexion and speed in Pasternak's sequence are beautifully calculated: . . .

'Will there be pity for me in the city squares?
Oh, if only you knew my anguish
When some hundred times in the course of a day
The street catches on the move your likeness!'

No mood is held for long. The note here between regard and insecure resignation turns rapidly in the next lyric to one of frenzied appeal to have his grief smothered. From the hurrying excitement of a passage that describes Actaeon in pursuit of Atalanta, the voice changes to an elaborate slow irony: . . .

You are disillusioned? You thought in peace
We should part over a swan requiem?

The poem's last quatrain (often quoted like the first lines of the series, and the second excerpt above, by Mayakovsky) places the personal disaster in a context of public confusion. The note is very restrained, and the final simile has a Roman ring: these are the times of Tacitus. . . .

I don't hold you. Go, do good works.
Be off to others. *Werther* has already been written,
And in our days the very air smells of death:
To open the window is to open your veins.

It is natural to set **'A Break'** over against **'Marburg'**, the poem of an earlier separation. A line such as *Poshchadyat li ploshchadi menya?* ['Will there be pity for me in the city squares?'] can be compared with this from **'Marburg'**: . . .

The flagstone glowed, and the street's forehead
Was swarthy, and at the sky glowered up
Cobblestones . . .

The tone of **'Marburg'**, however, is ecstatic: the poem flowers into fantasies more vivid than the grief it purports to express. In **'The Break'** an irrepressible feeling shapes every line. Not until *Second Birth* in 1931-2, and especially the love lyrics of its third section, does Pasternak write so evidently from the heart. The other poems of *Themes and Variations* are endlessly inventive, and they certainly cannot be called hollow. Yet their success is mainly a matter of technical triumph. They achieve a fusion of energy and control which only in **'The Break'** are used to articulate and make bearable a moment of intense passion.

More usual with Pasternak are those moments in which dislocation results not from emotional shock, the sudden

reversal of feelings, but rather from what he has called in the *Essay in Autobiography* a 'passion of creative contemplation' [*strast' tvorcheskogo sozertsaniya*]. There he applied the words to Tolstoy, who saw everything 'in its original freshness, newly, and as it were for the first time'. Tolstoy stripped away the conventional associations: he looked at the world with a deliberate *naïveté*, a dogmatic innocence. The *naïveté* in Pasternak is not something assumed: his self-consciousness is different from Tolstoy's, an artistic rather than a didactic need. But in the later as in the early poetry, he does resemble Tolstoy, whenever a whole scene is illuminated by 'the passion of creative contemplation'. The most striking example of this can be found in a short and very well known poem of 1918, which appears as the first one in a sequence entitled 'Spring' ['*Vesna*']: . . .

Spring, I've come from the street, where the popular is amazed,
Where the distance is scared, where the house
   fears to fall,
Where the air is dark blue, like the bundle of
   linen
Of one discharged from hospital.

Where evening is empty, like a broken-off story,
Left by a star without continuation
To the perplexity of a thousand loud eyes,
Fathomless and devoid of expression.

Tolstoy will interpret a scene in terms of a man's feeling: Prince Andrey sees the pledge of his own restoration in the old oak tree which has put forth leaves, Levin on his way to Kitty's house as her affianced lover is met by new and astonishing sights on every hand. In Pasternak's poem the speaker, at the moment he enters from the street, vanishes. The action takes place in the street where the poplar is amazed, and four times more the conjunction 'where' recurs. There, in the scene that has suddenly closed for him on leaving the street, his excited apprehensions live on, transferred to their objects. The novelty of vision here has not been contrived by syntax, although syntax, with the gradually lengthening adverbial clauses, has realised the vision in its singularity. The poem catches the sense of a spring evening, the emptiness in the air, the feeling of convalescence after a long winter, the unfulfilled hopes and inexpressible excitement. It builds up with a gathering momentum. The opening has the directness of Blok's famous lyric *Noch', ulitsa, fonar', apteka* . . . [*Night, the street, a lamp, the chemist's*]. In both poems the first word states the essence of the scene (it is spring or night); then the local particulars emerge (the street, houses, the quality of the lighting—in Blok's poem, 'meaningless and dull light' from a street lamp, in Pasternak's, the dark blue of the sky, the single star at the approach of evening). But whereas Blok's poem, also in two quatrains and eight lines, is locked into a circle of despair, ending with the same everlasting scene— . . .

Night, icy ripple of the canal,
   The chemist's, the street, the lamp

—Pasternak's with its expanding syntax follows an expanding movement that proceeds even when the story is broken off. There are two conceits in the poem (apart from that of the astonishment and fear that assail poplar, view and house): first, the comparison with a discharged patient from a hospital, the blue of whose bundle is the same colour as the evening sky; the second, the comparison of this moment with a story that is interrupted (and as Plank has suggested, the star that 'leaves it without continuation' may also be an asterisk). The first image of the discharged patient reflects back on the poplar's amazement (trembling of its leaves?), and the fear of the distance and the house that feels near toppling: they too share the surprise at recovery and the apprehensions of the invalid. In the second image Pasternak, as so often, merges nature and art: an experience for him exists through its telling. (Thus, in the last stanza of **'The Break'**, he protests '*Werther* has already been written': the pains of today are different and demand another form for them to be realised.) The 'thousand loud eyes' are perhaps the stars that come out in what should have been the continuation of the story, when darkness falls. They seem to bear some relation to Lermontov's figure—itself derived from Goethe's 'Willkommen und Abschied'—in *Mtsyry:* . . .

> And with a million dark eyes
> The obscurity of night looked
> Through the twigs of every bush.

The eyes are at once 'loud' and 'devoid of expression'—that is to say, not expressionless because they have nothing to declare but the opposite, *deprived* [*lishonnykh*] of expression. They are also described as *bezdonnykh,* 'fathomless'—the ordinary romantic term for the eyes of a mistress deep in significance. (Pasternak uses the phrase *zharkiy, bezdonnyy belok* ['hot, fathomless white of eye'] for Pushkin's Zemphira in *The Gipsies,* though the adjectives would be more appropriate to the pupil.) There is a fathomless depth of meaning in the spring nightfall which cannot be put into words because the poet has left the scene.

Pasternak wrote in *Safe Conduct* that the effect of art is to give all things an equal status in the eye of the impassioned artist.

> Focused upon a reality that is dislocated by feeling, art is the record of that dislocation . . . Particulars gain in vividness, while they lose their independent meaning. Each may be replaced by another. Any one is valuable. Any one you may choose serves as evidence of that condition in which reality is held after being shifted around.

Poetry so conceived will move easily from the palpable to the notional: . . .

> clear as marble
> The air in the woods and like a call forlorn.

(*Besprizoren,* here rendered 'forlorn', means 'neglected' and was the word applied to the thousands of homeless and fatherless children in the civil war. The poem dates from 1917; six years later, on its publication in 1923, this overtone would have been unavoidable.) Nothing in Pasternak's view need be excluded from poetry; and everything it draws upon may be read in terms of something quite different: 'Art is realistic as an activity, and symbolic as a fact. It is realistic in that it did not invent a metaphor

but found it in nature and piously reproduced it.' So in **'Poetry'** [**'Poeziya'**], a statement about his art written in 1923, Pasternak offers four metaphors that he has found in nature to express what poetry is: . . .

> Poetry, I shall swear
> By you and end up wheezing out:
> You are not the posture of the euphonist,
> You are summer with a seat travelling third,
> The edge of town, not a refrain.
> You are Yamskaya Street, stifling sweet like
> May,
> The Shevardino redoubt by night,
> Where the clouds utter moans
> And go their ways like drifting lumber.

He disclaims a mellifluous poetry that carries itself with a conscious dignity and grace, and here Pasternak is still the Futurist. Instead, poetry becomes a matter of overwhelming sensation, close to humanity: in a hot third-class railway carriage during summer, in a city suburb, or among the scents of a street crowded with prostitutes, or at night on the field of Borodino among the wounded and dying.

Characteristically at the head of these four incarnations there is an image from the railway. Journeys by train occur everywhere in Pasternak's art. The title poem of **My Sister Life** ends with a scattering of carriage doors over the steppe; the volume has many references to branch lines and stations in the Saratov region; another poem describes the rail journey back to Moscow. Every one of his first four stories in prose features the railway; a volume of poetry published in 1943 was called **On Early Trains** [**Na rannikh poezdakh**]; and the first part of *Doctor Zhivago* concludes with a memorable rail journey from Moscow to the Urals, while from the very start of the novel trains have been present, their whistles sounding in Yura's ears after his mother's funeral, and his father committing suicide on the 'five o'clock express'. And Pasternak has a love of wayside halts, and all the paraphernalia of railways; he is a master of the technical terms, so that one recalls Kipling in *007*. But Pasternak's interest takes another form than Kipling's: it is not as a way of life, another manifestation of human skill, that the railway fascinates him, but rather as a means to that 'dislocation' in which art consists. Roman Jakobson has suggested that the railway journey appeals to him as bringing a rapid change of place to the passive observer. Thus the girl Zhenya, in *The Childhood of Luvers,* looks out of the train window while 'the Urals goes on shaping and reshapes itself '; and thus in the *Essay in Autobiography* the train (at the beginning) circles round and the wayside halt is 'turned over slowly like a page that has been read', before disappearing from view. The train becomes emblematic of his poetry, in which the writer himself is often an excited and seemingly helpless observer. At the same time, with its chance meetings of strangers, 'a seat travelling third' allows a small-scale experience of city life, the main inspiration of Pasternak's poetry. In the carriage as in the street all is momentarily brought together, like Zhenya's mother and the fat man with asthma.

His strange formula in the next image, 'the edge of town, not a refrain' [*prigorod, a ne pripev*] is repeated in almost the same words two stanzas on: *Predmest'e, a ne perepev*

['A suburb, not a repetition']. The second term on each occasion (*pripev, perepev*) refers back to the mellifluous poetry of the third line, and the variation *perepev* makes it clear that such poetry repeats itself (like much work of the Symbolists in their decline). *Prigorod, predmest'e* both mean 'suburb'; but I have translated the first 'edge of town' since Pasternak's Moscow was not encircled by Wokings and Wembleys. The borderland of the city attracted him because, as he wrote in *Spektorsky,* it is the place . . .

> Where the horizon is far freer,
> And running across the border of the town
> Freely roams the woods' green contagion.

(This is the feeling of the city in the *Zhivago* poems.) The words *prigorod* and *predmest'e* (that which is beside or before the town or place) imply a nearness of relations such as he figures in a poem of 1931: *'Tesney, chem serdtse i predserd'e'* ['Closer than heart and auricle']. Poetry is that which surrounds the city, and mediates between it and the countryside.

About the 'diverse community' [*pyostroe obshchestvo*] in Yamskaya Street, near which Pasternak was born, he speaks in *Safe Conduct.* What he met there filled him with 'a pity for women frightening him out of his life' and Strelnikov denounces the conditions of the exploited in that quarter during his last talk with Zhivago. The note of pity becomes clear in the final image, recalling the night after the slaughter of Borodino, and with its evocation of *War and Peace* pointing the road for poetry to its fulfilment in epic.

This was the road that lay ahead of Soviet poetry in the 1920s, when there was a general turning towards narrative and an 'epic' breadth of conception. Nadezhda Mandelstam has written slightingly of this 'gigantomania', when the novel and the play—and outside literature the epic film—appeared the necessary forms in which to celebrate Soviet life. Pasternak could not remain indifferent to this call, which Mayakovsky had rushed to answer. At least one poem written by Pasternak in this period, **'Sailor in Moscow'** ['Matros v Moskve', 1919] looks in this direction, and was eventually published with half a dozen other poems mostly dating from the earlier 1920s, under the heading 'Epic motifs'. *The High Malady* [*Vysokaya bolezn',* 1924] which first appeared in *Lef* is preoccupied with an assault on the 'fortress' of epic; *Spektorsky,* a long narrative in verse which he had difficulty in shaping—it took six years to complete—began that same year, 1924. A lyric of 1921 opens the new perspective. Having described the life of a poet in Russia as going on . . .

> Under a grey moving crust
> Of rains, clouds and soldiers'
> Soviets, of verses and discussions
> On transport and on art

he continues . . .

> We were people. We are epochs

and there follows the image of a train whirling them across the tundra. More than one poem of *Themes and Variations* bears the traces of that period when private citizens were swept into a new and terrifying era. Pasternak, a lyric poet by vocation, gave much time to both prose and narrative verse, the latter particularly in the 1920s. The prose, as we shall see, remained at this stage an extension of the lyrical voice. But the narrative poetry, whatever the result, aimed to escape from the lyrical mode.

Themes and Variations is thus at the crossroads. On the one hand it recognises even in 1917 that a change must come— . . .

> I shall say *au revoir* to verses, my passion,
> I have arranged you should meet me in a novel.

But a poem of the same year calls childhood 'a ladle for the depths of the soul' [*Kovsh dushevnoy glubi*] and owns it to be 'my inspirer, my choirmaster' [*Moy vdokhnovitel', moy regent*]. And one of the most memorable achievements in this volume is the lines of 1919 that tell how the imagination grows with the growing child: . . .

> Thus they begin. At about two
> From the nurse they rush into a swarm of melo-
>   dies.

There is nothing here to adumbrate the civic poet, who was to write of the 1905 revolution. It goes on to describe how 'they begin to understand' [*nachinayut ponimat'*] and this is through the familiar process of alienation, childhood fears, Faustian exaltation. The poem, in its final stanza, arrives at a position that recalls Mayakovsky:

> So they start quarrels with the sun.

Then a single line follows:

> So they begin to live by verse.

What this meant Pasternak came fully to realise in the next decade. (pp. 67-83)

. . . . .

The closing decade of Pasternak's life was dominated by *Doctor Zhivago*—first the writing of it in those disheartening post-war years, when also the internment of Olga Ivinskaya drove him to seek relief in this personal testament and witness to his time; and then its reception. As early as June 1952 he reported to the Georgian poet Simon Chikovani and his wife that friends on the whole did not care for it and considered it a failure. The sense of isolation was already growing on him. By March 1947, as Gladkov records, his good standing in Soviet literary circles, much enhanced during the war, was beginning to totter; Fadeev, then secretary of the Writer's Union, from which Akhmatova and Zoshchenko had been expelled in the previous year, made a sharp attack on him. Ivinskaya, to whom he was deeply devoted and whose fate threatened to become that of Lara—to perish anonymously in one of the concentration camps in the north—was never during these last years of Pasternak's life safe for long from the K.G.B. And he understood well enough what would be the consequences of publishing his novel. In August 1957, three months before Feltrinelli released the Italian translation, he told Gladkov a cloud hung over him: 'They want to make me a second Zoshchenko.'

It was the award of the Nobel Prize for Literature in October 1958 that let loose the storm. This recognition did not ostensibly follow upon the appearance of *Doctor Zhivago,* yet most people in his own country and abroad assumed a connection. As one American critic [Herbert E. Bowman] puts it, 'Even in the years to come, it will remain impossible to read *Doctor Zhivago* with completely undivided attention' because 'we can never wash the finger marks of politics' from this as from any other work issuing from the Soviet Union. Pasternak had never sought fame: *Byt' znamenitym—nekrasivo*—'To be celebrated is an ugly thing', he wrote in a poem of 1956. Now suddenly the full horror of fame descended upon him—fame outside the Soviet Union, and at home notoriety and execration. The journal *Literaturnaya Gazeta* printed a long letter from the editorial board of *Novy Mir* which explains why they had not been willing to publish *Doctor Zhivago* when it was offered to them. He was expelled from the Writers' Union, and his own Moscow branch recommended that he should forfeit Soviet citizenship. Pasternak then declined the prize, and wrote to Khrushchev pleading that he might not be separated from his native land:

> For me that is impossible. I am bound to Russia by my birth, my life, my work.

> I cannot conceive my fate apart from and outside her.

Khrushchev relented; and Pasternak lived on for another year and a half, now publicly accounted a member of the 'internal emigration'. Overnight he had become a world figure like Tolstoy—similarly mistrusted by the authorities, no more the master of his own time, overwhelmed by correspondence, at once elated by the success of his novel and troubled that this might have come for the wrong reasons.

In the first agony of rejection he wrote a poem entitled **'The Nobel Prize'** [*'Nobelevskaya premiya'*] comparing himself to a hunted animal: . . .

> I am finished like a beast at the kill.
> Somewhere are people, freedom, light,
> But after me the din of pursuit,
> For me there is no way out.

> Dark forest and edge of pond,
> Timber of a fallen spruce.
> The path is cut off on every side.
> Come what may, it is all the same.

> What vile thing have I done,
> Am I a murderer and scoundrel?
> I have made the whole world weep
> Over the beauty of my land.

> But even so, nearly in my grave
> I believe the time is coming—
> The power of baseness and spite
> Will be mastered by the spirit of good.

> Ever more close is the ring of the battue,
> And I am to blame for another thing:
> I have not with me my right hand,
> The friend of my heart is not with me!

> With a noose like this at my throat
> I could still want it
> That my tears should be wiped away
> By my right hand.

There was a sense in which Pasternak had always felt himself to be irremovably at home in the world, even though—as when his close friend Meyerhold was arrested in 1939—he had at times faced extreme peril. Akhmatova wrote some lines after his death that called him 'a converser with the woods' [*sobesednik roshch*]. The tribute is characteristically precise: she saw that Pasternak's intimacy with the natural scene was unique and profound. Yet in this poem he feels for the first and only time estranged from it. The tree has fallen and turned to dead timber; the dark forest makes no response and the pond seems an alien element. Strong in the poem—despite the hope of its fourth stanza—is the conviction that his enemies have found their opportunity to destroy him. (pp. 214-16)

Pasternak's last collection of verse, **When the Weather Clears** [**Kogda razgulyaetsya**] spans the period from 1956 until 1959. These poems, together with an unfinished play, *The Blind Beauty* [*Slepaya krasavitsa*], form an epilogue to his work which had reached its climax in the prose and poetry of *Doctor Zhivago.*

For this book, not published in his lifetime, he had chosen an epigraph from Proust: *'Un livre est un grand cimetière où sur la plupart des tombes on ne peut plus lire les noms*

Pasternak, working in the vegetable garden in front of his dacha in 1958.

effacés.' Elsewhere Pasternak says that there are virtues in oblivion, which is helpful to the artist: 'To lose things in life is more necessary than to acquire them. The grain yields no shoot if it does not die. One should live without pause, look forward and nourish oneself on the living supplies which together with memory produce oblivion.' There he was referring to lost manuscripts. The peculiar creative oblivion he fostered can be understood from a poem **'The Soul'** ['**Dusha'**], which appears undated in the Michigan edition. It belongs to an unusual mode for Pasternak, the elegy with a theme of civic indignation, accompanied by a 'sobbing lyre': . . .

> My soul, sympathiser
> For all in my circle,
> You have become the burial-vault
> Of men tormented alive.
>
> Embalming their bodies,
> Dedicating to them verse,
> With a sobbing lyre
> Lamenting them,
>
> You in our self-seeking age
> For conscience and dread
> Stand like a funeral urn,
> Cherishing their dust.
>
> Their torments combined
> Have bowed you to the ground.
> You reek of decaying corpses
> In morgues and sepulchres.
>
> My soul, a vessel,
> Everything seen here
> Grinding down as a mill does
> You have mingled together.
>
> You must grind down farther
> All that has happened to me,
> For almost forty years,
> Into graveyard humus.

'The Soul' stands third in this volume. It speaks more directly of suffering at the hands of history than any poem outside the *Zhivago* cycle, and it offers a new definition of poetry, the process which makes 'graveyard humus' out of sorrow and disaster. In his novel Pasternak had observed that 'the kingdom of plants' is 'a very near neighbour to the kingdom of death'. 'The grain yields no shoot if it does not die.' Thus personal loss is made bearable in the 'broad serenity' that art achieves by its transformations; many of the names are effaced, but the pity remains.

This is a singular poem for Pasternak to have written, blending as it does the style of eighteenth-century formal ode [*Rydayushcheyu liroyu / Oplakivaya ikh . . . Stoish' mogil'noy urnoyu / Pokoyashchey ikh prakh . . .*] with the cadences and images of something much older and deeply traditional [*Dusha moya, pechal'nitsa / O vsekh v krugu moyom . . . Ikh muki sovokupnye / Tebya sklonili nits . . .*] The feeling of the poem and the consolation it provides bring it within range of Zhivago's last poem, **'The Garden of Gethsemane'.**

The two lyrics that precede it are both declarations of artistic principle. The first of them, making in its course yet another tribute to Chopin, ends with a brief formulation that describes this poem itself no less than the aim of poetry in general: . . .

> Of an achieved triumph
> the play and the torment—
> The tight stretched string
> Of a taut bow.

The second, 'To be celebrated is an ugly thing' [*'Byt' znamenitym-nekrasivo'*] proclaims the principles that had always governed Pasternak's writing: . . .

> The end of creating is to yield oneself up,
> And not making a stir, not success . . .
>
> To be alive, simply alive,
> Simply alive to the end.

The former statement is contrasted by Nadezhda Mandelstam with his earlier **'Definition of Poetry'** in *My Sister Life.* 'To my ear,' she remarks, 'it sounds a little like something from an official report', and she finds the word *tvorchestvo,* 'creation', too grand, while *samootdacha,* 'yielding oneself up', seems in her opinion to betray 'a secret desire to assert and promote oneself'. The comment is acute, as always with her, but too harsh. The moral stand taken by Pasternak is not, I maintain, suspect. Yielding himself up to his art had never in any way been difficult for him. But those who value more highly his earlier poetry than his later, as Nadezhda Mandelstam does, are bound to have noticed, and responded perhaps a little uneasily, to one feature. This final volume accentuates the liking for aphorism which had already shown here and there, for instance, in *Spektorsky.* The effect can be lapidary, as when in the poem **'Change'** ['**Peremena'**] explaining a shift in his attitude to what he had regarded as the special virtues of the poor and of working people, he declares:

> I have lost the human being
> Ever since he has been lost by all.

The poem **'Night'** ['**Noch' '**] ends with an exhortation to himself: . . .

> You must not sleep, artist,
> Nor yield to slumber:
> You are eternity's hostage
> By time held prisoner.

—the last couplet, . . . chiming with the philosophy of Rilke. Again, **'After the Storm'** ['**Posle grozy'**], leads up to another moral for the artist in particular: . . .

> It is not commotions and upheavals
> That clear a way to the new life,
> But the discoveries, storms and bounties
> Of some man's spirit on fire.

Statements like the last have their place in poetry, but one can detect in them a hint of something like 'an official report'. They correspond to some of the didactic passages in *Zhivago* when the voice of Uncle Nikolay can directly or indirectly be heard.

However, the characteristic poems in *When the Weather Clears* succeed not by their neat moral conclusions (which now seem more of a return visit than a discovery) but by their fidelity to a scene observed, or a mood caught and externalised.

His achievement is summed up best in the poem that closes the group, **'Unequalled Days'** ['**Edinstvennye dni'**]: . . .

> In the course of many winters
> I remember the days of the solstice,
> And every one was unrepeatable
> And repeated itself anew beyond counting.
>
> And their whole sequence
> Took form little by little—
> One of days unequalled, when
> It seemed to us time stood still.
>
> I remember them every one:
> Winter comes to its mid point,
> Roads are wet, roofs dripping,
> And the sun basks on the ice-block.
>
> And lovers, as in a dream,
> Draw together in more haste,
> And in the trees on high
> Starling-boxes sweat with the heat.
>
> And the dozing hands are unwilling
> To turn on the clock-face,
> And more than a century lasts the day,
> And there is no end to the embrace.

This might be a description of 'midwinter sun . . . its own season' like the passage in *Little Gidding*. Both Eliot and Pasternak are concerned with an experience out of time; and the ending of this poem might appear no less symbolical than the privileged moments of *Four Quartets*. Yet there is no philosophy, no religious doctrine lying under the surface here. The meaning of the poem is restricted to the notation which records not only particulars (the sun basking on the ice, the thaw that shows like sweat on the starling boxes) but also the relations between them established by the advance of the poem, as it also 'takes form little by little'. The result is completely satisfying, a surely held instant which the very movement of the verse shows to be continually building up anew to the final seemingly endless embrace. What Pasternak says about the winter solstice defines the quality of his perceptions as found in so many late poems: they are unrepeatable because unique, but for the same reason, since this poet lives by and through the unique, the series repeats itself 'beyond counting'.

In general these poems are about transformation: *Chto stalos' s mestnost'yu vsegdashney?* ['What has become of the everyday scene?'] one of them asks; and the question is implicit in all the rest. Their usual key, no longer as at the beginning of Pasternak's career raised to an ecstatic pitch, has become deliberately muted. These are so many visits to listening-posts: . . .

> Like a musical box
> The forest overhears it [a bird's twittering],
> Takes up the voice resonantly
> And waits long for the sound to vanish. . . .
>
> A cock gives his throaty cry,
> And then he is again long silent,
> As though taken with the reflection
> What this striking up could mean.
>
> But somewhere in a distant nook

> Away crows a neighbour;
> Like a sentry from the guardpost
> The cock calls in reply. . . .
>
> In the forest there is silence, stillness,
> As though life in the remote hollow
> Was not bewitched by the sun,
> But there was quite another reason.

The poem from which the last quotation comes actually has the name **'Stillness'** ['**Tishina'**], and it is stillness that characterises the late poetry of Pasternak quite as much as the simplicity of style does. Indeed, the two are inseparable. The restrained metres, the unobtrusive originality of the rhymes, the almost casual concatenation of sound effects—*Otchayannye kholoda / Zaderzhivayut tayan'e* ['Desperate cold spells/ Hold back the thaw']—and the mildness of the conceits—*Osen'. Skazochnyy chertog / Vsem otkrytyy dlya obzora* ['Autumn. A fabulous palace / Open for everyone to inspect']—all testify to an inner peace. It is a very rare thing for poetry in this age continually to celebrate happiness and to express gratitude for life wholly unbidden. Such an attitude scarcely seems believable in a serious artist. Yet in Pasternak it is habitual, and with the years this habit intensified: . . .

> 'O Lord, how perfect are
> Thy works', the sick man thought,
> 'The beds, and the people, the walls,
> The night of death and the city by night.'

Those lines are spoken by a man who supposes himself to be dying.

The poem from which they are taken bears the title **'In Hospital'** ['**V bol'nitse'**] and it is based on Pasternak's experience of a heart-attack in 1953. The entire work reads as follows: . . .

> They stood as before a shop-window,
> Almost damming up the pavement.
> The stretchers were thrust into the car,
> Into the cab leaped the orderly.
>
> And the ambulance, passing by
> Footwalks, doorways, idlers,
> The night confusion of the streets,
> Dived with its lights into the gloom.
>
> Policemen, streets, faces
> Flickered by in the lamplight.
> The attendant swayed
> With her ammonia phial.
>
> Rain fell, and in the casualty ward
> Forlornly sounded the gutter,
> As line after line
> They scribbled the questionnaire.
>
> He was put in the entry.
> The block had no room at all.
> There was a reek of iodine fumes,
> And in at the window blew the street.
>
> The window held in its square
> Part of the garden and a scrap of sky.
> At wards, floors and dressing gowns
> The newcomer looked closely.
>
> When suddenly from the nurse's questions

As she shook her head
He saw that out of this business
He would hardly come alive.

Then he glanced in gratitude
At the window, behind which the wall
Seemed, as by a spark of fire
From the city, lit up.

In the glare glowed the gate
And, illuminated from the city, a maple
Made with its gnarled branch
A farewell bow to the sick man.

'O Lord, how perfect are
Thy works', the sick man thought,
'The beds, and the people, the walls,
The night of death and the city by night.

I have taken my sleeping draught
And I weep, tugging at a handkerchief.
O God, tears of emotion
Hinder my sight of Thee.

It is sweet to me by the dim light
That scarcely falls on the bed
To acknowledge myself and my fate
As Thy gift beyond value.

Now at my end in a hospital bed
I feel the burning of Thy hands.
Thou holdest me as Thy handiwork
And dost hide me as a jewel in its case.'

The core of this poem is to be found in a letter that he wrote to Nina Tabidze on 17 January 1953 at the time of his illness:

> When it happened, and they took me away, and for five hours that evening I lay first in the casualty ward, and then for the night in the corridor of the usual vast and overcrowded city hospital, during the intervals between loss of consciousness and the onsets of nausea and vomiting I was possessed by such calm and bliss! . . . And nearby everything followed such a familiar course, objects grouped themselves so distinctly, shadows fell so sharply! The long corridor, a whole verst, with the bodies of sleepers, sunk in twilight and silence, finished at a window on to the garden, with the inky murk of a rainy night and the reflection of the glare from a city, the glare of Moscow, beyond the tops of the trees. And this corridor, and the green glow of the lampshade on the duty sister's table by the window, and the silence, and the shadows of the nurses, and the proximity of death beyond the window and at my back—all this in its concentration was such a fathomless and superhuman poem!

> In the minute that seemed the last of my life, more than ever before I wanted to talk with God, to glorify what I saw, to catch and imprint it. 'Lord', I whispered, 'I thank Thee for having laid the colours so thickly and for making life and death such that Thy language is majesty and music, that Thou hast made me an artist, that creation is Thy school, that all my life Thou hast prepared me for this night.' *And I rejoiced and wept* from happiness.

The Michigan editors give the date 'Summer 1956' for Pasternak's poem. This makes it more than three years after the experience. Akhmatova too had been told by him all he had undergone that night, so that, as Nadezha Mandelstam relating this observes, he was able to use 'an already existing account'. There seems therefore good reason to believe that the poem grew out of Pasternak's letter to Nina Tabidze, which must have 'caught and imprinted' the details of that time in their final clarity. Mrs. Mandelstam does not care for a poem with origins like these: 'I can always very closely distinguish between verse that wells by itself up from the depths of the mind and that which sets forth a preconceived idea.' For her it had 'too programmatic a ring', although Akhmatova had singled out this particular poem from the body of Pasternak's later verse.

The criticism does not seem entirely fair. Pasternak's letter to Nina Tabidze speaks of every element in the scene having been concentrated so as to form 'a fathomless and superhuman poem'. The window looking on the garden, the glare of Moscow outside, the rain, the tree (now identified as a maple) have been preserved in the poem that eventually records that night. However, the realisation in Pasternak's stanzas is more complete than in his letter. For one thing, we are made to sense the city that surrounds the hospital as inseparable from the scene within: even as he lies there, a gust of air comes in from the street. Now, apart from the nurse who explains the seriousness of his condition, the patient is left alone to confront the climax of a happy life. Gone are the sleepers, the shadows of the nurses; the green glow of the sister's lampshade no longer holds his attention. All that matters is the last sight of the city, its reflection upon the night sky as the maple gives a farewell bow, and his outpouring of gratitude to God. It may not be fanciful to see, in the statement that because the building was full they put him in the entry, an inverted image of the Nativity. Just as the child in Zhivago's poem was greeted by the Christmas star, so here the maple in the hospital garden bids the dying man goodbye. In his death he is cradled like Jesus at the beginning of life. I do not think that Pasternak is here arrogating more to himself than he would regard as the privilege of any believer—to be counted as a precious jewel in the sight of his God.

The poem **'In Hospital'** departs very little from the language and even the word-order of prose. Its narrative form is absolutely straightforward. And yet, while submitting so readily to these restraints, Pasternak has not for one moment slipped into banality as Wordsworth did in some of the *Lyrical Ballads*, or as many Soviet poets, including Yevtushenko, have done. This is partly because his diction never falters: it remains altogether natural, and can place a sleeping draught [*snotvornogo dozu*] in the context of language that is rising to the scriptural, because nowhere earlier has it sought to be consciously poetic. The transformation that makes this so unlike the prose account in its final effect comes about from the poet's parleying with language which even here, despite the scrupulous plainness, exerts a steady pressure to impose another design. Thus three things seen on the journey—policemen, streets, faces—are linked together as a single experience by affinities of sound: *Militsiya, ulitsy, litsa.* So are the sights that the sick man attends to in hospital—*K palatam, polam i khalatam*—wards, floors and dressing-gowns. The ninth stanza (about the maple) shows an intricacy of sound that recalls Pasternak's earlier style:

> Tam v zareve rdela zastava
> I, v otsvete goroda, klyon
> Otveshival vetkoy koryavoy
> Bol'nomy proshchal'nyy poklon.

This poem's simplicity is that of an ornate manner unwound, the legacy of which can be traced for example in the pleasing interest of many rhymes, and the alterations of pace governing the rhythm. The language retains the freedom asserted in Pasternak's earlier poetry to slide at will into extreme informality—*Chast' sada i neba klochok; On ponyal, chto iz peredelki/ Edva li on vyydet zhivoy.* The co-presence of these terms with a more elevated range is well illustrated in the final stanza, which opens with the most prosaic account of the poet's situation—*Konchayas' v bol'nichnoy posteli*—and and then glorifies it, as his feeling demands, with the eloquence that follows. This quatrain indeed can be seen to demonstrate the whole process of Pasternak's later poetry which turns the commonplace into revelation.

Pasternak in this last phase of his poetry is still writing out of the inspiration that first came into full tide forty years earlier. There are no love poems here apart from **'Nameless' ['Bez nazvaniya']** which is playful and detached; but the apprehension of the natural world, though calmer, remains what it had been; all is familiar to the reader who has found Pasternak to be essentially one of the most consistent poets in Russian literature, whatever the differences of tone and manner. A stanza of **'Music' ['Muzyka']**, written in the summer of 1956, recalls—but these things had never been lost for Pasternak—the sights, sounds and preoccupations of that revelatory summer in 1917:

> The roll of improvisations carried
> Night, flame, thunder of fire tenders.
> The avenue under a downpour, the clatter of
>   wheels,
> Street life, the fate of men by themselves.

(pp. 219-30)

> *Henry Gifford, in his* Pasternak: A Critical Study, *Cambridge University Press, 1977, 280 p.*

FURTHER READING

Biography

Barnes, Christopher. *Boris Pasternak: A Literary Biography, Volume One: 1890-1928.* New York: Cambridge University Press, 1990, 507 p.

First installment of a proposed two-volume set provid-

ing the most comprehensive portrait of Pasternak's early life and career.

Pasternak, Evgeny. *Boris Pasternak: The Tragic Years 1930-1960.* London: Collins Harvell, 1990, 278 p.

Translated from the Russian text by Pasternak's son, this volume recounts the author's rise to prominence in and subsequent rejection by the Soviet literary community.

Criticism

Bodin, Per-Arne. "God, Tsar and Man: Boris Pasternak's Poem *Artillerist.*" *Scottish Slavonic Review,* No. 6 (Spring 1986): 69-80.

Examines the biographical significance of "Artillerist" as well as its social and political commentary.

de Mallac, Guy. *Boris Pasternak: His Life and Art.* Norman: University of Oklahoma Press, 1981, 450 p.

Detailed chronicle of Pasternak's life that extensively analyzes his poetry and prose.

Erlich, Victor, ed. *Pasternak: A Collection of Critical Essays.* Englewood Cliffs, N.J.: Prentice-Hall, 1978, 192 p.

Collection of scholarly essays on Pasternak's poetry and prose, with an expository introduction by Erlich.

Fleishman, Lazar. *Boris Pasternak: The Poet and His Politics.* Cambridge, Mass.: Harvard University Press, 1990, 359 p.

Critical study of Pasternak's career.

France, Peter. "Pasternak and the English Romantics." *Forum for Modern Language Studies* XXVI, No. 4 (October 1990): 315-25.

Analyzes the influence of English Romantic poets on Pasternak's poetic style.

Hughes, Olga R. *The Poetic World of Boris Pasternak.* Princeton, N.J.: Princeton University Press, 1974, 192 p.

Provides a critical overview of Pasternak's poetic style, as well as his views on poetry and the role of the poet.

Jennings, Elizabeth. "Boris Pasternak: A Vision from Behind Barriers." In her *Seven Men of Vision: An Appreciation,* pp. 224-46. London: Vision Press, 1976.

Examination of the poems in *Doctor Zhivago,* focusing upon their religious themes and imagery.

Kayden, Eugene M. Introduction to *Poems,* by Boris Pasternak, translated by Eugene M. Kayden, pp. vii-xii. Ann Arbor: University of Michigan Press, 1959.

Evaluation of Pasternak's poetry, focusing upon his poetic innovations and compassionate portrayal of humanity.

MacKinnon, John Edward. "From Cold Axles to Hot: Boris Pasternak's Theory of Art." *The British Journal of Aesthetics* 28, No. 2 (Spring 1988): 145-61.

Outlines the central features of Pasternak's theory of creativity, including "movement and interaction," "transformation and re-union," and "naming and the lyric truth."

———. "Boris Pasternak's Concept of Realism." *Philosophy and Literature* 12, No. 2 (October 1988): 211-31.

Contends that "successful art, for Pasternak, is necessarily realist, issuing each time from a selfless regard toward and a sustained caring for the world, for objects, and memories."

Tarnaovsky, Kiril. "On the Poetics of Boris Pasternak." *Russian Literature* X, No. IV (15 November 1981): 339-58.

　　Examination of Pasternak's poetic technique, centering upon Pasternak's own description of his verse as "uniting the rapture with the ritual of everyday life."

Additional coverage of Pasternak's life and career is contained in the following sources published by Gale Research: *Contemporary Authors,* Vols. 116 [obituary], 127; *Contemporary Literary Criticism,* Vols. 7, 10, 18, 63; *Major 20th-Century Writers;* and *World Literature Criticism.*

Wallace Stevens

1879-1955

American poet, essayist, and playwright.

INTRODUCTION

Stevens is one of the most important poets of the twentieth century. Integrating such European influences as Symbolism, Imagism, and Romanticism into his distinctly American idiom, Stevens has been praised for his virtuosic use of language, superb craftmanship, and exploration of philosophical, metaphysical, and aesthetic concepts. Many of Stevens's works are concerned with the nature of reality, often exploring the relationship between human imagination and the physical world.

Stevens was born in Reading, Pennsylvania, to an upper-middle-class family of Dutch origins. His father, a prominent attorney, and his mother, a schoolteacher by training, encouraged their son's early interest in literature. As a student in the classical curriculum at Reading Boys High School, Stevens studied several languages and national literatures. In 1897 he enrolled at Harvard University, where he attended the lectures of the philosopher George Santayana and began writing lyric poetry in the style of the English Romantics. These early poems, which critics generally perceive as formally advanced and thematically derivative, were published in the *Harvard Advocate,* a student magazine that numbered Stevens as a staff member. In 1900 Stevens left Cambridge for New York City, where he pursued a career in journalism, eventually writing for the New York *Tribune.* His father persuaded Stevens to enroll at the New York Law School in 1901. He was admitted to the New York bar in 1904 and practiced law with several firms in New York City until 1908, when he accepted a position as an attorney with an insurance company. The following year Stevens married, wrote poetry and dramas when time permitted, and was in contact with the literary and artistic milieu of Greenwich Village. His New York poems were published in Harriet Monroe's *Poetry* magazine and in *Trend* in 1914. The next two years were a particularly fecund period of Stevens's poetic career; he published several poems in "little magazines," including "Sunday Morning," which appeared in *Poetry* in 1915.

Stevens moved to Hartford, Connecticut, in 1916, having accepted a position with the Hartford Accident and Indemnity Company. Stevens initially found his career in business stultifying, and once stated in a letter to his wife, "I certainly do not exist from nine to six, when I am at the office." However, his work not only ensured him the comfortable life-style that he desired but, as he told a reporter five years before his death, gave "a man character as a poet to have this daily contact with a job." Writing

in the evenings, on weekends, and while traveling on business in Florida and throughout the southern United States, Stevens published his New York poems along with several more recent endeavors as *Harmonium* in 1923. The imagistic and sensuous descriptions, orientalism, and exotic language of the volume were perceived by most reviewers as the work of a literary hedonist who ignored the "wasteland crisis" of modern society. After the publication of *Harmonium* and the birth of his daughter Holly in 1924, Stevens ceased writing poetry for the next six years. His next book, *Ideas of Order,* was not published until 1935 and was followed by *Owl's Clover,* which appeared in 1936. Stevens received some critical and popular recognition for the poems collected in *Ideas of Order* although he noted that "*Harmonium* was a better book than *Ideas of Order* notwithstanding the fact that *Ideas of Order* probably contains a small group of poems better than anything in *Harmonium.*" *Owl's Clover* departed more radically from Stevens's earlier poetry and he called the unstructured and prosaic work a complete failure. In *The Man with the Blue Guitar, and Other Poems,* published in 1937, Stevens reexamined his poetic style and returned to thematic and formal unity and a metered verse structure, traits that he had modified in *Owl's Clover*. In 1942 he published *Parts of a World* and, what many consider his greatest poetic and theoretical statement, *Notes toward a Supreme Fiction*. The late 1940s and early 1950s brought further recognition of Stevens's poetic achievements and the continued success of his career in business. The recipient of many awards and honorary degrees, he delivered several lectures on poetic theory and aesthetics, which were collected in *The Necessary Angel: Essays on Reality and the Imagination*. His *Collected Poems* was published in 1954 and he was offered the Charles Eliot Norton chair of poetry at Harvard University in 1955, which he refused, remaining with the Hartford Indemnity Company until his death that same year.

As a poet, Stevens was concerned with the relationship between human imagination and the physical world; he often maintained that it is only through the imagination that one can perceive the true nature of reality and acquire a sense of meaning in an apparently empty universe. Influenced by the secular humanism of Ralph Waldo Emerson and the aesthetic philosophy of Santayana, Stevens sought to counter the godlessness and skepticism of the modern age with a faith in art. In such early poems as "Sunday Morning," Stevens illustrated his proposition that "after one has abandoned a belief in god, poetry is that essence which takes its place as life's redemption." The stylized and evocative language of "Sunday Morning" describes the withering away of accepted religious rituals and icons—the Sabbath, the crown of thorns, the cross—and proposes new symbols and metaphors, which are now derived from secular artistic creations, as replacements for the old myths. Stevens further explores the role of art in the modern age in "Anecdote of the Jar in Tennessee," which Helen Vendler has deemed as important to the structuring of the American poetic imagination as John Keats's "Ode on a Grecian Urn" was to the English Romantic tradition. The speaker in "Anecdote of the Jar in Tennessee" discovers that order and meaning in nature must be derived from aesthetic form. Throughout Stevens's poetry his theoretical interests are balanced by a fascination with language. His interest in the sound, appearance, and etymologies of words is particularly evident in such poems as "The Comedian as the Letter C" and "Le Monocle de Mon Oncle."

Throughout the 1940s Stevens's theoretical and poetic investigations are centered on what he termed the "Supreme Fiction." Stevens introduced the phrase in his 1942 poem *Notes toward a Supreme Fiction*. Comprised of thirty short poems, a prologue, and coda, *Notes toward a Supreme Fiction* is considered by many to encapsulate the traits of Stevens's strongest poetry: colorful concrete images, a range of poetic diction, thematic unity, and playful language. According to Stevens, the "Supreme Fiction" or "Grand Poem" is an ideal fusion of reality and the imagination. In *Notes toward a Supreme Fiction,* which was written during World War II, Stevens illustrates this fusion by conflating the terms of war and artistic creation: "Soldier, there is a war between the mind / And sky, between thought and day and night. It is / For that the poet is always in the sun, / Patches the moon together in his room / To his Virgilian cadences, up down, / Up down. It is a war that never ends."

Stevens's mature works, such as *Esthétique du Mal* and *The Auroras of Autumn,* reiterate and refine the aesthetic philosophies that he had evolved in his earlier works. In the poem "An Ordinary Evening in New Haven," Stevens outlines his understanding of the relationship between art, life, and language: "the theory / Of poetry is the theory of life, / As it is, in the intricate evasions of as, / In things seen and unseen, created from nothingness, / The heavens, the hells, the worlds, the longed-for lands."

Some critics have found Stevens's solution to twentieth-century metaphysical uncertainties to be rarefied and impersonal, frequently derogating his poetry for its abstraction and paucity of recognizably human characters and situations. However, Stevens insisted that his interest was not in individual personalities or social issues, but in humanism, art, and epistemology. Believing that his poetry addressed the general human condition by asking that "men turn to a fundamental glory of their own and from that create a style of bearing themselves in reality," Stevens never perceived his poetry as existing simply in the realm of aesthetics. His theoretical acumen and poetic skill have appealed to a wide range of critical schools. Harold Bloom has called Stevens the heir to the Romantic tradition in America, while poststructuralist and deconstructionist critics have praised Stevens's investigations of pure poetry and language. The diverse influences in Stevens's work are united by his unique style and his ambition to define the role of art in an age of anxiety and skepticism. The poetry that grew out of this quest represents one of the major accomplishments in modern literature.

PRINCIPAL WORKS

POETRY

Harmonium   1923
Ideas of Order   1935
Owl's Clover   1936
The Man with the Blue Guitar, and Other Poems   1937
Notes toward a Supreme Fiction   1942
Parts of a World   1942
Esthétique du Mal   1945
Transport to Summer   1947
The Auroras of Autumn   1950
Collected Poems   1954

OTHER MAJOR WORKS

The Necessary Angel: Essays on Reality and the Imagination   (essays)   1951
Opus Posthumous   (poetry, dramas, and essays)   1957
Letters   (letters)   1966
The Palm at the End of the Mind   (poetry and drama)   1971

CRITICISM

Marianne Moore   (essay date 1924)

[*An American poet, essayist, and critic, Moore is considered one of the foremost American literary figures of the twentieth century. Winner of the Pulitzer and Bollingen Prizes and the National Book Award, she also edited* Dial *magazine from 1925 to 1929. In the following review of* Harmonium, *she considers structure, pattern, imagery, and emphasis on the imagination in Stevens's poetry.*]

It is not too much to say that some writers are entirely without imagination—without that associative kind of imagination certainly, of which the final tests are said to be simplicity, harmony, and truth. In Mr Stevens' work, however, imagination precludes banality and order prevails. In [*Harmonium*], he calls imagination "the will of things," "the magnificent cause of being," and demonstrates how imagination may evade "the world without imagination"; effecting an escape which, in certain manifestations of *bravura,* is uneasy rather than bold. One feels, however, an achieved remoteness as in Tu Muh's lyric criticism: "Powerful is the painting . . . and high is it hung on the spotless wall in the lofty hall of your mansion." There is the love of magnificence and the effect of it in these sharp, solemn, rhapsodic elegant pieces of eloquence; one assents to the view taken by the author, of Crispin whose

> . . . mind was free
> And more than free, elate, intent, profound.

The riot of gorgeousness in which Mr Stevens' imagination takes refuge, recalls Balzac's reputed attitude to money, to which he was indifferent unless he could have it "in heaps or by the ton." It is "a flourishing tropic he requires"; so wakeful is he in his appetite for colour and in perceiving what is needed to meet the requirements of a new tone key, that Oscar Wilde, Frank Alvah Parsons, Tappé, and John Murray Anderson seem children asleep in comparison with him. One is met in these poems by some such clash of pigment as where in a showman's display of orchids or gladiolas, one receives the effect of vials of picracarmine, magenta, gamboge, and violet mingled each at the highest point of intensity:

> In Yucatan, the Maya sonneteers
> Of the Caribbean amphitheatre
> In spite of hawk and falcon, green toucan
> And jay, still to the nightbird made their plea,
> As if raspberry tanagers in palms,
> High up in orange air, were barbarous.

One is excited by the sense of proximity to Java peacocks, golden pheasants, South American macaw feather capes, Chilcat blankets, hair seal needlework, Singalese masks, and Rousseau's paintings of banana leaves and alligators. We have the hydrangeas and dogwood, the "blue, gold, pink, and green" of the temperate zone, the hibiscus, "red as red" of the tropics.

> . . . moonlight on the thick, cadaverous bloom
> That yuccas breed . . .

> . . . with serpent-kin encoiled
> Among the purple tufts, the scarlet crowns.

and as in a shot spun fabric, the infinitude of variation of the colours of the ocean:

> . . . the blue
> And the colored purple of the lazy sea,

the emerald, indigos, and mauves of disturbed water, the azure and basalt of lakes; we have Venus "the centre of sea-green pomp" and America "polar purple." Mr Stevens' exact demand, moreover, projects itself from nature to human nature. It is the eye of no "maidenly greenhorn" which has differentiated Crispin's daughters; which characterizes "the ordinary women" as "gaunt guitarists" and issues the junior-to-senior mandate in Floral Decorations for Bananas:

> Pile the bananas on planks.
> The women will be all shanks
> And bangles and slatted eyes.

He is a student of "the flambeaued manner,"

> . . . not indifferent to smart detail . . .
> . . . hang of coat, degree
> Of buttons . . .

One resents the temper of certain of these poems. Mr Stevens is never inadvertently crude; one is conscious, however, of a deliberate bearishness—a shadow of acrimonious, unprovoked contumely. Despite the sweet-Clementine-will-you-be-mine nonchalance of the Apostrophe to Vincentine, one feels oneself to be in danger of unearthing the ogre and in **"Last Looks at the Lilacs,"** a pride in unserviceableness is suggested which makes it a microcosm of cannibalism.

Occasionally the possession of one good is remedy for not possessing another as when Mr Stevens speaks of "the young emerald, evening star," "tranquillizing . . . the torments of confusion." **"Sunday Morning"** on the other hand—a poem so suggestive of a masterly equipoise—gives ultimately the effect of the mind disturbed by the intangible; of a mind oppressed by the properties of the world which it is expert in manipulating. And proportionately; aware as one is of the author's susceptibility to the fever of actuality, one notes the accurate gusto with which he discovers the negro, that veritable "medicine of cherries" to the badgered analyst. In their resilience and certitude, the **"Hymn From a Watermelon Pavilion"** and the commemorating of a negress who

> Took seven white dogs
> To ride in a cab,

are proud harmonies.

One's humour is based upon the most serious part of one's nature. **"Le Monocle De Mon Oncle"; "A Nice Shady Home";** and **"Daughters With Curls":** the capacity for self-mockery in these titles illustrates the author's disgust with mere vocativeness.

Instinct for words is well determined by the nature of the liberties taken with them, some writers giving the effect merely of presumptuous egotism—an unavoided outlandishness; others, not: Shakespeare arresting one continually with nutritious permutations as when he apostrophizes the lion in *A Midsummer Night's Dream*—"Well moused, lion." Mr Stevens' "junipers shagged with ice," is properly courageous as are certain of his adjectives which have the force of verbs: "the spick torrent," "tidal skies," "loquacious columns"; there is the immunity to fear, of the good artist, in "the blather that the water made." His precise diction and verve are grateful as contrasts to the current vulgarizations of "gesture," "dimensions," and "intrigue." He is able not only to express an idea with mere perspicuity; he is able to do it by implication as in **"Thirteen Ways of Looking at a Blackbird"** in which the glass coach evolved from icicles; the shadow, from birds; it becomes a kind of aristocratic cipher. **"The Emperor of Icecream,"** moreover, despite its not especially original theme of poverty enriched by death, is a triumph of explicit ambiguity. He gets a special effect with those adjectives which often weaken as in the lines:

> . . . That all beasts should . . .
> . . . be beautiful
> As large, ferocious tigers are

and in the phrase, "the eye of the young alligator," the adjective as it is perhaps superfluous to point out, makes for activity. There is a certain bellicose sensitiveness in

> I do not know which to prefer . . .
> The blackbird whistling
> Or just after,

and in the characterization of the snow man who

> . . . nothing himself, beholds
> The nothing that is not there and the nothing
> that is.

In its nimbleness *con brio* with seriousness, moreover, **"Nomad Exquisite"** is a piece of that ferocity for which one values Mr Stevens most:

> As the immense dew of Florida
> Brings forth
> The big-finned palm
> And green vine angering for life.

Poetic virtuosities are allied—especially those of diction, imagery, and cadence. In no writer's work are metaphors less "winter starved." In **"Architecture"** Mr Stevens asks:

> How shall we hew the sun, . . .
> How carve the violet moon
> To set in nicks?
>
> Pierce, too, with buttresses of coral air
> And purple timbers,
> Various argentines

and **"The Comedian as the Letter C,"** as the account of the craftsman's un"simple jaunt," is an expanded metaphor which becomes as one contemplates it, hypnotically incandescent like the rose tinged fringe of the night blooming cereus. One applauds those analogies derived from an enthusiasm for the sea:

> She scuds the glitters,
> Noiselessly, like one more wave.
>
> The salt hung on his spirit like a frost,

The dead brine melted in him like a dew.

In his positiveness, aplomb, and verbal security, he has the mind and the method of China; in such conversational effects as:

> Of what was it I was thinking?
> So the meaning escapes,

and certainly in dogged craftsmanship. Infinitely conscious in his processes, he says

> Speak even as if I did not hear you speaking
> But spoke for you perfectly in my thoughts.

One is not subject in reading him, to the disillusionment experienced in reading novices and charlatans who achieve flashes of beauty and immediately contradict the pleasure afforded by offending in precisely those respects in which they have pleased—showing that they are deficient in conscious artistry.

Imagination implies energy and imagination of the finest type involves an energy which results in order "as the motion of a snake's body goes through all parts at once, and its volition acts at the same instant in coils that go contrary ways." There is the sense of the architectural diagram in the disjoined titles of poems with related themes. Refraining for fear of impairing its litheness of contour, from overelaborating felicities inherent in a subject, Mr Stevens uses only such elements as the theme demands; for example, his delineation of the peacock in **"Domination of Black,"** is austerely restricted, splendour being achieved cumulatively in **"Bantams in Pine-Woods," "The Load of Sugar-Cane," "The Palace of the Babies,"** and **"The Bird With the Coppery Keen Claws."**

That "there have been many most excellent poets that never versified, and now swarm many versifiers that need never answer to the name of poets," needs no demonstration. The following lines as poetry independent of rhyme, beg the question as to whether rhyme is indispensably contributory to poetic enjoyment:

> There is not nothing, no, no, never nothing,
> Like the clashed edges of two words that kill

and

> The clambering wings of black revolved,
> Making harsh torment of the solitude.

It is of course evident that subsidiary to beauty of thought, rhyme is powerful in so far as it never appears to be invented for its own sake. In this matter of apparent naturalness, Mr Stevens is faultless—as in correctness of assonance:

> Chieftan Iffucan of Ascan in caftan
> Of tan with henna hackles, halt!

The better the artist, moreover, the more determined he will be to set down words in such a way as to admit of no interpretation of the accent but the one intended, his ultimate power appearing in a selfsufficing, willowy, firmly contrived cadence such as we have in **"Peter Quince at the Clavier"** and in **"Cortège for Rosenbloom":**

> . . . That tread
> The wooden ascents

Of the ascending of the dead.

One has the effect of poised uninterrupted harmony, a simple appearing, complicated phase of symmetry of movements as in figure skating, tight-rope dancing, in the kaleidoscopically centrifugal circular motion of certain mediaeval dances. It recalls the snake in **"Far Away and Long Ago,"** "moving like quicksilver in a rope-like stream" or the conflict at sea when after a storm, the wind shifts and waves are formed counter to those still running. These expertnesses of concept with their nicely luted edges and effect of flowing continuity of motion, are indeed

> . . . pomps
> Of speech which are like music so profound
> They seem an exaltation without sound.

One further notes accomplishment in the use of reiteration—that pitfall of half-poets:

> Death is absolute and without memorial,
> As in a season of autumn,
> When the wind stops. . . .
> When the wind stops.

In brilliance gained by accelerated tempo in accordance with a fixed melodic design, the precise patterns of many of these poems are interesting.

> It was snowing
> And it was going to snow

and the parallelism in **"Domination of Black"** suggest the Hebrew idea of something added although there is, one admits, more the suggestion of mannerism than in Hebrew poetry. Tea takes precedence of other experiments with which one is familiar, in emotional shorthand of this unwestern type, and in **"Earthy Anecdote"** and the **"Invective Against Swans,"** symmetry of design is brought to a high degree of perfection.

It is rude perhaps, after attributing conscious artistry and a severely intentional method of procedure to an artist, to cite work that he has been careful to omit from his collected work. One regrets, however, the omission by Mr Stevens of **"The Indigo Glass In The Grass," "The Man Whose Pharynx Was Bad," "La Mort du Soldat Est Près des Choses Naturelles (5 Mars)"** and **"Comme Dieu Dispense de Graces":**

> Here I keep thinking of the primitives—
> The sensitive and conscientious themes
> Of mountain pallors ebbing into air.

However, in this collection one has eloquence. "The author's violence is for aggrandizement and not for stupor"; one consents therefore, to the suggestion that when the book of moonlight is written, we leave room for Crispin. In the event of moonlight and a veil to be made gory, he would, one feels, be appropriate in this legitimately sensational act of a ferocious jungle animal. (pp. 84-91)

> *Marianne Moore, "Well Moused, Lion," in* The Dial, *Chicago, Vol. 76, January, 1924, pp. 84-91.*

Percy Hutchison   (essay date 1931)

[*In the following review of* Harmonium, *Hutchison associates Stevens's verse with the concept of "pure poetry," which he berates for what he perceives as its failure to address ideas and evoke emotions.*]

More than one critic, and not a few poets, have toyed with the idea of what has been termed "pure poetry," which is to say, a poetry which should depend for its effectiveness on its rhythms and the tonal values of the words employed with as complete a dissociation from ideational content as may be humanly possible. Those who have argued for such "pure poetry" have frequently, if not always, been obsessed with some hazy notion of an analogy between music and poetry. As a shining example of this school take Sidney Lanier, who was a skilled musician as well as a notable poet. Lanier advanced the theory that every vowel has its color value. This was not an association of ideas; the letter "e" was not red because it is in the word red, or green because it is in the word green, but the hearer, experiencing the word should, on Lanier's theory, experience, simultaneously with the sound, a distinct sensation of color. In the second decade of this century—the movement began in the first decade—numerous poetic schools drove theory hard. Perhaps none strove especially to carry out Lanier's color hypothesis, but there were the Imagists, and there was Vorticism and Cubism, and many more "isms" besides. For the most part, these schools have died the death which could have been prophesied for them. Poetry is founded in ideas; to be effective and lasting, poetry must be based on life, it must touch and vitalize emotion. For proof, one has but to turn to the poetry that has endured. In poetry, doctrinaire composition has no permanent place.

Hence, unpleasant as it is to record such a conclusion, the very remarkable work of Wallace Stevens cannot endure. The verses which go to make up the volume *Harmonium* are as close to "pure poetry" as one could expect to come. And so far as rhythms and vowels and consonants may be substituted for musical notes, the volume is an achievement. But the achievement is not poetry, it is a tour de force, a "stunt" in the fantastic and the bizarre. From one end of the book to the other there is not an idea that can vitally affect the mind, there is not a word that can arouse emotion. The volume is a glittering edifice of icicles. Brilliant as the moon, the book is equally dead. Only when Stevens goes over to the Chinese does he score, and then not completely, for with all the virtuosity that his verse displays he fails quite to attain the lacqueur finish of his Oriental masters. The following, **"Hibiscus on the Sleeping Shores,"** is the piece that comes nearest to the Chinese, and this is marred by the intrusion in the last line of the critical adjective "stupid."

> I say now, Fernando, that on that day
> The mind roamed as a moth roams,
> Among the blooms beyond the open sand;
> And that whatever noise the motion of the waves
> Made on the sea-weeds and the covered stones
> Disturbed not even the most idle ear.
> Then it was that the monstered moth
> Which had lain folded against the blue
> And the colored purple of the lazy sea,

And which had drowsed along the bony shores,
Shut to the blather that the water made,
Rose up besprent and sought the flaming red
Dabbled with yellow pollen—red as red
As the flag above the old cafe—
And roamed there all the stupid afternoon.

For the full tonal and rhythmic effect of this it must be read aloud, chanted, as Tennyson and Swinburne chanted their verses. Then, within its limits, its very narrow limits, **"Hibiscus"** will be found to be a musical attainment not before guessed at. But it is not poetry in the larger meaning of the term. And it is not actually music that one has here, but an imitation of music. And if there is a mood conveyed, the mood could have been equally as well conveyed by other lines equally languid of rhythm. No doubt the theorists in poetry have enriched their craft, but at a disservice to themselves. Wallace Stevens is a martyr to a lost cause.

> *Percy Hutchison, "Pure Poetry and Mr. Wallace Stevens," in* The New York Times Book Review, *August 9, 1931, p. 4.*

Harriet Monroe   (essay date 1932)

[*As the founder and editor of* Poetry, *Monroe was a key figure in the American "poetry renaissance" which took place in the early twentieth century.* Poetry *was the first periodical devoted primarily to the works of new poets and to poetry criticism, and from 1912 until her death Monroe maintained an editorial policy of printing "the best English verse which is being written today, regardless of where, by whom, or under what theory of art it is written." Monroe was one of the first to publish Stevens's poems, with some of his verse appearing in* Poetry *as early as 1914. In this review, Monroe discusses Stevens's role as a philosopher and humorist.*]

The delight which one breathes like a perfume from the poetry of Wallace Stevens is the natural effluence of his own clear and untroubled and humorously philosophical delight in the beauty of things as they are. Others may criticize and complain, may long for more perfect worlds or search subliminal mysteries—for him it is enough to watch the iridescent fall of sunlight on blue sea-water and pink parasols, and meditate on the blessed incongruities which break into rainbow colors this earth of ours and the beings who people it. To him the whole grand spectacle is so amazing that no melodramatic upheaval of destiny could possibly increase his sense of awe and wonder, or disturb his philosophic calm. He is content to live profoundly in the beauty of a universe whose lightest, most transient phenomena are sufficient evidence, to a mind in tune with it, of harmonies magnificent to infinity.

For this reason his poems, even those which seem slight, become hints of this immutable perfection. Like a Japanese carver discovering a god in a bit of ivory, Wallace Stevens, in such a poem as the **"Paltry Nude"** or **"Peter Quince at the Clavier"** presents the ineffable serenity of beauty.

Man's interference with this serenity—an interference ineffectual in any ultimate sense—is the central theme of his longer poems. In the one-act play **"Three Travellers Watch a Sunrise,"** a poem exquisite and deeply moving beyond analysis, this interference brings about tragedy; but even tragedy is shown as ineffectual to contradict beauty, whose processional march of splendor demands agony along with joy. In **"The Comedian as the Letter C"** the interference brings the more bewildering frustration of comedy; but even this falls whimsically into the scheme, for beauty invincible and immortal accepts frustration just as music accepts discord—and, lo and behold, the symphony moves on enriched. The hero of **"Carlos Among the Candles"** may be confused and amazed, but he goes on lighting the candles and illuminating with beams from the human imagination the inexhaustible beauty of the world. (pp. 39-40)

[There] was never a more flavorously original poetic personality than the author of [*Harmonium*]. If one seeks sheer beauty of sound, phrase, rhythm, packed with prismatically colored ideas by a mind at once wise and whimsical, one should open one's eyes and ears, sharpen one's wits, widen one's sympathies to include rare and exquisite aspects of life, and then run for this volume of iridescent poems.

I should like to take my copy to some quiet sea-flung space in Florida, where a number of the poems were written. The sky, perhaps, is cobalt, with mauve-white clouds; the sea is sapphire, flicking into diamonds under the wind; the sand is a line of purplish rose, and there are gaudy bathers and loiterers on the beach. And here is a poet undaunted by all this splendor, a poet as sure of delight as nature herself, as serenely receptive of beauty. The bleak despairs of lesser men visit him not at all—his philosophy embraces the whole fantastic miracle of life. . . . (p. 41)

For the philosopher and the satirist temper the poet's rage in Wallace Stevens. Whether he ever writes his masterpiece or not—and that is always uncertain through the turmoil of conflicting claims which besets us all today—he is of the race of the great humorists, using the word in its most profound sense, the sense in which Cervantes, Shakespeare, Synge, Lincoln may be counted as great humorists. In such men agony sinks into depths dark, hidden and unconfessed. The hard black stone is there, but laughter washes over it, covers it up, conceals it. Tragedy is comedy with such men—they are aware of the laughter of the gods and the flaming splendor of man's fight against it. This poet is one of them; his work, however incomplete as yet, is haughty with their lineage.

Always, in his lightest play of whimsicalities as well as in his most splendid assertions of beauty, one feels this deeper note, this sense of ultimate vanities and ecstasies contending, in the human atom, against infinities that threaten it with doom. The play of whimsicalities may seem a mere banter of word-bubbles, as in **"Ordinary Women"**; the assertions of beauty may be as magical in pomp of color and sound as **"Le Monocle de Mon Oncle"** . . . or as **"The Paltry Nude Starts on a Spring Voyage"**. . . . But in either extreme of lovely or whimsical utterance one feels the larger rhythms, one measures the poet's sweep by spaces beyond our earthly inches.

Perhaps **"The Comedian as the Letter C"** is the most complete assertion of cosmic humor which Mr. Stevens has as yet confessed to the world. It is at least the presentment, probably more or less autobiographical, of the predicament of man in general, or of highly sensitized man—let us say the artist—in particular, as he tries to live gloriously, and finds his soul caught in the meshes of life's allurements. Many poets have made a tragedy of this situation, shouting their agonies of rebellion and despair in more or less effective verse. Mr. Stevens is perhaps more keenly inspired in making of it a comedy searching and profound, a comedy whose azure laughter ripples almost inaudibly over hushed and sombre depths.

His little human unit—this "Socrates of snails," this "wig of things," this "sovereign ghost," . . . in short, this Crispin, who was "washed away by magnitude"—is he not our modern exemplar of frustration, as Don Quixote was in his day? (pp. 42-4)

We must hope that the poem is not strictly autobiographical, that Mr. Stevens, unlike his baffled hero, will get his story uttered—to such a degree at least, as may be within the reach of poor mortality. For this poet, like a supersensitized plate, is aware of color-subtleties and sound-vibrations which most of us do not detect, and of happiness in fine degrees which most of us do not attain. He derives, so far as one may trace the less obvious origins, from no one; but like Napoleon he may say, *"Je suis ancêtre!"* ["I am an ancestor"] for shoals of young poets derive from him. Quite free of literary allegiances to period or place, he distils into a pure essence the beauty of his own world. And beauty's imperishable perfection among shifting mortal shows is the incongruity at the heart of life which this poet accepts with the kind of serene laughter that covers pain. (p. 45)

> *Harriet Monroe, "A Cavalier of Beauty," in her* Poets and Their Art, *revised edition, Macmillan Publishing Company, 1932, pp. 39-45.*

Babette Deutsch (essay date 1935)

[*Deutsch was an American poet, novelist, and respected critic, well known for her studies of modern poetry. Below, she discusses the vibrantly colorful imagery and musical quality of Stevens's poems in* Ideas of Order.]

Wallace Stevens's favorite among his own poems is **"The Emperor of Ice Cream,"** because it has what he calls "the essential gaudiness of poetry." Yet he praises his friend William Carlos Williams for the anti-poetic attitude of a Diogenes. In [*Ideas of Order*], Stevens is both gaudy and, to a lesser degree, anti-poetic. Consider his **"Dance of the Macabre Mice,"** which suggests a surréaliste painting, and begins:

> In the land of turkeys in turkey weather
> At the base of the statue, we go round and
> round.
> What a beautiful history, beautiful surprise!
> Monsieur is on horseback. The horse is covered
> with mice.

As the poem progresses the symbolism becomes clear, and the ornament, shall we say, functional:

> This dance has no name. It is a hungry dance.
> We dance it out to the tip of Monsieur's sword.
> Reading the lordly language of the inscription.
> Which is like zithers and tambourines combined:
>
> The Founder of the State. Whoever founded
> A state that was free, in the dead of winter, from
> mice?
> What a beautiful tableau tinted and towering,
> The arm of bronze outstretched against all evil!

The bizarre picture transforms itself into a sardonic commentary on civilization.

But though Stevens punctuates his observations with thought, though he gives sensation and sentiment a coloring of reflection, for the most part he is content to chronicle a mood, to embroider musically upon his responses to sunrise and twilight, the orchestra and the ocean, birds, fruits, landscapes. His poems are not so much "ideas of order" as order itself,—the pattern that the artist imposes upon nature. He is assisted by the fact that he sees nature in a state that is only semi-savage. He is assisted further by a nice ear and by a keen delight in color, preferably barbaric. There are moments when the present intrudes, as in **"Sad Strains of a Gay Waltz":**

> There are these sudden mobs of men,
> These sudden clouds of faces and arms,
> An immense suppression, freed,
> These voices crying without knowing for what.
> Except to be happy, without knowing how,
> Imposing forms they cannot describe,
> Requiring order beyond their speech.

Or again, in **"Mozart, 1935,"** which recalls, with a difference, MacLeish's "Men of My Century Have Loved Mozart":

> Poet, be seated at the piano.
> Play the present, its hoo-hoo-hoo,
> Its shoo-shoo-shoo, its ric-a-nic,
> Its envious cachinnation.
> If they throw stones upon the roof
> While you practice arpeggios,
> It is because they carry down the stairs
> A body in rags.
> Be seated at the piano.

Yet Stevens is not concerned with the present. He is too much engrossed with what is present peculiarly to himself. If one comes to these verses with a raw sense of the times in which we live—and more generally die—their delicate aloofness may offend. To surrender to them, however, is to be admitted to a world no more private than age and death, no more reprehensible than those moments of heightened being which poetry rescues from the black bag of age and death. For

> Poetry is a finikin thing of air
> That lives uncertainly and not for long
> Yet radiantly beyond much lustier blurs.

Stevens's work is not quite as finikin here as heretofore. He is, as ever, interested in Havana and its particular and rather trifling ornaments. But occasionally he draws a deep breath and fetches forth a more generous canvas, as for this resplendent image:

> In the far South the sun of autumn is passing
> Like Walt Whitman walking along a ruddy
>   shore.
> He is singing and chanting the things that are
>   part of him.
> The worlds that were and will be, death and day.
> Nothing is final, he chants. No man shall see the
>   end.
> His beard is of fire and his staff is a leaping flame.

Sometimes he denies his impulse to be gaudy and accepts a simple adequate metaphor, as when he speaks of "The ever-hooded, tragic-gestured sea." The Brave Man, the declamation of a sun worshiper, might be—except for the line describing the stars' "Pale helms and spiky spurs"—a translation of an Indian chant. There is a new sombreness, a new gravity, about the collection as a whole, so that if he is preoccupied with the Emperor of Ice Cream, who is death, the poet sees him in a more dignified if no less disturbing guise.

> Babette Deutsch, *"The Gaudiness of Poetry,"* in New York Herald Tribune Books, *December 15, 1935, p. 18.*

Ruth Lechlitner   (essay date 1936)

[*Lechlitner was an American poet and critic. In this excerpted review of Stevens's* Ideas of Order *and* Owl's Clover, *she emphasizes his continued focus on the power of the imagination and the primacy of the individual, and concludes that Stevens may be remembered more for his mastery of form than for his ideas.*]

Of the two volumes under review, *Ideas of Order* contains the poems that appeared last fall in the Alcestis Press limited edition, to which three new poems have been added: **"Farewell to Florida," "Ghosts as Cocoons"** and **"Postcard From the Volcano."** *Owl's Clover,* Wallace Stevens's latest work, is a group of poems, in blank verse, which may be read as a single long poem with a philosophic theme in symphonic structure.

In *Harmonium,* Stevens's first collection (1923), the poet's preoccupation with design—particularly with "the eccentric as the base of design"—was evident. An interwoven pattern repeating the color of hemlocks and the cry of peacocks might serve, or a recurrent death-sweet Oriental note with a phrase of acrid irony in careful counterpoint. And the gay perfection of his simple melodious lyrics (one recalls with delight **"Ploughing on Sunday"**) is nearer to pure poetry than anything Stevens has since done. A definite theme, however, underlies the work in *Harmonium:* that imagination is the "one reality" in this imagined world. It is a theme fulsomely elaborated by that autobiographical pilgrim, Crispin.

Ideas of Order, which carries on this premise, further sets forth the belief that the poet should be "the exponent of the imagination of society." Stevens is not concerned with the ideas of a political or social order, but of order arising from "individual concepts." The position of the poet

caught between the romantic and the factual, in **"Sailing After Lunch,"** gives rise to an idea of order in the practice of an art. **"Sad Strains of a Gay Waltz"** contemplates the non-existence of order both in nature (in a further poem, **"Marx has ruined Nature, for the moment"**) and in the masses of mankind:

> These sudden clouds of faces and arms,
> An immense suppression, freed,
> These voices crying without knowing for what,
> Except to be happy, without knowing how,
> Imposing forms they cannot describe,
> Requiring order beyond their speech.

As in *Harmonium,* Stevens continues with his fondness for epigram and metaphorical definition: "life is an old casino in a park," "One is most disclosed when one is most anonymous," and, of romantic decadence, "The twilight overfull of wormy metaphors." There is the further juxtaposition of contrasting images, the sun and death; and the two forms of motion, that fixed and suspended (stone, statue), that unbound and flowing (the wind, the sea).

> To stand here on the deck in the dark and say
> Farewell and to know that that land is forever
>   gone
> And that she will not follow in any word
> Or look, nor ever again in thought, except
> That I loved her once. . . .

But the poems retain music as feeling, music as the analysis of a mood; the brooding intensity of Brahms, the "essential prose wearing a poem's guise."

Owl's Clover contains a fusion of the themes established in the two previous collections: the all-pervading power of imagination as reality, and the function of imagination alone in creating a sense of order. And imagination, to Stevens, must be considered as an individual as opposed to a mass or collective concept. The poem itself (the title is cryptic) is built up . . . around a central symbol: a sculptured group of marble horses. As Marianne Moore has carefully noted, Stevens employs the "principle of dispersal" common to music, a classical building up and recapitulation of sections in the movement. The first poem, **"The Old Woman and the Statue,"** establishes the sculpture, an idea of order created by the imagination, in harmonious accord with the wind-blown, autumn-bronze trees surrounding it. This, as foreseen by the sculptor, makes for an ordered design, but there is an unforeseen intrusion: an old woman, black-cloaked, walking along the park path, seeing nothing but herself and her solitude. Hence, this intrusion reduces the mass of "winged stone" to "marble hulk"; light, confronted by "black thought," falls falsely.

"Mr. Burnshaw and the Statue" is in the nature of a reply to a review by Stanley Burnshaw of *Ideas of Order* [published in *New Masses,* 1 October 1935], in which the reviewer took Stevens to task for his anti-collective viewpoint and the confusion of his ideas. Starving again with his sculptured marble horses, from a rather lamely satiric statement that they are not even Russian animals, Stevens pretends a future replacement of the statue by stones on which shall be carved "The mass appoints these marbles of itself to be itself." He shudders at a time when politics will rule a poet's world—a world impossible for poets. In such a world, when the hopeless waste of the past merges with the waste to come, and from which the peacocks, doves and ploughman of yesterday are fled,

> . . . buzzards pile their sticks among the bones
> Of buzzards and eat the bellies of the rich,
> Fat with a thousand butters, and the crows
> Sip the wild honey of the poor man's life,
> The blood of his bitter brain: and there the sun
> Shines without fire on columns intercrossed,
> White slapped on white, majestic, marble heads
> Severed and tumbled into seedless grass,
> Motionless, knowing neither dew nor frost.

The cooler, graver "northward" moving voice of Stevens becomes predominant. His statue is a part of northern sky, the marble "imagined in the cold." His spiritual survey of modern Europe (in contrast to Africa, where death sits on the serpent's throne) is dispassioned analysis; the heaven of Europe is empty, the heaven that was once the "spirit's episcopate," in which man, walking alone, beheld truth. Here, again, imagination on singular wings achieves the "order" of solitude; the plural, or mass, represents chaos. The question as to the desirability of man thinking his separate thoughts, or of men thinking together as one, is further propounded. **"Somber Figuration,"** the concluding piece, is an apostrophe to the power of imagination transcending thought—imagination, "the man below," born within us as a second self. But

> Even imagination has an end
> When the statue is not a thing imagined, a stone
> That changed in sleep.

The somberly melodic final lines show the marked differences between Stevens's work in *Harmonium* and his present mood and technique:

> . . . to feel again
> The reconciliation, the rapture of a time
> Without imagination, without past
> And without future, a present time, is that
> The passion, indifferent to the poet's hum,
> That we conceal? A passion to fling the cloak,
> Adorned for a multitude, in a gesture spent
> In the gesture's whim, a passion merely to be
> For the gaudium of being, Jocundus instead
> Of the black-blooded scholar, the man of the
>   cloud, to be
> The medium man among other medium men.
> The cloak to be clipped, the night to be rede-
>   signed,
> Its land-breath to be stifled, its color changed,
> Night and the imagination being one.

By recognizing the importance of political and social change, but refusing to admit the desirability of the union of the mass in an "orderly" life, Stevens is obviously open to attack from the left. He takes his stand as a poet who prefers to suffer defeat by a cosmic rather than a Marxian law. He is aware that his is the philosophical liberal attitude; that he ironically admits his confusion and the anomaly of his position ("my old boat goes round on a crutch") is a point in his favor, but scarcely helps in resolving contradictions.

Stevens may well be remembered not so much for his ideas as for his superb mastery of form. In his present experi-

mentation with the possibilities of the iambic pentameter of blank verse as a flexible instrument for modern prosody, he has made expert use of word-stress, internal rhyme, occasional inverted phrasing and—as in the above-quoted passage—variation in the metrical line itself to gain a finely integrated verbal texture.

> *Ruth Lechlitner, "Imagination as Reality," in* New York Herald Tribune Books, *December 6, 1936, p. 40.*

Eda Lou Walton   (essay date 1937)

[*Walton was an American critic, anthologist, and poet. In the following review of* The Man with the Blue Guitar, *she praises the "leaner, more casual" quality of Stevens's poems, asserting that the collection departs from his previous focus on beauty to express an interrelationship between imagination and the real world.*]

In his last two books of poetry Wallace Stevens has been preoccupied with the relationship between the world of the imagination and the real world. *Owl's Clover* reprinted in this collection in briefer and more perfect form, emphasized the opposition between these two worlds. *The Man With the Blue Guitar,* even as Stevens himself says, is a series of poems indicating the "conjunctioning between things as they are and things imagined."

One of the finest American lyric poets, Stevens, like Yeats, has moved from richly harmonized reflections concerning beauty toward a leaner poetic analysis of the real world. All of his earlier poems were published under the single title *Harmonium.* Truly he has changed instruments: he has forsaken the organ of formal harmonized singing for the guitar, an instrument for the most informal improvisation. He calls his guitar "blue" because strummed it changes the recitative concerning actual life.

> They said, "You have a blue guitar
> You do not play things as they are."
>
> The man replied, "Things as they are
> Are changed upon the blue guitar."

In this new group of poems Stevens has avoided all embroideries of language. In rhythms that precisely approximate guitar playing and singing, he talks out his ideas. At times the singer is himself completely identified with his instrument, at times he and the instrument are in syncopation. But under the influence of the rhythm, the informal and contradictory effects of life as the poet observes them, seem to take on an art form.

> Poetry is the subject of the poem,
> From this the poem, issues and
>
> To this returns. Between the two,
> Between the issue and return, there is
>
> An absence in reality,
> Things as they are. Or so we say.

Wallace Stevens has always perceived the truth stated here, but in his earlier poems he saw the necessity of dwelling always, even though ironically, on beauty:

> Beauty is momentary in the mind—

The fitful tracing of a portal
But in the flesh it is immortal

The body dies; the body's beauty lives
So evenings die, in their green going,
A wave interminably flowing.

This new collection of poems indicates, in other words, that a fine poet has come to devote himself to proving an interrelationship between fact and vision. He has forsaken any desire to devote himself to building beauty apart from life. Therefore, though this poetry is leaner, more casual, the collection is a distinct advance in Stevens's work. The skill of these plucked and strummed-out improvisations proves him again the master of the most subtle rhythmical effects.

> *Eda Lou Walton, "Wallace Stevens's Two Worlds," in* The New York Times Book Review, *October 24, 1937, p. 5.*

Mary M. Colum　(essay date 1942)

[*In the following review of* Parts of a World, *Colum discusses the collection's emphasis on the role of imagination and human consciousness in the world and faults its intellectual, speculative quality as unpoetic.*]

Parts of a World is Wallace Stevens's latest book. There is no doubt that this is a poet with a following some of whom are certainly distinguished; and judging by the general nonsense that is written about him, some a little crack-brained. So impressive is the mind behind ***Parts of a World*** that one hesitates to express dissatisfaction with its product. The author, we are told on the jacket of the book, is concerned with the relation between the imagination and the world, but he himself tells us that in our time consciousness takes the place of the imagination. It seems to us that what Wallace Stevens is really concerned with is the relation between one man's consciousness and the world, but a world in which humanity and its problems, desires and affections have hardly any place. The mind that the author projects into such careful and measured language is the philosophic speculative mind where the passions are of the intellectual rather than the sensuous order. We can have no great poetry without intellectual brooding, but when the speculative intellect is too dominating, as it is now among a certain type of writer, the result, no matter what command he has over rhythms and words, is something other than poetry. Consider these lines from **"The Poems of Our Climate"**:

> Say even that this complete simplicity
> Stripped one of all one's torments, concealed
> The evilly compounded, vital I
> And made it fresh in a world of white.
> A world of clear water, brilliant-edged,
> Still one would want more, one would need
> 　　more,
> More than a world of white and snowy scents.

This is very accomplished writing, but one reader, anyway, gravely doubts if it has in it enough sensuous delight to be poetry. It reads a little like a piece of Thomas Aquinas. Wallace Stevens has been compared to a whole array of French poets, including Laforgue and Gautier. Actual-ly there is something of Gautier in Stevens, but temperamentally he seems to this reviewer to be the opposite of Laforgue, whose concern was with people and with objects permeated with a sense of people. Wallace Stevens's concern is with objects, and when he writes about people they are simply other objects. He seems to be aware of his separation from life as it is commonly lived:

> To think of a dove with an eye of grenadine
> And pines that are cornets, so it occurs,
> And a little island full of geese and stars:
> It may be that the ignorant man, alone,
> Has any chance to mate his life with life
> That is the sensual, pearly spouse, the life
> That is fluent in even the winteriest bronze.

> *Mary M. Colum, in a review of "Parts of a World," in* The New York Times Book Review, *November 29, 1942, p. 12.*

Gerard Previn Meyer　(essay date 1946)

[*Meyer was an American poet and critic. In the following review of* Esthétique du mal, *he praises the collection's language, balance between imagination and reality, and exploration of the problem of evil.*]

There are major poets in our midst, and Wallace Stevens is one of them. He is a major poet because he has come to grips with the really major concerns of life in any age, in any time—the conflict of the imagination with reality, the nature of reality itself—and, at every step, has shown the perfect control of the artist who is master of his craft, the musician who commands his instrument. This latter-day "Hartford Wit," however much he may remain caviare to the general, today stands clearly revealed as a talent that has survived the test of both coterie fame and public neglect and gone on to deepen toward a peculiar perfection.

Eloquent of his control, of his ability to "abstract reality," is the not altogether irrelevant circumstance that the diligent student of Stevens's poetry—now extended within the covers of seven books—will not discover, must search in vain to find any mention of the position (surely unique, for a poet!) of this man as a man of this world, not merely *in* it. He must go elsewhere to learn that Wallace Stevens is—to put the awful truth bluntly—vice-president of a large insurance company in the insurance capital of Hartford, Connecticut; that he is, by profession, lawyer; and that he has passed his sixty-sixth birthday. It takes an exceptional sort of man to keep his personal life so completely out of his poetry; a sort of man reticent, even shy, by nature, who is driven to speech—for he is a poet—but, being driven to it, does not begin to speak until he has chosen his words carefully.

That this is the kind of poet Stevens is suggested also by his publishing history. Sometime in 1917, or shortly thereafter, he wrote a letter to William Carlos Williams (with whom he had appeared in *Others,* together with T. S. Eliot, Alfred Kreymborg, Marianne Moore, Ezra Pound, and Carl Sandburg "and Others"), in which he observed: "Well, a book of poems is a damned serious affair." He proved that he meant this by waiting until 1923 to issue his own first volume, **Harmonium.** He was the last of his poetic generation to publish a book. The reader curious to learn the subsequent events of Stevens's life-in-print is referred to the excellent "Wallace Stevens Number" of *The Harvard Advocate* which appeared in December 1940; undoubtedly out of print, it may be found in the larger libraries. It tells the fascinating story of Stevens's gradual, but inevitable, emergence as much more than the "dandy," the exponent of a "bizarre," niggling sensuality" that early critics (Gorham Munson, Llewelyn Powys) thought him to be. In passing, it may be noted that the epithets "dandy," "bizarre," and "niggling" were touched off by his "exotic" vocabulary—the exoticism of which, R. P. Blackmur later pointed out in a careful essay [in the *Partisan Review,* May-June 1943], might have been traced to the extreme *care* with which Stevens chose the exact words he wanted for his purposes. In like measure, this poet, warned in the '20's [by John Gould Fletcher in his "The Revival of Estheticism," *Freeman,* December, 1923] that "he must either expand his range to take in more human experience, or give up writing altogether," has been disclosed, in his later works, to be acutely aware of "things as they are": his awareness has been so evident, his position towards other people and "the confusion in which they find themselves" so plainly stated, that his writings have been the focus of attack from the socially-minded critics.

Yet even they can never completely reject him, because—since he chooses his words carefully—he is one of the few living masters of the poetic idiom as a crystal ("tranquillizing with this jewel / the torments of our confusion")—and thus stands on unassailable ground, poetically. He is a master of what the semanticists call the plurisign—the connotative word that distinguishes poetry from prose; the resonances, both of sound and of feeling, in Stevens's language have been justly said to "extend indefinitely," to approach the infinite in fact.

Does this take him "out of this world," as his detractors (and some misguided admirers) have asserted? Not if you ponder and accept the Stevens view of reality—call it "a willing suspension of unbelief," if you will. Now, the nature of reality has certainly been narrowed unnecessarily by our pragmatic and materialistic writers. As Stevens said at Princeton, in a lecture delivered some four years ago, "Unreal things have a reality of their own, in poetry as elsewhere." In **Harmonium,** indeed, he had dared to go so far as to speak of "The imagination the one reality / in this imagined world." But Stevens is not an unreconstructed follower of Berkeley. "Reality is things as they are." It "includes all its natural images and its connotations are without limit." Stevens's reality, in short, is a reality for the atomic age. He has quoted with approval Dr. Joad's dictum:

> Every body, every quality of a body, resolves itself into an enormous number of vibrations, movements, changes. . . . Philosophy has long dismissed the notion of substance and modern physics has endorsed the dismissal. . . . How then does the world come to appear to us as a collection of solid, static objects extended in

space? Because of the intellect, which presents us with a false view of it.

Nevertheless, the primary concern of Stevens has always been poetry, which requires more than reality (even though reality be more than mere): in short, imagination. We must all be immensely grateful to Wallace Stevens for his consistency in asserting and proving the superior place of the imagination in the hierarchy of values. But this imagination is not the uncontrolled sort, though it may make use of the subconscious. "The imagination loses vitality as it ceases to adhere to what is real." The fact is that Stevens, a self-confessed romantic and escapist, even defiantly proud of it, though completely aware of reality is not thrown into emotional or intellectual confusion by it; he maintains an equilibrium between imagination and reality, being possessed of a profound understanding of both these factors.

His latest book, **Esthétique du Mal,** would seem to balance the two, and to reflect in its very title Stevens's preoccupation with the external problem: that of finding some answer—however much of an evasion it may *seem*—for the question of evil in the world has always challenged the explanations of religion. The very existence of pain, the poet seems to say, can be laid at the door of humankind; nature, on the other hand, is serenely indifferent:

> Except for us, Vesuvius might consume
> In solid fire the utmost earth and know
> No pain (ignoring the cocks that crow us up
> To die). This is a part of the sublime
> From which we shrink. And yet, except for us,
> The total past felt nothing when destroyed.
>   Pain, human pain
>   does not regard
> This freedom, this supremacy, and in
> Its own hallucination never sees
> How that which rejects it saves it in the end.

Here, truly, is a new, if less obvious, kind of salvation, perhaps no more difficult for the mind to accept today than the old kind based on the belief that nothing on earth is regarded with indifference in heaven—a belief sorely shaken by the existence of evil.

Stevens cannot, it appears, accept the orthodox, anthropomorphic Deity:

> The fault lies with an over-human god,
> Who by sympathy has made himself a man . . .

but chooses instead a salvation in

> "the health of the world":
>   It seems
> As if the health of the world might be enough.

The health of the world is closely tied up with the physical: it can be defeated by "the false engagements of the mind." And again:

> The greatest poverty is not to live
> In a physical world.

This is a theme the poet has celebrated for a long time, as far back as **"Peter Quince at the Clavier,"** in fact, with its "Beauty is momentary in the mind—/ The fitful tracing of a portal; / But in the flesh it is immortal." Because of the domination of this theme, his reaction to "ideological" revolutions might have been predicted:

> Revolution
> Is the affair of logical lunatics.

Nor is a compassion that can "take in more human experience" lacking in that noble elegy beginning, "How red the rose that is the soldier's wound," which has already been anthologized, and which, nevertheless, deserves quotation entire here, on its own merits alone and also because it gives the lie once more to the persistent fiction that Wallace Stevens's certainly special world is not tangential to the "commonal":

> How red the rose that is the soldier's wound,
> The wounds of many soldiers, the wounds of all
> The soldiers that have fallen, red in blood,
> The soldier of time grown deathless in great size.
>
> A mountain in which no ease is ever found,
> Unless indifference to deeper death
> Is ease, stands in the dark, a shadows' hill,
> And there the soldier of time has deathless rest.
>
> Concentric circles of shadows, motionless
> Of their own part, yet moving on the wind,
> From mystical convolutions in the sleep
> Of time's red soldier deathless on his bed.
>
> The shadows of his fellows ring him round
> In the high night, the summer breathes for them
> Its fragrance, a heavy somnolence, and for him,
> For the soldier of time, it breathes a summer
>   sleep,
>
> In which his wound is good because life was.
> No part of him was ever part of death.
> A woman smoothes her forehead with her hand
> And the soldier of time lies calm beneath that
>   stroke.

The flawless execution is peculiarly Stevens: the manipulation of sound and beat, the Rimbaudian utilization of vowel-color, the alliteration-rhyme, the delicate shadings of feeling, the sensitive mirror of nature.

But if the object continues to evade the search, may not the object itself be in the search? and what matter, if only the search "give pleasure," as Stevens has said "the supreme fiction" must? That certainly this poetry does, to a supreme degree. (pp. 7-8)

> *Gerard Previn Meyer, "Wallace Stevens: Major Poet," in* The Saturday Review of Literature, *Vol. XXIX, No. 12, March 23, 1946, pp. 7-8.*

Robert Lowell   (essay date 1947)

[*The winner of two Pulitzer Prizes and a National Book Award, Lowell is widely considered the premier American poet of his generation. One of the original proponents of the confessional school of poetry, he frequently voiced personal as well as social concerns, leading many to regard him as the prototypical liberal intellectual writer of his time. In the following essay, Lowell emphasizes the primacy of imagination and philosophy in*

Transport to Summer, *favorably comparing the volume to Stevens's previous collections.*]

The subject throughout Stevens's poems is the imagination, and its search for forms, myths, or metaphors that will make the real and the experienced coherent without distortion or simplification. . . . In his later poems Stevens often uses an elaborate machinery of abstractions, but what he is saying has changed very little. His world is an impartial, hedonistic, speculative world—he is closer to Plato than to Socrates, and closer to the philosophy and temperament of George Santayana than to Plato. Directly or indirectly much of his thought is derived from the dialectical idealism of Hegel. (p. 400)

His places are places visited on a vacation, his people are essences, and his passions are impressions. Many of his poems are written in a manner that is excessively playful, suave, careless, and monotonous. And their rhetoric, with its Tennysonian sound effects, its harmonious alliteration, and its exotic vocabulary, is sometimes no more than an enchanting inflection of the voice.

The [poems in *Transport to Summer*] are more philosophical, and consider many things in this world of darkness ("Lenin on a bench beside a lake disturbed / The swans. He was not the man for swans") which the Stevens of *Harmonium* would have excluded as unpoetic. His language is simpler and more mature. But structural differences make all that has been gained precarious. Nothing like the dense, large-scale organization of his **"Sunday Morning,"** or even the small perfection of his **"Peter Quince at the Clavier,"** is attempted. The philosophy is not exhaustive and marshaled as in Lucretius; and it is seldom human and dramatic as in Donne. When one first reads this poetry that juggles its terminology with such lightness and subtlety, one is delighted; but as one rereads, it too often appears muddled, thin, and repetitious. How willingly one would exchange much of it for the concrete, gaudy wit of *Harmonium.*

The points that I have been making are probably overstated, and they are necessarily simplified. But few poets of Stevens's stature have tossed off so many half-unfinished improvisations. Underneath their intellectual obscurity and whimsey, their loose structures, their rhetorical and imagistic mannerisms, and their tenuous subject matter, there seems to be something in the poet that protects itself by asserting that it is not making too great an effort.

The best poems in *Transport to Summer* are as good as anyone is writing in English. . . . In spite of a few beautiful sections—particularly *Begin, ephebe, by perceiving; The first idea was not our own; Not to be realized; It feels good as it is; The great statue;* and *A lasting visage*—and many fine moments, the whole [of *Notes Toward a Supreme Fiction*] seems to me to be unsuccessful. Its structure is sloppy, idiosyncratic, and repetitious. It rambles and rambles without gathering volume, and many of the sections are padded to fill out their twenty-one lines. Much of the rhetoric is extremely mannered. Certain details, such as Canon Asperin, and Nanzia Nunzio Confronting Ozymandias, seem written for Stevens's private amusement. Of the shorter poems, I think the best is **"No Pos-**

sum, No Sop, No Taters." It is objective and subtle in its rhythms and perceptions, and is certainly one of Stevens's most magical and perfect slighter pieces. Other small poems in *Transport to Summer* approach it in excellence but are imperfect, or have much less to them. **"Dutch Graves in Bucks County"** is much grander and more ambitious. The past and the present are opposed thematically. . . . It is written with tremendous feeling, pathos, and power. I think that no living poet would be able to match the magnificence of its rhetoric and resonance. A few lines are slightly mannered, and there is something a little long, formless, and vague about its development. But it is a very large undertaking wonderfully executed. (pp. 400-01)

[*Esthétique du Mal*] is about as good and important a poem as T. S. Eliot's "Four Quartets" or "Ash Wednesday." Its subject is: How shall the imagination act when confronted with pain and evil? The structure is not very tight, two or three sections are not particularly good, and several others have a great number of bad or overwritten lines. The good parts can be detached, but they lose some of their momentum. But *Esthétique du Mal* is more in the grand manner than any poetry since Yeats's; and it reminds one of parts of *Cymbeline* and *The Winter's Tale*—slow and rapid, joining the gorgeous with the very simple, wise, elaborate, open, tolerant without apathy, understanding with the understanding of having lived long. (p. 402)

> Robert Lowell, "Imagination and Reality," in The Nation, *New York, Vol. 164, No. 14, April 5, 1947, pp. 400-02.*

Victor Tejera   (essay date 1948)

[*In the following review of* Transport to Summer, *Tejera discusses the metaphysical and philosophical nature of Stevens's poetry.*]

The discussion of poetry, from the side of the philosophers, should address itself more directly to the poem, to the particularity of the poetic instance, at the same time that it bears in mind the philosophic implications of the concomitant insight and seeks its ontological ground. These implications widen the reference of what seemed a specific perception by giving status to the symbol that carried the perception. At the same time that, and to the degree in which, the symbol acquires status, the compresent emotion acquires perpetuity. The philosophic attitude, it is suggested, gives status to the poetic symbol by being involved in a two-way analysis of its transitivity. It discovers what, externally, made the bare bones of a situation amenable to emotive perception through the symbol. And it unfolds the internal, or psychological, ground of the congruity and color that lend felicity and pleasure to the instant vision provoked, conjured by that symbol. However this may be, it can at least be assumed that the philosophical attitude involves poetry—already a reflective process—in a further process of abstraction.

It is because Stevens' work is a unique attempt to bridge the above-mentioned gap that I do not think it a hardihood to recommend it as reading for philosophers. Wallace Stevens' work [*Transport to Summer*] evinces a large-

ly philosophical attitude to both experience as the matter of poetry, and to poetry as the best issue of experience (he has also written as a critic). This attitude can be read into, and accounts for, the abstract and reflective manner of his work. It also accounts for the freedom and conviction with which he creates inasmuch as in his critical statements he has taken, as the justification of his use of metaphor, an explicitly realistic epistemological position. He believes, like some interesting contemporary philosophers, in the objectivity of the relation of similarity. He sees metaphor as a way of things; his poetry is realism asserted, in operation.

> **[Stevens's] subject is the search for forms, myths, or metaphors that will reduce the chaos of man's experience to an interesting order.**
>
> —*Victor Tejera*

In this respect Stevens is symptomatic of the ever more keenly felt community of subject-matter between poetry and metaphysics. The methods of these two pursuits are obviously quite different; but can it be said that the purposes of poetry as implied by Stevens are so different from those of metaphysics as suggested in the work of Santayana, for example? It is a question of more than the coexistence, observable in both these men and in other poets and metaphysicians, of richly developed imagination with an explicit degree of ontological realism. It is a question of Stevens' novel way of handling metaphor and analogy in such a manner as to make them the bases of his view of the world.

Thus, if it can be said that metaphysics consists in the analysis of the differentiae of being, then it may also be said that poetry is the quest for similarities in the same domain. Seen in this light poetry becomes a complement, a transliteration of metaphysics. Stevens, of course, does not set out to illustrate in the denser, more vivid, medium of his poetry, philosophical theories. But while the relation of his poetry to metaphysics is not quite one of subalternation, he does avow that his subject is the search for forms, myths, or metaphors that will reduce the chaos of man's experience to an interesting order. He attempts, in other words, to invest the world with form for a practical as well as a purely esthetic purpose, i.e., his purpose is practical in the sense a working, say, skeptical or spectator, metaphysics is practical, and esthetic in the sense that his method of presentation is vivid and sensuous. This attempt has three stages, each of which to be effected successfully requires the exercise of a specific virtue. The first stage is Pyrrhonic: *skepticism* clears away the rubble of old and dead forms. The second is empirical and devoted to *observation* of the now naked and consequently stark reality. The third stage is the strictly poetic one and represents a reconstruing of experience through the *invention* of new and adequate forms; forms which are, to one reader at least, a guide to the feelings and a stimulus to the imagination. More important perhaps to other readers will be Stevens' habit, over and above the previously mentioned virtues, of reacting to the presented world with simultaneous irony and wonder. (pp. 137-39)

Victor Tejera, in a review of "Transport to Summer," in The Journal of Philosophy, *Vol. XLV, No. 5, February 26, 1948, pp. 137-39.*

John Ciardi   (essay date 1954)

[*Ciardi was a highly respected American poet, translator, critic, educator, and editor. In the following review of* Collected Poems, *he praises the musical quality of Stevens's verse and suggests that Stevens's lack of popularity among the public and critics is related to his insistence that imagination is more "real" than the material world.*]

No poet of real talent will find an audience ready for him in our time. To the extent that he has achieved his own way of seeing and of saying he will be entering areas for which few but the most devoted readers will be ready. Wallace Stevens is not unique in having outrun the "audience," but he is certainly our one poet of unquestionable major stature to have separated himself by so great a distance. As far as the general reader, whoever that may be, is concerned, Stevens is American poetry's Great Unread. For every fifty citizens who know of Robert Frost and have read a few Frost poems or who have at least heard him read, one or two at best will be aware that Stevens exists. To be sure, the last few years have brought Stevens the Bollingen Prize and the National Book Award. It still seems significant that despite the fact that he has published five of the best books of poetry ever written by an American—the first one as far back as 1923—he has never attracted the notice of the Pulitzer Prize Committee in Poetry. By this time I don't see that the committee has any choice: if Stevens doesn't win the Pulitzer for '54 the committee might as well turn the prize into a blue ribbon and award it at the National Horse Show, for any relevance it will have to poetry.

Stevens's failure to reach the "audience" is a direct consequence, in some part, of his refusal to be a salesman and platform stumper for his poems and, rather more, of his absolute insistence that imagination is more "real" than reality ("The world imagined is the absolute good") and his ascetic refusal to accept in his poems the reality of the "real" world. "I taste at the root of the tongue the unreal of what is unreal." Stevens not only prefers imagination; he denies the reality of the world's view of itself.

Joking with Robert Frost once in Florida (I report the exchange from Mr. Frost's account of it), Stevens said, "The trouble with you, Frost, is that you write on subjects." Frost replied, "The trouble with you is you write bric-à-brac."

The exchange was in play, but the center of the play locates a real difference. Some poets, Frost notable among them, write poems which have their references, at least in large part, in a recognizable external world; to the extent

> **It is not for such devices, or for the philosophy of the imagination, that one falls in love with Stevens, but for the magnificence of his ear.**
>
> **—*John Ciardi***

that we knew beforehand something at least about what they are describing, our understanding of the poems is made easier. Stevens, on the other hand, insists on the poem as its own imagination and subject; a thing made of itself in the saying; a self-entering, self-generating, self-sealing organism, a thing of its own nature.

> The sound of that slick sonata
> Finding its way from the house, makes
>   music seem
> To be a nature, a place in which itself
> Is that which produces everything else.

In the pursuit of that absolute music, that music which rises from itself and follows itself, Stevens has gone farther than any other man in English to achieve his sound effects. So in **"Bantams in Pine Woods"**:

> Chieftain Iffucan of Azcan in caftan
> Of tan with henna hackle, halt.

The reader who does not stay around long enough to realize that this is good play beginning with the comic effect of saluting a champion bantam rooster (significantly strutting about in a pine woods as if he meant to knock over the trees) by the ridiculous name he bears in the pedigree book—such a reader will simply find himself puzzled here, especially if he is one of those literalists who must always know at once where he stands. For that matter, even the most devoted admirer of Stevens is likely to find himself swallowing hard to take down some of the decorative French tags and quasi-Elizabethan lolly-lilly ricanic's Stevens so often runs in while pursuing his "absolute music."

It is not for such devices, or for the philosophy of the imagination, that one falls in love with Stevens, but for the magnificence of his ear. Let any reader begin with such a poem as **"Le Monocle de Mon Oncle"** or **"Sunday Morning,"** and simply ask himself if English or American speech has ever been made to overflow with such music as this. Stevens teaches the language its own singing possibilities.

Even in profoundest admiration, however, I cannot get rid of the feeling that Stevens's true golden period ended with *Transport to Summer.* His sixth book, *Auroras of Autumn,* and what must count as his seventh, being the section of new poems first published in this collection as **"The Rock,"** are still the work of the master, but of the master repeating himself, and just a bit wearily. Stevens is now seventy-five. The age is certainly no necessary limit to the imagination; William Carlos Williams is seventy-five too, and his last book contains some of his best things. Nevertheless, every poet past his first excitement is tempted to become talky and to borrow from himself, and of late Stevens seems to have succumbed to the temptation. The images and the rhythms that arrived to him once as to a marriage tend now simply to arrive to an anniversary, and to come not in an excitement but in a habituation. It is all there, all written, all made. He tends to assume too much from his own past performance. It seems more inviting to talk about his perceptions than to make them happen. It is, to be sure, rich talk. In such a recent poem as **"To an Old Philosopher in Rome"** it becomes almost the real thing again. But the total begins to tire. Even magnificence can grow late. But what matters is the magnificence, and that will be there as long as the language is spoken. (pp. 346-47)

> *John Ciardi, "Wallace Stevens's 'Absolute Music'," in* The Nation, *New York, Vol. 179, No. 16, October 16, 1954, pp. 346-47.*

> **It is easy to suppose that few people realize on that occasion, which comes to all of us, when we look at the blue sky for the first time, that is to say: not merely see it, but look at it and experience it and for the first time have a sense that we live in the center of a physical poetry, a geography that would be intolerable except for the non-geography that exists there—few people realize that they are looking at the world of their own thoughts and the world of their own feelings.**

> **—*Wallace Stevens, in his* The Necessary Angel: Essays on Reality and the Imagination, *1951*.**

Hayden Carruth   (essay date 1955)

[*Carruth is an American poet, novelist, critic, and editor. In the essay below, he praises* The Collected Poems of Wallace Stevens *for Stevens's masterly use of language and his "rhetorical genius."*]

Opulence—it is the quality which most of us, I expect, ascribe before all others to the poetry of Wallace Stevens: profusion, exotic abundance and luxuriance. We carry in our minds an image of poems which teem with rich, strange, somehow forbidden delights, omnifarious and prodigious. Just to read the titles of his poems [included in ***The Collected Poems of Wallace Stevens***] is to acquire again this sense of the extraordinary: **"Tea at the Palaz of Hoon," "The Bird with the Coppery, Keen Claws," "Sea Surface Full of Clouds," "The Man with the Blue Guitar," "Mrs. Alfred Uruguay," "The Owl in the Sarcophagus," "Angel Surrounded by Paysans," "The Irish Cliffs of Moher"**—and hundreds more, of course. They are everywhere, extending round one, as it were, like an incredible, incomparable gallery.

Nor is the idea of a gallery out of place in speaking of the collected edition of Mr. Stevens' poems. I was continually impressed, as I wandered—no other word will do—among the hundreds of poems in this volume, by the way in which they present to us the whole movement of this century in art; no exhibition of paintings could be more expressive of the modern artist's aims and methods. Of course, the poet's very graphic way with imagery reminds one naturally of painting; the bright, Mediterranean colors and the dramatic interiors, as in the opening lines of **"Sunday Morning,"** recall to me most clearly, I think, Matisse, though other readers undoubtedly have other associations. The chief point is, however, that in these poems the many influences on the art of our time can be seen clearly: French, pastoral, metaphysical, Homeric, etc.; and the many aims: to originate, to shock, to re-examine, to analyse, and above all to deal uncompromisingly with the realities of the contemporary world.

In point of time, Stevens' career as a writer has been co-extensive with the development of modern art, at least as it has occurred in this country, and the career itself, as recorded in these poems, reveals the stages through which we have come to believe the masters must always pass. The chronology is not definite and, for my purpose, perhaps not important. But there are the early masterpieces of conventional technique—**"Sunday Morning"** and a few shorter poems in regular but marvelously controlled blank verse. There are the poems in which this technique begins to shift under an experimental impetus; of many examples, **"The Comedian as the Letter C"** is one. There are the sheer experiments, often fragmentary and uncharacteristic. There are the variations on a constant theme—many of them apparently impromptu—of the middle period, when the poet was working toward a strong and individual style, a technique with which he could master any material, no matter how complex or "unpoetic." And there are the later poems which sometimes revert to an old simplicity. The progression has, of course, been accompanied—quickened, pervaded, impelled—by a relentless amendment and elaboration of the poet's theme, and the lavishness of his invention has never diminished.

But why? Why do we inevitably come back to this impression of opulence? One thinks immediately of the abounding images from the natural world, quick glimpses of land and water:

> The rocks of the cliffs are the heads of dogs
> That turn into fishes and leap
> Into the sea.

> It is true that the rivers went nosing like swine,
> Tugging at banks, until they seemed
> Bland belly-sounds in somnolent troughs.

> On an old shore, the vulgar ocean rolls
> Noiselessly, noiselessly, resembling a thin bird,
> That thinks of settling, yet never settles, on a
>   nest.

> The cricket in the telephone is still.
> A geranium withers on the window-sill.

But do they really abound? It was much more difficult than I had expected it would be to find these four detachable examples, and even they are not truly representative. The fact is, most of the poems are single metaphors, short, whole, compact, even spare; the images are used frugally and pointedly; they are never merely decorative. Even the long poems are generally composed of short sections, separated and numbered, which each conform to this pattern of lyric rigor, and the few long poems which do comprise sustained passages of narrative or exposition are surprisingly unadorned. In other words, the poems themselves, when we examine them without our preconceptions, contain neither denser nor more ornate imagery than we should expect to find in 534 pages of poetry by any other author, and in many cases the comparison, especially if it were with the work of his contemporaries, would show Stevens' poems to be the simpler in design, structure, and figuration.

Perhaps, then, it is a question of the poet's subject, his *materia*. Many of the poems, true enough, and especially the earlier ones, convey an exotic scene, a Caribbean radiance of sun-drenched seas and forests. **"Hibiscus on the Sleeping Shores," "The Idea of Order at Key West," "O Florida, Venereal Soil"**—these and many others, most of them from *Harmonium,* the poet's first book, are clearly visions of splendor. But the first poem in the second book is called **"Farewell to Florida,"** and thereafter Stevens' characteristic scene is not tropical but northern, and there are as many celebrations of drab and wintry occasions as of summer. Again I was surprised to find how few of the poems are in fact given to outright flourishes of terrestrial glitter.

The earlier poems, those which appeared in *Harmonium,* are undoubtedly the best known. They have been republished many times in anthologies and repeatedly discussed by the critics. They have become a regular part of university courses in modern literature. And many of them, of course, are undeniably brilliant; it is not surprising that they are used as displays. But they are not as good as the later poems, and emphatically they do not reveal the qualities of Stevens' whole accomplishment. The advantage of this collected edition is the prominence which it gives to the main body of poems.

I think we conclude finally that, in the texts themselves, the language is the only constant ratification of our sense of the poet's opulent invention. There is nothing new in the idea of Stevens as a master of language. But to explore the pages of this collection is to be astonished, quite literally, by the extraordinary range and intensity of his rhetorical genius. It is not virtuosity, for the virtuoso's superlative performance must be theoretically attainable by anyone, whereas Stevens excels at that which only he can do. It is a perfection, a pressing extension within the formulations of his own strict style and prosody, of the aptitude for naming which must be fundamental to any writer's talent. Someday, perhaps, an industrious scholar will count the number of different words Stevens has used; I hope so, for although I am sure his poems incorporate by far the largest vocabulary among contemporary poets, it would be instructive to have the difference measured. Stevens delights in odd words, archaic words, foreign words which he can wrest to an English meaning. In this respect he is like Whitman, but, to my ear, better than Whitman, for

I am never embarrassed by Stevens' importations: he dominates and controls the foreign words with an authority which Whitman could never achieve. More exactly, Stevens is Elizabethan in his attitude toward language, highhanded in the extreme. When all else fails, he derives words anew, gambling with the recognizable roots and associations:

> The grackles sing avant the spring
> Most spiss—oh! Yes, most spissantly.

Such delight in language is infectious, and we are convinced, as we should be, when Stevens says to us,

> Natives of poverty, children of malheur,
> The gaiety of language is our seigneur.

Stevens is the delighted craftsman whose delight is, in part, the access of gratification which comes upon the exercise of mastery. His pleasure is endless because it is part of his work, past and present; it is transmissible because we too, in reading his poems, share that mastery.

True poetry is instinct with this delight—and with much more, of course. With meaning which transcends its verbal properties. With a passion which makes whole the verbal elements. As it happens, Stevens' delight in language is concomitant to his entire vision, his argument. If there is space in this short tribute for only a glance at one or two technical aspects of his poetry, I think we can be sure that scholars and critics for many, many years will be engrossed by the problems of the larger content. As their work progresses and our appreciation grows, we shall see more and more clearly how *humane* is the desire which has given us, in these poems, a delight that is interpretative of our world. Even now, of course, we have in this book poems which are beautiful, impeccable, and famous, poems which are so intimate a part of our time and scene that we are almost persuaded to say, appropriatively: "This is what we have been able to do; by these works we are willing to be known." (pp. 288-93)

> *Hayden Carruth, "Without the Inventions of Sorrow," in* Poetry, *Vol. 85, No. 5, February, 1955, pp. 288-93.*

Elizabeth Jennings   (essay date 1960)

[*Jennings is an English poet and critic who established her literary reputation as a member of "the Movement," a group of writers that included Kingsley Amis, Thom Gunn, and Philip Larkin. In the following review of* Opus Posthumous, *Jennings asserts that Stevens was primarily a visionary writer whose works are introspective.*]

There is a quality in the best twentieth-century American poets which, though extremely difficult to define, gives their work an exciting air of foreignness. One sees words from new angles, as it were, casting strange lights, throwing unexpected shadows. This quality is partly a matter of language and texture but it goes deeper than just that. It is, I think, fundamentally a question of insight, of using poetry for tasks which are usually relegated to the philosopher. There has always, it is true, been a tradition of philosophical verse in England, but in such verse, whether it is that of Pope, Coleridge, Wordsworth or the Eliot of the *Four Quartets,* the philosophical content seems often to be something separate from the form of the poem. One sometimes feels, in fact, that the ideas could easily be extracted from the verse, that they are not essentially *poetic* ideas. In American verse, on the other hand, language seems to be entirely at the service of ideas and insights. And the result, paradoxically, is not an arid metaphysical verse but a poetry highly charged with scintillating imagery. This is as true of the pastoral meditations of Robert Frost as of the elegant inquiries of Richard Wilbur. But it is especially true of the work of Wallace Stevens.

All Stevens's poems are concerned with one overriding theme—the relation between imagination and reality, or imagination as a mode of knowledge. All his poems are, in a sense, about poetry; all of them test the validity of language as a vehicle of truth. The very *naming* of things, therefore, had for Stevens some kind of absolute value even though he usually regarded absolutes with an extreme suspicion.

In *Opus Posthumous,* Samuel French Morse has gathered together plays, poems, essays and aphorisms by Stevens, one third of which appear for the first time. The rest, notably the poems, have either been collected from magazines and anthologies or else taken from early volumes of verse. A number of the latter poems were omitted from the *Collected Poems.* This book represents, therefore, the hitherto scattered prose and verse writings of a major poet.

Wallace Stevens was, above all, a wholly dedicated writer. Although he spent his adult working life in an important job with a firm of insurance brokers, he was not an amateur, a dilettante, a 'Sunday poet'. On the contrary, his poetry, with its deceptive stillness and calm, its constant questioning and doubting, has an urgency which comes from the whole man. The note of alarm is seldom sounded but it is never far off. The elusiveness of this alarm, this agitation, has, I think, unfortunately led some critics into the belief that Stevens was fundamentally concerned with abstractions. Such a view springs, I believe, from a current misunderstanding about the nature of Stevens's verse. He is usually regarded as a metaphysician, a philosopher, whereas a truly accommodating reading of his work would, I am convinced, reveal him as essentially a *visionary* writer. He is a visionary poet, however, who has no belief in God and who searches for meaning and unity in an order both disclosed by and created in the human imagination. *Opus Posthumous* provides convincing evidence of the visionary character of Stevens's mind in the collection of aphorisms which are part of the contents of the book. Here are a few examples of what I mean: 'Reality is the spirit's true centre', 'The world of the poet depends on the world that he has contemplated', 'The man who asks questions seeks only to reach a point where it will no longer be necessary for him to ask questions.'

In such statements as these, as well as in his poems, Stevens shows himself to be a religious man who repudiated dogma, an agnostic who hungered for certainty. In his best-known and great poem, **"Sunday Morning"**, he discloses a world without God, a place where the senses are appeased but appeased only momentarily. Stevens's

poems are, it is true, crammed with religious language and symbols but these things are removed from their proper contexts and employed by him for his own private purposes. Like the paintings, still lifes and *objets d'art* which fill so much of his verse, these religious symbols are only springboards for Stevens's dominant preoccupation—his exploration of the limits of the imagination.

In all Stevens's best work there is a poignant sense of absence, together with a stoic determination to accept that absence. Against this poignancy, he sets a stylishness, a care for detail, a concern with subtleties and nuances. There is no full vision, only adumbrations. In the poems which Samuel French Morse has assembled in this book, the themes which constantly preoccupied Stevens are to be found in many forms and guises. If one predominant subject possessed Stevens all his life, he never ceased to examine that subject from different angles and in different lights. In **"A Mythology Reflects Its Region,"** which may well be the last poem he wrote, we find the same obsession which appears so vividly, so concretely in **"Credences of Summer"** and **"The Comedian as the Letter C."** In this late poem, however, imagery has been stripped down to its essence, simplified and laid bare:

> The image must be of the nature of its creator,
> It is the nature of its creator increased,
> Heightened. It is he, anew in a freshened youth
> And it is he in the substance of his region . . .

The plays printed in this book are interesting only for their insights and images since Stevens was never a dramatic poet. Nor, on the other hand, was he a personal poet in the sense that he passionately explored his own motives, feelings and reactions; he was interested in feeling at its source rather than in its countless manifestations. When he turned inward to examine himself, it was always his own imagination which he tested and probed. His poetry presents the delicate adjustment of that imagination to exterior things, tangible and intangible. In an essay here called *The Irrational Element in Poetry,* Stevens declares, ' . . . while it can lie in the temperament of very few of us to write poetry in order to find God, it is probably the purpose of each of us to write poetry to find the good which, in the Platonic sense, is synonymous with God'. This is an uncompromising affirmation and if *Opus Posthumous* contained nothing else but these essays in which Stevens makes himself wholly accessible to us, it would be of extreme value. But the poems and the aphorisms here are also useful and revealing; they are the products of a deeply reflective, subtle and dispassionate mind. There can surely be little doubt now that Wallace Stevens was a poet of extraordinary originality and splendid achievement. (pp. 85-7)

> *Elizabeth Jennings, in a review of "Opus Posthumous," in* London Magazine, *Vol. 7, No. 5, May, 1960, pp. 85-7.*

Helen Vendler   (essay date 1979)

[*Vendler is an American educator and critic who is widely praised as an outstanding critic of poetry. Her meticulous and rigorous studies of W. B. Yeats, John Keats,*

George Herbert, and Stevens influenced critical percep-
tions of each poet's works and development. Her writings
on Wallace Stevens include On Extended Wings: Wallace Stevens' Longer Poems *(1969) and* Wallace Stevens: Words Chosen Out of Desire *(1984). In the fol-*
lowing excerpt from the latter work, originally published
in the AWP Newsletter, *Vendler considers Stevens's po-*
etry as an expression of personal disappointment and
emotional pain.]

"The words of Mercury," Armado says at the close of
Love's Labor's Lost, "are harsh after the songs of Apollo."
Apollo's songs, like those of Orpheus, are conventionally
thought to be full "of linked sweetness long drawn out,"
but the criterion of sweetness or melodiousness has always
been questioned by our greater poets. On the whole, Wallace Stevens is still considered one of the euphonious,
"sweet," "aesthetic" poets, against whom the anthologies
range our modern realists and ironists. There is some truth
in the opposition, of course, or it would not have been
made: **"The Idea of Order at Key West"** sounds different
from *The Waste Land.* I choose here to enter Stevens'
work by way of an interrogation of his harsher poems,
those in which a brutality of thought or diction reveals
feelings obscured by playfulness or obliqueness in his more
decorative poems. I do this in part because I think the role
of feeling in Stevens' poems has not yet been clarified. It
is popularly believed that Stevens is a poet preoccupied by
the relations between the imagination and reality, and
there is good reason for the popular belief, since Stevens
so often phrased his own preoccupation in those unreveal-
ing words. The formula, properly understood, is not untrue; but we must ask what causes the imagination to be
so painfully at odds with reality. The cause setting the two
at odds is usually, in Stevens' case, passionate feeling, and
not merely epistemological query.

One poem by which to enter this topic is **"Chaos in Motion and Not in Motion"** (1947); the title is itself unnerving as a violation of the axiom that a thing cannot be and
not be in the same way at the same time:

> Oh, that this lashing wind was something more
> Than the spirit of Ludwig Richter . . .
>
> The rain is pouring down. It is July.
> There is lightning and the thickest thunder.
>
> It is a spectacle. Scene 10 becomes 11,
> In Series X, Act IV, et cetera.
>
> People fall out of windows, trees tumble down,
> Summer is changed to winter, the young grow
>   old,
>
> The air is full of children, statues, roofs
> And snow. The theatre is spinning round,
>
> Colliding with deaf-mute churches and optical
>   trains.
> The most massive sopranos are singing songs of
>   scales.
>
> And Ludwig Richter, turbulent Schlemihl,
> Has lost the whole in which he was contained,
>
> Knows desire without an object of desire,
> All mind and violence and nothing felt.

> He knows he has nothing more to think about,
> Like the wind that lashes everything at once.

The poem is composed of many reminiscences of former
poems; it treats its subject with a mixture of comedy,
irony, pathos, and brutality. I isolate Stevens' moments of
brutality toward himself and his life because brutality, in
Stevens (and in other poets as well), is usually a sign of extreme discomfort, misery, and self-hatred. Many of Stevens' poems—read from one angle, most of the best
poems—spring from catastrophic disappointment, bitter
solitude, or personal sadness. It is understandable that Stevens, a man of chilling reticence, should illustrate his suffering in its largest possible terms. That practice does not
obscure the nature of the suffering, which concerns the
collapse of early hopeful fantasies of love, companionship,
success, and self-transformation. As self and beloved alike
become, with greater or lesser velocity, the final dwarfs of
themselves, and as social awareness diminishes dreams of
self-transcendence, the poet sees dream, hope, love, and
trust—those activities of the most august imagination—
crippled, contradicted, dissolved, called into question, em-
bittered. This history is the history of every intelligent and
receptive human creature, as the illimitable claims on existence made by each one of us are checked, baffled, frustrated, and reproved—whether by our own subsequent perceptions of their impossible grandiosity, or by the accidents of fate and chance, or by our betrayal of others, or
by old age and its failures of capacity. In spite of the severe
impersonality of Stevens' style, in spite even of his (often
transparent) personae, it is himself of whom he writes. He
has been too little read as a poet of human misery.

The human problem—stated late but very baldly in
"Chaos in Motion and Not in Motion"—is that its hero
"Has lost the whole in which he was contained, / Knows
desire without an object of desire, / All mind and violence
and nothing felt." I do violence to these lines in detaching
them from what precedes and follows them, but I do so
for a reason. More often than not, the human pang in Stevens is secreted inconspicuously in the poem, instead of
being announced in the title or in the opening lines. It is
the usual, if mistaken, way of commentators to begin at
the beginning and to take Stevens' metaphysical or epistemological prolegomena as the real subject of the poem,
when in fact they are the late plural of the subject, whose
early candor of desire reposes further down the page. And
so I isolate what I take to be the psychological or human
"beginning" of the poem, its point of origin in feeling,
which, though it comes late in the poem, serves as the center from which the other lines radiate.

This center, which I have just quoted, tells us that the
worst thing that can happen to a poet has happened to its
hero: he has stopped having feelings. In Stevens' words,
he is "all mind and violence and nothing felt." Since feeling—to use Wordsworthian terms—is the organizing
principle of poetry (both narratively, insofar as poetry is
a history of feeling, and structurally, insofar as poetry is
a science or analysis of feeling), without feeling the world
of the poet is a chaos. As we know, as the poet knows, the
absence of feeling is itself—since the poet is still alive—a
mask for feelings too powerful to make themselves felt:
these manifest themselves in this poem as that paradoxical

"desire without an object of desire," libido unfocused and therefore churning out in all directions—like a wind, as the last line of the poem says, "that lashes everything at once." Unfocused and chaotic libido does not provide a channel along which thought can move. Once there is an object of desire, the mind can exert all its familiar diversions—decoration, analysis, speculation, fantasy, drama, and so on. But with no beloved object, the mind is at loss; the hero of the poem has "lost the whole in which he was contained . . . / He knows he has nothing more to think about." The landscape is the objective correlative to this state of mind: "There is lightning and the thickest thunder."

The poem, as I have so far described it, ought to be a poem of *sturm und drang,* beset by the turbulent wind of desire, surrounded by its attendant *donner und blitzen.* But the brutality of the poem is that it treats its own problem with indifferent irony. The hero is "Ludwig Richter, turbulent Schlemihl," and his sufferings are watched through a monocle:

> It is a spectacle. Scene 10 becomes 11,
> In Series X, Act IV, et cetera.

This passage is a self-quotation from **"Like Decorations in a Nigger Cemetery,"** in which inception itself is satirized:

> An opening of portals when night ends,
> A running forward, arms stretched out as
>   drilled.
> Act I, Scene I, at a German Staats-Oper.
>
> (XIX)

We all begin in the hope of romantic embrace: by the time **"Chaos in Motion"** is written we have moved on from Act I, Scene I, to the tenth series of performances in the Staats-Oper, and in that tenth series we are in the fourth act of some play, and in that fourth act we are moving from scene 10 to scene 11: in short, we are almost to Act V. And surely Series X is the last of the season. The poet has watched these operatic performances of desire too many times: like anyone middle-aged he has ceased to believe in the "running forward, arms stretched out"—but the wild thrashing of unfocused desire continues. It has preoccupied Stevens elsewhere; in **"Puella Parvula":**

> Keep quiet in the heart, O wild bitch. O mind
> Gone wild, be what he tells you to be. *Puella.*

In **"Chaos in Motion"** Stevens quotes another early poem, the triumphant **"Ploughing on Sunday."** There, while his docile neighbors troop off to church, the poet, violating the Sabbath, blasphemously harnesses his team to the plough and takes to the fields, full of indiscriminate joy in the sun and wind alike: in that poem, "the wind pours down," while now "the rain is pouring down." It is July, the month of credences of summer, when the plenitude of desire was felt in the past, and the mind could lay by its trouble. Now, in disbelief in the existence of any object of desire, the old seasonal myth of sun and love is abandoned, and with icy detachment Stevens enunciates all conceivable tragedies as though they could be watched with ultimate *froideur:* suicide, "people fall out of windows"; the decay of nature, "trees tumble down"; the ice age, "sum-

mer is changed to winter"; decline, "the young grow old"; violation of natural process in a chaotic upheaval of life and art, "the air is full of children, statues, roofs / And snow." The *theatrum mundi* itself collapses, its fall coincident with the collapse of its impotent institutions and its stage scenery: "The theatre is spinning round, / Colliding with deaf-mute churches and optical trains." In this Götterdämmerung, harmony itself is reduced to elemental monotony: "The most massive sopranos are singing songs of scales."

All of this is normally material for elegy, and most of it has been or will be material for elegy in Stevens:

> The last leaf that is going to fall has fallen.
>
> She is exhausted and a little old.
>
> The general was rubbish in the end.
>
> A cabin stands, deserted, on a beach.

A roof abandoned, a statue broken, a leafless tree, a fall of rain, a beloved grown old, a church of bird-nest arches and of rain-stained vaults, a theater or capitol collapsing—all can elicit lament, and do, except when Stevens is being brutal. In **"Chaos in Motion"** the unbearable acceleration and offhand inventory of the spectacle—"People fall out of windows, trees tumble down, / Summer is changed to winter, the young grow old"—borrows a common cinematic brutality (used in film for comic effect)—to reproduce the look of the *theatrum mundi* to the eyes of the old, who have seen the cycle too many times repeated. The old seraph in **Notes** has seen too many springs:

> The Italian girls wore jonquils in their hair
> And these the seraph saw, had seen long since,
> In the bandeaux of the mothers, would see again.

The seraph has gone through his own cycles of seraphic chastity and Saturnalian desire (when he turns to a satyr): he has desired the mothers and the daughters alike and has turned from both in surfeit and disbelief. Even in spring, the world, to this jaded Stevens, seems "a withered scene."

In spite of the severe impersonality of Stevens' style, in spite even of his (often transparent) personae, it is himself of whom he writes. He has been too little read as a poet of human misery.

—*Helen Vendler*

Stevens' grand claim on us in his later poems is his willingness to refuse lyric emotions. The truth is, he tells us, that the old detach themselves from empathy and, with a certain weary sense of déjà vu, see their grandchildren predictably rising to adolescent erotic idolatry and entrusting themselves to Summer's warmth, only, in their turn, to encounter failure, loss, cold, age, and death. One greets this spectacle, in middle age, without the tragic emotions with which one passed through the cycle oneself. And yet there is no diminution in desire: there is only a loss of belief in a possible object adequate to desire. The tonelessness with which Stevens recounts the disastrous events around him is meant to reflect his own sense of inevitable and repetitive human fate. And yet tonelessness is the ultimate lyric risk. The reader who can penetrate irony, brutality, rapidity, and tonelessness to see behind them a catastrophic loss of feeling, a fear of unleashed libido with no conceivable object, and the despair of a mind of genius that has nothing more to think about, will read **"Chaos in Motion and Not in Motion"** as a poem reflecting one of the fundamental miseries of the old.

The brutality of style I have dwelt on in **"Chaos in Motion"** has early roots in Stevens, but when it appears in *Harmonium* it is usually preceded or followed by some softening of perception. Two cases exhibiting this softening must suffice: in **"Anecdote of the Prince of Peacocks"** Stevens meets his own potential madness; in **"The Apostrophe to Vincentine"** he meets the unaccommodated object of desire before she has been clothed in the beauty of fantasy. Each poem is distanced by being given a rhetorical title—[**"Anecdote of a Jar," "Apostrophe to Vincentine"**]—so that, even though they are, unusually for Stevens, written in the first person, they scarcely share at all in the lyric convention of personal experience. The poet—here, the Prince of Peacocks, full of showiness and *superbia*—meets the Saxon-named Berserk: he meets him in the realm of poetry—sleep and moonlight. But Berserk is "sharp as the sleepless," a phrase suggesting that if the Prince of Peacocks should wake into the dread sunlight of experience, he would go mad. The impossibility of the poet's evading Berserk, even in dreams, is the purport of the colloquy between the two. When the poet asks, "Why are you red / In this milky blue? . . . / Why suncolored, / As if awake / In the midst of sleep?" Berserk answers that he sets his traps in the midst of dreams, forcing the poet to recognize the hazards of mentality even in the kingdoms of escape. At this point in the poem the diction turns brutal:

> I knew from this
> That the blue ground
> Was full of blocks
> And blocking steel.

However, Stevens' retreat from brutality into incantation is immediate:

> I knew the dread
> Of the bushy plain
> And the beauty
> Of the moonlight
> Falling there,
> Falling
> As sleep falls
> In the innocent air.

This is an unrewarding ending to a poem which began so promisingly as an exploration of the threats—reaching even to breakdown—posed by consciousness.

"The Apostrophe to Vincentine" is a bolder poem. The female, imagined naked, is nothing more to her poet than a lean, small, white, nameless animal, dwarfed by the magnitude of the scale of earth and sky. Nevertheless, the poem allows her to preexist this reductive imagining. She is already, in the poet's mind, Heavenly Vincentine; he is already enamored. Still, he engages in the deliberate aesthetic exercise of depriving her of all interiority and humanness and exterior garments, trying to see her as a purely visual object, an isolated biological phenomenon. This peculiar exercise prefigures Stevens' later enterprises of viewing the *ding-an-sich*. But it is one thing to try to see the sun or a March morning without evasion; to see the Platonic beloved in this way is in itself deeply repellent to Stevens. Melodramatically he affixes Roman numerals to each stage of Vincentine's appearance. Number I, though reserving the final repellency—animality—for later, otherwise presents the unadorned female figure in pure visuality:

> I figured you as nude between
> Monotonous earth and dark blue sky.
> It made you seem so small and lean
> And nameless
> Heavenly Vincentine.

In II, Vincentine is allowed warmth (that is to say, her poet is allowed to see her as flesh, not only as outline). She is given a dress to wear, a modified green (like that worn by the spring "queen . . . in slipper green") to contrast with the monotonous earth and dark blue sky. She is also given hair (as a modified brunette). Peculiarly, her other attribute besides warmth is cleanliness; one suspects the exigencies of rhyme:

> I saw you then, as warm as flesh,
> Brunette,
> But yet not too brunette,
> As warm, as clean
> Your dress was green,
> Was whited green,
> Green Vincentine.

In III, Vincentine is allowed, so to speak, a soul, exhibited in her independent motion; she is also placed in a society, so that her voice can be heard and so that she can express feeling:

> Then you came walking,
> In a group
> Of human others,
> Voluble.
> Yes: you came walking,
> Vincentine.
> Yes: you came talking.

In her progressive assumption of human attributes as she approaches the poet, Vincentine changes from a tiny animal outline in the cosmic scale to a living woman, around whom the cosmos falls into place. She becomes in fact the heavenly or Platonic axis on which all creation turns, rendering monotonous earth no longer monotonous but rather a place imbued with her reality. Or so we believe when the fourth stanza begins:

> And what I knew you felt
> Came then.
> Monotonous earth I saw become
> Illimitable spheres of you.

This transformatory rhetoric generally leaves behind the

STEVENS

POETRY CRITICISM, Vol. 6

original dwarfed state and leads to the language of apotheosis. Stevens, after accomplishing the apotheosis of earth, refuses to remain on the level of the glorified and re-does his apotheosis twice more, each time reiterating Vincentine's original state of nude leanness, but making her, as she was not at the beginning, a "white animal," in the uneasy phrase, "that white animal, so lean":

> Monotonous earth I saw become
> Illimitable spheres of you
> And that white animal, so lean,
> Turned Vincentine,
> Turned heavenly Vincentine,
> And that white animal, so lean,
> Turned heavenly, heavenly Vincentine.

Brutality and apotheosis end in a stalemate. We remember Vincentine at least as powerfully in her repellent incarnation as a white animal so lean as in her named and transfigured state, brunette, dressed, walking, talking, and feeling. The poem shows us a mind willing and welcoming the decor of thought and fancy, while unable to rid itself of primal reductiveness and visual disgust. The reductive diction, telling us in itself that poetry and apotheosis are *not* one, but remain in a problematic relation, marks the speaker as a man caught between the nameless lean, on the one hand, and illimitable spheres of the beloved, on the other. There is no diction equally appropriate to both.

In an altogether harsher poem from *Harmonium,* Stevens subjects his own idealizations to ridicule. **"The Virgin Carrying a Lantern,"** an unsettling poem with a Pre-Raphaelite title, embodies Stevens' brutality in the negress who watches malevolently the more seraphic and elegiac postures of life and supposes "things false and wrong" about "the lantern of the beauty / Who walks there." The poem pretends to ally itself unequivocally in its declarations with the innocent virgin:

> There are no bears among the roses,
> Only a negress who supposes
> Things false and wrong
>
> About the lantern of the beauty
> Who walks there, as a farewell duty,
> Walks long and long.
>
> The pity that her pious egress
> Should fill the vigil of a negress
> With heat so strong!

The simpering Victorian voice, reproving the negress' suppositions as "false and wrong," expressing indignation at the negress' strong "heat" ("The pity" of it!), and endorsing the "pious egress" of the virgin, is entirely contradicted by the brutal left-hand side, so to speak, of Stevens' diptych: if the negress supposes bears, it is because she is acquainted with bears, while the virgin knows only roses; the negress is in the dark, the virgin bears a lantern; the negress, with her strong "heat," is sexual, the virgin chaste; the negress an impious spy, the virgin a pious vestal. The trouble with the virgin's universe, which would be pleasing if it contained only roses, dutiful virgins, lanterns, and pious farewells, is that it contains the negress, her vigil, her heat, and her suppositions. The negress makes the virgin ridiculous; no one engaged in a "pious egress" can ever be poetically respectable. The negress' heat has the last

word. The poem may be seen as a rewriting of Blake's lamb and tiger: the virgin is what Melville would have called a radiant ninny, but there is none of Blake's admiration for his tiger embodied in Stevens' figure for the dark, for the heated, and for the bestial in himself.

These earliest examples from *Harmonium*—Berserk, the animal Vincentine, and the negress—show Stevens already aware of certain incompatibilities—between waking and dreaming, between the animal and the heavenly, between chaste piety and strong heat—against which his only defenses were a comic or ironic language, a rhetorical distance in entitling, a reduction of the lyric potential of the "I" who speaks, and, most of all, a rather tedious polar separation of imagery: the milky blue of moonlight opposed to the red of sunlight, the small animal Vincentine contrasted to the illimitable heavenly Vincentine, the pious virgin distinguished from the heated negress. Crispin thought placatingly that his life could be a voyaging "up and down between two elements," but the ranker element in **"The Comedian"** is described with too little of the brutality that honesty would dictate; instead, Stevens treats it with the same unchanged high rhetoric that is the vehicle for all of Crispin's experience. Crispin is not made sufficiently unhappy by the tension between his two elements: Berserk, who comes summoned by Stevens' incapacity to mediate between sun and moon, never invades **"The Comedian."**

If we turn our attention to the shape of Stevens' whole career, we can see three large phases in his management of this problem. (I would take **"Chaos in Motion"** as the harsh turning point between the second and third phases.) The first phase, represented by the poems I have instanced from *Harmonium,* resorted to certain concealments of tension, on the one hand, and to violent dislocations of sensibility, on the other. Both were attempts at accommodation, and brought Stevens to the state of misery in which he met the traditionally invulnerable Berserk, his traps, and his blocking steel.

The second phase finds Stevens attempting to exorcise these private tensions by resorting to a solution in the social order. As he tries to see depression as a social, rather than a personal, emotion, he thinks it may be ended by social cohesion rather than by interior resolution. An early example of a poem that goes wrong—though the number of these is legion among the war poems—is **"The Men That Are Falling."** This poem begins wonderfully, in private loss, as the moon "burns in the mind on lost remembrances." As the poet leans on his bed, he realizes that the pull he feels to it is not the pull of sleepiness, but of desire:

> This is not sleep. This is desire.
>
> Ah! Yes, desire . . . this leaning on his bed,
> This leaning on his elbows on his bed,
>
> Staring, at midnight, at the pillow that is black
> In the catastrophic room . . . beyond despair,
>
> Like an intenser instinct. What is it he desires?

Some confrontation with the erotic lost remembrances evoked by the empty pillow where the beloved should lie is in order, but Stevens places instead an imagined head,

310

a male one, on the pillow—"the head of one of the men that are falling," in part a double of himself, in part his opposite. A flicker of brutality is allowed to enter in the description of the iconic head, "thick-lipped from riot and rebellious cries," but the soldier is redeemed from the sub-human by the "immaculate syllables / That he spoke only by doing what he did." Stevens thinks to turn his attention here to those moral "words" of heroic action "that are life's voluble utterance," insisting that right action alone is the arena for the resolution of inner pain. But by turning the acts of soldiers into a form of utterance, he suggests that his own "immaculate syllables" spring as well from a form of death, symbolized by the absence of the inamorata on the pillow. Having died to her, he rises into syllables. The impotence he characteristically evokes in misery is "cured" in this poem by the dangerous example of the hero, always a seductive icon for Stevens. Just as he had tried in *Harmonium* for a euphony symbolized in the "**Infanta Marina**," binding together nature, thought, and art, so in *Parts of a World* he imagines a synthesis among flying birds, marching soldiers, and rolling drums—the motions of nature, the motions of social action, and the motions of the music of war. The consequent self-effacement represents the effacement of the psychic problem of private misery, and the poet's aversion from the corresponding aesthetic problem of the relation of that misery to both art and nature. The oppositions between euphony and cacophony, harmony and eccentricity, the seraphic and the satiric are in Stevens symbols for the discrepancy between the irresistible yearnings of desire and the irreversible misery at its failure. But the war poems turn the symbolic focus outward; as a result, they become forced.

In the notion, developed in several middle poems, of a contradictory plurality of "truths," Stevens began to solve conceptually the problem of the conflict between desire and loss. But the conceptual concession to plurality did not in itself invent a style representative of the several truths of appetite and failure. The evasions inherent in retaining an old style for new perceptions can be seen in the poem most clearly articulating the creed of plural truths, "**On the Road Home:**"

> It was when I said,
> "There is no such thing as the truth,"
> That the grapes seemed fatter.
> The fox ran out of his hole.
>
> You . . . You said,
> "There are many truths,
> But they are not parts of a truth."
> Then the tree, at night, began to change.

The two figures "said we stood alone." The man in "**Anglais Mort à Florence**" had stood at last "by God's help and the police," but here God and social institutions have disappeared. The narrator continues, in an argument against the Logos:

> "Words are not forms of a single word.
> In the sum of the parts, there are only the parts.
> The world must be measured by eye."

The "you" replies with a comparable indictment of idolatry:

> "The idols have seen lots of poverty,
> Snakes and gold and lice,
> But not the truth."

These sentiments are all very well; they are anti-Platonic, nominalist, iconoclastic. The poem asserts that the expression of such dry sentiments enhances nature:

> It was at that time that the silence was largest
> And longest, the night was roundest,
> The fragrance of the autumn warmest,
> Closest and strongest.

The "rhyming" superlatives here suggest a Platonic extension and extrapolation of nature, as well as a Platonic coherence of the parts of nature; this extension, extrapolation, and coherence represent Stevens' unresolved wish that the sum of the parts should be more than the parts. Brutality of language ought to appear in coincidence with the absence of Platonic reassurance; in this poem the nominalist theme is not allowed its appropriate style of closure.

It is one of Stevens' claims to greatness that he went on to invent a new style—the style of parts as parts, of words refusing to form a single word, of the many truths not part of "a" truth, the style of many of the most interesting late poems. For Stevens, one theoretical problem in inventing such a style lay in the suspicion that it would call metaphor into question. Metaphor implies analogy and resemblance, neither of which can be stable in a world of nonce effects. In *Harmonium* Stevens had decided, in "**Metaphors of a Magnifico**," to distinguish between fact (twenty men crossing a bridge into a village), distinctive individual experience (twenty men crossing twenty bridges into twenty villages), and collective perception (in which the twenty men become one man):

> Twenty men crossing a bridge,
> Into a village,
> Are twenty men crossing twenty bridges,
> Into twenty villages,
> Or one man
> Crossing a single bridge into a village.
>
> This is an old song
> That will not declare itself. . . .

Brute fact, in the second essay at the rendering of this sight, seems to win the upper hand: "Twenty men crossing a bridge / Into a village / Are / Twenty men crossing a bridge / Into a village." However, all speculation about the truths occurring on the far side of the copula is vanquished, finally, by the sensuous particulars of the scene, as the Magnifico ceases to be a philosopher of perception, ceases even to be a spectator, and becomes a participant:

> The boots of the men clump
> On the boards of the bridge.
> The first white wall of the village
> Rises through fruit-trees.
>
> Of what was it I was thinking?
>
> So the meaning escapes.
>
> The first white wall of the village . . .
> The fruit trees. . . .

At one point the Magnifico's view had been as "certain as

meaning," but in the sensual experience, "the meaning escapes." These separations between speculation and experience are still present in the absolute disjunction between the dispute on truth and the fat grapes of **"On the Road Home."**

The most strictly comparable poem in the later work to **"Metaphors of a Magnifico"** and **"On the Road Home"** is **"The Motive for Metaphor,"** a poem in which the interpenetration of thought (with its consequent vocabulary of words, things, metaphor, expression, obscurity, motive, and so on) and sense (with *its* vocabulary of seasonal change, colors, moonlight, trees, clouds, and birds) is almost except for the ending, complete. The partial truths, earlier so eagerly embraced as a solution for the absence of authority, now rightly take on the impoverished colors appropriate to them, instead of nostalgically imitating, in Platonic superlatives, the very consolations they were meant to forgo.

The degree of self-loathing Stevens felt in sacrificing his absolutist "Platonic" self—that which believed, with all an acolyte's sincerity, in religion, love, and art—is evident in the self-contempt at the beginning of **"The Motive for Metaphor"** with which he addresses his new, "partial" self:

> You like it under the trees in autumn
> Because everything is half dead.
> The wind moves like a cripple among the leaves
> And repeats words without meaning.
>
> In the same way, you were happy in spring,
> With the half colors of quarter-things,
> The slightly brighter sky, the melting clouds,
> The single bird, the obscure moon—
>
> The obscure moon lighting an obscure world
> Of things that would never be quite expressed,
> Where you yourself were never quite yourself
> And did not want nor have to be,
>
> Desiring the exhilarations of changes:
> The motive for metaphor, shrinking from
> The weight of primary noon,
> The ABC of being,
>
> The ruddy temper, the hammer
> Of red and blue, the hard sound—
> Steel against intimation—the sharp flash,
> The vital, arrogant, fatal, dominant X.

Whatever voice it is that speaks here, it speaks dismissively of the poet's love of half colors and quarter-things. He loves half-dead things in autumn and quarter-things in spring, the voice says, because such things represent change: a half-dead thing can die, a cripple was once healthy, a moon can wax and wane, a single bird can become a chorus, a cloud can melt, a sky can brighten. Spring and autumn are the seasons of change. But the speaking voice detests those exhilarations of changes which are the motive for metaphor. This new, self-contemptuous voice which opens **"The Motive for Metaphor"** sees the seductiveness of change as an evasion of the obdurate, blocking, trapping knowledge of the fatal and dominant self, the self that, under all the changes, one is. That is the self that the sharp light of noon, without any

shadows, would reveal. It is at once the ABC of being and also its X, the Alpha and Omega of self, that which the Prince of Peacocks had been afraid to face—Berserk and his traps of steel. In moonlight, says the self-accuser in **"The Motive for Metaphor,"** "you yourself were never quite yourself / And did not want nor have to be." You shrank from the weight of primary noon. But the speaker knows, now, with entire intimacy, "the hard sound— / Steel against intimation—the sharp flash / The vital, arrogant, fatal, dominant X." That steel is both vital and fatal, ABC and X, the infant self and its later hierophant. This is a very brutal poem, in which Stevens is much unkinder to his younger self than he will be in his last poems. But it is a relief, after earlier evasions, to hear him being so harsh.

The tonelessness with which Stevens recounts the disastrous events around him is meant to reflect his own sense of inevitable and repetitive human fate.

—*Helen Vendler*

The final hammer and knife-blade, the smith's hammer and the executioner's edge, are extremely beautiful, but just slightly overdone. The speaker has not yet been wooed entirely away from his more shrouded and nuanced haunts, in spite of his sortie into a contemptuous tone. The trouble with biding in autumn and spring after they no longer mediate adequate self-knowledge is that the words one writes about them cease to have any meaning, and the divine afflatus is crippled. Stevens—it is part of his greatness—was quick to see when he was being false and, in spite of the immense stubbornness of his slow nature, was willing to force himself unwillingly on to the next stage of discovery, even if it meant new desolation. **"The Motive for Metaphor"** finds him falling back on the natural ground of his own life and private misery, rather than looking toward the social order for a collective example of ethical escape. The misery in **"The Motive for Metaphor"** lies in the pain of the choices it offers: a crippled, half-dead, and meaningless life in autumn (it being now no longer possible to return to spring) or a submission to what one shrinks from: a brutal solar weight, a hard hammer, the surgical flash of the fatal X. Stevens dreads being exposed to that sun, being tempered by that hammer, finding that blocking steel against his intimations (though he no longer believes he will go mad under the trial, as he did when he was the Prince of Peacocks). With the dread there coexists a compelling attraction—the exhilaration of a new sort of self-knowledge, a change into the changelessness of a final, permanent self. Because the new phase incorporates the motive for all the previous ones, the desire for change (which is the motive for metaphor), it attracts. But the poem implies that the new self-knowledge that it implicitly recommends will be the last possible phase, the fatal phase, and therefore the end of poetry. This suspicion causes both the nostalgia for previous seasons of happiness, no matter how evasive, which the poem candidly exhibits, and the desire for the new.

Stevens' style in **"The Motive for Metaphor"** is, comparatively speaking, one of apparent simplicity. But the old Platonism, the desire for harmony, is smuggled in by way of two flurries of apposition, at the middle and end of the poem. Apposition is a figure which of itself implies that things can be aligned in meaningful parallels, that metaphorical equivalences are a portion of significance—that

> the weight of primary noon
> the ABC of being
> the ruddy temper
> the hammer of red and blue
> the hard sound
> steel against intimation
> the sharp flash
> the vital, arrogant, fatal, dominant X

can all be substituted, one for the other, to signify a dreadful exposure from which the earlier, more fugitive poet, shrinks. In this parallelism Stevens betrays his nostalgia for synthesis and system: brutality has extended to his self-perception and to his imagery without yet having reached his syntax. **"Chaos in Motion and Not in Motion"** extends this brutality to syntax, letting that crippled wind fully loose, allowing it to lash everything at once, changing the self-loathing of **"The Motive for Metaphor"** to self-irony, refusing soothing syntax in favor of rapid primary syntactical forms.

In his last years Stevens writes a poetry of powerful retrospective weight in which all the attitudes exhibited and assumed over a long life are admitted to the arena, each seen as something authentic in its time. The worst bitternesses, when they recur, as they do even in **"The Rock,"** subside. Brutality appears, and recedes. In the great and heartbreaking poem of self-evaluation, **"Things of August,"** Stevens forgives all his selves, remembers all of them, accedes to the unintelligibility of the world, and celebrates the new text of it he has created. He is now, as he will say in **"The Rock,"** the "silent rhapsodist" of the earth. Of all the poems I could choose to show the last stage of Stevens' harshness, I will turn to one about sexual feeling in old age, called **"The Dove in Spring":**

> Brooder, brooder, deep beneath its walls—
> A small howling of the dove
> Makes something of the little there,
>
> The little and the dark, and that
> In which it is and that in which
> It is established. There the dove
>
> Makes this small howling, like a thought
> That howls in the mind or like a man
> Who keeps seeking out his identity
>
> In that which is and is established . . . It howls
> Of the great sizes of an outer bush
> And the great misery of the doubt of it.
>
> Of stripes of silver that are strips
> Like slits across a space, a place
> And state of being large and light.

> There is this bubbling before the sun,
> This howling at one's ear, too far
> For daylight and too near for sleep.

The dove is Venus' bird, its absence mourned earlier in *Harmonium,* in **"Depression before Spring,"** when, though the cock has crowed, "ki-ki-ri-ki / Brings no rou-cou, No rou-cou-cou," and "no queen comes / In slipper green." It is the "tempestuous bird," the "dove in the belly" who "builds his nest and coos" when things of the world appear promising and bright. It is the dove that rises up every spring when the Italian girls wear jonquils in their hair. Stevens is seventy-four as he writes this poem, his last word almost on the persistence of desire. What is one to make of the voice of Venus' dove at seventy-four? Hatred, irony, and comedy can appear in the literature of sexual meditation in old age; one thinks of Yeats. But Stevens' meditation is entirely respectful and serious; he does not feel absurd or reprehensible for harboring the dove; what he feels is a sadness for the dove and for himself. The dove is imprisoned behind walls, in the dark. It can no longer coo; it can only howl. A howl is its singing, and it decides to sing even an unlovely song, rather than fall silent. The dove knows that somewhere outside there is a great bush that is its natural habitat; at the same time, it doubts that any such bush exists. This doubt causes its misery: it howls of "a place and state of being large and light," but all it has of that light is what it perceives in slits through its prison bars, in stripes of silver. The dove's small howling takes place at night. It prevents sleep, without presaging a new day. Spring's infuriations, the poem tells us, are never over. They take, in old age, forms that may seem degenerate—a dove displaced from a bough to a prison, a dove that does not coo but howls, a dove that cannot any longer see the undulating silver fans of any imaginable mate—but if truth is to be told, even degenerate forms must be allowed their pathos of expression.

I do not mean to sentimentalize Stevens in insisting that his poems are meditations on emotions of love, idolatry, loss, self-loathing, and self-forgiveness. He is so chaste in self-revelation that his emotions are easily passed over. A poem like **"The Dove in Spring,"** written in "the little and the dark," sees the sexual impulse, and all the love and idealization it gave rise to in life, as strictly parallel to the impulse to thought and the impulse to self-definition. In allowing a syntactic parallelism between these three impulses—the sexual, the intellectual, and the personal— Stevens is resorting not to Platonism but to memory, the memory of how his life had structured itself around three persistent shapings of identity. The grief of the ending of the poem is not the elegiac sorrow for the great bush or the large light state, but rather the grief of Tithonus, that one can neither die nor live, as one endures the last protests and affirmations of desire.

James Merrill once remarked in a *Paris Review* interview that Stevens "continues to persuade us of having had a private life, despite—or thanks to—all the bizarreness of his vocabulary and idiom." On the whole, criticism has avoided the evidences of that private life, but it is, as Merrill says, so inseparable from the incomparable style invented to express it that it is a failure of imagination to discuss the style without its subject. The lapses and failures of ide-

Caricature of Stevens that appeared in The New York Review of Books *December 1, 1966.*

alization—especially the idealization of romantic love, forced on us by nature, culture, and, above all, literature—press Stevens to an ever more stringent, and even harsh, analysis of the interrelation of emotion's flights and their eventual correction in time. It may be that the harshness or brutality which I have been describing is Stevens' defense against a Romantic sweetness, though I think not. It is rather, I feel sure, the expression of an anger that a mind so designed for adoration never found adoration and sensuality compatible; they remained locked compartments, a source of emotional confusion and bitterness. In the end, however, Stevens' unwillingness to abandon either of his two incompatible truths—the truth of desire and the truth of the failure of desire—led to a great amplitude of human vision not granted to those who live more comfortably in body and soul, and to a truth-telling ease not granted to those who have fewer difficulties to confess. (pp. 10-28)

> *Helen Vendler, "Apollo's Harsher Songs: 'Desire without an Object of Desire',"* in her Wallace Stevens: Words Chosen Out of Desire, *The University of Tennessee Press, Knoxville, 1984, pp. 10-28.*

Leonora Woodman   (essay date 1983)

[*In the following essay, Woodman discusses Stevens's concept of "pure poetry," the relationship between his poetry and philosophical ideas, and his idea of the "es-*

sential imagination" or humankind's "common God" as expressed in his verse, particularly in Owl's Clover.]

To begin a study of Stevens' work by exploring the sense of the "ultimate poem," a phrase that appears in the poetry only twice and even then does not arise until midpoint in the corpus, may strike the reader as somewhat eccentric. And well it might, if the phrase were viewed as singular—and aberrant intrusion bearing little or no relation to Stevens' work as a whole. This, of course, is questionable on two counts: the "poem" that Stevens invokes is one of his major motifs—indeed, as Samuel French Morse reminds us, Stevens' work "from the very beginning . . . [was] 'about' poetry; it is the one real subject of **Harmonium** and all the later work"—and the epithet is likewise representative, for in its suggestion of something fundamental and without peer, it is close in meaning to "supreme," "absolute," and "essential," frequently used in the poetry to suggest unconditioned rank. Indeed, the "supreme fiction," a major theme generally thought to mean poetry, bears a signification akin to that of the "ultimate poem." We may thus assume on both counts that the "ultimate poem," however seldom it arises, represents one of Stevens' major concerns.

The meaning Stevens intends in this perplexing phrase may be sought by attending to the sense of "ultimate," an hierarchical term implying degree. For an "ultimate poem" to exist, there must be "lesser" poems; and, indeed, this distinction between two levels of poetry is claimed in **"A Primitive Like an Orb,"** a poem of the forties which offers for consideration a "central poem" that is "seen and known in lesser poems." The sense that a lower form of poetry exists in which a higher form may be discerned or from which it may arise is similarly implied in a passage in **Notes toward a Supreme Fiction,** where the poet foresees the "fiction of an absolute" (something perfect and whole, the sense of "absolute") which is expected to arise from "crude compoundings," a phrase which suggests an impure amalgam from which something pure, presumably the poem or "fiction," is to be refined.

The notion of two levels of poetry—related, to be sure, but ultimately distinct—is crucial to the meaning Stevens intends when he proposes an "ultimate poem" that is somehow to evolve from "lesser poems." For it suggests, at the very least, a kind of linguistic legerdemain—a suspicion that the poet intends for the word "poetry" at least one meaning superior to its ordinary sense; and, at the very most, a sense that there exists for the poetic act a *terminus ad quem*—a conclusion beyond which it cannot go.

These distinctions appear in **"Extracts from Addresses to the Academy of Fine Ideas,"** the only poem in which the "ultimate poem" is mentioned in the poetic text itself. (The phrase also appears in the title of the late poem, **"The Ultimate Poem Is Abstract."**) Its appearance is embedded in the poet's consideration of two aspects of the mind, the first dismissed as merely "systematic thinking," the other offered as the "ultimate poem":

> That other one wanted to think his way to life,
> Sure that the ultimate poem was the mind,
> Or of the mind . . .

Affirmed as "the mind, / Or of the mind," the "ultimate poem" suggests both process and product—the mind that creates and the thing created. Except for the epithet, we might well concede that Stevens is proposing the "poem" in its ordinary sense, using as etymological guide for its double reference the Greek *poiein* which means "to make" and from which descends the modern meaning of "poem." When, however, the "poem" is prefaced by an epithet bearing the sense of stasis, we encounter the perplexing suggestion of a making—a process—which concludes in a product or "poem" beyond which there can be no further making. In short, "ultimate" suggests a closure that collides with the notion of process in which it lies embedded.

This perhaps overly-fastidious attention to Stevens' language has its point, namely, that when Stevens offers the "poem" or "poetry" qualified by "ultimate" or by equivalent epithets such as "central" or "high" or "pure"; or when, in another analogous construction, he suggests a "poem of pure reality," he is not, I shall urge, concerned with the poem as it is commonly understood, but is rather celebrating a spiritual entity which he chose to veil in the language of aesthetics. Poetry in its "ultimate" sense had a special meaning for Stevens, considerably different from what is usually referred to by that linguistic symbol; indeed, in Stevens' lexicon, "poetry" and the "idea of man" are synonymous, but not for the humanistic reasons commonly offered. Rather, Stevens believed in the evolution of a qualitatively different man shaped in the image of an archetypal prototype; and because art or the "lesser" poem expressed the features of this archetype—indeed, was the very medium which gave rise to his being—Stevens claimed him as the "ultimate poem." The linguistic means Stevens used to adapt the word *poetry* to his private purpose may be seen in his letters, essays, and the "Adagia," his commonplace book, where certain recurring concepts will provide the initial textual evidence for the thesis of this study.

We can best approach Stevens' "ultimate poem" by seeking the meaning of "pure poetry," a phrase that recurs with some frequency in his prose. Early references in several letters of the mid-thirties betray some uneasiness with the phrase. Not only does Stevens use it retrospectively, as if it were a concept once held but since discarded, but he appears to associate it with the first and apparently inferior half of a literature-life dichotomy. Asked by a correspondent whether the poems of *Harmonium* were "essentially decorative," he replies that he was on the point of responding negatively when he remembered his delight during the writing of *Harmonium* in the sensuous image and the musical phrase: "there was a time when I liked the idea of images and images alone, or images and the music of verse together. I then believed in *pure poetry,* as it was called." However, he continues, "life means a good deal more to us now-a-days than literature does. In the period of which I have just spoken, I thought literature meant most." Several months later he makes a distinction between "pure poetry" and "didactic poetry" but appears to assume that, while "pure poetry" remains his ultimate objective, "didactic poetry" or "didacticism in poetry" is a necessary stage in its evolution.

By the end of the thirties, Stevens' skepticism regarding the value of "pure poetry" seems to have been resolved, for he confidently announces to one correspondent that "I am, in the long run, interested in pure poetry" and writes to another that "pure poetry" should be "the highest objective of the poet." At the same time the phrase crops up in several essays and in glosses to two major poems. In these later references, however, Stevens uses the phrase in a different sense from the one noted above. There "pure poetry" is discussed in a commonly accepted linguistic context: that is, "pure poetry," however its formal and aesthetic properties may differ from "impure" poetry, designates something that has achieved an objective form. Stevens' subsequent references, however, subtly alter this meaning; not only does he refuse to identify "pure poetry" with the affective components of image and music, but he consistently distinguishes it from the poem itself.

> **Stevens' preoccupation with the idea of God as the supreme "poetic idea" accounts for his multiple definitions for poetry.**
>
> —*Leonora Woodman*

The distinction may be seen in the gloss Stevens provided in 1940 to poem xxii of *The Man with the Blue Guitar:* "Poetry is the spirit, as the poem is the body. Crudely stated, poetry is the imagination. But here poetry is used as the poetic, without the slightest pejorative innuendo. I have in mind pure poetry. The purpose of writing poetry is to attain pure poetry."

What is striking here are the shifting and distinctly different meanings Stevens attaches to poetry. In the first set of equivalencies—poetry—spirit—imagination—the meaning of poetry is internalized, becoming synonymous with an attribute of the human mind—the imagination. In the second set of equivalencies, Stevens departs from grammatical logic to propose that poetry (noun)—poetic (adjective)—pure poetry (adjective, noun). Stevens refuses to locate his evaluative adjective, but clearly he means to establish "poetic" as distinct from either poetry as imagination or poetry as poem. Finally, poetry is used as a referent for the poem, but the process (writing) of poetry is conceived instrumentally: that is, one writes poetry to attain pure poetry, an achievement further complicated by the fact that if, indeed, the "poetic" and "pure poetry" are synonymous, the goal of writing poetry is not the poem but a state produced by the poem.

Since Stevens identifies "pure poetry" with the "poetic," our task is next to trace the word "poetic" to see what can be further established about "pure poetry." Here we are led to a major Stevensian theme, his eagerness to develop a "theory of poetry" that would expand its relatively narrow, specialized meaning to one embracing the whole of human activity. This is the sense of his proposition that "the theory / Of poetry is the theory of life." His hope that such a venture would "disclose the truth about poetry" led Stevens in 1940 to urge a wealthy friend to establish a chair of poetry at Harvard for the study of "the history of poetic thought and of the theory of poetry," elaborated in a subsequent "Memorandum." His proposal clearly relegates poetry as genre to a minor place. A theory of poetry, he writes, should not confine itself to "specimens" of the genre that "are merely parts of a great whole," but should concern itself with the "poetic side of life, of the abstraction and the theory." "It [theory of poetry] does not mean verse any more than philosophy means prose. The subject-matter of poetry is the thing to be ascertained." The distinction between "poetic" and poetry as poem is repeated in the "Adagia": "The poetic view of life is larger than any of its poems (a larger thing than any poem); and to recognize this is the beginning of the recognition of the poetic spirit." Evidently, Stevens regarded poetry as genre as an instance of a larger principle transcending the literary form. Indeed, he seems to have held a hierarchical view of poetry, according "the poetic view of life" or "pure poetry" a generic status subsuming poetry as poem.

Although the "poetic view of life" is still vague (Stevens acknowledged that it "sounds rather mussy"), Stevens provides a significant clue when he narrows its appearance in poetry to subject matter, leading us to consider what he regarded as appropriate content for poetry. Here, the "Memorandum" may still suffice as text. It appears that the "poetic view of life" that depends on an "abstraction" is related in Stevens' mind to the idea of God, "the major poetic idea in the world." Acknowledging that current skepticism requires some modification of the traditional idea of God, he suggests that "the poetry that created the idea of God will either adapt it to our different intelligence, or create a substitute for it, or make it unnecessary." But in any case, he continues, the idea of God remains the primary "knowledge of poetry" as well as of philosophy and science.

The idea of God appears, then, to be linked to Stevens' concept of the "poetic" or "pure poetry." Let us investigate the precise relationship. Apparently disappointed in his effort to establish the study of the theory of poetry as a scholarly enterprise, Stevens attempted a formulation of his own, writing "A Collect of Philosophy" in 1951 as an example of what he meant by the "poetic view of life." Drawing on notes sent him by distinguished friends and a student's handbook of philosophy, Stevens sets out in this essay to demonstrate that the philosopher and the poet, however different their method and purpose, often "think alike" by virtue of the "inherently poetic" ideas they treat—that it is conception rather than form, or idea (abstraction) rather than mode of discourse, that unites two such seemingly contrasting pursuits.

No doubt Stevens' reading of philosophy is eccentric (one critic [Joseph N. Riddel] notes that he had "read in almost every modern philosopher and . . . understood almost none"), but to seek an accurate exposition of philosophical ideas in this essay is to miss Stevens' intent. Stevens is solely interested in developing his notion that the imagination

of the philosopher, like the imagination of the poet, contains an innate reservoir of poetic ideas (an "enormous a priori" in the mind, he says, is a potential "poetic . . . concept"), which compels the loftiest abstractions, chief of which is the idea of God. His purpose is not to argue ontologically for God's existence but rather to illustrate how the idea of God, as a purely psychic phenomenon, has inspired poetic ideas objectified in philosophical systems, and so he reads his philosophers in terms of this overriding objective. Thus, according to Stevens, Leibniz "thought like a poet" because "Monad by monad . . . he achieved God." Similarly, he reads Schopenhauer's *The World as Will* as a "cosmic poem of the ascent into heaven." Both, it appears, are examples of "ideas that are inherently poetic" because they agitate the imagination to conceive of an escape from human limitation—even, indeed, to aspire to godhead: "in a system of monads, we come, in the end, to a man who is not only a man but sea and mountain, too, and to a God who is not only all these: man and sea and mountain but a God as well." *The World as Will* permits a similar escape: "it is precisely the faults of life that this poem enables us to leave behind." Therefore, if the poem of the ascent into heaven is "unimpeachably divine," it is but a step removed from God, "the ultimate poetic idea." Indeed, Stevens clearly identifies poetry with the idea of God unwittingly discovered by the philosopher:

> Essentially what I intend is that it shall be as if the philosophers had no knowledge of poetry and suddenly discovered it in their search for whatever it is that they are searching for and gave the name of poetry to that which they discovered. Whether one arrives at the idea of God as a philosopher or as a poet matters greatly.

And it is precisely because the idea of God—the supreme abstraction—derives from the imagination rather than from man's logical or cognitive capacities, that Stevens urges the imagination's ascendancy over reason:

> Does not philosophy carry us to a point at which there is nothing left except the imagination? If we rely on the imagination (or, say, intuition), to carry us beyond that point, and if the imagination succeeds in carrying us beyond that point (as in respect to the idea of God, if we conceive of the idea of God as this world's capital idea), then the imagination is supreme, because its powers have shown themselves to be greater than the powers of the reason.

Even the most casual reading of Stevens' prose will reveal how extraordinarily drawn he was to the idea of God, yet the significance of this obsessive theme has never been fully appreciated. An aesthetic interpretation suggests that is it merely a metaphor for the creative possibilities of the imagination and, by synecdoche, of poetry, inasmuch as poetry provides the fulfilling integration—the order, or the search for the ideal—that the idea of God had formerly sustained. Such an interpretation seems compelling, given Stevens' hostility to traditional Christianity and his persistent effort to replace religious orthodoxy with something he called poetry. Nevertheless, the evidence appears to indicate otherwise: according to Stevens, the idea of God is an innate constituent of the imagination variously but compellingly objectified not only by the poet but by the philosopher and scientist as well. Any discourse that reveals the idea of God is, by this definition, "poetry," a word now so broadly conceived as to apply to any number of human pursuits.

Stevens' preoccupation with the idea of God as the supreme "poetic idea" accounts for his multiple definitions for poetry. He distinguishes the "poetic" from the poem *qua* poem because he wishes to separate form (poetry as genre) from content (poetry as poetic concept), as when he proposes that a poem is composed of "several poetries": "Poetry is a poetic conception, however expressed. A poem is poetry expressed in words. But in a poem there is a poetry of words. Obviously, a poem may consist of several poetries." The "Adagia" provides another example of this double event in the life of the poem: "Every poem is a poem within a poem: the poem of the idea within the poem of the words." The "poetic conception" and the "poem of the idea" echo the sense of the texts already explored, but another observation, provided in the essay "The Irrational Element in Poetry," clearly indicates that Stevens regarded the "poetic," "pure poetry," and the idea of God as closely related: "pure poetry is a term that has grown to be descriptive of poetry in which not the true subject but the poetry of the subject is paramount. All mystics approach God through the irrational. Pure poetry is both mystical and irrational."

Here we move forward considerably. Though Stevens has ostensibly shifted to the poem as artifact, he is, in fact, still insisting on the poem's doubleness, repeating his view that "pure poetry" arises only when the "poetry of the subject" or the idea of God is "paramount." It appears, moreover, that the idea of God is an irrational, noncognitive abstraction arising from largely instinctive and unconscious psychic realms. If this is so, and if we take seriously Stevens' belief that the idea of God is an imaginative abstraction that reveals the imagination's supremacy over reason, then we must assume that the imagination is also a largely unconscious psychic function.

A summary will clarify these relationships. Initially Stevens identified "pure poetry" with the "poetic." The "poetic," as elaborated in the "Memorandum" and elsewhere, provided an added set of equivalencies: the poetic—poetic view of life—abstraction—subject-matter—poetry of the subject—idea of God. These equivalencies were repeated in "A Collect of Philosophy," with the addition of the imagination. If, to borrow a Euclidean axiom, things equal to the same thing are equal to each other, we may conclude that "pure poetry" equals the imagination, the source of the idea of God. Furthermore, it should be stressed that at no point did Stevens identify "pure poetry" with the poem as objective artifact. When he refers to the poem he either conceives it instrumentally ("the purpose of writing poetry is to attain pure poetry"), or as an element subordinate to the "poetic view of life," or as a vehicle embodying a "poetic conception." "Pure poetry," according to Stevens' definitions, is consistently internalized, becoming synonymous with a construct of the imagination and eventually with the imagination itself.

In 1936 Stevens published his longest poem, **Owl's Clover,**

and later provided an extensive gloss to the poem in a series of letters to Hi Simons. These glosses provide the fullest explanation of what Stevens meant by "pure poetry," and, accordingly, I turn to them before examining the poem.

In his gloss to **"The Greenest Continent,"** the third canto of *Owl's Clover,* Stevens has this to say of "pure poetry":

> One way of explaining this poem is to say that it concerns the difficulty of imposing the imagination on those that do not share it. The idea of God is a thing of the imagination. We no longer think that God was, but was imagined. The idea of pure poetry, essential imagination, as the highest objective of the poet, appears to be, at least potentially, as great as the idea of God, and, for that matter, greater, if the idea of God is only one of the things of the imagination.

Of signal importance here is that Stevens is proposing *two levels of the imagination* in a hierarchy of ascending value. The secondary imagination constructs the myriad ideas of God, each of which convinces the believer of its absolute authority and compels him to reject a different view of the divine. However, as Stevens says here and was often to repeat, the idea of God is merely a human (imaginative) construct pointing not to God's objective existence but to a compelling human need to propose an object of veneration. Unfortunately, man has misunderstood this psychic need, converting it into a projected divine image when in reality he alone is the source and object of faith. The proof that the idea of God is merely the "idea of man," Stevens elsewhere says, lies in the fact that an objectified God always assumes an anthropomorphic form: "the gods of Greece are always Greeks and . . . all gods are created in the images of their creators." But in truth the gods are only projections of man's inner life, testifying to "the fundamental glory of men and women, who being in need of it create it, elevate it, without too much searching of its identity."

What this perpetual deification points to is not the form itself but the psychic structure that produced it. Man can entertain the idea of God because the image of divinity arises out of inherent qualities of the human mind for which no corresponding objective analogue need be postulated. The "essential imagination"—"pure poetry"—is thus the fountainhead of deity from which all images of deity—shadows of itself—spring.

In the second section of the gloss, Stevens further clarifies the distinction between the "idea of God" and "pure poetry." Since the idea of God, he writes, "partakes of consciousness," it unavoidably embodies extraneous and adventitious elements introduced by self-awareness, and so assumes multiple forms reflecting the peculiarities of race and nation. In contrast, the "essential imagination" is that deeper, irrational God the Father common to all: "This [idea of pure poetry] would be universally true if the imagination was the simple thing that it is commonly regarded as being. However, the imagination partakes of consciousness, and as the consciousness of West (Europe) differs from the consciousness of South (Africa), etc., so the imagination of West differs from that of South, and so the idea of God and the idea of pure poetry, etc. differ."

This distinction between two levels of the imagination accounts for Stevens' paradoxical view of divinity, excoriated on the one hand as merely a "postulate of the ego" and aggrandized on the other as the god within: "God is in me or else is not at all (does not exist)." The first proposition rejects the spurious objectified phantasies of the secondary imagination in favor of the inner "essential imagination"—man himself. The process by which Stevens arrived at this conclusion is given quasi-syllogistic form in the "Adagia": "Proposita: 1. God and the imagination are one. 2. The thing imagined is the imaginer. The second equals the thing imagined and the imaginer are one. Hence, I suppose, the imaginer is God."

Stevens' reluctance to identify "pure poetry" with poetry as poem is now understandable. "Pure poetry," or the "essential imagination," cannot be poetry as object but must be poetry as subject: man himself is "pure poetry" because his unconscious "essential imagination" that produces the "idea of God" is itself the prototype of all the gods. The need is thus to divert man from worshiping the "fictions" created by his imagination to worshiping the imagination itself, conceived as an archetypal principle of deity. But, as Stevens admits, this has "its difficulties." Logically, he writes, he "ought to believe in essential imagination" divested of all symbolic representations (logically, of course, the unconscious is a *Ding-an-Sich* that cannot be objectified), but since "it is easier to believe in a thing created by the imagination," he will offer a substitute "fiction" to represent the "essential imagination." This substitute "fiction," Stevens writes, is the mythological Ananke, mankind's "common god" introduced at the end of the third canto of *Owl's Clover:*

> Yet, the poem concludes with what is its point,
> that, if ideas of God are in conflict, the idea of
> pure poetry: imagination, extended beyond local
> consciousness, may be an idea to be held in com-
> mon by South, West, North and East. It would
> be a beginning, since the heaven in Europe is
> empty, to recognize Ananke, who, now more
> than ever, is the world's "starless crown."

In the final gloss to the **"The Greenest Continent,"** Stevens writes that Ananke is both created by and a symbol of the "essential imagination," that he is a substitute for the God that has been abjured, belief being necessary, and that he is a form of the fiction with which Stevens was grappling at the time (1940) the gloss was written.

It is my view that Ananke, Stevens' explicit symbol for the primary "essential imagination" (and for "pure poetry"), represents the single, most important element of Stevens' thought. This is not to say that this mythic figure receives extensive and explicit attention in the poetry. Indeed, apart from *Owl's Clover,* Ananke appears in his specific form only twice, first in a cryptic parable in **"Like Decorations in a Nigger Cemetery,"** included in the 1935 *Ideas of Order,* and later in an excised stanza intended for **"Examination of the Hero in a Time of War,"** a poem that appeared in the 1942 *Parts of a World.* Nevertheless, Ananke casts his shadow over all of Stevens' creative life.

The textual examples provided were written over a period of some sixteen years, yet they exhibit a remarkable uniformity in language and conception. Stevens' insistence on more than one kind of poetry, his repeated use of "poetic conception," "poetic ideas," "poetic view of life," his recurring attraction to the idea of God, all serve to make these observations timeless, so that violating his chronology does not distort his meaning. Consequently, when an investigation of "pure poetry" leads ultimately to Ananke, clearly identified as "pure poetry" and said to be "the highest objective of the poet," we may safely conclude that Ananke is the presiding assumption of Stevens' later effort to define this important concept.

There is further reason to insist on Ananke's importance. It is apparent that Stevens' use of the word "poetry" is decidedly various, bearing in its ultimate sense—"pure poetry"—only a tangential relationship to poetry as artifact. In this connection, Stevens' identification of "pure poetry" with Ananke casts considerable doubt on many of the assumptions that have governed the criticism of Stevens' poetry. I have noted that Stevens' proposition that "the theory / Of poetry is the theory of life" is closely linked to his concept of "pure poetry." If, indeed, this belief is a central and informing doctrine in the poetry, it would appear that Stevens' poems are primarily concerned with Ananke and only peripherally concerned with aesthetics (aesthetics is a minor concern, as I shall shortly note). Furthermore, without explicitly acknowledging that Ananke is the fiction with which he is currently preoccupied, Stevens nevertheless implies in his gloss that Ananke is a form of the fiction. The consequences of this admission are again significant, inasmuch as Stevens' "supreme fiction" is another poetic theme that spans a considerable portion of his poetic career. Finally, there is good reason to believe, given Stevens' lexical arbitrariness, that when he universalizes poetry by suggesting that it is to supplant religion ("Poetry / Exceeding music must take the place / Of empty heaven and its hymns"), or when he particularizes it as his poetic subject ("Poetry is the subject of the poem"), he is not talking about an art form at all but is referring to the deification of man's unconscious life—the "ultimate poem"—which is to supplant the obsolete idea of God. This may be illustrated more precisely.

In **"Sombre Figuration,"** the final canto of *Owl's Clover,* Stevens introduces an Ananke surrogate, a shadowy "subman" who is clearly a symbol of the subterranean collective unconscious said to be eternal and absolute:

> There is a man whom rhapsodies of change,
> Of which he is the cause, have never changed
> And never will, a subman under all
> The rest, to whom in the end the rest return,
> The man below the man below the man,
> Steeped in night's opium, evading day.

Now, if Ananke represents the "essential imagination" subsuming the secondary imagination that "partakes of consciousness," then plainly he and the subman are identical forces intended to represent the archaic contents of man's racial memory. This is what Stevens says of his "subman" in the gloss to **"Sombre Figuration":**

> The sub-conscious is assumed to be our begin-

ning and end (I). It follows that it is the beginning and end of the conscious. Thus, the conscious is a lesser thing than the sub-conscious.
The conscious is, therefore, inadequate. In another note I said that the imagination partakes
of the conscious. Here it is treated as an activity
of the sub-conscious: the imagination is the subconscious.

The importance of this gloss is not merely that Stevens
identifies his Ananke-subman with the collective unconscious (subconscious) but that he invests him with escha-
tological significance. If the subconscious is that fundamental psychic stratum that inspires the "lesser" secondary imagination, then it and not its shadow is the master
of man's psychic life, destined eventually to reassert its hegemony. In short, Ananke is the goal of human aspiration:
"our beginning and end." When Stevens, therefore, writes
that the "purpose of writing poetry is to attain pure poetry," we can only assume that Ananke and not the poem
is the *terminus ad quem* of the poetic act. Roy Harvey
Pearce has observed of Stevens' late poems that "poetry,
in being poetry, manifests the existence of a poetry beyond
poetry." Precisely. If man's Ananke-subconscious is "pure
poetry," then it is towards Ananke as a principle of being
that all human objectifications (projections of Ananke) actively strive and yearn. It is not merely that Ananke inspires all human endeavor but that all human endeavor actively strains to realize Ananke as a principle of life. We
write poetry because we are compelled to express our desire to *be* Ananke, an assumption that led Stevens to the
conclusion that a theory of poetry that would account for
Ananke's preeminence would also be a "theory of life."

Owl's Clover is a visionary poem, as William Van
O'Connor has correctly noted [in *The Shaping Spirit*].
The word *future* appears twelve times, and where explicit
statement will not do, Stevens resorts to the future-like infinitive "to be" or the predictive modal auxiliary "would
be" to prefigure a vision that seems imminent but as yet
inaccessible. Moreover, the poem is suffused with the rhetoric of prophetic exaltation: a mysterious portent appears
in the sky adumbrating "the form / Of a generation that
does not know itself"; "eternal vistas" appear on the horizon; "celestial paramours" perform ritualistic dances of
religious obeisance. Indeed, there is a persistent oracular
quality about the poem that leads one to suspect that it is
intended as a testament of faith.

**It is my view that Ananke, Stevens'
explicit symbol for the primary "essential
imagination" (and for "pure poetry"),
represents the single, most important
element of Stevens' thought.**

—*Leonora Woodman*

Inspired by a Marxist critic's charge that *Ideas of Order*
had failed to concern itself with the grave social and eco-

nomic issues of the depression, *Owl's Clover* is Stevens'
testimony that he was indeed concerned but that his concern and his solution were of an altogether different order.
Consequently, he refused to acknowledge his critic's assumptions that man's malaise stemmed from social and
economic dislocations that the socially committed poet
was morally bound to note and treat, and proposed instead
that man's difficulties were to be traced to a far more archetypal event for which contemporary problems were but
instances. That event, in Stevens' mind, was closely related to the origin and function of art; hence, each of the five
cantos hovers around a ring of white marble horses, a central symbol sometimes intended as a symbol for art.

Ananke, however, is Stevens' principal subject; this important personification of "pure poetry" provides the key
to the whole of *Owl's Clover.* Most readers, following Ananke's mythological original, have seen him as an external
god, "an utterly objective, transcendental force." Precedent exists of course for such an interpretation. The inflex-
ible order Ananke (a female divinity) represents in Par-
menides and Plato suggests a transcendent, immutable
world of Being distinct from the sensible and transitory
world of human experience. However, W. K. C. Guthrie
reminds us that the early natural philosophers often associated the principle of necessity with the concept of *physis:*
"*Physis* in the eyes of these men is a natural necessity inherent in each separate thing or substance, not a law of interaction between them. With each thing moving as its
own *physis* dictates, the clashes between them will be fortuitous though caused by necessity."

In this sense, Ananke is an internal principle of necessity,
compelling the organism to assert its inexorable nature.
That Stevens considers him equivalent to the "essential
imagination" similarly confirms him as a peerless interior
god. Mythological precedent, then, gives warrant for Ananke's two-fold domain: he is at once an invincible outer
deity controlling the destiny of the cosmos, and an equally
"fateful" (Stevens' instructive epithet) inner force directing the affairs of men.

Clearly, Stevens intends his Ananke to symbolize a first
principle subject to no other. Predictably, too, he appears
at the end of a canto whose focus is Africa. As the "Sultan
of African sultans," Ananke represents the primitive and
savage energy of man's instinctive life, revealed in the half-
brute "jaguar-men" and "lion-men" who populate the pri-
meval jungles of **"The Greenest Continent."** Predictably,
too, the canto focuses on the idea of God, beginning with
a rhetorical question on the nature of divine hegemony
eventually answered in the minatory and aggressive de-
claratives signalling Ananke's appearance:

> Large-leaved and many-footed shadowing,
> What god rules over Africa, what shape,
> What avuncular cloud-man beamier than
>   spears?

> Fatal Ananke is the common god.

> Sultan of African sultans, starless crown.

Ananke certainly satisfies all the requirements of divinity:
he is almighty, omniscient and eternal, totally without

human frailty, and invulnerable to human desire. Much like the sovereign God of Stevens' Protestant forebears, Ananke sits in "ether flamed," an "unmerciful pontifex" whose "ubiquitous will" directs human destiny. This universal god of Africa subsumes the myriad transitory gods worshipped in his name:

> He is that obdurate ruler who ordains
> For races, not for men, powerful beyond
> A grace to nature, a changeless element.

Evidently Stevens believed in an original and powerful substratum of the human psyche that he thought once enjoyed total hegemony. The "essential imagination" represents not only the universal or archetypal imagination, as some commentators have noted, but a unified condition of life antedating the development of consciousness. Ananke is the vestigial memory of that former life, arising when human consciousness severed man's organic ties. As a result, man assuaged his loneliness and fear by inventing compensatory gods, but in reality these gods are merely Ananke's voice in another guise expressing man's sense of loss. Consequently, Stevens hammers at epithets of estrangement:

> He dwells below, the man below, in less
> Than body and in less than mind, ogre,
> Inhabitant, in less than shape, of shapes
> That are dissembled in vague memory
> Yet still retain resemblances, remain
> Remembrances, a place of a field of lights . . .

Ananke is the force that agitates the imagination to retrieve its lost paradise. A portent of the future introduced in the final canto illustrates Stevens' regressive hopes. Said to be inspired by the "subman" ("An image of his making"), the portent is a Janus image, embodying both past and future, memory and time to come:

> The portent may itself be memory,
> And memory may itself be time to come
>   . . . . .
> And memory's lord is the lord of prophecy . . .

Stevens' gloss to this passage further emphasizes his conviction that mankind's future is closely tied to the contents of the collective unconscious: "The future must bear within it every past, not least the pasts that have become submerged in the sub-conscious, things in the experience of races."

From the belief that man's unconscious prods him to recapture a past condition of life, it is but a step to the further belief that man's imaginative constructions—his art and myth—objectify such yearnings. Evidently Stevens felt that mankind's expressive need and religious sentiment (the two are really one) arose only after the birth of consciousness, impelled by a consequent sense of isolation and solitariness. However, the imaginative constructions arising from these needs are derivative, originating in the reduced but germinal seeds of memory incubating in the subconscious. Thus art and myth have a single source of inspiration—vestigial memory, or Ananke:

> He thinks of the noble lives
> Of the gods and, for him, a thousand litanies
> Are like the perpetual verses in a poet's mind.

Therefore, the ubiquitous statue of *Owl's Clover* is said to be "A ring of horses rising from memory" and is directly attributed to Ananke's importunacy: "He, only, caused the statue to be made / And he shall fix the place where it will stand."

Since Ananke is a dynamic symbol important for the change he presages and initiates, the art that incarnates his image is equally an instrument of change. Hence, the statue of *Owl's Clover* in some instances represents man's *redemptive* imagination—the role Stevens assigned to the constructs of the secondary imagination. Art functions in this manner because it is animated by an idea of God (actually the idea of man) that agitates and revives a corresponding idea in the mind of its audience. Consequently, each imaginative construct has extraordinary significance, for behind its plastic or verbal facade lies the compelling Ananke-musician whose music "mimics" man's inner life:

> He turns us into scholars, studying
> The masks of music. We perceive each mask
> To be the musician's own and, thence, become
> An audience to mimics glistening
> With meanings, doubled by the closest sound,
> Mimics that play on instruments discerned
> In the beat of the blood.

Consequently, art has a job to do. It is functional rather than decorative, instructive rather than merely entertaining, the initially necessary but ultimately dispensable means of reawakening the "child asleep in its own life." Its instrumental function is clearly defined in the body of the poem.

Owl's Clover opens with a description of a ring of white, winged, marble horses arrested in mid-flight. Forelegs taut, bodies "contorted," poised for the "vivid plunge," the horses are charged with an extraordinary vigor on the point of exploding into motion. The image is an appropriate one, for Stevens means the statue to represent man's Ananke temporarily imprisoned in the lifeless artifact. Its dynamism, however, expresses the latent power of man's unconscious straining for the leap that is to assure Ananke's hegemony. Immediately after this description, Stevens introduces an Old Woman, a strange and haggard figure who represents man's current estrangement from his Ananke and his consequent sense of desolation. She is, however, searching for an alternative, which finds its focus in the "atmosphere" generated by the statue, but it is only after the statue's strange and sudden collapse that she experiences it as an exact duplication of her own agitations: "A change so felt, a fear in her so known, / Now felt, now known as this."

Stevens prepares us for the Old Woman's transformation through the incremental repetition of "black" and the destruction of the statue, both of which can be understood only in the context of his apotheosis of the collective unconscious. Stevens consistently uses black and its temporal analogue night to characterize his Ananke-subman-portent: the "dark-skinned" Ananke-serpent presides over Stevens' restored paradise, "the black sublime"; the "subman" is "Steeped in night's opium"; the form his portent takes "bears all darkness in its bulk." The final gloss to **"Sombre Figuration"** explicitly identifies night with the subconscious: "as the portent sank in the night of the sub-conscious, the night in which the trees were full of fare-wells became the perennial night of the sub-conscious." Therefore, when Stevens writes that the Old Woman's "musty mind / Lay black and full of black misshapen" and that her alteration in the wake of the statue's collapse takes the form of unity with night, he intends to affirm the latent power of the subconscious eventually asserting its supremacy.

The collapse of the statue also follows logically from Stevens' psychological assumptions. Stevens insists that the "atmosphere" of the statue corresponds to the "atmo-sphere" of the Old Woman's "musty mind" because he wishes to stress the abstraction embedded in the statue. He assumes that Ananke is the animating principle of art, but art is only incidental to Ananke. Indeed, art is only a kind of allegory—the "pinchings of an idea"—representing once removed the splendors of man's original divinity. True, its function is initially necessary; as paradigm it in-carnates, however faintly, man's original perfection; as catalyst, it impels the psychological transformation neces-sary for retrieval. Once it initiates the reconciliation of man to his Ananke, however, it loses its efficacy and ratio-nale, collapsing to "marble hulk."

Thus, the collapse of the statue in the fourth section of the first canto merely presages its unique resurrection in the fifth section, for its destruction marks the annihilation of art and the beginning of human renewal. Characteristical-ly turning to the future, Stevens predicts a state "beyond imagined trees" in which "the horses would rise again," this time not as a symbol of incipient and unconsummated power arrested in the static artifact, but as living beings finally capable of flight. The horses "Would flash in air," their hoofs would grind, their muscular bodies strain, until all would explode into motion as "The light wings lifted through the crystal space / Of night." No longer impris-oned in the cold and inanimate marbles of man's imagina-tive surrogates, the horses, vivid examples of Stevens' be-lief that "the theory / Of poetry is the theory of life," are now symbols of liberated mankind. The splendid powers of Ananke formerly projected onto the artifact have been redeemed; art has yielded to experience; and man himself is now the "ultimate poem."

The second canto, **"Mr. Burnshaw and the Statue,"** fur-ther develops Stevens' regressive cosmology. This time the statue is the symbol of a moribund civilization, part of an "immense detritus" to be swept aside in favor of "a hope-ful waste to come." But first its former powers must be ex-orcised; once a symbol of the viable artistic artifact, the statue is now an incubus discouraging the full maturation of man's inner divine life. Thus Stevens' mordant tone, the acrimony and contempt with which he speaks of art. The statue is, he writes, a paltry thing concocted by an artist-cook "that never rode the back / Of his angel through the skies." Continuing, he flays the statue as the product of in-significant men—"moonlit muckers" who fashioned "cre-puscular images" as surrogates for "a life they never lived." The horses "should go clattering," infinitely nobler in life than as the frozen mementoes of "the sculptor's fop-pishness." Indeed, the statue is the product of man's

"dank imagination," an "idea" considerably inferior to the original instinctive life it represents:

> much below
> Our crusted outlines hot and huge with fact,
> Ugly as an idea, not beautiful
> As sequels without thought.

The destruction of the statue is completed in a dance of exorcism performed by a group of "celestial paramours" whose dual function is to destroy the old order and usher in the new. Hence, they chant "sibilant requiems" while performing a "ballet infantine," meanwhile turning their backs on the statue now characterized as an "effigy." Foretelling a new day "Astral and Shelleyan," the dancers slowly circle the statue, symbolically enacting the trans-ference of art into life; and as they circle, the exchange takes place: "the statue falls, / The heads are severed, top-ple, tumble, tip," and men become "marble men," ap-pointing to themselves the power of their artifacts. The ep-itaph inscribed on the statue once and for all removes art from the realm of human experience:

> The stones
> That will replace it shall be carved, *"The Mass*
> *Appoints These Marbles Of Itself To Be*
> *Itself."* No more than that, no subterfuge,
> No memorable muffing, bare and blunt.

Between exorcism and annunciation Stevens predicts a modern Gomorrah called "the end of the world." It ap-pears that not only must man's art be destroyed to pave the way for Stevens' "new reality," but so too must all the earmarks of his present culture. Thus, the world is re-duced to a "trash can"; buzzards feed on the carrion of the rich and poor alike; both sculptor and statue lie decapitat-ed among the debris.

Having treated man in his fallen state (the metaphor of the Fall is of course naturalistically rather than Christologi-cally defined) and his consequent redemptive struggle given form and focus in the statue, Stevens turns in his third and central poetic sequence, **"The Greenest Conti-nent,"** to Africa, the symbol for mankind's original para-dise. Here man is ruled by the natural god of the instinc-tive self, offered in the image of a serpent whose province is "death":

> That was never the heaven of Africa, which had
> No heaven, had death without a heaven, death
> In a heaven of death. Beneath the heavy foils,
> Beneath the spangling greens, fear might placate
> And the serpent might become a god, quick-
>   eyed,
> Rising from indolent coils.

This "heaven of death" deifies no abstract, external god: the "black sublime" of Africa is twice invaded in the course of the canto, once by the missionary "angels" of Europe who would impose their idea of God as mytholo-gy, once by the statue of Europe, which would impose its idea of God as aesthetic object. Neither survives. The mis-sionaries return to "their tabernacles," the statue to the "northern sky." Twice returning to the subject of art, Ste-vens asks whether the statue could survive in primitive Af-rica, only to confirm the hostility of the earlier cantos. If it were indeed possible for the statue to arise in Africa, it would be quickly destroyed by man's serpent-Ananke, who has no need of it. Only where human life is characterized by a cultivated consciousness does it become necessary to project the idea of God in an artifact:

> If the statue rose,
> If once the statue were to rise, if it stood,
> Thinly, among the elephantine palms,
> Sleekly the serpent would draw himself across.
> The horses are part of a northern sky
> Too starkly pallid for the jaguar's light . . .

"A Duck for Dinner," the fourth and most explicitly social canto, addresses itself to the twin themes of change and the future, in both of which the artist and his artifact have a significant and central function. Here, however, Stevens' revolutionary ardor is tempered, his mood evolutionary rather than apocalyptic. Confident that in contrast to socialist ideology—a "Profound / Abortion"—the future promised by Ananke had universal validity, Stevens constructs his version of "everyman . . . rapt round / By dense unreason whom he sees rising "inch / By inch, Sunday by Sunday, many men." His masses act in concert, obedient to their Ananke who guarantees their psychic unity and identity of purpose:

> Is each man thinking his separate thoughts or,
>   for once,
> Are all men thinking together as one, thinking
> Each other's thoughts, thinking a single
>   thought,
> Disclosed in everything, transcended, poised
> For the syllable, poised for the touch?

While Stevens believes in universal change, he is yet doubtful about the capacity of "this mob" to effect change without the dynamic leadership of an authoritative figure—a "super-animal" who is to "dictate our fates." The man most likely to fulfill this function, it appears, is the orator-poet, upon whom the "future depends":

> What man of folk-lore shall rebuild the world,
> What lesser man shall measure sun and moon,
> What super-animal dictate our fates?
>
>   . . . . .
>
> It may be the future depends on an orator . . .

The language used here is instructive. Ananke, it will be recalled, wields absolute power: he is "fatal" and "fateful," our death and destiny. The "super-animal," then, cannot be other than Ananke in the guise of his most sensitive agent, the orator-poet. Hence, Stevens apotheosizes the poet in much the same hyperbolic rhetoric reserved for Ananke. Embodying sexual energy, tribal authority, and *Erde* mystique, the poet is a vatic figure whose "clairvoyant eye" discerns the shape of things to come:

> Don Juan turned furious divinity,
> Ethereal compounder, pater patriae,
> Great mud-ancestor, oozer and Abraham,
> Progenitor wearing the diamond crown of
>   crowns,
> He from whose beard the future springs, elect.

Since the poet's special task is to erase the legacy of estrangement by uniting the man to "the man below," he is indeed a figure of enormous prestige, like Ananke worthy of being crowned with the royal diadem. Not surprisingly,

Stevens addresses him as "Great mud-ancestor, oozer and Abraham," deliberately regressive images recalling the Ananke-god who arose when man became a "pale alien of the mud." For the artist, Ananke's most sensitive instrument, provides the articulated link between man and his original paradise.

The statue serves a similar instrumental function. More than an artifact designed to give aesthetic pleasure, it rather objectifies the aspirations of man's instinctive life, focusing in an explicit image of the idea of God what had previously rested on the threshold of consciousness. To its observers, it reflects:

> The metropolitan of mind, they feel
> The central of the composition, in which
> They live. They see and feel themselves, seeing
> And feeling the world in which they live.

Predictably, the statue adumbrates the future appearance of "another race, / Above our race, yet of ourselves transformed." Art, in short, is Stevens' intermediate version of the Incarnation. As man's inner divine life objectified, its effect is no less than human purification; it spiritualizes the race.

"Sombre Figuration," the final canto, promises to restore the loss of original innocence by ensuring the hegemony of "the man below." Beginning with a paean of praise to the Ananke-subman's powers, Stevens next turns to the impending apocalypse his advent heralds. The shape of this future looms in the heavens as a "sprawling portent" revealing "the form / Of a generation that does not know itself." Thrice insisting on the portent's impalpability to suggest it as the spiritual reality diffused in man and nature, Stevens nevertheless resorts to word picture to paint the intangible subman. What emerges is a gigantic "bulk" in Atlas-like support of the horizon, casting its prodigious shadow over the world's inhabitants, breathing upon them an "immense intent."

Predictably, the final lines of the poem foresee a future distinguished by the absence of the secondary imagination, a firm and logical conclusion given the assumptions Stevens brings to the nature of man. Insisting that "imagination has an end," Stevens envisions the "new reality" promised by the reconciliation between man and his Ananke. It is a life of sheer presentness and sensation. Having shed the temporal understanding by which consciousness mediates and orders experience, man is now relieved of history, free to enjoy the "gaudium of being," eternal and timeless:

> To flourish the great cloak we wear
> At night, to turn away from the abominable
> Farewells and, in the darkness, to feel again
> The reconciliation, the rapture of a time
> Without imagination, without past
> And without future, a present time, is that
> The passion, indifferent to the poet's hum,
> That we conceal?

Life is purposeless, desultory. Whatever gesture man is capable of is merely a "gesture's whim" without forethought or intent. Logically, neither the poet nor the statue intrude to disturb this regained paradisal home, for the poet is banished and the statue, having fulfilled its promise, "is not a thing imagined, a stone / That changed in sleep." Indeed, man no longer needs such supports, having supplanted them with himself, gay "Jocundus," acting out his comic inheritance in what Stevens was later to call an "unspotted imbecile revery." The promise fulfilled, Ananke restored to his supreme and undisputed status, man returns to the mindlessness of instinctive life, "Night and the imagination being one." (pp. 9-32)

> *Leonora Woodman, in her* Stanza My Stone: Wallace Stevens and the Hermetic Tradition, *Purdue University Press, 1983, 195 p.*

Richard Gray   (essay date 1984)

[*In the following excerpt, Gray discusses Stevens's "kinship" with English Romanticism, French Symbolism, and American literature and philosophy in an examination of the general characteristics of Stevens's poetry.*]

'Poetry is the subject of the poem', wrote Wallace Stevens in **'The Man with the Blue Guitar'.** 'From this the poem issues and / To this returns.' Characteristically, Stevens meant a number of things by this, if only because as he saw it and expressed it in his 'Adagia', 'Poetry and materia poetica are interchangeable terms.' 'Poetry' for him included 'that / Irrational moment' when the mind feels reconciled, at one with its surroundings as well as 'the gaiety . . . of language' or indeed any other means the mind might employ to achieve this feeling. On a more elementary level, however, by 'poetry' Stevens also meant the poetry of other people, or statements made about poetry by other people with whom, perhaps, he felt he had some kind of intellectual *rapport.* For like many artists in different fields during this century—like Joyce, for instance, or Picasso or Stravinsky—Stevens was fascinated by the nature of his own art, and felt compelled to explore its possibilities and limitations. His work is nothing if not self-conscious. It almost asks us to look for contents and antecedents; it virtually obliges us to see it, and its creator, in terms of a particular time and place. In seeing things in this way, of course, there is the danger of becoming the kind of reader that Stevens deplored in one of his letters, 'who spends his time dissecting what he reads for echoes, imitations, influences, as if no one was ever simply himself but is always compounded of a lot of other people'. Not to do so, though, or rather not to look for signs of *kinship,* of spiritual resemblance rather than influence, would be to ignore Stevens's centrality and, quite possibly, underestimate his importance. Stevens was a great original, certainly: as indeed anyone who believes that 'All poetry is experimental poetry' must be. But he was a great original precisely because he could absorb and cope with so much pressure—because he could gather up so many different threads and out of them weave something entirely personal, coherent and new.

The first and probably most obvious sign of kinship is to be found in Stevens's 'final belief', the impulse that shapes and gives life to all of his work, and which marks him as a true heir of the Romantics. 'I do very much have a dislike of disorder', he admitted once, 'One of the first things I do when I get home at night is to make people take things off radiator tops'. Put in a characteristically self-mocking way, this sums up the nature of the impulse: a 'rage for order', for form and a sense of meaning recovered, however temporarily, from the essential chaos of life. For Stevens, in fact, as for most of the great Romantic poets and philosophers, reality is not something given to us, which our minds receive passively, but is on the contrary something made, the product of an interchange, an interplay or dialectic between our minds and our given circumstances. We, or more accurately our consciousnesses, are not simply blank pieces of paper, Stevens felt, on which the world writes its messages, not just mirrors that reflect our environment; rather, they are lamps, active, creative things which illuminate that environment, helping to give it shape and perspective and so making it adequate, even if only momentarily, to ordinary human desires. 'The imagination', declared Stevens echoing Blake and Coleridge, 'is the power of the mind over the possibilities of things'; 'like light, it adds nothing, except itself'.

Stevens was sometimes irritated by references to the Romantics. 'The past is my own', he insisted in one of his letters, 'not something marked Coleridge, Wordsworth etc. I know of no one who has been particularly important to me'. Nevertheless, when one looks in detail at what Stevens terms his 'reality-imagination complex', it is not difficult to see several correspondences. 'Conceptions are artificial', Stevens argues; our world is always, in a sense, an imagined one, because as soon as we begin to think about it we begin to structure it according to some law—such as the scientific law of cause and effect. We begin, in effect, to 'read' and interpret it in the same way that, instinctively, we read and interpret a written text. On this level, the mind or imagination, as Stevens described it, broadly corresponds to what Coleridge, in *Biographia Literaria* called the primary imagination: 'the living power and prime agent of all human perception, and . . . a repetition in the finite mind of the eternal act of creation in the infinite I AM'. Much more important for Stevens, though, were those acts of the mind which made it correspond with what Coleridge termed the secondary imagination; that is to say, those acts whereby man attempts quite consciously to give significance to his life—to devise some moral or aesthetic order, however fragile or provisional, which can give coherence and a sense of purpose to things. This kind of order was what Stevens called a 'supreme fiction'; and for him, as for Coleridge, the prime creator of such fictions was the poet. The poet, according to Stevens, strives for a 'precise equilibrium' between the mind and its environment at any given moment in time; and then creates a fiction which is at once true to our experience of the world and true to his and our need for value and meaning.

It is worth emphasizing that Stevens was no different from Coleridge and other Romantics, either, in insisting on the fact of change. We are always altering, Stevens believed, our given circumstances alter too, and the fictive world created out of the synthesis or union of the two must invariably respond to this. We must be reassessing our personal needs and given circumstances continually so as to devise new ideas which do full justice to the dynamic nature of both mind and world; and the poet, in turn, must be writing new poems, new fictions all the time so as to pay his tribute to the metamorphic nature of things. Stevens's favourite metaphor for this was the seasons, with winter seen as the bare, icy reality void of all fictive covering; spring as the moment when the imagination and the world come together and embrace; summer as the period of fruition, when the marriage between the desires of the mind and the things of the world is complete and harmonious; and autumn as the moment when the fiction no longer suffices because the imagination that created it, and the world it was created for, have altered, requiring new fictions, fresh identities and relationships. As this rather bare outline indicates, perhaps, the imagery of sexual congress and conflict mingles with that of natural growth and decay to describe what Stevens, in one of his poems, termed the imagination's 'ancient cycle'; and in this respect, again, he was not so very different from a writer like Coleridge. Consider, for example, these two brief passages, one from 'Dejection: An Ode' and the other from *Notes toward a Supreme Fiction*:

> O Lady! we receive but what we give
> And in our life alone does Nature live. . . .
>
> Joy, Lady! is the spirit and the power
> Which wedding Nature to us gives in dower
> A new Earth and a new Heaven. . . .
>
> Two things of opposite natures seem to depend
> On one another, as a man depends
> On a woman, day on night, the imagined
>
> On the real. This is the origin of change.
> Winter and spring, cold copulars, embrace
> And forth the particulars of rapture come.

Mind and world, night and day, male and female: both writers see life here as a marriage of opposites. Joy, or a sense of meaning, is the offspring of this marriage. And what Coleridge called dejection, a sense of melancholy and futility, comes when the marriage fails; when, for example, the world is too much with us and the mind becomes a passive instrument—or, alternatively, when the mind escapes from the pressures of the world completely and withdraws into solipsism and day-dreaming.

'A poet looks at the world as a man looks at a woman.' This, from the 'Adagia', offers a variation on the sexual metaphor: and it is also a reminder of just how seductive, for Stevens, was the figure of the poet. For Stevens was no less of a Romantic in this, his tendency to see the fabulator, the maker of poems, as a latter-day prophet: someone who creates the myths that give meaning to people's lives and so enables them to survive—and who also offers an example to his audience, by showing them how to devise their own myths as well as listen to his. Stevens was quite categorical about this. For, whenever he discussed the task or function of the poet, the thrust of his argument was invariably the same. 'I think', he would say,

> . . . that he fulfills himself only as he sees his imagination become the light in the minds of others. His rôle, in short, is to help people to live their lives. ['Noble Rider and the Sound of Words']

In effect, Stevens returned the poet to his ancient rôle of bard or myth-maker, offering purpose and a sense of meaning to his tribe. And to this he added another, more peculiarly Romantic and American, dimension: which was that of hero. For the poet, Stevens suggested, is his own hero because his mind, his representative imagination, is the catalyst of events. Instead of a third person protagonist, the poet, the 'I' of the poem, occupies the centre of the stage; there, 'like an insatiable actor, slowly and / with meditation', he speaks words and acts out a drama to which

> an invisible audience listens,
> Not to the play, but to itself, expressed
> In an emotion as of two people, as of two
> Emotions becoming one.
>   ['Of Modern Poetry']

To the extent that Stevens did attribute such an extraordinarily powerful and central rôle to the poet, he was of course revealing a kinship with some of the later poets and philosophers in the Romantic tradition, like Matthew Arnold, Henri Bergson—and, above all, George Santayana. While he was still a student at Harvard, Stevens became acquainted with Santayana and was often invited to visit him; he read the older man some of his early poetry and then, much later, addressed one of his finest poems, **'To an Old Philosopher in Rome'**, to him. In a way, Stevens seems to have regarded Santayana as a saint—a type, anyway, of the imaginative man, who can use his mind to redeem the essential poverty of life—and Santayana's ideas served as a lamp and guide to the poet throughout his career, illuminating his way, his various poetic voyages, and giving him some hazy sense of a possible destination. This famous passage from the 'Adagia', for example, recalls Santayana's suggestion that 'religion and poetry are identical in essence', since both, ignoring 'matters of fact', 'repair to the material of existence . . . and then out of that . . . material . . . build new structures, richer, finer, fitted to the primary tendencies of our nature':

> The final belief is to believe in a fiction, which you know to be a fiction, there being nothing else. The exquisite truth is to know that it is a fiction and that you believe in it willingly.

'Poetry' said Stevens elsewhere, in **'The Man with the Blue Guitar'**, '. . . must take the place / Of empty heaven and its hymns.' For him, as for Santayana, the old religious myths had crumbled and poetry had now to act as a means of redemption. The poet had to replace the priest (or, alternatively, the priest had to accept the rôle of poet). Art had to replace the liturgy of the church. Imaginative belief, or what Coleridge called 'a willing suspension of disbelief', had to replace religious faith. And a possible earthly paradise, created here and now out of the marriage between mind and world, had to replace the vision of a heavenly paradise situated in some great hereafter. Beginning with an essentially Romantic belief in 'The imagination, the one reality / In this imagined world', and building slowly and meditatively on this, Stevens ended in fact with another centrally Romantic notion—that (to quote from the 'Adagia' again)

> in the absence of a belief in God, the mind turns to its own creations and examines them, not

alone from the aesthetic point of view, but for what they reveal, for what they validate and in- validate, for the support they give.

To dwell on Stevens's Romanticism, however, to the ex- clusion of other aspects of his poetic character would be to forget how very important to him both the French poets—and, in particular, the Symbolistes, their immedi- ate precursors and successors—and his own American background were. The kinship with the French was un- doubtedly less crucial than is often supposed; many com- mentators have exaggerated it, perhaps because it is fairly obvious—a matter, more often than not, of vocabulary and idiom. Nevertheless, it proved useful to Stevens in sev- eral respects, and not least in his efforts to distinguish him- self from the English tradition. 'Nothing could be more in- appropriate to American literature than its English source', he . . . declared [in the 'Adagia'], 'since the Americans are not British in sensibility'. And one way he chose to underline this in his early work was by adopting, on occasion, a self-consciously Gallic tone, with phrases from the French, a smattering of French words—or that demureness of statement combined with elegance of man- ner and the kind of sonorous, precious and witty language that is often associated with such poets of the late nine- teenth century as Verlaine and Laforgue. In turn, the later work often recalls more recent French poets like Valéry, in its openly philosophical approach, its confident use of large abstractions, and its extraordinarily complex net- work of figurative reference.

Perhaps the French poet with whom Stevens shared most, however, was not Verlaine, Laforgue, or even Valéry, but Baudelaire because, in this case at least, the sense of kin- ship operated on a rather deeper level. Certainly, the par- allels in technique are evident here as well. Both Baude- laire and Stevens manage, for instance, to combine rule and misrule in their poems. Their rhythms are elegantly exact; the movement of each line is measured and poised; and the structure of each of their longer pieces seems to be premeditated, precise, a matter of inherited rather than imitative form. And yet, on the other hand, their language can be bizarre; their imagery gaudy, intentionally star- tling; and, on closer inspection, it seems that their longer poems do not so much progress as stand still or go round in a circle—existing in space, really, rather than time. As several critics have observed, Baudelaire was at once a Ro- mantic writer and a Classical one, which is perhaps one of the reasons why he described the right to be inconsis- tent as 'a right in which everyone is interested'. Exactly the same could be said of Stevens, who openly admitted to a correspondent that he liked to move 'in many direc- tions at once'. 'No man of imagination is prim', he added defiantly, 'the thing is a contradiction in terms.'

'May it be', asked Stevens half-seriously when he was just 26, 'that I am only a New Jersey Epicurean?' That ques- tion leads indirectly to the other, deeper level on which Baudelaire and Stevens meet: which is their shared insis- tence on the artificial, figurative nature of their poetic worlds. Very often, this insistence led them to play the lit- erary dandy. Even if it did not, however, even when the tone was more agonized or philosophical, there was in- variably this emphasis on the poet as maker, inventing a

world rather than simply reporting one—and, in doing so, uncovering a possibility available to everyone. One of the most vivid and memorable descriptions of this activity— of the mind giving life whatever savour or meaning it pos- sesses—occurs in **'The Idea of Order at Key West'**. In it, the poet describes a woman whom he once heard singing by the sea (a traditional figure for raw experience), who becomes identified for him with the 'blessed rage for order', the need that singer, poet, and all of us must feel to discover form and significance in our lives. 'When she sang', the poet declares,

> the sea
> Whatever self it had, became the self
> That was her song, for she was the maker. Then
>   we,
> As we beheld her striding there alone,
> Knew that there never was a world for her
> Except the one she sang and, singing, made.

The stress on that final 'made' is enormous, reminding us of the infinite series of makings that add up to the experi- ence of the poem: the woman 'makes' or interprets the scene, and in turn each reader, each time he reads the piece, 'makes' or interprets what he sees and hears.

It may be worth pointing out that, in reminding us con- stantly of the figurative nature of poetic truth and the fic- tive nature of poetry, Stevens is (as so often) poised be- tween paradoxes. The world the poem creates is real, Ste- vens seems to be saying, because the material for it is dis- covered *in* reality; and yet it is unreal, a fiction in a way, because it depends on the mind then reshaping that mate- rial. It is true in the sense that it reproduces a true—that is to say, a true Romantic-Symboliste—version of things; but it is untrue in that it does not reflect 'the first idea', pure, unadorned fact. Above all, it is perfect and complete in so far as it represents a perfect marriage, a complete synthesis of mind and circumstance; and yet it is imper- fect, incomplete to the extent that, as mind and circum- stance change, the poet must go on to devise new mar- riages, new syntheses, and so in effect new poems. Of course, Stevens never tried to achieve a logical reconcilia- tion of these opposites because, like so many writers since the Romantic revolution, he realized that his beliefs stemmed from a profound illogic, a deep unreason. 'The poem', Stevens suggested [in the 'Adagia'], 'reveals itself only to the ignorant man' for the simple reason that it de- pends on contradictions which can never be explained or argued away—but which can perhaps be reconciled with the help, and under the 'miraculous influence', of the imagination.

'Do I contradict myself? / Very well then I contradict myself, / (I am large, I contain multitudes)' [Walt Whit- man, 'Song of Myself']. That would be one way of dis- missing any objections Stevens's paradoxes might raise: the lofty gesture of a poet like Walt Whitman who insists that his self-contradictions are part of his representative nature, his attempt to register the variety of his home- place. Which leads me, inevitably, to the native context; for all his kinship with the English Romantics and poets like Baudelaire, Stevens was nothing if not an American writer—and someone who believed that (to quote one of his very last poems) 'a mythology reflects its region'. 'The gods of China', Stevens declared, 'are always Chinese' ['Two or Three Ideas']; that is, the world the imagination embraces is always a specific, local one and the fictions created out of that embrace must bear the stamp of their locality. 'One turns with something like ferocity toward a land that one loves', he said elsewhere, in a revealing discussion of another poet, John Crowe Ransom, '. . . to demand that it surrender, reveal, that in itself which one loves' ['John Crowe Ransom: Tennessean']. As Stevens saw it, this consummation devoutly to be wished, this marriage between a particular person and place, was 'a vital affair, not an affair of the heart . . . , but an affair of the whole being, a fundamental affair of life'. It was not simply a matter of idiom and gesture, in other words, but of identity and vision. Of course, the paraphernalia of American culture is there in Stevens's poems—things like coffee, saxophones and large sombreros—and, like Whitman, Stevens shows that he has fallen in love with American names. But these things matter less, as a mark of origin, than the fact that Stevens chose as his starting-point what he called 'human loneliness / A part of space and solitude' [**The Sail of Ulysses**']; like every great American poet, in fact, he began with the isolated consciousness—Whitman's 'essential Me'—and then progressed from there to the new dimensions, the moments of self-assertion or communion, which that consciousness struggles gamely to create.

Here, however, we are confronted with another paradox in Stevens's work. Like so many American writers, Stevens began with the isolated self, the separate mind and its world; unlike most of them, though, he then moved in two quite different directions, which could perhaps be termed *centripetal* and *centrifugal*. The centripetal movement recalls that arch-egotist and solipsist, Edgar Allan Poe; and, to some extent, Stevens does sound very much like Poe. The self, he insists, creates its own world, and the poem presents us with a supreme version of that world—which is self-contained, fixed and (in a sense, as I have already suggested) perfect. The centrifugal movement, in turn, recalls Emily Dickinson. For Stevens can be quite as insistent as Dickinson was that the self is fragile, evanescent, dwarfed by its surroundings, and that the world it creates must—due to the limitations of its creator—be provisional and incomplete. In some respects, Stevens's poems resemble Poe's in that they drive inwards upon what Poe, in one of his reviews, called 'the circumscribed Eden' of the poet's dream. 'Pure' or 'closed' poems in a way, they are as autonomous and intangible as the worlds they describe; they exist in their own special dimension, or, as Stevens himself put it once, 'beyond the compass of change / Perceived in a final atmosphere' [**The Man with the Blue Guitar**']. In other respects, though, Stevens's poems seem far more like Dickinson's, edging out tentatively as they do towards the boundaries of perception. 'Open' poems of a kind, they tend to emphasize their arbitrariness, to offer themselves up to reinterpretation and reinvention—and so to remind us that they are (to quote Stevens [in *Notes toward a Supreme Fiction*]) 'inconstant objects of inconstant cause / In a universe of inconstancy'.

Just how Stevens manages to walk this tightrope between 'open' and 'closed' structures is beautifully illustrated by one of his most famous earlier pieces, **'Anecdote of the Jar'**. The animating conception in this poem is very simple: the jar serves as a point which orders all that surrounds it. It performs the function of the imagination just as its surroundings, organized for a moment into a series of significant relationships, perform the function of reality. What complicates things, however, and gives an additional dimension to the poem is its form, the way in which Stevens chooses to flesh out this conception. **'Anecdote of the Jar'** begins with a series of unrhymed couplets, continues with them until the eighth line, and then suddenly presents the reader with two end-stopped lines, set off for the first time by rhyme:

> It took dominion everywhere.
> The jar was gray and bare.

It sounds for a moment as if the argument is completed, the poem rounded off. But then, it turns out, it is not; and the premature finality of the lines I have quoted gives an air of *un*finality to the two lines which follow, and which form yet another unrhymed couplet. Even this, the feeling that things have not quite been rounded off, is not left unqualified, however, because the last line returns us to a word used in the first line: 'Tennessee'. Joining the end to the beginning, the poet still seems to be trying to round the poem off, to seal it; and we, the readers, cannot really be sure that he has failed. So we are made to feel that the work is at once complete *and* incomplete, that the argument has been concluded and yet that something has been missed out, left hanging loose. **'Anecdote of the Jar'** is, in effect, made to imitate in its form (as well as describe in its content) the continuing act of the imagination, by which worlds are created that are complete in themselves and yet subject to alteration. The mind behind the poem has apparently composed things for a moment, achieved an order 'beyond the compass of change'; and yet it intimates that it must give that order up soon and—casting aside 'the rotted names', obsolete forms and vocabulary—submit itself to 'a universe of inconstancy'.

'Anecdote of the Jar' is exemplary in several ways. The same essential structure, for instance, is used with a difference in **'Thirteen Ways of Looking at a Blackbird'**. Here, a blackbird serves as a focal point, a means of bringing out the significance of the context in which it is involved. The meaning of the bird depends on each context, just as the meaning of the context depends on it, with the result that there is exactly the same condition of interdependence between the bird and each of its settings as there is between the jar and its surroundings: a condition which (it need hardly be added) Stevens felt to be characteristic of the relationship between the imagination and its surroundings. In the first section of the poem, for example, the blackbird provides a focal point for the landscape it composes in the same way that a compositional centre composes a landscape painting; and, in doing so, it provides a paradigm of the way the mind orders reality by discovering significant relations in it.

> Among twenty snowy mountains,
> The only moving thing
> Was the eye of the blackbird.

In this case, the snowy surroundings are static, and the

eye/I of the blackbird offers the only motion. By contrast, in the final section the terms are reversed:

> It was evening all afternoon.
> It was snowing
> And it was going to snow.
> The blackbird sat
> In the cedar-limbs.

Now the blackbird is motionless in a world of swirling, snowy movement. The bird has become a still point; the imagination is, apparently, at rest; and the poet, making the last lines echo the first, seems to be bringing things full circle, rounding them off. Everything appears to be completed; that is, until we are reminded that, for Stevens, winter was a beginning as well as an end. This section concludes 'Thirteen Ways', certainly; but by reminding us of the process of decreation—what Stevens called [in a letter] 'getting rid of the paint to get at the world itself'—it also acts as a prelude to further imaginative activity, an opening to poems as yet to be written. Once again, things are complete and yet somehow incomplete, closed and at the same time open.

Quite apart from the structure, the tone and idiom of 'Anecdote of the Jar' are also characteristic. The tone is serio-comic as with so many of Stevens's poems, especially the earlier ones; here as in, say, 'Bantams in Pinewoods' or 'Le Monocle de Mon Oncle' the poet uses wit and irony to qualify and complicate matters further, and so prevent the reader from coming to too simple or final a conclusion. And the idiom, in turn, is characterized by repetition and echo ('round . . . Surround . . . around . . . round . . . ground'), a series of significant if often subterranean connections. This repetitive pattern becomes far more elaborate in some of the longer pieces, with the result that poems like (for example) 'Sunday Morning' or 'The Idea of Order at Key West' resemble mosaics, in which the poet seems to be trying to construct his own personal version of the imaginative fictions he celebrates. Complex designs of word, sound and image, they offer the reader a special world, in this case a verbal one, which may be abstracted from and so depend upon our given surroundings—but which has its own innate structure and system of cross-reference.

It would be wrong, however, to dwell on 'Anecdote of the Jar' as if it summed up the whole of Stevens's work, even in its paradoxes and ambiguities. No one poem can do that; and not merely because the later poetry is, on the whole, less spry and balletic than the earlier—more meditative and austere, more discursive and openly philosophical. It is also because Stevens rarely allowed himself to be contained by a particular idiom even within the space of one poem. Each of his pieces is complexly layered, moving almost casually and quite unpredictably between high rhetoric and the colloquial, book-words, foreign borrowings, and native slang. As a result, each seems unique in a way, with its own particular rhythms and adjustments—its own special way of turning the world into words. Of modern poetry, Stevens once said,

> It is like the voice of . . . some . . . figure concealed. . . . There is no accompaniment. If occasionally the poet touches the triangle or one of

the cymbals, he does it only because he feels like doing it. Instead of a musician we have an orator whose speech sometimes resembles music. ['Effects of Analogy']

This passage, from the poem that concludes the third section of *Notes toward a Supreme Fiction,* suggests something of what he meant. The poem is a hymn to the earth, which Stevens describes as a 'fat girl' and addresses in exactly the same way that earlier poets addressed God or their mistress. Like God, the poet suggests, the earth is mysterious, hidden, infinite in its surprises; like the traditional notion of the mistress she is also enticing but elusive, given to radically varying changes of mood. More important, perhaps: like both, she can only be understood through an act of the imagination, a poem or fiction of some kind—something in which her changeableness, her extraordinary vitality and variety, can be caught for a moment in a single, crystalline image.

> Fat girl, terrestrial, my summer, my night
> How is it I find you in difference, see you there
> In a moving contour, a change not quite completed?
>   . . . . .
>
> Even so when I think of you as strong or tired.
>
> Bent over work, anxious, content, alone,
> You remain the more than natural figure. You
> Become the soft-footed phantom, the irrational
>
> Distortion, however fragrant, however dear.
> That's it: the more than rational distortion,
> The fiction that results from feeling. Yes, that.
>
> They will get it straight one day at the Sorbonne.
> We shall return at twilight from the lecture
> Pleased that the irrational is rational.
>
> Until flicked by feeling, in a gildered street,
> I call you by name, my green, my fluent mundo.
> You will have stopped revolving except in crystal.

The image of the revolving crystal is, of course, an image of an image: a fictional embodiment of the kind of imaginative fiction that can at once recover the world about us, in all its brightness, plenitude, and vitality, and raise it to a higher power, a superior dimension of reality. And with this image we are back, really, where we began, at the centre of the Romantic-Symbolist tradition, which is the great tradition in modern poetry; since the forms of knowledge and vision that Stevens celebrates here are no different from those celebrated by the great Romantic poets and their successors when they have talked, for example, about the truth of the imagination, the power and suggestiveness of the deep image, or described the world as a forest of symbols. In its own way, the crystal corresponds to—which is to say, has the same basic significance and performs the same symbolic function as—Coleridge's moon imagery, Keats's nightingale and urn, or the memorable allusion to the dancer that concludes Yeats's 'Among School Children'. For it summarizes in the only way possible for Stevens (that is, in an imaginative way) what was for him the central fact of life: the ability of the mind to achieve a kind of redemption—by working *with* the world to abstract something of value out of that world, and so (as Stevens himself put it once) build a bridge between fact and miracle.

'Why do poets in particular resent the attribution of the influence of other poets?' asked Stevens in a letter to Richard Eberhart. 'It seems to me that the true answer is that with a true poet his poetry is the same thing as his vital self. It is not possible for anyone else to touch it'. This necessarily brief essay has been in no sense an attempt to deny the simple fact that Stevens states here; like every 'true poet', Stevens declared his own unique being in his work—developed his own personal sense of things, and of himself, using his own characteristic voice. Despite what some critics may assert, however, Stevens was not a solipsist, any more than he was an aesthete or a hedonist; he was 'a man speaking to men' (to borrow a familiar but nevertheless useful phrase from Wordsworth) preoccupied with 'what will suffice' and enable us all to live our lives. 'We can never have great poetry', Stevens insisted in one of his very last speeches, 'unless we believe that poetry serves great ends'; and, in pursuit of those ends, he willingly absorbed the best that had been thought and said by other writers—other people who had tried to make their imagination the light in the minds of their readers—to absorb it and then make it a part of his own meditations. He was a solitary poet, of course, and something of an eccentric visionary—aware, even while he sought knowledge, that 'always there is another life / A life beyond this present knowing' ['**The Sail of Ulysses**']. But his very solitude made him an heir of the Romantics, as well as a kinsman of Poe, Dickinson and Whitman; while his visions were shared ones, their eccentricity deriving not from any personal idiosyncrasies but from the fact that, in an age of disbelief, the truth can only be arrived at, he felt, by the most circuitous and stony of routes. The figure of Santayana perhaps best sums up this central paradox, of being apart from and yet a part of things. For in describing his former mentor, in '**To an Old Philosopher in Rome**', Stevens seems to be describing himself—or, to be more accurate, his own particular choices and best possibilities. 'Be orator', he implores Santayana,

> but with an accurate tongue
> And without eloquence . . .
>
> So that we feel, in this illumined large,
> The veritable small, so that each of us
> Beholds himself in you, and hears his voice
> In yours, master and commiserable man. . . .

Throughout his life, Stevens sought exactly the kind of dual rôle, of 'master and commiserable man', that he asks Santayana to assume here: which is why, in the end, his poetry bears so many signs of kinship with others, living and dead, while remaining utterly and unmistakably his own. (pp. 41-56)

Richard Gray, "Poetry and the Subject of the Poem: Wallace Stevens," in Modern American Poetry, *edited by R. W. (Herbie) Butterfield, London: Vision Press, 1984, pp. 41-57.*

Frank Lentricchia   (essay date 1988)

[*An American educator and critic, Lentricchia emphasizes the social aspect of literature and language in all of his writings. While Lentricchia's criticism has focused on the relationship between poetry and identity, as in* The Gaiety of Language: An Essay on the Radical Poetics of W. B. Yeats and Wallace Stevens *(1968), his more recent work has addressed the social responsibility of literature, theory, and criticism. His* Criticism and Social Change *(1984) addresses the responsibilities of the critic in society and further defines his understanding of the relationship between culture and society. In the following excerpt, Lentricchia examines the dual identities of Stevens as both businessman and poet, discusses the treatment of class concerns in his poetry, and places Stevens's work in the context of high modernist poetry.*]

The standard generalization about Wallace Stevens' poetic development is that as he grew older he put on the vocal weight which enabled him to transcend the mere aesthetic perfections of his earlier poems—so sensuously full, so exquisitely achieved, so intellectually empty. Aside from Yvor Winters and his few (and ever fewer) devotees it is hard to find serious readers of Stevens who don't believe that he actually grew up as he grew older and that the proof of his maturity lies in his later long poems where (so it goes) he at last achieved the requisite (churchly) tone of high seriousness and important human reference. That old contention of Stevens' critics is strongly echoed in a wider cultural dimension in the self-reflexive song of canonical modernism, in the full terror that modernists feel for their own social relevance. Beginning with aestheticist principles, modernists ask, with an art that presumably turns its back on the world, refuses representation, turns inward to sensation and impression, as Pater urged, how can we put art back in—give it connection, power, or, in Stevens' words, "a ministry in the world"? Whether they write poems, narratives of character, or narratives of ideas called critical theory, that's long been a panicky question of literary modernism. And the story I am telling about Stevens and his culture is maybe the most vivid example that I can give of an anxiety framed by this classic contradiction of the middle-class world: on the one hand, our retreat to the interior, whether of our homes, our families, or our writing—wherein we indulge the sentiment that our private life is our authentic life—and our concurrent disavowal of all possibility for happiness in the public sphere, or in relationships not sanctioned by the public sphere; a retreat, a disavowal, on the other hand, incessantly accompanied by an incipiently explosive dissatisfaction with all private (and aestheticizing) solutions to pains whose sources are not personal and which require keen attention to history's plots. Georg Lukács's excoriation of the subjective and plotless qualities of high-modernist literature is perfectly just as far as it goes. But what it leaves out is one of the most interesting things about high modernists—their pre-Lukácian discomfort with what they suspect as their own self-trivializing ahistoricism.

Reviewers of Stevens' first volume said over and again, in so many words, that he was a precious little aesthete—that he had nothing to say and, even worse, that his poems were on principle mindless: maybe gemlike, but also without point. These negative assessments bothered Stevens but not for the usual egoistic reasons. The fact is that he had heard it all before. His reviewers had only uttered publicly what he was telling his friends in letters in the months when he was deciding on the contents of *Harmonium,* reading over all he had written in the previous decade, thinking about what to keep in and what to keep out. He was saying in those painfully self-conscious days that his poems were "horrid cocoons from which later abortive insects had sprung"; they were "witherlings"; "debilitated." At best, "preliminary minutiae"; at worst, "garbage" from which no "crisp salad" could be picked. Stevens, at forty-four, would not be one of those writers who could by reading his old things over gather sustenance. He was one of those modernists who suffered from a severe originality neurosis whose sources were equally literary and economic, whose obsessive force was determined by equally decisive experiences of the literary avant-garde and the decadent edge of consumer capitalism. As his master category of value, originality simply makes nonsense of the conventional modernist opposition of aesthetics and economics because it not only prized the new as the different, the rare, and the strange, but could and did find triggering releases of pleasure equally in original poems and in exotic fruits bought at a specialty market for gourmet shoppers. He was one of those writers who find their old things just old—and psychically unprofitable to reencounter. And given the significant social role he had imagined and would imagine for poetry from his Harvard years on to the end of his life, his judgment upon what he had actually managed to produce from his late twenties through his early forties must have felt bitterly ironic. Yet, I think, not really despairing. For even as he condemned himself in self-disgust, he was allowing himself the hopeful fiction of organic growth. He might be looking at abortions but he could imagine and believe in the possibility of full-term birth and teleological perfection both for himself and for his poetic project—a distinction which became harder and harder to make as he absorbed the full failure of his marriage to Elsie Moll.

His project was not wrong from the start. The origin was in fact good. His beginning as an aesthete, if only a beginning, in the delights of pure perception and linguistic riot, was yet the right sort of beginning. For him the aesthetic was an isolated moment, withdrawn from the social mess and forever free from didactic and political translation. As he grew older and more critical of the canonical modernism he partly endorsed, he began to believe that if the autonomous aesthetic moment was to become the urgent and compelling moment he always felt it inherently to be, then it would somehow have to carry its purity beyond itself, back into the social mess, to his rhetorical target: the culturally and economically privileged readers who, like himself, needed to transform the basic joyless conditions of their existence. **"It Must Give Pleasure"** is the title of the final section of *Notes toward a Supreme Fiction. It* must give pleasure because little else does. He declared in a characteristic moment in the essays he wrote in the later years of his career that poetry helps us to live our lives, and lucky for us that it does—we get so little help from anyplace else. He once told his wife that the nine-to-five working-day Wallace was nothing—the sources of his authentic selfhood were at home, quite literally: the site of his marriage and (for this aesthetic burgher) the site of poetic activity. But when love and marriage parted, making his marriage an empty form, his writing became the final source of selfhood: his last resort. The fate of his poetic project turned out to be indistinguishable from the fate of pleasure. The most poignant and definitive image I've ever seen drawn of what Stevens became as a man, after his marriage collapsed, was drawn by Stevens himself in a letter written in his seventieth year: "We have a very good time here. We go upstairs at night long before dark. Nothing could be more exciting than to sit in the quiet of one's room watching the fireflies." The "we" referred to, Elsie and himself, is a "we" long limited to pronominal designation. In fact, "we" are not having a good time. As "we" fades to the impersonal "one," Stevens is relieved of the embarrassment of openly saying to his correspondent "my room." They go upstairs long before dark to separate bedrooms they'd chosen many years before—Elsie to do God knows what, he never tells us, he to watch the flashing of fireflies in their mating game, to feel excitement that he can't share except with his interior lover, his own creative impulse, whose power to bring him "vivid transparence" he defines as the power of peace itself: poetry, Stevens' ultimate mating game, a game best played with only one player in the game, a last resort but also a best resort because in this game reliance on another is not a possibility.

The idea of the long poem became attractive to Stevens in the prepublication period of *Harmonium* because it promised to resolve the painful and difficult-to-disentangle questions of his literary stature and his marriage (hard to call it his love life), neither of which he could separate from his economic role as a male, from the social disease that I have called econo-machismo. The long poem, not the small pleasures of minority—those little things he had praised of Dr. Campion and Verlaine—could be the signature at once of his maleness and of his cultural relevance, a figure of his emerging social prowess at a time when he began to have doubts about his sexual prowess.

"Witherlings," that coinage for his early poems was just right: a live thing too soon dead, dried up because unnourished by what it most needed but could not from itself generate—a sustaining environment of thought. "Witherlings": literary modernism's great ideal, autonomous life, as aborted life. And "witherlings" in another sense, a thing withered in the human sense of the metaphor: the thing in question, now, not a tender shoot of plant life but an intention to speak and to act—*the aesthete as minister*—stunned into silence and paralysis (as in: he was withered by her scorching tone). The long poem, which would speak discursively as well as be, could never be figured by a decoration on a trivial thing (like a fan) in the hand of a leisured woman—the decoration, like useless autonomous art, a signifier of leisured life; the fan, an indulgent necessity (like autonomous art) for those unused to and unwilling to sweat and whose cultural advantages (like the experience of autonomous art) presuppose economic advantages. Real men, like Gainsborough, paint landscapes and portraits, not decorations on fans; real men, if they write poetry, go for the long poem of public (epic) import, not the small lyric of bourgeois delight. The poet who in his thirties felt himself marginalized by his social context as a ladylike dabbler in after-hours verse writing would become in his imaginative life at least (or is it at most?) a Latin lover courting what has to seem for the male modernist a forbidden woman, the epic muse who not only inspired but also had been possessed by a special sort of man, the sort embodied by Homer, Virgil, Dante, Milton. With those types she was obviously well bedded; could she be persuaded to try somebody new and so apparently ill-endowed for the task of epic loving? Could ladylike Stevens become one of those he had once called "your man-poets"? He wasn't sure and he marked his doubts with a humor which is always the sign (if we can trust Robert Frost's surmise about this) of virtually unbearable and unshareable inner seriousness: "I find this prolonged attention to a single subject has the same result that prolonged attention to a senora has according to the authorities. All manner of favors drop from it. Only it requires a skill in the varying of the serenade that occasionally makes one feel like a Guatemalan when one particularly wants to feel like an Italian" [*Letters of Wallace Stevens*].

In the time between the publication of *Harmonium* (1923) and his second volume, *Ideas of Order* (1935), specifically in the period between 1923 and 1930 or so, or for about seven years, Stevens wrote hardly anything. His literary sterility in those years can't be explained by the largely indifferent and hostile reception of *Harmonium;* bad reviews didn't silence him because he was their virtual author. In **"The Comedian as the Letter C,"** his first attempt at a long poem, Stevens was a previewer of *Harmonium*'s reception, more harsh than any of his actual reviewers. The **"Comedian"** is a severe and hilarious reflection on a poet, like himself, who seemed to him to deserve the deflating mockery of epithets like "lutanist of fleas" and "Socrates of snails," as well as sexually caustic allegorization as a skinny sailor trying to conduct the sublimely frightening music of a sea storm with a pathetically inadequate little baton: as if poetic and sexual inadequacy were somehow each other's proper sign.

Self-disappointment and the need to think through self-revision are better but not sufficient explanations of his literary silence: if he was experimenting with new longer forms and new ambition, he was doing it in his head, or in drafts which no one will ever see. He certainly wasn't trying out his new self in the little magazine scene whose editors constantly requested his work and likely would have published pretty much anything he might have given them. By 1923 he was a respected avant-garde writer whose attractiveness was enhanced by his privacy and mysteriousness. He turned down many requests for poems; he had nothing to give. And while he was imagining but doing very little about earning his poetic manhood he was living out and doing a great deal about earning the sort of manhood that his American middle-class superego taught him to desire or pay the price in guilt.

From 1924 to 1932 he lived in a noisy two-family house, on a busy street in Hartford. In 1932, having saved up enough, he bought his first and only house (for $20,000, in cash). In this period he became a father who did what

typical working fathers do—exercise their fatherhood after supper and on weekends, or precisely during those times when this father, unlike most working fathers, wanted to but couldn't do the reading and writing which were the basis for his other career. One of the few poetic exhibits we have from this period is an occasional verse, done for Valentine's Day 1925. It is an offhanded, sweet little thing, as its genre demanded, but nevertheless an elegy for his recent poetic death dipped in bitters, in which he tries to rationalize his quotidian obligations as a new kind of poetry, expressed in doggerel, the perfect representation of the well-grooved routine his everyday life had become. Not the poetry of everyday life, but everyday life as poetry:

> Though Valentine brings love
> And Spring brings beauty
> They do not make me rise
> To my poetic duty
> But Elsie and Holly do
> And do it daily—
> Much more than Valentine or Spring
> And very much more gaily.

In this post-*Harmonium* period he seems to have made his greatest effort—in which he succeeded—to rise to the corporate top of his business world: the right sort of thing to do for a man with family responsibilities, who was sole source of the family's income, who wanted his own home, and who liked really nice things, like oriental rugs. But poetry was power and freedom over circumstances—Stevens, like most writers since the late eighteenth century, needed to believe that—and the more financially unstable the writer, the more he believes that proposition of aesthetic idealism, the promise that there will be refuge even in the filthy prison house of capitalism. Stevens undefensively knew and admitted and even celebrated another, more commonly held proposition: that money was power and freedom, too. Cultural capital, money of the mind, is good, even if it is the opium of the intellectuals: it is a *kind* of money. But money itself, ah! money itself, whatever it is, it certainly is not a *kind* of money. The logic, which Stevens never resisted, is that money is a kind of poetry. In 1935, the middle of the Depression, when he was earning $25,000 a year (roughly the equivalent of $200,000 a year in our terms), when, in other words, he'd made it financially—after 1935 his poetic production simply mushroomed—he wrote this to a business associate:

> Our house has been a great delight to us, but it is still quite incomplete inside. . . . It has cost a great deal of money to get it where it is and, while it is pleasant to buy all these things, and no one likes to do it more than I do, still it is equally pleasant to feel that you are not the creature of circumstances, but are (at least to a certain degree) the master of the situation, which can only be if you have the savings banks sagging with your money and the presidents of the insurance companies stopping their cars to ask the privilege of taking you to the office. For my part, I never really lived until I had a home, say, with a package of books from Paris or London. [*Letters*]

Unlike most writers in his romantic tradition he knew that feelings of power and freedom in imagination were precisely the sorts of effects produced by a capitalist economic context in those (writers and intellectuals) who hate capitalist economic contexts; he seemed to know that aesthetic purity was economically encased; that imaginative power was good, to be sure, but that economic power was a more basic good because it enables (as it makes us desire) both the aesthetic good and the aesthetic goods (books from Paris and London) that he required. Can cultural power, however acquired and whatever its origin, turn on its economic base, become a liberating and constructive force in its own right? Believing in that proposition is not the opium of intellectuals, it's our LSD. Yet it may not be completely naive to think that art and intellect are forces of social change. Marxists, of course, think so; on the other hand, the textbook critics on the Christian New Right, who practice a different sort of hermeneutics of suspicion, also think so; even T. S. Eliot thought so. It is possible that the addiction I allude to is a necessary addiction, a need of literary types to "turn on" politically because all the while we fear our political irrelevance. Stevens himself constantly chewed over the idea, and though he tended to reject the notion that literary force is also political force—the artist has no social role, he said more than once in his letters of the thirties and in his essays—it may be that the deep intellectual unity of his later career was produced by his encounter with radical thought in the thirties. Stevens emerged from that encounter thinking that Stanley Burnshaw's Marxist critique of his work was intelligent and probing—a fact contemptuously buried by [Harold] Bloom and [Joseph] Riddel, among other champions of the poet; he emerged believing in the social responsibility of his poetry, everything he says to the contrary notwithstanding. How more responsible (and guilty) can you get than, on the one hand, to write the rarefied lyric that Stevens writes, and, on the other, to assert that poets help people to live their lives?

What Burnshaw's critique of *Ideas of Order* did was to crystallize for Stevens his own class position and at the same time that of his ideal and (as it would seem to him) inevitable audience. Stevens found Burnshaw's review "most interesting" because it "placed" him in a "new setting." That new setting, the "middle ground" of the middle class, is the socio-economic space of those who are both potential allies and potential enemies of class struggle. Burnshaw's insight into this "contradiction," as he called it, of the middle class—into, really, the undemarcated and therefore (at best) confused quality of class struggle in the United States—is matched and one-upped by Stevens in a letter written shortly after he read Burnshaw in *The New Masses:*

> I hope I am headed left, but there are lefts and lefts, and certainly I am not headed for the ghastly left of *Masses.* The rich man and the comfortable man of imagination are not nearly so rich nor nearly so comfortable as he believes them to be. And, what is more, his poor men are not nearly so poor.

In the United States, the middle ground is vaster than Burnshaw thinks and the high and low grounds are narrower and not as melodramatically in opposition as the Manichean metaphors of Communist party rhetoric

would make them out to be. As the poet of the middle ground, of those not subject to revolutionary hunger (we need the pun), whose basic sustenance was more or less assured (the "more or less" assuring also a conservative anxiety, a willingness to rock the boat ever so gently), it was Stevens' "role to help people"—people: the middle class is easily universalized in American discourse—"to help people live their lives. [The poet] has had immensely to do with giving life whatever savor it possesses" [*The Necessary Angel: Essays on Reality and the Imagination*]. To supply savor is to supply aesthetic, not biological, necessity: to supply what Marx in *The German Ideology* called the "new needs" (or felt lacks) of women and men after their life-sustaining necessities have been met and they begin to produce not only their sustenance but also the means of reproducing their sustenance. At the point at which leisure becomes real and, in the same moment, really problematic, "we" need a civilized poet. Stevens believed it to be a need of cultural life and death whose satisfaction would determine our "happiness," or lack thereof, outside and irrespective of our political state (which for the middle class rhymes with fate).

It was also in this period of his economic growth and literary self-critique that one of the crueler jokes of literary history that I know was played out. Stevens, a major figure in the insurance business, according to those who know, the best in the field of surety bonds in the country, developed a serious case of rising-executive sickness: high blood pressure bad enough that he was advised not only to lose a great deal of weight but also to get to bed as early as possible on the faultless medical theory that a sleeping man's pressure can't help but be good. Stevens assented to the advice: so after supper there was the noise of a two-family house (the landlord had young children), there was the new baby, there were the domestic chores he regularly pitched in on, then lights out at nine. The joke is that the blood pressure problem was so serious that this well-connected insurance executive could not buy life insurance, not then, not ever—and the "then" I refer to was 1929, 1930, 1931, etc. One reason he worked well past retirement age, practically to the day he died, is that he liked his work (there can be no question about this). Another reason was that he had to because there was one part of his material context—the physiological part—over which he could not become master. Add to that his unquestioned and perhaps unquestionable feeling, which was something like an unavoidable affective accompaniment of his patriarchal formation, that it was his duty to take care of Elsie and Holly. And given the situation of those three, it could not have been otherwise. At these levels his brute material situation was not subject to his personal manipulation: his literary power could not touch it. (pp. 206-16)

Frank Lentricchia, "Writing after Hours: Penelope's Poetry—The Later Wallace Stevens," in his Ariel and the Police: Michel Foucault, William James, Wallace Stevens, *The University of Wisconsin Press, 1988, pp. 196-244.*

Von Edward Underwood   (essay date 1988)

[*In the following essay, Underwood discusses the impor-*

tance of nature and the concept of divinity in Stevens's life and poetry.]

Stevens' first poems to appear in print, with the exception of the juvenile poems published in the *Harvard Advocate,* appeared in 1914. Some of these are small and limited poems written for his wife (then fiancée) in 1909. The first really interesting poems begin to appear in 1915 and 1916, when Stevens was already thirty-six. His first full volume of poetry, *Harmonium,* appeared in 1923, and Stevens was forty-four. As a result, many of the characteristics of the crisis described in the work of [Stefan George, Hugo von Hofmannsthal, and William Carlos Williams, about whom the critic also writes in his book] (such as language skepticism, and an agnosticism and irony) are already presuppositions of Stevens' first book of poems. This is, however, only an aspect of the real difference that matters here. That is that Stevens' development as a poet is marked by several broad gaps in output before the mid-30's. These were not necessarily periods in which Stevens was silenced by a contradiction or a profound block through which he was compelled to struggle. He turned rather to practical concerns. When Stevens left Harvard in 1900 for New York, he entered a particularly bleak period of his life. He tried his hand at journalism, and then entered law school. When he began publishing poetry in 1914, he was married and a practicing attorney in the insurance world. After *Harmonium* appeared in 1923, Stevens was quiet, if not silent, as far as poetry is concerned, for almost ten years. His daughter, born in 1924, writes of this period in a note to his collected letters, [*Letters of Wallace Stevens,* edited by Holly Stevens], "His energy in this period between the ages of forty-four and fifty-two went largely into his work at the insurance company." Since two of the last poems written were **"Sea Surface Full of Clouds"** and **"Academic Discourse at Havana,"** there may have also been simply too much of a gap between the poetics Stevens had developed in the *Harmonium* years and the "everyday world" to which Stevens settled down in the 1920s. This will be clearer after some of the poems of *Harmonium* have been discussed. The important point here is that Stevens starts late, and that two large gaps in publication surround his first published book. That makes it difficult to trace the development of Stevens' poetry in these years in the same way we can trace the early works of the other poets. It is an interrupted development, and one that flowers with a more complex and exotic maturity.

The reader of Stevens will already have begun to guess the relevance of Stevens to the discussion of many of the central issues raised in the earlier essays. Suspicion of transcendent insight, whether divine insight or a sense of transcendence found in experience, word-skepticism, and close study of how former accomplishment loses its relevance for the contemporary imagination, and what that implies for modern poetry, all are hardly strange issues in Stevens' work. While I do not propose to fill in, or even to discuss in detail, the long gaps in Stevens' development, there are several points about the early years that cast an interesting light on the key issues of *Harmonium* and the later books of the 30's and early 40's with which I will be primarily concerned. These will introduce the sense of a

false start, or, as with the others poets, of a series of false starts, which can be found in Stevens' early books of poetry, and the kinds of agnostic and nominalistic investigations of poetry and reality Stevens found central to both his poetry and his theory of poetry. The objective of this essay, then, is to show how a now familiar quandary arose for a poet whose career had a different shape, and for whom poetry was an essential part of the good life, if not the whole of it.

There are three images of the young Stevens which are emblematic of others in the journals and letters and cast some useful light on the later work. Were it not for Stevens' insatiable intelligence, his keen sense of irony, and what he would later call "the pressure of reality," Stevens might have become a happy, romantic nature poet, a sort of latter-day bucolic Virgil of the Pennsylvania Dutch country. The first two images have to do with Stevens' early relationship with nature.

The first of these images comes from Stevens' journal of the summer of 1899, during the period in which he was a special student at Harvard. We must imagine the young Stevens lying in a field listening to birds singing as the sun sets, and staying through sunset and moonrise, and then going home to read Book III of *Endymion.* His journals show readings of poetry and criticism and discussion with his young friends and walks in the countryside in the summer near Reading, Pennsylvania. A few days before, he had met John Wily, a garrulous resident of rural Berkeley, Pennsylvania. Stevens had gotten to know the Wilys, who are descendants of a poet John Wily who published a book in 1719. Stevens' journal describes many "raptures" like that he felt lying in the field at evening. His journal entry was later used, almost word for word, in a piece for the *Harvard Advocate,* though the end is changed; in the latter, Stevens is sitting on a fence rather than lying in a field, and nearby "on a tall spray of black berry bushes a robin was swinging in the wind, his throat pouring forth a song of ravishing beauty." A farmer comes by, on his way home from ploughing the fields, still splotched with clay from his work. He stops to talk, but hears a robin, and turns to look at it "wonderingly," and then says "Just listen to that robin a' hollerin' over there." This is not promising as literature, but there is an appreciation of the happiness of the "natural man," emblemized for Stevens in the man of the land or the farmer.

One of the poems in **"The Little June Book,"** written for Stevens' future wife, Elsie, in 1909, attempts to capture some of this detailed, woodland pleasure:

> Here the grass grows
> And the wind blows,
> And in the stream,
> Small fishes gleam:
> Blood-red and hue
> Of shadowy blue,
> And amber sheen
> And water-green,
> And yellow flash
> And diamond ash;
> And the grass grows,
> And the wind blows.

The repetition and simplistic sing-song rhythms of this little poem (later published in *Trend* in 1914) remain a part of Stevens' later strategy for expressing the naive pleasures of the countryside, though his attitudes toward such pleasures change. Another poem of **"June Book"** seems to have our early image specifically in mind:

"Eclogue"

Lying in the mint,
I heard an orchard bell
Call the ploughman home,
To his minty dell.

I saw him pass along.
He picked a bough to jog
His single, loathful cow,
And whistled to his dog.

I saw him cross a field
I saw a window glint,
I heard a woman's voice,
Lying in the mint.

This poem is less interesting as a poem, and is too full of stock images, and far too "minty," but in it Stevens is at his ease in the country, sharing and admiring the joys of the ploughman. In *Harmonium,* Stevens has stopped writing what he thinks his girl will find pretty, but the same experiences in Pennsylvania are behind a much more complex and satisfying poem:

"Ploughing on Sunday"

The white cock's tail
Tosses in the wind.
The turkey-cock's tail
Glitters in the sun.

Water in the fields.
The wind pours down.
The feathers flare
And bluster in the wind.

Remus blow your horn!
I'm ploughing on Sunday,
Ploughing North America.
Blow your horn!

Tum-ti-tum,
Ti-tum-tum-tum!
The turkey-cock's tail
Spreads to the sun.

The white cock's tail
Streams to the moon.
Water in the fields.
The wind pours down.

This irreverent poem violates the sabbath for the sheer pleasure of ploughing and singing. We should remember that Stevens glimpses this land of boisterous celebration and naiveté on summer vacations, and amidst his thinking about "the difference between literary creations and natural men." In the sentence immediately prior to his description of his first encounter with John Wily, Stevens wrote:

Out in the open air with plenty of time and space I felt how different literary emotions were from natural feelings. On top of the hill I stood for about a quarter of an hour watching whatever color could break through the clouds, listening to the robins and other birds.

These "natural" moments are already "natural" only by contrast, and their simplicity is tinged with one of Stevens' arch enemies, sentimentality. While **"Ploughing on Sunday"** may result from a kind of "willed and artificial primitivism," [as suggested by Helen Vendler in her *On Extended Wings: Wallace Stevens' Longer Poems*], it does manage to overcome nostalgia, and to celebrate a naive, if boisterous, freshness of emotion that Stevens felt was a part of being a "man of the land." As a consequence, an occasional "Tum-ti-tum" sneaks into Stevens' later work as an emblem of this category of projected native happiness. It is a kind of naive relation to the rural countryside that would prove less and less natural to Stevens as he continued to write, though it remained a category, a possible way of feeling for his projected figures. The strain on his attitude toward this primitivism is already apparent in another poem of *Harmonium,* **"Life is Motion"**:

In Oklahoma
Bonnie and Josie,
Dressed in calico,
Danced around a stump.
They cried,
"Ohoyaho,
Ohoo" . . .
Celebrating the marriage
Of flesh and air.

This is sheer comedy, but the absurd effects create an irony in the last two lines. This is no mystical marriage, and, while Bonnie and Josie enjoy the dance, they have been duped. The seeming irony of the last two lines may be intentional on Stevens' part, but it more probably results from the strain Stevens felt embracing a naive, native energy that was not natural to his temperament. The "marriage" is born of a desire to dignify an energy of celebration in country life which Stevens could admire, or in fact invent, while reclining in the mint leaves, but in which he could never fully take part.

Stevens was a vigorous man, but that vigor took expression in nature in his long and solitary walks, especially after he moved to New York, in 1900. Only about half as many people lived in New York at the turn of the century, and the city was smaller though still crowded. It was, nonetheless, a hard and lonely life for Stevens, and he escaped the grim aspects of the city and the burdens of his day-to-day survival frequently by taking long walks up the Hudson, his route taking him up to forty miles in a single day. Also in this period, in the fall of 1903, Stevens made his one great expedition into the wilderness, a hunting trip in the Canadian Rockies with W. G. Peckham, in whose law firm Stevens was apprenticed as a clerk. Theodore Roosevelt, that bully outdoorsman (whom Stevens, incidentally, would meet in Washington in 1907), was serving his first term as President, and may have created something of a fashion for this sort of Canadian safari. The entries in Stevens' journals that deal with the hunting trip and his excursions into the wilds surrounding New York contain exaltations of the rugged life, but also elation and awe at the beauty and power of nature, which refreshed him and restored what the grind of law school and clerkship and loneliness were costing. On April 18, 1904, Stevens took one of his longest sweeps out of New York along the Hudson, and later recorded his elation in a lengthy entry in his journal. Stevens added a hasty note, which supplies our second image: the young Stevens on the train ride back from one of his long, solitary walks in nature:

> —One more word. I thought, on the train, how utterly we have forsaken the Earth, in the sense of excluding it from our thoughts. There are but few who consider its physical hugeness, its rough enormity. It is still a disparate monstrosity, full of solitudes & barrens & wilds. It still dwarfs & terrifies & crushes. The rivers still roar, the mountains still crash, the winds still shatter. Man is an affair of cities. His gardens & orchards & fields are mere scrapings. Somehow, however, he has managed to shut out the face of the giant from his windows. But the giant is there, nevertheless. And it is a proper question, whether or not the Lilliputians have tied him down. There are his huge legs, Africa & South America, still, apparently, free; and the rest of him is pretty rough and unhandy. But, as I say, we do not think of this. There was a girl on the train with a face like the under-side of a moonfish. *Her* talk was of dances & men. For her, Sahara had no sand; Brazil, no mud.

The central tension in this passage is between the vastness and potential violence of the natural world and the self-absorption of the comparatively tiny area ("mere scrapings") man has managed to domesticate for himself, and which, in 1904, could still be conceived of as surrounded by wilderness. This passage bears an interesting resemblance to a much later poem by a poet who is seldom thought of in relation to Stevens. Gary Snyder wrote "It Pleases" in Washington, D.C. in 1973:

> Far above the dome
> Of the capitol—
>   It's true!
> A large bird soars
> Against white cloud,
> Wings arced,
> Sailing easy in this
> humid Southern sun-blurred
>   breeze—
>   the dark policeman
>   watches tourist cars—
>
> And the center
> The center of power is nothing!
> Nothing here.
> Old white stone domes,
> Strangely quiet people,
>
> Earth-sky-bird patterns
>   idly interlacing
>
> The world does what it pleases.
>   (*Turtle Island*)

The powers of the capitol come to nothing compared to the power of these interlacing natural patterns. Snyder celebrates nature's independence and superiority to human authority in the kind of mindful, sparkling statement that characterizes the finest poems of *Turtle Island*. Stevens' passage has not the kind of dimension that a zen pun like

"The center of power is nothing!" brings to Snyder's poem, but then Stevens' passage is not developed to the full force of a poem either. Stevens' natural giant embodies a realization similar to Snyder's of the independence and strength of nature compared to the power at work in the self-absorbed city of man. Stevens' image is possessed of an intenser, more violent natural energy, perhaps because in 1904 nature seemed less threatened by the power of man, and less likely to be matched violence for violence by man. This is perhaps also why the realization the poem and the passage share seems more heroic and necessary in 1973.

The relief of his escape from the city, the memory of the hunting trip in the Rockies the previous fall, and the exhilaration of such a long walk (forty-two miles) contributed to Stevens' sense of the hugeness of the natural world, which he sees as a "disparate monstrosity, full of solitudes & barrens & wilds." Earlier in this entry in his journal, Stevens recorded his exaltations on hilltops, his fantasies in coves, his explorations of regions hospitable and inhospitable, complete with maps and drawings. The passage quoted is a kind of postscript about a realization he came to on his way home, as he returned toward that darker, smaller world of his life in New York. He wishes to record a difficulty in reconciling the sense of expansion he experiences before the power and beauty of nature with his inexorable return to that self-absorption by which man forsakes the natural world. As he turns to expressing the independence and scope of the natural world, however, he falls upon a spate of violent verbs: Nature still "dwarfs & terrifies & crushes" and the rivers, mountains, and winds still "roar" and "crash" and "shatter." As much as Stevens loves nature, and meets its physical challenges with a hardy vigor, it places his life in the city in perspective with a peculiar violence. It is at this point in the passage, amid the dwarfing, crushing and shattering, that Stevens' imagination invents the giant, the first such giant in his journals, lingering menacingly at the edge of town and lowering at the windows. By the end of the passage the giant has become a comic figure. He is beset by Lilliputians in the northern continents, who have not managed to tie him down. The image of Africa and South America as two huge legs makes the giant larger and gives him a shape, but becomes essentially a comic image. It is hard not to imagine the legs kicking. The projection of the giant at once embodies the idea of nature's strength and independence and also softens the menace of its power.

In the last few sentences of Stevens' passage, he turns his attention to the girl on the train. Imagining the giant has left Stevens with an odd enlargement of perspective that makes him seem a kind of menace, a threat to the naive self-absorption of this girl with "a face like the under-side of a moonfish." "*Her* talk was of dances and men," and she becomes an example of that smallness of scope, a contrast for his restored expansive sense of life. Stevens, himself, becomes a kind of awkward giant looming at the windows, made greater by the dwarfing and terrifying and crushing power of nature. In Stevens' attitude toward nature there is an odd mixture of awe and gratitude, and his experience of it is marked by this kind of "dwarfing" or humbling followed by an invented expansiveness.

Natural giants related to this figure appear in Stevens' mature work. The Old Seraph of *Notes Toward a Supreme Fiction,* other figures in **"Credences of Summer," "Chocorua to its Neighbor," "A Primitive like an Orb,"** and the "necessary angel of earth" in *Auroras of Autumn* belong to a single class of natural giants, each slightly differently conceived. They are distinct from the hero and from Major Men, like the Canon Aspirin and the MacCullough, all of which are exponents of man. There are also a number of gestures in the earlier books which are closely related to the odd, intimidating Naturalism of this passage, and the subsequent spiritual enlargements Stevens associated with it. Crispin's romantic voyage in the **"The Comedian as the Letter C"** will be discussed more fully below, but along his way the "celestial sneering" that accompanies the stripping away of his former self, and the reference to "the ruses that were shattered by the large" have much to do with Stevens' troubled life in New York and his long solitary walks and returns. The ennobling power of the natural world, its power to uplift and expand the spirit is one of the central fascinations of the poems in *Ideas of Order.* After *Ideas of Order,* however, Stevens' naturalism, as ever controlled by temperament and intelligence, is, in a sense, displaced as his central theme. As Stevens later wrote in "Imagination as Value":

> A generation ago we should have said that the imagination is an aspect of the conflict between man and nature. Today we are more likely to say it is an aspect of the conflict between man and organized society. It is part of our security. It enables us to live our lives. We have it because we do not have enough without it.

The pressure to which the acts of Stevens' imagination were a response may simply have been conceived in terms of the calamities of organized societies in the 30's and 40's. If the natural giants drop out of sight in his poetry for a time, it is only for a time, and in *The Whole of Harmonium* (as Stevens wanted to entitle his collected poems) they return again, fleshed out and changed by this thought on other issues.

Stevens' naturalism and his long walks were not unrelated in his own mind to his thoughts on religion. One Sunday, April 10, 1902, Stevens walked seventeen-and-a-half miles out to Paterson and took the trolley back. His journal reads:

> I love to walk along with a slight wind playing in the trees about me and think over a thousand and one odds and ends. Last night I spent an hour in the dark transept of St. Patrick's Cathedral where I go now and then in my more lonely moods. An old argument with me is that the true religious force in the world is not the church but the world itself: The mysterious callings of Nature and our responses. What incessant murmurs fill that ever-laboring, tireless church! But to-day in my walk I thought that after all there is no conflict of forces but rather a contrast. In the cathedral I felt one presence; on the highway I felt another. Two different deities presented themselves; and though I have only cloudy visions of either, yet I know the distinction between them. The priest in me worshipped one

God at one shrine; the poet another God at another shrine. The priest worshipped Mercy and Love; the poet Beauty and Might. In the shadows of the church I could hear the prayers of men and women; in the shadows of the trees nothing human mingled with Divinity. As I sat dreaming with the Congregation I felt how the glittering altar worked on my senses stimulating and consoling them; and as I went tramping through the fields and woods I beheld every leaf and blade of grass revealing or rather betokening the Invisible.

In the contrast between the two "religious forces" in the world, Stevens makes out two Gods, one of Mercy and Love, the other of Beauty and Might, each with its own "mysterious" callings, evoking a religious response. Yet the priest and the poet, both worshippers, are Stevens, and the contrast makes both callings and responses aspects of the Religious, to follow Stevens' penchant for capitalization. As a result, it is "Divinity" Stevens experiences in the trees, though there it is "mingled" with nothing human. This Divinity, betokened in every leaf and blade of grass, Stevens also calls the "Invisible." This journal entry represents one of the few instances in which Stevens' search for transcendence is untinged by irony or skeptical intelligence. It is weighted heavily toward the natural, toward Beauty, Might and the Invisible, and tells us that Stevens' naturalism was an aspect of religious response that he preferred to the human side.

This brings us to the third and final image of the young Stevens: Stevens sitting quietly in the back of a cathedral at an odd hour meditating about religion, nature, and his reading at the Astor Library. On another Sunday morning, May 2, 1909, Stevens dropped into a different church, again not to attend regular services. He wrote to his fiancée:

> . . . Today I have been roaming about town. In the morning I walked down-town—stopping once to watch three flocks of pigeons circling in the sky. I dropped in to St. John's chapel an hour before the service and sat in the last pew and looked around. It happens that last night at the Library I read a life of Jesus and I was interested to see what symbols of that life appeared in the chapel. I think there were none at all excepting the gold cross on the altar. When you compare that poverty with the wealth of symbols, of remembrances, that were created and revered in times past, you appreciate the change that has come over the church. The church should be more than a moral institution, if it is to have the influence that it should have. The space, the gloom, the quiet mystify and entrance the spirit. But that is not enough.—And one turns from this chapel to those built by men who felt the wonder of the life and death of Jesus—temples full of sacred images, full of the air of love and holiness—tabernacles hallowed by worship that sprang from the noble depths of men familiar with Gethsemane, familiar with Jerusalem.—I do not wonder that the church is so largely a relic. Its vitality depended on its association with Palestine, so to speak.

This particular blend of imagery (Sunday morning, pigeons circling, the quiet, empty chapel) and meditation on how the church or the altar calls to its congregation, and wakes or fails to awake a religious response, would stay with Stevens for a long time. As we have already seen, the notion of the call of the church was contrasted in Stevens' mind with those other callings of nature, and there was both a priest and a poet in Stevens to respond. Much of the rest of the letter to Elsie deals with their walks together on the previous weekend, and other letters make it clear that the following weekend, Stevens made another of his solitary rambles. Both the imagery and the meditations recorded here are recalled in **"Sunday Morning,"** which was written in November, 1915, and is one of the first and finest poems that mark the quantum leap from Stevens' juvenilia to the level of accomplishment of *Harmonium.* Since it is Sunday morning, Stevens' protagonist, even lounging in her rooms with her cockatoo and her oranges, hears the call of " . . . Palestine, / Dominion of the blood and sepulchre" across the "wide water" of time and space. In the second canto, the failing call of the church, the "gloom and quiet" that "mystify and entrance the spirit" but are "not enough" are brought into contrast again with the living, natural calls that can wake a religious response:

> Why should she give her bounty to the dead?
> What is divinity if it can come
> Only in silent shadows and in dreams?
> Shall she not find in comforts of the sun,
> In pungent fruit and bright, green wings, or else
> In any balm or beauty of the earth,
> Things to be cherished like the thought of heaven?
> Divinity must live within herself:
> Passions of rain, or moods in falling snow;
> Grievings in loneliness, or unsubdued
> Elations when the forest blooms; gusty
> Emotions on wet roads on autumn nights;
> All pleasures and all pains, remembering
> The bough of summer and the winter branch.
> These are the measures destined for her soul.

The canto suggests that looking for divinity in an image of a remote land and the imagery of death may amount to searching through shadows and dreams. Divinity, mercy, consolation, reside in life, and in human responses to life. The first item in Stevens' list of possible sources for this "balm," the gaudy exoticism of rare birds and bright colors, will be best discussed in relation to the rest of *Harmonium.* The remainder of the list, however, is drawn from Stevens' long walks, the experiences that awake in him a sense of elevation and "betoken the Invisible."

The priest in me worshipped one God at one shrine; the poet another God at another shrine. The priest worshipped Mercy and Love; the poet Beauty and Might.

—*Wallace Stevens*

Another passage from the letter to Elsie shows that the priest-scholar in Stevens has also been at work in the Astor Library, spending his Saturday evening reading a life of Christ. The letters of May and April are heavy with descriptions of long walks in nature, some with Elsie, and with notes from his very energetic reading in the library. Later in the letter of May 3, he wrote "I wish I could spend the whole season out of doors, walking by day, reading in the evenings. I feel a tremendous capacity for enjoying that kind of life—but it's all over, and I acknowledge 'the fell clutch of circumstance'." It was a vigorous and ascetic period of Stevens' life in which he was rediscovering the life of the mind and, since he had finally found his way to the insurance world, was planning his life so as to have time to write poetry. His particular research, and his particular meditation in the passage quoted concerns the "poverty" of St. John's Chapel compared to "the wealth of symbols, of remembrances, that were created and revered in times past" and the "change that has come over the church." Without necessarily noting it as a general principle, Stevens finds in the failure of Christian symbology that same dependence of the imagination upon reality that is his theme in "The Noble Rider and the Sound of Words." He writes, "I do not wonder that the church is so largely a relic. Its vitality depended on its association with Palestine, so to speak." In **"Sunday Morning,"** the "wide water" of time and space that cuts off his protagonist, and her quiet, complacent room, from Palestine, surrounds and isolates her world from that former "wealth of symbols" made by "men who felt the wonder of the life and death of Jesus." That broken connection to the reality of Palestine is behind the symbolic poverty of the church and the failure of its call. The meditation on Jesus in the letter to Elsie continues in a later passage. Stevens wrote:

> Before today I do not think that I have realized that God was distinct from Jesus. It enlarges the matter almost beyond comprehension. People doubt the existence of Jesus—at least, they doubt incidents of his life, such as, say, the Ascension into Heaven after his death. But I do not understand that they deny God. I think everyone admits that in some form or other.—The thought makes the world sweeter—even if God be no more than the mystery of Life.

It may be that Stevens is approaching these religious questions somewhat coyly, not wanting to shock or dismay his considerably younger and less educated fiancée. Nonetheless, Stevens separates the thought of God from the thought of Jesus (and from the question of His immortality) and in the end seems more concerned with the role of the idea than with its referent. God, released from Palestine in the temporal stream, may be "only the mystery of Life," an unfortunate lapse into cliché that hides a presence and a call for human response.

All of these meditations, and the pigeons as well, come together in the last canto of **"Sunday Morning."** As Helen Vendler has shown [in *On Extended Wings*], the language of the last canto owes a great deal to Keats' "Ode to Autumn," and the poem was in fact written in Autumn-November, 1915. It is fascinating, however, to see how the long walks, the pigeons, and the meditations in the back of St. John's chapel are refracted in the language of Keats' "Ode":

> She hears, upon that water without sound,
> A voice that cries, "The tomb in Palestine
> Is not the porch of spirits lingering.
> It is the grave of Jesus, where he lay."
> We live in an old chaos of the sun,
> Or old dependency of day and night,
> Or island solitude, unsponsored, free,
> Of that wide water, inescapable.
> Deer walk upon our mountains, and the quail
> Whistle about us their spontaneous cries;
> Sweet berries ripen in the wilderness;
> And, in the isolation of the sky,
> At evening, casual flocks of pigeons make
> Ambiguous undulations as they sink,
> Downward to darkness on extended wings.

When the pigeons return it is evening, and rather than circling, as Stevens saw them outside St. John's, they descend. They are, nevertheless, like Snyder's "Earth-sky-bird" patterns, symbols of a natural presence, admittedly a little citified, but a natural presence nonetheless. Their descent on outstretched wings does represent, as Helen Vendler puts it, "Stevens' rare acquiescent drift in the temporal stream." They also awake, however, something like the "gusty / Emotions on wet roads in Autumn nights" of the second canto. Their descent, like the descent of the eagle in **"Some Friends from Pascagoula,"** is the kind of natural experience that humbles, consoles, and finally ennobles the human spirit, and thus belonged for Stevens to the realm of religious response, as a kind of visual call to evoke a sense of the invisible. Perhaps what they betoken may be "only the mystery of Life," glimpsed after a long walk in the country, while entering a quiet church that barely survives at an impossible distance from the events in which it had its origin.

The same cluster of images and meditations, though regrettably without the pigeons, was still present in Stevens' mind in 1937 when he wrote *The Man with the Blue Guitar.* In canto XXIX, Stevens wrote:

> In the cathedral, I sat there, and read,
> Alone, a lean Review and said,
>
> "These degustations in the vaults
> Oppose the past and festival,
>
> What is beyond the cathedral, outside,
> Balances with nuptial song.
>
> So it is to sit and to balance things
> To and to and to the point of still,
>
> To say of one mask it is like,
> To say of another it is like,
>
> To know the balance does not quite rest,
> That the mask is strange however like."
>
> The shapes are wrong and the sounds are false.
> The bells are the bellowing of bulls.
>
> Yet Franciscan don was never more
> Himself than in this fertile glass.

In *The Man with the Blue Guitar,* other meditations had disturbed Stevens' sense of a direct relationship with na-

ture. The roles of poet and priest in the back of St. Patrick's and St. John's seem masks he was trying to balance, and to see as being alike. But in both masks, "the shapes are wrong and the sounds are false," or so the meditation on the relationship between imagination and reality in *The Man with the Blue Guitar* has led him to believe. Yet Stevens, the Franciscan don (the monkish scholar-poet) was never more himself. When we return to *The Man with the Blue Guitar,* it will be much clearer that the ambivalence of the young Franciscan don is not introduced in the canto simply out of nostalgia and sentimentality. The ambivalence of the young Stevens is brought into the context of the paradoxes and ambivalences that haunt the relationship between poet, poem, and "things as they are."

The three images of Wallace Stevens—lying in a field watching the farmer turn homeward in 1899, riding the train back into New York from one of his long walks in 1904, and sitting in the back of St. John's chapel in 1909—sum up, in a way, a number of important directions in Stevens' thought which came to bear, poetically speaking, in the writing of *Harmonium.* This last passage from *The Man with the Blue Guitar* already indicates that "false notes" arose as Stevens pursued these directions. The first blush of these problems became clear as Stevens turned his mind to seriously writing poetry for the poems of *Harmonium,* and were taken up again when he decided to write *Ideas of Order* at the request of Ronald Lane Latimer of Alcestis Press. (pp. 300-17)

> *Von Edward Underwood, "Wallace Stevens,"*
> *in his* A History That Includes the Self: Essays on the Poetry of Stefan George, Hugo von Hofmannsthal, William Carlos Williams and Wallace Stevens, *Garland Publishing, Inc., 1988, pp. 299-357.*

Barbara M. Fisher   (essay date 1990)

[*In the following essay, Fisher discusses the affinity for nature and rural regionalism Stevens expressed in his poetry.*]

Within the profusion of notions having to do with place and space, three ideas stand forth as having the most direct bearing on Stevens's poetry: (1) the seduction of landscape; (2) nativity, in the sense of belonging to a region; and (3) Stevens's treatment of metaphor both as "region" in itself and as a method of transport. The first primarily calls up sensuality; the second, rootedness; the third, motion. These appear to have a correspondence with the three ontological premises of Stevens's promised land—the modes of pleasure, abstraction (what remains the same), and change (what moves). As three musical themes may be woven together and yet retain their original melodic form, so each of these "place" themes governs a conceptual area distinct from the others while each is capable of acting upon or with the others. The *transport* of metaphor, for example, suggests the motion of a figural vehicle in Stevens's poetics of place, but also the ecstatic stillness of rapture.

The sense of affectionate relation between poet and planet is particularly explicit in the final canto of [*Notes toward a Supreme Fiction*]. Stevens names the great round globe of earth "my green, my fluent mundo," and addresses the circular and encircling beloved teasingly: "Fat girl, terrestrial, my summer, my night." Is Stevens's apostrophe to earth, one wonders in passing, a half-revealed notice of identification with the "Fat girl"? For "my fluent mundo" can be read "my fluent *world*" or "my fluent *mind*"—both revolving, and both creatively, voluptuously green. The analogy of turning world and turning mind will be set forth explicitly in **"The Sail of Ulysses:"**

> Round summer and angular winter and winds,
> Are matched by other revolutions
> In which the world goes round and round
> In the crystal atmospheres of the mind.

In **"Description without Place,"** the mind-world analogue occurs in its most concise form: "Her green mind made the world around her green." It would appear that Stevens's "Fat girl," his Marvell-ous Green Queen, and his "fluent mundo" are a gracefully linked triad. In **"An Ordinary Evening in New Haven,"** a brilliant orchestration of blowing winds, changing color and light, "eloquent" mountains, and a shivering dark-gleaming sea is again summed up in amorous terms: "These lineaments were the earth, / Seen as inamorata, of loving fame."

While "lineaments" suggests a courteous nod in the direction of Blake (the famous "lineaments of desire"), Stevens's sense of intimacy with the physical world goes deeper than rhetoric. There is evidence that it begins in early boyhood. "He possessed a familiarity with his region that a discerning native alone can boast," observes Thomas F. Lombardi in an account of Stevens's Pennsylvania years [in "Wallace Stevens: At Home in Pennsylvania," in the *Wallace Stevens Journal,* Spring 1978]. Lombardi describes the young man's solitary rambles over miles of country, noting his affinity for the mountains. When we think of Stevens's great emblem of the rock, as well as poems like **"Valley Candle,"** the passage is illuminating: "Many of the country roads that Stevens traveled wound high into the mountains. . . . At times, he would climb the Pinnacle. . . . alone or with friends he would scale Pulpit Rock. . . . afterward meandering downward through hillsides thick with spruce. When Stevens was not hiking to the tops of mountains or hills, he was trekking below them . . . or simply wandering down the Great Valley."

Impressions from the Pennsylvania years crop up in the poetry, particularly (as Holly Stevens notes in *Letters*) in poems of the 1940s. Stevens often imparts to these scenes a simple warmth that is unique in the canon. Here one finds the "inherited garden" of childhood, the home attached to the land, the ground where one's ancestors are both buried and remembered:

> The mother ties the hair-ribbons of the child
> And she has peace. *My Jacomyntje!*
> *Your great-grandfather was an Indian fighter.*

Under the most unlikely titles one is introduced to the particulars of rural Pennsylvania at the turn of the century: "The cool sun of the Tulpehocken"; the bass that "lie deep" in the Perkiomen, "looking ahead, upstream"; the "puddles of Swatara / And Schuylkill"; the hay "Baked through long days" and "piled in mows" in the Oley Valley. The "natural tower of all the world" in **"Credences"** owes something, surely, to the "Tower" of Mount Penn that Stevens climbed when he was nineteen, while the chilled retrospect of **"The Auroras of Autumn"** contains more than Stevens's "master of the maze" and the nest "where the serpent lives." It contains scenes of ghostly warmth: "The mother's face, / The purpose of the poem, fills the room. / They are together, here, and it is warm." This is Stevens's version of "memory mixed with desire," remembrance tinged with nostalgia. It is genuine sentiment, genuinely devoid of sentimentality.

"These lineaments were the earth, / Seen as inamorata . . . " Stevens's sense of intimacy with the physical world bespeaks an affair of long standing, and an intensely private affair. A letter to Elsie some eighteen months before their marriage describes a "before breakfast" tramp in the woods near East Orange. "There was pussy-willow everywhere—and mud and mist, today. The wind drove the mist in sheets over the fields. . . . Once I stopped and smelled the earth and the rain and looked about me—and recognized it all as the face of my dearest friend." What strikes one is that Stevens presents this muddy ground, this March weather, to his bride-to-be, not merely as seductive but as a serious rival for his affections: "The sheets of mist, the trees swallowed up at a little distance . . . the driving cold wind, the noisy solitude, the clumps of ice and patches of snow—the little wilderness all my own, shared with nobody, not even with you—it made me myself. It was friendly, so much deeper than anything else could be." This full-hearted communion in the "noisy solitude" of a March woods can be "shared with nobody, not even with you," Stevens tells the girl he plans to marry. It is a possessive passion, the claiming of a "little wilderness all my own."

What should not be passed over in Stevens's letter to Elsie are his impressions of friendliness and of ownership. Here we see the conjunction of two major themes, for precisely these attributes of the seductive landscape—possession and friendliness—constitute the primal sense of belonging in, or to, a place. The feeling that a place is one's own and friendly is the essential condition of nativeness, and, it may be, a precondition of identity. To the young Stevens at least, the experience of the terrain as "all my own"— even temporarily—seems to have been enough to have "made me myself."

The idea of nativity opens out in Stevens's poetry from a pointlike center into expanding rings or ripples, changing as it does from a stabilizing to a dynamic force. Native feeling moves from the boyhood world to the idea of existence on the planet as a thinking human being to the adopted region of the mature years. And always, thoughts of place initiate dynamic transfers: the notion of *where one lives* skips in and out of the physical world and glides into the geography of metaphor. At the heart of things is the almost animal sense of *home*. There is a strength, a folklore, a powerful mythology that attaches to the particular region, a visceral relation to home territory. John N. Serio has discerningly cited Stevens's appreciation of the poems of John Crowe Ransom. Taking into account Stevens's usual reserve and lawyerlike neutrality, it is almost unnerving to enter into the passion of his attachment to place: "One turns with something like ferocity toward a land that one loves, to which one is really and essentially native, to demand that it surrender, reveal, that in itself which one loves. . . . One's cry of O Jerusalem becomes little by little a cry of something a little nearer and nearer until at last one cries out to a living name, a living place, a living thing" [*Opus Posthumous*]. One is reminded that while the poem is always the "cry of its occasion" for Stevens, the maker of the poem remains "the intelligence of his soil."

Stevens's poetry is studded with place-names that are part of the map of America. Many refer to the eastern seaboard, from Monhegan and Pemaquid down to Indian River and Key West. The ranging walks of the young man exploring the Pennsylvania countryside—hiking in the Canadian Rockies during college vacation—are paralleled in maturity by the travels of the insurance lawyer sent to investigate bond claims in various states. Stevens loved to vacation in Florida where the tropical heat and color, flora and fauna, sea surface and cloud structures presented a stimulating contrast to northern scenes: "rings in the nets around the racks by the docks of Indian River," and "the red-bird breasting the orange-trees"; "pine and coral and coraline sea"; "lights in the fishing boats at anchor" off Key West. "The big-finned palm / And green vine angering for life . . . the young alligator." The early poem **"O Florida, Venereal Soil"** adds an ominous note to the catalogue of the South: "Convulvolus and coral / Buzzards and live-moss," "crayfish," and "corpses," alternate with "bougainvilleas" and "the guitar."

Much as he loves the South, home territory exerts an intense pull on the poet. In 1955, the year of his death, Stevens wrote a short piece about his adopted region. A trip by rail from Hartford to Boston stands in contrast to all things tropical, but Stevens describes the austerity, and the monotony, of the late winter landscape with the same precision he accords its fragile beauty: "Everything seemed gray, bleached and derelict. . . . The soil everywhere seemed thin and difficult, and every cutting and open pit disclosed gravel and rocks in which only the young pine trees seemed to do well." But he begins to see farms, cow barns, apple and peach orchards, and to reflect upon the approach of the "spare" New England spring: "The man who loves . . . the spare region of Connecticut, loves it precisely because of the spare colors, the thin light, the delicacy and slightness and beauty of the place. The dry grass on the thin surface would soon change to a lime-like green and later to an emerald brilliance in a sunlight never too full." Stevens concludes, "It is not that I am a native, but that I feel like one," and he observes that "coming home" is an experience that "nothing can ever change or remove."

John Malcolm Brinnin, introducing Stevens at a reading of his poetry at the YMHA in 1954, observed that one had to read Wallace Stevens to know what America was like. Peter Brazeau records Brinnin's remarks [in his *Parts of a World*]: "When you're very young and you come to

Wallace Stevens and you begin to look at those sources, they seem all to come out of a European connection—except for a few little programmatic jars in Tennessee, or whatnot. But after a while . . . I began to see that this guy was as American as Walt Whitman or Frank Lloyd Wright or Gertrude [Stein]—or any of our home-grown, impossible people. That cranky, marvelous genius is really an American thing." Brinnin concludes that "it has something to do with both inheriting Europe and getting rid of it."

In this, Brinnin is absolutely on target. For Stevens, the richly diverse European inheritance must be absorbed into the cranky American genius before it can be transmuted, or turned away from. Certainly for the young Stevens, the idea of nativity continues to expand. "Belonging" ripples out from a regional to a global sense of citizenship. This notion of expanded citizenship, with its socioeconomic overtones of independence and free exchange between nations, is expressed in Goethe's notion of *Der Weltbürger* in *Hermann und Dorothea* (1797)—the "citizen of the world." It is a citizenship framed in the French Revolution's triad of *liberté, égalité, fraternité*. Its code was not "God and Country" but "Humanity"; its ethic, a civilized, humane commerce with others.

But the notion of world citizenship extends from purely political and military issues to the idea of an international fraternity of art and thought. Stevens reflects this latter meaning, although it is my impression that he intends the other senses as well, in *The Man with the Blue Guitar* (1936) when he claims the right to think as a "native in the world":

> I am a native in this world
> And think in it as a native thinks,
>
> Gesu, not native of a mind
> Thinking the thoughts I call my own,
>
> Native, a native in the world
> And like a native think in it.

Is this a dialectic involving the right to live where one pleases and think as one chooses? Or does it, perhaps, take up a Heideggerian kind of challenge—that a thinking being must strive to attain an authentic being-in-the-world? From such a position, the very fact of *dwelling* necessarily conducts one to the act of *thinking*. On the other hand, Stevens may be strumming a variation on a theme by Coleridge in these verses from *Blue Guitar,* the belief that great poetry requires serious thought. The romantic compressed this idea into a phrase: "native Passion." "The truth is," wrote Coleridge, reassessing a poet of whom he had once thought highly, "Bowles has indeed the *sensibility* of a poet; but he has not the *Passion* of a great poet. . . . He has not native Passion, because he is not a Thinker."

Perhaps Stevens's verses on belonging and thinking, in *Blue Guitar,* should not be ascribed to any single philosophic stance. What remains perfectly clear is that the word *native* is repeated six times in as many lines, while the changing forms of *to think* ("think . . . thinks . . . thinking . . . thoughts") occur with almost the same frequency. Here we may recognize another thematic nexus, as the sense of nativity moves between the "Cis-Alpine" and "Trans-Alpine" ranges of thought, although Stevens's thinker is blessed with synoptic vision: "The pensive man . . . He sees that eagle float / For which the intricate Alps are a single nest."

Coleridge's "native Passion," the philosophical poet's ferocity of response, skyrockets into an "exhilaration of changes," Stevens's motive for metaphor. This is the mode of transport, of delight, and of vision. The sense of belonging becomes detached from "a living name, a living place, a living thing"—from the physical, phenomenal universe—and attaches to familiar topoi or to unfamiliar "things beyond resemblance." One has arrived at the realm of metaphor, the poet's country of invisible bridges, where nativity no longer means stability, rootedness, the Home Office, but instantaneous motion, lightning-flash conversion; where a thing exists as itself at the same precise moment it transforms into another thing, and continues its primary existence. One is in a *paysage,* that is to say, where ordinary continuities of time and space are suspended, where the command to "Beam me up, Scottie!" effects an instantaneous transfer and reformation of particles. It is a place of formidable creative energies, disciplined by an elementary "A B C" proposition and remaining, eerily, a mystery. "We laymen have always wondered greatly," Freud remarked, "how that strange being, the poet, comes by his material. What makes him able to carry us with him in such a way and to arouse emotions in us of which we thought ourselves perhaps not even capable?" Stevens's country of metaphor suggests a ground where this happens, a place where "nativity" truly means bringing to birth in the wonderful; a place, says Stevens in **"The Motive for Metaphor,"**

> Where you yourself were never quite yourself
> And did not want nor have to be,
>
> Desiring the exhilarations of changes:
> The motive for metaphor, shrinking from
> The weight of primary noon,
> The A B C of being,
>
> The ruddy temper, the hammer
> Of red and blue, the hard sound—
> Steel against intimation—the sharp flash,
> The vital, arrogant, fatal, dominant X.

Vendler has recorded the sense of loss felt in the opening measures, and the "harshness" of this poem—but not the exhilaration of change that closes **"The Motive for Metaphor"** on a *dominant* chord. This is the hardware of the uncanny—"Steel against intimation"—a universe hammered out of syllable and sound. It seems to me, although I do not know exactly why, that an anecdote recounted by Delmore Schwartz serves as the best gloss of Stevens's motivations for metaphor. Perhaps because it is as far from the "weight of primary noon" as one can get. Perhaps because it records the quality of experience that Stevens spoke of as "accessible only in the extreme ranges of sensibility"—the sensibility of genius. "In 1936," the younger poet recalls, "I first heard Wallace Stevens . . . read his poetry at Harvard: it was the first time Stevens had ever read his poetry in public, and this first reading was at once an indescribable ordeal and a precious event to Stevens. . . . Before and after reading each poem, Stevens

spoke of the nature of poetry . . . and he said, among other things, that the least sound counts, the least sound and the least syllable. He illustrated this observation by telling of how he had awakened after midnight the week before and heard the sounds of a cat walking delicately and carefully on the crusted snow outside his house."

This record of the occasion shows that Delmore Schwartz was himself finely tuned, not only to the delicacy of Stevens's acoustical perception, but to the stress of the older man's "indescribable ordeal." How good it must have been for Stevens, at home again at night, to prepare for bed in the frame of the house and move round the rooms, which do not ever seem to change. (pp. 120-27)

> *Barbara M. Fisher, in her* Wallace Stevens: The Intensest Rendezvous, *University Press of Virginia, 1990, 185 p.*

FURTHER READING

Bibliography

Edelstein, J. M. *Wallace Stevens: A Descriptive Bibliography.* Pittsburgh: University of Pittsburgh Press, 1973, 429 p.
   Includes both primary and secondary sources.

Biography

Brazeau, Peter. *Parts of a World: Wallace Stevens Remembered.* Berkeley: North Point Press, 1983, 330 p.
   "Oral portrait" of Stevens compiled through interviews with his contemporaries.

Richardson, Joan. *Wallace Stevens: A Biography, The Early Years, 1879-1923.* New York: William Morrow, 1986, 591 p.
   Studies Stevens's life from birth to the publication of *Harmonium.*

———. *Wallace Stevens: The Later Years 1923-1955.* New York: William Morrow, 1988, 462 p.
   Documents the life and career of Stevens from the publication of *Harmonium* until his death.

Weiss, Theodore. "Wallace Stevens: Lunching with Hoon." In his *The Man from Porlock: Engagements 1944-1981,* pp. 58-98. Princeton: Princeton University Press, 1982.
   Recounts the circumstances of Weiss's visit with Stevens and reflects on the diverse components of Stevens's life.

Criticism

Alter, Robert. "Borges, Stevens, and Post-Symbolist Writing." In his *Motives for Fiction,* pp. 134-43. Cambridge: Harvard University Press, 1984.
   Compares the works of the Argentinean author Jorge Luis Borges and Stevens, noting the paradoxical and unstable meanings of symbols in the writings of both authors.

Arensberg, Mary. "White Mythology and the American Sublime: Stevens' Auroral Fantasy." In *The American Sublime,*

edited by Mary Arensberg, pp. 153-72. Albany: State University of New York Press, 1986.
    Freudian reading of Stevens's early poems.

Axelrod, Steven Gould, and Deese, Helen, eds. *Critical Essays on Wallace Stevens.* Boston: G. K. Hall, 1988, 265 p.
    Collects representative criticism on Stevens's poetry and poetic theory.

Bahti, Timothy. "End and Ending: On the Lyric Technique of Some Wallace Stevens Poems." *Modern Language Notes* 105, No. 5 (December 1990): 1046-62.
    Examines the semantic and rhetorical qualities of Stevens's poems in a discussion that stresses the importance of linguistic construction over thematic content.

Baker, Carlos. "Wallace Stevens: *La vie antérieure* and *Le bel aujourd'hui.* " In his *The Echoing Green: Romanticism, Modernism, and the Phenomena of Transference in Poetry,* pp. 277-309. Princeton: Princeton University Press, 1984.
    Traces the influence of the English Romantics in Stevens's work.

Bates, Milton J. *Wallace Stevens: A Mythology of Self.* Berkeley: University of California Press, 1985, 319 p.
    Historical study of Stevens's life and works.

Beehler, Michael. *T. S. Eliot, Wallace Stevens, and the Discourses of Difference.* Baton Rouge: Louisiana State University Press, 1987, 182 p.
    Compares the strategies of representation used by Stevens and Eliot in order to clarify the differences between their poetry and poetics.

Benamou, Michel. *Wallace Stevens and the Symbolist Imagination.* Princeton: Princeton University Press, 1972, 154 p.
    Discusses the influence of the French Symbolist poets Jules Laforgue, Charles Baudelaire, and Stephane Malarmé and analyzes the importance of pictorial language in Stevens's poetry.

Berger, Charles. *Forms of Farewell: The Late Poetry of Wallace Stevens.* Madison: University of Wisconsin Press, 1985, 198 p.
    Offers a reading of the major poems of Wallace Stevens's last decade and "provides a shape, or a plot, to the final movement of his career."

Bevis, William W. *Mind of Winter: Wallace Stevens, Meditation, and Literature.* Pittsburgh: University of Pittsburgh Press, 1988, 343 p.
    Examines meditative moments in Stevens's poetry.

Blackmur, R. P. "The Substance That Prevails." In *Outsider at the Heart of Things,* edited by James T. Jones, pp. 148-60. Urbana: University of Illinois Press, 1989.
    Examines the complementary relationship between lyricism and theory in Stevens's poetry.

Blasing, Mutlu Konuk. "Wallace Stevens: The Exquisite Errors of Time." In his *American Poetry: The Rhetoric of Its Forms,* pp. 84-100. New Haven, Conn.: Yale University Press, 1987.
    Reconsiders the influence of English and American Romanticism on Stevens's poetry.

Blessington, Francis C., and Rotella, Guy, eds. *The Motive for Metaphor: Essays on Modern Poetry.* Boston: Northeastern University Press, 1983, 171 p.
    Collection of biographical and critical essays that in-

cludes Samuel French Morse's essay on Stevens's descriptions of landscape and his years in Hartford; Frank Doggett and Dorothy Emerson's analysis of Stevens's poetic theory; Peter Brazeau's discussion of Stevens's relationship to his extended family; and Robert Buttel's comparison of the treatment of old age in the poetry of W. B. Yeats and Stevens.

Bloom, Harold. *Wallace Stevens: The Poems of Our Climate.* Ithaca, N.Y.: Cornell University Press, 1977, 413 p.
    Overview of Stevens's poetry and poetics and interpretation of Stevens's place within the American literary canon.

Bové, Paul A. "Fiction, Risk, and Destruction: The Poetry of Wallace Stevens." In his *Destructive Poetics: Heidegger and Modern American Poetry,* pp. 181-97. New York: Columbia University Press, 1980.
    Analyzes identity, language, and the role of the imagination in Stevens's poetry.

Brogan, Jacqueline Vaught. *Stevens and Simile: A Theory of Language.* Princeton: Princeton University Press, 1986, 214 p.
    Discusses wordplay, paranomasia, and figurative language in Stevens's poetry.

Bromwich, David. "Stevens and the Idea of the Hero." *Raritan* VII, No. 1 (Summer 1987): 1-27.
    Analyzes the hero of several of Stevens's poems in light of his interest in the pragmatist philosophy of William James and the nihilistic philosophy of Friedrich Nietzsche.

Carroll, Joseph. *Wallace Stevens' Supreme Fiction: A New Romanticism.* Baton Rouge: Louisiana State University Press, 1987, 361 p.
    Traces the influence of the English Romantics in Stevens's poetry by analyzing his treatment of such Romantic topics as the imagination, nature, and identity.

Cook, Eleanor. "Directions in Reading Wallace Stevens: Up, Down, Across." In *Lyric Poetry: Beyond New Criticism,* edited by Chaviva Hosek and Patricia Parker, pp. 298-309. Ithaca, N.Y.: Cornell University Press, 1985.
    Exegesis of the themes and images in the poem "An Ordinary Evening in New Haven."

———. *Poetry, Word-Play, and Word-War in Wallace Stevens.* Princeton: Princeton University Press, 1988, 325 p.
    Relates Stevens's wordplay to the themes, images, and plots of his poems.

Daiches, David. "The American Experience, From Puritanism through Post-Puritanism to Agnosticism: Edward Taylor, Emily Dickinson, Wallace Stevens." In his *God and the Poets: The Gifford Lectures, 1983,* pp. 153-75. Oxford: Oxford University Press, 1984.
    Places Stevens's poetry in the context of the agnostic tradition in America.

Doggett, Frank. *Wallace Stevens: The Making of the Poem.* Baltimore: Johns Hopkins University Press, 1980, 160 p.
    Discusses Stevens's poetry with respect to the poetic theory outlined in his letters.

Donoghue, Denis. "Stevens's Gibberish." In his *Reading America: Essays on American Literature,* pp. 158-74. New York: Alfred Knopf, 1987.
    Assesses to what degree Stevens is a philosophical poet

by analyzing the relationship between rationality and the imagination in several poems.

Dotterer, Ronald L. "The Fictive and the Real: Myth and Form in the Poetry of Wallace Stevens and William Carlos Williams." In *The Binding of Proteus: Perspectives on Myth and the Literary Process,* edited by Marjorie W. McCune, Tucker Orbison, and Philip M. Withim, pp. 221-48. Lewisburg, Pa.: Bucknell University Press, 1980.
> Formalist analysis that compares Williams's *Paterson* and Stevens's *Notes toward a Supreme Fiction,* concentrating on the relationship between reality and fictionality in each work.

Dougherty, Jay. " 'Sunday Morning' and 'Sunday Morning'." *English Language Notes* XXVII, No. 1 (September 1989): 61-8.
> Compares the two published versions of "Sunday Morning," which vary in length and in the sequence of the stanzas.

Doyle, Charles, ed. *Wallace Stevens: The Critical Heritage.* London: Routledge & Kegan Paul, 1985, 503 p.
> Collects essays and reviews on Stevens's work written by his contemporaries.

Ehrenpreis, Irvin. "Stevens." In *Poetries of America: Essays on the Relation of Character to Style by Irvin Ehrenpreis,* edited by Daniel Albright, pp. 26-41. Charlottesville: University Press of Virginia, 1989.
> Analyzes wordplay, punning, and humor in Stevens's poetry.

Estrin, Barbara L. "Seeing through the Woman in Wallace Stevens's *Notes toward a Supreme Fiction.*" *Contemporary Literature* 31, No. 2 (Summer 1990): 208-26.
> Examines the interplay of genus, gender, and nature in *Notes toward a Supreme Fiction.*

Fisher, Barbara M. *Wallace Stevens: The Intensest Rendezvous.* Charlottesville: University Press of Virginia, 1990, 185 p.
> Proposes that "erotic energy is the key to Stevens's work and, further, that it is these dynamics—that is, the presence of eros and the transformations of eros—that determine the vital structures and the configuration of the entire [Stevens] canon."

Gelpi, Albert, ed. *Wallace Stevens: The Poetics of Modernism.* Cambridge: Cambridge University Press, 1985, 165 p.
> Collects essays that address Stevens's relationship to modernism.

Halliday, Mark. "Stevens and Solitude." *Essays in Literature* 16, No. 1 (Spring 1989): 85-111.
> Examines Stevens's treatment of solipsism and community.

Jarraway, David R. "Crispin's Dependent 'Airs': Psychic Crisis in Early Stevens." *Wallace Stevens Journal* 14, No. 1 (Spring 1990): 21-32.
> Traces the "active-passive" dynamic of Freud's Oedipal triangle in the poem "The Comedian as the Letter C."

Keller, Lynn. " 'Thinkers without Final Thoughts': The Continuity between Stevens and Ashbery." In her *Re-making It New: Contemporary American Poetry and the Modernist Tradition,* pp. 15-41. Cambridge: Cambridge University Press, 1987.
> Discusses Stevens's influence on American poet John Ashbery and the latter poet's divergence from the modernist and surrealist strains in Stevens's verse.

Kermode, Frank. *Wallace Stevens.* 1960. Reprint. New York: Chip's Bookshop, 1979, 135 p.
> Overview of the stylistic, thematic, and philosophical characteristics of Stevens's poetry.

Leggett, B. J. *Wallace Stevens and Poetic Theory: Conceiving the Supreme Fiction.* Chapel Hill: University of North Carolina Press, 1987, 224 p.
> Analyzes critical interpretations of the relationship between poetic theory and practice in Stevens's poetry.

Leonard, J. S., and Wharton, C. E. *The Fluent Mundo: Wallace Stevens and the Structure of Reality.* Athens: University of Georgia Press, 1988, 208 p.
> Examines the relationship between imagination and reality in Stevens's poetry.

MacLeod, Glen. "Surrealism and the Supreme Fiction: 'It Must Give Pleasure'." *Wallace Stevens Journal* 14, No. 1 (Spring 1990): 33-8.
> Examines Stevens's treatment of the irrational in the last section of *Notes toward a Supreme Fiction* and in the essay "The Irrational Element in Poetry" in order to trace the influence of Surrealism in his poetry.

Mariani, Paul. "Williams and Stevens: Storming the Edifice." In his *A Usable Past: Essays on Modern & Contemporary Poetry,* pp. 95-104. Amherst: University of Massachusetts Press, 1984.
> Discusses the relationship between William Carlos Williams and Stevens, the terms of their friendship, and the ways in which the poetry of each responds to the work of the other.

Mollinger, Robert N. "The Literary Symbol: Wallace Stevens's Archetypal Hero" and "The Literary Oeuvre—Levels of Meaning: Wallace Stevens's Poetry." In his *Psychoanalysis and Literature: An Introduction,* pp. 61-72, 121-34. Chicago: Nelson-Hall, 1981.
> Jungian analyses of the hero and literary symbol in Stevens's poetry.

Nyquist, Mary. "Musing on Susanna's Music." In *Lyric Poetry: Beyond New Criticism,* pp. 310-27, edited by Chaviva Hosek and Patricia Parker. Ithaca, N.Y.: Cornell University Press, 1985.
> Discusses Stevens's poetic technique and his understanding of his poetic vocation.

Parkinson, Thomas. "Wallace Stevens on Sunday Morning." In his *Poets, Poems, Movements,* pp. 107-16. Ann Arbor, Mich.: UMI Research Press, 1987.
> Reflects on the images, style, themes, and import of "Sunday Morning."

Patke, Rajeev S. *The Long Poems of Wallace Stevens: An Interpretative Study.* Cambridge: Cambridge University Press, 1985, 263 p.
> Contends that Stevens's long poems bring "to focus in a single, extended and homogeneous form the problems he encountered and the strategies he evolved in using poetry as a means of making sense of his experience of living."

Pearce, Roy Harvey. "The Cry and the Occasion: Rereading

Stevens." In his *Gesta Humanorum: Studies in the Historicist Mode,* pp. 121-55. Columbia: University of Missouri Press, 1987.

> Discusses what Pearce calls the dialectical process of "Invention, Decreation, and Re-creation" in Stevens's poetry.

————, and Miller, J. Hillis, eds. *The Act of the Mind: Essays on the Poetry of Wallace Stevens.* Baltimore: Johns Hopkins University Press, 1965, 287 p.

> Collects essays that address thematic, structural, and theoretical aspects of Stevens's work.

Perloff, Marjorie. "Pound/Stevens: Whose Era?" In her *The Dance of the Intellect: Studies in the Poetry of the Pound Tradition,* pp. 1-32. Cambridge: Cambridge University Press, 1985.

> Contrasts the poetry of Stevens and Ezra Pound. Perloff contends that the discord that exists between their two styles and aesthetic theories evidences the existence of various strands of modernism.

Quinn, Sister Bernetta. "Wallace Stevens: 'The Peace of the Last Intelligence'." *Renascence* XLI, No. 4 (Summer 1989): 191-208.

> Rebukes critics who have dismissed the relevance of Stevens's death-bed conversion to Catholicism and stresses the importance of the event to an overall interpretation of Stevens's life and works.

Riddel, Joseph N. *The Clairvoyant Eye: The Poetry and Poetics of Wallace Stevens.* Baton Rouge: Louisiana State University Press, 1965, 308 p.

> Considers each period of Stevens's poetic development in a discussion of general characteristics of his poetry and poetics.

Robinson, Fred Miller. "Wallace Stevens: The Poet as Comedian." In his *The Comedy of Language: Studies in Modern Comic Literature,* pp. 89-126. Amherst: University of Massachusetts Press, 1980.

> Examines comic elements in relation to plot, drama, and character in Stevens's poetry.

Schaum, Melita. *Wallace Stevens and the Critical Schools.* Tuscaloosa: University of Alabama Press, 1988, 199 p.

> Explores vicissitudes in the critical reception of Stevens's poetry, perceiving Stevens's poems as a "literary *arena* . . . in which major critical assumptions continue to be determined and debated."

Scott, Nathan A., Jr. "Stevens's Route—Transcendence Downward." In his *The Poetics of Belief: Studies in Coleridge, Arnold, Pater, Santayana, Stevens, and Heidegger,* pp. 115-45. Chapel Hill: University of North Carolina Press, 1985.

> Discusses Stevens as a religious poet, who, in seeking to replace a faith in transcendence with an understanding of reality, creates a spiritual humanism.

Smith, Lyle H., Jr. "The Argument of 'Sunday Morning'." *College Literature* XIII, No. 3 (Fall 1986): 254-65.

> Contrasts the weak formal structure of "Sunday Morning" with the poem's imagistic strengths and explicates the secular humanist argument thematized in the poem.

Steinman, Lisa M. "Wallace Stevens: Getting the World Right." In her *Made in America: Science, Technology, and American Modernist Poets,* pp. 133-68. New Haven, Conn.: Yale University Press, 1987.

> Compares Stevens's relationship to American culture with those attitudes held by other American Modernist writers and investigates the influence of scientific theories on Stevens's poetry.

Vendler, Helen. *On Extended Wings: Wallace Stevens' Longer Poems.* Cambridge: Harvard University Press, 1969, 334 p.

> Interprets the long poems in relation to literary and theoretical concerns evident throughout Stevens's oeuvre.

Wagner, C. Roland. "Wallace Stevens: The Concealed Self." *Wallace Stevens Journal* XII, No. 2 (Fall 1988): 83-101.

> Reevaluates Stevens's mature poetry with reference to his "susceptivity to the nurturing female others of his mind—his wife, his mother, his secret childhood divinities," and discusses his alleged death-bed conversion to Catholicism.

Walker, David. *The Transparent Lyric: Reading and Meaning in the Poetry of Stevens and Williams.* Princeton: Princeton University Press, 1984, 203 p.

> Examines several poems by Stevens and William Carlos Williams and compares their styles "within the broader context of an investigation of a modern lyric genre."

Wallace, Ronald. "Wallace Stevens: The Revenge of Music on Bassoons." In his *God Be with the Clown: Humor in American Poetry,* pp. 141-168. Columbia: University of Missouri Press, 1984.

> Discusses humorous interludes in Stevens's poetry and stresses the importance of comedy throughout Stevens's oeuvre.

Woodman, Leonora. *Stanza My Stone: Wallace Stevens and the Hermetic Tradition.* West Lafayette, Ind.: Purdue University Press, 1983, 193 p.

> Analyzes the concordance of Stevens's concepts of self, imagination, and nature with the religious philosophy of Hermeticism.

Woodward, Kathleen. "Wallace Stevens and *The Rock:* Not Ideas about Nobility but the Thing Itself." In her *At Last, The Real Distinguished Thing: The Late Poems of Eliot, Pound, Stevens, and Williams,* pp. 99-131. Columbus: Ohio State University Press, 1980.

> Examines the manner in which changes in Stevens's attitudes toward religion, aging, and aesthetics are reflected in his mature poetry.

Zukofsky, Louis. "For Wallace Stevens." *Prepositions: The Collected Critical Essays of Louis Zukofsky,* rev. ed., pp. 24-38. Berkeley: University of California Press, 1981.

    Reflections on Stevens's poetry and life.

Additional coverage of Stevens's life and career is contained in the following sources published by Gale Research: *Concise Dictionary of American Literary Biography 1929-1941; Contemporary Authors,* **Vols. 104, 124;** *Dictionary of Literary Biography,* **Vol. 54;** *Major 20th-Century Writers;* **and** *Twentieth-Century Literary Criticism,* **Vols. 3, 12, 45.**

Alfred, Lord Tennyson

1809-1892

English poet and playwright.

INTRODUCTION

Tennyson is considered one of the greatest poets in the English language. He was immensely popular in his lifetime, especially in the years following the publication of his lengthy elegiac poem *In Memoriam.* Epitomizing Tennyson's art and thought, this work was embraced by readers as a justification of their religious faith amid doubt caused by the scientific discoveries and speculations of the time. While many critics have since found his poetry excessively moralistic, Tennyson is widely acclaimed as a lyricist of unsurpassed skill.

The fourth of twelve children, Tennyson was born in Somersby, Lincolnshire. Tennyson's father was virtually disinherited by his family, and his bitterness led him to indulge in drugs and alcohol, creating a harmful domestic atmosphere often exacerbated by his violent temper. Each of his children suffered to some extent from drug addiction or mental illness, promoting the family's grim speculation on the "black blood" of the Tennysons, whose history of mental and physical debilities—epilepsy prominent among them—had become a distressing part of their family heritage. Biographers speculate that the general melancholy and morbidity expressed in much of Tennyson's verse is rooted in the unhappy environment at Somersby.

Tennyson's first volume of poetry, *Poems by Two Brothers,* included the work of his two elder brothers and was published in 1827. Later that year, Tennyson enrolled at Trinity College, Cambridge, where in 1829 he won the chancellor's gold medal for his poem "Timbuctoo." *Poems, Chiefly Lyrical,* published in 1830, was well received and marked the beginning of Tennyson's literary career; another collection, *Poems,* appeared in 1832 but was less favorably reviewed, many critics praising Tennyson's artistry but objecting to what they considered an absence of intellectual substance. This latter volume was published at the urging of Arthur Hallam, a Cambridge undergraduate who had become Tennyson's closest friend and an ardent admirer of his poetry. Hallam's enthusiasm was welcomed by Tennyson, whose personal circumstances had led to a growing despondency: his father died in 1831, leaving Tennyson's family in debt and forcing his early departure from Trinity College; one of Tennyson's brothers suffered a mental breakdown and was institutionalized; and Tennyson himself was morbidly fearful of falling victim to epilepsy or madness. Hallam's untimely death in 1833, which prompted the series of elegies later comprising *In Memoriam,* contributed greatly to Tennyson's despair. In describing this period, he wrote: "I suffered what seemed to

me to shatter all my life so that I desired to die rather than to live."

For nearly a decade after Hallam's death Tennyson published no further poetry. During this period he became engaged to Emily Sellwood, but financial difficulties and Tennyson's persistent anxiety over the condition of his health resulted in their separation. In 1842, yielding to a friend's insistence, Tennyson published his two-volume collection *Poems,* which won virtually unanimous praise. That same year an unsuccessful financial venture cost Tennyson nearly everything he owned, causing him to succumb to a deep depression that required medical treatment. In 1845 he was granted a government pension in recognition of both his poetic achievement and his apparent need. Contributing to his financial stability, the first edition of his narrative poem *The Princess: A Medley,* published in 1847, sold out within two months. Tennyson resumed his courtship of Sellwood in 1849, and they were married the following year.

The timely success of *In Memoriam,* published in 1850, ensured Tennyson's appointment as poet laureate succeeding William Wordsworth. *Idylls of the King,* considered by Tennyson's contemporaries to be his masterpiece, and *Enoch Arden, Etc.,* which sold more than forty thousand copies upon publication, increased both his popularity and his wealth, and earned him the designation "the people's poet." Tennyson completed several well-received collections of poems in the last decade of his life, and in 1883 became the first poet awarded a peerage strictly on the basis of his literary achievement. Tennyson died in 1892 and was interred in Westminster Abbey.

In Memoriam expressed Tennyson's personal grief over Hallam's death while examining the nature of death and bereavement in relation to contemporary scientific issues, especially those involving evolution and the geologic dating of the earth's history, that brought into question traditional religious beliefs. Largely regarded as an affirmation of faith, *In Memoriam* was especially valued for its reflections on overcoming bereavement. Comprising 132 sections written over the course of nearly two decades, the poem progresses from despair to joy and concludes with a marriage celebration, symbolically expressing Tennyson's faith in the moral evolution of humanity and reflecting the nineteenth-century ideal of social progress. *Maud, and Other Poems* was the first collection Tennyson published as laureate, but only his 1832 volume, *Poems,* elicited a more negative response. *Maud* is a "monodrama" in which the changing consciousness of the narrator is traced through a series of tragedies that result in his insanity. Confined to an asylum, the protagonist is cured of his madness and asserts his love for humanity by serving his country in the Crimean War. George Eliot and William Gladstone denounced the poem as morbid and obscure, and were among many who disapproved of Tennyson's apparent glorification of war, which he depicted as an ennobling enterprise essential to the cleansing and regeneration of a morally corrupt society. Modern critics largely agree with Christopher Ricks that *Maud* was for Tennyson an "exorcism"; as Ricks explains, "*Maud* was an intense and precarious attempt . . . to encompass the bitter experiences of four decades of a life in which many of the formative influences had also been deformative." Thus madness, suicide, familial conflict, shattered love, death and loss, and untempered mammonism, all central grievances in Tennyson's life, are attacked openly and passionately in *Maud,* with war cultivating the spirit of sacrifice and loyalty which Tennyson felt essential to avert the self-destruction of a selfishly materialistic society.

Tennyson's epic poem *Idylls of the King* followed the controversial *Maud* by examining the rise and fall of idealism in society. "I tried in my *Idylls,*" Tennyson wrote, "to teach men the need of an ideal." F. E. L. Priestley has observed that Tennyson used the "Arthurian cycle as a medium for discussion of problems which [were] both contemporary and perennial" and concluded that the *Idylls* "represent one of Tennyson's most earnest and important efforts to deal with the major problems of his time." Tennyson was concerned with what he considered to be a growing tendency toward hedonism in society and an attendant rejection of spiritual values. *Idylls of the King* expresses his ideal of the British empire as an exemplar of moral and social order: the "Table Round / A glorious company" would "serve as a model for the mighty world." However, when individual acts of betrayal and corruption

result from adultery committed by Queen Guinevere and Lancelot, the ensuing disorder destroys the Round Table, symbolizing the effects of moral decay which were Tennyson's chief concern for the society of his day.

Describing Tennyson's verse as "poised and stationary," Henry James presaged twentieth-century criticism when he stated in 1876 that "a man has always the qualities of his defects, and if Tennyson is . . . a static poet, he at least represents repose and stillness and the fixedness of things, with a splendour that no poet has surpassed." Other critics contended that Tennyson's vision of a spiritually elevated world was betrayed by his concessions to a smug and materialistic Victorian ethic. Recent critics, however, have dismissed the generalizations of their predecessors as part of a post-World War I reaction against the Victorian era and supposed Victorian hypocrisy and narrow-mindedness, and Tennyson has once again come to be viewed, not as "the surface flatterer of his time," as T. S. Eliot described him, but as the embodiment of his age, a poet who reflected both the thoughts and feelings of his generation. The skill with which he did so has been the focus of a wealth of modern criticism, and much of the luster of Tennyson's early reputation has been restored, so that a present-day critic may well pose a question similar to that of Henry Van Dyke, who wrote shortly before Tennyson's death: "In the future, when men call the role of poets who have given splendour to the name of England, they will begin with Shakespeare and Milton—and who shall have the third place, if it be not Tennyson?"

PRINCIPAL WORKS

POETRY

Poems by Two Brothers [with Frederick and Charles Tennyson] 1827
"Timbuctoo" 1829
Poems, Chiefly Lyrical 1830
Poems 1832
Poems 2 vols. 1842
The Princess: A Medley 1847
In Memoriam 1850
"Ode on the Death of the Duke of Wellington" 1852
Maud, and Other Poems 1855
Idylls of the King 1859; enlarged edition, 1874
Enoch Arden, Etc. 1864
The Holy Grail, and Other Poems 1869
Gareth and Lynette, Etc. 1872
Ballads and Other Poems 1880
Tiresias, and Other Poems 1885
Locksley Hall Sixty Years After, Etc. 1886
Demeter, and Other Poems 1889
The Death of Oenone, Akbar's Dream, and Other Poems 1892

OTHER MAJOR WORKS

Queen Mary: A Drama (drama) 1875
Harold: A Drama (drama) 1876
Becket (drama) 1884

The Cup and The Falcon (drama) 1884
The Foresters, Robin Hood and Maid Marian (drama)
  1892

CRITICISM

Arthur Henry Hallam   (essay date 1831)

[*Hallam was an English poet, essayist, and critic who is
primarily remembered as the subject of Tennyson's elegy*
In Memoriam. *In the following excerpt, Hallam offers
a favorable assessment of* Poems, Chiefly Lyrical.]

Mr. Tennyson belongs decidedly to the class we [de-
scribe] . . . as Poets of Sensation. He sees all the forms of
nature with the "*eruditis oculus,*" and his ear has a fairy
fineness. There is a strange earnestness in his worship of
beauty, which throws a charm over his impassioned song,
more easily felt than described, and not to be escaped by
those who have once felt it. We think he has more definite-
ness, and soundness of general conception, than the late
Mr. Keats, and is much more free from blemishes of diction, and hasty capriccios of fancy. He has also this advantage over that poet, and his friend Shelley, that he comes
before the public, unconnected with any political party, or
peculiar system of opinions. Nevertheless, true to the theory we have stated, we believe his participation in their
characteristic excellencies is sufficient to secure him a
share in their unpopularity. The volume of ***Poems, Chiefly
Lyrical,*** does not contain above 154 pages; but it shews us
much more of the character of its parent mind, than many
books we have known of much larger compass, and more
boastful pretensions. The features of original genius are
clearly and strongly marked. The author imitates nobody;
we recognise the spirit of his age, but not the individual
form of this or that writer. His thoughts bear no more resemblance to Byron or Scott, Shelley or Coleridge, than
to Homer or Calderon, Ferdusi or Calidas. We [note] . . .
five distinctive excellencies of his own manner. First, his
luxuriance of imagination, and at the same time his control over it. Secondly, his power of embodying himself in
ideal characters, or rather moods of character, with such
extreme accuracy of adjustment, that the circumstances of
the narration seem to have a natural correspondence with
the predominant feeling, and, as it were, to be evolved
from it by assimilative force. Thirdly, his vivid, picturesque delineation of objects, and the peculiar skill with
which he holds all of them *fused,* to borrow a metaphor
from science, in a medium of strong emotion. Fourthly,
the variety of his lyrical measures, and exquisite modula-
tion of harmonious words and cadences to the swell and
fall of the feelings expressed. Fifthly, the elevated habits
of thought, *implied* in these compositions, and imparting
a mellow soberness of tone, more impressive, to our
minds, than if the author had drawn up a set of opinions
in verse, and sought to instruct the understanding, rather
than to communicate the love of beauty to the heart. (pp.
620-21)

"**Recollections of the Arabian Nights!**" What a delightful,
endearing title! How we pity those to whom it calls up no
reminiscence of early enjoyment, no sentiment of kindli-
ness as towards one who sings a song they have loved, or
mentions with affection a departed friend! But let nobody
expect a multifarious enumeration of Viziers, Barmecides,
Fireworshippers, and Cadis; trees that sing, horses that
fly, and Goules that eat rice pudding! Our author knows
what he is about: he has, with great judgment, selected our
old acquaintance, "the good Haroun Alraschid," as the
most prominent object of our childish interest, and with
him has called up one of those luxurious garden scenes,
the account of which, in plain prose, used to make our
mouths water for sherbet, since luckily we were too young
to think much about Zobeide! We think this poem will be
the favourite among Mr. Tennyson's admirers; perhaps
upon the whole it is our own; at least we find ourselves recurring to it oftener than to any other, and every time we
read it, we feel the freshness of its beauty increase, and are
inclined to exclaim with Madame de Sevigné, "*a force
d'être ancien, il m'est nouveau*" ["by force of being ancient, it is new to me"]. (p. 621)

The poems towards the middle of the volume seem to have
been written at an earlier period than the rest. They display more unrestrained fancy, and are less evidently pro-
portioned to their ruling ideas, than those which we think
of later date. Yet in the "**Ode to Memory**"—the only one
which we have the poet's authority for referring to early
life—there is a majesty of expression, united to a truth of
thought, which almost confounds our preconceived distinctions. The "**Confessions of a Second-Rate, Sensitive
Mind,**" are full of deep insight into human nature, and
into those particular trials, which are sure to best men who
think and feel for themselves at this epoch of social development. The title is perhaps ill chosen: not only has it an
appearance of quaintness, which has no sufficient reason,
but it seems to us incorrect. The mood pourtrayed in this
poem, unless the admirable skill of delineation has deceived us, is rather the clouded reason of a strong mind,
than the habitual condition of one feeble and "second-
rate." Ordinary tempers build up fortresses of opinion on
one side or another; they will see only what they choose
to see; the distant glimpse of such an agony as is here
brought out to view, is sufficient to keep them for ever in
illusions, voluntarily raised at first, but soon trusted in
with full reliance as inseparable parts of self. Perhaps,
however, Mr. Tennyson's mode of "rating" is different
from ours. He may esteem none worthy of the first order,
who has not attained a complete universality of thought,
and such trustful reliance on a principle of repose, which
lies beyond the war of conflicting opinions, that the grand
ideas, "*qui planent sans cesse au dessus de l'humanité*"
["which ever hover above humanity"], cease to affect him
with bewildering impulses of hope and fear. We have not
space to enter farther into this topic; but we should not despair of convincing Mr. Tennyson, that such a position of
intellect would not be the most elevated, nor even the most
conducive to perfection of art. "**The How and the Why**"
appears to present the reverse of the same picture. It is the
same mind still; the sensitive sceptic, whom we have
looked upon in his hour of distress, now scoffing at his own
state with an earnest mirth that borders on sorrow. It is

exquisitely beautiful to see in this, as in the former portrait, how the feeling of art is kept ascendant in our minds over distressful realities, by constant reference to images of tranquil beauty, whether touched pathetically, as the Ox and the Lamb in the first piece, or with fine humour, as the "great bird" and "little bird" in the second. The **"Sea Fairies"** is another strange title; but those who turn to it with the very natural curiosity of discovering who these new births of mythology may be, will be unpardonable if they do not linger over it with higher feelings. A stretch of lyrical power is here exhibited, which we did not think the English language had possessed. The proud swell of verse, as the harp tones "run up the ridged sea," and the soft and melancholy lapse, as the sounds die along the widening space of waters, are instances of that right imitation which is becoming to art, but which in the hands of the unskilful, or the affecters of easy popularity, is often converted into a degrading mimicry, detrimental to the best interests of the imagination. A considerable portion of this book is taken up with a very singular, and very beautiful class of poems, on which the author has evidently bestowed much thought and elaboration. We allude to the female characters, every trait of which presumes an uncommon degree of observation and reflection. Mr. Tennyson's way of proceeding seems to be this. He collects the most striking phenomena of individual minds, until he arrives at some leading fact, which allows him to lay down an axiom, or law, and then, working on the law thus attained, he clearly discerns the tendency of what new particulars his invention suggests, and is enabled to impress an individual freshness and unity on ideal combinations. These expressions of character are brief and coherent nothing extraneous to the dominant fact is admitted, nothing illustrative of it, and, as it were, growing out of it, is rejected. They are like summaries of mighty dramas. We do not say this method admits of such large luxuriance of power, as that of our real dramatists; but we contend that it is a new species of poetry, a graft of the lyric on the dramatic, and Mr. Tennyson deserves the laurel of an inventor, an enlarger of our modes of knowledge and power. (pp. 626-27)

One word more, before we have done, and it shall be a word of praise. The language of this book, with one or two rare exceptions, is thorough and sterling English. A little more respect, perhaps, was due to the "*Jus et norma loquendi*" ["proper and normal language"], but we are inclined to consider as venial a fault arising from generous enthusiasm for the principles of sound analogy, and for that Saxon element, which constitutes the intrinsic freedom and nervousness of our native tongue. We see no signs in what Mr. Tennyson has written of the Quixotic spirit which has led some persons to desire the reduction of English to a single form, by excluding nearly the whole of Latin and Roman derivatives. Ours is necessarily a compound language; as such alone it can flourish and increase; nor will the author . . . be likely to barter for a barren appearance of symmetrical structure that fertility of expression, and variety of harmony, which "the speech, that Shakspeare spoke," derived from the sources of southern phraseology. (p. 628)

Arthur Henry Hallam, "On Some of the Char-

acteristics of Modern Poetry, and on the Lyrical Poems of Alfred Tennyson," *in* The Englishman's Magazine, *Vol. I, August, 1831, pp. 616-28.*

John Wilson Croker   (essay date 1833)

[*Croker made extensive contributions to the* Quarterly Review, *the most prominent conservative periodical of the early nineteenth century. While Croker was a noteworthy critic of literature and historical writings, he had a greater role in guiding the political direction of the* Quarterly Review. *Croker, who was First Secretary of the Admiralty and a friend to Tory leaders in the English government, so effectively channeled the government's views into the* Review *that, from 1830 to 1850, the journal was considered the voice of the old Tory party. In the following excerpt, Croker presents a sarcastic review of Tennyson's second collection,* Poems.]

[*Poems*] is, as some of his marginal notes intimate, Mr. Tennyson's second appearance. By some strange chance we have never seen his first publication, which, if it at all resembles its younger brother, must be by this time so popular that any notice of it on our part would seem idle and presumptuous; but we gladly seize this opportunity of repairing an unintentional neglect, and of introducing to the admiration of our more sequestered readers a new prodigy of genius—another and a brighter star of that galaxy or *milky way* of poetry of which the lamented Keats was the harbinger. . . . (p. 81)

[It] is very agreeable to us, as well as to our readers, that our present task will be little more than the selection, for their delight, of a few specimens of Mr. Tennyson's singular genius, and the venturing to point out, now and then, the peculiar brilliancy of some of the gems that irradiate his poetical crown.

A prefatory sonnet opens to the reader the aspirations of the young author, in which, after the manner of sundry poets, ancient and modern, he expresses his own peculiar character, by wishing himself to be something that he is not. The amorous Catullus aspired to be a sparrow; the tuneful and convivial Anacreon . . . wished to be a lyre and a great drinking cup; a crowd of more modern sentimentalists have desired to approach their mistresses as flowers, tunicks, sandals, birds, breezes, and butterflies;— all poor conceits of narrow-minded poetasters! Mr. Tennyson (though he, too, would, as far as his true-love is concerned, not unwillingly be 'an earring,' 'a girdle,' and 'a necklace,') in the more serious and solemn exordium of his works ambitions a bolder metamorphosis—he wishes to be—*a river!*

"SONNET"
Mine be the strength of spirit fierce and free,
    Like some broad river rushing down *alone*—

rivers that travel in company are too common for his taste—

With the self-same impulse wherewith he was
    thrown—

a beautiful and harmonious line—

From his loud fount upon the echoing lea:—
Which, with *increasing* might, doth *forward
    flee*—

Every word of this line is valuable—the natural progress of human ambition is here strongly characterized—two lines ago he would have been satisfied with the *self-same* impulse—but now he must have *increasing* might; and indeed he would require all his might to accomplish his object of *fleeing forward,* that is, going backwards and forwards at the same time. Perhaps he uses the word *flee* for *flow;* which latter he could not well employ in *this* place, it being, as we shall see, essentially necessary to rhyme to *Mexico* towards the end of the sonnet—as an equivalent to *flow* he has, therefore, with great taste and ingenuity, hit on the combination of *forward flee*—

> —doth forward flee
> By town, and tower, and hill, and cape, and isle,
> And in the middle of the green *salt* sea
> Keeps his blue waters fresh for many a mile.

A noble wish, beautifully expressed, that he may not be confounded with the deluge of ordinary poets, but, amidst their discoloured and briny ocean, still preserve his own bright tints and sweet savor. He may be at ease on this point—he never can be mistaken for any one else. We have but too late become acquainted with him, yet we assure ourselves that if a thousand anonymous specimens were presented to us, we should unerringly distinguish his by the total absence of any particle of *salt.* But again, his thoughts take another turn, and he reverts to the insatiability of human ambition:—we have seen him just now content to be a river, but as he *flees forward,* his desires expand into sublimity, and he wishes to become the great Gulf-stream of the Atlantic.

> Mine be the power which ever to its sway
> Will win *the wise at once*—

We, for once, are wise, and he has won *us*—

> Will win the wise at once; and by degrees
> May into uncongenial spirits flow,
> Even as the great gulphstream of Flor*ida*
> Floats far away into the Northern seas
> The lavish growths of southern Mexi*co!*

And so concludes the sonnet.

The next piece is a kind of testamentary paper, addressed 'To—,' a friend, we presume, containing his wishes as to what his friend should do for him when he (the poet) shall be dead—not, as we shall see, that he quite thinks that such a poet can die outright.

> Shake hands, my friend, across the brink
> Of that deep grave to which I go.
> Shake hands once more; I cannot sink
> So far—far down, but I shall know
> Thy voice, and answer from below!

Horace said 'non omnis moriar,' meaning that his fame should survive—Mr. Tennyson is still more vivacious, 'non *omnino* moriar,'—'I will not die at all; my body shall be as immortal as my verse, and however *low I may go,* I warrant you I shall keep all my wits about me,— therefore'

When, in the darkness over me,
The four-handed mole shall scrape,
Plant thou no dusky cypress tree,
Nor wreath thy cap with doleful crape,
But pledge me in the flowing grape.

Observe how all ages become present to the mind of a great poet; and admire how naturally he combines the funeral cypress of classical antiquity with the crape hatband of the modern undertaker.

He proceeds:—

> And when the sappy field and wood
> Grow green beneath the *showery gray,*
> And rugged barks begin to bud,
> And through damp holts, newflushed with May,
> Ring sudden *laughters* of the jay!

Laughter, the philosophers tell us, is the peculiar attribute of man—but as Shakspeare found 'tongues in trees and sermons in stones,' this true poet endows all nature not merely with human sensibilities but with human functions—the jay *laughs,* and we find, indeed, a little further on, that the woodpecker *laughs* also; but to mark the distinction between their merriment and that of men, both jays and woodpeckers laugh upon melancholy occasions. We are glad, moreover, to observe, that Mr. Tennyson is prepared for, and therefore will not be disturbed by, human laughter, if any silly reader should catch the infection from the woodpeckers and jays.

> Then let wise Nature work her will,
> And on my clay her darnels grow,
> Come only when the days are still,
> And at my head-stone whisper low,
> And tell me—

Now, what would an ordinary bard wish to be told under such circumstances?—why, perhaps, how his sweetheart was, or his child, or his family, or how the Reform Bill worked, or whether the last edition of the poems had been sold—*papœ!* our genuine poet's first wish is

> And tell me—*if the woodbines blow!*

When, indeed, he shall have been thus satisfied as to the *woodbines,* (of the blowing of which in their due season he may, we think, feel pretty secure,) he turns a passing thought to his friend—and another to his mother—

> If *thou* art blest, my *mother's* smile
> Undimmed—

but such inquiries, short as they are, seem too commonplace, and he immediately glides back into his curiosity as to the state of the weather and the forwardness of the spring—

> If thou art blessed—my mother's smile
> Undimmed—*if bees are on the wing?*

No, we believe the whole circle of poetry does not furnish such another instance of enthusiasm for the sights and sounds of the vernal season!—The sorrows of a bereaved mother rank *after* the blossoms of the *woodbine,* and just before the hummings of the *bee;* and this is *all* that he has any curiosity about; for he proceeds—

> Then cease, my friend, a little while

That I may—

'send my love to my mother,' or 'give you some hints about bees, which I have picked up from Aristæus, in the Elysian Fields,' or 'tell you how I am situated as to my own personal comforts in the world below'?—oh no—

> That I may—hear the *throstle sing*
> His bridal song—the boast of spring.
> Sweet as the noise, in parchèd plains,
> Of bubbling wells that fret the stones,
> (*If any sense in me remains*)
> Thy words will be—thy cheerful tones
> As welcome to—my *crumbling bones!*

'*If any sense in me remains*'!—This doubt is inconsistent with the opening stanza of the piece, and, in fact, too modest; we take upon ourselves to re-assure Mr. Tennyson, that, even after he shall be dead and buried, as much 'sense' will still remain as he has now the good fortune to possess.

We have quoted these two first poems in *extenso,* to obviate any suspicion of our having made a partial or delusive selection. We cannot afford space—we wish we could—for an equally minute examination of the rest of the volume, but we shall make a few extracts to show—what we solemnly affirm—that every page teems with beauties hardly less surprising.

'The Lady of Shalott' is a poem in four parts, the story of which we decline to maim by such an analysis as we could give, but it opens thus—

> On either side the river lie
> Long fields of barley and of rye,
> That clothe the world and *meet the sky*—
> And *through* the field the road runs *by.*

The Lady of Shalott was, it seems, a spinster who had, under some unnamed penalty, a certain web to weave.

> Underneath the bearded barley,
> The reaper, reaping late and early,
> Hears her ever chanting cheerly,
> Like an angel singing clearly. . . .
> No time has she to sport or play,
> A charmèd web she weaves alway;
> A curse is on her if she stay
> Her weaving either night or day. . . .
> She knows not—

Poor lady, nor we either—

> She knows not what that curse may be,
> Therefore she weaveth steadily;
> Therefore no other care has she,
>   The Lady of Shalott.

A knight, however, happens to ride past her window, coming

> —from Camelot;
> From the bank, and *from* the *river,*
> He flashed *into* the crystal *mirror*—
> "Tirra lirra, tirra *lirra*," (*lirrar?*)
>   Sang Sir Launcelot.

The lady stepped to the window to look at the stranger, and forgot for an instant her web:—the curse fell on her,

and she died; why, how, and wherefore, the following stanzas will clearly and pathetically explain:—

> A long drawn carol, mournful, holy,
> She chanted loudly, chanted lowly,
> Till her eyes were darkened *wholly,*
> And her smooth face *sharpened slowly,*
>   Turned to towered Camelot.

> For ere she reached upon the tide
> The first house on the water side,
> Singing in her song she died,
>   The Lady of Shalott!

> Knight and burgher, lord and dame,
> To the plankèd wharfage came;
> Below *the stern* they read her name,
>   The Lady of Shalott.

We pass by two—what shall we call them?—tales, or odes, or sketches, entitled **'Mariana in the South'** and **'Eleänore,'** of which we fear we could make no intelligible extract, so curiously are they run together into one dreamy tissue—to a little novel in rhyme, called **'The Miller's Daughter.'** Miller's daughters, poor things, have been so generally betrayed by their sweethearts, that it is refreshing to find that Mr. Tennyson has united himself to *his* miller's daughter in lawful wedlock, and the poem is a history of his courtship and wedding. He begins with a sketch of his own birth, parentage, and personal appearance—

> My father's mansion, mounted high,
> Looked down upon the village-spire;
> I was a long and listless boy,
> And son and heir unto the Squire.

But the son and heir of Squire Tennyson often descended from the 'mansion mounted high;' and

> I met in all the close green ways,
> While walking with my line and rod,

A metonymy for 'rod and line'—

> The wealthy miller's mealy face,
> Like the *moon in an ivytod.*
> He looked so jolly and so good—
> While fishing in the mill-dam water,
> I laughed to see him as he stood,
> And dreamt not of the miller's daughter.

He, however, soon saw, and, need we add, loved the miller's daughter, whose countenance, we presume, bore no great resemblance either to the 'mealy face' of the miller, or 'the moon in an ivy-tod;' and we think our readers will be delighted at the way in which the impassioned husband relates to his wife how his fancy mingled enthusiasm for rural sights and sounds, with a prospect of the less romantic scene of her father's occupation.

> How dear to me in youth, my love,
> Was everything about the mill;
> The black, the silent pool above,
> The pool beneath that ne'er stood still;
> The meal-sacks on the whitened floor,
> The dark round of the dripping wheel,
> *The very air about the door,*
> *Made misty with the floating meal!*

The accumulation of tender images in the following lines appears not less wonderful:—

> Remember you that pleasant day
> When, after roving in the woods,
> ('Twas April then) I came and lay
> Beneath those *gummy* chestnut-buds?
> A water-rat from off the bank
> Plunged in the stream. With idle care,
> Downlooking through the sedges rank,
> I saw your troubled image there.
> If you remember, you had set,
> Upon the narrow casement-edge,
> A *long green box* of mignonette,
> And you were leaning on the ledge.

The poet's truth to Nature in his 'gummy' chestnut-buds, and to Art in the 'long green box' of mignonette—and that masterly touch of likening the first intrusion of love into the virgin bosom of the Miller's daughter to the plunging of a water-rat into the mill-dam—these are beauties which, we do not fear to say, equal anything even in Keats. We pass by several songs, sonnets, and small pieces, all of singular merit, to arrive at a class, we may call them, of three poems derived from mythological sources—Œnone, deserted by

> Beautiful Paris, evilhearted Paris,

sings a kind of dying soliloquy addressed to Mount Ida, in a formula which is *sixteen* times repeated in this short poem.

> Dear mother Ida, hearken ere I die.

She tells her 'dear mother Ida,' that when evilhearted Paris was about to judge between the three goddesses, he hid her (Œnone) behind a rock, whence she had a full view of the *naked* beauties of the rivals, which broke her heart.

> *Dear mother Ida, hearken ere I die:*—
> It was the deep mid noon: one silvery cloud
> Had *lost his way* among the pined hills:
> They came—*all three* the Olympian goddesses.
> Naked they came—
>
> . . . . .
>
> How beautiful they were! too beautiful
> To look upon; but Paris was to me
> *More lovelier* than all the world beside.
> *O mother Ida, hearken ere I die.*

In the place where we have indicated a pause, follows a description, long, rich, and luscious—Of the three naked goddesses? Fye for shame—no—of the 'lily flower violet-eyed,' and the 'singing pine,' and the 'overwandering ivy and vine,' and 'festoons,' and 'gnarlèd boughs,' and 'tree tops,' and 'berries,' and 'flowers,' and all the *inanimate* beauties of the scene. It would be unjust to the *ingenuus pudor* of the author not to observe the art with which he has veiled this ticklish interview behind such luxuriant trellis-work, and it is obvious that it is for our special sakes he has entered into these local details, because if there was one thing which 'mother Ida' knew better than another, it must have been her own bushes and brakes. We then have in detail the tempting speeches of, first—

> The imperial Olympian,

> With archèd eyebrow smiling sovranly,
> Full-eyèd Here;

secondly of Pallas—

> Her clear and barèd limbs
> O'er-thwarted with the brazen-headed spear,

and thirdly—

> Idalian Aphrodite ocean-born,
> Fresh as the foam, new-bathed in Paphian
> *wells*—

for one dip, or even three dips in one well, would not have been enough on such an occasion—and her succinct and prevailing promise of—

> The fairest and most loving *wife* in Greece;—

upon evil-hearted Paris's catching at which prize, the tender and chaste Œnone exclaims her indignation, that she herself should not be considered fair enough, since only yesterday her charms had struck awe into—

> A wild and wanton pard,
> Eyed like the evening star, with playful tail—

and proceeds in this anti-Martineau rapture—

> *Most* loving is *she?*
> Ah me! my mountain shepherd, that my arms
> Were wound about thee, and my hot lips prest
> Close—close to thine in that quick-falling dew
> Of *fruitful* kisses . . . .
> Dear mother Ida! hearken ere I die!

After such reiterated assurances that she was about to die on the spot, it appears that Œnone thought better of it, and the poem concludes with her taking the wiser course of going to town to consult her swain's sister, Cassandra—whose advice, we presume, prevailed upon her to live, as we can, from other sources, assure our readers she did to a good old age.

In the **'Hesperides'** our author, with great judgment, rejects the common fable, which attributes to Hercules the slaying of the dragon and the plunder of the golden fruit. Nay, he supposes them to have existed to a comparatively recent period—namely, the voyage of Hanno, on the coarse canvas of whose log-book Mr. Tennyson has judiciously embroidered the Hesperian romance. The poem opens with a geographical description of the neighbourhood, which must be very clear and satisfactory to the English reader; indeed, it leaves far behind in accuracy of topography and melody of rhythm the heroics of Dionysius *Periegets.*

> The north wind fall'n, in the new-starrèd night.

Here we must pause to observe a new species of *metabolé* with which Mr. Tennyson has enriched our language. He suppresses the E in *fallen,* where it is usually written and where it must be pronounced, and transfers it to the word *new-starrèd,* where it would not be pronounced if he did not take due care to superfix a *grave* accent. This use of the grave accent is, as our readers may have already perceived, so habitual with Mr. Tennyson, and is so obvious an improvement, that we really wonder how the language has hitherto done without it. We are tempted to suggest, that if analogy to the accented languages is to be thought of, it is rather the acute (ˊ) than the grave (ˋ) which should be employed on such occasions; but we speak with profound diffidence; and as Mr. Tennyson is the inventor of the system, we shall bow with respect to whatever his final determination may be.

> The north wind fall'n, in the new-starrèd night
> Zidonian Hanno, voyaging beyond
> The hoary promontory of Soloë,
> Past Thymiaterion in calmèd bays.

We must here note specially the musical flow of this last line, which is the more creditable to Mr. Tennyson, because it was before the tuneless names of this very neighbourhood that the learned continuator of Dionysius retreated in despair, . . . but Mr. Tennyson is bolder and happier—

> Past Thymiaterion in calmèd bays,
> Between the southern and the western Horn,
> Heard neither—

We pause for a moment to consider what a sea-captain might have expected to hear, by night, in the Atlantic ocean—he heard

> —neither the warbling of the *nightingale*
> Nor melody o' the Libyan lotusflute,

but he did hear the three daughters of Hesper singing the following song:—

> The golden apple, the golden apple, the hal-
>   lowèd fruit,
> Guard it well, guard it warily,
> Singing airily,
> Standing about the charmèd root,
> Round about all is mute—

mute, though they sung so loud as to be heard some leagues out at sea—

> —all is mute
> As the snow-field on mountain peaks,
> As the sand-field at the mountain foot.
> Crocodiles in briny creeks
> Sleep, and stir not: all is mute.

How admirably do these lines describe the peculiarities of this charmèd neighbourhood—fields of snow, so talkative when they happen to lie at the foot of the mountain, are quite out of breath when they get to the top, and the sand, so noisy on the summit of a hill, is dumb at its foot. The very crocodiles, too, are *mute*—not dumb but *mute.* The 'red-combèd dragon curl'd' is next introduced—

> Look to him, father, lest he wink, and the golden
>   apple be stolen away,
> For his ancient heart is drunk with overwatch-
>   ings night and day,
> Sing away, sing aloud evermore, in the wind,
>   without stop.

The north wind, it appears, had by this time awaked again—

> Lest his scalèd eyelid drop,
> For he is older than the world—

older than the *hills,* besides not rhyming to 'curl'd,' would hardly have been a sufficiently venerable phrase for this most harmonious of lyrics. It proceeds—

> If ye sing not, if ye make false measure,
> We shall lose eternal pleasure,
> Worth eternal want of rest.
> Laugh not loudly: watch the treasure
> Of the wisdom of the west.
> In *a corner* wisdom whispers. Five and three
> (*Let it not be preached abroad*) make an awful
>   mystery.

This recipe for keeping a secret, by singing it so loud as to be heard for miles, is almost the only point, in all Mr. Tennyson's poems, in which we can trace the remotest approach to anything like what other men have written, but it certainly does remind us of the 'chorus of conspirators' in the Rovers.

Hanno, however, who understood no language but Punic—(the Hesperides sang, we presume, either in Greek or in English)—appears to have kept on his way without taking any notice of the song, for the poem concludes,—

> The apple of gold hangs over the sea,
> Five links, a golden chain, are we,
> Hesper, the Dragon, and sisters three;
> Daughters three,
>
> Bound about
> All round about
> The gnarlèd bole of the charmèd tree,
> The golden apple, the golden apple, the hal-
>   lowèd fruit.
> Guard it well, guard it warily,
> Watch it warily,
> Singing airily,
> Standing about the charmèd root.

We hardly think that, if Hanno had translated it into Punic, the song would have been more intelligible.

The '**Lotuseaters**'—a kind of classical opium-eaters—are Ulysses and his crew. They land on the 'charmèd island,' and eat of the 'charmèd root,' and then they sing—

> Long enough the winedark wave our weary bark
>   did carry.
> This is lovelier and sweeter,
> Men of Ithaca, this is meeter,
> In the hollow rosy vale to tarry,
> Like a dreamy Lotuseater—a delicious Lotus-
>   eater!
> We will eat the Lotus, sweet
> As the yellow honeycomb;
> In the valley some, and some
> On the ancient heights divine,
> And no more roam,
> On the loud hoar foam,
> To the melancholy home,
> At the limits of the brine,
> The little isle of Ithaca, beneath the day's de-
>   cline.

Our readers will, we think, agree that this is admirably characteristic, and that the singers of this song must have made pretty free with the intoxicating fruit. How they got home you must read in Homer:—Mr. Tennyson—himself, we presume, a dreamy lotus-eater, a delicious lotus-eater—leaves them in full song.

Next comes another class of poems,—Visions. The first is the **'Palace of Art,'** or a fine house, in which the poet *dreams* that he sees a very fine collection of well-known pictures. An ordinary versifier would, no doubt, have followed the old routine, and dully described himself as walking into the Louvre, or Buckingham Palace, and there seeing certain masterpieces of painting:—a true poet dreams it. We have not room to hang many of these *chefs-d'œuvre*, but for a few we must find space.—'**The Madonna'**—

> The maid mother by a crucifix,
> In yellow pastures sunny warm,
> Beneath branch work of costly sardonyx
> Sat smiling—*babe in arm.*

The use of this latter, apparently, colloquial phrase is a deep stroke of art. The form of expression is always used to express an habitual and characteristic action. A knight is described '*lance in rest*'—a dragoon, '*sword in hand*'—so, as the idea of the Virgin is inseparably connected with her child, Mr. Tennyson reverently describes her conventional position—'*babe in arm.*'

His gallery of illustrious portraits is thus admirably arranged:—The Madonna—Ganymede—St. Cecilia—Europa—Deep-haired Milton—Shakspeare—Grim Dante—Michael Angelo—Luther—Lord Bacon—Cervantes—Calderon—King David—'the Halicarnassëan' (*quære,* which of them?)—Alfred, (not Alfred Tennyson, though no doubt in any other man's gallery *he* would have had a place) and finally—

> Isaïah, with fierce Ezekiel,
> Swarth Moses by the Coptic sea,
> Plato, *Petrarca,* Livy, and Raphaël,
> And eastern Confutzee!

We can hardly suspect the very original mind of Mr. Tennyson to have harboured any recollections of that celebrated Doric idyll, 'The groves of Blarney,' but certainly there is a strong likeness between Mr. Tennyson's list of pictures and the Blarney collection of statues—

> Statues growing that noble place in,
> All heathen goddesses most rare,
> Homer, Plutarch, and Nebuchadnezzar,
> All standing naked in the open air!

In this poem we first observed a stroke of art (repeated afterwards) which we think very ingenious. No one who has ever written verse but must have felt the pain of erasing some happy line, some striking stanza, which, however excellent in itself, did not exactly suit the place for which it was destined. How curiously does an author mould and remould the plastic verse in order to fit in the favourite thought; and when he finds that he cannot introduce it, as Corporal Trim says, *any how,* with what reluctance does he at last reject the intractable, but still cherished offspring of his brain! Mr. Tennyson manages this delicate matter in a new and better way; he says, with great candour and simplicity, 'If this poem were not already too long, *I should have added* the following stanzas,' and *then he adds them*—or, 'the following lines are manifestly superfluous, as a part of the text, but they may be allowed to stand as a separate poem,' *which they do;*—or, 'I intend-

ed to have added something on statuary, but I found it very difficult;'—(he had, moreover, as we have seen, been anticipated in this line by the Blarney poet)—'but I had finished the statues of *Elijah* and *Olympias*—judge whether I have succeeded,'—and then we have these two statues. This is certainly the most ingenious device that has ever come under our observation, for reconciling the rigour of criticism with the indulgence of parental partiality. It is economical too, and to the reader profitable, as by these means

> We lose no drop of the immortal man.

The other vision is **'A Dream of Fair Women,'** in which the heroines of all ages—some, indeed, that belong to the times of 'heathen goddesses most rare'—pass before his view. We have not time to notice them all, but the second, whom we take to be Iphigenia, touches the heart with a stroke of nature more powerful than even the veil that the Grecian painter threw over the head of her father.

> —dimly I could descry
> The stern blackbearded kings with wolfish eyes,
> Watching to see me die.
> The tall masts quivered as they lay afloat;
> The temples, and the people, and the shore;
> One drew a sharp knife through my tender
>   throat—
> Slowly,—and *nothing more!*

What touching simplicity—what pathetic resignation—he cut my throat—'*Nothing more!*' One might indeed ask, 'what *more*' she would have?

But we must hasten on; and to tranquillize the reader's mind after the last affecting scene, shall notice the only two pieces of a lighter strain which the volume affords. The first is elegant and playful; it is a description of the author's study, which he affectionately calls his **'Darling Room.'**

> O darling room, my heart's delight;
> Dear room, the apple of my sight;
> With thy two couches, soft and white,
> There is no room so exqui*site;*
> No little room so warm and bright,
> Wherein to read, wherein to write.

We entreat our readers to note how, even in this little trifle, the singular taste and genius of Mr. Tennyson break forth. In such a dear *little* room a narrow-minded scribbler would have been content with *one* sofa, and that one he would probably have covered with black mohair, or red cloth, or a good striped chintz; how infinitely more characteristic is white dimity!—'tis as it were a type of the purity of the poet's mind. He proceeds—

> For I the Nonnenwerth have seen,
> And Oberwinter's vineyards green,
> Musical Lurlei; and between
> The hills to Bingen I have been,
> Bingen in Darmstadt, where the *Rhene*
> Curves towards Mentz, a woody scene.
> Yet never did there meet my sight,
> In any town, to left or right,
> A little room so exqui*site,*
> With *two* such couches soft and white;
> Not any room so warm and bright,

Wherein to read, wherein to write.

A common poet would have said that he had been in London or in Paris—in the loveliest villa on the banks of the Thames, or the most gorgeous chateau on the Loire—that he had reclined in Madame de Staël's boudoir, and mused in Mr. Roger's comfortable study; but the *darling room* of the poet of nature (which we must suppose to be endued with sensibility, or he would not have addressed it) would not be flattered with such common-place comparisons;—no, no, but it is something to have it said that there is no such room in the ruins of the Drachenfels, in the vineyard of Oberwinter, or even in the rapids of the *Rhene,* under the Lurleyberg. We have ourselves visited all these celebrated spots, and can testify, in corroboration of Mr. Tennyson, that we did not see in any of them anything like *this little room so exquis*ITE. (pp. 82-95)

> *John Wilson Croker, in an originally unsigned essay titled "Poems by Alfred Tennyson," in* The Quarterly Review, *Vol. 49, No. XCVII, April, 1833, pp. 81-96.*

George Eliot   (essay date 1855)

[*Considered one of the greatest English novelists of the nineteenth century, Eliot was also an essayist, poet, editor, short story writer, and translator. Her work, including the novels* The Mill on the Floss *(1860) and* Middlemarch: A Study of Provincial Life *(1871-72), is informed by penetrating psychological analysis and profound insight into human character. In the following excerpt, Eliot, while expressing a high appraisal of Tennyson's overall poetic achievement, attacks* Maud *for its "morbid" tone and apparent advocation of warfare.*]

If we were asked who among contemporary authors is likely to live in the next century, the name that would first and most unhesitatingly rise to our lips is that of Alfred Tennyson. He, at least, while belonging emphatically to his own age, while giving a voice to the struggles and the far-reaching thoughts of this nineteenth century, has those supreme artistic qualities which must make him a poet for all ages. As long as the English language is spoken, the word music of Tennyson must charm the ear; and when English has become a dead language, his wonderful concentration of thought into luminous speech, the exquisite pictures in which he has blended all the hues of reflection, feeling, and fancy, will cause him to be read as we read Homer, Pindar, and Horace. Thought and feeling, like carbon, will always be finding new forms for themselves, but once condense them into the diamonds of poetry, and the form, as well as the element, will be lasting. This is the sublime privilege of the artist—to be present with future generations, not merely through the indirect results of his work, but through his immediate creations; and of all artists the one whose works are least in peril from the changing conditions of humanity, is the highest order of poet. . . . (p. 596)

Such a poet, by the suffrage of all competent judges among his countrymen, is Tennyson. His **"Ulysses"** is a pure little ingot of the same gold that runs through the ore of the Odyssey. It has the "large utterance" of the early epic, with

that rich fruit of moral experience which it has required thousands of years to ripen. The **"Morte d'Arthur"** breathes the intensest spirit of chivalry in the pure and serene air of unselfish piety; and it falls on the ear with the rich, soothing melody of a *Dona nobis* swelling through the aisles of a cathedral. **"Locksley Hall"** has become, like Milton's minor poems, so familiar that we dare not quote it; it is the object of a sort of family affection which we all cherish, but think it is not good taste to mention. Then there are his idyls, such as the **"Gardener's Daughter,"**—works which in their kind have no rival, either in the past or present. But the time would fail us to tell of all we owe to Tennyson, for, with two or three exceptions, every poem in his two volumes is a favourite. The *Princess,* too, with all that criticism has to say against it, has passages of inspiration and lyrical gems imbedded in it, which make it a fresh claim on our gratitude. But, last and greatest, came **In Memoriam,** which to us enshrines the highest tendency of this age, as the Apollo Belvedere expressed the presence of a free and vigorous human spirit amidst a decaying civilization. Whatever was the immediate prompting of **In Memoriam,** whatever the form under which the author represented his aim to himself, the deepest significance of the poem is the sanctification of human love as a religion. If, then, the voice that sang all these undying strains had remained for ever after mute, we should have had no reason to reproach Tennyson with gifts inadequately used; we should rather have rejoiced in the thought that one who has sown for his fellow-men so much—

> generous seed,
> Fruitful of further thought and deed,

should at length be finding rest for his wings in a soft nest of home affections, and be living idyls, instead of writing them.

We could not prevail on ourselves to say what we think of *Maud,* without thus expressing our love and admiration of Tennyson. For that optical law by which an insignificant object, if near, excludes very great and glorious things that lie in the distance, has its moral parallel in the judgments of the public: men's speech is too apt to be exclusively determined by the unsuccessful deed or book of today, the successful doings and writings of past years being for the moment lost sight of. And even seen in the light of the most reverential criticism, the effect of *Maud* cannot be favourable to Tennyson's fame. Here and there only it contains a few lines in which he does not fall below himself. With these slight exceptions, he is everywhere saying, if not something that would be better left unsaid, something that he had already said better; and the finest sentiments that animate his other poems are entirely absent. We have in *Maud* scarcely more than a residuum of Alfred Tennyson; the wide-sweeping intellect, the mild philosophy, the healthy pathos, the wondrous melody, have almost all vanished, and left little more than a narrow scorn which piques itself on its scorn of narrowness, and a passion which clothes itself in exaggerated conceits. While to his other poems we turn incessantly with new distress that we cannot carry them all in our memory, of *Maud* we must say, if we say the truth, that excepting only a few passages, we wish to forget it as we should wish to

Tennyson's close friend Arthur Henry Hallam, circa 1830.

forget a bad opera. And this not only because it wants the charms of mind and music which belong to his other poetry, but because its tone is throughout morbid; it opens to us the self-revelations of a morbid mind, and what it presents as the cure for this mental disease is itself only a morbid conception of human relations.

> As long as the English language is spoken, the word music of Tennyson must charm the ear; and when English has become a dead language, his wonderful concentration of thought into luminous speech, the exquisite pictures in which he has blended all the hues of reflection, feeling, and fancy, will cause him to be read as we read Homer, Pindar, and Horace.
>
> —*George Eliot*

But we will abstain from general remarks, and make the reader acquainted with the plan and texture of the poem. It opens, like the gates of Pandemonium, "with horrible discord and jarring sound,"—with harsh and rugged hexameters, in which the hero, who is throughout the speaker, tells us something of his history and his views of society. It is impossible to suppose that, with so great a master of rhythm as Tennyson, this harshness and ruggedness are

otherwise than intentional; so we must conclude that it is a device of his art thus to set our teeth on edge with his verses when he means to rouse our disgust by his descriptions; and that, writing of disagreeable things, he has made it a rule to write disagreeably. These hexameters, weak in logic and grating in sound, are undeniably strong in expression, and eat themselves with phosphoric eagerness into our memory, in spite of our will. The hero opens his story by telling us how "long since" his father was found dead in "the dreadful hollow behind the little wood," supposed to have committed suicide in despair at the ruin entailed on him by the failure of a great speculation; and he paints with terrible force that crisis in his boyhood:—

> I remember the time, for the roots of my hair
>   were stirr'd
> By a shuffled step, by a dead weight trail'd, by
>   a whisper'd fright,
> And my pulses closed their gates with a shock
>   on my heart as I heard
> The shrill-edged shriek of a mother divide the
>   shuddering night.

An old neighbour "dropt off gorged" from that same speculation, and is now lord of the broad estate and the hall. These family sorrows and mortifications the hero regards as a direct result of the anti-social tendencies of Peace, which he proceeds to expose to us in all its hideousness; looking to war as the immediate curative for unwholesome lodging of the poor, adulteration of provisions, child-murder, and wife-beating—an effect which is as yet by no means visible in our police reports. It seems indeed that, in the opinion of our hero, nothing short of an invasion of our own coasts is the consummation devoutly to be wished:—

> For I trust if an enemy's fleet came yonder round
>   by the hill,
> And the rushing battle-bolt sang from the three-
>   decker out of the foam,
> That the smoothfaced snubnosed rogue would
>   leap from his counter and till,
> And strike, if he could, were it but with his
>   cheating yardwand, home.

From his deadly hatred of retail traders and susceptibility as to the adulteration of provisions, we were inclined to imagine that this modern Conrad, with a "devil in his sneer," but not a "laughing devil," had in his reduced circumstances taken a London lodging and endured much peculation in the shape of weekly bills, and much indigestion arising from unwholesome bread and beer. But no: we presently learn that he resides in a lone house not far from the Hall, and can still afford to keep "a man and a maid." And now, he says, the family is coming home to the Hall; the old blood-sucker, with his son and a daughter, Maud, whom he remembers as a little girl, "with her sweet purse-mouth, when my father dangled the grapes." He is determined not to fall in love with her, and the glance he gets of her as she passes in her carriage, assures him that he is in no danger from her "cold and clear-cut face,"—

> Faultily faultless, icily regular, splendidly null,
> Dead perfection, no more.

However, he does not escape from this first glance without

the "least little touch of the spleen," which the reader foresees is the germinal spot that is to develop itself into love. The first lines of any beauty in the poem are those in which he describes the "cold and clear-cut face," breaking his sleep, and haunting him "star-sweet on a gloom profound," till he gets up and walks away the wintry night in his own dark garden. Then Maud seems to look haughtily on him as she returns his bow, and he makes fierce resolves to flee from the cruel madness of love, and more especially from the love of Maud, who is "all unmeet for a wife;" but presently he hears her voice, which has a more irresistible magic even than her face. By-and-by she looks more benignantly on him, but his suspicious heart dares not sun itself in her smile, lest her brother—

> That jewell'd mass of millinery,
> That oil'd and curl'd Assyrian Bull,

may have prompted her to this benignity as a mode of canvassing for a vote at the coming election. A fresh circumstance is now added in the form of a new-made lord, apparently a suitor of Maud's—

> a captain, a padded shape,
> A bought commission, a waxen face,
> A rabbit mouth that is ever agape.

Very indignant is our hero with this lord's grandfather, for having made his fortune by a coal-mine, though the consideration that the said grandfather is now in "a blacker pit," is somewhat soothing to his chafed feelings. In the denunciations we have here of new-made fortunes, new titles, new houses, and new suits of clothes, it is evidently Mr. Tennyson's aversion, and not merely his hero's morbid mood, that speaks; and we must say, that this immense expenditure of gall on trivial social phases, seems to us intrinsically petty and snobbish. The gall presently overflows, as gall is apt to do, without any visible sequence of association, on Mr. Bright, who is denounced as—

> This broad-brimm'd hawker of holy things,
> Whose ear is stuft with his cotton, and rings
> Even in dreams to the chink of his pence.

In a second edition of *Maud,* we hope these lines will no longer appear on Tennyson's page: we hope he will by that time have recovered the spirit in which he once wrote how the "wise of heart"

> Would love the gleams of good that broke
> From either side, nor veil his eyes.

On the next page, he gives us an agreeable change of key in a little lyric, which will remind the German reader of Thekla's song. Here is the second stanza:—

> Let the sweet heavens endure,
> Not close and darken above me,
> Before I am quite, quite sure
> That there is one to love me;
> Then let come what come may
> To a life that has been so sad,
> I shall have had my day.

At length, after many alternations of feeling and metre, our hero becomes assured that he is Maud's accepted lover, and atones for rather a silly outburst, in which he requests the sky to

> Blush from West to East,
> Blush from East to West,
> Till the West is East,
> Blush it thro' the West,

by some very fine lines, of which we can only afford to quote the concluding ones:—

> Is that enchanted moan only the swell
> Of the long waves that roll in yonder bay?
> And hark the clock within, the silver knell
> Of twelve sweet hours that past in bridal white,
> And died to live, long as my pulses play;
> But now by this my love has closed her sight
> And given false death her hand, and stol'n away
> To dreamful wastes where footless fancies dwell
> Among the fragments of the golden day.
> May nothing there her maiden grace affright!
> Dear heart, I feel with thee the drowsy spell.
> My bride to be, my evermore delight,
> My own heart's heart and ownest own, farewell.
> It is but for a little space I go:
> And ye meanwhile far over moor and fell
> Beat to the noiseless music of the night!
> Has our whole earth gone nearer to the glow
> Of your soft splendours that you look so bright?
> *I* have climb'd nearer out of lonely Hell.
> Beat, happy stars, timing with things below,
> Beat with my heart more blest than heart can tell,
> Blest, but for some dark undercurrent woe
> That seems to draw—but it shall not be so:
> Let all be well, be well.

We are now approaching the crisis of the story. A grand dinner and a dance are to be held at the Hall, and the hero, not being invited, waits in the garden till the festivities are over, that Maud may then come out and show herself to him in all the glory of her ball-dress. Here occurs the invocation, which has been deservedly admired and quoted by every critic:—

> Come into the garden, Maud,
> For the black bat, night, has flown,—
> Come into the garden, Maud,
> I am here at the gate alone;
> And the woodbine spices are wafted abroad,
> And the musk of the roses blown.
>
> For a breeze of morning moves,
> And the planet of Love is on high,
> Beginning to faint in the light that she loves
> On a bed of daffodil sky,
> To faint in the light of the sun she loves,
> To faint in his light, and to die.

Very exquisite is that descriptive bit, in the second stanza, where the music of the verse seems to faint and die like the star. Still the whole poem, which is too long for us to quote, is very inferior, as a poem of the Fancy, to the **"Talking Oak."** We do not, for a moment, believe in the sensibility of the roses and lilies in Maud's garden, as we believe in the thrills felt to his "inmost ring" by the **"Old Oak of Summer Chace."** This invocation is the topmost note of the lover's joy. The interview in the garden is disturbed by the "Assyrian Bull" and the "padded shape." A duel follows, in which the brother is killed. And now we find the hero an exile on the Breton coast, where, from delivering some stanzas of Natural Theology *à propos* of a shell, he proceeds to retrace the sad memories of his love, until he becomes mad. We have then a Bedlam soliloquy, in which he fancies himself dead, and mingles with the images of Maud, her father, and her brother, his early-fixed idea—the police reports. From this madness he is recovered by the news that the Allies have declared war against Russia; whereupon he bursts into a pæan, that

> the long, long canker of Peace is over and done.

It is possible, no doubt, to allegorize all this into a variety of edifying meanings; but it remains true, that the ground-notes of the poem are nothing more than hatred of peace and the Peace Society, hatred of commerce and coal-mines, hatred of young gentlemen with flourishing whiskers and padded coats, adoration of a clear-cut face, and faith in War as the unique social regenerator. Such are the sentiments, and such is the philosophy embodied in **Maud;** at least, for plain people not given to allegorizing; and it, perhaps, speaks well for Tennyson's genius, that it has refused to aid him much on themes so little worthy of his greatest self. Of the smaller poems, which, with the well-known **"Ode,"** make up the volume, **"The Brook"** is rather a pretty idyl, and **"The Daisy"** a graceful, unaffected recollection of Italy; but no one of them is remarkable enough to be ranked with the author's best poems of the same class. (pp. 596-601)

> *George Eliot, in an originally unsigned essay titled "Belles Lettres," in* The Westminster and Foreign Quarterly Review, *Vol. LXIV, No. CXXVI, October, 1855, pp. 596-615.*

Walt Whitman   (essay date 1887)

[*Considered one of America's greatest poets, Whitman was a literary innovator whose poetry decisively influenced the development of modern free verse. His masterpiece, the poetry collection* Leaves of Grass *(1855), focused on themes of death, immortality, and democracy, and was controversial during the author's lifetime for its frank treatment of sexuality and lack of such conventional poetic devices as rhyme, regular meter, and uniform length of line and stanza. In the following essay, he reviews Tennyson's poetry from an American perspective.*]

Beautiful as the song was, the original **'Locksley Hall'** of half a century ago was essentially morbid, heart-broken, finding fault with everything, especially the fact of money's being made (as it ever must be, and perhaps should be) the paramount matter in worldly affairs.

> Every door is barr'd with gold, and opens but to
> golden keys.

First, a father, having fallen in battle, his child (the singer)

> Was left a trampled orphan, and a selfish uncle's
> ward.

Of course love ensues. The woman in the chant or monologue proves a false one; and as far as appears the ideal of woman, in the poet's reflections, is a false one, at any rate for America. Woman is *not* 'the lesser man.' (The heart

is not the brain.) The best of the piece of fifty years since is its concluding line:

> For the mighty wind arises roaring seaward and
> I go.

Then for this current 1886-7, a just-out sequel, which (as an apparently authentic summary says) 'reviews the life of mankind during the past sixty years, and comes to the conclusion that its boasted progress is of doubtful credit to the world in general and to England in particular. A cynical vein of denunciation of democratic opinions and aspirations runs throughout the poem, in marked contrast with the spirit of the poet's youth.' Among the most striking lines of this sequel are the following:

> Envy wears the mask of love, and, laughing
> sober fact to scorn,
> Cries to weakest as to strongest, 'Ye are equals,
> equal-born.'
> Equal-born! Oh yes, if yonder hill be level with
> the flat.
> Charm us, orator, till the lion look no larger
> than the cat;
> Till the cat, through that mirage of overheated
> language, loom
> Larger than the lion Demos—end in working its
> own doom.
>   . . . . .
>
> Tumble nature heel over head, and, yelling with
> the yelling street,
> Set the feet above the brain and swear the brain
> is in the feet.
> Bring the old Dark Ages back, without the faith,
> without the hope
> Beneath the State, the Church, the throne, and
> roll their ruins down the slope.

I should say that all this is a legitimate consequence of the tone and convictions of the earlier standards and points of view. Then some reflections, down to the hard-pan of this sort of thing.

The course of progressive politics (democracy) is so certain and resistless, not only in America but in Europe, that we can well afford the warning calls, threats, checks, neutralizings, in imaginative literature, or any department, of such deep-sounding and high-soaring voices as Carlyle's and Tennyson's. Nay, the blindness, excesses, of the prevalent tendency—the dangers of the urgent trends of our times—in my opinion, need such voices almost more than any. I should, too, call it a signal instance of democratic humanity's luck that it has such enemies to contend with—so candid, so fervid, so heroic. But why do I say enemy? Upon the whole is not Tennyson—and was not Carlyle (like an honest and stern physician)—the true friend of our age?

Let me assume to pass verdict, or perhaps momentary judgment, for the United States on this poet—a removed and distant position giving some advantages over a nigh one. What is Tennyson's service to his race, times, and especially to America? First, I should say, his personal character. He is not to be mentioned as a rugged, evolutionary, aboriginal force—but (and a great lesson is in it) he has been consistent throughout with the native, personal, healthy, patriotic spinal element and promptings of him-self. His moral line is local and conventional, but it is vital and genuine. He reflects the upper-crust of his time, its pale cast of thought—even its *ennui*. Then the simile of my friend John Burroughs is entirely true, 'his glove is a glove of silk, but the hand is a hand of iron.' He shows how one can be a royal laureate, quite elegant and 'aristocratic,' and a little queer and affected, and at the same time per-fectly manly and natural. As to his non-democracy, it fits him well, and I like him the better for it. I guess we all like to have (I am sure I do) some one who presents those sides of a thought, or possibility, different from our own—different, and yet with a sort of home-likeness—a tartness and contradiction offsetting the theory as we view it, and construed from tastes and proclivities not at all our own.

To me, Tennyson shows more than any poet I know (per-haps has been a warning to me) how much there is in finest verbalism. There is such a latent charm in mere words, cunning collocations, and in the voice ringing them, which he has caught and brought out, beyond all others—as in the line,

> And hollow, hollow, hollow, all delight,

in 'The Passing of Arthur,' and evidenced in 'The Lady of Shalott,' 'The Deserted House,' and many other pieces. Among the best (I often linger over them again and again) are 'Lucretius,' 'The Lotos Eaters,' and 'The Northern Farmer.' His mannerism is great, but it is a noble and wel-come mannerism. His very best work, to me, is contained in the books of *The Idylls of the King,* all of them, and all that has grown out of them. Though indeed we could spare nothing of Tennyson, however small or however pe-culiar—not 'Break, Break, Break' nor 'Flower in the Crannied Wall' nor the old, eterally-told passion of 'Ed-ward Gray:'

> Love may come and love may go,
> And fly like a bird from tree to tree
> But I will love no more, no more
> Till Ellen Adair come back to me.

Yes, Alfred Tennyson's is a superb character, and will help give illustriousness, through the long roll of time, to our Nineteenth Century. In its bunch of orbic names, shining like a constellation of stars, his will be one of the brightest. His very faults, doubts, swervings, doublings upon himself, have been typical of our age. We are like the voyagers of a ship, casting off for new seas, distant shores. We would still dwell in the old suffocating and dead haunts, remembering and magnifying their pleasant expe-riences only, and more than once impelled to jump ashore before it is too late, and stay where our fathers stayed, and live as they lived.

May-be I am non-literary and non-decorous (let me at least be human, and pay part of my debt) in this word about Tennyson. I want him to realize that here is a great and ardent Nation that absorbs his songs, and has a re-spect and affection for him personally, as almost for no other foreigner. I want this word to go to the old man at Farringford as conveying no more than the simple truth; and that truth (a little Christmas gift) no slight one either. I have written impromptu, and shall let it all go at that.

The readers of more than fifty millions of people in the New World not only owe to him some of their most agree-able and harmless and healthy hours, but he has entered into the formative influences of character here, not only in the Atlantic cities, but inland and far West, out in Mis-souri, in Kansas, and away in Oregon, in farmer's house and miner's cabin.

Best thanks, anyhow, to Alfred Tennyson—thanks and appreciation in America's name. (pp. 1-2)

> *Walt Whitman, "A Word about Tennyson," in* The Critic, *New York, Vol. 10, January 1, 1887, pp. 1-2.*

George Saintsbury   (essay date 1895)

[*Saintsbury has been called the most influential English literary historian and critic of the late nineteenth and early twentieth centuries. As a critic of poetry and drama, Saintsbury was a radical formalist who fre-quently asserted that subject is of little importance, and that "the so-called 'formal' part is of the essence." In the following excerpt, he praises the descriptive and rhyth-mic elements of Tennyson's verse.*]

[We] have quite recently found some persons saying that "Tennyson is as great as Shakespeare," and other people going into fits of wrath, or smiling surprise with calm dis-dain, at the saying. If what the former mean to say and what the latter deny is that Tennyson has a supreme and peculiar poetic charm, then I am with the former and against the latter. He has: and from the very fact of his having it he will not necessarily be appreciated at once, and may miss appreciation altogether with some people.

The recent publication anew of the earliest *Poems by Two Brothers* has been especially useful in enabling us to study this charm. In these poems it is absolutely nowhere: there is not from beginning to end in any verse, whether attri-buted to Alfred, Frederick, or Charles, one suggestion even of the witchery that we Tennysonians associate with the work of the first-named. It appears dimly and distant-ly—so dimly and distantly that one has to doubt whether we recognise it by anything but a "fallacy of looking back"—in **"Timbuctoo,"** in **"The Lovers' Tale"** quite dis-tinctly, but uncertainly; and with much alloy in the pieces which the author later labelled as "Juvenilia."

It is true that these "Juvenilia" have been a good deal re-touched, and that much of the really juvenile work on which the critics were by no means unjustly severe has been left out. But the charm is there. Take the very first stanza of **"Claribel."** You may pick holes in the conceit which makes a verb "I low-lie, thou low-liest, she low-lieth," and you may do other things of the same kind if you like. But who ever wrote like that before? Who struck that key earlier? Who produced anything like the slow, dreamy music of the variations in it? Spenser and Keats were the only two masters of anything in the remotest de-gree similar in English before. And yet it is perfectly inde-pendent of Spenser, perfectly independent of Keats. It is Tennyson, the first rustle of the "thick-leaved, ambrosial" murmuring which was to raise round English lovers of poetry a very Broceliande of poetical enchantment for sixty years to come during the poet's life, and after his death for as long as books can speak and readers hear. (pp. 28-30)

I believe that, in so far as the secret of a poet can be discovered and isolated, the secret of Tennyson lies in that slow and dreamy music . . . and I am nearly sure that my own admiration of him dates from the time when I first became aware of it. **"Claribel,"** of course, is by no means a very effective example; though the fact of its standing in the very forefront of the whole work is excessively interesting. The same music continued to sound—with infinite variety of detail, but with no breach of general character—from **"Claribel"** itself to **"Crossing the Bar."** At no time was Tennyson a perfect master of the quick and lively measures; and in comparison he very seldom affected them. He cannot pick up and return the ball of song as Praed—another great master of metre if not quite of music, who preceded him by seven years at Trinity—did, still less as Praed partly taught Mr. Swinburne to do. There is nothing in Tennyson of the hurrying yet never scurrying metre of "At a Month's End," or the Dedication to Sir Richard Burton. His difficulty in this respect has not improved **"The Charge of the Light Brigade,"** and it is noticeable that it impresses a somewhat grave and leisurely character even on his anapæsts,—as for instance in the **"Voyage of Maeldune."** If you want quick music you must go elsewhere, or be content to find the poet not at his best in it.

But in the other mode of linked and long-drawn out sweetness he has hardly any single master and no superior:

> At midnight the moon cometh
> And looketh down alone.

There again the despised **"Claribel"** gives us the cue. And how soon and how miraculously it was taken up, sustained, developed, varied, everybody who knows Tennyson knows. **"Mariana"** is the very incarnation, the very embodiment in verse of spell-bound stagnation, that is yet in the rendering beautiful. The **"Recollections of the Arabian Nights"** move something sprightlier, but the **"Ode to Memory,"** by far the greatest of the "Juvenilia," relapses into the visionary gliding. Even in **"The Sea Fairies"** and **"The Dying Swan,"** the occasional dactyls and anapæsts rather slide than skip; and the same is the case with the best lines in **"Oriana"** and (naturally enough) with the whole course of the **"Dirge."** All the ideal girl-portraits except **"Lilian"** (the least worthy of them) have this golden languor, which is so distinctly the note of the earlier poems that it is astonishing any one should ever have missed it. Yet, as I have said, I believe I missed it myself for some time, and certainly, judging from their criticisms, contemporaries of the poet much cleverer than I never seem to have heard it at all.

When the great collection came it must have been hard still to miss it; yet how little the English public even yet was attuned is shown by the fact that both then and since one of the most popular things has been *The May Queen,* which, if anything of Tennyson's could be so, I should myself be disposed to call trumpery. **"The Lady of Shalott"** is very far from trumpery, and perhaps the poet's very happiest thing not in a languid measure; but even **"The Lady of Shalott"** does not count among the poems that

established Tennyson's title to the first rank among English poets. **"The Lotos-Eaters," "The Palace of Art," "A Dream of Fair Women," "Œnone," "Ulysses,"** (though perhaps it will be said that I ought not to include blank verse pieces,) all have the trailing garments of the night, not the rush and skip of dawn; and though there are some exceptions among the rightly famous lyrics, such as **"Sir Galahad"** and the admirable piece of cynicism in **"The Vision of Sin,"** they are exceptions. Even **"Locksley Hall"** canters rather than gallops, and the famous verses in **"The Brook"** are but a *tour de force.*

But it would be impossible here to go through the whole of the poet's work. He can do many things; but he always (at least to my taste) does his best in lyric to slow music. And I doubt whether any one will again produce this peculiar effect as he has produced it. It must be evident, too, how much this faculty of slow and stately verse adds to the effect of *In Memoriam.* If the peculiar metre of that poem is treated (as I have known it treated by imitators) in a light and jaunty fashion—to quick time, so to speak— the effect is very terrible. But Tennyson has another secret than this for blank verse. This is the secret of the paragraph, which he alone of all English poets shares with Milton in perfection. There is little doubt that he learnt it from Milton, but the effect is quite different, though the means resorted to are necessarily much the same in both cases, and include in both a very careful and deliberate disposition of the full stop which breaks and varies the cadence of the line; the adoption when it is thought necessary of trisyllabic instead of disyllabic feet; and the arrangement of a whole block of verses so that they lead up to a climax of sense and sound in the final line. Almost the whole secret can be found in one of the earliest and perhaps the finest of his blank verse exercises, the **"Morte d'Arthur,"** but examples were never wanting up to his very last book.

These two gifts, that of an infinitely varied slow music and dreamy motion in lyric and that of concerted blank verse, with his almost unequalled faculty of observation and phrasing as regards description of nature, were, I think, the things in Tennyson which first founded Tennyson-worship in my case. And these, I am sure, are what have kept it alive in my case, though I have added to them an increasing appreciation of his wonderful skill in adjusting vowel values. His subjects matter little: I do not know that subject ever does matter much in poetry, though it is all important in prose. But if I have been right in my selection of his chief gifts, it will follow almost as the night the day that the vague, the antique, and to some extent the passionate, must suit him better than the modern, the precise, the meditative. Not that Tennyson is by any means as some misguided ones hold, a shallow poet; the exquisite perfection of his phrase and his horror of jargon have deceived some even of the elect on that point, just as there have been those who think that Plato is shallow because he is nowhere unintelligible, and that Berkeley cannot be a great philosopher because he is a great man of letters. But art, romance, distant history (for history of a certain age simply becomes romance), certainly suit him better than science, modern life, or argument. Vast efforts have been spent on developing schemes of modernised Christianity out of *In Memoriam;* but the religious element in that poem is as consistent with an antiquated orthodoxy as with anything new and undogmatic; and the attraction of the poem is in its human affection, in its revelation of the House of Mourning, and above all in those unmatched landscapes and sketches of which the poet is everywhere prodigal.

It is perhaps (if I may refine still further on the corrections of impressions which years of study have left) in the combination of the faculty of poetical music with that of poetical picture drawing that the special virtue of Tennyson lies. There have been poets, though not many, who could manage sound with equal skill; and there have been those, though not many, who could bring with a few modulated words a visual picture before the mind's eye and almost the eye of the body itself with equal sureness and success. But there have hardly been any, outside the very greatest Three or Four, who could do both these things at the same time in so consummate a fashion. The very musical poets are too apt to let the sharp and crisp definition of their picture be washed away in floods of sound; the very pictorial poets to neglect the musical accompaniment. Tennyson never commits either fault. The wonderful successions of cartoons in the **"Palace"** and the **"Dream"** exhibit this in his very earliest stage. If any one has ever in this combination of music, draughtsmanship, and colour equalled him who wrote,

> One seemed all dark and red, a tract of sand,
> And some one pacing there alone,
> Who paced for ever in a glimmering land,
> Lit with a low large moon,

I do not know him. The first stanza of **"The Lotos-Eaters"** has the same power of filling eye and ear at once, so that it is almost impossible to decide whether you hear the symphony or see the picture most clearly. And at the very other extreme of the poet's poetical life, in those famous lines which united all competent suffrages (though one egregious person I remember called them "homely" and divers wiseacres puzzled over the identity of the "pilot" and the propriety of his relation of place toward the "bar"), this master faculty again appeared.

> With such a tide as moving seems asleep,
> Too full for sound or foam,

are words which make the very picture, the very foamless swirl, the very soundless volume of sound, which they describe.

No! In the impressions given by such a poet as this, when they have been once duly and fairly received, there can be no correction, except a better and better appreciation of him as time goes on. The people who have liked what was not best, or have not liked what was best, may grow weary of well admiring. Those who look rather at the absence of faults than at the presence of beauties may point to incongruities and mediocrities, to attempts in styles for which the poet had little aptitude, to occasional relapses from the grand manner to the small mannerism, and so forth. But those whose ears and eyes (if not, alas! their lips) Apollo has touched, will never make any mistake about him. They may as in other—as in all—cases be more or fewer

as time goes on: there may be seasons when the general eye grows blind and the general ear deaf to his music and his vision. But that will not matter at all. So long as the unknown laws which govern the presentation of beauty in sight and sound last, beauty will be discovered here just as we ourselves after two thousand years find it in the ancient tongues which we cannot even pronounce with any certainty that we are nearer to the original than Mr. Hamerton's little French boy was when he tried to vocalise that very stanza of **"Claribel"**, to which I have referred above. (pp. 31-40)

> George Saintsbury, "Tennyson" and "Tennyson (Concluded)," in his Corrected Impressions: Essays on Victorian Writers, *Dodd, Mead and Company, 1895, pp. 21-30, 31-40.*

Harold Nicolson   (essay date 1925)

[*Nicolson was an English diplomat, politician, author, and critic who wrote prolifically on literature, history, and politics. In the following excerpt, he analyzes the strengths and weaknesses of Tennyson's poetry.*]

Were an anthology of Tennyson's poetry to be compiled for the purpose of including only such poems as can appeal directly to the literary taste of to-day, the result might well be both curious and illuminating. Such a volume would, in the first place, be far more bulky than might be imagined. And, in the second place, it would be found, I think, that in any honest and intelligent process of rejection and selection a great many of the more famous and popular poems would be discarded—it would be found, that is, that in the end the Victorian Tennyson, the didactic and the narrative Tennyson, had disappeared, and that someone quite different had emerged in his place. Were I myself to make such a selection, I should from the first be tempted to reject the **Idylls of the King,** the **Idylls of the Hearth,** or at any rate **Enoch Arden,** **"Dora"** and **"Sea Dreams,"** the "Keepsake" verses, most of the ballads and dramatic pieces, and some of the later theological compositions. I should also, I think, reject both the **"Locksley Halls."** On the other hand, I should include all the "Classical" poems, with the exception of **"Lucretius"** and **"The Death of Oenone"**; I should include nearly all the early Romantic poems, together with the **"Kraken"** and the **"Ode to Memory"**; I should give **"The Vision of Sin"** and **"The Palace of Art"** in their entirety; I should include **"The Northern Farmer,"** while rejecting the other dialect poems; I should give the lyrics from *The Princess* while omitting the main narrative; I should include the whole of **"The Two Voices"** and *Maud* and nearly the whole of *In Memoriam;* I should give **"Boädicea"** and the other experiments in quantity; and finally, I should retain practically all the occasional poems, the dedications, epitaphs and such pieces as **"The Daisy"** and **"Will Waterproof's Lyrical Monologue."**

Such a selection would doubtless be arbitrary and personal. I do not think, however, that, as regards the two general categories of the selected and the rejected, there would to-day be much dispute. For these categories do actually represent a basic divergence of taste between the nineteenth and the twentieth century; they represent, that is, the divergence between absolute or if you prefer it, "pure," poetry and applied poetry. For whereas the Victorians cared mainly for applied poetry, for poetry as a vehicle, either of instruction or diversion, for poetry either as a sermon or a novel; we, caring less for the object or even the form of a poem, insist that it shall possess an "absolute" quality, that it shall be an end unto itself. And it is because of this conviction of "poetry for poetry's sake," that we are particularly apt to resent the intrusion of any extraneous purpose. Now, the great mass of Tennyson's poetry is . . . "applied" poetry; nor, even as such, is it of a very high quality. His didactic poetry suffers from a lack of intellect and education, his dramatic poetry is marred by the fact that, unlike Browning, he was not a creative analyst of character. But if we can isolate this great mass of his "applied," of his didactic and narrative, poetry, there remains a very important residue of "absolute" poetry, and it is because of the value, of the very remarkable value, of this "absolute" poetry that he will survive.

For should anyone doubt the real importance of this distinction between the "absolute" and the "applied" poetry of Tennyson, let him cast a glance at the many incidental or occasional poems which figure in the collected works. Although these poems constitute applied poetry to the extent that they are written for the avowed purpose of conveying some compliment or message, yet the object of the poem is in effect subsidiary to the subject. The occasional verses of Tennyson stand, that is, midway between his subjective and his objective poetry. For whereas in the latter we are continually disconcerted by the suspicion that the thing could be done far better either in the form of a novel with a purpose or in a volume of philosophical or religious essays, in the former, in his lyrical poetry, we are convinced that verse alone offers the accordance form of expression. In the intermediary category of his occasional verses we may feel, of course, that he could as well have put it all into a letter, yet we must admit that his choice of the forms of verse has raised the communication to a far higher and more memorable level. And the fact that we are so pleasurably surprised by the quality of Tennyson's occasional verse shows, I think, that the moment he can rid himself of the obsession of his "message" and his mission, from that moment he begins to write very good poetry indeed. And if so slight a thing as incidental and often perfunctory versification can cause us pleasure, how far more penetrating should be the effect of those subjective emotions which forced him, almost against his will, to give them lyrical expression! (pp. 272-74)

Tennyson's occasional verses are, as I have said, of considerable interest, not only because of their intrinsic quality, but also because they are generally exempt from the intention of striking some particular attitude or conveying some particular moral. They are taken, so to speak, in his stride, and they show, better than his didactic poems or his cautionary tales, how wide, and indeed lavish, was his range of interest. They show him, moreover, in a pleasant light as a quite human, quite urbane, almost genial man of culture. They are an invaluable antidote to the Victorian fog which obscures so many of his poems. Even the odes which he would write from time to time in his official

capacity as Poet Laureate are better than those of his predecessors, infinitely better than those of his immediate successor and imitator in that office. They produce the same pleasurable feeling of satisfaction at the achievement of something intricate and deliberate, as is conveyed by a polished copy of Latin verses; and, of course, the Wellington ode is in a class by itself. But apart from the official poems, there is a great mass of incidental verse, dedications, epitaphs and the like, which, whether they be incised with the stately condensation of some Roman inscription, or composed with the flowing lucidity of some of the lighter odes of Horace, carry with them a very welcome and a very mellow savour of the humanities.

Take this, for instance, from the lines to F. D. Maurice:—

> You'll have no scandal while you dine,
> But honest talk and wholesome wine,
> And only hear the magpie gossip
> Garrulous under a roof of pine:
>
> For groves of pine on either hand,
> To break the blast of winter, stand;
> And further on, the hoary Channel
> Tumbles a billow on chalk and sand;
>
> Where, if below the milky steep
> Some ship of battle slowly creep,
> And on thro' zones of light and shadow
> Glimmer away to the lonely deep,
>
> We might discuss the Northern sin
> Which made a selfish war begin;
> Dispute the claims, arrange the chances;
> Emperor, Ottoman, which shall win.

Even better, perhaps, are the lines to FitzGerald, in which, after recalling his visit to Woodbridge in 1876, and the pigeons and the vegetarianism of it all, Tennyson sends his friend **"Tiresias"**:—

> which you will take
> My Fitz, and welcome, as I know,
> Less for its own than for the sake
> Of one recalling gracious times,
> When, in our younger London days,
> You found some merit in my rhymes,
> And I more pleasure in your praise.

One is pleased by the urbanity of this, by the supple Horatian felicity with which the last line closes the movement; and, indeed, there is a real place in poetry for the urbane. (pp. 274-76)

Equally intermediate in character is Tennyson's treatment of Nature. For although much of his Nature poetry is, it must be owned, written with the old desire to instruct, with the wish, even, to display his powers of observation, or his peculiar felicity in condensing such observation into accurate and concentrated expression, yet one has but to read through any of the longer poems to be pleasantly stimulated at recurrent intervals by some chance simile or illustration of Nature such as opens a sudden rift of blue in the heavy clouds which hang so often upon his poetry. It is not that Tennyson's Nature poetry is as a rule more subjective or more "absolute" than his other themes—it is that, in approaching the eternal and illimitable inspiration of Nature, the emotional ecstasy depends perhaps more upon the temperament of the reader than upon the imaginative impulse of the poet himself. For if the reader is at all sensitive to the inspiration of Nature, it will require but the slightest stimulus of "recognition," some incidental allusion vivid or merely accurate, in order to inflame his own imaginative recollection, and to afford him that startled realisation of the identity of the personal with the eternal which is, in effect, the essence of the highest poetic appreciation. As a theme, Nature herself contains all the necessary elements for such appreciation: she combines, in a perpetual surprise, the minute and the infinite, the precise and the unknowable, the momentary and the eternal. One has but to feel assured that the poet is himself sensitive to these sublime contrasts for his Nature poetry to be affected almost automatically, and by processes which, if applied to other themes, might well fail to produce any nervous vibration. And with Tennyson at least you have such an assurance. One of the few subjective poems which he wrote on this theme figures fittingly upon the base of his most appropriate statue, that rugged masterpiece of Watts which stands in shambling untidiness under the Lincolnshire sky and in the shadow of the three cathedral towers which grace and dominate the wide, sad county of his birth:—

> Flower in the crannied wall,
> I pluck you out of the crannies,
> I hold you here, root and all, in my hand,
> Little flower—but *if* I could understand
> What you are, root and all, and all in all,
> I should know what God and man is.

It is not, however, merely this sense of the spirituality of Nature which gives to Tennyson's treatment of the subject so peculiar an interest. It is also that his observation of Nature is curiously concentrated and detailed. This concentration arises, not only from his unwillingness to record facts which he had not actually experienced, or to describe phenomena which he had not actually examined, but also from the more practical cause of his extreme short sight. The result is that the Nature poetry of Tennyson so often deals, on the one hand, with the tiny and incidental phenomena of the foreground, and, on the other, with the vast and illimitable movements in the background: there is no middle distance. And, as a result, the essential contrast of Nature—the contrast between the microscopic and the illimitable, between the speedwell and the stars—is continually, even if only indirectly, emphasised. And the emotional reality of this contrast gives to Tennyson's Nature poetry, whether he be speaking of the minute or of the infinite, a very peculiar significance.

It is important, in discussing Tennyson's powers of observation, to keep in mind this emotional reality, since there are moments when his habits of accuracy, his method of storing and "working up later" some observed phenomena—the rippled shadow on a cow's neck when drinking, the foam flakes scudding along the beach at Mablethorpe, the flat leaves of water-lilies tugging at their stems in a gust of wind, the little tufts of thrift upon some Cornish headland—might savour otherwise of the perfunctory, or even of the prosaic. And it must be admitted that at times Tennyson's habits of accuracy, his predilection for the scientific, his sudden relapses into botany, his interest in pond

life, are apt to throw the shadow of "Madam How and Lady Why" over some of his most stimulating references to Nature. It is unfortunate, for instance, on reading in Section X of *In Memoriam* lines as good as:—

> Than if with thee the roaring wells
> Should gulf him fathom-deep in brine;
> And hands so often clasp'd in mine
> Should toss with tangle and with shells,

to turn to the note and find the following:—

> Section X, verse v, *tangle,* or "oar-weed" (*Laminaria digitata*).

But then the notes to the Eversley Edition should in any case be read only by the healthy-minded.

If we are resolved, therefore, to steel ourselves against these relapses into the accurate, and to bear in mind Tennyson's essentially emotional attitude towards Nature, his powers of observation and portrayal will then become for us of great value and interest. For how often, and with what economy of language, does he set before us such penetrating touches as the soft smell of the earth after rain, as the colours of the autumn woods reeling behind the smoke of burning weeds, as the crumpled leaf of a poppy when first liberated from its sheath, as the rustle of the poplar leaves like the patter of rain, as the breeze of early dawn stirring the flowers of a garden, or as the sound in every mood of falling waters? It may be said, of course, that his pictures of Nature savour too much of the Rectory garden, of the soft, steaming monochrome of the Isle of Wight, of the trim complacency of Surrey; that they recall a little too vividly the water-colours of Mrs. Allingham.

There are moments when this is true enough, such as the description of the cottage-gardens, in **"Aylmer's Field"**:—

> Her art, her hand, her counsel all had wrought
> About them: here was one that, summer-
>   blanch'd,
> Was parcel-bearded with the traveller's-joy
> In autumn, parcel ivy-clad; and here
> The warm-blue breathings of a hidden hearth
> Broke from a bower of vine and honeysuckle:
> One look'd all rosetree, and another wore
> A close-set robe of jasmine sown with stars:
> This had a rosy sea of gillyflowers
> About it; this. . . .
> A lily-avenue climbing to the doors;
> One, almost to the martin-haunted eaves
> A summer burial deep in hollyhocks.

All this perhaps is too sweet to be wholly true. But in the main the Nature poetry of Tennyson, restricted as it is to his actual range of observation, is a faithful and stimulating picture of English country scents and sounds and habits. (pp. 277-80)

If Tennyson's appreciation of the more tender processes of Nature has, perhaps, too domestic a flavour, his sense of the infinities of sea and sky is on a larger, and indeed a sterner, scale. Ever since his schoolboy days, the sense of water, the sound of water, had meant a great deal to him, and his earlier poems abound with impressions of the great North Sea rollers booming along the flat beach at Mablethorpe. The Isle of Wight, when it came, furnished him with other scenes and echoes, and with the scream of the shingle sucked back by the retreating wave. His visits to Cornwall gave him one simile, at least, of arresting truth and beauty:—

> So dark a forethought roll'd about his brain
> As on a dull day in an Ocean cave
> The blind wave feeling round his long sea-hall
> In silence.

His voyage to Norway in 1858 remains in one of his few deep-sea similes:—

>   as a wild wave in the wide North Sea
> Green-glimmering toward the summit, bears, with all
> Its stormy crests that smoke against the skies
> Down on a bark, and overbears the bark . . .

And finally it was the slow movement of Lymington harbour-mouth which inspired what is perhaps the finest of all his references to the sea:—

> But such a tide as moving seems asleep,
> Too full for sound and foam,
> When that which drew from out the boundless deep
> Turns again home.

Of his sense of the infinity of space I have already spoken, but some further mention must here be made of the many striking passages in which he speaks of the stars. His knowledge of astronomy was slightly above that of the ordinary amateur, and we hear of him in the 'sixties going down frequently to Fairfax road to look through Lockyer's six-inch equatorial. And after dinner, sometimes, at Farringford, he would take them all on to the roof and point out Venus. "Can you imagine," he would say, as he said later in the second **"Locksley Hall,"** "roaring London and raving Paris *there* in that point of peaceful light?" "While I said *there*," he would add, "the earth has whirled twenty miles." Scattered throughout his poems there are many passages which show how deep was the feeling which possessed him for the majesty and the distance of the stars. As early as the first **"Locksley Hall"** we hear of "great Orion sloping slowly to the West," or we find him watching the Pleiades:—

>   rising thro' the mellow shade,
> Glitter like a swarm of fire-flies tangled in a silver braid.

And later, when his renown had grown to wider proportions, he would gaze at the Nebula in the sword of Orion and be filled with dismay at the insignificance of human fame:—

> A single misty star
> Which is the second in a line of stars
> That seem a sword beneath a belt of three,
> I never gazed upon it but I dreamt
> Of some vast charm concluded in that star
> To make fame nothing.

If, therefore, we can find in the felicitous humanism of Tennyson's incidental verses a relief from the heavy shallowness of his didactic and narrative poetry; if we can discover in his loving and precise observation of Nature an interest which is quite detached from the usual conception of him as devoted only to the applied purposes of poetry; we can also, I think, look to his technical proficiency as a master of the English language to provide a genuine stirring of purely literary enjoyment.

I have not the aptitude, nor indeed the space, to discuss in detail the technical aspects of Tennyson's prosody and language. Much has been written on the subject. . . . It may be said, perhaps, that he never fully justified the prosodic promise of his early poems, which, tentative as they were, yet showed a metrical originality such as causes us to wonder at the contemporary strictures of Coleridge and the later criticisms of Swinburne. The extraordinary dexterity with which, by the shifting of the stress, by the interchange of vowel sounds, and by the use, and sometimes the abuse, of alliteration, he was able to vary the inherent monotony of **In Memoriam;** the mastery which he abundantly displayed in the trochaic measure—a measure so naturally adapted to the English language; the success of his experiments in quantity, of such pieces as the Phalaecian hendecasyllables, or **"The Battle of Brunanburh,"** make one regret that he was not more often, as in **"The Daisy,"** tempted to adopt original verse forms, and that he confined himself predominantly to blank verse, in which, proficient as he indubitably was, he did not possess the skill of Browning or the mellow movement even of Matthew Arnold. One has only to read the panting, spasmodic interjections of **Maud,** or the frenzied sweep of **"Boädicea,"** the rattling galliambics of which, so unlike the effeminacy of the **"Attis,"** have all the fire of Borodin's *Igor,* to realise what a remarkable talent Tennyson possessed for accommodating the movement of his verse to its subject, for marking the gradations of his theme by the subtlest changes of key or intonation.

His skill in this important and intricate branch of his art is conveniently illustrated by his famous lines to Catullus. He had, in the summer of 1880, been travelling in the Dolomites with his son, Hallam Tennyson. They had gone down to Garda and had rowed out one evening to the peninsula of Sirmio. As they rowed across the lake the poignant movement of the old Catullan choriambics, fused with the elegiacs to his brother, mingled in the poet's consciousness with the rhythmic beating of the oar:—

> Paene insularum, Sirmio, insularumque.

and he produced the following famous stanza:—

> Row us out from Desenzano, to your Sirmione row!
> So they row'd, and there we landed—"O venusta Sirmio"—
> There to me thro' all the groves of olive in the summer glow,
> There beneath the Roman ruin where the purple flowers grow,
> Came the "Ave atque Vale" of the Poet's hopeless woe,
> Tenderest of the Roman poets, nineteen hundred years ago,
> "Frater Ave atque Vale"—as we wandered to and fro
> Gazing at the Lydian laughter of the Garda Lake below

> Sweet Catullus' all-but-island, olive-silvery Sir-
>   mio!

The subtlety with which these lines are constructed, in-stinctive and subconscious as they probably were, merits some analysis. For, of the two currents of emotion which gave birth to the poem, the first is the actual beauty of the moment—the flat lake, the encircling mountains and the Italian boatmen, singing, doubtless, to their oars—and the second is the plangent recollection of Catullus—of how, so many years ago, he had looked upon this little jutting strip of olives as his own, how he had come so gaily back to it from Bithynia, and how he had lost the brother whom he loved. There are therefore two musical *motifs* in the poem—the *motif* of the rowers, represented by the vowel "o," and the *motif* of Catullus, represented by the broad Roman "a." The music is set to eight rhythmic beats, as is general in all such water songs from the Volga to the Elbe, and in the first line, as well as in the first two beats of the second, the rowing motif predominates. With the broader vowel of "landed," however, it ceases to ob-trude—becomes indeed an undertone to what follows and passes in recurrent echoes among the hills. The transition between the "o" motif and the "a" motif is marked by the intermediately broad vowel of "there," which word is re-peated and echoed predominantly in the two lines that fol-low. In the fifth line, the "a" *motif* is definitely introduced by the "Ave atque Vale," which is repeated in the opening of the seventh line, and echoed in the lesser tones of "wan-dered," "at," "Lydian," "laughter," "Garda" in the verse that follows. And the poem ends with the sighing rustle of the concluding line, in which the two dominant *motifs* are fused in a crowd of gentler vowels. (pp. 282-86)

This very dexterous manipulation of vowel sounds can be illustrated from other poems of Tennyson, and might be said, indeed, to constitute his most original contribution to the harmonics of the English language. We have the au-thority of Sir C. Stanford that "it was his perfection of vowel balance which made his poetry so difficult to set to music," and he was himself fully aware of his talent in this direction, and would at times exploit it somewhat unduly. He would take infinite trouble to exclude the harsher gut-turals and sibilants from his verse, and he had a prejudice against the vowels "i" and "ē." He even went so far on one occasion as to inform Rawnsley that "the finest line he had ever written" was:—

> The mellow ouzel fluted in the elm.

It must be admitted, indeed, that Tennyson was apt to ex-aggerate the importance of harmonics, and to rely a little too often and too lavishly upon the mere devices of verse—upon onomatopœia, epanaphora and alliteration. (pp. 286-87)

[Tennyson's use of the onomatopœic device] was a talent which was inherent in him, and as early as **"Mariana"** we find:—

> The sparrow's chirrup on the roof,
> The slow clock ticking, and the sound
> Which to the wooing wind aloof
> The poplar made. . . .

In later years the thing became a habit, and of almost irri-tating frequency. For while one can well admire the "moan of doves in immemorial elms," the "murmuring of innumerable bees," and the "long wash of Australasian seas," one cannot wholly welcome such expressions as "oilily bubbled up the mere," or such a simile as:—

> like an iron-clanging anvil banged
> With hammers.

Nor can the device be wholly legitimate when applied to visual and not to aural impressions, as in the following:—

> And I rode on and found a mighty hill
> And on the top a city wall'd: the spires
> Prick'd with incredible pinnacles into heaven.

But at its best the use which Tennyson makes of ono-matopœia is effective enough, and one cannot but respect the skill with which the introduction of the four leading labials in the last two lines of the following passage marks the transition from the preceding gutturals:—

> Dry clashed his harness in the icy caves
> And barren chasms, and all to left and right
> The bare black cliff clang'd round him as he
>   based
> His feet on juts of slipping crag that rang
> Sharp-smitten with the dint of armed heels—
> And on a sudden, lo! the level lake
> And the long glories of the winter moon.

Coupled with Tennyson's use of onomatopœia must be mentioned his employment of the devices of epanaphora, or repetition, and alliteration. The former he could use, at times, with great effect, as when:—

> The rain of heaven and their own bitter tears,
> Tears, and the careless rain of heaven mixt
> Upon their faces;

or even when:—

> The lizard, with his shadow on the stone
> Rests like a shadow;

but in his narrative poems, and with the purpose of giving an impression of speed and continuity to his blank verse, he is apt to employ the device with too much frequency, and we find, for instance, in a passage of **The Princess,** fourteen out of seventeen consecutive lines beginning with the same word: "and."

His abuse of the trick of alliteration has been severely commented on. He derived it, doubtless, as he derived his onomatopœia, from too appreciative a study of the *Æneid.* But at times, and in combination with onomatopœia, he can use it with almost miraculous effect, as in the inter-change of the letters "d," "s" and "h" in the famous Wye passage of **In Memoriam:**—

> The Danube to the Severn gave
> The darken'd heart that beat no more;
> They laid him by the pleasant shore,
> And in the hearing of the wave.
>
> There twice a day the Severn fills;
> The salt sea-water passes by,
> And hushes half the babbling Wye,
> And makes a silence in the hills.
>
> The Wye is hush'd nor moved along,

And hush'd my deepest grief of all,
When fill'd with tears that cannot fall,
I brim with sorrow drowning song.

I have dealt hitherto with the more technical aspects of Tennyson's style, its general beauties being sufficiently obvious and familiar. The development of his style was, in truth, as has been said, a progression "from the luxuriant to the heroic." The early affectations, the lispings of **"Claribel,"** the abundance of epithets, the abuse of double or archaic words disappeared with his increasing power of selection and condensation. This power of condensation, which was indeed remarkable, led him at times into irritating tricks of periphrasis and elaboration. The sea becomes "the ocean mirrors rounded large," a poacher appears as "the nightly wirer of the innocent hare," and "the foaming grape of Eastern France" is, I suppose, to be interpreted as champagne. Such tricks are harmless enough, and have their precedent in even greater poetry, but there are occasions when Tennyson's use of periphrasis is illegitimate, in that it deliberately produces a false sense of beauty. The lines, for instance:—

Or where the kneeling hamlet drains
The chalice of the grapes of God,

do not, as one vaguely hopes, refer to some village in the Alban hills, but to early service at Clevedon parish church; and the simplicity essential to his meaning is marred by the elaboration of the language in which that meaning is conveyed. Nor am I one of those who relish the verbal contortions in which the game-pie of **"Audley Court"** is so intricately involved; for food, apart from drink, is a subject for epic poetry alone.

Such elaboration is not, however, the dominant characteristic of Tennyson's maturer style, and indeed, one can observe in his later poems a determined endeavour to prefer the direct to the elaborate, and even the Anglo-Saxon to the Latin word. Nor does he indulge over-much in the device, so popular with English poets from Milton to Flecker, of enlivening the grey colours of our native speech by the introduction of resonant and flamboyant foreign names. He is at his best, and he knows that he is at his best, in the flow of direct and simple narrative, as in the nine initial lines with which the scenery of the sea-village is sketched as the introduction to *Enoch Arden.* And indeed the impression which emerges from any unbiassed reading of Tennyson is not that of his many tricks and affectations, but of a very outright simplicity, continuity and stateliness; more definitely, perhaps, of a remarkable gift of condensation, of a condensation which could produce such lines as the following:—

And one, the reapers at their sultry toil.
In front they bound the sheaves. Behind
Were realms of upland, prodigal in oil,
And hoary to the wind,

and of a directness which could evolve:—

Not wholly in the busy world, nor quite
Beyond it, blooms the garden that I love.
News from the humming city comes to it
In sound of funeral or of marriage bells;
And, sitting muffled in dark leaves, you hear

Tennyson at about 30 years of age.

The windy clanging of the Minster clock;
Although between it and the garden lies
A league of grass, wash'd by a slow broad
    stream,
That, stirred with languid pulses of the oar,
Waves all its lazy lilies, and creeps on,
Barge-laden, to three arches of a bridge,
Crown'd with the Minster towers.

The fields between
Are dewy-fresh, browsed by deep-udder'd kine,
And all about the large lime-feathers blow,
The lime a summer home of murmurous
    wings. . . .

(pp. 288-92)

In its technical and narrow sense lyrical poetry implies a form of words written to be sung to the lyre or other accompaniment; in its applied and extended meaning it is interpreted as the poetry of personal experience or emotion. The latter interpretation is the more comprehensive and important. The former, however, is not without its interest and its instances. For the songs of Tennyson, written separately as interludes to break the flow of narrative, are among the best in the English language, and in them we find, as rarely in his other poems, the absolute vatic ecstasy; the "purest" poetry, perhaps, which he ever composed. For in his songs, and predominantly in the songs incorporated in *The Princess,* his poetic energy was concentrated wholly on the magic of words. He sang, for once, "but as the linnets sing"; he sang, for once, "without a conscience and an aim." The result comes to one with a shock of delight. For they vibrate, these songs of Tennyson, with something vague and poignant, with:—

> I knew not what of wild and sweet,
> Like that strange song I heard Apollo sing
> While Ilion like a mist rose into towers.

And they vibrate with more than this—they vibrate, at last, with that "divine excess," with that glimpse of the Dionysiac, that unmistakable sense of impulsive continuity falling haphazard upon the right, the only word; they vibrate with that conviction of the inevitable and the inimitable, with that conviction of the inspired, which only the greatest lyric poets can achieve in the moments when they feel the force and beauty of their own genius:—

> For Love is of the valley, come thou down
> And find him; by the happy threshold, he,
> Or hand in hand with Plenty in the maize,
> Or red with spirted purple of the vats,
> Or fox-like in the vine; nor cares to walk
> With Death and Morning or the silver horns,

or again:—

> Now sleeps the crimson petal, now the white;
> Nor waves the cypress in the palace walk;
> Nor winks the gold fin in the porphyry font:
> The fire-fly wakens: waken thou with me.
>
> Now droops the milk-white peacock like a ghost,
> And like a ghost she glimmers on to me.
>
> Now lies the earth all Danäe to the stars,
> And all thy heart lies open unto me.
>
> Now slides the silent meteor on, and leaves
> A shining furrow, as thy thoughts in me.
>
> Now folds the lily all her sweetness up,
> And slips into the bosom of the lake:
> So fold thyself, my dearest, thou, and slip
> Into my bosom and be lost in me.

This poem is clearly beyond criticism and even elucidation. The sheer melody of the verse, unaided as it is by the agency of rhyme, is by itself remarkable. The poem can stand, I think, second only to the odes of Keats, to which, in the quality of its inspiration, it bears a resemblance, faint but unmistakable. And unconscious, also. For although the critic may find in the skill with which the word "up" is placed at the end of the last stanza an echo of the even greater skill which induced Keats to construct the Ruth stanza of the "Nightingale" upon the corner-stone of "hath," yet with Tennyson it is evident and welcome that this song at least came all unconsciously, and with such elaboration only as is given to something born already essentially completed from the soul.

Nor are his other songs, although they seldom reel to the same drunken sense of beauty, much inferior in quality. The first verse, at least, of **"Ask Me No More,"** with the sad echo of the hollow-toned vowels in which he so delighted, and with the skilful shifting of the stress in the fourth line, is haunting enough:—

> Ask me no more: the moon may draw the sea;

> The cloud may stoop from heaven and take the
>   shape,
> With fold to fold, of mountain or of cape;
> But O too fond, when have I answer'd thee?
>
>   Ask me no more.

Nor can I see how the two following verses, familiar as they are, can fail to be classed in the first rank of lyrical poetry:—

> Ah, sad and strange as in dark summer dawns
> The earliest pipe of half-awaken'd birds
> To dying ears, when unto dying eyes
> The casement slowly grows a glimmering
>   square;
> So sad, so strange, the days that are no more.
>
> Dear as remember'd kisses after death,
> And sweet as those by hopeless fancy feigned
> On lips that are for others; deep as love,
> Deep as first love, and wild with all regret;
> O Death in Life, the days that are no more.

And with what relief from the panting spasms of *Maud* do we slide into:—

> There has fallen a splendid tear
> From the passion flower at the gate.
> She is coming, my dove, my dear;
> She is coming, my life, my fate;
> The red rose cries, "She is near, she is near,"
> And the white rose weeps, "She is late."
> The larkspur listens, "I hear, I hear,"
> And the lily whispers, "I wait."

Few indeed are the occasions when Tennyson rises to his own poetic level, when the tremulous intensity of his emotion wells up suddenly within him and passes into that plangent wistfulness to which his lyre was so perfectly attuned. "A little flash" will come to him at moments, "a mystic hint," and, suddenly, he will write songs such as these, or let fall a verse such as:—

> Between the loud streams and the trembling
>   stars,

or conceive **"Ulysses,"** and the inspired line:—

> And see the great Achilles whom we knew,

or strike upon the infinite beauty of the conclusion to **"Tithonus":**—

> Thou seest all things, thou wilt see my grave:
> Thou wilt renew thy beauty morn by morn;
> I earth in earth forget these empty courts,
> And thee returning on thy silver wheels.

It is with an almost melancholy satisfaction that one cites these scattered instances of poetic ecstasy, regretting, as one cannot but regret, how few they are, how seldom they occur, how rarely—how very rarely—the wide and continuous middle level of his poetry is relieved even by the swallow-flights of song. One feels that, like the youthful horseman of the **"Vision of Sin":**—

> He rode a horse with wings, that would have
>   flown,
> But that his heavy rider kept him down.

This may be so. But even if we are of those who resent the

fact that Tennyson was so emphatically not "of the howling dervishes of song," we must admit, I think, that his "middle level" is in itself a remarkable achievement of stately continuity and craftsmanship. (pp. 293-96)

And then there is *In Memoriam.* Not that artificially constructed synthesis which appeard in 1850, with its prologue and its epilogue, with its three arbitrary divisions of Despair, Regret and Hope, ticked off symmetrically by the successive Christmas Odes; not the theological treatise on the conflict between faith and doubt, religion and dogma, belief and science; but the original Μηνισ; those plangent elegies which were scribbled in the old account-book, scribbled in odd unhappy moments during the seven years from 1833 to 1840; those lonely, wistful, frightened elegies. (pp. 296-97)

For the most durable impression of *In Memoriam* is that of a poem which renders, with an infinitely subtle melody, the "muffled motions" of a human soul overwhelmed by some immense personal disaster, of a soul crushed suddenly by irreparable grief. There is the first numbed insensibility to what has happened—his mind dwells only on the physical aspect, the dumb thought that "he is gone," the instinctive fusion of Arthur Hallam with the ship sailing slowly with his coffin from Trieste; the relief at feeling that he is at last in England; the incredible fact that one so vivid and so intimate should suddenly have become speechless and unreveal'd—the cry "Where wert thou, brother, those four days?" And, on the heels of this, the identification of his own blind sorrow with the dumb movements of Nature:—

> But Summer on the steaming floods,
> And Spring that swells in narrow brooks,
> And Autumn, with a noise of rooks,
> That gather in the waning woods,
>
> And every pulse of wind and wave
> Recalls, in change of light or gloom,
> My old affection of the tomb,
> And my prime passion in the grave.

In section after section we have the sensitive response of his bruised and languid nerves to the moods of Nature. Whether it be that first sad October:—

> Calm is the morn without a sound,
> Calm as to suit a calmer grief,
> And only thro' the faded leaf
> The chestnut pattering to the ground:
>
> Calm and deep peace on this high wold,
> And on these dews that drench the furze,
> And all the silvery gossamers
> That twinkle into green and gold:
>
> Calm and still light on yon great plain
> That sweeps with all its autumn bowers,
> And crowded farms and lessening towers,
> To mingle with the bounding main:
>
> Calm and deep peace in this wide air,
> These leaves that redden to the fall;
> And in my heart, if calm at all,
> If any calm, a calm despair,

or the wilder month that followed:—

> To-night the winds begin to rise
> And roar from yonder dropping day;
> The last red leaf is whirl'd away,
> The rooks are blown about the skies;
>
> The forest crack'd, the waters curl'd,
> The cattle huddled on the lea;
> And wildly dash'd on tower and tree
> The sunbeam strikes along the world:
>
> And but for fancies, which aver
> That all thy motions gently pass
> Athwart a plane of molten glass,
> I scarce could brook the strain and stir
>
> That makes the barren branches loud;
> And but for fear it is not so,
> The wild unrest that lives in woe
> Would dote and pore on yonder cloud
>
> That rises upward always higher,
> And onward drags a labouring breast,
> And topples round the dreary west,
> A looming bastion fringed with fire.

With this despair mingles the galling sense of waste, of resentment almost, that he who bore "the weight of all the hopes of half the world," that so radiant a promise, should have been quenched as if gratuitously. Such thoughts flit sombrely, with sad, incessant wings pulsating in the dim recesses of the poet's grief, and

> circle moaning in the air
> Is this the end? Is this the end?

They kill within him the interest of life itself, the joy even of the coming spring, the love of home; they "make a desert in the mind"; the "purple from the distance dies"; the "bases of his life" are drowned in tears. And through this veil of tears looms gradually the great problem of immortality, the agonised faith in ultimate reunion, the struggling hope, the torturing doubt, the dread of Nature's vicious cruelty:—

> I falter where I firmly trod,
> And falling with my weight of cares
> Upon the great world's altar stairs
> That slope thro' darkness up to God
>
> I stretch lame hands of faith, and grope,
> And gather dust and chaff, and call
> To what I feel is Lord of all,
> And faintly trust the larger hope.

In the pauses of such bitter spasms he dwells with almost morbid insistence on the past: he forces himself to recall the features and the accents of his friend, he visualises little vivid incidents in that dawn-golden time, he traces lovingly the course of those four years of friendship, the "tracts that pleased us well," the "path by which we twain did go"; and in an agony he cries:—

> How changed from when it ran
> Thro' lands where not a leaf was dumb;
> But all the lavish hills would hum
> The murmur of a happy Pan.

And thus gradually, through bitter reactions and long pauses of uncertainty, he works out his conviction of love and immortality. But the interest of *In Memoriam,* to me at least, centres not in the triumphant notes of its conclusions, but in the moods of terror and despair through which the ultimate conviction is attained.

Again and again this terror would seize and rack him, leaving him with quivering pulses sobbing as:—

> An infant crying in the night,
> An infant crying for the light
> And with no language but a cry.

There are moments, such as the first anniversary of Hallam's death, when the wan hopelessness of it all descends upon him as a cloud:—

> Risest thou thus, dim dawn, again,
> And howlest, issuing out of night,
> With blasts that blow the poplar white,
> And lash with storm the streaming pane?
>
> Day, when my crown'd estate begun
> To pine in that reverse of doom,
> Which sicken'd every living bloom,
> And blurr'd the splendour of the sun;
>
> Who usherest in the dolorous hour
> With thy quick tears that make the rose
> Pull sideways, and the daisy close
> Her crimson fringes to the shower, . . .
>
> Lift as thou may'st thy burthen'd brows
> Thro' clouds that drench the morning star,
> And whirl the ungarner'd sheaf afar,
> And sow the sky with flying boughs,
>
> And up thy vault with roaring sound
> Climb thy thick noon, disastrous day;
> Touch thy dull goal of joyless gray,
> And hide thy shame beneath the ground.

And there are moments, "in the dead unhappy night, and when the rain is on the roof," when he is in the dark and alone, when he lies there with the moon upon his bed, and the sense of night around him—moments when his nerves ache with fear and loneliness; moments when he sees:—

> A gulf that ever shuts and gapes,
> A hand that points, and palled shapes
> In shadowy thoroughfares of thought;
>
> And crowds that stream from yawning doors,
> And shoals of pucker'd faces drive;
> Dark bulks that tumble half alive,
> And lazy lengths on boundless shores.

It was at moments such as this, when "the blood creeps and the nerves prick," that he would yearn with passionate intensity for Hallam, that he would lie there crushed by his own fear and loneliness, and that he would cry out in agony:—

> Speak to me from the stormy sky!
> The wind is loud in holt and hill,
> It is not kind to be so still,
> Speak to me, dearest, lest I die.

This haunting wail of fear and loneliness piercing at moments through the undertones of **In Memoriam,** echoes a note which runs through all the poetry of Tennyson, and which, when once apprehended, beats with pitiful persistence on the heart. It proceeds from that grey region between the conscious and the unconscious; from that dim glimmering land where mingle the "Voices of the Dark" and the "Voices of the Day"; from the uncertain shadow-edges of consciousness in which stir the evanescent memories of childhood or the flitting shapelessness of half-forgotten dreams. It is a cry that mingles with the mystery of wide spaces, of sullen sunsets or of sodden dawns; the cry of a child lost at night time; the cry of some stricken creature in the dark; "the low moan of an unknown sea":—

> The first gray streak of earliest summer-dawn
> The last long stripe of waning crimson gloom,
> As if the late and early were but one—
> A height, a broken grange, a grove, a flower
> Had murmurs "Lost and gone and lost and
>   gone":
> A breath, a whisper—Some divine farewell—
> Desolate sweetness—far and far away.

And thus, in that "ever-moaning battle in the mist" which was the spiritual life of Tennyson, there were sudden penetrating moments when he would obtain:—

> A glimpse of that dark world where I was born;

when, once again, the "old mysterious glimmer" would steal into his soul, and when, in a sombre flash of vision, he would see his life:—

> all dark and red—a tract of sand,
> And someone pacing there alone,
> Who paced for ever in a glimmering land,
> Lit with a low large moon.

To the vibration of so sad a cadence I should wish to leave him, trusting that the ultimate impression, thus attuned, will prove more poignant and more durable than any hollow reverence for what was once admired. The age of Tennyson is past; the ideals which he voiced so earnestly have fallen from esteem. The day may come, perhaps, when the conventions of that century will once again inspire the thoughtful or animate the weak. But, for the moment, it is not through these that any interest can be evoked. And thus, we consider it reasonable and right that Tennyson should also stand among the poets, let us, for the present, forget the delicate Laureate of a cautious age; the shallow thought, the vacant compromise; the honeyed idyll, the complacent ode; let us forget the dulled monochrome of his middle years, forget the magnolia and the roses, the indolent Augusts of his island-home; forget the laurels and the rhododendrons.

Let us recall only the low booming of the North Sea upon the dunes; the grey clouds lowering above the wold; the moan of the night wind on the fen; the far glimmer of marsh-pools through the reeds; the cold, the half-light, and the gloom. (pp. 297-303)

Harold Nicolson, in his Tennyson: Aspects of His Life, Character and Poetry, *Houghton, Mifflin Company, 1925, 308 p.*

Michael Wheeler on Tennyson's theology:

Like Arthur Hallam, [Tennyson] believed that mankind could partake of God's loving nature, and that this was made possible in the incarnation. Claims that his hopes for the development of mankind are confused with his Christian hope of personal immortality take no account of his theomorphic conception of mankind, of which Hallam was the principal exemplum. The better world for which Hallam was created—and here was the final and most fruitful ambiguity associated with his death—is both here and elsewhere. He was taken before the time was ripe from a world which he would have made better had he survived, but he represented to Tennyson a sign of God's loving nature, made in God's image, which gave the poet hope for the future of the race and for continued development in heaven. Tennyson's larger hope was for the endurance of individuality after death, for the eventual salvation of the whole world, and, linked with the latter, a broader kind of Christianity, grounded in love.

Michael Wheeler, in his Death and the Future Life in Victorian Literature and Theology, *1990.*

Patrick Greig Scott   (essay date 1980)

[*An English educator, editor, and critic, Scott is author of* Tennyson's "Enoch Arden": A Victorian Best-Seller *(1970). In the following essay, he illustrates how Tennyson's style offers insight into the poet's views on the nature of language.*]

Perhaps one of the most notable, and certainly one of the most interesting, trends in recent Tennyson criticism has been renewed attention to Tennyson's style. Titles like F. E. L. Priestley's *Language and Structure in Tennyson's Poetry* (1973), Alan Sinfield's *The Language of Tennyson's "In Memoriam"* (1971), or W. D. Shaw's *Tennyson's Style* (1976) reflect a new emphasis very different from that of the previous generation of Tennyson critics, who were concerned with alien visions, themes and symbols, and the growth of the poet's mind. Even the more general books of the 1970's, such as the biographically oriented studies by Christopher Ricks and Paul Turner, show a new fascination with the detail of the Tennysonian idiolect. Little of this new criticism (apart from Alan Sinfield's book on *In Memoriam*) makes much technical use of modern linguistics, but it has shown the enormous sophistication in Tennyson's use of language, and has shared with the linguisticians the conviction that it is in the idiosyncrasies of the syntactic structures of a work that we come closest to recognizing the individuality of an author's mind.

What is striking, however, is how relatively silent the recent studies have been about Tennyson's own view of language, and about the kinds of linguistic awareness he might have expected of his readers. While the nineteenth-century philologists clearly recognized the importance of grammatical structure for the classification of the various languages, the predominant concern in most Victorian discussion of language was not so much syntactic, as phonological or lexical; Tennyson developed his poetic style

at a time when there was considerable debate about the nature of language, but through all the debates etymology still held center stage in public awareness. The emphasis placed by Augustus and Julius Hare, in their influential book *Guesses at Truth by Two Brothers* (1827), is typical of the whole early nineteenth century: "Words," they wrote, "have a meaning and a history, and . . . when used according to their historical meaning they have also life and power." Even though the Victorian development of a more scholarly sense of "history" made the older search for "real meanings" in linguistic origins seem less possible, Victorian readers remained unusually sensitive to the "life and power" which a knowledge of word-roots could bring. The shift in the way language is studied, between the nineteenth and twentieth centuries, is part of a much broader shift in intellectual attitudes. The key science of the twentieth century might be said to be nuclear physics, highly aware of its own fictiveness, using highly-developed, and essentially timeless or ahistorical, conceptual models, while the key sciences of the nineteenth century were the historical, time-bound disciplines of geology and evolutionary biology, where each landscape and each animal showed the vestiges of continuing change. Victorian language study, or philology, was much less kin to modern theoretical linguistics than to the contemporary geologist or biologist, as largely amateur scholars turned over the strata and fossil-life of language, and classified the cognate forms and families of speech. Tennyson followed closely the developments in Victorian philology through his friendships with philologists and through his reading, and his responsiveness to the linguistic ideas of his time had a direct influence in the poetry he wrote. (pp. 371-72)

The changing attitudes in Victorian philology might seem, on first sight, to be reflected directly in Tennyson's own references to language. In an early poem, **"The Poet,"** he radiates confidence about the connection between the lightning-flash of wisdom and meaning, and the subsequent reverberant thunder of the historical language; in *In Memoriam,* in his middle period, the emphasis is on the problematic relationship of words to inner or ultimate meanings, for "words, like Nature, half reveal / And half conceal the Soul within"; in the later *Idylls of the King,* a revealing simile suggests a deep skepticism about the early Victorian readiness to explain the power of language through its roots:

> we dwell upon a word we know,
> Repeating, till the word we know so well
> Becomes a wonder, and we know not why.

In Tennyson's early poems, as J. F. A. Pyre long ago pointed out, he appropriates words "to special poetic use" by employing "latinisms in a special or primitive sense," a procedure entirely consonant with the philological attitudes of the earlier, Richardsonian, period. By contrast, one of the major linguistic innovations of Tennyson's later years, his poems in mid-Lincolnshire dialect, as well as his experiments with such Celtic and Anglo-Saxon based poems as **"The Voyage of Maeldune"** and **"The Battle of Brunanburh,"** parallel the more limitedly British interests of most later Victorian philology.

However, in the realm of language as in many other areas

of his thought, Tennyson's modernization was far from complete: what goes on in his poetry with regard to language, as with religion and so much else, is a continuing dialogue or interplay between the attitudes of his formative years, with their strongly romantic or idealist bent, and the disturbing, skeptical empiricism of Victorian "scientific" scholarship. It is, I would suggest, broadly true that in his earlier poems Tennyson uses the etymological root of a word forcefully and directly for his own meaning, while in his later poems such etymological "meanings" seem rather to be possibilities, potential explications to be held in tension with the overlay of modern usage. But one must not exaggerate the change; though Tennyson's attitude towards such root meanings for words is modified under the influence of the new philology, throughout his life he retained a sense, in the Richardsonian fashion, that behind each word lay an older, more forceful original. In a very significant poem from late in his life, Tennyson wrote, of Virgil, that in his poetry one finds "All the charm of all the Muses often flowering in a lonely word" (**"To Virgil"**), and that line was, I suggest, a projection of his own response to language. Fully to read Tennyson's poetry, we need to add to the modern concern with syntax the early Victorian sensitivity that, as R. C. Trench once argued, we can find "boundless stores of moral and historical truth, and no less of passion and imagination" in *"words contemplated singly."*

Such a sensitivity to single words can add considerably to our understanding of Tennyson's artistic achievement. A simple example comes in one of the most moving sections of **In Memoriam:**

> What am I?
> An infant crying in the night:
> An infant crying for the light:
> And with no language but a cry.

A modern student of style would, quite properly, point out how the effect of these lines is built up through a parallelism of syntax ("crying in the night," "crying for the light") which on closer inspection involves a shift in the meaning of "crying" from mere reaction to possibly purposive utterance. He might also, more conjecturally, note how the stanza moves from a construction of noun + adjectival phrase (repeated) to one of an adjectival phrase left nounless, and infer that Tennyson is expressing the loss of identity inherent in the inability to have meaningful expression of ideas. A student of prosody might point out how the wistfulness of the final rhyme-word "cry" rests on its being an uncompleted rhyme to the "night" and "light" of the middle lines. But, as Christopher Ricks notes, much of the force of the passage for a Victorian reader would have come from the root meaning of "infant," from Latin *infans,* unable to speak.

This sort of reading is suspect to many modern language scholars. Pyles and Algeo, for instance, would condemn as the "etymological fallacy" any attempt to suppose that the true or real meaning of a word is revealed by its derivation and history rather than by its actual usage. But the "actual usages" we already know when we hear or read anyone else's language are necessarily more or less historical, and what the Victorian poet was conscious of were the

subtle discrepancies that a writer could exploit between past and present usages. Margaret Schlauch has suggested that the old etymological model for explaining such word-use as "infant," in the example above, can be assimilated to a more modern semantic model through "semantic rejuvenation." She argues that a poet uses the contextual network in provoking a reader's recognition of those earlier meanings which have passed from currency: because of a context, the reader relearns, or even teaches himself, meanings additional to modern usage. This is a particularly useful idea for the reading of Tennyson, as his use of etymology often relies on extended networks of etymological allusion, and these sustain the impact of the single word, validating the reader's initial sense that the root-meaning might be relevant and so greatly sophisticating the reading-responses for which the poet can hope.

An example of such a network of etymologies occurs in **"The Palace of Art."** If one reads the passage in the light, say, of Miltonic use of Latin original-meanings, the Latinism seems merely playful or witty, but if it is viewed as a network of root-possibilities, then etymology becomes central to the interpretation of the passage. In these lines, one star has seemed to stand still while the heavens revolve around it, and Tennyson describes how the central star

> with the choral starry dance
> Joined not, but stood, and standing saw
> The hollow orb of moving Circumstance
> Rolled round by one fixed law.

What appears on first reading to be a synaesthetic compound ("choral dance"), blending sound and sight, really rests on the Greek root for *chorus,* a dance in a circle: it is the familiar Tennysonian repetition at work. Secondly, as W. David Shaw points out, the central paradox in the lines, between fixity and movement, comes from a punning conflict between the modern sense of *circumstance* as fluid, chancy, and changing, and the Latin root-meaning, "standing around," an image of stability. But we can go further, if we let ourselves be tempted, as a reader used to the wilder conjectures of early nineteenth-century etymologists would have been tempted, by the phonological similarity between *stood, standing, stance,* and *star* itself: the sentence holds out the temptation of linking the fixed star to Latin *stare,* to stand. (Just this wild conjecture in fact appears as a serious etymological explanation in the writings of the medieval Latinist Isidore of Seville.)

Of course, such an etymology is false; the shock comes if we replace it with the etymology newly favored by the early Victorian lexicographers. Richardson derives the word "star" from Old English *stiran,* to stir or move, which he claims was applied to the more distant or "glittering luminaries of the sky" because of their "apparent perpetual motion" or "perpetual quivering." The polarity of motion and fixity is rooted, therefore, in the etymology of most of the major words, Greek, Latin, or English, in the stanza. Tennyson's own comments add still another element to the linguistic complexity of the passage, and suggest the way he hoped the lines would be read: he noted, "Some old writer calls the Heavens 'the Circumstance.' . . . Here it is more or less a play on the word."

Sometimes Tennyson's use of etymology is not so much

additional as essential to the understanding of his imagery. Lines which have seemed inflated in diction or even vague in meaning may in fact conceal a lively metaphor. In section CIX of *In Memoriam,* Tennyson describes Arthur Hallam's conversational exuberance as "Heart-affluence in discursive talk / From household fountains never dry." Alan Sinfield, one of the most careful recent students of Tennyson's style, comments that "one wonders just what 'heart-affluence' is," and uses the passage as an example of "vague and uninspired" diction.

"Affluence" had, of course, long before acquired something like its modern meaning in English, for both of the eighteenth-century dictionaries that Tennyson possessed gloss the word in terms of wealth or plenty, suggesting a reference to Hallam offering emotional riches, "heart-affluence." Johnson notes an older, scientific usage, when Harvey, the seventeenth-century physiologist, had used the word for the outflow of blood from the heart. But Richardson's early Victorian dictionary approached the word rather differently, for it made the "flow" idea primary and the riches secondary, and tried to retain, even in the definition of modern usage, a sense of the original Latin root of the word, *affluentia,* "flowing"; "affluence," Richardson insisted, was only applied metaphorically to wealth, riches, or opulence, and really meant "flowing with the fullness of a flood." "Effluence" might be the Modern English equivalent of the force which the word had for an early Victorian reader, and in fact Tennyson originally wrote in his draft "heart-effluence," presumably revising it because he wanted to avoid the new and nasty Victorian sanitational overtones of his first choice. If we can read with Victorian eyes, therefore, far from finding these lines vague, we discover a consistently developed water-image in the heart's affluence or over-flowing; in the discursive, or running, talk; and in the source for conversational topics, the household fountains. Even the final word becomes a witty pun, for not only did Hallam's conversation never run dry, but it was never dull or recondite either.

Etymology can be a clue to the complexity of Tennyson's meaning, as well as to the richness of his metaphor. In the final book of *The Princess,* a remark by the Prince about the nature of womanhood has not excited much modern admiration: "For woman," he says, "is not undevelopt man, / But diverse." Kate Millett comments that the sentiment is "of course wonderfully familiar—*vive la différence,*" and says that Tennyson is passing "off traditional inequalities as interesting variety." Even if the idea is not to be admired, however, Tennyson's expression of it is far from simple-minded. The assonance or phonological similarity between "undevelopt" and "diverse" offers the first clue to the contrast Tennyson is setting up. This is the only occasion when Tennyson uses the word "diverse" in his poetry, though he sometimes uses the cognate "divers" elsewhere. Again, we find a striking variation between the way the eighteenth-century dictionaries define the word, more or less in its modern sense of "different or various," and the way Richardson defines it, through its Latin origin, as "turned aside or diverted." Tennyson's contrast is between an idea he rejects, that woman is undeveloped or not turned out to full growth (from Latin, *devolvere*), and

the idea he endorses, that woman has instead developed by an alternative route. This second idea would seem particularly cogent if the reader had also in mind the etymology of "woman" given by Richardson and others, as coming from Old English *wiþman,* where the word itself is a diverse development of the word "man."

In at least one instance, Tennyson's very language can be understood only if one has etymological knowledge. In the first "Old Yew" section of *In Memoriam,* Tennyson describes how the somberness of the yew-tree and the churchyard will never change: "Nor branding summer suns avail / To touch thy thousand years of gloom." All Tennyson's dictionaries concur in giving much the modern definition for "branding," as "burning with a hot iron, as a mark of ownership or guilt." But what relevance has that sort of brand to the sun in the churchyard? One has to connect the word, not with current Victorian usage, but to its root in Old English, *brinnan* or *byrnan,* "to scorch or burn." Tennyson himself had a copy of the recent Anglo-Saxon dictionary by Joseph Bosworth; but only a confidence that his readers would have a very developed sensitivity to metathesis as a guide to cognate words can explain the sheer eccentricity of Tennyson's usage here. (In face, the eccentric denotation leaves the reader with some of the overtones of the more common usage, and so with the feeling that the churchyard bears painful visible evidence that the world and the dead are owned by time, even if it also witnesses to the timeless outrage death is felt to be at this point in the poem. To identify with the mourner, the reader must reject the modern overtones for an outdatedness as apparently perverse as the mourner's attitude to death.)

In short, I am arguing that to read Tennyson we have to know, not so much the scrupulous, historically based achievements of the late Victorian lexicographers, but the whole philological ethos of his age, where "words contemplated singly" carried the special force and meaning of their often rather conjectural origins. It is, I think, significant that in his later life Tennyson was attracted, not so much to the activities of the Philological Society, which busied itself with doggedly empirical word-histories, as to two rather singular comparative philologists. In F. W. Farrar, he would find the interjectional or onomatopoeic theories of the origins of speech—which had previously been considered utilitarian theories and over which he had despaired in *In Memoriam*—miraculously transformed through Farrar's rhetorical sleight of hand into an argument for the emotive and imaginative nature of language, a theory which we would regard with more sympathy. In Max Müller, Tennyson found a philologist who still retained an almost mystical reverence for the ultimate Indo-European roots of language, and who still believed such roots to be irreducible realities for the mind: in Müller, virtually alone of late-Victorian language theorists, a German Idealist philosophy preserved the magic of words from merely historical and relativistic research. In his attitude to language, as in so much else, Tennyson was both involved with the developing thought of his age and in an uneasy tension with the ultimate tendency of that thought towards an historical relativism. Through careful use of the various Victorian dictionaries, we can recapture, not just some fascinating individual Victorian word-meanings, but something also of the typical Victorian mode of response to language. Tennyson's is a highly verbal art, but the detailed artifice of its allusions can be recognized only if we bring to the poems a Victorian way of reading. (pp. 375-81)

Patrick Greig Scott, " 'Flowering in a Lonely Word': Tennyson and the Victorian Study of Language," in Victorian Poetry, *Vol. 18, No. 4, Winter, 1980, pp. 371-81.*

William E. Buckler   (essay date 1980)

[*Buckler is an American educator, critic, and author of* Man and His Myths: Tennyson's "Idylls of the King" in Critical Context *(1984). In the following excerpt from his 1980 study of Victorian literature, he delineates Tennyson's variations on the theme of madness in his poetry.*]

Tennyson's fascination with "The abysmal deeps of Personality" is pervasive in his poetry. From his earliest known poem (**"The Devil and the Lady"**) to the last poem he finished (**"The Dreamer"**), he was a poet of human experience, perpetually probing distinctive, often strange, states of being through the placement of an imaginary *persona* at the heart of a processive human action that enables that character to gain an original perspective on the human condition and enables the poet thereby to purify and strengthen the imagination of the reader. Tennyson, of course, experimented with almost every turning of the poetic art as exemplified in both the English and the Classical literary traditions, and hence one would hesitate to characterize too broadly and simply such a large, experimental, and varied canon. Still, the human consciousness in motion is a fair phrasing of that central imaginative current in which Tennyson's chief poetic successes flow.

Madness is one of the "abysmal deeps" to which the human psyche is vulnerable, and we know that to Tennyson the man it was an ever present reality, a defining, cautioning outcropping in the Tennyson family. But it is curious how little of this deep personal experience of madness finds its way into the work of a poet who has been so persistently searched for autobiographical implants. Instead, Tennyson very early distanced his acute awareness of this special vulnerability of the human spirit to an imaginative construct on which he worked many variations in his long poetry-writing career. The chief lineaments of that imaginative construct and the process through which it gradually passes in the Tennyson canon can be clarified through a comparative look at an early and a late poem, **"Sense and Conscience"** (written in the late 1820s) and **"Rizpah"** (written in 1878).

"Sense and Conscience," called an "unfinished allegory," is an ambitious Miltonic imitation. The poem is narrated by the unidentified Spirit of Man, the minister or steward of Time. The contention is between Spirit and Sense; and man woos "the Arch-Enemy *Sense*," who prospers "at the court of Time," by stealth drugging "Great Conscience," "boldest of the warriors of Time," offspring of "*Reason* and *Will!*" Though drugged by Sense, Conscience cannot

die, but lying helpless in "deep shades," he struggles subconsciously in an all-enveloping atmosphere of sensuous invasion. Finally, Memory, now in mourning weeds, comes upon him, and he is reminded of what a "fair vision" she once was:

(The woof of Earth Heaven-dipt, in orient hues
Storying the Past which charactered in fire
Burned from its inmost folds). . . .

But Conscience is too weak to rise, and he merely wreaks havoc among the images of beauty in this unwanted Bower of Blissless Bliss. He does at last escape into the deep interior, where he lives on "bitter roots which Memory / Dug for him round his cell." Finally, he is caught up in the rhythms of madness:

One solemn night
He could not sleep, but on the bed of thorns,
Which Memory and Pain had strown for him,
Of brambles and wild thistles of the wood,
Lay tossing, hating light and loathing dark,
And in his agony his heart did seem
To send up to his eyes great drops of blood,
Which would not fall because his burning eyes
Did hiss them into drought. Aloud he wept,
Loud did he weep, for now the iron had come
Into his soul: the hollow-vaulted caverns
Bore out his heavy sobs to the waste night,
And some the low-browed arch returned unto
His ear; so sigh from sigh increasing grew.

Here we have a simple paradigm of madness as it surfaces repeatedly in the Tennyson canon. A *persona* of considerable emprise is caught in a collision of forces—a distinctive individual in a conflict of motives and actions—between which he struggles and at the center of which is the subtler conflict of desire and an unyielding recognition of the falseness of the desire, creating in the *persona* a magnified psychic collision. This leads to madness, but it is a madness made inevitable by the very refinement of the *persona*'s imaginative sensibility. Memory, a raw but imperious presence in the early poetry of Tennyson, will be later integrated and submerged into the texture of poetic action, but its role as "Mother of the Muses" and chief igniter of the imagination will, though subdued, persist.

"Rizpah" is a penetratingly sad poem, but its effects are positively exhilarating too. Here madness is not just a crippled state, but a heroic solution. A mad, impersonal society is confronted in a mad personal way, as Rizpah works out for herself and her son a "supreme Dénouement" that functions for her so successfully that the murky waters of a debilitating pathos are cleansed by her diminutive but relentless grandeur. **"Rizpah"** is thus a fit illustration of how Tennyson maintained the Aristotelian, Wordsworthian, Arnoldian principle "that the feeling therein developed gives importance to the action and situation, and not the action and situation to the feeling. . . ." The central irony of the poem is that Rizpah outwits a brutally dehumanized socio-ethical system through coordinates of that same system in which she is herself imprisoned. She rectifies the gross injustice of society's hanging of her son in chains, high for the world to see and for "the hell-black raven and horrible fowls of the air" to pick clean, by gathering his bones as they fall and laying "him in holy ground." She thus makes an imaginative transfer from "the cursèd tree" upon which Willy was hung to the blessed tree upon which Christ was hung. Ironic, too, is the discrepancy between the milder predestinate fundamentalism of her Methodist-Calvinist visitor and the desperate faith and unlimited courage of mad Rizpah.

Any number of forces could, in the course of the events, account for the initial madness of Rizpah—overwhelming grief, monstrous injustice, devastating shame. But the poem itself pinpoints the boy's last-minute cry that leaves her with a haunting and unbearable sense of incompleteness—the "something further" that he had to say which she "never shall know" but which her memory and imagination cannot relinquish. That memory / imagination is what torments her unremittingly through years of confinement and beatings (the eighteenth century's version of shock treatment) until she grows "stupid and still." That memory / imagination, too, is what shapes her furtive apostolate: maybe what he was going to say was, " 'Mother, O mother!—[see that I am buried in holy ground!]' " But even if that was not it, the possibility thereof becomes her only way, by the mad internalization of the mad belief of the times, of ever getting to know. The frantic strategy built on that possibility by Rizpah, isolated from the world's understanding and sympathy and carrying on only when protected from the world's spying by the extreme darkness and inclemency in which the most furtive of body-snatchers work, becomes the action by which she effects a tenuous truce with the mighty collisions in her imaginative consciousness.

The grim bardic quality that is domesticated in Rizpah's cunningly imaginative madness seems to translate into the structure and movement of this poem Merlin's "Riddling of the Bards" in **"Gareth and Lynette"**:

> " 'Confusion, and illusion, and relation,
> Elusion, and occasion, and evasion.' "

"Rizpah" is monitored by this "bardic subtext" as follows. Faced with an infinity of insuperably chaotic conflicts *(confusion)*, the protagonist creates a private myth or fable *(illusion)* by which she can script into her real-life dilemma a manageable order *(relation)* and thereby sidestep the crushing effects of a shapeless chaos *(elusion)* by creating an action *(occasion)* in which something can be done instead of yielding to circumstances in which everything is to be endured *(evasion)*.

The simple, early paradigm persists: the imagination, fed by memory, attempts to cope with such turbulent inner conflict that the *persona* is driven mad. In **"Sense and Conscience,"** there is a complete failure to cope; in **"Rizpah,"** the efforts of the mad old woman to cope are notably successful through the evocation of and perseverance in a private myth that enables her to achieve a grim "salvation" for herself and her son. And although Tennyson did not slavishly subordinate his poetic structures to these two models, both have relevance to all his poems of madness.

In **"The Lover's Tale,"** for example, a poem of strange imaginative energy and fascinating in the way Browning's *Pauline* is fascinating, the strained, unsuccessful efforts of the poet-protagonist to create a truly functional bardic

subtext—or the duplicity with which he attempts to insinuate a false subtext—seem to explain the state of exacerbated vagueness in which he exists. And while one would not call it a successful poem, **"The Lover's Tale"** establishes an extraordinary space in the young Tennyson's poetic history that otherwise would not be poetically defined. The poet-protagonist of **"The Lover's Tale,"** for all his lyrical resource, fails through his incapacity to shape an action by which, like the protagonists of **"Rizpah"** and *Maud,* to achieve at least an eclipsed success. Despite his ingenious psychic maneuvering, he does not evade a situation in which everything is to be endured and nothing is to be done: he merely repeats forever the telling of his tale, the "telling" thus becoming the central metaphor of the "tale's" experience.

Madness is a pervasive insinuation rather than an explicit declaration of **"The Lover's Tale,"** and this fascinating inconclusiveness is one of the tantalizing, almost subliminal aspects of the poet's imaginative apprehension, as if the highly gifted teller has ingeniously suspended the tale at an indifference point between madness and sanity. At some junctures, the reader is even led to wonder if the tale is really true, if Camilla is not one of the "witching fantasies" to which Conscience is subjected in **"Sense and Conscience,"** and this haunting suspicion is reenforced by the imaginative inflation of the speaker's language, the impreciseness of the narrative situation—place, time, audience, occasion—and the peculiar way in which he selects his narrative episodes. For example, he magnifies in the most erotic way the cradle-cuddling about which he admittedly has no personal memory, and yet he omits entirely, except for a disturbing reference to the death of her father and "how we found / The dead man cast upon the shore," the eighteen-year period when young love would presumably have been in flower.

After the collapse of the myth of romantic love, which he has created with such imaginative flamboyance and "fantastical merriment" in Part I, Julian attempts to implant in his story the first *illusion* by which to ground his psychic turbulence *(confusion)* and to bring the coordinates of his life into supportable *relation:*

> Love's arms were wreathed about the neck of Hope,
> And Hope kissed Love, and Love drew in her breath
> In that close kiss, and drank her whispered tales.
> They said that Love would die when Hope was gone,
> And Love mourned long, and sorrowed after Hope;
> At last she sought out Memory, and they trod
> The same old paths where Love had walked with Hope,
> And Memory fed the soul of Love with tears.

It will not hold, of course, since it is an attempt to substitute a state of feeling for an action; and although it is effectively said, it is so abstracted beyond flesh and blood that it suffers from a haughty imaginative hysteria, the "mock-disease," perhaps, of the schizophrenic manic-depressive.

At the center of Julian's consciousness is a mighty imaginative collision. His love for Camilla is incestuous, not so much literally as by imaginative conversion. He has refined their closeness in every possible way, prevented only by the historical facts themselves from making them issue simultaneously from the same womb; but his frenzied imagination will not consciously accept the taboo against romantic incestuous love. It is as though he would give Hermaphroditus erotic as well as aesthetic privilege:

> Why were we one in all things, save in that
> Where to have been one had been the cope and
> crown
> Of all I hoped and feared?—if that same near-
> ness
> Were father to this distance, and that *one*
> Vauntcourier to this *double?* if Affection
> Living slew Love, and Sympathy hewed out
> The bosom-sepulchre of Sympathy?

Thus the nightmarish visions that he suffers after being hopelessly separated from his love-object are all filled with psychosexual images of love and death, weddings interwoven with funerals, bacchanals rising from biers, sexual aggression met with horrified rejection, his efforts to imprint "Colour and life" upon Camilla's "naked forms" resulting in a wild surrealistic turbulence:

> round and round
> A whirlwind caught and bore us; mighty gyres
> Rapid and vast, of hissing spray and wind-
> driven
> Far through the dizzy dark. Aloud she shrieked;
> My heart was cloven with pain; I wound my
> arms
> About her: we whirled giddily; the wind
> Sung; but I clasped her without fear: her weight
> Shrank in my grasp, and over my dim eyes,
> And parted lips which drank her breath, down-
> hung
> The jaws of Death: I, groaning, from me flung
> Her empty phantom: all the sway and whirl
> Of the storm dropt to windless calm and I
> Down weltered through the dark ever and ever.

Thus the guilt which Julian has so imaginatively masked from his consciousness surfaces in nightmares impregnated by both unyielding desire and relentless conscience.

Part IV (**"The Golden Supper,"** called "the sequel") relates Julian's efforts to modify the bardic subtext by creating a genuine action, but this, too, fails since the action is rooted in a haughty imaginative self-deception which he cannot quite hide even from himself; and this forces him to abandon the role of "teller" and reenforces the centrality of the metaphor of telling. The key to the explicit falseness of the action (*occasion,* "event") by which he hopes to rise above the darkening chaos of his life (*elusion*) and avoid an unendurable future (*evasion*) resides in the parable by which Julian traps Lionel into affirming that Camilla, "by all the laws of love and gratefulness" is his "body and soul / And life and limbs, all his to work his will." The sexual imperiousness has clearly not abated, and the parallel between the master and his servant and Lionel and Camilla is patently false, as is that between Julian and the savior-figure of the parable. But it is on such falseness that he erects his new myth (*illusion*) of material and spiritual grandeur, in which he actually arrogates to himself the godlike role of taking into his hands the destinies of others, as in Part I he had attempted to mythicize a god-goddess role above human imperatives for him and Camilla. His "action" in Part IV is a mere inversion of his own guilt and psychic turbulence into an ornate grandeur that does not cleanse him of his flamboyant hubris, but only compounds it.

Thus the connection between madness and imagination is made explicit in **"The Lover's Tale."** Julian's imaginative frenzy is an attempt to reorder moral imperatives in violation of his own attenuated moral conscience, and it leaves him ultimately companioned with his mental sickness. His theory of the imagination is intact enough:

> Alway the inaudible invisible thought,
> Artificer and subject, lord and slave,
> Shaped by the audible and visible,
> Moulded the audible and visible. . . .

But such a theory is morally neutral, and when Julian uses it to support essentially immoral willfulness and aggression, it creates a mighty collision in his imagination that, by the very keenness of his sensibilities, drives him mad.

Looking again to the later Tennyson, to **Idylls of the King,** we find variations on the same imaginative construct. In **Idylls of the King,** which is too frequently read as a morally apothegmatical poem, characters are in fact measured by the quality and force of their imaginations. Thus Arthur's love-epiphany, by which he suddenly inscapes himself and his universe, imprints its truth upon him so indelibly that he can see his world explode around him without ultimately betraying that initial vision. Leodogran resolves his weighty dilemma by rising above a sea of conflicting testimony and making an act of faith engendered by imagination. Gareth brings to his *rite de passage* a highly self-cultured imagination that enables him to overcome his collusion in deception and to persevere, becoming true Prince, true Knight. Geraint begins with a tawdry self-myth, and his treatment of Enid is so blunt and stupid because his imagination is incapable of anything beyond a low-grade theatricality.

The madness of Elaine, Guinevere, Lancelot, Pelleas, and Balin turns variously upon this central issue. Elaine's case is simple and horrifying. She is the delicate bearer of a fatal either-or imagination—the tender, ingratiating metaphor of an excruciating pathos and of a monotonic, devastating inevitability; and when the two parts of her naked dichotomy between sweet death and sweeter but frozen and unavailable love clash together in her finely tuned but childishly inexperienced imagination, her madness rises momentarily to the shrill, wailing note of a banshee's piercing shriek:

> High with the last line scaled her voice, and this,
> All in a fiery dawning wild with wind
> That shook her tower, the brothers heard, and
> thought
> With shuddering, "Hark the Phantom of the
> house
> That ever shrieks before a death," and called
> The father, and all three in hurry and fear
> Ran to her, and lo! the blood-red light of dawn
> Flared on her face, she shrilling, "Let me die!"

The "action" for which she opts represents her despair of

a bardic subtext by which her torn but simplistic psyche can ever be healed. She becomes the victim of an initial self-myth that, being fatal, allows no chance of mythic transformation. Her memory has no resources beyond its current drama, and hence she has nothing but the present to draw upon in the shaping of what might have been an alternative future.

Guinevere's case is so complex and her brush with madness is so lightly sketched that one can hardly speak of her in the present context without a sense of massive disproportion. But the threshold-to-madness moment is there and cannot be ignored. It is recorded in her idyll after Lancelot has discovered Modred spying for hard evidence, and although she is not brought to the depths of madness experienced by the soul in **"The Palace of Art,"** the parallel is unmistakable:

> Henceforward . . . the powers that tend the
>   soul,
> To help it from the death that cannot die,
> And save it even in extremes, began
> To vex and plague her. Many a time for hours,
> Beside the placid breathings of the King,
> In the dead night, grim faces came and went
> Before her, or a vague spiritual fear—
> Like to some doubtful noise of creaking doors,
> Heard by the watcher in a haunted house,
> That keeps the rust of murder on the walls—
> Held her awake: or if she slept, she dreamed
> An awful dream; for then she seemed to stand
> On some vast plain before a setting sun,
> And from the sun there swiftly made at her
> A ghastly something, and its shadow flew
> Before it, till it touched her, and she turned—
> When lo! her own, that broadening from her
>   feet,
> And blackening, swallowed all the land, and in
>   it
> Far cities burnt, and with a cry she woke.

Guinevere is being traumatized by guilt, of course, but this period occupies a peculiar segment in a complex life-story. Guinevere has become so inured in her alternative fantasy, her self-myth of life as a May-game radiating outward from her, that she cannot conscientiously indict herself at the conscious level for her particular sin. Being fearful of disclosure but not morally self-disclosed, she cannot break out of her self-myth. She can hypothesize action and, when caught *flagrante delicto,* take action of despair, but she has as yet no worthy insight into the real truth. Hence, "the powers that tend the soul" can only "vex and plague her" with a real but uncomprehended distress. Were she not a great lady with imaginative resources numbed but real, she would simply break under the strain and spin off into irremediable madness. But it is her good fortune at the critical hour to reach beyond the memory of the pleasure-myth that began with Lancelot's initial mission and touch a time, obliquely configurated by the little novice, in which her values were shaped and monitored by an exemplary father-king, Leodogran; and out of this self-renewal, this reinitiation into earlier patterns of personality and value, she becomes available to the Arthurian insight and constructs for herself an Arthurian bardic subtext that saves her from suicidal madness. At the final mo-

ment, she accepts the Arthurian myth that she has heretofore rejected *(illusion)* and thereby brings her life into a new creative order *(relation)* by which her desperate *confusion* is resolved. She is thus enabled to undertake a simple life-work *(occasion)* that enables her to rise above a chaotic past but lately recognized *(elusion)* and avoid a catastrophic future *(evasion).*

Lancelot's situation has analogues in those of Elaine and Guinevere. Indeed, it is through a juxtaposition of the images of the two of them, a concentration of the life-experience summed up in his efforts to cope with them both, that he is led to the self-harrowing soliloquy that enables us to understand the basic nature of his dilemma and to believe that he "should die a holy man." Like "Elaine the fair" and Guinevere "the fairest of all flesh on earth," Lancelot is "fair . . . / As a king's son." Schooled in this very special sense of self by the Lady of the Lake, Lancelot mythicizes that self and aspires to be a king. On the one hand, his loyalty to Arthur the King is inviolable; but when Guinevere falls in love with him, he can yet realize an approximation of his myth, a king-*manqué* with a queen who is his, *manqué.* His experience of Elaine shows him how tender and endearing and fatal mythic self-deception can be; and Guinevere's turbulent rage, casting into the river the diamond-symbols of his fabricated kingship, shows him what a fool's paradise he has been living in. And though he has not yet discovered the myth-based action by which to evade self-destruction (the bardic subtext), he recognizes that life under these circumstances is unsustainable:

> "I needs must break
> These bonds that so defame me: not without
> She wills it: would I, if she willed it? nay
> Who knows? but if I would not, then may God,
> I pray him, send a sudden Angel down
> To seize me by the hair and bear me far,
> And fling me deep in that forgotten mere,
> Among the tumbled fragments of the hills."

Lancelot discovers the myth and the action by which to evade self-destruction through the wild madness of his near-despairing quest for the Holy Grail, his metaphoric journey into the hell of the existential self which he just barely survives. It is his vow-within-a-vow that saves him, the vow to follow on his quest the counsel of "the one most holy saint." Through all his turbulent, surreal madness, his irreducible minimum of hope enables him to maintain faith in that counsel and, having faced the rampant lions projected from his own shield without yielding to doubt, he hears, standing in the bare, cloistral, tomblike hall of Carbonek, the lark of Hope singing in the tower toward the rising sun and can believe in his own eventual resurrection and redemption. Thus his new myth *(illusion)* is validated: he is worthy of salvation. His old fabricated myth, which has self-destructed and almost carried him into chaos, can now be abandoned because, like Guinevere, his naked existential self has been touched by authentic hope. But this is only a preliminary part of the bardic subtext; like Guinevere, Lancelot must yet perform a thousand individual acts of self-renewal and undergo, with faith but without certainty, countless experiences of jeopardy:

> "up I climbed a thousand steps

> With pain: as in a dream I seemed to climb
> For ever: at last I reached a door,
> A light was in the crannies, and I heard,
> 'Glory and joy and honour to our Lord
> And to the Holy Vessel of the Grail.'
> Then in my madness I essayed the door;
> It gave; and through a stormy glare, a heat
> As from a seventimes-heated furnace, I,
> Blasted and burnt, and blinded as I was,
> With such a fierceness that I swooned away—
> O, yet methought I saw the Holy Grail,
> All palled in crimson samite, and around
> Great angels, awful shapes, and wings and
>   eyes."

Thus, Lancelot's story, like Guinevere's, is made both complex and representative by his need to dismantle one deeply interwoven myth and to erect upon the remnant of the authentic self a subtext of salvation.

Set against the austerely muted successes of Guinevere and Lancelot are the gothic failures of Pelleas and Balin. Their madness outruns all expectation of order and implants in *Idylls of the King* intimations as terrifying as those of the Spirit of the Years in Hardy's *The Dynasts:*

> where the roars and plashings of the flames
> Of earth-invisible suns swell noisily,
> And onwards into ghastly gulfs of sky,
> Where hideous presences churn through the
>   dark—
> Monsters of magnitude without a shape,
> Hanging amid deep wells of nothingness.

Their efforts are, within the limits of their capacities, heroic; but their personal resources are so fragile and the circumstances with which they contend so brutal that their minds are blown in a manner that tumbles all sense even of a tragic order.

Pelleas' madness must be witnessed in the overlapping curve that includes both young Sir Pelleas of the Isles in **"Pelleas and Ettarre"** and the Red Knight in **"The Last Tournament."** For all his simple charm that makes Arthur love him immediately, Sir Pelleas is an ill-fated figure. He comes riding out of his wasteland like a Don Quixote with the hooves of Pan, and he makes a supreme effort that is poignantly sad to live knighthood to the letter and to love. It is a delicate transformation, the conversion of one ontological state into another. Even in the face of the bestial treachery of Gawain and Ettarre, this gentle son of Pan and Arthurian fundamentalist goes by the book; and he rises, in the face of measurable personal catastrophe, to genuine tragic stature, indicting the world that has betrayed him, but indicting himself even more. It is Percivale who, inadvertently and ineptly, converts catastrophe into chaos for Sir Pelleas. Tragically bruised by his personal empirical knowledge of infidelity within the knighthood, Sir Pelleas extrapolates Percivale's shabby innuendo concerning Guinevere and Lancelot into global, atheistic, abstract condemnation of the whole Order in which he has been such an exemplary novice-knight. The after-shocks of his fractured literalism leave his world in ruins. He has made of Arthurianism a total myth of self-fulfillment, a textbook way of transforming a barren spiritual wasteland into a magnificent imaginative reality, and when that

myth fails him, he is catapulted into despair that reaches an insanely generalized level:

> "No name, no name," he shouted, "a scourge
>   am I
> To lash the treasons of the Table Round."
> "Yea, but thy name?" "I have many names," he
>   cried:
> "I am wrath and shame and hate and evil fame,
> And like a poisonous wind I pass to blast
> And blaze the crime of Lancelot and the
>   Queen."

With the collapse of Arthurianism, Pelleas' imagination, buoyed up by Arthurianism, collapses too, and the only bardic subtext he can manage is a brutal inversion of Arthurianism with a line-by-line literalness. He founds his "Round Table in the North," and as a maddened rebel against the community that has failed to render him its promised justice, he becomes the center of the " 'flat confusions and brute violences' " of a revenge tragedy in which orderly justice itself is beyond the reach of human expectation. So when the offended community, in the persons of the young men lately knighted, takes its revenge upon the rebel against community, it creates an image which the imagination itself finds almost unendurable. The drunken Pelleas, alias the Red Knight, has fallen headlong into the swamp:

> then the knights, who watched him, roared
> And shouted and leapt down upon the fallen;
> There trampled out his face from being known,
> And sank his head in mire, and slimed them-
>   selves:
> Nor heard the King for their own cries, but
>   sprang
> Through open doors, and swording right and
>   left
> Men, women, on their sodden faces, hurled
> The tables over and the wines, and slew
> Till all the rafters rang with woman-yells,
> And all the pavement streamed with massacre:
> Then, echoing yell with yell, they fired the
>   tower. . . .

Mankind has itself gone mad, and in the "lazy-plunging sea" with which the incident is glossed, we hear "The voice of days of old and days to be," the tidal voice that preceded the coming of man and that will roll "far along the gloomy shores" aeons after his passing.

The Pelleas-Red Knight story comes late in *Idylls of the King* and has reverberations of a chaos more macrocosmic than that seeded in the story of Balin. But **"Balin and Balan"** brings a different generative quality to *Idylls of the King.* By its explicit use of the doppelgänger formula, it centers the chaos within, and to the degree that that metaphor of inwardness pervades our sense of the total poem, **"Balin and Balan"** becomes a fundamental imaginative pressure on our full experience of Tennyson's chief poetic accomplishment.

It is not surprising that **"Balin and Balan"** confirms to an extraordinary degree the relevance of the bardic subtext to Tennyson's imaginative method as a whole and to his specific treatment of the theme of madness: the idyll was begun soon after the completion of **"Gareth and Lynette,"** in which Merlin's "Riddling" appears. And although the rich imaginative details with which Tennyson works it out in this gothic tale of personal devastation can hardly be more-than hinted at here, its relevance as a monitoring construct can be briefly suggested.

What happens in **"Balin and Balan"** is that a young knight, after being "sent down" by Arthur for three years as a result of his rageful violation of the code of gentilesse, returns with his model brother (his "other"), tries vigorously to "move / To music with [the] Order and the King," breaks out again into discord, and ends in a mad symbolic desecration of the Order and the King and the violent destruction of himself and his "other." The poetic process by which this action is worked out in implicit response to the inevitable question "Why?" suspends the moral issue as not really relevant and focuses instead on the imaginative authenticity of that process.

Balin exists in a welter of inner and outer *confusions.* Ever prone to a self-depreciation so intense that it perpetually hovers around images of suicide, he can hardly ground the least hint of a slight from an external source, while at the same time he habitually treats himself to torrents of self-abuse. After witnessing a moment of soul-crisis between Guinevere and Lancelot, he translates a disturbing half-realization about them into an intense flagellation of himself:

> "My father hath begotten me in his wrath.
> I suffer from the things before me, know,
> Learn nothing; am not worthy to be knight;
> A churl, a clown!"

When Vivien hypocritically asks his guidance to Arthur's court, he defames himself unmercifully:

> "here I dwell
> Savage among the savage woods, here die—
> Die: let the wolves' black maws ensepulchre
> Their brother beast, whose anger was his lord."

When Balan (the "other") goes in quest of the "demon of the woods," Balin, despairing of even the strictest efforts to "learn what Arthur meant by courtesy, / Manhood, and knighthood," hits upon an *illusion,* the myth that if the Queen will allow him to substitute her crown-royal for the red-tongued beast "toothed with grinning savagery" upon his shield, things will bear a different *relation* to each other and he can avoid *(elusion)* the catastrophic results of his "heats and violences" and "live afresh." The favor granted as a harmless humoring of his boyish eagerness but still threatened with raging impulses, Balin, "mad for strange adventure," undertakes an action *(occasion)* in hopes of finding his "other" and escaping *(evasion)* his own self-fulfilling prophecy of doom. It doesn't work, of course; and after a series of gothic episodes—horrible episodes that sap the strength without exhilarating the soul—he is himself taken for the "demon of the woods" by his "other," and they clash in ignorance and die "either locked in either's arm."

Thus, the bardic subtext works very differently from the way it works in **"Rizpah,"** but the difference is not one of authenticity. Balin fails miserably, but he processes himself through the imaginative formula to his own inevitable,

Self-portraits by Tennyson.

imaginatively just, end; and the aesthetic result is neither pathetic nor tragic, but startlingly and disquietingly gothic. Even the mad act of desecration that triggers his and his "other's" destruction reflects the poet's wholly steady imagination:

> his evil spirit upon him leapt,
> He ground his teeth together, sprang with a yell,
> Tore from the branch, and cast on earth, the
>   shield,
> Drove his mailed heel athwart the royal crown,
> Stampt all into defacement, hurled it from him
> Among the forest weeds, and cursed the tale,
> The told-of, and the teller.

It is the inevitable result of his initiating illusion as his illusion is the inevitable result of his initiating nature; and there is no possibility of any crucial might-have-beens unless one would write quite a different tale of madness and self-destruction. All Balin's memories are of a failed nature: that is the self-myth which he simply cannot dismantle. Thus, the myth that he adopts and the action he undertakes are evasions, not of the confusions of his life or of the catastrophe to which they point, but of the issue itself. All of Balin's inner resources are consumed by self-doubt and brutal anguish, so that he has no capacity for inner transformation. He can only bring his self-doomed destiny to its inevitable term.

"Lucretius," the only other major poem of madness in the later Tennyson canon, also deals with the process of self-mythic metamorphosis. Here the issue is not, as in the cases of Guinevere and Lancelot, the dismantling of a patently false self-myth, but what one does when the perceptual rules are all changed. Lucretius has worked out for himself a wholly conscientious theory of the nature of man and his universe, has created a graceful, poetic rendering of those "truths," and has reached a personal point of "divine Tranquility." That is both his urbane myth of nature and his self-myth. But Lucilia's love-potion changes all that, creating in Lucretius a horrible confusion that must itself be dealt with:

> the wicked broth
> Confused the chemic labor of the blood,
> And tickling the brute brain within the man's
> Made havock among those tender cells, and
>   checked
> His power to shape: he loathed himself. . . .

Lucretius' imagination is whiplashed between his remembered myth of philosophic calm and this new experiential reality for which a new, wholly personal myth must be created and acted upon.

The chief keys to Lucretius' experience of madness and suicide as generically human are the two levels at which his dreams function: the impossibility, intellectually or imaginatively, of being sure that what seems to be a violent aberration is not a true truth; and his personal unwillingness to live with the latter even if it is only a genuine possibility. At one level, Lucretius names and claims his dream. Although it is an explosive contradiction of his theory of nature, its images are only perceptual inversions and, as a student of the mind as well as of the universe, he can easily ground in the human understanding this playfulness of consciousness. At a second level, however, in which "colour and life" are added to the "naked forms" of nature in the aspect of carnal bestiality, he refuses to claim the dream as his own because here there is havoc rather than correspondence, introducing intolerable possibilities about the nature of man and Lucretius' own nature as a man. The fire that shoots out from the standing breasts of Helen scorches him at a deep inner level that negates the very concept of a gradually evolving, ever stabilizing state of human civilization. Moreover, what appears to be so self-horrifying may in fact be self-revealing. Although Lucretius does not claim this deeper dream as his own, he is caught in his own homocentricity and cannot wholly excuse himself from personal complicity. " 'How should the mind, except it loved them, clasp / These idols to herself?' " Nature may be self-cleansing, but is man? Nor can he be quite sure that his horror is unmixed with desire: " 'do I wish— / What?—that the bush were leafless? or to whelm / All of them in one massacre?' "

At the beginning of his monologue, Lucretius has not decided to kill himself; the process by which he articulates his distress leads him to that resolution and act. And the naked horror of the experience is not the primary cause. He is led closer to it by the effects on his mind of the expe-

rience: " 'my mind / Stumbles, and all my faculties are lamed.' " But it is his long-habituated mental realism, the ingrained habit of his mind to accept whatever is, that is decisive. Though this experience is unprecedented for him, he does not deny its reality as an experience, and the acceptance of its horrible truth even at that ungeneralized level loosens his light if graceful hold on life.

Lucretius confronts this new and intolerable *confusion* in his life by creating a new myth *(illusion)* upon which he then founds an action *(occasion)*; and both the myth and the action do have the effect of enabling him to *elude* an insufferable situation and to *evade* a progressive degradation. The order *(relation)* which he thereby gives to his existence is necessarily a conjectural one, but it is undertaken without triviality or cowardice. On the premise that a civilized man has the right to a life of civilized dignity, he bases his myth of suicide on very simple and cogent grounds: it is a peculiarly human privilege; there is the very noblest precedent for it; nature can be depended on to recycle him in her own fashion; in the end, all things will return to "atom and void," no longer sensuously apprehensible as man defines sensuousness; and Plato's argument against it is effectively set aside on the grounds that "the Gods are careless. . . ." Thus, **"Lucretius"** follows other models of madness in the Tennyson canon. It is the very refinement of the protagonist's imagination that makes him incapable of coping with a life controlled by this awful collision within the imagination. The reasons he gives for self-destruction are impeccably thoughtful, but that rational train is set in motion by a thundering awareness of intolerable possibilities within the self that he despairs of reconciling.

> In Tennyson's poetry . . . madness is a
> metaphor, not only of the most devastating
> human distress, but also of the very
> greatest aesthetic challenge, a challenge
> which Tennyson successfully met and
> thereby changed dramatically the course
> of modern English poetry.
>
> —*William E. Buckler*

"The Lady of Shalott", "The Palace of Art," and **"The Vision of Sin,"** all from the earlier Tennyson canon, touch the theme of madness, myth, and action in very different ways. The Lady's moment of madness is clearly formulaic according to the basic formula suggested in this essay: she invokes the curse as a result of the imaginative collision brought on in her developed suceptibilities by the peculiar way in which she suddenly perceives Lancelot ("From the bank and from the river / He flashed into the crystal mirror") as a magnificent emblem of cosmic reality. And although, being cursed, she does not create either her original self-myth or that myth's transformation, she seems fully reconciled to the fated conclusion. **"The Palace of Art"** projects a more dynamic process. Here, as in the cases of Guinevere and Lancelot, there is the dismantling of a complexly developed self-myth and the substitution of an alternative myth. But the proportions of the poem make it clear that the poet's primary centers of interest were in the creation of the self-myth and the madness that results from the faulted character of that myth, and **"The Palace of Art"** is one of the three most extensive dramatizations in the Tennyson canon of the progress of madness.

First there is confusion, the mind's coordination falling into division. Then follows "dread and loathing of her solitude," which gives birth to self-scorn and the threshold hysteria of scorn of self-scorn: she tries to justify the way she has been acting by finding it rooted in her deepest sense of an authentic self. Next, nightmarish images begin to invade the "dark corners" of her mind, ghastly images of the humanity she has been so proudly aloof from— "white-eyed phantoms weeping tears of blood," hollow shadows with "hearts of flame," standing corpses with their foreheads worm-fretted. She perceives herself in a lonely human backwash, cut off from the rhythms and laws of life. The isolation of which she had been so proud now has a serpent-sting to it, the medium of aesthetic exaltation turns to mud, and instead of being "as God," she is "exilèd from eternal God." The perpetuation motif that she had found in art ("So wrought, they will not fail") now mocks her as "dreadful time, dreadful eternity" in which her fearful loneliness takes on the character of a perpetual unrelief, as the palace becomes a tomb, the artifacts no more than the "blackness" of "a solid wall," and the footsteps of humanity in the distance a grand discovery made too late.

It is a complete reversal of the bardic subtext by which the monstrous distortions and dehumanizations of the original myth are laid bare. The false *relation* which her arrogant *illusion* has sought to establish between art and life makes art itself monstrous, and life stripped of art as an authentic ordering principle becomes a mad bedlam of *confusion,* an infinity of incoherence. Such a myth translated into action *(occasion)* induces rather than avoids chaos *(elusion)* and leads inevitably, not to salvation, but to the very self-destruction that art is intended to help men prevent *(evasion).* What enables the "soul" of the poem to reverse the reversed sub-text in the brief coda to the main action of the poem is the hellish harrowing that she has experienced and the faint memory of "the riddle of the painful earth" which "Flashed through her" and never allowed her wholly to forget the "moral instinct." The poem thus reaches backward toward the *persona* in **"The Lover's Tale"** and forward toward Guinevere. (pp. 64-84)

At the chronological middle of the Tennyson canon is the centerpiece of his poetry of madness, *Maud.* The subject of *Maud* is madness in an all-encompassing way unparalleled elsewhere in Tennyson except in the superb miniature **"Rizpah"** and, in a vague and inadequate way, in **"The Lover's Tale."** The speaker in "Maud or the Madness" never achieves genuine sanity: whether he is "fantastically merry" or suffering from the dark "suspicion that all the world is against him" [Hallam Tennyson, *Alfred Tennyson: A Memoir*] *(passim),* his psyche remains even at his best moments "a little shattered." He is "a morbid

poetic soul" and "the heir of madness" who strategizes life with only a deeply faulted success. Despite the intensity of his yearnings, his myths collapse all around him, and even those in which he invests the greatest imaginative energy reward him with only a doomed embrace.

Like Tennyson's other supremely distinctive poems (*In Memoriam* and *Idylls of the King*), *Maud* was allowed to evolve over a very long period of time. Being a consciousness-in-motion poem, it could not be turned upon a thematic perception but had to wait upon such moments of intuitive insight as had the ring of authentic experiential truth to them. Nor could that authenticity be threatened by an externally imposed story-line and structure: it had to be allowed to evolve from within, emerging out of the idiosyncratic inner logic of a protagonist observed unawares, the continuity being only implicit and the white spaces between dramatic moments being either sufficiently imaginable or negligible. Thus madness surfaces and submerges in a poetic text, a linguistic artifact, that is itself a metaphoric awareness rather than an intellectual concept of madness. And the protagonist's madness is a dimension of this Apollo-gift: his capacity for pain is a measure of his capacity for pleasure. The psychic collisions that finally drive him into the asylum are magnified and rarefied by his own imagination (see especially Part II, Canto IV); the asylum lyric itself (Part II, Canto V) orchestrates in the most imaginative way fragments of memory and judgment into an illusion or myth, rather tentatively held, that he lies in an unquiet grave; and it would seem that he regains a shattered sanity by concentrating on and enlarging his imaginative memory of "the one bright thing to save / [His] yet young life in the wilds of Time."

From the beginning, the speaker suffers from such a polluted imagination that he stands on the edge of chaos. Visually intense, his memory saturated with vivid horror, terrified that he may go mad, pervaded with an acute sense of his lonely, unloved state, he spasms frantically in search of a myth. Fable-clutching is a defining characteristic of his consciousness: Echo (and Narcissus), Cain, Mammon, Timour, the Devil, Orion, the "monstrous eft . . . of old, the Sultan, the Maker, Isis, Death, Honor, Cleopatra, Viziers, Oreads, the crest of Juno's peacock, the laurel of Pyramus and Thisbe, the cedars of Lebanon, the "Forefathers of the thornless garden," and so on. It is a habit of his mind to translate experience into myth. His sense of chaos is the result of his having been so long without a personal cohering myth, his previous childhood myth having been shattered with his father's plunge into the pit. Thus he has turned his myth-making energy upon his age, and in the piercing confrontal language which is a persistent index both to his imaginative gifts and his psychic imbalance, he pins it like a scorpion to the wall. He also creates for himself a cluster of inadequate mythic actions: he will go away (but won't); he will bury himself in himself (but doesn't); he will become a stoic or "a wiser epicurean," leading a "philosopher's life in the quiet woodland ways" (but can't).

A genuine myth finally becomes available to him, and after some initial and inevitable psychic stalking, he translates it into action. Thus, the bardic subtext becomes fully operative as his way of "climb[ing] nearer out of lonely Hell." The chaotic *confusion* of his life is brought into meaningful *relation* by the myth of romantic love *(illusion)*; and by translating that myth into action *(occasion)*, he avoids the devastating effects of a life of chaos *(elusion)* and prevents his ultimate self-destruction *(evasion)*. It is not a perfectly idyllic episode because he does not quite succeed in cleansing his psyche of the sense of being, like his Hamlet prototype, "splenetic, personal, base," and thus purging his destiny of the specter of "some dark undercurrent woe"; but it is, on the whole, a remarkably successful mythic action.

The protagonist's myth of romantic love explodes in a personal storm that results in the death of Maud's brother and of Maud herself. This places the protagonist once more on the threshold of madness, and he does in fact go mad. Part II of *Maud* is a richly economical revelation of his slide into madness. The extraordinary thing about the speaker in this sequence is that he never contemplates suicide. He asks God to "Strike dead the whole weak race of venomous worms"; but he still nurses in his "dark heart / However weary, a spark of will / Not to be trampled out," and this enables him, in an exquisite lyric, to identify with "a lovely shell" on the Breton coast that, however "Frail," has had the "force to withstand, / Year upon year, the shock / Of cataract seas. . . ."

There are two new forces at work in the speaker in Part II that were not present in this threshold-to-madness situation at the beginning of Part I. One is his personal complicity in "the Christless code": he himself is guilty of "the red life spilt for a private blow—." The other is the imaginative knowledge, indelibly lodged in his memory, of

> where a garden grows.
> Fairer than ought in the world beside,
> All made up of the lily and rose
> That blow by night, when the season is good,
> To the sound of dancing music and flutes. . . .

Deprived of all possibility of mythic restoration at this point, unable, as he says,

> After long grief and pain
> To find the arms of my true love
> Round me once again!

the protagonist becomes the powerless victim of a mighty collision within his imagination—restorative memories of an almost perfect love and erosive memories of an almost unforgivable sin—and succumbs to madness.

If it is fair to conjecture, as I have, that the protagonist of *Maud* regains a shattered sanity by concentrating on and enlarging his imaginative memory of "the one bright thing to save / [His] yet young life in the wilds of Time," and if the bardic subtext upon which the thesis of this essay is largely based has cogency, then one is justified in taking a view of Part III of *Maud* in which war as such and the Crimean War specifically have very little critical relevance. What we have rather is a compulsive mythmaker trying to give some order to his stripped existential state. He gathers into the needs of his fragile sanity old memories and old patterns. The glory that he finally found in

Maud is rooted deep in "A martial song like a trumpet's call," and his ingrained habit of giving body to his ever passionate perceptions through exaggerative language is in visible flow again. He combines these two tendencies of his imagination in the adoption of a new myth *(illusion)* that will bring order *(relation)* out of chaos *(confusion)* and make available to him an action *(occasion)* which will free him from the erosive effects of a purposeless life *(elusion)* and save him from a selfish grave *(evasion)*. That there is something of the deathwish in his mythic idealism seems clear enough; but it does provide a singular opportunity, in his mythic consciousness, to be reconciled to his fellow man and reunited with his beloved.

In conclusion, then: (1) Madness is one of the most "abysmal deeps of Personality" to which the human psyche is vulnerable, and Tennyson explored its experiential coordinates from youth to old age, *in* youth and *in* old age. (2) In *Maud* there is the hint of hereditary susceptibility to madness, but in *Maud* as elsewhere, Tennyson saw madness and imagination as very closely allied, madness being the result of a mighty collision in the imagination of a gifted *persona* with which the imagination itself could not cope. The madness may be thunderous but "momentary," as in **"The Lady of Shalott"** and Guinevere; recurrent and of long standing, as in Lancelot; grotesquely inflated, self-enclosed, and static, as in **"The Lover's Tale;"** tenuously redemptive, as in **"The Palace of Art," *Maud*,** and **"Lucretius;"** catastrophic beyond even the tragic vision, as in Pelleas; both penetratingly sad and positively heroic, as in Rizpah. But without exception, sanity is traumatized by a sudden collision of mighty contraries in the consciousness or pulverized by the self-grindings of a dilemma from which there seems to be no escape. (3) The way out of the paralyzing effects of madness is through an *action* that, being rooted deeply in the authentic self, measures that self and provides the *persona* with something to be done beyond the mere endurance of pain. It is the presence of an action that converts the exacerbated consciousness into the moral being, merges *expressiveness* and *mimesis* into a new species of psychological poetry, and draws the terrifyingly intense metaphor of madness into the mainstream of human experience. We are all susceptible to madness; but madness, being imaginative rather than moral, is itself susceptible to every species of moral outcropping. Guinevere and Lancelot discover an action that is self-cleansing and enables them to establish an authentic if muted moral grandeur. Julian, in **"The Lover's Tale,"** does not: he is the slave of an imperiously arrogant romantic imagination who cannot or will not subject himself to moral imperatives external to the self-inflations of that imagination. Pelleas also fails, but his failure, unlike Julian's, fills us with a near-unmanageable sadness. He is of that penetrating company of Judge Fawley—a young person who embarks upon the Daedalian fabrication of a new self in the labyrinth of life and for whom the issue quickly shifts from *what* he will be to *if* he will be at all. As Elaine, with an almost unendurably excruciating pathos, threatens our capacity to cling to a stabilizing tragic vision, so Pelleas nearly overwhelms our classical sense of justice and challenges tragedy as the ultimate gloss on the truth of human experience. Finally (4), each of Tennyson's poems of madness is an experiment in narrative form and feeling, and each positions madness in a different relationship to story-telling. Tennyson was the first of the modern psychological poets, and he altered the art of narrative poetry by discovering not just *a* way to process action in character, though **"Rizpah"** is a superb dramatic monologue. *Each* of his poems is a new way of setting the distressed consciousness in motion, and Tennyson never probes the abysmal deeps of personality in quite the same way twice. His narrative structures are as variable as his *personae,* and each of his poems brings both variables into a new and fascinating combination. In Tennyson's poetry, then, madness is a metaphor, not only of the most devastating human distress, but also of the very greatest aesthetic challenge, a challenge which Tennyson successfully met and thereby changed dramatically the course of modern English poetry. (pp. 85-90)

> William E. Buckler, "Tennysonian Madness: Mighty Collisions in the Imagination," in his The Victorian Imagination: Essays in Aesthetic Exploration, *New York University Press, 1980, pp. 64-91.*

L. M. Findlay   (essay date 1981)

[*In the following essay, Findlay demonstrates that studying the interaction of sensation and memory in "Ulysses" offers thematic analysis of the poem.*]

Consciousness is an arena where past and present, memory and sensation interact. This situation affords opportunities for creation and control of "reality" that were as evident to classical adepts of ars memoria as they are to modern students of psychology and phenomenology. However, awareness of the conditions of consciousness does not mean that we can fully comprehend and control its processes. Tennyson, struggling to come to terms with the death of Hallam, was painfully aware of his own mental frailty and the accommodations made by consciousness to grief. The reality of personal loss had to be placed in some wider context lest it cloud his mind forever.

In **"Ulysses"** Tennyson adopts a persona famed for his shrewdness and ability to survive, though now close to the end of his life. Will physical extremity induce a comparable mental extremity, or will heroic tough-mindedness intercede? We are all familiar with the ambiguity of Tennyson's answer. The present essay attempts a fresh resolution of this ambiguity according to the consciousness activated in **"Ulysses"** by spatial and other sensory references, and by their interaction with memory in Ulysses, Tennyson, and ourselves. Ulysses' perceptions and recollections are vivid, impressive, rich in resonance. However, their details are not uniformly attractive, nor are their resonances entirely under his control. We participate in Ulysses' mental life with increasing vigilance and are eventually led beyond him by allusion to alternative versions of the Ulysses theme.

Sense experience in **"Ulysses"** is grounded in the four elements, but it is never value-free. References to earth, air, fire, and water convey mood and express judgment. The expansive ocean is firmly established as Ulysses' element, in contrast to the confining crags of Ithaca. Ulysses sees his life in terms of drinking "delight of battle," and the ocean as a possible final resting place. Appetite and elemental affinity are as closely matched in him as in the land-bound Ithacans who "hoard, and sleep, and feed." This much is apparent to any attentive reader of the poem.

References to sound and hearing are more equivocal, especially when linked to reputation as in the double-edged hyperbole of "I am become a name," or the ominously vague hope of "Some work of noble note." There is a disquieting contrast between the reassuringly specific sounds from Ulysses' past—the ringing clash of arms at Troy, the smack of oars in "sounding furrows"—and the ultimate ambiguity of death, "that eternal silence." The present mediation between past and future is ambiguously animistic: "the deep / Moans round with many voices." Ulysses' element communicates with him in a way unmatched by Penelope and Telemachus, but in a way that may not be entirely to his credit.

Tactile references reinforce the contrast between Ulysses and the Ithacans. Their ruggedness will gradually be worn away by the "soft degrees" of Telemachus' reform, whereas Ulysses and his mariners have savored more violent and fleeting encounters. They have moved through the vexations of the sea and the clash of battle, and Ulysses now conceives himself as "a part of all that [he has] met," apparently oblivious to the burden of self-diffusion in his words. The sense of touch is significantly emptied of physical reference in the psychic metaphor of "my purpose holds," preparing us for the pathos of "It may be we shall touch the Happy Isles." The potentially emotive verb "touch" suggests the intensity of Ulysses' desire to relive his past experience with Achilles, but the dominant navigational sense of the term here indicates that renewal of human acquaintance may not be granted to a man who has shown himself neither capable nor desirous of more than casual contact.

Hearing and touch make an important contribution to the rich texture of **"Ulysses,"** but the preponderant sensory detail is visual or spatial, a fitting emphasis in a poem where memory is so prominent. Most adepts of ars memoria support Cicero's contention that sight, as the strongest of the senses, plays the major role in re-creating the past. In **"Ulysses"** the visual-spatial dimension manifests itself on all levels from syntax and prosody through a full range of lexical and symbolic effects.

A consideration of the "spatial form" of the poem indicates that the movement of each section creates a spatial equivalent for the situation it presents. This is evident in the opening lines of **"Ulysses,"** where the unequivocal subject of the first sentence ("I") is placed in medias res, but not in furtherance of some briskly epic purpose. Ulysses is syntactically immured at the center of hostile circumstance, flanked on one side by stultifying things and on the other by equally distasteful activities. The second section of the poem is essentially linear in effect. Elan is a matter of memory for Ulysses now. His past is presented in an episodic measure, sometimes staccato or fractured, sometimes fluent through several lines, but always enforcing the notion of the hero's appetite for adventure and the obstacles facing him. The third section is much smoother than the second. The apostrophe to Telemachus is prosodically apt: seven of the ten lines are enjambed, and less strenuously than elsewhere in the poem, thereby supporting the idea of a smooth transition of power from father to son and the need to pursue a gradualist course. The final section of the poem reverts to the episodic measure of the second, but there is a further complication. The contradictions of Ulysses' situation are more manifest than ever and are expressed by the contest among will, precedent, possibility, and the palpable inertia of the present. These tensions are maintained till the final line, where the forces that oppose Ulysses' resolve are given the last word: "To strive, to seek, to find, and not to yield."

Inferences based on prosodic evidence are necessarily provisional. However, the sense of movement in the four sections of the poem and the spatial configurations suggested by each are greatly strengthened by Tennyson's use of locations. The main contrast is between the closed, stable environment associated with the circle, and the very different environment associated with infinite linearity. The poem opens with Ulysses trapped at the center of domestic and political obligation. "By this still hearth, among these barren crags." Ulysses' sense of entrapment contrasts starkly with Telemachus, "centred in the sphere / Of common duties," and the more noticeably so because of the affinities with the linear established in the second section of the poem. Ulysses' restlessness is well captured in the contrast between the topography of Ithaca and Troy: the congested skies of the one, the spacious plains and uncluttered horizons of the other. But Ulysses is most at home on the "dark broad seas," kinesis made measureless.

Descriptions of movement across the seas abound in the poem, and their details and resonance furnish important clues to the nature and justification of Ulysses' wanderlust. One of the most striking of these references takes the form of an axiom:

> Yet all experience is an arch where through
> Gleams that untravelled world, whose margin
>   fades
> For ever and for ever when I move.

This spatial stylization might have used the term "arc," thereby pointing to navigation and the fact that Ulysses' metaphor is shaped by the experiences of his odyssey. By preferring "arch" Tennyson evokes further associations: through architecture with the pillars of Hercules and the limits of the known world; through Homeric *arche* with the past and the onset of death. The arch of years is also to be found in Dante's *Purgatorio,* where Sapia describes herself as "già discendendo l'arco d'i miei anni", that is, at the stage in her life when, to be sapient, she ought to have turned her thoughts to God. But it is Sapia herself who describes a parabola, whereas Ulysses moves and sees through a parabolic vista, steering a course towards the regressive horizon. Whether or not Tennyson intended us to see a veiled reference here to optical possibilities in a railway tunnel, he seems to be making full use of the *"eruditus oculos"* ascribed to him by Arthur Hallam, and we are certainly invited to ponder Ulysses' spatial metaphor for life. Changes in perception due to movement do not promote in Ulysses a chastening sense of the relativity of his views.

His eyes continue to stare avidly ahead. Not for him the cloistered vision of **"The Palace of Art"** with its "shadowed grots of arches interlaced." But does he at this stage offer us more than man as projectile, life as compulsive tourism?

The image of the arch is supported by another striking passage a few lines later:

> And this gray spirit yearning in desire
> To follow knowledge like a sinking star,
> Beyond the utmost bound of human thought.

The key question here is whether Ulysses can point to knowledge as the justification for his wandering. The syntax invites us to connect the "sinking star" with Ulysses as well as with knowledge. The ambiguity seems deliberate: Ulysses' capacity to know dwindles with his vital powers rather than providing consolation in old age. But is following knowledge certainly equivalent to knowing? The uneasiness of Ulysses' formulation is sustained in the notion of going beyond "human thought." The transcendence involved is more than intellectual swagger. The "bound" in question may mean a boundary or a leap. The sense of a margin or limit clearly dominates, but signifies metahuman stamina, not apotheosis. Ulysses' ambition is horizontal, not vertical, its emphasis quantitative rather than qualitative, despite his opening attempt to distinguish between stagnation and real living. The secondary suggestion of thought as a series of leaps reminds us that Ulysses' mind has bounded back and forth throughout the poem.

However, we are still not certain about the nature and value of Ulysses' thinking and knowledge. He himself has pointed to the limited awareness of the Ithacans who "know not" him, unlike the mariners with whom he has "toiled, and wrought, and thought." One might expect "fought" instead of "thought" here; the cerebral substitution is uneasy, like all such references in the poem. But the Tennyson canon contains numerous explorations of epistemology that distinguish between true and false, ephemeral and lasting knowledge. After indicating his son in a rather wooden way Ulysses gestures more expansively, "There lies the port," and follows this with the third version of the spatial image that is central to his conception of cognition and life:

> for my purpose holds
> To sail beyond the sunset, and the baths
> Of all the western stars, until I die.

The exceeding of the bounds of human thought is now translated into navigational terms, and we feel the incremental force, physical and metaphysical, of "beyond." There seems at first sight no way of being surer about this passage than about its two predecessors. However, the obvious Homeric allusion helps clarify matters. In his annotated edition of *The Poems of Tennyson* Christopher Ricks states that the poet is adapting *Odyssey* v. 270-275 at this point, but misses Tennyson's irony. The baths of Ocean (*loetron Okeanoio*) figure once only in the *Odyssey,* and the crucial circumstance is that Ulysses sets out *alone* from Calypso's isle after showing great caution and shrewdness in determining whether Calypso had set a trap for him on his hazardous journey. Ulysses is prepared to "endure, with a heart within . . . patient of affliction," but nevertheless builds his raft with great care and takes the helm vigilantly while Calypso summons a warm breeze to waft him on his way. The main implications of this Homeric echo seem clear. Ulysses is on his own, despite his invocation of the mariners, but is incapable of the careful calculation and vigorous self-reliance of earlier days. He acknowledges his loss of strength but not the full measure of his isolation. His visionary capacities, such as they are, are hobbled to his own needs. The affirmation, "Much have I seen and known," is subtly questioned by Tennyson. Ulysses may be wide-ranging and synthetic in his perceptions, fitting past and present detail to his image for resolute advance—unlike the analytical Telemachus "discerning to fulfil"—but this does not of itself make him a "lord of large experience" like Hallam, one who knows neither entrapment nor anomie because his "faith has centre everywhere, / Nor cares to fix itself to form."

A fuller appreciation of the interplay of sensation and memory in the poem can be gained by considering the nature of Ulysses' imagination, as revealed in his use of figurative language. The most sustained figures in the poem are, of course, not epic similes but those spatial images already discussed. Puns and animistic devices have also been mentioned. The latter may be partially defended as true to the Homeric world, consistent with the impulses behind the naming of the Happy Isles, though they also reveal Ulysses' displacement of humanity from his family and nation to the milieu of his heroic endeavors. The reliance on synecdoche and metonymy is almost inevitable in a poem whose persona is a part of all that he has met, intently manipulating details rich in personal association. These devices can be used pejoratively—"As though to breathe were life"—but more often they show Ulysses focusing on the salient virtues of himself and his crew: "My mariners, / Souls . . . Free hearts, free foreheads . . . We are not now that strength . . . One equal temper of heroic hearts." But what is the status of such a "free" heart? How does it sit with Ulysses' "hungry heart," and is the freedom involved the kind that comes with wisdom, as Cicero reminds us in *Paradoxa Stoicorum?* It may be a dubious form of detachment, like the "heart-free" hero's in **Maud.** Furthermore, the "free foreheads" seem to have little in common with the brows that witness so much grief in Homer. The Virgilian and Ciceronian *frons* is certainly the mirror of feeling, and hearts and foreheads will thus register the same in any trusting company. But in this case such unanimity of the inner and outer man ought not to obscure Ulysses' gift for craftiness. Ulysses affirms his kinship in idealized terms. Idealization is itself akin to euphemism, and it is not surprising to see a euphemistic element in the references to death that outnumber the unequivocal admission, "until I die": "that eternal silence . . . When I am gone . . . It may be that the gulfs will wash us down." The forces of negation and privation are also apparent, in the incidences of litotes, for example: "I cannot rest from travel . . . not least, but honoured of them all . . . decent not to fail . . . Not unbecoming men that strove with Gods." The use of this form of emphasis keeps the alternatives to Ulysses' chosen course constantly before us.

However, a more important source of the imaginative energies in the poem lies in another cluster of related devices: antithesis, tautology, repetition, and redundancy. The basis of the poem in contrast occasions such apparently balanced propositions as "To rust unburnished, not to shine in use . . . all times I have enjoyed / Greatly, have suffered greatly . . . Though much is taken, much abides . . . He works his work, I mine." The sense of measured discrimination is deceptive. Closer scrutiny discloses a self-glorifying impulse, confirming the suspicion that Ulysses' greatness has more quantity than quality, while the reference to Telemachus is damnably neat, the kind of sundering that might gratify a martial mind addicted to swift decisions but not a devotee of thought and knowledge. This particular antithesis is also tautologous ("He works his work") and underscores the self-referring insularity of different philosophies of life. (Sound is evaluative here too, pedestrian and ugly repetition giving way to the rising assonance of "I mine.") Redundancy may strike us at first as simple emphasis, as in the "barren crags" at the beginning of the poem. But there is a definite cumulative effect to formulations such as these: "For ever and for ever . . . to pause, to make an end . . . all times . . . always . . . all experience . . . something more, / A bringer of new things . . . to store and hoard myself . . . yearning in desire . . . my son, mine own . . . slow prudence . . . toiled, and wrought . . . old; / Old age . . . old days . . . something . . . Some work . . . that which we are, we are." These are surely the accents of self-persuasion. Ulysses' repetition and *circular* logic are deeply ironic in a poem that strives to establish his affinities with the new and the infinitely linear.

The illusory progress of such restatement suggests that the gratifications of Ulysses' "hungry heart" and mind are at least in part deceptive. Not surprisingly, he cannot steer clear of hyperbole either, but again Tennyson uses ironic echo to aid our interpretation. When Ulysses declares that "Life piled on life / Were all too little," it is difficult not to think of death: corpses heaped on the battlefield, and the barrows of the dead; or the titanic stratagem of piling Ossa on Olympus, Pelion on Ossa. Homer points to the foolishness of such overreaching through the blighting of the youthful promise of Ephialtes and Otus. [In *Inferno*] Dante mentions only Ephialtes (Fialte), but stresses the fact that his weapons are now immobile: "le braccia ch'el menò, già mai non move. Ulysses' ambitions are horizontal, but the language wherein he expresses them has admonitory associations with illegitimate revolt and a doom designed to terrify one who would "shine in use." A similar process is at work in the concluding reference to "that strength which in old days / Moved earth and heaven." There seems to be a titanic force again in mind, but the reader's first connection may not be with Ulysses and his crew but with the power of their greatest foe, constantly referred to as the Earth-Shaker (*Poseidaon enosichthon*). Misled by memory, Ulysses seems intent on giving Poseidon another chance, now that he is no longer under the protection of Pallas Athene nor accompanied by his crew.

"**Ulysses**" is a richly ambivalent poem, nor would one wish to reduce its meaning to one narrowly programmatic reading. However, one needs somehow to come to terms with the contradictions in the poem, whether or not Tennyson ever did—or Hallam ever could have:

> But a still deeper feeling is caused by that immediate knowledge of the past which is supplied by memory. . . . I fear these expressions will be thought to border on mysticism. Yet I must believe that if any one, in the least accustomed to analyse his feelings, will take the pains to reflect on it, he may remember moments in which the burden of this mystery has lain heavy on him; in which he has felt it miserable to exist, as it were, piecemeal, and in the continual flux of a stream; in which he has wondered, as at a new thing, how we can be, and have been, and not be that which we have been. But the yearnings of the human soul for the irrecoverable past are checked by a stern knowledge of impossibility. So also in its eager rushings towards the future, its desire of that mysterious something which now is not, but which in another minute we shall be, the soul is checked by a lesson of experience, which teaches her that she cannot carry into that future the actual mode of her existence. But were these impossibilities removed, were it conceivable that the soul in one state should co-exist with the soul in another, how impetuous would be that desire of reunion, which even the awful laws of time cannot entirely forbid!

The imagery and sentiments of Hallam's prose have much in common with Tennyson's poem. However, Hallam checks his impetuous urge to recover the irrecoverable, though vividly aware of the allure of such an enterprise. Ulysses in old age has forsaken discretion for valor, a shift of allegiance more understandable than admirable.

Homer and Dante have already been invoked in an attempt to clarify some of Tennyson's ambiguities. Such a procedure is always hazardous, but Tennyson seems deliberately to activate our memories of the *Odyssey* and *Divine Comedy* in order to suggest the most appropriate response to Ulysses' nostalgia. A concluding comparison of Tennyson and Dante may shed further light on the question of Ulysses' nobility and the probity of Tennyson's entwining of memory and truth.

Two passages from Dante recommend themselves in this connection, one well known to commentators on **"Ulysses,"** the other not. The general situation of Ulysses by the seashore at dusk, a "gray spirit yearning in desire" to be embarked again on his endless quest but physically incapable of such motion, offers an ironic parallel to the eagerness of the true pilgrims in Dante:

> Noi eravam lunghesso mare ancora,
> come gente che pensa a suo cammino,
> che va col cuore e col corpo dimora.

> Meanwhile, we linger'd by the water's brink,
> Like men, who, musing on their road, in thought
> Journey, while motionless the body rests.

Pious eagerness is appeased by the Angel of Faith whose swift bark has no need of sail or oar. This is divine transcendence not egotistic distortion of the facts of nature. Tennyson could not explicitly introduce a Christian moral

context into his poem without violating its special nature. **"Ulysses"** implicates such a context with great tact.

The second apposite passage from Dante is the account of the last voyage of Ulisse in *Inferno.* It is rich in poetic justice. Ulisse suffers as the larger tongue of a double flame shared with Diomedes because of their fraudulent acquisition of the Palladium. Dante is relentlessly censorious, despite his eagerness to learn more about Ulisse ("redi che del disio ver' lei mi piego!"). The witlessness of the last voyage ("folle volo") will end with Poseidon having the last word: " 'I mar fu sovra noi richiuso." Ulisse takes the form most graphically epitomizing his verbal trickery:

> Lo maggior corno de la fiamma antica
> cominciò a crollarsi mormorando,
> pur come quella cui vento affatica;

> indi la cima qua e là menando,
> come fosse la lingua che parlasse,
> gittò voce di fuori e disse.

> Of the old flame forthwith the greater horn
> Began to roll, murmuring, as a fire
> That labours with the wind, then to and fro
> Wagging the top, as a tongue uttering sounds,
> Threw out its voice and spake.

Tongue and breath were the favorite instruments of Ulisse when alive, and they are the symbols of his torture in hell. As if this were not enough for Dante's allegorical purposes, he has Ulisse dramatize his talent for silvertongued deception. He persuades his crew to go beyond the pillars of Hercules, appealing to them as brothers who share his lofty ideals. Then comes a damaging admission:

> Li miei compagni fec' io sì aguti,
> con questa orazion picciola, al cammino,
> che a pena poscia li avrei ritenuti.

> With these few words I sharpened for the voyage
> The mind of my associates, that I then
> Could scarcely have withheld them.

The *frati* have now become *compagni,* and Ulisse mockingly confesses to the uncertainty of his control over those whom he has just fatally manipulated. He is alone, having wilfully turned the poop of his vessel to the morning (and the known world). His true kin are neither his crew nor his family, but other arch-deceivers like Diomedes.

It seems possible that Tennyson followed the principle at work in Dante's portrayal of Ulisse. The form of Ulisse embodies a moral judgment, and his brilliant, hollow rhetoric justifies his condemnation. Tennyson's Ulysses is as much alone as Ulisse. Ulysses' notions of knowledge and truth are distorted, if not entirely specious; his desires now mock his failing physical powers; and, the most pathetic plague of all, his dazzling powers of persuasion now play upon himself. He is convinced by his *orazion picciola,* and his frustrations increase commensurately; we need not be won over by his words and may thus increase our obligation to Tennyson as moral tutor and master poet.

Sensory references and figurative language collaborate effectively to give this poem immediacy and unity and to encourage our participation in Ulysses' mental life; but our memories are not identical with his. The allusive fabric of the poem controls its larger meanings—one might say its ethical import in an aptly unobtrusive way that curbs the claims of Ulysses. Memory can create the present and future in the image of the past, but only at a price. It allows Ulysses to sustain the galling illusion of heroic quest, just as it undermines Tennyson's resolve to go on living after the death of Hallam. In **"Ulysses"** there is a vivid dramatization of tendencies Tennyson shares with his persona, but the pains and consolations of personal memory are placed in the cautionary context of that collective literary memory where Homer and Dante reign. (pp. 139-49)

> *L. M. Findlay, "Sensation and Memory in Tennyson's 'Ulysses',"* in *Victorian Poetry, Vol. 19, No. 2, Summer, 1981, pp. 139-49.*

Timothy Peltason   (essay date 1984)

[*In the following essay, Peltason examines Tennyson's depiction of nature in relation to that of English Romantic poets.*]

Tennyson prided himself on his powers of observation and on the care with which he rendered in his poems the familiar forms of external nature. Anecdotes tell of his falling to the ground in the course of rural walks, that he might more closely examine the petals of a flower or the wings of a dragonfly. When Ruskin suggested that the lines from **"Maud,"** "For her feet have touched the meadows / And left the daisies rosy," were an example of the pathetic fallacy, Tennyson was indignant: "Why . . . the very day I wrote it, I saw the daisies rosy in Maiden's Croft, and thought of enclosing one to Ruskin labelled 'A pathetic fallacy.' " This scrupulous fidelity to natural appearances was notorious among Tennyson's contemporaries and earned him both the respect of the scientific community and the appreciation of the Victorian public, who felt that he was showing them for the first time the beauty of nature's every minute creation. Writing in 1940, Edmund Wilson chose to distinguish Michelet's passages of natural description by ascribing to them "an accuracy almost Tennysonian."

For all his descriptive powers, however, Tennyson wrote remarkably little descriptive poetry, a paradox that is easily resolved by distinguishing poetic devices from poetic aims. Tennyson was indeed the master of the vividly rendered detail, but such details, as they appear in finished poems, are characteristically discrete, removed from natural context or obviously manipulated in the service of some more than descriptive end. Of course, there is probably no major poetry in English whose ends are simply descriptive, certainly not that of Tennyson's immediate predecessors and most imposing models, the great Romantics. But Tennyson's poetic means, too, differ significantly from those of Wordsworth and Coleridge, Shelley and Keats, and in his memorable early lyrics he addresses the concerns of what M. H. Abrams has named the greater Romantic lyric in a significantly and purposefully modified poetic form.

In the familiar lyric form that Abrams has named, a first-person figure with whom we readily identify the poet engages in a dialectic encounter with the object world, commonly a landscape or a figure of nature. This encounter is both the subject and the occasion of a poem that enacts its own genesis and so reports the experience, whether of natural piety or imaginative usurpation, from which it arises. Even when the encounter with the natural world is a self-conscious exercise in the pathetic fallacy, as in Keats's "Ode to a Nightingale," even when the poet knows, as Coleridge does in his "Dejection," that "We receive but what we give," the experience is structured and presented as an encounter between the speaking imagination and the world. There is at least the fiction of immediacy, the fiction of an achieved continuity between the creative imagination of the poet, the language of the poem, and the world of our own experience. But Tennyson dispenses with this fiction. His early poems make use of natural observation and clearly emanate from a distinctive sensibility, but they hold themselves at a knowing distance from experience and do not pretend to report directly the career of a particular self in a particular place or circumstance.

In the *Poems, Chiefly Lyrical* of 1830, Tennyson makes his debut as a younger Romantic poet whose distinctive contribution to the tradition is a lyric form that, while it separates the poet and the reader from each other and from the familiarly observed world, gives shape to a lyric voice that binds the world, the poet, and the reader together in the space of the poem.

This, of course, is only to repeat the insight of one of the earliest and still the most astute reviewer of *Poems, Chiefly Lyrical,* Arthur Hallam, who listed as one of Tennyson's "distinctive excellencies," his "vivid, picturesque delineation of objects, and the peculiar skill with which he holds all of them fused, to borrow a metaphor from science, in a medium of strong emotion." As Hallam does not say, Tennyson rarely writes sustained passages of description. Even when he does, however, Hallam's comment remarks the way in which description is secondary to emotional effect. The 1830 poem **"Elegiacs"** (reprinted in 1884 and subsequently as **"Leonine Elegiacs"**) offers a characteristic example:

> Low-flowing breezes are roaming the broad valley dimmed in the gloaming:
> Through the black-stemmed pines only the far river shines.
> Creeping through blossomy rushes and bowers of rose-blowing bushes,
> Down by the poplar tall rivulets babble and fall.
> Barketh the shepherd-dog cheerly; the grasshopper carolleth clearly,
> Deeply the wood-dove coos; shrilly the owlet halloos;
> Winds creep; dews fall chilly: in her first sleep earth breathes stilly:
> Over the pools in the burn water-gnats murmur and mourn.
> Sadly the far kine loweth: the glimmering water outfloweth:
> Twin peaks shadowed with pine slope to the dark hyaline.

As Valerie Pitt has observed, the passage only appears to be descriptive and is, in fact, more concerned with its own metrical and phonic inventiveness and with creating an atmosphere of mystery and melancholy, than with present-ing an observed scene. The poem continues with a conventional lament for a lost love, Rosalind, moving further from natural description and closer to the emotional concerns signaled by its title:

> Low-throned Hesper is stayed between the two
>   peaks: but the Naiad
> Throbbing in mild unrest holds him beneath in
>   her breast.
> The ancient poetess singeth, that Hesperus all
>   things bringeth,
> Smoothing the wearied mind: bring me my love,
>   Rosalind.
> Thou comest morning or even; she cometh not
>   morning or even.
> False-eyed Hesper, unkind, where is my sweet
>   Rosalind?

This imaginative structure recalls in crude outline the practice of those Romantic lyrics in which perceived natural landscape provides the means to important self-revelation, except that here both the scene and the self-revelation have undergone their Romantic transformation before entering the poem. Whatever vague sense of loss the poem attempts to record has been conventionalized into the lament for a fictitious beloved, and the natural scene has given way to the personifications of the last six lines. Furthermore, the poet's reflections are now drawn not from nature but from a song of "the ancient poetess," Sappho.

Even in the first ten lines natural detail seems strangely unnatural. True, the natural noises that begin at line five are suddenly distinct, as if the sounds of nature, more than its sights, are able to reach through to the poet untransformed by the "medium of strong emotion." Perhaps that is why these sounds seem oddly out of place. Gradually, however, the poem draws them back into its world. The dog's cheerful bark, coming first, is at once the most prosaically rendered of these sounds and the least in keeping with the poem's predominant mood. Dogs bark both in and out of poems, but the caroling grasshopper that comes next, whatever its emotional quality, draws us back into the artifice of poetic language. "Carolleth," far from capturing the actual sound of a grasshopper, distracts the reader from natural reference. Then, with the deep-cooing dove, the poem's dominant sound textures and emotional atmosphere have returned and nature has receded. The sound the bird makes is less important than the sound the word makes, and this impression is only strengthened by the murmur and mourn of the water-gnats a few lines later. For this, as Tennyson's younger contemporary William Allingham later noted, cannot have come from the natural scene at the late hour described, and derives instead from line 27 of Keats's "To Autumn," "Then in a wailful choir the small gnats mourn." The sequence of natural sounds, culminating in the literary allusion, repeats in small the process by which nature becomes poeticized.

Both landscape and feeling have been de-naturalized, filtered through the same very literary sensibility before being allowed to enter the poem, where they may meet on common ground. Thus, the important transition in the poem is not from the landscape to the poet's consciousness, but from the putatively observed scene of the first ten lines to the clearly conventionalized one of the last six, a transition that repeats the originating movement of the poem, a movement away from nature into language. The familiar closing device, contrasting the infinite renewability of nature to human mortality, enforces a distinct, but related, point about the inalterable difference between man and nature and the resultant failure of natural consolation, an issue that receives greater emphasis in those later poems in which the poet has greater need of consolation.

Here it takes its part in an odd mixture. The poem laments the difference of the natural from the human world, but at the same time exploits images of nature in the effort to express human emotion, a procedure made both necessary and possible by the condition of language, which is itself unlike the world, but which alone permits the pathetic fallacies that render the natural and the human in terms of one another. This poem about separation is itself separated from the natural and human worlds, which can enter it only by being translated—that is, by receiving expression in words that are as interested in their own sounds as in their powers of reference, or that are drawn from other texts. These words have not renounced, but they have self-consciously qualified, their powers of reference. It is a truism that there is nothing in poetry except words, but a poem as poetical as **"Leonine Elegiacs"** draws attention to this truth by exaggeration.

But **"Leonine Elegiacs"** is hardly one of Tennyson's finest poems, and this reading may seem to do no more than convict Tennyson once again of the artificiality for which, among other things, an earlier generation dismissed him. By looking at other poems of the period and by referring to the practice of the Romantic poets, we can offer against this reduction of Tennyson the argument that his characteristic practice does not represent a regression from Wordsworthian heroic naturalism or egotistical sublimity, either one, but rather a critical development of high Romantic practice.

William K. Wimsatt's important essay on "The Structure of Romantic Nature Imagery" advanced the thesis that "The common feat of the Romantic nature poets was to read meanings into the landscape," and that this feat was accomplished by combining a close attention to observed nature with what Wordsworth termed in his 1815 Preface the "*modifying* powers of the imagination." Perception and imagination are partners in the experience of nature, or, from "Tintern Abbey,"

> . . . of all the mighty world
> Of eye and ear,—both what they half create,
> And what perceive;

so that the meaning generated by any reading of landscape is the product equally of the reader-poet and of the landscape itself, and is thus a witness to the achieved relationship between them. A tension, or better yet a balance, obtains between "reading" and "reading into." For Tennyson, too, nature presented itself as an object of interpretation. The poet remembered all his life how, in earliest boyhood, he would hold his arms open to stormy weather and cry, "I hear a voice that's speaking in the wind." He wrote to Emily Sellwood in 1837, near the beginning of their long courtship: "A known landskip is to me an old friend that continually talks to me of my own youth and half-forgotten things, and indeed, does more for me than many an old friend that I know." Pleasant as this seems, however, it already threatens to compromise the independent significance of nature and to reduce the landscape to a repository of private human meanings.

In Tennyson's poetry the delicate balance between perception and imagination is further tipped, and when nature speaks it is characteristically the evidence of dementia. *Maud* offers many examples, perhaps the best in its opening lines:

> I hate the dreadful hollow behind the little
>   wood;
> Its lips in the field above are dabbled with blood-
>   red heath,
> The red-ribb'd ledges drip with a silent horror
>   of blood,
> And Echo there, whatever is ask'd her, answers
>   "Death."

Nature's voice has become an echo, independent here of any particular utterance, but wholly dependent upon the speaker's own obsession.

When Ruskin first defined and discussed the pathetic fallacy in Volume 3 of *Modern Painters,* he intended to describe an imaginative limitation of the modern age—Scott and Turner were the two exceptions—and he had Tennyson in mind as the characteristic poet of the day. He was surely right to discern in Tennyson a certain high-handedness with nature, a frankly exploitative interest in the visual accuracy that Tennyson and Ruskin valued equally. But as Josephine Miles's survey of the *Pathetic Fallacy in the Nineteenth Century* confirms, Tennyson's use of the pathetic fallacy was something quite different from that of the Romantics and sprang from psychological and poetic motives quite other than those that Ruskin had posited.

> Tennyson, [says Josephine Miles] contrary to my expectation at least, used the [pathetic fallacy] far less than the established standard of fifty lines to a bestowal. His frequency was about one in ninety lines. His thought regarding natural objects, still deeply full of qualities, scenes, and parallels as before, nevertheless concerned itself with a fundamentally different structure of relationship between nature and man . . . for the first time the pathetic fallacy consistently expresses a new vision of things. The vision is one of sensed qualities, not objects, as the associates of human emotions. Immediately felt color and atmosphere take the place of representative objects and arrangements. The adjective rather than the noun is clue to the emotion.

Here is a description, reached by much counting and comparison, of the "medium of strong emotion" from Hallam's early review. The distance between subject and object is bridged by the distributive quality of the adjective which applies equally to both. The distinct realms of consciousness and nature, interdependent in Romantic poet-

ry, are now intermingled. They have grown less distinct through occupying a common emotional ground, as in **"Leonine Elegiacs."**

Miles marks this process in another way by observing that Tennyson is the first major poet in whose work uses of the pathetic fallacy, attributing human emotion to nature, are equalled by uses of "objectification," rendering human qualities in terms of natural objects. Such an exchange of qualities produces natural description like this from **"Isabel,"** another of the 1830 poems:

> The mellowed reflex of a winter moon;
> A clear stream flowing with a muddy one,
> Till in its onward current it absorbs
> With swifter movement and in purer light
> The vexed eddies of its wayward brother:
> A leaning and upbearing parasite,
> Clothing the stem, which else had fallen quite
> With clustered flower-bells and ambrosial orbs
> Of rich fruit bunches leaning on each other—
> Shadow forth thee.

Pathetic fallacy is contained within a larger structure of objectification. Natural objects act like humans—streams are vexed and have brothers—but they are present in the poem only to shadow forth the human subject. This odd reversal is itself shadowed forth in the image of the "up-bearing" parasite that supports its host plant. Nature comes first in the passage, which begins as description, but it comes second in importance and is explicitly subordinated to the human world.

The increased interpenetration of natural and human qualities has resulted, in fact, in the estrangement of nature. It is one thing to hear a voice in the wind as the four-year old Tennyson did, and the experience may be one of communion with a greater spirit. When nature speaks only of the hearer's own obsessions, however, there is no dialogue, but only delusion. Likewise, the pathetic fallacy may have begun in witness to a sympathetic or an analogical relationship between man and nature, but its use by Tennyson, coupled with his use of objectification, only serves to denote a nature that is de-natured and put in service of other ends. The medium of strong emotion in which man and nature are fused is itself too recognizably the product of a human sensibility.

But Tennyson does not succumb to solipsism in his poems or think that nature bends to his will. While it is true that Mariana thinks the whole world as dreary as her own life, **"Mariana"** knows more than Mariana and takes the estrangement of the world as a starting point. Unlike Ruskin's sample modern poet, Tennyson is not carried away by his own emotions into the weak-willed belief that nature shares them with him. Indeed, the malleability of a nature that readily takes the shape of the poet's mind or of Isabel's or Mariana's character is precisely the evidence that the poet confronts not nature itself, but a phantasm. Nature is intransigent, outside the poet's mind, but also outside his poem, present only in his figures. Tennyson's poetic artifice is thus an imaginative choice, rather than an imaginative limitation, the expression of the bookishness of the youthful poet, but also of an exacting scepticism about the relationship between human experience and the world of objects.

We may return, then, in an altered vocabulary, to the question of Tennyson's relations to Romantic poetry, saying now that Tennyson writes about nature allegorically, using that charged term as it is used by Paul de Man in his influential essay, "The Rhetoric of Temporality." "Allegory," according to de Man, is the poetic means of true Romanticism, specifically of Rousseau and Wordsworth. In de Man's special usage, the allegorical is distinguished from the symbolic as the mode of language that knows and acknowledges its own difference from the world, the world to which it may seem to refer and with which it can never truly coincide. Allegorical language thus confesses its irrecoverable distance from experience, and this distance corresponds to that which separates the flux and contingency of consciousness from the permanence of nature. The character of this correspondence, which relates a linguistic situation to a human one, is not, however, developed by de Man, though it is precisely this correspondence that reopens the question of referentiality.

In "The Rhetoric of Temporality" and in other essays, especially in his reviews of the work of Harold Bloom, de Man takes a stand against Wimsatt in the continuing debate over whether the Romantics, and especially Wordsworth, were nature poets in any meaningful or essential way, and, in so doing, he describes a use of language similar to that I have been attributing to Tennyson. Yet the differences between Tennyson's poetic strategies and Wordsworth's are evident, and in Wimsatt's scheme or de Man's, Tennyson appears regressive. To de Man, post-Romantic writers reveal a failure of nerve, a retreat from the imaginative heroism that he describes in an earlier essay as "a possibility for consciousness to exist entirely by and for itself, independently of all relationship with the outside world, without being moved by an intent aimed at any part of this world." The Romantics are "the first modern writers to have put into question, in the language of poetry, the ontological priority of the sensory object."

But de Man himself retreats from this position in his later work, recognizing—as Tennyson had a century before—the logical contradiction in a scheme that separates language from the world and then empowers it to make ontological determinations. Putting the world into question in language will never alter its priority, as Tennyson acknowledges in his use of a poetic diction that does not describe nature directly, yet relies on nature for its images. Where a traditional view objects to Tennyson's abandonment of the natural for the poetical, de Man would likely fault him for a nostalgic involvement with both nature and consciousness and with the possibility of adequate reference. Yet if the first of these positions underestimates the anti-natural, anti-mimetic element in Romanticism, the second underestimates the extent to which Tennyson was himself an advanced reader of the Romantics whose work anticipates the insights of modern criticism and, if only indirectly, has helped to shape them.

Tennyson's boyhood enthusiasm for Byron is well known, as is his mature admiration for Wordsworth, whom he considered "on the whole the greatest English poet since Milton," and his special affection for Keats, whose reputation George Ford credits Tennyson with reviving. Thus, in the progress and character of his tastes is reflected the history of Romantic reputation in the nineteenth and twentieth centuries. More important, Tennyson's poetry seems to develop from an extreme moment in the Romantic dialectic, specifically from the recognition of an antithetical relationship between imagination and nature that is adumbrated in several of Tennyson's early poems.

Long before the famous speculations of *In Memoriam* on "Nature, red in tooth and claw," before Tennyson evidenced any anxiety over the findings of the geologists or the evolutionists, his poems offered a vision of the human and the natural as distinct, if not antipathetic, realms. In **"Leonine Elegiacs"** natural and human processes are at odds, and in the earlier landscape meditation **"Ode: O Bosky Brook,"** the young poet explicitly denies any reciprocity of man and nature. Indeed, the nature he addresses is hardly natural, and **"Ode: O Bosky Brook"** leaves the observed scene behind almost immediately to address a personified moon and then the Egyptian goddess of the darkness.

> I savour of the Egyptian and adore
> Thee, venerable dark! august obscure!
>   Sublimest Athor!
>   It is not that I doat upon
> Thy glooms, because the weary mind is fraught
>   With fond comparison
> Of thy deep shadow to is inward strife,
>   But rather,
>   That as thou wert the parent of all life,
> Even so thou art the mother of all thought,
> Which wells not freely from the mind's recess
>   When the sharp sunlight occupies the sense
> With this fair world's exceeding comeliness.
>   . . . Not that the mind is edged,
>   Not that the spirit of thought is freshlier
>   fledged
> With stillness like the stillness of the tomb
> And grossest gloom,
> As it were of the inner sepulchre.
> Rare sound, spare light will best address
> The soul for awful muse and solemn watchfulness.

Once past the exclamation points and the Gothic manners, this is a fascinating passage. For de Man, the moments at which Wordsworth most clearly reveals his allegorical consciousness—the moments at which he is most surely and powerfully himself—are those in which the light of sense goes out, and it is such a moment that Tennyson celebrates here. The imagination takes flight as the light of nature fades. But the speaker does not invoke a darkness that comes after nature. Athor, the name of Tennyson's goddess of darkness, "did not mean that privation of light which succeeds sunset; but the darkness of Chaos before creation." Those creepy familiars, the grave and the sepulchre, are rejected here because they are images of lateness, and the poem seeks to recover the imaginatively potent absence before creation. Imagination is prior to nature, for its darkness prepares a dawn. The "rare sound" and "spare light" that close the poem are an odd qualification, perhaps a suggestion of dawn and its quickening, or perhaps the sign of an unwillingness or an inability to conceive an entire absence of nature.

"Ode: O Bosky Brook" was probably written before Tennyson had read Wordsworth, but these opening lines from **"Timbuctoo"** almost certainly were not:

> I stood upon the Mountain which o'erlooks
> The narrow seas, whose rapid interval
> Parts Afric from green Europe, when the Sun
> Had fallen below the Atlantick, and above
> The silent Heavens were blenched with faery
>   light.

In the first movement of this visionary poem, the light of nature once again goes out, to be replaced by the uncertain "faery light" of imagination. The passage from nature to imagination is thus located not in the center of the poem, as it would have been in Wordsworth, but at the beginning, before the beginning really, because the sun already "had fallen" at the first moment that the poem describes. The imagination stands forth independently, and its light, as Wordsworth asserted before him and as Tennyson was still asserting in the very late poem **"Merlin and the Gleam,"** was "Not of the sunlight, / Not of the moonlight, / Not of the starlight." Tennyson attempts to begin his career at the frontier to which Romantic poetry has conducted him, where nature is left behind for the grander forms of vision.

But it is not an easy matter to write poetry on the far side of this rupture. Both **"Timbuctoo"** and **"Ode: O Bosky Brook"** put forth a poetic "I" whose consciousness will supplant nature, but the latter poem ends with this announcement, while the former can only release the imagination from the world to tell a story in which the world returns to triumph. As the poem closes, the magical city of "Timbuctoo" is preparing to yield its magic to "keen *Discovery,*" and at the last the faery light cannot be sustained:

> . . . and I
> Was left alone on Calpe, and the Moon
> Had fallen from the night, and all was dark!

A poetry wholly beyond the world has lost its sustaining tensions, tensions that were maintained in Wordsworth by highlighting the passage from the natural to the visionary that was revelatory of the imagination's power.

In the poems of the 1830 volume that begin to define Tennyson's characteristic practice, nature returns in a new way, as the raw material for poetic language. **"Recollections of the Arabian Nights"** transplants the natural sights and sounds of Lincolnshire into the exuberantly artificial kingdom of Haroun Alraschid, a proto-Yeatsian paradise of art. The lush vegetation of **"The Kraken"** surrounds a mythical beast in a closely, but impossibly, observed undersea landscape, necessarily the willed fancy of the author. And in **"Mariana,"** the richly particular description of the moated grange hardly distinguishes between natural and man-made evidences of decay and dreariness. But this is not the sign of an achieved intimacy. It is rather that Mariana's spiritual disease and the author's intention to portray it determine a marshalling of descriptive detail that never pretends to arise from a lived episode. Only the

poplar refuses to signify Mariana's mood for her, signifying instead the uncontrolled and excluded world of nature that enters the poem only as an allegorical sign.

I would like to offer a fuller reading here of another 1830 poem, because it is less celebrated than it should be, I think, and also because it is exemplary and suggestive in its relationships to nature and to Romantic nature poetry. **"The Dying Swan"** is a poem about a legendary and literary bird that begins in the midst of a calm and expectant and peculiar natural scene:

> The plain was grassy, wild and bare,
> Wide, wild, and open to the air,
> Which had built up everywhere
> An under-roof of doleful gray.
> With an inner voice the river ran,
> Adown it floated a dying swan,
> And loudly did lament.
> It was the middle of the day.
> Ever the weary wind went on,
> And took the reed-tops as it went.

The natural setting, wild and far from man, grows slowly in its isolation into something stranger, more than natural. A first line of simple description is oddly repeated in the sound and sense of line two, as the bare plain is opened up and then closed in by the under-roof of gray. The river appears in line five as if we were supposed to know already that it was there. Its inner voice reinforces the sense of enclosure, a sense that the elements of this landscape keep to themselves. The dying swan, a creature of legend, removes the landscape still further from simple rural description, and it, too, seems separated from the other elements of the scene. It floats on the river, yet swan and river have each their separate voices, and there is no evidence yet that the swan's song is heeded. Dying at midday, the swan is out of harmony with its place, and the perpetual, weary wind is as indifferent to the swan as to time. Nor is the rest of the landscape more attentive:

> Some blue peaks in the distance rose,
> And white against the cold-white sky,
> Shone out their crowning snows.
>   One willow over the river wept,
> And shook the wave as the wind did sigh;
> Above in the wind was the swallow,
>   Chasing itself at its own wild will,
>   And far through the marish green and still
>   The tangled water-courses slept
>   Shot over with purple, and green, and yellow.

The scene gradually fills up with a host of animal, vegetable, and mineral objects, each discrete and isolated, or involved at most in some small, contained interaction. The mountains form a group apart, distant, inaccessible, their whiteness distinct from the white sky. Their light is not even reflected, but shines out. Then a single willow, a single bird that is chasing itself, and finally the unexpected bright colors of a new network of water ways. By a process of gradual accretion the bare landscape has become full, almost lush. Yet it lacks the coherence of a perceived scene, for its elements are not in discernible relation with one another.

A normal act of perception organizes a visual field and holds all of its elements present simultaneously. The sequential appearance of the elements of this landscape has been more than just a concession to the limitations of language. Had it been presented as an object of the speaker's perception, the scene might from the start have arranged itself—or have been arranged by the act of perception—around the swan. Instead, its elements have seemed one by one to come into existence only as they entered the poem, as if language did not copy them from the world, but were their only mode of existence. Nothing at present binds them together, save their presence in the same poem.

The landscape of **"The Dying Swan"** is a reduced and off-key version of the beautifully self-sufficient natural scene that opens Wordsworth's "Resolution and Independence." A single verbal echo suggests a linkage that tone and narrative situation help to justify. Tennyson's swallow, chasing itself "at its own wild will," recalls Wordsworth's line "Over his own sweet voice the Stock-dove broods." But Wordsworth's stock-dove is answered by a jay, and his landscape celebrates the joyful community into which the poem's narrator will arrive from the melancholy world of men. Tennyson's landscape is already melancholy and still awaits the power that will establish its community. No human narrator will arrive, and instead it is the swan who organizes the landscape and whose movement stands in for the movement of a narrative consciousness through the busy, but unmoving, scene. Yet another clear echo here is of the river that "glideth at his own sweet will" in Wordsworth's sonnet, "Composed Upon Westminster Bridge," where, again, a calm and contained power is evoked, but where the "mighty heart" of the city is evenly matched with the mighty heart of the poet. Ten-

Tennyson in 1857.

nyson's poem is younger, less self-possessed, far less ready to claim imaginative dominion. The poet appears only as the swan and the swan appears only in two lines of the first twenty, and not at all in the second section. Thus the lines that follow are striking, a sudden description and a sudden evidence of power:

> The wild swan's death hymn took the soul
> Of that waste place with joy
> Hidden in sorrow: at first to the ear
> The warble was low and full and clear;
> And floating about the under sky,
> Prevailing in weakness, the coronach stole
> Sometimes afar, and sometimes anear;
> But anon her awful jubilant voice,
> With a music strange and manifold,
> Flowed forth on a carol free and bold;

The bird's song transforms the bleak landscape, gaining strength as the bird itself spends it, partaking of the paradoxical power of the imagination, which can bring joy from sorrow and prevail in weakness. What is more, the landscape, under the influence of the song, coalesces into a single responsive organism. It has a soul to be moved by song and, oddly, an ear to hear it. The single voice of the swan becomes a manifold music as the discrete elements of the landscape join in to form a community of song, but not until another community has been introduced in a magisterial simile. I quote the remainder of the poem:

> As when a mighty people rejoice
> With shawms, and with cymbals, and harps of
>   gold,
> And the tumult of their acclaim is rolled
> Through the open gates of the city afar,
> To the shepherd who watcheth the evening star.
> And the creeping mosses and clambering weeds,
>
> And the willow-branches hoar and dank,
> And the wavy swell of the soughing reeds,
> And the wave-worn horns of the echoing bank,
> And the silvery marish-flowers that throng
> The desolate creeks and pools among,
> Were flooded over with eddying song.

Like the swan's song, the poem steadily gains power, not stopping to note the beginning of a fourth ten-line section and then overflowing the mark to reach its end at line forty-two. In the profuse accounting of a suddenly animated and intermingled landscape, the poet himself floods over with song and sound, but his continuous flow contains a sharp discontinuity in the "as" that forces an imaginative shift away from the natural scene to the vaguely biblical human city. Thus the human and natural scenes are related only through simile and through the excited and simile-making power of the poet's imagination. They are alike in witnessing the power of a manifold music to create a community, even to join separate realms, as the city song rolls out to the pastoral shepherd, but their two musics do not reach one another. The countryside into which the sounds of the city carry is different altogether from that in which the swan sings. The rush of the verse seems at first to be following the human sounds back into the wild scene of the first thirty lines. But that scene, as the final line makes clear, resides still in the past tense, where it was midday, and the shepherd watching his evening star exists in another world. The natural scene comes alive here far from man, in the fashion of a fantastic children's tale in which all the inanimate objects of a household cavort and dance while their owners sleep.

But where is the poet in relation to these objects that he describes? Is he hiding in the rushes, and was that perhaps his ear that sneaked for a moment into the picture? The answer, of course, is that the poet is nowhere in the imagined scene, precisely because it is an imagined scene. The poem separates the human and natural worlds from one another and separates itself from both. The natural scene, for all its wealth of perceived detail, is evidently not a perceived scene, any more than those shawms and cymbals and harps of gold are the ordinary accouterments of an early nineteenth-century English town festival. Both of the poem's locales derive from legendary or literary sources, the clamorous city from the fourth book of the *Iliad,* and come into being anew here as the poet speaks them. The poet himself does not emerge as a speaker in the poem because the events and scenes he presents were never a part of his experience in the world, and so he does not present himself in the act of perceiving them. The simile of the city, which gives to the poem its vision of two separated realms, further serves to separate the speaker from the poem, by making it impossible to construct a single situation of utterance, a single place for any speaker to stand. The poet is as much in one place as another, as his ability to extend the simile makes clear, and both scenes are thus revealed as the un-observed products of the imagination.

Although the elements of landscape in **"The Dying Swan"** are drawn from the English countryside, the poem shares an imaginative structure with such purely imagined poems as **"The Kraken"** or **"Mariana."** These poems describe things never seen, yet without presenting themselves as the act or utterance of a particular imagination who appears in the text. Instead they draw attention to some imagined figure who does not speak the poem itself, but who is at least a tempting figure for the poet. Like so many Romantic poems, these are poems about the poetic imagination, but they speak indirectly, through fable, and this indirection is itself a problem that the poetic imagination confronts.

In its presentation of the natural and the human orders as parallel and separate, **"The Dying Swan"** suggests yet another version of the poet's separation from the world. Yet the poem is also a tribute to the power of voice to create a community, and we must ask whether its vision of discontinuity places or is placed by its vision of continuity. Is there not a third music, that of the verse itself, which connects the city and the wild plain? To the degree that the poem is not mimetic, it does not matter that the two are not represented as coming into contact with one another, for they do not exist anywhere except in the poem and there they are not only contiguous but clearly the product of the same voice, fused once again in the medium of strong emotion. But here the problem of discontinuity reappears, for how does the poem touch the world if it is neither mimetic nor expressive, if its voice is disembodied, not continuous with the experience of a human speaker?

One answer lies in Tennyson's acknowledged linguistic mastery, which has compelled us already to speak of voice and music. In spite of its self-conscious literariness and its failure to claim the presence of a human speaker or the immediacy of speech, the poem demands to be read aloud and to be heard. Its richness is so evidently auditory that it calls the ear into play just as the swan's song magically generated an ear in the midst of a wild landscape. Tennyson's language is always personalized, humanized in this way, always unmistakably Tennysonian. But the familar and lovely Tennyson music is not enough. The poems pursue meaning as well as music, and they do so by means of an allegory that signifies the gap between self and language, imagination and utterance, poet and reader, even as it attempts to bridge it.

Imagination and nature, the grand opposed terms of high Romantic writing, virtually disappear from Tennyson's vocabulary, but not because they are no longer of importance. Rather, nature cannot appear as an integrated force, or even as the spirit of a particular landscape, because it has ceased to be a single presence and has dissolved into fragments. Meanwhile, the power that reassembles these fragments does so in the effort to project an image of itself, an image in which it cannot be represented as a single element, because it has no background of externality against which to appear. De Man has said of Romantic literature that "the very fact that the relationship [between matter and consciousness] has to be established within the medium of language indicates that it does not exist in actuality." This is the case, however, only if one assumes what has not been proved, that the language of this literature is anti-mimetic, that it represents only what is not. In Tennyson the case is clearer and more extreme, because the interaction of man and nature appears only in a language that is obviously figural, rendering the poems as a whole allegorical.

The result is a poetry that does not move from nature to imagination, but from one realm of artifice to another. Instead of presenting a reading of landscape that is also a self-revelation, Tennyson's poems present a linguistic landscape that the reader must read and that the poet has written. The drama of perception and imagination has preceded the poem and is represented only in its product, which proceeds explicitly as a drama of writing and reading, or, rather of the written and the to-be-read. The writer who has perceived and imagined is not shown in the process of doing either.

Tennyson's career thus discovers and develops an apocalyptic and anti-natural—that is, a very modern—version of Romanticism: first, in its subordination, through allegorical landscape, of structures of nature to structures of consciousness; second, in its concern with the difficulties of rendering those structures of consciousness in a language that threatens to violate their integrity. For Tennyson's poetry is allegorical with respect not only to nature, but to the self. The concern with poetic origins, the absence from the strongest early poems of the first person singular, the recurring images of separation and discontinuity, all point to this recognition. The poems continually imagine their own origins, but they do so by means of an indirection that signifies a separation from any creative source in the self. The crucial index of difficulty is what Wordsworth called "the sad incompetence of human speech"; the possible result is the painful isolation of a self that must remain hidden behind a veil of language, cut off from nature and other men, yet unable to celebrate its autonomy in a truly expressive speech.

Of course, it is not only the self, but the whole world, that has in some sense been lost to these poems, a fact that may explain the feeling of objectless regret that many readers have discerned in them. In a sensitive and little-noticed essay, J. H. Prynne remarks in Tennyson "the sense of loss [that] is not essentially loss of some definable object or person, but a purely intransitive version of this," and goes on to say that "once the elegiac mind has excluded the external world . . . this itself becomes an added motive: the loss of significant externality can be added to the other springs of regret." To this I would add only that the empirical self is now a part of that excluded externality, the Romantic tension between the "inside" of consciousness and the "outside" of the world having yielded to a new tension between the language that is inside the poem and the world of subjects and objects both that lies beyond it. A first person claiming this poetic language as his own would provide at least the image of a link between poem and world, but such a first person appears in only a very few of the 1830 poems, and those not the poems for which the volume is remembered.

And yet these early poems are oddly calm in their imaginative isolation. All the pains of separated personality have been displaced onto their protagonists, as all the distinctive evidences of the poet's personality have been displaced into a poetic style that is only covertly expressive. Tennysonian protagonists may die into song, as the dying swan does, as the kraken does, as the lady of Shalott will do, but these deaths are curiously emotionless, because they are so obviously figurative. And they are balanced by the linguistic and figurative life of a poet who is feeling out the darker implications of the liberated Romantic imagination, of a poetry that threatens to flourish beyond mere experience.

If such a threat were to be made good, the resultant poetry would be a structuralist's delight, self-contained, self-sufficient, self-aware. Only the last of these truly describes Tennyson's poetry, however, for against the first two conditions the poems offer both their music—the powerful, if indirect, evocation of a deep subjectivity—and the allegorical evidences of an active intelligence. They ask, in other words, to be read and, thus, whatever prison house of language they constitute, to take their part in a human exchange. Tennyson learned from the Romantic poets before him the impossibility of any simple naturalism or supernaturalism, and his poetry does not describe a regression from Romantic practice, but the form of its survival. Acknowledging the necessity of a mediated vision of human experience, Tennyson's early lyrics explore new strategies of indirection and fragmentation and thus form an indispensable link in the chain of example and imitation that connects the Romantic lyric with its twentieth century heirs. (pp. 75-92)

Timothy Peltason, "Tennyson, Nature, and Romantic Nature Poetry," in Philological Quarterly, *Vol. 63, No. 1, Winter, 1984, pp. 75-93.*

Peter M. Sacks (essay date 1985)

[*Sacks is a South-African born American educator, critic, and poet. In the following excerpt from his* The English Elegy: Studies in the Genre from Spenser to Yeats, *he analyzes* In Memoriam *as an elegy, outlining the poem's themes and structure.*]

"Adonais" was first printed in Pisa on 13 July 1821, and copies were sent to the Ollier brothers to distribute in London. It was not, however, until 1829, seven years after Shelley's own death, that the poem was first printed in England. Two Cambridge undergraduates were responsible for this act of homage and salvage. Despite his unpopularity in England, Shelley impressed them and their intellectual club, The Apostles, as having been one of the greatest poets of the preceding decades, and the club was soon to defend this estimate in a debate against the Oxford admirers of Wordsworth. One of the two sponsors of the reprint was Richard Monckton Milnes, later to become Lord Houghton, Keats's first biographer and an influential friend to many poets and writers of the century. The other was the promising young scholar and critic Arthur Hallam, whose sudden death four years later at the age of twenty-two would move his closest friend, Tennyson, to work for seventeen years on one of the most extraordinary elegies ever written.

Despite both Hallam's and Tennyson's reverence for Shelley, *In Memoriam* is strikingly different from "Adonais." Tennyson lacked little of Shelley's technical skill. Indeed, he could imitate the Romantic poet so convincingly that during their debate at Oxford his fellow Apostles were able to pass off some of his lines as being Shelley's own. But as we have remarked, Shelley had driven the elegy to an extremity that few succeeding poets, least of all a poet of the Victorian period, could match.

There were many reasons why "Adonais" would have been a difficult example for a *Victorian* elegist, in particular, to follow. The later poets were more skeptical with regard not only to religious or philosophical beliefs but also to the nature and products of the poetic imagination. Shelley had doubted the means rather than the sources or objects of poetic expression, whereas for the Victorians even the latter were suspect. This far-reaching doubt subverted more than the poet's confidence in his particular works or in his vocation. Unable to rely, as the Romantics had, on idealist assurances that individual reason or imagination might participate in a realm beyond that of the merely empirical, the Victorian poet found it no less difficult to rely on notions of an ideal self or soul, an entity to which the merely personal could be subsumed. When the self was regarded as something idiosyncratic—in short, as personality—how was one to imagine some transpersonal element of identity that would survive an individual's death? Whereas "Adonais" celebrated the return of Keats's soul to the universal fountain of its origins, Tennyson resists precisely this sacrifice of the narrowly defined personality of Hallam:

> That each, who seems a separate whole,
>   Should move his rounds, and fusing all
>   The skirts of self again, should fall
> Remerging in the general Soul,
>
>   Is faith as vague as all unsweet:

How, then, was one to mourn? If the self and its attachments were uniquely and hence irreplaceably personal, how could they be transformed or displaced? How could the deceased or the survivor be submitted to that process of self-purification or to versions of that universalizing myth of the martyred and reborn deity that we have come to regard as so essential to the search for consolation? Amidst the proliferating details and furnishings of Victorian funerary practices, behind the crepe and the highly personalized souvenirs, the very mainspring of the work of mourning had weakened. As Matthew Arnold complained, "The nobleness of grief is gone— / Ah, leave us not the fret alone."

In Memoriam presents many reflections of this general predicament, exaggerated as it was by Tennyson's own temperament and by the immense personal significance to him of Hallam's death. We have already glanced, for example, at Tennyson's insistence on a highly personalized sense of identity. Before exploring this and other thematic examples, we should look at the formal reflections of the problem. There is, first of all, the poem's extreme length, close to three thousand lines. Written during seventeen years, the poem narrates an almost three-year-long mourning period, a period unprecedentedly long for any elegy. The poem's length, moreover, represents no smoothly unfolding process, no *strictly* unified development to which all parts are organically subordinated:

> The sections were written at many different places, and as the phases of our intercourse came to my memory and suggested them. I did not write them with any view of weaving them into a whole, or for publication, until I found that I had written so many. The different moods of sorrow as in a drama are dramatically given. . . .

Refusing to submit the idiosyncrasy of his grief to the shape of conventional ceremony, the poet is concerned rather to accentuate each moment and nuance, each erratic fluctuation of response. Elements of the elegiac conventions are certainly evident, as we shall see, and Tennyson did later rearrange his sections so that they might broadly conform to the general structure of an elegy. But these elements are thoroughly dispersed among details of personal narrative and reflection, which heavily overscore and often contradict the poem's general trend.

Perhaps more important than the poem's length or the way in which the highly personalized moments tend to fracture any strict generic coherence is the fact that *In Memoriam* is created precisely by an *accretion* of moments. Tennyson in fact works against the very dictates of mourning: he collects and elaborates rather than strips or refines; he accumulates rather than lets go. As Verlaine complained, "He had many reminiscences." By their

"drama," these "Fragments of an Elegy," as Tennyson once thought of entitling the poem, tend to interfere not only with the elegy's narrative progress but with the very movement of time itself.

For it is against the unfolding of time that Tennyson struggles here, as elsewhere in his poetry. He is not merely trying to cling to the lost object of his love; he is also resisting the very passage of time that makes loss so irreversible. The accretions may therefore be seen as attempts to congeal the flow of time in order to preserve personalities or moments whose definitions are threatened by change. Arthur Hallam himself had spoken of the Victorian "poetic impulse" as "a check acting for conservation against a propulsion towards change."

Reinforcing the slow, accretive structure of the poem is the actual form of its 133 sections. These sections are variously long accumulations of iambic tetrameter quatrains. The relative terseness of the line, together with an *abba* rhyme scheme, gives each stanza a self-encysted quality, an effect of being withheld from time, in a unit whose end echoes its beginning. Each stanza thus seems to cancel out its motion, to bury or seal itself in a past on which it seeks to confer a timeless presence. One is reminded of Henry James's acute remark: "When Tennyson wishes to represent movement, the phrase always seems to me to pause and slowly pivot upon itself, or at most to move backwards."

Clearly, these formal features—the slow and lengthy accretiveness; the stress on disjointed, self-enclosed fragments; the resistance to time or narrative—reflect an attitude that we recognize as melancholia; and the poem certainly justifies Auden's observation that there was very little that Tennyson did not know about that condition. Throughout, *In Memoriam* reveals the melancholic's self-love and self-doubt, his guilt and self-contempt, his insistence on personality and on the discrete particulars of experience, his distrust of mediation, especially that of his own language, and his reluctance to accept any remedy for grief. And yet *In Memoriam* does eventually represent a successful work of mourning, one whose most intriguing aspect is not Tennyson's skepticism—"the quality of his doubt"—but rather the unique if tortuous way in which he achieves consolation by *revising* rather than rejecting the constraints of his own melancholia. To assess that achievement, the reader must ask such questions as the following: How can Tennyson's resistance to time allow for the consoling belief in evolution? How does that allowance itself depend on precisely the kind of figurative language that the melancholy poet distrusts? And how is Tennyson's acceptance of such language an important part of his work of mourning? What inherited symbols and elements of ritual do survive in this poem, and how do they enable the elegist to perform his idiosyncratic version of the mourner's task?

The prologue to *In Memoriam* is itself a perplexing introduction, raising several issues beyond those that we have begun to note. By at once offering and discussing what follows, it resembles a dedication to a patron or reader, in this case the "Strong Son of God, immortal Love," whose existence is, however, immediately presented as a problematic object of belief rather than knowledge ("Believing where we cannot prove"). *In Memoriam* is famous for its noncognitive faith. But what has not been remarked is the fact that Tennyson's very manner of proposing this faith conforms to what we have come to regard as the elegiac process of self-chastisement. For as we shall see, Tennyson closely associates knowledge with an anarchic desire that brooks no detour, precisely the kind of desire that the elegist must quell or reform. The way in which Knowledge is rebuked in section 114, and replaced there by Wisdom or faith, is thus inseparable not only from the way in which the physical presence of Hallam is gradually supplanted by its more spiritual successor but also from the elegist's displacement of his own desires.

Returning to the prologue, we recognize that the entire poem to come is thus addressed to an auditor whose presence is both invisible and unprovable. Almost all elegies have shown variants of this strategy whereby the act of address invents the presence of an addressee. And we have seen how many elegies begin and continue in the mode of address. But seldom has the elegist so immediately and so explicitly drawn attention to the unverifiable nature of his audience. And seldom has the latter been more than an admissible fiction such as that of the nymphs, the Muses, or the spirit of the dead. Here, it is no less than the "Son of God."

The problem of addressing his poem to an unverifiable audience must have affected Tennyson more severely than any elegist. For him, there was not only the matter of having to posit a supreme being, or of having to write out of a painful, Victorian sense of private isolation from an unprecedentedly large and faceless reading public. For Tennyson, the very object of his grief, Arthur Hallam, had in fact been his invaluably attuned personal audience. It was Hallam who had written the brilliant and sympathetic review of Tennyson's early poems in 1831 and who had continued to appreciate and find publishers for his friend's work at a time when Tennyson felt most crushed by hostile critics. The influential Lockhart and Croker had abused the *Poems* of 1832, and even though Tennyson wrote some of his finest poems in 1833, he would not publish another volume until 1842. According to his son, Tennyson "was so far persuaded that the English people would never care for his poetry, that, had it not been for the intervention of his friends, he declared it not unlikely that after the death of Hallam he would not have continued to write." That "silent" decade was certainly marked by sheer grief and solitude, but there is little doubt that a crucial element of distress was the loss of his assured and admiring reader.

In Memoriam is in large part a quest to repair that particular loss, and it is in this light that one should note the great incidence and variety of address throughout the poem. Of the 133 sections, no less than 80 contain some act of address. And these extend to almost 30 different objects, ranging from a yew tree to a ship, from the poet's heart to Time itself. We shall see more fully how this quest for a restored audience is part of the poet's quest to repair a wounded narcissism. The desperate succession of addresses represents the poet's need to bring himself back into the presence of some entity that will reflect his own image. Already in the prologue we note that Tennyson has chosen to regard the "Son of God" as being curiously conflated with Tennyson's ideal reader.

It is before this reader that the poet criticizes himself and his poem:

> Forgive these wild and wandering cries,
>   Confusions of a wasted youth,
>   Forgive them where they fail in truth,
> And in thy wisdom make me wise.

We are familiar with the mourner's impulse to self-abasement. As addressed to God, but also to the dead, this is partly the mourner's penitence for having survived, for choosing to live on, for having been unable to protect the dead, or simply for being unable to mourn him more effectively. As part of a quest for readership, the plea works especially well, for it entreats the kind of active scrutiny that must enter into relation with the poet and poem and respond with an actual judgment. The plea thus posits a superior reader who will somehow complete the poem.

As an introduction, this request is strangely proleptic, in the original sense of the term—it seeks to ward off, or at least preempt, criticism. What is more important, it is a defense that works against time itself by seeking to cancel or outleap time's process. The prologue, which was, in fact, written after the entire poem, in 1849, speaks in retrospect about the poem that it nevertheless precedes. One of the most curious examples of an elegy's conventional self-commentary, this coda-prologue calls for an act of improvement that requires time, even while the call outleaps temporality with respect to the poem itself. The problem is central to the entire poem, and lies behind the first section.

> I held it truth, with him who sings
>   To one clear harp in divers tones,
>   That men may rise on stepping-stones
> Of their dead selves to higher things.
>
> But who shall so forecast the years
>   And find in loss a gain to match?
>   Or reach a hand thro' time to catch
> The far-off interest of tears?
>
> Let Love clasp Grief lest both be drown'd,
>   Let darkness keep her raven gloss:
>   Ah, sweeter to be drunk with loss,
> To dance with death, to beat the ground,
>
> Than that the victor Hours should scorn
>   The long result of love, and boast,
>   'Behold the man that loved and lost,
> But all he was is overworn.'

If the prologue implied a complicated attitude toward time, the first section of the poem proper immediately confronts the relation between that attitude and the work of mourning. Rather than accept the Goethean notion of constant self-surpassal, related as it is to the mourner's task, the poet clings to a self-definition that will not admit of change. Complaining precisely of his inability to overcome time by forecasting its yield, he chooses instead to defeat it by sheer resistance. At the very outset of the poem, these lines spell out the poet's greatest concern: not merely the loss of his friend but the threatened survival, in time, of his own selfhood. The question for the poet is how to mourn while retaining a sense of self.

In view of the Victorian passion for collectibles, for tangible guarantees of the unchanging and the idiosyncratic, it is interesting to note how Tennyson presents his struggle by images of physical touch or possession. He cannot "hold" Goethe's truth because he cannot reach a hand through time to catch the interest of tears. So he chooses to "clasp" Grief instead. This fierce insistence on something to hold is similar to the demand for empirical knowledge, for proof positive, and relates, as we have seen, to the desire that must be broken and redirected during the process of mourning. Only thus can the poet relinquish his fixation on a certain attachment or knowledge and look instead to the more speculative rewards of time.

At this point, however, the poet's obsession with an unchanging identity is too strong. The second section therefore follows with an envious address to the yew tree, emblem not only of melancholy fixation and millennial constancy but also of physically apprehended connections ("Old Yew, which graspest at the stones . . . Thy fibres net the dreamless head, / Thy roots are wrapt about the bones"). Like the stifling, encrusted world of Mariana in her moated grange, this is a form of anti-pastoral, cutting against the grain of a conventional elegy. So, too, the recognizably elegiac images of texture here serve neither to conceal nor redress mortality nor to fabricate a substitute for the lost; rather, they serve as a literal bond, an integument that weaves the living to the dead. Instead of a consoling text we have a fibrous knot, in the place of a symbol of natural growth we find a stubborn stump with which the poet yearns to identify.

As though troubled by elements of projection in his address to the yew, the poet goes on to criticize an explicit case of projection, exposing it as a self-imprisoning danger besetting any griever. As in the previous section, images of texture do not suggest consoling fabrics. Rather, the poet continues, albeit via the distanced figure of Sorrow, to multiply negative versions of the elegiac craft. According to Sorrow, a web obscures the sky; Nature itself is a "hollow echo," a "hollow form" projected by Sorrow herself. The recognition that these expressions are themselves lies only carries us further into the melancholic's distrust of any expressions of grief. And the poet now thinks of repressing this figure of sorrow: "shall I . . . crush her, like a vice of blood, / Upon the threshold of the mind?" The language is psychologically precise, stressing both the prohibition from consciousness and the stifling, rather than displacement, of natural vitality.

In sleep, however, the censorship is lifted to the point where the poet can at least admit that the heart's melancholia involves not only a repression of grief but also another prominent feature of melancholy—what Freud termed unconscious loss:

> O heart, how fares it with thee now,
> That thou should'st fail from thy desire,
> Who scarcely darest to inquire,
> 'What is it makes me beat so low?'

> Something it is which thou hast lost,
> Some pleasure from thine early years.

To pass from melancholia to mourning, this "nameless loss," as Tennyson goes on to call it, must be defined and confronted. The congealment of affection must be broken and set in movement. So, too, the melancholic must overcome his icy resistance to the conventional expressions of grief: "Break, thou deep vase of chilling tears, / That grief hath shaken into frost!"

But the griever still distrusts his language, and although admitting its use as a narcotic, he once again stresses its opacity: "In words, like weeds, I'll wrap me o'er . . . / But that large grief which these enfold / Is given in outline and no more." We catch the similarity to Hamlet's rejection of the "suits of woe" in favor of an inexpressible inwardness, and the resemblance deepens in section 6 as the poet echoes Hamlet's mockery ("Ay, madam, it is common") of any consoling thoughts of grief's commonality. He does, however, allow several self-comparisons to other grievers—a father, a mother, and a young woman expecting her lover. But despite this apparent broadening of reference, the burden of the last comparison is one of extreme self-absorption, and it confirms our suspicion regarding the narcissistic element of the poet's grief.

The woman admires herself in the mirror, and "glad to find herself so fair," prepares specifically for her visitor's admiration. She expects him to reinforce the mirror's complimentary imaging of her. As if to stress the somewhat compulsive attraction to the mirror, there is the detail not only of her turning to it a second time but of this turn being carefully associated with the instant of her visitor's death. By inversion, the scenario mirrors that of **"The Lady of Shalott,"** confirming the incompatibility between the constraints of the mirror and the call of the outside world. In the earlier poem, a turn from the mirror destroyed the self, while here a return to the mirror destroys the other. In both poems, the incompatibility had hung in the air, as a "curse," waiting to fall. And in both, the woman had been immersed in creating artful textures—a magic web or an arrangement of golden ringlets. Tennyson's choice of this elaborate comparison suggests more than a continued assault on mediating texture. Now he seems also to express the guilt of one who was himself immersed in the self-reflection of his craft and who waited, like the woman, for the beloved's approval.

Both narcissism and guilt dominate the following section, in which the poet creeps "like a guilty thing" to Hallam's house in Wimpole Street and asks the house and doors to "behold" him as if they could substitute for the mirroring friend. The present thwarting of past anticipations, the frustrated desire for a physical welcome, the sleepless haunting of a limbo hour before dawn, the desperate placement of the poet not only on a barred threshold but on a middle ground between contemptuous attachment to the self and an equally contemptuous and melancholy detachment from the outside world—these all contribute to the impact of this section. Its close is especially powerful:

> He is not here; but far away
> The noise of life begins again,
> And ghastly thro' the drizzling rain

On the bald street breaks the blank day.

The poet gazes through a despised veil of rain onto a scene that his extreme detachment has rendered unreal but haunting, ghastly, as though a mocking substitute for the true ghost. The "noise" of life suggests nuisance as well as sound, and the unpleasant insistence of sound is itself caught by the near-mindless alliteration of the last line. Associated with time, the daybreak is hatefully "bald" and "blank," words whose connotations of barrenness, exposure, and ashen nullity apply as much to the poet as to the scene.

Section 8 pursues these themes and brings them to the kind of temporary resolution necessary for the poem's continuance. Once again, like one who loses an admiring lover ("her that loves him well"), the poet is instantly disenchanted. "He saddens, all the magic light / Dies off at once. . . . " But now, instead of unadorned blankness, he seems to "find" his verse, or rather its value as an object like the flower once admired and fostered by his dead friend. The need for that fostering is as great as ever, but the poet is able to displace its focus slightly from himself ("my forsaken heart") to his poetry. And with the stress still on having "pleased a vanish'd eye," he offers his verse to the dead. Tentatively, the gesture hints at the ancient rites of tribute, and more specifically of sowing and hence of possible resurrection ("I go to plant it on his tomb, / That if it can it there may bloom, / Or dying, there at least may die").

As if to belie the notion of organic development, however, the poem shifts to a goup of sections addressing the ship that bears home the remains of Hallam. (The first of these sections was in fact written earlier than the sections discussed above.) It is interesting that the stress now falls concertedly on calm sureness of motion. In describing what he desires, the poet gives his very lines the kind of ceremonious fluency that both he and his poem require. Instead of the melancholic's resistance to mobility and time, the ship moves so evenly in time that its "favorable speed" seems to tame or becalm time itself within its motion. Like the flower, and like the evolutionary myth that is to follow, the image of the ship's voyage thus indicates the kind of resolution that Tennyson will achieve. He soon describes how the sails appear to "linger weeping on the marge"; the waves will seem to "sway themselves in rest." Here—and later—Tennyson converts the melancholy fascination with the fixed instant to an assertion of a temporal flow that is somehow consonant with the fulness of any moment.

As yet, the poet falls far short of this achievement. He is still skeptical regarding the power or truth of his "idle dreams"; and he frames his "home bred fancies" of a quiet resting place for the dead with harsher references to the "vanish'd life" and to the often-clasped hands now tossing with tangle and with shells. So, too, his evocations of calm are imperiled by their own potential for a mere return to the fixity of despair and to the calmness of the dead. The fair ship yields easily to the poet's explicitly self-reflective image of an "unhappy bark" that "strikes by night a craggy shelf." In this description of traumatic shock, the conquest over time is only the nightmarish product of a deliri-

um that fuses old and new. The poem is still marked by negative versions of its eventual success and by a repeated alternation, even within individual sections of hope and despair, resignation and protest.

Section 19 initiates a further series of doubts about craft. By way of a beautiful description of the tidal Severn, Tennyson repeats the melancholy preference for an unexpressed and supposedly inexpressible fulness rather than for the shallow mourner's empty vocalizing. With similar effect, he contrasts the volubility of servants to the silence of their master, and to the immobilized children with their "other griefs within / And tears that at their fountain freeze." Again, the poem seems to seize up, as the melancholy poet discredits his own utterance; and in section 21 the skepticism turns specifically against the very genre of elegy, attacking this poet, who "take[s] the grasses of the grave, / And make[s] them pipes whereon to blow." Against charges of enervation, paraded constancy, and selfish opposition to an age of progress, the poet defends himself with a rather weak plea for the poetry of natural impulse: "I do but sing because I must, / And pipe but as the linnets sing." The simplistic terms of the defense surely strengthen the charges, while further depleting the reserves of traditional pastoral consolation.

And yet the generic conventions do allow moments of retrospect, in which the poet evokes the traditional idyll of shared joy. Here, with Pan and the flutes of Arcady, the survivor can at least surmise images of well-being while also submitting himself and his friend to the impersonal figures of Theocritean pastoral. The sections are, however, overshadowed by Death and by the poet's relentless skepticism, which characteristically turns to attack the idyll as mere idealization: "is it that the haze of grief / Makes former gladness loom so great?" Once again, an intervening texture is distrusted rather than recognized as the potential medium of consolation. Similarly, in this section the traditional elegiac images of sun and star are robbed of their solacing effect by mention of sunspots and the distortive effects of distance. The poet appears to have adopted the disenchanted perspective of Sorrow's bitter claims, thus returning to the tone of section 3, while making ever deeper inroads into the resources of the genre.

Although section 26 confirms the element of guilt in the poet's melancholy, his paralyzing sensitivity to accusations of inconstancy or betrayal, the following section brings a crucial alteration:

> I envy not the beast that takes
> His license in the field of time,
> Unfetter'd by the sense of crime,
> To whom a conscience never wakes,
>
> Nor, what may count itself as blest,
> The heart that never plighted troth
> But stagnates in the weeds of sloth;
> Nor any want-begotten rest.
>
> I hold it true, whate'er befall,
> I feel it, when I sorrow most;
> 'Tis better to have loved and lost
> Than never to have loved at all.

This momentary casting out of remorse, like that of

Yeats's Self in "A Dialogue of Self and Soul," enables more than an act of *amor fati.* As Walter Benjamin suggested, a conviction of guilt, or of being unredeemably fallen, partly determined the melancholy fear that language could be no more than a fabric of opaque and unfulfillable signs. The poet's affirmative revision of his "sense of crime" may, therefore, allow a more positive attitude toward the formal expression of grief. This is indeed what we discover in the immediately subsequent sections. As we know, they form one of the major dividing points of the elegy, marking the first of three Christmases. But the true nature of the crux should, I think, be seen in this altering attitude toward the forms of grief, and hence toward the medium of the poem itself.

At first, the poet's resistance blocks out the Christmas bells, "as if a door / Were shut between me and the sound." He admits to having wished that his own death might have forestalled his hearing them again. But as the nature of mourning requires, the suicidal desire yields to an everlasting "canon gainst self-slaughter," and the poet does in fact submit to the bells, hearing them now as figures of an almost parental sway.

> But they my troubled spirit rule,
>   For they controll'd me when a boy;
>   They bring me sorrow touch'd with joy,
> The merry, merry bells of Yule.

We have already begun to note how heavily Tennyson's consolation will depend on this achievement of an attitude whose childlike nature establishes a comforting relation to a superior authority. Here, the submission also works positively against, yet with, Time, bridging the gulf between boyhood and adulthood, allaying the poet's fear that time defeats identity. What might otherwise have been regarded as mere hollow sound thus yields a certain fullness. And this submissive revaluation of ritual forms and figures continues even more thoroughly in what follows.

Resembling a miniature elegy in itself, section 30 narrates how a nervous and faltering observance of traditional forms wins through to an affirmative crescendo. The elegiac images of weaving and of echoing song—it is as though the antiphonal bells ring on within the voices—are certainly those of Sorrow in section 3. But the attitude toward them is now utterly different. What at first rang hollow now takes on an impetuously released charge, and with a ceremonious recommencement so typical of the genre, the song rises, like Virgil's "Eclogue IV" or "Lycidas," to a "higher range":

> Our voices took a higher range;
>   Once more we sang: 'They do not die
>   Nor lose their mortal sympathy,
> Nor change to us, although they change,
>
> 'Rapt from the fickle and the frail
>   With gather'd power, yet the same,
>   Pierces the keen seraphic flame
> From orb to orb, from veil to veil.'
>
> Rise, happy morn, rise, holy morn,
>   Draw forth the cheerful day from night:
>   O Father, touch the east, and light
> The light that shone when Hope was born.

This denial of death addresses the precise terms of the mourner's fear by asserting that a given identity may sustain rather than suffer change. There will be many relapses before this position is consolidated, but for the moment, much is gained; and the poet can turn to the Father, which his boyhood has implied, and encourage Him to advance the passage of once-hated Time. The images of light and sphere are now repaired. And whereas it had earlier been spurned, the motif of dawn is heralded in a typically elegiac note of triumphant elevation. Even the "touch" so often mourned, and again so tentatively hinted at by the "trembling fingers" of the poet, is here recuperated and augmented in a figure of regenerative power.

We should not, however, overlook the fact that the poet's celebration of the "happy morn" contains a powerful defense against the mere unfolding of time. The welcomed light is, after all, the same light that shone in the past. And the temporal rebirth of Christ counters the very passage of time by revealing a persistent identity, making the very motion of time a circular rather than an irrevocably linear process. This will be an essential element of the poet's consolation and will determine the very category of rhetoric that he will employ. For as we may already suspect, the ground is being prepared for a consoling use of typology, or *figura,* which will allow the poet to reconcile his antipathy to temporal change with his myth of evolution. Unlike metaphor, which depends on the very substitution that Tennyson resists, and unlike metonymy, whose comforting contiguities Tennyson would accept were not all links felt to have been broken, a *type* appears to allow the retention of an identity that is as changeless in form and as fixed in time as Tennyson desires and yet that also participates in a higher existence fulfilled and revealed in time.

Hence the positive reappraisal of ritual and poetic forms continues, with specific attention to the principal figure of Christ as "type." And dominated by this figure, the surrounding sections' defense of religious fable and of the incarnation of the Word should be read as crucial elements of the poet's partial reconciliation with the devices of his mourning and his poem.

Tennyson will not use typology fully until later in the poem, and he characteristically interrupts the incipient mood of acceptance. His guilt disrupts the positive attitude toward language that has been so painstakingly gathering force. Regarding the muse of Shelley and Milton as an aloof and hostile judge, the poet's saturnine Melpomene deprecates herself for having "darken'd sanctities with song." Nevertheless, not all the ground is surrendered, and with spring, the poet's songs offer a "doubtful gleam of solace." Similarly, in section 39, his revised description of the yew ("To thee too comes the golden hour / When flower is feeling after flower") is meant at least to suggest an alternative to Sorrow's continuing stress on gloomy fixation. With more success than in the harshly repressive section 3, the poet is still seeking to accommodate the univocal distress of melancholy within the antiphonal or eclogic form of elegy. But the following sections reveal how strongly melancholia continues to dictate the terms of the poet's grief.

Spring offers the image of a young bride, but the poet rejects the analogy between her departure from home and Hallam's death. He has introduced the figure only to lament "the difference" between its rhetorical nature and the reality that he discerns. The rejection of the image is thus itself a melancholy act, but the terms involved are even more significant. In fact, they are vital to an understanding of the poem.

The bride would become "A link among the days, to knit / The generations each with each." In other words, the bride represents the kind of mediation ("knit" reminds us of the textual fabric) and evolution that might allow a happier relation to linear time. By contrast, the poet and his dead friend are held incommunicado, with no language, no "tidings," to connect them. The poet has "lost the links that bound Thy changes." Contradicting section 30, he complains that Hallam has not remained "the same" but rather has "turn'd to something strange." And having denied the possibility of linkage, he desires to "leap the grades of life and light, / And flash at once, my friend, to thee." Again, the bias is against both the "stepping-stones" of intervening grades and a linked progression into the "secular to-be." The urge is for an *instantaneous* and unmediated leap or flash, an obliteration of grades, barriers, intervals, or links. The language is that of rebellious desire itself, which, as noted earlier, is associated with the passionate attachment to the dead and also with the urge for immediate, apprehensible knowledge—in particular, knowledge of what lies beyond the boundaries of the living and beyond the fabric of time or language.

It is precisely this melancholy desire that forms the subject of **"Ulysses,"** which, as Tennyson admitted, "was more written with the feeling of [Hallam's] loss upon me than many poems in *In Memoriam.*" There, too, a griever rejects all "slow degrees" and rules, as well as all generational linkage, choosing instead a suicidal quest in which forbidden knowledge is again associated with the (lost) object of desire:

> And this grey spirit yearning in desire
> To follow knowledge like a sinking star,
> Beyond the utmost bound of human thought.

Within **"Ulysses,"** the proleptic reverie itself seems to narcotize and hence safely retard forever the destructive quest that it envisions. But *In Memoriam* faces the issue more directly. The poet analyses more fully the relation between knowledge and unchecked desire, and he also spells out the mourner's need to subdue that wild urge:

> Who loves not Knowledge? Who shall rail
>   Against her beauty? May she mix
>   With men and prosper! Who shall fix
> Her pillars? Let her work prevail.
>
> But on her forehead sits a fire:
>   She sets her forward countenance
>   And leaps into the future chance,
> Submitting all things to desire.
>
> Half-grown as yet, a child, and vain—
>   She cannot fight the fear of death.
>   What is she, cut from love and faith,
> But some wild Pallas from the brain
>
> Of Demons? fiery-hot to burst

> All barriers in her onward race
> For power. Let her know her place;
> She is the second, not the first.
>
> A higher hand must make her mild,
>   If all be not in vain, and guide
>   Her footsteps, moving side by side
> With wisdom, like the younger child:
>
> For she is earthly of the mind,
>   But Wisdom heavenly of the soul.

As we have learned to expect in an elegy, these terms are close to those of oedipal submission. We have already suspected that much of Tennyson's consolation will depend on his assuming the position of a chastened child. These lines only confirm how closely that self-humbling is related to the mourner's necessary shift from the "earthly" to the "heavenly," from Knowledge to Wisdom, from an insistence on the timeless moment to a reconciliation with the gradual passage of time, and finally from a wilful rage for the immediate and graspable, to an acceptance of what the mediate can at best suggest.

Of course, this shift occurs neither smoothly nor by any single turning point. But we do see it gathering as an intermittent tendency that after several reversals and successes yields its rewards and allows a programmatic statement such as that in section 114. Returning to the earlier passage, in which the poet still yearns for the sudden leap, we do find, for example, that it is followed, in section 42, by a self-rebuke ("I vex my heart with fancies dim: / He still outstript me in the race") and a disavowal of knowledge ("one that loves but knows not"). In section 43, he would willingly concede not only to a period of delay, of "interval gloom," but also to the highly literary device of a "figured leaf" on which the persisting identity of the dead would be inscribed and thus preserved until their final rebirth.

The poet also works now to replace the wilful desire for full knowledge by the chastened, more passive receptions of fragmentary "hints." Instead of the single and ultimate flash or leap into certainty, he now images "a little flash, a mystic hint," such as the remembering Hallam may receive "he knows not whence." Apart from being diminished, the once-and-for-all singularity of the flash is dispersed over time—it is given out "at times." Both the diminution and the fracturing submission to time are crucial elements of the mourner's acquiescence. The word *hint* itself suggests the attendant shift from physical *bent* to mental apprehension, and this chastening of touch is emphasized in the succeeding lines ("some dim touch . . . such a dreamy touch"). So, too, the self-castrative nature of this entire acquiescence is emphasized by further images of fragmentation and of mediating textures that are both childlike and fragile:

> From art, from nature, from the schools,
>   Let random influences glance,
>   Like light in many a shiver'd lance
> That breaks about the dappled pools:
>
> The lightest wave of thought shall lisp,
>   The fancy's tenderest eddy wreathe,
>   The slightest air of song shall breathe
> To make the sullen surface crisp.

And look thy look, and go thy way,
    But blame not thou the winds that make
    The seeming-wanton ripple break,
The tender-pencil'd shadow play.

These terms of the mourner's admission do more than describe his accommodation to language. They describe the very form of his particular poem—its fragmentary, intermittent "hoarding" of self-encircling but incomplete eddies or wreaths of song. This accurate self-commentary should not, however, lead us to suppose that the poet is happily at one with himself or with his poem. For even as he is setting forth the ideological vindication of its form and content, he is pointing, in melancholy fashion, to the essentially superficial nature of his own language: the eddy, the ripple, and the play of light on the crispening surface of the pool. And it is from just these characterizations of his own song that the last stanza of this section withholds assent:

Beneath all fancied hopes and fears
    Ay me, the sorrow deepens down,
    Whose muffled motions blindly drown
The bases of my life in tears.

With this reversal, we are back to the complaints of section 5, the Hamlet-like dismissal of language and the "forms of grief" as an inky cloak that muffles the inner life. While it is fair to speak of some "progress" in the poem thus far, we are forced to regard it as one of continuing debate, the antiphonal division that marks a grieving mind as surely as it structures any elegy's eclogic form. That division is of unusual depth, and as I have already suggested, it is rendered especially problematic because the resolution will depend more on an interpenetration of melancholia and mourning than on a sheer replacement of one by the other.

Pursuing its argument, therefore, the melancholy voice of section 50 requests the closeness of the dead ("Be near me") and rages against both the tyranny of "Time, a maniac scattering dust," and the texture of human life ("men . . . weave their petty cells and die"). Instead, this voice hankers for the "twilight of eternal day," which marks "the low dark verge of life." In addition, the melancholic again raises the question of his guilt, "some hidden shame," which is once more associated with his narcissistic attachment to the dead ("he for whose applause I strove"). And although he does establish the "clear eye" of the dead, the "larger other eyes than ours," this totemic power which Hallam now shares with God as ideal audience is primarily menacing: "the dead shall look me thro' and thro.'" There is the tentative hope for a milder attitude, an "allowance," but this is still far from the more complete prayer for a forgiving criticism such as he will make in the prologue. The poet has yet to argue more effectively against his own guilt and particularly against his conviction that recourse to language is itself a sin.

We have noted how the melancholy contempt for representation is associated with a distrust of Time and it is not surprising to find how much the continuing defense against the poet's self-prosecution entails an explicit defense of Time. Thus, although section 52 begins with the familiar attack on the superficiality and opacity of words

("My words are only words, and moved / Upon the topmost froth of thought"), the counterargument ("blame not thou thy plaintive song") opposes the image of maniacal Time by one of Time as the agent who will have "sunder'd shell from pearl."

But even as the poet seeks to consolidate this optimistic defense, this hope "that somehow good / Will be the final goal of ill," his argument breaks down in a combination of ruptured syntax, cliché, self-doubt, and explicit attack on the inadequacy of his own language:

Behold, we know not anything;
    I can but trust that good shall fall
    At last—far off—at last, to all,
And every winter change to spring.

So runs my dream: but what am I?
    An infant crying in the night:
    An infant crying for the light:
And with no language but a cry.

As mentioned before, this self-chastening return to childhood is essential to the poem's consolation. Indeed, we have speculated earlier on the relation between elegy and the infant's cry of abandonment. But here this cry is one of sheer desolation: only later will it evoke the comforting presence of a parental figure. The cry now introduces one of the poem's most bitter and most famous passages.

Sections 55 and 56 are familiar to all readers of the poem, but it is essential to recognize how the great denunciation of Nature, "red in tooth and claw," derives its force and function from the psyche of a mourner. From Theocritus's "First Idyl" to "Lycidas" and "Adonais," we have noted not only the place of anger in elegies but the relation of that anger to the mourner's loss of a mother figure. In each case, that loss is associated with images of castration, as though the mourner were being forced to recapitulate a moment of original separation, as well as the later moment in which he voluntarily renounced or curbed his own desire to abolish that separation. Section 55, therefore, follows the image of the abandoned infant with images of sharply attenuated physical strength ("I falter where I firmly trod, / And falling with my weight of cares / Upon the great world's altar stairs . . . I stretch lame hands . . . And faintly trust. . . . ") It is this drastically subdued questor who is crushed by the juxtaposed images of futile, frail mankind and of an at best indifferently ravenous Mother Nature. Here, then, is *In Memoriam*'s version of such passages as those in which a stricken Daphnis cursed his implacable tormentor Aphrodite; or Milton despaired, "What could the Muse herself" for her decapitated Orpheus? or Shelley set the figure of dead Adonais against that of the oblivious mother, Urania, sitting in paradise "with veiled eyes." As we have asked before, how but in relation to an immortal matrix should man most suffer his mortality? And how can the mourner avoid repeating his own necessary separation from that matrix?

Unable to merge or identify in an immediate way with such a source or setting, the poet must artificially weave what once had seemed a natural bond. And this woven fabric must interpose between him and the object of knowledge or desire. Hence the imagery in a soothing yet also frustrating answer to the poet's anguish in section 55: "What hope of answer, or redress? / Behind the veil, behind the veil." As the word *redress* suggests, the veil will be a necessary part of any answer. It is there, not to be torn aside, but to be used precisely as a medium. And as we shall see, succeeding sections of the poem, particularly the moments of solacing vision, confirm how thoroughly any consolation must depend upon the texture of language. The very next words of the poem suggest as much: "Peace; come away: the song of woe / Is after all an earthly song."

Here, in the calm with which so many elegies have followed anger, song's earthliness is meant to refer not only to its sphere of reference but to its materiality. And after several intervening passages that imagine Hallam looking back at the "dimly character'd" script and fading legend of his past, the poet arrives at the first of those consoling trances that so explicitly depend on the physical properties of language. Section 64 depicts the poet as one who "ploughs," "reaps," and "muses" in the earthly "furrow" of his song. The following section speaks of "painful phases wrought" to yield happiness. And section 66 defends an apparent gaiety as follows:

> The shade by which my life was crost,
>   Which makes a desert in the mind,
>   Has made me kindly with my kind,
> And like to him whose sight is lost;
>
> Whose feet are guided thro' the land,
>   Whose jest among his friends is free,
>   Who takes the children on his knee,
> And winds their curls about his hand:
>
> He plays with threads, he beats his chair
>   For pastime, dreaming of the sky,
>   His inner day can never die,
> His night of loss is always there.

Pursuing his observance of the veiled ("shade") and earthly ("desert") quality of his mind, the poet shows an unusual acceptance of positive self-comparison. Blindness, as we know, suggests the chastened condition of a mourner, and the image "plays with threads" describes so many elegists, from Virgil to Stevens. "Winds their curls" takes the physical image of spinning or weaving further (we may recall by contrast the self-admiring virgin arranging her ringlets in section 6) and adds to it the important suggestion of an old man braiding his affectionate linkage to the younger generation. Similarly, "beats his chair / For pastime" drives home the physicality of the poet's rhythmic art while again stressing its potential reconciliation, or rather alliance with time.

In section 67, darkness is again an essential element. Indeed, it is as though the poet were now obeying such ancient elegiac rites as those at Eleusis, where revelations were received only by those who had descended into the dark. At night, he imagines (he is not there to see) how the moonlight illuminates the memorial tablet of his friend.

> Thy marble bright in dark appears,
>   As slowly steals a silver flame
>   Along the letters of thy name,
> And o'er the number of thy years.

> The mystic glory swims away;
>   From off my bed the moonlight dies;
>   And closing eaves of wearied eyes
> I sleep till dusk is dipt in gray:
>
> And then I know the mist is drawn
>   A lucid veil from coast to coast,
>   And in the dark church like a ghost
> Thy tablet glimmers to the dawn.

Apart from the "marble bright in dark" or the tablet glimmering under a "lucid veil" of mist, the emphasis on a physical script is striking. In fact, the slow passage of moonlight over the individual letters suggests the deliberate movement of the mind over the material nature of words. The script's emergence out of darkness thus figures not only the resurrection of the dead into a world of light but also the resurrection of language itself as the medium of that event. From our knowledge of the poem thus far, we could say that language itself is emerging from the darkness of the poet's melancholy disapproval. Furthermore, the "silver flame," which shines without burning, surely indicates that language is being not only resurrected but also transfigured. The meaning is clear: not transcendence nor ascension but rather transfiguration in which the mediating form is preserved but glorified.

This cluster of images and concerns helps to explain what is, nevertheless, the rather banal dream in section 69, and the more interesting dream in section 70. In the first, the poet weaves himself a crown of thorns which a glorious hand transforms to leaf. Similarly, in the following dream, after the poet seeks to "paint" Hallam's face on the fabric of "the gloom," the imperfect representation is transfigured to a perfect semblance. With consistent acuity, the poet stresses that this consoling image is still mediated by a woven screen ("thro' a lattice on the soul / Looks thy fair face"). It is significant that this apparition is said to occur "beyond the will," as if to emphasize how these acceptances of mediation depend on a chastening of the will. Later visions will return to this with programmatic clarity.

Before considering those later passages, we should note how the debate continues to allow melancholy its voice. There are the angry denunciation of the first anniversary of Hallam's death, the complaint that poetry can neither describe the dead nor in itself survive, and the bitter lament that Death prevents all speech between the living and the dead. But interspersed with these are counterarguments in favor of continuing song, the familiar rituals, and the passage of time. Only with section 85 does the balance shift conclusively away from melancholia. The section is the longest in the entire poem, and in its struggling oscillation of mood it seems to recapitulate much of the poem at large.

Indeed, this elegy within the elegy begins by quoting from an early section and goes on to narrate the poet's shock at hearing of Hallam's death, the pain of survival, and the difficult necessity of breaking the fixation of this first attachment and "transfer[ring]" his affection to a new object. Despite the impossibility of conversation, the poet feigns responses from the dead, conceding that in this manner "shall grief with symbols play." Not only does he

seem unusually at ease with his own devices but the answer he projects is a positive restatement of those ultimate
rewards that he had rejected in section 1 ("I triumph in
conclusive bliss, / And that serene result of all"). Finally,
in response both to this reassurance and to Hallam's advice that he should form a new attachment, the poet offers
his affections to his sister Cecilia's fiancé, Edmund Lush-
ington. The description of this offer is as beautiful as it is
canny:

> Ah, take the imperfect gift I bring,
>   Knowing the primrose yet is dear,
>   The primrose of the later year,
> As not unlike to that of Spring.

Although he offers a lesser version of an original gift, this
offering is of the same *type* of flower. Once again, the poet
approximates the mode of rhetoric that we have expected
to become the chief consoling device of the poem—that of
typology (here, however, reversing its eventual movement
from diminished to fulfilled identity). A single name or
type identifies two individual flowers from different times.
Once again, the *figura* thus works in time but against
time's dissolution of identity, while the specific type, prim-
rose, stresses the firstness whose conservation the poet has
so highly prized.

This use of type introduces a series of sections marked by
recollection, by an establishment of what is still "The
same, but not the same." And from recollection the
mourner moves to invocation, courting a return of the
dead. Of interest here is the self-chastening quality of this
courtship—the stress that any manifestation will depend
on the mourner's purity at heart, his ascetic receptivity to
the unseen spirit, rather than his wilful grasping after any
visible form. In fact, the mourner must strive for a level
of spirituality matching that of the dead:

> No visual shade of some one lost,
>   But he, the Spirit himself, may come
>   Where all the nerve of sense is numb;
> Spirit to Spirit, Ghost to Ghost.
>   . . . . .
>   That in this blindness of the frame
>   My Ghost may feel that thine is near.

And at the beginning of section 94:

> How pure at heart and sound in head,
>   With what divine affections bold
>   Should be the man whose thought would hold
> An hour's communion with the dead.

By this preparation, reminiscent of the self-refining rituals
of the elegiac cults, the poet approaches the celebrated
trance of section 95:

> By night we linger'd on the lawn,
>   For underfoot the herb was dry;
>   And genial warmth; and o'er the sky
> The silvery haze of summer drawn;
>
> And calm that let the tapers burn
>   Unwavering: not a cricket chirr'd:
>   The brook alone far-off was heard,
> And on the board the fluttering urn:
>
> And bats went round in fragrant skies,

> And wheel'd or lit the filmy shapes
>   That haunt the dusk, with ermine capes
> And woolly breasts and beaded eyes;
>
> While now we sang old songs that peal'd
>   From knoll to knoll, where, couch'd at ease,
>   The white kine glimmer'd, and the trees
> Laid their dark arms about the field.

If we allow the conjunction of line 9 ("And bats . . . ")
to erase the preceding period, these stanzas are all part of
a single sentence, which in fact extends beyond them
("But when . . . "). There is, therefore, an unusual syntactic inclusiveness within these lines, a sense of their par-
ticipating in one "linger'd" moment that becomes more
scene than time. The unifying effect is reinforced by a subtle mesh of imagery: the "silvery haze," which shares its
light with the tapers, fluttering urn, filmy moths, and glimmering kine—almost all of which represent the poet's
mind, that delicate yet uncertain source of light that depends on the surrounding gloom for its definition and that,
as we now recognize, is a light invariably associated with
some veil or texture.

The atmosphere and elements are those of near-religious
rites: tapers, urn, old songs that peal like bells. The word
knoll is itself an inspired choice, offering its associated root
meaning of "knot" (hence adding to the images of texture)
while also blending *knell* and *toll*. But the heart of the ritual begins with the ceremonious departure "one by one" of
the poet's companions and the extinction, "light after
light," of all sources of illumination other than those already associated with the poet's mind. As in Gray's elegy,
the poet is left in solitary custody of the night, a custody
close to identification (compare Tennyson's "Withdrew
from me and night" with "And leaves the world to darkness and to me"). This repetition of the mourner's earlier
experience of abandonment brings a predictable pang ("A
hunger seized my heart") and forces him to search once
more for consolation.

Although we have been following the poet's struggle to accept his dependence on language, it is still perhaps a shock
to see how directly he now turns to the very medium that
his earlier imagery of lucid veils and illuminated scripts
implied: "A hunger seized my heart; I read. . . . " Like
Gray in the churchyard, he, too, reads, in this case the letters of his friend, the "fallen leaves which kept their
green." (The metaphor only drives home the substitution
of the literary for the natural.) His friend survives as a
script whose silence is enforced despite the oxymoronic
straining for voice:

> And strangely on the silence broke
>   The silent-speaking words, and strange
>   Was love's dumb cry defying change
> To test his worth;

This dependence on the written letter is even more firmly
emphasized in what follows:

> So word by word, and line by line,
>   The dead man touch'd me from the past,

The physical touch so long desired, and so reluctantly
spiritualized, has finally become a literary impression, and

TENNYSON   *POETRY CRITICISM, Vol. 6*

Tennyson and his family. From left: Hallam, Alfred, Emily, and Lionel.

the recovered presence of the dead in letters suggests the poet's own recovery of Hallam in the lines of his elegy.

For a moment, the communion rises to a height that apparently transcends mere letters:

> And all at once it seem'd at last
> The living soul was flash'd on mine,
>
> And mine in this was wound, and whirl'd
>   About empyreal heights of thought,
>   And came on that which is, and caught
> The deep pulsations of the world,
>
> Aeonian music measuring out
>   The steps of Time—the shocks of Chance—
>   The blows of Death.

Here "at last" is the instantaneous flash that fulfills the poet's desire not so much for reunion with Hallam as for the revelation of an eternal pattern ("that which is") in which the adversary, Time, is accommodated to measures of music. What he sees, or rather hears, is an ideal version of his own poem, a reconciliation of the timebound with the timeless in a music that smoothly encompasses the occasions of grief.

But with the mention of Death, the reverie breaks up with

a specific reminder of its textual nature: "At length my trance / Was cancell'd, stricken thro' with doubt." It is as though the trance were no more than a canceled page of script. But now the poet's admission of his "matter-moulded forms of speech" coexists with an apparently residual faith in the vision to which these forms seem to have led. *Returning* to the "vague words" and to the materiality of language may finally be the poet's way of conceding the "word by word" ground from which the vision sprang. Hence, too, the return to the surrounding scene, the knolls, the trees, the kine now glimmering in the uncertain light before dawn. This time, a gentle breeze animates the scene and issues into the language of proclamation:

> 'The dawn, the dawn,' and died away;
>   And East and West, without a breath,
>   Mixt their dim lights, like life and death,
> To broaden into boundless day.

Apart from the assurance with which language now seems to usher in the time of day, something of the all-encompassing trance persists in the medley of lights. Like the Aeonian music, the twilight seems to overcome what may otherwise appear to be the discontinuities of day and night, life and death. The poet celebrates the passage of time, but within a chordlike compounding of its divisions.

As always, the lights are dim. And in the following section, the poet makes his most explicit defense of this essential obscurity. The darkness, or veil, is now meant to refer also to doubt, an easy extension, since we have all along been associating darkness with accepted limitation, blindness, or the material, "earthly" nature of language. The poet praises one who, like Hallam or himself, has found a "stronger faith":

> And Power was with him in the night,
> Which makes the darkness and the light,
> And dwells not in the light alone,
>
> But in the darkness and the cloud,
>   As over Sinaï's peaks of old,
>   While Israel made their gods of gold,
> Altho' the trumpet blew so loud.

Intriguingly, the passage combines a defense of a mediating veil or cloud like that of language with an allusion to the figure of Moses, who in himself represents mediation and is, moreover, a prime example of the very kind of mediation, the precise mode of rhetoric, that most enables the consoling resolution of this poem—*figura* or type. For Moses, *the* type of the mediator, is himself a type prefiguring Christ. Milton had captured this in his account of the Sinaitic instruction "by types / And shadows":

> . . . he grants what they besought,
> Instructed that to God is no access
> Without Mediator, whose high Office now
> Moses in figure bears, to introduce
> One greater, of whose day he shall foretell.

Earlier, we began to suggest that the device of *figura* was particularly helpful to a poet who was struggling to reconcile the instantaneous with the passage of time and who needed to preserve an assurance of identity despite temporal change. We had remarked how fully Tennyson subscribed to the Victorian insistence on a self defined as idiosyncratic personality and how completely he therefore shunned the traditional displacements by which a mourned self gave way to some new substitute. The appeal of *figura* is that it requires neither an alteration of identity nor a submission to time conceived as merely horizontal metamorphic linkage. Rather, it offers a preservation and fulfillment of any discrete moment or identity by a revelation of its higher, timeless character. As Erich Auerbach put it:

> In this way the individual earthly event is not regarded as . . . a link in a chain of development in which single events or combinations of events perpetually give rise to new events, but viewed primarily in immediate vertical connection with a divine order which encompasses it [Tennyson's "that which is"], which on some future day will itself be concrete reality. . . .
>
> For Dante the literal meaning or historical reality of a figure stands in no contradiction to its profounder meaning, but precisely "figures" it; the historical reality is not annulled, but confirmed and fulfilled by the deeper meaning.

It is precisely this avoidance of the much doubted and much dreaded transformation or substitution that must have so appealed to the poet of *In Memoriam.* And in the remaining sections of the poem, he exploits the resources of *figura* with varied amplitude. For example, the consoling dream that attends the departure from his childhood home at Somersby centers upon successive encounters with the figure of Hallam. At first the figure is

> A statue veil'd, to which they sang;
>
> And which, tho' veil'd, was known to me,
>   The shape of him I loved, and love
> For ever.

Like the first term of the *figura,* this is the shape that conceals within itself its true and essentially unchanging identity. In Auerbach's similar terms, "Thus, history, with all its concrete force, remains forever a figure, cloaked and needful of interpretation." As statue, the shape is emphatically immobile. It has the frozen aspect that we earlier associated with the statuesque attitudes of melancholy. As we know, however, Tennyson retains yet revises the elements of his melancholy. The veiled statue is, after all, interpretable, and it is succeeded by a revelation and enlargement of its identity. And the poet himself increases to gigantic size as he is ferried with his poems to meet his friend.

Elsewhere, the figures of typology are more straightforwardly employed:

> Till at the last arose the man;
>
> Who throve and branch'd from clime to clime,
>   The herald of a higher race,
>   And of himself in higher place,
> If so he type this work of time
>
> Within himself, from more to more;

According to Tennyson's idiosyncratic blend of typology and evolution, a historical individual may have within himself an identity that resembles a veiled statue while on earth but would be fully apparent now and forever in heaven, or, in the fullness of time, by way of evolution, here on earth. By regarding evolution as a movement toward a manifestation of what certain types on earth have already prefigured, and of what exists already outside of time, Tennyson tempers what would otherwise be a merely linear series of substitutions. He maintains his stress on a lasting identity as surely as he continues his "check" against the "propulsion towards change." The final expression of this particular use of typology, in which Hallam himself is seen as the type of human perfection, will bring the poem to its conclusion.

Before turning to the epilogue, however, we should note some features of the preceding sections, particularly those that pursue and resolve such previously mentioned issues as the poet's melancholy narcissism, his adoption of a childlike posture, his need to repair a sense of audience, and his related need to conserve a stable image of his *own* identity.

The departure from Somersby is interestingly described, for the poet clearly displaces onto Somersby the wounded narcissism that he himself suffered at Hallam's death. By a series of repeated negations, he suggests that Somersby had no existence apart from its relation to Hallam or himself. His departure now seems, therefore, to repeat the devastating effect of Hallam's then: "And, leaving these, to pass away, / I think once more he seems to die." By leaving Somersby, he enacts his own abandonment by Hallam, not unlike the child who brings about a symbolic version of its mother's departure in order to master the experience. Somersby precisely represents the poet's forsaken self, a self deprived of love and audience: "Unwatch'd . . . Unloved . . . Uncared for."

For Somersby, the only redress will be a new tenant, a substitute for the departing lover. And similarly, for the poet, redress will depend on the regained presence of his approving friend. An essential part, therefore, of the "departure dream" in section 103 is Hallam's welcome, extended both to the poet and to his works. Significantly, the poet cannot bid his own poems to enter. It is the ideal reader, Hallam, who must save them from neglect (" 'And wilt thou leave us now behind?' ")

In the light of this dream, the departure from Somersby thus takes on added complexity. The poet not only leaves behind his youth but detaches himself from that youth defined as a scenario of abandonment. In other words, the mourner is making that crucial movement beyond a prior state of desolation, beyond a melancholy fixation on the dead and on his own forsaken self. Tennyson frees himself from the ego on to which his affections had refastened after Hallam's death—the ego that nevertheless had unconsciously, and melancholically, been associated with Hallam as a lost object. The poet's own sense of enlargement in the dream reflects his surpassal of that younger, arrested self. But it also represents his arrival at a repaired and enlarged narcissistic relation to the dead. As he had previously identified with the lost, so he now reidentifies with the found Hallam. And as the found Hallam is enlarged and unveiled, so the poet himself mirrors this new state.

Finally, by the images of the summons, the shallop-ferry, and the waters broadening to a grand "flood," the poet confirms that this dream passage prefigures his own death. And as in "Adonais," but without Shelley's blazing extinction of personality, it is the resource of transformed narcissism that enables the poet to use his new image of the dead as a mirror image of his own surviving self. Once again, the elegy yields its archaic reward—the elegist's invention and rehearsal of his immortality.

This augmentative mirroring, in which the poet projects and then tries to match a higher self-image or ideal ego, continues with the poet's attempts to imitate the wisdom of the dead. The reflective device is captured by approximate echoes: " 'Tis held that sorrow makes us wise, / Whatever wisdom sleep with thee;" "High wisdom holds my wisdom less;" "And in thy wisdom make me wise." And the culmination of this entire strategy is reached in the epilogue, where the poet describes himself in terms similar to those of the dream in section 103:

> No longer caring to embalm
>   In dying songs a dead regret,
>   But like a statue solid-set,
> And moulded in colossal calm.

Regret is dead, but love is more
  Than in the summers that are flown,
  For I myself with these have grown
To something greater than before;

While he retains the motif of enlargement, he has also carried over the image of the statue. That is, he imitates not only the fulfilled, colossal figure of the refound Hallam but also the statuesque figure of the dead Hallam in his life-size, shrouded state before fulfillment. So intent is the poet not to lose his or Hallam's familiar form that he clings, even in the midst of imaging his higher self, to the conservative condition of the statue. He thus carefully preserves the prior, historical figure within its later fulfillment. There could be no better example of his overall retention yet revision of his melancholia.

Throughout these last sections the poet is thus devising images that represent both Hallam and himself as being "the same, yet not the same," enlarged but not transformed. The masterful Hesper-Phosphor image in section 121 is one such image, relying yet again on a version of *figura* ("double name / For what is one, the first, the last"). And it is the inherent conservatism of such a passage, like that regarding the statue in the epilogue, that may make the reader a little skeptical of the apparent upsurge of belief, for the first time in the poem, in an impersonal version of immortality:

> What art thou then? I cannot guess;
>   But tho' I seem in star and flower
>   To feel thee some diffusive power,
> I do not therefore love thee less.
>
> My love involves the love before;
>   My love is vaster passion now;
>   Tho' mix'd with God and Nature thou,
> I seem to love thee more and more.

Even if one were not a little skeptical, one should at least note how these assertions are situated in clauses that are not only subordinate but concessional. The emphasis throughout this and the surrounding sections bears firmly on the stable, obsessively stressed identity of the poet and of his still extremely possessive love: "Dear heavenly friend that canst not die, / Mine, mine, for ever, ever mine."

The last section of the poem proper—before the epilogue—returns to several essential themes:

> O living will that shalt endure
>   When all that seems shall suffer shock,
>   Rise in the spiritual rock,
> Flow thro' our deeds and make them pure,
>
> That we may lift from out of dust
>   A voice as unto him that hears,
>   A cry above the conquer'd years
> To one that with us works, and trust,
>
> With faith that comes of self-control,
>   The truths that never can be proved
>   Until we close with all we loved,
> And all we flow from, soul in soul.

The "living will," by which is meant "Free will, the higher and enduring part of man," is here assimilated, by way of the elegiac image of liquidity, to the will of Christ. The allusion is to 1 Corinthians 10.4: "For they drank of the spiritual Rock that followed them: and the Rock was Christ." This is itself a perfect example of *figura,* fulfilling the type in Exodus 17.6: "and thou shalt smite the rock, and there shall come water out of it, that the people may drink." And this in turn takes us back to section 96, the defense of darkness, mediation, and *figura* in the reference to Moses. Like the Scriptures, the poem itself appears to be fulfilling its own prefigurations, exemplifying the very process on which its consolation depends.

The second stanza continues the image of miraculous liquidity, now mingling it with a representation of voice or cry. Since the beginnings of elegy, in which a shepherd's voice accompanied a murmuring stream, we have grown accustomed to this mingling. And since discussing how the earliest images for the spirit and the enduring will, or the powers of song, were drawn from images of an originally sexual force, we have come to recognize the complex nature of this figure. As his specific use of the above *figura* suggests, however, Tennyson has done far more than merely rely on a given convention. His cry has a highly individual character. It refers us back to the cry of the infant abandoned by its mother Nature in section 54 and to the entire issue of the poet's need for a regained sense of almost parental audience. In section 124, the achievement of just such a cry is carefully linked to the mourner's work of self-chastisement. And once again, that work seems to involve an oedipal resolution:

> And like a man in wrath the heart
> Stood up and answer'd, 'I have felt.'
>
> No, like a child in doubt and fear:
>   But that blind clamor made me wise;
>   Then was I as a child that cries,
> But, crying, knows his father near;

The abandoning and abandoned mother is thus replaced by a father, under whose aegis the mourning poet has apparently unmanned himself, but with consoling effects. Hence the final submission in section 131 of the "free will" to that of Christ, himself a martyr, and the replacement of the rebellious desire for knowledge with a milder attitude of "trust" and "faith that comes of self-control." Only in this way can the poet raise a voice "as unto him that hears." The use of simile hints at poignant uncertainty, a symptom of the continuing deferral of knowledge.

The epilogue, as Tennyson admitted, carries the poem from funeral to marriage, thereby concluding with the ancient rituals of sexual reunion and rebirth. But the marriage itself is described as though it were somehow a funeral in which the poet is compelled to give away or surrender his sister to her new life. Section 40 suggested some of the similarity between a bride and the newly deceased, and while the epilogue does repair the dissatisfaction of the earlier section, it nonetheless retains something of a mourner's resignation. There is the recollected idyll framed by its own fate:

> For I that danced her on my knee,
>   That watch'd her on her nurse's arm,
>   That shielded all her life from harm,
> At last must part with her to thee;

The presence of the dead surrounds her: "Their pensive tablets round her head." The marriage inscription, by contrast with the "living words of life," takes on an epitaphic cast ("Now sign your names, which shall be read, / Mute symbols of a joyful morn"). And the unavoidable moment of departure, however delayed, is abrupt and final:

> But they must go, the time draws on,
>   And those white-favour'd horses wait;
>   They rise, but linger; it is late;
> Farewell, we kiss, and they are gone.

In the wake of this farewell, the poet is repeatedly shadowed ("A shade falls on us . . . the shade of passing through") until he is left alone, as in section 95, with the night. But the dark sets off the "shining vapour" of moonlight which moves like the poet's mind to bless his sister's marriage: "And breaking let the splendour fall / To spangle all the happy shores." True to its original sense, the blessing would grant a procreative strength, which yields the consoling figure of the reborn child. Whereas earlier in the poem the poet lamented the absence of linkage, the child now serves to connect "Betwixt us and the crowning race." But as always, the sheer linearity of linkage is modified by the insistence that Hallam had been "a noble type," prefiguring such a race, and that he continues to exist, to "live" as such, "in God." The "one far-off divine event, / To which the whole creation moves," is therefore not exclusively the product of evolution. It is also the revelation of what has been and of that which is. Along with the elegiac image of vegetative ripening, merged now with the final use of *figura,* the poet draws his friend into the Aeonian music, which, like the poem's extraordinarily long final sentence, seems to envelop in itself the far-off reaches of time to which it points and moves.

Or rather *seems* to move. Like so many of Tennyson's resolutions, the end is a postponement. The final lines not only stave off consummation but seem to fall into a self-involved trance in which motion of any kind is laid to sleep or drugged. The syntactic advance is so exhausting that one tends to collapse upon the final word rather than advance according to its meaning. More precisely, the almost agglutinative caution with which the clauses are attached one to another ensures that the entire mass will move together if it moves at all. The motion is therefore as hard to perceive as that of the globe itself. And for all its splendidly climactic cadence, the poem ends with a suspended approach to, rather than a decisive apprehension of, the "far-off divine event." Certainly, elegies often end with an indication of further movement—the shepherd's rise and departure from the place of song, the uncouth swain's prospect of pastures new, Shelley's self-consuming drive beyond mortality. But these endings usually clinch or go beyond the culmination of the elegiac achievement, whereas ***In Memoriam*** remains at a long remove from the culmination to which it points. And although the poem ends by creating the illusion that the act of pointing itself may sound or feel like an arrival, the prologue is there, as if it were the poem's true coda, to remind us of the poet's residual and no doubt comforting sense of incompletion in regard to both himself and his elegy:

> Forgive these wild and wandering cries,

Confusions of a wasted youth;
　Forgive them where they fail in truth,
　And in thy wisdom make me wise.

Any appreciation of *In Memoriam* must recognize that its length is essential to its success. With such a burden of skepticism and such a passionate clinging to the empirical and personal, there was little chance of Tennyson's finding genuine consolation in an elegy of conventional length. Only the prolonged accretion, the ebb and flow of inner dialogue, the patient piecing together of visionary fragments, and the necessarily gradual deployment of typology could resist the tremendous counterpressure of melancholy. And yet we may wonder whether too much ground has been ceded to that counterpressure and whether the poem's length robs it of the energetic, processional drive that is so important to elegy. *In Memoriam* does not perform the kind of single, unified ceremony that pretends to accomplish the work of mourning in one action. Reading this poem in fact shows up the importance of the condensation and intense thrust of other elegies—how those poems leave the reader invigorated as well as comforted. (pp. 166-202)

> *Peter M. Sacks, "Tennyson: 'In Memoriam',"
> in his* The English Elegy: Studies in the Genre
> from Spenser to Yeats, *Johns Hopkins University Press, 1985, pp. 166-203.*

Seamus Heaney on Tennyson's achievement and influence:

That Tennyson's death should have occurred in the same year as Christopher Grieve/Hugh MacDiarmid's birth is a nice coincidence. Once the drunk man looked at the thistle, and Finnegan woke, and Hopkins hove to, the Lawn Tennyson game was up. Rhythm sprang, tundish ruled and the vowels and consonants of Boeotia (as Les A. Murray calls the land of relegation) came swarming in like rug-headed kernes. Of course, Tennyson did write in dialect on occasion, and there does seem to have been something robust and unassimilable about him, at a personal level; but every time I come to that **"Northern Farmer, Old Style"**, I feel like the man in the old story who was unsure who was taking the micky out of whom once his companion (hitherto, like himself, the apparent victim of a speech impediment) began to mimic the impeccable accents of the barman. Even so, what is unmistakably the real thing is Tennyson's strong hypnotic frequency, a note somewhere between that of the banshee and the turbine. The *In Memoriam* stanza, with its unique combination of accelerating voice and metrical brake-lining, is still a potent chanter; it has wonderful tonal verity, capable of maintaining a purchase on the endured and a thrust into the desired. Tennyson's perfect pitch may have been a penalty as well as a gift, but it served him well as long as it stayed in contention with a countervailing, sluggard undervoice that was the poetic earnest of a suffered melancholy in himself, and in the order of things as he experienced it.

> *Seamus Heaney, in* The Times Literary Supplement,
> *1992.*

Rhoda L. Flaxman   (essay date 1987)

[*In the following excerpt from her* Victorian Word-Painting and Narrative: Toward the Blending of Genres, *Flaxman examines Tennyson's innovations in poetic form and style and his development throughout his career.*]

In a demonstration of imaginative originality equal to the contrast between Wordsworth's *Descriptive Sketches* and his *Lyrical Ballads of 1798,* Tennyson burst upon the literary scene in 1830 with **Poems, Chiefly Lyrical.** This volume includes outstanding poems such as **"Mariana"** and **"The Kraken,"** along with interesting, if flawed, lesser works such as **"Supposed Confessions of a Second-Rate Sensitive Mind"** and **"Recollections of the Arabian Nights."** Although some of the poems in this collection continue to rely on the picturesque imagination we have noticed in Tennyson's juvenilia, **"Mariana"** and **"The Kraken"** announce the deepening suggestiveness of Tennyson's poetic descriptions. **"Mariana"** includes both simple visual images—the least complex kind of poetic description—and visually oriented materials that serve simultaneously to illuminate the object being described and the sensibility perceiving it. **"The Kraken,"** on the other hand, is a fine early example of Tennyson's interest in visionary poetry. A fourth level of complexity for visually oriented description—visual images that appeal simultaneously to sensuous and intellectual understanding (such as Metaphysical poetry)—will appear much later in Tennyson's poetry, and I will note it in the discussion of *Idylls of the King.*

In contrast to the generalized landscapes of the sublime word-paintings that dominate Tennyson's early poetic efforts, **"Mariana"** announces an approach to landscape description that is severely fragmented, deriving its effect from the specificity of close examination of ordinary objects often considered too insignificant to mention. Instead of expansive vista, **"Mariana"** opens with an exceedingly contractive enumeration of eight disconnected objects in a landscape whose principle of organization is not at first clear.

> With blackest moss the flower-plots
> 　Were thickly crusted, one and all:
> The rusted nails fell from the knots
> 　That held the pear to the gable-wall.
> The broken sheds look'd sad and strange:
> 　Unlifted was the clinking latch;
> 　Weeded and worn the ancient thatch
> Upon the lonely moated grange.
> 　She only said, 'My life is dreary,
> 　　He cometh not,' she said;
> 　She said, 'I am aweary, aweary,
> 　　I would that I were dead!'

Flower-plots, nails, gable wall, shed, latch, thatch, and grange suggest a narrow focus and introduce the structural model for the poem: eight lines of sensuous description followed by a four-line balladic refrain that varied slightly to suggest Mariana's despair. The idiosyncratic visual perspective evokes curiosity in the reader concerning both the psychological state of this particular observer and the narrative explanation for her present state. Tennyson's use of word-painting to raise questions concerning psychological and narrative truths in a poem constitutes a maturing so-phistication in this poet's technique.

Although Tennyson narrates the poem in the third person, Culler and others argue that the particular way in which the landscape is described convinces us that the entire poem is spoken by Mariana. Culler's explanation of the technique by which Tennyson achieves this perspective admirably summarizes recent critical thinking about the poem.

> It is her perception of the grange, the phenome-nology of it, that we are given. Partly this is done through the images of brokenness and decay, of darkness and shadow, of emptiness and desola-tion, which are also the images of her mind. But partly, too, it is done through a prolonged sense of interior time. . . . The technical means by which this is done—chiefly the alternation of night and day, the use of verbs in the customary or habitual mode, the slight variations in the re-frain which but emphasize its essential same-ness, and the retardation of the meter—are deft-ly handled. But the chief resource in fusing sub-ject and object is the utter absence in the poem of any guiding, organizing, or generalizing intel-ligence. The description consists entirely of iso-lated, atomistic detail.

Culler's last point echoes the more narrowly focused study by Carol Christ (*The Finer Optic*), who studies the rela-tionship between particularization and generalization in the poetry of Tennyson, Rossetti, Browning, and Hopkins. And both critics are indebted to the early work of Harold Bloom, who argued some years ago that the visual intensi-ty of description in **"Mariana"** forces the reader to deduce heightened emotional states in the speaker to account for an "unnatural" vividness and intensity in the descriptive materials. Bloom's work, which restates Ruskin's "pathet-ic fallacy," notes the displacement of unusual emotion from individual to landscape. Bloom also points to a simi-lar use of sensuous images in *In Memoriam,* such as the description of the yew. He suggests Tennyson's skill at ar-ticulating static states of being such as ennui, lethargy, melancholy, and inertia.

Picturesque detail in **"Mariana"** takes on new significance when simple visual impressions suggest both phenomeno-logical and psychological truths. Christ argues that in the case of **"Mariana"** and *Maud* (the only Tennyson poems she studies in detail), visually oriented specificity is meant to suggest the "morbid emotion" of the viewer. The way in which objects are intensely visualized symbolizes "the loss of balance and proportion, the inability to integrate and order experience, and a consequent isolation in purely subjective perception." The fragmented word-painting that largely composes **"Mariana,"** in other words, is far from a merely picturesque landscape—which Christ de-fines in general as "an emphasis on the pleasures of vision apart from any truth value they might contain"—but is, rather, a correlative for the incoherence of despair.

The "story" of Mariana is deliberately indeterminate. Nothing "happens" in the poem, but the refrain suggests that she wishes to die. Like many literary ballads—for ex-ample, Keats's *La Belle Dame sans merci*—this poem sug-gests a state of despair or death-in-life. But Tennyson sac-rifices specificity of event to depiction of a generalized psy-chological state. Paradoxically, he succeeds in eliciting this generalized state by reference to extremely specific de-tails in a desolate landscape. Word-painting in this poem simultaneously convinces the reader to accurately picture what Mariana sees and hears ("The blue fly sung in the pane," for example) and to feel her languor. The landscape accurately registers her stagnation and despair.

This poem represents Tennyson's first successful effort to use word-painting both to suggest a psychological state and to relate uniquely to the story that explains that state. Although **"Mariana"** cannot really be termed a "narra-tive," narrative fragments imply the woman's story, and word-painting here is more symbolic and visionary than picturesque. How delightful it would have been for the present writer, had **"Mariana"** been the product of Tenny-son's middle or late years. Then, the poem might have been an example of Tennyson's developmental progres-sion from picturesque to symbolic landscapes. But, so far, this close study of Tennyson's word-paintings indicates the consistency of motifs and his early appreciation of the usefulness of word-paintings to depict simultaneously the object perceived and the quality of the perceiver. As Ten-nyson masters technique, he will become increasingly suc-cessful at word-paintings and narrative in later poems.

Another of Tennyson's favorite subjects for word-paintings also appears in both his juvenilia and in *Poems, Chiefly Lyrical.* The visionary, the third kind of descrip-tive poetry previously mentioned, offers word-paintings that describe other-worldly visions whose outlines we have never seen. Yet the descriptions convince us of the possibilities for such visionary landscapes through a tech-nique that fuses deliberate vagueness of some elements in the landscape with acute specificity of other details.

Tennyson paints many such visionary landscapes in the course of his career, from **"Armageddon"** and **"Timbuc-too"** through **"The Kraken,"** to **"The Holy Grail"** and other visionary landscapes from *Idylls of the King.* Even some of his very last lyrics such as **"The Ancient Sage"** and **"Merlin and the Gleam"** incorporate allusions to other-worldly visions.

John D. Rosenberg asserts that **"The Kraken"** stakes out Tennyson's essential subject: "the twilight world of myth in which consciousness and unconsciousness intersect." Tennyson's compositional method varies from poem to poem, but the critic Valerie Pitt notices that a peculiar combination of vivid foreground detail and background blurriness occurs in all. She attributes this feature to the poet's poor eyesight and conjectures that Tennyson really saw the world this way. Yet in writing visionary poetry, Tennyson may simply combine traditional attitudes to-ward the visionary with his own keen interest in contem-porary scientific discoveries concerning geological time and the enormity of Darwinian cycles of life. Certainly, Tennyson's visionary landscapes sometimes share the technique we have examined in the visionary passages from Wordsworth's *The Prelude,* where a dramatic use of misted and clarified vision illuminates both an external and internal landscape of thought and feeling. A similar treatment of visionary landscape is notable in ***Idylls of the King.***

"Armageddon" represents an early version of a visionary landscape upon which Tennyson later drew for details in **"The Coming of Arthur."** The young poet vividly captures the hallucinatory acuteness of an other-worldly experience:

> . . . my mental eye grew large
> With such a vast circumference of thought,
> That, in my vanity, I seemed to stand
> Upon the outward verge and bound alone
> Of God's omniscience. Each failing sense,
> As with a momentary flash of light,
> Grew thrillingly distinct and keen. I saw
> The smallest Grain that dappled the dark Earth,
> The indistinctest atom in deep air,
> The Moon's white cities, and the opal width
> Of her small, glowing lakes, her silver heights
> Unvisited with dew of vagrant cloud,
> And the unsounded, undescended depth
> Of her black hollows.

Tennyson pays relatively more attention to the structure of the description here than he did in the earlier passage from **"The Devil and the Lady"** with which it shares certain iconographical motifs. This attention makes the passage from **"Armageddon"** more visually acute than the earlier passage, even though it describes a private vision. In order to anchor the visionary moment in **"Armageddon,"** Tennyson attempts to direct the viewer's mental eye to "circumference" and "verge," presenting the vision in terms that clearly contrast darkness and light, form and formlessness. The visual rationale in this passage is clear, for the description moves coherently from earth to air, to the moon with its "white cities," its lakes, mountains, and hollows. And, when Tennyson later reworks the passage from **"Armageddon"** for **"Timbuctoo,"** he augments the beautiful distinctness with lines describing the galaxy and its supernatural lights in order to intensify even further the dramatic interplay of light and dark:

> The clear Galaxy
> Shorn of its hoary lustre, wonderful,
> Distinct and vivid with sharp points of light,
> Blaze within blaze, an unimagined depth
> And harmony of planet-girded Suns
> And moon-encircled planets, wheel in wheel,
> Arched the wan Sapphire.

Paden notes that this passage "is apparently the first of Tennyson's references to that mystical experience which, occurring throughout his life, formed the personal basis of his faith." Tennyson himself noted of such a moment that, "It is no nebulous ecstasy, but a state of transcendent wonder, associated with absolute clearness of mind." On such a moment will the climax of ***In Memoriam*** later depend.

The examples cited thus far attest to Tennyson's continuing interest in visionary landscapes throughout his career. One of the most successful of these appears in the collection of 1830. **"The Kraken"** suggests apocalypse in a brief fifteen-line description of the fabled sea-monster who slumbers in the depths of the sea. James Welch points out that, here, landscape images two sorts of time: static and dynamic. The poem's brevity and careful selection of significant detail help Tennyson avoid the structural excesses of the other early visionary poems I have just discussed.

> Below the thunders of the upper deep;
> Far, far beneath in the abysmal sea,
> His ancient, dreamless, uninvaded sleep
> The Kraken sleepeth: faintest sunlights flee
> About his shadowy sides: above him swell
> Huge sponges of millennial growth and height;
> And far away into the sickly light,
> From many a wondrous grot and secret cell
> Unnumbered and enormous polypi
> Winnow with giant arms the slumbering green.
> There hath he lain for ages and will lie
>
> Battening upon huge seaworms in his sleep,
> Until the latter fire shall heat the deep;
> Then once by man and angels to be seen,
> In roaring he shall rise and on the surface die.

Images of surface and depths, of sunlight and shadow, of oceanic movement combined with the absolute stasis of the sea-monster build a sense of dread in the reader, who may remember the moment predicted in Rev. 13:1, "And I stood upon the sand of the sea, and saw a beast rise up out of the sea." The description of objects around the kraken (the sponges and polypi) attracts our attention away from a precise visualization of the sea creature, which adds to its sense of mystery. The combination of clarity and void helps account for the description's powerfully enigmatic effect. The kraken, mythological, becomes a symbol to link past prophecy with future catastrophe.

While post-Modernist critics concentrate on poems such as **"Mariana"** and **"The Kraken,"** it is important to remember that ***Poems, Chiefly Lyrical*** contains mostly picturesque word-paintings. Indeed, it is fascinating to realize that Hallam, Tennyson's first and most important critic, fails even to mention these two poems in his first, appreciative review. Discussing Tennyson as a picturesque poet, and linking him with Keats and Shelley as "poets of sensation," Hallam concentrates, instead, on **"Recollections of the Arabian Nights"**! Important comments on Tennyson's use of the picturesque—an approach to landscape that concerns this study, since it represents the first stage in the history of word-painting—began with Arthur Henry Hallam's insightful early evaluation of Tennyson's art, "On Some of the Characteristics of Modern Poetry, and on the Lyrical Poems of Alfred Tennyson." Here Hallam sketches "the five distinctive excellencies of Tennyson's manner."

> First, his luxuriance of imagination, and at the same time his control over it. Secondly, his power of embodying himself in ideal characters, or rather moods of character, with such extreme accuracy of adjustment, that the circumstances of the narration seem to have a natural correspondence with the predominant feeling, and, as it were, to be evolved from it by assimilative force. Thirdly, his vivid, picturesque delineation of objects, and the peculiar skill with which he holds all of them fused, to borrow a metaphor from science, in a medium of strong emotion. Fourthly, the variety of his lyrical measures, and exquisite modulation of harmonious words and

cadences to the swell and fall of the feelings expressed. Fifthly, the elevated habits of thought,
implied in these compositions.

The passage reminds one of the qualities Tennyson's contemporaries praised in his work. Hallam assumes that
"Recollections of the Arabian Nights" will be the favorite
poem from the collection of 1830, and, sounding the highest praise, calls the poem "a perfect gallery of pictures,"
because of the poet's "concise boldness, with which in a
few words an object is clearly painted."

The two stanzas that Hallam singles out to demonstrate
Tennyson's skill in painting "pictures," are the two outstanding visually oriented passages in this work which, in
Hallam's words, captures the "mood" of childhood with
the "solemn distinctness in every image." As the speaker
glides down the Tigris in a dream vision on the "tide of
time," he views with pleasure the panorama unfolding on
the shore:

> Above through many a bowery turn
> A walk with vary-coloured shells
> Wandered engrained. On either side
> All round about the fragrant marge
> From fluted vase, and brazen urn
> In order, eastern flowers large,
> Some dropping low their crimson bells
> Half-closed, and others studded wide
> With disks and tiars, fed the time
> With odour in the golden prime
> Of good Haroun Alraschid.

The structure provided by narrating a journey down the
Tigris organizes a series of brightly colored scenes, with
their exotic shapes and eastern fragrances, but the journey
structure is distinctly secondary to the word-pictures
themselves. In this poem, sight fuses with the sense of
smell to produce a pleasing mixture of sensations. Later
in the poem, when the speaker walks through the gardens
of Haroun Alraschid, he gazes, transfixed ("with dazed vision") at a glorious fairy-tale architecture (stanza 12) in
which flame-lit windows contrast with "hollow-vaulted
dark" and the streaming glory of a crescent-decorated
roof. The poem culminates in a vision of the Caliph and
a strangely alluring Persian girl, after which, in silence,
the poem breaks off, denying narrative. The poem's movement, in keeping with childlike dreams, is disconnected,
focusing neither on coherent narrative nor on psychological complexity. Both structure and imagery suggest elements that will reappear in later Tennyson poems such as
"The Palace of Art" and parts of *The Princess* and *In
Memoriam.* But word-painting in **"Recollections of the
Arabian Nights"** looks back to the picturesque tradition
I have been sketching, rather than forward to a more inte-
grally related symbolic technique.

One last example from *Poems, Chiefly Lyrical* indicates
a future direction for visually oriented poetry in Tennyson. In the long, tormented monologue, **"Supposed Confessions of a Second-Rate Sensitive Mind,"** formlessness—a traditional image of sublimity—becomes fearful
as an image of self:

> What if
> Thou pleadest still, and seest me drive

> Through utter dark a full-sailed skiff,
> Unpiloted i' the echoing dance
> Of reboant whirlwinds, stooping low
> Unto the death, not sunk!
> . . . . .
> I think that pride hath now no place
> Nor sojourn in me. I am void,
> Dark, formless, utterly destroyed.

Again one notes the iconography of sea and skiff, sounding
like similar visual motifs from **"The Devil and the Lady,"**
but, in a dramatic tightening of word-painting and narrative, the pilotless boat has become internalized as a motif
of self-doubt.

Thus far, this study of Tennyson has established basic features of his early word-paintings and has asserted that the
essential elements of his visually oriented descriptions are
present fairly early. His juvenilia and *Poems, Chiefly Lyrical* contain at least three of the four basic kinds of descriptive poetry: simple visual images, images suggestive of a
state of mind (**"Mariana"**), and visionary landscapes
(**"The Kraken"**). Now that some of the basic features of
Tennyson's word-paintings have been established here,
subsequent discussion will focus on their relationship to
narrative (which increasingly interested the poet in his
mature years).

A brief examination of those major poems published first
in 1832—but extensively revised for the collection published after Tennyson's "ten-year's silence," in 1842—
indicates how the poet trimmed some of the excesses characteristic of his early word-paintings in order to integrate
description with narration. Increasingly, Tennyson moves
away from long set pieces of descriptive poetry and toward
briefer, but more suggestive, description that contributes
important material both to form and content of particular
poems. "By 1842," Edgar F. Shannon notes, "Tennyson
was in complete control of his poetic purpose and resources." Poems important to the argument that his control shapes both description and narration in Tennyson's
work include **"The Lady of Shalott,"** **"The Lotos-Eaters,"**
"The Palace of Art," **"Ulysses,"** **"Morte d'Arthur"** and
English Idylls. (pp. 78-85)

. . . [For Tennyson], the repetition of a
single simple phrase could reconcile
thoughts of past and present into hints of
preexistence and immortality. The result
is a feeling of sudden elevation, a
manifestation of a central process of mind
which, by working imaginatively on the
raw materials of sensation, turns them
into images of significance and
permanence.

—*Ashton Nichols, in his* "The Epiphanic
Trance Poem: Why Tennyson Is Not a
Mystic," *1986.*

"The Lady of Shalott" represents Tennyson's most concentrated recounting of a fairy-tale narrative in four brief sections. Again, he relies primarily on the visual sense, but augments this with the auditory. The figure overlooking a prospect from a high cliff has been replaced here by the immured maiden who views an exterior scene only obliquely. Like Mariana, she is isolated, but there is no brooding, internalized landscape in **"The Lady of Shalott."** Instead, the poem opens with a picturesque landscape scene which later readers of the poem called "Pre-Raphaelite," because of its preternatural brightness and clarity and its deliberately archaic syntax.

> On either side the river lie
> Long fields of barley and of rye,
> That clothe the wold and meet the sky;
> And through the field the road runs by
>   To many-towered Camelot;
> And up and down the people go,
> Gazing where the lilies blow
> Round an island there below,
>   The island of Shalott.

In this ballad, perspective determines both scale and theme. The Lady, high in her tower, mirrors reality, turning it into a series of tapestry pictures. At the poem's climax, when (lured by her own loneliness and the sight of Sir Lancelot) she turns to look directly out the window, she loses the ordering of her perceptions and must die, cursed by some indeterminate fate. Shannon's interesting article tries to reconcile the many interpretations of this poem by following the ambiguity of images associated with the Lady (e.g. the suggestion that appearances deceive in the opening landscape, the self-indulgent aspects of the Lady's bower, and her life-denying service to art) and contrasting them with primarily positive religious and visual images associated with Lancelot. Nothing that "light, Lancelot's primary attribute, is in Tennyson's poetry invariably the image for a spiritual state of perfection or for the manifestation of Divinity," Shannon concludes that, "The Lady's final vision resolves the ambiguity of appearance and reality posed by the opening landscape of the poem. Passing from sight to insight through three stages of perception in ascending order of truth—indirect, direct and mystical—she grasps behind the phenomena the reality of which Tennyson himself was certain." Thus, Shannon argues convincingly that the poem celebrates "commitment over detachment and expressive over mimetic art."

The opening word-painting at once announces Tennyson's mastery of suggestive detail and strongly patterned rhythmical structure. The first section of the poem gives an external perspective on the Lady's environs, narrated in the iterative present tense. Much like a medieval emblem book, a peaceful rural scene stretches before the reader, and details like "willows whiten," turning up their leaves in the breeze, convince us of the sharp focus of the verbal picture. Section II brings the reader within "four gray walls, and four gray towers" where one shares the Lady's perspective on the scene. The same landscape, introduced in Section I, appears only through a mirror that reflects "shadows of the world." Color from this outside world is bright and primary: red, yellow, blue. Although these vi-

sual pictures are clear, the Lady herself remains shadowy, for, like the technique in **"The Kraken,"** we never look directly at her in her tower, but only at her accessories. Section II ends with her announcement that she is "half sick of shadows."

This psychological state prepares both Lady and reader for the appearance of Lancelot in Section III. He enters the poem, dazzling in flame and gold, like a star in the purple night. His strong, cheerful song combines with her fairy song in the first part of the poem to dramatize the fusion of sound and sight in this deceptively simple ballad. Sight, however, is still primary, and causes the denouement: when the Lady looks directly at world of man and nature, "the curse is come upon" her.

Section IV begins with a brief word-painting to balance the cheerful summer landscape of the poem's opening. With the curse, the Lady enters the world of time and death, and the cycle of nature turns from summer to autumn:

> In the stormy east-wind straining,
> The pale yellow woods were waning,
> The broad stream in his banks complaining,
> Heavily the low sky raining
>   Over towered Camelot

Descending from her tower, she embarks by boat upon the river of time, singing her expressive death song. The poem's action concludes when Lancelot, not knowing who she is, nevertheless is touched by something in her lovely face, and muses upon her death.

The pared-down simplicity of stanzaic structure and the tight rhyme scheme (aaaabccb) enhances Tennyson's control over both description and the forward narration of the action in this poem. Clear, visually oriented descriptive materials balance perfectly with the requirements of vivid story telling in the balladic tradition, in which individual moments create a structure of discrete sections whose interconnections are left unstated. By moving the story from late summer to fall, the landscape suggests the approach of death and mirrors human actions in nature's sympathies. By threading a number of sharply realized visual pictures through the poem, Tennyson causes word-painting to contribute significantly to the evocation of an earlier, simpler oral poetry.

"Oenone" and **"The Lotos-Eaters,"** like **"The Lady of Shalott,"** rely on a dramatic story to keep the poem moving along; but in the case of these two contemporaneous poems, Tennyson increasingly leans upon the structure of myth. Both mythic poems successfully incorporate extended visual pictures into their narrations, but with opposite narrative effects. **"Oenone"** emphasizes the story of how Paris abandons Oenone for Helen of Troy (a narrative that progresses in a linear fashion), whereas all the images in **"The Lotos-Eaters"** reinforce a mood of inaction, stasis, and stagnation. Both poems, however, center upon a single decisive moment of choice. And in both poems, word-painting mirrors theme.

"Oenone" represents both Tennyson's reworking of what Rick calls "the pastoral love-lament—hopeless lover, loved one, setting," and an early experiment with mythic retelling in the form of a dramatic monologue. Interestingly, of the other important Tennysonian dramatic monologues, only **"The Lotos-Eaters"** and **"Tithonus"** include extended visually oriented description. **"St. Simeon Stylites," "Ulysses,"** and **"Rizpah"** include no word-painting at all, focusing, instead, on the depiction of the unique inner state of the speaker. **"Ulysses"** contains memorable flashes of visual imagery—for example, the lines, "to follow knowledge like a sinking star" or "The lights begin to twinkle from the rocks / The long day wanes: the slow moon climbs: the deep / Moans round with many voices." This suggestion of setting, enormously successful because so carefully selected and so rhythmically appropriate, is not allowed to flower into a fully developed description. This strategy maintains the focus upon the aged, stoical hero, Ulysses. Word-painting does not participate in this mythic retelling.

But it participates significantly in both **"Oenone"** and **"The Lotos-Eaters." "Oenone"** opens with a beautiful description by the nameless narrator of the vale of Ida, seen from a high perspective, another prospect vision, but here in classical, not Biblical context. The poem, Tennyson's first important classical idyll (defined as a little picture in verse) owes its form to Theocritus: opening setting, following by the love-lament of the abandoned nymph.

> There lies a vale in Ida, lovelier
> Than all the valleys of Ionian hills.
> The swimming vapour slopes athwart the glen,
> Puts forth an arm, and creeps from pine to pine,
> And loiters, slowly drawn. On either hand
> The lawns and meadow-ledges midway down
> Hang rich in flowers, and far below them roars
> The long brook falling through the cloven ravine
> In cataract after cataract to the sea.
> Behind the valley topmost Gargarus
> Stands up and takes the morning: but in front
> The gorges, opening wide apart, reveal
> Troas and Ilion's columned citadel,
> The crown of Troas.

Again, a dramatic landscape opens a narrative poem, but this word-painting is the most visually coherent we have yet examined. The coherence comes both from the underlying personification of the waters as a loitering spirit, and a clear organization reflective of how the eye progresses over a view. The landscape itself is unusually dramatic, and the passage vividly captures the valley of Cauteretz through which Tennyson and Hallam journeyed during the summer of 1830. Moving, falling water echoes and introduces active story telling. The mind's eye follows the descent of the water from glen to lawns and meadow-ledges to cloven ravine until it crashes into the sea far below. One can easily visualize the steps from high piney-glen downward "midway" where the flowers hang, and, finally, to the opening gorges through which one can glimpse Troy. This progression of the eye anticipates a similar movement in the poem from word-painting to narrative and from Oenone's isolation to her descent into the city to speak with Cassandra at the poem's end, a movement from nature to the human community.

Lush mountains which frame the realms of man represent peaceful harmony in the poem. Oenone, a nymph of Troy,

is the daughter of Ida, and the nature imagery through the poem appropriately suggests her identity with the natural world. Word-painting, not limited to the opening prospect, suggests this identity at key points in the narrative of her betrayal by Paris. Fragments of vision that augment the opening word-painting here suggest a viewer sensitive to beauty, one who, in contrast with Mariana's fragmented vision, can put together the pieces of the external world in a coherent vision. Oenone notices, with unsentimental clarity:

> For now the noonday quiet holds the hill:
> The grasshopper is silent in the grass:
> The lizard, with his shadow on the stone,
> Rests like a shadow, and the winds are dead.

Music sings in these assonant and rhythmical lines. They are appropriate to Oenone because she is the spirit of the Vale; and both her acute observation of tiny creatures and the way in which the shadow falls on the land to suggest the time of day convince us of her perfect sympathy with Nature. The gods come, bringing sorrow, but the pictures of her mountain home are the elements one retains from the poem. One such frozen picture, for example, presents Oenone, sitting solitarily as Paris approaches:

> Far-off the torrent called me from the cleft:
> Far off the solitary morning smote
> The streaks of virgin snow. With down-dropt
>   eyes
> I sat alone: white-breasted like a star
> Fronting the dawn he moved:

The passage evokes Oenone's vulnerability and innocence, as the one who will represent her doom approaches through a landscape whose spirit she represents.

A series of elaborate frames contains the story of the Judgment of Paris. First, the narrator describes the vale, and then Oenone describes the time before her fateful meeting with Paris, the Judgment of Paris itself, and the disaster to come. Like the knights who see the Holy Grail and are changed forever, Oenone cannot return to the peaceful life she lived before she saw Paris, and the poem ends with imagery of fire which replaces the water and earth of the opening description. A familiar mythic narrative amply supports the lusciousness of the natural descriptions in this poem. Word-painting, beautifully developed in **"Oenone,"** adequately balances the elaboration of frames, the character of the speakers, and the clear narrative progression.

Similarly, in **"The Lotos-Eaters,"** a landscape of gorgeous proportions which shares many features of the landscape in **"Oenone"** carries thematic meaning. Tennyson's descriptive opening stanzas in both poems derive from the same trip through the Pyrenees in 1830, but he uses them with opposite effect. **"The Lotos-Eaters,"** far from placing us within an ongoing narrative, presents a mood very close to that of **"Mariana,"** a state of lassitude and stasis which represents one of the trials of the *Odyssey*. In the *Odyssey*, the mariners resist the death-lure of the Lotos-Eaters, but Tennyson chooses to dramatize those who fail to do so. The poet sets out to convince us by imagery and music that "slumber" is more sweet than toil." Tennyson does so by what Langbaum calls, "an over-richness of land-scape, imagery and . . . enervated cadence."

In spite of the richness of its word-painting, this poem keeps landscape description distinctly secondary to the enactment of a state of being. By beginning the poem, not with his standard set piece, but, rather, with four lines of narrative, Tennyson indicates his awareness of the need for balance between narrative and descriptive materials in this mythic recounting.

> 'Courage!' he said, and pointed toward the land,
> 'This mounting wave will roll us shoreward
>   soon.'
> In the afternoon they came unto a land
> In which it seemed always afternoon.
> All round the coast the languid air did swoon,
> Breathing like one that hath a weary dream.
> Full-faced above the valley stood the moon;
> And, like a downward smoke, the slender stream
> Along the cliff to fall and pause and fall did
>   seem.

The opening lines, which thrust the reader into a story already in progress, establish the dominant motif of gently rolling movement and rhythm. The terms of the opening word-painting create an enervating sense of inertia which continues through the five Spenserian stanzas with which Tennyson introduces the eight-stanza Choric song of the becalmed mariners. Rolling waves, languid air, and a stuttering stream that appears to stop and start again as it descends the cliff substitute for **"Oenone"**'s movement of descending waters.

The second stanza reinforces the mood of becalming enchantment, with its repeating rhyme scheme of ababbcbcc and its long lines stretched out with the sounds of o and s.

> A land of streams! some, like a downward
>   smoke,
> Slow-dropping veils of thinnest lawn, did go;
> And some through wavering lights and shadows
>   broke,
> Rolling a slumbrous sheet of foam below.
> They saw the gleaming river seaward flow
> From the inner land; far off, three mountain-
>   tops,
> Three silent pinnacles of agèd snow,
> Stood sunset-flushed: and, dewed with showery
>   drops,
> Up-clomb the shadowy pine above the woven
>   copse.

The landscape, slow-moving and rolling gently, echoes the mood of the Lotos-Eaters themselves, who soon appear to lure the mariners toward the land, as the sun sets.

> The charmèd sunset lingered low adown
> In the red West: through mountain clefts the
>   dale
> Was seen far inland, and the yellow down
> Bordered with palm, and many a winding vale
> And meadow, set with slender galingale;
> A land where all thngs always seemed the same!
> And round about the keel with faces pale,
> Dark faces pale against that rosy flame,
> The mild-eyed melancholy Lotos-eaters came.

Nature conspires with the mood of the men to swerve the heroes from their path, in another thwarted quest pattern. In this poem, Tennyson uses word-painting to suggest the attraction of the sensual and the present, as opposed to the goal-oriented life of duty, toil, and death.

"Oenone" and **"The Lotos-Eaters"** exemplify mythic poems that successfully integrate word-painting with a coherent narrative. **"The Palace of Art"** proves instructive as an example of what happens to a poem's structure when gorgeous visually oriented pictures in the text overload a poem lacking a strong narrative substructure. Undoubtedly, Tennyson meant to provide a narrative structure, but it is buried in descriptive stanzas. **"The Palace of Art"** is very important as one of Tennyson's first experiments with the panel structure he was to use with great success in *In Memoriam,* but both 1832 and 1842 versions of the shorter poem demonstrate the pitfalls of overemphasizing word-painting. Unintentionally, the poem's structure gives a feeling of stasis equal to that of **"The Lotos-Eaters."** However, in the latter poem it is appropriate, whereas in the former it indicates a structural breakdown.

When the reader encounters "I built my soul a lordly pleasure-house" in the opening lines of **"The Palace of Art,"** he may well expect a narrative poem to follow. But the poem actually describes the abode of a particular soul. The first two hundred lines lay out gardens, exterior, interior rooms with their pictures and galleries, and central hall, decorated with busts of great men from Dante to Milton and mosaics depicting the cycles of man's life. By the time one hears again of the "she" in the poem, the reader may not be blamed for having forgotten who "she" is! Having introduced the "soul" in the opening lines, Tennyson fails to mention her in the sheer exuberance with which he details the descriptive panels of the "pleasure-house." When the poet returns to the narrative material, he hurries through the recounting of the soul's hubris, her subsequent fall, and her resolution to leave the palace for a simple cottage, though she may one day return.

Clearly, Tennyson was more interested in word-paintings than in narrative in **"The Palace of Art."** The subject of the poem partly justifies descriptive technique here, for he enumerates an entire history of the arts in describing a single architectural structure. But the last one-third of the poem must carry all the narrative, and in such a way that it is possible to overlook the story line altogether. The lack of balance between word-painting and narrative in this work partly accounts for its structural weakness.

Even so, no examination of Tennyson's word-painting could ignore **"The Palace of Art."** Individual stanzas present superb examples of Tennyson's verbal visualizations. Part II of the poem, for example, begins:

> Four courts I made, East, West and South and
>   North,
>   In each a squared lawn, wherefrom
> The golden gorge of dragons spouted forth
>   A flood of fountain-foam.

The section ends:

> Likewise the deep-set windows, stained and
>   traced,

Would seem slow-flaming crimson fires
From shadowed grots of arches interlaced,
And tipt with frost-like spires.

These passages demonstrate Tennyson's mastery at using language to evoke the object intensely seen. The integration of skillful word-paintings with a narrative structure represents the chief remaining aesthetic challenge for Tennyson in his mature period. (pp. 85-92)

> *Rhoda L. Flaxman, "Tennyson," in her* Victorian Word-Painting and Narrative: Toward the Blending of Genres, *UMI Research Press, 1987, pp. 73-124.*

Herbert F. Tucker (essay date 1988)

[*In the following excerpt from his* Tennyson and the Doom of Romanticism, *Tucker surveys "Timbuctoo" and "Armageddon," emphasizing Tennyson's shifting views on the nature of myth and the human mind.*]

"Nothing of mine after the date of '**Timbuctoo**' was imitative," the poet rightly boasted, because in **"Timbuctoo"** he had learned from his Romantic models how to imitate originally. The poem presents a greatly altered version of the pulsating, visionary **"Armageddon"**; and the best way to appreciate the difference between the two poems is to take their pulses. The pulse of **"Timbuctoo"** is not the timeless sympathy of the individual heart with the universal soul, as in **"Armageddon,"** but the historically conditioned give and take of myth, as made and remade in cultural transmission. Toward the end of the revised poem the seraph sums up the sensuous intimations of **"Armageddon"** when he says, "Few there be / So gross of heart who have not felt and known / A higher than they see." As in **"Armageddon,"** the seraph has helped Tennyson to transcend the visual, "to feel / My fullness," and "with ravished sense" to hear "the lordly music flowing from / The illimitable years." But these last words suggest something new. Tennyson's wisdom of feeling now has a temporal habitation and a name—even as the seraph now names himself:

I am the Spirit,
The permeating life which courseth through
All the intricate and labyrinthine veins
Of the great vine of Fable.

The life that coursed through the poet's own literal, physical veins in **"Armageddon"** now permeates the metaphorical veins of fable. Tennyson has changed the focus of his poem from the energies of the body, as a fundamental pattern of individual consciousness, to the embodiment of those energies in products of the collective human imagination that creates myths, builds labyrinths, and indeed makes such metaphors as "the great vine of *Fable*." The mythmaking faculty, the mind's ability to give its intuitions concrete and public form, now receives the homage Tennyson earlier paid to the intuitive mind alone.

We can see how explicitly **"Timbuctoo"** repudiates **"Armageddon"** if we recall the repudiation of "fabled" tradition with which the earlier poem pushes off: "No fabled Muse / Could breathe into my soul such influence" as

might "express / Deeds inexpressible by loftiest rhyme." Like most repudiations of influence and tradition, this gesture is highly traditional. The allusion in its last line to Milton's allusion to Ariosto, "Things unattempted yet in prose or rhyme," affiliates **"Armageddon"** not just with Milton but with the tradition of eighteenth-century originalism, in which a series of Miltonides crested by Gray and Young had taken aim at the sublime by taking their stand on the inexpressible. Although something like this posture has been taken as the essence of Romanticism, in fact the Romantics' attitudes toward the literary past exhibit much more flexibility than their immediate predecessors'. It is not eighteenth-century originalism but a critically reconstructive, Romantic perspective on tradition that we find Tennyson adopting in **"Timbuctoo."** Having proudly fabled about himself in **"Armageddon,"** here he bends his pride and fables about fabling instead. Contracting the visionary span and swollen girth of his earlier narcissistic apocalypse, he enters as an equal partner into a lifetime contract with that great benefactor of imagination, the sense of the cultural past, a once and future power that most enriches those who know best how to pay it deference.

Of course, this change of focus and attitude is just the kind of revision that looks designed to please a panel of university examiners who might have been unfriendly to the self-celebration of **"Armageddon."** Still, Tennyson's revisions in **"Timbuctoo"** are thorough and searching enough to warrant a belief that he was writing less to please academic judges than to clinch a maturing conviction that the sources of his poetic power were to lie in a confrontation with literary tradition—particularly with the Romantic poetry he had been reading since his arrival at Cambridge. In other words, while Tennyson was writing **"Timbuctoo"** the truly severe judges at his elbow were Wordsworth, Coleridge, Shelley, and Keats; and in addressing himself to the vicissitudes of fable, the erosion and regeneration of the mind's faith in its own fictions, Tennyson knowingly addressed Romantic themes on the Romantics' ground. Furthermore, in acknowledging that the Romantics had been there before him, Tennyson first encountered the exacerbated dilemma of Victorian Romanticism, whereby a poet's sense of belatedness is compounded by the realization that belatedness itself may already have become a shopworn theme for modern art.

The poet of **"Timbuctoo"** begins with the mountain prospect of **"Armageddon"**; but while visual imagery still predominates, his earlier crisis of perception has now become a crisis of belief. He looks for the fabled pillars of Hercules but finds them "Long time erased from Earth." Likewise Atlantis and Eldorado are "Shadows" to which "Men clung with yearning Hope" in days gone by, as they clung to "legends quaint and old / Which whilome won the hearts of all on Earth." The lacquered diction serves, as in Keats's comparable account of first reading Chapman's Homer, to antique a belief no longer available. Tennyson is disarmingly ready to concede the fictive character of belief: even in the heyday of faith the faithful clung to "Shadows," not substances. In its glory Atalantis was but a "Memory" invested with significance by the faith of its vo-

Chalk sketch of Tennyson, circa 1890.

taries. Tennyson analyzes this dialectic of fetishistic belief with a protracted simile:

> As when in some great City where the walls
> Shake, and the streets with ghastly faces
>   thronged
> Do utter forth a subterranean voice,
> Among the inner columns far retired
> At midnight, in the lone Acropolis,
> Before the awful Genius of the place
> Kneels the pale Priestess in deep faith, the while
> Above her head the weak lamp dips and winks
> Unto the fearful summoning without:
> Nathless she ever clasps the marble knees,
> Bathes the cold hand with tears, and gazeth on
> Those eyes which wear no light but that where-
>   with
> Her phantasy informs them.

Half Athens, half Atalantis, this city of no special place or time—first of the poet's many civic images for what the Victorians would soon be calling an age of transition—suffers not an invasion but an insurrection from within. The priestess worships an idol that is long since stone dead ("the marble knees," "the cold hand"), as is the phase of naively receptive faith it stands for. Taking the fall from orthodoxy for granted, Tennyson concerns himself instead with a second-order lapse: the loss of demicroyance. The "ghastly faces thronged" of this cultural revolution are modeled on Milton's "dreadful Faces throng'd" from *Paradise Lost*, XII.644, because "the fearful summoning" of the "subterranean voice" of modernity threatens an expulsion from even the belated, artificial paradise that a religion in retreat has made for itself. For Tennyson the old legends drew all hearts "Toward their brightness, even as flame draws air; / But had their being in the heart of Man / As air is the life of flame." His crisis of faith therefore stems less from unworthiness in the demystified object of belief than from atrophy of the will to believe.

This last comparison, between the believing heart and air drawn by the flame it feeds, comes from a simile in Shelley's "Hymn to Intellectual Beauty": "Thou—that to human thought art nourishment, / Like darkness to a dying flame!" Shelley's Spirit of Beauty will reappear in **"Timbuctoo"** as Tennyson's Spirit of Fable, and the recollection of a Romantic precursor suggests a diagnosis of Tennyson's disorder of faith: it is a symptom of the Romantic poet's constitutional incapacity to assimilate anything but what he himself has made. An undeniable symptom of this disorder heads the poem, in the form of a mellifluously Tennysonian epigraph from "Chapman" that no scholar has yet verified: *"Deep in that lion-haunted inland lies / A mystick city, goal of high emprise."* Arthur Hallam, who met Tennyson as a friendly contestant for the 1829 Chancellor's Gold Medal at Cambridge, and who claimed to have originated the theme of Romantic faith with which both their entries approached the set topic of Timbuctoo, wrote a poem far more explicitly derivative of Romantic texts than Tennyson's; its epigraph, typically, comes straight from Wordsworth's "Yarrow Unvisited." Tennyson, unlike Hallam, has confected a text to put before his poem; this minor invention of a precursor bespeaks a larger Romantic intention to have no other texts before him.

The poem's opening crisis of faith is thus, in Romantic terms, the poet's creative opportunity. The ostensible lament for earlier, happier days is charged with the deferred gratification of a poet who would make the void fruitful on his own.

> Where are ye
> Thrones of the Western wave, fair Islands green?
> Where are your moonlight halls, your cedarn
>   glooms,
> The blossoming abysses of your hills?

"Where are ye?" is Tennyson's version of Wordsworth's "Where is it now?," Shelley's "Where art thou gone?," and Keats's "Where are the songs of Spring?." Like his Romantic forebears, Tennyson asks the question in the confidence that he will grieve not, that there is a harmony in autumn, that he has his music too. The old poet's remark about the originality of **"Timbuctoo,"** quoted at the outset of this discussion, registers the memorable experience of self-conscious innovation, within an acknowledged tradition, which he had inscribed into the poem. For what is distinctively Romantic about the confidence of **"Timbuctoo"** is precisely its engagement with the prior texts of the Romantics, texts that themselves engaged the poetic past with a view to proclaiming the originality of the latecomer.

"Blossoming abysses," in the lines just quoted, offers a resounding image of the paradoxical process of belief Tennyson's long first paragraph has discussed, and also of the Romantic resolve we can read behind his refusal to participate in such a process too quickly. These lines introduce a passage that looks back to a paradise of palpable, liquid light, "Filled with Divine effulgence, circumfused, / Flowing." The paragraph manifestly corresponds to the **"Armageddon"** passage in which "Eve came down," with a reminder of lost paradisal perception; but the Miltonic allusion of that passage has been subsumed by a Romantic allusion, to Coleridge's "Kubla Khan." Tennyson's "blossoming abysses" suggests the "deep Romantic chasm which slanted / Down the green hill athwart a cedarn cover" in Coleridge's poem; the allusion comes to a head with the rare form "cedarn," which Coleridge himself learned to use, Ricks points out, from its first appearance in Milton's *Comus*. "Kubla Khan" was a poem multiply indebted to Milton; and as Tennyson must have discovered with dismay, it had already done the post-Miltonic work of rendering visionary dejection—and of rendering dejection visionary—rather more successfully than had part I of **"Armageddon."** Finding himself preempted by an earlier poetic son of Milton, and perhaps remembering how in the chasm of "Kubla Khan" an abandoned woman wails by moonlight, Tennyson executes a fine recovery and makes of desolation an opening for voice:

> Then I raised
> My voice and cried, "Wide Afric, doth thy Sun
> Lighten, thy hills enfold a City as fair
> As those which starred the night o' the elder
>   World?
> Or is the rumour of thy Timbuctoo
> A dream as frail as those of ancient Time?"

In "Kubla Khan" Coleridge envisioned "an Abyssinian

maid" singing of "Mount Abora," with an allusion to the false paradise of *Paradise Lost,* IV.280-282: "Where *Abassin* Kings their issue Guard, / Mount *Amara,* though this by some suppos'd / True Paradise under the *Ethiop* Line." It is worth conjecturing that Tennyson had caught this allusion, and that he was taking the Cambridge Chancellor's set topic of **"Timbuctoo"** as an occasion for building a visionary city in a blossoming Abyss-inia of his own.

The necessity that the young poet be his own master builder forms a new theme of the seraph's revised message. Instead of asking why Tennyson is not making ready for the battle of Armageddon, the seraph now chides him for musing on "the dreams of old," with their "passing loveliness" and "odours rapt from remote Paradise," in lines recalling those that Wordsworth published in 1815 as a "Prospectus" to *The Recluse:*

> Paradise, and groves
> Elysian, Fortunate Fields—like those of old
> Sought in the Atlantic Main—why should they
>   be
> A history only of departed things,
> Or a mere fiction of what never was?

While this passage seems one probable source for the "fair Islands green," "Elysian solitudes," and "Atalantis" that we meet in **"Timbuctoo,"** Tennyson will never find his paradise, early or late, in the terms of Wordsworth's naturalism as a "simple produce of the common day" ("Prospectus"). He does, however, borrow Wordsworth's insistence that the poet wean himself from regressive dependence on the past; the visionary city Tennyson goes on to behold will be an ornate "fiction of what never was" before.

On his way to the apparition of that city, Tennyson undergoes a more darkly Wordsworthian rite of passage to poetic maturity. The poet designing to celebrate not his own feelings but the embodiment of feeling in the currency of fable must first weather the fall from sensation into abstraction that Wordsworth commemorated in "Tintern Abbey" and the "Intimations" ode. Lines 113-157 of **"Timbuctoo"** replace the apotheosis of sensation we have met in **"Armageddon,"** II.40-50. Yet Tennyson's newly Wordsworthian project of exchanging feelings for ideas, percepts for concepts, turns out disastrously; and he knows it. The new passage he wrote in lines 113-130 is far from satisfactorily clear, but it does establish clearly Tennyson's dissatisfaction with the kind of experience it describes. Visionary sensations of the **"Armageddon"** type now emit *thoughts,* which tend, unlike the harmonic impulses of sense, to collide and strike each other out. The bizarre Lake District simile Tennyson finds for this process—bizarre in itself, and certainly atypical of his oceanic repertoire—shows that the conversion of feelings into ideas leaves him feeling more than a little stricken:

> as when in some large lake
> From pressure of descendant crags, which lapse
> Disjointed, crumbling from their parent slope
> At slender interval, the level calm
> Is ridged with restless and increasing spheres
> Which break upon each other.

Thought thus begins as a ruin and ends in a confusion of

"interpenetrated arc" that baffles the mental eye. In the **"Armageddon"** passage that this one replaces, the mind given over to sensation can mix and burn "with its parent fire," but here the mind's thoughts, "descendants" of sensation, suffer a primal divorce and crumble "from their parent slope."

With this lapse from perceptual integrity into reflective chaos come doubts about the mind as a reflector, as Tennyson wonders whether "I entwine / The indecision of my present mind / With its past clearness." This patently Wordsworthian gambit underscores Tennyson's conscious failure to realize the Wordsworthian mode of creative recollection. A part of Tennyson wanted to share in the melioristic faith that informed Wordsworth's transition from childlike sensation to the philosophical mind—the belief that fired the authentic if programmatic optimism of his contemporary Browning and that was to constitute a tenet of the Victorian orthodoxy for which Tennyson would soon be expected to speak. But his spirit could never lend itself wholly to this progressive belief, least of all when asked to arise from sensation to discursive thought. On the contrary, when Tennyson was most himself he imagined that movement not as an ascent but as a lapse, a betrayal of primal experience and of his genuine gift; and **"Timbuctoo"** shows that he knew it quite early, before Hallam declared it to the world in a review of the 1830 *Poems* that was to become a classic of Victorian criticism.

In that essay Hallam made the now famous distinction between the Wordsworthian poet of "reflection" and the Tennysonian poet of "sensation." *In Memoriam* repeatedly praises Hallam for being a penetrating reader, and if he was as faithful a critic as he was a friend, he may well have derived his categories of reflection and sensation from an attentive reading of what Tennyson had written by 1830. **"Timbuctoo"** furnishes the most obvious instance of the distinction of thought from feeling, but a divide between reflective and sensuous poetry fissures all the juvenilia, to the consistent advantage of the latter. For example, while Tennyson ranks among the greatest Romantic exponents of the pathetic fallacy, a predominantly sensuous device for rendering the play between mind and nature, he is awfully clumsy when he comes to the related projective device of personification, which he evidently admired in Collins and others. The hypostasis of an emotion or ideal into a formal emblem was a process he could not clearly feel. For this reason—and also because his imagination of personal interaction remained peculiarly abstract—Tennyson rarely attempted allegorical personification with any success in fusing its intellectual and sensuous components.

Tennyson was never at home with the abstractions of philosophy; and **"Timbuctoo"** reaches its nadir with his blunt confession of inability to ride the torrent of experience and yet "muse midway," like a self-consoling Wordsworth or mediating Kubla Khan, "with philosophic calm." Apparently the seraphic Spirit of Fable, a more sly master than his seraphic predecessor from **"Armageddon,"** is ready to let his pupil work through a false start and learn for himself that the proper source of his power as a fabling poet lies in the improvement of sensual enjoyment:

I play about his heart a thousand ways,
Visit his eyes with visions, and his ears
With harmonies of wind and wave and wood,
—Of winds which tell of waters, and of waters
Betraying the close kisses of the wind.

As this cordial intercommunion of the senses should suggest, the pulsing music of **"Armageddon"** is about to burst into the revised poem, though with a difference. The embodiment of feeling in fable calls for translation of some kind; in **"Timbuctoo,"** however, the proper medium of translation is not reflective thought but the poetic image.

Liberation from reflective thought into imaginative sensation brings its own reward with the disclosure of Timbuctoo, which is—like Tennyson's later Bagdat, Palace of Art, and Camelot—the verbal capital of a state of pure image:

Then first within the South methought I saw
A wilderness of spires, and chrystal pile
Of rampart upon rampart, dome on dome,
Illimitable range of battlement
On battlement, and the Imperial height
Of Canopy o'ercanopied.

In **"Armageddon"** sound mediated between the outwardness of sight and the inwardness of feeling, but with this vision Tennyson so arrogates all sound to himself that the only mediating music we hear is in the verse. Balancing architectural terms on each other and, more subtly, reshaping their elements of sound ("spires" comes back transformed in "chrystal pile," as does "Illimitable" in "battlement"), Tennyson has rebounded from the "wild unrest" of fallen reflection into the aspiring "wilderness of spires" that build themselves, like living things with their own principle of organization. The passage recalls the self-begetting exuberance of language that we found in **"The Devil and the Lady,"** but Tennyson has now tamed his verbal energies to the service of an imaginative power that is more than merely verbal.

Paden has shown how this Timbuctoo is a city of the sun that recalls Miltonic visions of paradise. It recalls as well Tennyson's own earlier "blossoming abysses," paradises once lost but now regained at the zenith of vision: "wheeling Suns, or Stars, or semblances / Of either, showering circular abyss / Of radiance." In the tradition of metaphysical reflection since Plato, the distinction between the sun and its "semblance" forms a crucial trope for the making of fundamental discriminations between reality and appearance. Tennyson respects that distinction at some of the most poignant moments of his career; but, at the height of the Romantic tradition into which **"Timbuctoo"** marks Tennyson's initiation, poesy and not the sun must be what Keats had called "A drainless shower / Of light." At this height the distinction between what is and what seems simply does not matter, not to an imagination that figures its creative faith with the oxymoron "abyss / Of radiance," and that figures the conversion of doubt into faith with the return of the "ghastly faces" from line 29, there thronged against belief, but now redeemed as "multitudes of multitudes" who minister around a fiery central throne. Tennyson can now assume the part of his earlier "pale Priestess"—the part of "pale-mouth'd Prophet

dreaming" that Keats played before him in the "Ode to Psyche"—because now he ministers to an idol of his own making and not just to some prevenient "Genius of the place." The vision fades as Tennyson staggers and falls beneath its weight; and his fall repays comparison with the climax of **"Armageddon,"** which read: "I could have fallen down / Before my own strong soul and worshipped it." The difference between revering one's own strong soul and being overpowered by a visionary projection from that soul, the difference between worshiping Self and worshiping the goddess Psyche, corresponds to the difference between feeling and fable that Tennyson highlights with his revision of **"Armageddon"** into **"Timbuctoo."** In the former text, the visionary numen of the self arose to combat an ominous onslaught of ambiguous signifiers; the latter text inverts this procedure, rejecting numinous self-absorption in order to reclaim the omen as a mode of signification within a tradition of secular creativity—religion with a Romantic difference.

This difference forms the topic of the seraph's long final speech. The ministry of Fable is to teach the poet, and through the poet humankind, "to attain / By shadowing forth the Unattainable." As Browning's Paracelsus or Tennyson's own King Arthur might read these lines, "attain" would be an intransitive verb, and the vision of "the Unattainable" would serve as an incentive to present work. But these lines also bear a transitive construction that implies a more properly fabulous doctrine: to shadow forth the unattainable is somehow to attain it after all, on the shadowy ground of vision, as Tennyson has attained it in building his Timbuctoo. The seraph explores a related paradox later in announcing, "Lo! I have given *thee* / To understand my presence, and to feel / My fullness." To be singled out to "understand" a "presence" is to do what Tennyson left undone in **"Armageddon"**: it is to penetrate the ideal of presence as indeed a myth, albeit a fulfilling one once myth is understood as the representation or cultural rehearsal of what, without representation in some sensuous form, would remain the merely and abstractly "Unattainable." The condition toward which the Spirit of Fable directs Tennyson, then, is both empty and full—an abyss of radiance.

To a poet so conditioned, the seraph's prophetic lamentation over the approach of "keen *Discovery*" may come as the friendliest gesture of all. Readers of intellectual-historical bent have seized on this passage as if it contained the entire point of **"Timbuctoo"**; in a sense it does, but in order to grasp the point in its subtlety we have to connect it with the complex Romantic argument that has come first. Foreseeing that the Enlightenment spirit of scientific inquest will drain away the splendor of Timbuctoo, his "latest Throne"—something that had already occurred in 1828, when a French expedition reached Timbuctoo and found it a shambles—the seraph leaves the poet alone and darkling, but poised above the distinctively poetic potential that this clearing operation holds forth. Though much is taken from the spirit by scientific and intellectual advance, much abides; according to the logic of elegy that motivates most of Tennyson's best writing, whatever the cutting edge of "keen *Discovery*" may pare away from fable has never really been fable's to begin with.

Tennyson accordingly ends his disingenuous seraph's lament in an intertextual affirmation of solidarity with the most aggressively elegiac voice in the English poetic tradition. With the seraph's farewell to a proleptically dwindled Timbuctoo, "How changed from this fair City!," Tennyson reaches all the way back to the first words of that archetypal Romantic poet, Milton's Satan:

> If thou beest hee; But O how fall'n! how chang'd
> From him, who in the happy Realms of Light
> Cloth'd with transcendent brightness didst out-
>   shine
> Myriads though bright.

The poet of **"Timbuctoo"** stands with Satan in the abyss he would replenish with his own light. It is a fitting close to a poem that has been, like the inland of its ghostly "Chapman," "lion-haunted" by Romantic poets it deeply respects but refuses to lionize. We might observe in closing how changed is this layered allusiveness from the Miltonic mannerism that makes **"Armageddon"** so comparatively innocent a text. The change is, of course, that Tennyson has come to "understand" the "presence" of the Romantics. The return to Milton at this stage is in effect an act of generational violence urging Tennyson's claim to be the Romantics' peer in imagining the city that is never built at all, and therefore built forever. Byron's Satanic hero Manfred insisted that "The Tree of Knowledge is not that of Life"—and neither is the vine of Fable, quite, for Tennyson. But he grows into his own, exceptionally tradition-bred species of Romanticism with an answering realization that the vine of Fable bears what life we have. (pp. 53-64)

> *Herbert F. Tucker, in his* Tennyson and the Doom of Romanticism, *Cambridge, Mass.: Harvard University Press, 1988, 481 p.*

FURTHER READING

Bibliography

Shaw, Marion. *An Annotated Critical Bibliography of Alfred, Lord Tennyson.* New York: St. Martin's Press, 1989, 134 p.
    Contains an extensive bibliography and an introduction summarizing historical critical response to Tennyson.

Biography

Martin, Robert Bernard. *Tennyson: The Unquiet Heart.* Oxford: Clarendon Press, 1980, 643 p.
    Authoritative biography of Tennyson.

Criticism

Beasley, Violet E. "A Centered, Glory-Circled Memory: Memory in Tennyson's Early Poems." *The Tennyson Research Bulletin* 5, No. 3 (November 1989): 121-29.
    Outlines Tennyson's use of memory in his early poems to evoke a superficial melancholy and to serve as an occasion to present his descriptive verse.

Berglund, Lisa. " 'Faultily Faultless': The Structure of Tennyson's *Maud.*" *Victorian Poetry* 27, No. 1 (Spring 1989): 45-59.
    Examines the significance of Tennyson's combination of verse styles in *Maud.*

Bristow, Joseph. "Nation, Class, and Gender: Tennyson's *Maud* and War." *Genders* 9 (November 1990): 93-111.
    Assesses Tennyson's treatment of conflict between emotion and gender in *Maud.*

Faas, Ekbert. "Alfred Tennyson." In his *Retreat into the Mind: Victorian Poetry and the Rise of Psychiatry,* pp. 72-81. Princeton, N.J.: Princeton University Press, 1988.
    Discusses Tennyson's use of the concepts of self and consciousness in his poetry.

Fertel, Randy J. "Antipastoral and the Attack on Naturalism in Tennyson's *Idylls of The King.*" *Victorian Poetry* 19, No. 4 (Winter 1981): 337-50.
    Illustrates Tennyson's "ironic treatment of the pastoral genre" and "his thematic treatment of philosophical naturalism" in *Idylls of the King.*

Fulweiler, Howard W. "The Argument of 'The Ancient Sage': Tennyson and the Christian Intellectual Tradition." *Victorian Poetry* 21, No. 3 (Autumn 1983): 203-16.
    Argues that Tennyson's religious faith was rooted in "the Christian philosophical tradition"—opposing the prevalent view that it was strictly intuitive.

——. "Tennyson's *In Memoriam* and the Scientific Imagination." *Thought* LIX, No. 234 (September 1984): 296-318.
    Examines Tennyson's complex relation to the scientific imagination depicted in *In Memoriam.*

——. "Tennyson's 'The Holy Grail': The Representation of Representation." *Renascence* XXXVIII, No. 3 (Spring 1986): 144-59.
    Uses "The Holy Grail" to exemplify Tennyson's treatment of such broad issues as Christianity, morality, and social decline in *Idylls of the King.*

Hair, Donald S. " 'Matter-Moulded Forms of Speech.' " *Victorian Poetry* 27, No. 1 (Spring 1989): 1-15.
    Asserts that the origin of the phrase "matter-moulded forms of speech" in *In Memoriam* relates directly to English philosopher John Locke's theory that "language . . . makes it hard for the poet to frame his experience in speech."

Hinchcliffe, Peter. "Elegy and Epithalamium in *In Memoriam.*" *University of Toronto Quarterly* 52, No. 3 (Spring 1983): 241-62.
    Argues that *In Memoriam* evinces structural and thematic coherence.

Johnston, Eileen Tess. "This Were a Medley: Tennyson's *The Princess.*" *ELH* 51, No. 3 (Fall 1984): 549-74.
    Explores how Tennyson's style and wordplay illuminate intent and meaning in *The Princess.*

Joseph, Gerhard. "Tennyson's Sword: From 'Mungo the American' to *Idylls of the King.*" In *Sex and Death in Victorian Literature,* edited by Regina Barreca, pp. 60-8. Indianapolis: Indiana University Press, 1990.
    Studies Tennyson's use of the sword as a symbol of sexual indulgence.

Manning, Sylvia. "Death and Sex from Tennyson's Early Poetry to *In Memoriam.*" In *Sex and Death in Victorian Literature,* edited by Regina Barreca, pp. 194-210. Indianapolis: Indiana University Press, 1990.

Outlines Tennyson's representations of death and sex in his early poetry through *In Memoriam.*

Nichols, Ashton. "The Epiphanic Trance Poem: Why Tennyson Is Not a Mystic." *Victorian Poetry* 24, No. 2 (Summer 1986): 131-48.

Asserts that Tennyson's emotional or spiritual sensitivity should not be confused with mysticism.

Saunders, Mary. "Tennyson's 'Ulysses' as Rhetorical Monologue." *The Victorian Newsletter,* No. 60 (Fall 1981): 20-4.

Maintains that questions of setting and audience in "Ulysses" can be answered by studying the poem's rhetorical elements.

Shires, Linda M. "*Maud,* Masculinity and Poetic Identity." *Criticism* XXIX, No. 3 (Summer 1987): 269-90.

Characterizes *Maud* as Tennyson's attempt to resolve conflicts of gender and determine his own identity as a poet.

Slinn, E. Warwick. "Absence and Desire in *Maud.*" In his *The Discourse of Self in Victorian Poetry,* pp. 64-89. Charlottesville: University Press of Virginia, 1991.

Analyzes the interplay between absence and desire in *Maud.*

Stevenson, Catherine Barnes. "Tennyson's Dying Swans: Mythology and the Definition of the Poet's Role." *Studies in English Literature 1500-1900* XX, No. 4 (Autumn 1980): 621-35.

Outlines Tennyson's use of the classical myth of the dying swan in his poetry.

Wheeler, Michael. "Tennyson: *In Memoriam.*" In his *Death and the Future Life in Victorian Literature and Theology,* pp. 221-64. Cambridge: Cambridge University Press, 1990.

Interprets Tennyson's views on theology, physiology, and psychology as expressed in *In Memoriam.*

Poetry Criticism
INDEXES

Literary Criticism Series
Cumulative Author Index

Cumulative Nationality Index

Cumulative Title Index

How to Use This Index

The main references

Calvino, Italo
     1923-1985.....CLC **5, 8, 11, 22, 33, 39,**
                            73; SSC 3

---

list all author entries in the following Gale Literary Criticism series:

CLC = *Contemporary Literary Criticism*
CLR = *Children's Literature Review*
CMLC = *Classical and Medieval Literature Criticism*
DC = *Drama Criticism*
LC = *Literature Criticism from 1400 to 1800*
NCLC = *Nineteenth-Century Literature Criticism*
PC = *Poetry Criticism*
SSC = *Short Story Criticism*
TCLC = *Twentieth-Century Literary Criticism*

The cross-references

See also CANR 23; CA 85-88;
   obituary CA 116

---

list all author entries in the following Gale biographical and literary sources:

AAYA = *Authors & Artists for Young Adults*
AITN = *Authors in the News*
BLC = *Black Literature Criticism*
BW = *Black Writers*
CA = *Contemporary Authors*
CAAS = *Contemporary Authors Autobiography Series*
CABS = *Contemporary Authors Bibliographical Series*
CANR = *Contemporary Authors New Revision Series*
CAP = *Contemporary Authors Permanent Series*
CDALB = *Concise Dictionary of American Literary Biography*
CDBLB = *Concise Dictionary of British Literary Biography*
DLB = *Dictionary of Literary Biography*
DLBD = *Dictionary of Literary Biography Documentary Series*
DLBY = *Dictionary of Literary Biography Yearbook*
HW = *Hispanic Writers*
MAICYA = *Major Authors and Illustrators for Children and Young Adults*
MTCW = *Major 20th-Century Writers*
SAAS = *Something about the Author Autobiography Series*
SATA = *Something about the Author*
WLC = *World Literature Criticism, 1500 to the Present*
YABC = *Yesterday's Authors of Books for Children*

Aleichem, Sholom . . . . TCLC 1, 35
See also Rabinovitch, Sholem

Aleixandre, Vicente 1898-1984 . . . CLC 9, 36
See also CA 85-88; 114; CANR 26;
DLB 108; HW; MTCW

Alepoudelis, Odysseus
See Elytis, Odysseus

Aleshkovsky, Joseph 1929-
See Aleshkovsky, Yuz
See also CA 121; 128

Aleshkovsky, Yuz . . . . CLC 44
See also Aleshkovsky, Joseph

Alexander, Lloyd (Chudley) 1924- . . CLC 35
See also AAYA 1; CA 1-4R; CANR 1, 24,
38; CLR 1, 5; DLB 52; MAICYA;
MTCW; SATA 3, 49

Alfau, Felipe 1902- . . . . CLC 66
See also CA 137

Alger, Horatio Jr. 1832-1899 . . . . . NCLC 8
See also DLB 42; SATA 16

Algren, Nelson 1909-1981 . . . . CLC 4, 10, 33
See also CA 13-16R; 103; CANR 20;
CDALB 1941-1968; DLB 9; DLBY 81,
82; MTCW

Ali, Ahmed 1910- . . . . CLC 69
See also CA 25-28R; CANR 15, 34

Alighieri, Dante 1265-1321 . . . . CMLC 3

Allan, John B.
See Westlake, Donald E(dwin)

Allen, Edward 1948- . . . . CLC 59

Allen, Roland
See Ayckbourn, Alan

Allen, Woody 1935- . . . . CLC 16, 52
See also CA 33-36R; CANR 27, 38;
DLB 44; MTCW

Allende, Isabel 1942- . . . . CLC 39, 57
See also CA 125; 130; HW; MTCW

Alleyn, Ellen
See Rossetti, Christina (Georgina)

Allingham, Margery (Louise)
1904-1966 . . . . CLC 19
See also CA 5-8R; 25-28R; CANR 4;
DLB 77; MTCW

Allingham, William 1824-1889 . . . NCLC 25
See also DLB 35

Allston, Washington 1779-1843 . . . . NCLC 2
See also DLB 1

Almedingen, E. M. . . . . CLC 12
See also Almedingen, Martha Edith von
See also SATA 3

Almedingen, Martha Edith von 1898-1971
See Almedingen, E. M.
See also CA 1-4R; CANR 1

Alonso, Damaso 1898-1990 . . . . CLC 14
See also CA 110; 131; 130; DLB 108; HW

Alta 1942- . . . . CLC 19
See also CA 57-60

Alter, Robert B(ernard) 1935- . . . . . . CLC 34
See also CA 49-52; CANR 1

Alther, Lisa 1944- . . . . CLC 7, 41
See also CA 65-68; CANR 12, 30; MTCW

Altman, Robert 1925- . . . . CLC 16
See also CA 73-76

Alvarez, A(lfred) 1929- . . . . CLC 5, 13
See also CA 1-4R; CANR 3, 33; DLB 14,
40

Alvarez, Alejandro Rodriguez 1903-1965
See Casona, Alejandro
See also CA 131; 93-96; HW

Amado, Jorge 1912- . . . . CLC 13, 40
See also CA 77-80; CANR 35; DLB 113;
MTCW

Ambler, Eric 1909- . . . . CLC 4, 6, 9
See also CA 9-12R; CANR 7, 38; DLB 77;
MTCW

Amichai, Yehuda 1924- . . . . . . CLC 9, 22, 57
See also CA 85-88; MTCW

Amiel, Henri Frederic 1821-1881 . . NCLC 4

Amis, Kingsley (William)
1922- . . . . . . CLC 1, 2, 3, 5, 8, 13, 40, 44
See also AITN 2; CA 9-12R; CANR 8, 28;
CDBLB 1945-1960; DLB 15, 27, 100;
MTCW

Amis, Martin (Louis)
1949- . . . . CLC 4, 9, 38, 62
See also BEST 90:3; CA 65-68; CANR 8,
27; DLB 14

Ammons, A(rchie) R(andolph)
1926- . . . . CLC 2, 3, 5, 8, 9, 25, 57
See also AITN 1; CA 9-12R; CANR 6, 36;
DLB 5; MTCW

Amo, Tauraatua i
See Adams, Henry (Brooks)

Anand, Mulk Raj 1905- . . . . CLC 23
See also CA 65-68; CANR 32; MTCW

Anatol
See Schnitzler, Arthur

Anaya, Rudolfo A(lfonso) 1937- . . . . CLC 23
See also CA 45-48; CAAS 4; CANR 1, 32;
DLB 82; HW; MTCW

Andersen, Hans Christian
1805-1875 . . . . NCLC 7; SSC 6
See also CLR 6; MAICYA; WLC; YABC 1

Anderson, C. Farley
See Mencken, H(enry) L(ouis); Nathan,
George Jean

Anderson, Jessica (Margaret) Queale
. . . . CLC 37
See also CA 9-12R; CANR 4

Anderson, Jon (Victor) 1940- . . . . CLC 9
See also CA 25-28R; CANR 20

Anderson, Lindsay (Gordon)
1923- . . . . CLC 20
See also CA 125; 128

Anderson, Maxwell 1888-1959 . . . . . TCLC 2
See also CA 105; DLB 7

Anderson, Poul (William) 1926- . . . . CLC 15
See also AAYA 5; CA 1-4R; CAAS 2;
CANR 2, 15, 34; DLB 8; MTCW;
SATA 39

Anderson, Robert (Woodruff)
1917- . . . . CLC 23
See also AITN 1; CA 21-24R; CANR 32;
DLB 7

Anderson, Sherwood
1876-1941 . . . . . . TCLC 1, 10, 24; SSC 1
See also CA 104; 121; CDALB 1917-1929;
DLB 4, 9, 86; DLBD 1; MTCW; WLC

Andouard
See Giraudoux, (Hippolyte) Jean

Andrade, Carlos Drummond de . . . . . . CLC 18
See also Drummond de Andrade, Carlos

Andrade, Mario de 1893-1945 . . . . . TCLC 43

Andrewes, Lancelot 1555-1626 . . . . LC 5

Andrews, Cicily Fairfield
See West, Rebecca

Andrews, Elton V.
See Pohl, Frederik

Andreyev, Leonid (Nikolaevich)
1871-1919 . . . . TCLC 3
See also CA 104

Andric, Ivo 1892-1975 . . . . CLC 8
See also CA 81-84; 57-60; MTCW

Angelique, Pierre
See Bataille, Georges

Angell, Roger 1920- . . . . CLC 26
See also CA 57-60; CANR 13

Angelou, Maya 1928- . . . . CLC 12, 35, 64
See also AAYA 7; BLC 1; BW; CA 65-68;
CANR 19; DLB 38; MTCW; SATA 49

Annensky, Innokenty Fyodorovich
1856-1909 . . . . TCLC 14
See also CA 110

Anon, Charles Robert
See Pessoa, Fernando (Antonio Nogueira)

Anouilh, Jean (Marie Lucien Pierre)
1910-1987 . . . . . . CLC 1, 3, 8, 13, 40, 50
See also CA 17-20R; 123; CANR 32;
MTCW

Anthony, Florence
See Ai

Anthony, John
See Ciardi, John (Anthony)

Anthony, Peter
See Shaffer, Anthony (Joshua); Shaffer,
Peter (Levin)

Anthony, Piers 1934- . . . . CLC 35
See also CA 21-24R; CANR 28; DLB 8;
MTCW

Antoine, Marc
See Proust,
(Valentin-Louis-George-Eugene-)Marcel

Antoninus, Brother
See Everson, William (Oliver)

Antonioni, Michelangelo 1912- . . . . . CLC 20
See also CA 73-76

Antschel, Paul 1920-1970 . . . . . . CLC 10, 19
See also Celan, Paul
See also CA 85-88; CANR 33; MTCW

Anwar, Chairil 1922-1949 . . . . TCLC 22
See also CA 121

Apollinaire, Guillaume . . . . TCLC 3, 8
See also Kostrowitzki, Wilhelm Apollinaris
de

Appelfeld, Aharon 1932- . . . . CLC 23, 47
See also CA 112; 133

Apple, Max (Isaac) 1941- . . . . CLC 9, 33
See also CA 81-84; CANR 19

Appleman, Philip (Dean) 1926- . . . . . CLC 51
See also CA 13-16R; CANR 6, 29

Benet, Juan 1927-................ **CLC 28**

Benet, Stephen Vincent
1898-1943 .... **TCLC 7; SSC 10**
See also CA 104; DLB 4, 48, 102; YABC 1

Benet, William Rose 1886-1950 ... **TCLC 28**
See also CA 118; DLB 45

Benford, Gregory (Albert) 1941-.... **CLC 52**
See also CA 69-72; CANR 12, 24;
DLBY 82

Bengtsson, Frans (Gunnar)
1894-1954 .... **TCLC 48**

Benjamin, Lois
See Gould, Lois

Benjamin, Walter 1892-1940..... **TCLC 39**

Benn, Gottfried 1886-1956........ **TCLC 3**
See also CA 106; DLB 56

Bennett, Alan 1934-.............. **CLC 45**
See also CA 103; CANR 35; MTCW

Bennett, (Enoch) Arnold
1867-1931 .... **TCLC 5, 20**
See also CA 106; CDBLB 1890-1914;
DLB 10, 34, 98

Bennett, Elizabeth
See Mitchell, Margaret (Munnerlyn)

Bennett, George Harold 1930-
See Bennett, Hal
See also BW; CA 97-100

Bennett, Hal .... **CLC 5**
See also Bennett, George Harold
See also DLB 33

Bennett, Jay 1912-.............. **CLC 35**
See also CA 69-72; CANR 11; SAAS 4;
SATA 27, 41

Bennett, Louise (Simone) 1919-..... **CLC 28**
See also BLC 1; DLB 117

Benson, E(dward) F(rederic)
1867-1940 .... **TCLC 27**
See also CA 114

Benson, Jackson J. 1930-......... **CLC 34**
See also CA 25-28R; DLB 111

Benson, Sally 1900-1972 .... **CLC 17**
See also CA 19-20; 37-40R; CAP 1;
SATA 1, 27, 35

Benson, Stella 1892-1933........ **TCLC 17**
See also CA 117; DLB 36

Bentham, Jeremy 1748-1832 ..... **NCLC 38**
See also DLB 107

Bentley, E(dmund) C(lerihew)
1875-1956 .... **TCLC 12**
See also CA 108; DLB 70

Bentley, Eric (Russell) 1916-....... **CLC 24**
See also CA 5-8R; CANR 6

Beranger, Pierre Jean de
1780-1857 .... **NCLC 34**

Berger, Colonel
See Malraux, (Georges-)Andre

Berger, John (Peter) 1926- ...... **CLC 2, 19**
See also CA 81-84; DLB 14

Berger, Melvin H. 1927- .... **CLC 12**
See also CA 5-8R; CANR 4; SAAS 2;
SATA 5

Berger, Thomas (Louis)
1924- .... **CLC 3, 5, 8, 11, 18, 38**
See also CA 1-4R; CANR 5, 28; DLB 2;
DLBY 80; MTCW

Bergman, (Ernst) Ingmar
1918- .... **CLC 16, 72**
See also CA 81-84; CANR 33

Bergson, Henri 1859-1941....... **TCLC 32**

Bergstein, Eleanor 1938-.......... **CLC 4**
See also CA 53-56; CANR 5

Berkoff, Steven 1937-............. **CLC 56**
See also CA 104

Bermant, Chaim (Icyk) 1929- ...... **CLC 40**
See also CA 57-60; CANR 6, 31

Bernanos, (Paul Louis) Georges
1888-1948 .... **TCLC 3**
See also CA 104; 130; DLB 72

Bernard, April 1956- .... **CLC 59**
See also CA 131

Bernhard, Thomas
1931-1989 .... **CLC 3, 32, 61**
See also CA 85-88; 127; CANR 32;
DLB 85; MTCW

Berrigan, Daniel 1921-............. **CLC 4**
See also CA 33-36R; CAAS 1; CANR 11;
DLB 5

Berrigan, Edmund Joseph Michael Jr.
1934-1983
See Berrigan, Ted
See also CA 61-64; 110; CANR 14

Berrigan, Ted.................... **CLC 37**
See also Berrigan, Edmund Joseph Michael
Jr.
See also DLB 5

Berry, Charles Edward Anderson 1931-
See Berry, Chuck
See also CA 115

Berry, Chuck.................... **CLC 17**
See also Berry, Charles Edward Anderson

Berry, Jonas
See Ashbery, John (Lawrence)

Berry, Wendell (Erdman)
1934- .... **CLC 4, 6, 8, 27, 46**
See also AITN 1; CA 73-76; DLB 5, 6

Berryman, John
1914-1972 ..... **CLC 1, 2, 3, 4, 6, 8, 10,
13, 25, 62**
See also CA 13-16; 33-36R; CABS 2;
CANR 35; CAP 1; CDALB 1941-1968;
DLB 48; MTCW

Bertolucci, Bernardo 1940- .... **CLC 16**
See also CA 106

Bertrand, Aloysius 1807-1841 .... **NCLC 31**

Bertran de Born c. 1140-1215 ..... **CMLC 5**

Besant, Annie (Wood) 1847-1933 ... **TCLC 9**
See also CA 105

Bessie, Alvah 1904-1985.......... **CLC 23**
See also CA 5-8R; 116; CANR 2; DLB 26

Bethlen, T. D.
See Silverberg, Robert

Beti, Mongo.................... **CLC 27**
See also Biyidi, Alexandre
See also BLC 1

Betjeman, John
1906-1984 .... **CLC 2, 6, 10, 34, 43**
See also CA 9-12R; 112; CANR 33;
CDBLB 1945-1960; DLB 20; DLBY 84;
MTCW

Betti, Ugo 1892-1953............. **TCLC 5**
See also CA 104

Betts, Doris (Waugh) 1932-.... **CLC 3, 6, 28**
See also CA 13-16R; CANR 9; DLBY 82

Bevan, Alistair
See Roberts, Keith (John Kingston)

Beynon, John
See Harris, John (Wyndham Parkes Lucas)
Beynon

Bialik, Chaim Nachman
1873-1934 .... **TCLC 25**

Bickerstaff, Isaac
See Swift, Jonathan

Bidart, Frank 19(?)-............. **CLC 33**

Bienek, Horst 1930-............. **CLC 7, 11**
See also CA 73-76; DLB 75

Bierce, Ambrose (Gwinett)
1842-1914(?) ..... **TCLC 1, 7, 44; SSC 9**
See also CA 104; CDALB 1865-1917;
DLB 11, 12, 23, 71, 74; WLC

Billings, Josh
See Shaw, Henry Wheeler

Billington, Rachel 1942-.......... **CLC 43**
See also AITN 2; CA 33-36R

Binyon, T(imothy) J(ohn) 1936- .... **CLC 34**
See also CA 111; CANR 28

Bioy Casares, Adolfo 1914-.... **CLC 4, 8, 13**
See also CA 29-32R; CANR 19; DLB 113;
HW; MTCW

Bird, C.
See Ellison, Harlan

Bird, Cordwainer
See Ellison, Harlan

Bird, Robert Montgomery
1806-1854 .... **NCLC 1**

Birney, (Alfred) Earle
1904- .... **CLC 1, 4, 6, 11**
See also CA 1-4R; CANR 5, 20; DLB 88;
MTCW

Bishop, Elizabeth
1911-1979 ..... **CLC 1, 4, 9, 13, 15, 32;
PC 3**
See also CA 5-8R; 89-92; CABS 2;
CANR 26; CDALB 1968-1988; DLB 5;
MTCW; SATA 24

Bishop, John 1935-.............. **CLC 10**
See also CA 105

Bissett, Bill 1939-............... **CLC 18**
See also CA 69-72; CANR 15; DLB 53;
MTCW

Bitov, Andrei (Georgievich) 1937-... **CLC 57**

Biyidi, Alexandre 1932-
See Beti, Mongo
See also BW; CA 114; 124; MTCW

Bjarme, Brynjolf
See Ibsen, Henrik (Johan)

Bjornson, Bjornstjerne (Martinius)
1832-1910 .... **TCLC 7, 37**
See also CA 104

Carlyle, Thomas 1795-1881 ...... **NCLC 22**
See also CDBLB 1789-1832; DLB 55

Carman, (William) Bliss
1861-1929 .... **TCLC 7**
See also CA 104; DLB 92

Carossa, Hans 1878-1956........ **TCLC 48**
See also DLB 66

Carpenter, Don(ald Richard)
1931- .... **CLC 41**
See also CA 45-48; CANR 1

Carpentier (y Valmont), Alejo
1904-1980 .... **CLC 8, 11, 38**
See also CA 65-68; 97-100; CANR 11;
DLB 113; HW

Carr, Emily 1871-1945.......... **TCLC 32**
See also DLB 68

Carr, John Dickson 1906-1977 ...... **CLC 3**
See also CA 49-52; 69-72; CANR 3, 33;
MTCW

Carr, Philippa
See Hibbert, Eleanor Burford

Carr, Virginia Spencer 1929-....... **CLC 34**
See also CA 61-64; DLB 111

Carrier, Roch 1937- .... **CLC 13**
See also CA 130; DLB 53

Carroll, James P. 1943(?)-......... **CLC 38**
See also CA 81-84

Carroll, Jim 1951- .... **CLC 35**
See also CA 45-48

Carroll, Lewis .... **NCLC 2**
See also Dodgson, Charles Lutwidge
See also CDBLB 1832-1890; CLR 2, 18;
DLB 18; WLC

Carroll, Paul Vincent 1900-1968.... **CLC 10**
See also CA 9-12R; 25-28R; DLB 10

Carruth, Hayden 1921- .... **CLC 4, 7, 10, 18**
See also CA 9-12R; CANR 4, 38; DLB 5;
MTCW; SATA 47

Carson, Rachel Louise 1907-1964... **CLC 71**
See also CA 77-80; CANR 35; MTCW;
SATA 23

Carter, Angela (Olive)
1940-1991 .... **CLC 5, 41**
See also CA 53-56; 136; CANR 12, 36;
DLB 14; MTCW; SATA 66; SATO 70

Carter, Nick
See Smith, Martin Cruz

Carver, Raymond
1938-1988 ... **CLC 22, 36, 53, 55; SSC 8**
See also CA 33-36R; 126; CANR 17, 34;
DLBY 84, 88; MTCW

Cary, (Arthur) Joyce (Lunel)
1888-1957 .... **TCLC 1, 29**
See also CA 104; CDBLB 1914-1945;
DLB 15, 100

Casanova de Seingalt, Giovanni Jacopo
1725-1798 .... **LC 13**

Casares, Adolfo Bioy
See Bioy Casares, Adolfo

Casely-Hayford, J(oseph) E(phraim)
1866-1930 .... **TCLC 24**
See also BLC 1; CA 123

Casey, John (Dudley) 1939-........ **CLC 59**
See also BEST 90:2; CA 69-72; CANR 23

Casey, Michael 1947-............. **CLC 2**
See also CA 65-68; DLB 5

Casey, Patrick
See Thurman, Wallace (Henry)

Casey, Warren (Peter) 1935-1988 ... **CLC 12**
See also CA 101; 127

Casona, Alejandro .... **CLC 49**
See also Alvarez, Alejandro Rodriguez

Cassavetes, John 1929-1989....... **CLC 20**
See also CA 85-88; 127

Cassill, R(onald) V(erlin) 1919-... **CLC 4, 23**
See also CA 9-12R; CAAS 1; CANR 7;
DLB 6

Cassity, (Allen) Turner 1929- .... **CLC 6, 42**
See also CA 17-20R; CAAS 8; CANR 11;
DLB 105

Castaneda, Carlos 1931(?)-........ **CLC 12**
See also CA 25-28R; CANR 32; HW;
MTCW

Castedo, Elena 1937-............. **CLC 65**
See also CA 132

Castedo-Ellerman, Elena
See Castedo, Elena

Castellanos, Rosario 1925-1974..... **CLC 66**
See also CA 131; 53-56; DLB 113; HW

Castelvetro, Lodovico 1505-1571..... **LC 12**

Castiglione, Baldassare 1478-1529 ... **LC 12**

Castle, Robert
See Hamilton, Edmond

Castro, Guillen de 1569-1631........ **LC 19**

Castro, Rosalia de 1837-1885 ..... **NCLC 3**

Cather, Willa
See Cather, Willa Sibert

Cather, Willa Sibert
1873-1947 ...... **TCLC 1, 11, 31; SSC 2**
See also CA 104; 128; CDALB 1865-1917;
DLB 9, 54, 78; DLBD 1; MTCW;
SATA 30; WLC

Catton, (Charles) Bruce
1899-1978 .... **CLC 35**
See also AITN 1; CA 5-8R; 81-84;
CANR 7; DLB 17; SATA 2, 24

Cauldwell, Frank
See King, Francis (Henry)

Caunitz, William J. 1933-......... **CLC 34**
See also BEST 89:3; CA 125; 130

Causley, Charles (Stanley) 1917-..... **CLC 7**
See also CA 9-12R; CANR 5, 35; DLB 27;
MTCW; SATA 3, 66

Caute, David 1936-............... **CLC 29**
See also CA 1-4R; CAAS 4; CANR 1, 33;
DLB 14

Cavafy, C(onstantine) P(eter)...... **TCLC 2, 7**
See also Kavafis, Konstantinos Petrou

Cavallo, Evelyn
See Spark, Muriel (Sarah)

Cavanna, Betty .... **CLC 12**
See also Harrison, Elizabeth Cavanna
See also MAICYA; SAAS 4; SATA 1, 30

Caxton, William 1421(?)-1491(?)..... **LC 17**

Cayrol, Jean 1911-............... **CLC 11**
See also CA 89-92; DLB 83

Cela, Camilo Jose 1916-...... **CLC 4, 13, 59**
See also BEST 90:2; CA 21-24R; CAAS 10;
CANR 21, 32; DLBY 89; HW; MTCW

Celan, Paul .... **CLC 53**
See also Antschel, Paul
See also DLB 69

Celine, Louis-Ferdinand
.... **CLC 1, 3, 4, 7, 9, 15, 47**
See also Destouches, Louis-Ferdinand
See also DLB 72

Cellini, Benvenuto 1500-1571 .... **LC 7**

Cendrars, Blaise
See Sauser-Hall, Frederic

Cernuda (y Bidon), Luis
1902-1963 .... **CLC 54**
See also CA 131; 89-92; HW

Cervantes (Saavedra), Miguel de
1547-1616 .... **LC 6**
See also WLC

Cesaire, Aime (Fernand) 1913-... **CLC 19, 32**
See also BLC 1; BW; CA 65-68; CANR 24;
MTCW

Chabon, Michael 1965(?)- .... **CLC 55**

Chabrol, Claude 1930-............ **CLC 16**
See also CA 110

Challans, Mary 1905-1983
See Renault, Mary
See also CA 81-84; 111; SATA 23, 36

Chambers, Aidan 1934- .... **CLC 35**
See also CA 25-28R; CANR 12, 31;
MAICYA; SAAS 12; SATA 1, 69

Chambers, James 1948-
See Cliff, Jimmy
See also CA 124

Chambers, Jessie
See Lawrence, D(avid) H(erbert Richards)

Chambers, Robert W. 1865-1933... **TCLC 41**

Chandler, Raymond (Thornton)
1888-1959 .... **TCLC 1, 7**
See also CA 104; 129; CDALB 1929-1941;
DLBD 6; MTCW

Chang, Jung 1952-............... **CLC 71**

Channing, William Ellery
1780-1842 .... **NCLC 17**
See also DLB 1, 59

Chaplin, Charles Spencer
1889-1977 .... **CLC 16**
See also Chaplin, Charlie
See also CA 81-84; 73-76

Chaplin, Charlie
See Chaplin, Charles Spencer
See also DLB 44

Chapman, Graham 1941-1989 ...... **CLC 21**
See also Monty Python
See also CA 116; 129; CANR 35

Chapman, John Jay 1862-1933 ..... **TCLC 7**
See also CA 104

Chapman, Walker
See Silverberg, Robert

Chappell, Fred (Davis) 1936-....... **CLC 40**
See also CA 5-8R; CAAS 4; CANR 8, 33;
DLB 6, 105

Char, Rene(-Emile)
1907-1988 .... CLC 9, 11, 14, 55
See also CA 13-16R; 124; CANR 32;
MTCW

Charby, Jay
See Ellison, Harlan

Chardin, Pierre Teilhard de
See Teilhard de Chardin, (Marie Joseph)
Pierre

Charles I 1600-1649 .... LC 13

Charyn, Jerome 1937- .... CLC 5, 8, 18
See also CA 5-8R; CAAS 1; CANR 7;
DLBY 83; MTCW

Chase, Mary (Coyle) 1907-1981 ...... DC 1
See also CA 77-80; 105; SATA 17, 29

Chase, Mary Ellen 1887-1973 .... CLC 2
See also CA 13-16; 41-44R; CAP 1;
SATA 10

Chase, Nicholas
See Hyde, Anthony

Chateaubriand, Francois Rene de
1768-1848 .... NCLC 3
See also DLB 119

Chatterje, Sarat Chandra 1876-1936(?)
See Chatterji, Saratchandra
See also CA 109

Chatterji, Bankim Chandra
1838-1894 .... NCLC 19

Chatterji, Saratchandra .... TCLC 13
See also Chatterje, Sarat Chandra

Chatterton, Thomas 1752-1770 .... LC 3
See also DLB 109

Chatwin, (Charles) Bruce
1940-1989 .... CLC 28, 57, 59
See also AAYA 4; BEST 90:1; CA 85-88;
127

Chaucer, Daniel
See Ford, Ford Madox

Chaucer, Geoffrey 1340(?)-1400 ..... LC 17
See also CDBLB Before 1660

Chaviaras, Strates 1935-
See Haviaras, Stratis
See also CA 105

Chayefsky, Paddy .... CLC 23
See also Chayefsky, Sidney
See also DLB 7, 44; DLBY 81

Chayefsky, Sidney 1923-1981
See Chayefsky, Paddy
See also CA 9-12R; 104; CANR 18

Chedid, Andree 1920- .... CLC 47

Cheever, John
1912-1982 ..... CLC 3, 7, 8, 11, 15, 25,
64; SSC 1
See also CA 5-8R; 106; CABS 1; CANR 5,
27; CDALB 1941-1968; DLB 2, 102;
DLBY 80, 82; MTCW; WLC

Cheever, Susan 1943- .... CLC 18, 48
See also CA 103; CANR 27; DLBY 82

Chekhonte, Antosha
See Chekhov, Anton (Pavlovich)

Chekhov, Anton (Pavlovich)
1860-1904 ...... TCLC 3, 10, 31; SSC 2
See also CA 104; 124; WLC

Chernyshevsky, Nikolay Gavrilovich
1828-1889 .... NCLC 1

Cherry, Carolyn Janice 1942-
See Cherryh, C. J.
See also CA 65-68; CANR 10

Cherryh, C. J. .... CLC 35
See also Cherry, Carolyn Janice
See also DLBY 80

Chesnutt, Charles W(addell)
1858-1932 .... TCLC 5, 39; SSC 7
See also BLC 1; BW; CA 106; 125; DLB 12,
50, 78; MTCW

Chester, Alfred 1929(?)-1971 ...... CLC 49
See also CA 33-36R

Chesterton, G(ilbert) K(eith)
1874-1936 .... TCLC 1, 6; SSC 1
See also CA 104; 132; CDBLB 1914-1945;
DLB 10, 19, 34, 70, 98; MTCW;
SATA 27

Chiang Pin-chin 1904-1986
See Ding Ling
See also CA 118

Ch'ien Chung-shu 1910- .... CLC 22
See also CA 130; MTCW

Child, L. Maria
See Child, Lydia Maria

Child, Lydia Maria 1802-1880 .... NCLC 6
See also DLB 1, 74; SATA 67

Child, Mrs.
See Child, Lydia Maria

Child, Philip 1898-1978 .... CLC 19, 68
See also CA 13-14; CAP 1; SATA 47

Childress, Alice 1920-........... CLC 12, 15
See also AAYA 8; BLC 1; BW; CA 45-48;
CANR 3, 27; CLR 14; DLB 7, 38;
MAICYA; MTCW; SATA 7, 48

Chislett, (Margaret) Anne 1943-.... CLC 34

Chitty, Thomas Willes 1926-....... CLC 11
See also Hinde, Thomas
See also CA 5-8R

Chomette, Rene Lucien 1898-1981 .. CLC 20
See also Clair, Rene
See also CA 103

Chopin, Kate .... TCLC 5, 14; SSC 8
See also Chopin, Katherine
See also CDALB 1865-1917; DLB 12, 78

Chopin, Katherine 1851-1904
See Chopin, Kate
See also CA 104; 122

Chretien de Troyes
c. 12th cent. - .... CMLC 10

Christie
See Ichikawa, Kon

Christie, Agatha (Mary Clarissa)
1890-1976 ...... CLC 1, 6, 8, 12, 39, 48
See also AAYA 9; AITN 1, 2; CA 17-20R;
61-64; CANR 10, 37; CDBLB 1914-1945;
DLB 13, 77; MTCW; SATA 36

Christie, (Ann) Philippa
See Pearce, Philippa
See also CA 5-8R; CANR 4

Christine de Pizan 1365(?)-1431(?) .... LC 9

Chubb, Elmer
See Masters, Edgar Lee

Chulkov, Mikhail Dmitrievich
1743-1792 .... LC 2

Churchill, Caryl 1938- .... CLC 31, 55
See also CA 102; CANR 22; DLB 13;
MTCW

Churchill, Charles 1731-1764........ LC 3
See also DLB 109

Chute, Carolyn 1947- .... CLC 39
See also CA 123

Ciardi, John (Anthony)
1916-1986 .... CLC 10, 40, 44
See also CA 5-8R; 118; CAAS 2; CANR 5,
33; CLR 19; DLB 5; DLBY 86;
MAICYA; MTCW; SATA 1, 46, 65

Cicero, Marcus Tullius
106B.C.-43B.C. .... CMLC 3

Cimino, Michael 1943-............ CLC 16
See also CA 105

Cioran, E(mil) M. 1911-........... CLC 64
See also CA 25-28R

Cisneros, Sandra 1954-............ CLC 69
See also AAYA 9; CA 131; DLB 122; HW

Clair, Rene...................... CLC 20
See also Chomette, Rene Lucien

Clampitt, Amy 1920- .... CLC 32
See also CA 110; CANR 29; DLB 105

Clancy, Thomas L. Jr. 1947-
See Clancy, Tom
See also CA 125; 131; MTCW

Clancy, Tom..................... CLC 45
See also Clancy, Thomas L. Jr.
See also AAYA 9; BEST 89:1, 90:1

Clare, John 1793-1864............ NCLC 9
See also DLB 55, 96

Clarin
See Alas (y Urena), Leopoldo (Enrique
Garcia)

Clark, (Robert) Brian 1932-........ CLC 29
See also CA 41-44R

Clark, Eleanor 1913- .... CLC 5, 19
See also CA 9-12R; DLB 6

Clark, J. P.
See Clark, John Pepper
See also DLB 117

Clark, John Pepper 1935- .... CLC 38
See also Clark, J. P.
See also BLC 1; BW; CA 65-68; CANR 16

Clark, M. R.
See Clark, Mavis Thorpe

Clark, Mavis Thorpe 1909- .... CLC 12
See also CA 57-60; CANR 8, 37; MAICYA;
SAAS 5; SATA 8

Clark, Walter Van Tilburg
1909-1971 .... CLC 28
See also CA 9-12R; 33-36R; DLB 9;
SATA 8

Clarke, Arthur C(harles)
1917- ...... CLC 1, 4, 13, 18, 35; SSC 3
See also AAYA 4; CA 1-4R; CANR 2, 28;
MAICYA; MTCW; SATA 13, 70

Clarke, Austin C(hesterfield)
1934-..................... CLC 8, 53
See also BLC 1; BW; CA 25-28R;
CAAS 16; CANR 14, 32; DLB 53

Clarke, Austin 1896-1974......... **CLC 6, 9**
See also CA 29-32; 49-52; CAP 2; DLB 10, 20

Clarke, Gillian 1937- .... **CLC 61**
See also CA 106; DLB 40

Clarke, Marcus (Andrew Hislop)
1846-1881 .... **NCLC 19**

Clarke, Shirley 1925-............. **CLC 16**

.... **CLC 30**
See also Headon, (Nicky) Topper; Jones, Mick; Simonon, Paul; Strummer, Joe

Claudel, Paul (Louis Charles Marie)
1868-1955 .... **TCLC 2, 10**
See also CA 104

Clavell, James (duMaresq)
1925- .... **CLC 6, 25**
See also CA 25-28R; CANR 26; MTCW

Cleaver, (Leroy) Eldridge 1935-.... **CLC 30**
See also BLC 1; BW; CA 21-24R; CANR 16

Cleese, John (Marwood) 1939- ..... **CLC 21**
See also Monty Python
See also CA 112; 116; CANR 35; MTCW

Cleishbotham, Jebediah
See Scott, Walter

Cleland, John 1710-1789 .... **LC 2**
See also DLB 39

Clemens, Samuel Langhorne 1835-1910
See Twain, Mark
See also CA 104; 135; CDALB 1865-1917;
DLB 11, 12, 23, 64, 74; MAICYA;
YABC 2

Clerihew, E.
See Bentley, E(dmund) C(lerihew)

Clerk, N. W.
See Lewis, C(live) S(taples)

Cliff, Jimmy....................... **CLC 21**
See also Chambers, James

Clifton, (Thelma) Lucille
1936- .... **CLC 19, 66**
See also BLC 1; BW; CA 49-52; CANR 2,
24; CLR 5; DLB 5, 41; MAICYA;
MTCW; SATA 20, 69

Clinton, Dirk
See Silverberg, Robert

Clough, Arthur Hugh 1819-1861.. **NCLC 27**
See also DLB 32

Clutha, Janet Paterson Frame 1924-
See Frame, Janet
See also CA 1-4R; CANR 2, 36; MTCW

Clyne, Terence
See Blatty, William Peter

Cobalt, Martin
See Mayne, William (James Carter)

Coburn, D(onald) L(ee) 1938- ...... **CLC 10**
See also CA 89-92

Cocteau, Jean (Maurice Eugene Clement)
1889-1963 .... **CLC 1, 8, 15, 16, 43**
See also CA 25-28; CAP 2; DLB 65;
MTCW; WLC

Codrescu, Andrei 1946- .... **CLC 46**
See also CA 33-36R; CANR 13, 34

Coe, Max
See Bourne, Randolph S(illiman)

Coe, Tucker
See Westlake, Donald E(dwin)

Coetzee, J(ohn) M(ichael)
1940- .... **CLC 23, 33, 66**
See also CA 77-80; MTCW

Cohen, Arthur A(llen)
1928-1986 .... **CLC 7, 31**
See also CA 1-4R; 120; CANR 1, 17;
DLB 28

Cohen, Leonard (Norman)
1934- .... **CLC 3, 38**
See also CA 21-24R; CANR 14; DLB 53;
MTCW

Cohen, Matt 1942-............... **CLC 19**
See also CA 61-64; DLB 53

Cohen-Solal, Annie 19(?)- .... **CLC 50**

Colegate, Isabel 1931- .... **CLC 36**
See also CA 17-20R; CANR 8, 22; DLB 14;
MTCW

Coleman, Emmett
See Reed, Ishmael

Coleridge, Samuel Taylor
1772-1834 .... **NCLC 9**
See also CDBLB 1789-1832; DLB 93, 107;
WLC

Coleridge, Sara 1802-1852....... **NCLC 31**

Coles, Don 1928- .... **CLC 46**
See also CA 115; CANR 38

Colette, (Sidonie-Gabrielle)
1873-1954 ...... **TCLC 1, 5, 16; SSC 10**
See also CA 104; 131; DLB 65; MTCW

Collett, (Jacobine) Camilla (Wergeland)
1813-1895 .... **NCLC 22**

Collier, Christopher 1930-........ **CLC 30**
See also CA 33-36R; CANR 13, 33;
MAICYA; SATA 16, 70

Collier, James L(incoln) 1928- ..... **CLC 30**
See also CA 9-12R; CANR 4, 33;
MAICYA; SATA 8, 70

Collier, Jeremy 1650-1726.......... **LC 6**

Collins, Hunt
See Hunter, Evan

Collins, Linda 1931-............. **CLC 44**
See also CA 125

Collins, (William) Wilkie
1824-1889 .... **NCLC 1, 18**
See also CDBLB 1832-1890; DLB 18, 70

Collins, William 1721-1759 .... **LC 4**
See also DLB 109

Colman, George
See Glassco, John

Colt, Winchester Remington
See Hubbard, L(afayette) Ron(ald)

Colter, Cyrus 1910- .... **CLC 58**
See also BW; CA 65-68; CANR 10; DLB 33

Colton, James
See Hansen, Joseph

Colum, Padraic 1881-1972........ **CLC 28**
See also CA 73-76; 33-36R; CANR 35;
MAICYA; MTCW; SATA 15

Colvin, James
See Moorcock, Michael (John)

Colwin, Laurie (E.)
1944-1992 .... **CLC 5, 13, 23**
See also CA 89-92; CANR 20; DLBY 80;
MTCW

Comfort, Alex(ander) 1920-........ **CLC 7**
See also CA 1-4R; CANR 1

Comfort, Montgomery
See Campbell, (John) Ramsey

Compton-Burnett, I(vy)
1884(?)-1969 ...... **CLC 1, 3, 10, 15, 34**
See also CA 1-4R; 25-28R; CANR 4;
DLB 36; MTCW

Comstock, Anthony 1844-1915 .... **TCLC 13**
See also CA 110

Conan Doyle, Arthur
See Doyle, Arthur Conan

Conde, Maryse .... **CLC 52**
See also Boucolon, Maryse

Condon, Richard (Thomas)
1915- .... **CLC 4, 6, 8, 10, 45**
See also BEST 90:3; CA 1-4R; CAAS 1;
CANR 2, 23; MTCW

Congreve, William
1670-1729 .... **LC 5, 21; DC 2**
See also CDBLB 1660-1789; DLB 39, 84;
WLC

Connell, Evan S(helby) Jr.
1924- .... **CLC 4, 6, 45**
See also AAYA 7; CA 1-4R; CAAS 2;
CANR 2, 39; DLB 2; DLBY 81; MTCW

Connelly, Marc(us Cook)
1890-1980 .... **CLC 7**
See also CA 85-88; 102; CANR 30; DLB 7;
DLBY 80; SATA 25

Connor, Ralph .... **TCLC 31**
See also Gordon, Charles William
See also DLB 92

Conrad, Joseph
1857-1924 ...... **TCLC 1, 6, 13, 25, 43;**
SSC 9
See also CA 104; 131; CDBLB 1890-1914;
DLB 10, 34, 98; MTCW; SATA 27; WLC

Conrad, Robert Arnold
See Hart, Moss

Conroy, Pat 1945-............. **CLC 30, 74**
See also AAYA 8; AITN 1; CA 85-88;
CANR 24; DLB 6; MTCW

Constant (de Rebecque), (Henri) Benjamin
1767-1830 .... **NCLC 6**
See also DLB 119

Conybeare, Charles Augustus
See Eliot, T(homas) S(tearns)

Cook, Michael 1933- .... **CLC 58**
See also CA 93-96; DLB 53

Cook, Robin 1940- .... **CLC 14**
See also BEST 90:2; CA 108; 111

Cook, Roy
See Silverberg, Robert

Cooke, Elizabeth 1948- .... **CLC 55**
See also CA 129

Cooke, John Esten 1830-1886..... **NCLC 5**
See also DLB 3

Cooke, John Estes
See Baum, L(yman) Frank

Cooke, M. E.
See Creasey, John

Cooke, Margaret
See Creasey, John

Cooney, Ray .... CLC 62

Cooper, Henry St. John
See Creasey, John

Cooper, J. California.............. CLC 56
See also BW; CA 125

Cooper, James Fenimore
1789-1851 .... NCLC 1, 27
See also CDALB 1640-1865; DLB 3;
SATA 19

Coover, Robert (Lowell)
1932- .... CLC 3, 7, 15, 32, 46
See also CA 45-48; CANR 3, 37; DLB 2;
DLBY 81; MTCW

Copeland, Stewart (Armstrong)
1952- .... CLC 26
See also The Police

Coppard, A(lfred) E(dgar)
1878-1957 .... TCLC 5
See also CA 114; YABC 1

Coppee, Francois   1842-1908 ...... TCLC 25

Coppola, Francis Ford   1939-....... CLC 16
See also CA 77-80; DLB 44

Corcoran, Barbara   1911-.......... CLC 17
See also CA 21-24R; CAAS 2; CANR 11,
28; DLB 52; SATA 3

Cordelier, Maurice
See Giraudoux, (Hippolyte) Jean

Corman, Cid...................... CLC 9
See also Corman, Sidney
See also CAAS 2; DLB 5

Corman, Sidney   1924-
See Corman, Cid
See also CA 85-88

Cormier, Robert (Edmund)
1925- .... CLC 12, 30
See also AAYA 3; CA 1-4R; CANR 5, 23;
CDALB 1968-1988; CLR 12; DLB 52;
MAICYA; MTCW; SATA 10, 45

Corn, Alfred   1943-............... CLC 33
See also CA 104; DLB 120; DLBY 80

Cornwell, David (John Moore)
1931- .... CLC 9, 15
See also le Carre, John
See also CA 5-8R; CANR 13, 33; MTCW

Corrigan, Kevin.................. CLC 55

Corso, (Nunzio) Gregory   1930-... CLC 1, 11
See also CA 5-8R; DLB 5,16; MTCW

Cortazar, Julio
1914-1984 ..... CLC 2, 3, 5, 10, 13, 15,
33, 34; SSC 7
See also CA 21-24R; CANR 12, 32;
DLB 113; HW; MTCW

Corwin, Cecil
See Kornbluth, C(yril) M.

Cosic, Dobrica   1921- .... CLC 14
See also CA 122; 138

Costain, Thomas B(ertram)
1885-1965 .... CLC 30
See also CA 5-8R; 25-28R; DLB 9

Costantini, Humberto
1924(?)-1987 .... CLC 49
See also CA 131; 122; HW

Costello, Elvis   1955-............. CLC 21

Cotter, Joseph S. Sr.
See Cotter, Joseph Seamon Sr.

Cotter, Joseph Seamon Sr.
1861-1949 .... TCLC 28
See also BLC 1; BW; CA 124; DLB 50

Coulton, James
See Hansen, Joseph

Couperus, Louis (Marie Anne)
1863-1923 .... TCLC 15
See also CA 115

Court, Wesli
See Turco, Lewis (Putnam)

Courtenay, Bryce   1933-.......... CLC 59
See also CA 138

Courtney, Robert
See Ellison, Harlan

Cousteau, Jacques-Yves   1910-...... CLC 30
See also CA 65-68; CANR 15; MTCW;
SATA 38

Coward, Noel (Peirce)
1899-1973 .... CLC 1, 9, 29, 51
See also AITN 1; CA 17-18; 41-44R;
CANR 35; CAP 2; CDBLB 1914-1945;
DLB 10; MTCW

Cowley, Malcolm   1898-1989 .... CLC 39
See also CA 5-8R; 128; CANR 3; DLB 4,
48; DLBY 81, 89; MTCW

Cowper, William   1731-1800....... NCLC 8
See also DLB 104, 109

Cox, William Trevor   1928- ... CLC 9, 14, 71
See also Trevor, William
See also CA 9-12R; CANR 4, 37; DLB 14;
MTCW

Cozzens, James Gould
1903-1978 .... CLC 1, 4, 11
See also CA 9-12R; 81-84; CANR 19;
CDALB 1941-1968; DLB 9; DLBD 2;
DLBY 84; MTCW

Crabbe, George   1754-1832....... NCLC 26
See also DLB 93

Craig, A. A.
See Anderson, Poul (William)

Craik, Dinah Maria (Mulock)
1826-1887 .... NCLC 38
See also DLB 35; MAICYA; SATA 34

Cram, Ralph Adams   1863-1942.... TCLC 45

Crane, (Harold) Hart
1899-1932 .... TCLC 2, 5; PC 3
See also CA 104; 127; CDALB 1917-1929;
DLB 4, 48; MTCW; WLC

Crane, R(onald) S(almon)
1886-1967 .... CLC 27
See also CA 85-88; DLB 63

Crane, Stephen (Townley)
1871-1900 ..... TCLC 11, 17, 32; SSC 7
See also CA 109; CDALB 1865-1917;
DLB 12, 54, 78; WLC; YABC 2

Crase, Douglas   1944-............. CLC 58
See also CA 106

Craven, Margaret   1901-1980....... CLC 17
See also CA 103

Crawford, F(rancis) Marion
1854-1909 .... TCLC 10
See also CA 107; DLB 71

Crawford, Isabella Valancy
1850-1887 .... NCLC 12
See also DLB 92

Crayon, Geoffrey
See Irving, Washington

Creasey, John   1908-1973.......... CLC 11
See also CA 5-8R; 41-44R; CANR 8;
DLB 77; MTCW

Crebillon, Claude Prosper Jolyot de (fils)
1707-1777 .... LC 1

Credo
See Creasey, John

Creeley, Robert (White)
1926- .... CLC 1, 2, 4, 8, 11, 15, 36
See also CA 1-4R; CAAS 10; CANR 23;
DLB 5, 16; MTCW

Crews, Harry (Eugene)
1935- .... CLC 6, 23, 49
See also AITN 1; CA 25-28R; CANR 20;
DLB 6; MTCW

Crichton, (John) Michael
1942- .... CLC 2, 6, 54
See also AITN 2; CA 25-28R; CANR 13;
DLBY 81; MTCW; SATA 9

Crispin, Edmund .... CLC 22
See also Montgomery, (Robert) Bruce
See also DLB 87

Cristofer, Michael   1945(?)- .... CLC 28
See also CA 110; DLB 7

Croce, Benedetto   1866-1952 ...... TCLC 37
See also CA 120

Crockett, David   1786-1836 .... NCLC 8
See also DLB 3, 11

Crockett, Davy
See Crockett, David

Croker, John Wilson   1780-1857 .. NCLC 10
See also DLB 110

Crommelynck, Fernand   1885-1970 .. CLC 75
See also CA 89-92

Cronin, A(rchibald) J(oseph)
1896-1981 .... CLC 32
See also CA 1-4R; 102; CANR 5; SATA 25,
47

Cross, Amanda
See Heilbrun, Carolyn G(old)

Crothers, Rachel   1878(?)-1958..... TCLC 19
See also CA 113; DLB 7

Croves, Hal
See Traven, B.

Crowfield, Christopher
See Stowe, Harriet (Elizabeth) Beecher

Crowley, Aleister................. TCLC 7
See also Crowley, Edward Alexander

Crowley, Edward Alexander   1875-1947
See Crowley, Aleister
See also CA 104

Crowley, John   1942-............. CLC 57
See also CA 61-64; DLBY 82; SATA 65

Crud
See Crumb, R(obert)

de Beauvoir, Simone (Lucie Ernestine Marie
    Bertrand)
  See Beauvoir, Simone (Lucie Ernestine
    Marie Bertrand) de

de Brissac, Malcolm
  See Dickinson, Peter (Malcolm)

de Chardin, Pierre Teilhard
  See Teilhard de Chardin, (Marie Joseph)
    Pierre

Dee, John 1527-1608 .... LC 20

Deer, Sandra 1940-.............. CLC 45

De Ferrari, Gabriella .... CLC 65

Defoe, Daniel 1660(?)-1731 .... LC 1
  See also CDBLB 1660-1789; DLB 39, 95,
    101; MAICYA; SATA 22; WLC

de Gourmont, Remy
  See Gourmont, Remy de

de Hartog, Jan 1914-............ CLC 19
  See also CA 1-4R; CANR 1

de Hostos, E. M.
  See Hostos (y Bonilla), Eugenio Maria de

de Hostos, Eugenio M.
  See Hostos (y Bonilla), Eugenio Maria de

Deighton, Len .... CLC 4, 7, 22, 46
  See also Deighton, Leonard Cyril
  See also AAYA 6; BEST 89:2;
    CDBLB 1960 to Present; DLB 87

Deighton, Leonard Cyril 1929-
  See Deighton, Len
  See also CA 9-12R; CANR 19, 33; MTCW

de la Mare, Walter (John)
  1873-1956 .... TCLC 4
  See also CA 110; 137; CDBLB 1914-1945;
    CLR 23; DLB 19; MAICYA; SATA 16;
    WLC

Delaney, Franey
  See O'Hara, John (Henry)

Delaney, Shelagh 1939-........... CLC 29
  See also CA 17-20R; CANR 30;
    CDBLB 1960 to Present; DLB 13;
    MTCW

Delany, Mary (Granville Pendarves)
  1700-1788 .... LC 12

Delany, Samuel R(ay Jr.)
  1942-................. CLC 8, 14, 38
  See also BLC 1; BW; CA 81-84; CANR 27;
    DLB 8, 33; MTCW

Delaporte, Theophile
  See Green, Julian (Hartridge)

De La Ramee, (Marie) Louise 1839-1908
  See Ouida
  See also SATA 20

de la Roche, Mazo 1879-1961 ..... CLC 14
  See also CA 85-88; CANR 30; DLB 68;
    SATA 64

Delbanco, Nicholas (Franklin)
  1942-.................... CLC 6, 13
  See also CA 17-20R; CAAS 2; CANR 29;
    DLB 6

del Castillo, Michel 1933-......... CLC 38
  See also CA 109

Deledda, Grazia (Cosima)
  1875(?)-1936 .... TCLC 23
  See also CA 123

Delibes, Miguel .... CLC 8, 18
  See also Delibes Setien, Miguel

Delibes Setien, Miguel 1920-
  See Delibes, Miguel
  See also CA 45-48; CANR 1, 32; HW;
    MTCW

DeLillo, Don
  1936- .... CLC 8, 10, 13, 27, 39, 54
  See also BEST 89:1; CA 81-84; CANR 21;
    DLB 6; MTCW

de Lisser, H. G.
  See De Lisser, Herbert George
  See also DLB 117

De Lisser, Herbert George
  1878-1944 .... TCLC 12
  See also de Lisser, H. G.
  See also CA 109

Deloria, Vine (Victor) Jr. 1933- .... CLC 21
  See also CA 53-56; CANR 5, 20; MTCW;
    SATA 21

Del Vecchio, John M(ichael)
  1947-.................... CLC 29
  See also CA 110; DLBD 9

de Man, Paul (Adolph Michel)
  1919-1983 .... CLC 55
  See also CA 128; 111; DLB 67; MTCW

De Marinis, Rick 1934-........... CLC 54
  See also CA 57-60; CANR 9, 25

Demby, William 1922-............ CLC 53
  See also BLC 1; BW; CA 81-84; DLB 33

Demijohn, Thom
  See Disch, Thomas M(ichael)

de Montherlant, Henry (Milon)
  See Montherlant, Henry (Milon) de

de Natale, Francine
  See Malzberg, Barry N(athaniel)

Denby, Edwin (Orr) 1903-1983 ..... CLC 48
  See also CA 138; 110

Denis, Julio
  See Cortazar, Julio

Denmark, Harrison
  See Zelazny, Roger (Joseph)

Dennis, John 1658-1734........... LC 11
  See also DLB 101

Dennis, Nigel (Forbes) 1912-1989.... CLC 8
  See also CA 25-28R; 129; DLB 13, 15;
    MTCW

De Palma, Brian (Russell) 1940-.... CLC 20
  See also CA 109

De Quincey, Thomas 1785-1859 ... NCLC 4
  See also CDBLB 1789-1832; DLB 110

Deren, Eleanora 1908(?)-1961
  See Deren, Maya
  See also CA 111

Deren, Maya .... CLC 16
  See also Deren, Eleanora

Derleth, August (William)
  1909-1971 .... CLC 31
  See also CA 1-4R; 29-32R; CANR 4;
    DLB 9; SATA 5

de Routisie, Albert
  See Aragon, Louis

Derrida, Jacques 1930-............ CLC 24
  See also CA 124; 127

Derry Down Derry
  See Lear, Edward

Dersonnes, Jacques
  See Simenon, Georges (Jacques Christian)

Desai, Anita 1937- .... CLC 19, 37
  See also CA 81-84; CANR 33; MTCW;
    SATA 63

de Saint-Luc, Jean
  See Glassco, John

de Saint Roman, Arnaud
  See Aragon, Louis

Descartes, Rene 1596-1650 .... LC 20

De Sica, Vittorio 1901(?)-1974 ..... CLC 20
  See also CA 117

Desnos, Robert 1900-1945....... TCLC 22
  See also CA 121

Destouches, Louis-Ferdinand
  1894-1961 .... CLC 9, 15
  See also Celine, Louis-Ferdinand
  See also CA 85-88; CANR 28; MTCW

Deutsch, Babette 1895-1982 .... CLC 18
  See also CA 1-4R; 108; CANR 4; DLB 45;
    SATA 1, 33

Devant, William 1606-1649 .... LC 13

Devkota, Laxmiprasad
  1909-1959 .... TCLC 23
  See also CA 123

De Voto, Bernard (Augustine)
  1897-1955 .... TCLC 29
  See also CA 113; DLB 9

De Vries, Peter
  1910- .... CLC 1, 2, 3, 7, 10, 28, 46
  See also CA 17-20R; DLB 6; DLBY 82;
    MTCW

Dexter, Pete 1943-............ CLC 34, 55
  See also BEST 89:2; CA 127; 131; MTCW

Diamano, Silmang
  See Senghor, Leopold Sedar

Diamond, Neil 1941- .... CLC 30
  See also CA 108

di Bassetto, Corno
  See Shaw, George Bernard

Dick, Philip K(indred)
  1928-1982 .... CLC 10, 30, 72
  See also CA 49-52; 106; CANR 2, 16;
    DLB 8; MTCW

Dickens, Charles (John Huffam)
  1812-1870 .... NCLC 3, 8, 18, 26
  See also CDBLB 1832-1890; DLB 21, 55,
    70; MAICYA; SATA 15

Dickey, James (Lafayette)
  1923- .... CLC 1, 2, 4, 7, 10, 15, 47
  See also AITN 1, 2; CA 9-12R; CABS 2;
    CANR 10; CDALB 1968-1988; DLB 5;
    DLBD 7; DLBY 82; MTCW

Dickey, William 1928-.......... CLC 3, 28
  See also CA 9-12R; CANR 24; DLB 5

Dickinson, Charles 1951-......... CLC 49
  See also CA 128

Dickinson, Emily (Elizabeth)
  1830-1886 .... NCLC 21; PC 1
  See also CDALB 1865-1917; DLB 1;
    SATA 29; WLC

Dickinson, Peter (Malcolm)
1927- .... **CLC 12, 35**
See also AAYA 9; CA 41-44R; CANR 31;
DLB 87; MAICYA; SATA 5, 62

Dickson, Carr
See Carr, John Dickson

Dickson, Carter
See Carr, John Dickson

Didion, Joan 1934-..... **CLC 1, 3, 8, 14, 32**
See also AITN 1; CA 5-8R; CANR 14;
CDALB 1968-1988; DLB 2; DLBY 81,
86; MTCW

Dietrich, Robert
See Hunt, E(verette) Howard Jr.

Dillard, Annie 1945-............ **CLC 9, 60**
See also AAYA 6; CA 49-52; CANR 3;
DLBY 80; MTCW; SATA 10

Dillard, R(ichard) H(enry) W(ilde)
1937- .... **CLC 5**
See also CA 21-24R; CAAS 7; CANR 10;
DLB 5

Dillon, Eilis 1920-............... **CLC 17**
See also CA 9-12R; CAAS 3; CANR 4, 38;
CLR 26; MAICYA; SATA 2

Dimont, Penelope
See Mortimer, Penelope (Ruth)

Dinesen, Isak.......... **CLC 10, 29; SSC 7**
See also Blixen, Karen (Christentze
Dinesen)

Ding Ling....................... **CLC 68**
See also Chiang Pin-chin

Disch, Thomas M(ichael) 1940-... **CLC 7, 36**
See also CA 21-24R; CAAS 4; CANR 17,
36; CLR 18; DLB 8; MAICYA; MTCW;
SAAS 15; SATA 54

Disch, Tom
See Disch, Thomas M(ichael)

d'Isly, Georges
See Simenon, Georges (Jacques Christian)

Disraeli, Benjamin 1804-1881 .. **NCLC 2, 39**
See also DLB 21, 55

Ditcum, Steve
See Crumb, R(obert)

Dixon, Paige
See Corcoran, Barbara

Dixon, Stephen 1936-............. **CLC 52**
See also CA 89-92; CANR 17

Doblin, Alfred .... **TCLC 13**
See also Doeblin, Alfred

Dobrolyubov, Nikolai Alexandrovich
1836-1861 .... **NCLC 5**

Dobyns, Stephen 1941-............ **CLC 37**
See also CA 45-48; CANR 2, 18

Doctorow, E(dgar) L(aurence)
1931- ..... **CLC 6, 11, 15, 18, 37, 44, 65**
See also AITN 2; BEST 89:3; CA 45-48;
CANR 2, 33; CDALB 1968-1988; DLB 2,
28; DLBY 80; MTCW

Dodgson, Charles Lutwidge 1832-1898
See Carroll, Lewis
See also CLR 2; MAICYA; YABC 2

Doeblin, Alfred 1878-1957....... **TCLC 13**
See also Doblin, Alfred
See also CA 110; DLB 66

Doerr, Harriet 1910- .... **CLC 34**
See also CA 117; 122

Domecq, H(onorio) Bustos
See Bioy Casares, Adolfo; Borges, Jorge
Luis

Domini, Rey
See Lorde, Audre (Geraldine)

Dominique
See Proust,
(Valentin-Louis-George-Eugene-)Marcel

Don, A
See Stephen, Leslie

Donaldson, Stephen R. 1947-....... **CLC 46**
See also CA 89-92; CANR 13

Donleavy, J(ames) P(atrick)
1926- .... **CLC 1, 4, 6, 10, 45**
See also AITN 2; CA 9-12R; CANR 24;
DLB 6; MTCW

Donne, John 1572-1631 .... **LC 10; PC 1**
See also CDBLB Before 1660; DLB 121;
WLC

Donnell, David 1939(?)-........... **CLC 34**

Donoso (Yanez), Jose
1924- .... **CLC 4, 8, 11, 32**
See also CA 81-84; CANR 32; DLB 113;
HW; MTCW

Donovan, John 1928-1992 .... **CLC 35**
See also CA 97-100; 137; CLR 3;
MAICYA; SATA 29

Don Roberto
See Cunninghame Graham, R(obert)
B(ontine)

Doolittle, Hilda
1886-1961 .... **CLC 3, 8, 14, 31, 34, 73;**
PC 5
See also H. D.
See also CA 97-100; CANR 35; DLB 4, 45;
MTCW; WLC

Dorfman, Ariel 1942-............. **CLC 48**
See also CA 124; 130; HW

Dorn, Edward (Merton) 1929-... **CLC 10, 18**
See also CA 93-96; DLB 5

Dorsan, Luc
See Simenon, Georges (Jacques Christian)

Dorsange, Jean
See Simenon, Georges (Jacques Christian)

Dos Passos, John (Roderigo)
1896-1970 ... **CLC 1, 4, 8, 11, 15, 25, 34**
See also CA 1-4R; 29-32R; CANR 3;
CDALB 1929-1941; DLB 4, 9; DLBD 1;
MTCW; WLC

Dossage, Jean
See Simenon, Georges (Jacques Christian)

Dostoevsky, Fedor Mikhailovich
1821-1881 .... **NCLC 2, 7, 21, 33; SSC 2**
See also WLC

Doughty, Charles M(ontagu)
1843-1926 .... **TCLC 27**
See also CA 115; DLB 19, 57

Douglas, Ellen
See Haxton, Josephine Ayres

Douglas, Gavin 1475(?)-1522........ **LC 20**

Douglas, Keith 1920-1944 .... **TCLC 40**
See also DLB 27

Douglas, Leonard
See Bradbury, Ray (Douglas)

Douglas, Michael
See Crichton, (John) Michael

Douglass, Frederick 1817(?)-1895 .. **NCLC 7**
See also BLC 1; CDALB 1640-1865;
DLB 1, 43, 50, 79; SATA 29; WLC

Dourado, (Waldomiro Freitas) Autran
1926- .... **CLC 23, 60**
See also CA 25-28R; CANR 34

Dourado, Waldomiro Autran
See Dourado, (Waldomiro Freitas) Autran

Dove, Rita (Frances) 1952- ... **CLC 50; PC 6**
See also BW; CA 109; CANR 27; DLB 120

Dowell, Coleman 1925-1985........ **CLC 60**
See also CA 25-28R; 117; CANR 10

Dowson, Ernest Christopher
1867-1900 .... **TCLC 4**
See also CA 105; DLB 19

Doyle, A. Conan
See Doyle, Arthur Conan

Doyle, Arthur Conan 1859-1930 .... **TCLC 7**
See also CA 104; 122; CDBLB 1890-1914;
DLB 18, 70; MTCW; SATA 24; WLC

Doyle, Conan
See Doyle, Arthur Conan

Doyle, John
See Graves, Robert (von Ranke)

Doyle, Sir A. Conan
See Doyle, Arthur Conan

Doyle, Sir Arthur Conan
See Doyle, Arthur Conan

Dr. A
See Asimov, Isaac; Silverstein, Alvin

Drabble, Margaret
1939- .... **CLC 2, 3, 5, 8, 10, 22, 53**
See also CA 13-16R; CANR 18, 35;
CDBLB 1960 to Present; DLB 14;
MTCW; SATA 48

Drapier, M. B.
See Swift, Jonathan

Drayham, James
See Mencken, H(enry) L(ouis)

Drayton, Michael 1563-1631........ **LC 8**

Dreadstone, Carl
See Campbell, (John) Ramsey

Dreiser, Theodore (Herman Albert)
1871-1945 .... **TCLC 10, 18, 35**
See also CA 106; 132; CDALB 1865-1917;
DLB 9, 12, 102; DLBD 1; MTCW; WLC

Drexler, Rosalyn 1926- .... **CLC 2, 6**
See also CA 81-84

Dreyer, Carl Theodor 1889-1968.... **CLC 16**
See also CA 116

Drieu la Rochelle, Pierre(-Eugene)
1893-1945 .... **TCLC 21**
See also CA 117; DLB 72

Drop Shot
See Cable, George Washington

Droste-Hulshoff, Annette Freiin von
1797-1848 .... **NCLC 3**

Drummond, Walter
See Silverberg, Robert

Edwards, Jonathan 1703-1758 . . . . **LC 7**
See also DLB 24

Efron, Marina Ivanovna Tsvetaeva
See Tsvetaeva (Efron), Marina (Ivanovna)

Ehle, John (Marsden Jr.) 1925- . . . . **CLC 27**
See also CA 9-12R

Ehrenbourg, Ilya (Grigoryevich)
See Ehrenburg, Ilya (Grigoryevich)

Ehrenburg, Ilya (Grigoryevich)
1891-1967 . . . . **CLC 18, 34, 62**
See also CA 102; 25-28R

Ehrenburg, Ilyo (Grigoryevich)
See Ehrenburg, Ilya (Grigoryevich)

Eich, Guenter 1907-1972 . . . . **CLC 15**
See also CA 111; 93-96; DLB 69

Eichendorff, Joseph Freiherr von
1788-1857 . . . . **NCLC 8**
See also DLB 90

Eigner, Larry . . . . **CLC 9**
See also Eigner, Laurence (Joel)
See also DLB 5

Eigner, Laurence (Joel) 1927-
See Eigner, Larry
See also CA 9-12R; CANR 6

Eiseley, Loren Corey 1907-1977 . . . . . **CLC 7**
See also AAYA 5; CA 1-4R; 73-76;
CANR 6

Eisenstadt, Jill 1963- . . . . **CLC 50**

Eisner, Simon
See Kornbluth, C(yril) M.

Ekeloef, (Bengt) Gunnar
1907-1968 . . . . **CLC 27**
See also Ekelof, (Bengt) Gunnar
See also CA 123; 25-28R

Ekelof, (Bengt) Gunnar . . . . **CLC 27**
See also Ekeloef, (Bengt) Gunnar

Ekwensi, C. O. D.
See Ekwensi, Cyprian (Odiatu Duaka)

Ekwensi, Cyprian (Odiatu Duaka)
1921- . . . . **CLC 4**
See also BLC 1; BW; CA 29-32R;
CANR 18; DLB 117; MTCW; SATA 66

Elaine . . . . **TCLC 18**
See also Leverson, Ada

El Crummo
See Crumb, R(obert)

Elia
See Lamb, Charles

Eliade, Mircea 1907-1986 . . . . **CLC 19**
See also CA 65-68; 119; CANR 30; MTCW

Eliot, A. D.
See Jewett, (Theodora) Sarah Orne

Eliot, Alice
See Jewett, (Theodora) Sarah Orne

Eliot, Dan
See Silverberg, Robert

Eliot, George 1819-1880 . . . . **NCLC 4, 13, 23**
See also CDBLB 1832-1890; DLB 21, 35,
55; WLC

Eliot, John 1604-1690 . . . . **LC 5**
See also DLB 24

Eliot, T(homas) S(tearns)
1888-1965 . . . . **CLC 1, 2, 3, 6, 9, 10, 13,
15, 24, 34, 41, 55, 57; PC 5**
See also CA 5-8R; 25-28R;
CDALB 1929-1941; DLB 7, 10, 45, 63;
DLBY 88; MTCW; WLC 2

Elizabeth 1866-1941 . . . . **TCLC 41**

Elkin, Stanley L(awrence)
1930- . . . . **CLC 4, 6, 9, 14, 27, 51**
See also CA 9-12R; CANR 8; DLB 2, 28;
DLBY 80; MTCW

Elledge, Scott . . . . **CLC 34**

Elliott, Don
See Silverberg, Robert

Elliott, George P(aul) 1918-1980 . . . . . **CLC 2**
See also CA 1-4R; 97-100; CANR 2

Elliott, Janice 1931- . . . . **CLC 47**
See also CA 13-16R; CANR 8, 29; DLB 14

Elliott, Sumner Locke 1917-1991 . . . **CLC 38**
See also CA 5-8R; 134; CANR 2, 21

Elliott, William
See Bradbury, Ray (Douglas)

Ellis, A. E. . . . . **CLC 7**

Ellis, Alice Thomas . . . . **CLC 40**
See also Haycraft, Anna

Ellis, Bret Easton 1964- . . . . **CLC 39, 71**
See also AAYA 2; CA 118; 123

Ellis, (Henry) Havelock
1859-1939 . . . . **TCLC 14**
See also CA 109

Ellis, Landon
See Ellison, Harlan

Ellis, Trey 1962- . . . . **CLC 55**

Ellison, Harlan 1934- . . . . **CLC 1, 13, 42**
See also CA 5-8R; CANR 5; DLB 8;
MTCW

Ellison, Ralph (Waldo)
1914- . . . . **CLC 1, 3, 11, 54**
See also BLC 1; BW; CA 9-12R; CANR 24;
CDALB 1941-1968; DLB 2, 76; MTCW;
WLC

Ellmann, Lucy (Elizabeth) 1956- . . . . **CLC 61**
See also CA 128

Ellmann, Richard (David)
1918-1987 . . . . **CLC 50**
See also BEST 89:2; CA 1-4R; 122;
CANR 2, 28; DLB 103; DLBY 87;
MTCW

Elman, Richard 1934- . . . . **CLC 19**
See also CA 17-20R; CAAS 3

Elron
See Hubbard, L(afayette) Ron(ald)

Eluard, Paul . . . . **TCLC 7, 41**
See also Grindel, Eugene

Elyot, Sir Thomas 1490(?)-1546 . . . . . **LC 11**

Elytis, Odysseus 1911- . . . . **CLC 15, 49**
See also CA 102; MTCW

Emecheta, (Florence Onye) Buchi
1944- . . . . **CLC 14, 48**
See also BLC 2; BW; CA 81-84; CANR 27;
DLB 117; MTCW; SATA 66

Emerson, Ralph Waldo
1803-1882 . . . . **NCLC 1, 38**
See also CDALB 1640-1865; DLB 1, 59, 73;
WLC

Eminescu, Mihail 1850-1889 . . . . . **NCLC 33**

Empson, William
1906-1984 . . . . **CLC 3, 8, 19, 33, 34**
See also CA 17-20R; 112; CANR 31;
DLB 20; MTCW

Enchi Fumiko (Ueda) 1905-1986 . . . . **CLC 31**
See also CA 129; 121

Ende, Michael (Andreas Helmuth)
1929- . . . . **CLC 31**
See also CA 118; 124; CANR 36; CLR 14;
DLB 75; MAICYA; SATA 42, 61

Endo, Shusaku 1923- . . . . . **CLC 7, 14, 19, 54**
See also CA 29-32R; CANR 21; MTCW

Engel, Marian 1933-1985 . . . . **CLC 36**
See also CA 25-28R; CANR 12; DLB 53

Engelhardt, Frederick
See Hubbard, L(afayette) Ron(ald)

Enright, D(ennis) J(oseph)
1920- . . . . **CLC 4, 8, 31**
See also CA 1-4R; CANR 1; DLB 27;
SATA 25

Enzensberger, Hans Magnus
1929- . . . . **CLC 43**
See also CA 116; 119

Ephron, Nora 1941- . . . . **CLC 17, 31**
See also AITN 2; CA 65-68; CANR 12, 39

Epsilon
See Betjeman, John

Epstein, Daniel Mark 1948- . . . . **CLC 7**
See also CA 49-52; CANR 2

Epstein, Jacob 1956- . . . . **CLC 19**
See also CA 114

Epstein, Joseph 1937- . . . . **CLC 39**
See also CA 112; 119

Epstein, Leslie 1938- . . . . **CLC 27**
See also CA 73-76; CAAS 12; CANR 23

Equiano, Olaudah 1745(?)-1797 . . . . . . **LC 16**
See also BLC 2; DLB 37, 50

Erasmus, Desiderius 1469(?)-1536 . . . . **LC 16**

Erdman, Paul E(mil) 1932- . . . . **CLC 25**
See also AITN 1; CA 61-64; CANR 13

Erdrich, Louise 1954- . . . . **CLC 39, 54**
See also BEST 89:1; CA 114; MTCW

Erenburg, Ilya (Grigoryevich)
See Ehrenburg, Ilya (Grigoryevich)

Erickson, Stephen Michael 1950-
See Erickson, Steve
See also CA 129

Erickson, Steve . . . . **CLC 64**
See also Erickson, Stephen Michael

Ericson, Walter
See Fast, Howard (Melvin)

Eriksson, Buntel
See Bergman, (Ernst) Ingmar

Eschenbach, Wolfram von
See Wolfram von Eschenbach

Eseki, Bruno
See Mphahlele, Ezekiel

Esenin, Sergei (Alexandrovich)
1895-1925 . . . . TCLC 4
See also CA 104

Eshleman, Clayton 1935- . . . . CLC 7
See also CA 33-36R; CAAS 6; DLB 5

Espriella, Don Manuel Alvarez
See Southey, Robert

Espriu, Salvador 1913-1985 . . . . CLC 9
See also CA 115

Espronceda, Jose de 1808-1842 . . . NCLC 39

Esse, James
See Stephens, James

Esterbrook, Tom
See Hubbard, L(afayette) Ron(ald)

Estleman, Loren D. 1952- . . . . CLC 48
See also CA 85-88; CANR 27; MTCW

Evans, Mary Ann
See Eliot, George

Evarts, Esther
See Benson, Sally

Everett, Percival
See Everett, Percival L.

Everett, Percival L. 1956- . . . . CLC 57
See also CA 129

Everson, R(onald) G(ilmour)
1903- . . . . CLC 27
See also CA 17-20R; DLB 88

Everson, William (Oliver)
1912- . . . . CLC 1, 5, 14
See also CA 9-12R; CANR 20; DLB 5, 16;
MTCW

Evtushenko, Evgenii Aleksandrovich
See Yevtushenko, Yevgeny (Alexandrovich)

Ewart, Gavin (Buchanan)
1916- . . . . CLC 13, 46
See also CA 89-92; CANR 17; DLB 40;
MTCW

Ewers, Hanns Heinz 1871-1943 . . . TCLC 12
See also CA 109

Ewing, Frederick R.
See Sturgeon, Theodore (Hamilton)

Exley, Frederick (Earl) 1929- . . . . CLC 6, 11
See also AITN 2; CA 81-84; 138; DLBY 81

Eynhardt, Guillermo
See Quiroga, Horacio (Sylvestre)

Ezekiel, Nissim 1924- . . . . CLC 61
See also CA 61-64

Ezekiel, Tish O'Dowd 1943- . . . . CLC 34
See also CA 129

Fagen, Donald 1948- . . . . CLC 26

Fainzilberg, Ilya Arnoldovich 1897-1937
See Ilf, Ilya
See also CA 120

Fair, Ronald L. 1932- . . . . CLC 18
See also BW; CA 69-72; CANR 25; DLB 33

Fairbairns, Zoe (Ann) 1948- . . . . CLC 32
See also CA 103; CANR 21

Falco, Gian
See Papini, Giovanni

Falconer, James
See Kirkup, James

Falconer, Kenneth
See Kornbluth, C(yril) M.

Falkland, Samuel
See Heijermans, Herman

Fallaci, Oriana 1930- . . . . CLC 11
See also CA 77-80; CANR 15; MTCW

Faludy, George 1913- . . . . CLC 42
See also CA 21-24R

Faludy, Gyoergy
See Faludy, George

Fanon, Frantz 1925-1961 . . . . CLC 74
See also BLC 2; BW; CA 116; 89-92

Fanshawe, Ann . . . . LC 11

Fante, John (Thomas) 1911-1983 . . . CLC 60
See also CA 69-72; 109; CANR 23;
DLBY 83

Farah, Nuruddin 1945- . . . . CLC 53
See also BLC 2; CA 106

Fargue, Leon-Paul 1876(?)-1947 . . . TCLC 11
See also CA 109

Farigoule, Louis
See Romains, Jules

Farina, Richard 1936(?)-1966 . . . . CLC 9
See also CA 81-84; 25-28R

Farley, Walter (Lorimer)
1915-1989 . . . . CLC 17
See also CA 17-20R; CANR 8, 29; DLB 22;
MAICYA; SATA 2, 43

Farmer, Philip Jose 1918- . . . . CLC 1, 19
See also CA 1-4R; CANR 4, 35; DLB 8;
MTCW

Farquhar, George 1677-1707 . . . . LC 21
See also DLB 84

Farrell, J(ames) G(ordon)
1935-1979 . . . . CLC 6
See also CA 73-76; 89-92; CANR 36;
DLB 14; MTCW

Farrell, James T(homas)
1904-1979 . . . . CLC 1, 4, 8, 11, 66
See also CA 5-8R; 89-92; CANR 9; DLB 4,
9, 86; DLBD 2; MTCW

Farren, Richard J.
See Betjeman, John

Farren, Richard M.
See Betjeman, John

Fassbinder, Rainer Werner
1946-1982 . . . . CLC 20
See also CA 93-96; 106; CANR 31

Fast, Howard (Melvin) 1914- . . . . . . CLC 23
See also CA 1-4R; CANR 1, 33; DLB 9;
SATA 7

Faulcon, Robert
See Holdstock, Robert P.

Faulkner, William (Cuthbert)
1897-1962 . . . . CLC 1, 3, 6, 8, 9, 11, 14,
18, 28, 52, 68; SSC 1
See also AAYA 7; CA 81-84; CANR 33;
CDALB 1929-1941; DLB 9, 11, 44, 102;
DLBD 2; DLBY 86; MTCW; WLC

Fauset, Jessie Redmon
1884(?)-1961 . . . . CLC 19, 54
See also BLC 2; BW; CA 109; DLB 51

Faust, Irvin 1924- . . . . CLC 8
See also CA 33-36R; CANR 28; DLB 2, 28;
DLBY 80

Fawkes, Guy
See Benchley, Robert (Charles)

Fearing, Kenneth (Flexner)
1902-1961 . . . . CLC 51
See also CA 93-96; DLB 9

Fecamps, Elise
See Creasey, John

Federman, Raymond 1928- . . . . . . CLC 6, 47
See also CA 17-20R; CAAS 8; CANR 10;
DLBY 80

Federspiel, J(uerg) F. 1931- . . . . CLC 42

Feiffer, Jules (Ralph) 1929- . . . . CLC 2, 8, 64
See also AAYA 3; CA 17-20R; CANR 30;
DLB 7, 44; MTCW; SATA 8, 61

Feige, Hermann Albert Otto Maximilian
See Traven, B.

Fei-Kan, Li
See Li Fei-kan

Feinberg, David B. 1956- . . . . CLC 59
See also CA 135

Feinstein, Elaine 1930- . . . . CLC 36
See also CA 69-72; CAAS 1; CANR 31;
DLB 14, 40; MTCW

Feldman, Irving (Mordecai) 1928- . . . . CLC 7
See also CA 1-4R; CANR 1

Fellini, Federico 1920- . . . . CLC 16
See also CA 65-68; CANR 33

Felsen, Henry Gregor 1916- . . . . CLC 17
See also CA 1-4R; CANR 1; SAAS 2;
SATA 1

Fenton, James Martin 1949- . . . . CLC 32
See also CA 102; DLB 40

Ferber, Edna 1887-1968 . . . . CLC 18
See also AITN 1; CA 5-8R; 25-28R; DLB 9,
28, 86; MTCW; SATA 7

Ferguson, Helen
See Kavan, Anna

Ferguson, Samuel 1810-1886 . . . . . NCLC 33
See also DLB 32

Ferling, Lawrence
See Ferlinghetti, Lawrence (Monsanto)

Ferlinghetti, Lawrence (Monsanto)
1919(?)- . . . . CLC 2, 6, 10, 27; PC 1
See also CA 5-8R; CANR 3;
CDALB 1941-1968; DLB 5, 16; MTCW

Fernandez, Vicente Garcia Huidobro
See Huidobro Fernandez, Vicente Garcia

Ferrer, Gabriel (Francisco Victor) Miro
See Miro (Ferrer), Gabriel (Francisco
Victor)

Ferrier, Susan (Edmonstone)
1782-1854 . . . . NCLC 8
See also DLB 116

Ferrigno, Robert . . . . CLC 65

Feuchtwanger, Lion 1884-1958 . . . . . TCLC 3
See also CA 104; DLB 66

Feydeau, Georges (Leon Jules Marie)
1862-1921 . . . . TCLC 22
See also CA 113

Ficino, Marsilio 1433-1499 . . . . LC 12

Fiedler, Leslie A(aron)
1917- . . . . CLC 4, 13, 24
See also CA 9-12R; CANR 7; DLB 28, 67;
MTCW

Field, Andrew 1938-.............. **CLC 44**
  See also CA 97-100; CANR 25

Field, Eugene 1850-1895 .... **NCLC 3**
  See also DLB 23, 42; MAICYA; SATA 16

Field, Gans T.
  See Wellman, Manly Wade

Field, Michael .... **TCLC 43**

Field, Peter
  See Hobson, Laura Z(ametkin)

Fielding, Henry 1707-1754 .... **LC 1**
  See also CDBLB 1660-1789; DLB 39, 84,
  101; WLC

Fielding, Sarah 1710-1768 .... **LC 1**
  See also DLB 39

Fierstein, Harvey (Forbes) 1954- ... **CLC 33**
  See also CA 123; 129

Figes, Eva 1932-................. **CLC 31**
  See also CA 53-56; CANR 4; DLB 14

Finch, Robert (Duer Claydon)
  1900- .... **CLC 18**
  See also CA 57-60; CANR 9, 24; DLB 88

Findley, Timothy 1930- .... **CLC 27**
  See also CA 25-28R; CANR 12; DLB 53

Fink, William
  See Mencken, H(enry) L(ouis)

Firbank, Louis 1942-
  See Reed, Lou
  See also CA 117

Firbank, (Arthur Annesley) Ronald
  1886-1926 .... **TCLC 1**
  See also CA 104; DLB 36

Fisher, Roy 1930-................. **CLC 25**
  See also CA 81-84; CAAS 10; CANR 16;
  DLB 40

Fisher, Rudolph 1897-1934 .... **TCLC 11**
  See also BLC 2; BW; CA 107; 124; DLB 51,
  102

Fisher, Vardis (Alvero) 1895-1968.... **CLC 7**
  See also CA 5-8R; 25-28R; DLB 9

Fiske, Tarleton
  See Bloch, Robert (Albert)

Fitch, Clarke
  See Sinclair, Upton (Beall)

Fitch, John IV
  See Cormier, Robert (Edmund)

Fitgerald, Penelope 1916- .... **CLC 61**

Fitzgerald, Captain Hugh
  See Baum, L(yman) Frank

FitzGerald, Edward 1809-1883 .... **NCLC 9**
  See also DLB 32

Fitzgerald, F(rancis) Scott (Key)
  1896-1940 .... **TCLC 1, 6, 14, 28; SSC 6**
  See also AITN 1; CA 110; 123;
  CDALB 1917-1929; DLB 4, 9, 86;
  DLBD 1; DLBY 81; MTCW; WLC

Fitzgerald, Penelope 1916-...... **CLC 19, 51**
  See also CA 85-88; CAAS 10; DLB 14

FitzGerald, Robert D(avid)
  1902-1987 .... **CLC 19**
  See also CA 17-20R

Fitzgerald, Robert (Stuart)
  1910-1985 .... **CLC 39**
  See also CA 1-4R; 114; CANR 1; DLBY 80

Flanagan, Thomas (James Bonner)
  1923- .... **CLC 25, 52**
  See also CA 108; DLBY 80; MTCW

Flaubert, Gustave
  1821-1880 ..... **NCLC 2, 10, 19; SSC 11**
  See also DLB 119; WLC

Flecker, (Herman) James Elroy
  1884-1915 .... **TCLC 43**
  See also CA 109; DLB 10, 19

Fleming, Ian (Lancaster)
  1908-1964 .... **CLC 3, 30**
  See also CA 5-8R; CDBLB 1945-1960;
  DLB 87; MTCW; SATA 9

Fleming, Thomas (James) 1927- .... **CLC 37**
  See also CA 5-8R; CANR 10; SATA 8

Fletcher, John Gould 1886-1950 ... **TCLC 35**
  See also CA 107; DLB 4, 45

Fleur, Paul
  See Pohl, Frederik

Flying Officer X
  See Bates, H(erbert) E(rnest)

Fo, Dario 1926-................. **CLC 32**
  See also CA 116; 128; MTCW

Fogarty, Jonathan Titulescu Esq.
  See Farrell, James T(homas)

Folke, Will
  See Bloch, Robert (Albert)

Follett, Ken(neth Martin) 1949- .... **CLC 18**
  See also AAYA 6; BEST 89:4; CA 81-84;
  CANR 13, 33; DLB 87; DLBY 81;
  MTCW

Fontane, Theodor 1819-1898 ..... **NCLC 26**

Foote, Horton 1916-.............. **CLC 51**
  See also CA 73-76; CANR 34; DLB 26

Foote, Shelby 1916-.............. **CLC 75**
  See also CA 5-8R; CANR 3; DLB 2, 17

Forbes, Esther 1891-1967......... **CLC 12**
  See also CA 13-14; 25-28R; CAP 1;
  CLR 27; DLB 22; MAICYA; SATA 2

Forche, Carolyn (Louise) 1950-..... **CLC 25**
  See also CA 109; 117; DLB 5

Ford, Elbur
  See Hibbert, Eleanor Burford

Ford, Ford Madox
  1873-1939 .... **TCLC 1, 15, 39**
  See also CA 104; 132; CDBLB 1914-1945;
  DLB 34, 98; MTCW

Ford, John 1895-1973............. **CLC 16**
  See also CA 45-48

Ford, Richard 1944-.............. **CLC 46**
  See also CA 69-72; CANR 11

Ford, Webster
  See Masters, Edgar Lee

Foreman, Richard 1937-.......... **CLC 50**
  See also CA 65-68; CANR 32

Forester, C(ecil) S(cott)
  1899-1966 .... **CLC 35**
  See also CA 73-76; 25-28R; SATA 13

Forez
  See Mauriac, Francois (Charles)

Forman, James Douglas 1932-...... **CLC 21**
  See also CA 9-12R; CANR 4, 19;
  MAICYA; SATA 8, 70

Fornes, Maria Irene 1930-...... **CLC 39, 61**
  See also CA 25-28R; CANR 28; DLB 7;
  HW; MTCW

Forrest, Leon 1937-.............. **CLC 4**
  See also BW; CA 89-92; CAAS 7;
  CANR 25; DLB 33

Forster, E(dward) M(organ)
  1879-1970 .... **CLC 1, 2, 3, 4, 9, 10, 13,
                    15, 22, 45**
  See also AAYA 2; CA 13-14; 25-28R;
  CAP 1; CDBLB 1914-1945; DLB 34, 98;
  DLBD 10; MTCW; SATA 57; WLC

Forster, John 1812-1876 .... **NCLC 11**

Forsyth, Frederick 1938-...... **CLC 2, 5, 36**
  See also BEST 89:4; CA 85-88; CANR 38;
  DLB 87; MTCW

Forten, Charlotte L. .... **TCLC 16**
  See also Grimke, Charlotte L(ottie) Forten
  See also BLC 2; DLB 50

Foscolo, Ugo 1778-1827.......... **NCLC 8**

Fosse, Bob .... **CLC 20**
  See also Fosse, Robert Louis

Fosse, Robert Louis 1927-1987
  See Fosse, Bob
  See also CA 110; 123

Foster, Stephen Collins
  1826-1864 .... **NCLC 26**

Foucault, Michel
  1926-1984 .... **CLC 31, 34, 69**
  See also CA 105; 113; CANR 34; MTCW

Fouque, Friedrich (Heinrich Karl) de la Motte
  1777-1843 .... **NCLC 2**
  See also DLB 90

Fournier, Henri Alban 1886-1914
  See Alain-Fournier
  See also CA 104

Fournier, Pierre 1916-............ **CLC 11**
  See also Gascar, Pierre
  See also CA 89-92; CANR 16

Fowles, John
  1926- .... **CLC 1, 2, 3, 4, 6, 9, 10, 15, 33**
  See also CA 5-8R; CANR 25; CDBLB 1960
  to Present; DLB 14; MTCW; SATA 22

Fox, Paula 1923-................. **CLC 2, 8**
  See also AAYA 3; CA 73-76; CANR 20,
  36; CLR 1; DLB 52; MAICYA; MTCW;
  SATA 17, 60

Fox, William Price (Jr.) 1926- ..... **CLC 22**
  See also CA 17-20R; CANR 11; DLB 2;
  DLBY 81

Foxe, John 1516(?)-1587 .... **LC 14**

Frame, Janet .... **CLC 2, 3, 6, 22, 66**
  See also Clutha, Janet Paterson Frame

France, Anatole .... **TCLC 9**
  See also Thibault, Jacques Anatole Francois
  See also DLB 123

Francis, Claude 19(?)- .... **CLC 50**

Francis, Dick 1920- .... **CLC 2, 22, 42**
  See also AAYA 5; BEST 89:3; CA 5-8R;
  CANR 9; CDBLB 1960 to Present;
  DLB 87; MTCW

Francis, Robert (Churchill)
  1901-1987 .... **CLC 15**
  See also CA 1-4R; 123; CANR 1

Gard, Roger Martin du
See Martin du Gard, Roger

Gardam, Jane 1928-............. **CLC 43**
See also CA 49-52; CANR 2, 18, 33;
CLR 12; DLB 14; MAICYA; MTCW;
SAAS 9; SATA 28, 39

Gardner, Herb................... **CLC 44**

Gardner, John (Champlin) Jr.
1933-1982 .... **CLC 2, 3, 5, 7, 8, 10, 18, 28, 34; SSC 7**
See also AITN 1; CA 65-68; 107;
CANR 33; DLB 2; DLBY 82; MTCW;
SATA 31, 40

Gardner, John (Edmund) 1926-..... **CLC 30**
See also CA 103; CANR 15; MTCW

Gardner, Noel
See Kuttner, Henry

Gardons, S. S.
See Snodgrass, William D(e Witt)

Garfield, Leon 1921-.............. **CLC 12**
See also AAYA 8; CA 17-20R; CANR 38;
CLR 21; MAICYA; SATA 1, 32

Garland, (Hannibal) Hamlin
1860-1940 .... **TCLC 3**
See also CA 104; DLB 12, 71, 78

Garneau, (Hector de) Saint-Denys
1912-1943 .... **TCLC 13**
See also CA 111; DLB 88

Garner, Alan 1934-.............. **CLC 17**
See also CA 73-76; CANR 15; CLR 20;
MAICYA; MTCW; SATA 18, 69

Garner, Hugh 1913-1979 .... **CLC 13**
See also CA 69-72; CANR 31; DLB 68

Garnett, David 1892-1981 .... **CLC 3**
See also CA 5-8R; 103; CANR 17; DLB 34

Garos, Stephanie
See Katz, Steve

Garrett, George (Palmer)
1929- .... **CLC 3, 11, 51**
See also CA 1-4R; CAAS 5; CANR 1;
DLB 2, 5; DLBY 83

Garrick, David 1717-1779 .... **LC 15**
See also DLB 84

Garrigue, Jean 1914-1972 .... **CLC 2, 8**
See also CA 5-8R; 37-40R; CANR 20

Garrison, Frederick
See Sinclair, Upton (Beall)

Garth, Will
See Hamilton, Edmond; Kuttner, Henry

Garvey, Marcus (Moziah Jr.)
1887-1940 .... **TCLC 41**
See also BLC 2; BW; CA 120; 124

Gary, Romain .... **CLC 25**
See also Kacew, Romain
See also DLB 83

Gascar, Pierre .... **CLC 11**
See also Fournier, Pierre

Gascoyne, David (Emery) 1916-.... **CLC 45**
See also CA 65-68; CANR 10, 28; DLB 20;
MTCW

Gaskell, Elizabeth Cleghorn
1810-1865 .... **NCLC 5**
See also CDBLB 1832-1890; DLB 21

Gass, William H(oward)
1924- .... **CLC 1, 2, 8, 11, 15, 39**
See also CA 17-20R; CANR 30; DLB 2;
MTCW

Gasset, Jose Ortega y
See Ortega y Gasset, Jose

Gautier, Theophile 1811-1872 ..... **NCLC 1**
See also DLB 119

Gawsworth, John
See Bates, H(erbert) E(rnest)

Gaye, Marvin (Penze) 1939-1984 ... **CLC 26**
See also CA 112

Gebler, Carlo (Ernest) 1954-....... **CLC 39**
See also CA 119; 133

Gee, Maggie (Mary) 1948-......... **CLC 57**
See also CA 130

Gee, Maurice (Gough) 1931-....... **CLC 29**
See also CA 97-100; SATA 46

Gelbart, Larry (Simon) 1923- ... **CLC 21, 61**
See also CA 73-76

Gelber, Jack 1932-........... **CLC 1, 6, 14**
See also CA 1-4R; CANR 2; DLB 7

Gellhorn, Martha Ellis 1908- ... **CLC 14, 60**
See also CA 77-80; DLBY 82

Genet, Jean
1910-1986 ... **CLC 1, 2, 5, 10, 14, 44, 46**
See also CA 13-16R; CANR 18; DLB 72;
DLBY 86; MTCW

Gent, Peter 1942-................ **CLC 29**
See also AITN 1; CA 89-92; DLBY 82

George, Jean Craighead 1919-...... **CLC 35**
See also AAYA 8; CA 5-8R; CANR 25;
CLR 1; DLB 52; MAICYA; SATA 2, 68

George, Stefan (Anton)
1868-1933 .... **TCLC 2, 14**
See also CA 104

Georges, Georges Martin
See Simenon, Georges (Jacques Christian)

Gerhardi, William Alexander
See Gerhardie, William Alexander

Gerhardie, William Alexander
1895-1977 .... **CLC 5**
See also CA 25-28R; 73-76; CANR 18;
DLB 36

Gerstler, Amy 1956-.............. **CLC 70**

Gertler, T. .... **CLC 34**
See also CA 116; 121

Ghalib 1797-1869 .... **NCLC 39**

Ghelderode, Michel de
1898-1962 .... **CLC 6, 11**
See also CA 85-88

Ghiselin, Brewster 1903-.......... **CLC 23**
See also CA 13-16R; CAAS 10; CANR 13

Ghose, Zulfikar 1935-............. **CLC 42**
See also CA 65-68

Ghosh, Amitav 1956- .... **CLC 44**

Giacosa, Giuseppe 1847-1906 ...... **TCLC 7**
See also CA 104

Gibb, Lee
See Waterhouse, Keith (Spencer)

Gibbon, Lewis Grassic .... **TCLC 4**
See also Mitchell, James Leslie

Gibbons, Kaye 1960- .... **CLC 50**

Gibran, Kahlil 1883-1931........ **TCLC 1, 9**
See also CA 104

Gibson, William (Ford) 1948-... **CLC 39, 63**
See also CA 126; 133

Gibson, William 1914-............ **CLC 23**
See also CA 9-12R; CANR 9; DLB 7;
SATA 66

Gide, Andre (Paul Guillaume)
1869-1951 .... **TCLC 5, 12, 36**
See also CA 104; 124; DLB 65; MTCW;
WLC

Gifford, Barry (Colby) 1946-....... **CLC 34**
See also CA 65-68; CANR 9, 30

Gilbert, W(illiam) S(chwenck)
1836-1911 .... **TCLC 3**
See also CA 104; SATA 36

Gilbreth, Frank B. Jr. 1911-....... **CLC 17**
See also CA 9-12R; SATA 2

Gilchrist, Ellen 1935-.......... **CLC 34, 48**
See also CA 113; 116; MTCW

Giles, Molly 1942-.............. **CLC 39**
See also CA 126

Gill, Patrick
See Creasey, John

Gilliam, Terry (Vance) 1940-....... **CLC 21**
See also Monty Python
See also CA 108; 113; CANR 35

Gillian, Jerry
See Gilliam, Terry (Vance)

Gilliatt, Penelope (Ann Douglass)
1932- ....CLC **2, 10, 13, 53**
See also AITN 2; CA 13-16R; DLB 14

Gilman, Charlotte (Anna) Perkins (Stetson)
1860-1935 .... **TCLC 9, 37**
See also CA 106

Gilmour, David 1944-............. **CLC 35**
See also Pink Floyd
See also CA 138

Gilpin, William 1724-1804....... **NCLC 30**

Gilray, J. D.
See Mencken, H(enry) L(ouis)

Gilroy, Frank D(aniel) 1925-....... **CLC 2**
See also CA 81-84; CANR 32; DLB 7

Ginsberg, Allen
1926- ..... **CLC 1, 2, 3, 4, 6, 13, 36, 69;**
PC 4
See also AITN 1; CA 1-4R; CANR 2;
CDALB 1941-1968; DLB 5, 16; MTCW;
WLC 3

Ginzburg, Natalia
1916-1991 .... **CLC 5, 11, 54, 70**
See also CA 85-88; 135; CANR 33; MTCW

Giono, Jean 1895-1970......... **CLC 4, 11**
See also CA 45-48; 29-32R; CANR 2, 35;
DLB 72; MTCW

Giovanni, Nikki 1943- ..... **CLC 2, 4, 19, 64**
See also AITN 1; BLC 2; BW; CA 29-32R;
CAAS 6; CANR 18; CLR 6; DLB 5, 41;
MAICYA; MTCW; SATA 24

Giovene, Andrea 1904-............ **CLC 7**
See also CA 85-88

Gippius, Zinaida (Nikolayevna) 1869-1945
See Hippius, Zinaida
See also CA 106

Graham, Tom
See Lewis, (Harry) Sinclair

Graham, W(illiam) S(ydney)
1918-1986 . . . . CLC 29
See also CA 73-76; 118; DLB 20

Graham, Winston (Mawdsley)
1910- . . . . CLC 23
See also CA 49-52; CANR 2, 22; DLB 77

Granville-Barker, Harley
1877-1946 . . . . TCLC 2
See also Barker, Harley Granville
See also CA 104

Grass, Guenter (Wilhelm)
1927- . . CLC **1, 2, 4, 6, 11, 15, 22, 32, 49**
See also CA 13-16R; CANR 20; DLB 75;
MTCW; WLC

Gratton, Thomas
See Hulme, T(homas) E(rnest)

Grau, Shirley Ann 1929- . . . . CLC **4, 9**
See also CA 89-92; CANR 22; DLB 2;
MTCW

Gravel, Fern
See Hall, James Norman

Graver, Elizabeth 1964- . . . . CLC 70
See also CA 135

Graves, Richard Perceval 1945- . . . . CLC 44
See also CA 65-68; CANR 9, 26

Graves, Robert (von Ranke)
1895-1985 . . . . . CLC **1, 2, 6, 11, 39, 44,
45; PC 6**
See also CA 5-8R; 117; CANR 5, 36;
CDBLB 1914-1945; DLB 20, 100;
DLBY 85; MTCW; SATA 45

Gray, Alasdair (James) 1934- . . . . . . CLC 41
See also CA 126; MTCW

Gray, Amlin 1946- . . . . CLC 29
See also CA 138

Gray, Francine du Plessix 1930- . . . . CLC 22
See also BEST 90:3; CA 61-64; CAAS 2;
CANR 11, 33; MTCW

Gray, John (Henry) 1866-1934 . . . . TCLC 19
See also CA 119

Gray, Simon (James Holliday)
1936- . . . . CLC **9, 14, 36**
See also AITN 1; CA 21-24R; CAAS 3;
CANR 32; DLB 13; MTCW

Gray, Spalding 1941- . . . . CLC 49
See also CA 128

Gray, Thomas 1716-1771 . . . . LC 4; PC 2
See also CDBLB 1660-1789; DLB 109;
WLC

Grayson, David
See Baker, Ray Stannard

Grayson, Richard (A.) 1951- . . . . CLC 38
See also CA 85-88; CANR 14, 31

Greeley, Andrew M(oran) 1928- . . . . CLC 28
See also CA 5-8R; CAAS 7; CANR 7;
MTCW

Green, Brian
See Card, Orson Scott

Green, Hannah . . . . CLC 3
See also CA 73-76

Green, Hannah
See Greenberg, Joanne (Goldenberg)

Green, Henry . . . . CLC **2, 13**
See also Yorke, Henry Vincent
See also DLB 15

Green, Julian (Hartridge)
1900- . . . . CLC **3, 11**
See also CA 21-24R; CANR 33; DLB 4, 72;
MTCW

Green, Julien 1900-
See Green, Julian (Hartridge)

Green, Paul (Eliot) 1894-1981 . . . . . . CLC 25
See also AITN 1; CA 5-8R; 103; CANR 3;
DLB 7, 9; DLBY 81

Greenberg, Ivan 1908-1973
See Rahv, Philip
See also CA 85-88

Greenberg, Joanne (Goldenberg)
1932- . . . . CLC **7, 30**
See also CA 5-8R; CANR 14, 32; SATA 25

Greenberg, Richard 1959(?)- . . . . CLC 57
See also CA 138

Greene, Bette 1934- . . . . CLC 30
See also AAYA 7; CA 53-56; CANR 4;
CLR 2; MAICYA; SATA 8

Greene, Gael . . . . CLC 8
See also CA 13-16R; CANR 10

Greene, Graham (Henry)
1904-1991 . . . CLC **1, 3, 6, 9, 14, 18, 27,
37, 70, 72**
See also AITN 2; CA 13-16R; 133;
CANR 35; CDBLB 1945-1960; DLB 13,
15, 77, 100; DLBY 91; MTCW;
SATA 20; WLC

Greer, Richard
See Silverberg, Robert

Greer, Richard
See Silverberg, Robert

Gregor, Arthur 1923- . . . . CLC 9
See also CA 25-28R; CAAS 10; CANR 11;
SATA 36

Gregor, Lee
See Pohl, Frederik

Gregory, Isabella Augusta (Persse)
1852-1932 . . . . TCLC 1
See also CA 104; DLB 10

Gregory, J. Dennis
See Williams, John A(lfred)

Grendon, Stephen
See Derleth, August (William)

Grenville, Kate 1950- . . . . CLC 61
See also CA 118

Grenville, Pelham
See Wodehouse, P(elham) G(renville)

Greve, Felix Paul (Berthold Friedrich)
1879-1948
See Grove, Frederick Philip
See also CA 104

Grey, Zane 1872-1939 . . . . TCLC 6
See also CA 104; 132; DLB 9; MTCW

Grieg, (Johan) Nordahl (Brun)
1902-1943 . . . . TCLC 10
See also CA 107

Grieve, C(hristopher) M(urray)
1892-1978 . . . . CLC **11, 19**
See also MacDiarmid, Hugh
See also CA 5-8R; 85-88; CANR 33;
MTCW

Griffin, Gerald 1803-1840 . . . . NCLC 7

Griffin, John Howard 1920-1980 . . . . CLC 68
See also AITN 1; CA 1-4R; 101; CANR 2

Griffin, Peter . . . . CLC 39

Griffiths, Trevor 1935- . . . . CLC **13, 52**
See also CA 97-100; DLB 13

Grigson, Geoffrey (Edward Harvey)
1905-1985 . . . . CLC **7, 39**
See also CA 25-28R; 118; CANR 20, 33;
DLB 27; MTCW

Grillparzer, Franz 1791-1872 . . . . . . NCLC 1

Grimble, Reverend Charles James
See Eliot, T(homas) S(tearns)

Grimke, Charlotte L(ottie) Forten
1837(?)-1914
See Forten, Charlotte L.
See also BW; CA 117; 124

Grimm, Jacob Ludwig Karl
1785-1863 . . . . NCLC 3
See also DLB 90; MAICYA; SATA 22

Grimm, Wilhelm Karl 1786-1859 . . NCLC 3
See also DLB 90; MAICYA; SATA 22

**Grimmelshausen, Johann Jakob Christoffel
von** 1621-1676 . . . . LC 6

Grindel, Eugene 1895-1952
See Eluard, Paul
See also CA 104

Grossman, David . . . . CLC 67
See also CA 138

Grossman, Vasily (Semenovich)
1905-1964 . . . . CLC 41
See also CA 124; 130; MTCW

Grove, Frederick Philip . . . . TCLC 4
See also Greve, Felix Paul (Berthold
Friedrich)
See also DLB 92

Grubb
See Crumb, R(obert)

Grumbach, Doris (Isaac)
1918- . . . . CLC **13, 22, 64**
See also CA 5-8R; CAAS 2; CANR 9

Grundtvig, Nicolai Frederik Severin
1783-1872 . . . . NCLC 1

Grunge
See Crumb, R(obert)

Grunwald, Lisa 1959- . . . . CLC 44
See also CA 120

Guare, John 1938- . . . . CLC **8, 14, 29, 67**
See also CA 73-76; CANR 21; DLB 7;
MTCW

Gudjonsson, Halldor Kiljan 1902-
See Laxness, Halldor
See also CA 103

Guenter, Erich
See Eich, Guenter

Guest, Barbara 1920- . . . . CLC 34
See also CA 25-28R; CANR 11; DLB 5

Hargrave, Leonie
See Disch, Thomas M(ichael)

Harlan, Louis R(udolph) 1922- ..... **CLC 34**
See also CA 21-24R; CANR 25

Harling, Robert 1951(?)- .... **CLC 53**

Harmon, William (Ruth) 1938- ..... **CLC 38**
See also CA 33-36R; CANR 14, 32, 35;
SATA 65

Harper, F. E. W.
See Harper, Frances Ellen Watkins

Harper, Frances E. W.
See Harper, Frances Ellen Watkins

Harper, Frances E. Watkins
See Harper, Frances Ellen Watkins

Harper, Frances Ellen
See Harper, Frances Ellen Watkins

Harper, Frances Ellen Watkins
1825-1911 .... **TCLC 14**
See also BLC 2; BW; CA 111; 125; DLB 50

Harper, Michael S(teven) 1938- .. **CLC 7, 22**
See also BW; CA 33-36R; CANR 24;
DLB 41

Harper, Mrs. F. E. W.
See Harper, Frances Ellen Watkins

Harris, Christie (Lucy) Irwin
1907- .... **CLC 12**
See also CA 5-8R; CANR 6; DLB 88;
MAICYA; SAAS 10; SATA 6

Harris, Frank 1856(?)-1931 ...... **TCLC 24**
See also CA 109

Harris, George Washington
1814-1869 .... **NCLC 23**
See also DLB 3, 11

Harris, Joel Chandler 1848-1908 ... **TCLC 2**
See also CA 104; 137; DLB 11, 23, 42, 78,
91; MAICYA; YABC 1

Harris, John (Wyndham Parkes Lucas)
Beynon 1903-1969 .... **CLC 19**
See also CA 102; 89-92

Harris, MacDonald
See Heiney, Donald (William)

Harris, Mark 1922- .... **CLC 19**
See also CA 5-8R; CAAS 3; CANR 2;
DLB 2; DLBY 80

Harris, (Theodore) Wilson 1921- .... **CLC 25**
See also BW; CA 65-68; CAAS 16;
CANR 11, 27; DLB 117; MTCW

Harrison, Elizabeth Cavanna 1909-
See Cavanna, Betty
See also CA 9-12R; CANR 6, 27

Harrison, Harry (Max) 1925- ...... **CLC 42**
See also CA 1-4R; CANR 5, 21; DLB 8;
SATA 4

Harrison, James (Thomas) 1937-
See Harrison, Jim
See also CA 13-16R; CANR 8

Harrison, Jim .... **CLC 6, 14, 33, 66**
See also Harrison, James (Thomas)
See also DLBY 82

Harrison, Kathryn 1961- .... **CLC 70**

Harrison, Tony 1937- .... **CLC 43**
See also CA 65-68; DLB 40; MTCW

Harriss, Will(ard Irvin) 1922- ...... **CLC 34**
See also CA 111

Harson, Sley
See Ellison, Harlan

Hart, Ellis
See Ellison, Harlan

Hart, Josephine 1942(?)- .... **CLC 70**
See also CA 138

Hart, Moss 1904-1961 .... **CLC 66**
See also CA 109; 89-92; DLB 7

Harte, (Francis) Bret(t)
1836(?)-1902 .... **TCLC 1, 25; SSC 8**
See also CA 104; CDALB 1865-1917;
DLB 12, 64, 74, 79; SATA 26; WLC

Hartley, L(eslie) P(oles)
1895-1972 .... **CLC 2, 22**
See also CA 45-48; 37-40R; CANR 33;
DLB 15; MTCW

Hartman, Geoffrey H. 1929- .... **CLC 27**
See also CA 117; 125; DLB 67

Haruf, Kent 19(?)- .... **CLC 34**

Harwood, Ronald 1934- .... **CLC 32**
See also CA 1-4R; CANR 4; DLB 13

Hasek, Jaroslav (Matej Frantisek)
1883-1923 .... **TCLC 4**
See also CA 104; 129; MTCW

Hass, Robert 1941- .... **CLC 18, 39**
See also CA 111; CANR 30; DLB 105

Hastings, Hudson
See Kuttner, Henry

Hastings, Selina .... **CLC 44**

Hatteras, Amelia
See Mencken, H(enry) L(ouis)

Hatteras, Owen
See Mencken, H(enry) L(ouis)

Hatteras, Owen .... **TCLC 18**
See also Nathan, George Jean

Hauptmann, Gerhart (Johann Robert)
1862-1946 .... **TCLC 4**
See also CA 104; DLB 66, 118

Havel, Vaclav 1936- .... **CLC 25, 58, 65**
See also CA 104; CANR 36; MTCW

Haviaras, Stratis .... **CLC 33**
See also Chaviaras, Strates

Hawes, Stephen 1475(?)-1523(?) ..... **LC 17**

Hawkes, John (Clendennin Burne Jr.)
1925- ...... **CLC 1, 2, 3, 4, 7, 9, 14, 15,**
27, 49
See also CA 1-4R; CANR 2; DLB 2, 7;
DLBY 80; MTCW

Hawking, S. W.
See Hawking, Stephen W(illiam)

Hawking, Stephen W(illiam)
1942- .... **CLC 63**
See also BEST 89:1; CA 126; 129

Hawthorne, Julian 1846-1934 ..... **TCLC 25**

Hawthorne, Nathaniel
1804-1864 .... **NCLC 39; SSC 3**
See also CDALB 1640-1865; DLB 1, 74;
WLC; YABC 2

Haxton, Josephine Ayres 1921- .... **CLC 73**
See also CA 115

Hayaseca y Eizaguirre, Jorge
See Echegaray (y Eizaguirre), Jose (Maria
Waldo)

Hayashi Fumiko 1904-1951 ...... **TCLC 27**

Haycraft, Anna
See Ellis, Alice Thomas
See also CA 122

Hayden, Robert E(arl)
1913-1980 ...... **CLC 5, 9, 14, 37; PC 6**
See also BLC 2; BW; CA 69-72; 97-100;
CABS 2; CANR 24; CDALB 1941-1968;
DLB 5, 76; MTCW; SATA 19, 26

Hayford, J(oseph) E(phraim) Casely
See Casely-Hayford, J(oseph) E(phraim)

Hayman, Ronald 1932- .... **CLC 44**
See also CA 25-28R; CANR 18

Haywood, Eliza (Fowler)
1693(?)-1756 .... **LC 1**

Hazlitt, William 1778-1830 ...... **NCLC 29**
See also DLB 110

Hazzard, Shirley 1931- .... **CLC 18**
See also CA 9-12R; CANR 4; DLBY 82;
MTCW

Head, Bessie 1937-1986 .... **CLC 25, 67**
See also BLC 2; BW; CA 29-32R; 119;
CANR 25; DLB 117; MTCW

Headon, (Nicky) Topper 1956(?)- ... **CLC 30**
See also The Clash

Heaney, Seamus (Justin)
1939- .... **CLC 5, 7, 14, 25, 37, 74**
See also CA 85-88; CANR 25;
CDBLB 1960 to Present; DLB 40;
MTCW

Hearn, (Patricio) Lafcadio (Tessima Carlos)
1850-1904 .... **TCLC 9**
See also CA 105; DLB 12, 78

Hearne, Vicki 1946- .... **CLC 56**

Hearon, Shelby 1931- .... **CLC 63**
See also AITN 2; CA 25-28R; CANR 18

Heat-Moon, William Least .... **CLC 29**
See also Trogdon, William (Lewis)
See also AAYA 9

Hebert, Anne 1916- .... **CLC 4, 13, 29**
See also CA 85-88; DLB 68; MTCW

Hecht, Anthony (Evan)
1923- .... **CLC 8, 13, 19**
See also CA 9-12R; CANR 6; DLB 5

Hecht, Ben 1894-1964 .... **CLC 8**
See also CA 85-88; DLB 7, 9, 25, 26, 28, 86

Hedayat, Sadeq 1903-1951 .... **TCLC 21**
See also CA 120

Heidegger, Martin 1889-1976 ...... **CLC 24**
See also CA 81-84; 65-68; CANR 34;
MTCW

Heidenstam, (Carl Gustaf) Verner von
1859-1940 .... **TCLC 5**
See also CA 104

Heifner, Jack 1946- .... **CLC 11**
See also CA 105

Heijermans, Herman 1864-1924 ... **TCLC 24**
See also CA 123

Heilbrun, Carolyn G(old) 1926- ..... **CLC 25**
See also CA 45-48; CANR 1, 28

Heine, Heinrich 1797-1856 .... **NCLC 4**
See also DLB 90

Heinemann, Larry (Curtiss) 1944- .. **CLC 50**
See also CA 110; CANR 31; DLBD 9

449

Hirsch, Edward 1950- .... **CLC 31, 50**
See also CA 104; CANR 20; DLB 120

Hitchcock, Alfred (Joseph)
1899-1980 .... **CLC 16**
See also CA 97-100; SATA 24, 27

Hoagland, Edward 1932- .... **CLC 28**
See also CA 1-4R; CANR 2, 31; DLB 6;
SATA 51

Hoban, Russell (Conwell) 1925- .. **CLC 7, 25**
See also CA 5-8R; CANR 23, 37; CLR 3;
DLB 52; MAICYA; MTCW; SATA 1, 40

Hobbs, Perry
See Blackmur, R(ichard) P(almer)

Hobson, Laura Z(ametkin)
1900-1986 .... **CLC 7, 25**
See also CA 17-20R; 118; DLB 28;
SATA 52

Hochhuth, Rolf 1931- .... **CLC 4, 11, 18**
See also CA 5-8R; CANR 33; MTCW

Hochman, Sandra 1936- .... **CLC 3, 8**
See also CA 5-8R; DLB 5

Hochwaelder, Fritz 1911-1986 ...... **CLC 36**
See also Hochwalder, Fritz
See also CA 29-32R; 120; MTCW

Hochwalder, Fritz .... **CLC 36**
See also Hochwaelder, Fritz

Hocking, Mary (Eunice) 1921- ..... **CLC 13**
See also CA 101; CANR 18

Hodgins, Jack 1938- .... **CLC 23**
See also CA 93-96; DLB 60

Hodgson, William Hope
1877(?)-1918 .... **TCLC 13**
See also CA 111; DLB 70

Hoffman, Alice 1952- .... **CLC 51**
See also CA 77-80; CANR 34; MTCW

Hoffman, Daniel (Gerard)
1923- .... **CLC 6, 13, 23**
See also CA 1-4R; CANR 4; DLB 5

Hoffman, Stanley 1944- .... **CLC 5**
See also CA 77-80

Hoffman, William M(oses) 1939- ... **CLC 40**
See also CA 57-60; CANR 11

Hoffmann, E(rnst) T(heodor) A(madeus)
1776-1822 .... **NCLC 2**
See also DLB 90; SATA 27

Hofmann, Gert 1931- .... **CLC 54**
See also CA 128

Hofmannsthal, Hugo von
1874-1929 .... **TCLC 11**
See also CA 106; DLB 81, 118

Hogan, Linda 1947- .... **CLC 73**
See also CA 120

Hogarth, Charles
See Creasey, John

Hogg, James 1770-1835 .... **NCLC 4**
See also DLB 93, 116

Holbach, Paul Henri Thiry Baron
1723-1789 .... **LC 14**

Holberg, Ludvig 1684-1754 .... **LC 6**

Holden, Ursula 1921- .... **CLC 18**
See also CA 101; CAAS 8; CANR 22

Holderlin, (Johann Christian) Friedrich
1770-1843 .... **NCLC 16; PC 4**

Holdstock, Robert
See Holdstock, Robert P.

Holdstock, Robert P. 1948- .... **CLC 39**
See also CA 131

Holland, Isabelle 1920- .... **CLC 21**
See also CA 21-24R; CANR 10, 25;
MAICYA; SATA 8, 70

Holland, Marcus
See Caldwell, (Janet Miriam) Taylor
(Holland)

Hollander, John 1929- ...... **CLC 2, 5, 8, 14**
See also CA 1-4R; CANR 1; DLB 5;
SATA 13

Hollander, Paul
See Silverberg, Robert

Holleran, Andrew 1943(?)- .... **CLC 38**

Hollinghurst, Alan 1954- .... **CLC 55**
See also CA 114

Hollis, Jim
See Summers, Hollis (Spurgeon Jr.)

Holmes, John
See Souster, (Holmes) Raymond

Holmes, John Clellon 1926-1988 .... **CLC 56**
See also CA 9-12R; 125; CANR 4; DLB 16

Holmes, Oliver Wendell
1809-1894 .... **NCLC 14**
See also CDALB 1640-1865; DLB 1;
SATA 34

Holmes, Raymond
See Souster, (Holmes) Raymond

Holt, Victoria
See Hibbert, Eleanor Burford

Holub, Miroslav 1923- .... **CLC 4**
See also CA 21-24R; CANR 10

Homer c. 8th cent. B.C.- .... **CMLC 1**

Honig, Edwin 1919- .... **CLC 33**
See also CA 5-8R; CAAS 8; CANR 4;
DLB 5

Hood, Hugh (John Blagdon)
1928- .... **CLC 15, 28**
See also CA 49-52; CANR 1, 33; DLB 53

Hood, Thomas 1799-1845 .... **NCLC 16**
See also DLB 96

Hooker, (Peter) Jeremy 1941- ...... **CLC 43**
See also CA 77-80; CANR 22; DLB 40

Hope, A(lec) D(erwent) 1907- .... **CLC 3, 51**
See also CA 21-24R; CANR 33; MTCW

Hope, Brian
See Creasey, John

Hope, Christopher (David Tully)
1944- .... **CLC 52**
See also CA 106; SATA 62

Hopkins, Gerard Manley
1844-1889 .... **NCLC 17**
See also CDBLB 1890-1914; DLB 35, 57;
WLC

Hopkins, John (Richard) 1931- ...... **CLC 4**
See also CA 85-88

Hopkins, Pauline Elizabeth
1859-1930 .... **TCLC 28**
See also BLC 2; DLB 50

Horatio
See Proust,
(Valentin-Louis-George-Eugene-)Marcel

Horgan, Paul 1903- .... **CLC 9, 53**
See also CA 13-16R; CANR 9, 35;
DLB 102; DLBY 85; MTCW; SATA 13

Horn, Peter
See Kuttner, Henry

Horovitz, Israel 1939- .... **CLC 56**
See also CA 33-36R; DLB 7

Horvath, Odon von
See Horvath, Oedoen von
See also DLB 85

Horvath, Oedoen von 1901-1938... **TCLC 45**
See also Horvath, Odon von
See also CA 118

Horwitz, Julius 1920-1986......... **CLC 14**
See also CA 9-12R; 119; CANR 12

Hospital, Janette Turner 1942- ..... **CLC 42**
See also CA 108

Hostos, E. M. de
See Hostos (y Bonilla), Eugenio Maria de

Hostos, Eugenio M. de
See Hostos (y Bonilla), Eugenio Maria de

Hostos, Eugenio Maria
See Hostos (y Bonilla), Eugenio Maria de

Hostos (y Bonilla), Eugenio Maria de
1839-1903 .... **TCLC 24**
See also CA 123; 131; HW

Houdini
See Lovecraft, H(oward) P(hillips)

Hougan, Carolyn 19(?)- .... **CLC 34**

Household, Geoffrey (Edward West)
1900-1988 .... **CLC 11**
See also CA 77-80; 126; DLB 87; SATA 14,
59

Housman, A(lfred) E(dward)
1859-1936 .... **TCLC 1, 10; PC 2**
See also CA 104; 125; DLB 19; MTCW

Housman, Laurence 1865-1959 ..... **TCLC 7**
See also CA 106; DLB 10; SATA 25

Howard, Elizabeth Jane 1923- ... **CLC 7, 29**
See also CA 5-8R; CANR 8

Howard, Maureen 1930- ..... **CLC 5, 14, 46**
See also CA 53-56; CANR 31; DLBY 83;
MTCW

Howard, Richard 1929- ...... **CLC 7, 10, 47**
See also AITN 1; CA 85-88; CANR 25;
DLB 5

Howard, Robert Ervin 1906-1936... **TCLC 8**
See also CA 105

Howard, Warren F.
See Pohl, Frederik

Howe, Fanny 1940- .... **CLC 47**
See also CA 117; SATA 52

Howe, Julia Ward 1819-1910 ..... **TCLC 21**
See also CA 117; DLB 1

Howe, Susan 1937-................ **CLC 72**
See also DLB 120

Howe, Tina 1937-................. **CLC 48**
See also CA 109

Howell, James 1594(?)-1666 .... **LC 13**

Howells, W. D.
See Howells, William Dean

Howells, William D.
See Howells, William Dean

Ishiguro, Kazuo 1954- ...... **CLC 27, 56, 59**
See also BEST 90:2; CA 120; MTCW

Ishikawa Takuboku
1886(?)-1912 .... **TCLC 15**
See also CA 113

Iskander, Fazil 1929- .... **CLC 47**
See also CA 102

Ivan IV 1530-1584 .... **LC 17**

Ivanov, Vyacheslav Ivanovich
1866-1949 .... **TCLC 33**
See also CA 122

Ivask, Ivar Vidrik 1927- .... **CLC 14**
See also CA 37-40R; CANR 24

Jackson, Daniel
See Wingrove, David (John)

Jackson, Jesse 1908-1983 .... **CLC 12**
See also BW; CA 25-28R; 109; CANR 27;
CLR 28; MAICYA; SATA 2, 29, 48

Jackson, Laura (Riding) 1901-1991 .. **CLC 7**
See also Riding, Laura
See also CA 65-68; 135; CANR 28; DLB 48

Jackson, Sam
See Trumbo, Dalton

Jackson, Sara
See Wingrove, David (John)

Jackson, Shirley
1919-1965 .... **CLC 11, 60; SSC 9**
See also AAYA 9; CA 1-4R; 25-28R;
CANR 4; CDALB 1941-1968; DLB 6;
SATA 2; WLC

Jacob, (Cyprien-)Max 1876-1944 ... **TCLC 6**
See also CA 104

Jacobs, Jim 1942- .... **CLC 12**
See also CA 97-100

Jacobs, W(illiam) W(ymark)
1863-1943 .... **TCLC 22**
See also CA 121

Jacobsen, Jens Peter 1847-1885 .. **NCLC 34**

Jacobsen, Josephine 1908- .... **CLC 48**
See also CA 33-36R; CANR 23

Jacobson, Dan 1929- .... **CLC 4, 14**
See also CA 1-4R; CANR 2, 25; DLB 14;
MTCW

Jacqueline
See Carpentier (y Valmont), Alejo

Jagger, Mick 1944- .... **CLC 17**

Jakes, John (William) 1932- .... **CLC 29**
See also BEST 89:4; CA 57-60; CANR 10;
DLBY 83; MTCW; SATA 62

James, Andrew
See Kirkup, James

James, C(yril) L(ionel) R(obert)
1901-1989 .... **CLC 33**
See also BW; CA 117; 125; 128; MTCW

James, Daniel (Lewis) 1911-1988
See Santiago, Danny
See also CA 125

James, Dynely
See Mayne, William (James Carter)

James, Henry
1843-1916 ..... **TCLC 2, 11, 24, 40, 47;
SSC 8**
See also CA 104; 132; CDALB 1865-1917;
DLB 12, 71, 74; MTCW; WLC

James, Montague (Rhodes)
1862-1936 .... **TCLC 6**
See also CA 104

James, P. D. .... **CLC 18, 46**
See also White, Phyllis Dorothy James
See also BEST 90:2; CDBLB 1960 to
Present; DLB 87

James, Philip
See Moorcock, Michael (John)

James, William 1842-1910 ..... **TCLC 15, 32**
See also CA 109

James I 1394-1437 .... **LC 20**

Jami, Nur al-Din 'Abd al-Rahman
1414-1492 .... **LC 9**

Jandl, Ernst 1925- .... **CLC 34**

Janowitz, Tama 1957- .... **CLC 43**
See also CA 106

Jarrell, Randall
1914-1965 ...... **CLC 1, 2, 6, 9, 13, 49**
See also CA 5-8R; 25-28R; CABS 2;
CANR 6, 34; CDALB 1941-1968; CLR 6;
DLB 48, 52; MAICYA; MTCW; SATA 7

Jarry, Alfred 1873-1907 .... **TCLC 2, 14**
See also CA 104

Jarvis, E. K.
See Bloch, Robert (Albert); Ellison, Harlan;
Silverberg, Robert

Jeake, Samuel Jr.
See Aiken, Conrad (Potter)

Jean Paul 1763-1825 .... **NCLC 7**

Jeffers, (John) Robinson
1887-1962 .... **CLC 2, 3, 11, 15, 54**
See also CA 85-88; CANR 35;
CDALB 1917-1929; DLB 45; MTCW;
WLC

Jefferson, Janet
See Mencken, H(enry) L(ouis)

Jefferson, Thomas 1743-1826 .... **NCLC 11**
See also CDALB 1640-1865; DLB 31

Jeffrey, Francis 1773-1850 .... **NCLC 33**
See also DLB 107

Jelakowitch, Ivan
See Heijermans, Herman

Jellicoe, (Patricia) Ann 1927- ...... **CLC 27**
See also CA 85-88; DLB 13

Jen, Gish .... **CLC 70**
See also Jen, Lillian

Jen, Lillian 1956(?)-
See Jen, Gish
See also CA 135

Jenkins, (John) Robin 1912- .... **CLC 52**
See also CA 1-4R; CANR 1; DLB 14

Jennings, Elizabeth (Joan)
1926- .... **CLC 5, 14**
See also CA 61-64; CAAS 5; CANR 8, 39;
DLB 27; MTCW; SATA 66

Jennings, Waylon 1937- .... **CLC 21**

Jensen, Johannes V. 1873-1950 .... **TCLC 41**

Jensen, Laura (Linnea) 1948- ...... **CLC 37**
See also CA 103

Jerome, Jerome K(lapka)
1859-1927 .... **TCLC 23**
See also CA 119; DLB 10, 34

Jerrold, Douglas William
1803-1857 .... **NCLC 2**

Jewett, (Theodora) Sarah Orne
1849-1909 .... **TCLC 1, 22; SSC 6**
See also CA 108; 127; DLB 12, 74;
SATA 15

Jewsbury, Geraldine (Endsor)
1812-1880 .... **NCLC 22**
See also DLB 21

Jhabvala, Ruth Prawer
1927- .... **CLC 4, 8, 29**
See also CA 1-4R; CANR 2, 29; MTCW

Jiles, Paulette 1943- .... **CLC 13, 58**
See also CA 101

Jimenez (Mantecon), Juan Ramon
1881-1958 .... **TCLC 4**
See also CA 104; 131; HW; MTCW

Jimenez, Ramon
See Jimenez (Mantecon), Juan Ramon

Jimenez Mantecon, Juan
See Jimenez (Mantecon), Juan Ramon

Joel, Billy .... **CLC 26**
See also Joel, William Martin

Joel, William Martin 1949-
See Joel, Billy
See also CA 108

John of the Cross, St. 1542-1591 .... **LC 18**

Johnson, B(ryan) S(tanley William)
1933-1973 .... **CLC 6, 9**
See also CA 9-12R; 53-56; CANR 9;
DLB 14, 40

Johnson, Charles (Richard)
1948- .... **CLC 7, 51, 65**
See also BLC 2; BW; CA 116; DLB 33

Johnson, Denis 1949- .... **CLC 52**
See also CA 117; 121; DLB 120

Johnson, Diane (Lain)
1934- .... **CLC 5, 13, 48**
See also CA 41-44R; CANR 17; DLBY 80;
MTCW

Johnson, Eyvind (Olof Verner)
1900-1976 .... **CLC 14**
See also CA 73-76; 69-72; CANR 34

Johnson, J. R.
See James, C(yril) L(ionel) R(obert)

Johnson, James Weldon
1871-1938 .... **TCLC 3, 19**
See also BLC 2; BW; CA 104; 125;
CDALB 1917-1929; DLB 51; MTCW;
SATA 31

Johnson, Joyce 1935- .... **CLC 58**
See also CA 125; 129

Johnson, Lionel (Pigot)
1867-1902 .... **TCLC 19**
See also CA 117; DLB 19

Johnson, Mel
See Malzberg, Barry N(athaniel)

Johnson, Pamela Hansford
1912-1981 .... **CLC 1, 7, 27**
See also CA 1-4R; 104; CANR 2, 28;
DLB 15; MTCW

Johnson, Samuel 1709-1784 .... **LC 15**
See also CDBLB 1660-1789; DLB 39, 95,
104; WLC

aymor, Patrice Maguilene
See Senghor, Leopold Sedar

azan, Elia 1909-........... CLC 6, 16, 63
See also CA 21-24R; CANR 32

azantzakis, Nikos
1883(?)-1957 .... TCLC 2, 5, 33
See also CA 105; 132; MTCW

azin, Alfred 1915- .... CLC 34, 38
See also CA 1-4R; CAAS 7; CANR 1;
DLB 67

eane, Mary Nesta (Skrine) 1904-
See Keane, Molly
See also CA 108; 114

Keane, Molly................. CLC 31
See also Keane, Mary Nesta (Skrine)

Keates, Jonathan 19(?)-........... CLC 34

Keaton, Buster 1895-1966 .... CLC 20

Keats, John 1795-1821...... NCLC 8; PC 1
See also CDBLB 1789-1832; DLB 96, 110;
WLC

Keene, Donald 1922- .... CLC 34
See also CA 1-4R; CANR 5

Keillor, Garrison .... CLC 40
See also Keillor, Gary (Edward)
See also AAYA 2; BEST 89:3; DLBY 87;
SATA 58

Keillor, Gary (Edward) 1942-
See Keillor, Garrison
See also CA 111; 117; CANR 36; MTCW

Keith, Michael
See Hubbard, L(afayette) Ron(ald)

Kell, Joseph
See Wilson, John (Anthony) Burgess

Keller, Gottfried 1819-1890....... NCLC 2

Kellerman, Jonathan 1949- .... CLC 44
See also BEST 90:1; CA 106; CANR 29

Kelley, William Melvin 1937-...... CLC 22
See also BW; CA 77-80; CANR 27; DLB 33

Kellogg, Marjorie 1922-............ CLC 2
See also CA 81-84

Kellow, Kathleen
See Hibbert, Eleanor Burford

Kelly, M(ilton) T(erry) 1947-....... CLC 55
See also CA 97-100; CANR 19

Kelman, James 1946-............ CLC 58

Kemal, Yashar 1923- .... CLC 14, 29
See also CA 89-92

Kemble, Fanny 1809-1893 .... NCLC 18
See also DLB 32

Kemelman, Harry 1908-............ CLC 2
See also AITN 1; CA 9-12R; CANR 6;
DLB 28

Kempe, Margery 1373(?)-1440(?) ..... LC 6

Kempis, Thomas a 1380-1471 .... LC 11

Kendall, Henry 1839-1882....... NCLC 12

Keneally, Thomas (Michael)
1935- ...... CLC 5, 8, 10, 14, 19, 27, 43
See also CA 85-88; CANR 10; MTCW

Kennedy, Adrienne (Lita) 1931- .... CLC 66
See also BLC 2; BW; CA 103; CABS 3;
CANR 26; DLB 38

Kennedy, John Pendleton
1795-1870 .... NCLC 2
See also DLB 3

Kennedy, Joseph Charles 1929-...... CLC 8
See also Kennedy, X. J.
See also CA 1-4R; CANR 4, 30; SATA 14

Kennedy, William 1928-.. CLC 6, 28, 34, 53
See also AAYA 1; CA 85-88; CANR 14,
31; DLBY 85; MTCW; SATA 57

Kennedy, X. J..................... CLC 42
See also Kennedy, Joseph Charles
See also CAAS 9; CLR 27; DLB 5

Kent, Kelvin
See Kuttner, Henry

Kenton, Maxwell
See Southern, Terry

Kenyon, Robert O.
See Kuttner, Henry

Kerouac, Jack ..... CLC 1, 2, 3, 5, 14, 29, 61
See also Kerouac, Jean-Louis Lebris de
See also CDALB 1941-1968; DLB 2, 16;
DLBD 3

Kerouac, Jean-Louis Lebris de 1922-1969
See Kerouac, Jack
See also AITN 1; CA 5-8R; 25-28R;
CANR 26; MTCW; WLC

Kerr, Jean 1923-................. CLC 22
See also CA 5-8R; CANR 7

Kerr, M. E. .... CLC 12, 35
See also Meaker, Marijane (Agnes)
See also AAYA 2; SAAS 1

Kerr, Robert .... CLC 55

Kerrigan, (Thomas) Anthony
1918- .... CLC 4, 6
See also CA 49-52; CAAS 11; CANR 4

Kerry, Lois
See Duncan, Lois

Kesey, Ken (Elton)
1935- ...... CLC 1, 3, 6, 11, 46, 64
See also CA 1-4R; CANR 22, 38;
CDALB 1968-1988; DLB 2, 16; MTCW;
SATA 66; WLC

Kesselring, Joseph (Otto)
1902-1967 .... CLC 45

Kessler, Jascha (Frederick) 1929-.... CLC 4
See also CA 17-20R; CANR 8

Kettelkamp, Larry (Dale) 1933- .... CLC 12
See also CA 29-32R; CANR 16; SAAS 3;
SATA 2

Kherdian, David 1931-........... CLC 6, 9
See also CA 21-24R; CAAS 2; CANR 39;
CLR 24; MAICYA; SATA 16

Khlebnikov, Velimir .... TCLC 20
See also Khlebnikov, Viktor Vladimirovich

Khlebnikov, Viktor Vladimirovich 1885-1922
See Khlebnikov, Velimir
See also CA 117

Khodasevich, Vladislav (Felitsianovich)
1886-1939 .... TCLC 15
See also CA 115

Kielland, Alexander Lange
1849-1906 .... TCLC 5
See also CA 104

Kiely, Benedict 1919-........... CLC 23, 43
See also CA 1-4R; CANR 2; DLB 15

Kienzle, William X(avier) 1928- .... CLC 25
See also CA 93-96; CAAS 1; CANR 9, 31;
MTCW

Kierkegaard, Soeren 1813-1855... NCLC 34

Kierkegaard, Soren 1813-1855.... NCLC 34

Killens, John Oliver 1916-1987..... CLC 10
See also BW; CA 77-80; 123; CAAS 2;
CANR 26; DLB 33

Killigrew, Anne 1660-1685.......... LC 4

Kim
See Simenon, Georges (Jacques Christian)

Kincaid, Jamaica 1949- .... CLC 43, 68
See also BLC 2; BW; CA 125

King, Francis (Henry) 1923- ..... CLC 8, 53
See also CA 1-4R; CANR 1, 33; DLB 15;
MTCW

King, Stephen (Edwin)
1947- .... CLC 12, 26, 37, 61
See also AAYA 1; BEST 90:1; CA 61-64;
CANR 1, 30; DLBY 80; MTCW;
SATA 9, 55

King, Steve
See King, Stephen (Edwin)

Kingman, Lee.................. CLC 17
See also Natti, (Mary) Lee
See also SAAS 3; SATA 1, 67

Kingsley, Charles 1819-1875 ..... NCLC 35
See also DLB 21, 32; YABC 2

Kingsley, Sidney 1906-............ CLC 44
See also CA 85-88; DLB 7

Kingsolver, Barbara 1955-......... CLC 55
See also CA 129; 134

Kingston, Maxine (Ting Ting) Hong
1940- .... CLC 12, 19, 58
See also AAYA 8; CA 69-72; CANR 13,
38; DLBY 80; MTCW; SATA 53

Kinnell, Galway
1927- .... CLC 1, 2, 3, 5, 13, 29
See also CA 9-12R; CANR 10, 34; DLB 5;
DLBY 87; MTCW

Kinsella, Thomas 1928- .... CLC 4, 19
See also CA 17-20R; CANR 15; DLB 27;
MTCW

Kinsella, W(illiam) P(atrick)
1935- .... CLC 27, 43
See also AAYA 7; CA 97-100; CAAS 7;
CANR 21, 35; MTCW

Kipling, (Joseph) Rudyard
1865-1936 .... TCLC 8, 17; PC 3; SSC 5
See also CA 105; 120; CANR 33;
CDBLB 1890-1914; DLB 19, 34;
MAICYA; MTCW; WLC; YABC 2

Kirkup, James 1918- .... CLC 1
See also CA 1-4R; CAAS 4; CANR 2;
DLB 27; SATA 12

Kirkwood, James 1930(?)-1989 ...... CLC 9
See also AITN 2; CA 1-4R; 128; CANR 6

Kis, Danilo 1935-1989 .... CLC 57
See also CA 109; 118; 129; MTCW

Kivi, Aleksis 1834-1872 .... NCLC 30

Kizer, Carolyn (Ashley) 1925-... CLC 15, 39
See also CA 65-68; CAAS 5; CANR 24;
DLB 5

Klabund 1890-1928............. **TCLC 44**
See also DLB 66

Klappert, Peter 1942-............ **CLC 57**
See also CA 33-36R; DLB 5

Klein, A(braham) M(oses)
1909-1972 .... **CLC 19**
See also CA 101; 37-40R; DLB 68

Klein, Norma 1938-1989 .... **CLC 30**
See also AAYA 2; CA 41-44R; 128;
CANR 15, 37; CLR 2, 19; MAICYA;
SAAS 1; SATA 7, 57

Klein, T(heodore) E(ibon) D(onald)
1947- .... **CLC 34**
See also CA 119

Kleist, Heinrich von 1777-1811.... **NCLC 2**
See also DLB 90

Klima, Ivan 1931-................ **CLC 56**
See also CA 25-28R; CANR 17

Klimentov, Andrei Platonovich 1899-1951
See Platonov, Andrei
See also CA 108

Klinger, Friedrich Maximilian von
1752-1831 .... **NCLC 1**
See also DLB 94

Klopstock, Friedrich Gottlieb
1724-1803 .... **NCLC 11**
See also DLB 97

Knebel, Fletcher 1911-........... **CLC 14**
See also AITN 1; CA 1-4R; CAAS 3;
CANR 1, 36; SATA 36

Knickerbocker, Diedrich
See Irving, Washington

Knight, Etheridge 1931-1991...... **CLC 40**
See also BLC 2; BW; CA 21-24R; 133;
CANR 23; DLB 41

Knight, Sarah Kemble 1666-1727 ..... **LC 7**
See also DLB 24

Knowles, John 1926- ...... **CLC 1, 4, 10, 26**
See also CA 17-20R; CDALB 1968-1988;
DLB 6; MTCW; SATA 8

Knox, Calvin M.
See Silverberg, Robert

Knye, Cassandra
See Disch, Thomas M(ichael)

Koch, C(hristopher) J(ohn) 1932- ... **CLC 42**
See also CA 127

Koch, Christopher
See Koch, C(hristopher) J(ohn)

Koch, Kenneth 1925- .... **CLC 5, 8, 44**
See also CA 1-4R; CANR 6, 36; DLB 5;
SATA 65

Kochanowski, Jan 1530-1584....... **LC 10**

Kock, Charles Paul de
1794-1871 .... **NCLC 16**

Koda Shigeyuki 1867-1947
See Rohan, Koda
See also CA 121

Koestler, Arthur
1905-1983 ...... **CLC 1, 3, 6, 8, 15, 33**
See also CA 1-4R; 109; CANR 1, 33;
CDBLB 1945-1960; DLBY 83; MTCW

Kohout, Pavel 1928-............. **CLC 13**
See also CA 45-48; CANR 3

Koizumi, Yakumo
See Hearn, (Patricio) Lafcadio (Tessima
Carlos)

Kolmar, Gertrud 1894-1943...... **TCLC 40**

Konrad, George
See Konrad, Gyoergy

Konrad, Gyoergy 1933- ...... **CLC 4, 10, 73**
See also CA 85-88

Konwicki, Tadeusz 1926-..... **CLC 8, 28, 54**
See also CA 101; CAAS 9; CANR 39;
MTCW

Kopit, Arthur (Lee) 1937- .... **CLC 1, 18, 33**
See also AITN 1; CA 81-84; CABS 3;
DLB 7; MTCW

Kops, Bernard 1926-.............. **CLC 4**
See also CA 5-8R; DLB 13

Kornbluth, C(yril) M. 1923-1958.... **TCLC 8**
See also CA 105; DLB 8

Korolenko, V. G.
See Korolenko, Vladimir Galaktionovich

Korolenko, Vladimir
See Korolenko, Vladimir Galaktionovich

Korolenko, Vladimir G.
See Korolenko, Vladimir Galaktionovich

Korolenko, Vladimir Galaktionovich
1853-1921 .... **TCLC 22**
See also CA 121

Kosinski, Jerzy (Nikodem)
1933-1991 ... **CLC 1, 2, 3, 6, 10, 15, 53,
70**
See also CA 17-20R; 134; CANR 9; DLB 2;
DLBY 82; MTCW

Kostelanetz, Richard (Cory) 1940-.. **CLC 28**
See also CA 13-16R; CAAS 8; CANR 38

Kostrowitzki, Wilhelm Apollinaris de
1880-1918
See Apollinaire, Guillaume
See also CA 104

Kotlowitz, Robert 1924-........... **CLC 4**
See also CA 33-36R; CANR 36

Kotzebue, August (Friedrich Ferdinand) von
1761-1819 .... **NCLC 25**
See also DLB 94

Kotzwinkle, William 1938- ... **CLC 5, 14, 35**
See also CA 45-48; CANR 3; CLR 6;
MAICYA; SATA 24, 70

Kozol, Jonathan 1936-........... **CLC 17**
See also CA 61-64; CANR 16

Kozoll, Michael 1940(?)-.......... **CLC 35**

Kramer, Kathryn 19(?)-........... **CLC 34**

Kramer, Larry 1935- .... **CLC 42**
See also CA 124; 126

Krasicki, Ignacy 1735-1801....... **NCLC 8**

Krasinski, Zygmunt 1812-1859 .... **NCLC 4**

Kraus, Karl 1874-1936........... **TCLC 5**
See also CA 104; DLB 118

Kreve (Mickevicius), Vincas
1882-1954 .... **TCLC 27**

Kristofferson, Kris 1936-......... **CLC 26**
See also CA 104

Krizanc, John 1956-............. **CLC 57**

Krleza, Miroslav 1893-1981........ **CLC 8**
See also CA 97-100; 105

Kroetsch, Robert 1927- ...... **CLC 5, 23, 5**
See also CA 17-20R; CANR 8, 38; DLB 53
MTCW

Kroetz, Franz
See Kroetz, Franz Xaver

Kroetz, Franz Xaver 1946- .... **CLC 4**
See also CA 130

Kroker, Arthur 1945-............ **CLC 7**

Kropotkin, Peter (Aleksieevich)
1842-1921 .... **TCLC 3**
See also CA 119

Krotkov, Yuri 1917-............. **CLC 19**
See also CA 102

Krumb
See Crumb, R(obert)

Krumgold, Joseph (Quincy)
1908-1980 .... **CLC 12**
See also CA 9-12R; 101; CANR 7;
MAICYA; SATA 1, 23, 48

Krumwitz
See Crumb, R(obert)

Krutch, Joseph Wood 1893-1970.... **CLC 24**
See also CA 1-4R; 25-28R; CANR 4;
DLB 63

Krutzch, Gus
See Eliot, T(homas) S(tearns)

Krylov, Ivan Andreevich
1768(?)-1844 .... **NCLC 1**

Kubin, Alfred 1877-1959 .... **TCLC 23**
See also CA 112; DLB 81

Kubrick, Stanley 1928-........... **CLC 16**
See also CA 81-84; CANR 33; DLB 26

Kumin, Maxine (Winokur)
1925- .... **CLC 5, 13, 28**
See also AITN 2; CA 1-4R; CAAS 8;
CANR 1, 21; DLB 5; MTCW; SATA 12

Kundera, Milan
1929- .... **CLC 4, 9, 19, 32, 68**
See also AAYA 2; CA 85-88; CANR 19;
MTCW

Kunitz, Stanley (Jasspon)
1905- .... **CLC 6, 11, 14**
See also CA 41-44R; CANR 26; DLB 48;
MTCW

Kunze, Reiner 1933-............. **CLC 10**
See also CA 93-96; DLB 75

Kuprin, Aleksandr Ivanovich
1870-1938 .... **TCLC 5**
See also CA 104

Kureishi, Hanif 1954(?)-.......... **CLC 64**

Kurosawa, Akira 1910-........... **CLC 16**
See also CA 101

Kuttner, Henry 1915-1958........ **TCLC 10**
See also CA 107; DLB 8

Kuzma, Greg 1944-.............. **CLC 7**
See also CA 33-36R

Kuzmin, Mikhail 1872(?)-1936 .... **TCLC 40**

Kyd, Thomas 1558-1594............ **DC 3**
See also DLB 62

Kyprianos, Iossif
See Samarakis, Antonis

La Bruyere, Jean de 1645-1696...... **LC 17**

Lacan, Jacques (Marie Emile)
    1901-1981 . . . . **CLC 75**
    See also CA 121; 104

Laclos, Pierre Ambroise Francois Choderlos
    de 1741-1803 . . . . **NCLC 4**

La Colere, Francois
    See Aragon, Louis

Lacolere, Francois
    See Aragon, Louis

La Deshabilleuse
    See Simenon, Georges (Jacques Christian)

Lady Gregory
    See Gregory, Isabella Augusta (Persse)

Lady of Quality, A
    See Bagnold, Enid

La Fayette, Marie (Madelaine Pioche de la
    Vergne Comtes 1634-1693 . . . . . . **LC 2**

Lafayette, Rene
    See Hubbard, L(afayette) Ron(ald)

Laforgue, Jules 1860-1887 . . . . **NCLC 5**

Lagerkvist, Paer (Fabian)
    1891-1974 . . . . **CLC 7, 10, 13, 54**
    See also CA 85-88; 49-52; MTCW

Lagerkvist, Par
    See Lagerkvist, Paer (Fabian)

Lagerloef, Selma (Ottiliana Lovisa)
    1858-1940 . . . . **TCLC 4, 36**
    See also Lagerlof, Selma (Ottiliana Lovisa)
    See also CA 108; CLR 7; SATA 15

Lagerlof, Selma (Ottiliana Lovisa)
    See Lagerloef, Selma (Ottiliana Lovisa)
    See also CLR 7; SATA 15

La Guma, (Justin) Alex(ander)
    1925-1985 . . . . **CLC 19**
    See also BW; CA 49-52; 118; CANR 25;
    DLB 117; MTCW

Laidlaw, A. K.
    See Grieve, C(hristopher) M(urray)

Lainez, Manuel Mujica
    See Mujica Lainez, Manuel
    See also HW

Lamartine, Alphonse (Marie Louis Prat) de
    1790-1869 . . . . **NCLC 11**

Lamb, Charles 1775-1834 . . . . **NCLC 10**
    See also CDBLB 1789-1832; DLB 93, 107;
    SATA 17; WLC

Lamb, Lady Caroline 1785-1828 . . **NCLC 38**
    See also DLB 116

Lamming, George (William)
    1927- . . . . **CLC 2, 4, 66**
    See also BLC 2; BW; CA 85-88; CANR 26;
    MTCW

L'Amour, Louis (Dearborn)
    1908-1988 . . . . **CLC 25, 55**
    See also AITN 2; BEST 89:2; CA 1-4R;
    125; CANR 3, 25; DLBY 80; MTCW

Lampedusa, Giuseppe (Tomasi) di . . . **TCLC 13**
    See also Tomasi di Lampedusa, Giuseppe

Lampman, Archibald 1861-1899 . . **NCLC 25**
    See also DLB 92

Lancaster, Bruce 1896-1963 . . . . **CLC 36**
    See also CA 9-10; CAP 1; SATA 9

Landau, Mark Alexandrovich
    See Aldanov, Mark (Alexandrovich)

Landau-Aldanov, Mark Alexandrovich
    See Aldanov, Mark (Alexandrovich)

Landis, John 1950- . . . . **CLC 26**
    See also CA 112; 122

Landolfi, Tommaso 1908-1979 . . . **CLC 11, 49**
    See also CA 127; 117

Landon, Letitia Elizabeth
    1802-1838 . . . . **NCLC 15**
    See also DLB 96

Landor, Walter Savage
    1775-1864 . . . . **NCLC 14**
    See also DLB 93, 107

Landwirth, Heinz 1927-
    See Lind, Jakov
    See also CA 9-12R; CANR 7

Lane, Patrick 1939- . . . . **CLC 25**
    See also CA 97-100; DLB 53

Lang, Andrew 1844-1912 . . . . **TCLC 16**
    See also CA 114; 137; DLB 98; MAICYA;
    SATA 16

Lang, Fritz 1890-1976 . . . . **CLC 20**
    See also CA 77-80; 69-72; CANR 30

Lange, John
    See Crichton, (John) Michael

Langer, Elinor 1939- . . . . **CLC 34**
    See also CA 121

Langland, William 1330(?)-1400(?) . . . **LC 19**

Langstaff, Launcelot
    See Irving, Washington

Lanier, Sidney 1842-1881 . . . . **NCLC 6**
    See also DLB 64; MAICYA; SATA 18

Lanyer, Aemilia 1569-1645 . . . . **LC 10**

Lao Tzu . . . . **CMLC 7**

Lapine, James (Elliot) 1949- . . . . **CLC 39**
    See also CA 123; 130

Larbaud, Valery (Nicolas)
    1881-1957 . . . . **TCLC 9**
    See also CA 106

Lardner, Ring
    See Lardner, Ring(gold) W(ilmer)

Lardner, Ring W. Jr.
    See Lardner, Ring(gold) W(ilmer)

Lardner, Ring(gold) W(ilmer)
    1885-1933 . . . . **TCLC 2, 14**
    See also CA 104; 131; CDALB 1917-1929;
    DLB 11, 25, 86; MTCW

Laredo, Betty
    See Codrescu, Andrei

Larkin, Maia
    See Wojciechowska, Maia (Teresa)

Larkin, Philip (Arthur)
    1922-1985 . . . **CLC 3, 5, 8, 9, 13, 18, 33,**
                              39, 64
    See also CA 5-8R; 117; CANR 24;
    CDBLB 1960 to Present; DLB 27;
    MTCW

Larra (y Sanchez de Castro), Mariano Jose de
    1809-1837 . . . . **NCLC 17**

Larsen, Eric 1941- . . . . **CLC 55**
    See also CA 132

Larsen, Nella 1891-1964 . . . . **CLC 37**
    See also BLC 2; BW; CA 125; DLB 51

Larson, Charles R(aymond) 1938- . . . **CLC 31**
    See also CA 53-56; CANR 4

Latham, Jean Lee 1902- . . . . **CLC 12**
    See also AITN 1; CA 5-8R; CANR 7;
    MAICYA; SATA 2, 68

Latham, Mavis
    See Clark, Mavis Thorpe

Lathen, Emma . . . . **CLC 2**
    See also Hennissart, Martha; Latsis, Mary
    J(ane)

Lathrop, Francis
    See Leiber, Fritz (Reuter Jr.)

Latsis, Mary J(ane)
    See Lathen, Emma
    See also CA 85-88

Lattimore, Richmond (Alexander)
    1906-1984 . . . . **CLC 3**
    See also CA 1-4R; 112; CANR 1

Laughlin, James 1914- . . . . **CLC 49**
    See also CA 21-24R; CANR 9; DLB 48

Laurence, (Jean) Margaret (Wemyss)
    1926-1987 . . **CLC 3, 6, 13, 50, 62; SSC 7**
    See also CA 5-8R; 121; CANR 33; DLB 53;
    MTCW; SATA 50

Laurent, Antoine 1952- . . . . **CLC 50**

Lauscher, Hermann
    See Hesse, Hermann

Lautreamont, Comte de
    1846-1870 . . . . **NCLC 12**

Laverty, Donald
    See Blish, James (Benjamin)

Lavin, Mary 1912- . . . . . . **CLC 4, 18; SSC 4**
    See also CA 9-12R; CANR 33; DLB 15;
    MTCW

Lavond, Paul Dennis
    See Kornbluth, C(yril) M.; Pohl, Frederik

Lawler, Raymond Evenor 1922- . . . . **CLC 58**
    See also CA 103

Lawrence, D(avid) H(erbert Richards)
    1885-1930 . . . . . . **TCLC 2, 9, 16, 33, 48;**
                                SSC 4
    See also CA 104; 121; CDBLB 1914-1945;
    DLB 10, 19, 36, 98; MTCW; WLC

Lawrence, T(homas) E(dward)
    1888-1935 . . . . **TCLC 18**
    See also Dale, Colin
    See also CA 115

Lawrence Of Arabia
    See Lawrence, T(homas) E(dward)

Lawson, Henry (Archibald Hertzberg)
    1867-1922 . . . . **TCLC 27**
    See also CA 120

Laxness, Halldor . . . . **CLC 25**
    See also Gudjonsson, Halldor Kiljan

Layamon fl. c. 1200- . . . . **CMLC 10**

Laye, Camara 1928-1980 . . . . **CLC 4, 38**
    See also BLC 2; BW; CA 85-88; 97-100;
    CANR 25; MTCW

Layton, Irving (Peter) 1912- . . . . . **CLC 2, 15**
    See also CA 1-4R; CANR 2, 33; DLB 88;
    MTCW

Lazarus, Emma 1849-1887 . . . . **NCLC 8**

Lazarus, Felix
    See Cable, George Washington

Lord Byron
See Byron, George Gordon (Noel)

Lord Dunsany .... TCLC 2
See also Dunsany, Edward John Moreton
Drax Plunkett

Lorde, Audre (Geraldine)
1934- .... CLC 18, 71
See also BLC 2; BW; CA 25-28R;
CANR 16, 26; DLB 41; MTCW

Lord Jeffrey
See Jeffrey, Francis

Lorenzo, Heberto Padilla
See Padilla (Lorenzo), Heberto

Loris
See Hofmannsthal, Hugo von

Loti, Pierre .... TCLC 11
See also Viaud, (Louis Marie) Julien
See also DLB 123

Louie, David Wong 1954- .... CLC 70

Louis, Father M.
See Merton, Thomas

Lovecraft, H(oward) P(hillips)
1890-1937 .... TCLC 4, 22; SSC 3
See also CA 104; 133; MTCW

Lovelace, Earl 1935- .... CLC 51
See also CA 77-80; MTCW

Lowell, Amy 1874-1925 .... TCLC 1, 8
See also CA 104; DLB 54

Lowell, James Russell 1819-1891 .. NCLC 2
See also CDALB 1640-1865; DLB 1, 11, 64,
79

Lowell, Robert (Traill Spence Jr.)
1917-1977 ... CLC 1, 2, 3, 4, 5, 8, 9, 11,
15, 37; PC 3
See also CA 9-12R; 73-76; CABS 2;
CANR 26; DLB 5; MTCW; WLC

Lowndes, Marie Adelaide (Belloc)
1868-1947 .... TCLC 12
See also CA 107; DLB 70

Lowry, (Clarence) Malcolm
1909-1957 .... TCLC 6, 40
See also CA 105; 131; CDBLB 1945-1960;
DLB 15; MTCW

Lowry, Mina Gertrude 1882-1966
See Loy, Mina
See also CA 113

Loxsmith, John
See Brunner, John (Kilian Houston)

Loy, Mina .... CLC 28
See also Lowry, Mina Gertrude
See also DLB 4, 54

Loyson-Bridet
See Schwob, (Mayer Andre) Marcel

Lucas, Craig 1951- .... CLC 64
See also CA 137

Lucas, George 1944- .... CLC 16
See also AAYA 1; CA 77-80; CANR 30;
SATA 56

Lucas, Hans
See Godard, Jean-Luc

Lucas, Victoria
See Plath, Sylvia

Ludlam, Charles 1943-1987 ..... CLC 46, 50
See also CA 85-88; 122

Ludlum, Robert 1927- .... CLC 22, 43
See also BEST 89:1, 90:3; CA 33-36R;
CANR 25; DLBY 82; MTCW

Ludwig, Ken. .... CLC 60

Ludwig, Otto 1813-1865......... NCLC 4

Lugones, Leopoldo 1874-1938 ..... TCLC 15
See also CA 116; 131; HW

Lu Hsun 1881-1936 .... TCLC 3

Lukacs, George .... CLC 24
See also Lukacs, Gyorgy (Szegeny von)

Lukacs, Gyorgy (Szegeny von) 1885-1971
See Lukacs, George
See also CA 101; 29-32R

Luke, Peter (Ambrose Cyprian)
1919- .... CLC 38
See also CA 81-84; DLB 13

Lunar, Dennis
See Mungo, Raymond

Lurie, Alison 1926-........ CLC 4, 5, 18, 39
See also CA 1-4R; CANR 2, 17; DLB 2;
MTCW; SATA 46

Lustig, Arnost 1926-.............. CLC 56
See also AAYA 3; CA 69-72; SATA 56

Luther, Martin 1483-1546 .... LC 9

Luzi, Mario 1914-................ CLC 13
See also CA 61-64; CANR 9

Lynch, B. Suarez
See Bioy Casares, Adolfo; Borges, Jorge
Luis

Lynch, David (K.) 1946-........... CLC 66
See also CA 124; 129

Lynch, James
See Andreyev, Leonid (Nikolaevich)

Lynch Davis, B.
See Bioy Casares, Adolfo; Borges, Jorge
Luis

Lyndsay, SirDavid 1490-1555 .... LC 20

Lynn, Kenneth S(chuyler) 1923-.... CLC 50
See also CA 1-4R; CANR 3, 27

Lynx
See West, Rebecca

Lyons, Marcus
See Blish, James (Benjamin)

Lyre, Pinchbeck
See Sassoon, Siegfried (Lorraine)

Lytle, Andrew (Nelson) 1902-...... CLC 22
See also CA 9-12R; DLB 6

Lyttelton, George 1709-1773........ LC 10

Maas, Peter 1929- .... CLC 29
See also CA 93-96

Macaulay, Rose 1881-1958 ..... TCLC 7, 44
See also CA 104; DLB 36

MacBeth, George (Mann)
1932-1992 .... CLC 2, 5, 9
See also CA 25-28R; 136; DLB 40; MTCW;
SATA 4; SATO 70

MacCaig, Norman (Alexander)
1910- .... CLC 36
See also CA 9-12R; CANR 3, 34; DLB 27

MacCarthy, (Sir Charles Otto) Desmond
1877-1952 .... TCLC 36

MacDiarmid, Hugh..... CLC 2, 4, 11, 19, 6
See also Grieve, C(hristopher) M(urray)
See also CDBLB 1945-1960; DLB 20

MacDonald, Anson
See Heinlein, Robert A(nson)

Macdonald, Cynthia 1928-...... CLC 13, 1
See also CA 49-52; CANR 4; DLB 105

MacDonald, George 1824-1905..... TCLC
See also CA 106; 137; DLB 18; MAICYA;
SATA 33

Macdonald, John
See Millar, Kenneth

MacDonald, John D(ann)
1916-1986 .... CLC 3, 27, 4
See also CA 1-4R; 121; CANR 1, 19;
DLB 8; DLBY 86; MTCW

Macdonald, John Ross
See Millar, Kenneth

Macdonald, Ross..... CLC 1, 2, 3, 14, 34, 4
See also Millar, Kenneth
See also DLBD 6

MacDougal, John
See Blish, James (Benjamin)

MacEwen, Gwendolyn (Margaret)
1941-1987 .... CLC 13, 55
See also CA 9-12R; 124; CANR 7, 22;
DLB 53; SATA 50, 55

Machado (y Ruiz), Antonio
1875-1939 .... TCLC 3
See also CA 104; DLB 108

Machado de Assis, Joaquim Maria
1839-1908 .... TCLC 10
See also BLC 2; CA 107

Machen, Arthur................... TCLC 4
See also Jones, Arthur Llewellyn
See also DLB 36

Machiavelli, Niccolo 1469-1527 ...... LC 8

MacInnes, Colin 1914-1976...... CLC 4, 23
See also CA 69-72; 65-68; CANR 21;
DLB 14; MTCW

MacInnes, Helen (Clark)
1907-1985 .... CLC 27, 39
See also CA 1-4R; 117; CANR 1, 28;
DLB 87; MTCW; SATA 22, 44

Mackenzie, Compton (Edward Montague)
1883-1972 .... CLC 18
See also CA 21-22; 37-40R; CAP 2;
DLB 34, 100

Mackintosh, Elizabeth 1896(?)-1952
See Tey, Josephine
See also CA 110

MacLaren, James
See Grieve, C(hristopher) M(urray)

Mac Laverty, Bernard 1942-....... CLC 31
See also CA 116; 118

MacLean, Alistair (Stuart)
1922-1987 ....CLC 3, 13, 50, 63
See also CA 57-60; 121; CANR 28; MTCW;
SATA 23, 50

MacLeish, Archibald
1892-1982 .... CLC 3, 8, 14, 68
See also CA 9-12R; 106; CANR 33; DLB 4,
7, 45; DLBY 82; MTCW

MacLennan, (John) Hugh
1907- .... **CLC 2, 14**
See also CA 5-8R; CANR 33; DLB 68;
MTCW

MacLeod, Alistair 1936- .... **CLC 56**
See also CA 123; DLB 60

MacNeice, (Frederick) Louis
1907-1963 .... **CLC 1, 4, 10, 53**
See also CA 85-88; DLB 10, 20; MTCW

MacNeill, Dand
See Fraser, George MacDonald

Macpherson, (Jean) Jay 1931- ...... **CLC 14**
See also CA 5-8R; DLB 53

MacShane, Frank 1927- .... **CLC 39**
See also CA 9-12R; CANR 3, 33; DLB 111

Macumber, Mari
See Sandoz, Mari(e Susette)

Madach, Imre 1823-1864 .... **NCLC 19**

Madden, (Jerry) David 1933- .... **CLC 5, 15**
See also CA 1-4R; CAAS 3; CANR 4;
DLB 6; MTCW

Maddern, Al(an)
See Ellison, Harlan

Madhubuti, Haki R.
1942- .... **CLC 6, 73; PC 5**
See also Lee, Don L.
See also BLC 2; BW; CA 73-76; CANR 24;
DLB 5, 41; DLBD 8

Madow, Pauline (Reichberg) .... **CLC 1**
See also CA 9-12R

Maepenn, Hugh
See Kuttner, Henry

Maepenn, K. H.
See Kuttner, Henry

Maeterlinck, Maurice 1862-1949 ... **TCLC 3**
See also CA 104; 136; SATA 66

Maginn, William 1794-1842 .... **NCLC 8**
See also DLB 110

Mahapatra, Jayanta 1928- .... **CLC 33**
See also CA 73-76; CAAS 9; CANR 15, 33

Mahfouz, Naguib (Abdel Aziz Al-Sabilgi)
1911(?)-
See Mahfuz, Najib
See also BEST 89:2; CA 128; MTCW

Mahfuz, Najib .... **CLC 52, 55**
See also Mahfouz, Naguib (Abdel Aziz
Al-Sabilgi)
See also DLBY 88

Mahon, Derek 1941- .... **CLC 27**
See also CA 113; 128; DLB 40

Mailer, Norman
1923- ...... **CLC 1, 2, 3, 4, 5, 8, 11, 14,
28, 39, 74**
See also AITN 2; CA 9-12R; CABS 1;
CANR 28; CDALB 1968-1988; DLB 2,
16, 28; DLBD 3; DLBY 80, 83; MTCW

Maillet, Antonine 1929- .... **CLC 54**
See also CA 115; 120; DLB 60

Mais, Roger 1905-1955 .... **TCLC 8**
See also BW; CA 105; 124; MTCW

Maitland, Sara (Louise) 1950- ...... **CLC 49**
See also CA 69-72; CANR 13

Major, Clarence 1936- .... **CLC 3, 19, 48**
See also BLC 2; BW; CA 21-24R; CAAS 6;
CANR 13, 25; DLB 33

Major, Kevin (Gerald) 1949- .... **CLC 26**
See also CA 97-100; CANR 21, 38;
CLR 11; DLB 60; MAICYA; SATA 32

Maki, James
See Ozu, Yasujiro

Malabaila, Damiano
See Levi, Primo

Malamud, Bernard
1914-1986 ..... **CLC 1, 2, 3, 5, 8, 9, 11,
18, 27, 44**
See also CA 5-8R; 118; CABS 1; CANR 28;
CDALB 1941-1968; DLB 2, 28;
DLBY 80, 86; MTCW; WLC

Malcolm, Dan
See Silverberg, Robert

Malherbe, Francois de 1555-1628 ..... **LC 5**

Mallarme, Stephane
1842-1898 .... **NCLC 4; PC 4**

Mallet-Joris, Francoise 1930- ...... **CLC 11**
See also CA 65-68; CANR 17; DLB 83

Malley, Ern
See McAuley, James Phillip

Mallowan, Agatha Christie
See Christie, Agatha (Mary Clarissa)

Maloff, Saul 1922- .... **CLC 5**
See also CA 33-36R

Malone, Louis
See MacNeice, (Frederick) Louis

Malone, Michael (Christopher)
1942- .... **CLC 43**
See also CA 77-80; CANR 14, 32

Malory, (Sir) Thomas
1410(?)-1471(?) .... **LC 11**
See also CDBLB Before 1660; SATA 33, 59

Malouf, (George Joseph) David
1934- .... **CLC 28**
See also CA 124

Malraux, (Georges-)Andre
1901-1976 ...... **CLC 1, 4, 9, 13, 15, 57**
See also CA 21-22; 69-72; CANR 34;
CAP 2; DLB 72; MTCW

Malzberg, Barry N(athaniel) 1939- ... **CLC 7**
See also CA 61-64; CAAS 4; CANR 16;
DLB 8

Mamet, David (Alan)
1947- .... **CLC 9, 15, 34, 46**
See also AAYA 3; CA 81-84; CABS 3;
CANR 15; DLB 7; MTCW

Mamoulian, Rouben (Zachary)
1897-1987 .... **CLC 16**
See also CA 25-28R; 124

Mandelstam, Osip (Emilievich)
1891(?)-1938(?) .... **TCLC 2, 6**
See also CA 104

Mander, (Mary) Jane 1877-1949 ... **TCLC 31**

Mandiargues, Andre Pieyre de ...... **CLC 41**
See also Pieyre de Mandiargues, Andre
See also DLB 83

Mandrake, Ethel Belle
See Thurman, Wallace (Henry)

Mangan, James Clarence
1803-1849 .... **NCLC 27**

Maniere, J.-E.
See Giraudoux, (Hippolyte) Jean

Manley, (Mary) Delariviere
1672(?)-1724 .... **LC 1**
See also DLB 39, 80

Mann, Abel
See Creasey, John

Mann, (Luiz) Heinrich 1871-1950... **TCLC 9**
See also CA 106; DLB 66

Mann, (Paul) Thomas
1875-1955 ... **TCLC 2, 8, 14, 21, 35, 44;
SSC 5**
See also CA 104; 128; DLB 66; MTCW;
WLC

Manning, Frederic 1887(?)-1935 ... **TCLC 25**
See also CA 124

Manning, Olivia 1915-1980 ...... **CLC 5, 19**
See also CA 5-8R; 101; CANR 29; MTCW

Mano, D. Keith 1942- .... **CLC 2, 10**
See also CA 25-28R; CAAS 6; CANR 26;
DLB 6

Mansfield, Katherine... **TCLC 2, 8, 39; SSC 9**
See also Beauchamp, Kathleen Mansfield
See also WLC

Manso, Peter 1940- .... **CLC 39**
See also CA 29-32R

Mantecon, Juan Jimenez
See Jimenez (Mantecon), Juan Ramon

Manton, Peter
See Creasey, John

Man Without a Spleen, A
See Chekhov, Anton (Pavlovich)

Manzoni, Alessandro 1785-1873 .. **NCLC 29**

Mapu, Abraham (ben Jekutiel)
1808-1867 .... **NCLC 18**

Mara, Sally
See Queneau, Raymond

Marat, Jean Paul 1743-1793 .... **LC 10**

Marcel, Gabriel Honore
1889-1973 .... **CLC 15**
See also CA 102; 45-48; MTCW

Marchbanks, Samuel
See Davies, (William) Robertson

Marchi, Giacomo
See Bassani, Giorgio

Marie de France c. 12th cent. -.... **CMLC 8**

Marie de l'Incarnation 1599-1672.... **LC 10**

Mariner, Scott
See Pohl, Frederik

Marinetti, Filippo Tommaso
1876-1944 .... **TCLC 10**
See also CA 107; DLB 114

Marivaux, Pierre Carlet de Chamblain de
1688-1763 .... **LC 4**

Markandaya, Kamala .... **CLC 8, 38**
See also Taylor, Kamala (Purnaiya)

Markfield, Wallace 1926- .... **CLC 8**
See also CA 69-72; CAAS 3; DLB 2, 28

Markham, Edwin 1852-1940 ...... **TCLC 47**
See also DLB 54

Markham, Robert
See Amis, Kingsley (William)

Marks, J
See Highwater, Jamake (Mamake)

Marks-Highwater, J
See Highwater, Jamake (Mamake)

Markson, David M(errill) 1927- .... **CLC 67**
See also CA 49-52; CANR 1

Marley, Bob. .... **CLC 17**
See also Marley, Robert Nesta

Marley, Robert Nesta 1945-1981
See Marley, Bob
See also CA 107; 103

Marlowe, Christopher 1564-1593 ..... **DC 1**
See also CDBLB Before 1660; DLB 62;
WLC

Marmontel, Jean-Francois
1723-1799 .... **LC 2**

Marquand, John P(hillips)
1893-1960 .... **CLC 2, 10**
See also CA 85-88; DLB 9, 102

Marquez, Gabriel (Jose) Garcia. ..... **CLC 68**
See also Garcia Marquez, Gabriel (Jose)

Marquis, Don(ald Robert Perry)
1878-1937 .... **TCLC 7**
See also CA 104; DLB 11, 25

Marric, J. J.
See Creasey, John

Marrow, Bernard
See Moore, Brian

Marryat, Frederick 1792-1848 .... **NCLC 3**
See also DLB 21

Marsden, James
See Creasey, John

Marsh, (Edith) Ngaio
1899-1982 .... **CLC 7, 53**
See also CA 9-12R; CANR 6; DLB 77;
MTCW

Marshall, Garry 1934- .... **CLC 17**
See also AAYA 3; CA 111; SATA 60

Marshall, Paule 1929- .. **CLC 27, 72; SSC 3**
See also BLC 3; BW; CA 77-80; CANR 25;
DLB 33; MTCW

Marsten, Richard
See Hunter, Evan

Martha, Henry
See Harris, Mark

Martin, Ken
See Hubbard, L(afayette) Ron(ald)

Martin, Richard
See Creasey, John

Martin, Steve 1945- .... **CLC 30**
See also CA 97-100; CANR 30; MTCW

Martin, Webber
See Silverberg, Robert

Martin du Gard, Roger
1881-1958 .... **TCLC 24**
See also CA 118; DLB 65

Martineau, Harriet 1802-1876.... **NCLC 26**
See also DLB 21, 55; YABC 2

Martines, Julia
See O'Faolain, Julia

Martinez, Jacinto Benavente y
See Benavente (y Martinez), Jacinto

Martinez Ruiz, Jose 1873-1967
See Azorin; Ruiz, Jose Martinez
See also CA 93-96; HW

Martinez Sierra, Gregorio
1881-1947 .... **TCLC 6**
See also CA 115

Martinez Sierra, Maria (de la O'LeJarraga)
1874-1974 .... **TCLC 6**
See also CA 115

Martinsen, Martin
See Follett, Ken(neth Martin)

Martinson, Harry (Edmund)
1904-1978 .... **CLC 14**
See also CA 77-80; CANR 34

Marut, Ret
See Traven, B.

Marut, Robert
See Traven, B.

Marvell, Andrew 1621-1678......... **LC 4**
See also CDBLB 1660-1789; WLC

Marx, Karl (Heinrich)
1818-1883 .... **NCLC 17**

Masaoka Shiki. .... **TCLC 18**
See also Masaoka Tsunenori

Masaoka Tsunenori 1867-1902
See Masaoka Shiki
See also CA 117

Masefield, John (Edward)
1878-1967 .... **CLC 11, 47**
See also CA 19-20; 25-28R; CANR 33;
CAP 2; CDBLB 1890-1914; DLB 10;
MTCW; SATA 19

Maso, Carole 19(?)- .... **CLC 44**

Mason, Bobbie Ann
1940- .... **CLC 28, 43; SSC 4**
See also AAYA 5; CA 53-56; CANR 11,
31; DLBY 87; MTCW

Mason, Ernst
See Pohl, Frederik

Mason, Lee W.
See Malzberg, Barry N(athaniel)

Mason, Nick 1945-............... **CLC 35**
See also Pink Floyd

Mason, Tally
See Derleth, August (William)

Mass, William
See Gibson, William

Masters, Edgar Lee
1868-1950 .... **TCLC 2, 25; PC 1**
See also CA 104; 133; CDALB 1865-1917;
DLB 54; MTCW

Masters, Hilary 1928- .... **CLC 48**
See also CA 25-28R; CANR 13

Mastrosimone, William 19(?)-...... **CLC 36**

Mathe, Albert
See Camus, Albert

Matheson, Richard Burton 1926- ... **CLC 37**
See also CA 97-100; DLB 8, 44

Mathews, Harry 1930-......... **CLC 6, 52**
See also CA 21-24R; CAAS 6; CANR 18

Mathias, Roland (Glyn) 1915-...... **CLC 45**
See also CA 97-100; CANR 19; DLB 27

Matsuo Basho 1644-1694........... **PC**

Mattheson, Rodney
See Creasey, John

Matthews, Greg 1949- .... **CLC 4**
See also CA 135

Matthews, William 1942-......... **CLC 4**
See also CA 29-32R; CANR 12; DLB 5

Matthias, John (Edward) 1941-...... **CLC**
See also CA 33-36R

Matthiessen, Peter
1927- .... **CLC 5, 7, 11, 32, 6**
See also AAYA 6; BEST 90:4; CA 9-12R;
CANR 21; DLB 6; MTCW; SATA 27

Maturin, Charles Robert
1780(?)-1824 .... **NCLC**

Matute (Ausejo), Ana Maria
1925- .... **CLC 1**
See also CA 89-92; MTCW

Maugham, W. S.
See Maugham, W(illiam) Somerset

Maugham, W(illiam) Somerset
1874-1965 .... **CLC 1, 11, 15, 67; SSC**
See also CA 5-8R; 25-28R;
CDBLB 1914-1945; DLB 10, 36, 77, 100;
MTCW; SATA 54; WLC

Maugham, William Somerset
See Maugham, W(illiam) Somerset

Maupassant, (Henri Rene Albert) Guy de
1850-1893 .... **NCLC 1; SSC**
See also DLB 123; WLC

Maurhut, Richard
See Traven, B.

Mauriac, Claude 1914-............ **CLC**
See also CA 89-92; DLB 83

Mauriac, Francois (Charles)
1885-1970 .... **CLC 4, 9, 56**
See also CA 25-28; CAP 2; DLB 65;
MTCW

Mavor, Osborne Henry 1888-1951
See Bridie, James
See also CA 104

Maxwell, William (Keepers Jr.)
1908- .... **CLC 19**
See also CA 93-96; DLBY 80

May, Elaine 1932- .... **CLC 16**
See also CA 124; DLB 44

Mayakovski, Vladimir (Vladimirovich)
1893-1930 .... **TCLC 4, 18**
See also CA 104

Mayhew, Henry 1812-1887 ...... **NCLC 31**
See also DLB 18, 55

Maynard, Joyce 1953-........... **CLC 23**
See also CA 111; 129

Mayne, William (James Carter)
1928- .... **CLC 12**
See also CA 9-12R; CANR 37; CLR 25;
MAICYA; SAAS 11; SATA 6, 68

Mayo, Jim
See L'Amour, Louis (Dearborn)

Maysles, Albert 1926- .... **CLC 16**
See also CA 29-32R

Maysles, David 1932-........... **CLC 16**

Nin, Anais
1903-1977 ..... **CLC 1, 4, 8, 11, 14, 60; SSC 10**
See also AITN 2; CA 13-16R; 69-72; CANR 22; DLB 2, 4; MTCW

Nissenson, Hugh 1933- .... **CLC 4, 9**
See also CA 17-20R; CANR 27; DLB 28

Niven, Larry .... **CLC 8**
See also Niven, Laurence Van Cott
See also DLB 8

Niven, Laurence Van Cott 1938-
See Niven, Larry
See also CA 21-24R; CAAS 12; CANR 14; MTCW

Nixon, Agnes Eckhardt 1927- ...... **CLC 21**
See also CA 110

Nizan, Paul 1905-1940.......... **TCLC 40**
See also DLB 72

Nkosi, Lewis 1936- .... **CLC 45**
See also BLC 3; BW; CA 65-68; CANR 27

Nodier, (Jean) Charles (Emmanuel)
1780-1844 .... **NCLC 19**
See also DLB 119

Nolan, Christopher 1965- .... **CLC 58**
See also CA 111

Norden, Charles
See Durrell, Lawrence (George)

Nordhoff, Charles (Bernard)
1887-1947 .... **TCLC 23**
See also CA 108; DLB 9; SATA 23

Norman, Marsha 1947- .... **CLC 28**
See also CA 105; CABS 3; DLBY 84

Norris, Benjamin Franklin Jr.
1870-1902 .... **TCLC 24**
See also Norris, Frank
See also CA 110

Norris, Frank
See Norris, Benjamin Franklin Jr.
See also CDALB 1865-1917; DLB 12, 71

Norris, Leslie 1921- .... **CLC 14**
See also CA 11-12; CANR 14; CAP 1; DLB 27

North, Andrew
See Norton, Andre

North, Captain George
See Stevenson, Robert Louis (Balfour)

North, Milou
See Erdrich, Louise

Northrup, B. A.
See Hubbard, L(afayette) Ron(ald)

North Staffs
See Hulme, T(homas) E(rnest)

Norton, Alice Mary
See Norton, Andre
See also MAICYA; SATA 1, 43

Norton, Andre 1912- .... **CLC 12**
See also Norton, Alice Mary
See also CA 1-4R; CANR 2, 31; DLB 8, 52; MTCW

Norway, Nevil Shute 1899-1960
See Shute, Nevil
See also CA 102; 93-96

Norwid, Cyprian Kamil
1821-1883 .... **NCLC 17**

Nosille, Nabrah
See Ellison, Harlan

Nossack, Hans Erich 1901-1978 ..... **CLC 6**
See also CA 93-96; 85-88; DLB 69

Nosu, Chuji
See Ozu, Yasujiro

Nova, Craig 1945- .... **CLC 7, 31**
See also CA 45-48; CANR 2

Novak, Joseph
See Kosinski, Jerzy (Nikodem)

Novalis 1772-1801 .... **NCLC 13**
See also DLB 90

Nowlan, Alden (Albert) 1933-1983 .. **CLC 15**
See also CA 9-12R; CANR 5; DLB 53

Noyes, Alfred 1880-1958 .... **TCLC 7**
See also CA 104; DLB 20

Nunn, Kem 19(?)- .... **CLC 34**

Nye, Robert 1939- .... **CLC 13, 42**
See also CA 33-36R; CANR 29; DLB 14; MTCW; SATA 6

Nyro, Laura 1947- .... **CLC 17**

Oates, Joyce Carol
1938- ..... **CLC 1, 2, 3, 6, 9, 11, 15, 19, 33, 52; SSC 6**
See also AITN 1; BEST 89:2; CA 5-8R; CANR 25; CDALB 1968-1988; DLB 2, 5; DLBY 81; MTCW; WLC

O'Brien, E. G.
See Clarke, Arthur C(harles)

O'Brien, Edna
1936- ... **CLC 3, 5, 8, 13, 36, 65; SSC 10**
See also CA 1-4R; CANR 6; CDBLB 1960 to Present; DLB 14; MTCW

O'Brien, Fitz-James 1828-1862... **NCLC 21**
See also DLB 74

O'Brien, Flann .... **CLC 1, 4, 5, 7, 10, 47**
See also O Nuallain, Brian

O'Brien, Richard 1942- .... **CLC 17**
See also CA 124

O'Brien, Tim 1946- .... **CLC 7, 19, 40**
See also CA 85-88; DLBD 9; DLBY 80

Obstfelder, Sigbjoern 1866-1900... **TCLC 23**
See also CA 123

O'Casey, Sean
1880-1964 .... **CLC 1, 5, 9, 11, 15**
See also CA 89-92; CDBLB 1914-1945; DLB 10; MTCW

O'Cathasaigh, Sean
See O'Casey, Sean

Ochs, Phil 1940-1976............ **CLC 17**
See also CA 65-68

O'Connor, Edwin (Greene)
1918-1968 .... **CLC 14**
See also CA 93-96; 25-28R

O'Connor, (Mary) Flannery
1925-1964 ... **CLC 1, 2, 3, 6, 10, 13, 15, 21, 66; SSC 1**
See also AAYA 7; CA 1-4R; CANR 3; CDALB 1941-1968; DLB 2; DLBY 80; MTCW; WLC

O'Connor, Frank .... **CLC 23; SSC 5**
See also O'Donovan, Michael John

O'Dell, Scott 1898-1989.......... **CLC 30**
See also AAYA 3; CA 61-64; 129; CANR 12, 30; CLR 1, 16; DLB 52; MAICYA; SATA 12, 60

Odets, Clifford 1906-1963 .... **CLC 2, 28**
See also CA 85-88; DLB 7, 26; MTCW

O'Donnell, K. M.
See Malzberg, Barry N(athaniel)

O'Donnell, Lawrence
See Kuttner, Henry

O'Donovan, Michael John
1903-1966 .... **CLC 14**
See also O'Connor, Frank
See also CA 93-96

Oe, Kenzaburo 1935- .... **CLC 10, 36**
See also CA 97-100; CANR 36; MTCW

O'Faolain, Julia 1932- .... **CLC 6, 19, 47**
See also CA 81-84; CAAS 2; CANR 12; DLB 14; MTCW

O'Faolain, Sean
1900-1991 .... **CLC 1, 7, 14, 32, 70**
See also CA 61-64; 134; CANR 12; DLB 15; MTCW

O'Flaherty, Liam
1896-1984 .... **CLC 5, 34; SSC 6**
See also CA 101; 113; CANR 35; DLB 36; DLBY 84; MTCW

Ogilvy, Gavin
See Barrie, J(ames) M(atthew)

O'Grady, Standish James
1846-1928 .... **TCLC 5**
See also CA 104

O'Grady, Timothy 1951- .... **CLC 59**
See also CA 138

O'Hara, Frank 1926-1966 ..... **CLC 2, 5, 13**
See also CA 9-12R; 25-28R; CANR 33; DLB 5, 16; MTCW

O'Hara, John (Henry)
1905-1970 .... **CLC 1, 2, 3, 6, 11, 42**
See also CA 5-8R; 25-28R; CANR 31; CDALB 1929-1941; DLB 9, 86; DLBD 2; MTCW

O Hehir, Diana 1922- .... **CLC 41**
See also CA 93-96

Okigbo, Christopher (Ifenayichukwu)
1932-1967 .... **CLC 25**
See also BLC 3; BW; CA 77-80; MTCW

Olds, Sharon 1942-............ **CLC 32, 39**
See also CA 101; CANR 18; DLB 120

Oldstyle, Jonathan
See Irving, Washington

Olesha, Yuri (Karlovich)
1899-1960 .... **CLC 8**
See also CA 85-88

Oliphant, Margaret (Oliphant Wilson)
1828-1897 .... **NCLC 11**
See also DLB 18

Oliver, Mary 1935-............ **CLC 19, 34**
See also CA 21-24R; CANR 9; DLB 5

Olivier, Laurence (Kerr)
1907-1989 .... **CLC 20**
See also CA 111; 129

Olsen, Tillie 1913- ..... **CLC 4, 13; SSC 11**
See also CA 1-4R; CANR 1; DLB 28; DLBY 80; MTCW

Olson, Charles (John)
  1910-1970 ..... CLC 1, 2, 5, 6, 9, 11, 29
  See also CA 13-16; 25-28R; CABS 2;
  CANR 35; CAP 1; DLB 5, 16; MTCW

Olson, Toby 1937- .... CLC 28
  See also CA 65-68; CANR 9, 31

Olyesha, Yuri
  See Olesha, Yuri (Karlovich)

Ondaatje, Michael 1943- .... CLC 14, 29, 51
  See also CA 77-80; DLB 60

Oneal, Elizabeth 1934-
  See Oneal, Zibby
  See also CA 106; CANR 28; MAICYA;
  SATA 30

Oneal, Zibby .... CLC 30
  See also Oneal, Elizabeth
  See also AAYA 5; CLR 13

O'Neill, Eugene (Gladstone)
  1888-1953 .... TCLC 1, 6, 27
  See also AITN 1; CA 110; 132;
  CDALB 1929-1941; DLB 7; MTCW;
  WLC

Onetti, Juan Carlos 1909- .... CLC 7, 10
  See also CA 85-88; CANR 32; DLB 113;
  HW; MTCW

O Nuallain, Brian 1911-1966
  See O'Brien, Flann
  See also CA 21-22; 25-28R; CAP 2

Oppen, George 1908-1984 .... CLC 7, 13, 34
  See also CA 13-16R; 113; CANR 8; DLB 5

Oppenheim, E(dward) Phillips
  1866-1946 .... TCLC 45
  See also CA 111; DLB 70

Orlovitz, Gil 1918-1973 .... CLC 22
  See also CA 77-80; 45-48; DLB 2, 5

Orris
  See Ingelow, Jean

Ortega y Gasset, Jose 1883-1955 ... TCLC 9
  See also CA 106; 130; HW; MTCW

Ortiz, Simon J(oseph) 1941- .... CLC 45
  See also CA 134; DLB 120

Orton, Joe .... CLC 4, 13, 43; DC 3
  See also Orton, John Kingsley
  See also CDBLB 1960 to Present; DLB 13

Orton, John Kingsley 1933-1967
  See Orton, Joe
  See also CA 85-88; CANR 35; MTCW

Orwell, George .... TCLC 2, 6, 15, 31
  See also Blair, Eric (Arthur)
  See also CDBLB 1945-1960; DLB 15, 98;
  WLC

Osborne, David
  See Silverberg, Robert

Osborne, George
  See Silverberg, Robert

Osborne, John (James)
  1929- .... CLC 1, 2, 5, 11, 45
  See also CA 13-16R; CANR 21;
  CDBLB 1945-1960; DLB 13; MTCW;
  WLC

Osborne, Lawrence 1958- .... CLC 50

Oshima, Nagisa 1932- .... CLC 20
  See also CA 116; 121

Oskison, John M(ilton)
  1874-1947 .... TCLC 35

Ossoli, Sarah Margaret (Fuller marchesa d')
  1810-1850
  See Fuller, Margaret
  See also SATA 25

Ostrovsky, Alexander
  1823-1886 .... NCLC 30

Otero, Blas de 1916- .... CLC 11
  See also CA 89-92

Otto, Whitney 1955- .... CLC 70

Ouida .... TCLC 43
  See also De La Ramee, (Marie) Louise
  See also DLB 18

Ousmane, Sembene 1923- .... CLC 66
  See also BLC 3; BW; CA 117; 125; MTCW

Ovid 43B.C.-18th cent. (?)... CMLC 7; PC 2

Owen, Wilfred 1893-1918 ...... TCLC 5, 27
  See also CA 104; CDBLB 1914-1945;
  DLB 20; WLC

Owens, Rochelle 1936- .... CLC 8
  See also CA 17-20R; CAAS 2; CANR 39

Oz, Amos 1939- ... CLC 5, 8, 11, 27, 33, 54
  See also CA 53-56; CANR 27; MTCW

Ozick, Cynthia 1928- ...... CLC 3, 7, 28, 62
  See also BEST 90:1; CA 17-20R; CANR 23;
  DLB 28; DLBY 82; MTCW

Ozu, Yasujiro 1903-1963 .... CLC 16
  See also CA 112

Pacheco, C.
  See Pessoa, Fernando (Antonio Nogueira)

Pa Chin
  See Li Fei-kan

Pack, Robert 1929- .... CLC 13
  See also CA 1-4R; CANR 3; DLB 5

Padgett, Lewis
  See Kuttner, Henry

Padilla (Lorenzo), Heberto 1932- ... CLC 38
  See also AITN 1; CA 123; 131; HW

Page, Jimmy 1944- .... CLC 12

Page, Louise 1955- .... CLC 40

Page, P(atricia) K(athleen)
  1916- .... CLC 7, 18
  See also CA 53-56; CANR 4, 22; DLB 68;
  MTCW

Paget, Violet 1856-1935
  See Lee, Vernon
  See also CA 104

Paget-Lowe, Henry
  See Lovecraft, H(oward) P(hillips)

Paglia, Camille 1947- .... CLC 68

Pakenham, Antonia
  See Fraser, Antonia (Pakenham)

Palamas, Kostes 1859-1943 .... TCLC 5
  See also CA 105

Palazzeschi, Aldo 1885-1974 .... CLC 11
  See also CA 89-92; 53-56; DLB 114

Paley, Grace 1922- .... CLC 4, 6, 37; SSC 8
  See also CA 25-28R; CANR 13; DLB 28;
  MTCW

Palin, Michael (Edward) 1943- ..... CLC 21
  See also Monty Python
  See also CA 107; CANR 35; SATA 67

Palliser, Charles 1947- .... CLC 65
  See also CA 136

Palma, Ricardo 1833-1919 .... TCLC 29

Pancake, Breece Dexter 1952-1979
  See Pancake, Breece D'J
  See also CA 123; 109

Pancake, Breece D'J .... CLC 29
  See also Pancake, Breece Dexter

Papadiamantis, Alexandros
  1851-1911 .... TCLC 29

Papadiamantopoulos, Johannes 1856-1910
  See Moreas, Jean
  See also CA 117

Papini, Giovanni 1881-1956 ...... TCLC 22
  See also CA 121

Paracelsus 1493-1541 .... LC 14

Parasol, Peter
  See Stevens, Wallace

Parfenie, Maria
  See Codrescu, Andrei

Parini, Jay (Lee) 1948- .... CLC 54
  See also CA 97-100; CAAS 16; CANR 32

Park, Jordan
  See Kornbluth, C(yril) M.; Pohl, Frederik

Parker, Bert
  See Ellison, Harlan

Parker, Dorothy (Rothschild)
  1893-1967 .... CLC 15, 68; SSC 2
  See also CA 19-20; 25-28R; CAP 2;
  DLB 11, 45, 86; MTCW

Parker, Robert B(rown) 1932- ...... CLC 27
  See also BEST 89:4; CA 49-52; CANR 1,
  26; MTCW

Parkes, Lucas
  See Harris, John (Wyndham Parkes Lucas)
  Beynon

Parkin, Frank 1940- .... CLC 43

Parkman, Francis Jr. 1823-1893 .. NCLC 12
  See also DLB 1, 30

Parks, Gordon (Alexander Buchanan)
  1912- .... CLC 1, 16
  See also AITN 2; BLC 3; BW; CA 41-44R;
  CANR 26; DLB 33; SATA 8

Parnell, Thomas 1679-1718 .... LC 3
  See also DLB 94

Parra, Nicanor 1914- .... CLC 2
  See also CA 85-88; CANR 32; HW; MTCW

Parson Lot
  See Kingsley, Charles

Partridge, Anthony
  See Oppenheim, E(dward) Phillips

Pascoli, Giovanni 1855-1912 ...... TCLC 45

Pasolini, Pier Paolo
  1922-1975 .... CLC 20, 37
  See also CA 93-96; 61-64; MTCW

Pasquini
  See Silone, Ignazio

Pastan, Linda (Olenik) 1932- ...... CLC 27
  See also CA 61-64; CANR 18; DLB 5

Pasternak, Boris (Leonidovich)
  1890-1960 ..... CLC 7, 10, 18, 63; PC 6
  See also CA 127; 116; MTCW; WLC

Patchen, Kenneth 1911-1972 ... CLC 1, 2, 18
  See also CA 1-4R; 33-36R; CANR 3, 35;
  DLB 16, 48; MTCW

Pater, Walter (Horatio)
1839-1894 .... NCLC 7
See also CDBLB 1832-1890; DLB 57

Paterson, A(ndrew) B(arton)
1864-1941 .... TCLC 32

Paterson, Katherine (Womeldorf)
1932- .... CLC 12, 30
See also AAYA 1; CA 21-24R; CANR 28;
CLR 7; DLB 52; MAICYA; MTCW;
SATA 13, 53

Patmore, Coventry Kersey Dighton
1823-1896 .... NCLC 9
See also DLB 35, 98

Paton, Alan (Stewart)
1903-1988 .... CLC 4, 10, 25, 55
See also CA 13-16; 125; CANR 22; CAP 1;
MTCW; SATA 11, 56; WLC

Paton Walsh, Gillian   1939-
See Walsh, Jill Paton
See also CANR 38; MAICYA; SAAS 3;
SATA 4

Paulding, James Kirke   1778-1860.. NCLC 2
See also DLB 3, 59, 74

Paulin, Thomas Neilson   1949-
See Paulin, Tom
See also CA 123; 128

Paulin, Tom .... CLC 37
See also Paulin, Thomas Neilson
See also DLB 40

Paustovsky, Konstantin (Georgievich)
1892-1968 .... CLC 40
See also CA 93-96; 25-28R

Pavese, Cesare   1908-1950 .... TCLC 3
See also CA 104

Pavic, Milorad   1929- .... CLC 60
See also CA 136

Payne, Alan
See Jakes, John (William)

Paz, Gil
See Lugones, Leopoldo

Paz, Octavio
1914- ...... CLC 3, 4, 6, 10, 19, 51, 65;
PC 1
See also CA 73-76; CANR 32; DLBY 90;
HW; MTCW; WLC

Peacock, Molly   1947-............. CLC 60
See also CA 103; DLB 120

Peacock, Thomas Love
1785-1866 .... NCLC 22
See also DLB 96, 116

Peake, Mervyn   1911-1968 ...... CLC 7, 54
See also CA 5-8R; 25-28R; CANR 3;
DLB 15; MTCW; SATA 23

Pearce, Philippa .... CLC 21
See also Christie, (Ann) Philippa
See also CLR 9; MAICYA; SATA 1, 67

Pearl, Eric
See Elman, Richard

Pearson, T(homas) R(eid)   1956- .... CLC 39
See also CA 120; 130

Peck, John   1941- .... CLC 3
See also CA 49-52; CANR 3

Peck, Richard (Wayne)   1934- ...... CLC 21
See also AAYA 1; CA 85-88; CANR 19,
38; MAICYA; SAAS 2; SATA 18, 55

Peck, Robert Newton   1928-........ CLC 17
See also AAYA 3; CA 81-84; CANR 31;
MAICYA; SAAS 1; SATA 21, 62

Peckinpah, (David) Sam(uel)
1925-1984 .... CLC 20
See also CA 109; 114

Pedersen, Knut   1859-1952
See Hamsun, Knut
See also CA 104; 119; MTCW

Peeslake, Gaffer
See Durrell, Lawrence (George)

Peguy, Charles Pierre
1873-1914 .... TCLC 10
See also CA 107

Pena, Ramon del Valle y
See Valle-Inclan, Ramon (Maria) del

Pendennis, Arthur Esquir
See Thackeray, William Makepeace

Pepys, Samuel   1633-1703.......... LC 11
See also CDBLB 1660-1789; DLB 101;
WLC

Percy, Walker
1916-1990 ... CLC 2, 3, 6, 8, 14, 18, 47,
65
See also CA 1-4R; 131; CANR 1, 23;
DLB 2; DLBY 80, 90; MTCW

Perec, Georges   1936-1982 .... CLC 56
See also DLB 83

Pereda (y Sanchez de Porrua), Jose Maria de
1833-1906 .... TCLC 16
See also CA 117

Pereda y Porrua, Jose Maria de
See Pereda (y Sanchez de Porrua), Jose
Maria de

Peregoy, George Weems
See Mencken, H(enry) L(ouis)

Perelman, S(idney) J(oseph)
1904-1979 ... CLC 3, 5, 9, 15, 23, 44, 49
See also AITN 1, 2; CA 73-76; 89-92;
CANR 18; DLB 11, 44; MTCW

Peret, Benjamin   1899-1959 .... TCLC 20
See also CA 117

Peretz, Isaac Loeb   1851(?)-1915... TCLC 16
See also CA 109

Peretz, Yitzhok Leibush
See Peretz, Isaac Loeb

Perez Galdos, Benito   1843-1920 ... TCLC 27
See also CA 125; HW

Perrault, Charles   1628-1703 .... LC 2
See also MAICYA; SATA 25

Perry, Brighton
See Sherwood, Robert E(mmet)

Perse, Saint-John
See Leger, (Marie-Rene) Alexis Saint-Leger

Perse, St.-John .... CLC 4, 11, 46
See also Leger, (Marie-Rene) Alexis
Saint-Leger

Peseenz, Tulio F.
See Lopez y Fuentes, Gregorio

Pesetsky, Bette   1932-............. CLC 28
See also CA 133

Peshkov, Alexei Maximovich   1868-1936
See Gorky, Maxim
See also CA 105

Pessoa, Fernando (Antonio Nogueira)
1888-1935 .... TCLC 27
See also CA 125

Peterkin, Julia Mood   1880-1961.... CLC 31
See also CA 102; DLB 9

Peters, Joan K.   1945-............. CLC 39

Peters, Robert L(ouis)   1924-........ CLC 7
See also CA 13-16R; CAAS 8; DLB 105

Petofi, Sandor   1823-1849....... NCLC 21

Petrakis, Harry Mark   1923-........ CLC 3
See also CA 9-12R; CANR 4, 30

Petrov, Evgeny .... TCLC 21
See also Kataev, Evgeny Petrovich

Petry, Ann (Lane)   1908- ...... CLC 1, 7, 18
See also BW; CA 5-8R; CAAS 6; CANR 4;
CLR 12; DLB 76; MAICYA; MTCW;
SATA 5

Petursson, Halligrimur   1614-1674 .... LC 8

Philipson, Morris H.   1926-........ CLC 53
See also CA 1-4R; CANR 4

Phillips, David Graham
1867-1911 .... TCLC 44
See also CA 108; DLB 9, 12

Phillips, Jack
See Sandburg, Carl (August)

Phillips, Jayne Anne   1952- ..... CLC 15, 33
See also CA 101; CANR 24; DLBY 80;
MTCW

Phillips, Richard
See Dick, Philip K(indred)

Phillips, Robert (Schaeffer)   1938-... CLC 28
See also CA 17-20R; CAAS 13; CANR 8;
DLB 105

Phillips, Ward
See Lovecraft, H(oward) P(hillips)

Piccolo, Lucio   1901-1969.......... CLC 13
See also CA 97-100; DLB 114

Pickthall, Marjorie L(owry) C(hristie)
1883-1922 .... TCLC 21
See also CA 107; DLB 92

Pico della Mirandola, Giovanni
1463-1494 .... LC 15

Piercy, Marge
1936- .... CLC 3, 6, 14, 18, 27, 62
See also CA 21-24R; CAAS 1; CANR 13;
DLB 120; MTCW

Piers, Robert
See Anthony, Piers

Pieyre de Mandiargues, Andre   1909-1991
See Mandiargues, Andre Pieyre de
See also CA 103; 136; CANR 22

Pilnyak, Boris .... TCLC 23
See also Vogau, Boris Andreyevich

Pincherle, Alberto   1907-1990 ... CLC 11, 18
See also Moravia, Alberto
See also CA 25-28R; 132; CANR 33;
MTCW

Pineda, Cecile   1942-............. CLC 39
See also CA 118

Pinero, Arthur Wing   1855-1934 ... TCLC 32
See also CA 110; DLB 10

Pinero, Miguel (Antonio Gomez)
1946-1988 .... CLC 4, 55
See also CA 61-64; 125; CANR 29; HW

Priestley, J(ohn) B(oynton)
1894-1984 ....**CLC 2, 5, 9, 34**
See also CA 9-12R; 113; CANR 33;
CDBLB 1914-1945; DLB 10, 34, 77, 100;
DLBY 84; MTCW

Prince, F(rank) T(empleton) 1912- .. **CLC 22**
See also CA 101; DLB 20

Prince 1958(?)- ....**CLC 35**

Prince Kropotkin
See Kropotkin, Peter (Aleksieevich)

Prior, Matthew 1664-1721...........**LC 4**
See also DLB 95

Pritchard, William H(arrison)
1932- ....**CLC 34**
See also CA 65-68; CANR 23; DLB 111

Pritchett, V(ictor) S(awdon)
1900- ....**CLC 5, 13, 15, 41**
See also CA 61-64; CANR 31; DLB 15;
MTCW

Private 19022
See Manning, Frederic

Probst, Mark 1925- ....**CLC 59**
See also CA 130

Prokosch, Frederic 1908-1989....**CLC 4, 48**
See also CA 73-76; 128; DLB 48

Prophet, The
See Dreiser, Theodore (Herman Albert)

Prose, Francine 1947-............**CLC 45**
See also CA 109; 112

Proudhon
See Cunha, Euclides (Rodrigues Pimenta) da

Proust,
(Valentin-Louis-George-Eugene-)Marcel
1871-1922 ....**TCLC 7, 13, 33**
See also CA 104; 120; DLB 65; MTCW;
WLC

Prowler, Harley
See Masters, Edgar Lee

Prus, Boleslaw..................**TCLC 48**
See also Glowacki, Aleksander

Pryor, Richard (Franklin Lenox Thomas)
1940- ....**CLC 26**
See also CA 122

Przybyszewski, Stanislaw
1868-1927 ....**TCLC 36**
See also DLB 66

Pteleon
See Grieve, C(hristopher) M(urray)

Puckett, Lute
See Masters, Edgar Lee

Puig, Manuel
1932-1990 ....**CLC 3, 5, 10, 28, 65**
See also CA 45-48; CANR 2, 32; DLB 113;
HW; MTCW

Purdy, A(lfred) W(ellington)
1918- ....**CLC 3, 6, 14, 50**
See also Purdy, Al
See also CA 81-84

Purdy, Al
See Purdy, A(lfred) W(ellington)
See also DLB 88

Purdy, James (Amos)
1923- ....**CLC 2, 4, 10, 28, 52**
See also CA 33-36R; CAAS 1; CANR 19;
DLB 2; MTCW

Pure, Simon
See Swinnerton, Frank Arthur

Pushkin, Alexander (Sergeyevich)
1799-1837 ....**NCLC 3, 27**
See also SATA 61; WLC

P'u Sung-ling 1640-1715 ....**LC 3**

Putnam, Arthur Lee
See Alger, Horatio Jr.

Puzo, Mario 1920- ....**CLC 1, 2, 6, 36**
See also CA 65-68; CANR 4; DLB 6;
MTCW

Pym, Barbara (Mary Crampton)
1913-1980 ....**CLC 13, 19, 37**
See also CA 13-14; 97-100; CANR 13, 34;
CAP 1; DLB 14; DLBY 87; MTCW

Pynchon, Thomas (Ruggles Jr.)
1937- .. **CLC 2, 3, 6, 9, 11, 18, 33, 62, 72**
See also BEST 90:2; CA 17-20R; CANR 22;
DLB 2; MTCW; WLC

Qian Zhongshu
See Ch'ien Chung-shu

Qroll
See Dagerman, Stig (Halvard)

Quarrington, Paul (Lewis) 1953-....**CLC 65**
See also CA 129

Quasimodo, Salvatore 1901-1968 ...**CLC 10**
See also CA 13-16; 25-28R; CAP 1;
DLB 114; MTCW

Queen, Ellery..................**CLC 3, 11**
See also Dannay, Frederic; Davidson,
Avram; Lee, Manfred B(ennington);
Sturgeon, Theodore (Hamilton); Vance,
John Holbrook

Queen, Ellery Jr.
See Dannay, Frederic; Lee, Manfred
B(ennington)

Queneau, Raymond
1903-1976 ....**CLC 2, 5, 10, 42**
See also CA 77-80; 69-72; CANR 32;
DLB 72; MTCW

Quin, Ann (Marie) 1936-1973 ......**CLC 6**
See also CA 9-12R; 45-48; DLB 14

Quinn, Martin
See Smith, Martin Cruz

Quinn, Simon
See Smith, Martin Cruz

Quiroga, Horacio (Sylvestre)
1878-1937 ....**TCLC 20**
See also CA 117; 131; HW; MTCW

Quoirez, Francoise 1935-...........**CLC 9**
See also Sagan, Francoise
See also CA 49-52; CANR 6, 39; MTCW

Raabe, Wilhelm 1831-1910 ....**TCLC 45**

Rabe, David (William) 1940-...**CLC 4, 8, 33**
See also CA 85-88; CABS 3; DLB 7

Rabelais, Francois 1483-1553 ....**LC 5**
See also WLC

Rabinovitch, Sholem 1859-1916
See Aleichem, Sholom
See also CA 104

Radcliffe, Ann (Ward) 1764-1823 .. **NCLC 6**
See also DLB 39

Radiguet, Raymond 1903-1923 ....**TCLC 29**
See also DLB 65

Radnoti, Miklos 1909-1944 ......**TCLC 16**
See also CA 118

Rado, James 1939-...............**CLC 17**
See also CA 105

Radvanyi, Netty 1900-1983
See Seghers, Anna
See also CA 85-88; 110

Raeburn, John (Hay) 1941-........**CLC 34**
See also CA 57-60

Ragni, Gerome 1942-1991 ....**CLC 17**
See also CA 105; 134

Rahv, Philip....................**CLC 24**
See also Greenberg, Ivan

Raine, Craig 1944-...............**CLC 32**
See also CA 108; CANR 29; DLB 40

Raine, Kathleen (Jessie) 1908- ...**CLC 7, 45**
See also CA 85-88; DLB 20; MTCW

Rainis, Janis 1865-1929 ....**TCLC 29**

Rakosi, Carl.....................**CLC 47**
See also Rawley, Callman
See also CAAS 5

Raleigh, Richard
See Lovecraft, H(oward) P(hillips)

Rallentando, H. P.
See Sayers, Dorothy L(eigh)

Ramal, Walter
See de la Mare, Walter (John)

Ramon, Juan
See Jimenez (Mantecon), Juan Ramon

Ramos, Graciliano 1892-1953 .....**TCLC 32**

Rampersad, Arnold 1941-.........**CLC 44**
See also CA 127; 133; DLB 111

Rampling, Anne
See Rice, Anne

Ramuz, Charles-Ferdinand
1878-1947 ....**TCLC 33**

Rand, Ayn 1905-1982........**CLC 3, 30, 44**
See also CA 13-16R; 105; CANR 27;
MTCW; WLC

Randall, Dudley (Felker) 1914-......**CLC 1**
See also BLC 3; BW; CA 25-28R;
CANR 23; DLB 41

Randall, Robert
See Silverberg, Robert

Ranger, Ken
See Creasey, John

Ransom, John Crowe
1888-1974 ....**CLC 2, 4, 5, 11, 24**
See also CA 5-8R; 49-52; CANR 6, 34;
DLB 45, 63; MTCW

Rao, Raja 1909- ....**CLC 25, 56**
See also CA 73-76; MTCW

Raphael, Frederic (Michael)
1931- ....**CLC 2, 14**
See also CA 1-4R; CANR 1; DLB 14

Ratcliffe, James P.
See Mencken, H(enry) L(ouis)

Rathbone, Julian 1935- ....**CLC 41**
See also CA 101; CANR 34

Rattigan, Terence (Mervyn)
1911-1977 ....**CLC 7**
See also CA 85-88; 73-76;
CDBLB 1945-1960; DLB 13; MTCW

Riley, Tex
See Creasey, John

Rilke, Rainer Maria
1875-1926 ..... **TCLC 1, 6, 19; PC 2**
See also CA 104; 132; DLB 81; MTCW

Rimbaud, (Jean Nicolas) Arthur
1854-1891 ..... **NCLC 4, 35; PC 3**
See also WLC

Ringmaster, The
See Mencken, H(enry) L(ouis)

Ringwood, Gwen(dolyn Margaret) Pharis
1910-1984 ..... **CLC 48**
See also CA 112; DLB 88

Rio, Michel 19(?)- ..... **CLC 43**

Ritsos, Giannes
See Ritsos, Yannis

Ritsos, Yannis 1909-1990 ..... **CLC 6, 13, 31**
See also CA 77-80; 133; CANR 39; MTCW

Ritter, Erika 1948(?)- ..... **CLC 52**

Rivera, Jose Eustasio 1889-1928 ... **TCLC 35**
See also HW

Rivers, Conrad Kent 1933-1968 ..... **CLC 1**
See also BW; CA 85-88; DLB 41

Rivers, Elfrida
See Bradley, Marion Zimmer

Riverside, John
See Heinlein, Robert A(nson)

Rizal, Jose 1861-1896 ..... **NCLC 27**

Roa Bastos, Augusto (Antonio)
1917- ..... **CLC 45**
See also CA 131; DLB 113; HW

Robbe-Grillet, Alain
1922- ..... **CLC 1, 2, 4, 6, 8, 10, 14, 43**
See also CA 9-12R; CANR 33; DLB 83;
MTCW

Robbins, Harold 1916- ..... **CLC 5**
See also CA 73-76; CANR 26; MTCW

Robbins, Thomas Eugene 1936-
See Robbins, Tom
See also CA 81-84; CANR 29; MTCW

Robbins, Tom ..... **CLC 9, 32, 64**
See also Robbins, Thomas Eugene
See also BEST 90:3; DLBY 80

Robbins, Trina 1938- ..... **CLC 21**
See also CA 128

Roberts, Charles G(eorge) D(ouglas)
1860-1943 ..... **TCLC 8**
See also CA 105; DLB 92; SATA 29

Roberts, Kate 1891-1985 ..... **CLC 15**
See also CA 107; 116

Roberts, Keith (John Kingston)
1935- ..... **CLC 14**
See also CA 25-28R

Roberts, Kenneth (Lewis)
1885-1957 ..... **TCLC 23**
See also CA 109; DLB 9

Roberts, Michele (B.) 1949- ..... **CLC 48**
See also CA 115

Robertson, Ellis
See Ellison, Harlan; Silverberg, Robert

Robertson, Thomas William
1829-1871 ..... **NCLC 35**

Robinson, Edwin Arlington
1869-1935 ..... **TCLC 5; PC 1**
See also CA 104; 133; CDALB 1865-1917;
DLB 54; MTCW

Robinson, Henry Crabb
1775-1867 ..... **NCLC 15**
See also DLB 107

Robinson, Jill 1936- ..... **CLC 10**
See also CA 102

Robinson, Kim Stanley 1952- ..... **CLC 34**
See also CA 126

Robinson, Lloyd
See Silverberg, Robert

Robinson, Marilynne 1944- ..... **CLC 25**
See also CA 116

Robinson, Smokey ..... **CLC 21**
See also Robinson, William Jr.

Robinson, William Jr. 1940-
See Robinson, Smokey
See also CA 116

Robison, Mary 1949- ..... **CLC 42**
See also CA 113; 116

Roddenberry, Eugene Wesley 1921-1991
See Roddenberry, Gene
See also CA 110; 135; CANR 37; SATA 45

Roddenberry, Gene ..... **CLC 17**
See also Roddenberry, Eugene Wesley
See also AAYA 5; SATO 69

Rodgers, Mary 1931- ..... **CLC 12**
See also CA 49-52; CANR 8; CLR 20;
MAICYA; SATA 8

Rodgers, W(illiam) R(obert)
1909-1969 ..... **CLC 7**
See also CA 85-88; DLB 20

Rodman, Eric
See Silverberg, Robert

Rodman, Howard 1920(?)-1985 ..... **CLC 65**
See also CA 118

Rodman, Maia
See Wojciechowska, Maia (Teresa)

Rodriguez, Claudio 1934- ..... **CLC 10**

Roelvaag, O(le) E(dvart)
1876-1931 ..... **TCLC 17**
See also CA 117; DLB 9

Roethke, Theodore (Huebner)
1908-1963 ..... **CLC 1, 3, 8, 11, 19, 46**
See also CA 81-84; CABS 2;
CDALB 1941-1968; DLB 5; MTCW

Rogers, Thomas Hunton 1927- ..... **CLC 57**
See also CA 89-92

Rogers, Will(iam Penn Adair)
1879-1935 ..... **TCLC 8**
See also CA 105; DLB 11

Rogin, Gilbert 1929- ..... **CLC 18**
See also CA 65-68; CANR 15

Rohan, Koda ..... **TCLC 22**
See also Koda Shigeyuki

Rohmer, Eric ..... **CLC 16**
See also Scherer, Jean-Marie Maurice

Rohmer, Sax ..... **TCLC 28**
See also Ward, Arthur Henry Sarsfield
See also DLB 70

Roiphe, Anne Richardson 1935- ... **CLC 3, 9**
See also CA 89-92; DLBY 80

Rolfe, Frederick (William Serafino Austin
Lewis Mary) 1860-1913 ..... **TCLC 12**
See also CA 107; DLB 34

Rolland, Romain 1866-1944 ..... **TCLC 23**
See also CA 118; DLB 65

Rolvaag, O(le) E(dvart)
See Roelvaag, O(le) E(dvart)

Romain Arnaud, Saint
See Aragon, Louis

Romains, Jules 1885-1972 ..... **CLC 7**
See also CA 85-88; CANR 34; DLB 65;
MTCW

Romero, Jose Ruben 1890-1952 ... **TCLC 14**
See also CA 114; 131; HW

Ronsard, Pierre de 1524-1585 ..... **LC 6**

Rooke, Leon 1934- ..... **CLC 25, 34**
See also CA 25-28R; CANR 23

Roper, William 1498-1578 ..... **LC 10**

Roquelaure, A. N.
See Rice, Anne

Rosa, Joao Guimaraes 1908-1967 ... **CLC 23**
See also CA 89-92; DLB 113

Rosen, Richard (Dean) 1949- ..... **CLC 39**
See also CA 77-80

Rosenberg, Isaac 1890-1918 ..... **TCLC 12**
See also CA 107; DLB 20

Rosenblatt, Joe ..... **CLC 15**
See also Rosenblatt, Joseph

Rosenblatt, Joseph 1933-
See Rosenblatt, Joe
See also CA 89-92

Rosenfeld, Samuel 1896-1963
See Tzara, Tristan
See also CA 89-92

Rosenthal, M(acha) L(ouis) 1917- ... **CLC 28**
See also CA 1-4R; CAAS 6; CANR 4;
DLB 5; SATA 59

Ross, Barnaby
See Dannay, Frederic

Ross, Bernard L.
See Follett, Ken(neth Martin)

Ross, J. H.
See Lawrence, T(homas) E(dward)

Ross, (James) Sinclair 1908- ..... **CLC 13**
See also CA 73-76; DLB 88

Rossetti, Christina (Georgina)
1830-1894 ..... **NCLC 2**
See also DLB 35; MAICYA; SATA 20;
WLC

Rossetti, Dante Gabriel
1828-1882 ..... **NCLC 4**
See also CDBLB 1832-1890; DLB 35; WLC

Rossner, Judith (Perelman)
1935- ..... **CLC 6, 9, 29**
See also AITN 2; BEST 90:3; CA 17-20R;
CANR 18; DLB 6; MTCW

Rostand, Edmond (Eugene Alexis)
1868-1918 ..... **TCLC 6, 37**
See also CA 104; 126; MTCW

Roth, Henry 1906- ..... **CLC 2, 6, 11**
See also CA 11-12; CANR 38; CAP 1;
DLB 28; MTCW

Roth, Joseph 1894-1939 ..... **TCLC 33**
See also DLB 85

Sanchez, Sonia 1934-............. **CLC 5**
See also BLC 3; BW; CA 33-36R;
CANR 24; CLR 18; DLB 41; DLBD 8;
MAICYA; MTCW; SATA 22

Sand, George 1804-1876......... **NCLC 2**
See also DLB 119; WLC

Sandburg, Carl (August)
1878-1967 ... **CLC 1, 4, 10, 15, 35; PC 2**
See also CA 5-8R; 25-28R; CANR 35;
CDALB 1865-1917; DLB 17, 54;
MAICYA; MTCW; SATA 8; WLC

Sandburg, Charles
See Sandburg, Carl (August)

Sandburg, Charles A.
See Sandburg, Carl (August)

Sanders, (James) Ed(ward) 1939-... **CLC 53**
See also CA 13-16R; CANR 13; DLB 16

Sanders, Lawrence 1920-......... **CLC 41**
See also BEST 89:4; CA 81-84; CANR 33;
MTCW

Sanders, Noah
See Blount, Roy (Alton) Jr.

Sanders, Winston P.
See Anderson, Poul (William)

Sandoz, Mari(e Susette)
1896-1966 .... **CLC 28**
See also CA 1-4R; 25-28R; CANR 17;
DLB 9; MTCW; SATA 5

Saner, Reg(inald Anthony) 1931-.... **CLC 9**
See also CA 65-68

Sannazaro, Jacopo 1456(?)-1530...... **LC 8**

Sansom, William 1912-1976....... **CLC 2, 6**
See also CA 5-8R; 65-68; MTCW

Santayana, George 1863-1952..... **TCLC 40**
See also CA 115; DLB 54, 71

Santiago, Danny .... **CLC 33**
See also James, Daniel (Lewis); James,
Daniel (Lewis)
See also DLB 122

Santmyer, Helen Hooven
1895-1986 .... **CLC 33**
See also CA 1-4R; 118; CANR 15, 33;
DLBY 84; MTCW

Santos, Bienvenido N(uqui) 1911-... **CLC 22**
See also CA 101; CANR 19

Sapper .... **TCLC 44**
See also McNeile, Herman Cyril

Sappho fl. 6th cent. B.C.-.... **CMLC 3; PC 5**

Sarduy, Severo 1937-.............. **CLC 6**
See also CA 89-92; DLB 113; HW

Sargeson, Frank 1903-1982........ **CLC 31**
See also CA 25-28R; 106; CANR 38

Sarmiento, Felix Ruben Garcia 1867-1916
See Dario, Ruben
See also CA 104

Saroyan, William
1908-1981 ..... **CLC 1, 8, 10, 29, 34, 56**
See also CA 5-8R; 103; CANR 30; DLB 7,
9, 86; DLBY 81; MTCW; SATA 23, 24;
WLC

Sarraute, Nathalie
1900- .... **CLC 1, 2, 4, 8, 10, 31**
See also CA 9-12R; CANR 23; DLB 83;
MTCW

Sarton, (Eleanor) May
1912- .... **CLC 4, 14, 49**
See also CA 1-4R; CANR 1, 34; DLB 48;
DLBY 81; MTCW; SATA 36

Sartre, Jean-Paul
1905-1980 ... **CLC 1, 4, 7, 9, 13, 18, 24,
44, 50, 52; DC 3**
See also CA 9-12R; 97-100; CANR 21;
DLB 72; MTCW; WLC

Sassoon, Siegfried (Lorraine)
1886-1967 .... **CLC 36**
See also CA 104; 25-28R; CANR 36;
DLB 20; MTCW

Satterfield, Charles
See Pohl, Frederik

Saul, John (W. III) 1942- .... **CLC 46**
See also BEST 90:4; CA 81-84; CANR 16

Saunders, Caleb
See Heinlein, Robert A(nson)

Saura (Atares), Carlos 1932-....... **CLC 20**
See also CA 114; 131; HW

Sauser-Hall, Frederic 1887-1961.... **CLC 18**
See also CA 102; 93-96; CANR 36; MTCW

Savage, Catharine
See Brosman, Catharine Savage

Savage, Thomas 1915- .... **CLC 40**
See also CA 126; 132; CAAS 15

Savan, Glenn .... **CLC 50**

Saven, Glenn 19(?)- .... **CLC 50**

Sayers, Dorothy L(eigh)
1893-1957 .... **TCLC 2, 15**
See also CA 104; 119; CDBLB 1914-1945;
DLB 10, 36, 77, 100; MTCW

Sayers, Valerie 1952-............. **CLC 50**
See also CA 134

Sayles, John Thomas 1950-... **CLC 7, 10, 14**
See also CA 57-60; DLB 44

Scammell, Michael .... **CLC 34**

Scannell, Vernon 1922- .... **CLC 49**
See also CA 5-8R; CANR 8, 24; DLB 27;
SATA 59

Scarlett, Susan
See Streatfeild, (Mary) Noel

Schaeffer, Susan Fromberg
1941-.................. **CLC 6, 11, 22**
See also CA 49-52; CANR 18; DLB 28;
MTCW; SATA 22

Schary, Jill
See Robinson, Jill

Schell, Jonathan 1943-............ **CLC 35**
See also CA 73-76; CANR 12

Schelling, Friedrich Wilhelm Joseph von
1775-1854 .... **NCLC 30**
See also DLB 90

Scherer, Jean-Marie Maurice 1920-
See Rohmer, Eric
See also CA 110

Schevill, James (Erwin) 1920-....... **CLC 7**
See also CA 5-8R; CAAS 12

Schiller, Friedrich 1759-1805 .... **NCLC 39**
See also DLB 94

Schisgal, Murray (Joseph) 1926-..... **CLC 6**
See also CA 21-24R

Schlee, Ann 1934-................ **CLC 35**
See also CA 101; CANR 29; SATA 36, 44

Schlegel, August Wilhelm von
1767-1845 .... **NCLC 15**
See also DLB 94

Schlegel, Johann Elias (von)
1719(?)-1749 .... **LC 5**

Schmidt, Arno (Otto) 1914-1979.... **CLC 56**
See also CA 128; 109; DLB 69

Schmitz, Aron Hector 1861-1928
See Svevo, Italo
See also CA 104; 122; MTCW

Schnackenberg, Gjertrud 1953-..... **CLC 40**
See also CA 116; DLB 120

Schneider, Leonard Alfred 1925-1966
See Bruce, Lenny
See also CA 89-92

Schnitzler, Arthur 1862-1931 ...... **TCLC 4**
See also CA 104; DLB 81, 118

Schor, Sandra (M.) 1932(?)-1990 ... **CLC 65**
See also CA 132

Schorer, Mark 1908-1977 .... **CLC 9**
See also CA 5-8R; 73-76; CANR 7;
DLB 103

Schrader, Paul Joseph 1946-....... **CLC 26**
See also CA 37-40R; DLB 44

Schreiner, Olive (Emilie Albertina)
1855-1920 .... **TCLC 9**
See also CA 105; DLB 18

Schulberg, Budd (Wilson)
1914- .... **CLC 7, 48**
See also CA 25-28R; CANR 19; DLB 6, 26,
28; DLBY 81

Schulz, Bruno 1892-1942.......... **TCLC 5**
See also CA 115; 123

Schulz, Charles M(onroe) 1922- .... **CLC 12**
See also CA 9-12R; CANR 6; SATA 10

Schuyler, James Marcus
1923-1991 .... **CLC 5, 23**
See also CA 101; 134; DLB 5

Schwartz, Delmore (David)
1913-1966 .... **CLC 2, 4, 10, 45**
See also CA 17-18; 25-28R; CANR 35;
CAP 2; DLB 28, 48; MTCW

Schwartz, Ernst
See Ozu, Yasujiro

Schwartz, John Burnham 1965- .... **CLC 59**
See also CA 132

Schwartz, Lynne Sharon 1939-..... **CLC 31**
See also CA 103

Schwartz, Muriel A.
See Eliot, T(homas) S(tearns)

Schwarz-Bart, Andre 1928-....... **CLC 2, 4**
See also CA 89-92

Schwarz-Bart, Simone 1938-........ **CLC 7**
See also CA 97-100

Schwob, (Mayer Andre) Marcel
1867-1905 .... **TCLC 20**
See also CA 117; DLB 123

Sciascia, Leonardo
1921-1989 .... **CLC 8, 9, 41**
See also CA 85-88; 130; CANR 35; MTCW

Scoppettone, Sandra 1936-........ **CLC 26**
See also CA 5-8R; SATA 9

Sheldon, Alice Hastings Bradley
1915(?)-1987
See Tiptree, James Jr.
See also CA 108; 122; CANR 34; MTCW

Sheldon, John
See Bloch, Robert (Albert)

Shelley, Mary Wollstonecraft (Godwin)
1797-1851 . . . . **NCLC 14**
See also CDBLB 1789-1832; DLB 110, 116;
SATA 29; WLC

Shelley, Percy Bysshe
1792-1822 . . . . **NCLC 18**
See also CDBLB 1789-1832; DLB 96, 110;
WLC

Shepard, Jim 1956- . . . . **CLC 36**
See also CA 137

Shepard, Lucius 19(?)- . . . . **CLC 34**
See also CA 128

Shepard, Sam
1943- . . . . **CLC 4, 6, 17, 34, 41, 44**
See also AAYA 1; CA 69-72; CABS 3;
CANR 22; DLB 7; MTCW

Shepherd, Michael
See Ludlum, Robert

Sherburne, Zoa (Morin) 1912- . . . . . . **CLC 30**
See also CA 1-4R; CANR 3, 37; MAICYA;
SATA 3

Sheridan, Frances 1724-1766 . . . . **LC 7**
See also DLB 39, 84

Sheridan, Richard Brinsley
1751-1816 . . . . **NCLC 5; DC 1**
See also CDBLB 1660-1789; DLB 89; WLC

Sherman, Jonathan Marc . . . . **CLC 55**

Sherman, Martin 1941(?)- . . . . **CLC 19**
See also CA 116; 123

Sherwin, Judith Johnson 1936- . . . **CLC 7, 15**
See also CA 25-28R; CANR 34

Sherwood, Robert E(mmet)
1896-1955 . . . . **TCLC 3**
See also CA 104; DLB 7, 26

Shiel, M(atthew) P(hipps)
1865-1947 . . . . **TCLC 8**
See also CA 106

Shiga, Naoya 1883-1971 . . . . **CLC 33**
See also CA 101; 33-36R

Shimazaki Haruki 1872-1943
See Shimazaki Toson
See also CA 105; 134

Shimazaki Toson . . . . **TCLC 5**
See also Shimazaki Haruki

Sholokhov, Mikhail (Aleksandrovich)
1905-1984 . . . . **CLC 7, 15**
See also CA 101; 112; MTCW; SATA 36

Shone, Patric
See Hanley, James

Shreve, Susan Richards 1939- . . . . . . **CLC 23**
See also CA 49-52; CAAS 5; CANR 5, 38;
MAICYA; SATA 41, 46

Shue, Larry 1946-1985 . . . . **CLC 52**
See also CA 117

Shu-Jen, Chou 1881-1936
See Hsun, Lu
See also CA 104

Shulman, Alix Kates 1932- . . . . . . **CLC 2, 10**
See also CA 29-32R; SATA 7

Shuster, Joe 1914- . . . . **CLC 21**

Shute, Nevil . . . . **CLC 30**
See also Norway, Nevil Shute

Shuttle, Penelope (Diane) 1947- . . . . . **CLC 7**
See also CA 93-96; CANR 39; DLB 14, 40

Sidney, Mary 1561-1621 . . . . **LC 19**

Sidney, Sir Philip 1554-1586 . . . . **LC 19**
See also CDBLB Before 1660

Siegel, Jerome 1914- . . . . **CLC 21**
See also CA 116

Siegel, Jerry
See Siegel, Jerome

Sienkiewicz, Henryk (Adam Alexander Pius)
1846-1916 . . . . **TCLC 3**
See also CA 104; 134

Sierra, Gregorio Martinez
See Martinez Sierra, Gregorio

Sierra, Maria (de la O'LeJarraga) Martinez
See Martinez Sierra, Maria (de la
O'LeJarraga)

Sigal, Clancy 1926- . . . . **CLC 7**
See also CA 1-4R

Sigourney, Lydia Howard (Huntley)
1791-1865 . . . . **NCLC 21**
See also DLB 1, 42, 73

Siguenza y Gongora, Carlos de
1645-1700 . . . . **LC 8**

Sigurjonsson, Johann 1880-1919 . . . **TCLC 27**

Sikelianos, Angelos 1884-1951 . . . . **TCLC 39**

Silkin, Jon 1930- . . . . **CLC 2, 6, 43**
See also CA 5-8R; CAAS 5; DLB 27

Silko, Leslie Marmon 1948- . . . . **CLC 23, 74**
See also CA 115; 122

Sillanpaa, Frans Eemil 1888-1964 . . . **CLC 19**
See also CA 129; 93-96; MTCW

Sillitoe, Alan
1928- . . . . **CLC 1, 3, 6, 10, 19, 57**
See also AITN 1; CA 9-12R; CAAS 2;
CANR 8, 26; CDBLB 1960 to Present;
DLB 14; MTCW; SATA 61

Silone, Ignazio 1900-1978 . . . . **CLC 4**
See also CA 25-28; 81-84; CANR 34;
CAP 2; MTCW

Silver, Joan Micklin 1935- . . . . **CLC 20**
See also CA 114; 121

Silverberg, Robert 1935- . . . . **CLC 7**
See also CA 1-4R; CAAS 3; CANR 1, 20,
36; DLB 8; MAICYA; MTCW; SATA 13

Silverstein, Alvin 1933- . . . . **CLC 17**
See also CA 49-52; CANR 2; CLR 25;
MAICYA; SATA 8, 69

Silverstein, Virginia B(arbara Opshelor)
1937- . . . . **CLC 17**
See also CA 49-52; CANR 2; CLR 25;
MAICYA; SATA 8, 69

Sim, Georges
See Simenon, Georges (Jacques Christian)

Simak, Clifford D(onald)
1904-1988 . . . . **CLC 1, 55**
See also CA 1-4R; 125; CANR 1, 35;
DLB 8; MTCW; SATA 56

Simenon, Georges (Jacques Christian)
1903-1989 . . . . **CLC 1, 2, 3, 8, 18, 47**
See also CA 85-88; 129; CANR 35;
DLB 72; DLBY 89; MTCW

Simic, Charles 1938- . . . **CLC 6, 9, 22, 49, 68**
See also CA 29-32R; CAAS 4; CANR 12,
33; DLB 105

Simmons, Charles (Paul) 1924- . . . . . **CLC 57**
See also CA 89-92

Simmons, Dan 1948- . . . . **CLC 44**
See also CA 138

Simmons, James (Stewart Alexander)
1933- . . . . **CLC 43**
See also CA 105; DLB 40

Simms, William Gilmore
1806-1870 . . . . **NCLC 3**
See also DLB 3, 30, 59, 73

Simon, Carly 1945- . . . . **CLC 26**
See also CA 105

Simon, Claude 1913- . . . . . . **CLC 4, 9, 15, 39**
See also CA 89-92; CANR 33; DLB 83;
MTCW

Simon, (Marvin) Neil
1927- . . . . **CLC 6, 11, 31, 39, 70**
See also AITN 1; CA 21-24R; CANR 26;
DLB 7; MTCW

Simon, Paul 1942(?)- . . . . **CLC 17**
See also CA 116

Simonon, Paul 1956(?)- . . . . **CLC 30**
See also The Clash

Simpson, Harriette
See Arnow, Harriette (Louisa) Simpson

Simpson, Louis (Aston Marantz)
1923- . . . . **CLC 4, 7, 9, 32**
See also CA 1-4R; CAAS 4; CANR 1;
DLB 5; MTCW

Simpson, Mona (Elizabeth) 1957- . . . **CLC 44**
See also CA 122; 135

Simpson, N(orman) F(rederick)
1919- . . . . **CLC 29**
See also CA 13-16R; DLB 13

Sinclair, Andrew (Annandale)
1935- . . . . **CLC 2, 14**
See also CA 9-12R; CAAS 5; CANR 14, 38;
DLB 14; MTCW

Sinclair, Emil
See Hesse, Hermann

Sinclair, Mary Amelia St. Clair 1865(?)-1946
See Sinclair, May
See also CA 104

Sinclair, May . . . . **TCLC 3, 11**
See also Sinclair, Mary Amelia St. Clair
See also DLB 36

Sinclair, Upton (Beall)
1878-1968 . . . . **CLC 1, 11, 15, 63**
See also CA 5-8R; 25-28R; CANR 7;
CDALB 1929-1941; DLB 9; MTCW;
SATA 9; WLC

Singer, Isaac
See Singer, Isaac Bashevis

Southern, Terry 1926- .... CLC 7
See also CA 1-4R; CANR 1; DLB 2

Southey, Robert 1774-1843 .... **NCLC 8**
See also DLB 93, 107; SATA 54

Southworth, Emma Dorothy Eliza Nevitte
1819-1899 .... **NCLC 26**

Souza, Ernest
See Scott, Evelyn

Soyinka, Wole
1934- .... **CLC 3, 5, 14, 36, 44; DC 2**
See also BLC 3; BW; CA 13-16R;
CANR 27, 39; MTCW; WLC

Spackman, W(illiam) M(ode)
1905-1990 .... CLC 46
See also CA 81-84; 132

Spacks, Barry 1931- .... CLC 14
See also CA 29-32R; CANR 33; DLB 105

Spanidou, Irini 1946- .... CLC 44

Spark, Muriel (Sarah)
1918- ...... **CLC 2, 3, 5, 8, 13, 18, 40;
SSC 10**
See also CA 5-8R; CANR 12, 36;
CDBLB 1945-1960; DLB 15; MTCW

Spaulding, Douglas
See Bradbury, Ray (Douglas)

Spaulding, Leonard
See Bradbury, Ray (Douglas)

Spence, J. A. D.
See Eliot, T(homas) S(tearns)

Spencer, Elizabeth 1921- .... CLC 22
See also CA 13-16R; CANR 32; DLB 6;
MTCW; SATA 14

Spencer, Leonard G.
See Silverberg, Robert

Spencer, Scott 1945- .... CLC 30
See also CA 113; DLBY 86

Spender, Stephen (Harold)
1909- .... **CLC 1, 2, 5, 10, 41**
See also CA 9-12R; CANR 31;
CDBLB 1945-1960; DLB 20; MTCW

Spengler, Oswald (Arnold Gottfried)
1880-1936 .... TCLC 25
See also CA 118

Spenser, Edmund 1552(?)-1599 .... **LC 5**
See also CDBLB Before 1660; WLC

Spicer, Jack 1925-1965 ...... **CLC 8, 18, 72**
See also CA 85-88; DLB 5, 16

Spielberg, Peter 1929- .... CLC 6
See also CA 5-8R; CANR 4; DLBY 81

Spielberg, Steven 1947- .... CLC 20
See also AAYA 8; CA 77-80; CANR 32;
SATA 32

Spillane, Frank Morrison 1918-
See Spillane, Mickey
See also CA 25-28R; CANR 28; MTCW;
SATA 66

Spillane, Mickey .... **CLC 3, 13**
See also Spillane, Frank Morrison

Spinoza, Benedictus de 1632-1677 .... **LC 9**

Spinrad, Norman (Richard) 1940-... CLC 46
See also CA 37-40R; CANR 20; DLB 8

Spitteler, Carl (Friedrich Georg)
1845-1924 .... TCLC 12
See also CA 109

Spivack, Kathleen (Romola Drucker)
1938- .... CLC 6
See also CA 49-52

Spoto, Donald 1941-.............. CLC 39
See also CA 65-68; CANR 11

Springsteen, Bruce (F.) 1949- ...... CLC 17
See also CA 111

Spurling, Hilary 1940-........... CLC 34
See also CA 104; CANR 25

Squires, Radcliffe 1917-.......... CLC 51
See also CA 1-4R; CANR 6, 21

Srivastava, Dhanpat Rai 1880(?)-1936
See Premchand
See also CA 118

Stacy, Donald
See Pohl, Frederik

Stael, Germaine de
See Stael-Holstein, Anne Louise Germaine
Necker Baronn
See also DLB 119

Stael-Holstein, Anne Louise Germaine Necker
Baronn 1766-1817 .... **NCLC 3**
See also Stael, Germaine de

Stafford, Jean 1915-1979... **CLC 4, 7, 19, 68**
See also CA 1-4R; 85-88; CANR 3; DLB 2;
MTCW; SATA 22

Stafford, William (Edgar)
1914- .... **CLC 4, 7, 29**
See also CA 5-8R; CAAS 3; CANR 5, 22;
DLB 5

Staines, Trevor
See Brunner, John (Kilian Houston)

Stairs, Gordon
See Austin, Mary (Hunter)

Stannard, Martin................. CLC 44

Stanton, Maura 1946- .... CLC 9
See also CA 89-92; CANR 15; DLB 120

Stanton, Schuyler
See Baum, L(yman) Frank

Stapledon, (William) Olaf
1886-1950 .... TCLC 22
See also CA 111; DLB 15

Starbuck, George (Edwin) 1931-.... CLC 53
See also CA 21-24R; CANR 23

Stark, Richard
See Westlake, Donald E(dwin)

Staunton, Schuyler
See Baum, L(yman) Frank

Stead, Christina (Ellen)
1902-1983 .... **CLC 2, 5, 8, 32**
See also CA 13-16R; 109; CANR 33;
MTCW

Stead, William Thomas
1849-1912 .... TCLC 48

Steele, Richard 1672-1729.......... **LC 18**
See also CDBLB 1660-1789; DLB 84, 101

Steele, Timothy (Reid) 1948-....... CLC 45
See also CA 93-96; CANR 16; DLB 120

Steffens, (Joseph) Lincoln
1866-1936 .... TCLC 20
See also CA 117

Stegner, Wallace (Earle) 1909-... **CLC 9, 49**
See also AITN 1; BEST 90:3; CA 1-4R;
CAAS 9; CANR 1, 21; DLB 9; MTCW

Stein, Gertrude
1874-1946 .... **TCLC 1, 6, 28, 48**
See also CA 104; 132; CDALB 1917-1929;
DLB 4, 54, 86; MTCW; WLC

Steinbeck, John (Ernst)
1902-1968 ..... **CLC 1, 5, 9, 13, 21, 34,
45, 75; SSC 11**
See also CA 1-4R; 25-28R; CANR 1, 35;
CDALB 1929-1941; DLB 7, 9; DLBD 2;
MTCW; SATA 9; WLC

Steinem, Gloria 1934-............. CLC 63
See also CA 53-56; CANR 28; MTCW

Steiner, George 1929-............. CLC 24
See also CA 73-76; CANR 31; DLB 67;
MTCW; SATA 62

Steiner, Rudolf 1861-1925........ TCLC 13
See also CA 107

Stendhal 1783-1842............ **NCLC 23**
See also DLB 119; WLC

Stephen, Leslie 1832-1904........ TCLC 23
See also CA 123; DLB 57

Stephen, Sir Leslie
See Stephen, Leslie

Stephen, Virginia
See Woolf, (Adeline) Virginia

Stephens, James 1882(?)-1950...... **TCLC 4**
See also CA 104; DLB 19

Stephens, Reed
See Donaldson, Stephen R.

Steptoe, Lydia
See Barnes, Djuna

Sterchi, Beat 1949-............... CLC 65

Sterling, Brett
See Bradbury, Ray (Douglas); Hamilton,
Edmond

Sterling, Bruce 1954-............. CLC 72
See also CA 119

Sterling, George 1869-1926....... TCLC 20
See also CA 117; DLB 54

Stern, Gerald 1925- .... CLC 40
See also CA 81-84; CANR 28; DLB 105

Stern, Richard (Gustave) 1928-... CLC 4, 39
See also CA 1-4R; CANR 1, 25; DLBY 87

Sternberg, Josef von 1894-1969..... CLC 20
See also CA 81-84

Sterne, Laurence 1713-1768......... **LC 2**
See also CDBLB 1660-1789; DLB 39; WLC

Sternheim, (William Adolf) Carl
1878-1942 .... TCLC 8
See also CA 105; DLB 56, 118

Stevens, Mark 1951- .... CLC 34
See also CA 122

Stevens, Wallace
1879-1955 .... **TCLC 3, 12, 45; PC 6**
See also CA 104; 124; CDALB 1929-1941;
DLB 54; MTCW; WLC

Stevenson, Anne (Katharine)
1933- .... **CLC 7, 33**
See also CA 17-20R; CAAS 9; CANR 9, 33;
DLB 40; MTCW

Stevenson, Robert Louis (Balfour)
1850-1894 .... **NCLC 5, 14; SSC 11**
See also CDBLB 1890-1914; CLR 10, 11;
DLB 18, 57; MAICYA; WLC; YABC 2

Stewart, J(ohn) I(nnes) M(ackintosh)
1906- .... **CLC 7, 14, 32**
See also CA 85-88; CAAS 3; MTCW

Stewart, Mary (Florence Elinor)
1916- .... **CLC 7, 35**
See also CA 1-4R; CANR 1; SATA 12

Stewart, Mary Rainbow
See Stewart, Mary (Florence Elinor)

Still, James 1906-............... **CLC 49**
See also CA 65-68; CANR 10, 26; DLB 9;
SATA 29

Sting
See Sumner, Gordon Matthew

Stirling, Arthur
See Sinclair, Upton (Beall)

Stitt, Milan 1941-............... **CLC 29**
See also CA 69-72

Stockton, Francis Richard 1834-1902
See Stockton, Frank R.
See also CA 108; 137; MAICYA; SATA 44

Stockton, Frank R................. **TCLC 47**
See also Stockton, Francis Richard
See also DLB 42, 74; SATA 32

Stoddard, Charles
See Kuttner, Henry

Stoker, Abraham 1847-1912
See Stoker, Bram
See also CA 105; SATA 29

Stoker, Bram................... **TCLC 8**
See also Stoker, Abraham
See also CDBLB 1890-1914; DLB 36, 70;
WLC

Stolz, Mary (Slattery) 1920-....... **CLC 12**
See also AAYA 8; AITN 1; CA 5-8R;
CANR 13; MAICYA; SAAS 3;
SATA 10, 70, 71

Stone, Irving 1903-1989............ **CLC 7**
See also AITN 1; CA 1-4R; 129; CAAS 3;
CANR 1, 23; MTCW; SATA 3; SATO 64

Stone, Oliver 1946-............... **CLC 73**
See also CA 110

Stone, Robert (Anthony)
1937-.................. **CLC 5, 23, 42**
See also CA 85-88; CANR 23; MTCW

Stone, Zachary
See Follett, Ken(neth Martin)

Stoppard, Tom
1937-... **CLC 1, 3, 4, 5, 8, 15, 29, 34, 63**
See also CA 81-84; CANR 39;
CDBLB 1960 to Present; DLB 13;
DLBY 85; MTCW; WLC

Storey, David (Malcolm)
1933-.................. **CLC 2, 4, 5, 8**
See also CA 81-84; CANR 36; DLB 13, 14;
MTCW

Storm, Hyemeyohsts 1935-......... **CLC 3**
See also CA 81-84

Storm, (Hans) Theodor (Woldsen)
1817-1888 .... **NCLC 1**

Storni, Alfonsina 1892-1938 .... **TCLC 5**
See also CA 104; 131; HW

Stout, Rex (Todhunter) 1886-1975 ... **CLC 3**
See also AITN 2; CA 61-64

Stow, (Julian) Randolph 1935- .. **CLC 23, 48**
See also CA 13-16R; CANR 33; MTCW

Stowe, Harriet (Elizabeth) Beecher
1811-1896 .... **NCLC 3**
See also CDALB 1865-1917; DLB 1, 12, 42,
74; MAICYA; WLC; YABC 1

Strachey, (Giles) Lytton
1880-1932 .... **TCLC 12**
See also CA 110; DLBD 10

Strand, Mark 1934- ...... **CLC 6, 18, 41, 71**
See also CA 21-24R; DLB 5; SATA 41

Straub, Peter (Francis) 1943- ...... **CLC 28**
See also BEST 89:1; CA 85-88; CANR 28;
DLBY 84; MTCW

Strauss, Botho 1944- .... **CLC 22**

Streatfeild, (Mary) Noel
1895(?)-1986 .... **CLC 21**
See also CA 81-84; 120; CANR 31;
CLR 17; MAICYA; SATA 20, 48

Stribling, T(homas) S(igismund)
1881-1965 .... **CLC 23**
See also CA 107; DLB 9

Strindberg, (Johan) August
1849-1912 .... **TCLC 1, 8, 21, 47**
See also CA 104; 135; WLC

Stringer, Arthur 1874-1950 .... **TCLC 37**
See also DLB 92

Stringer, David
See Roberts, Keith (John Kingston)

Strugatskii, Arkadii (Natanovich)
1925-1991 .... **CLC 27**
See also CA 106; 135

Strugatskii, Boris (Natanovich)
1933-.................. **CLC 27**
See also CA 106

Strummer, Joe 1953(?)- .... **CLC 30**
See also The Clash

Stuart, Don A.
See Campbell, John W(ood Jr.)

Stuart, Ian
See MacLean, Alistair (Stuart)

Stuart, Jesse (Hilton)
1906-1984 .... **CLC 1, 8, 11, 14, 34**
See also CA 5-8R; 112; CANR 31; DLB 9,
48, 102; DLBY 84; SATA 2, 36

Sturgeon, Theodore (Hamilton)
1918-1985 .... **CLC 22, 39**
See also Queen, Ellery
See also CA 81-84; 116; CANR 32; DLB 8;
DLBY 85; MTCW

Sturges, Preston 1898-1959 .... **TCLC 48**
See also CA 114; DLB 26

Styron, William
1925- .... **CLC 1, 3, 5, 11, 15, 60**
See also BEST 90:4; CA 5-8R; CANR 6, 33;
CDALB 1968-1988; DLB 2; DLBY 80;
MTCW

Suarez Lynch, B.
See Bioy Casares, Adolfo; Borges, Jorge
Luis

Suarez Lynch, B.
See Borges, Jorge Luis

Su Chien 1884-1918
See Su Man-shu
See also CA 123

Sudermann, Hermann 1857-1928 .. **TCLC 15**
See also CA 107; DLB 118

Sue, Eugene 1804-1857 .... **NCLC 1**
See also DLB 119

Sueskind, Patrick 1949-.......... **CLC 44**

Sukenick, Ronald 1932-..... **CLC 3, 4, 6, 48**
See also CA 25-28R; CAAS 8; CANR 32;
DLBY 81

Suknaski, Andrew 1942- .... **CLC 19**
See also CA 101; DLB 53

Sullivan, Vernon
See Vian, Boris

Sully Prudhomme 1839-1907...... **TCLC 31**

Su Man-shu .... **TCLC 24**
See also Su Chien

Summerforest, Ivy B.
See Kirkup, James

Summers, Andrew James 1942-..... **CLC 26**
See also The Police

Summers, Andy
See Summers, Andrew James

Summers, Hollis (Spurgeon Jr.)
1916-...................... **CLC 10**
See also CA 5-8R; CANR 3; DLB 6

Summers, (Alphonsus Joseph-Mary Augustus)
Montague 1880-1948........ **TCLC 16**
See also CA 118

Sumner, Gordon Matthew 1951-.... **CLC 26**
See also The Police

Surtees, Robert Smith
1803-1864 .... **NCLC 14**
See also DLB 21

Susann, Jacqueline 1921-1974....... **CLC 3**
See also AITN 1; CA 65-68; 53-56; MTCW

Suskind, Patrick
See Sueskind, Patrick

Sutcliff, Rosemary 1920-.......... **CLC 26**
See also CA 5-8R; CANR 37; CLR 1;
MAICYA; SATA 6, 44

Sutro, Alfred 1863-1933........... **TCLC 6**
See also CA 105; DLB 10

Sutton, Henry
See Slavitt, David R.

Svevo, Italo .... **TCLC 2, 35**
See also Schmitz, Aron Hector

Swados, Elizabeth 1951- .... **CLC 12**
See also CA 97-100

Swados, Harvey 1920-1972 .... **CLC 5**
See also CA 5-8R; 37-40R; CANR 6;
DLB 2

Swan, Gladys 1934- .... **CLC 69**
See also CA 101; CANR 17, 39

Swarthout, Glendon (Fred) 1918- ... **CLC 35**
See also CA 1-4R; CANR 1; SATA 26

Sweet, Sarah C.
See Jewett, (Theodora) Sarah Orne

Swenson, May 1919-1989..... **CLC 4, 14, 61**
See also CA 5-8R; 130; CANR 36; DLB 5;
MTCW; SATA 15

Swift, Augustus
See Lovecraft, H(oward) P(hillips)

Swift, Graham 1949- .... **CLC 41**
See also CA 117; 122

Swift, Jonathan 1667-1745.......... **LC 1**
See also CDBLB 1660-1789; DLB 39, 95,
101; SATA 19; WLC

Swinburne, Algernon Charles
1837-1909 ....**TCLC 8, 36**
See also CA 105; CDBLB 1832-1890;
DLB 35, 57; WLC

Swinfen, Ann................... **CLC 34**

Swinnerton, Frank Arthur
1884-1982 .... **CLC 31**
See also CA 108; DLB 34

Swithen, John
See King, Stephen (Edwin)

Sylvia
See Ashton-Warner, Sylvia (Constance)

Symmes, Robert Edward
See Duncan, Robert (Edward)

Symonds, John Addington
1840-1893 .... **NCLC 34**
See also DLB 57

Symons, Arthur 1865-1945 ...... **TCLC 11**
See also CA 107; DLB 19, 57

Symons, Julian (Gustave)
1912-...................**CLC 2, 14, 32**
See also CA 49-52; CAAS 3; CANR 3, 33;
DLB 87; MTCW

Synge, (Edmund) J(ohn) M(illington)
1871-1909 ....**TCLC 6, 37; DC 2**
See also CA 104; CDBLB 1890-1914;
DLB 10, 19

Syruc, J.
See Milosz, Czeslaw

Szirtes, George 1948-............ **CLC 46**
See also CA 109; CANR 27

Tabori, George 1914-............ **CLC 19**
See also CA 49-52; CANR 4

Tagore, Rabindranath 1861-1941.... **TCLC 3**
See also CA 104; 120; MTCW

Taine, Hippolyte Adolphe
1828-1893 .... **NCLC 15**

Talese, Gay 1932-............ **CLC 37**
See also AITN 1; CA 1-4R; CANR 9;
MTCW

Tallent, Elizabeth (Ann) 1954- ..... **CLC 45**
See also CA 117

Tally, Ted 1952-................ **CLC 42**
See also CA 120; 124

Tamayo y Baus, Manuel
1829-1898 .... **NCLC 1**

Tammsaare, A(nton) H(ansen)
1878-1940 .... **TCLC 27**

Tan, Amy 1952- .... **CLC 59**
See also AAYA 9; BEST 89:3; CA 136

Tandem, Felix
See Spitteler, Carl (Friedrich Georg)

Tanizaki, Jun'ichiro
1886-1965 .... **CLC 8, 14, 28**
See also CA 93-96; 25-28R

Tanner, William
See Amis, Kingsley (William)

Tao Lao
See Storni, Alfonsina

Tarassoff, Lev
See Troyat, Henri

Tarbell, Ida M(inerva)
1857-1944 .... **TCLC 40**
See also CA 122; DLB 47

Tarkington, (Newton) Booth
1869-1946 .... **TCLC 9**
See also CA 110; DLB 9, 102; SATA 17

Tarkovsky, Andrei (Arsenyevich)
1932-1986 .... **CLC 75**
See also CA 127

Tasso, Torquato 1544-1595 .... **LC 5**

Tate, (John Orley) Allen
1899-1979 .... **CLC 2, 4, 6, 9, 11, 14, 24**
See also CA 5-8R; 85-88; CANR 32;
DLB 4, 45, 63; MTCW

Tate, Ellalice
See Hibbert, Eleanor Burford

Tate, James (Vincent) 1943- ... **CLC 2, 6, 25**
See also CA 21-24R; CANR 29; DLB 5

Tavel, Ronald 1940-............ **CLC 6**
See also CA 21-24R; CANR 33

Taylor, Cecil Philip 1929-1981 ..... **CLC 27**
See also CA 25-28R; 105

Taylor, Edward 1642(?)-1729....... **LC 11**
See also DLB 24

Taylor, Eleanor Ross 1920-......... **CLC 5**
See also CA 81-84

Taylor, Elizabeth 1912-1975 ... **CLC 2, 4, 29**
See also CA 13-16R; CANR 9; MTCW;
SATA 13

Taylor, Henry (Splawn) 1942-...... **CLC 44**
See also CA 33-36R; CAAS 7; CANR 31;
DLB 5

Taylor, Kamala (Purnaiya) 1924-
See Markandaya, Kamala
See also CA 77-80

Taylor, Mildred D. .... **CLC 21**
See also BW; CA 85-88; CANR 25; CLR 9;
DLB 52; MAICYA; SAAS 5; SATA 15,
70

Taylor, Peter (Hillsman)
1917-..... **CLC 1, 4, 18, 37, 44, 50, 71;
SSC 10**
See also CA 13-16R; CANR 9; DLBY 81;
MTCW

Taylor, Robert Lewis 1912-........ **CLC 14**
See also CA 1-4R; CANR 3; SATA 10

Tchekhov, Anton
See Chekhov, Anton (Pavlovich)

Teasdale, Sara 1884-1933.......... **TCLC 4**
See also CA 104; DLB 45; SATA 32

Tegner, Esaias 1782-1846........ **NCLC 2**

Teilhard de Chardin, (Marie Joseph) Pierre
1881-1955 .... **TCLC 9**
See also CA 105

Temple, Ann
See Mortimer, Penelope (Ruth)

Tennant, Emma (Christina)
1937-.................. **CLC 13, 52**
See also CA 65-68; CAAS 9; CANR 10, 38;
DLB 14

Tenneshaw, S. M.
See Silverberg, Robert

Tennyson, Alfred
1809-1892 .... **NCLC 30; PC 6**
See also CDBLB 1832-1890; DLB 32; WLC

Teran, Lisa St. Aubin de .... **CLC 36**
See also St. Aubin de Teran, Lisa

Teresa de Jesus, St. 1515-1582...... **LC 18**

Terkel, Louis 1912-
See Terkel, Studs
See also CA 57-60; CANR 18; MTCW

Terkel, Studs.................... **CLC 38**
See also Terkel, Louis
See also AITN 1

Terry, C. V.
See Slaughter, Frank G(ill)

Terry, Megan 1932-.............. **CLC 19**
See also CA 77-80; CABS 3; DLB 7

Tertz, Abram
See Sinyavsky, Andrei (Donatevich)

Tesich, Steve 1943(?)-.......... **CLC 40, 69**
See also CA 105; DLBY 83

Teternikov, Fyodor Kuzmich 1863-1927
See Sologub, Fyodor
See also CA 104

Tevis, Walter 1928-1984 .... **CLC 42**
See also CA 113

Tey, Josephine................... **TCLC 14**
See also Mackintosh, Elizabeth
See also DLB 77

Thackeray, William Makepeace
1811-1863 .... **NCLC 5, 14, 22**
See also CDBLB 1832-1890; DLB 21, 55;
SATA 23; WLC

Thakura, Ravindranatha
See Tagore, Rabindranath

Tharoor, Shashi 1956-............ **CLC 70**

Thelwell, Michael Miles 1939- ..... **CLC 22**
See also CA 101

Theobald, Lewis Jr.
See Lovecraft, H(oward) P(hillips)

The Prophet
See Dreiser, Theodore (Herman Albert)

Theroux, Alexander (Louis)
1939-.................. **CLC 2, 25**
See also CA 85-88; CANR 20

Theroux, Paul (Edward)
1941- .... **CLC 5, 8, 11, 15, 28, 46**
See also BEST 89:4; CA 33-36R; CANR 20;
DLB 2; MTCW; SATA 44

Thesen, Sharon 1946-............ **CLC 56**

Thevenin, Denis
See Duhamel, Georges

Thibault, Jacques Anatole Francois
1844-1924
See France, Anatole
See also CA 106; 127; MTCW

Thiele, Colin (Milton) 1920- .... **CLC 17**
See also CA 29-32R; CANR 12, 28;
CLR 27; MAICYA; SAAS 2; SATA 14

Thomas, Audrey (Callahan)
1935-.................. **CLC 7, 13, 37**
See also AITN 2; CA 21-24R; CANR 36;
DLB 60; MTCW

Tristan
See Gomez de la Serna, Ramon

Tristram
See Housman, A(lfred) E(dward)

Trogdon, William (Lewis) 1939-
See Heat-Moon, William Least
See also CA 115; 119

Trollope, Anthony 1815-1882 .. NCLC 6, 33
See also CDBLB 1832-1890; DLB 21, 57;
SATA 22; WLC

Trollope, Frances 1779-1863 ..... NCLC 30
See also DLB 21

Trotsky, Leon 1879-1940 .... TCLC 22
See also CA 118

Trotter (Cockburn), Catharine
1679-1749 .... LC 8
See also DLB 84

Trout, Kilgore
See Farmer, Philip Jose

Trow, George W. S. 1943- .... CLC 52
See also CA 126

Troyat, Henri 1911- .... CLC 23
See also CA 45-48; CANR 2, 33; MTCW

Trudeau, G(arretson) B(eekman) 1948-
See Trudeau, Garry B.
See also CA 81-84; CANR 31; SATA 35

Trudeau, Garry B. .... CLC 12
See also Trudeau, G(arretson) B(eekman)
See also AITN 2

Truffaut, Francois 1932-1984 ...... CLC 20
See also CA 81-84; 113; CANR 34

Trumbo, Dalton 1905-1976 .... CLC 19
See also CA 21-24R; 69-72; CANR 10;
DLB 26

Trumbull, John 1750-1831 ...... NCLC 30
See also DLB 31

Trundlett, Helen B.
See Eliot, T(homas) S(tearns)

Tryon, Thomas 1926-1991 ...... CLC 3, 11
See also AITN 1; CA 29-32R; 135;
CANR 32; MTCW

Tryon, Tom
See Tryon, Thomas

Ts'ao Hsueh-ch'in 1715(?)-1763 ...... LC 1

Tsushima, Shuji 1909-1948
See Dazai, Osamu
See also CA 107

Tsvetaeva (Efron), Marina (Ivanovna)
1892-1941 .... TCLC 7, 35
See also CA 104; 128; MTCW

Tuck, Lily 1938- .... CLC 70

Tunis, John R(oberts) 1889-1975 ... CLC 12
See also CA 61-64; DLB 22; MAICYA;
SATA 30, 37

Tuohy, Frank .... CLC 37
See also Tuohy, John Francis
See also DLB 14

Tuohy, John Francis 1925-
See Tuohy, Frank
See also CA 5-8R; CANR 3

Turco, Lewis (Putnam) 1934- ... CLC 11, 63
See also CA 13-16R; CANR 24; DLBY 84

Turgenev, Ivan
1818-1883 .... NCLC 21; SSC 7
See also WLC

Turner, Frederick 1943- .... CLC 48
See also CA 73-76; CAAS 10; CANR 12,
30; DLB 40

Tusan, Stan 1936- .... CLC 22
See also CA 105

Tutuola, Amos 1920- .... CLC 5, 14, 29
See also BLC 3; BW; CA 9-12R; CANR 27;
MTCW

Twain, Mark
.... TCLC 6, 12, 19, 36, 48; SSC 6
See also Clemens, Samuel Langhorne
See also DLB 11, 12, 23, 64, 74; WLC

Tyler, Anne
1941- .... CLC 7, 11, 18, 28, 44, 59
See also BEST 89:1; CA 9-12R; CANR 11,
33; DLB 6; DLBY 82; MTCW; SATA 7

Tyler, Royall 1757-1826 .... NCLC 3
See also DLB 37

Tynan, Katharine 1861-1931 ...... TCLC 3
See also CA 104

Tytell, John 1939- .... CLC 50
See also CA 29-32R

Tyutchev, Fyodor 1803-1873 ..... NCLC 34

Tzara, Tristan .... CLC 47
See also Rosenfeld, Samuel

Uhry, Alfred 1936- .... CLC 55
See also CA 127; 133

Ulf, Haerved
See Strindberg, (Johan) August

Ulf, Harved
See Strindberg, (Johan) August

Unamuno (y Jugo), Miguel de
1864-1936 .... TCLC 2, 9; SSC 11
See also CA 104; 131; DLB 108; HW;
MTCW

Undercliffe, Errol
See Campbell, (John) Ramsey

Underwood, Miles
See Glassco, John

Undset, Sigrid 1882-1949 .... TCLC 3
See also CA 104; 129; MTCW; WLC

Ungaretti, Giuseppe
1888-1970 .... CLC 7, 11, 15
See also CA 19-20; 25-28R; CAP 2;
DLB 114

Unger, Douglas 1952- .... CLC 34
See also CA 130

Updike, John (Hoyer)
1932- ...... CLC 1, 2, 3, 5, 7, 9, 13, 15,
23, 34, 43, 70
See also CA 1-4R; CABS 1; CANR 4, 33;
CDALB 1968-1988; DLB 2, 5; DLBD 3;
DLBY 80, 82; MTCW; WLC

Upshaw, Margaret Mitchell
See Mitchell, Margaret (Munnerlyn)

Upton, Mark
See Sanders, Lawrence

Urdang, Constance (Henriette)
1922- .... CLC 47
See also CA 21-24R; CANR 9, 24

Uris, Leon (Marcus) 1924- .... CLC 7, 32
See also AITN 1, 2; BEST 89:2; CA 1-4R;
CANR 1; MTCW; SATA 49

Urmuz
See Codrescu, Andrei

Ustinov, Peter (Alexander) 1921- .... CLC 1
See also AITN 1; CA 13-16R; CANR 25;
DLB 13

V
See Chekhov, Anton (Pavlovich)

Vaculik, Ludvik 1926- .... CLC 7
See also CA 53-56

Valenzuela, Luisa 1938- .... CLC 31
See also CA 101; CANR 32; DLB 113; HW

Valera y Alcala-Galiano, Juan
1824-1905 .... TCLC 10
See also CA 106

Valery, (Ambroise) Paul (Toussaint Jules)
1871-1945 .... TCLC 4, 15
See also CA 104; 122; MTCW

Valle-Inclan, Ramon (Maria) del
1866-1936 .... TCLC 5
See also CA 106

Vallejo, Antonio Buero
See Buero Vallejo, Antonio

Vallejo, Cesar (Abraham)
1892-1938 .... TCLC 3
See also CA 105; HW

Valle Y Pena, Ramon del
See Valle-Inclan, Ramon (Maria) del

Van Ash, Cay 1918- .... CLC 34

Vanbrugh, Sir John 1664-1726 ...... LC 21
See also DLB 80

Van Campen, Karl
See Campbell, John W(ood Jr.)

Vance, Gerald
See Silverberg, Robert

Vance, Jack .... CLC 35
See also Vance, John Holbrook
See also DLB 8

Vance, John Holbrook 1916-
See Queen, Ellery; Vance, Jack
See also CA 29-32R; CANR 17; MTCW

Van Den Bogarde, Derek Jules Gaspard Ulric
Niven 1921-
See Bogarde, Dirk
See also CA 77-80

Vandenburgh, Jane .... CLC 59

Vanderhaeghe, Guy 1951- .... CLC 41
See also CA 113

van der Post, Laurens (Jan) 1906- ... CLC 5
See also CA 5-8R; CANR 35

van de Wetering, Janwillem 1931- .. CLC 47
See also CA 49-52; CANR 4

Van Dine, S. S. .... TCLC 23
See also Wright, Willard Huntington

Van Doren, Carl (Clinton)
1885-1950 .... TCLC 18
See also CA 111

Van Doren, Mark 1894-1972 ..... CLC 6, 10
See also CA 1-4R; 37-40R; CANR 3;
DLB 45; MTCW

Wakoski, Diane
1937- . . . . CLC 2, 4, 7, 9, 11, 40
See also CA 13-16R; CAAS 1; CANR 9;
DLB 5

Wakoski-Sherbell, Diane
See Wakoski, Diane

Walcott, Derek (Alton)
1930- . . . . . . CLC 2, 4, 9, 14, 25, 42, 67
See also BLC 3; BW; CA 89-92; CANR 26;
DLB 117; DLBY 81; MTCW

Waldman, Anne 1945- . . . . CLC 7
See also CA 37-40R; CANR 34; DLB 16

Waldo, E. Hunter
See Sturgeon, Theodore (Hamilton)

Waldo, Edward Hamilton
See Sturgeon, Theodore (Hamilton)

Walker, Alice (Malsenior)
1944- . . . . . . CLC 5, 6, 9, 19, 27, 46, 58;
SSC 5
See also AAYA 3; BEST 89:4; BLC 3; BW;
CA 37-40R; CANR 9, 27;
CDALB 1968-1988; DLB 6, 33; MTCW;
SATA 31

Walker, David Harry 1911-1992. . . . CLC 14
See also CA 1-4R; 137; CANR 1; SATA 8;
SATO 71

Walker, Edward Joseph 1934-
See Walker, Ted
See also CA 21-24R; CANR 12, 28

Walker, George F. 1947- . . . . CLC 44, 61
See also CA 103; CANR 21; DLB 60

Walker, Joseph A. 1935- . . . . CLC 19
See also BW; CA 89-92; CANR 26; DLB 38

Walker, Margaret (Abigail)
1915- . . . . CLC 1, 6
See also BLC 3; BW; CA 73-76; CANR 26;
DLB 76; MTCW

Walker, Ted. CLC 13
See also Walker, Edward Joseph
See also DLB 40

Wallace, David Foster 1962- . . . . CLC 50
See also CA 132

Wallace, Dexter
See Masters, Edgar Lee

Wallace, Irving 1916-1990. . . . . . . CLC 7, 13
See also AITN 1; CA 1-4R; 132; CAAS 1;
CANR 1, 27; MTCW

Wallant, Edward Lewis
1926-1962 . . . . CLC 5, 10
See also CA 1-4R; CANR 22; DLB 2, 28;
MTCW

Walpole, Horace 1717-1797. . . . . LC 2
See also DLB 39, 104

Walpole, Hugh (Seymour)
1884-1941 . . . . TCLC 5
See also CA 104; DLB 34

Walser, Martin 1927- . . . . CLC 27
See also CA 57-60; CANR 8; DLB 75

Walser, Robert 1878-1956 . . . . TCLC 18
See also CA 118; DLB 66

Walsh, Jill Paton. . . . . CLC 35
See also Paton Walsh, Gillian
See also CLR 2; SAAS 3

Walter, Villiam Christian
See Andersen, Hans Christian

Wambaugh, Joseph (Aloysius Jr.)
1937- . . . . CLC 3, 18
See also AITN 1; BEST 89:3; CA 33-36R;
DLB 6; DLBY 83; MTCW

Ward, Arthur Henry Sarsfield 1883-1959
See Rohmer, Sax
See also CA 108

Ward, Douglas Turner 1930- . . . . CLC 19
See also BW; CA 81-84; CANR 27; DLB 7,
38

Warhol, Andy 1928(?)-1987. . . . . . . CLC 20
See also BEST 89:4; CA 89-92; 121;
CANR 34

Warner, Francis (Robert le Plastrier)
1937- . . . . CLC 14
See also CA 53-56; CANR 11

Warner, Marina 1946- . . . . CLC 59
See also CA 65-68; CANR 21

Warner, Rex (Ernest) 1905-1986. . . . CLC 45
See also CA 89-92; 119; DLB 15

Warner, Susan (Bogert)
1819-1885 . . . . NCLC 31
See also DLB 3, 42

Warner, Sylvia (Constance) Ashton
See Ashton-Warner, Sylvia (Constance)

Warner, Sylvia Townsend
1893-1978 . . . . CLC 7, 19
See also CA 61-64; 77-80; CANR 16;
DLB 34; MTCW

Warren, Mercy Otis 1728-1814. . . NCLC 13
See also DLB 31

Warren, Robert Penn
1905-1989 . . . CLC 1, 4, 6, 8, 10, 13, 18,
39, 53, 59; SSC 4
See also AITN 1; CA 13-16R; 129;
CANR 10; CDALB 1968-1988; DLB 2,
48; DLBY 80, 89; MTCW; SATA 46, 63;
WLC

Warshofsky, Isaac
See Singer, Isaac Bashevis

Warton, Thomas 1728-1790. . . . . LC 15
See also DLB 104, 109

Waruk, Kona
See Harris, (Theodore) Wilson

Warung, Price 1855-1911. . . . . TCLC 45

Warwick, Jarvis
See Garner, Hugh

Washington, Alex
See Harris, Mark

Washington, Booker T(aliaferro)
1856-1915 . . . . TCLC 10
See also BLC 3; BW; CA 114; 125;
SATA 28

Wassermann, (Karl) Jakob
1873-1934 . . . . TCLC 6
See also CA 104; DLB 66

Wasserstein, Wendy 1950- . . . . . . CLC 32, 59
See also CA 121; 129; CABS 3

Waterhouse, Keith (Spencer)
1929- . . . . CLC 47
See also CA 5-8R; CANR 38; DLB 13, 15;
MTCW

Waters, Roger 1944- . . . . CLC 35
See also Pink Floyd

Watkins, Frances Ellen
See Harper, Frances Ellen Watkins

Watkins, Gerrold
See Malzberg, Barry N(athaniel)

Watkins, Paul 1964- . . . . CLC 55
See also CA 132

Watkins, Vernon Phillips
1906-1967 . . . . CLC 43
See also CA 9-10; 25-28R; CAP 1; DLB 20

Watson, Irving S.
See Mencken, H(enry) L(ouis)

Watson, John H.
See Farmer, Philip Jose

Watson, Richard F.
See Silverberg, Robert

Waugh, Auberon (Alexander) 1939- . . CLC 7
See also CA 45-48; CANR 6, 22; DLB 14

Waugh, Evelyn (Arthur St. John)
1903-1966 . . . CLC 1, 3, 8, 13, 19, 27, 44
See also CA 85-88; 25-28R; CANR 22;
CDBLB 1914-1945; DLB 15; MTCW;
WLC

Waugh, Harriet 1944- . . . . CLC 6
See also CA 85-88; CANR 22

Ways, C. R.
See Blount, Roy (Alton) Jr.

Waystaff, Simon
See Swift, Jonathan

Webb, (Martha) Beatrice (Potter)
1858-1943 . . . . TCLC 22
See also Potter, Beatrice
See also CA 117

Webb, Charles (Richard) 1939- . . . . . . CLC 7
See also CA 25-28R

Webb, James H(enry) Jr. 1946- . . . . CLC 22
See also CA 81-84

Webb, Mary (Gladys Meredith)
1881-1927 . . . . TCLC 24
See also CA 123; DLB 34

Webb, Mrs. Sidney
See Webb, (Martha) Beatrice (Potter)

Webb, Phyllis 1927- . . . . CLC 18
See also CA 104; CANR 23; DLB 53

Webb, Sidney (James)
1859-1947 . . . . TCLC 22
See also CA 117

Webber, Andrew Lloyd. . . . . CLC 21
See also Lloyd Webber, Andrew

Weber, Lenora Mattingly
1895-1971 . . . . CLC 12
See also CA 19-20; 29-32R; CAP 1;
SATA 2, 26

Webster, John 1579(?)-1634(?) . . . . DC 2
See also CDBLB Before 1660; DLB 58;
WLC

Webster, Noah 1758-1843 . . . . NCLC 30

Wedekind, (Benjamin) Frank(lin)
1864-1918 . . . . TCLC 7
See also CA 104; DLB 118

Weidman, Jerome 1913- . . . . CLC 7
See also AITN 2; CA 1-4R; CANR 1;
DLB 28

PC Cumulative Nationality Index

PC Cumulative Title Index

Tristram (Robinson) **1**:470-72, 474-75, 481, 489

"Tristram and Iseult" (Arnold) **5**:9, 12, 33-4, 42, 49, 64

Triumphal March (Eliot) **5**:168, 185

"The Tropics in New York" (McKay) **2**:228

"Trouble in De Kitchen" (Dunbar) **5**:146

Troy Park (Sitwell) **3**:293-94, 298, 301, 303, 307-08, 320

"The Truce of the Bear" (Kipling) **3**:171, 182

"Truck-Garden-Market Day" (Millay) **6**:232

"True Confessional" (Ferlinghetti) **1**:187

"True Romance" (Kipling) **3**:161

"True Tenderness" (Akhmatova) **2**:14

"Trumpet Player: 52nd Street" (Hughes) **1**:241, 247, 249

"Truth" (McKay) **2**:215

"Truth and Error" (Goethe) **5**:228

"Truth Is Not the Secret of a Few" (Ferlinghetti) **1**:186

"The Truth the Dead Know" (Sexton) **2**:346, 361

"Tulips" (Plath) **1**:390, 395, 399-401, 405, 407, 409, 414

Tulips and Chimneys (Cummings) **5**:74-5, 77-8, 86, 91, 93-4, 104

"Tumbling-Hair" (Cummings) **5**:104

"The Tunnel" (Crane) **3**:86, 88-90, 106-07, 110-11

"The Turn of the Moon" (Graves) **6**:154, 156

"The Turncoat" (Baraka) **4**:5, 14

"Turning" (Rilke) **2**:280-81

"The Twa Dogs" ("Dialogues of the Dogs") (Burns) **6**:51, 78, 83-4, 88

"The Twa Herds" (Burns) **6**:85

"The Twelve Dancing Princesses" (Sexton) **2**:365

Twentieth Century Harlequinade (Sitwell) **3**:299-300, 302

Twenty-five Poems (Thomas) **2**:378, 389

"Twenty-four Years" (Thomas) **2**:383

Twenty Love Poems and a Desperate Song (Neruda)
   See *Veinte poemas de amor y una canción desesperada*

Twenty Love Poems and a Song of Despair (Neruda)
   See *Veinte poemas de amor y una canción desesperada*

Twenty Love Poems and One Song of Despair (Neruda)
   See *Veinte poemas de amor y una canción desesperada*

Twenty-One Love Poems (Rich) **5**:384, 395

Twenty Poems (Neruda)
   See *Veinte poemas de amor y una canción desesperada*

Twice or thrice had I loved thee (Donne)
   See "Aire and Angels"

"Twicknam Garden" (Donne) **1**:124, 130, 134

The Twilight Book (Neruda)
   See *Crepúsculario*

"Twilight Reverie" (Hughes) **1**:255

The Twin In the Clouds (Pasternak)
   See *Bliznets v tuchakh*

"Two Amsterdams" (Ferlinghetti) **1**:183

"Two-an'-Six" (McKay) **2**:208-09

"The Two April Mornings" (Wordsworth) **4**:374

"Two Children" (Graves) **6**:156

"Two Egyptian Portrait Masks" (Hayden) **6**:185

"Two Hands" (Sexton) **2**:371

"Two in the Campagna" (Browning) **2**:68

"Two Little Boots" (Dunbar) **5**:122, 129

"Two Look at Two" (Frost) **1**:194, 229, 231

"Two Night Pieces" (Sitwell) **3**:293

"Two Poems" (Madhubuti) **5**:321

"Two Scavengers in a Truck, Two Beautiful People in a Mercedes" (Ferlinghetti) **1**:183, 188

"Two Songs" (Rich) **5**:365

"The Two Thieves" (Wordsworth) **4**:374, 388

"Two Tramps in Mud Time" (Frost) **1**:198, 221

"Two Views of a Cadaver Room" (Plath) **1**:389

"The Two Voices" (Tennyson) **6**:360

"The Typical American?" (Masters) **1**:343

Tyrannus Nix? (Ferlinghetti) **1**:174

U samovo morya (*At the Very Edge of the Sea*; |*By the Seashore*) (Akhmatova) **2**:15

"Uber Das Werden im Vergehen" (Holderlin) **4**:147

"Ulalume" (Poe) **1**:425-26, 428, 431, 434, 436, 439-40, 442-43, 447, 453

"The Ultimate Poem Is Abstract" (Stevens) **6**:314

"Ulysses" (Graves) **6**:130, 137

"Ulysses" (Tennyson) **6**:354, 359, 366, 381, 383-84, 398, 409, 411

"Un-American Investigators" (Hughes) **1**:252

"The Unbeliever" (Bishop) **3**:48

"The Uncle Speaks in the Drawing Room" (Rich) **5**:359, 392

"Uncollected Poems" (Crane) **3**:90

"Under" (Sandburg) **2**:300

"Under Sirius" (Auden) **1**:23

"Under the Olives" (Graves) **6**:155-56

"Under the Viaduct" (Dove) **6**:110

"Understanding but not Forgetting" (Madhubuti) **5**:337-38, 340

"Underwear" (Ferlinghetti) **1**:183

"Unequalled Days" (Pasternak)
   See "Edinstvennye dni"

"The Unexplorer" (Millay) **6**:235

"The Unfaithful Married Woman" (Garcia Lorca)
   See "La casada infiel"

"Ungratefulnesse" (Herbert) **4**:119, 133-34

"Unidentified Flying Object" (Hayden) **6**:196

"The Unions at the Front" (Neruda)
   See "Los Grernios en el frente"

"The United Fruit Company" (Neruda)
   See "La United Fruit Company"

"La United Fruit Company" ("The United Fruit Company") (Neruda) **4**:296

"U.S. 1946 King's X" (Frost) **1**:200

"Unknown Girl in the Maternity Ward" (Sexton) **2**:349, 355

"Les uns et les autres" (Verlaine) **2**:416

"An Unsaid Word" (Rich) **5**:359, 393

"Unsleeping City (Brooklyn Bridge Nocturne)" ("Brooklyn Bridge Nocturne") (Garcia Lorca) **3**:139-40

"Unsounded" (Rich) **5**:359

"The Unsung Heroes" (Dunbar) **5**:131

"Unto the Whole—How Add?" (Dickinson) **1**:103

"Up at a Villa-Down in the City, as Distinguished by an Italian Person of Quality" (Browning) **2**:38

"The Up Rising" (Duncan) **2**:104

"Upon Meeting Don L. Lee in a Dream" (Dove) **6**:104-05, 108

"Upon the Annunciation and Passion" (Donne) **1**:139

"Upon Your Held-Out Hand" (Thomas) **2**:406

"Uptown" (Ginsberg) **4**:47

"The Urals" (Pasternak) **6**:268

"Urania" ("Excuse") (Arnold) **5**:43

"Us" (Sexton) **2**:352

"Used Up" (Sandburg) **2**:303

"Ustica" (Paz) **1**:355, 360-61

"V bol'nitse" ("In Hospital") (Pasternak) **6**:266, 269, 286-87

"V lesu" ("In the Forest") (Pasternak) **6**:280

"Vagabonds" (Rimbaud) **3**:261

"Vain and Careless" (Graves) **6**:141, 150

"Vaivén" (Paz) **1**:359

Vale Ave (H. D.) **5**:282

"The Vale of Esthwaite" (Wordsworth) **4**:41

"A Valediction: forbidding mourning" ("As virtuous men pass mildly away") (Donne) **1**:124, 126, 130, 135

"A Valediction Forbidding Mourning" (Rich) **5**:371, 395

"A Valediction: of my name, in the window" (Donne) **1**:152

"A Valediction: of the booke" ("I'll tell thee now (dear love) what thou shalt doe") (Donne) **1**:128, 130

"A Valediction: of weeping" (Donne) **1**:124, 130, 153

"A Valentine" (Poe) **1**:445

"Valentine I" (Bishop) **3**:36

"Valley Candle" (Stevens) **6**:338

"The Valley of the Shadow" (Robinson) **1**:490

"The Valley of Unrest" (Poe) **1**:438

"Values in Use" (Moore) **4**:261

"The Vampire" (Kipling) **3**:166

"Van Winkle" (Crane) **3**:100, 109

"Vandracour" (Wordsworth) **4**:399

"Vanitie" (Herbert) **4**:120

"Vanitie I" (Herbert) **4**:132

"Variations on Two Dicta of William Blake" (Duncan) **2**:103

Vecher (*Evening*) (Akhmatova) **2**:3, 5-6, 11, 17

Veinte poemas de amor y una canción desesperada (*Twenty Love Poems and a Desperate Song*; *Twenty Love Poems and a Song of Despair*; *Twenty Love Poems and One Song of Despair*; *Twenty Poems*) (Neruda) **4**:276, 282, 284, 291, 299-305, 307

Venetian Epigrams (Goethe) **5**:223

"Venice" (Pasternak) **6**:276

"The Venice Poem" (Duncan) **2**:105-06

Venture of the Infinite Man (Neruda)
   See *Tentativa del hombre infinito*

"Vénus anadyomène" (Rimbaud) **3**:255

"Venus and the Ark" (Sexton) **2**:355

"Veracruz" (Hayden) **6**:193-94

"Vermächtnis" (Goethe) **5**:248

Vers et Prose (Mallarme) **4**:207

"Vers nouveaux et chansons" (Rimbaud) **3**:285

"Vertigo" (Rich) **5**:360

"Vertue" ("Virtue") (Herbert) **4**:100-01, 110, 113, 132-34

"Les veuves" (Baudelaire) **1**:44, 58-9

Title Index

Title Index

ISBN 0-8103-8334-9